Biographical Dictionary of Tang Dynasty Literati

Biographical Dictionary of Tang Dynasty Literati

William H. Nienhauser, Jr., Editor
Michael E. Naparstek, Associate Editor

Indiana University Press

This book is a publication of

Indiana University Press
Office of Scholarly Publishing
Herman B Wells Library 350
1320 East 10th Street
Bloomington, Indiana 47405 USA

iupress.org

© 2022 by Indiana University Press

All rights reserved
No part of this book may be reproduced or utilized in any form or by any means, electronic or mechanical, including photocopying and recording, or by any information storage and retrieval system, without permission in writing from the publisher. The paper used in this publication meets the minimum requirements of the American National Standard for Information Sciences—Permanence of Paper for Printed Library Materials, ANSI Z39.48-1992.

Manufactured in the United States of America

First Printing 2022

Library of Congress Cataloging-in-Publication Data

Names: Nienhauser, William H., editor author. | Naparstek, Michael E., editor.
Title: Biographical dictionary of Tang dynasty literati / William H. Nienhauser, Jr, editor ; Michael E. Naparstek, associate editor.
Description: Bloomington : Indiana University Press, 2022.
Identifiers: LCCN 2021043279 (print) | LCCN 2021043280 (ebook) | ISBN 9780253060266 (hardback) | ISBN 9780253060273 (ebook)
Subjects: LCSH: Authors, Chinese—Biography—Dictionaries. | Chinese literature—Bio-bibliography—Dictionaries. | Chinese literature—Tang dynasty, 618-907—Bio-bibliography—Dictionaries. | LCGFT: Dictionaries. | Biographies
Classification: LCC PL2265 .N54 2022 (print) | LCC PL2265 (ebook) | DDC 895.109/003—dc23/eng/20220203
LC record available at https://lccn.loc.gov/2021043279
LC ebook record available at https://lccn.loc.gov/2021043280

THIS VOLUME IS DEDICATED TO

My Students

Table of Contents

Acknowledgments xiii

List of Contributors xv

On Using this Book xvii

List of Abbreviations xix

Tang Emperors xxv

Introduction: An Overview of Tang Literature xxvii

Biographical Entries

Amoghavajra (Bukong 不空)+ 3

Bo Juyi 白居易 8

Bo Xingjian 白行簡 18

Cao Tang 曹唐+ 21

Cen Shen 岑參 24

Chang Gun 常袞+ 28

Chang Jian 常建 30

Chen Zi'ang 陳子昂 32

Cheng Xuanying 成玄英+ 35

Chu Guangxi 儲光羲 38

Cui Hao 崔顥 40

Cui Zhongrong 崔仲容+ 42

Dai Shulun 戴叔倫+ 43

Daoshi 道世+ 46

Du Fu 杜甫 48

Du Guangting 杜光庭 63

Du Mu 杜牧 68

Du Shenyan 杜審言 74

Du Xunhe 杜荀鶴 77

Dugu Ji 獨孤及 80

Falin 法琳+ 82

Table of Contents

Feng Su 馮宿+ 85

Gao Shi 高適 87

Geng Wei 耿湋+ 91

Gu Feixiong 顧非熊+ 93

Gu Kuang 顧況 95

Guanxiu 貫休 98

Han Hong 韓翃+ 101

Han Wo 韓偓 104

Han Yu 韓愈 107

Hanshan 寒山 115

He Zhizhang 賀知章+ 120

Huangfu Ran 皇甫冉+ 124

Huangfu Shi 皇甫湜+ 126

Jia Dao 賈島 129

Jia Zhi 賈至 134

Jiao Ran 皎然 136

Judun 居遁+ 140

Li Ao 李翱 142

Li Bo 李白 145

Li Deyu 李德裕+ 159

Li Duan 李端+ 163

Li Gongzuo 李公佐 165

Li Guan 李觀 167

Li He 李賀 170

Li Hua 李華 176

Li Jiao 李嶠 179

Li Jilan 李季蘭+ 181

Li Pin 李頻+ 184

Li Qi 李頎+ 187

Li Rong 李榮+ 190

Li Shangyin 李商隱 193

viii

Li Shen 李紳+	199
Li Yi 李益+	203
Liang Su 梁肅	207
Lingche 靈澈+	210
Linghu Chu 令狐楚+	212
Lingyou 靈祐+	215
Liu Cha 劉叉+	218
Liu Fangping 劉方平+	221
Liu Mian 柳冕	224
Liu Yuxi 劉禹錫	227
Liu Zhangqing 劉長卿	232
Liu Zhiji 劉知幾	235
Liu Zongyuan 柳宗元	240
Lu Guimeng 陸龜蒙	247
Lu Lun 盧綸	251
Lu Tong 盧仝+	253
Lu Zhaolin 盧照鄰	256
Lu Zhi 陸贄	260
Lü Wen 呂溫+	263
Luo Binwang 駱賓王	266
Luo Yin 羅隱	269
Ma Dai 馬戴+	272
Meng Haoran 孟浩然	274
Meng Jiao 孟郊	278
Ouyang Zhan 歐陽詹+	282
Pei Xing 裴鉶+	285
Pi Rixiu 皮日休	288
Qiji 齊己	293
Qian Qi 錢起	296
Qingjiang 清江+	301
Qiwu Qian 綦毋潛	303

Table of Contents

Quan Deyu 權德輿+ 306
Rong Yu 戎昱+ 309
Shangguan Wan'er 上官婉兒+ 312
Shangguan Yi 上官儀+ 317
Shen Jiji 沈既濟 322
Shen Quanqi 沈佺期 325
Shen Yazhi 沈亞之 327
Shi Jianwu 施肩吾+ 331
Sikong Shu 司空曙+ 333
Sikong Tu 司空圖 335
Sima Chengzhen 司馬承禎 340
Song Zhiwen 宋之問 343
Su Ting 蘇頲 345
Sun Qiao 孫樵+ 348
Sun Simiao 孫思邈+ 351
Wang Bo 王勃 354
Wang Changling 王昌齡 359
Wang *Fanzhi* 王梵志 363
Wang Ji 王績 366
Wang Jian 王建 369
Wang Wei 王維 373
Wang Zhihuan 王之渙 380
Wei Yingwu 韋應物 383
Wei Zhuang 韋莊 386
Wen Tingyun 溫庭筠 390
Wuke 無可+ 395
Wu Yuanheng 武元衡+ 398
Wu Yun 吳筠+ 401
Xiao Yingshi 蕭穎士 406
Xu Hun 許渾+ 410
Xu Jingzong 許敬宗+ 413

Xuanjue 玄覺+	416
Xuantai 玄泰+	420
Xue Tao 薛濤	423
Xuzhong 虛中+	425
Yan Shigu 顏師古+	427
Yang Jiong 楊炯	430
Yang Juyuan 楊巨源+	432
Yang Ning 楊凝+	434
Yao He 姚合+	437
Yu Shinan 虞世南+	439
Yu Xuanji 魚玄機	442
Yuan'an 元安+	448
Yuan Chun 元淳+	451
Yuan Jie 元結	452
Yuan Zhen 元稹	457
Zhang Ben 張賁+	462
Zhang Hu 張祜+	465
Zhang Ji 張繼	467
Zhang Ji 張籍	469
Zhang Jiuling 張九齡	473
Zhang Ruoxu 張若虛	477
Zhang Wei 張謂+	480
Zhang Yue 張說	482
Zhang Zhuo 張鷟	485
Zhao Gu 趙嘏+	489
Zhu Kejiu 朱可久+	491
Appendix I: Official Titles and Ranks	494
Official Titles, Alphabetized by English Translation	496
Official Titles, Alphabetized by Pinyin Romanization	502
Appendix II: Literary Timeline of the Tang	508

Acknowledgments

The idea for much of the material in this volume began in the late 1970s when Joseph S. M. Lau encouraged me to compile a dictionary of traditional Chinese literature. That encouragement led to the *Indiana Companion to Traditional Chinese Literature* (2 volumes, published by Indiana University Press in 1986 and 1998). Shortly after the publication of the first volume, it occurred to me that material from the *Companion* might provide the basis for a dictionary of Tang literati. Other projects interrupted this and then the T'ang Studies Society began a similar work.

In the past few years various projects (foremost David R. Knechtges and Taiping Chang's *Ancient and Early Medieval Chinese Literature, A Reference Guide,* in four volumes) convinced me that such a work is still needed. Although there are sixty-three new entries in this volume, including entries on Buddhists, Daoists and women, seventy-seven have been revised from entries that originally appeared in the *Companion*. Aided by students, undergraduate and graduate, at the University of Wisconsin, these entries have been thoroughly revised (including a change to Pinyin Romanization), the bibliographies all updated. Each entry also contains a translation and short analysis of a work or works typifying each author, hoping to appeal both to specialists in the field of Tang literature as well as to those interested in medieval prose and verse.

Most of the entries are listed as co-authored. The authors who wrote entries for the *Companion* were contacted, but many were otherwise occupied. The first listed author for each entry is normally the person who penned the original entry, the second (or sometimes third) authors are those who revised the biographies in light of the most recent scholarship and added the representative work in translation with a brief close reading of that text. The addition of translations of literary works to a reference work on literature seems essential to give readers a complete sense of the author. In this way, our dictionary differs from all other similar western-language works on Chinese literature or history.

Several pages would be needed to thank all the people who have helped put this volume together, since the work has gone on for nearly ten years and represents the work of many minds and hands. I had early assistance of various sorts from Jingyi Qu at Nanyang Technical University. Over the next few years new entries were drafted by graduate students from my department at the University of Wisconsin: Shuxiang You, Yiwen Shen, Han Yan, Amelia Ying Qin, Chen Wu, and Ji Wang. Aaron Reich helped put many entries in proper format. Masha Kobzeva, aside from writing or revising many entries, also helped translating poems and providing assistance wherever needed. Yuyang Zhang read some draft translations offering useful suggestions. Ji Wang also looked carefully at many of the translations and proofread a draft of the entire text; he was instrumental in countless corrections. Cheng Liu, who was in Madison as a post-doc, was consulted on many Tang prose passages. Zheyu Su also assisted in revising translations.

We are grateful for the Scholarly Production Grant the Tang Studies society provided. The greatest debt is, however, clearly to my Associate Editor, Michael Naparstek, who has read and reread these entries with me, written or revised many of the texts, handled all matters concerning formatting, and has been a steadfast friend throughout the past decade.

William H. Nienhauser, Jr.

List of Contributors

Xue Bai
Zhaojie Bai
Richard Bodman
Daniel Bryant
Megan Cai
Yixuan Cai
Marie Chan
Timothy Wai Keung Chan
Po-hui Chuang
Charles H. Egan
Sebastian Eicher
Michael B. Fishlen
Craig Fisk
Douglas Gjertson
Charles Hartman
Richard M. W. Ho
Sharon S. J. Hou
Chenxi Huang
Wenting Ji
Jinhua Jia
Volker Klöpsch
Masha Kobzeva
Paul W. Kroll
Wolfgang Kubin

Li Kun
S. F. Lai
C. Bradford Langley
David Lattimore
Oscar Lee
Martin Lehnert
Gonghuang Liu
James J. Y. Liu
Ziyun Liu
Clara Luhn
Nan Ma
Y.W. Ma
David L. McMullen
Michael E. Naparstek
Douglas Nielson
William H. Nienhauser, Jr.
Thomas Donnelly Noel
Marc Nürnberger
Steven Owen
Angela Jung Palandri
Jakob Pöllath
Ying Qin
Jingyi Qu
Tamotsu Satō

Edward H. Schafer
Yiwen Shen
Wilfried Spaar
Madeline Spring
Josiah Stork
Beth Upton
Marsha Wagner
Jan W. Walls
Rui Wang
Ji Wang
Christine Welch
Catherine Witzling
Timothy Wong
Chen Wu
Yanwen Wu
Han Yan
Cordell Yee
Sarah Yim
Shuxiang You
Chunli Yu
Pauline Yu
Ying Zhan
Xin Zou

On Using this Book

All references to the Tang dynastic histories refer to the *Jiu Tang shu* and *Xin Tang shu* published by Zhonghua Shuju. For the *Quan Tang shi* we have used the 2014 edition that includes all the recent supplements. For the *Quan Tang wen* we have used Zhou Shaoliang 周紹良, ed. *Quan Tang wen xinbian* 全唐文新編 (Changchun: Jilin Wenshi, 1999–2000).

Asterisks* following a person's dates, as in Du Fu 杜甫 (712–770),* indicates that there is a separate entry for that person. Plus signs (+) following a name in the Table of Contents indicates the entry was written especially for this volume and added to those originating in the *Indiana Companion to Traditional Chinese Literature*. In entries, *zi* following a person's name indicates his or her stylename. *Juan* 卷 is untranslated and is roughly equivalent to a chapter.

The *jinshi* 進士 (presented scholar) examination, which most scholars attempted, was basically a test of literary talent (requiring the composition of both *shi*-poetry and *fu* written on assigned topics). It was begun under the Sui dynasty (581–618), but greatly expanded under Empress Wu (r. 690–705).

There were several types of poetry during the Tang, all rhymed, usually on the even-numbered lines. *Shi* 詩 (traditional poetry) can be further divided into *gushi* 古詩 (old-style poetry) and *jinti shi* 近體詩 (new-style poetry). New-style poetry also has two subdivisions: *jueju* 絕句 (quatrains) in four lines of five or seven characters (pentasyllabic and heptasyllabic) and *lüshi* 律詩 (regulated poems) in eight lines each also with five or seven characters. All new-style verse was subject to prosodic rules including parallelism in the second and third couplets and tonal patterns for each line. New-style poetry was written during the Early Tang (618-712) but came into its own during the High Tang (713-779). *Yuefu* 樂府 (music-bureau poems or ballads) traditionally were poems on a particular theme tied to the title; they had originally been collected by the Music Bureau (Yuefu) during the Han dynasty (206 BC–CE 8), thus the name. Du Fu (712–770)* initiated *xin yuefu* 新樂府, new music-bureau poems, which were then popularized during the early ninth century by Li Shen 李紳 (772–846),* Bo Juyi 白居易 (772–846),* and Yuan Zhen 元稹 (779–831).* *Ci* 詞 or *ci*-lyrics were poems written to a tune pattern, originally sung. There were two types: *xiaoling* 小令 which had only one stanza and *manci* 慢詞 which were longer, usually with two stanzas. *Fu* 賦 (rhapsodies or prose-poems) were prosimetric works, usually with a prose preface followed by a long poetic section and concluded with a coda in prose.

For dates of persons we have generally used Fu Xuancong's *Tang, Wudai wenxue biannian shi* 唐五代文学编年史 (4v.; Shenyang: Liaohai, 1998) which was also the basis of many entries in the "Literary Timeline of the Tang" appended to this volume.

List of Abbreviations

ACQ—*Asian Culture Quarterly*

Articulated Ladies—Paul Rouzer, *Articulated Ladies, Gender and the Male Community in Early Chinese Texts*. Cambridge: Harvard University Asia Center, 2001.

Barnstone, *Chinese Poetry*—Tony Barnstone and Chou Ping. *The Anchor Book of Chinese Poetry*. New York: Anchor Books, 2005.

Bauer, *Golden Casket*—Wolfgang Bauer and Herbert Franke, eds. *The Golden Casket*. Christopher Levenson, translator. Baltimore: Penguin, 1967.

Baibu—*Baibu congshu jicheng* 百步叢書集成. *Baibu congshu jicheng* 百部叢書集成. Also known as *Congshu jicheng zhengbian* 叢書集成正編. Rpt. Taibei, 1965–1970.

Birch, *Anthology*—Cyril Birch. *Anthology of Chinese Literature*. 2v. New York: Grove, 1965.

Bodman, "Poetics"—Richard Bodman. "Poetics and Prosody in Early Medieval China: A Study and Translation of Kūkai's *Bunkyō hifuron*." Unpublished Ph.D. dissertation, Cornell University, 1978.

Bol—Bol, Peter K. *This Culture of Ours, Intellectual Transitions in T'ang and Sung China*. Stanford: Stanford University, 1992.

Buswell, *Dictionary*—Robert E. Buswell, Jr. and Donald S. Lopez Jr. *The Princeton Dictionary of Buddhism*. Princeton: Princeton University, 2014.

Bynner, *Jade Mountain*—Witter Bynner (1881–1968) and Kiang Kang-hu 江亢虎 (1883–1954). *The Jade Mountain*. New York: Knopf, 1929. Rpt. New York: Vintage Books, 1972.

CSJC—*Congshu jicheng chubian* 叢書集成初編. Shanghai: Shangwu Yinshuguan, 1935–1937.

Chang, *Women Writers*—Chang Sun Kang-i, Haun Saussy, and Charles Yim-tze Kwong, eds.. *Women Writers of Traditional China: An Anthology of Poetry and Criticism*. Stanford: Stanford University, 1999.

Chinese Fiction—Winston L.Y. Yang and Curtis P. Adkins, eds. *Critical Essays on Chinese Fiction*. Hong Kong: Chinese University, 1980.

Critical Essays—William H. Nienhauser, Jr., ed. *Critical Essays on Chinese Literature*. Hong Kong: Chinese University of Hong Kong, 1976.

Davis, *Penguin*—A. R. Davis, ed. *The Penguin Book of Chinese Verse*. Translations by Robert Kotewall and Norman L. Smith. Baltimore: Penguin Books, 1962.

Debon, *Mein Haus*—Günther Debon, translator. *Mein Haus liegt Menschen fern doch nah den Dingen. Dreitausend Jahre chinesischer Poesie*. Munich: Eugen Diedrichs, 1988.

Debon, *Tang-Zeit*—Günther Debon, translator. *Chinesische Dichter der Tang-Zeit*. Stuttgart: Reclam, 1975.

Demiéville, *Anthologie*—Paul Demiéville. *Anthologie de la poésie chinoise classique*. Paris: Gallimard, 1962.

DZ—*Zhengtong Daozang* 正統道藏.

Edwards, *Prose Literature*—E. D. Edwards, *Chinese Prose Literature of the T'ang Period: A.D. 618–906* 2v. London: Arthur Probsthain, 1974.

Egan, *Clouds*—Charles Egan. *Clouds Thick, Whereabouts Unknown, Poems by Zen Monks of China*. New York: Columbia University, 2010.

List of Abbreviations

Field, "Taking Up the Plow"—Stephen Field. "Taking Up the Plow: Real and Ideal Version of the Farmer in Chinese Literature." Unpublished Ph.D. dissertation, University of Texas, 1985.

Frankel, *Palace Lady*—Hans H. Frankel. *The Flowering Plum and the Palace Lady*. New Haven: Yale University, 1976.

Fu, *Shiren*—Fu Xuancong 傅璇琮. *Tangdai shiren congkao* 唐代詩人叢考. Beijing: Zhonghua Shuju, 1980.

Fu, *Tang caizi zhuan*—Fu Xuancong 傅璇琮. *Tang caizi zhuan jiaojian* 唐才子傳校箋. 6v. Beijing: Zhonghua, 1987.

Graham, *Late T'ang*—A. C. Graham. *Poems of the Late T'ang*. Middlesex and Baltimore: Penguin Books, 1965.

Gundert, *Lyrik*—Wilhelm Gundert, ed. *Lyrik des Ostens: China*. München: C. Hanser, 1958.

Hanan, *Vernacular Story*—Patrick Hanan. *The Chinese Vernacular Story*. Cambridge, Mass..: Harvard University, 1981.

HJAS—*Harvard Journal of Asiatic Studies*

Hsü, *Anthologie*—S. N. Hsü. *Anthologie de la littérature chinoise des origines à nos jours*. Paris: Librairie Delagrave, 1933.

Hu-Sterk, Florence. *Ainsi bat l'autre cœur—Anthologie commentée de poèmes d'amour chinois*. Paris: Éditions Yorku-feng, 2008.

Iriya—Irya Kyōju Ogawa Kyōju taikyū kinen Chūgoku bungaku gogaku ronshū 入矢教授小川教授退休記念中國文學語學論集. Tokyo: Hatsubaimoto Chikuma Shobō, 1974.

Jaeger, *Anthologie*—Georgette Jaeger. *L'Anthologie des Trois Cents Poèmes de la Dynastie des Tang*. Beijing: Société des éditions culturelles internationales, 1987.

Jakob, *Poètes*—Paul Jakob. *Poètes bouddhistes des Tang*. Connaissance de l'Orient 58. Paris: Gallimard, 1987.

Jakob, *Vacances*—Paul Jakob. *Vacances du pouvoir—Poèmes des Tang*. Connnaissance de l'Orient 53. Paris: Gallimard, 1983.

JAOS—*Journal of the American Oriental Society*

JCR—*Journal of Chinese Religions*

JOS—*Journal of Oriental Studies*

Jiu Tang shu—*Jiu Tang shu* 舊唐書. Beijing: Zhonghua, 1975.

Kroll, "Recalling Xuanzong"—Paul W. Kroll. "Recalling Xuanzong and Lady Yang: A Selection of Mid- and Late-Tang Poems," *TS* 35 (2017): 1–19.

Levy, *Narrative Poetry*—Levy, Dore J. *Chinese Narrative Poetry: The Late Han Through T'ang Dynasties*. Durham, N.C.: Duke University, 1988.

Lin and Owen, *Vitality*—Shuen-fu Lin and Stephen Owen, eds. *The Vitality of the Lyric Voice, Shih Poery from the Late Han to the T'ang*. Princeton: Princeton University, 1986.

Liu, *Classical Prose*—Shih Shun Liu, trans. *Chinese Classical Prose: The Eight Masters of the T'ang-Sung Period*. Hong Kong: Chinese University, 1979.

Luo, *Lunwen xuan*—Luo Liantian 羅聯添, ed. *Zhongguo wenxue shi lunwen xuan* 中國文學史論文選. 4v. Taibei: Taiwan Xuesheng, 1979.

Mair, *Anthology*— Victor H. Mair, ed. *The Columbia Anthology of Traditional Chinese Literature*. New York: Columbia University, 1994.

Mair, "Tang Poems"—Denis Mair. "Tang Poems as Vehicles for Ideas," in *Hawai'i Reader in Traditional Chinese Culture*. Victor H. Mair, Nancy S. Steinhardt and Paul Goldin, eds. Honolulu: University of Hawai'i, 2005, pp. 340–48.

Margouliès, *Anthologie*—Georges Margouliès. *Anthologie raisonnée de la littérature chinoise*. Paris: Payot, 1948.

Margouliès, *Kou-wen*—Georges Margouliès, ed. and trans. *Le Kou-wen chinois; recueil de textes avec introduction et notes*. Paris: Paul Geuthner, 1925.

Margouliès, *Prose*—Georges Margouliès. *Histoire de la littérature chinoise: prose*. Paris: Payot, 1949.

McMullen, "Literary Theory"—David L. McMullen. "Historical and Literary Theory in the Middle-Eighth Century." In Arthur F. Wright and Denis Twitchett, ed. *Perspectives on the T'ang*. New Haven: Yale University, 1973. pp. 307–342.

Miao, *Studies*—Ronald C. Miao, ed. *Studies in Chinese Poetry and Poetics*. V. 1. San Francisco: Chinese Materials Center, 1978.

Miao, "T'ang Quatrains"—Ronald C. Miao, "Poetics of the T'ang Quatrains." In *Excursions in Chinese Culture*. Marie Chan et al., eds. Hong Kong: The Chinese University, 2002, pp. 47–97.

Minford and Lau—John Minford and Joseph S. M. Lau, eds. *An Anthology of Translations, Classical Chinese Literature, Volume I: From Antiquity to the Tang Dynasty*. New York and Hong Kong: Columbia University Press, Chinese University, 2000.

MS—*Monumenta Serica*.

New *Directions*—*The New Directions Anthology of Classical Chinese Poetry*. Eliot Weinberger, ed. New York: New Directions, 2003. Translations by William Carlos Williams, Ezra Pound, Kenneth Rexroth, Gary Snyder, and David Hinton.

Nienhauser, *Liu*—William H. Nienhauser, Jr. et al. *Liu Ts'ung-yüan*. New York: Twayne 1973.

Nienhauser, *Tang Dynasty Tales*—William H. Nienhauser, Jr., ed. *Tang Dynasty Tales, A Guided Reader*. Singapore: World Scientific, 2010.

Ōgawa, *Tōdai*—Ōgawa Tamaki 小川環樹, comp. *Tōdai no shijin—sono denki* 唐代の詩人 — その傳記. Tokyo: Taishūkan Shoten, 1975.

Orchid Boat—Kenneth Rexroth and Ling Chung, trans. *Orchid Boat*. New York: McGraw-Hill, 1972.

Owen, "Deadwood"—Stephen Owen. "Deadwood: The Barren Tree from Yü Hsin to Han Yü." *CLEAR*, 1.2 (July 1979) pp. 157–179.

Owen, *Early T'ang*— Stephen Owen, *The Poetry of the Early T'ang*. New Haven: Yale University, 1977.

Owen, *High T'ang*— Stephen Owen, *The Great Age of Chinese Poetry: The High T'ang*. New Haven: Yale University, 1981.

Owen, *Late Tang*— Stephen Owen, *The Late Tang: Chinese Poetry of the Mid-Ninth Century (827–860)*. Cambridge, Mass.: Harvard University Asia Center, 2006.

Owen, *Meng Chiao*—Stephen Owen, *The Poetry of Meng Chiao and Han Yü*. New Haven: Yale University, 1975.

Owen, *Middle Ages*—Stephen Owen, *The End of the Chinese 'Middle Ages': Essays in Mid-Tang Literary Culture*. Stanford: Stanford University, 1996.

Owen, *Omen*—Stephen Owen, *Traditional Chinese Poetry and Poetics: Omen of the World*. Madison: University of Wisconsin, 1985.

List of Abbreviations

Owen, *Remembrances*—Stephen Owen, *Remembrances, The Experience of the Past in Classical Chinese Literature.* Cambridge, Mass.: Harvard University, 1986.

P—Pelliot Chinois manuscript collection, Biblioteque Nationale.

Perspectives—Denis Twitchett and Hans H. Frankel, eds. *Perspectives on the T'ang.* New Haven: Yale University, 1973.

Pimpaneau—Jacques Pimpaneau. *Anthologie de la littérature chinoise classique.* Arles: Pilippe Picquier, 2004.

Pindu cidian—Li Jianguo 李劍國. *Tang Song chuanqi pindu cidian* 唐宋傳奇品讀辭典. 2v. Beijing: Xinshijie, 2007.

Quan Tang shi—*Quan Tang shi* 全唐詩. 12v. Beijing: Zhonghua, 1960.

Quan Tang wen—*Qinding quan Tang wen* 欽定全唐文. 20v. Taibei: Qiwen, 1961. Facsimile reproduction of 1814 edition.

Reading Du Fu– Xiaofei Tian, ed. *Reading Du Fu: Nine Views.* Hong Kong: Hong Kong University, 2020.

S—Stein Chinois manuscript collection, Biblioteque Nationale.

Schafer, *Golden Peaches*—Edward H. Schafer. *The Golden Peaches of Samarkand: A Study of T'ang Exotics.* Berkeley: University of California, 1963.

Schafer, *Vermilion Bird*—*The Vermilion Bird: T'ang Images of the South.* Berkeley: University of California, 1967.

SKQS—*Siku quanshu* 四庫全書.

SBBY—*Sibu beiyao* 四部備要. Shanghai, 1927–1937. Rpt. Taibei, 1966.

SBCK—Zhang Yuanji 張元濟, ed. *Sibu congkan* 四部叢刊. 3rd series. Shanghai: Shangwu Yinshuguan, 1919–1937.

Sunflower—*Sunflower Splendor: Three Thousand Years of Chinese Poetry.* Wu-chi Liu and Irving Yucheng Lo, eds. Garden City, NY: Anchor Books, 1975.

Suzuki, *Tōdai*—Suzuki Shūji. *Todāi shijin ron* 唐代詩人論. 2v. Tokyo: Ōtori Shuppan, 1973.

Tangren xiaoshuo—Wang Pijiang 汪辟疆, ed. *Tangren xiaoshuo* 唐人小說. Shanghai: Shanghai Gudian Wenxue, 1983.

Tangshi yanjiu—*Tangshi yanjiu lunwen ji* 唐詩研究論文集. Beijing: Renmin Wenxue, 1959.

Tangwen shiyi—Lu Xinyuan 陸心源, ed. *Tangwen shiyi* 唐文拾遺. 3v. Taibei: Wenhai, 1962.

T—*Taishō Shinshū Daizōkyō* 大正新脩大藏經 (Taishō Canon).

TDCS—*Tangdai congshu* 唐代叢書.

THM—*T'ien-hsia Monthly.*

Traditional Chinese Stories—Y. W. Ma and Joseph S. M. Lau, eds. *Traditional Chinese Stories: Themes and Variations.* New York: Columbia University, 1978.

TS—*Tang Studies*

Waley, *Chinese Poems*—Arthur Waley. *Chinese Poems: Selected from 170 Chinese Poems.* London: George Allen and Unwin, 1962.

Waley, *More*—Arthur Waley. *More Translations from the Chinese, The Temple and The Book of Songs.* London: George Allen and Unwin, 1946.

Waley, *Po Chü-i*—*The Life and Times of Po Chü-i.* London: George Allen and Unwin, 1949.

Waley, *The Temple*—*The Temple, and Other Poems.* New York: Persee, 1926.

Waley, *Translations*—*Translations from the Chinese.* New York: A.A. Knopf, 1941.

Watson, *Columbia*—Burton Watson, trans. and ed. *The Columbia Book of Chinese Poetry from Early Times to the Thirteenth Century*. New York: Columbia University, 1984.

Watson, *Lyricism*—Burton Watson. *Chinese Lyricism*. New York: Columbia University, 1971.

White Pony—*The White Pony: An Anthology of Chinese Poetry*. Robert Payne, ed. New York: Mentor, 1960.

Wu, *Decadence*—Fusheng Wu. *The Poetics of Decadence: Chinese Poetry of the Southern Dynasties and Late Tang Periods*. Albany: SUNY, 1998.

Xin Tang shu—*Xin Tang shu* 新唐書. Beijing: Zhonghua, 1975.

XXSKQS—*Xuxiu Siku quanshu* 續修四庫全書.

Yang Xianyi, *Poetry and Prose*—Yang Xianyi and Gladys Yang, translators. *Poetry and Prose of the Tang and Song*. Beijing: Panda Books, 1984.

Yu, *Imagery*—Pauline Yu. *The Reading of Imagery in the Chinese Poetic Tradition*. Princeton: Princeton University, 1987.

von Zach, *Han Yü*—Erwin von Zach. *Han Yü's poetische Werke*. Cambridge, MA: Harvard-Yenching Institute Studies, 1952.

Zan Ning—Zan Ning 贊寧 (919–1001), compiler. *Song Gaoseng zhuan* 宋高僧傳. Fan Xiangyong 范祥雍, ed. Beijing: Zhonghua, 1987.

Zhan, *Daojiao*—Zhan Shichuang 詹石窗. *Daojiao wenxue shi* 道教文學史. Shanghai: Shanghai Wenyi, 1992.

Zhenben—*Siku quanshu zhenben* 四庫全書珍本.

Tang Emperors

Gaozu 高祖 (Li Yuan 李淵, 565–635), r. 618–626
Taizong 太宗 (Li Shimin 李世民, 597–649), r. 626–649
Gaozong 高宗, Li Zhi 李治, later Li Zhe 李哲 (628–683, r. 649–683)
Zhongzong 中宗 (Li Xian 李顯, 656–710), r. 684
Ruizong 睿宗 (Li Dan 李旦, 662–716), r. 684–690
Zhou 周 Dynasty, 690–705 (Wu Zetian 武則天, 624–705), r. 690–705
Zhongzong, r. 705–710
Shangdi 殤帝 (Li Chongmao 李重茂, 695–714), r. 710
Ruizong, r. 710–712
Xuanzong 玄宗 (Li Longji 李隆基, 685–762), r. 712–756
Suzong 肅宗 (Li Heng 李亨, 711–762), r. 756–762
Daizong 代宗 (Li Yu 李豫, 727–779), r. 762–779
Dezong 德宗 (Li Kuo 李适, 742–805), r. 779–805
Shunzong 順宗 (Li Song 李誦, 761–806), r. 805
Xianzong 憲宗 (Li Chun 李純, 778–820), r. 806–820
Muzong 穆宗 (Li Heng 李恆, 795–824), r. 820–824
Jingzong 敬宗 (Li Zhan 李湛, 809–826), r. 824–827
Wenzong 文宗 (Li Ang 李昂, 809–840), r. 827–840
Wuzong 武宗 (Li Yan 李炎, 814–846), r. 840–846
Xuanzong 宣宗 (Li Chen 李忱, 810–859), r. 846–859
Yizong 懿宗 (Li Cui 李漼, 843–873), r. 859–873
Xizong 僖宗(Li Xuan 李儇, 862–888), r. 873–888
Zhaozong 昭宗 (Li Ye 李曄, 867–904), r. 888–904
Aidi 哀帝 or Zhaoxuandi 昭宣帝 (Li Zhu 李柷, 892–908), r. 904–907

Introduction: An Overview of Tang Literature

The Tang (618–907) dynasty is the only era for which no western-language biographical dictionary is available. Yet the period is one of the most important in Chinese literary history. Tang culture encompasses the interactions between the scholarship of the South, inherited from the preceding regimes, and that of the North, that the new rulers represented. The Tang pits the new literate class of families rising slowly on the social scale against the hereditary aristocrats lingering from the previous dynasties whom this new group hoped to replace. It juxtaposes the foreigners who flowed into the Tang capital Chang'an from all directions to those Han Chinese born or drawn to the city, all set upon an intellectual topography grounded by popular religion, Daoism, Buddhism and Confucianism. In short, it is one of the most diverse and fascinating periods of Chinese history.

Tang literature varied from traditional verse (*shi* 詩) and the legendarium of tales written in classical Chinese to the lyrics (*ci* 詞) of the wine shops and the stories of the marketplace that enlivened Buddhist proselytizing. The era is best known for its traditional poems of which nearly fifty thousand are extant. The Tang is also distinguished by new genres besides the tale and the lyric, such as the discursive essay (*lun* 論), derived from Buddhist writings in the century prior to the Tang, and the prose *fu* (*wenfu* 文賦); and by innovations in style, including both refinement of parallel-style prose (*pianwen* 駢文) and the advancement of ancient-style prose (*guwen* 古文). Most of these styles and genres became dominant in the subsequent Song 宋 dynasty (960–1269). Religious writings, such as records of immortals (*xianlu* 仙錄), transformation texts (*bianwen* 變文 –which also included secular narratives), Buddhist scriptures (notably those translated by Xuanzang 玄奘 [602–664] and Amoghavajra [Bukong 不空, 705–774]*),[1] as well as hymns and songs adapted especially by Chan Buddhists, expressed the experiences and inspirations of their authors, all written under the growing influence of vernacular language.

This volume offers critical, short biographies of 140 literati who lived between the seventh and tenth centuries, including all major literary figures of this period. Of these biographies 63 have been written for this volume (indicated by a plus sign "+" following their name in the Table of Contents); the remaining 77 are based upon entries that originally appeared in the two volumes of the *Indiana Companion to Traditional Chinese Literature*. Those earlier accounts, moreover, have been revised, removing errors in fact and form, and adding translations and short close readings of exemplary selections from their literary corpus, many examples appearing in translation for

---

[1] Those authors marked with asterisks have entries in the main text below.

Introduction

the first time. Since the biographies of these men and women in official histories, when they exist, are court-centered political narratives, it is through poetry and the more personal prose genres (prefaces and letters) that the personalities of these writers can been seen more clearly.

The dynasty in which these men and women wrote began by consolidating much that the preceding short-lived Sui 隨 dynasty (581–617) had achieved. The first Tang rulers like their predecessors were descended from the northwestern aristocracy and had heavily intermarried with the Turkic nobilities. They claimed descent from Laozi and worked to unify the empire that had been split internally by the various rebels against the Sui and threatened externally by the Turks themselves. They also worked to reduce the power of the northwestern great clans by appointing members of the houses from the east and south to balance the court. Following the brief interregnum of Empress Wu Zetian's 武則天 Zhou 周 dynasty (684–705), this unification was completed by Emperor Xuanzong 玄宗 (r. 713–756). Xuanzong also further reduced the power of the great clans by employing more officials who had passed the civil-service exams. Through the first three decades his rule, he mentored a cultural effluence that many believe has never been matched. He abdicated at the onset of the An Lushan Rebellion (756–763), a revolt that his own neglect of government had precipitated. His successors oversaw the dismemberment of its empire, a process which accelerated after the reign of Xianzong 顯宗 (806–820). Yet the legacy established in the first century of the Tang in government administration, law, and culture extended well beyond its final years. The technical accomplishments in fields such as sculpture, ceramics, metalworking, and textiles, and, most significantly, the literary arts, are unique in Chinese history. The Tang also marked the largest Chinese empire before the Qing dynasty (1644–1911), encompassing significant parts of what are now Kyrghstan and Vietnam, overseen by the local governments of nearly 1600 *xian* 縣 or counties.

The Tang was also religiously diverse, with both Buddhism and Daoism influencing the common people, the literati, and the royal house. The population, supported by extensive new lands opened to agriculture in the Yangzi Valley, reached more than 50,000,000, and the cosmopolitan capital, Chang'an, was one of the largest cities in the world and swollen in part by the literati who flocked there. Other than a few major cities, the prefectural cities and towns were much less desirable sites for a residence or an official post.

Most of the literati featured in this volume lived what could be considered a typical career. This would involve service both in the capital and in provincial administrations. There they were charged with—among other things—maintenance of law and order, record keeping, written communications with the throne and central government, and, increasingly after 820, with the defense of the realm. This provincial service enhanced the close ties between literary skills and work at the county (*xian* 縣), prefectural (*zhou* 州), and circuit (*dao* 道) levels. These literary skills were honed by members of all strata of the elite and tested in over twenty types of examinations, the most prestigious begin the presented-scholar (*jinshi* 進士) examination, held annually in the capital. The examination in part required composition in two poetic genres, the traditional *shi* 詩 (poem) and the euphuistic *fu* 賦 (sometimes rendered "rhapsody"—see also "On Using This Book"). Up to 2000 candidates competed, most recommended by prefects; they were known as "local tribute," *xianggong* 鄉貢. On average only 1–2% of the candidates passed each year (around 30 men). There were also two examinations focusing on the classics, the "clarifying the classics" (*mingjing* 明經), which had a higher rate of success (15%) but which few literati took (the best known of them was Yuan Zhen 元積 [779–831]*) and the "nine-classics" (*jiujing* 九經) examinations, the latter passed by Du Guangting 杜光庭 (850–933).* Success in these preliminary selection examinations did not always lead immediately to an official position, but passing the subsequent promotional examinations (such as the "preeminent talent" or *bacui* 拔萃 examination) increased the likelihood of gaining a position either in or near the capital, Chang'an. Life in this city of nearly 2,000,000 people and service in the central administration there were the goal of all literati-officials.

Successful candidates often found themselves appointed as Editors in the Palace Library, a choice entry position. This was the case for Jia Zhi 賈至 (718–772),* Li Duan 李端 (d. ca. 787),* Li Pin 李頻 (d. ca. 876),* Liu Yuxi 劉禹錫 (772–842),* Liu Zongyuan 柳宗元 (773–819),* and Zhu Kejiu 朱可久 (fl. 826),* although Zhu, like many others, had to struggle for several years before he was appointed to office. Bo Juyi 白居易 (772–846)* and Yuan Zhen also first served as Editors, albeit after passing an advanced promotional examination. Gu Kuang 顧況 (ca. 725–ca. 814)* was made Editor as the result of the support of Liu Hun 柳渾 (715–789) without passing any examination. Zhu Kejiu attained the same position because of Zhang Ji's 張籍 (ca. 766–829)* support. Other successful candidates like Du Shenyan 杜審言 (ca. 645–708),* Dugu Ji 獨孤及 (725–777),* and Geng Wei 耿湋 (*jinshi* 763, d. after 787) were made commandants (*wei* 尉) in areas close to the capital. Sikong Shu 司空曙 (ca. 720–790)* was appointed Reminder on the Left in the period following the An Lushan Rebellion when it seems higher ranks were available to these young scholars. Li Shen 李紳 (772–846),* after passing the *jinshi*, became an Instructor in the National University. Sun Qiao 孫樵 (*jinshi* 855)* was appointed Secretariat Drafter after his examination success.

There were, however, other means to become an official. Especially after the An Lushan Rebellion, when the staffs of military commissioners had grown, some literati sought positions working for these provincial officials: Cen Shen 岑參 (ca. 715–770),* Du Mu 杜牧 (803–ca. 852),* Li Ao 李翱 (774–836),* Li Shangyin 李商隱 (ca. 813–858), and Ouyang Zhan 歐陽詹 (ca. 755–ca. 800)* are notable examples. Li Shangyin's early career was then promoted by his patron, Linghu Chu 令狐楚 (ca. 766–837), much as Zhang Yue 張說 (667–731)* advanced He Zhizhang 賀知章 (ca. 659–744).* Still other literati found positions via the protection privilege (*yin* 蔭), which allowed sons and grandsons of officials to be conferred official status, but not necessarily appointments: Luo Binwang, who became a companion to Prince Dao 道王, Wang Zhihuan 王之渙 (688–742),* who was appointed an Assistant Magistrate, and Wei Yingwu 韋應物 (737–ca. 791),* who first served as an imperial guard for Emperor Xuanzong, all used this privilege to start their careers.

After these initial positions and decisions, literati-officials were often appointed to posts far from their homes and the capital. Moreover, they were regularly moved from one area to another, assuring that separation and longing for loved ones were major themes in both poetry and prose. Indeed, a position in the provinces often provided the opportunity for periods of great literary accomplishment; Bo Juyi, Du Fu 杜甫 (712–770),* Han Yu 韓愈 (768–824),* and Liu Zongyuan are prime examples of authors whose major works were produced away from the capital.

The constant movement and search for official careers prompted many literati to exchange letters, many of which remain extant to form a genre of Tang writing all its own. Traditional Chinese letters are of two types: personal communications and those epistles meant to be shared with the reading public—that is, other scholar-officials. Although many dealt with questions of historical (see Liu Zhiji 劉知集 [661–721]* for an example) or literary composition (see Liu Mian

Introduction

柳冕 [d. 804],* **Sikong Tu** 司空圖 [837–908],* Wang Wei 王維 [ca. 699–761]*), and some simply passed on news to old friends (see Bo Juyi [772–846]*), a great number were written by scholars seeking preferment from a powerful official for the writer himself (Li Bo 李白 [701–762],* Li Guan 李觀 [766–794],* and Xiao Yingshi 蕭穎士 [717–760]*) or for a friend or colleague (Han Yu 韓愈 [768–824]*). Some letters expressed the frustration of years spent in exile (Liu Zongyuan 柳宗元 [773–819]*).

An alternative to a secular official career was to escape from the mundane to the world of Buddhism, as Amoghavajra (Amuqubazheluo 阿目佉跋折羅, also known by his courtesy name Bukong 不空), Falin 法琳 (571–640),* Guanxiu 貫休 (832–912),* Jiao Ran 皎然 (ca. 730–799),* Judun 居遁 (835–923),* Lingche 靈澈 (746–816),* Lingyou 靈祐 (771–853),* Qiji 齊己 (fl. 881),* Qingjiang 清江 (d. ca. 806), Wuke 無可 (fl. 825–827),* Xuanjue 玄覺 (665/675–713),* Xuantai 玄泰 (ca. 850–ca. 912),* and Xuzhong 虛中 (fl. 897–942)* did. Similarly, many literati, including Cao Tang 曹唐 (ca. 797–ca. 866),* Cheng Xuanying 成玄英 (fl. 631–653),* Cui Zhongrong 崔仲容 (8th century), Daoshi 道世 (597–683),* Du Guangting 杜光庭 (850–933),* Gu Feixiong 顧非熊 (ca. 795–ca. 854),* Gu Kuang, Lu Guimeng 陸龜蒙 (ca. 836–881),* Luo Yin 羅隱 (833–909),* Sima Chengzhen 司馬承禎 (647–735),* Sun Simiao 孫思邈 (ca. 581–682),* Zhang Ben 張賁 (fl. ca. 850),* and Yu Xuanji 魚玄機 (705–774),* espoused Daoism and withdrew from society. Yu was a Daoist nun and poet and Cui a priestess in the Shangqing 上清 (Highest Clarify) tradition, joining Li Jilan 李季蘭 (d. 784),* Shangguan Wan'er 上官婉兒 (664–710),* Xue Tao 薛濤 (768–831),* and Yuan Chun 元淳 (ca. 720–ca. 779)* in representing the distaff in this volume.

Those depicted in these pages for the most part did not view themselves as literati, but rather as government officials. The Chinese term *shi dafu* 士大夫 means both "literatus" and "official." The intricate link between the presented-scholar examination, which was the main means of entry to officialdom, and the literary works required by that examination, allowed almost all educated Chinese of the Tang era the ability to compose poetry; thus most officials could also be considered literati. This examination system also served to break the monopoly that the great clans had held on the highest offices of the state for previous centuries, especially after the examination system was expanded in the last half of the seventh century under Empress Wu 武后 (624–705, r. 690–705). Concomitant with this expansion was the increase in poets and poetry, since the examinations stressed, in addition to mastery of Confucian and Daoist texts, literary skill, especially in the *shi* (poetry) and *fu* (prose-poetry) genres (as noted above). Estimates for poetry written in the centuries before the Tang range from 4000 to 5000 works, but the Tang alone left us nearly 50,000 poems by almost 2200 poets. The major poets include (in chronological order) Wang Wei 王維 (ca. 699–761),* Li Bo 李白 (also known as Li Bai, 李白, 701–762),* Du Fu, Meng Haoran 孟浩然 (689–740),* Wei Yingwu 韋應物 (737–792), Han Yu, Meng Jiao 孟郊 (751–814),* Bo Juyi, Liu Yuxi 劉禹錫 (772–842),* Yuan Zhen, Li He 李賀 (791–817),* Li Shangyin, Du Mu, Wen Tingyun 溫庭筠 (ca. 812–870),* and Wei Zhuang 韋莊 (ca. 836–910).* Although many of their works have been lost, over 12,000 poems by these 15 poets remain.[2]

Despite the emphasis on *shi* poetry, Tang verse varied in style and genre. In the Early Tang (618–712) court poetry reflected the legacy of the euphuistic styles of the preceding Qi and Liang

---

[2] The top five are Bo Juyi (around 3,000 extant poems), Du Fu (nearly 1500), Li Bo (nearly 1000), Yuan Zhen (nearly 900) and Qiji 齊己 ([fl. 881],* over 800).

dynasties and with many poems written at imperial order (see the entries on Xu Jingzong 許敬宗 [592–672],* Shangguan Yi 上官儀 [ca. 607–ca. 665],* Shen Quanqi 沈佺期 [656–716],* Song Zhiwen 宋之問 [656–ca. 712],* Li Jiao 李嶠 [ca. 644–ca. 714],* and Su Ting 蘇頲 [670–727]).* A century later saw the first literati examples of the *ci*-lyric. Poets such as Li Bo and Gao Shi 高適 (700–765),* also wrote songs (*ge* 歌). Those with court connections (Liu Zongyuan, for example) wrote hymns and texts for court ritual. Two transitional figures, Chen Zi'ang 陳子昂 (659–ca. 699) and Zhang Yue, stepped away from the limited vocabularies and themes of court verse, preparing the way for the famous generation of High Tang (713-779) poets led by Wang Wei, Li Bo and Du Fu. Wang Wei combined his study of Chan Buddhism with an interest in the natural world in his verse (see also Meng Haoran, Qian Qi 錢起 [720–ca. 783],* and Wei Yingwu). In Du Fu's hands the eight-lined "regulated verse" (*lüshi* 律詩, see "On Using This Book" and entries for Song Zhiwen, Shangguan Yi, and Shen Quanqi) was perfected. Li Bo excelled at the shorter version, *jueju* 絕句 (quatrains). Li's traditional *yuefu* 樂府 (music-bureau songs or ballads), which called for content related to the original Han-dynasty tunes; see also Shen Quanqi, Gao Shi, Linghu Chu, and Meng Jiao) gave way to Du Fu's new style of socially-critical ballads (see also Wang Jian 王建 [ca. 766–ca. 830]*). The Tang was also an encyclopedic era that saw the compilation of several anthologies of poetry and prose (see Daoshi and Xu Jingzong, for example).

The new-ballad movement in poetry was in part tied to the social and intellectual changes brought about by the gradual influx of men from the lower-level elite into officialdom (chiefly via the presented-scholar examination). These men inherited the intellectual changes brought about by the ideas of the court-appointed historians who produced a number of dynastic histories in the mid-seventh century, as well as by the reaction to their work by the historiographer Liu Zhiji in his *Shitong* 史通 (Generalities on Historiography). Liu laid the groundwork for what later became a distinction between history and fiction. The new-ballad poets of the early ninth century were already creating fictional narratives in which they would encounter a peasant who would then comment eloquently on some social ill (see Du Fu, Zhang Ji, Wang Jian, Bo Juyi, Yuan Zhen, Li Shen, and Pi Rixiu 皮日休 (ca. 834–ca. 883).*

At about the same time—the early years of the Mid Tang (780–835)—iconoclastic thinkers like Lu Chun 陸淳 (d. 805), calling for a rejection of intervening commentaries and a return to the texts of the classics themselves, spawned the *fugu* 復古 or "return-to-antiquity movement." Soon thereafter, writers like Han Yu and Liu Zongyuan were crafting fictional "pseudo-biographies" of invented protagonists such as Liu's "Bushezhe shuo" 捕蛇者說 (The Argument of the Snake Catcher) or allegories like Han's "Maoying zhuan" 毛穎傳 (An Account of Tip of the Writing Brush). Meanwhile, other scholars—many involved in official historical projects—wrote some of the first Tang tales (*chuanqi* 傳奇). The term *chuanqi* is a modern invention and the corpus of the several hundred narratives that have been identified under this term vary in theme, length, and technique. The earliest Tang tale was "Gujing ji" 古鏡記 (Record of an Ancient Mirror) which is a pastiche of different sources probably written by Wang Du 王度 (fl. 620) and then revised by later hands. Some of these works can be considered the first created works of fiction (as opposed to the *zhiguai* 志怪, records of the strange) which preceded them in the pre-Tang era. The authors of the *chuanqi* often sat together, rehearsing stories they had heard and then turning them into polished tales in what was then the classical language (see Shen Yazhi 沈亞之 [781–832]*). Whether or not they are the first creative fictional works, they are certainly the first records of

Introduction

entertainment literature and they continued to provide material for later related entertainment genres such as drama and vernacular-language fiction. Other tales such as Bo Xinjian's 白行簡 (776–826)* "Li Wa zhuan" 李娃傳 (An Account of Beauty Li) were love tales of young scholars and courtesans, some tragic, some melodramatic. Jiang Fang's 蔣防 (fl. 820) "Huo Xiaoyu zhuan" 霍小玉傳 (An Account of Huo Xiaoyu) and Yuan Zhen's 元稹 (773–831)* "Yingying zhuan" 鶯鶯傳 (An Account of Yingying) directly or indirectly criticize the way scholars sometimes took advantage of these women. Another early tale, "Youxian ku" 遊仙窟 (The Grotto of Wandering Transcendents) by Zhang Zhuo 張鷟 (ca. 657–730),* contains scenes of erotic intensity involving the narrator and two fairy-like women he discovered while traveling. Shen Jiji's 沈既濟 (ca. 740–ca. 800)* "Renshi zhuan" 任氏傳 (Account of Ms. Ren), on the other hand, reveals how a female fox-spirit demonstrates morals that put to shame her real-life sisters. Other tales record fantastic dreams, such as Li Gongzuo 李公佐 (ca. 770–ca. 848)* "Nanke Taishou zhuan" 南柯太守傳 or Shen Yazhi's "Qin meng ji" 秦夢記 (Record of a Dream of Qin). Shen also wrote a narrative about a knight-errant, "Feng Yan zhuan" 馮燕傳 (An Account of Feng Yan) that seems to be based on fact. The late eighth and early ninth century marked the apex of these works. After 830 most of the tales were shorter, often involved the supernatural, and were collected by compilers such as Pei Xing 裴鉶 (ca. 825–ca. 880)* and Li Deyu 李德裕 (787–850).* Their collections, *Chuanqi* 傳奇 (The Tales) and *Xuanguai lu* 玄怪錄 (Records of the Mysterious and Strange), are the best known. But authors such as Du Guangting 杜光庭 (850–933),* who also compiled Daoist hagiographies, left us a few notable stories such as his "Qiuran Ke zhuan" 虬髯客傳 (An Account of the Curly-bearded Stranger). Although we know little about many of the authors of these tales, it seems that almost as many scholars were involved in transmitting or recording the oral versions of these texts as there were Tang poets (see also Luo Yin 羅隱 [833–909]* and Han Hong 韓翃 [fl. 754].*

The same iconoclasm that led to a differentiation between the historical and the fictive, also fostered the ancient-style-prose movement (*guwen yundong* 古文運動) led by Xiao Yingshi 蕭穎士 (717–760),* Liang Su 梁肅 (753–793),* Liu Mian, Liu Zongyuan, Han Yu, and Han's followers. Despite the popularity of the new prose style among these major writers, parallel prose (*pianwen* 駢文) remained the medium for all court documents (see Wang Bo 王勃 [650–676],* Luo Binwang, Su Ting, Zhang Yue, Chang Gun 常袞 [729–783],* Jia Zhi, Lu Zhi 陸贄 [754–805],* and Quan Deyu 權德興 [761–818]*).

Two major poets of the Mid Tang, Bo Juyi and Yuan Zhen, established a subgenre in the 810s known as the Yuanhe Style 元和體 after the then current reign era (Yuanhe, 806–820). Bo Juyi intended his verse to be understood by a wider audience and argued that one of the goals of writing should be to foster social change (as did Yuan Jie 元結 [719–772])* and Pi Rixiu. Frontier verse (*biansai shi* 邊塞詩), which had begun in the High Tang in the works of Cen Shen, Gao Shi and Wang Changling 王昌齡 (ca. 690–ca. 756),* continued in the Mid Tang especially with Lu Lun 盧綸 (748-ca. 798)* and Lü Wen 呂溫 (772–811).* Li He and Li Shangyin, in diametric opposition to Bo and Yuan, favored allusive poems and allegories (see Chen Zi'ang) that even their peers found difficult to comprehend. The politics of this era were often tied to factions and which benefitted, at least for a time, men like Li Shangyin (on Li's patron see Linghu Chu; on patrons in general see also Zhang Yue and Zhang Jiuling 張九齡 [678–740]).*

Li Shangyin's life spanned the Mid and the Late Tang (836–907). While Li is probably the best-known poet of the period, Du Mu can be considered a peer. Du's quatrains and longer poems were often tied by allusion to historical parallels, while many of his works were clearly autobiographical. Moreover, despite the suppression of Buddhism in 845, many monks continued to contribute to both religious and secular literature (see Jia Dao 賈島 [779–843],* Jiao Ran, Qiji, Guanxiu, Qingjiang, Wuke, Xuantai, Xuzhong, Xuanjue, and Yuan'an 元安 (835–899]*). As the Tang central government continued to weaken in the second half of the ninth century, reclusion and Daoist themes became more prominent in works by Lu Guimeng, Du Guangting, and Zhang Ben (see also Li Jilan, Li Rong 李榮 [fl. 660–669],* Shi Jianwu 施肩吾 [fl. 820],* Sima Chengzhen, Sun Simiao, and Wu Yun 吳筠 [d. 778]*).

The Late Tang also saw significant changes in the language of literature. Responding to the tunes and musical instruments from Central Asia that had gained popularity among the populace in general, the *ci*-lyric 詞, which Li Bo, Liu Yuxi, and Bo Juyi had experimented with earlier, was established as a literary genre by Wen Tingyun and Wei Zhuang. These two poets created "roomscapes" which often featured a young woman as persona living in luxury but nearly immobilized by her loneliness. Self-indulgence also marks the early verse of Pi Rixiu, who turned radically, as the Tang House faltered, to socially critical poems written in a simple language. The collections of "Hanshan" 寒山* and "Wang *Fanzhi* 王梵志 poems"* span much of the dynasty, but their use of the vernacular accompanies the rise of the *ci*-lyric and adumbrates much of the literature that would characterize the succeeding Song dynasty.

As noted at the start of this essay, this is the first western-language biographical dictionary for the Tang. It is hoped that this volume will not only serve as an accessible introduction to the lives and works of those literati who created what has been called the Golden Age of Chinese literature, but also will provide scholars looking to further their knowledge of these authors, and thus expand on more general overviews like Stephen Owen's *Anthology of Chinese Literature* (W. W. Norton, 1996). The entries and bibliographies in this volume, along with the "Literary Timeline of the Tang" and the references in this Introduction, should provide an outline for further reading on the major Tang literati for readers at any level. It is also hoped that this book will provide the impetus for other reference volumes on Tang political, military, and religious figures.

The Tang is, however, a complex era that rewards broader, interdisciplinary study. To that end, readers are also recommended to consult the following: the "Introduction" to *Perspectives on the T'ang* (Yale, 1973), Denis Twitchett's "Forward" to *Essays on T'ang Society* (Brill, 1976), the "Introduction" to *Tales from the Tang Dynasty* edited by Sarah M. Allen, Alexei Kamran Ditter, and Jessey Choo (Hackett, 2017), Charles Benn's *Daily Life in Traditional China: The Tang Dynasty* (Greenwood, 2002), Mark Edward Lewis's *China's Cosmopolitan Empire, The Tang Dynasty* (Harvard, 2009), and the forthcoming *Cambridge History of China, Volume 4: The Tang Dynasty, Part Two*.

William H. Nienhauser, Jr.
20 June 2021 in Madison

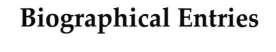

Amoghavajra (Amuqubazheluo 阿目佉跋折羅, *zi*, Bukongjingang 不空金剛 or Bukong 不空, posthumous dharma name Zhizang 智藏, 705–774) is considered one of the most prolific and influential Buddhist monks of the Tang. The scope of his literary production and the range of his activities includes services as a liturge, imperial envoy, and preceptor under the reign of three succeeding emperors, Xuanzong (r. 713–756), Suzong (r. 756–762), and Daizong (r. 762–779).

Biographical sources differ with respect to his ancestry and the circumstances under which he came to China. Of non-Han and probably Sogdian origin, Amoghavajra became a disciple of Vajrabodhi (671–741) in his youth, though there are conflicting accounts on the location where they li Chang'an together. Recognized as a polyglot, Amoghavajra took part in an imperial mission to the kingdom of Sri Lanka shortly after Vajrabodhi's death in 741, and subsequently travelled the southern Indic regions. Amoghavajra outlined his aims in a memorial (dated 771) included in Yuanzhao's 圓照 (727–809) *Daizong chao zeng sikong Da Bianzheng Guangzhi sanzang heshang biaozhi ji* 代宗朝贈司空大辨正廣智三藏和上表制集 (Collection of Documents of the Tripiṭaka monk [Amoghavajra] entitled Great Corrector and Extensive Wisdom, posthumously appointed a Minister of Works by the court of Emperor Daizong; T 2120):

> Then I went to the five parts of India seeking for [the doctrine] that I had not been taught, in order to study again the *sūtras* and *śāstras*. I collected more than five hundred Sanskrit works, *sūtras* and *śāstras* on *yoga* and *mantra*, to have them respectfully offered to the state and to have them translated carefully into imperial language, extensively venerating prosperity and protection. In the fifth year of Tianbao (746) I returned to the capital.
>
> 後遊五夫尋求所未受者并諸經論, 更重學習。凡得梵本瑜伽真言經論五百餘部。奉為國家詳譯聖言, 廣崇福祐。天寶五載却至上都。(T 2120.52.840a)

Upon his return, Amoghavajra was ordered by Emperor Xuanzong to grant him consecration. In response, Amoghavajra received the Purple Robe (*Ziyi* 紫衣), the highest dignity bestowed upon a monk by an emperor, granting the right to access the Imperial Chapel and to participate in governmental assemblies. Such recognition demarcates the scope and character of his future activities: Amoghavajra was repeatedly commissioned to perform consecration ceremonies for officials and military leaders, and in 754 the governor-general Geshu Han 哥舒翰 (d. 757) ordered him to consecrate his troops and to translate the *Sarvatathāgatā-tattva-saṃgraha* (The Compendium of Truth of All the Tathāgatas; T 865). The following paragraph may give an impression of the unwieldy grandeur of this scripture:

> As soon as it had come forth from the hearts of All the Tathāgatas, he, the Lord Vajradhara, became a multitude of wisdom-swords. When they had appeared, they entered the heart of the World-honored One, the Buddha Vairocana, where they combined and became One, producing the form of an adamantine sword, which settled in the Buddha's palm. From this form of an adamantine sword there appeared the figures of Tathāgatas equal [in number] to the dust-motes of all world-systems, and they performed the play of the supernatural powers of all the Buddhas, such as the knowledge-wisdom of All the Tathāgatas.

從一切如來心。纔出已。即彼婆伽梵持金剛。為眾多慧劍。出已。入世尊毘盧遮那佛心。聚為一體。生金剛釰形。住佛掌中。則從彼金剛劍形。出一切世界微塵等如來身。一切如來智慧等。作一切佛神通遊戲。(T 865.18.211b, tr. Giebel 2001, 41)

Amoghavajra based his authority on this scripture, a purportedly fragmentary version of the "first assembly" (*hui* 會) of a legendary full-length text consisting of eighteen assemblies and 100,000 verses, the content of which he summarized in his treatise *Jin'gangding jing yuqie shibahui zhigui* 金剛頂經瑜伽十八會指歸 (Indications of the Goals of the Eighteen Assemblies of the Yoga of the Adamantine Pinnacle Scripture, T 869):

> The Eighteen Assemblies of the Yoga Teachings have either four thousand verses, five thousand verses or seven thousand verses—in all they consist of one hundred thousand verses. They have Five Divisions, four kinds of *maṇḍalas* and four seals, and have thirty-seven deities.... If the practitioner properly masters this general purport of *yoga*, he will be like the Buddha Vairocana... proclaiming the Buddha's teaching of *yoga* not shared with the Two Vehicles.... This enables one to suddenly benefit and delight all sentient beings, bodhisattvas, auditors (*śrāvaka*), dependently enlightened ones (*pratyekabuddha*) and non-Buddhists.

> 瑜伽教十八會, 或四千頌或五千頌或七千頌, 都成十萬頌。具五部四種曼荼羅四印。具三十七尊。(...) 修行者善達此瑜伽中大意。如遍照佛。(...) 演說瑜伽二乘不共佛法。(...) 是能頓作利樂一切有情諸菩薩聲聞緣覺及諸外道。(T 869.18.287b, tr. Giebel 1995, 200)

Presenting himself as the sole authority in possession of the whole teaching, its ritual efficacy was subject to his exclusive expertise therein: such textual policy warranted him a position in close relation to the sumptuous ceremonies commanded by the court, for which he provided the doctrinal, mythical and technical framework in further scriptures. During the An Lushan 安祿山 Rebellion (756–763), he was detained at the capital and stationed in the Daxingshan Monastery 大興善寺, secretly keeping contacts with Tang loyalists and the heir apparent Li Heng 李亨 (711–762), who in 756 declared himself emperor (Suzong) and restored the Tang rule. In 759, Amoghavajra was commanded to consecrate him as *cakravartin*, propagating an unstable regimen as reappearance of universal dominion.

While the succeeding emperor, Daizong, still struggled to consolidate the political and economic control after the demise of the rebellion, Amoghavajra gained access to influential circles at the imperial court. Supported by high officials, powerful eunuchs and military commanders such as Yuan Zai 元載 (d. 771), Wang Jin 王縉 (700–782), Du Hongjian 杜鴻漸 (709–769), and Yu Chaoen 魚朝恩 (722–770), many of them pious Buddhists, Amoghavajra was able to monopolize three basic functions of religious authority: the authentic transmission of doctrine and praxis, directing the liturgy, and the mediation of divine force on behalf of imperial order. During this period, he introduced to the court his teachings of the *Jiaoling lun* 教令論 (Wheel of Instruction and Command), promising control over wrathful deities such as the *Budong mingwang* 不動明王 (*vidyārāja* Acala, Unmoveable King of Clarity), who he had established as a prominent deity since the An Lushan Rebellion. In 765, Amoghavajra's ritual command of Acala and the salvific power of his "translation" of the *Renwang boreboluomi jing* 仁王般若波羅密經 (Scripture on Perfect Insight for Humane Kings, T 245, cf. T 246) was credited for causing the sudden split of a Tibetan-Uigur military alliance that was threatening the Tang.

Amoghavajra rewrote the extant late fifth-century apocryph falsely ascribed to Kumārajīva (344–413) in order to bolster his ritual services of state protection in a moment of imminent crisis. Following the instructions propounded in this scripture, Emperor Daizong ordered one hundred monks to perform the proper rituals whenever a threat occurred, and that a copy be carried ahead of him as soon as he left the palace. Amoghavajra's influence became more and more conspicuous as he gained free access to the inner palace and the license to dispute the ordinances of high officials.

In 767, rituals referring to the *vajradhātu-maṇḍala* and its thirty-seven basic deities were institutionalized all over the country in order to establish imperial dominion as a "field of merit" (*futian* 福田) while the government introduced tax exemptions for Buddhist monasteries. The costly construction work on the palatial Golden Monastery (*Jinge si* 金閣寺) on Mt. Wutai was completed despite the ruinous condition of the state finances. In 769, Amoghavajra, vested with the title Preceptor of State, had his scriptures distributed among the Buddhist clergy to be memorized and recited by imperial decree, and he installed a liturgy dedicated to the bodhisattva Mañjuśrī as a tutelary deity.

Serving in the Imperial Chapel and in monasteries affiliated with the imperial household, he created a comprehensive arsenal of apotropaic and purificatory rituals, rituals for the prolongation of the emperor's life and salvation of the dynastic ancestry, for controlling the weather and for dealing with celestial phenomena. As a result, a large part of his literary work consists of (supposedly translated) ritual manuals, excerpts and supplements indicating the use of practices taught in the sūtras in addition to scriptures that provide doctrinal and mythological contexts.

Combining translation, redaction, compilation, excerption, rewriting, and exegesis, Amoghavajra's wide range of literary production served apotropaic and therapeutic aims for which he organized and directed a sumptuous liturgy that systematically linked Buddhist soteriology with the imperial household, and especially with services of state protection promising control over disorder and the extinction of the enemy. Amoghavajra not only laid claim to privileged access to divine force, but also explicitly referred to the "nine tastes" (Skt. *navarasa*), a concept of Indian dramaturgy, implying close connections between the soteriological and the performative dimension:

> [This liturgy] expounds extensively the principle of reality, as well as explaining the root source of the Five Divisions and explaining the method of *yoga*, which are endowed with the nine tastes: namely, "splendour" (Vajrasattva), "valor" (Vairocana), "great compassion" (Vajradhara), "mirth" (Avalokiteśvara), "anger" (Vajrateja), "terror" (Trailokyavijaya), "disgust" (Śakyamuni Buddha), "wonder" (Vajrahāsa), and tranquility (Vairocana in *yoga*). It explains how the Bodhisattva Samantabhadra and so forth up to Vajramuṣṭi each explain the four kinds of *maṇḍalas*, a ritual for inducting the disciple . . . . It also explains the rituals of song, praise and dance for the Five Divisions.

> 廣說實相理, 并說五部根源, 并說瑜伽法, 具九味。所謂華麗(金剛薩埵)勇健(毘盧遮那)大悲(持金剛)喜笑(觀自在)瞋怒(金剛光)恐怖(降三世)厭患(釋迦牟尼佛)奇特(金剛笑)寂靜(瑜伽中毘盧遮那)說普賢菩薩等, 至金剛拳。各說四種曼荼羅。及引入弟子儀。(...) 并說五部中歌讚舞儀。 (T 869.18.286c, tr. Giebel 1995, 180)

Such scriptural and ceremonial politics allowed him to present himself as a liturge and thaumaturge of universal command able to mediate between the imperial court, military leaders, and the domain of divine force according to the political interests of his supporters. Accorded with honors, titles, official ranks, and fiefs, Amoghavajra depended in particular on the personal recognition he obtained from Emperor Daizong. He clearly understood the politics of his position to address the difficult situation of the embattled state and the crisis of imperial order by establishing a specific body of occult hermeneutics and ritual services for the ruling elite.

Amoghavajra's death in 774 marked the loss of a trusted imperial preceptor and proficient expert whose command of divine forces safeguarded the rule of the Tang in difficult times, a status reflected in the official mourning period of three days and the honorific titles posthumously conferred upon him. Amoghavajra's conception of Buddhist liturgy for state protection influenced later Buddhist masters, notably the eminent Japanese monk Kūkai 空海 (774–835) who claimed to be a heir of Amoghavajra's lineage. In China, however, possibly under the political influence of a growing Confucian opposition in concert with worrisome economic concerns, the costly liturgical services in the Imperial Chapel were halted under the reign of Emperor Dezong (r. 780–805). Amoghavajra's model of Buddhist ritual remained influential though, as it provided a blueprint for subsequent Buddhist practices that ultimately empower the chosen ritual master to compel divine force to defend imperial order and to vanquish its enemies.

BIBLIOGRAPHY

Editions:

The exact number of Amoghavajra's works and the status of his "authorship" are uncertain. According to his own account included in a memorial (d. 771), he "translated 77 works" but the appended catalogue actually lists 71 titles. Some other works may have been produced in the following years or by his disciples. The consecutive editions of the Chinese Tripiṭaka however attribute to Amoghavajra a growing bulk of works of unknown origin up to the total number of 171 works included in the Taishō Tripiṭaka.

Taishō shinshū daizōkyō 大正新修大藏經. Takakusu Junjirō 高楠順次郎 and Watanabe Kaigyoku 渡邊海旭, *et al.* (eds.), 100 vols. Tokyo: Taishō Issaikyō Kankōkai 大正一切經刊行會, 1924–34.

Yamada Isshi 山田一止. *Sarva-tathāgata-tattva-saṅgraha nāma mahāyāna-sūtra: A Critical Edition Based on the Sanskrit Manuscript and Chinese and Tibetan Translations*. New Dehli: Mrs. Sharada Rani, 1981.

Biographical Sources:

Zan Ning, 1:6–16.

Translations:

Astley-Kristensen, Ian. *The Rishukyō. The Sino-Japanese Tantric Prajñāpāramitā in 150 Verses (Amoghavajra's Version)*. Tring: The Institute of Buddhist Studies, 1991.

___. "An Annotated Translation of Amoghavajra's Commentary on the *Liqu jing* (*Rishukyō*) - Part I." *Studies in Central and East Asian Religions* 7 (1994): 27–53.

Giebel, Rolf W. "The *Chin-kang-ting ching* yü-ch'ieh shih-pa-hui chih-kuei: An Annotated Translation." *Journal of Naritasan Institute for Buddhist Studies* 18 (1995): 107–201.

___. *Two Esoteric Sutras: The Adamantine Pinnacle Sutra and the Susiddhikara Sutra*. Berkeley: Numata Center for Buddhist Translation and Research, 2001.

Orzech, Charles D. "The Legend of the Iron Stūpa," in Donald S. Lopez, Jr., ed., *Buddhism in Practice*. Princeton: Princeton University, 1995, pp. 314–17.

___. *Politics and Transcendent Wisdom: The Scripture for Humane Kings in the Creation of Chinese Buddhism*. University Park: Penn State, 1998.

For Japanese translations see the *Kokuyaku issaikyō Indo senjubutsu* 國譯一切經印度撰述部. Iwano Masao 岩野真雄 (ed.), 155 vols. Tokyo: Daitō 大東, 1933–36.

Studies:

Chen, Jinhua. "The Tang Buddhist Palace Chapels."*JCR* 32 (2004): 101–73.

Chou, I-liang. "Tantrism in China." *HJAS* 8 (1945): 241–332.

Goble, Geoffrey C. *Chinese Esoteric Buddhism: Amoghavajra, the Ruling Elite, and the Emergence of a Tradition*. New York: Columbia University Press, 2019.

Hasegawa Takeshi 長谷川岳史. "Fukū yaku kyōten no busshinkan 不空訳経典の仏身観." *Ryūkoku Daigaku ronshū* 龍谷大学論集 453 (1999): 24–40.

Kiyota, Minoru. *Tantric Concept of Bodhicitta: A Buddhist Experiential Philosophy (An Exposition Based upon the Mahāvairocana-sūtra, Bodhicitta-śāstra and Sokushin-jōbutsu-gi)*. Madison: University of Wisconsin-Madison, 1982.

Lehnert, Martin. "Myth and Secrecy in Tang-period Tantric Buddhism," in Bernhard Scheid, Mark Teeuwen (eds.). *The Culture of Secrecy in Japanese Religion*. London, New York: Routledge, 2006, pp. 78–104.

___. "Amoghavajra: His Role in and Influence on the Development of Buddhism," in Charles Orzech, Richard Payne and Henrik Sørensen, eds., *Esoteric Buddhism and the Tantras in East Asia*. Leiden: Brill, 2011, pp. 351–59.

Lü Jianfu 呂建福. *Zhongguo mijiao shi* 中國密教史. Beijing: Zhongguo Shehui Kexue, 1995.

___. "Lun Bukong de zhengjiao sixiang" 論不空的政教思想, in *Shijie zongjiao yanjiu* 世界宗教研究 4 (2010): 39–46.

Matsunaga Yūkei 松長有慶. *Mikkyō no sōjōsha–sono kōdō to shisō* 密教の相承者– その行動と思想. Tokyo: Hyōronsha 評論社, 1973.

McBride, Richard D. "Dhāraṇī and Spells in Medieval Sinitic Buddhism." *Journal of the International Association of Buddhist Studies* 28.1 (2005): 85–114.

Nakata Mie 中田美繪. "Tōchō seijishijō no 'Ninnokyō' honyaku to hōhe" 唐朝政治史上の'仁王經'翻譯と法会. *Shigaku zasshi* 史学雑誌 115.3 (2006): 322–47.

Orlando, Raffaello. "A Study of Chinese Documents Concerning the Life of the Tantric Buddhist Patriarch Amoghavajra (A.D. 705–774)." Unpublished Ph.D. dissertation, Princeton University, 1981.

Orzech, Charles D. "Metaphor, Translation, and the Construction of Kingship in the *Scripture for Humane Kings* and the *Mahāmāyūrī Vidyārājñīsūtra*," *Cahiers d'Extrême-Asie* 13 (2002–2003): 55–83.

___. "The 'Great Teaching of Yoga,' the Chinese Appropriation of the Tantras, and the Question of Esoteric Buddhism." *JCR* 34 (2006): 29–78.

___. "Esoteric Buddhism in the Tang: From Atikūṭa to Amoghavajra (651–780)," in Charles Orzech, Richard Payne and Henrik Sørensen, eds. *Esoteric Buddhism and the Tantras in East Asia*. Leiden: Brill, 2011, pp. 263–85.

Sharf, Robert. "On Esoteric Buddhism in China." Appendix to *Coming to Terms with Chinese Buddhism. A Reading of the Treasure Store Treatise*. Honolulu: University of Hawai'i, 2002, pp. 263–78.

Strickmann, Michel. *Mantras et mandarins. Le bouddhisme tantrique en Chine*. Paris: Éditions Gallimard, 1996.

Wang Yarong 王亞榮. *Daxingshan si* 大興善寺. Xi'an: Sanqin 三秦, 1986.

Amoghavajra

Yoritomi Motohiro 賴富本宏. *Chūgoku mikkyō no kenkyū* 中國密教の研究. Tokyo: Daitō 大東, 1979.
Yu Xin 余欣, "Zuo tu you shu: Bukong suo jin hupo baosheng rulai xiang jikao" 左圖右書: 不空所進虎魄寶生如來像稽考 in Yu Xin, Bowang mingsha: Zhongguo Xieben Yanjiu yu Xiandai Zhongguo Xueshushi zhi huitong 博望鳴沙: 中古寫本研究與現代中國學術史之會通. Shanghai: Shanghai Guji, 2012, pp. 322–37.

Martin Lehnert

Bo Juyi 白居易 (also known as Bai Juyi; *zi*, Letian 樂天, *hao*, Xiangshan 香山, 772–846) was one of the most popular Tang poets. He was born in Xinzheng 新鄭 (modern Henan) to an impoverished scholarly family originally from Taiyuan 太原 (Shanxi). Before his birth, the family had lived in Xiagui 下邽, on the south bank of the Wei River 渭水, not far from Chang'an, the Tang capital. When Bo Juyi was about ten, his father took the family to Pengcheng 彭城 (modern Xuzhou, Jiangsu) where he served as a magistrate. Bo Juyi, however, was sent to live with some relatives in Xiagui, possibly to be educated. A precocious child, it is said he could read before he was two and knew the rules of prosody when he was seven; nevertheless, he did not pass the *jinshi* examination until 800, when he was twenty-eight. In 802 he passed the *Bacui* 拔萃, a selective-placement examination. Among the eight successful candidates was Yuan Zhen 元稹 (779–831),* who became his lifelong friend. Their names became linked because of their many joint literary ventures. Bo and Yuan were also appointed as Editors in the Palace Library following the examination. During their tenures as editors, the pair prepared themselves for a special palace examination. They cloistered themselves for six months, studying, discussing current events, and trying to find solutions to problems concerning the affairs of the state in anticipation of possible examination questions. Seventy-five essays, which resulted from their studies are preserved in Bo Juyi's collected works under the title "Ce lin" 策林 (Forest of Plans). Although the questions they had anticipated were not asked, they both passed with flying colors. Both passed with flying colors.

Perhaps the most famous letter of the Tang era testifies to their close friendship. Written in 817 when Bo was exiled to Xunyang 潯陽 (modern Jiujiang City 九江市 in Jiangxi) and Yuan Zhen was serving in a remote post in what is modern Sichuan, Bo speaks of his concern over having heard Yuan was ill, their fate to be separated often, the poems Yuan sent him, and then lapses into a poetic account of his recent excursions to nearby Mount Lu 廬山:

> Weizhi, Weizhi (Yuan's stylename)! It has been three years since I have seen your face, going on two years since I have your letter... When I first arrived in Xunyang, Xiong Rudeng happened by and gave me your letter from the year before when you were so sick. At the start you reported on the condition of your illness, then you told about your mood in your sickness, and closed by commenting on our lifelong friendship. You also said 'This is a point of crisis for me and I don't have time to speak of other things. I have only collected several of my writings, sealed them and written on them 'To be sent sometime to Master Bo the Twenty-second to allow me to have them take the place of a letter.'
>
> In the autumn of last year I began to roam about Mount Lu, reaching the Eastern and Western Monasteries beneath Incense-burner Peak, seeing clouds and streams, springs and rock formations, all the most extraordinary. I cherished it so I could not abandon it and

therefore built a thatched hut there. Before it are dozens of soaring pines and more than a thousand tall bamboos. Green creepers are its garden walls and white rocks form its paths and bridges. Flowing waters are all about below the hut and cascades from springs fall over its eaves. Red azaleas and white lotus spread on the pond and stones—it is basically like this, but I cannot express it all by writing it down...

> 微之微之, 不見足下面, 已三年矣, 不得足下書, 欲二年矣 ... 僕初到潯陽時, 有熊孺登來, 得足下前年病甚時一札, 上報疾狀, 次序病心, 終論平生交分, 且雲危惙之際, 不暇他及, 唯收數日報導, 封題其上曰, "他日送達白二十二郎", 便請以代書。
> 僕去年秋, 始遊廬山, 到東西二林間、香爐峰下, 見雲水泉石, 勝絕第一, 愛不能舍, 因置草堂。 前有喬松十餘株, 修竹千餘竿, 青蘿為牆垣, 白石為橋道, 流水周於舍下, 飛泉落於檐間, 紅榴白蓮, 羅生池砌, 大抵若是, 不能殫記.

Although Yuan later held high office in the capital, their literary reputations were matched during their lifetimes. After their deaths, however, Bo's fame was unparalleled. But his political career never reached the heights attained by Yuan Zhen, although neither man realized his youthful dreams of effecting social reform. The nearest Bo Juyi ever came to the emperor was when he was a member of the Hanlin Academy and served concurrently as Reminder of the Left (807–815). Because of his outspoken criticism of governmental policies and his remonstrances against injustice, especially that done to Yuan Zhen (who was banished in 809), Bo was exiled from Chang'an in 815. Although he held several desirable positions afterwards—Prefect of Hangzhou (822–825) and Prefect of Suzhou (825–827)–he was never in a position to exercise his influence in the central government. Disappointed in politics in later years, Bo Juyi turned to Buddhism for consolation. After retiring from an honorary post as Junior Mentor of the Heir Apparent, he remained in Luoyang until his death at the age of seventy-four.

A prolific writer, Bo Juyi wrote more than three thousand poems, taking pains to preserve his works for posterity, which may account in part for his lasting fame. When he was banished to Jiangzhou 江州 (modern Jiujiang City 九江市 in Jiangxi) in 815 he sent fifteen *juan* of his writings, classified under different categories, to Yuan Zhen. In 824 and 825, Yuan Zhen edited and compiled a collection of Bo's works, *Boshi Changqing ji* 白氏長慶集. In his introduction to this volume, dated the twelfth month of the fourth year of the Changqing 長慶 reign period (January 825), Yuan Zhen gives a full account of Bo's life, the popularity of Bo's poetry and his international reputation (Bo's verse was especially prized in Japan–see below). He speaks of their joint endeavor in promoting the new *yuefu* style (*xin yuefu* 新樂府) and the long poems in regulated verse (*pailü* 排律). These poems, with hundreds of rhymes devised by the two friends, became known to posterity as *Yuanhe shi* 元和詩 (Yuanhe Poems, after the Yuanhe reign period, 806–820, during which much of this verse was written) or *Yuan Bo ti* 元白體 (Yuan and Bo Style). Two years before he died, Bo Juyi added twenty-five more *juan* to this collection, for a total of seventy-five *juan*. He then made five copies and housed them in different locales to insure their preservation. One of his best known poems is "Cao" 草 (Grasses):

> Boundless bend the grasses on the plain,
> Drying up, then sprouting anew with each passing year.
> Wildfires can't burn them up,
> For the spring wind blows them alive again.

Bo Juyi

> Their far-reaching fragrance overruns the old road,
> Their clear emerald color stretches to the ruined walls.
> Again I see off a noble friend,
> These lush greens teem with my parting thoughts.

> 離離原上草,一歲一枯榮。
> 野火燒不盡,春風吹又生。
> 遠芳侵古道,晴翠接荒城。
> 又送王孫去,萋萋滿別情。

This poem was written when Bo first came to the capital to sit for examinations. Gu Kuang 顧況 (ca. 727–ca. 814)* read it and through his comments offered both the poem and the poet renown. Ironically this was merely a poetic exercise as evidenced by the alternate title "Fude guyuan cao songbie" 賦得古原草送別 (Written on the Theme 'Parting by the Grasses on the Ancient Plain'). The imagery is in part borrowed from "Zhao yinshi" 招隱士 (Summoning a Recluse) in the *Chu ci* 楚辭 (Songs of the South). It was two lines from that poem—"A prince went wandering and did not return, / In spring the grass grows lush and green" 王孫游兮不歸,春草生兮萋萋—that first associated the thick grasses of the plain with the sadness of parting.

Bo Juyi, however, most treasured his *fengyu shi* 諷喻詩 (satirical and allegorical poems) and the new *yuefu* poems, such as "Xinfeng zhebi weng" 新豐折臂翁 (An Old Man with a Broken Arm), an attack on militarism, "Maitan weng" 賣炭翁 (The Old Charcoal Vendor), a plaint against official harassment, and "Shangyang baifa ren" 上陽白髮人 (The White-haired Person of Shangyang Palace), a lament on the fate of palace ladies. Although these poems can seem prosaic in translation, they represent Bo's spirit, while also expressing the didactic tendencies of the *fugu* 複古 (return to antiquity) sentiments of the times. "Mai hua" 買花 (Purchasing Flowers), one of the series titled "Qinzhong yin" 秦中吟 (Songs from Qin), is typical:

> In the Imperial City spring is about to end,
> Rumbling, rumbling–coaches and horses pass by.
> Everyone is talking about the peony season,
> Following the crowd to purchase flowers.
> Cheap or dear, no standard price,
> The cost matches the merits of the blossoms.
> So brilliant the red, one hundred flowers,
> So much the price, five bolts of white silk.
> Above an awning shields them,
> Alongside a wattle-fence protects them.
> Sprayed with water and coated with mud,
> After transport, their beauty does not fade.
> In each household it's become a custom,
> Everyone continues to be obsessed.
> An old farmer fellow,
> Who happened by the flower fair,
> Head bowed, only uttered a deep sigh,
> A sigh that nobody understood.

One bouquet of those deep-colored flowers,
Would pay taxes for ten common households.

帝城春欲暮，喧喧車馬度。
共道牡丹時，相隨買花去。
貴賤無常價，酬直看花數。
灼灼百朵紅，戔戔五束素。
上張幄幕庇，旁織巴籬護。
水灑復泥封，移來色如故。
家家習為俗，人人迷不悟。
有一田舍翁，偶來買花處。
低頭獨長歎，此歎無人喻。
一叢深色花，十戶中人賦。

For posterity, however, the most popular of his poems are his romantic ballads such as "Changhen ge" 長恨歌 (Song of Everlasting Sorrow), which narrates the love story of the Emperor Xuanzong (r. 713–756) and his consort Yang Guifei 楊貴妃 (d. 756), and "Pipa xing" 琵琶行 (Song of the Pipa), which describes the sad life of a female entertainer, whom the poet encountered during his exile in Jiangzhou.

Bo Juyi's greatest literary contribution was to popularize literature and make it readily accessible to the masses. Bo strove for clarity and simplicity of language and beauty and harmony in rhythm in occasional poems like the following "Weishang ou diao" 渭上偶釣 (Idly Fishing on the Wei River):

The waters of the Wei as if a mirror,
Therein are carp and bream.
Idly with bamboo rod in hand,
I drop my hook by its banks.
A light breeze blows my fishing gear,
Bobbing up and down, my ten feet of line.
Who knows when I'll sit as if I'm fishing
Whether my heart wandered to a place where there is nothing else.
Of old a white-haired man,
Also fished on the north side of the Wei.
He was fishing for men, not fish—
At age seventy he caught King Wen.
But my intent in dropping a line
Is to forget all about both men and fish.
With no opportunity to catch either one,
I just play with the autumn water's reflection.
When I lose interest, my fishing will also stop;
I'll go home to drink my cup of wine.

渭水如鏡色，中有鯉與魴。
偶持一竿竹，懸釣在其傍。
微風吹釣絲，嫋嫋十尺長。
誰知對魚坐，心在無何鄉。

> 昔有白頭人，亦釣此渭陽。
> 釣人不釣魚，七十得文王。
> 況我垂釣意，人魚又兼忘。
> 無機兩不得，但弄秋水光。
> 興盡釣亦罷，歸來飲我觴。

Two allusions augment Bo's text. In line 8 the "place where there is nothing else" refers to the final lines of the "Xiaoyao you" 逍遙遊 chapter of *Zhuang Zi* where Zhuang Zi explains to Hui Zi that he should plant his large, useless tree in "where there is nothing else" so that he can roam about in non-action beside it and sleep with no cares beneath it. Line 12 alludes to Lü Shang 呂尚 who sat idly fishing and thereby won the notice of King Wen of the Zhou for whom he became and advisor. Bo invokes Lü Shang so that he can make clear that his intention in fishing is more a platform for reflection on the life of reclusion.

Bo's poems were widely read, sung, and admired by people from all walks of life, from schoolboys and peasant women to courtesans and palace ladies; they were also often written on walls of temple and inns. Copies were sold in marketplaces and some made their way to Heian Japan where his popularity spread quickly. Today through the pioneering translations by Arthur Waley (see Bibliography), Bo's poetry is better known in the West than that of his contemporaries.

Bo Juyi's "Song of Everlasting Sorrow" provides a good example of how poetry and fiction mutually influenced each other in Tang times. As noted above, the poem depicts the ill-fated love affair between Emperor Xuanzong and his favorite concubine, Yang Guifei. It portrays the emperor's sorrow after her death and their final meeting, arranged by a Daoist adept who summoned her soul for a final tryst. After the song had been circulated, Chen Hong 陳鴻 (*jinshi*, 805), a close friend of Bo, read it and wrote a tale (*chuanqi* 傳奇) based on it. The combined influence of the tale and the poem has been enormous, especially in the field of drama, and the Yang Guifei theme has become a major tradition in Chinese popular literature.

BIBLIOGRAPHY

Editions:

Bo Kong liu tie: wai sanzhong 白孔六帖: 外三種. Shanghai: Shanghai Guji, 1992.

Bo Xiangshan shiji: Changqing ji ershi juan, houji shiqi juan, bieji yi juan, buyi erjuan, nianpu er juan 白香山詩集: 長慶集二十卷, 後集十七卷, 別集一卷, 補遺二卷, 年譜二卷. Taibei: Shijie Chuju Gufen, 2006.

Bo Xiangshan shiji 白香山詩集. *SBBY*.

Boshi Changqing ji 白氏長慶集. *SBCK* edition.

Ding Ruming 丁如明 and Nie Shimei 聶世美, eds. *Bo Juyi quan ji* 白居易全集. Shanghai: Shanghai Guji, 1999.

Fu Tonghua 傅東華, ed. and comm. *Bo Juyi shi* 白居易詩. Taibei: Taiwan Shangwu, 1990.

Gu Xuejie 顧學頡, ed. *Bo Juyi ji* 白居易集. 4v. Beijing: Zhonghua, 1979. Appends a *nianpu*.

He Ming 鶴鳴. *Tang Song ba da mingjia. 3, Bo Juyi jingdian zuopin xuan* 唐宋八大名家. 3, 白居易經典作品選. Chongqing: Xinan Shifan Daxue, 1996.

Hiraoka Takeo 平岡武夫 and Imai Kiyoshi 今井清, eds. *Hakushi bunshū kasha sakuin* 白氏文集歌詩索引. 3v. Tokyo: Dōhōsha, 1980.

Luan Guiming 欒貴明 et al., eds. *Quan Tang shi suoyin: Bo Juyi juan* 全唐詩索引: 白居易卷. Qinhuangdao: Xiandai, 1994.

Quan Tang shi, 7: 4665–5292, 8: 10051–52, 11: 8989–991, 14: 10658, 15: 11298–308.
Quan Tang wen, 656–83.7419–724.
Sun Anbang 孫安邦, ed. *Bo Juyi ji* 白居易集. Taiyuan: Shanxi Guji, 2003.
Sun Mingjun 孫明君. *Bo Juyi shi* 白居易詩. Beijing: Renmin Wenxue, 2005.
Tokuharu Kamitaka 神鷹德治. *Hakushi monjū wa monjū ka bunshū ka: monjū kandan* 白氏文集は<もんじゅう>か<ぞんしゅう>か: "文集"閒談. Tokyo: Yūgakusha, 2012.
Wang Rubi 王汝弼. *Bo Juyi xuanji* 白居易選集. Shanghai: Shanghai Guji, 2012.

Annotations:
Chen Caizhi 陳才智. *Zhongguo gudian shici jingpin shang du, Bo Juyi* 中國古典詩詞精品賞讀, 白居易. Beijing: Wuzhou Chuanbo, 2005.
Chen Youqin 陳友琴. *Bo Juyi ji qi zuopin xuan: Bo Juyi; Bo Juyi shiwen xuanzhu* 白居易及其作品選: 白居易; 白居易詩文選注. Shanghai: Shanghai Guji, 1998.
Chu Binjie 褚斌傑. *Bo Juyi shige shangxi ji* 白居易詩歌賞析集. Chengdu: Ba Shu, 1990.
Fei Ruming 費如明. *Shuojin xinzhong wuxian shi: Bo Juyi shixuan* 說盡心中無限事: 白居易詩選. Taibei: Yeqiang, 1995.
Ge Peiling 葛培嶺. *Bo Juyi* 白居易. Taibei: Zhishufang, 2001.
Gong Kechang 龔克昌. *Zhongguo shiyuan yinghua. Bo Juyi juan* 中國詩苑英華. 白居易卷. Jinan: Shandong Daxue, 1997.
Guo Jie 郭傑. *Yuan Bo shi zhuan* 元白詩傳. Changchun: Jilin Renmin, 2000.
Jian Changchun 蹇長春. *Bo Juyi ping zhuan: fu Yuan Zhen ping zhuan* 白居易評傳: 附元稹評傳. Nanjing: Nanjing Daxue, 2002.
Juan Xueyan 雋雪豔. *Wenhua de chongxie: Riben gudian zhongde Bo Juyi xingxiang* 文化的重寫: 日本古典中的白居易形象. Beijing: Qinghua Daxue, 2010.
___. and Hisao Takamatsu 高松壽夫. *Bo Juyi yu Riben gudai wenxue* 白居易與日本古代文學. Beijing: Beijing Daxue, 2012.
Kōji Akiya 秋谷幸治. *Haku Kyoi bungakuron kenkyū: dentō no keishō to kakushin* 白居易文學論研究: 伝統の繼承と革新. Tokyo: Kyūko, 2012.
Li Gui 李貴. *Zhong Tang zhi bei Song de dianfan xuanze yu shige yinge* 中唐至北宋的典範選擇與詩歌因革. Shanghai: Fudan Daxue, 2012.
Liao Meiyun 廖美雲. *Yuan Bo xin yuefu yanjiu* 元白新樂府研究. Taibei: Taiwan Xuesheng, 1989.
Liu Longkai 劉隆凱. *Chen Yinke"Yuan Bo shi zheng shi" jiangxi ce ji* 陳寅恪"元白詩證史" 講席側記. Wuhan: Hubei Jiaoyu, 2005.
Liu Yisheng 劉逸生. *Bo Juyi shi xuan* 白居易詩選. Hong Kong: Sanlian, 1985.
Ma Minghao 馬銘浩. *Tangdai shehui yu YuanBo wenxue jituan guanxi zhi yanjiu* 唐代社會與元白文學集團關係之研究. Taibei: Taiwan Xuesheng, 1991.
Mo Lifeng 莫礪鋒. *Mo Lifeng ping shuo Bo Juyi* 莫礪鋒評說白居易. Hefei: Anhui Wenyi, 2010.
Qiao Lizhi 喬立智. *Bo Juyi shige cihui yanjiu* 白居易詩歌詞彙研究. Beijing: Renmin, 2012.
Qiu Xieyou 邱燮友. *Bo Juyi: Zhongtang shidai zui weida shiren*. 白居易: 中唐時代最偉大詩人. Taibei: Xinfeng Wenhua Shiye Gongsi, 1990.
Shi Changtai 師長泰. *Bo Juyi shi xuanping* 白居易詩選評. Xi'an: Sanqin, 2008.
Shi Rong 施蓉 and Su Jianke, 蘇建科. *Bo Juyi shi jingxuan jingzhu* 白居易詩精選精注. Guilin: Guangxi Shifan Daxue, 1996.
Takagi Hiroshi 高木博. *Chōkonka zakki* 長恨歌襍記. Tokyo: Sōbunsha, 1988.
Wang Ling 王玲. *Bo Juyi shici* 白居易詩詞. Jinan: Jinan, 2007.
Wang Yunxi 王運熙. *Tangdai wuda wenhao: Liu Zongyuan, Bo Juyi, Han Yu, Du Fu, Li Bo* 唐代五大文豪: 柳宗元, 白居易, 韓愈, 杜甫, 李白. Shanghai: Shanghai Guji, 1996.

Bo Juyi

Wu Dakui 吳大逵 and Ma Xiujuan 馬秀娟. *Yuan Zhen, Bo Juyi shi xuan yi* 元稹白居易詩選譯. Nanjing: Fenghuang, 2011.

Wu Weibin 吳偉斌. *Bo Juyi quanzhuan: Wenzhang yi man xingren er* 白居易全傳: 文章已滿行人耳. Changchun: Changchun, 1997.

Xiao Ruifeng 肖瑞峰. *Liu Yuxi, Bo Juyi shi xuanping* 劉禹錫白居易詩選評. Shanghai: Shanghai Guji, 2002.

Xiao Weitao 肖偉韜. *Bo Juyi yanjiu de fansi yu pipan* 白居易研究的反思與批判. Lanzhou: Gansu Renmin, 2008.

___. *Bo Juyi shengcun zhexue benti yanjiu* 白居易生存哲學本體研究. Nanjing: Daxue, 2009.

Xie Siwei 謝思煒. *Bo Juyi ji zonglun* 白居易集綜論. Beijing: Zhongguo Shehui Kexue, 1997.

___. *Bo Juyi shiji jiaozhu* 白居易詩集校註. Beijing: Zhonghua, 2006.

___. *Bo Juyi wenji jiaozhu* 白居易文集校注. Beijing: Zhonghua, 2011.

Yang Zhixian 楊志賢. *Zhong Tang. Xianshi zhuyi shiren: Bo Juyi, 772–846.* 中唐. 現實主義詩人: 白居易, 772–846. Shenzhen: Haitian, 1999.

Zhan, *Daojiao*, pp. 327–50.

Zhang Qian 張黔. *Bo Juyi shi shang du* 白居易詩賞讀. Beijing: Xianzhuang, 2007.

Zhang Jian 張健. *Da Tang shi mo: Bo Juyi shixuan* 大唐詩魔: 白居易詩選. Taibei: Wunan, 1998.

Zheng Yongxiao 鄭永曉. *Bo Juyi shige shangxi* 白居易詩歌賞析. Nanning: Guangxi Jiaoyu, 1990.

___. *Xiangfeng hebi ceng xiangshi: Bo Juyi zuopin shangxi* 相逢何必曾相識: 白居易作品賞析. Taibei: Kaijin Wenhua Shiye Youxian Gongsi, 1993.

Zhu Jincheng 朱金城, ed. and comm. *Bo Juyi ji jiaojian* 白居易集校箋. 6v. Shanghai: Shanghai Guji, 1988. Contains prefaces, biographical and bibliographical information, and an index.

Biographical Sources:
Fu, *Tang caizi*, 3:1–22, 5:270.
Jiu Tang shu, 166:4340–58.
Xin Tang shu, 119.4300–07.

Translations:
Alley, Rewi, trans. *Bo Juyi, 200 Selected Poems*. Peking: New World, 1983. Lightly annotated translations.
Articulated Ladies, pp. 195–99.
Birch, *Anthology*, pp. 266–78.
Bynner, *Jade Mountain*, pp. 92–103.
Costantini, Vilma, ed. *Coppe di giada*. Turin, 1985. Contains translations of nearly forty poems by Bo Juyi.
Cryer, James M. "Bo Chu–i," in Seaton, Jerome P. and Denni Maloney, eds. *A Drifting Boat: An Anthology of Chinese Zen Poetry*. Fredonia, NY: White Pine Press, 1994, pp. 64–68.
Davis, Timothy M. "Lechery, Substance Abuse, and . . . Han Yu?" *JAOS*, 135 (2015): 71-92.
Demièville, *Anthologie*, pp. 307–25.
Frankel, *Palace Lady*, p. 98.
Fuller, Michael A. *An Introduction to Chinese Poetry: From the* Canon of Poetry *to the Lyrics of the Song Dynasty*. Cambridge: Harvard University Press, 2018, pp. 274–89.
Hinton, David. *The Selected Poems of Po Chü-I*. New York: New Directions, 1999.
Hinton, *Anthology*, pp. 265–85.
Hoizey, Dominique. *Bo Juyi, poèms*. Paris: Albédo, 1985.
Idema, W.L. *Gans, Papegaii en kraanvogel-Gedichten uit het oude China*. Amsterdam: Meulenhoff, 1986.
Jaeger, Georgette. *Bo Juyi, Chant des regrets étenels et autre poèmes*. Paris: Editions Orphée La différence, 1992.
Levy, Howard S., et al. *Translations from Bo Chü-i's Collected Works*. 4v. New York: Paragon Reprint Book Corp., 1971–1978.
Lin and Owen, *Vitality*, pp. 239–42.

New Directions, pp. 128–38.

Mair, *Anthology*, pp. 304, 477–87.

Margoulies, *Anthologie*, pp. 351–53, 386–88.

Minford and Lau, pp. 871–902.

Owen, *High T'ang*, pp. 147–61.

Okamura Shigeru 岡村繁. *Hakushi bunshū* 白氏文集. 13v. Tokyo: Meiji, 1988–1993. *Shinshaku kanbun taikei*, 97–109.

Owen. *Late Tang*, pp. 45–67, 69, 71, 89–90.

___. *Middle Ages*, pp. 21–22, 27–28, 81–111.

___, *Mi-Lou*, pp. 147–50, 159–60.

___. *Omen*, pp. 188–90, 233–36, 274–77.

___, *Remembrances*, pp. 74–79.

Payne, *White Pony*, pp. 205–19.

Shields, Anna. *Crafting a Collection, The Cultural Contexts and Poetic Practice of the Huajian ji* 花間集 *(Collection from Among the Flowers)*. Cambridge: Harvard University Asia Center, 2006, pp. 17–18, 44–45.

Sunflower, pp. 201–11.

Takeshi Shizunaga 靜永健 and Liu Weizhi 劉維治, trans. *Bo Juyi xiefeng yushi de qianqian houhou* 白居易寫諷喻詩的前前後後. Beijing: Zhonghua, 2007.

Tao Min 陶敏 and Lu Qian 魯茜. *Xinyi Bo Juyi shiwen xuan* 新譯白居易詩文選. Taibei: Sanmin, 2009.

Zach, Erwin von. *Han Yü's Poetische Werke*. Cambridge, Mass.: Harvard University, 1952, pp. 318–47.

Waley, Arthur. *A Hundred and Seventy Poems from the Chinese*. London: Constable, 1918.

___. *More Poems from the Chinese*. New York: Alfred A. Knopf, 1919.

___. *Translations from the Chinese*. New York: Alfred A. Knopf, 1941, pp. 126–273.

___. *Waiting for the Moon: Poems of Bo Juyi*. Mount Jackson, Virginia: Axios, 2012.

Wang, Elizabeth Te-chen 王德箴. "Story of Everlasting Sorrow," in Elizabeth Te-chen, Wang, *Ladies of the T'ang*, Taibei, 1961, pp. 107–32. English translation of "Changhen ge zhuan."

Watson, *Columbia*, pp. 243–58.

___. *Lyricism*, pp. 184–88.

Yang Xianyi, *Poetry and Prose*, pp. 107–34.

Studies:

Cha Zhengxian 查正賢. "Lun zizhu suoshi Bo Juyi shige chuangzuo de ruogan tezheng yu yiyi" 論自注所示白居易詩歌創作的若干特徵與意義, *Wenxue yichan* 2015.2: 85–93.

Chan Chiu-ming. "Between the World and the Self-Orientations of Pai Chü-i's (772–846) Life and Writings." Unpublished Ph.D. dissertation, University of Wisconsin, 1991.

Chen Jiahuang 陳家煌. *Bo Juyi shiren zijue yanjiu* 白居易詩人自覺研究. Gaoxiong: Guoli Zhongshan Daxue Wenxueyuan, 2009.

Chen Jinxian 陳金現. *Song shi yu Bo Juyi de huwen xing yanjiu* 宋詩與白居易的互文性研究. Taibei: Wenjin, 2010.

Ch'iu Hsieh-yu 邱燮友. *Bo Juyi* 白居易. Taibei, 1978.

Chu Binjie 褚斌傑. *Bo Juyi* 白居易. Shenyang: Chunfeng Wenyi, 1999.

Dagdanov, G. B. "Vliianie chan'buddizma na tvorchestvo tanskikh poetov. Na primere Van Veia (701–761) i Bo Tsziu-ii (772–846)." Unpublished Ph.D. dissertation, Institut Vostokovedeniia Akademiinauk SSSR, 1980.

DeBlasi, Anthony Augustine. *Reform in the Balance: The Defense of Literary Culture in mid-Tang China*. Albany: State University of New York, 2002, *passim*.

Bo Juyi

Du Xuexia 杜學霞. *Wenxue zhuanxing shiye xia de Bo Juyi shixue sixiang* 文化轉型視野下的白居易詩學思想. Ph. D. Diss., Beijing Shifan Daxue, 2007.

Feifel, Eugene. "Biography of Bo Juyi 白居易: Annotated Translation from *Chüan* 166 of the *Chiu T'ang-shu* 舊唐書." *MS* 17 (1958): 255–311.

Field, Stephen Lee. "Taking Up the Plow: Real and Ideal Versions of the Farmer in Chinese Literature." Unpublished Ph.D. dissertation, University of Texas, 1985. Ch. 6 and Ch. 7 (pp. 106–48) deal with Bo Juyi and other Tang poets.

Goldin, Paul Rakita. "Reading Po Chü-i." *TS* 12 (1994): 57–96.

Gu Xuejie. "Bo Juyi shixi jiazu kao" 白居易世系家族攷. *Wenxue pinglun congkan* 文學評論叢刊 13 (May, 1982): 131–68.

Hanabusa Hideiki. 花房英樹. *Haku Kyoi kenkyū* 白居易研究. Kyoto, 1971.

___. *Hakushi monjū no hihanteki kenkyū* 白氏文集の批評的研究. Kyoto, 1974.

___. *Haku Rakuten* 白楽天. Tokyo: Shimizu, 1990.

Hiraoka Takeo 平岡武夫. *Haku Kyoi* 白居易. Tokyo: Chikuma, 1977.

___. "*Hakushi monjū no sōrisu*" 白氏文集の成立. in *Tōhō gakkai sōrisu 15 shūnen kinen tōhōgaku ronshū* 東方學會成立十五週年紀念東方學論集, Tokyo, 1962, pp. 260–75.

Hirakawa Sukehiro 平川佑弘. "Chinese Culture and Japanese Identity: Po Chü-i in a Peripheral Country." *TkR* 16.1–4 (Autumn 1984–Summer 1985): 201–20.

Jian Changchun 塞长春. *Bo Juyi pingzhuan* 白居易評傳. Nanjing: Nanjing Daxue, 2002.

Jian Jinsong 簡錦松. "Bo Juyi 'Chu chu lantian lu zuo' shixian de yanjiu: Tang Shangzhou wuguan yilu lantianduan xinyi" 白居易 '初出藍田路作' 詩現地研究-唐商州武關驛路藍田段新譯, in *Han Xue Yan Jiu*, 30 (2012): 167–204.

Kominami Ichirō 小南一郎. "Gen Haku bungaku shūdan no shōsetsu: 'Ōōden' o chūshin ni shite" 元白文學集集団の小説–鶯鶯伝を中心にして. *Nippon Chūgoku Gakkaihō* 47 (1995): 63–74.

Kondō Haruo 近籐春雄. *Chōkonka to Yō Kihi* 長恨歌と楊貴妃. Tokyo: Meiji, 1993.

___. *Hakushi bonshū to kokubun gaku* 白氏文集と国文學. Tokyo: Meiji, 1990. *Shin gafu shin chūgin no kenkyū*.

Li Jingyi 李敬一. "Bo Juyi shige de sanda zhuti yanjiu" 白居易詩歌的三大主題研究. Unpublished Ph.D. Dissertation, Beijing Daxue, 2001.

Lin Wen-yüeh 林文月. "'Changhen ge' dui 'Changhen ge zhuan' yu *Yuanshi wuyu* ('t'ung-hu') de yingxiang" 長恨歌對長恨歌傳與源氏物語的影響, in *Zhongguo gudian wenxue yanjiu congkan: Xiaoshuo zhibu* 中國古典文學研究叢刊：小說之部 1, Taibei, 1977, pp. 191–216.

Liu Ning 劉寧. *Tang Song zhi ji shige yanbian yanjiu: yi yuanbo zhi yuanheti de chuangzuo wei zhongxin* 唐宋之際詩歌演變研究：以元白之元和體的創作影響為中心. Beijing: Beijing Shifan Daxue, 2002.

Ma Gedong 馬歌東. *Riben Bo Juyi yanjiu lunwen xuan* 日本白居易研究論文選. Xi'an: Sanqin, 1995.

Mao Yanjun 毛妍君. *Bo Juyi xianshi shi yanjiu* 白居易閒適詩研究. Ph. D. Dissertation, Shanxi Shifan Daxue, 2006.

Mizuno Heiji 水野平次. *Haku Rakuten to Nihon bungaku* 白楽天と日本文學. Tokyo: Daigakudō, 1982.

Nienhauser, William H., Jr. "Po Chü-i Studies in English, 1916–1992." *Asian Culture Quarterly* XXII. 3 (Autumn 1994): 37–50.

Nishimura Tomiko 西村富美子. *Haku Rakuten* 白楽天. *Kanshō Chūgoku no koten*, 18. Tokyo: Kadokawa, 1988.

Ōta Tsugio 太田次郎. *Chū Tō bunjin kō–Kan Yu, Ryū Sōgen, Haku Kyoi* 中唐文人考–韓愈, 柳宗元, 白居易. Tokyo: Kenbun, 1993.

___, et al., eds. *Haku Kyoi kenkyū kōza* 白居易研究講座. 7v. Tokyo: Benseisha, 1994. Treats Bo's life and works, Japanese and foreign studies, editions and his reputation in Japan. Excellent bibliography.

Shang Yongliang 尚永亮. *Yuanhe wu da shiren yu bianzhe wenxue kaolun* 元和五大詩人與貶謫文學考論. Taibei: Wenjin, 1993.

Shields, Anna M. "Remembering When: The Uses of Nostalgia in the Poetry of Bo Juyi and Yuan Zhen," *HJAS* 66 (2006): 321–61.

___. *One Who Knows Me: Friendship and Literary Culture in Mid-Tang China*. Cambridge and London: Harvard University Asia Center, 2015, pp. 115–31, 173–99, and *passim*.

Shimosada Masahiro 下定雅弘. *Haku Kyoi to Ryū Sōgen: konmei no yo ni sei no sanka o* 白居易と柳宗元：混迷の世に生の讃歌を. Tokyo: Iwanami, 2015.

Spring, Madeline K. "The Celebrated Cranes of Po Chü-i." *JAOS* 111 (1991): 8–18.

Tanaka Katsumi 田中克己 (1911–1992). *Haku Rakuten* 白楽天. Tokyo: Shūeisha, 1964.

Thilo, Thomas. "Aspekte der arbeitenden Volkes in den späteren Werken des Dichters Bo Juyi." *Altorientalische Forschungen* 16 (1989): 153–81.

Twichett, Dennis. "Po Chü-i's 'Government Ox,'" *T'ang Studies* 7 (1989): 23–38.

Ueki Hisayuki 植木久行. "Tōdai kakka shin ginen roku (5): Gi Chō, Gu Seinan, Jōkan Shōyō, Tei Ryōshi, Haku Kyoi, Haku Gyōkan, Gō Hō, Ra In, Ri Riran, Raku Shi, Ryū Ushaku" 唐代作家新疑年錄 (5)-魏徵, 虞世南, 上官昭容, 鄭良士, 白居易, 白行簡, 鮑防, 羅隱, 李李蘭, 陸贄，劉禹錫. *Bunkei Ronsō* 37.3 (1992).

Umeda Shigeo 埋田重夫. *Haku Rakuten kenkyū: shigo to shūji* 白居易研究：詩語修辭. Tokyo: Kyūko, 2020.

Waley, Arthur. *Life and Times of Po Chü-i*. London: G. Allen and Unwin, 1949.

Wang, Ao. "The Fashioning of a Poetic Genius: Yuan Zhen and Mid-Tang Imperial Culture." Unpublished Ph.D. dissertation, Yale University, 2008. Chapter 3 examines Yuan Zhen and Bo Juyi's mutual fashioning in both their exchanged poems and cultural performance.

Wang Meng-ou 王夢鷗. *Tangren xiaoshuo yanjiu siji* 唐人小説研究四集. Taibei, 1978, pp. 213–38. Clarifies much of the controversy concerning Chen Hong and his authorship of "Changhen ge zhuan" and other writings.

Wang Shiyi 王拾遺. *Bo Juyi yanjiu* 白居易研究. Shanghai: Shanghai Renmin, 1954.

Wang, Ernestine H. "Po Chü-i: The Man and His Influence in Chinese Poetry." Unpublished Ph.D. dissertation, Georgetown University, 1987.

Watson, Burton, "Buddhism in the Poetry of Po Chu-i," *The Eastern Buddhist* (New Series) 21-1 1988 :1–22.

___. "Buddhist Poet-Priests of the T'ang," *The Eastern Buddhist* (New Series) 25-2 (1992): 30–58.

Wen Yanrong 文豔蓉. *Bo Juyi shengping yu chuangzuo shizheng yanjiu* 白居易生平與創作實證研究. Ph. D. Dissertation, Zhejiang Daxue, 2009.

Xie Siwei 謝思煒. "Riben guchaoben *Bo shi wenji* de yuanliu ji jiaokan jiazhi" 日本古本白氏文集的源流及校勘價值, *Zhongguo guji yanjiu* 中國古籍研究. v1. Shanghai: Shanghai Guji, 1996, pp. 371–89.

___. *Bo Juyi ji zonglun* 白居易集綜論. Peking: Shehui Kexue, 1997.

___. "Cong Zhang Wang *yuefu* shi kan Yuan Bo xin *yuefu* gainian" 從張王樂府詩看元白新樂府概念, in *Tang Song shixue lunji* 唐宋詩學論集. Beijing: Shangwu, 2003, pp. 170–82.

Yamada Yūhei. 山田侑平. *Haku Kyoi* 白居易. Tokyo: Nicchû, 1985.

Yang Xiaoshan. "Money Matters: Bai Juyi's Self-Image as a Septuagenarian," *MS* 48 (2000): 39–66.

___. "Having It Both Ways; Manor and Manners in Bo Juyi's Poetry" *HJAS* 56 (1996): 123–49.

Yu, *Imagery*, pp. 177–84.

Yu Pingbo 俞平伯. "'Changhen ge' ji 'Changhen ge zhuan' de zhiyi" 長恨歌及長恨歌傳的質疑. *Xiaoshuo yuebao* 20.2 (February 1929): 357–61.

Zhang Hong 張弘. *Milu xin hui yin xiangfo: Bo Juyi yu fo chan* 迷路心回因向佛：白居易與佛禪. Zhengzhou: Henan Renmin, 2001.

Zhang Rongqing 張榮慶. *Xianda shiren Bo Juyi yu "Boshi Changqing ji" qi'erge huizhi* 賢達詩人白居易與《白氏長慶集》七二個慧知. Beijing: Zhonghua Gongshang Lianhe, 2004.

Zhang Zhongyu 張中宇. *Bo Juyi "Changheng ge" yanjiu* 白居易長恨歌研究. Beijing: Zhonghua, 2005.

Zhongguo shehui kexueyuan. Wenxue yanjiusuo 中國社會科學院. 文學研究所. *Bo Juyi shi pingshu huibian* 白居易詩評述彙編. Beijing: Zhishi Chanquan, 2006.

Zhou Lüjing 周履靖 (fl. 16th–17th c.), ed. *Xiangshan jiusong* 香山酒頌. Beijing: Zhonghua, 1985.

Zhu Jincheng 朱金城. *Bo Juyi nianpu* 白居易年譜. Shanghai: Shanghai Guji, 1982.

___. *Bo Juyi yanjiu* 白居易研究. Xi'an: Shanxi Renmin, 1987.

Zou Xin, Angela Jung Palandri, Y. W. Ma, and William H. Nienhauser, Jr.

Bo Xingjian 白行簡 (also known as Bai Xingjian; *zi*, Zhitui 知退, 776–826) was the younger brother of Bo Juyi 白居易 (772–846).* His ancestral home was in Taiyuan 太原 (part of modern Shanxi), but he was born in Xinzheng 新鄭 (modern Henan) and later moved to Pengcheng 彭城 (modern Xuzhou, Jiangsu—see the preceding entry on Bo Juyi). He passed the *jinshi* examination in 807, held several provincial posts, and late in life (beginning in 820) served as Reminder of the Right and then Vice Director of the Bureau of Receptions. He was a talented writer whose collected corpus amounted to twenty *juan*, most of it now lost. His poetic style has been compared to that of his elder and better-known brother, with whom he lived until 814. Among his extant works, his *chuanqi* 傳奇 are the most well-known, including the highly regarded "Li Wa zhuan" 李娃傳 (Tale of Li Wa).

This tale celebrates Miss Li, a courtesan of Chang'an in the Tianbao 天寶 period (742–756). She becomes the lover of a young man of good family, the Zhengs of Xingyang 滎陽 (just west of modern Zhengzhou 鄭州 in Henan), who has come to Chang'an to study for the examinations. After a year, the young man's money is exhausted, and Miss Li and her "mother" desert him. Bewildered and despairing, he falls ill, eventually finding employment as a singer of chants at a funeral home. By chance his father hears him sing in a contest. Enraged he beats his son with a whip and leaves him to die. Rescued by his fellow employees, he winds up homeless and begging for food. In a snowstorm he happens on the house to which Miss Li had fled; she recognizes his voice and realizes that she loves him. She buys her freedom, rents a house, and nurses the young man back to health. Under her direction he takes up his studies again and is able to pass a special examination as the top candidate. He wins an important official assignment, marries Miss Li, holds a succession of high offices and has four sons all of whom became high officials. The tale is remarkable among Tang *chuanqi* for the details used to describe the various settings that reveal the dynamism between social and intimate relationships within the demimonde of the capital. In the scene when the young man suggests that night has fallen and as he is too far from home, he should spend the night:

> The young man glanced several times at the old lady [Miss Li's "mother"]. "Yes," the old lady said, "yes." Only then did the young man summon his own family servants to bring a pair of rolls of fine silk to provide for the evening's food and drink. Miss Li smiled and stopped him, saying, "The etiquette between host and guest is not like that. This evening's expenses we should like to take from our humble household, as well as what shoddy fare we can offer."

生數目姥，姥曰：「唯唯。」生乃召其家僮，持雙縑，請以備一宵之饌。娃笑而止之曰：「賓主之儀，且不然也。今夕之費，願以貧窶之家，隨其粗糲以進之。

Some modern scholars have argued that the piece is a veiled attack on a member of the Zheng family. Regardless of its allegorical force, the tale remains one of the gems of the genre.

"Li Wa zhuan" first appeared in *Taiping guangji* 太平廣記, *juan* 484, which attributes it to the Tang collection *Yiwen ji* 異文集. However, it seems also to have circulated in independent versions during the ninth century and was well known in later periods. At least two dramas from later periods were based on it.

Bo was also the author of tale "Sanmeng ji" 三夢記 (A Record of Three Dreams), in which he claims there are three kinds of extraordinary dreams: (1) someone dreams of something and another person encounters it; (2) someone does something and someone else dreams of it; and (3) two people dream the same dream. In three short stories reminiscent of *zhiguai* 志怪 (records of anomalies) genre he strives to provide actual examples of such dream types.

Only seven of his *shi* 詩 poems are extant along with nineteen *fu* 賦 (prose-poems), the genre which first gained him a reputation in the early ninth century. Among this later corpus is the "Dale fu" 大樂賦 (Prose-poem on the Greatest Pleasure), a text discovered at Dunhuang (Pelliot 2539) which depicts various historical and practical aspects of traditional sexual life.

Although his verse is not widely recognized (in part because most of it has been lost), the remaining corpus illustrates, through its allusions and imagery, a certain talent for poetry as well. The following poem, "Jin zai rong" 金在鎔 (Bronze Being Smelted), probably an exercise to prepare for the *jinshi* examination, is typical. The poem is replete with puns that defy translation:

> Within the forge bellows it is being smelted into an object
> In a vast furnace about to become patterned bronze.
> From the purple gleam it can be seen to gradually emerge,
> In the crimson air one gazes even more deeply.
> In the blazing heat clouds in the clear sky change,
> Under the drifting smoke, the light of day darkens.
> The firm and the hard originate in my nature—
> The blowing and smelting depend upon your heart.
> Leaping up is in vain and will only signal you are different,
> Hiding deep away you can naturally command respect.
> When can the "utensil" be brought to completion?
> It must wait to consult one who really understands it.

> 巨橐方鎔物，洪爐欲範金。
> 紫光看漸發，赤氣望逾深。
> 焰熱晴雲變，煙浮晝景陰。
> 堅剛由我性，鼓鑄任君心。
> 踴躍徒標異，沈潛自可欽。
> 何當得成器，待叩向知音。

The poem establishes the analogy between the master metalsmith and his smelting of bronze to the poet and someone who "understands him" (with a possible allusion in lines 9–10 to the "Da zong" 大宗師 [The Great Revered Teacher] chapter of *Zhuang Zi* 莊子 where the creator is compared to a master smith). Critical of those who would "leap in vain" to win attention, the author here opts for the more authentic, more "natural," of being recognized by those worthy of appreciating his talents. The trope of hidden and unrecognized talent here is brought out by the wait for the true utility of the "utensil" to be finished in the forged. Only when once who can truly appreciate, truly "understand" the utility of the tool will it be completed. Thus, the poem seems to have been written to attract a patron (or impress the examiner) who could help Bo attain an official position.

BIBLIOGRAPHY

Editions:

Bo Xiangshan ji 白香山集. 2v. Taibei: Taibei Shangwu, 1960.
Lu Xun 魯迅. *Tang Song chuanqi ji* 唐宋傳奇集. Rpt. Hong Kong, 1967.
Quan Tang shi, 7: 5335–36.
Quan Tang wen, 692.7828–45.
Tangshi jishi 唐詩紀事, *juan* 41.
Wang Guoyuan 汪國垣, ed. *Tangren xiaoshuo* 唐人小說. Hong Kong: Zhonghua, 1966, pp. 100–12. The *chuanqi* tales.

Translations:

Bauer, *Golden Casket*, pp. 118–36.
Birch, *Anthology*, v. 1, pp. 300–12.
Dudbridge, Glen. *The Tale of Li Wa, Study and Critical Edition of a Chinese Story from the Ninth Century*. London: Ithica, 1983.
Idema, W. L. *Het hoogste genot [Dale fu]. Cahiers van De Lantaarn, No. 19*. Leiden, 1983.
Iida Yoshirō 飯田吉郎. *Haku Kōkan Tairaku fu* 白行簡太樂賦. Tokyo: Kyūko, 1995.
Okamura Shigeru 岡村繁. *Hakushi bunshū* 白氏文集. 13v. *Shinshaku kanbun taikei*, Tokyo: Meiji, 1988-93. pp. 97–109.
Traditional Chinese Stories, pp. 163–71.

Studies:

Bian Xiaoxuan 卞孝萱. "'Li Wa zhuan' xintan" 李娃傳新探, *Yantai Shifanyuan xuebao* 煙臺師範院學報 4 (1991): 12–19.
Chan Chiu-ming. "Between the World and the Self-Orientations of Pai Chü-i's (772–846) Life and Writings." Unpublished Ph.D. dissertation, University of Wisconsin, 1991.
Cheng Guofu 程國賦. "'Li Wa zhuan' yanjiu zongshu" 李娃傳研究綜述. *Jianghan luntan* 4 (1993): 73–75.
Dai Wangshu 戴望舒. "Du Li Wa zhuan" 讀李娃傳, in his *Xiaoshuo xiqu lunji* 小說戲曲論集, Beijing, 1958, pp. 7–26.
DeBlasi, Anthony Augustine. *Reform in the Balance: The Defense of Literary Culture in mid-Tang China*. Albany: State University of New York, 2002, *passim*.
Dudbridge, Glen. *The Tale of Li Wa*.
Fang Shiming 方詩銘. "Tang Bo Xingjian 'Sanmeng ji' kaobian" 唐白行簡三夢記考辨. *Zhonghua wenshi luncong* 53 (1994): 168–84.
Fu Xiren 傅錫壬. "Shi tan 'Li Wa zhuan' de xiezuo dongji ji shidai" 試探李娃傳的寫作動機及時代. *Tamkang Review* 20 (1983): 211–20.
Huang Dahong 黃大宏. "Bo Xingjian nianpu" 白行簡年普, *Wenxian* 文獻 3 (July 2002): 65–78.

Huang Jiaying 黃加應. "'Li Wa zhuan' chuantong pinglun zhiyi" 李娃傳傳統評論質疑 *Hangzhou Daxue xuebao*, 17.1 (March 1987): 49–53 and 84.

Idema, Wilt. Review of Glen Dudbridge, *The Tale of Li Wa*, *TP* 71 (1985): 279–82.

Kominami Ichirō 小南一郎. "'Ri Ai den' no kōzō" 李娃伝の構造, *Tōhō gakuhō* 62 (1990): 271–309.

Lee Yuhua. *Fantasy and Realism in Chinese Fiction: Tang Love Themes in Contrast*. San Francisco: Chinese Material Center, 1984.

Li Jianguo 李劍國. "'Li Wa zhuan' yiwen kaobian ji qita—jian yi Taiping guangji yin wen tili" 李娃傳疑文考辨及其他—兼議太平廣記的引文體例, *Wenxue yichan* 3 (2007): 73–79.

___. "Zhulin shen, Pingkang li, Xuanyang li—guanyu 'Li Wa zhuan' de yi chu quewen" 竹林神, 平康里, 宣陽里—關於李娃傳的一處闕文, *Wenshi baiti* 6 (2007): 33–38.

Liu Guozhong 劉國忠. "Du Deqiao de 'Li Wa zhuan' yanjiu" 杜德僑的李娃傳研究, *Shupin* 書品, 1999.1: 70–74.

Nienhauser, William H., Jr. Review of Glen Dudbridge, *The Tale of Li Wa*, *JAOS*, 106 (1986): 400–01.

___. "A Third Look at 'Li Wa zhuan,'" *TS* 25 (2008): 91–110.

Uchiyama Chinari 內山知也. "Haku Kōkan to 'Ri Ai den'" 白行簡と李娃傳, *Daku kiyō* 10 (March 1972): 169–97.

Van Gulik, Robert H. *Sexual Life in Ancient China*. Leiden: Brill, 1974. A summary (partly in Latin) and discussion of the "Dale fu" is on pp. 203–208.

Wang Meng'ou 王夢鷗. "'Li Wa zhuan' xiecheng niandai de shangque" 李娃傳寫成年代的商榷, *Zhongwai wenxue* 1.4 (September 1972): 32–39.

Zheng Qiaofang 鄭喬方. "Li Wa gushi de yanbian" 李娃故事的演變. *Fuda Zhongyansuo xuekan* 輔大中研所學刊 4 (1995): 307–19.

Zhu Jincheng 朱金城. *Bo Juyi nianpu* 白居易年譜. Shanghai: Shanghai Guji, 1982.

Sarah Yim and William H. Nienhauser, Jr.

Cao Tang 曹唐 (*zi*, Yaobin 堯賓, ca. 797–ca. 866), Daoist poet, was a native of Guizhou 桂州 (modern Guilin) or Chenzhou 郴州 (modern Hunan). Not much is known about Cao's life. A Daoist adept in his youth, Cao later returned to secular life. Traditional accounts say this was during the Dahe reign (827–835), but the modern scholar Liang Chaoran 梁超然 (b. 1936) has surmised that this happened in 821 at the latest, since Cao spent three years (ca. 822–825) as a Retainer (*Congshi* 從事) in Shaozhou 邵州 (modern Shaoyang, Hunan). Cao also served again as Retainer in Rongzhou 容州 (modern Rong County, Guangxi) in the late 820s, and possibly also in Yuezhou 岳州 (modern Yueyang, Hunan) in the early 850s.

Cao spent at least thirty years (roughly 820s–850s) traveling between the capital and remote locations, taking the exams and seeking employment. He took the imperial examination some time during the Dazhong reign (847–860), and possibly also once or several times in the 820s and 830s when he spent time on and off in the capital. There are differing accounts regarding Cao's success in these exams, but since he only held the minor position of Retainer, he most likely failed. The posts Cao did hold were probably obtained due to the notoriety he enjoyed for his wandering-immortal poetry (*youxianshi* 遊仙詩), which was popular in the capital and beyond.

With 130 surviving wandering-immortal poems, Cao Tang boasts the greatest number of poems in this genre of any Tang poet. Although only ninety-nine of Cao's "Xiao youxianshi" 小

Cao Tang

遊仙詩 (Minor Wandering-Immortal Poems) survive, he most likely wrote a cycle of one-hundred poems, as was the fashion in the Tang.

Cao's minor wandering-immortal poems, for the most part, describe the life and romantic musings of transcendent women. He uses popular Daoist figures and imagery to express themes typical to poetry of the Tang, such as the frailty of life and frustrated love. The sensual way in which the transcendent women in Cao's poems are portrayed is often compared to the depiction of elite women in palace-style lyrics (*gongti ci* 宮體詞).

Seventeen of an original fifty "Dayouxianshi" 大遊仙詩 (Grand Wandering-Immortal Poems) are extant. Written in seven-syllable regulated verse (*qilü* 七律), these seventeen poems differ from earlier poems in this genre, which described the poet's journey to an immortal realm and his ingestion of various life-extending herbs or elixirs. Cao's other poems, on the other hand, relate vignettes from eleven popular tales, such as the Emperor Wu of the Han's (Han Wudi 漢武帝, r. 141–87) encounter with the Queen Mother of the West (Xiwangmu 西王母) and the star-crossed lovers, the Herder Boy (Niulang 牛郎) and Weaving Girl (Zhinü 織女).

Some scholars have posited that Cao's grand wandering immortal poems were intended as companion pieces for oral-storytelling performances. One set of five poems, for example, neatly progresses through the main scenes in a story about Liu Chen 劉晨 and Ruan Zhao 阮肇 that is preserved in Liu Yiqing's (403–444) *Youming lu* 幽明錄 (*Record of the Hidden and Visible*). In this story, Liu and Ruan stumble upon an immortal's grotto while picking herbs on Mount Tiantai 天臺山. They meet and fall in love with two immortal women who reside there. Growing homesick after half a year, Liu and Ruan return home to find that seven generations had already passed. When they try to return to the grotto, they are unable to find the entrance.

The language of this set of poems is clear and simple, and two of them end with a couplet that foreshadows the next scene. "Liu Chen Ruan Zhao You Tiantai" 劉晨阮肇遊天台 (Liu Chen and Ruan Zhao Wander on [Mount] Tiantai" Liu Chen and Ruan Zhao Wander on [Mount] Tiantai), for example, ends with the lines: "They do not know where this place will lead, / In a moment they will go to the Peach Blossom Font and ask the host" 不知此地歸何處，須就桃源問主人. There might have originally been more poems describing Liu and Ruan's encounter with the immortals, but these are now missing from the cycle. "Xianzi Dongzhong You Huai Liu Ruan" 仙子洞中有懷劉阮 (The Immortals in the Grotto Long for Liu and Ruan) is representative of Cao's grand wandering-immortal poems:

> She does not take up the clear zither to play "Rainbow Skirts,"
> How could mortals' dusty dreams know how long immortal crane dreams last?
> The grotto has its own heaven, springtime is quiet and lonely,
> There is no path to the world of men, the moon is vast and distant.
> Jade sand and jasper plants link with the creek's green,
> Peach blossoms on the flowing water fill the ravine with fragrance.
> Morning dew and hurricane lamps wane, disappear completely,
> In this lifetime she has no way to visit Master Liu.

不將清瑟理霓裳，塵夢那知鶴夢長。
洞裏有天春寂寂，人間無路月茫茫。

玉沙瑤草連溪碧，流水桃花滿澗香。
曉露風燈零落盡，此生無處訪劉郎。

Unable to search for Liu Chen in the dusty world, his immortal lover can only pine for him in her grotto of endless springtimes. Time continues to pass in the mortal world, and she knows that he will be unable to return to her in his lifetime. The title suggests that there was originally another poem that describes the longing of the other immortal lover for Ruan Zhao.

Cao's remaining poems explore such topics as buying swords and seeing someone off. Of these, the series of five poems titled "Bing Ma" 病馬 (A Sick Horse) has garnered the most attention and is thought to reflect the poet's disappointment with his official career, similar to Li He's 李賀 (790–816)* cycle of horse poems. The recipients of Cao's occasional poems are minor officials, Daoists, and recluses.

Cao Tang's wandering-immortal poetry was well received by his contemporaries. His poems inspired imitations by a number of later poets, including Wang Zi 王鎡 (early 13th c.), Zhang Zhu 張翥 (1287–1368), Xu Teng 徐熥 (ca. 1580–ca. 1637), and Li E 厲鶚 (1692–1752). By the Qing dynasty, Cao Tang's name had become synonymous with wandering-immortal poetry. Cao did not put together his own collection of poetry. Some of his poems were included in poetry anthologies as early as the late-Tang, such as Wei Zhuang's 韋莊 (ca. 836–910)* *You Xuan Ji* 又玄集 (Another Compilation of the Mysterious).

BIBLIOGRAPHY

Editions:
Cao Ye 曹鄴 (*jinshi* 850). Jiang Mian 蔣冕 (1463–1533), ed. *Cao Ci bu ji* 曹祠部集, SKQS ed.
Hong Mai 洪邁 (1123–1202), ed. *Wanshou Tangren jueju* 萬首唐人絕句. Beijing: Wenxue Guji Kanxingshe, 1955, 3:1859–1888. (Photolithograph of Ming Jiajing edition, *juan* 61, 1a–15b). (98 poems)
Qian Qianyi 錢謙益 (1582–1664) and He Zhuo 何焯 (1661–1722). *Tangshi guchui pingzhu* 唐詩鼓吹評注. Punctuated and collated by Han Chengwu 韓成武, et al. Baoding: Hebei Daxue, 2000, pp. 169–182.
Quan Tang shi, 10: 7386–404.

Annotations:
Chen Jiming 陳繼明. *Cao Tang shi zhu* 曹唐詩注. Shanghai: Shanghai Guji, 1996.
Wanshou Tangren jueju jiaozhu ji ping 萬首唐人絕句校註集評. Huo Songlin 霍松林, ed. Taiyuan: Shanxi Renmin, 1991, 3:1051–1074.
Wen Yiduo 聞一多 (1899–1946). "Tangshi daxi" 唐詩大係 in *Wen Yiduo quanji* 聞一多全集. Zhu Ziqing 朱自清 (1898–1948), et al. eds. Shanghai: Kaiming, 1948, 4:421–23. (28 poems)
Xi Qiyu 席啓寓 (d. 1703). *Cao Congshi ji* 曹從事集. *Tangshi baimingjia quanji* 唐詩百名家全集, vol. 31. Shanghai: Saoye Shanfang, 1920.
Yuan Haowen 元好問 (1190–1257). Notations by Hao Tianting 郝天挺 (1247–1313), explicated by Liao Wenbing 廖文炳 (fl. 1579). *Tangshi guchui* 唐詩鼓吹. SKQS ed. (18 poems)

Biographical Sources:
Fu, *Tang caizi*, 3:489–508, 5:427–30.

Cao Tang

Translations:

Owen, *Late Tang*, pp. 315–34.

Schafer, Edward H. *Mirages on the Sea of Time: The Taoist Poetry of Ts'ao T'ang*. Berkeley: University of California, 1985, *passim*.

Studies:

Bai Xiuye 柏秀葉. "Cao Tang 'Dayouxianshi' de xushi tese tanxi" 曹唐〈大遊仙詩〉的敘事特色探析, *Chongqing Gongshang Daxue xuebao (Shehui kexue ban)* 4.22 (2005): 111–15.

Chen Jiming 陳繼明. "Cao Tang shige lüelun" 曹唐詩歌略论, *Zhongnan Minzu Xueyuan xuebao (Shehui kexue ban)* 4 (1986): 84–89.

Chen Lili 陈丽丽. "'Cao Tang shiyu' chengshu niandai ji bianzhe zaikao bian" '草堂诗余'成书年代及编者再考辨, *Zhongguo wenxue yanjiu* 2 (2013): 41–64.

Chen Zhiqiang 陳志強. "Cao Ye, Cao Tang shige yongyun zai kao" 曹鄴、曹唐詩歌用韻再考, *Guangxi Jiaoyu Xueyuan xuebao (Shehui kexue ban)* 1 (1999): 58–62.

Cheng Qianfan 程千帆. "Guo Jingchun, Cao Yaobin 'Youxian' shi bianyi" 郭景純、曹堯賓〈遊仙〉詩辨異. *Gushi kaosuo* 古詩考索. Shanghai: Shanghai Guji, 1984, pp. 166–79.

Fu Xuancong 傅璇琮, ed. *Zhongguo gudai shiwen mingzhu tiyao (Han Tang Wudai juan)* 中國古代詩文名著提要. Shijiazhuang: Hebei Jiaoyu, 2009, pp. 465–67.

Huang Nanjin 黃南津. "Cao Ye, Cao Tang shige yongyun kao" 曹鄴、曹唐詩歌用韻考, *Guangxi Jiaoyu Xueyuan xuebao (Shehui kexue ban)* 2 (1996): 46–52.

Jin Bingyan 金丙燕. "Cao Tang ji qi shige yanjiu" 曹唐及其詩歌研究. Unpublished M.A. thesis, Nanjing Shifan Daxue, 2008.

Li Fengmao 李豐楙. "Cao Tang dayouxianshi yu Daojiao chuanshuo" 曹唐大遊仙詩與道教傳說, *Tangdai wenxue yanjiu* 唐代文學研究, vol. 3. Guilin: Guangxi Shifan Daxue, 1992, pp. 442–75.

___. "Cao Tang 'xiaoyouxianshi' de shenxian shijie chutan" 曹唐〈小遊仙詩〉的神仙世界初探. *You yu you: Liuchao Sui Tang youxianshi lunji* 優與遊—六朝隋唐遊仙詩論集. Taibei: Xuesheng, 1996, pp. 175–256.

Li Nailong 李乃龍. "Lun Cao Tang xiao youxianshi de wenxue yiyi" 論曹唐小遊仙詩的文學意義, *Guangxi Shehui Kexue* 6 (1998): 98–101.

Li Yongping 李永平 and Gao Hui 高慧. "Wan Tang Cao Tang youxianshi zhong de xiandong yuanxing jianji lishi yanjin zhong de wutuobang dingshi" 晚唐曹唐遊仙詩中的仙洞原型—兼及歷史演進中的烏托邦定勢, *Ningxia Shehui Kexue* 3 (2006): 153–55.

Liang Chaoran 梁超然. "Wan Tang shiren Cao Tang jiqi shige" 晚唐詩人曹唐及其詩歌, *Tangdai wenxue* 1 (1982): 72–79.

___. "Wan Tang Guilin shiren Cao Tang kaolüe" 晚唐桂林诗人曹唐考略, *Guangxi Shifan Daxue xuebao (Zhexue shehui kexue ban)* 4 (1989): 30–34.

Schafer, *Mirages* (see translations above).

Zhao Hongkui 趙洪奎. "Cao Tang shige jianlun" 曹唐詩歌簡論, *Xueshu luntan* 4 (2005): 172–74.

Meghan Cai

Cen Shen 岑參 (715–770) was a major poet during the High Tang era. He was born in Jiangling 江陵 County of Jingzhou 荊州 prefecture (southwest of modern Wuhan in Hubei) and was a member of the famous Cen Clan of Nanyang 南陽 (modern Hunan). His grandfather, Cen Wenben 岑文本 (595–645), was an important scholar, writer and official under Tang Taizong (r. 626–649). Cen Shen, however, was orphaned at an early age and spent his youth in the Song

Mountains 嵩山 near Luoyang (modern Henan). He passed the *jinshi* examination in 744 and was appointed an Adjutant in the office of the heir apparent's bodyguard. After languishing in that position for four years, he found a patron in the powerful general Gao Xianzhi 高仙芝 (d. 755). Appointed Gao's secretary, he accompanied the general to Kucha in Central Asia in 749, returning to Chang'an in 751 after Gao's disastrous defeat in the Battle of Talas. That year Cen joined Gao Shi 高適 (700–765),* Du Fu 杜甫 (712–770),* Chu Guangxi 儲光羲 (ca. 706–ca. 762),* and Xue Ju 薛據 (*jinshi* 731) in a visit to the Temple of Compassionate Mercy 慈恩寺 in the capital, where the group composed what would later become a much anthologized collection of poems celebrating the pagoda of the famous temple. In 754, Cen returned to Central Asia, where he served General Feng Changqing 封常清 (d. 756) as Administrative Assistant.

The eight years between 749 and 757 spent in Central Asia were perhaps Cen's most creative period. He returned to China after the An Lushan 安祿山 Rebellion had erupted, arriving in 757 at Emperor Suzong's (r. 756–762) temporary court in Fengxiang 鳳翔 (near modern Baoji 寶雞, Shaanxi). There, on the recommendation of his friend Du Fu, he was appointed Rectifier of Omissions of the Right. When the emperor returned to Chang'an, Cen suffered the same fate as Du Fu: he was dismissed from court and sent to Guozhou 虢州 (Lushi County 盧氏縣 in modern Henan). Unlike Du Fu, however, Cen was recalled to the capital in 762 where he held a series of posts including Imperial Diarist; he also accompanied the future Emperor Dezong (r. 779–805) on a campaign against Shi Chaoyi 史朝義 (d. 763). In 765 he became Prefect of Jiazhou 嘉州 (modern Leshan City 樂山市 in Sichuan; Cen is also known as Cen Jiazhou). A local rebellion delayed his departure until 766, when he accompanied Du Hongjian 杜鴻漸 (709–769) campaign to put down the insurgency. By 767 he was able to take his post at Jiazhou. In the summer of 768 he headed homeward again, but his route was cut off by yet another local rebellion. He died in Chengdu 成都 in 770.

Cen Shen is now chiefly remembered for the "frontier" poetry he composed during his two sojourns in Central Asia. His achievement in this subgenre may be viewed both as a departure from, as well as the culmination of the poetic tradition. Writing after the great frontier songs such as Gao Shi's "Yange xing" 燕歌行 (Song of Yan), Wang Han's 王翰 (fl. 713) "Liangzhou ci" 涼州詞 (Lyrics of Liangzhou) and Wang Changling's 王昌齡 (ca. 690–ca. 756)* exquisite quatrains, Cen's most memorable poems may be considered the apogee of a vigorous tradition. On the other hand, his personal knowledge of a region that hitherto had been only the stuff of poetic convention allowed him to extend the tradition. Recent studies have shown that Cen's knowledge of the geography of Central Asia far exceeded that of the other poets who wrote on the frontier; poems on such topics as the hot volcanic lakes explore subjects previously unknown in Chinese poetry.

Yet this identification of Cen Shen with the poetry of the frontier and martial exploits is a late critical emphasis that may be misleading. Of Cen's more than four hundred poems, only a small number has the frontier as its subject, and these were written during only an eight-year period of the poet's life. Contemporary scholars pay little attention to the nature and eremitic works of the poet's early years or the artistically mature pieces written after 757. A more balanced critical perspective, perhaps, is to consider Cen Shen as a master of the craft of poetry, a stylist who creates daring, original, and ingenious effects with the most ordinary of themes. As testament to Cen's craftsmanship, traditional critics cite couplets that are among the most felicitous in Tang poetry. They also observe that Cen's mastery of his poetic art is not matched by the strength of his emotion. However, Cen's works are a triumph of art over feeling; in them technical cunning and brilliant ornamentation mask pedestrian sentiments, such as that on display in his "Zouma Chuan xing—feng song chushi xizheng" 走馬川行—奉送出師西征 (A Song of the Surging Horses River: Respectfully Seeing off the Army on Campaign to the West):

> Don't you see
> At Surging Horses River by the banks of the Snowy Sea,
> The yellow storm swirling up into Heaven on the desert plain?
> Over Luntai in the ninth month the wind howls at night;
> A river of loose pebbles and bushel-basket size stones
> Rush with the wind and dash all over the ground.
> The Xiongnu's grasses turn yellow, just as their horses grow fat;
> To the west of the Golden Mountains the rolling dust [of enemy riders],
> Heading west the Grand General of the House of Han sends out its host.
> Never removing his armor even at night;
> Mid through the night the soldiers' halberds clatter as they knock together.
> The wind cuts like a knife blade, as if their faces were slashed;
> With snow clinging to the horses' hair, sweat steams up,
> And quickly becomes ice on the dappled and piebald hides;
> The ink in the stone congeals as an urgent dispatch is drafted in the general's tent,
> Hearing of this, the caitiff cavalry should quiver in fear;
> We know that they dare not meet us face to face,
> So at the west gate of Jushi we wait for prisoners to be presented.

> 君不見，
> 走馬川行雪海邊，平沙莽莽黃入天。
> 輪台九月風夜吼，一川碎石大如鬥，
> 隨風滿地石亂走。匈奴草黃馬正肥，
> 金山西見煙塵飛，漢家大將西出師。
> 將軍金甲夜不脫，半夜軍行戈相撥，
> 風頭如刀面如割。馬毛帶雪汗氣蒸，
> 五花連錢旋作冰，幕中草檄硯水凝。
> 虜騎聞之應膽懾，料知短兵不敢接，
> 車師西門佇獻捷。

Chen's poem offers the timeless depiction of Chinese soldiers in their struggle with the nomadic peoples of the steppe that had become something of a literary trope. Allusions to the grand military campaigns of one the great generals of the Han dynasty (perhaps Li Guang 李廣) and the stalwart soldiers who accompanied him is set amidst the place names of that era—their memory conjured as the poet looks out over Xuehai 雪海, (the Snowy Sea). "Snowy Sea" is a lake located in present-day Russia about thirty miles from Lake Isykukul, a place Cen Shen would himself visit while attached to the Tang armies. Here, out on his own frontier, the author deploys war imagery—the clattering weapons and the steam of war horses—rising from the frozen Chinese camp in the wilderness. Pride for the intimidating presence of the imperial army recalls the longstanding tension between the center and periphery that continued to define imperial attitudes towards the steppe from ancient times to his own.

BIBLIOGRAPHY

Editions:
Cen Jiazhou shi 岑嘉州詩. SBCK.
Quan Tang shi, 3: 2028–110, 14: 11112.
Quan Tang wen, 358.4099–100.

Reference Works:
Shimmen Keiko 新免惠子. *Shin Shin kashi sakuin* 岑參歌詩索引. Hiroshima: Chūgoku Chūsei Bungaku Kenkyūkai, 1978.

Annotations:
Chen Tiemin 陳鐵民 and Hou Zhongyi 侯忠義. *Cen Shen ji jiaozhu* 岑參集校注. Shanghai: Shanghai Guji, 1981.
Lin Maoxiong 林茂雄. *Cen Jiazhou shi jiao zhu yu ping jian* 岑嘉州詩校注與評箋. Taibei: Wanjuan Lou Tushu Gufen 萬卷樓圖書股份, 2013.
Liu Kaiyang 劉開揚. *Cen Shen shi xuan* 岑參詩選. Shanghai: Shanghai Guji, 1983.
Ruan Tingyu 阮廷瑜. *Cen Jiazhou shi jiaozhu* 岑嘉州詩校注. Taibei: Guoli Bianyi Guan Zhonghua Congshu Bianshen Weiyuanhui, 1980.
Tu Yuanqu 涂元渠. *Gao Shi, Cen Shen shi xuanzhu* 高適，岑參詩選注. Shanghai: Shanghai Guji, 1983.
Zhang Hui 張輝, ed. *Cen Shen biansai shi xuan* 岑參邊塞詩選. Beijing: Renmin Wenxue, 1981. Contains over 70 poems, with lengthy annotations.

Biographical Sources:
Fu, *Tang Caizi*, 3:439–45, 5:80–81.

Translations:
Bynner, *Jade Mountain*, pp. 108–12.
Demiéville, *Anthologie*, p. 294.
Mair, *Anthology*, p. 220.
Margoulies, *Anthologie*, pp. 232, 317, 375, 415.
Owen, *High T'ang*, pp. 165–82.
Payne, *White Pony*, pp. 179–81.
Sunflower, pp. 143–49.

Studies:
Chan, Marie. "The Frontier Poems of Ts'en Shen," *JAOS*, 97.4 (1979): 420–37.
Lai Yihui 賴義輝. *Cen Shen nianpu* 岑參年譜. Beijing: Beijing Tushuguan, 1999.
Li Jiayan 李嘉言. "Cen shi xianian" 岑詩系年, *Wenxue yichan zengkan* 3 (1956): 119–54.
Liao Li 廖立. *Cen Shen shiji zhuozuo kao* 岑參事蹟著作考. Zhengzhou: Zhongzhou Guji, 1997.
Liu Kaiyang 劉開揚. "Lüetan Cen Shen he ta de shi" 略談岑參和他的詩, in his *Tang shi lunwen ji* 唐詩論文集, Shanghai: Shanghai Guji, 1979, pp. 68–82.

Nakano, Miyoko 中野美伐子. "Shih Shin no saigai shi" 岑參の塞外詩, *Nihon Chūgoku Gakkai-hō* 12 (1960): 38–54.
Owen, *High Tang,* pp. 169–82.
Shi Moqing 史墨清. *Cen Shen yanjiu* 岑參研究. Taibei: Shangwu, 1966.
Sugaya Shōgo 菅谷省吾. "Shih Shin no koshi ni tsuite" 岑參の古詩について, *Shinagaku kenkyū* 24–25 (1960): 152–62.
Sun Zhi 孫植, "Sun Shen shengnian zhushuo bianyi" 岑參生年諸說辨疑. *Hainan Shifan Daxue xuebao (Shehui kexue ban),* 26.9 (2013): 7–11.
Suzuki, *Tōdai,* pp. 393–451.
Waley, Arthur. "A Chinese Poet in Central Asia," in *The Secret History of the Mongols,* London: George Allen & Unwin, 1963, pp. 30–46. On Cen Shen's life and verse; contains translations of seven poems.
Wang Su 王素. "Tubo Wenshu zhong youguan Cen Shen de yixie ziliao" 吐蕃文書中有關岑參的一些資料, *Wenshi* 文史, 32 (1992): 185–98.
Xu Baicheng 徐百成. *Cen Shen xiyu shi xinshi* 岑參西域詩新釋. Wulumuqi: Xinjiang Renmin, 1992.
Zhan, *Daojiao,* pp. 241–48.

Marie Chan and William H. Nienhauser, Jr.

Chang Gun 常袞 (zi, Yifu 夷甫, 729–783) was born in the Tang capital, Chang'an, during the heyday of Emperor Xuanzong's reign (r. 712–756). His great-grandfather, Chang Xu 常緒, grandfather Chang Yi 常毅, and father Chang Wuwei 常無為, all served as minor officials, and he also had at least one older brother, Chang Jie 常皆. The timing of his official career was optimal, as he passed the *jinshi* examination as the top graduate in 755, just before the outbreak of the An Lushan Rebellion. He was made Proofreader in the Secretariat of the Heir Apparent, Li Heng 李亨 (711–762), who was to become Emperor Suzong (r. 756–762) a few years later, but held no higher position until Suzong's eldest son, Li Yu 李豫 (726–779, r. 763–779), became emperor in 763 upon Suzong's death. That year Chang was appointed a Supernumerary in the Bureau of Evaluations and concurrently a Hanlin Scholar. In 765 he was promoted to become Secretariat Drafter and a Scholar in the Academy of Scholarly Worthies. Chang seems to either have had a talent for documentary writing or developed one in these positions.

In 774 he made Vice-minister of the Ministry of Rites, a significant promotion; in this role was the Chief Examiner for the *jinshi* from 775 to 777. Following the demotion of the powerful ministers Yuan Zai 元載 (d. 777) and Wang Jin 王縉 (700–782) early in 777, he became Vice-Director of the Chancellery and concurrently a Jointly Manager of Affairs with the Secretariat-Chancellery, i.e. one of the Grand Councilors. After the fall of Yuan and Wang there was a hiatus during which official positions were left empty. Once Chang took power he is said to have made 800 appointments in 200 days, stressing the importance of candidates' literary skills. He was often at odds, especially over matters of ritual, with his colleague Cui Youfu 崔祐甫 (721–780), the son of Cui Mian 崔沔 (673–739), and thus the descendant of a distinguished, old elite family. The friction between them was in part due to their opposing backgrounds, since Chang was a member of the literary elite who had risen through the *jinshi* examination. Chang was a staunch Confucian who opposed the Buddhist and Daoist elements at Daizong's (r. 762–779) court. He instituted some reforms and cleared much of the corruption that characterized the years Yuan Zai was in power. He and Yang Yan 楊炎 (727–781) were the two key rescript writers of the 770s; a reading of Chang's over 250 memorials and rescripts provides an excellent insight into the workings of the central government in the later part of this decade. His "Xie jin chengzi ci cha biao" 謝進橙子賜茶表 (Memorial Giving Thanks for Being Conferred Tea after Presenting Oranges [to the Emperor]) was probably written during these years (perhaps the "military alert" refers to the problems with Tibetan incursions which went on into the 770s):

> Your subject, a certain person, states: the messenger from the palace [i.e. a eunuch] has arrived at a certain time and he was ordered to proclaim the decree of the universal sage [i.e. the emperor]: because of the orange trees that your subject presented before the Sagely Ancestor Hall [of Laozi] in the Great Purity Palace [of the Heir Apparent], one hundred cakes of tea were conferred on me. This honorable reward is beyond what I deserve and I am fearful and anxious in accepting your command. Your Majesty's reverence for the Original Ancestor in the palace has caused the root and branches to flourish, sending down a sweet fragrance over the beautiful trees, and the fruits have become treasures, often causing those in charge to collect and protect the fruit with wrappings. When the time was right they collected them to present them, but just as your subject wrongly took the lead to offer them as tribute, it was in a time of military alert, how could I expect that your imperial favor would arrive, bestowing favor with this humble official's private present. What I fear is that I claimed Heaven's credit in this. I tread lightly in trepidation, incapable of fulfilling my official duties.
>
> 臣某言：中使某至，奉宣聖旨。 以臣所進太清宮聖祖殿前橙子，賜茶百串，榮齋非次，承命兢惶。 伏以陛下尊元元于上宮，本枝既盛，降馨香于嘉木，果實自珍，常令護領之司，及時采摘以進。 臣謬當率職，正在戎期，豈望皇澤之曲臨，寵及下臣之私獻。 貪天是懼，踏地載惶。 無任。

In the final years of Daizong's reign, Chang enjoyed great power. Feeling that he should have a noble title, he induced the famous general and statesman Guo Ziyi 郭子儀 (697–781) to support him and was given the honorific title Duke of Henei 河內公. In 779 after Emperor Dezong (r. 779–805) took the throne, but still during the mourning period for Daizong, Chang argued with Cui Youfu over the number of days the officials should wear mourning. He was able to have Cui exiled, but soon overstepped his authority by signing a document that required the approval of the other two Grand Councilors and in turn was banished to become Vice Governor of Henan and then further exiled to serve as Prefect of Chaozhou 潮州 (modern Guangdong). Despite the reforms Chang instituted under Daizong to prevent the purchasing of official positions, he had preferred his own men for appointments, would jealously attack some of his former colleagues too vigorously, and had made enemies among the eunuchs. Nevertheless, after Yang Yan was made a Grand Councilor in 780, Yang was able to have Chang promoted to become Surveillance Commissioner of Fujian. Chang established the first schools in Fujian and promoted Confucian education there, where his efforts would result in the first scholar from the area passing the *jinshi* examinations. He died in 783 while serving in Fujian.

Although we have only nine extant poems from Chang Gun (some of these are attributed to Lu Lun 盧綸 [748-ca. 798]*), his reputation as a man of letters and the fact that he knew many of the famous poets of the Dali era (766–779) suggests he was also an active poet.

BIBLIOGRAPHY

Editions:
Quan Tang shi, 4: 2851–53, 14: 11136.
Quan Tang wen, 410–20.4825–916.

Biographical Sources:
Jiu Tang shu, 119.3445–47.
Xin Tang shu, 150.4809.

Studies:
Chen Ye 陳曄. "Tabo yu xianxiang: Chang Gun xiangye de Songdai shushi" 毊伯與賢相: 常衮相業的宋代敘事, *Jiangxi shehui kexue*, 2019.1: 135–44
Yang Wenxin 杨文新, "Tangdai Fujian Guanchashi Chang Gun shiji shuping" 唐代福建觀察使常衮事迹述評, *Fujian Jiaoyu Xueyuan xuebao* 7 (2002): 33–35.

William H. Nienhauser, Jr.

Chang Jian 常建 (fl. 727) grew up in Chang'an, where he pursued his studies and passed the *jinshi* examination in 727 along with Wang Changling 王昌齡 (ca. 690–ca. 756).* Although he must have been part of the capital poetic scene at the time, we know nothing of his career until he served much later as Commandant of Xuyi 盱眙 (modern Jiangsu) during the Tianbao 天寶 era (742–756) and then went into reclusion at West Mountain on Ezhu 鄂渚 (E Islet, near modern Wuchang in Hubei) where he kept company for a time with Wang Changling, composing such poems such as "Ezhu zhao Wang Changling zhangfen" 鄂渚招王昌齡張僨 (At Ezhu, beckoning Wang Changling to my Expansive Ruin). Separated from the capital, he developed his own poetic style. Consequently, he is noted for his recluse poetry as well as his frontier poetry. Fewer than sixty of his poems survive (one *juan*) but these show great variety and originality. His verse and that of Wang Changling make up much of Yin Fan's 殷璠 famous anthology, *Heyue yingling ji* 河岳英靈集. "Poshan Si hou chanyuan" 破山寺後禪院 (The Meditation Court behind Broken-Mountain Temple) is a fine example of the pure, impersonal nature poetry at which Chang Jian excelled:

> Early morning I enter the ancient temple;
> the first light illuminating the towering forest.
> A bamboo path leads to a secluded abode;
> the meditation cell is deep in flowers and trees.
> The mountain's radiance brings joy to the birds;
> A pond's reflection empties human minds.
> All kinds of sounds become still,
> but for the chiming of the ritual bell and chime stone.

> 清晨入古寺，初日照高林。
> 竹徑通幽處，禪房花木深。

山光悅鳥性，潭影空人心。
萬籟此都寂，但餘鐘磬音。

BIBLIOGRAPHY

Editions:
Chang Jian shi 常建詩. 3 *juan*. Taibei: Taiwan Shangwu, 1983–1986.
Chang Jian shiji 常建詩集. 2 *juan*. Beijing: Beijing Tushuguan, 2004.
Quan Tang shi, 2: 1456–67.
Quan Tang wen, 334.3827.
Song Lin'an ben Chang Jian shiji 宋臨安本常建詩集. 2 *juan*. Beijing: Gugong Bowuyuan, 1932.

Biographical Sources:
Fu, *Tang caizi*, 1:263–69, 5:68.

Translations:
Frankel, Hans, *Palace Lady*, pp. 115–16.
Minford and Lau, p. 841.
Owen, *High T'ang*, pp. 88–90.
Payne, *White Pony*, pp. 232–33.
Sunflower, p. 101.

Studies:
Fu Xuanzong 傅璇琮. "Chang Jian kao" 常建考 in *Tangdai shiren congkao* 唐代詩人叢考. Beijing: Zhonghua, 1980, pp. 78–87.
Harada, Ken'yu 原田憲雄. "Jo Ken shishu kochu" 常建詩集校注, *Jimbun ronso,* 13 (1966): 1–38.
Mou Chenyi 牟臣益. "Chang Jian biansaishi de beiku yishi" 常建边塞诗的悲苦意识, *Xinan shifan daxue xuebao* (*Renwen shehui kexue ban*) 2 (1990): 121–26.
Sun Lijun 孙丽君. "Yinyue yu shige de shentou–jiantan Chang Jian shige de yinyue xing" 音乐与诗歌的渗透—浅谈常建诗歌的音乐性, *Jinri nanguo* (*lilun chuangxin ban*) 9 (2009): 122.
Tang Zhuang 谭庄. "Chang Jian shengzunian kaobian" 常建生卒年考辨, *Wenhua xuekan* 3 (May, 2009): 147–51.
Wang Tinjiu 王锡九. "Chang Jian shige jianlun" 常建诗歌浅论, *Yangzhou shiyuan xuebao* (*Shehui kexue ban*) 1 (1988): 27–31.
Wu Heqing 吴河清. "'Chang Jian shiji' banben yuanliu kaoshu" 《常建詩集》版本源流考述, *Suzhou daxue xuebao* (*Zhexue shehui kexue ban*) 5 (2007): 74–78.
Wu Zhefu 吳哲夫. "Song ban Chang Jian shiji" 宋版常建詩集, *Gugong Tushu jikan* 1.2 (1970): 79–80.
Yang Lin 杨霖, "TangSong shixue zhuanguan shiyexia de Chang Jian shige lun" 唐宋诗学转关视野下的常建诗歌论, *Anhui wenxue* 5 (2015): 1–3.
Zhang Haoxun 张浩逊. "Chang Jian shi 'Tangyin kong renxin' xinjie" 常建诗"潭影空人心"新解, 1 (1996): 16.
Zhang Maoyuan 马茂元, "Chang Jian kaolüe buzheng" 常建考略补正, *Shanghai shishifan daxue xuebao* (*Zhexue shehui kexue ban*) 2 (1980): 106.
Zhang Xuezhong 張學忠. "Cong Tangshi kao Chang Jian jiguan" 从唐诗考常建籍贯, *Shaanxi shifan daxue xuebao* (*Zhexue shehui kexue ban*), 2 (1997).

___. "Chang Jian wannian yin yu Qinzhong bian" 常建晚年隱於秦中辨, *Wenxue yichan* 5 (1989): 63–67.
Zhao Yiwen 赵亦文. "Lun Chang Jian shige de yishu mei" 论常建诗歌的艺术美, *Xueshu jiaolu* 2 (2009).

Michael E. Naparstek and William H. Nienhauser, Jr.

Chen Zi'ang 陳子昂 (*zi*, Boyu 伯玉, 659–ca. 699, formerly believed to be 661–702), a native of Shehong 射洪 County in Zizhou 梓州 (Shehong County in modern Sichuan), he was among the first poets in Tang dynasty to openly express discontent over the effeteness of contemporary poetry and to advocate a return to the seriousness of the Han-Wei Style 漢魏體.

Chen passed the *jinshi* examination held in Luoyang in 684, after an unsuccessful attempt in 682. He assumed the post of Proofreader in the Palace Library, but his progress up the official ladder was slow. In 688 he seems to have returned to Shu. In 693 he became Reminder of Omissions of the Right at the age of thirty-three. Chen had been a critic of Wu Sansi's harsh governmental measures, and in probably late 699, while he was in mourning for his father in Sichuan, he died as a result of persecution by the district magistrate, Duan Jian 段簡, acting under instructions from Wu Sansi 武三思 (d. 707), a cousin of Empress Wu (Wu Zhao 武曌 [ca. 624–705]).

Chen Zi'ang's extant literary views are contained in the introduction to his poem "Xiuzhu pian" 修竹篇 (The Tall Bamboo). In it he criticizes the poetry of the Southern Dynasties for its obsession with formal beauty at the expense of profound feelings and advocates a return to more serious themes. He was later recognized for the remainder of the Tang as an innovative poet who set an example for those poets of later ages concerned with social issues. Writers such as Li Bo 李白 (701–762),* Du Fu 杜甫 (712–770),* Han Yu 韓愈 (768–824),* Bo Juyi 白居易 (772–846),* Liu Zongyuan 柳宗元 (773–819),* and Yuan Zhen 元稹 (779–831)* were admirers of Chen Zi'ang.

Chen Zi'ang's poetic reputation rests mainly on his cycle of thirty-eight poems entitled "Ganyu" 感遇 (Stirred by My Experiences, probably begun in 689). The following is the sixth poem in the cycle:

> When I observe the changes of the dragon,
> I know the zenith of the *yang* power.
> No matter how dark and thick the stone forests,
> Or how deep the caves, they cannot bar its passage.
> Of old, those who acquired the immortal's way
> Must indeed have been in harmony with the workings of nature.
> Such subtle inspirations are not for the dull to perceive,
> Which of them can plumb such fathomless depths?
> Men are bound by what they see with their eyes,
> Warm with wine, they laugh at the book of the elixir.
> On the Kunlun is the jasper tree,
> How can they ever gather its blossoms?

> 吾觀龍變化，乃知至陽精。
> 石林何冥密，幽洞無留行。
> 古之得仙道，信與元化并。
> 玄感非蒙識，誰能測淪冥。

世人拘目見，酣酒笑丹經。
崑崙有瑤樹，安得采其英。

This cycle was seen by Du Fu as a paragon of "loyalty and righteousness," because many of the hidden accusations in the poems were directed at the usurper, Empress Wu. The poem quoted above, for example, is full of mythical references. It begins with the dragon, the supreme creature in Chinese geomancy and the embodiment of the *yang* power. As heavenly-mandated emperors have always been symbolized by dragons, this should refer to the displaced royal house of Li. "Stone forests," mentioned in Qu Yuan's 屈原 (ca. 340–ca. 278 BC) "Tianwen" 天問 (Questions to Heaven) and Zuo Si's 左思 (ca. 250–ca. 305) "Wudu fu" 吳都賦 (Rhyme-prose on the Capital of Wu), were apparently a characteristic of the southern landscape. The deposed emperor (Zhongzong, r. 684 and 705–710) was then in exile in what had been the state of Chu 楚 in South China, so both the dragon and the *yang* power might well refer to him. Thus, if one day this supreme symbol of the *yang*, the dragon, were to free itself of all its tethers, it would not brook hindrance by dark stone forests or deep caves, which belong to the *yin* category. In this poem, as in many others of the same cycle, Chen expresses his belief in the revival of the house of Li.

However, the uncommon diction of these poems, probably deliberate to avoid political persecution, veiled the contents, so that by the close of the Tang dynasty, readers no longer understood the allegorical flavor of these texts and, in an ironic twist, appraised them in terms of the style in which they were written. Song Qi 宋祁 (998–1061), who wrote Chen's biography in the *Xin Tang shu*, mistook the "Ganyu" for poetic exercises of Chen's early years. Some later critics even dismissed the poems as meaningless utterances clad in Daoist mysticism. It was not until the Qing dynasty that Chen Hang 陳沆 (1785–1826) realized the allegorical qualities of the poems and attempted to decode the whole cycle in his *Shi bixing jian* 詩比興箋 (Commentary on Selected Allegorical Poems).

BIBLIOGRAPHY

Editions:
Andō Shunroku 安東俊六. *Chin Shikō shi sakuin* 陳子昂詩索引. Nagoya: Saika Shorin, 1976.
Chen Boyu wenji 陳伯玉文集. 10 *juan*. SBCK. Shanghai: Shangwu, 1922.
Chen Zi'ang ji 陳子昂集. Beijing: Zhonghua, 1960. Contains a *nianpu*.
Jiu Tang shu, 190 中.5018–25 (pp. 1281–83).
Luan Guiming 欒貴明 et al., eds. *Quan Tang shi suoyin: Chen Zi'ang, Zhang Yue juan* 全唐詩索引:陳子昂, 張說卷. Qinhuangdao: Xiandai, 1994.
Quan Tang shi, 2: 887–913, 14: 10601.
Quan Tang wen, 134.1510–14.
Xinjiao Chen Zi'ang ji 新校陳子昂集. Taibei: Shijie, 1964.
Xu Peng 徐鵬. *Chen Zi'ang ji* 陳子昂集. Beijing: Zhonghua, 1980. Revised edition, Shanghai: Shanghai Guji, 2013. Standard modern critical edition.

Annotations:
Peng Qingsheng 彭慶生. *Chen Zi'ang shizhu* 陳子昂詩注. Xining: Qinghai Renmin, 1980; Chengdu: Sichuan Renmin, 1981. Reprint Hefei: Huangshan, 2015.

Chen Zi'ang

Biographical Sources:
Fu, *Tang caizi,* 1:101–13.
Jiu Tang shu, 190B.5018–25.
Xin Tang shu, 107.4067–78.

Translations:
Bynner, *Jade Mountain,* p. 10.
Demiéville, *Anthologie,* p. 231.
Frankel, *Palace Lady,* pp. 108–11.
Fuller, Michael A. *An Introduction to Chinese Poetry: From the* Canon of Poetry *to the Lyrics of the Song Dynasty.* Cambridge: Harvard University Press, 2018, pp. 186–87.
Ho, Richard M. W. (see Studies below)
Owen, *Vitality,* pp. 163–64.
Mair, *Anthology,* p. 192.
Miller, Bradford S. *Selections from the Kanyu.* Thousand Oaks, California: Imp Press, 2001.
Minford and Lau, pp. 690–93.
White Pony, p. 150.
Sunflower, pp. 88–89.
Watson, *Columbia,* p. 272.

Studies:
Andō Shunroku 安東俊六. "Chin Shikō no Kangūshi o sasaeru shisō ni tsuite" 陳子昂の「感遇詩」を支える思想について, *Chūgoku bungei zadankai nōto* 6 (1967): 1–15.
___. "Chin Shikō no shiron to sakuhin" 陳子昂の詩論と作品, *Kyūshū Chūgoku gakkaihō* 14 (1968): 47–62.
___. "Shotō bungakushi ni okeru Chin Shikō no ichizuke" 初唐文學史における陳子昂の位置づけ, *Kyūshū Chūgoku gakkaihō* 15 (1969): 16–28.
Bai Zongde 白宗德. *Chen Zi'ang shige yanjiu* 陳子昂詩歌研究. Singapore: Xinjiapo Huawen Jiaoshi Zonghui, 2005.
Bi Wanchen 畢萬忱. "Lun Chen Zi'ang shige lilun de chuantong tezhi" 論陳子昂詩歌理論的傳統特質, *Wenxue yichan* 3 (1990): 42–49.
Cai Maoxiong 蔡茂雄. *Chen Zi'ang* 陳子昂. Taibei: Linbai, 1979.
Chan, Tim. "The 'Ganyu' of Chen Zi'ang: Questions on the Formation of a Poetic Genre," *TP* 87 (2001): 14–42.
Chen Hang. "Chen Zi'ang shijian" 陳子昂詩箋, in *Shi bixing jian* 詩比興箋. Shanghai: Shanghai Guji, 1981, pp. 95–116.
Chen Zi'ang yanjiu lunji 陳子昂研究論集. Beijing: Zhongguo Wenlian Chuban Gongsi, 1989.
Han Lizhou 韓理洲. *Chen Zi'ang pingzhuan* 陳子昂評傳. Xi'an: Xibei Daxue, 1987.
___. *Chen Zi'ang yanjiu* 陳子昂研究. Shanghai: Shanghai Guji, 1988.
Ho, Richard M. W. 何文匯. *Chen Zi'ang Ganyu shijian* 陳子昂感遇詩箋. Hong Kong: Xuejin, 1978. Appended is an article on Chen Zi'ang's controversial memorials written by C. C. Chan.
___. *Ch'en Tzu-ang, Innovator in T'ang Poetry.* London and Hong Kong: School of Oriental and African Studies, University of London and the Chinese University, 1993.
Liu Mau-Tsai. "Der Dichter und Staatsman Chen Zi'ang (661–702) und sein *jen-chi*-Konzept," *OE* 24 (1977): 179–85.
Liu Shi 劉石. "Chen Zi'ang xinlun" 陳子昂新論, *Wenxue pinglun* 2 (1988): 131–37.
Liu Yuanzhi 劉遠智. *Chen Zi'ang jiqi Ganyu shi yanjiu* 陳子昂及其感遇詩研究. Taibei: Wenjin, 1987.

Luo Yong 羅庸 (1900–1950). *Tang Chen Zi'ang xiansheng Boyu nianpu* 唐陳子昂先生伯玉年譜. Taibei: Taiwan Shangwu, 1986.

Mair, Victor H. *Four Introspective Poets: A Concordance to Selected Poems by Roan Jyi, Chern Tzyy-arng, Jang Jeouling, and Lii Bor*. Tempe: Center for Asian Studies, Arizona State University, 1987.

Mori Hiroyuki 森博行. "Chin Shikō Kangūshi sanjuhachi shu no sekai" 陳子昂感遇詩三十八首の世界. *Chūgoku bungakuhō* 36 (1985): 15–46.

Nohara Takurō 野原卓郎. *Chūgoku Tōdaishi ronshū: Chin Shikō Kangūshi, To Ho no kotaishi o yomu* 中国唐代詩論集：陳子昂「感遇」詩，杜甫の古体詩を読む. N.p.: No publisher given, 1989.

Owen, Stephen. "Ch'en Tzu-ang," in *Early T'ang*, pp. 151–223.

Qu Zhen 曲辰. *Chen Zi'ang zhuan* 陳子昂傳. Shenyang: Liaohai, 2018.

Seaton, Jerome P. *The Shambhala Anthology of Chinese Poetry*. Boston: Shambhala, 2008, p. 83.

Shen Huile 沈惠樂 and Qian Huikang 錢惠康. *Chu Tang sijie he Chen Zi'ang* 初唐四傑和陳子昂. Shanghai: Shanghai Guji, 1987.

Sichuan Shehong xian Chen Zi'ang yanjiu lianluozu 四川射洪縣陳子昂研究聯絡組, ed. *Chen Zi'ang yanjiu lunji* 陳子昂研究論集. Beijing: Zhongguo Wenlian Chuban Gongsi, 1989.

Sun Ziyun 孫自筠. *Chen Zi'ang* 陳子昂. Beijing: Renmin Wenxue, 2003.

Takagi Masakazu 高木正一. "Chin Shikō to shi no kakushin" 陳子昂と詩の革新, in *Yoshikawa Hakushi taikyū kinen Chūgoku bungaku ronshū* 吉川博士退休記念中國文學論集, Tokyo, 1968, pp. 353–72.

Wang Guo'an 王國安 and Wang Youmin 王幼敏, ed. *Chu Tang sijie yu Chen Zi'ang shiwen xuanzhu*. 初唐四傑與陳子昂詩文選注. Shanghai: Shanghai Guji, 1995.

Wang Yunxi 王運熙 and Wu Chengxue 吳承學. "Lun Chen Zi'ang de lishi gongxian" 論陳子昂的歷史貢獻, *Xuchang Shizhuan xuebao* 3 (1989): 33–38.

Wu Mingxian 吳明賢. *Chen Zi'ang lunkao* 陳子昂論考. Chengdu: Bashu, 1995.

Xu Wenmao 徐文茂. *Chen Zi'ang lunkao* 陳子昂論考. Shanghai: Shanghai Guji, 2002.

Zhang Buyun 張步雲. "Shi ping chu Tang shiren Chen Zi'ang" 試評初唐詩人陳子昂, *Shanghai Shifan Daxue xuebao* 3 (1988): 51–56.

Zhou Xiaotian 周嘯天. "Wuhou shidai yu Chen Zi'ang de zhengzhi fengci shi" 武后時代與陳子昂的政治諷刺詩, *Chengdu Shizhuan xuebao* 1 (1986): 22–26.

Richard M. W. Ho

Cheng Xuanying 成玄英 (*zi*, Zishi 子實, *hao* Xihua 西華, fl. 631–653) was a Daoist priest-theorist active in the early Tang period. He was a native of Shanzhou 陝州 (modern Shan county in Henan), where he developed an excellent command of Confucian and Daoist classics at a young age. He lived in seclusion in Donghai 東海 (modern eastern Shandong) until he was summoned to the capital, where he was bestowed the title of Xihua fashi 西華法師 (Master of the Western Florescence) in 631. There, Cheng served as abbot of the Xihua Abbey, where Daoist texts were copied for dissemination throughout the empire. In 636, he led the court debate with Buddhists and took part in the Sanskrit translation project in 647. Six years later, Emperor Gaozong (r. 649–683) banished Cheng to Yuzhou 郁州 (modern Lianyungang city in Jiangsu) where he lived in reclusion on Mount Yuntai 雲臺山, focusing on writing commentaries to Daoist classics and scriptures.

Many of Cheng's commentaries are recorded in Song dynasty catalogs: *Lao Zi Daode jing shu* 老子道德經疏 (A Subcommentary on Lao Zi's *Daode jing*) in 2 *juan*, *Lao Zi kaiti xujue yishu* 老子開題序訣義疏 (A Subcommentary and Topical Introduction to the *Lao Zi*) in 7 *juan*, *Zhuang Zi zhu*

Cheng Xuanying

莊子注 (A Commentary on *Zhuang Zi*) in 30 *juan*, and *Zhuang Zi shu* 莊子疏 (Subcommentary on *Zhuang Zi*) in 12 *juan*. Chen Jingyuan's 陳景元 (d. 1094) later commentary entitled *Yuanshi wuliang Duren shangpin miaojing sizhu* 元始無量度人上品妙經四注 (Four Commentaries on the *Book of Salvation*) includes fragments of Cheng Xuanying's *Durenjing zhu* 度人經注 (Commentary on the *Book of Salvation*). Song-Yuan catalogs also attribute works of divination to Cheng, but they are likely later creations.

Later scholars combined Cheng Xuanying's *Zhuang Zi shu* and Guo Xiang's 郭象 (252–312) *Zhuang Zi zhu* 莊子注 (Commentary on *Zhuang Zi*) into a single work titled *Nanhua zhenjing zhushu* 南華真經注疏 (Commentaries on the True Scripture of the Southern Florescence). That combined work later served as the basis for Cao Chuji 曹礎基 and Huang Lanfa's 黃蘭發 modern critical edition titled *Zhuangzi zhushu* 莊子注疏 (Combined Commentaries to Zhuangzi). Unfortunately, Cheng Xuanying's commentary to the *Lao Zi*, *Lao Zi Daode jing shu* was lost, but some fragments appear in the Dunhuang manuscript P. 2517 and Qiang Siqi's 強思齊 (fl. 920) *Daode zhenjing xuande zuanshu* 道德真經玄德纂疏 (Compendium of Commentaries on the Mysterious Virtue of the *Daode jing*). Meng Wentong 蒙文通 (1894–1968) collected the fragments to compile the "Jijiao Cheng Xuanying Daode jing yishu" 輯校成玄英道德經義疏 (Collection and Collation of Cheng Xuanying's Subcommentary on the *Daode jing*).

Cheng Xuanying was one of the most important figures of the Early Tang to promote the theory of Twofold Mystery Learning (Chongxuanxue 重玄學). This theory interprets the Dao by applying the four propositions of Buddhist Mādhyamika philosophy. Cheng illumined this theory through his commentary to *Daode jing*. He interprets the phrase *xuan zhi you xuan* 玄之又玄 (mysterious and again mysterious) in chapter one as follows:

> A person with desires is hindered only by his [one-sided clinging to] being. The gentleman without desires is instead hindered by his [one-sided clinging to] nonbeing. Thus when [Lao Zi] speaks of the first "mysterious," it is to eliminate these two [one-sided] views. However, he is then afraid that the adept may be hindered by this [conception of] "mysterious." Then he says, "again mysterious," and eliminates this last hindrance. Thus he not only obtains a state where there are no more hindrances, but also realizes a state where being without hindrances does not become a hindrance in itself. This is the rejection. This is why he says "mysterious and again mysterious" (translation revised from Assandri, p. 208).

> 有欲之人, 唯滯於有; 無欲之士, 又滯於無. 故說一玄, 以遣雙執. 又恐行者滯于此玄, 今說又玄, 更袪後病. 既而非但不滯於滯, 亦乃不滯於不滯, 此則遣之又遣, 故曰玄之又玄.

Cheng Xuanying connects whether one understands the Dao as being or nonbeing with one's sense of desire or being void of desire: a person with desires clings to the view of the being of Dao, while a person without desires clings to the view of the nonbeing of Dao. Both understandings are one-sided, and therefore it is necessary to use the "first mysterious" to eliminate these two views of hindrance. Non-hindrance itself, however, is also a kind of hindrance. Therefore, it is also necessary to use the "again mysterious" to eliminate the thinking of non-hindrance, in order to eventually reach the absolute oneness with Dao. Cheng's interpretation had exerted a profound influence on the Twofold Mystery theory of Daoism.

Cheng Xuanying's commentary to *Zhuang Zi* presents many other concepts and theories of early Tang Daoism. For example, in his commentary to the chapter "Zhi beiyou" 知北遊 (Knowledge Wanders North), he discusses the relation between Dao and things. He starts with the Daoist cosmogony that Dao is the origin of the myriad things in the universe: "The Dao without form can give birth to things with form" 夫無形之道, 能生有形之物. Then he indicates that, because the myriad things are produced by Dao, both sentient beings and non-sentient objects possess parts of Dao. As a result, "Dao and things are neither the same nor different but detached from the Dao there are no things" 道物不一不異, 而離道無物. Thus, Cheng's discussions of the relation between Dao and things are not limited to the scope of cosmogony but intertwine the theory of Dao-nature. As such, Cheng's interpretations stand as an example of what some modern scholars see as the influence of Buddhist philosophy in the development of Daoist discourse during the Early Tang.

BIBLIOGRAPHY

Editions:

Cao Chuji 曹礎基 and Zhuang Lanfa 莊蘭發, eds. *Zhuang Zi zhushu* 莊子注疏. Beijing: Zhonghua, 2011.

Cao Chuji and Huang Lanfa 黃蘭發, eds. *Nanhua zhenjing zhushu* 南華真經疏 in *Daojiao dianji xuankan* 道教典籍選刊, Beijing: Zhonghua, 1998.

Chen Jingyuan 陳景元 (d. 1094), ed. DZ (*Daozang*) 87 *Yuanshi wuliang duren shangpin miaojing sizhu* 元始無量度人上品妙經四注.

Cheng Xuanying 成玄英. *Nanhua zhenjing shu* 南華真經疏. *Guyi Congshu* 古逸叢書 ed., vol. 15.

Fan Yingyuan 范應元 (fl. 1265–1275), ed. *Lao Zi Daodejing guben jizhu* 老子道德經古本集注. Shanghai: Huadong Shifandaxue, 2010.

Guo Qingfan 郭慶藩, ed. *Zhuang Zi jijie* 莊子集釋. Beijing: Zhonghua, 2006.

Guo Xiang 郭象 (252–312) and Cheng Xuanying 成玄英 (fl. 631–653). DZ 745 *Nanhua zhenjing zhushu* 南華真經注疏.

Meng Wentong 蒙文通 (1894–1968), ed. "Jijiao Cheng Xuanying *Daodejing yishu*" 輯校成玄英道德經義疏, in *Meng Wentong wenji* 蒙文通文集, vol. 6. Chengdu: Bashu, 1998.

Qiang Siqi 強思齊 (fl. 920), ed. DZ 711 *Daode zhenjing xuande zuanshu* 道德真經玄德纂疏.

Translations:

Assandri, Friederike. *Beyond the Daode jing: Twofold Mystery in Tang Daoism.* Magdalena: Three Pines, 2009.

Yu, Shiyi. *Reading the Chuang-tzu in the T'ang Dynasty: The Commentary of Ch'eng Hsüan-ying (fl. 631–652).* Bern: Peter Lang, 2000.

Studies:

Fujiwara Takeo 藤原高男. "Sei Gen'ei hon Dōto ku kyō nit suite" 成玄英本道德經について, *Kagawa daigaku kyōiku gakubu kenkyū hōkō* 50 (1980): 137–72; 52 (1980): 1–45.

Gong Pengcheng 龔鵬程. "Cheng Xuanying Zhuangzishu chutan" 成玄英庄子疏初探, in *Fojiao xinjie* 佛教新解. Beijing: Beijing Daxue, 2009, pp. 31–55.

Kohn, Livia. *Taoist Mystical Philosophy: The Scripture of Western Ascension.* Albany: State University of New York, 1991.

Kohn, Livia and Russell Kirkland. "Daoism in the Tang." In Livia Kohn, ed., *Daoism Handbook*, Boston and Leiden: Brill, 2004, pp. 339–83.

LaFargue, Michael. *Tao and Method: A Reasoned Approach to the Tao Te Ching*. Albany: State University of New York, 1994.

Lu Guolong 盧國龍. *Zhongguo Chongxuanxue* 中國重玄學. Beijing: Renmin Zhongguo, 1993.

Luo Zhongshu 羅中樞. *Chongxuan zhisi: Cheng Xuanying de chongxuan fangfa he renshilun yanjiu* 重玄之思: 成玄英的重玄方法和認識論研究. Chengdu: Bashu, 2010.

Ōfuchi, Ninji 大淵忍爾. *Tonkō Dōkyō* 敦煌道經. Tokyo: Kokubu, 1979.

Qiang Yu 強昱. *Cheng Xuanying pinghzuan* 成玄英評傳. Nanjing: Nanjing daxue, 2006.

Robinet, Isabelle. *Les commentaries du Tao to king jusqu'au VIIe siècle*. Paris: Collège de France, Institut des Hautes Études Chinoises, 1977.

___. "Nanhua zhenjing zhushu" in Kristofer Schipper and Fransiscus Verellen, eds. *The Taoist Canon: A Historical Companion to the Daozang*, vol. 1, Chicago: University of Chicago, 2004, pp. 294–96.

Sharf, Robert H. *Coming to Terms with Chinese Buddhism: A Reading of the Treasure Store Treatise*. Honolulu: University of Hawaii, 2002.

Sunayama, Minoru 砂山稔. *Zui Tō Dōkyō shisōshi kenkyū* 隋唐道教思想史研究. Tokyo: Hirakawa, 1990.

Wang Zhongmin 王重民. "Laozi Daodejing shu" 老子道德經義疏, in *Dunhuang guji xulu* 敦煌古籍敘錄. Beijing: Shangwu, 1958, pp. 236–42.

Yan Lingfeng 嚴靈峰. *Jingzi congzhu* 經子叢著. Taibei: Guoli Bianyiguan, 1983.

Yu Qiang 强昱. *Cheng Xuanying pingzhuan* 成玄英评传. Nanjing: Nanjing Daxue, 2006.

Yu Shiyi. *Reading the Chuang-tzu in the T'ang Dynasty: The Commentary of Ch'eng Hsüan-ying (fl. 631–652)*. Bern: Peter Lang, 2000.

Jinhua Jia and Zhaojie Bai

Chu Guangxi 儲光羲 (ca. 706–ca. 762) was a poet from Yanling 延陵 County, Runzhou 潤州 (modern Jiangsu) who spent his early life as a prominent figure in Chang'an society. He knew and exchanged poems with Wang Wei 王維 (692–761 or 699–759),* Cui Hao 崔顥 (d. 754),* and others. Chu studied in the National University 太學 in 724 and passed the *jinshi* in 726. Thereafter he held minor positions in the south before retiring to his home in 733. By the early 740s he was living in reclusion at Zhongnan Mountain 終南山 south of the capital. Within a few years he had returned to court serving as an Investigating Censor. He was later captured by the An Lushan rebels in 755–756 and forced to serve under them. After the restoration he was first imprisoned, then officially pardoned for his collaboration with the rebels but banished to the south where he died.

Though his court poetry is quite conventional, Chu Guangxi's more relaxed old-style poetry in the style of Tao Qian 陶潛 (365–427), such as his poems on farming that praise the joys of country life, were well known. One such example is "Tianjia zaxing, di bashou" 田家雜興, 第八 (Impromptu Songs of a Farmer, Number 8), in which the content is also reminiscent of Tao Qian:

> I've planted over a hundred mulberry trees,
> Planted thirty acres of millet;
> So of food and clothing I've plenty.
> From time to time I meet close friends.
> When summer comes we have wild rice,
> Once autumn arrived there's chrysanthemum wine.
> My wife gladly welcomes them,

My children know to tiptoe about.
At sunset we sit idly in the garden,
Under the spreading shade of elm and willow.
Dead drunk they ride home at night,
As a cool breeze blows through my window.
I gaze at the River of Stars so clear and close,
Watch the Dipper rise and set.
I've a couple of jars not yet opened—
Will we be able to drink them tomorrow?

種桑百餘樹，種黍三十畝。
衣食既有餘，時時會親友。
夏來菰米飯，秋至菊花酒。
孺人喜逢迎，稚子解趨走。
日暮閑園裡，團團蔭榆柳。
酩酊乘夜歸，涼風吹戶牖。
清淺望河漢，低昂看北斗。
數甕猶未開，明朝能飲否。

Some of his poems describe immortals, and Chu Guangxi's "gift for vignette"–sketches of a significant human situation, mostly in extended old-style but also in quatrain form–has also received praise. Seventy *juan* of Chu Guangxi's poems were originally collected, but only four remain.

BIBLIOGRAPHY

Editions:
Chu Guangxi shiji 儲光羲詩集. 5 *juan*. Shanghai: Shanghai Guji, 1992. Reprint of *SKQS* edition.
Quan Tang shi, 2: 1373–1419.

Biographical Sources:
Fu, *Tang caizi*, 1:211–23; 5:37–39

Translations:
Articulated Ladies, pp. 190–91.
Field, "Taking Up the Plow," pp. 125–27.
Mair, *Anthology*, p. 206.
Minford and Lau, pp. 837–38.
Margoulies, *Anthologie*, p. 250–51.
New Directions, p. 94.
Owen, *High Tang*, pp. 63–70.
Payne, *White Pony*, p. 153.
Sunflower, pp. 99–100.
Watson, *Columbia*, pp. 275–76.

Studies:

Cao Chenchen 曹晨晨. "Chu Guangxi tianyuanshi yanjiu" 储光羲田园诗研究. M.A. thesis, Kashi Daxue, 2015.

Chen Tiemin 陳鐵民. "Chu Guangxi shengping shiji kaobian" 储光羲生平事迹考辨, *Wenshi* 12 (September 1981): 195–210.

Li Jinkun 李金坤. "Chu Guangxi liguan, shenzunian kaobian" 储光羲里貫, 生卒年考辨, *Wenxue yichan* 2 (1991): 44–50.

Liu Yan 刘燕. "Chu Guangxi yanjiu shuping" 储光羲研究述评. *Huangshi Ligong Xueyuan xuebao (Renwen shehui kexue ban)* 27.2 (2010): 19–22.

Liu Yu 刘蔚. "Lun Su Zhe dui Chang Guangxi de faxian yu tuizun" 论苏辙对储光羲的发现与推尊, *Shehui kexue zhanxian* 11 (2014): 163–69.

Tang Huanhuan 唐欢欢. "Chu Guangxi wugu yanjiu" 储光羲五古研究. M.A. thesis, Xinjiang Shifan Daxue, 2013.

Wang Yingxue 王莹雪. "Chu Guangxi shige yanjiu" 储光羲诗歌研究. M.A. thesis, Sichuan Daxue, 2007.

Zhu Jifa 竺济法. "Chu Guangxi yanjiu santi" 储光羲研究三题, *Changzhou gongxueyuan xuebao (Sheke ban)* 3 (2007).

William H. Nienhauser, Jr. and Marsha Wagner

Cui Hao 崔顥 (d. 754), hailed from Bianzhou 汴州 (modern Kaifeng in Henan) and received his *jinshi* degree in 723 after joining Wang Wei 王維 (692–761 or 699–759)* and others in the prestigious literary salon of Li Fan 李範 (d. 726), the Prince of Qi 岐王 a few years earlier. There he perfected the early Tang court-poetic style of regulated verse (*lüshi* 律詩). Although Cui Hao continued his friendship with Wang Wei, he broke away from this decorous style. He later served under Zhang Jiuling 張九齡 (678–740),* but earned a reputation largely for wild and reckless behavior, gambling, and drinking; he married several times and remained in Chang'an until his death in 754.

In his early years, Cui Hao's poems used flowery and pompous language. But after much traveling and service in the frontier areas, his poetic style changed significantly. His poems became vigorous and passionate, especially those about border fortresses and landscapes, poems which dominate his later works and typify his late style. He composed poems in the *yuefu* 樂府 and heptasyllabic-song forms; his regulated verse frequently violated rules for parallelism. He is also well known for his quatrains, such as the folksong imitations, "Changgan xing" 長干行 (Song of Changgan). His regulated poem "Huanghe Lou" 黃鶴樓 (Yellow Crane Tower) is one of the most famous of the High Tang period:

> Where the ancient sage departed on a yellow crane,
> Nothing is left but the Yellow Crane Tower.
> Once gone, the yellow crane has not returned again,
> Only the white clouds sail aimlessly for a thousand years.
> By the sun-lit stream, the Hanyang trees are clear and bright,
> On the Parrot Islet, grasses grow lush and green.
> As the sun sets, I wonder where my native place is,
> This river of misty waves saddens a man.

昔人已乘黃鶴去，此地空餘黃鶴樓。
黃鶴一去不復返，白雲千載空悠悠。
晴川歷歷漢陽樹，芳草萋萋鸚鵡洲。
日暮鄉關何處是，煙波江上使人愁。

The first four lines of the poem depict the history of the Yellow Crane Tower (on a hill on the north side of the Yangzi River near modern Wuhan). Legend says there was an old man who came to an inn nearby and drank there without paying his bill. The owner generously allowed him to do so for some time. One day the old man came into the inn and painted a huge crane on the wall. Patrons discovered that the crane would dance whenever anyone played a tune and the inn prospered. Ten years later the old man came back, summoned the crane from the wall, and rode it away to immortality. The last four lines help up to locate the persona atop Mount Yellow Crane looking across to Parrot Islet in the river and Hanyang on the south bank. The scene seems to remind Cui Hao of his own home place, Bianzhou, on the southern bank of the Yellow River far to the north but in the mist over the river both his view and his hopes are thwarted.

Li Bo 李白 (701–762),* who admired Cui Hao for his free spirit and his unrestrained style, conferred the greatest honor on him by deriving the ending for his famous "Deng Jinling Fenghuang Tai" 登金陵鳳凰台 (Climbing Phoenix Terrace at Jinling) from Cui's closure to "Yellow Crane Tower." According to a famous anecdote recorded in the *Tangshi jishi* 唐詩紀事, Li Bo planned to write a poem when he visited Yellow Crane Tower in 725, but after he read Cui Hao's "Huanghe Lou" inscribed there on the wall, he felt he could not better this poem. He gave up and sighed: "The scenery before my eyes I cannot describe, since Cui Hao's poem is inscribed high up [on the wall]" 眼前有景道不得, 崔顥題詩在上頭.

BIBLIOGRAPHY

Editions:
Quan Tang shi, 2: 1321–30, 14: 11076.
Quan Tang wen, 330.3756–57.

Annotations:
Wan Jingjun 萬竟君, ed. *Cui Hao shizhu* 崔顥詩注, *Tangshi xiaoji*. Shanghai: Shanghai Guji, 1985. pp. 1–4.

Biographical Sources:
Fu, *Tang caizi*, 1:196–206; 5:35.
Jiu Tang shu, 190.5047–48.

Translations:
Bynner, *Jade Mountain*, pp. 142–43.
Demièville, *Anthologie*, p. 280.
Fuller, Michael A. *An Introduction to Chinese Poetry: From the* Canon of Poetry *to the Lyrics of the Song Dynasty*. Cambridge: Harvard University, 2018, pp. 202–03.
Margoulies, *Anthologie*, p. 437.
Minford and Lau, p. 827.

Cui Hao

Owen, *High T'ang*, pp. 60–63.
___. *Late Tang*, p. 194.

Studies:

Chen Youqin 陳友琴. "Guanyu Cui Hao de Huanghe lou shi" 關於崔顥的黃鶴樓詩, *Guangming ribao*, May 12, 1958; included in Chen's *Wengu ji* 溫故集. Beijing: Zhonghua, 1959, pp. 172–76.
Fu Xuancong 傅璇琮. "Cui Hao kao" 崔顥考, in *Tangdai shiren congkao* 唐代詩人叢考. Beijing: Zhonghua, 1980, pp. 66–77.
Fu Zengxiang 傅增湘. "Cui Hao shiji ba" 崔顥詩集跋. *Beiping Tushuguan guankan*, 6.2 (April 1932).
Ji Yougong 計有功. *Tangshi jishi* 唐詩紀事, *juan*. 21. Shanghai: Shanghai Guji, 2008, pp. 310–11.
Sha Yuanwei 沙元偉. "Ping Cui Hao Huanghe lou he Li Bo Fenghuang tai" 評崔顥 "黃鶴樓" 和李白 "鳳凰台," *Wenxue Yichan* 3 (2001): 117–18.
Yu, Pauline. "Charting the Landscape of Chinese Poetry," *CLEAR* 20 (1998): 71–87.

William H. Nienhauser, Jr. and Marsha Wagner

Cui Zhongrong 崔仲容 (fl. 8th century) was a Daoist priestess-poet. Her poems appear in the *Yaochi xinyong ji* 瑤池新詠集 (Collection of New Songs from the Turquoise Pond), an anthology of Tang female poets' works compiled by Cai Xingfeng 蔡省風 (fl. ninth century). In Cai's arrangement, Cui Zhongrong's works were placed after Li Jilan 李季蘭 (d. 784),* Yuan Chun 元淳 (ca. 720–ca. 779),* and Lady Zhang 張夫人 (fl. 766–788), possibly indicating that she was their younger contemporary.

There are no other early records about Cui's life, but her extant three poems and four couplets provide clues about her identity, life experience, and emotional world. She was apparently ordained within the Highest Clarity (Shangqing 上清) Daoist tradition. Meanwhile, the majority of her work reflects amorous encounters, or the allusion to such possibilities. In a five-syllabic regulated verse titled "Zeng suosi" 贈所思 (Presented to My Beloved), Cui actively pursues a true, though unrequited, love:

> It's good fortune that we live near each other,
> meeting each other, but not intimate–
> like the moon amidst in clouds,
> like a reflection in the mirror.
> To see you is to sorrow in vain,
> hard to be broken-hearted in spring.
> I wish I were a swallow dwelling on your beams –
> but have no means to transform this body.

所居幸接鄰, 相見不相親. 一似雲間月, 何殊鏡裡人.
目成空有恨, 腸斷不禁春. 願作梁間燕, 無由變此身.

In the opening lines the poet reveals her love for the man next door and makes clear that he does not seem to share her feelings. Their proximity causes her anguish—in the second couplet she compares their relationship to the moon above and a reflection in the mirror—both clearly visible, but physically unattainable. In the final couplet, by evoking the image of the swallow, which has been portrayed in poetry since the *Book of Odes* to represent conjugal happiness, she dreams of transcending the distance between them. Like her fellow priestess-poets Li Jilan and Yu Xuanji 魚玄機 (ca. 844–868),* Cui articulated women's own voices and transformed the traditional image of women from the object of desire into a subject with desire.

In addition to love poems, Cui Zhongrong has a poem titled "Zeng geji" 贈歌姬 (Presented to a Singing Girl), which describes and admires a singing girl's beautiful appearance, graceful performance, and her feelings. This poem is among the earliest exchanges between female writers or at least between female writers and readers.

BIBLIOGRAPHY

Editions:
Chen Yingxing 陳應行 (fl. 1194), ed. *Yinchuang zalu* 吟窗雜錄. Beijing: Zhonghua, 1997.
Quan Tang shi, 2: 762–66.
Xu Jun. *Dunhuang shiji canjuan jikao* 敦煌詩集殘卷輯考. Beijing: Zhonghua, 2001.

Translations:
Jia, Jinhua 賈晉華. "The Life and Poetry of Cui Zhongrong." In Jinhua Jia, *Gender, Power, and Talent, the Journey of Daoist Priestesses in Tang China*. New York: Columbia University, 2018, pp. 158–61.
___. "New Poetry from the Turquose Pond: Women Poets in Eight and Ninth-century China," *Tang Studies*, 37 (2019): 59–80.
___. "The *Yaochi ji* and Three Daoist Priestess-Poets in Tang China," *Nan Nü: Men, Women and Gender in China* 13 (2011): 205–43.
Kelen, Christopher et al., trans. *Fragrance of Damask: Women Poets of the Tang Dynasty*. Macau: Association of Stories in Macau, 2009.

Studies:
Jia, Jinhua. "The *Yaochi ji* and Three Daoist Priestess-Poets in Tang China." *Nan Nü: Men, Women and Gender in China* 13 (2011): 205–43.
Rong Xinjiang 榮新江 and Xu Jun 徐俊. "Xinjian E cang Dunhuang Tangshi xieben sanzhong kaozheng ji jiaolu" 新見俄藏敦煌唐詩寫本三種考證及校錄. *Tang yanjiu* 唐研究 5 (1999): 59–80.
___. "Tang Cai Xingfeng bian *Yaochi xinyong* chongyan" 唐蔡省風編瑤池新詠重研. *Tang yanjiu* 7 (2001): 125–44.

Jinhua Jia

Dai Shulun 戴叔倫 (*zi*, Yougong 幼公, Cigong 次公, 732–789) was one of the "lost generation" of authors that reached maturity during the rebellions of the 750s, and like so many others he foundered in their aftermath. While his more celebrated contemporaries are remembered as the last generation of "High Tang" poets, Dai Shulun's surviving corpus remains stylistically at odds with the traditional periodization favored by historians of Tang literature and is often read as a precursor to the lyricism of the Mid-Tang.

Dai Shulun

His biographies in the official histories are terse, offering little more than litanies of official posts and few of the anecdotes that often flavor the accounts of literary careers. A native of Jintan 金壇 (now a district of the municipality of Changzhou 常州 in modern Jiangsu) and the son of a proud family of some local prominence, his political and literary fortunes rose and fell with the careers of the men he most closely aligned himself with. Among his forbears he counted Dai Kui 戴逵 (ca. 331–398), a master of many literary and plastic arts noted for pioneering amateur literati painting and championing scholarly eremitism. That Dai Shulun would even choose to pursue a career in the imperial bureaucracy is surprising given his family's history; almost nothing is known of his grandfather Dai Xiuyu 戴修譽 and his father Dai Shenyong 戴眘用, for both had shunned the imperial bureaucracy and devoted much of their lives to reclusion and private study. Dai Shulun however planned to follow his elder brother into public life, though recognition for his talents in *belles-lettres* was hindered by political turmoil. Fleeing the chaos of the 750s, his family removed further southward and his entry into the civil service was further delayed. Success in the imperial examinations thus came later in his life, as he likely did not earn the prestigious *jinshi* degree until the early 760s.

His literary pedigree was beyond reproach, however. He is counted among the many pupils who prepared for the examinations under the exacting tutelage of Xiao Yingshi 蕭穎士 (717–760),* a brilliant scholar remembered for his moral didacticism and reverence for ancient literary styles, and this in turn played no small part in establishing Dai Shulun's posthumous reputation as a writer and thinker ahead of his time. Unlike his teacher, Dai was able to secure patronage of powerful men during his youth and Liu Yan 劉晏 (ca. 715–780) in particular took interest in his early career. Dai Shulun first served directly under Liu as a Proofreader in the Palace Library, and later on Liu's recommendation he rose to the position of Investigating Censor in what is now modern Hunan. This assignment to the provinces, ostensibly a temporary stint away from the capital in anticipation of further advancement, sadly foretold a decade of partial exile following Liu Yan's demotion and execution in 780.

At the height of his powers, Dai Shulun the poet was a far cry from the public functionary. Of the three hundred odd pieces that have survived into the present era, many have a bucolic flavor that faintly recalls the verse of Tao Yuanming. Other pieces that touch on the plights of peasant women and the common soldiery offer veiled critiques of the political climes, and these may be read as heralds of the more overtly scathing reproaches of the "new *yuefu*" that came to fruition early in the following century. Nearly all betray a remarkable propensity for carefully crafted lyrical imagery. Due to its inclusion in the influential *Three Hundred Tang Poems* anthology, the regulated octave "Keshe yu guren yuji" 客舍與故人偶集 (A Chance Gathering with a Friend at a Guesthouse) remains the well-known of Dai Shulun's surviving works:

> The weather autumnal, the moon once again full,
> watchtowers on the city's walls, in evening countless stories deep.
> We returned for a "South of the River" meeting,
> yet I suspect we've come on another in a dream.
> Windblown branches startle the hushed magpies,
> dewy grasses cover the cold's crickets.
> Travelers at an inn, lingering drunken stupor,
> bidding each other remain, fearing the dawn's bells.

天秋月又滿, 城闕夜千重.
還作江南會, 翻疑夢裏逢.
風枝驚暗鵲, 露草覆寒蛩.
羈旅長堪醉, 相留畏曉鐘.

While the exact date of composition remains unknown, critics have consistently assumed that this was written beyond the walls of the capital, either preceding or following one Dai's many appointments to the provinces. Seemingly yet another octave on the popular theme of "chance meetings," this piece offers readers a glimpse at a rare evening encounter with a distinctly southern flavor. As the year begins to wain and the capital's walls and watch towers seem to loom higher in the evening, a sudden reunion of two acquaintances hailing from the faraway lands "South of the River" seems almost beyond belief. As the cold signs of a coming autumn envelop the scenery around this guesthouse, their reverie continues through the night with neither traveler willing to take his leave, though both know well that bells will toll at daybreak to waken them at last. In a poem that could have easily lapsed into overtrodden cliché, "Keshe yu guren yuji" remains a stirring testament to Dai's gifts for striking lyrical imagery and his difficulty in balancing private inclination and public duty.

Dai Shulun was eventually rehabilitated once the emperor began to realize his benefactor had been a victim of slander, though reprieve has once again come over late. By 789, the long years of loyal service in the provinces had finally taken their toll when Dai Shulun's health began to fail him. He appealed to be released from the emperor's service and submitted a memorial requesting ordination as a Daoist priest. While his petitions were granted by the throne, the long journey home proved too much. Dai Shulun died a few months after setting out, on the mountain roads of Sichuan, and it was only in the following year that he was brought home to rest at least. He is likely to remain an understudied figure, though his place in the tradition as a premonition of the literary stylings of the early 9th century will remain secure.

BIBLIOGRAPHY

Editions:
Dai Shulun shi ji jiao zhu 戴叔倫詩集校注. Yin Jiang 蔣寅, editor and compiler. Shanghai: Shanghai Guji, 2010.
Fu, *Tang caizi zhuan*, 5.518–26.
Quan Tang shi, 5: 3061–111, 14: 11149–50.
Quan Tang wen, 510.5189.

Biographical Sources :
Xin Tang shu, 143.4690–91.

Translations:
Minford and Lau, p. 844. Includes a translation, by Stephen Owen, entitled "Su Creek Pavilion."
Bynner, *Jade Mountain*, pp. 135–36. One translation of the same selection rendered in this entry.

Dai Shulun

Sunflower Splendor, pp. 152–53. Translations of three of Dai's best known poems, including the piece rendered in the entry above.

Studies:

Wang Dianqi. Dai Shulun ruogan shizuo bianwei buzheng" 戴叔倫若干詩作變為補正. *Zhongguo Shehui Kexue Yanjiusheng Xueyuan xuebao*, 27.3 (2006): 126–29.

Xiong, Fei. "Dai Shulun nianpu jianbian" 戴叔倫年譜簡編. *Fuzhou Shizhuan xuebao*, 4 (1992): 13–19.

___, "Dai Shulun nianpu jianbian (du)" 戴叔倫年譜簡編(讀). *Fuzhou Shizhuan xuebao*, 1 (1993): 33–38.

___, "Dai Shulun zaishi kao" 戴叔倫雜詩考. *Tangdu xuekan*, 3 (1994): 18–20.

Yin Jiang. "Lun Dai Shulun shi" 論戴叔倫詩. *Wenxue yichan*, 1 (1988): 64–74.

Thomas Donnelly Noel

Daoshi 道世 (secular surname Han Shi 韓世, *zi*, Xuanhui 玄惲, 597–683) was a prominent monk and the author or editor two important works concerned with Buddhism, the *Zhujing yaoji* 諸經要集 and the *Fayuan zhulin* 法苑珠林 (A Grove of Pearls in the Dharma Garden). A native and life-long resident of the Tang capital of Chang'an, Daoshi was noted even as a youth for his intelligence and piety: he left home to become a monk when only eleven. Both his teacher, Zhishou 智首 (567–635), and one of his fellow students, Daoxuan 道宣 (596–667), are considered principal figures in the Chinese *lü* 律 or "discipline" school of Buddhism. Daoshi lived for several years in the same monastery as Daoxuan, who has also been associated with the Discipline School.

Daoshi first extracted phrases from the available literature and compiled a chrestomathy called *Zhujing jiyao* 諸經集要 (Collection of the Essentials of All Sutras). The central theme of the *Zhujing jiyao* is karmic retribution for good and evil acts, and it cites passages not only from sutras, but also from non-Buddhist literature and thus can be useful to scholars from other fields. Thereafter, he put together the *Fayuan zhulin* to cover a broader understanding of Buddhist tenets. According to a preface by Li Yen 李儼 (d. ca. 675), it was completed in 668, though there is some evidence that it was in limited circulation earlier, perhaps in a preliminary draft. Divided topically into one hundred "units" (*pian* 篇) and subdivided into numerous "sections" (*bu* 部), the encyclopedia attempts to provide a comprehensive introduction to major aspects of Buddhist doctrine through explanations by the compiler combined with quotations from translated Buddhist scriptures and non-canonical indigenous works. The first unit begins the encyclopedia with a description of the *kalpa* or "eon" ("Jieliang pian" 劫量篇), a term central to the Buddhist cosmological system, while the final unit is devoted to Buddhist bibliography; in between are units on such topics as "Liudao pian" 六道篇 (The Six Paths, Unit 5), "Jingseng pian" 敬僧篇 ("Honoring Monks, Unit 8), "Sheli pian" 舍利篇 (Relics of the Buddha, Unit 37), and "Shoubao pian" 受報篇 (Retribution, Unit 79).

Appended to many units or sections of the encyclopedia are what Daoshi called *ganying yuan* 感應緣 (stories of response) intended to provide concrete illustration of how the Buddhist doctrine being explained in that particular section was manifested in everyday life. There are ninety-four "stories of response" sections in the *Fayuan zhulin*; overall the collection contains hundreds of anecdotes and tales from earlier works of philosophical, historical, biographical, geographical, and tale literature, all drawn from indigenous Chinese sources, both Buddhist and non-Buddhist. Within each section the cited texts are arranged chronologically according to when the events they relate occurred. Daoshi added collational notes at the end of many items or groups of items usually giving the original sources. Although his annotation has suffered at the hands of copyists and editors across the centuries, it remains remarkably accurate. Comparison of his quotations with works which survive also shows him to have been quite faithful to the original texts, seldom significantly altering or abridging the passages he quoted. Among the more than seventy-five titles mentioned in the "stories of response" sections are more than two dozen collections of strange and miraculous tales that had been compiled during the Six Dynasties and Early Tang periods. There are also several stories of events that Daoshi had witnessed personally or heard about from participants, which are recorded by Daoshi for the first time. Although the *Fayuan zhulin* was neither the first Chinese Buddhist work to make use of quotations from the translated Buddhist canon nor the first to include passages from non-canonical works to illustrate Buddhist concepts, its scope went far beyond any of its predecessors. Sometimes the relationship between the quoted text and canonical Buddhism is tenuous, as in the following passage on *gui* 鬼 "ghosts" cited from the *Han Shi waizhuan* 韓詩外傳 (Outer Tradition of the Han Version of the Book of Odes), but not included in the received edition of that text:

> When you die you become a ghost. "Ghost" means to revert. The essential pneuma reverts to Heaven. Flesh reverts to earth, blood reverts to water, arteries revert to pools, voices revert to thunder, motion reverts to wind, eyes revert to the sun and moon, bone revert to wood, sinew reverts to mountains, teeth revert to stone, fat returns to dew, hair returns to grass, inhaling and exhaling pneuma, reverts again to human beings.

> 死為鬼，鬼者，歸也。精氣歸於天，肉歸於土，血歸於水，脉歸於澤，聲歸於雷，動作歸於風，眼歸於日月，骨歸於木，筋歸於山，齒歸於石，膏歸於露，髮歸於草，呼吸之氣，復歸於人。

The commonly used modern edition contains a total text of over one million characters. In addition to its obvious importance as a source on early Chinese Buddhism, the *Fayuan zhulin* is also of great value to students of Chinese tale literature, because of its use of earlier collections of Chinese tales, many now lost.

BIBLIOGRAPHY

Editions and References:

Fayuan zhulin 法苑珠林, in *Taishō shinshū daizōkyō* 大正新修大藏經. Tokyo: Taishō Issaikyō Kankōkai, 1928; rpt. Tokyo: Taishō shinshū Daizōkyō Kankōkai, 1962. V. 53, no. 2122. A variorum edition based on the Korean edition of 1151, collated against a Song edition of 1239, a Yuan edition of 1290, a Ming edition of 1601, and an old Song edition of 1104–1148 from the Library of the Japanese Imperial Household..
___. *SBCK*. Follows a Ming edition of 1591.
Paper, Jordan D. *An Index to Stories of the Supernatural in the Fayuan zhulin*. Taibei: Chinese Materials Center, 1975.
Quan Tang shi, 14: 10943.
Quan Tang wen, 912.12390–91.

Daoshi

Annotations:

Fayuan zhulin jiaozhu 法苑珠林校注. 6v. Zhou Shujia 周叔迦 and Su Jinren 蘇晉仁, eds. Beijing: Zhonghua, 2003. Excellent introductory material; now the standard edition.

Biographical Sources:

Zan Ning, 4.66–67.

Translations

Cheung, Martha P. Y., ed. *An Anthology of Chinese Discourse on Translation. Volume 1: From Earliest Times to the Buddhist Period.* Rpt. London and New York: Routledge, 2014 (2006), pp. 148–52.

Studies:

Dong Zhiqiao 董志翹. "*Fayuan zhulin jiaozhu* kuangbu"《法苑珠林校注》廣補. *Guji zhengli yanjiu xuekan*, 2 (2007): 26–31.

Kawaguchi Gishō 川口義照. "*Hōon jurin* ni mirareru isson, besson kyō ni tsuite" 法苑珠林にみられる逸存, 別存經について, *Nanto bukkyō*, 37 (November 1976): 82–101.

___. "Kyōroku kenkyū yori mita *Hōon jurin* Dōsei ni tsuite" 經錄研究より見た法苑珠林道世について, *Indogaku Bukkyōgaku kenkyū*, 24.2 (1976): 794–97.

Satō Kiyoji 佐藤喜代治. "*Hōon jurin* to kirokutai"《法苑珠林》と記錄體, *Chūgoku kankei ronsetsu shiryō*, 21 (1979): 415–20.

William H. Nienhauser, Jr.

Du Fu 杜甫 (*zi*, Zimei 子美, 712–770) was one of the great geniuses of world literature. As a poet he drove himself to develop every potentiality, strenuously harmonizing some tendencies that we might regard as contrary–bookish allusiveness, for example, and creative spontaneity:

> Reading, I've tattered ten thousand scrolls,
> Setting brush to paper, I was like a god–

> 讀書破萬卷，下筆如有神.

or beauty of versification and earnestness of appeal to social conscience:

> Though by nature rustic, I craved a lovely line,
> With words I'd stir mankind, or I'd die yet never sleep.

> 為人性僻耽佳句，語不驚人死不休。

Du Fu's enormous range of talents was equaled by the range of men and matters, exalted and humble, that woke his curiosity and his human sympathy–hence his modern fame as a literary "realist" and as a "people's poet."

But his great powers of admiration and compassion hardly won a response in his own time:

All my hundred years a song of sorrow
Never meeting any who'd "know my tune."

百年歌自苦，未見有知音.

These passages of self-assessment, from "Fengzeng Wei Zuocheng Zhang, ershier yun" 奉贈韋左丞丈，二十二韻 (Twenty-two Rhymes Respectfully Presented to My Elder Friend, Assistant Director [of the Department of State Affairs], Wei [Ji] 韋[濟]), "Jiangshang zhi shui ruhai shi liao duanshu" 江上值水入海勢聊短述 (Some Lines While Standing on the Bank of the River Just As Its Strength Is Like That When It Enters the Sea), and "Nanzheng" 南征久客 (March to the South) respectively are well known to students of Du Fu.

Like other synthesists, Du Fu made a too-ambiguous exemplar for any particular school of art or thought to champion immediately. Although he claimed early renown as a prodigy of letters and mingled with the writers of his time, he led no coterie–indeed his ambitions, however delusive they may have been, lay in the realm of real and not literary politics. Du Fu's works were scattered, and many of them probably lost after his death in provincial obscurity, during a time of warlordism and foreign invasions following An Lushan Rebellion. No poem by him appears in known anthologies earlier than the *Youxuanji* 又玄集 (dated 900). While now generally considered the greatest of Chinese poets, Du Fu was not established as preeminent until the eleventh century. Part of the fascination for Du Fu has always been the drama of his neglect and rediscovery. In literary sinology the millennial effort to reassemble, date, and interpret Du Fu's surviving works has been a labor of ingenuity and controversy rivaled only by the scholarship on the novel *Hongloumeng* 紅樓夢 (Dream of the Red Chamber).

Du Fu belonged to the aristocracy, but during much of his life in the status of a poor relation. The old ruling class of the Six Dynasties, which had temporarily recouped its political power during his years of maturity, in the long term yielded place to the new gentry of scholar-bureaucrats, more dependent for entry to office upon the examination system.

Du Fu always referred to himself as a man of Jingzhao 京兆 (the prefecture including Chang'an); of Duling 杜陵, a place in the south of Jingzhao associated with Du clans; or of Shaoling 少陵, in Duling. His ancestors served the southern courts through most of the Six Dynasties. Du Fu's places of birth and education are unknown (the standard histories associate him with Xiangyang 襄陽 [modern Hubei], probably an error due to the prominence of the Du clan of that place). The family seems to have owned property at Duling–in the neighborhood were many of their graveyard poplars–also at Yanshi 偃師, burial-place of the great scholar Du Yu 杜預 (222–285), near the secondary Tang capital, Luoyang. Du Fu's many occasional poems, restored where possible to their original sequence, permit us to reconstruct much of the poet's detailed self-portrayal during and after the An Lushan Rebellion.

There is no comparable testimony regarding his earlier years. By his forties, Du Fu claimed to have written over one thousand pieces, yet only a small percentage of them survive. Perhaps none of his poems antedates 735. It nevertheless seems clear that Du Fu was groomed from an early age for the examination career–like that of his grandfather, Du Shenyan 杜審言 (ca. 645–708),* a *jinshi* of 670–which could lead relatively quickly to literary and advisory posts in the capital, rather than for a more pedestrian career of provincial administration such as his father had entered, probably by hereditary privilege. The pattern thus set was to endure for life. When not living in retirement or engaged upon his restless travels, Du Fu sought government employment only by examination or by submission of writings. His routine provincial appointments were limited to a minor police position, which he declined, and one in provincial education, which he quickly resigned. Unfortunately, Du Fu was no better suited to the advisory-admonitory posts he sought than to the ordinary administrative posts he avoided. His employment of Reminder of the Right under Emperor Suzong (r. 756–762) led within days to his arrest and trial for outspokenness (his message of thanks for pardon remained obdurately outspoken).

Du Fu's adult life may be envisaged as a triptych, each panel representing a period with a different geographical center. The first period (ca. 731–745), in the East and Southeast, was largely given over to his wanderings as a young bachelor devoted (by his account) to furs and silks, archery, falconry, and revelry. After travels down the coast as far as Zhejiang, he journeyed to Chang'an to take part in the *jinshi* examination of 736. Despite his favorable position as an entrant of the capital prefecture, Du Fu failed, for unknown reasons. Thereafter he traveled in the Northeast, perhaps at that time becoming family-head following his father's death. At Chenliu 陳留 (modern Kaifeng) in 744 and the next year at Lujun 魯郡 south of Taishan occurred the only actual meetings between the famous literary friends Du Fu and Li Bo 李白 (701–762).* What reality may have underlain the odd coupling of the elder Li Bo, Daoist "immortal of poetry" (*shixian* 詩仙), and Du Fu, Confucian "sage of poetry" (*shisheng* 詩聖), is hard to judge. The ascription of intimate friendship to pairs of persons named Li and Du is formulaic, with a number of instances ascending to Latter Han times (Li Gu 李固 [94–147] and Du Qiao 杜喬, [d. 147]). Du Fu's friendship for the romantic older celebrity has been termed one-sided, yet Du Fu himself claimed Li Bo had shown a liking for him.

Du Fu's poetry of the first person already exhibits some of the peculiarities of his later work. An example can be found in what is perhaps one of the earliest poems in Du Fu's corpus, "Ye yan Zuoshi zhuang" 夜宴左氏莊 (Evening Banquet at the Zuo Family Grange, possibly written in 735), which imparts some of the experiences of a northerner traveling for the first time in the South:

> Trees wind-blown, as a slender new moon sets,
> Our robes dew-damp, while a clear zither sounds.
> Unseen waters flow by flower-strewn paths,
> Spring stars wreathe the thatched hall.
> I look through books till the candles burn down,
> Examine swords as I draw deep on my cup.
> When my poem is done, I chance to hear Wu songs–
> Unforgettable memories of my time in a lone boat.

> 風林纖月落，衣露淨琴張。
> 暗水流花徑，春星帶草堂。
> 檢書燒燭短，看劍引杯長。
> 詩罷聞吳詠，扁舟意不忘。

Du Fu's indifference to the decorum of subgenres and their themes–perhaps the reason for his slow acceptance in the literary world–is already evident in this poem, which may well be simultaneously a poem of meeting for a drinking party on the Double Third and of parting on a journey. Also evidenced here, and related to his characteristic hyperbole, is Du Fu's penchant for contrasts of sublime magnitude (here between a rustic grange and the Milky Way) compressed into a single line: "Spring stars wreathe a thatched hall." The line is famous primarily for its use of the verb *dai* 帶, literally "to gird," here "wreathe." The progression of the night is presented here through vivid images: the new moon setting, the early darkness of the second couplet, and the late-night scene of candles sputtering. Du Fu's balanced concern for the book and the sword makes its appearance, acknowledging the dual ideals of the civil (*wen* 文) and of the martial (*wu* 武) that mark officialdom, as does his celebrated arrogance–here the hint (conveyed in a double allusion) that the poet, in his twenty-fourth year, has completed a literary conquest of the Wu Region comparable to the military conquest of Wu by Fan Li 范蠡 in the time of Confucius (after Fan guided the victory over Wu, he sailed off in a single boat).

Du Fu's second period (745–756) belonged to the capital region. Now fatherless and (from a late but uncertain date) himself a husband and father, he spent the first ten of these years in a frustrating search for the financial security of government employment. Unfortunately, Emperor Xuanzong (r. 712–756), preoccupied with Daoism, Tantrism, and his beloved consort Yang Guifei 楊貴妃, had in old age left practical affairs in the hands of despotic ministers. From 744 his Grand Councilor, Li Linfu 李林甫 (d. 753), had engaged in vendettas against potential rivals. On arriving in the capital Du Fu had come under the politically harmless patronage of the Prince of Ruyang 汝陽, a favorite nephew of the emperor. But he also maintained multiple connections to the entourage of the heir apparent, including Fang Guan 房琯 (696–763), Li Shizhi 李適之 (694–747), and Du Fu's early mentor Li Yong 李邕 (678–747), all hated and feared by Li Linfu. All three of these connections fell in the purges of 746–747. Du Fu's family tie to Li Linfu (his nephew Du Wei 杜位 [fl. 766] was married to one of Li's daughters) may possibly have protected the poet from harm, but it could hardly obtain him advancement. With all other entrants (including Yuan Jie 元結 [719–772]*), Du Fu failed a special examination to discover neglected talent (747). Three times in the ensuing years he approached the emperor directly with virtuosic works of the *fu* 賦 genre, accompanied by pleas for favor. On one occasion (751) he won Xuanzong's attention with three *fu* on major rites. A special examination was set for him, which he passed, being then enrolled among those awaiting office; yet two years went by without further result. During this time Du Fu seems to have played the role of small gentleman-farmer and village-elder in Duling. Owing to a local famine in 754 he removed his family to Fengxian 奉先 (modern Pucheng 蒲城縣 about 40 miles northeast of the Tang capital). In 755 he objected to the offer of a somewhat demeaning post and received instead a sinecure in the heir apparent's household. The appointment ironically became a dead letter, owing to the outbreak of the An Lushan Rebellion.

Returning to Fengxian, Du Fu found that his infant son had died, he believed of starvation. In the face of the rebellion Du Fu conveyed his family, under conditions of great hardship, to a more remote retreat (Fuzhou 鄜州) in what is now northern Shaanxi. Meanwhile the rebels seized Chang'an and Luoyang, causing Xuanzong to flee to Sichuan, then to abdicate. En route he had been forced to allow members of his military escort to execute Yang Guifei. Leaving his family, Du Fu apparently sought to join the former heir apparent, now ruling from exile in the far

Du Fu

Northwest as Emperor Suzong but was captured by rebels. In the fall of 756, while thinking of his family in Fuzhou, he wrote "Yue ye" 月夜 (Moonlit Night):

> For the Fuzhou moon tonight,
> My wife can only keep watch alone.
> I pity my little ones far away,
> They can't understand why she would miss Chang'an.
> A mist she made fragrant moistens her piled high hair,
> The clear moonlight chills her jade-like arms.
> When will we be able to lean on an open window
> And let the moon shine on us both, drying our tears?

> 今夜鄜州月，閨中只獨看。
> 遙憐小兒女，未解憶長安。
> 香霧雲鬟濕，清輝玉臂寒。
> 何時倚虛幌，雙照淚痕乾？

The poem is not only a rare mention of Du Fu's wife, but also contains a level of sensuality (in the fifth and sixth lines) uncommon in Du's corpus. The uncharacteristic intimacy shown here in expressions of longing reveal Du Fu's mastery of allusion. Trapped in the familiar environs of the capital now turned a prison, Du Fu's longing comes to be embodied by the image of his wife left back in Fuzhou. The desire to see her once again in the cold and distant moonlight parallels her desire, and through her, the poet's hope to once again see Chang'an in its former glory. The poem concludes with an ambiguous sense of irony, as we are left to wonder if the open window on which the poet desires to lean once again with his beloved, is back in Fuzhou, or rather in a restored Chang'an.

After a year's detention in Chang'an he escaped to Suzong's court and received the ceremonial office of Reminder of the Right. He erred by taking literally the formal designation of this post, coming too vehemently to the defense of his friend Fang Guan. He was arrested but pardoned. After revisiting his family, he probably joined Suzong's triumphal entry into liberated Chang'an, where he continued to serve as Reminder, until in 758 with the rest of the Fang Guan group he suffered a mild degree of banishment.

In Du Fu's poetry of this second period the syncretism of poetic subgenres, seen already earlier, became a syncretism of poetry (*shi* 詩) with *fu* 賦 and prose: words and themes previously confined to *fu*, to prose, or even to common speech, are now admitted to his poetry. From the viewpoint of traditional decorum this can be rephrased negatively: Du Fu, having violated accepted boundaries of poetic subgenres, now violated those of poetry as such. One result is that his *shi* addressed the homely and traditionally "unpoetic" details of everyday private life. It also addressed the equally "unpoetic" details of public life, political, military, or economic–beginning with his "Bingju xing" 兵車行 (Ballad of the Army Carts) of 750 (*Concordance*, pp. 9–10), a *yuefu* ballad belonging to the *fugu* 復古 revival of poetry as remonstrance. This poem, rather than expressing a generalized sympathy for soldiers and their families or a generalized antimilitarism, presents an ethical judgment of specific events (the Tibetan campaigns of 747–750), probably reflecting the views of General Wang Zhongsi 王忠嗣 (706–750), another person in the ambiance of the heir-apparent, and placing blame squarely on Xuanzong. Du Fu's style in such poems embodies an additional syncretism too: namely, of *fugu* seriousness with a minute concreteness derived from the synecdochic circumlocutions of court poetry, as it had been written, for example, by his grandfather, Du Shenyan. (On Du Fu's then-unfashionable taste for court poetry, balanced against his contrary taste for the plain style, see his six *jueju* 絕句, "Xiwei" 戲為 [Done in Jest]). Finally, Du Fu's crowning syncretism of this period, as first fully evident in "Zi jing fu Fengxianxian yonghuai wubaizi" 自京赴奉先縣詠懷五百字 (Five Hundred Words Expressing My Feelings on a Journey from the Capitol to Fengxian), is that of the public combined with the private "realism" or unpoeticism, and interweaving of national and personal joys and sorrows. It is harmony that the poet–now in his own estimation aged–himself beautifully characterizes in "Dui xue" 對雪 (Facing the Snow):

Weeping in wartime, many new ghosts, Sadly chanting, a lone old man.

戰哭多新鬼，愁吟獨老翁。

Du Fu's third period (759–770) belonged to the West and the South: modern Gansu, Sichuan, and Hunan. Quitting his employment at Huazhou 華州 (modern Hua County about 50 miles east of the capital) and with the eastward route to Luoyang closed by the rebel Shi Siming 史思明 (703–761), Du Fu headed west to Qinzhou 秦州 (modern Tianshui 天水) and then Tonggu 同谷 (modern Chengxian 成縣) in what is now Gansu. In the winter of the same year (759), joining a considerable flow of southbound refugee intelligentsia, he moved to Chengdu. From this time the ailing Du Fu and his small family were permanent charges upon their friends, relatives, and admirers. They moved repeatedly, no doubt as the available local literary commissions and charity were exhausted or, sometimes, to avoid rebellions or outbreaks of banditry. Nonetheless, a certain serenity came as Du Fu no longer needed to contemplate so seriously the duty of public service or excuse himself from it on the pretext (unconvincing, at least in later life) of practicing Daoist arts. Now he had the more natural excuse of physical illness–lung trouble (asthma?) and chronic cough from 754 onward, summer malarial fevers from 757, then rheumatism, headaches, deafness in one ear. An almost idyllic retreat in 760–762 was his "thatched hut" near Chengdu. There, probably in 760 shortly after his arrival, he wrote "Ke zhi" 客至 (A Guest Arrives):

Springtime waters north and south of my dwelling
Only flocks of gulls come daily to call.
My flower-strewn path unswept for the visitor,
My wicker gate first opens for you today.
The market's far away so I have few dishes,
My poor household has only jars from an old brew.
If you are willing to sit and drink with my old neighbor,
I'll call him over the fence to come help us finish the remaining cupfuls.
舍南舍北皆春水，但見群鷗日日來。
花徑不曾緣客掃，蓬門今始為君開。
盤飧市遠無兼味，樽酒家貧只舊醅。
肯與鄰翁相對飲？隔籬呼取盡余杯。

Du Fu

The *locus classicus* of the relationship between gulls and men is the *Liezi* 列子, which makes it clear that gulls will only visit those pure of heart. The "wicker gate" (*peng men* 蓬門) in the fifth line recalls another poet who referred to himself as "the wicker-hut gentleman" (*penglu shi* 蓬廬士), Tao Qian 陶潛 (365–427), and who also wrote about entertaining his neighbors in a simple fashion such as we have here. The best home-made wines were fresh and had been filtered. Here it seems Du Fu can only offer a stale brew. Du Fu's own note tells us the visitor was Prefect Cui 崔, who may have been his uncle. Perhaps he came to coax Du Fu out of retirement. In any case, the poem seems to be a proclamation that for the time being the poet was learning to be content in retirement.

Chengdu was also where Du Fu's old friend and patron, Yan Wu 嚴武 (726–765), soon became Military Commissioner 節度使, while Gao Shi 高適 (700–765),* Fang Guan, and a cousin numbered among the magistrates of nearby prefectures. In 764–765 he served as a military adviser under Yan, a post he soon resigned because of illness. "Deng lou" 登樓 (On Climbing the Tower) was written at this time.

> Flowers near the high tower sadden the visitor's heart.
> Troubles everywhere, I've climbed up to see the view.
> The spring scene on the Brocade River puts all the world before me;
> The floating clouds above Jade Fortress have witnessed the changes of all eras.
> The court of the Northern Star remains unaltered.
> Let not the bandits from the Western Mountains raid us!
> The poor Second Ruler still has his shrine.
> As evening falls I can do nothing but sing the "Song of Liang-fu."

> 花近高樓傷客心，萬方多難此登臨。
> 錦江春色來天地，玉壘浮雲變古今；
> 北極朝廷終不改，西山寇盜莫相侵；
> 可憐後主還祠廟，日暮聊為梁甫吟。

This is one of many poems Du Fu wrote in the topos of "ascent and contemplation of the past"; it dates from the spring of 764, a little later than "A Guest Arrives," after the capital had been retaken from the invading Tibetans allowing the new Emperor Daizong to return to the palace. But the Tibetans still occupied parts of Western Sichuan, hence the gay spring scene revealed to Du Fu as he gazes down from his tower fills him not with elation but with gloomy concern for the Chengdu region. The first line sets the mood and recalls Du Fu's famous line "moved by the times flowers bring tears to my eyes" (*ganshi hua jianlei* 感時花濺淚) from his "Chun wang" 春望 (Spring Prospect), a poem that laments a similarly dark time in Tang history. The Jade Fortress (line 4) overlooks a fortified border-crossing between Tibetan and Tang territory established during the early years of the dynasty. The floating clouds that emerge from the mountains usually suggest the ephemeral, but here Du Fu turns them to symbols of what recurs eternally, perhaps intending them to suggest the sycophants at court who obscure the ruler's judgment (as they do in the "Jiu bian" 九辯, "The Nine Arguments" in the *Chuci* 楚辭). In the third couplet Du Fu notes that the Imperial government (the court of the Northern Star) has returned to Chang'an after the brief interregnum in 763 when the Tibetans set up a puppet emperor in the capital city, and the emperor has been restored to his throne. Though this leads to a convincingly enhanced reading, it is possible that the second line of this couplet may be stronger, something like "Let not the marauders from the Western Mountains raid the borders."

The final couplet continues the dichotomy between the past and the present with a pair of historical allusions. The first is the "Second-Ruler" from line seven—literally "last ruler"—that refers to Liu Shan 劉禪 (207–271), the last ruler of the state of Shu 蜀 (modern Sichuan), who ruled from 223 to 271 after succeeding his famous father, Liu Bei 劉備 (161–223). Liu Shan was first guided by the famous councilor Zhuge Liang 諸葛亮 (181–234), who had proven an invaluable advisor to his father. But Zhuge died in an attack on the northern state of Wei. After his death, Liu Shan came to rely more on the advice of the eunuch Huang Hao 黃皓 and as a result, Shu was quickly conquered by Wei. The second historical allusion—to the "Liangfu yin" 梁甫吟 (Song of Liangfu) found in line eight—alludes again to Zhuge Liang. The original "Song of Liangfu" depicted how Yan Zi 晏子 (Yan Ying 晏嬰, ca. 578–500 BCE), the chief advisor to Duke Jing of Qi 齊景公 (r. 547–490 BCE), devised a plan to trick three powerful men who were threatening to overthrow the state of Qi into taking their own lives. Zhuge Liang sang the song when he was out of office as an indirect criticism of Huang Hao and other advisors on whom the Second Ruler was relying. Du Fu was no doubt aware of how the histories tell of Shu's swift downfall following the succession of a less capable ruler, and the lessons from the past must have weighed heavily upon his mind amidst the political upheaval of his own time. In addition, the shrine to Liu Shan was located in Chengdu and Du Fu certainly visited it during his sojourn in the region. Thus, these final lines form a veiled criticism of the current Emperor Daizong, himself a "Second Ruler" after the abdication of his famous father, Xuanzong, and the recapture of Chang'an after the An Lushan Rebellion. Daizong's misplaced confidence in eunuch advisers (especially Cheng Yuanzhen 程元振 (d. ca. 764) and Yu Chao'en 魚朝恩 (722–770), much like Li Shan's confidence in Huang Hao so lamented in the "Song of Liangfu," was held responsible for many of the empire's difficulties at the time.

The death of Du Fu's patron Yan Wu in 765 lessened the attraction of staying in Chengdu, and Du Fu then traveled down the Yangzi, staying two years in Kuizhou 夔州 (modern Fengjie 奉節, Sichuan), where he found a generous patron in the local prefect. The poet's last three years were spent largely in boat-travel, thoughts of return to Chang'an being thwarted by Tibetan invasions. In 769 he journeyed southward across Lake Dongting 洞庭湖 and up the Xiang River 湘水. In 770 he returned to Tanzhou 潭州 (modern Changsha), where he died.

Du Fu's poems of the third period are by far his most numerous. With characteristic tenacity, though ill and isolated from literary centers, he undertook works of ever greater technical difficulty and perfection. In its time his grandfather Du Shenyan's lengthy *pailü* 排律 (extended *lüshi* 律詩 or regulated poem of forty couplets) had been unprecedented; his grandson now produced a tour-de-force of one hundred couplets (cf. "Qiuri Kuaizhou yonghuai ji Zheng Jian, Li Binke, yibai yun" 秋日夔州詠懷寄鄭監[審]李賓客[之芳] [Singing What's In My Heart on an Autumn Day in Kuizhou, to be sent to Director Zheng [Shen] and Master of Ceremonies to the Heir Apparent, Li [Zhifang]). Artistically more significant are his carefully unified *lüshi* series such as "Qiuxing, ba shou" 秋興八首 (Autumn Sentiments, Eight Poems). In this and other masterpieces he wrote while in Kuizhou, the playful representationalism of his earlier "thatched hut" poems is countered by a somber richness of symbolism scarcely rivaled in Chinese poetry. Despite their classical precision of versification, these works share the free idiosyncratic inwardness of the greatest artistic masters (such as Michelangelo or Beethoven) in their late periods. Especially noteworthy is Du Fu's syntax, which becomes at once more tortuous and more ambiguous; realism becomes surrealism as line after line invites construal in a variety of complementary ways. This ambiguity in the "Autumn Sentiments" reinforces Du Fu's ability to fuse the sorrow of his own personal situation with passionate concern for the larger agony of his country. In these poems the poet's own age and approaching death parallel his vision of the decimated population and ruined country. The series is without doubt Du Fu's crowning masterpiece and among the greatest poems in the Chinese language.

BIBLIOGRAPHY

Editions:

Cai Mengbi 蔡夢弼. *Du Gongbu Caotang shijian: wushi juan* 杜工部草堂詩箋: 五十卷. Beijing: Beijing Tushuguan, 2006.

Caotang shijian 草堂詩箋 [caption title: *Du Gongbu Caotang shijian* 杜工部草堂詩箋]. 2v. 40 *juan* plus *Waiji* 外集 1 *juan*, with *Du Gongbu Caotang shihua* 杜工部草堂詩話 in 2 *juan* appended. Taibei: Guangwen, 1971. A photolithographic reprint of the edition edited by Lu Yin 魯訔 (1100–1176), with a commentary by Cai Mengbi 蔡夢弼 (fl. 1247); one contains a preface by Lu (dated 1153) and one by Cai (dated 1204) respectively.

Chen Chaishan 陳茝珊. *"Qianjian Dushi" yanjiu* "錢箋杜詩"研究. Beijing: Xueyuan, 2011.

Du Fu shiji 杜甫詩集. Changchun: Jilin Daxue, 2011.

Du Gongbu ji 杜工部集. 2v. 20 *juan*. Taibei: Taiwan Xuesheng, 1967. A photolithographic reprint of Wang Zhu's 王洙 edition, with a preface by Wang dated 1039.

Du Gongbu ji 杜工部集. Beijing: Beijing Tushuguan, 2004.

Du Gongbu shiji 杜工部詩集. Yangzhou: Guangling, 2009.

Dushi yan zhi: [16 juan] 杜詩言志: [16 卷]. Shanghai: Shanghai Guji, 2002. Based on the Song-dynasty edition of Guo Zhida 郭知達.

Jin Shengtan 金聖嘆 (1610–1661). *Du shi jie* 杜詩解. Zhong Lai'en 鐘來恩, ed. Shanghai: Shanghai Guji, 1984.

Lu Guochen 盧國琛. *Du Fu shichun* 杜甫詩醇. Hangzhou: Zhejiang Daxue, 2006.

Pu Qilong 浦起龍 (1679–ca. 1762), comm. *Du Duxinjie* 讀杜心解. 3v. Beijing: Zhonghua, 1978.

Qian Qianyi 錢謙益 (1582–1664), comm. *Qian Muzhai xiansheng jianzhu Dushi* 錢牧齋先生箋註杜詩. Taibei: Datong, 1974.

___, comm. *Qian zhu Dushi* 錢注杜詩. Shanghai: Shanghai Guji, 2009.

Qiu Zhao'ao 仇兆鰲 (1638–1713), comm. *Dushi xiangzhu* 杜詩詳注. 5v. Beijing: Zhonghua, 1979. Best modern critical edition.

Quan Tang shi, 4: 2252–586, 11: 8970, 13: 10045, 14: 10629, 11113.

Quan Tang wen, 359–60.4111–31.

Yang Lun 楊倫 (1747–1803), comm. *Dushi jingquan* 杜詩鏡銓. 2v. Shanghai: Shanghai Guji, 1980.

Zhao Cigong 趙次公 (Song dynasty), comm.; Lin Jizhong 林繼中, ed. *Du shi Zhao Cigong xianhou jiejijiao* 杜詩趙次公先後解輯校. Shanghai: Shanghai Guji, 1994.

References:

Cao Shuming 曹樹銘. *Du Fu congjiao* 杜甫叢校. Beijing: Zhonggua, 1978. Critical studies of various traditional editions.

Du Fu caotang lishi wenhua congshu 杜甫草堂歷史文化叢書. Chengdu: Sichuan Wenyi, 1997.

Hung, William. *Dushi yinde* 杜詩引得 (A Concordance to the Poetry of Du Fu). Harvard-Yenching Insitute Sinological Index Series, Supplement, no. 14. 3v. Beijing: Hafo Yanjing Xueshe, 1940.

Luan Guiming 欒貴明, ed. *QuanTangshi suoyin: Du Fu juan* 全唐詩索引:杜甫卷. 2v. Beijing: Zhonghua, 1997.

Wang Shijing 王士菁. *Du Fu cidian* 杜甫詞典. Zhengzhou: Henan Daxue, 2011.

Zhang Yuan 張遠. *Du shi huicui* 杜詩會粹. 24 *juan*. 1688.

Zhang Zhonggang 張忠剛. *Du Fu dacidian* 杜甫大辭典. Jinan: Shandong Jiaoyu, 2009.

___. *Du ji xu lu* 杜集敘錄. Jinan: Qilu, 2008.

Zheng Qingdu 鄭慶篤, et al., eds. *Du shi shumu tiyao* 杜詩書目提要. Jinan: Qi Lu, 1986. A thorough study of editions with a 120-page bibliography of modern studies appended.

Zhong Fu 鐘夫 and Tao Jun 陶鈞, eds. *Du Fu wuzhong suoyin* 杜甫五種索引. Shanghai: Shanghai Guji, 1992.

Zhou Caiquan 周采泉, ed. *Du ji shulu* 杜集書錄. 2v. Shanghai: Shanghai Guji, 1986. The most extensive biography of editions, commentaries, studies, etc.; with indexes.

Annotations:

Du Fu shixuan 杜甫詩選. Changsha: Hunan Renmin, 2009.

Fang Shendao 方深道 (Song dynasty). *Zhujia Lao Du shiping* 諸家老杜詩評. Zhang Zhongwang 張忠網, ed. Beijing: Shumu Wenxian, 1994.

Ge Xiaoyin 葛曉音. *Du Fu shi xuanping* 杜甫詩選評. Shanghai: Shanghai Guji, 2011.

Hai Bing 海兵. *Du Fu shiwen xiangzhu* 杜甫詩文詳注. Wulumuqi: Xinjiang Renmin, 2000.

Huang Sheng 黃生 (fl. 1650). *Du Gongbu shi shuo* 杜工部詩說. Yimutang 一木堂. 1696.

Li Shousong 李壽松. *Quan Dushi xinshi* 全杜詩新釋. Beijing: Zhongguo, 2002.

Nie Shiqiao 聶石樵 and Deng Kuiying 鄧魁英. *Du Fu xuanji* 杜甫選集. Shanghai: Shanghai Guji, 1983. Carefully annotated versions of about 200 poems following a fine introduction to Du Fu. May be seen as a companion volume to that on Li Bo by Yu Xianhao 郁賢浩 (also published by Shanghai Guji in 1990).

Shan Fu 單復. *Du Fu yude* 杜甫愚得. 1696. Rpt. *Du shih congkan* 杜詩叢刊, 2nd series, no. 11. 3v. Taibei: Datung, 1974.

Shi Hongbao 施鴻保 (d. 1871). *Du Du shi shuo* 讀杜詩說. 1890. Rpt. Hong Kong: Zhonghua, 1964.

Wang Sishi 王嗣奭. *Du yi* 杜臆. 1870. Rpt. Beijing: Zhonghua, 1963.

Wu Gengshun 吳庚舜. *Du Fu shi xuanzhu* 杜甫詩選注. Shanghai: Shanghai Yuandong, 2011.

Wu Jiansi 吳見思. *Du shi lunwen* 杜詩論文. 1672. Rpt. *Du shih congkan* 杜詩叢刊, 3rd series, no. 27. 4v. Taibei: Datung, 1974.

Wu Shuling 吳淑玲. *Dushi xiang zhu yanjiu* 杜詩詳注研究. Jinan: Qi Lu, 2011. A meticulous study of Qiu Zhao'ao's edition, *Du shi xiangzhu*.

Xiao Difei 蕭滌非 (1906–1991), ed. *Du Fu quanji jiaozhu* 杜甫全集校注 12v. Beijing: Renmin, 2014.

Yuan Huiguang 袁慧光. *Du Fu Xiangzhong shiji zhu* 杜甫湘中詩集註. Changsha: Yuelu, 2010.

Zhang Zhonggang 張忠剛. *Xinyi Du Fu shixuan* 新譯杜甫詩選. Taibei: Sanmin, 2009.

___. *Du Fu shixuan* 杜甫詩選. Beijing: Zhonghua, 2005.

Zhu Heling 朱鶴齡 (1606–1683). *Du Gongbu shiji ji zhu* 杜工部詩集輯注. ca. 1667. Rpt. Baoding: Hebei Daxue, 2009.

Biographical Sources:

Fu, *Tang caizi*, 1:395–404.

Jiu Tang shu, 190B.5053–54.

Xin Tang shu, 201.5735–36.

Du Fu

Translations:

Alley, Rewi. *Du Fu Selected Poems*. Beijing: Waiwen, 2000.

Ayscough, Florence. Vol. I: *Tu Fu, The Autobiogrpahy of a Chinese Poet*. Vol. II: *Travels of a Chinese Poet: Tu Fu, Guest of Rivers and Lakes, A.D. 712–770*. Boston: Houghton Mifflin Company, 1929–1934.

Azarova, Natalya, trans. *Du Fu*. Moscow: OGI, 2012. Lightly annotated translations of about hundred poems. Also includes a selection of poems with several versions of translation done by poets in Moscow.

Birch, *Anthology*, pp. 235–41.

Chapuis, Nicolas. *Du Fu, poèmes de jeunesse; Ouvre poétique I*. Paris: Les Belles Lettres, 2015. A heavily annotated rendition of Du Fu's early poems.

___. *La Guerre civile (755-759); Ouvre poétique II*. Paris: Les Belles Lettres, 2018.

Cheng Qianfan. "One Sober and Eight Drunk; Du Fu's 'Song of the Eight Drunken Immortals.'" Song Zianchun, trans. *Social Sciences in China* 6.4 (1985): 83–94.

Cheng Wing-fun and Hervé Collet, trans. *Tu Fu, dieux det diable spleurent*. Millemont, France: Moundarren, 1987. Free, unannotated versions of about 70 poems preceded by a 14-page introduction.

Cooper, Arthur. *Li Po and Tu Fu*. London: Penguin Books, 1973.

Costantini, Vilma, ed. *Coppe di giada*. Turin: UTET, 1985. Contains translations of about forty poems each by Li Bo, Du Fu and Bo Juyi.

Demiéville, *Anthologie*, pp. 260–273.

Egan, *Clouds*, p. 41.

Frankel, *Palace Lady*, pp. 116–24.

Fuller, Michael A. *An Introduction to Chinese Poetry: From the* Canon of Poetry *to the Lyrics of the Song Dynasty*. Cambridge: Harvard University Press, 2018, pp. 224–68.

Graham, A.C. "Late Poems of Tu Fu (712–70)," in *Poems of the Late T'ang*, Middlesex and Baltimore: Penguin Books, 1965, pp. 39–56.

Hawkes, David. *A Little Primer of Tu Fu*. London: Clarendon, 1967.

Hinton, David. *Anthology*, pp. 190–212.

___. *The Selected Poems of Du Fu*. New York: New Directions, 1989.

Hu-Sterk, Florence. *L'Apogeé de la poésie chinoise—Li Bai et Du Fu*. Paris: Éditions You-feng, 2000.

Hung, William. *Tu Fu: China's Greatest Poet*. 2v. Cambridge, Mass.: Harvard University, 1952.

Idema, W. L. *De verweesde boot–klassieke Chinese gedicten*. Amsterdam: Meulenhoff, 1989. Translations of 144 poems with explanatory notes.

Mair, *Anthology*, pp. 208–18.

Mair, "Tang Poems," pp. 342–45.

Margoulies, *Anthologie*, pp. 189, 231–32, 253–54, 279–80, 375, 436.

Minford and Lau, pp. 765–816. A collection of renditions by various translators with useful notes.

Murphy, James R. *Murphy's Du Fu*. 4v. CreateSpace Independent Publishing Platform, 2008–2009.

New Directions, pp. 96–115.

Owen, *Anthology*, pp. 285–78, 413–40, 468–69, 472–75.

___, *Mi-Lou*, pp. 106–10, 161–62.

___, *High T'ang*, pp. 183–224.

___, *Late Tang*, pp. 72–73.

___, *Middle Ages*, pp. 90–94.

___, *Omen*, pp. 12–17, 23–27, 35–39, 46–47, 74–77, 90–91, 101–07, 116–21, 125–25, 212–18, 220–22, 237–42, 272–74, 282–83.

___. *The Poetry of Du Fu*. 6v. Boston and Berlin: Walterde Gruyter, 2016. The definitive translation of the complete œuvre, annotated, with a critical introduction, and Chinese texts of the poems.

___, *Remembrances*, pp. 3–7.
Payne, *White Pony*, pp. 182–204.
Pimpaneau, pp. 428–434.
Watson, Burton. *The Selected Poems of Du Fu*. New York: Columbia University, 2003.
Yang Xianyi, *Poetry and Prose*, pp. 37–63.
Yoshikawa Kojiro 吉川幸次郎. *To Ho shizhu* 杜甫詩注, up to vol. 10 (1026) now edited by Kōzen Hiroshi 興膳宏. Tokyo: Chikuma Shobo, 1977–2016.
Young, David. *Du Fu—A Life in Poetry*. New York: Alfred P. Knopf, 2010.
Yu, *Imagery*, pp. 195–97.
Zach, Erwin von. *Tu Fu's Gedichte*. 2v. Cambridge, Mass: Harvard University, 1952. A complete translation of all poems attributed to Du Fu.

Studies:
Akinobu Gotō 後藤秋正. *Tōzai nanboku no hito* 東西南北の人: 杜甫の詩と詩語. Tokyo: Kenbun Shuppan, 2011.
Bender, Lucas Rambo. "Du Fu: Poet Historian, Poet Sage." Unpublished Ph.D. dissertation, Harvard University, 2016.
___. "Ironic Empires," in *Reading Du Fu*, pp. 56–72.
Bezin, Leonid E. *Du Fu*. Moscow: Molodaja Gvardija, 1987.
Bu Jinshan 卜進善. *Du Fu zai Longyou* 杜甫在隴右. Lanzhou: Dunhuang Wenyi, 2010.
Cai Jinfang 蔡錦芳. *Dushi banben ji zuopin yanjiu* 杜詩版本及作品研究. Shanghai: Shanghai Daxue, 2007.
Cai Zhennian 蔡振念. *Dushi Tang Song jieshou shi* 杜詩唐宋接受史. Taibei: Wunan Tushu Chuban Gufen Xouxian Gongsi, 2002.
Cao Mufan 曹慕樊. *Du shi zashuo* 杜詩雜說. Chengdu: Sichuan Renmin, 1984. A collection of essays and notes by a traditional-style scholar.
Chan, Timothy Wai Keung. "Wall Carvings, Elixirs and the Celestial King: An Exegetic Exercise on Du Fu's Poems on Two Palaces," *JAOS* 127 (2007): 471–89.
Chen, Jack W. "Foundings of Home: On Du Fu and Poetic Success," in *Reading Du Fu*, pp. 15–26.
Chen, Jue. "The Tang Poet in Song Poetics—Song Poetics in the Tang Poet: The Construction of Du Fu's Image as Verbal Master," *TP* 109 (2018): 537–71.
___. "Making China's Greatest Poet: The Construction of Du Fu in the Poetic Culture of the Song Dynasty (960–1279)." Unpublished Ph. D. dissertation, Princeton University, 2016..
Chen Meizhu 陳美朱. *Qingchu Dushi shiyi chanshi yanjiu* 清初杜詩詩意闡釋研究. Tainan: Han Jia, 2007.
Chen Shaozhi 陳少志. *Shisheng Du Fu yu xianshizhuyi shige* 詩聖杜甫與現實主義詩歌. Changchun: Jilin Wenshi, 2010.
Chen Yixin 陳貽焮. *Du Fu ping zhuan* 杜甫評傳. 3v. Shanghai: Shanghai Guji, 1982 and 1988. A careful biography of over 1300 pages.
Chen Wei 陳偉. *Du Fu shixue tanwei* 杜甫詩學探微. Taibei: Wenshizhe, 1985.
Chen Wenhua 陳文華. *Du Fu zhuanji Tang Song ziliao kaobian* 杜甫傳記唐宋資料考辨. Taibei: Wenshizhe, 1987.
Chen Yaoji 陳瑤璣. *Dushi tezhi yuanyuan kao* 杜詩特質淵源考. Taibei: Zongjingxiao Hongdao Wenhua Shiye Youxian Gongsi, 1978.
Cheng Taoguang 程韜光. *Shisheng Du Fu* 詩聖杜甫. Zhengzhou: Henan Wenyi, 2010.
Cherniack, Susan. "Three Great Poems by Du Fu: 'Five Hundred Words: A Song of My Thoughts on Travelling from the Capital to Fengxian,' 'Journey North,' and 'One Hundred Rhymes: A Song of My Thoughts on an Autumn Day in Kuifu, Respectfully Sent to Director Zheng and Adviser to the Heir Apparent Li.'" Unpublished Ph.D. dissertation, Yale University, 1988.

Chou, Eva Shan. "Allusion and Periphrasis as Modes of Poetry in Tu Fu's Eight Laments." *HJAS* 45 (1985): 77–128.

___. *Reconsidering Tu Fu, Literary Greatness and Cultural Context*. New York and Cambridge: Cambridge University, 1996.

___. "Tu Fu's 'Eight Laments': Allusion and Imagery as Modes of Poetry." Unpublished Ph. D. dissertation, Harvard University, 1984.

___. "Tu Fu's Social Conscience: Compassion and Topicality in His Poetry." *HJAS* 51 (1991): 5–53.

Chung Ling. "This Ancient Man is I: Kenneth Rexroth's Versions of Tu Fu." *Renditions* 21 and 22 (Spring and Autumn 1984), pp. 307–30. A study of Rexroth's (1905–1982) critically regarded renditions of Du Fu.

Davis, A.R. "'The Good Lines of the World are a Common Possession': A Study of the Effect of Tu Fu upon Su Shih." In *Zhongyang Yanjiu Yuan Guoji Hanxue huiyi lunwenji*. Taibei: Zhongyang Yanjiu Yuan, 1981, pp. 471–504. Although the focus is on Su Shi, a number of poems by Du Fu and Li Bo are discussed.

___. "The Poetry of Tu Fu (712–770)." *Journal of the Australasian Universities Language and Literature Association* 22 (November 1964): 208–220.

___. *Tu Fu*. New York: Twayne Publishers, 1971.

Du Fu yanjiu xuekan 杜甫研究學刊. Chengdu: Du Fu Yanjiu Xuekan Bianjibu, 1981, V. 1– .

Egan, Ronald. "Ming-Qing Paintings Inscribed by Du Fu's Poetic Lines," in *Reading Du Fu*, pp. 129–42.

Fang Boren 方泊荏. *Zhonghua shisheng-Du Fu* 中華詩聖-杜甫. Guiyang: Guizhou Jiaoyu, 2011.

Fan Zhenwei 范震威. *Yigeren de shishi: Piaobo yu shenghua de gezhe Du Fu dazhuan* 一個人的史詩：漂泊與圣化的歌者杜甫大傳. Baoding: Hebei Daxue, 2009.

Feng Ye 封野. *Du Fu Kuizhou shi shulun* 杜甫夔州詩疏論. Nanjing: Dongnan Daxue, 2007.

Feng Zhi 馮至. *Du Fu zhuan* 杜甫傳. Tianjin: Baihua Wenyi, 1999.

Fisk, Craig. "On the Dialectics of the Strange and Sublime in the Historical Reception of Tu Fu." In *Proceedings of the Ninth Congress of the International Comparative Literature Association*," Innsbruck, 1980, v. 2, pp. 75–82.

Fu Gengsheng 傅庚生. *Du Fu shilun* 杜甫詩論. Shanghai: Shanghai Guji, 1985.

Gao Tianyou 高天佑. *Du Fu Long Shu jixing shi zhuxi* 杜甫隴蜀紀行詩注析. Lanzhou: Gansu Minzu, 2002.

Ge Jingchun 葛景春. *Du Fu yu zhongyuan wenhua* 杜甫與中原文化. Zhengzhou: Henan Renmin, 2008.

Ge Xiaoyin. "Prose within the Poem" (*Shi Zhong You Wen*): Du Fu's Creative Breakthrough in the Light of *Wugu* Narrative Rhythm," *Chinese Literature and Culture*, 2 (2015): 481–514.

Guo Moruo 郭沫若 (1892–1978). *Li Bo yu Du Fu* 李白與杜甫. 1971. Rpt. Beijing: Zhongguo Chang'an, 2010.

Han Chengwu 韓成武. *Du Fu xinlun* 杜甫新論. Baoding: Hebei Daxue, 2007.

___. *Shisheng: youhuan shijie zhong de Du Fu* 詩聖：憂患世界中的杜甫. Baoding: Hebei Daxue, 2000.

Hao Ji. *The Reception of Du Fu (712–770) and His Poetry in Imperial China*. Leiden and Boston: Brill, 2017.

Hao Runhua 郝潤華. *Dushi xue Dushi wenxian* 杜詩學與杜詩文獻. Chengdu: Ba Shu, 2010.

Hartman, Charles. "Du Fu in the Poetry Standards (*Shige* 詩格) and the Origins of the Earliest Du Fu Commentary," *T'ang Studies* 28 (2010): 61–76.

___. "The Tang Poet Du Fu and the Song Dynasty Literati," *CLEAR* 30 (2008): 43–74.

Hasebe Tsuyoshi 長谷部剛. *To Ho shunbunshū no keisei ni kansuru bunken gakuteki kenkyū* 杜甫詩文集の形成に関する文献学的研究. Suita: Kansai Daigku, 2019.

Hsieh, Daniel. "Du Fu's 'Gazing at the Mountain,'" *CLEAR* 16 (1994): 1–18.

___. "Fragrant Rice and Green Pawlonia: Notes on a Couplet in Du Fu's 'Autumn Meditations,'" *CLEAR* 31 (2009): 71–95.

___. "Meeting through Poetry: Du Fu's 杜甫 (712–770) "Written in Accord with Prefect Yuan's 'Ballad of Chongling.'" *Tang Studies*, 32 (2014): 1–20.

Hu Lingyan 胡凌燕. "Zhengcang Yuan (Shōsōyin) *Wang Bo shixu* yu shixu wenti de dulixing" 正倉院藏《王勃詩序》與詩序文體的獨立性, *Wenxue yichan*, 2020.2: 184–87.

Huang Yizhen 黃奕珍. *Du Fu zi Qian ru Shu shige xiping* 杜甫自秦入蜀詩歌析評. Taibei: Li Ren, 2005.
Huang Yufeng 黃玉峰. *Shuo Dufu* 說杜甫. Shanghai: Shanghai Cishu, 2008.
Jaeger, Georgette. *Du Fu: Il y a homme errant*. Paris: La Différence, 1989.
Jian Mingyong 簡明勇. *Du Fu Qilü yanjiu yu jianzhu* 杜甫七律研究與箋注. Taibei: Wuzhou, 1973.
Jiang Ruizao 蔣瑞藻. *Xu Du Gongbushihua* 續杜工部詩話. Zhang Zhongwang 張忠網, ed. Beijing: Shumu Wenxian, 1994.
Jin Qihua 金啟華. *Du Fu shiluncong* 杜甫詩論叢. Shanghai: Shanghai Guji, 1985.
___ and Hu Wentao 胡問濤. *Du Fu ping zhuan* 杜甫評傳. Xian: Shanxi Renmin, 1984.
Jin Shengtan 金聖歎 (1610–1661). *Jin Shengtan pi Tang caizi shi: Dushi jie* 金聖歎批唐才子詩: 杜詩解. Beijing: Zhonghua, 2010.
Jing You 競游. *Du Fu-shisheng* 杜甫-詩聖. Huhehaote: Neimenggu Renmin, 2007.
Kan Mitsu 韓美津, *et al. To Ho –shi to shogai* 杜甫-詩と生涯. Tokyo: Tokuma, 1992.
Kurokawa Yoichi 黑川洋一. *To Ho* 杜甫. Tokyo: Kadokawa, 1987.
___. *To Ho shi sen* 杜甫詩選. Tokyo: Iwanami, 1991.
Li Yi 李誼. *Du Fu Caotang shi zhu* 杜甫草堂詩注. Chengdu: Sichuan Renmin, 1982.
Li Limin 李利民. *An Shi zhiluan yu san da shiren yanjiu* 安史之亂與三大詩人研究. Beijing: Zhongguo Shehui Kexue, 2010.
Liang Guifang 梁桂芳. *Du Fu yu Songdai wenhua* 杜甫與宋代文化. Chongqing: Chongqing Daxue, 2011.
Lin Minghua. *Du Fu xiuci yishu* 杜甫修辭藝術. Zhengzhou: Zhongzhou Guji, 1991.
Lin Jizhong 林繼中. *Du Fu yanjiu xudiao* 杜甫研究續貂. Taizhong: Tiankong Shuwei Tushu Youxiangongsi, 2010.
___. *Dushi xuanping* 杜詩選評. Xi'an: Sanqin, 2004.
Liu Fenggao 劉鳳誥 (1761–1830). *Du Gongbu shihua* 杜工部詩話. Zhang Zhongwang 張忠網, ed. Beijing: Shumu Wenxian, 1994.
Liu Jianhui 劉健輝 *et al.*, eds. *Du Fu zai Kuizhou* 杜甫在夔州. Chongqing: Chongqing, 1992.
Liu Minghua 劉明華. *Du Fu yanjiu lunji* 杜甫研究論集. Chongqing: Chongqing, 2005.
Liu Wan. "Poetics of Allusion: Tu Fu, Li Shang-yin, Ezra Pound, and T.S. Eliot." Unpublished Ph. D. dissertation, Princeton University, 1992.
Lu Kebing 魯克兵. *Du Fu yu fojiao guanxi yanjiu* 杜甫與佛教關係研究. Ph. D. Dissertation, Fudan Daxue, 2007.
Ma Chongqi 馬重奇. *Du Fu gushi yundu* 杜甫古詩韻讀. Beijing: Zhongguo Zhanwang, 1985.
Ma Xu 馬旭. "*Ji qianjia zhu fenlei Du Gongbu shi* leibian tixi chuyi" 《集千家注分類杜工部詩》類編體系芻議. *Wenxue yichan* 2020.4: 70–75.
McCraw, David R., "Review of Stephen Owen, translator, *The Poetry of Du Fu*," *HJAS* 79 (2019): 378-85.
___. *Du Fu's Laments from the South*. Honolulu: University of Hawaii, 1992.
McMullen, David L. "Du Fu's Political Perspectives : His Outlook on Governorships and his Response to Yuan Jie's Daozhou Verses," *Tang Studies* 37 (2019): 81–110.
___. "Recollection without Tranquility: Du Fu, the Imperial Gardens, and the State," *Asia Major, Third Series* 14 (2001): 189–252.
Mei Tsu-lin and Yu-kung Kao. "Tu Fu's 'Autumn Meditations': An Exercise in Linguistic Criticism." *HJAS* 28 (1968): 44–80.
Mekada Makoto 目加田誠. *To Ho no shi to shogai* 杜甫の詩と生涯. Tokyo: Ryukei Shosha, 1983.
Mo Lifeng 莫礪鋒. *Du Fu ping zhuan* 杜甫評傳. Nanjing: Nanjing Daxue, 1993. *Zhongguo sixiangjia pingzhuan congshu*, 66.
___. *Du Fu* 杜甫. Nanjing: Nanjing Daxue, 2010.
___. "Wenxue shi shiye zhong de Du Fu pailü" 文學史視野中的杜甫排律, *Wenxue yichan* 2018.1: 60–72.
Mori Kainan 森槐南. *To Ho kogi* 杜甫講義. 4v. Tokyo: Heibonsha, 1993.
Morino Shigeo 森野繁夫. *Chinutsu shijin To Ho* 沈鬱詩人杜甫. Tokyo: Shueisha, 1982.

Motsch, Monika. *Mit Bambusrohr und Ahle, von Qian Zhongshus Guanzhuibian zu einer Neubetrachtung Du Fus*. Frankfurt: Peter Lang, 1994.

Mukōjima Shigeyoshi 向島成美, ed. *Ri Haku to To Ho no jiten* 李白と杜甫の事典. Tokyo: Taishukan, 2019.

Naoto Uno 宇野直人 and Masashi Ebara 江原正士. *To Ho: Idainaru yuutsu* 杜甫: 偉大なる憂鬱. Tokyo: Heibonsha, 2009.

Nienhauser, William H., Jr. "You Had to Be There: A Call for an Uncommon Poetics." *Asian Cultural Quarterly* 14.3 (Autumn 1986): 41–62. Focuses on Du Fu's "Du zhou" 獨酌.

Nugent, Christopher M. B. "Sources of Difficulty, Reading and Understanding Du Fu," in *Reading Du Fu*, pp. 111–28.

Ou Lijuan 歐麗娟. *Tangdai shige yu xingbie yanjiu: yi Du Fu wei zhongxin* 唐代詩歌與性別研究: 以杜甫為中心. Taibei: Liren, 2008.

Owen, Stephen. *Traditional Chinese Poetry and Poetics: Omen of the World*. Madison: University of Wisconsin, 1985. Much of the discussion is based on poems by Du Fu.

___. "Thinking through Poetry: Du Fu's 'Getting Rid of the Blues' (*Jie men*)," in *Reading Du Fu*, pp. 27–40.

Pan Deyu 潘德輿 (1785–1839). *Yangyi Zhai Li, Du shihua* 養一齋李杜詩話. Zhang Zhongwang 張忠網, ed. Beijing: Shumu Wenxian, 1994.

Patterson, Gregory. "Elegies for Empire: The Poetics of Memory in the Late Work of Du Fu." Unpublished Ph.D. dissertation, Columbia University, 2013.

___. "Du Fu's Ethnographic Imagination: Local Culture and Its Contexts in Kuizhou Poetry," *CLEAR* 37 (2015): 29–65.

___."History Channels: Commemoration and Communication in Du Fu's Kuizhou Poems," in *Reading Du Fu*, pp. 41–55.

Peng Xing 朋星. *Du Fu yu Xianqin wenhua* 杜甫與先秦文化. Ph. D. Dissertation, Shandong Daxue, 2005.

Peng Yan 彭燕. "Du Fu yanjiu yibainian" 杜甫研究一百年, *Du Fu yanjiu xuekan* 3 (2015): 105–25.

___. "Lun Han fu dui Du Fu chuangzuo de yingxiang" 論漢賦對杜甫創作的影響, *Wenxue yichan* 2016.10: 40–44.

Rouzer, Paul. "Du Fu and the Failure of Lyric," *CLEAR* 33 (2011): 27–53.

___. "Refuges and Refugees, How Du Fu Writes Buddhism," in *Reading Du Fu*, pp. 75–92.

Shimosada Masahiru 下定雅弘. "To Ho ni okeru senkyō to sendō e no shōkei 杜甫における仙境と仙道への憧憬," *Chūgoku bungaku hō*, 91(2018): 1–27.

Song Kaiyu 宋開玉. *Dushi shidi* 杜詩釋地. Shanghai: Shanghai Guji, 2004.

Suet-ching Whitty Bui 貝雪菁. *A Study of Du Fu's (712–770) War Poems* 杜甫 (712–770) 戰爭詩研究. Ph. D. Dissertation, University of Hongkong, 2009.

Sun Liyao 孫立堯. "Du Fu qilü yuxu chanwei" 杜甫七律語序闡微, *Wenxue yichan* 2018.4: 62–74.

Sun Wei 孫微. *Dushi wenxian yanjiu lungao* 杜詩文獻研究論稿. Baoding: Hebei Daxue, 2010.

___. *Qingdai Dushi xue wenxian kao* 清代杜詩學文獻考. Nanjing: Fenghuang, 2007.

___. *Qingdai Dushi xueshi* 清代杜詩學史. Jinan: Qi Lu, 2004.

Tagawa Junzo 田川純三. *To Ho no tabi* 杜甫の旅. Tokyo: Shinchosha, 1991.

Tao Daoshu 陶道恕. *Du Fu shige shangxi ji* 杜甫詩歌賞析集. Chengdu: Ba Shu, 1993.

Tian Xiaofei, ed. *Reading Du Fu (712–770): Nine Views*. Hong Kong: Hong Kong University, 2020.

___. "Feeding the Phoenix, Du Fu's Qinzhou-Tonggu Series," in *Reading Du Fu*, pp. 93–108.

Tillman, Hoyt Cleveland. "Reassessing Du Fu's Line on Zhuge Liang," *MS* 50 (2002): 295–313.

Wang Dingzhang 王定璋. *Ru Shu shiren xieying: sijie, Du Fu, Lu You ji qita* 入蜀詩人擷英. Chengdu: Ba Shu, 2009.

Wang Huibin 王輝斌. *Du Fu yanjiu xintan* 杜甫研究新探. Hefei: Huangshan, 2011.

Wang Peizhong 王培中. *Du Fu Tonggu shi zhu kaobian* 杜甫同谷詩注考辨. Lanzhou: Dunhuang Wenyi, 2010.

Wang Shijing 王士菁. *Du shi bian lan* 杜詩便覽. Chengdu: Sichuan Wenyi, 1986.

Williams, Nicholas Morrow. "Sashimi and History: On a New Translation of Du Fu, *The Poetry of Du Fu* by Stephen Owen," *China Review International* 21 (2014): 201–44.

Wu Huaidong 吳懷東. *Shishi yundong yu zuojia chuangzao: Du Fu yu Liuchao shige guanxi yanjiu* 詩史運動與作家創造: 杜甫與六朝詩歌關係研究. Hefei: Anhui Jiaoyu, 2004.

Wu Jilu 吳繼路. *Qiannian shisheng-Du Fu* 千年詩聖-杜甫. Beijing: Shoudu Shifan Daxue, 2010.

Wu Jinwei 吳瑾瑋. *The Metrics of Du Fu: An Optimality Theory Approach* 從優選理論分析杜甫近體詩律. Taibei: Wen He, 2007.02.

Wu Mingxian 吳明賢. *Dushi lunxi* 杜詩論析. Chengdu: Sichuan Daxue, 2010.

Wu Zhuanzheng. "A Comparative Study of the Poetic Sequence: Tu Fu and W.B. Yeats." Unpublished Ph. D. dissertation, University of Washington, 1989.

Xia Songliang 夏松涼. *Du shi jianshang* 杜詩鑑賞. Shenyang: Liaoning Jiaoyu Xueyuan, 1986. Interesting close readings of nearly forty poems.

Xiao Lihua 肖麗華. *Lun Dushi chenyuduncuo zhi fengge* 論杜詩沉鬱頓挫之風格. Taibei: Huamulan, 2008.

Xie Siwei 謝思煒, ed. *Du Fu ji jiaozhu* 杜甫集校注. Shanghai: Shanghai Guji, 2015.

Xin Xiaojuan 辛曉娟. *Du Fu qiyan gexing yishu yanjiu* 杜甫七言歌行藝術研究. Ph. D. dissertation, Beijing Daxue, 2012.

Xu Guoneng 徐國能. *Qingdai shilun yu Dushi piping: yi shenyun, gediao, jili, xingling wei lunshu zhongxin* 清代詩論與杜詩批評: 以神韻, 格調, 肌理, 性靈為論述中心. Taibei: Liren, 2009.

Xu Xiping 徐希平 and Peng Chao 彭超. "Yuan Jie yu Du Fu guanxi zaitan" 元結與杜甫關係再探, *Zhongguo wenxue yanjiu*, 2020.4: 77–84.

Xu Yongzhang 許永璋. *Du shi mingpian xinxi* 杜詩名篇新析. Nanjing: Nanjing Daxue, 1989.

Yang Jinghua 楊經華. *Songdai Dushi chanshixue yanjiu* 宋代杜詩闡釋學研究, Beijing: Zhongguo Shehui Kexue, 2011.

Yang, Michael V. "Man and Nature: A Study of Du Fu's Poetry," *MS* 50 (2002): 315–36.

Yang Zhi 楊志. *Fengzhi he Du Fu shige bijiao yanjiu* 馮至和杜甫詩歌比較研究. Ph. D. Dissertation, Beijing Shifan Daxue, 2005.

Ye Jiaying 葉嘉瑩. *Du Fu Qiuxing bashou ji shuo* 杜甫秋興八首集說. Taibei: Zhonghua Congshu Bianshen Weiyuanhui, 1966.

___. *Ye Jiaying shuo Du Fu shi* 葉嘉瑩說杜甫詩. Beijing: Zhonghua, 2008.

Yoshikawa Kojiro 吉川幸次郎. *To Ho shizhu* 杜甫詩注, up to vol. 10 (1026) now edited by Kōzen Hiroshi 興膳宏. Tokyo: Chikuma Shobo, 1977–2016.

Yu Nianhu 于年湖. *Dushi yuyan yishu yanjiu* 杜詩語言藝術研究. Jinan: Qi Lu, 2007.

Zang Xiaofei 臧笑菲. *Shizhong shengzhe-Du Fu* 詩中聖哲—杜甫. Changchun: Jilin Wenshi, 2010.

Zeng Xiangbo 曾祥波. *Du Gongbu Cangtang shijian* zhuwen de laiyuan 《杜工部草堂詩箋》注文的來源、改寫与冒认, *Wenxue yichan* 2020.2: 81–91.

Zhao Hailing 趙海菱. *Du Fu yu Rujia wenhua chuantong yanjiu* 杜甫與儒家文化傳統研究. Jinan: Qi Lu, 2007.

Zhang Qiugui 張丘奎. *Tangmo Du Fu shige yanjiu yi Luo Yin, Wei Zhuang, Han Wo sanren wei tantao* 唐末杜甫詩歌研究以羅隱韋莊韓偓三人為探討. Taibei: Huamulan, 2020.

Zhang Wei 張巍. *Dushi ji zhongwan tang shi yanjiu* 杜詩及中晚唐詩研究. Jinan: Qi Lu, 2011.

Zuo Jiang 左江. *Li Zhi Dushi pi jie yanjiu* 李植杜詩批解研究. Beijing: Zhonghua, 2007.

David Lattimore and William H. Nienhauser, Jr.

Du Guangting 杜光庭 (*zi*, Binsheng 賓聖 or Binzhi 賓至, *hao*, Dongyin zi 東瀛子 and Huadiang Yuren 華頂羽人, 850–933) was a member of the Du clan of Duling 杜陵 in the capital area. At an early age he went to Guacang 括蒼 (or Jinyun 縉雲) in Chuzhou 處州 (modern Zhejiang). After failing the examination on the nine classics, he went to Mount Tiantai 天台, where he prepared himself for the Daoist priesthood. He was invited to join the court of Emperor Xizong (r. 874–888) in 875 and followed that sovereign into exile in Chengdu in 881, during the insurrection of Huang Chao 黃巢 (d. 884). During this period Du served the heir and after being summoned by the emperor to be conferred a Purple Robe 紫衣, he returned to the capital with him in 885. In 886 he again fled the capital with the emperor, then went on alone to Chengdu. Xizong died in 888. Meanwhile his captain Wang Jian 王建 (847–918) was bringing Sichuan under his personal control. He was supreme there by 891 and later created a kingdom (known to posterity as the Former Shu 前蜀) out of the province. Du Guangting was affably received at this splendid new court and was awarded high authority and magnificent titles, including the Daoist one of *Guangcheng Xiansheng* 廣成先生 (Prior Born of Broad Achievement). Later, after further honors under the second ruler of Shu, Wang Yan 王衍 (r. 919–925), who conferred on him the title *Chuanzhen Tianshi* 傳真天師 (Heavenly Master who Transmits the Truth); in 896 he resigned his posts and retired to Qingcheng Mountain 青城山, the summit of the Minshan 岷山 complex, which had been held in high regard by Daoists since the time of the first Celestial Masters of Later Han times. In 903 he declined an invitation to edit Wei Zhuang's 韋莊 (ca. 836–910)* works.

A considerable number of Du Guangting's prose writings survive. Three of these deserve special mention because of their length and the importance of their contents. One is *Yongcheng jixian lu* 墉城集仙錄 (Register of the Transcendents Gathered at Yongcheng), devoted to the careers, both mortal and immortal, of Daoist women and goddesses. These are both edifying examples of devotion, piety, and miracles, and also–differently considered–specimens of the typical wonder tale of the late Tang, saturated with mystery, exoticism, and the evidence of unseen worlds. In short, this is hagiography assimilated to the literary short story: its author clearly intended his readers to take his histories seriously as representations of religious truths. (The version of this collection preserved in the early Song Daoist anthology, *Yunji qiqian* 雲笈七籤, which appears to be close to Du Guangting's original, omits a number of exalted beings of the pantheon of Highest Clarity [*Shangqing* 上清] who appear in full panoply in the Ming version of the *Daozang* 道藏; on the other hand, a number of ladies in the former gallery are conspicuously absent from the latter.)

Another major contribution by Du Guangting to the history of medieval religion is his *Dongtian fudi yuedu mingshan ji* 洞天福地嶽瀆名山記 (A Record of Grotto Heavens, Paradisal Spots, Marchmount Caverns and Famous Mountains), a spiritual baedeker for the subterranean worlds styled "grotto heavens" (*dongtian* 洞天), hidden in the lowest roots of China's sacred mountains and equipped with their own skies, planets, sun, and moon. An elegant preface to this work describes also the cities of the sky, the high counterparts of those dreamlike underworlds, whose palaces and basilicas were shaped from coagulated clouds and frozen mists. There is also his *Lidai chong Dao ji* 歷代崇道記 (A Historical Record of Honoring the Dao), an account of the honors conferred on the Daoist religion and its adherents by the royal court from the earliest times down to the tenth century. This reverent relation of benefactions, promotions, preferments, architectural endowments, celebrations, and honors is particularly rich in information about the rulers of the Tang, above all Emperor Xuanzong (r. 712–756).

Prominent among the many shorter prose compositions of Du Guangting is a considerable number of highly formalized texts outlining the procedures of Daoist rituals. These fall chiefly into two groups: *zhaici* 齋詞 (texts for purgation) and *jiaoci* 醮詞 (texts for cosmodramas). The former category of scenario refers to rites conducted in special theaters on holy occasions. The second group outlines the plots and purposes of triumphal proceedings which often marked the climax of preparatory days of purgation.

Many other prose writings survive, some of them concerned with court business, some related to religious affairs. Virtually all are in some measure concerned with cosmic or metaphysical matters. To judge from such compositions as these, Du Guangting appears as a conservative thinker, and adherent of fashionable orthodoxy, which implies that, like his associate Guanxiu 貫休 (832–912),* he was a religious syncretist.

The rather small corpus of his extant poems, however, gives a different view of his creative talents. Almost all of them have a purely Daoist content, but they are by no means merely reverent and ceremonial. Their themes range from allusions to holy grottoes and sacred mountains, to holy men, perennial cranes, and spectral apes, to the divine spectacles presented by radiant clouds and blazing stars. Like other Daoist writers he lets his fancy roam throughout space in faery fantasies: He harnesses the moon toad, he actualizes divine birds in his personal microcosm, he finds infinity in the inner space of his mind. His writing, always competent, in such instances seems inspired. For example, in "Zeng ren" 贈人 (Sent to a Certain Person):

Soul quiet, thoughts in focus—looking up into the blue abyss;
This very evening the enduring sky let down an auspicious star.
Last night, out on the sea, I heard the plumed wings of the *peng* bird,
Just now, here among men, I see the figure of a crane.

靜神凝思仰青冥，此夕長天降瑞星。
海上昨聞鵬羽翼，人間初見鶴儀形。

Here Du sees, in the hidden landscape of his own mind, the divine birds, potential vehicles for a longed-for journey to paradise. Their advent is betokened by a symbolic star sent for his eyes alone. The appearance of the crane in the final line, a symbol of imminent departure to immortality, confirms his poetic augury that he is not long for the world of men.

To those outside the Daoist circle, Du Guangting is best remembered as the author of a remarkable Tang story "Qiuranke zhuan" 虬髯客傳 (The Curly-bearded Stranger). Set at the end of the Sui dynasty (589–618), the story purports to be a reconstruction of some of the events behind the rise of Li Shimin 李世民 (599–649), who later became the Tang emperor Taizong (r. 626–649). The narrative follows the travels of Li Jing 李靖 (571–649)–later a high-ranking military officer under Li Shimin–after eloping with a maid in the household of the Sui minister Yang Su 楊素 (d. 606). The minister declines Li Jing's offer to counsel him, but the maid Hongfu 紅拂 recognizes Li's merit and decides to run away to him. The love affair is not allowed to develop much further. On their way eastward Li Jing and Hongfu meet a brazen, curly-bearded stranger at an inn. The "curly-bearded stranger" is a common trope for those from a foreign land, and thus the encounter at the inn can be seen as an encounter with the Other. After they have shared their meal with him, the stranger asks:

Du Guangting

"Is there wine?" "To our west is a wine shop," replied Li Jing. He [went to] get a jug of wine. After a round of drinking, the stranger said, "I have a little something to go with the wine. Would you, Master Li, share it with me?" Li Jing replied, "It would be my honor." At this the stranger opened his colorful sack and took out a human head, heart and liver. He put the head back into the sack and cut up the heart and liver, eating them together with Li Jing. The stranger said, "This is the heart of an unfaithful friend. For ten years I held this against him. Just now I was not able to capture him. Now I'm relieved and have no regrets."

曰："有酒乎？"靖曰：主人西則酒肆也。靖取酒一剉。酒既巡，客曰："吾有少下酒物，李郎能同之乎？"靖曰："不敢。"於是開華囊，取出一人頭並心肝。卻收頭囊中，以匕首切心肝共食之。曰："此人乃天下負心者心也，銜之十年，今始獲，吾憾釋矣。"

The stranger then asks Li Jing whether he knows of any men of worth. Li Jing responds that he knows of only one man–Li Shimin–worthy of becoming emperor and later arranges a meeting. When they meet, the stranger immediately recognizes that Li Shimin is destined to become emperor and gives up his own ambitions. He bequeaths his considerable fortune to Li Jing and Hongfu and then disappears, eventually becoming a ruler in another land.

At one level of interpretation the story illustrates the importance of the custom of *bao* 報 (reciprocation)–the stranger repays Li Jing and Hongfu for the favors they have done him. But the story's explicit didactic purpose is to illustrate the futility of rebellion, of striving against the will of Heaven. This aim is only at the expense of historical fact: Li Shimin won the throne after killing his older brother, the heir apparent. The story's idealization of Li Shimin's rise to power accords with the political mood toward the end of the Tang. To those living in that time of fragmentation, Li Shimin's prosperous reign seemed a golden age. "Qiuran ke zhuan" has been interpreted as an expression of this late Tang nostalgia–as a political protest expressing the hope that a true emperor would appear to restore order. This interpretation, however, is difficult to fit to Du's political ideas, though in some poems he does lament a lack of social order.

The tale's textual history indicates that there may have been some uncertainty about its intended meaning–perhaps on the author's own part. The story is extant in two basic versions. What is considered the earlier text appears in Du Guangting's *Shenxian ganyu zhuan* 神仙感遇傳 (Encounters with Divine Transcendents, 904), under the title "Qiuxu ke" 虯鬚客 (The Curly-whiskered Stranger). In this version the political allegory seems to be emphasized: The stranger is mentioned at the beginning as the narrative's focus, and Li Jing's elopement with Hongfu is only briefly sketched. In the later text, included in the *Taiping guangji* 太平廣記 (Extensive Gleanings of the Reign of Great Tranquility) and believed by some to contain Du Guangting's own revisions, the emphasis changes. The stranger is not introduced until about one-fourth through the story, and the romance between Hongfu and Li Jing is described in greater detail. More stress is placed on Hongfu's courage as manifested by her escape from Yang Su's household and by her equanimity in dealing with a stranger who lies down beside her without warning to watch her comb her hair. Li Jing's characterization changes too: a colorless character to begin with, he recedes further into the background, serving as a foil to both Hongfu and the stranger and as a mere plot device for bringing together various characters.

Whoever revised the story seems to have realized that the relationships established in the first half–Hongfu's interaction with Li Jing and the stranger–would overshadow the political lesson drawn in the second. To compensate for this, passages stressing the story's political import were added–for example, an insertion that reads: "A subject who foolishly thinks of rebellion is a mantis trying to stop a rolling wheel with its arms." Nevertheless it is the trio of Li Jing, Hongfu, and the stranger–later referred to as "the three well-traveled gallants" (*fengchen sanxia* 風塵三俠)– that inspired later writers. The characters served as subjects of Ming drama: for example, Ling Mengchu's 凌濛初 (1580–1644) *Qiuran weng* 虬髯翁 (The Curly-bearded Old Man) and Zhang Fengyi's 張風翼 (1527–1613) *Hongfu ji* 紅拂記 (Record of the Red Whisk).

BIBLIOGRAPHY

Editions:

Wang Meng'ou 王夢鷗. *Tangren xiaoshuo jiaoshi* 唐人小說校釋. Taibei: Zhengzhong, 1983, pp. 319–38. Excellent annotated version of "Qiuran ke zhuan."

"Qiuran ke zhuan" in Li Fang 李昉. *Taiping guangji* 太平廣記, Beijing: Zhonghua, 1986, ch. 193, pp. 1445–48. Reliable text of the later version.

___, *Tang Song chuanqi xuan* 唐宋傳奇選, Shi Yan 師言, ed. Beijing, 1963, pp. 124–30. A heavily annotated text.

Quan Tang shi, 14: 10755.

Quan Tang wen, 929–44.12753–880.

Zhengtong Daozang 正統道藏. Rpt. Taibei, 1976. (Individual works may be located by reference to Weng Dujian 翁獨健, *Combined Indices to the Author and Titles of Books in Two Collections of Taoist Literature* [Harvard-Yenching Institute Sinological Index Series, No. 25], rpt. Taibei: Chengwen, 1966. For instance, No. 599 is *Dontian fudi yuedu mingshan ji*, and No. 782 is *Yongcheng jixianlu*.)

Translations:

Birch, Cyril. "The Curly-bearded Hero," in *Anthology of Chinese Literature*. Vol. 1, New York: Grove, 1965, pp. 314–322.

Cahill, Suzanne E, trans. *Divine Traces of the Daoist Sisterhood: Records of the Assembled Transcendents of the Fortified Walled City*. Magdalna, NM: Three Pines, 2006.

Chai Ch'u (1906–1986) and Winberg Chai. "The Curly-bearded Guest," in *A Treasury of Chinese Literature: A New Prose Anthology Including Fiction and Drama*, New York: Appleton-Century, 1965, pp. 117–24.

Chavannes, Édouard. *Le Jet des Dragons* (*Mémoires concernant l'Asie Orientale*, 3 [1919]), pp. 172–214 (translation of *Taishang ling bayou guiming zhenda zhai yan gongyi* 太上靈寶玉匱明真大齋言功儀 [Weng Dujian, No. 521]).

___. "Les lieux célestes profondes" (translation of *Dongtian fudi yuedu mingshan ji*), Ibid., pp. 131–68.

Lévy, André. "L'étranger à la barbe et aux favoris bouclés," in *Histoires extraordinaires et récits fantastiques de la Chine ancienne*. V. 2. Paris: Aubier, 1993, pp. 186–95.

Schafer, Edward H. "Three Divine Women of South China," *CLEAR* 1 (1979): 31–42. Translations from *Yongcheng jixian lu*.

Wang Jing. "The Tale of the Curly-Bearded Guest." In William H. Nienhauser, Jr. *Tang Dynasty Tales: A Guided Reader*. Singapore and Hackensack, New Jersey: World Scientific, 2010, pp. 189–222.

Yang Xianyi and Gladys Yang. "The Man with the Curly Beard," in *The Dragon King's Daughter*. 2nd printing; Beijing: Waiwen, 1962, pp. 92–99.

Studies:

Chavannes, Édouard. "Biographie de Tou Kouang-t'ing," *Le Jet des Dragons, Mémoires concernant l'Asie Orientale* 3 (1919): 130 ff.

Imaetd Jiro 今枝二郎. "To Kotei shoko" 杜光庭小考. In *Yoshioka Hakase kanreki kinen Dokyō kenkyū ronshu–Dokyō no shisō to bunka* 吉岡博士還歷記念道教研究記 – 道教の思想と文化. Tokyo, 1977, pp. 523–32.

Li Dahua 李大華 et al. "Du Guangting Daojiao zhexue sixiang tixi" 杜光庭哲學思想體系 in *Sui Tang Daojia yu Daojiao* 隋唐道家與道教. Beijing: Renmin, 2011, pp. 474–536.

Ling Zi 凌子. "Tan 'Qiuran ke zhuan' de yishu shijiao" 談虯髯客傳的藝術視角. *Wenshi zhishi* 1 (1992): 56–60.

Luo Zhengming 羅爭鳴. 2002a. *Du Guangting liangdu ru Shu kao* 杜光庭兩度入蜀考 [A Textual Study of Du Guangting's Two Trips to Shu]. *Zongjiaoxue Yanjiu* 宗教學研究 1: 100–3.

Liu, James J.Y. *The Chinese Knight-Errant*. Chicago: University of Chicago, 1967, pp. 87–88.

Liu Kairong 劉開榮. *Tangdai xiaoshuo yanjiu* 唐代小說研究, rev. ed. Hong Kong: Shangwu, 1964, pp. 187–215.

Liu Ying 劉瑛. *Tangdai chuanqi yanjiu* 唐代傳奇研究. Taibei: Lianjing, 1994, pp. 376–83. Study of "Qiuran ke zhuan."

Rao Zongyi 饒宗頤. "Qiuran ke zhuan kao" 虯髯客傳考. *Dalu zazhi* 18.1 (1959): 1–4.

Swatek, Catherine. "The Self in Conflict: Paradigms of Change in a Tang Legend." In *Expressions of Self in Chinese Literature*, Robert E. Hegel and Richard C. Hessney, eds. New York: Columbia University, 1985, 153–88. A comparison of "Qiuran ke zhuan" and "Hongfu ji."

Sun Yiping 孫亦平. *Du Guangting sixiang yu Tang Song daojiao de zhuanxing* 杜光庭思想與唐宋道教的轉型. Nanjing: Nanjing Daxue, 2004.

Suanyama Minoru 石少山稔. "To Kōtei no shisō ni tsuite" 杜光庭の思想について, *Shūkan Tōyōgaku* 集刊東洋學 54 (1985): 297–316.

Verellen, Franciscus. *Du Guangting (850–933): Taoist de cour à la fin de la Chine médiévale*. Paris: Collège de France, Institut des Hautes Études Chinoises, 1989. *Mémoires del'Institut des Hautes Études Chinoises*, 30.

___. "Green Memorials: Daoist Ritual Prayers in the Tang-Five Dynasties Transition," *Tang Studies*, 35 (2017): 51–86.

Wang Yunxi 王運熙. "Du 'Qiuran ke zhuan' zhaji" 讀虯髯客傳札記. *Xuelin manlu* 11 (1985): 130–36.

Wu Renchen 吳任臣 (ca. 1628–1689). *Shiguo chunqiu* 十國春秋. Taibei: Taiwan Shangwu, 1972, ch. 47, pp. 5b–8a.

Zhan, *Daojiao*, pp. 386–95.

Edward H. Schafer, Cordell Yee, and William H. Nienhauser, Jr.

Du Mu 杜牧 (*zi*, Muzhi 牧之, 803–852 or 853) is a late Tang poet-essayist traditionally known for his lyrical, romantic quatrains and for similar qualities attributed to his life. The romantic image is due largely to the tale "Yangzhou meng ji" 揚州夢記 (Record of Yangzhou Dream), and embellished summation of anecdotes and legends compiled shortly after Du Mu's death by Yu Ye 于鄴 (fl. 867). Until recent years, his many lengthy narrative poems were neglected for the popular quatrains, but it is primarily in the longer poems, as in his letters and essays, that Confucian issues are raised and that he invariably provides testimony on the politics of his age.

Born in Chang'an at the home of his grandfather, the noted author and high official Du You 杜佑 (735–812), Du Mu spent his childhood amid the culture and opulence of Grand Councilors's estate. However, the family fortunes dwindled rapidly after the death of Du You, and Du Mu's father died some years later, so that Du Mu could describe his youth as a time when servants deserted the household and the family survived only by selling off property. It is implied that because of the domestic imperatives, he did not begin to study the classics until he was twenty, but he must have learned fast, for he was writing letters to high officials and *fu* 賦 (prose-poems) at twenty-three, and he passed the *jinshi* at twenty-five.

The "Afang gong fu" 阿房宮賦 (Prose-poem on the Afang Palace), composed in 825, supposedly presaged his success in the *jinshi* examination. Ostensibly it is a critique of the excesses of Qin Shi Huangdi 秦始皇帝 (First Emperor of the Qin Dynasty), but its Confucian judgments are really aimed at the brief reign of Emperor Jingzong (r. 825–827). The *fu* is his earliest poetic effort; it is considered stylistically original and a precursor of the *wenfu* 文賦 (prose *fu*) of the Song dynasty. His first datable poem was written in 827, the year before he passed the examination, and it, too, is a lengthy, moralistic self-advertisement entitled "Gan huai shi" 感懷詩 (Deep-seated Feelings); the title and format have been used by many poets.

His career began well enough: from 828 to 833, after serving as an Editor in the Institute for the Advancement of Literature, he became an Adjutant Left Militant Guard in the Military Service Section (of the Palace), then was a clerk for Shen Chuanshi 沈傳師 (769–827), before moving to the staff of Niu Sengru 牛僧孺 (ca. 779–ca. 848) in Yangzhou. He returned to Chang'an early in 835 as an Investigating Censor and by mid-year had himself transferred to Luoyang, where he marked time for two years before retiring to take care for his younger brother, Du Yi 杜顗 (806–851), who was going blind. Various minor positions in Chang'an between 838 and 842 ended with a series of prefectships in the southeast, which he considered a six-year exile. Du Mu returned to Chang'an to a post too lowly to support his and his brother's families, and after much lobbying he was made Prefect of Huzhou 湖州 in 850. His brother died in 851; Du Mu then returned to capital.

The expression of frustration is constant in Du Mu's writings, and it raises the question of who or what kept him from high office. Thanks to Du You, the Du family had good connections with both sides in the Niu-Li factional dispute; Du Mu eventually worked for both. His relations with Niu were particularly warm, and he seemed to have had an almost continuous correspondence with Li Deyu 李德裕 (787–850).* Evidence from his poetry suggests that 835 actually was the turning point in his career, when he joined those opposed to the appointments of Zheng Zhu 鄭注 (d. 835) and Li Xun 李訓 (d. 835) as Grand Councilors. The backlash took the life of one good friend and affected several careers; Du Mu found it the better part of valor to lie low in Luoyang. In that year he wrote "Li Gan" 李甘, more obscurely in "Xi shi Wen Huangdi, sanshier yun" 昔事文皇帝三十二韻 (Formerly in the Service of Emperor Wen, Thirty-two Rhymes), and in several poems on the family estate at the Vermilion Slope 朱坡 (in the Southern Mountains outside the capital), describing the events of 835, arguing his somewhat shameful innocence, grieving over friends, and generally mourning the impact on his career. The Sweet Dew Incident 甘露之變, an abortive attempt to assassinate powerful eunuchs which ended in a massacre of officials, occurred at the end of the year but seems not to have had the same relevance for Du Mu as the earlier conflict.

Throughout his life Du Mu wrote letters to those in high places, telling them what was wrong with policy and military strategy and what was right about his own credentials for advancement. A prime example is his "Zui yan" 罪言 (Guilty Words) of 834; the title refers to his presumption in criticizing policy from his lowly position, but he does so anyway, offering an inventory of Confucian ideals. His claim to be a military strategist was belatedly lent credence by his widely accepted commentary to the *Sunzi* 孫子 (Art of War), completed sometime before 849. He wrote Li Deyu frequently in the 840s, when Li was a Grand Councilor, to offer strategies, and his ideas were once followed (with positive results). The single-mindedness of such pieces, pedantic, formal, and lyrical by turns, reflects Du Mu's public concern and personal ambition. They remind the reader of the link between *guwen* 古文 prose and Confucian ideals, but Du Mu's style is really best described as eclectic.

His "Jinguyuan" 金谷園 (The Garden of Golden Valley) reveals some of his artistry:

The splendors of the past scattered in fragrant dust,
The flowing waters heartless, the grasses turn to spring on their own.
At sunset the east wind, causes the birds to cry mournfully—
The fallen flowers resemble that girl who threw herself from the tower.

繁華事散逐香塵，流水無情草自春。
日暮東風怨啼鳥，落花猶似墮樓人。

The poem contrasts the vanity of worldly glory with the constancy of nature in the context of an allusion. The title refers to the garden where Shi Chong 石崇 (249–300), a wealthy courtier, constructed his villa northwest of modern Luoyang. By Du Mu's time the villa was in ruins where only the grasses renewed themselves unaided by the waters which represent time's relentless flow. Du Mu recalls that Shi Chong had a beautiful concubine named Lüzhu 綠珠 (Green Pearl). When Sun Xiu 孫秀, a member of the Wu royal family who had taken refuge in Luoyang, sought to obtain Green Pearl, Shi Chong refused, and Sun took offense. While banqueting with Green Pearl high in a tower, Shi complained to her that he had offended a powerful man on her behalf. Just then Sun Xiu brought troops to surround the garden. Green Pearl, realizing her dilemma, threw herself from the tower to express her loyalty to Shi Chong. Sun then executed Shi and his entire clan. The poem laments time's erasure of human creations, while recalling Green Pearl's exemplary loyalty.

Du Mu's work is often autobiographical, as in "Dayu xing" 大雨行 (Ballad of Heavy Rain), or in "Zhang Haohao shi" 張好好事 (The Affair of Zhang Haohao), where he poignantly tells the story of a singsong girl, Zhang Haohao, from the happy times when he first met her to her consequent fates as a barmaid and refugee. Other poems treat partings, travel as a metaphor, and the vicissitudes of public life.

Du Mu's quatrains tend to be more subdued than his longer poems, although internal rhyme, alliteration, repetition, and allusion still are abundant. He favors the Later Han dynasty as the source for parallels with the late Tang. Irony is an often-used vehicle of expression, as in his "Chi Bi" 赤壁 (Red Cliff) and "Bo Qinhuai" 泊秦淮 (Mooring on the Qinhuai River). His romantic-erotic quatrains also provided material for the stories in the "Yangzhou meng ji." Reference is commonly made to his "Zeng bie" 贈別 (Offered at Parting) which described a thirteen-year-old beauty; "Qian huai" 遣懷 (Chasing Cares Away), which mentions a ten-year Yangzhou dream; and "Tan hua" 歎花 (Singing over Flowers), which tells of his coming too late to find a flower, it having already gone to fruit (metaphorically referring to a woman). The dominant tone of much of his verse is understatement.

His lifelong search for high office ended in 852 when he was made a Secretariat Drafter; he died a few months later. That a great number of his poems (524) remain is in part the result of his careful editing, particularly of his earlier poems. It is difficult to say who the ultimate influences were for his poetry; early models and his respect for masters like Du Fu 杜甫 (712–770),* Li Bo 李白 (701–762),* Han Yu 韓愈 (768–824),* and Liu Zongyuan 柳宗元 (773–819)* do not fully explain his style, but anticipate his acquaintance with allegory.

BIBLIOGRAPHY

Editions:

Chaoxian keben Fanchuan wenji jiazhu 朝鮮刻本樊川文集夾注. Beijing: Zhonghua Quanguo Tushuguan Wenxian Suowei Fuzhi Zhongxin, 1997.
Chen, Yunji 陳允吉, ed. *Du Mu quanji* 杜牧全集. Shanghai: Shanghai Guji, 1997.
Du Mu 杜牧. *Fanchuan shiji zhu* 樊川詩集注 (*Sibu beiyao* 四部備要). Shanghai: Zhonghua, 1936.
___. *Fanchuan shiji* 樊川詩集. Shanghai: Shanghai Guji, 2005.
Quan Tang shi, 8: 5980–6084, 11: 9007, 13: 9903, 9924, 10673, 14: 10673, 15: 11317–18.
Quan Tang wen, 748–56.8802–98.
Zhu Yishi 朱一是 (1610–1671) et al. *Du Fanchuan ji shiqijuan* 杜樊川集十七卷. Wushi Xishuang Tang 吳氏西爽堂, between 1621 and 1644.

References:

Luan Guiming 欒貴明, ed. *Quan Tangshi suoyin: Du Mu juan* 全唐詩索引: 杜牧卷. Beijing: Zhonghua, 1992.
Yamauchi Haruo 山內春夫, ed. *To Boku shi sakuin* 杜牧詩索引. Kyōto: Ibundo, 1972 and 1986.

Annotations:

Feng Jiwu 馮集梧 (*jinshi* 1781). *Fanchuan shiji zhu* 樊川詩集注. Beijing: Zhonghua, 1962.
Miao Yue 繆鉞, comp. *Du Mu shixuan* 杜牧詩選. Beijing: Renmin Wenxue, 1957.
Ouyang Zhuo 歐陽灼. *Du Mu ji* 杜牧集. Changsha: Yuelu, 2001.
Wu Zaiqing 吳在慶. *Du Mu ji xinian jiaozhu* 杜牧集系年校注. Beijing: Zhonghua, 2013.
Zhang Houyu 張厚余, comm. *Du Mu ji* 杜牧集. Taiyuan: Shanxi Guji, 2004.
Zhang Songhui 張松輝. *Xinyi Du Mu shiwen ji* 新譯杜牧詩文集. Taibei: Sanmin, 2002.
Zhu Bilian 朱碧蓮 and Wang Shujun 王淑均, eds. *Du Mu shiwen xuanzhu* 杜牧詩文選注. Shanghai: Shanghai Guji, 1982.

Biographical Sources:

Fu, *Tang caizi*, 3:191–210.
Jiu Tang shu, 147.3978–88.
Xin Tang shu, 166.5085–98.

Translations:

Arai Ken 荒井健. *To Boku* 杜牧. Tokyo: Chikuma Shobō, 1974.
Burton, R. F., trans. *Plantains in the Rain: Selected Chinese Poems of Du Mu*. London: Wellsweep, 1990.
Demiéville, *Anthologie*, pp. 315–316.

Fuller, Michael A. *An Introduction to Chinese Poetry: From the* Canon of Poetry *to the Lyrics of the Song Dynasty*. Cambridge: Harvard University Press, 2018, pp. 334–40.
Graham, A. C. *Poems of the Late T'ang*. Baltimore: Penguin Books, 1965, pp. 121–40.
Kroll, "Recalling Xuanzong," pp. 14–18.
Kubin, Wolfgang. *Das lyrische Werk des Tu Mu (803–852), Versuch eine Deutung*. Wiesbaden: Harrassowitz, 1976.
Mair, *Anthology*, p. 236.
Margoulies, *Anthologie*, pp. 143–44, 317, 376.
Minford and Lau, pp. 915–19.
New Directions, p. 141.
Owen, *Middle Ages*, p. 35.
___, *Mi-Lou*, pp. 147–50, 159–60.
___, *Omen*, pp. 181–82.
___, *Remembrances*, pp. 51–54, 120–21.
Pimpaneau, pp. 454–6.
Sukys, Gail Ellen. "'Formerly in the Service of Emperor Wen, 32 Rhymes' by Tu Mu (803–852): Translation and Interpretation." Unpublished M.A. thesis. University of Oregon, 1982.
Watson, *Columbia*, p. 286.
___, *Lyricism*, p. 121.
Wu Ou 吳鷗, trans. and comm. *Du Mu shiwen xuanyi* 杜牧詩文選譯. Chengdu: Shushe, 1991. *Gudai wenshi mingzhu xuanyi congshu*.
___, trans. and comm. *Du Mu shiwen* 杜牧詩文. Taibei: Jinxiu Chuban Shiye Gefen Youxian Gongsi, 1993. *Zhongguo mingzhu xuanyi congshu*, 60.

Studies:
Aikō Hiroshi 愛甲弘志. "To Boku to Kan Yu to no Kankei" 杜牧と韓愈との關係. *Chugokū bungaku ronshū* 中國文學論集, 10 (1982): 73–94.
Cao Zhongfu 曹中孚. *Wan Tang shiren Du Mu* 晚唐詩人杜牧. Xian: Shanxi Renmin, 1985.
___. *Du Mu shi shangxi* 杜牧詩賞析. Guangzhou: Guangdong Renmin, 2003.
Chen Guang 陳光. *Du Mu shi shang du* 杜牧詩賞讀. Beijing: Xianzhuang, 2007.
Chen Yongji 陳永吉 and Zhongshan Hu 胡中山. *Shuangye hong ye eryue hua: Du Mu shige shangxi* 霜葉紅於二月花: 杜牧詩歌賞析. Taibei: Yeqiang, 1997.
Chen Xiang 陳香. *Du Mu de jueju shi* 杜牧的絕句詩. Taibei: Taiwan Shangwu, 1984.
Deng Shaoji 鄧紹基 and Xiucai Zhou 周秀才 et al. *Du Mu* 杜牧. Dalian: Dalian, 1997.
Feng Hairong 冯海榮. *Du Mu* 杜牧. Shanghai: Shanghai Guji, 1991.
Fish, Michael B. "The Tu Mu and Li Shangyin Prefaces to the Collected Poems of Li Ho." In *Chinese Poetry and Poetics*, Vol.1, by R.C. Miao, ed., San Francisco: Chinese Materials Center, 1978, pp. 231–286.
___. "Tu Mu's Poems on the Vermilion Slope: Laments on a Meager Career." *OE* 25.2 (1978): 190–205.
Fishlen, Michael [Michael B. Fish]. "Wine, Poetry and History: Du Mu's 'Pouring Alone in the Prefectural Residence.'" *TP* 80 (1994): 260–97.
Ge Liang 葛亮. *Du Mu shi* 杜牧詩. Hongkong: Shangwu, 2003.
Ge Zhaoguang 葛兆光 and Yan Dai 戴燕. *Wan Tang Fengyun: Du Mu yu Li Shangyin* 晚唐風韻: 杜牧與李商隱. Hongkong: Zhonghua, 1990.
Hong, Yue. "Celebrating Sensual Indulgence: Du Mu 杜牧 (803–852), His Readers, and the Making of a New *Fengliu* 風流 Ideal," *JAOS*, 139 (2019): 143–64.
Hsiao Ching-song Gene. "Semiotic Interpretation of Chinese Poetry: Du Mu's Poetry as Example." Unpublished Ph. D. dissertation, University of Arizona, 1985.

Hu Kexian 胡可先. *Du Mu yanjiu conggao* 杜牧研究叢稿. Beijing: Renmin Wenxue, 1993.

___. *Yan long hanshui yue long sha* 煙籠寒水月笼沙. Zhengzhou: Henan Wenyi, 2002.

Hu Yunyi 胡雲翼. *Langman shiren Du Mu* 浪漫詩人杜牧. Taibei: Taiwan Wenhua, 1957.

Hu Kexian 胡可先. *Du Mu yanjiu conggao* 杜牧研究叢稿. Beijing: Renmin Wenxue, 1993. An important collection of basic scholarly studies.

___. *Xiao Li Du* 小李杜. Beijing: Zhonghua, 2010.

Ichinosawa Torao 市野澤寅雄. *To Boku* 杜牧. Tokyo: Shūeisha, 1965.

Kirishima Kaoruko 桐島薫子. *Bantō shijin kō: Ri Shōin, On Teiin, To Boku no hikaku to kōsatsu* 晚唐詩人考: 李商隱. 溫庭筠. 杜牧の比較と考察. Fukuoka: Chūgoku, 1998.

Kou Yanghou 寇養厚. "Du Mu de wenxue sixiang" 杜牧的文學思想. *Wenshizhe* 6 (1993): 64–73.

Kroll, Paul W. "Recalling Xuanzong and Lady Yang: A Selection of Mid- and Late Tang Poems," *Tang Studies*, 35 (2017): 1–19.

Kubin, Wolfgang (see Translations above).

Kung, Wen-k'ai. "The Official Biography of Tu Mu (803–852) in the *Old T'ang History*." *Chinese Culture* 29 (1987): 87–99.

___. *Tu Mu (803–852): His Life and Poetry*. San Francisco: Chinese Materials Center, 1990. *Asian Library Series*, 38.

___. "Tu Mu's Poetry of Social Criticism and the Historical Past." *Chinese Culture* 26.1 (March 1985): 47–77.

Li Quan 李全. *Tang Song shici shi da jia. Du Mu shiji* 唐宋詩詞十大家. 杜牧詩集. Jinan: Jinan, 1995.

Lin Zhongxiang 林仲湘, "Du Mu shiwen yongyun kao" 杜牧詩文用韻考, *Guangxi Daxue xuebao* 廣西大學學報 2 (1990): 88–97.

Liu Gang 劉剛. *Du Mu, Li Shangyin* 杜牧, 李商隱. Shenyang: Chunfeng Wenyi, 1999.

Lu Yonglin 盧永璘. *Xiao Li Du shi zhuan* 小李, 杜詩傳. Changchun: Jilin Renmin, 2003.

Lü Wuzhi 呂武志. *Du Mu sanwen yanjiu* 杜牧散文研究. Taibei: Taiwan Xuesheng, 1994.

Miao Yue 繆鉞. "Luetan Du Mu yongshishi" 略談杜牧詠史詩. *Wenshi zhishi* 7 (1985): 8–13.

___. *Du Mu nianpu* 杜牧年譜. Shijiazhuang: Hebei Jiaoyu, 1999.

___. *Du Mu shi xuan* 杜牧詩選. Beijing: Renmin Wenxue, 1957.

___. *Du Mu xingnian jianpu* 杜牧行年簡譜. Beijing: Renmin Wenxue, 1957.

___. *Du Mu zhuan* 杜牧傳. Beijing: Renmin Wenxue, 1977.

___. *Du Mu zu nian kao* 杜牧卒年考. Beijing: Zhonghua, 1962.

___. *Miao Yue quanji di wu juan Du Mu yanjiu* 繆鉞全集第五卷杜牧研究. Shijiazhuang: Hebei Jiaoyu, 2004.

Pilière, Marie-Christine Verniau. "Du Mu: Comment render justice à la homme er à l'oeuvre?" *Études Chinoises* 6 (1987): 47–71.

___. "Les Thèmes de la poésie de 'Du Mu' (803–852)." Unpublished thesis/dissertation, Paris, 1984.

Qi Liantao 齊連濤 et al. *Du Mu Juan* 杜牧卷. Dalian: Dalian, 1997.

Shigeru Saitō 齋藤茂. *To Boku* 杜牧. Tokyo: Meiji, 2020.

Su Yinghui 蘇瑩輝. *Shilun Du Mu Fanchuan ji zhong He Huang zhushi de niandai* 試論杜牧樊川集中河湟諸詩的年代, N.p., n.d.

Takahashi Miki 高橋未来. *To Boku kenkyū: To boku ni okeru seiji to bungaku* 杜牧研究 : 杜牧における政治と文学 / 高橋未来著. Tokyo: Tokyo University, 2016.

Tan-Li Zongmu 譚黎宗慕. *Du Mu yanjiu ziliao huibian* 杜牧研究資料彙編. Taibei: Yiwen, 1972.

Tao Ruizhi 陶瑞芝. *Du Fu, Du Mu shi luncong* 杜甫, 杜牧詩論叢. Shanghai: Xuelin, 2005.

Teng Young-sheng. "Tu Mu as a Literary Critic: Gleanings from the Villa on Fan Stream." Unpublished Ph.D. dissertation, Indiana University, 1987.

Tomohisa Matsūra et al. *To boku shisen* 杜牧詩選. Tokyo: Iwanami, 2004.

Wang Jingni 王景霓. *Du Mu jiqi zuopin* 杜牧及其作品. Changchun: Shidai Wenyi, 1985.

Wang Xiping 王西平 and Tian Zhang 張田. *Du Mu ping chuan* 杜牧評傳. Xian: Shanxi Renmin, 1987.

___ and Gao Yunguang 高雲光. *Du Mu shimei tansuo* 杜牧詩美探索. Xian: Shanxi Renmin, 1993. Appends an index to scholarly works on Du Mu published between 1985 and 1990.
Wen Zheng. "Myth and Reality: A Reconsideration of Du Mu (803–852)." Unpublished Ph.D. dissertation, University of Wisconsin, 2015.
Wu Zaiqing 吳在慶. *Du Mu jixi nian jiaozhu* 杜牧集繫年校注. Beijing: Zhonghua, 2008.
___. *Du Mu lungao* 杜牧論稿. Amoy: Xiamen Daxue, 1991.
___. *Du Mu quanzhuan* 杜牧全傳. Changchun: Changchun, 1998.
___. *Du Mu shiwen xuanping* 杜牧詩文選評. Shanghai: Shanghai Guji, 2002.
___. *Shui cong jiangla yinzheng di, bie shi tan bing Du Muzhi: shilun Du Mu de yingxiang deng youguan wenti* 誰從絳臘銀箏底, 別識談兵杜牧之: 試論杜牧的影響等有關問題. Nanjing: Jiangsu Jiaoyu, 1994.
Xie-Jin Guiyu 謝錦桂毓. *Du Mu yanjiu* 杜牧研究. Taibei: Shangwu, 1976.
Xiong Jiangping 熊江平. "Du Mu shiyun kao" 杜牧詩韻考. *Qinghai Shifan Daxue xuebao* 青海師範大學學報 1 (1995): 83–92.
Yamauchi Haruo 山內春夫. *To Boku no kenkyū* 杜牧の研究. Kyoto: Ibundo, 1985.
Yan Kunyang 顏昆陽. *Du Mu* 杜牧. Taibei: Guojia, 1982.
Zhan Mei 張梅. *Du Mu* 杜牧. Beijing: Wuzhou Chuanbo, 2006.
Zhang Huoyu 張厚余. *Du Mu ji* 杜牧集. Taiyuan: Shanxi Guji, 2004.
Zhang Jinhai 張金海. *Du Mu ziliao huibian* 杜牧資料彙編. Beijing: Zhonghua, 2006.
Zhang Shuqiong 張淑瓊. *Tu Mu* 杜牧. Taibei: Diqiu, 1989.
Zheng Naixin 鄭乃新 and Wu Changfa 吳昌發. *Du Mu yu Huangzhou* 杜牧與黃州. Wuhan: Wuhan Daxue, 2020.
Zhong Shuhe 鍾叔河 and Yuan, Dachuan 袁大川. *Tangshi baijia quanji: Du Mu* 唐詩百家全集: 杜牧. Haikou: Hainan, 1992.
Zhou Xifu 周錫复. *Du Mu shixuan* 杜牧詩選. Hong Kong: Sanlian, 1980.
Zhuang Rufa 庄如發. *Lun Ruti bingyong de Du Mu* 論儒體兵用的杜牧. Hong Kong: Huoyi Chuban Shiye Youxian Gongsi, 1999.
Zhu Bilian 朱碧蓮. *Du Mu xuanji* 杜牧選集. Shanghai: Shanghai Guji, 1995.
___. "Lun Du Mu yu niuli dangzheng" 論杜牧與牛李黨爭. *Wenxue yichan* 2 (1989): 69–78.
___, and Wang Shujun 王淑均. *Du Mu shiwen xuanzhu* 杜牧詩文選注. Shanghai: Shanghai Guji, 1982.
Zhu Chuanyu 朱傳譽. *Du Mu shengping ji nianpu* 杜牧生平及年譜. Taibei: Tianyi, 1982.
___. *Du Mu shiwen jiqi jiaoyou* 杜牧詩文及其交遊. Taibei: Tianyi, 1982.
___. *Du Mu zhuanji ziliao* 杜牧傳記資料. Taibei: Tianyi, 1982.

Michael B. Fishlen and William H. Nienhauser, Jr.

Du Shenyan 杜審言 (*zi*, Bijian 必簡, ca. 645–708) was a native of Xiangyang 襄陽 in Xiangzhou 襄州 (modern Hubei) and the grandfather of Du Fu 杜甫 (712–770).* After passing the *jinshi* examination in 670 and a short assignment as Commandant of Xicheng 隰城尉 (modern Shanxi), he went on to an erratic career in the central administration at Luoyang. In 697 he was exiled for a time as Revenue Manager in Jizhou 吉州 (modern Ji'an 吉安 in Jiangxi) where he fell out with local officials, was framed, and imprisoned. In retaliation Du's son, Du Bing 杜并 (682–697), attacked the Vice Prefect, Zhou Jitong 周季童, who died from his wounds. Du Bing himself was killed immediately by guards. These events nevertheless led to Du Shenyan's release and his return to Luoyang where Empress Wu appointed him Assistant Editorial Director, in effect serving as a court poet. He quickly rose to Vice Director of the Catering Bureau and in the late

690s found favor with the notorious Zhang brothers (Zhang Yizhi 張易之 [d. 705] and Zhang Changzong 張昌宗 [d. 705], favorites of the Empress). In 705, just before the death of Wu Zhao, he was exiled to Fengzhou 峯州 (modern Hanoi in Vietnam), accused of complicity in a political conspiracy. His compulsory residence was a precarious frontier outpost, whose garrison was responsible for the behavior of the Cuan 爨 barbarians, a Tibeto-Burman people, centered in what is now Yunnan. This fortified settlement, aside from its strategic value, benefited the distant aristocracy by annual tribute of areca nuts, cardamoms, iridescent kingfisher feathers, and rhinoceros horn. Two years later he was recalled and made Recorder in the National University and an Auxiliary Academician in the Institute for the Cultivation of Literature. He died in his sixties and was awarded posthumous honors at the insistence of Li Jiao 李嶠 (ca. 644–ca. 714)* and others.

This biographical sketch is a stereotype of the official record of the career of any gifted writer cast in the role of a minor court functionary in the seventh century. It helps us little, if at all, in understanding what was good about his writing. The small fraction of the ten *juan* of verse that are said to have circulated after his death provides a rather flimsy basis for evaluation. His contemporaries, we are told, recognized his talents, especially his skill in contriving five-syllable verses, and he numbered excellent writers among his intimates—notably the poets Li Jiao, Cui Rong 崔融 (653–706), and Su Weidao 蘇味道 (648–705). Perhaps these associations count for more than his reported boast that his literary craft was superior to that of Qu Yuan 屈原 (340–278 BCE) and Song Yu 宋玉 (ca. 290–ca. 223 BCE), and that his calligraphy exceeded that of Wang Xizhi 王羲之 (321–379).

Most of his surviving poems are expressions of his courtly responsibilities, command performances, specifically compositions contrived for grand occasions at royal request (*ying zhi* 應制). Often these were composed at parties for ambassadors and newly appointed provincial magistrates about to leave the capital; some were occasioned by garden parties, picnics, moon-watching meets, and "Seventh Eve" celebrations. Two are in honor of the great public festivals called Da pu 大酺 (Great Bacchanals), for which free wine was provided to the whole citizenry. Astrological allusions are not uncommon in Du's verse, and these, understandably, favor starry omens of prosperity and stability for the realm. A few stanzas are more personal and reveal his affection for his friends. For instance, there are two addressed to Cui Rong, one to Su Weidao, and some replying to others. All of these poems show inventiveness—often cooled by the formality of the occasion. One of the best poems in this kind is his regulated poem "He Jinling Lucheng zaochun youwang" 和晉陵路丞早春遊望 (In Reply to Jinling Assistant Magistrate Lu's Poem: An Excursion in Early Spring):

> Alone, officials on their way from home,
> Startle at nature made new by time and clime.
> Rosy clouds rising out of the sea are the dawn,
> Plums and willows here across the river mark the spring.
> Warm air urges on the yellow orioles,
> Bright sunlight coils the green watergrass.
> Suddenly I hear an old tune of yours—
> Missing home, tears wet my handkerchief.

Du Shenyan

獨有宦遊人, 偏驚物候新.
雲霞出海曙, 梅柳渡江春.
淑氣催黃鳥, 晴光轉綠蘋.
忽聞歌古調, 歸思欲沾巾.

This poem, probably written in 689 in what is now modern Changzhou 常州 (Jiangsu), is about the passage of time, its effects on nature and man, and the difference in climate between the north of Tang China and Du Shenyan's position south of the Yangzi. In line two the poet admits to being doubly startled: first by the sudden arrival of spring and second by its coming so early there in the south. The second couplet may suggest the excursion of the title was to somewhere nearer the sea: there the rosy clouds, like the plums and willows with spring, presage the dawn. Spring's arrival also seems to engender life in both the singing orioles and the dancing watergrass. The "old tune" may refer to a poem by Magistrate Lu 陸, to whom Du's verse is a reply; in any case it breaks the mood, reminding the poet of his distance from home.

The poems written in exile, however miserable Du Shenyan may have been, benefit from the absence of such restraints. Although Du Shenyan's period of banishment is given only perfunctory treatment in his official biographies, that episode looms large in what remains of his poetry. The verses written at that time show, as do the comparable ones of Shen Quanqi 沈佺期 (656–716)* and Song Zhiwen 宋之問 (656–ca. 712),* the beginning of a new awareness of the deep south during the second half of the seventh century. They display a sense of personal tragedy, but also point the way to the full-blown exoticism of the eighth century and the true assimilation of the South in the ninth and tenth centuries. In short, they lack entirely the exuberance of the tropical verses of men like Li Xun 李珣 (fl. 896) and Ouyang Jiong 歐陽炯 (896–971). Du Shenyan expresses amazement at the lack of true seasonal divisions and at the disorderly wildness of the countryside–which for him was ameliorated in some measure by the glorious and even violent colors of both the mineral substrata and the organic life. But unlike Liu Zongyuan 柳宗元 (773–819),* he lacked a truly flexible and adaptable spirit, always yearning for his northern homeland, with its familiar garden birds and flowers and the company of sophisticated men.

It is possible to detect magical images in many of his poems, but hard to make an overall estimate of his writing that would justify—or confute—the high reputation he earned. This is the inevitable result of the scantiness of the extant relics of his writing.

BIBLIOGRAPHY

Editions:
Du Shenyan shiji 杜審言詩集. Beijing: Beijing Tushuguan, 2004.
Quan Tang shi, 2: 729–37.

Annotations:
Xu Dingxiang 徐定祥, comm. *Du Shenyan shizhu* 杜審言詩注. Shanghai: Shanghai Guji, 1982.

Biographical Sources:
Fu, *Tang caizi*, 1:66–75, 5:8.

Jiu Tang shu, 190A.4998–5000.
Xin Tang shu, 201.5735–36.

Translations:
Bynner, *Jade Mountain*, p. 146.
Minford and Lau, pp. 694–95.
Owen, *Early Tang*, pp. 327–37.
Schafer Edward. *The Vermilion Bird: T'ang Images of the South*. Berkeley: University of California, 1967, pp. 126, 258.

Studies:
Chen Guangming 陳冠明. "Du Shenyan nianpu" 杜審言年譜. *Du Fu yanjiu xuekan* 杜甫研究學刊, 2001.9.
Fu Xuancong 傅璇琮. "Du Shenyan kao" 杜審言考, in *Tangdai shiren congkao* 唐代詩人叢考. Beijing: Zhonghua, 1980, pp. 23–36.
Ji Yougong 計有功. *Tangshi jishi* 唐詩紀事, *juan*. 21. Shanghai: Shanghai Guji, 2008, pp. 77–78.
Owen, *Early Tang*, pp. 325–38.
Pan Yue 潘玥. "Xiaoyi Du Shenyan dui Du Fu shige chuangzuo de yingxiang" 小議杜審言對杜甫詩歌創作的影響, *Du Fu yanjiu xuekan* 杜甫研究學刊, 2011.12: 27–32.
Shi Youming 施由明. "Lun Du Shenyan yu Ganzhong wenfeng de kaiqi" 論杜審言與贛中文風的開啟, *Jiangsi Shehui Kexue*, 2011.5: 131–34.
Tang Jun 湯軍. "Lun Du Shenyan dui Tangshi fazhan de yishu gongxian" 論杜審言對唐詩發展的藝術貢獻, *Qianyan* 前沿, 2010.12: 166–69.
Xiao Difei 蕭滌非. "Du Shenyan 'Jingxing Lanzhou' jianshang" 杜審言'經行嵐州' 鑒賞, *Guoxue* 國學, 2012.3: 39.
Zhang Qinghua 張清華. "Du Shenyan pingzhuan" 杜審言評傳, *Yindu xuekan* 殷都學刊, 1984.7.

Edward H. Schafer

Du Xunhe 杜荀鶴 (*zi*, Yanzhi 彥之, *hao*, Jiuhua Shan ren 九華山人, 846–ca. 907), a poet-official who was also skilled in music, was born in Chizhou 池州 (Shitai County 石台縣 in modern Anhui). Several Southern Song accounts claim his father was Du Mu 杜牧 (803–ca. 852).* These narratives relate that during Du Mu's service in Chizhou one of his concubines became pregnant. Du Mu's wife, out of jealousy, forced the woman out of the household to be married to a local, Du Yun 杜筠. In any case, Du Xunhe seems to have grown up in a family of rather limited means.

His adult life encompassed the gradual collapse of the Tang dynasty, from the army revolt of 868, through the devastating Huang Chao 黃巢 Rebellion of the late 870s and early 880s, to the chaos of the final years of the Tang house. It was the approach of the rebel army under Huang Chao (835–884) that led Du to move to Jiuhua Shan 九華山 (Nine Flowers Mountain), about twenty miles southeast of the Yangzi River and Chizhou. He lived and studied there for fifteen years. The region served as a refuge for scholars. Du studied and wrote verse with other literati there—Gu Yun 顧雲 (*jinshi* 874; d. ca. 895), Yin Wengui 殷文圭, Zhang Qiao 張喬 (*jinshi* 860–873), all three natives of Chizhou, and Li Zhaoxiang 李昭象, a Buddhist whose father had served in Chizhou. He also exchanged poems with Luo Yin 羅隱 (833–909),* who visited Nine Flowers Mountain. Although the group was considered eremitic, most of these men, including Du, sought

Du Xunhe

a patron through their writings. This goal was perhaps the reason for the extensive travels in the Yangzi and southern eastern littoral regions which are documented in Du's verse. One such night on the road is portrayed in his "Lü she yuyu" 旅舍遇雨 (At an Inn, Encountering Rain)":

    Moon magnificent, stars brilliant, I sit taking it all in;
    The hue of the peaks, the sound of the river, secretly wrap me in sorrow.
    Midnight before the lamp, ten years of my affairs
    In time with the rain fall onto my heart.

    月華星彩坐來收，岳色江聲暗結愁。
    半夜燈前十年事，一時和雨到心頭。

In 891 at the rather advanced age of forty-five Du finally passed the *jinshi* examination. He returned to his home for a short time, before he and Yin Wengui became retainers of Tian Jun 田君 (d. 903), a general in the Huainan Region. It is possible that this was the time he wrote one of his best known poems, "Zaijing Huchengxian" 再經胡城縣 (Again Passing by Hucheng County), on a visit to his home northwest of Fuyang County 阜陽縣 in Anhui:

    Last year when I passed this country seat
    Not a single person who didn't cry out over injustices.
    Now I come again to find the magistrate has just added a red sash
    That is simply dyed in the blood of the local people.

    去歲曾經此縣城，縣民無口不冤聲。
    今來縣宰加朱紱，便是生靈血染成。

The red sash was a reward given to magistrates for outstanding service, a reward that Du turns on its head in his powerful, ironic final line.

    Following Tian's defeat in 903, Du entered the service of Zhu Wen 朱溫 (852–912), a former lieutenant of Huang Chao turned warlord. Under Zhu's aegis, Du rose to several high positions including Academician in the Hanlin Academy (903). Zhu was the virtual ruler during the last decade of the Tang; he had the penultimate emperor executed and kept a tight rein on his successor. Because of Du's service to Zhu, some Tang loyalists reportedly plotted to murder Du. Before this plan could be carried out, Du Xunhe fell ill and died (another tradition says he died in 904) in 907, the same Zhu chose to formally overthrow the Tang.

    All of Du's surviving poetry—about three hundred *shi* in the modern style—antedate his success in the examinations. He collected this corpus himself under the title *Tang feng ji* 唐風集, "*feng*" referring both to the style (the "Tang style") and to the content ("criticism of the Tang") of his verse. This is a poetry of lament: the two primary subjects are the common people, who suffered in the disorders which plagued these years, and Du himself, who had been unsuccessful in passing the examinations and in finding a patron. It is also an unusual corpus in that the medium for socially critical poetry was normally old-style verse.

    The general pattern of a large corpus of socially conscious verse before beginning an official career, followed by virtual silence thereafter (none of Du Xunhe's writings after 891 are extant), can be seen in the lives of several of Du's contemporaries, Pi Rixiu 皮日休 (ca. 834–ca. 883),* for example. Scholar-officials of the late Tang hoped to serve the state—poetry was the means to achieve that goal. The didactic verse written by many late Tang poets was intended more to garner a position or a patron, than it was to establish a poetic reputation. The social fabric had been shaken by rebellion so that it was significantly easier for a relatively unknown literatus to rise quickly through the ranks in the late ninth century than ever before under the Tang.

Du's literary career may also serve to illustrate the regional tendency of late Tang poetry which centered more and more on a local literary group or patron. Analogous to Stephen Owen's concept of a "capital poetry" during the mid-eighth century, the late ninth could be viewed as one of "provincial verse." This can be seen in the two poems discussed above, as well as in the well-known "Chun gong yuan" 春宮苑 (A Lament in a Springtime Palace), and "Mashang xing" 馬上行 (Lines Written on Horseback), which bemoaned his personal lot. The last mentioned is also an example of Du's use of a more vernacular style, an attribute which has invited comparison with Luo Yin's works.

Several of Du Xunhe's works appeared already in Tang anthologies and Hong Mai 洪邁 (1123–1202) writes that his poetry was popular during the Song. "A Lament in a Springtime Palace" appears in the *Tangshi sanbaishou* 唐詩三百首. Although relatively neglected thereafter, recent critics in China have shown a renewed interest in his socially relevant verse.

BIBLIOGRAPHY

Editions:
Du Xunhe wenji 杜荀鶴文集. Shanghai: Guji, 1980. Photolithic reprint of a Song edition.
Du Xunhe shixuan 杜荀鶴詩选. Hefei: Huangshan, Xinhua Shudian Jingxiao, 1988.
Nie Yizhong shi, Du Xunhe shi 聶夷中詩, 杜荀鶴詩. Shanghai: Zhonghua, 1959.
Tang feng ji 唐風集. Taibei: Taiwan Shangwu, 1983.
Quan Tang shi, 10: 7995–8055.

Biographical Sources:
Fu, *Tang caizi*, 4:262–77; 5:469–70.

Translations:
Bynner, *Jade Mountain*, p. 143.
Li, Teresa, "A Nocturne," *THM* 8 (1940): 75.
Owen, *Omen*, pp. 94–96.
___, *Late Tang*, pp. 154–55.
Sunflower, p. 288.
Watson, *Lyricism*, pp. 83–84, p. 122.

Studies:
Hu Wentao 胡問濤. *Du Xunhe jiqi "Tangfeng ji" yanjiu* 杜荀鶴及其《唐風集》研究. Chengdu: Ba Shu, 2005.
Kamio Ryūsuke 上尾龍, "Tō Junkaku no shi" 杜荀鶴詩社會性, *Nihon Chūgoku gakkai hō* 20 (Oct 1968).
Xiao Wenyuan 肖文苑. "Du Xunhe de shenghuo daolu ji chuangzuo" 杜荀鶴的生活道路及創作, *Beijing Shida Xuebao*, 1979.3.

Xu Xiaoxing 徐曉星. "Wan Tang shiren Du Xunhe" 晚唐詩人杜荀鶴, *Wenxue yichan zengkan*, 1956.2: 141–56.

Zhang Shuqiong 張淑瓊. *Du Xunhe* 杜荀鶴. 2nd ed. Taibei: Diqiu, 1992.

William H. Nienhauser, Jr

Dugu Ji 獨孤及 (*zi*, Zhizhi 至之, 725–777) is known mainly as a literary critic, an advocate of *guwen* 古文 (ancient-style) prose, and an early, though indirect, influence on the great ancient-style prose master Han Yu 韓愈 (768–824).* Dugu came from an aristocratic Turkic clan that married into the imperial families of both the Sui and the Tang. After being successful in a Daoist-decree examination of 754, he served just before the An Lushan Rebellion as Commandant of Huayin 華陰, not far east of Chang'an. After the rebellion and a period of service in the southeast, his most important posts were under Daizong (r. 762–779) as Reminder of the Left, Erudite in the Court of Imperial Sacrifices, and Vice Director of the Bureau of Personnel. Two provincial prefectships, those of Haozhou 濠州 and Shuzhou 舒州 (both modern Anhui), followed. His final posting, to the prefectship of the strategically important prefecture of Changzhou 常州 (in modern Jiangsu), was particularly sought by administrators because of its prestige. After his death he received the canonization Xian 憲 "Exemplary."

Dugu's views on literature were close to those of Jia Zhi 賈至 (718–772),* Li Hua 李華 (715–774),* and Xiao Yingshi 蕭穎士 (717–760),* with whom he was acquainted. He emphasized the primacy of the Confucian canon and the moral function of writing, condemning ornamental or euphuistic style, and endorsed the traditional Confucian theory of poetic composition that saw it as the patterned expression of feelings from within. Despite his purism, he recognized, as did most of his contemporaries, merit in some of the developments in tonality that had taken place in verse writing earlier in the eighth century.

Much of Dugu's prose writing was occasioned by his official career. Two early works, the "Xianzhang ming" 仙掌銘 (Inscription for the Immortal's Handprint) and "Gu Hangu Guan ming" 古函谷關銘 (Inscription for the Ancient Hangu Pass), prove that he could use the high-flown and hyperbolic style that was valued for such monumental pieces. After the rebellion, as an Erudite in the Court of Imperial Sacrifices, he composed examples of one of the minor but much respected genres of Tang bureaucratic writing, the *Shiyi* 謚議 (Discussion of Canonization), in which he argued the appropriateness of canonization titles proposed for recently deceased officials. He also wrote a large number of epitaphs (both for members of his own family and for others), sacrificial prayers, inscriptions for institutions, texts for monasteries, and occasional verse.

Dugu's "Wu Ji Zi Zha lun" 吳季子札論 (Essay on Ji Zi Zha) reflects both his mastery of the classical tradition and the iconoclastic spirit shared by many of the *fugu* 復古 (return to antiquity) prose writers. Ji Ji Zha 姬季札 (Ji Zha the Younger, 576–484 BC) was the fourth son of Shoumeng 壽夢, King of Wu 吳王 (r. 585–561 BC). His father deemed him worthy of succeeding him, but Ji Zha yielded the throne, first retiring to "till the land," and then fleeing two successive appeals to rule Wu by fleeing to the Man tribes of the south. He served as Wu's ambassador to Lu 魯, Qi 齊, and Zheng 鄭 in an effort to win allies against Wu's traditional enemy, Chu 楚, and he is best known for his ability to discern the future of these states by listening to their music. But Dugu's emphasis in this essay is on Ji Zha's thrice refusing the throne and the resulting chaos in Wu which eventually led to its defeat and extinction by Yue 越 a decade after Ji Zha's death. The essay begins:

I humbly claim that in discarding the order of his late lord, Ji Zha was not acting filially; in adhering to the righteousness of Zicang [of Cao 曹, who also renounced the throne], he was not acting in the public interest; in strictly following the rites and maintaining the standards, in causing his state to be conquered and his lord to be killed, he was not acting with humanity; in leaving [Wu] to be able to observe the barbarians of the south, and returning but not suppressing chaos, he was not acting wisely. Zuo Qiuming [in the *Zuo zhuan* 左傳] and His Honor the Grand Scribe [Sima Qian 司馬遷 in the *Shiji* 史記] by writing of him without indirect criticism, caused me to have such strong feelings about him.

竊謂廢先君之命，非孝也；附子臧之義，非公也；執禮全節，使國簒君弒，非仁也；出能觀變，入不討亂，非智也。左邱明、太史公書而無譏，余有惑焉。

Herein Dugu Ji, like a number of his contemporaries, called for a reassessment of the *Chunqiu* 春秋 (Spring and Autumn Annals) that would relate more to contemporary readings, thereby moving beyond the *Zuo zhuan* or the *Shiji*. Towards his conclusion to this essay Dugu emphasizes how Ji Zha's acceptance of the throne of Wu could have propped up the weakened Zhou dynasty, in a analogous political situation to that of the late eighth century when provincial satraps were increasingly working to undermine the Tang regime. Had Ji Zha accepted the throne, Du argues:

he would certainly have been able to bring luster to the Zhou Way and to hold hegemony over the Jing and Man barbarians. Thus through his might many difficulties in the great enterprise [of ruling the empire] would not have occurred.

必能光啟周道，以霸荊蠻。則大業用康，多難不作。

Among Dugu's admirers were Cui Youfu 崔祐甫 (721–780), Grand Councilor and director of the dynastic history at the start of Dezong's reign (r. 779–805), and Quan Deyu 權德輿 (761–818),* an influential, eclectic intellectual of the reigns of Dezong and Xianzong (r. 805–820). But Dugu's most important close pupil was Liang Su 梁肅 (753–793),* whom he taught when he was Prefect of Changzhou and who edited his literary collection. Liang Su in turn influenced the great Han Yu. Han was also said to have been influenced by Dugu, whom he cannot have known personally. One of Dugu Ji's sons, Dugu Yu 獨孤鬱 (778–816), however, was a long-term friend of Han Yu.

Extant editions of Dugu Ji's literary collection, the *Piling ji* 毗陵集, which consists of seventeen *juan* of prose and three of verse, derive from a manuscript copy made in the Palace Library by Wu Guan 吳琯 (1436–1504). Much of his writing was also contained in the major early Song anthologies.

BIBLIOGRAPHY

Editions:
Piling Ji 毗陵集. Preface 1791. *SBCK*.
Quan Tang shi, 4: 2753–72, 14: 10632, 11123–24.
Quan Tang wen, 384–93.4414–509.

Dugu Ji

Biographical Sources:
Fu, Tang caizi, 1:577–87.
Xin Tang shu, 162.4990–94.

Studies:
Bol, pp. 116–22.
DeBlasi, Anthony. *Reform in the Balance, The Defense of Literary Culture in Mid-Tang China*. Albany: SUNY, 2002, passim.
Dong Guodong 凍國棟. "Du Dugu Ji 'Diao dao jin wen bing xu' Shu Hou 讀獨孤及"吊道饉文並序"書后, *Wei Jin Nan Bei chao Sui Tang shi ziliao* 22 (2005): 69–74.
Jiang Yin 蔣寅. "Dugu Ji wen xinian buzheng" 獨孤及文係補正, *Taiyuan Shifan Xueyuan xuebao* 1 (1996): 6–12.
___. "Zuowei shiren de Dugu Ji" 作為詩人的獨孤及, *He'nan Daxue xuebao* 4 (1996): 47–51.
Guo Shuwei 郭樹偉. "Dugu Ji yu zhong Tang guwen yundong" 獨孤及與中唐古文運動, *Zhongzhou xuekan* 4 (2012): 166–69.
Luo Liantian 羅聯添. "Dugu Ji kaozheng" 獨孤及考證, *Dalu zazhi* 48.3 (March 15, 1974): 117–38.
___. "Dugu Ji nianpu" 獨孤及年譜, in Luo Liantian, *Tangdai shiwen liujia nianpu* 唐代詩文六家年譜. Taibei: Xuehai, 1986, pp. 5–74.
Wu Fengzhen 吳逢箴. "Tan Dugu Ji 'Chi yu Tubo Zanpu shu'" 談獨孤及 "敕與吐蕃贊普書," *Xizang minzu xueyuan xuebao* 3 (1986): 87–93.

David L. McMullen and William H. Nienhauser, Jr.

Falin 法琳 (secular surname Chen 陳, 571–640), was a learned monk famous for his defense of Buddhism in the early years of the Tang Dynasty. His ancestral home was Yingchuan 潁川 (modern Xuchang 許昌, Henan), where his forefather Chen Qun 陳群 (d. 237) had served as an important minister to the Wei courts of Cao Cao 曹操 (155–220) and Cao Pi 曹丕 (187–226). His family had taken up residence in Xiangyang 襄陽 (modern Xiangfan 襄樊, Hubei). By the time of the Sui Dynasty.

Early in life, he became a monk at the Yuquan Monastery 玉泉寺 at Qingxi 青溪 in Jingzhou 荊州 (modern Yuan'an 遠安, Hubei), where he studied Buddhist and non-Buddhist scriptures intensely. According to one source, he was fond of mountains and waters, wandered about, and chose the life of a hermit in the Guigudong 鬼谷洞 (Ghost Valley Grotto) in the Qingxi Mountains, where he composed the now lost *Qingxi shan ji* 青溪山記 (Record of the Qingxi Mountains). He may have been a student of Zhiyi 智顗 (538–597), the founder of the Tiantai School 天台 and also a native of Yingchuan. He may have had contact with Jizang 吉藏 (549–623), whose terminology he sometimes seems to have adopted in his later essays.

Falin entered the capital Daxing 大興 (modern Xi'an) during the Renshou era (601–604). In the first year of the Yining era (617), he decided to study the Daoists and their teachings. He even donned their cloth, only to return to the Sangha in 618, living at the local Jifa Monastery 濟法寺.

In the fourth year of the Wude era (621) the Director of the Astrologers, Fu Yi 傅奕 (555–639), handed in a memorial to disregard Buddhism on the grounds of its danger to the state and failure to benefit the people. Although Falin was able to change the Emperor's mind on the issue, Fu Yi did not stop his propaganda, calling the Buddhists "Tuding" 禿丁 (Baldies) and the Buddha "Hugui" 胡鬼 (Barbarian Ghost)—much to the detriment of their standing at court and in the streets. While other Buddhist monks and laymen would turn to the Buddhist canon to counter Fu Yi's attacks, Falin tasked himself in his *Po xie lun* 破邪論 (Essay on the Destruction of Wrong Views) with a head-on defense, arguing that Confucius and other teachers of the past respected the Buddhist sayings and that there had been revolutions and uprisings in the empire long before Buddhism arrived, as pre-Han history amply showed. When the essay began to circulate, the great calligrapher and later follower of Li Shimin 李世民 (598–649), Yu Shinan 虞世南 (558–638),* attached a supportive foreword to it. In the fifth year of the Wude era (622), Falin's essay was presented to the then heir, Li Jiancheng 李建成 (589–626). In 623 it was presented to Li Shimin himself, who later became Emperor Taizong (r. 626–649). Yet, Emperor Gaozu 高祖 (Li Yuan 李淵, r. 618–626) acquiesced in 626 to further pressure from Fu Yi, thereby reducing the number of temples and monks in the capital.

Although these measures were repealed that same year after Li Shimin forced his father to abdicate, the power struggle between the factions at court did not cease. Soon thereafter, the ambitious Daoist, Li Zhongqing 李仲卿, wrote his *Shiyi jiumi lun* 十異九迷論 (Essay on the Ten Differences and Nine Confusions), a further assault on Buddhism, that presented an unfavorable comparison between Laozi and Shakyamuni and ridiculed nine common Buddhist views. Falin prepared an immediate response. His *Bian zheng lun* 辯正論 (Essay on the Distinguishing the Correct [Beliefs]) in eight *juan*, with a preface and commentary by Chen Zi'ang 陳子昂 (659–ca. 699),* not only refuted Li Zongqing's theses, but also expounded various arguments to demonstrate the superiority of Buddhism over Daoism (and Confucianism). Therein, he meticulously gathered valuable historic information about the worship of Buddha from the Jin to the Tang Dynasty, declaring Buddha to be Laozi's teacher and accusing the Daoists in general of fraudulently incorporating Buddhist ideas and achievements into their teachings.

At the beginning of the Zhenguan era (627–649), the Longtian Monastery 龍田寺 was established in the Zhongnan Mountains 終南山, south of the capital. Falin, fond of the quietude of the valleys, went there and became the head of the temple. During the following years, he joined the group of monks around Prabhākaramitra (波羅頗迦羅蜜多羅, 565–633) and devoted his efforts towards the translation of Buddhist scriptures such as the *Baoxing duoluoni jing* 寶星陀羅尼經 (Ratnaketudhāraṇī Sūtra).

In the thirteenth year of the Zhenguan era (639), another Daoist, Qin Shiying 秦世英, accused Falin of *lèse majesté*, claiming that his former *Bian zheng lun* insulted the ancestors of the Tang imperial family (possibly by not concealing their relation to the Tuoba 拓跋 of the Yuan Wei 元魏 Dynasty, and not foreseeing that Taizong would declare Li Er 李耳, i.e. Laozi, as the grand ancestor of his Li Clan in 637). When Taizong learned of this, he became enraged. Falin was arrested, interrogated and found guilty of a crime deserving the death penalty. Taizong gave him seven days to meditate upon the Bodhisattva Guanyin, in order to "test" his claim that prayers could render a human invulnerable to swords. When he was due for execution, he was asked again, if he had gained any insights from his exercise. Falin responded that in the whole seven days he had not once meditated upon Guanyin, but only on the Emperor. This reply and his following explanation, that the Emperor (for all his kindness to the common people) was Guanyin, earned him the reduction of his sentence to exile to a monastery in Yizhou 益州 (a prefecture with its center at Chengdu, modern Sichuan).

On his way to the West, he composed the "Dao Qu Yuan pian" 悼屈原篇 (Mourning Qu Yuan) to demonstrate one last time his true intentions, as the opening lines evince:

> Why had the Heavenly Way become so beclouded,
> the stars lost their proper place
> and the loyal and upright Qu Yuan
> been sent into exile?
> Slanderers and favorites followed the will of the ruler,
> received eminent positions and maintained shining reputations,
> while forthright speech with nothing taboo
> led to his encounter with calamity.

> 何天道之幽昧兮，乖張列宿。
> 使忠正之屈原兮，而見放逐。
> 讒佞從旨兮，位顯名彰。
> 直言不諱兮，遂焉逢殃。

Falin died on his way into exile in the fourteenth year of the Zhenguan era (640), having reached the Puti Monastery 菩提寺 at the Baiyu Pass 百宇關 (modern Mian 勉 County, Shaanxi). Only the above-mentioned essays and a handful of poems and extracts from his hagiographies have survived from his original broad literary oeuvre that once counted 30 *juan*.

BIBLIOGRAPHY

Editions:
Falin 法琳. *Po xie lun* 破邪論. *Taishō Shinshū Daizōkyō*, no. 2109, vol. 52.
___. *Bian zheng lun* 辯正論. *Taishō Shinshū Daizōkyō*, no. 2110, vol. 52.
Quan Tang shi, 14: 10895.
Quan Tang wen, 904.12305–15.

Translations:
Hōrin 法琳. *Hajaron / Benshōron* 破邪論 / 辯正論. *Kokuyaku issaikyō, Wakan senjutsu* 97 (*Gokyōbu* 4 *ge*) 國訳一切経, 和漢撰述 97 (護教部4下).

Studies:
Jülch, Thomas. *Die apologetischen Schriften des buddhistischen Tang-Mönchs Falin*. München: Herbert Utz, 2010. Contains partial translations.
Miwa Hareo 三輪晴雄. "Tō gohō shamon Hōrin ni tsuite" 唐護法沙門法琳について. *Indogaku bukkyōgaku kenkyū* 22.2 (1974): 290–95.
Nakanishi Hisami 中西久味. "Hōrin no sankyōron ni yosete" 法琳の三教論によせて. *Chūgoku shisōshi kenkyū* 24 (2001): 77–108.
___. "Hōrin zō shi" 法琳雜誌. *Hikaku shūkyō shisō kenkyū* 比較宗教思想研究 2 (2002): 1–17, and 4 (2004): 1–29.

Nishiyama Fukiko 西山蕗子. Hōrin 'Hajaron' ni tsuite 法琳『破邪論』について. *Suzuki Gakujutsu Zaidan kenkyū nenpō* 9 (1973): 69–86.

Nose Keijiro 野瀬慶治郎. "'Benshōron' totatoe hen no bun ni tsuite" 「弁正論」十喩篇の文について. *Ashiya daigaku ronsō* 16 (1988): 197–210.

Ōfuchi Ninji 大淵忍爾 and Ishii Masako 石井昌子, eds. *Rikuchō Tō Sō no kobunken shoin Dōkyō tenseki mokuroku, sakuin* 六朝唐宋の古文献所引道教典籍目録, 索引. Tokyo: Kokusho Kankōkai, 1988.

Pan Guiming 潘桂明. "Tang chu Fodao zhi zheng de shizhi he yinxiang" 唐初佛道之爭的實質和影響. *Anhui Shifan Daxue bao* 安徽師大學報 1 (1990): 54–66.

Shōno Masumi 庄野眞澄. "Tō shamon Hōrin den ni tsuite" 唐沙門法琳傳について. *Shien* 14 (1936).

Taira Hidemichi 平秀道. "'Benshōron' shoin no ishin sho ni tsuite" 「弁正論」所引の讖緯書について. *Ryūkoku daigaku ronshū* 392 (1969): 48–62.

Takeuchi Hajime 竹内肇. "Hōrin ni okeru ja to sei no ishiki—'Haja ron' to 'Benshō ron' wo chūshin to shite" 法琳における邪と正の意識—破邪論と弁正論を中心として. *Nihon bukkyō gakkai nenpō* 48 (1982): 193–208.

Wright, Arthur F. "Fu I and the Rejection of Buddhism." *Journal of the History of Ideas*. 12.1 (1951): 33–47.

Zong Shulin 鐘書林. "'Dazang jing zongmu tiyao' zhi 'Tang hufa shamen Falin biezhuan' zuozhe bianzheng—jian lun Suichao Yancong, Tangchao Yancong, Tangchao Yancong" "大藏經總目提要" 之 "唐護法沙門法琳別傳" 作者辨正-兼論隋朝彥琮、唐朝彥琮、唐朝彥驚. *Wenxian* 1 (2012): 153–62.

Marc Nürnberger

Feng Su 馮宿 (*zi* Gongzhi 拱之, 767–837) was a native from Dongyang 東陽 in Yuzhou 婺州 (near modern Jinhua city 金華市 in Zhejiang), whose family claimed descent from Feng Fengshi 馮奉世 (d. ca. 39 BC), the Han General to the Left and Chamberlain for Attendants). Feng Su's cousin, Feng Shen 馮審 (d. ca. 870) passed the *jinshi* in 796 and held a series of high positions including Chancellor of the Directorate of Education. Feng's younger brother, Feng Ding 馮定 (d. 845), was also successful in the *jinshi* sometime during the Zhenyuan era (785–805); he also held many court positions, serving for a time Director of Studies of the Directorate of Education.

A noted writer of poetry and prose, he attracted Emperor Wenzong's personal attention. Feng Su's cousins, Feng Kuan 馮寬 and his son Feng Jian 馮緘 were also *jinshi* graduates. Feng Su himself passed the *jinshi* examination in 792, together with notable literati and statesmen like Han Yu 韓愈 (768–824),* Ouyang Zhan 歐陽詹 (ca. 755–ca. 801),* and Li Jiang 李絳 (764–830). The inscription on Feng Su's *bei* 碑 (grave stele) states that he also sat for the Erudite Literatus Examination, in which he composed the "Baibu chuan yangye fu" 百步穿楊葉賦 (*Fu on Piercing Poplar Leaves from a Hundred Feet*). This *fu*, now lost, is described as model *fu* for later generations.

Feng Su then entered service as Secretary in the staff of Zhang Jianfeng 張建封 (745–800), the Military Commissioner of Xuzhou 徐州 (in modern Jiangsu). After Zhang Jianfeng had passed away, Feng Su briefly continued to serve under his son Zhang Yin 張愔 (fl. 800) and mediated between him, Wang Wujun 王武俊 (735–801) and Li Shigu 李師古 (778–806) to avoid a military confrontation in Xuzhou. Feng Su's "Yu Wang Wujun shu" 與王武俊書 (Letter to Wang Wujun) is incorporated in his biography in the *Xin Tang shu* as well as the *Jiu Tang shu*. When Zhang Yin found out about Feng Su's plans to leave his service, he caused him to be demoted to a minor military position in Quanzhou 泉州 (in modern Fujian).

Feng Su

In 808 Feng Su was summoned to the capital and by 817 had advanced to the position of Vice Director of the Criminal Administration Bureau. That same year he was part of Grand Councilor Pei Du's 裴度 (765–839) staff for the punitive expedition against Huaixi 淮西. After the expedition's victorious return in 819, Feng Su was promoted to the position of Director of the Bureau of Review. In the wake of Han Yu's "Lun fogu biao" 論佛骨表 (Memorial on the Buddha Relic), he was briefly demoted to the position of Prefect of Shezhou 歙州 (modern She 歙 County in south-east Anhui), but returned to Chang'an 長安 the year after as Director of the Ministry of Justice. He advanced in office to the position of Policy Adviser to the Left (825) before he was sent to take office as Administrator of Henan (828).

The poem "Chou Bo Letian Liu Mengde" 酬白樂天劉夢得 (In Response to Bo Letian and Liu Mengde) was written on the occasion of Feng's departure as an answer to farewell poems by Bo Juyi 白居易 (772–846)* and Liu Yuxi 劉禹錫 (772–842)*:

Together we praise Luo City for not taking the selection lightly,
But how could I be favored with a heavenly decree that employs a fool?
In the distant future a gentle breeze shall renew the grasses and trees,
And let fresh snow settle the dust.
At the crossroads I'm ashamed that all the Three Departments have come out,
At the farewell party no one refrains from getting drunk on a hundred cups.
Next year scholars will gather under the blossoms in the Apricot Garden,
Assured that the spring scene will come from the east.

共稱洛邑難其選，何幸天書用不才。
遙約和風新草木，且令新雪靜塵埃。
臨岐有愧傾三省，別酌無辭醉百杯。
明歲杏園花下集，須知春色自東來。

Having passed the selection examination and having been promoted to Administrator of Henan, Feng humbly claims that he is unworthy of this position in line 2. His biography tells us he was able to reject the position and be demoted back to a more normal bureaucratic path. The repetition of *xin* 新 (used as a verb in line 3 and an adjective in line 4) emphasizes both his new start while it may also refer to contemporary political events, since Emperor Wenzong has been enthroned just the year before—the snow in line four seems to be both part of the scene (Bo Juyi mentions it in his poem seeing off Feng) as well as symbolizing the fresh start of the new regime. The third couplet reveals that most of the officials in the capital have come out to see him off. The last two lines express the hope that he will join them back in Chang'an as the new *jinshi* scholars gather in the Apricot Garden south of the capital. The "spring scene" of the final line seems to refer to Feng's hopes for a renewed, successful career path, news of which he hopes to bring back to his friends in Chang'an the following year.

In 830, Feng Su became Vice Director of the Ministry of Works and two years later Vice Director of the Ministry of Justice. At that time, he edited a collection of official documents titled "Ge hou chi" 格後敕, which Feng's biographies of *Xin Tang shu* and *Jiu Tang* claim to have consisted of 30 *juan* but is mentioned in Feng Su's grave stele with 50 *juan*. The work is lost. In 835, Feng Su was appointed Military Commissioner of Dongchuan 東川 (near modern

Dongchuan qu 東川區 in Yunnan), a position he held until his death in 837. Three of his sons, Feng Yuan 馮園, Feng Tao 馮陶, and Feng Tao 馮韜, were all successful in the *jinshi* examinations. Feng Su and Han Yu crossed paths several times in their life. They passed the *jinshi* examination in the same year and served together under Zhang Jianfeng and Pei Du. Two letters of Han Yu to Feng Su still exist, most importantly Han Yu's "Yu Feng Su lun wen shu" 與馮宿論文書 (Letter to Feng Su Discussing Literature), but none of Feng Su's writings to Han Yu are extant. Feng Su himself was known as a talented prose writer. He wrote more than 600 works, but today only three of his *fu*, three *shi*, and a handful of prose works survive. Wang Qi 王起 (760–847) composed the text for Feng Su's grave stele and its calligraphy was done by Liu Gongquan 柳公權 (778–865).

BIBLIOGRAPHY

Editions:
Quan Tang shi, 5: 3115; *Quan Tang wen*, 624.7060–66.

Biographical Sources:
Jiu Tang shu, 168.4389–90.; *Xin Tang shu*, 177.5277–78.

Studies
Bian Xiaoxuan 卞孝萱. *Liu Yuxi congkao* 劉禹錫從考. Chengdu: Ba Shu, 1988, pp. 90–92.

Clara Luhn

Gao Shi 高適 (*zi*, Dafu 達夫, 700–765), a contemporary of Du Fu 杜甫 (712–770)* and Li Bo 李白 (701–762),* was one of the major poets of the High Tang. A native of Bohai 渤海 (modern Hebei), Gao came from an impoverished official family. His father, Gao Chongwen 高崇文 (653–719), had been Chief Scribe of Shaozhou 韶州. Biographical sources claim that as a youth Gao was forced to live with another family in the Song 宋 region (modern Henan). After failing to find advancement in the capital around 720, he set off for the northeastern frontier, likely in search of a military appointment. In 735 he was back in Chang'an in the company of Wang Zhihuan 王之渙 (679–742),* Wang Changling 王昌齡 (ca. 690–ca. 756),* and other poets, but did not find success in the examinations. After spending some time in Suiyang 睢陽 (modern Shangqiu 商丘, Henan), Gao in 744 met Li Bo and Du Fu and wrote poems with them. In 749 he passed a Daoist examination and was made Commandant of Fengqiu 封丘 (in modern Henan north of Kaifeng). His fortunes began to rise when he attracted the notice of Geshu Han 哥舒翰 (d. 757), one of the most important generals of the day. Gao Shi accompanied him to Central Asia in 753. The following year when Geshu was decisively defeated by An Lushan's troops, thus losing the Tong Pass that guards the road to Chang'an, Gao Shi presented a spirited defense of his superior before Emperor Xuanzong (r. 712–756) and won an appointment as Grand Master of Remonstrance in Xuanzong's exile government.

Gao Shi

Gao's fortunes continued to rise in the court of Emperor Suzong (r. 756–762). He vigorously opposed the policy of appointing imperial princes to key military commands and was vindicated when the Prince of Yong 永王 (Li Lin 李璘 [ca. 721–757]) revolted in 756. Appointed Military Commissioner of Huainan, Gao was charged with helping to crush this rebellion (which involved Li Bo). Shortly after, Gao found himself ousted from the court of the restored Tang house, the result, according to the histories, of the enmity of the eunuch Li Fuguo 李輔國 (704–762). He was assigned to the heir apparent's household in Luoyang and then in 760 was appointed Prefect of Pengzhou 彭州 (modern Sichuan). There he proved his considerable military acumen by putting down two local rebellions. In recognition, Gao was appointed Military Commissioner of Jiannan and Xichuan 劍南西川 in 762. The following year he failed to subdue a Tibetan incursion and was recalled to Chang'an. Despite this failure, Gao was enfeoffed and appointed Vice Director in the Bureau of Justice. He died shortly thereafter. The *Jiu Tang shu* (*juan* 111) claims that Gao was the only well-known poet in the Tang who had an eminent political career.

Gao Shi's talent for military matters and his dedication to public affairs are reflected in his works. Traditional critics describe his poetry as *bei zhuang* 悲壯 (robust and sad) and filled with *qi* 氣 (vigorous spirit) and *feng gu* 風骨 (form and élan), terms are all associated with Jian'an 建安 period (196–220) poetry and suggesting the poet's indebtedness to that tradition. The *Fugu* 復古 (Return to Antiquity) Movement had taken Jian'an poetry as its model in its attempt to free poetry from the *gongti* 宮體 (courtly style) which had been dominant from the Six Dynasties to the early Tang. Gao Shi may be regarded as inheriting Chen Zi'ang's 陳子昂 (659–ca. 699)* legacy; Chen was widely considered the foremost poet of the early Tang identified with the movement. His series of five poems "Jimen" 薊門 (Ji Gate) is written in the same form and style as Chen Zi'ang's "Jiqiu langu" 薊丘覽古 (Observing the Past at Ji Heights). The following is the fifth poem in the series:

> Gloomy and dark beyond the Great Wall;
> the sun sets to even more smoke, more dust.
> Though the tartar horsemen invaded, then overran,
> the soldiers of Han gave no thought to their lives.
> Ancient trees fill the empty fortifications,
> Before yellow clouds of sand the sorrow overwhelms one.

> 黯黯長城外，日沒更煙塵。
> 胡騎雖憑陵，漢兵不顧身。
> 古樹滿空塞，黃雲愁殺人。

Gao Shi is now chiefly remembered by his masterpiece, "Yan ge xing" 燕歌行 (Song of Yan). Although "Yan ge xing" was a Han *yuefu* title, no early version of it survives. The earliest text written to the title was Cao Pi's 曹丕 (187–226) poem, which depicts the sorrows of a lady pining for her absent husband. Gao Shi must have known this poem and acknowledges it by including an unhappy wife in his piece. But in the best tradition of the literary *yuefu*, Gao infuses the song with his own spirit:

Gao Shi

For the House of Han, smoke and dust lie in the northeast,
The Han general leaves home to crush the remaining brigands.
On real men who by nature value long expeditions,
The Son of Heaven casts an exceedingly kind countenance.
Striking kettledrums, beating tambours, as they descend Elm Pass—
Pennons twisting, banners twining, within the Tablet Rocks.
Dispatches from the colonels fly across Sea of Sand,
The Chanyu's hunting fires shine on Wolf Mountain.
Gloom through mountain and stream on the far borderlands,
The menace of the Tartar horsemen mixes with wind and rain.
The vanguard of our warriors betwixt life and death,
While lovely maidens still dance and sing in the commanders' tents.
Grasses wilt on the great desert at this end of autumn,
As the sun sets, battling troops at a lone fortress dwindle.
Having personally tasted imperial favor they make light of the foe,
Their strength spent in at the mountain passes they have not broken the siege.
Mail coats at distant garrisons have long endured toil,
Jade hairpins respond in tears after they have parted.
A young wife south of the fortress her heart about to break,
On campaign a husband north of Ji looks back in vain.
Border winds whipping back and forth, how can they cross the frontier?
In this limitless land there is only an indistinct vastness.
Arduous air for three seasons forms clouds of phalanxes,
Cold sounds all night long pass along the watch beat.
Face to face with bare blades, blood spatters
Resolved to die, they have never cared for rewards.
Haven't you seen the suffering on the sandy battlefields?
But even today we still recall General Li.

漢家煙塵在東北，漢將辭家破殘賊。
男兒本自重橫行，天子非常賜顏色。
摐金伐鼓下榆關，旌旗逶迤碣石間。
校尉羽書飛瀚海，單于獵火照狼山。
山川蕭條極邊土，胡騎憑凌雜風雨。
戰士軍前半死生，美人帳下猶歌舞。
大漠窮秋塞草衰，孤城落日鬥兵稀。
身當恩遇常輕敵，力盡關山未解圍。
鐵衣遠戍辛勤久，玉箸應啼別離後。
少婦城南欲斷腸。征人薊北空回首。
邊風飄飄那可度，絕域蒼茫更何有。
殺氣三日作陣雲，寒聲一夜傳刁鬥。
相看白刃血紛紛，死節從來豈顧勳。
君不見沙場征戰苦，至今猶憶李將軍。

The virile tone, from which Gao Shi is known is established in the opening couplet where the Han armies leave on a punitive expedition against the Xiongnu and their ruler, the Chanyu. Although the martial tone can be read throughout, Tang poems depicting events in the Han are often indirectly pointing to contemporary parallels. Thus the clear criticism of the commanders who are entertained by young girls in their tents while the troops risk their lives may reflect on the situation in the Tang. The cumulative effect of imagery like the "arduous air" forming "clouds of phalanxes" and the passing of the watch beat only in "cold sounds" is striking and portrays an atmosphere that conveys the border regions as well as any Tang author has. The final line alludes to the Han general Li Guang 李廣 (ca. 184–199 BC). Li Guang was both one of the most successful commanders to fight the Xiongnu while at the same time the recipient of jealous critiques that led to his demotion to the status of a commoner. The poem therefore may exalt the Tang armies fighting in the same regions while warning of the dangers of factionalism.

On the basis of this one brilliant poem, later critics have often designated him a *Biansai ti* 邊塞體 (frontier-style) poet, although only a portion of his 250 poems treat border subjects. He is often paired with Cen Shen 岑參 (715–770),* a contemporary who also wrote extensively of his experience on the frontier. Comparisons between the works of the two men have not been to Gao's advantage; the younger Cen was regarded a greater master of the poetic craft and his brilliant, often flamboyant style has instantaneous appeal. Gao, on the other hand, is the more somber and intellectual poet and his works are considered less accessible.

BIBLIOGRAPHY

Editions:
Gao Changshi shiji 高常侍詩集. 8 *juan*. The text is found in several editions, the most reliable and accessible being the *SBCK*, which is the reprint of a movable-type edition of the Ming.
Gao Guangfu 高光復, ed. *Gao Shi, Cen Shen shi yishi* 高適岑參詩譯釋. Harbin: Heilongjiang Renmin, 1984.
Liu Kaiyang 劉開揚, ed. *Gao Shi shiji biannian jianzhu* 高適詩集編年箋注. Taibei: Hanjing Wenhua Shiye, 1983.
Quan Tang shi, 3: 2189–243, 14: 10621, 11101.
Xie Chufa 謝楚發, ed. *Gao Shi, Cen Shen shi* 高適岑參詩. Taibei: Jinxiu, 1993.

Annotations:
Ruan Tingyu 阮廷瑜, comp. *Gao Changshi shi jiaozhu* 高常侍詩校注. Taibei: Zhonghua Congshu Bianshen Weiyuanhui, 1965. Punctuated and annotated.
Sun Qinshan 孫欽善, annot. *Gao Shi ji jiaozhu* 高適集校註. 2nd ed. Shanghai: Shanghai Guji, 2014 (1984).

Biographical Sources:
Fu, *Tang caizi*, 1:414–25.
Jiu Tang shu, 111.3328–31.
Xin Tang shu, 143.4679–81.

Translations:
Chan, Marie. *Kao Shih* (see below).
Demiéville, *Anthologie*, pp. 257–58.
Margoulies, *Anthologie*, pp. 189, 231, 375.
Minford and Lau, pp. 835–37.

Owen, *High T'ang*, pp. 147–61.
Sunflower, pp. 114–15.

Studies:
Allen, Joseph Roe III. "From Saint to Singing Girl: The Rewritng of the Lo-fu Narrative in Chinese Literati Poetry." *HJAS* 48.2 (December 1988): 321–41. Contains a translation and discussion of a Lo-fu poem by Gao Shi.
Bian Xiaoxuan 卞孝萱. "Gao, Cen yitong lun" 高岑異同論. *Wenshi jilin*, 1985.4: 151–73.
Cai Zhennian 蔡振念. *Gao Shi shi yanjiu* 高適詩研究. Taibei: Hua Mulan Wenhua, 2008.
Chan, Marie. *Kao Shih*. Boston: Twayne, 1978.
Fu Xuancong, "Gao Shi nianpu zhong de jige wenti" 高適年譜中的幾個問題, in Fu, *Shiren*, pp. 142–70.
Kawaguchi Yoshiharu 川口喜治. "Ko Teki kenkyū no genjo to tenbo" 高適研究の現狀と展望. *Chūgoku gakushi* 3 (1988): 15–28.
McMullen, David. "Boats Moored and Unmoored: Reflections on the Dunhuang Manuscripts of Gao Shi's Verse." *HJAS* 73 (2013): 83–145.
She Zhengsong 佘正松. *Gao Shi yanjiu* 高適研究. Chengdu: Ba Shu, Sichuan Sheng Xinhua Shudian Jingxiao, 1992.
Sun Qinshan 孫欽善. "*Gao Shi ji* jiao Dunhuang can*juan* ji" 高適集校敦煌殘卷記. *Wen xian* 17 (1983): 35–55.
Yu Zhengsong 佘正松. *Gao Shi yanjiu* 高適研究. Chengdu: Ba Shu, 1992.
Zhang Xinxin 张馨心. "Gao Shi yanjiu shuping" 高适研究述评. *Gansu shehui kexue* (January, 2011): 133–37.
Zhou Xunchu 周勛初. *Gao Shi nianpu* 高適年譜. Shanghai: Shanghai Guji, 1980.
___ and Yao Song 姚松. *Gao Shi he Cen Shen* 高適和岑參. Shanghai: Shanghai Guji, 1991.
Zuo Yunlin 左雲林. *Gao Shi zhuan lun* 高適傳論. Beijing: Renmin Wenxue, 1985.

Marie Chan and William H. Nienhauser, Jr.

Geng Wei 耿湋 (*zi*, Hongyuan 洪源, *jinshi* 763, d. ca. 787) was from Hedong 河東 (modern Shanxi). He was one of the *Dali shi caizi* 大曆十才子 (Ten Talents of the Dali Era [766–779]; see also Lu Lun 盧綸 [748–ca. 798]),* perhaps the least ornate writer of the group. After passing the *jinshi* in 763 he became Commandant of Zhouzhi 盩厔 County (about twenty-five miles west of the capital). A year or two later he was called to court and appointed Reminder on the Left, a position he shared for a time with Sikong Shu 司空曙 (ca. 720–790).* In the late-760s he went to the Lower Yangze Region as a Reminder on the Left and Acting Editor of the Palace Library. At the start of the Zhenyuan era (785–805) he became Administrator for Law Enforcement and died shortly after.

His poetry concentrates on personal themes, but often lacks detachment, making him less of a "nature poet" than his colleague Sikong Shu. He also wrote many heptasyllabic verses with realistic, descriptive passages reflecting the social disturbances of the latter half of the eighth century, such as "Lupang laoren" 路旁老人 (The Old Man by the Roadside).

> An old man sits alone, leaning on a tree by the roadside,
> He bursts into tears before he can say anything.
> Wishing to return to rural home, but he has no property.
> Some relatives are buried in the soldiers' cemetery near the city wall.
> The rest of his life will still be difficult, hard days,
> Those he meets on the long road are unreliable.

Geng Wei

Though the clear waters and green mountains are as of old,
What he can do now after falling into poverty?

老人獨坐倚官樹，欲語潸然淚便垂。
陌上歸心無產業，城邊戰骨有親知。
餘生尚在艱難日，長路多逢輕薄兒。
綠水青山雖似舊，如今貧後復何為。

These pieces, along with his "frontier poetry," were often set in desolate landscapes which accord with the generally melancholy mood of many of his over 170 extant poems.

BIBLIOGRAPHY

Editions:
Quan Tang shi, 4: 2966–97, 11: 8982.

Annotations:
Zhang Dengdi 張登第, Jiao Wenbin 焦文彬 and Lu Anshu 魯安澍. *Dali shi caizi shixuan* 大曆十才子詩選. Xi'an: Shaanxi Renmin, 1988.

Biographical Sources:
Fu, *Tang caizi*, 2:30–35, 5:166–67.
Xin Tang shu, 203.5785–86.

Translations:
Minford and Lau, p. 844.
Owen, *High Tang*, pp. 274–80.

Studies:
Deng Jian 邓建, "Geng Wei Shige Chuangzuo Yishu Xieyao" 耿湋詩歌創作藝術擷要, *Leshan Shifan Xueyan Xuebao* 27.2 (Feb. 2008): 25–27.
___, "Lun Geng Wei Shige zai Tangshi Yanjin zhongde Juese he Yingxiang" 論耿湋詩歌在唐詩演進中的角色和影響, *Guangong Haiyang Daxue Xuebao* 2 (April 2007): 70–73.
___, "Dali Caizi Geng Wei Shige de Qinggan Shijie" 大歷才子耿湋詩歌的情感世界, *Zhongguo Yunwen Kan* 21.3 (Sept. 2007): 38–42.
Fu Xuancong 傅璇琮. "Geng Wei kao" 耿湋考, *Tangdai shiren congkao* 唐代詩人叢考. Beijing: Zhonghua, 1980, pp. 493–501.
Jiang Yin 蔣寅. *Dali shiren yanjiu* 大曆詩人研究. Beijing: Zhonghua, 1995.
Liu Yanyan 刘燕燕, "Dali Shicaizi de Shige Chuangzuo" 大歷十才子的詩歌創作, *Qianyan* 7 (2008): 182–84.
Ogawa, Shoichi 小川昭一. "Taireki no shijin" 大曆の詩人, *Shibun* 24 (1959): 22–33.

William H. Nienhauser, Jr.

Gu Feixiong

Gu Feixiong 顧非熊 (ca. 795–ca. 854) was a native of Suzhou 蘇州 and son of the famous literatus, Gu Kuang 顧況 (ca. 725–ca. 814).* Duan Chengshi 段成式 (ca. 800–863) reports in the *Youyang zazu* 酉陽雜俎 that Gu Feixiong was regarded as the reincarnation of another beloved son of Gu Kuang, whose death his father lamented.

Gu Feixiong is said to have displayed precocious literary gifts, but his attempts over many years to win certification as a *jinshi* graduate proved fruitless until, in 845, when he failed again, Emperor Wuzong (r. 840–846) personally read his examination papers and compelled the examiners to pass him. His official life was brief and has hardly been reported. He served in two minor positions in Xuyi County 盱眙縣 (about forty miles north of modern Nanjing in Jiangsu). He is reputed to have shared in some degree his father's wit and insolence, and this may explain his early departure to Mount Mao 茅山 (about thirty miles southeast of Nanjing), where, as had his father, he spent what is known of the rest of his life. A poem by Wang Jian 王建 (ca. 766–ca. 830)* speaks of Gu's departure from the capital.

Only about seventy of Gu Feixiong's poems survive. They are mainly about persons and events in his own life, like the following "Qiuye Chang'an binghou zuo" 秋夜長安病後作 (Written on an Autumn Night in Chang'an after Being Sick):

> Mid-autumn in the imperial city, ten days of rain have passed;
> Even after clearing the cicada's song is still not heard.
> All alone in my quiet courtyard, just up from a recent sickness:
> Geese form a flock and head south to my hometown.

> 秋中帝里經旬雨，晴後蟬聲更不聞。
> 牢落閒庭新病起，故鄉南去雁成群。

Although this poem cannot be dated, the sadness of a southerner sojourning in the capital while struggling to pass the examinations comes through clearly. The extended rainfall may have hindered visits by friends. The silence of his courtyard reminds the reader not only of the absence of the usual chirping of the cicadas in the fall, but also the poet's isolation. All this stands in contrast to the geese which gather and fly south, calling to mind Gu's hometown of Suzhou.

Although he knew many poets including Wang Jian 王建 (ca. 766–ca. 830),* Yao He 姚合 (ca. 779–ca. 849),* and Jia Dao 賈島 (779–843),* many of his poems are addressed to Buddhist monks. The latter show appreciation of the devotion and fortitude of these men, but little concern with their beliefs. Sometimes a wry skepticism or even an occasional crankiness shows through. Like the poems of his father, his verse employs a rather plain diction. But unlike his father's, Gu's Feixiong's Mao Shan poems have little of the supernatural or religious in them. The writer honors the gentlemen-priests he met there, and he appreciates the advantages of the slow, peaceful rhythm of life on the mountain. The following "Ti Juezhen Shangren yuan" 題覺真商人院 (Written on the Courtyard Wall of Monk Juezhen) is typical:

> Chang'an is a place of carriages and horses—
> This courtyard shuts in the sounds of pines.
> Recently you left lecturing in the palace,
> Formerly you have wandered every mountain.

Gu Feixiong

> Adept at verse, thus you write gāthās,
> Fond of guests, how could this be related to your fame.
> You appointed me to come this Mid-autumn night
> To watch together as the moon grows bright.

> 長安車馬地，此院閉松聲。
> 新罷九天講，舊曾諸岳行。
> 能詩因作偈，好客豈關名。
> 約我中秋夜，同來看月明。

The poem contains the sort of praise that is typical for a guest to honor his host. The sixth line emphasizes that Juezhen's goals in seeking friendship is not to forward his career, unlike many men Gu must have met. Although Gu confronts his failure in the world of practical affairs, he cannot shake off his bitterness. He may pose as a gentleman reconciled to exile in a well-pruned landscape, but even the sound of a spring dripping down the face of a cliff reminds him of the palace clepsydra and the splendid but ritualized life it governed. The attention to pines, wild deer, monkeys, unusual birds, and cold mountain water seems little more than the arranging of stage properties: his father's sense of the numinous in nature remains absent. The following "Jing Hangzhou" 經杭州 (Passing through Hangzhou) nevertheless reveals a skillful use of imagery while also reflecting his conflicted emotions:

> Ramparts of the commandery seat wind along the banks of the river,
> People's houses seem close to the white clouds.
> I watch the waves in the evening from a railing,
> The sound of oars beyond the city wall are heard.
> Mountains start to disappear out around the inlet,
> A rainbow bends yet the rain has not year cleared away.
> Is there anyone to understand my thoughts?
> As my mind drives away a flock of gulls.

> 郡郭繞江濆，人家近白雲。
> 晚濤臨檻看，夜櫓隔城聞。
> 浦轉山初盡，虹斜雨未分。
> 有誰知我意，心緒逐鷗群。

The poem opens with a view of the tidal bore of the Qiantang River in the early evening. The breadth of the bay beyond Hangzhou can be sensed as the poet looks out to see houses in the distance that appear to be touching the clouds and mountains fading from sight in the declining light. The final couplet alludes to the belief first expressed in the *Lie Zi* that gulls will only approach someone with a pure mind—Gu admits that the birds easily sense his unfulfilled personal ambitions.

Surprisingly, the single piece of his imaginative prose to survive, the "Miaonü zhuan" 妙女傳 (An Account of a Marvelous Woman), a popular tale of the supernatural in a Buddhist setting with some Daoist elements, displays a rather charming dreamlike atmosphere, quite unlike that of his more down-to-earth poems.

BIBLIOGRAPHY

Editions:
Chen Bohai 陳伯海. *Tangshi huiping* 唐詩彙評. Hangzhou: Zhejiang Jiaoyu, 1995, v. 2, pp. 2293–95.
Gu Feixiong ji 顧非熊集. 1 *juan*. Shanghai: Saoye Shanfang, 1920.
Huanghe Shanzhuang 黃鶴山莊, ed. *Guozuogong buyi* 國佐公補遺, 1, 1839.
Leimin zhuan 雷民傳. Beijing: Zhonghua, 1985 (1935).

Miaonü zhuan 妙女傳. Taibei: Yiwen, 1968.
Quan Tang shi, 8: 5822–34, 15: 11321.

Biographical Sources:
Fu, *Tang caizi*, 3:351–56, 380–82; *Jiu Tang shu*, 130.3625.

Translations:
Edwards, Evangeline D. *Chinese Prose Literature of the T'ang Period, A.D. 618–906: Fiction*. New York: AMS, 1974, pp. 183–85. Translation of "Miaonü zhuan."
Owen, *Omen*, pp. 97–98.
___, *Late Tang*, pp. 135–36.

Studies:
Zeng Yuxia 曾羽霞 and Jing Xiadong 景遐东. "Tangdai Jiangnan diqu Gushi jiaxue jingshen yu wenxue chuangzuo" 唐代江南地区顾氏家学精神与文学创作. *Xueshujie* 176.1 (January 2013): 124–32.

Edward H. Schafer, Ji Wang, and William H. Nienhauser, Jr

Gu Kuang 顧況 (*zi*, Buweng 逋翁, ca. 725–ca. 814), a painter, poet, and calligrapher, was a native of Suzhou 蘇州. He passed the *jinshi* examination in 757 and held two minor positions in Hangzhou. From 771–774 he served as Supervisor in the Salt Monopoly in Yongjia 永嘉 County (near modern Wenzhou in Zhejiang). Thereafter he wandered through the lower Yangzi Valley, eventually attracting the attention of the powerful politicians Liu Hun 柳渾 (715–789) and especially Li Bi 李泌 (722–789) who were in the area at this time. Li Bi became his patron, possibly, like himself, Gu Kuang was devoted to Daoist studies. But it was Liu Hun who enabled Gu to move to the capital where he became a Rectifier in the Court of Judicial Rule. By 787, Gu was an Editor in the Palace Library and the following year he was promoted to become Editorial Director. That summer he won fame for poems he wrote together with Liu Hun and Liu Taizhen 劉太真 (725–792). But the next year Liu Hun died and Gu Kuang, exposed to the attacks of enemies he had made with his notoriously sarcastic wit, was degraded to a minor post in Raozhou 饒州, which he soon deserted to spend the rest of his life in retirement on Mao Shan 茅山, the sacred center of the dominant Daoist sect of Shangqing (Highest Clarity 上清) during Tang times. The Tang chronicler Li Chuo 李綽 avers that the popular view of Gu Kuang's "expulsion" is erroneous. Perhaps he was too "relaxed and uninhibited" for most courtiers, but Gu left Chang'an voluntarily, rejecting preferment and patronage in favor of a contemplative life in reclusion. During his retirement he styled himself Huayang Zhenyi 華陽真逸 (Realized and Unconfined

Gu Kuang

One of Huayang) and lived out his peaceful days at Heishi Chi 黑石池 (Black-stone Pool), overlooking an herb garden from a pine-shaded window near the home of his fellow-poet Qin Xi 秦系 (724–after 804).

It is difficult to find traces of Gu Kuang's reputed sarcasm in his poetry. His "old style" compositions, much concerned with man's predicament, are often pathetic, occasionally tinged with irony. But his work as a whole—a substantial corpus—is most characteristically engaged with supernatural themes and shows a sense of wonder at the mysterious forces working beyond the phenomenal world. The conventional figures who serve as foci for these musings include the star goddess known as Zhi Nü 織女 (Weaving Girl), the goddess of the Han River, and the familiar spirits of Lake Dongting 洞庭湖. There are often glimpses of shamanistic rites or echoes of antiquity in the voice of the ghost-king of ancient Chu. More specifically, Daoist allusions to astral powers are revealed through gemmy images of powerful entities behind the stars (the sun and moon are "jade discs"; the five planets are "pearls"). His most interesting poems were written in his congenial retreat at Mao Shan. There his love of nature is finally fused with his otherworldly aspirations. The delights of a carefully selected or cultivated landscape are impregnated with both literary and religious attitudes. The following "Yezhong wang xianguan" 夜中望仙觀 (Looking at the Immortal Belvedere Midway through the Night) was probably written at Mao Shan:

> Flowers in beaks, with setting of the sun, flying birds return;
> Where the moon shines above the torrent, I see blue mountains.
> From afar I am aware of a tree before the window of a Jade Woman:
> But unless one is a transcendent person, one is not allowed to climb it.

> 日暮銜花飛鳥還，月明溪上見青山。
> 遙知玉女窗前樹，不是仙人不得攀。

Beyond nature lies super-nature. The moonlit blue hills resemble the palaces of the moon. The persona of the poem aspires to the company of the Jade Woman, custodian of the secrets of the Upper World—but he is still inadequately prepared for the perilous flight: the feathers, like those of angels, are metaphorical. The flight is also represented as a climb, hauling oneself up the World Tree.

His other ostensible themes range widely, from verses about trees, flowers, wild birds, and mountain scenery, in artfully arranged diction, to others addressed to priests or responding to musical performances. Looking out over the lush prospect of Willow Valley, he ponders the secrets of the *Huangting Jing* 黃庭經 (Yellow Court Classic); he has intimations of immortality in the shadows of moonlit fanes which suggest the starry mansions of the gods; he is entranced by visions of holy but untouchable priestesses, and by the uncanny bugling of sacred cranes. One of his Daoist poems, "Buxu ci" 步虛詞 (Canto on Pacing the Void), based on an old Mao Shan ritual, was written during his joyless residence in the capital; he composed it at the Taiqing Gong 太清宮 (Palace of Grand Clarity), a temple founded by Xuanzong (r. 712–756) in honor of Taishang Laojun 太上老君 (All Highest Lord Lao, i.e. Lao Zi).

A small collection of Gu Kuang's prose survives. The most noteworthy works are a number of *ji* 記 (records) which show a deep familiarity with nature, sometimes tinged with a haunting sense of divine presences. The unornamented but sensitive style recalls some of the compositions of Liu Zongyuan 柳宗元 (773–819).*

Huangfu Shi 皇甫湜 (776–ca. 835),* the author of the preface to Gu Kuang's collected works, finds both poet and poetry well-suited to the rich and strange land of Wu, marked by the weird rocks of Lake Tai 太湖, the fantastic calls of the cranes, and the great Buddhist establishments. Huangfu even asserts that the poet's use of language was beyond the attainment of ordinary mortals–indeed, he finds him the only poet of his generation ranking with Li Bo 李白 (701–762)* and Du Fu 杜甫 (712–770).*

In early 770s Gu wrote linked poems with Jiao Ran 皎然 (720–799)* and others, but his best known poem is the "Gongti" 宮詞 (Palace Poem) that is also included in the *Tang shi sanbaishou* 唐詩三百首:

> In the jade tower halfway to heaven a flute song arises,
> The wind twines the palace girls' laughter within.
> In the Moonlit Hall as shadows form, a water clock drips:
> Crystal curtains open wide, bringing closer the River of Stars.

> 玉樓天半起笙歌，風送宮嬪笑語和。
> 月殿影開聞夜漏，水精簾卷近銀河。

Gu brings the scene inside the harem (the Moonlit Hall was actually part of the palace of Emperor Jianwen 建文 of the Liang dynasty, r. 503–551) as night falls and the young women are perhaps thinking of the love between the Weaver Girl and the Herder Boy, lovers who are represented by stars on either side of the Milky Way (i.e. River of Stars) and who can only meet once a year.

BIBLIOGRAPHY

Editions:
Gu Huayang ji 古華陽集. Huanghe Shanzhuang Cang Ban 黃鶴山莊藏板, 1839.
Gu Kuang shiji 顧况诗集. Nanchang: Jiangxi Renmin, 1983.
Quan Tang shi, 4: 2920–65.
Quan Tang wen, 528–530.6144–65.

Annotations:
Wang Qixing 王啟興 and Zhang Hong 張虹, eds. *Gu Kuang shiji zhu* 顧况詩集注. Shanghai: Shanghai Guji, 1994.

Biographical Sources:
Fu, *Tang caizi*, 1:633–54, 5:141–43.
Jiu Tang shu, 130.3625.

Translations:
Hsü, *Anthologie*, pp. 167–68.

Gu Kuang

Minford and Lau, pp. 842–43.
Schafer, E. H. *Mao Shan in T'ang Times* (Society for the Study of Chinese Religions, Monograph No. I). Boulder, Colorado, 1980, pp. 39–40, p. 43, p. 50.
Sunflower, pp. 150–51.

Studies:
Feng Shuran 馮淑然. "Gu Kuang shiwen zhulu yu banben kaoshu" 顧況詩文著录與版本考述. *Tushuguan zazhi* 28.12 (2009): 63–73.
Fu, *Shiren*, pp. 379–408.

Edward H. Schafer and William H. Nienhauser, Jr.

Guanxiu 貫休 (secular surname, Jiang 姜; *zi*, Deyin 德陰, 832–912), was a native of Lanqi 蘭溪 in Wuzhou 婺州 (modern Zhejiang). Orphaned at an early age, he was sent to live in a Buddhist monastery in his hometown, where he showed early promise as a poet, painter, and calligrapher. During the later years of the Xiantong era (860–874) he traveled to Hongzhou 洪州 (modern Nanchang in Jiangxi) and then for four or five years lived in the neighboring Zhongling Mountains 鍾陵山. Having returned to Wuzhou, the late 870s found him in Changzhou 常州 (modern Jiangsu) and then Hangzhou 杭州—to avoid Huang Chao's 黃巢 rebel troops—returning to Wuzhou only in 884. In 894 he traveled to Hangzhou to visit Qian Liu 錢鏐 (r. 907–932), the future king of Wu-Yue 吳越 who was already firmly in control of the area.

During this period, when he was a resident of Hangzhou, he painted the celebrated pictures of sixteen arhats. These are said to have been inspired by a dream (a poetic version of the affair was composed by Ouyang Jiong 歐陽炯 [896–971], later his colleague in Sichuan). Each painting shows an austere saint seated under an overhanging rock or in a stony niche. Critical opinion differs as to which of the paintings of arhats attributed to him are authentic; the set in the Imperial Household Collection in Tokyo is particularly well regarded.

Guan's career as a court poet came to an end when he took offense at Qian Liu's suggestion that he reword a laudatory poem to make it even more flattering. The poet–so the tale goes–made an impertinent reply, casting doubt on the prince's qualifications as a literary critic. Guanxiu then moved up the Yangzi to the domain of the warlord Cheng Rui 成汭 (d. 903) who was his patron for a brief period. Here he became the friend of the poet Wu Rong 吳融 (850–903), with whom he could speak seriously about philosophic and literary matters. Cheng Rui's court proved no more satisfactory than that of Wu-Yue. At the beginning of the ninth century, Guan continued westward into Sichuan, where he was given a suitably-honorable welcome by Wang Jian 王建 (877–943), founder of the new kingdom of Shu 蜀. In 907, already an ornament of the brilliant court at Chengdu and celebrated both as priest and prelate, he was invested with the title of *Chanyue Dashi* 禪月大師 (Great Master of the Chan Moon). There he ended his days, full of years and glory. Guanxiu put together the first collection of his writings in 896, while he was still with Cheng Rui in Jiangling 江陵. It was titled *Xiyue Ji* 西岳集 (Collection from the Western Peak), a name which reflects a period in the 850s when the poet resided at Hua Shan 華山. (Wu Rong wrote a prefatory essay for this collection.) This was superseded by a new collection made posthumously by his disciple Tanyu 曇域 (b. ca. 865)–a version which now circulates as *Chanyue ji* 禪月集 (Wu Rong's preface remains attached to some editions).

In the most characteristic of his works, Guanxiu reveals himself as a dreamer and visionary. Even his portrayals of the courts and gardens of this world are couched in the language of illusion and elegant hallucination. His symbols of immortality are largely drawn from the color spectrum and the many-faceted mineralogical world. An aristocratic pleasance is subtly transformed into a crystalline paradise, whose trees tinkle with leaves of gold and silver, through which shine gemmy fruits and jeweled flowers. Through all, a luminous atmosphere intimates the white light of eternity. Such visions characterize his courtly odes and lauds as much as they do his religious verses–chiefly occasional stanzas on Buddhist monasteries and Daoist ecclesiastics. Yet he also left poems, such as the series of twenty-four poems titled "Shanju" 山居 (Living in the Mountains) written while he was living at Zhongling 鍾陵 (near modern Nanchang 南昌 in Jiangxi) in 863–864 in which his predilection for Buddhism is clear, here is the second of that series:

> Difficult to speak of retiring and then immediately to retire;
> At the head of an jade-green stream I sit solitary and clearly intone.
> No one comes to the three-room thatched hut,
> I wander alone ten-*li* under the shade of pines.
> The bright moon, the cool wind at Zong Bing's community,
> The setting sun, the fall colors at Master Yu's pavilion.
> Cultivating the mind I have not yet reached the status of no-mind,
> The ten thousand things, the thousand sorts, pursue the flowing waters.

> 難是言休即便休，清吟孤坐碧溪頭。
> 三間茆屋無人到，十里松陰獨自遊。
> 明月清風宗炳社，夕陽秋色庾公樓。
> 修心未到無心地，萬種千般逐水流。

Since Zhongling is close to Mount Lu, the title may refer to it specifically. The poem depicts Guanxiu's attempts to attain a state of "no-mind," (*wuxin* 無心) with no troubling thoughts or desires "Retire" here in the sense of retire from the world. Sitting alone and intoning a sutra are part of the regime (although it is also possible Guanxiu was chanting his own poem). Guanxiu knows his goal. Lines 6 and 7 allude to the Lotus Society 蓮社 set up by Hui Yuan 慧遠 (334–416) on Mount Lu during the Taiyuan era (376–397) that included Zong Bing 宗炳 (375–433). All the community members vowed to be reborn in Amitaba's Western Pure Land, and here Guanxiu shows his yearning to join them. Master Yu is Yu Liang 庾亮 (289–340), a man who held temporal power for most of his life; while governing a region near Mount Lu where he had a pavilion built. The mixed allusions here seem to reflect Guanxiu's own political interest. The final two lines return to the theme of attaining "no-mind," the final line either suggesting his lack of success as time passes, or more likely that he is able to release his ties to the worldly.

Still, Guan was not an ecstatic poet like that dedicated star-traveler Wu Yun 吳筠 (d. 778).* He saw religion as a civilizing agency; the life of this world was very much in his mind. He was, in fact, a syncretist, both in thought and in verse. He employed the imagery of Daoism, Buddhism, and "Confucianism" (the secular idealism inherited from antiquity) interchangeably. His ideas on this theme are summarized in a poem entitled "Daxing Sanjiao" 大興三教 (Greatly Exalted Are the Three Doctrines). Beyond this, he believed that the brilliant culture of Shu might, under his guidance, bring together men of all kinds and all traditions into a variegated but harmonious whole. Such utopian and apostolic beliefs are expressed in another poem named "Shou zai Xi Yi" 守在四夷 (Our Guard Lies with the Four Aliens), in which appears a typical transformational antithesis: "The incenses of Java seem to be snow; the horses of the Uighurs are like a forest" 闍婆香似雪，回鶻馬如林–that is, the northern wastes and the tropical jungles are identical when considered beyond phenomenal illusion. His "Gusai xia qu" 古塞下曲 (Song Written Beneath the Ancient Fortifications) allows a further look into opposition to traditional frontier policy:

> Battlefield bones trampled into dust,
> Fly into the eyes of those on campaign.
> Yellow clouds turn suddenly black,
> Battlefield ghosts wail as they form ranks:
> Sinister winds howl on the Great Desert,
> Signal fires that no one will come forth to answer.
> Who will step before the Son of Heaven
> To sing this song of the border walls?

> 戰骨踐成塵，飛入征人目。
> 黃雲忽變黑，戰鬼作陣哭。
> 陰風吼大漠，火號出不得。
> 誰為天子前，唱此邊城曲。

In the estimation of literary persons of his era, Guanxiu rated very highly. His name was linked with that of his Sichuanese contemporary, the poetical *śramaṇa* Qi Ji 齊己 (fl. 883).* His old friend Wu Rong thought him the only worthy successor to Li Bo 李白 (701–762)* and Bo Juyi 白居易 (772–846).* The Buddhist hagiographer Zan Ning 贊寧 (919–1001) held him to be the peer of Li Bo and Li He 李賀 (790–816).* After the Song dynasty, however, his reputation declined.

BIBLIOGRAPHY

Editions:
Chanyue ji 禪月集. SBCK.
Chanyue ji 禪月集 (26 *juan*). Taibei: Taiwan Xuesheng, 1975 (photolithographic reprint).
Quan Tang shi, 12: 9386–515.
Quan Tang wen, 921.12630–31.

Annotations:
Hu Dajun 胡大浚, ed. *Guanxiu geshi jinian jianzhu* 貫休歌詩繫年箋注. Beijing: Zhonghua, 2011.
Lu Yongfeng 陆永峰, ed. *Chanyueji jiaozhu* 禪月集校注. Chengdu: Ba Shu, 2006.

Biographical Sources:
Fu, *Tang caizi*, 4:428–43.
Zan Ning, 30.749–50.

Translations:
Egan, *Clouds*, pp. 89–93.
Mazanec, Thomas J. "Guanxiu's 'Mountain-Dwelling Poems': A Translation." *Tang Studies* 34 (2016): 99–123.
Minford and Lau, p. 985.
Owen, Stephen. "How Did Buddhism Matter in Tang Poetry?" *TP* 103 (2017): 394–95.
Sanford, James H. and Jerome P. Seaton, "Kuan Hsiu," in Seaton, Jerome P. and Denni Maloney, eds. *A Drifting Boat: An Anthology of Chinese Zen Poetry*. Fredonia, NY: White Pine Press, 1994, pp. 77–79.
Schafer, E. H. "Mineral Imagery in the Paradise Poems of Kuan-hsiu," *AM* 10 (1963), 73–102.

Studies:
Buswell, *Dictionary*, pp. 178–79.
Cui Baofeng 崔寶峰. "Shiseng Guanxiu yanjiu zongshu" 詩僧貫休研究綜述. *Shanxin Shida xuebao (Shehui kexue ban)* 1 (2013): 84–86.
Fan Zhimin 范志民. *Guanxiu*. Shanghai: Shanghai Renmin Meishu, 1981.
Kobayashi Taichirō 小林太市郎. *Zengetsu daichi no shōgai to geijutsu* 禪月大師の生崖と藝術. Tokyo: Sōgensha, 1947.
Lu Chen 路振 (957–1014). *Jiuguo zhi* 九國志. *Shoushan Ge congshu* 守山閣叢書.
Ouyang Jiong 歐陽炯. "Guanxiu ying meng luohan hua ge" 貫休應夢羅漢畫歌, *Quan Tang shi*, v. 11, juan 761, pp. 8638–8639.
Schafer, E. H., "Mineral Imagery."
Wu Jiyu 吳其昱. "Le séjour de Kouan-hieou au Houa chan et Ie titre du recueil de ses poèmes: Si-yo tsi," *Melanges publiés par l'Institut des Hautes Etudes Chinoise*, 2 (1960): 159–78.
———. "Trois poèmes inédits de Kouan-hieou." *JA*, 247 (1959): 349–78.
Wu Renchen 吳任臣. *Shi guo chun qiu* 十國春秋 (ed. of 1793), juan 47, pp. 1b–4b.
Wu Rong 吳融. "Chanyue ji xu" 禪月集序, *Quan Tang wen*, v. 17, juan 820, p. 10892..

Edward H. Schafer

Han Hong 韓翃 (*zi*, Junping 君平, fl. 754), a native of Nanyang 南陽 (modern Nanyang in Henan), was one of the group of poets known as the "Dali shi caizi" 大歷十才子 (Ten Talents of the Dali Era). He passed the *jinshi* examination in 754. In 762, he became a Retainer to Hou Xiyi 侯希逸, the Military Commissioner of Ziqing 淄青 (in modern Shandong). In 765, Hou was driven out by his subordinates, and Han went back to Chang'an with Hou. In Chang'an Han became friends with some of the most eminent poets of the age, among them Qian Qi 錢起 (720–ca. 783)* and Lu Lun 盧綸 (739–799).* In 774, Han was a Retainer to Tian Shenyu 田神玉 (d. 776), the Military Commissioner of Biansong 汴宋 (stretching over modern eastern Henan and northwestern Anhui). Two years later, Tian passed away, and there was a rebellion in Bianzhou 汴州 (modern Kaifeng). After the rebellion was put down, Li Zhongchen 李忠臣 (716–784) became the new Military Commissioner, with Han continuing to serve him as Retainer. In 779, when Li Xilie 李希烈 (d. 786), Li Zhongchen's subordinate, forcibly replaced Li Zhongchen, Han moved his

Han Hong

allegiance to Li Xilie. Later when the imperial government sent Li Mian 李勉 (717–788) to replace Li Xilie, Han joined the staff of Li Mian.

One of Han Hong's most famous poems is "Hanshi" 寒食 (Cold Food Day):

Throughout the royal city fly flowers of spring,
On Cold Food Day in the eastern wind the willows swing.
At dusk the court of Han will waxen candles send
To the homes of the "Five Marquises" where light and incense softly blend.

春城無處不飛花，寒食東風御柳斜。
日暮漢宮傳蠟燭，輕煙散入五侯家。

On "Cold Food" day, fire of any sort was forbidden, and no smoke would appear from the chimneys of ordinary people. At dusk, however, the imperial court would send candles to the senior officials as a gesture of imperial favor. The final line refers to the five eunuchs who were all made marquises on the same day by Emperor Xuan 宣 of the Han (r. 98–41 BCE) dynasty. The final couplet is therefore read as a veiled criticism of the eunuchs who were in control of much of the government under the reign of Emperor Dezong (r. 779–805).

The poem is said to have made an impression on the emperor, for when the post of Participant in the Drafting of Proclamations became vacant, Dezong wanted to assign this post to Han Hong. At that time, there was a namesake who was the Prefect of Jianghuai 江淮. The Grand Councilor asked which Han Hong should take the position, and the emperor replied, "the one who wrote 'Throughout the royal city fly flowers of spring.'" Han Hong took the position and later was appointed Secretariat Drafter, from which position he retired.

"Liushi zhuan" 柳氏傳 [The Tale of Liushi] recorded the love story of a certain Han Yi 韓翊 and his concubine Liushi. In the tale, when Han Yi is thought to have represented Han Hong. Having just come to Chang'an, he befriended a man whose surname was Li 李 and had a singing girl named Liushi. She and Han fell in love and Li gave Liushi to Han as a present. After Han passed the *jinshi* examination in 754, he went back to his hometown to visit his parents and left Liushi in Chang'an. The next year, before Han had returned to the capital, the An Lushan Rebellion broke out and Liushi took refuge in a temple. At that time, Han was a Retainer in Ziqing 淄青. When Han finally came back to Chang'an, Liushi had been snatched by a foreign general, Sha Zhali 沙吒利. But an officer of Ziqing named Xu Jun 許俊 was able to get Liushi back through a stratagem. Fearing Sha Zhali's revenge, Xu, Han and their colleagues asked Hou Xiyi 侯希逸 (d. 781) for help. Hou was moved by Xu Jun and wrote a memorial to Emperor Daizong. In the end, Emperor Daizong bestowed many rolls of silk on Sha Zhali as compensation and let Liushi stay with Han Yi. While Han was separated from Liushi, he wrote a poem which he sent to her with some gold:

Willow of Zhang Pavilion, Willow of Zhang Pavilion,
Have you still the beauty of your youth?
Even though your slender branches may still hang as of old,
They must have been picked by someone else's hand.

章台柳，章台柳，
顏色青青今在否？
縱使長條似舊垂，
也應攀折他人手。

And Liushi replied:

Green branches of a willow—so fragrant and graceful
How sad to see year after year you gift parting lovers.
One leaf falling in the wind suddenly announces autumn
Even though you return, what is left to pick?

楊柳枝，芳菲節，
可恨年年贈離別。
一葉隨風忽報秋，
縱使君來豈堪折.

Many scholars believe there was some historical basis for this tale. Though we have no records of Sha Zhali or Xu Jun, Hou Shiyi was an important general and official of the time. Although the protagonist in "Liushi zhuan" is called Han Yi, he and Han Hong shared the same hometown and life experiences.

BIBLIOGRAPHY

Editions:
Chen Wanghe 陳王和. *Han Hong shiji jiaozhu* 韓翃詩集校注. Taibei: Wenshizhe, 1973.
Han Hong 韓翃. *Han Junping ji: 3 Juan* 韓君平集 3卷. Rare books National Library Peiping; reel 499–500, [publisher not identified], [date of publication not identified].
Quan Tang shi, 4: 2718–61.
Xi Qiyu 席啓寓. *Han Junping Shiji: 1 Juan, Buyi 1 Juan* 韓君平詩集: 一卷, 補遺一卷. China: Dongshan Xishi Qinchuan Shuwu 東山席氏琴川書屋, 1708.
___. *Han Sheren Shiji: 1 Juan* 韓舍人詩集: 1卷. Shanghai: Saoye Shanfang 掃葉山房, 1920.

Biographical Sources:
Fu, *Tang caizi*, 1:20–30.
Xin Tang shu, 203.5786.

Translations:
Bynner, *Jade Mountain*, pp. 26–27.
Edwards, Evangeline Dora. "Chang-t'ai Liu chuan," in Edwards, *Chinese Prose Literature of the Tang Period A.D. 618–906*. London: Probsthain, 1938, v. 2, pp. 170–73.
Herdan, Innes. *300 T'ang Poems*. Taibei: Taibei Far East Book Company, 1973, p. 276, p. 344, p. 427.
Jenyns, Soame. *A Further Selection from the Three Hundred Poems of the T'ang Dynasty*. London: John Murray, 1944, pp. 72–73.
Lévy, André. "Triomphe de l'amour, Relation de l'affaire dame Saule," in Lévy, *Histoires d'amour et de mort de la Chine ancienne*. Paris: Aubier, 1992, pp. 53–67.

Owen, *Late Tang*, p. 201.

Ts'ai T'ing-kan 蔡廷幹 [Cai Tinggan]. *Chinese Poems in English Rhyme*. Chicago, Ill.: The University of Chicago, 1932, p. 56.

Wang, Elizabeth Te-chen. "Madam Willow" [Liushi zhuan 柳氏傳], in Wang, *Ladies of the Tang, 22 Classical Stories*. Taibei: Mei Ya, 1973, pp. 1–13.

Waters, Geoffrey R, Michael Farman, David Lunde and Jerome P Seaton. *Three Hundred Tang Poems*. Buffalo, N.Y.: White Pine, 2011, p. 141, p. 168, p. 197.

Xu Yuan-zhong 許淵沖, Loh Bei-yei 陸佩弦 and Wu Juntao 吳鈞陶 eds. *300 Tang Poems: A New Translation*. Hong Kong: The Commercial, 1987, pp. 225–27.

Studies:

Bao Junqin 鮑俊琴. "Han Hong ji qi shige yanjiu" 韓翃及其詩歌研究 [A Study of Han Hong and his Poems]. M.A. thesis, Nanjing Normal University, 2009.

Ju Fei 鞠飛. "Han Hong shengping kaoshu" 韓翃生平考述 [A Study of Han Hong's Life], *Journal of Kaili University* 凱里學院學報, 2011.4: 124–27.

___. "Han Hong shengping kaoshu" 韓翃生卒年考 [A Study of Han Hong's Dates of Birth and Death], *Journal of Suihua University* 綏化學院學報, 2011.8: 116–18.

Lei Jinyu 雷金玉. "Han Hong shige yanjiu" 韓翃詩歌研究 [A Study of Han Hong's Poems]. M.A. thesis, Hebei University, 2007.

Luo Yaojun 駱耀軍. "Lun sheng Tang yuyun li Han Hong shige de 'feng' yixiang" 論盛唐餘韻裡韓翃詩歌的"楓"意象 [The Image of the Maple in Han Hong's Poetry as a Reflection of the High Tang]. *Central China Normal University Journal of Postgraduates* 華中師範大學研究生學報. 2012.2: 76–80.

Wang Mengou 王夢鷗. *Tang Ren Xiaoshuo Jiaoshi* 唐人小說校釋 [Proofreading and Explanation for Tang Tales]. Taibei: Zhengzhong, 1983, pp. 73–79.

Wang Pijiang 汪辟疆. *Tang Ren Xiaoshuo* 唐人小說 [Tang Tales]. Shanghai: Shanghai Guji, 1978, pp. 52–55.

Xing Zhenxia 邢振霞. "Han Hong ji qi shige yanjiu" 韓翃及其詩歌研究 [The Study of Han Hong and His Poems]. M.A. thesis, Qufu Normal University, 2009.

Yang Lihua 楊麗花. 柳氏故事文本演变及文化意蕴 [Textual evolution and cultural implication of Liushi's story]. M.A. theis, Nankai University, 2007.

Zhang Ying 張穎. "Han Hong yanjiu" 韓翃研究 [Study of Han Hong]. M.A. theis, Sichuan Normal University, 2010.

Zhou Chan 周嬋. "Wenzhang he wei shi er zhu, ge shi he wei shi er zuo: dali shi caizi xianshi ticai zuopin yanjiu" 文章合為時而著 歌詩合為事而作：大曆十才子現實題材作品研究 [Creative Articles and Poems to Reflect the Social Reality: The Research of Practical Subjects Works of Ten Wets in Tang Dynasty-ta-li]. M.A. thesis, Guizhou University, 2009.

Zhou Zuzhuan 周祖譔. *Zhongguo Wenxuejia Da Cidian Tang Wu Dai Juan* 中國文學家大辭典唐五代卷 [Thesaurus of Chinese Literati, Volume of Tang and Five Dynasties]. Beijing: Zhonghua, 1992, p. 744.

Rui Wang

Han Wo 韓偓 (*zi*, Zhiyao 致堯 or Zhiyuan 致元 or Zhiguang 致光, 842–923; called himself Yushan Jiaoren 玉山樵人 [The Woodcutter of Mount Yu]), is traditionally remembered as a statesman and poet who remained loyal to the Tang in its final decade. Han was born in the capital, Chang'an. His father, Han Zhan 韓瞻 (fl. 837), was related by marriage to Li Shangyin 李商隱 (ca. 813–858),* and the elder poet cast an approving eye on the poetry of preadolescent Han Wo. Little is known of Han's life until he passed the *jinshi* examination in 889, at the age of 47, and entered government service at court. His career coincides with the reign of Zhao Zong (r. 888–904), the last Tang sovereign. He held a number of high positions and was made a Hanlin Academician in 901. Biographers dwell on how Han gained the emperor's favor by defending the sovereign's title and person from would-be usurpers, at great personal cost. Han was finally driven from court in 903 by Zhu Quanzhong 朱全忠 (852–912), who became the first sovereign of Liang. After a succession of minor positions that moved him further and further from the capital, Han fled to the semi-autonomous state of Min 閩 on the southeast coast. Tradition has it that he spent the remaining fourteen years of his life in poverty, devoting his time to the study of Daoist alchemy.

The two historical stereotypes of Han Wo seen in biographies have greatly influenced critical perception of his poetry. He is usually cast as a lesser Du Fu 杜甫 (712–770)* or Tao Qian 陶潛 (365–427), a tragic elder statesman lamenting political disaster, or seen as a youthful romantic rake, a protégé of Li Shangyin. His extant work is now divided into two collections: the *Han Hanlin ji* 韓翰林集 (Collection of Academician Han) with 226 poems, and the *Xiang lian ji* 香奩集 (Fragrant Trousseau Collection) with 95 poems. The former collection is praised and accepted as the work of the loyal statesman; the latter is either faulted as steeped in voluptuous emotion, its diction devoted to graceful beauties, or defended as allegorical criticism, or rejected as spurious. This latter opinion, alive since Song times, has been laid to rest on internal evidence by modern scholars. While the compilation of the *Fragrant Trousseau* and its preface are probably from a later writer, most of the poems in both collections are Han Wo's.

Despite critical ambivalence, Han Wo's poetry has always attracted a small but enthusiastic audience. Han is praised for his clear style and ability to convey events and emotions convincingly. Living at the end of a literary golden age, he managed to assimilate completely a variety of influences. His work contains fewer images and allusions than that of many Tang poets. His relatively loose style, use of repetition and grammatical particles, and creative manipulation of standard tonal patterns bothers some critics and impresses others. The human emotional response to loss and change is one of his favorite themes.

Few of Han Wo's poems are well-known. His seven-syllable quatrain "Yi liang" 已涼 (Already Cool), included in the *Tangshi sanbaishou*, is probably the most renowned:

Outside the jade-green railings, embroidered curtains hang;
Her scarlet screen painted with branches of trees.
On her eight-foot dragon-beard mat, are brocaded squares of quilt:
The weather is already cool, but not yet cold.

碧闌干外繡帘垂，猩色屏風畫折枝。
八尺龍鬚方錦褥，已涼天氣未寒時。

Here as in many of Han's poems the ostensible scene is a woman's boudoir. The poem depicts that period of early autumn when the nights are already cool, the bamboo curtains used in the summer having already been replaced by heavier curtains. A screen in the painting style used to depict only the interlocking branches (not the entire tree) would also have suggested not only the transition of seasons, but the loneliness of the occupant and a sense of incompleteness. The mat made of the soft rush known as "dragon beard" is like the curtains designed for cooler nights. While the poet's familiarity with the roomscape suggests he may have been a visitor. But aside from the mild erotic tone, the poem also suggests the decline of the year and, perhaps, as some critics have argued, the decline of the Tang house itself.

Han is also known for his ability to recreate a scene in more powerful language, portraying the sounds and sights of the complete cycle of a summer storm in his "Xia ye" 夏夜 (Summer Night):

Wild wind under flashes of lightning—black clouds are born.
Splashing, splashing in tall woods—the sound of dense rain.
Night lengthens, rain stops, and the wind, too, is settled.
From broken clouds a floating moon once more slants down its light.

猛風飄電黑雲生，霎霎高林簇雨聲。
夜久雨休風又定，斷雲流月卻斜明。

BIBLIOGRAPHY

Editions:
Haishan ji 海山記. Taibei: Yiwen (photolithographic reprint), 1966.
Han Hanlin ji 韓翰林集. Wu Rulun 吳汝綸 (1840–1903), commentator. 3 *juan*. Taibei: Taiwan Xuesheng, 1967. Appended the *Xiang lian ji* 香奩集 in 3 *juan*. The most comprehensive collection of Han Wo's writings, with occasional brief annotations.
Milou ji 迷樓記. Taibei: Yiwen, four folios (photolithographic reprint), 1966.
Quan Tang shi, 10: 7851–915.
Quan Tang wen, 829.10439–42.
Tang liu mingjia ji 唐六名家集. Shanghai, 1926 facsimile of *Wumen hansong tang* 吳門寒松堂 reproduction of Jigu ge edition of Mao Jin 毛晉 (1599–1659). Contains *Han Neihan bie ji* 韓內翰別集.
Wu Tangren shi ji 五唐人詩集. Shanghai, 1926 facsimile of Mao Jin edition, as above. Contains *Xiang lian ji* 香奩集.

Annotations:
Chen Jilong 陳繼龍. *Han Wo shi zhu* 韓偓詩注. Shanghai: Xuelin, 2001.
Qi Tao 齊濤. *Han Wo shiji jianzhu* 韓偓詩集箋注. Ji'nan: Shandong Jiaoyu, 2000.

Biographical Sources:
Fu, *Tang caizi*, 4:232–47.
Xin Tang shu, 183.5387–90.

Translations:
Bynner, *Jade Mountain*, p. 18.
Demiéville, *Anthologie*, p. 344.
Minford and Lau, p. 987.
Sunflower, pp. 291–92.

Upton, Beth. "The Poetry of Han Wo." Unpublished Ph.D. dissertation, University of California, Berkeley, 1980. A study of Han's work and an in-depth translation of thirty-three poems.

Wilson, Graeme. "Letter to a Zen Master," in Minford and Lau, pp. 987–98.

Studies:

Ashidate Ichiro 芦立一郎. "Tōmatsu no enjōshi ni tsuite" 唐末の艶情詩について. *Bulletin of Graduate School of Social and Cultural Systems at Yamagata University* 1 (2005): 31–42.

Cao Lifeng 曹丽芳. "Lun Han Wo shige zai Tang Song shiqi de chuancun yu jieshou" 论韩偓诗歌在唐宋时期的传存与接受. *Nanjing Shifan Daxue Wenxueyuan xuebao* 2 (2013): 106–22.

Chen Bohai 陳伯海. "Han Wo shengping jiqi shizuo jianlun" 韓偓生平及其詩作簡論, *Zhonghua wenshi luncong* 中華文史論叢 1981.4: 125–42.

Chen Hong 陳鴻. "Han Wo shiyun yanjiu: Wudai shiyun yanjiu zhiyi" 韓偓詩韻研究–五代詩韻研究之一. *Fujian shifan Daxue xuebao* 福建師範大學學報 124 (2004.1): 127–31.

Chen Jilong 陳繼龍. *Han Wo shiji kaolue* 韓偓事跡考略. Shanghai: Shanghai Guji, 2004.

Chen Xiang 陳香. *Wan Tang shiren Han Wo* 晚唐詩人韓偓. Taibei: Guojia, 1993.

Gao Wenxian 高文顯. *Han Wo* 韓偓. Taibei: Xinwenfeng Chuban Gongsi, 1985.

Huo Songlin 霍松林, Deng Xiaojun 鄧小軍. "Han Wo nian pu (shang, zhong, xia)" 韓偓年譜（上、中、下）. *Shanxi Shifan Daxue xuebao* 陝西師範大學學報 1988.3: 95–103, 1988.4: 46–55, 1989.1: 116–24.

Jia Jinhua 賈晉華. "Han Wo he Yan Renyu" 韓偓和顏仁郁, in Jia Jinhua, *Tangdai jihui zhongji yu shirenqun yanjiu* 唐代集會總集與詩人群研究. Beijing: Beijing Daxue, 2001, pp. 544–46.

Miao Quansun 繆荃孫. *Han Hanlin shi pu lue* 韓翰林詩譜略. Beijing: Beijing Tushuguan, 1999.

Shi Zhecun 施蟄存. "Du Han Wo ci zhaji" 讀韓偓詞札記, *Zhonghua wenshi luncong* 中華文史論叢 1979.4: 273–82.

Sun Keqiang 孙克强 and Chen Lili 陈丽丽. "Han Wo shige dui citi de yingxiang" 韩偓诗歌对词体的影响. *Shantou Daxue xuebao* 2005.5: 56–60.

Wang Dajin 王達津. "'Gong liu shi' he Han Wo de sheng zu nian" 〈宮柳詩〉和韓偓的生卒年 in *Tangshi congkao* 唐詩叢考. Shanghai: Shanghai Guji, 1986, pp. 196–98.

Xu Fuguan 徐復觀. "Han Wo shi yu *Xiang lian ji* lun kao" 韓偓詩與〈香奩集〉論考 in *Zhongguo wenxue lunji* 中國文學論集. Taibei: Taiwan Xuesheng, 2001, pp. 255–96.

Yan Jianbi 閻簡弼. "*Xiang lian ji* gen Han Wo" 香奩集跟韓偓. *Yanjing xuebao* 燕京學報 38 (1950): 179–228.

Zhang Qiugui 張丘奎. *Tangmo Du Fu shige yanjiu yi Luo Yin, Wei Zhuang, Han Wo sanren wei tantao* 唐末杜甫詩歌研究以羅隱韋莊韓偓三人為探討. Taibei: Huamulan, 2020.

Zhen Jun 震鈞. *Xianglian ji fa wei* 香奩集發微. Shanghai: Saoye Shanfang, 1914.

Zhou Zuzhuan 周祖譔. "Han Wo shi de bianji, liuchuan yu banben" 韓偓詩的編集、流傳與版本. *Wenxue yichan* 文學遺產 2000.1: 74–83.

Beth Upton and William H. Nienhauser, Jr.

Han Yu 韓愈 (*zi*, Tuizhi 退之, 768–824) was a major figure in the history of Chinese literature, comparable in stature to Dante, Shakespeare, or Goethe in their respective literary traditions. He was among that small group of writers whose works not only became classics of the language–required reading for all those with claims to literacy in succeeding generations—but whose writings define and change the course of the tradition itself. Although Han Yu is best-known as a prose-stylist—the master shaper of the so-called *guwen* 古文 (ancient-style prose) style—he was a stylistic innovator in the many genres in which he wrote, including poetry. And he was a major

Han Yu

influence on the literary and intellectual life of his time, an important spokesman for a rejuvenated traditionalism that later emerged as Song Neo-Confucianism.

Han Yu was born into a family of scholars and minor officials in the area of modern Mengxian 孟縣 in Henan. He was orphaned at the age of two and raised in the family of his older brother Han Hui 韓會 (740–781), from whom he received his early education and his disdain for the current literary style descended from Six Dynasties *pianwen* 駢文 (parallel prose). The family endured southern exile in 777, and in the early 780s the provincial rebellion in the Northeast caused further dislocation. Han Yu seems to have spent these early years in the provinces studying. He came to Chang'an in 786, and after four attempts passed the *jinshi* examination in 792. He failed three times, however, to pass the Erudite Literatus examination, which would have meant an immediate appointment in the central government. In desperation, he accepted employment in 796 on the staff of Dong Jin 董晉 (724–799), the Military Commissioner at Bianzhou, and remained there until Dong's death in 799. These were important years for Han Yu's intellectual development. For in Bianzhou he formed lasting friendships with Li Ao 李翱 (774–836),* Meng Jiao 孟郊 (751–814),* Zhang Ji 張籍 (ca. 776–829),* and a number of lesser figures who formed the nucleus of "Han Yu's disciples" (*Hanmen dizi* 韓門弟子), a literary coterie that looked to Han Yu as their leader. Han was loyal to these men as his letter to Meng Jiao, written in 800 or 801 testifies:

> I have been separated from you for a long time…When I speak, who listens? When I chant a poem, who matches it?… you know if in my heart if I am happy! Your talent is lofty and your vital essence pure; you follow the ancient Way but reside in the present day; you have no fields [and you need to worry about] clothing and food, and yet you serve your mother left and right without disobeying and your concern is constant, putting yourself to labor and suffer! Your body whirled about in the turbid murk of this age, your heart alone pursues and follows the ancients. Your Way, it truly causes me sorrow!
>
> 與足下別久矣...吾言之而聽者誰歟？吾倡之而和者誰歟？...足下知吾心樂否也。足下才高氣清，行古道，處今世，無田而衣食，事親左右無違，足下之用心勤矣，足下之處身勞且苦矣。混混與世相濁，獨其心追古人而從之，足下之道，其使吾悲也。

Aside from the overt praise for Meng, Han Yu's letter alludes twice to the *Analects* of Confucius in depicting Meng's filial behavior and his diligence and closes with language resonating with the claim in "Yu fu" 漁夫 (The Fisherman) in the *Chuci* in which the narrator claims only he is pure in the turbid world.

He eventually secured his first position in the central government in 802, as Erudite of the National University, an institution with which he maintained a sporadic lifelong association, eventually becoming Chancellor of the National University in 820. In 803 he refused to join the political faction formed by Wang Shuwen 王叔文 (753–806) in support of the heir apparent, Li Song 李誦 (761–806), and was exiled to Yangshan 陽山 in the far South (modern Guangdong). When this faction, which included Liu Zongyuan 柳宗元 (773–819)* and Liu Yuxi 劉禹錫 (772–842),* was vanquished in 805, Han Yu's political fortunes also turned, and he was recalled to Chang'an. His anticipation during the trip and the joy of reunion with literary friends in the capital, where the new government of Emperor Xianzong (r. 806–820) was being formed, found expression in his works of the year 806, Han Yu's *annus mirabilis.* Two of his most important poems—the "Nanshan shi" 南山詩 (Poem on the Southern Mountains) and the "Yuanhe Shengde shi" 元和聖德詩 (Poem on the Sagacious Virtue of the Age of Primal Harmony), both extolling the virtue of the new emperor, date from this year. So probably too does the "Qiuhuai" 秋懷 (Autumn Sentiments), perhaps his most successful poems, and "Yuan dao" 原道 (On the Origin of the Way), his most famous agenda for a revived Confucianism.

The "Autumn Sentiments" are a suite of eleven poems whose interlocking allusions and themes explore eternal issues of life, time, and relevance. The second poem reads:

> White dews drop on the hundred grasses
> Brushwood and orchid fade together;
> But vibrant green under the hedgerows
> Will bloom again and cover the ground.
> Cold cicadas for an instant still,
> Crickets sing out to self-content.
> The cosmos turns in endless periods
> And the essence given everything bitterly differs;
> Yet each, attuned to time, attains its place—
> No need to treasure the evergreen.

> 白露下百草，蕭蘭共雕悴。
> 青青四牆下，已復生滿地。
> 寒蟬暫寂寞，蟋蟀鳴自恣。
> 運行無窮期，稟受氣苦異。
> 適時各得所，松柏不必貴。

But, despite such poetic expressions of acceptance, factional jealousies made life difficult and thwarted his hopes for quick success in the new government. He requested transfer to Luoyang in 807, remaining there until 811, when he again returned to Chang'an. Han Yu was an ardent royalist and supporter of the use of military power to extend central government control over the autonomous provinces of the Northeast. In this cause, he was a partisan of the great Grand Councilor Pei Du 裴度 (765–839), the architect of Emperor Xianzong's eventual suppression of the separatist forces. Han Yu took part in the campaigns against the separatists in Huaixi province in 817 and recorded the events in his famous "Ping Huaixi bei" 平淮西碑 (Inscription on the Pacification of Huaixi), a text that well demonstrates the intimate connection between his literary, philosophical, and political concerns.

In 819, perhaps lulled by the success of his patron Pei Du and misguided by excessive devotion to the emperor, he wrote the infamous "Lun Fogu biao" 論佛骨表 (Memorial on the Bone-Relic of the Buddha), in which he intimated that Xianzong's participation in the veneration of a relic of the Buddha would shorten the sovereign's life. This was a severe act of *lèse majesté*, and only the intervention of Han Yu's powerful patrons saved him from the death penalty. He was exiled to Chaozhou 潮州 on the South China coast (modern Guangdong). He was back in the capital by 820, however, where he served in a series of upper echelon posts, including that of Metropolitan Governor, until his death in 824.

Han Yu

Han Yu's "ancient-style" prose was an attempt to replace the contemporary *pianwen* with a less florid, looser style better suited to the needs of a more flexible, utilitarian prose. Han Yu's *guwen* was thus not an imitation of the ancient prose, but rather a new style based on the ancient (pre-Qin and Han) ideals of clarity, conciseness, and utility. To this end, he incorporated elements of colloquial rhythm, diction, and syntax into both prose and poetry, while at the same time reaffirming the Confucian classics as the basis of education and good writing. His most successful *guwen* compositions fuse these classical ideals with contemporary realities, and the flexibility of their style furnished an example to later generations of how to relate the classical tradition to contemporary literary needs. Han Yu is appropriately the first of the *Tang Song bada sanwen jia* 唐宋八大散文家 (Eight Great Prose Masters of the Tang and Song).

The style of Han Yu's poetry is governed by the same passion for clarity that pervades his prose. He strives always for an accuracy and clarity appropriate to the content of the poem and its social context. Some critics have labeled the intricate style of the "Southern Mountains" 'baroque.' But this intricacy is not pursued for its own sake; rather the verbal complexity reinforces the actual terrain of the mountains themselves. The style becomes an accurate and appropriate reflection of the reality. On the other hand, Han Yu's poetic corpus contains a great number of seemingly casual, conversational poems whose style seems quite close to popular speech. Some critics have postulated that these two styles present a contradiction and constitute a conflict with Han Yu himself. Yet both styles are governed by the twin principles of accuracy and appropriateness. Han Yu articulated these principles several times in his letters, stating that "the language of composition should be in accord with reality" 其文章言語，與事相侔, and that "to adhere to reality in forming expressions was precisely what the ancient authors did" 因事以陳辭，古之作者正如是爾.

Han Yu's theory and practice of literary style is an extension of his drive to rejuvenate Confucianism as a viable intellectual concern. Intellectual life during the Tang was largely dominated by the great monastic schools of Buddhist scholasticism. In the eighth century, the Chan school gained in popularity by virtue of its direct appeal to intuition and experience rather than by looking to commentary and book learning as sources of wisdom. This movement rapidly gained ground after the An Lushan Rebellion of 755, and Han Yu was exposed to its influence from an early age. Although violently opposed to monasticism and monkish exploitation of a superstitious peasantry, his drive to rejuvenate Confucianism by encouraging personal master-disciple relationships and by establishing an orthodox line of transmission for Confucian teaching owes much to contemporary Chan practice.

Politically, Han Yu favored a strong central government. This explains the special affection he maintained for Emperor Xianzong, known historically as the "restorer" of the Tang's political fortunes. Han Yu deplored the political and cultural fragmentation that had been tolerated in order to hold together the multiracial and cosmopolitan Tang state. He was not *per se* anti-Buddhist and xenophobic, but he desired a central state that vigorously promoted a cultural orthodoxy that was to be identical to his own rejuvenated Confucianism. When the emperor revealed himself to be more anxious to promote raw central power than to propagate cultural orthodoxy, Han Yu responded with the sense of outrage and betrayal that exuded from between the lines of the "Memorial on the Bone-Relic of the Buddha."

BIBLIOGRAPHY

Editions:

Fang Sunqin 方崧卿 (1135–1194). *Han ji ju zheng* 韓集舉正. Tokyo: Kyūko, 2002.

Hanabusa Hideki 花房英樹. *Kan Yu shika sakuin* 韓愈詩歌索引. Kyoto, 1964. A useful concordance to Han Yu's poetry.

Hartman, Charles. "Preliminary Bibliographical Notes on the Sung Editions of Han Yü's *Collected Works*," in *Critical Essays*, pp. 89–100. A study of the traditional editions and their relationship to each other.

Ma Qichang 馬其昶 (1855–1930), ed. *Han Changli wenji jiaozhu* 韓昌黎文集校註. Rpt. Hong Kong: Zhonghua, 1972. The basic edition of Han Yu's prose.

Qian Zhonglian 錢仲聯. *Han Changli shi xinian jishi* 韓昌黎詩繫年集釋. Shanghai: Gudian Wenxue, 1957. A chronologically-arranged modern edition of the poetry with an excellent selection of commentary.

Quan Tang shi, 5: 3763–881, 11: 8983–9003, 14: 10648.

Quan Tang wen, 547–68.6329–519.

Xin kan wu bai jia zhuyin bian Changli xiansheng wenji 新刊五百家註音辯昌黎先生文集. 40 *juan*. *Wai ji* 外集 10 *juan*. *Xu* 序, *Zhuan* 傳, *Bei* 碑, *Ji* 記 1 *juan*. *Hanwen leipu* 韓文類譜 10 *juan*. Beijing: Beijing Tushuguan, 2006.

Zhu Qichen 朱啓成. *Xin yi Changli xiansheng wenji* 新譯昌黎先生文集. Taibei: Sanmin, 1999.

Zhu Wengong jiao Changli xiansheng wenji 朱文公校昌黎先生文集. 40 *juan*. *Waiji* 外集 8 *juan*. Beijing: Beijing Tushuguan, 2006.

Zhu Xi 朱熹 (1130–1200). *Hui'an Zhu shi jiang xiansheng Han wen kao yi* 晦庵朱侍講先生韓文考異. 10 *juan*. Beijing: Beijing Tushuguan, 2006.

Annotations:

Gu Sili 顧嗣立, ed. *Changli xiansheng shiji zhu* 昌黎先生詩集註. 11 *juan* with a biography and chronicle of Han Yu. Beijing: Beijing Tushuguan, 2006.

Liu Zhenhun 劉真倫 and Yue Zhen 岳珍, comm. *Han Yu wenji hui jiao jian zhu* 韓愈文集匯校箋注. Beijing: Zhonghua, 2010.

Luo Liantian 羅聯天, comm. *Han Yu guwen jiaozhu huibian* 韓愈古文校注彙編. Taibei: Guoli Bianyiguan, 2003.

Meng Er'dong 孟二東, comm. *Han Meng shi xuan*. 韓孟詩選. Changchun: Jilin Renmin, 2003.

Qu Shouyuan 屈守元 and Chang Sichun 常思春, eds. *Han Yu quanji jiaozhu* 韓愈全集校注. Chengdu: Sichuan Daxue, 1996.

Sun Changwu 孫昌武. *Han Yu shi wen xuan ping* 韓愈詩文選評. Shanghai: Shanghai Guji, 2002.

Tong Dide 童第德. *Han Yu wenxuan* 韩愈文選. Beijing: Renmin Wenxue, Xinhua Shudian Beijing Faxing Suo Faxing, 1980.

Wen Tang 文儻, ed. *Xinkan jing jin xiangzhu Changli Xiansheng wen* 新刊經進詳註昌黎先生文. Beijing: Beijing Tushuguan, 2006.

Wu Xiaolin 吳小林. *Han Yu xuanji* 韓愈選集. Beijing: Renmin Wenxue, 2001.

Yan Qi 閻琦. *Han Changli wenji zhushi* 韓昌黎文集註釋. Xi'an: San Qin, 2004.

___. *Han Changli wenxue zhuan lun* 韓昌黎文學傳論. Xi'an: San Qin, 2003.

Zhi Shui 止水, comp. *Han Yu Shixuan* 韓愈詩選. Hong Kong, 1980.

Biographical Sources:

Fu, *Tang caizi*, 2:434–58, 242–43.

Jiu Tang shu, 160.4195–204.

Xin Tang shu, 176.5255–65.

Han Yu

Translations:
Birch, *Anthology*, vol. 1, pp. 244–57, 262–64.
Bynner, *Jade Mountain*, pp. 19–25.
Demièville, *Anthologie*, pp. 305–06.
Elling O. Eide, "Another Go at the *Mao Ying chuan*," *T'ang Studies*, 8/9 (1990–1): 107–11.
Frankel, *Palace Lady*, pp. 41–43, 47–49.
Fuller, Michael A. *An Introduction to Chinese Poetry: From the* Canon of Poetry *to the Lyrics of the Song Dynasty*. Cambridge: Harvard University Press, 2018, pp. 290–301.
Graham, *Late T'ang*, pp. 71–79.
Harada Kenyū 原田憲雄. *Kan Yu* 韓愈. Tokyo: Shūeisha, 1972. A selection of Han Yu's poetry with Japanese annotation and translation.
Hinton, *Anthology*, pp. 251–64.
Kaderas, Christoph. "Das Yuan Dao des Han Yu (768–824): Analyse und vollständige Übersetzung." *Zeitschrift der Deutschen Morgenländischen Gesellschaft* 150 (2000): 243–67.
Kawai Kōzō 川合康三 et al. *Kan Yu shi yakuchū* 韓愈詩訳注. 2v. Tokyo: Kenbun, 2015 and 2017.
Lin and Owen, *Vitality*, p. 230.
Liu, *Classical Prose*, pp. 23–98.
Mair, *Anthology* pp. 222–23, 580–88.
Margoulies, *Anthologie raisonnèe de la littérature chinoise*. Paris: Payot, 1948. Contains numerous translations of Han Yu's best known prose pieces.
McCraw, David. "Yuanhe Poetry Sequences: A New Look." *JAOS* 136 (2016): 69-97. An important new reading of Han Yu's "Qiu huai" 秋懷 (Autumn Sentiments) series.
Nienhauser, William H., Jr. "The Biography of Fur Point," in Mair, *Anthology*, pp. 747–50.
___. "The Biography of Ge Hua, Marquis of Xiapi 下邳侯革華傳," *Tang Tales: A Guided Reader, Volume 2*. Singapore: World Scientific, 2016, pp. 207–34.
Owen, Stephen, *Anthology*, 368–69, 484–89.
___, *Late Tang*, pp. 105–06.
___, *Middle Ages*, pp. 8–15 and passim. Numerous prose and poetry renditions.
___, *Omen*, pp. 51–52, 279–80.
___. *The Poetry of Meng Chiao and Han Yü*. New Haven and London: Yale University, 1975.
Shields, Anna M. *One Who Knows Me: Friendship and Literary Culture in Mid-Tang China*. Cambridge and London: Harvard University Asia Center, 2015, pp. 159–99, 310–39, and passim.
Shimizu Shigeru 清水茂, *Kan Yu* 韓愈. Tokyo, 1959. A good, selected anthology of Han Yu's poetry with Japanese annotation and translation.
___. *Tōsō hakkabun* 唐宋八家文, Tokyo, 1966. Japanese translations with annotation and discussion of Han Yu's major prose texts.
Sunflower, pp. 165–90.
Watson, *Columbia*, pp. 237–41.
Watson, *Lyricism*, pp. 179–84.
Von Zach, Erwin (1872–1942). *Han Yü Poetische Werke*. Edited by James R. Hightower. Cambridge: Harvard-Yenching, 1952. A complete translation into German of Han Yu's poetry.
Yang Xianyi, *Poetry and Prose*, pp. 63–98.

Studies:
Bol, pp. 23–27, 123–31, and 165–85.
Cai Shoufu 蔡寿福. "Han Yu, Li Zongyuan he Tangdai guwen yundong," 韓愈、柳宗元和唐代的古文运动, *Yunnan jiaoyu*, (September 1980), 26–29.

Chen Yinke. "Han Yü and the T'ang Novel," *HJAS*, 1 (1936): 39–43.

___. "Lun Han Yu" 論韓愈, *Lishi yanjiu* 2 (1954), 105–14. Still important article.

Davis, Timothy M. "Lechery, Substance Abuse, and . . . Han Yu?" *JAOS*, 135 (2015): 71–92.

DeBlasi, Anthony. *Reform in the Balance, The Defense of Literary Culture in Mid-Tang China*. Albany: SUNY, 2002, *passim*.

Fang Jie 方介. *Han Liu xin lun* 韓柳新論. Taibei: Taiwan Xuesheng, 1999.

Hartman, Charles. *Han Yü and the T'ang Search for Unity*. Princeton, 1985.

Hatamura Manabu 畑村学. "Kan Yu shikan shūnin shinkō" 韓愈史官就任新考 in *Chūgoku chūsei bungaku kenkyū: shijisshūnen kinen ronbunshū* 中國中世文學研究: 四十周年記念論文集. Tokyo: Hakuteisha, 2001.

Hightower, James R. "Han Yü as Humorist," *HJAS*, 44.1 (June 1984), 5–27.

Ji Zhenghuai 季鎮淮. "Han Yu de shilun he shizuo" 韓愈的詩論和詩作, in *Zhonghua xueshu lunwen ji* 中華學術論文集, Zhonghua, ed., Peking, 1981, pp. 437–59.

Jia Jinhua 賈晉華. "Lun Han-Meng shirenqun" 論韓孟詩人群, in Jia Jinhua, *Tangdai jihui zhongji yu shirenqun yanjiu* 唐代集會總集與詩人群研究. Beijing: Beijing Daxue, 2001, pp. 499–518.

Kawai Kōzō 川合康三. *Shūnanzan no hen'yō: Chūtō bungaku ronshū* 終南山の変容: 中唐文学論集. Tokyo: Kenbun Shuppan, 1999. Contains three articles on Han Yu's literary thought.

Kawai Kōzō 川合康三 et al. *Kan Yu shi yakuchū* 韓愈詩訳注. 2v. Tokyo: Kenbun, 2015 and 2017.

Li Jiankun 李建崑. *Han Yu shi tanxi* 韓愈詩探析. Taibei: Hua Mulan Wenhua, 2009.

___. *Han Meng shi lun cong* 韓孟詩論叢. Taibei: Xiu Wei Zixun Keji Gufen Youxian Gongsi, 2005.

Li Zhuofan 李卓藩. *Han Yu shi chutan* 韓愈詩初探. Taibei: Wenshizhe, 1999.

Liu Guoying 劉国盈. *Han Yu cong kao* 韓愈叢考. Beijing: Wenhua Yishu, 1999.

Liu Ning 劉寧. Han Yu langzhong wenfeng de xingchen yu Yuanhe shiqi de wen wu guanxi" 韓愈狠重文風的形成與元和時期的文武關系, *Wenxue yichan* 2020.1 4–15.

Liu Zhenlun 劉真倫. *Han Yu ji Song Yuan chuanben yanjiu* 韓愈集宋元傳本研究. Beijing: Zhongguo Shehui Kexue, 2004.

Luo Liantian 羅聯添. *Han Yu yanjiu* 韓愈研究. Taibei: Xuesheng, 1977. Reprints all of Luo's studies on Han Yu's biography, contains a useful collection of traditional critical opinion on the prose.

___. comm. *Han Yu guwen jiaozhu huibian* 韓愈古文校注彙編. Taibei: Guoli Bianyiguan, 2003.

Ma, Y. W. "Prose Writings of Han Yü and *Ch'uan-ch'i* Literature," *JOS* 7 (1969): 195–223. Discusses the relationship of the *guwen* style to Tang *chuanqi* fiction.

Maeno Naoaki 前野直彬. *Kan Yu no shōgai* 韓愈の生涯. Tokyo, 1976. A full-length biography of Han Yu.

Nienhauser, William H., Jr. "An Allegorical Reading of Han Yü's 'Mao-Ying Chuan' (Biography of Fur Point)," *OE*, 23.2 (December 1976), 153–74.

___. "Han Yü, Liu Tsung-yüan and the Boundaries of Literati Piety," *Journal of Chinese Religions,* 19 (1991): 75–104.

___. "The Reception of Han Yü in America, 1936–1992," *ACQ,* XXI.1 (1993): 18–48.

Owen, Stephen. *The Poetry of Han Yü and Meng Chiao*. New Haven: Yale University, 1975. Also contains numerous translations.

Pollack, David. "Han Yü and the 'Stone Cauldron Linked-verse Poem," *J. of Chinese Studies*, 1 (1984): 171–201.

___. "Linked-verse Poetry in China: A Study of Associative Linking in 'Lien-chü' Poetry with Emphasis on the Poems of Han Yü and His Circle." Unpublished Ph.D. dissertation, U. of California-Berkeley, 1976.

Pulleyblank, E. G. "Liu K'o, a Forgotten Rival of Han Yü," *AM*, 7 (1959): 145–60.

Qian Deyun 錢德運. "'Hanmen dizi' kaolun" 韓門弟子考論, *J. of Chinese Studies*, 59 (2014): 165–80.

Satō Tamotsu 佐藤保解. *Shōrei sensei shū* 昌黎先生集. Tokyo: Iwanami, 2019.

Schmidt, Jerry D. "Han Yü and His *Ku-shih* Poetry." Unpublished M.A. thesis. University of British Columbia, 1969.

Shi Chuankan 市川勘. *Han Yu yanjiu xin lun* 韓愈研究新論. Taibei: Wenjin, 2004.

Shields, Anna. "The Limits of Knowledge: Three Han Yu Letters to Friends, 799–802." *Tang Studies* 22 (2004): 41–80.

Spring, Madeline K. *Animal Allegories in T'ang China.* New Haven: American Oriental Society, 1993. *American Oriental Series*, v. 76.

___. "A Stylistic Study of Tang *Guwen*: The Rhetoric of Han Yu and Liu Zongyuan." Unpublished Ph.D. dissertation, University of Washington, 1983.

___. "Tang Landscape of Exile." *JAOS* 117 (1997): 312–23.

Sun Changwu 孫昌武. "Lun Han Yu de Ruxue yu wenxue" 論韓愈的儒學與文學, *Wenxue pinglun congkan*, 13 (May 1982): 239–62.

Sun Yujin 孫羽津. "Han Yu 'Mao Yingzhuan' xinlun" 韓愈毛穎傳新論, *Wenxue yichan* 2018.4: 75–84.

Tan, Mei Ah. "Han Yu's 'Za shuo' 雜說 (Miscellaneous Discourse): A Three-tier System of Government," *JAOS* 140 (2020): 859–74.

Tschen, Yinkoh [陳寅恪]. "Han Yü and T'ang Novel," *HJAS* 1.1 (April 1936): 39–43.

Virag, Curie K. "That Which Encompasses the Myriad Cares: Subjectivity, Knowledge, and the Ethics of Emotion in Tang and Song China." Ph. D. diss., Harvard University, 2004.

Wang Han 王涵. "Kan Yu kenkyū shinron: sono shisō to bunshō sōsaku" 韓愈研究新論: その思想と文章創作. Ph. D diss., Keio University, 2004.

Wong, Kwok-yiu. "Re-discovering Literature in Medieval China: Mid-Tang Literary Theories and Political Discourse." Ph. D. diss., University of Toronto, 2002.

Wu Wenzhi 吳文治. *Han Yu ziliao huibian* 韓愈資料彙編. Beijing: Zhonghua, 1983.

Yan Qi 閻琦. *Han Changli wenxue zhuan lun* 韓昌黎文學傳論. Xi'an: San Qin, 2003.

Yang Ziyi 楊子儀. *Han Yu cichao yu Su Shi yuhui bijiao yanjiu* 韓愈刺潮與蘇軾寓惠比較研究. Chengdu: Bashu, 2008.

Ye Baifeng 葉百豐. *Han Changli wen huiping* 韓昌黎文彙評. Taibei: Zhongzheng, 1990.

Ye Xiucheng 業修成. "Han Yu's *Huang ling miao bei* bian wu" 韓愈黃陵廟碑辨誤, *Wenxue yichan* 文學遺產, 2008.3: 30.

Yoshikawa, Kōjirō 吉川幸次郎. "Kan Yu bun" 韓愈文, in *Tōdai no shi to sambun* 唐代の詩と散文, Tokyo: Kōbundō Shobō, 1967, pp. 53–122.

Yu Shucheng 餘恕誠. "Shige: cong Han Yu dao Li Shangyin" 詩歌: 從韓愈到李商隱, *Wenxue yichan* 1999.4: 39–41.

Zeng Jincheng 曾金承. *Han Yu shige Tang Song jieshou yanjiu* 韓愈詩歌唐宋接受研究. Taibei: Hua Mulan Wenhua, 2010.

Zhang Anzu 張安祖. "Han Yu *guwen* hanyi bianxi" 韓愈"古文"含義辨析, *Wenxue yichan* 1998.6: 97–99.

Zhang Huilian 張慧蓮. *Han Yu shiguan ji qi shi* 韓愈詩觀及其詩. Taibei: Hua Mulan Wenhua, 2009.

Zhang Qinghua 張清華, et al., eds. *Han Yu yu Lingnan wenhua* 韓愈與嶺南文化. Beijing: Xueyuan, 2006.

___. *Han Yu yu Zhongyuan wenhua* 韓愈與中原文化. Beijing: Xueyuan, 2005.

___. *Han Yu da zhuan* 韓愈大傳. Zhengzhou: Zhongzhou Guji, 2003.

___. *Han Yu ping zhuan* 韓愈評傳. Nanjing: Nanjing Daxue, 1998.

___. *Han xue yanjiu* 韓學研究. Nanjing: Jiangsu Jiaoyu, 1998.

Zhang Renfu 張仁福. *Zhongguo nanbei wenhua de fancha: Han Yu he Ouyang Xiu de wenhua toushi* 中國南北文化的反差: 韓愈和歐陽修的文化透視. Beijing: Zhongguo Shehui Kexue, 2009.

Zhou Kangxie 周康燮, comp. *Han Yu yanjiu lun cong* 韓愈研究論叢. Hong Kong, 1978. An extremely useful collection of major twentieth-century scholarship on Han Yu along with a reprinting of the traditional *nianpu*. An essential book.

Charles Hartman

Hanshan

Hanshan 寒山 (Cold Mountain) has traditionally been considered the name of a poet. Yet there is no reliable material proving the existence of a person with this name. Moreover, the stylistic differences of the poetical works associated with this name are considerable and suggest that they were created by more than one hand. The most that can be claimed for the more than three hundred poems handed down under Hanshan's name is that they were written during the Tang dynasty (618–907). It is possible that there was a poet Hanshan who wrote poems that were combined by a later editor with imitators of his work. E. G. Pulleyblank (1978) has used linguistic evidence to show that the poems date from two periods: the early Tang and towards the end of the dynasty. The collection was ostensibly put together by a certain Lüqiu Yin 閭丘胤, purportedly a high official who became acquainted with Hanshan while serving as prefect of Taizhou 台州 (modern Taizhou in Zhejiang), which in anecdotal literature was Hanshan's home. The preface Lüqiu wrote has become the main source of biographical information on Hanshan. Although the preface seems to date from the late Tang, the style suggests that it could not have been written by someone with the literary knowledge demanded of a Tang official. Scholars have argued that Daoqiao 道翹, an undistinguished local monk in Taizhou, who is said in the Lüqiu preface to have compiled the poems, may well be the author of many of them. Another candidate is the Buddhist monk Zhi Yan 智巖. Nevertheless, during the Tang legendary narratives of Hanshan evolved, perhaps the best known is that recorded by Du Guangting 杜光庭 (850–933)* in his *Xianzhuan shiyi* 仙傳拾遺 (Collected Fragments of the Biographies of Immortals; as recorded in *Taiping guangji*, *juan* 55):

> This Master of Cold Mountain, no one knows his name. During the Dali era (766–779), he lived in reclusion on the Cuiping Shan 翠屏山 (Mount Green Screen) in Tiantai 天臺 County (modern Taizhou in Zhejiang). This mountain ran so deep and high that in summer there was snow. It was also called Hanyan 寒岩 (Cold Crag or Cold Cliff). Accordingly he gave himself the sobriquet Master of Cold Mountain. He was fond of writing poetry and whenever he could come up with a verse or a line, he would immediately write it on a rock amidst the trees. Those men who were fond of such unusual things, would immediately record them, in all more than three hundred poems. Most of them depicted the feelings of living in seclusion, or criticized the political situation of the times, enabling him to awaken the common people.

寒山子者，不知其名氏。大曆中，隱居天臺翠屏山。其山深邃，當暑有雪，亦名寒岩，因自號寒山子。好為詩，每得一篇一句，輒題於樹間石上。有好事者，隨而錄之，凡三百余首，多述山林幽隱之興，或譏諷時態，能警勵流俗。

Regardless of their origins, the poems, of varied metrical patterns and prosody, differ from most Tang verse in their lively use of colloquial-influenced language and their wit. As befitting their likely disparate origins, they deal with quite different topics. Many can be understood as containing a basic tension between ideas and reality or between asceticism and secularization; they often reflect a view of life as an unchangeable decline and depict the endless human sorrow at the transience of existence. This gives rise to two conflicting responses: on the one hand there is the traditional tendency toward *carpe diem* and the desire for longevity; on the other, an attempt to solve this contradiction by self-negation and retreat into the mountains, where enlightenment in the *Dao* and in Chan (Zen) meditation can be sought. Nature plays here a double role: it appears

Hanshan

as evil and dangerous—the mountains are unreachable—then becomes the ideal place for insights into Zen. Finally, in a new state of mind, *becoming* Zen. The view of nature as dangerous still implies a consciousness of the body that can be traced back to the hermit poetry (*zhaoyin shi* 招隱詩) of the third and fourth century. But when enlightenment makes nature a home for the Chan Buddhist, the landscape takes on a religious aspect that can be traced to Six Dynasties predecessors.

The Chan Buddhist impact on the Hanshan corpus is apparent in both its form and content. Poetry becomes a medium for propagating Chan and for attacking wrong attitudes towards life and learning. It often makes use of the spirit and technique of Buddhist didactic verse (*ji* 偈). Its admonitions are not meant only for the gentry and fellow Buddhists, but also for the common people. Thus, perhaps for the first time, poetry was directed towards educating the uneducated and the poor. Things represented in colloquial and vulgar language are themselves–they do not necessarily have metaphoric or symbolic values. In this respect the outer world became the passage of the poet's consciousness into Chan. At the same time, a new lyrical expression made its appearance in Chinese literature: simplicity and the advocacy of it brought the plain things of life into the foreground as the ultimate goals of existence. The following poems may illustrate such attitudes as well as the breadth in the poems now attributed to Hanshan:

> I've heard of Emperor Wu of the Han,
> as well as the First Emperor of Qin;
> Both were fond of techniques of immortality,
> in extending life, they didn't last long after all.
> The Golden Tower of the first already crumbled,
> the other finally met his end at Sandy Mound.
> On Mouling and Liyue [the mausoleums of these emperors]
> the grasses spread far and wide today.

Here the two most powerful classical rulers are recalled along with a debunking of their belief in finding a way to live forever.

> 常聞漢武帝，爰及秦始皇。
> 俱好神仙術，延年竟不長。
> 金臺既摧折，沙丘遂滅亡。
> 茂陵與驪岳，今日草茫茫。

> Human life in this cloud of dust–
> Just like a bug in a bowl.
> Till day's end we go round and round,
> Never leaving our bowl.
> Immortality we cannot reach,
> Worries we count without end.
> Months and years are like flowing water,
> And in a moment we've become old men.

人生在塵蒙，恰似盆中蟲。
終日行繞繞，不離其盆中。
神仙不可得，煩惱計無窮。
歲月如流水，須臾作老翁。

This little poem turns on "round and round" (*raorao* 繞繞), which also suggests entanglement; but here probably just referring to the repetitive, useless activity of daily life. It is a trope that Hanshan returns to several times in his poems.

> In Luoyang there are lots of young girls,
> on spring days flaunting their gorgeous beauty.
> Together they break off roadside blossoms,
> each placing some in their lofty chignons.
> Their lofty chignons bound with blossoms,
> men look and watch them out of the corners of their eyes.
> "Don't seek any tender love from us–
> we're about to return to see our husbands."

洛陽多女兒，春日逞華麗。
共折路邊花，各持插高髻。
髻高花匝匝，人見皆睥睨。
別求醉醉憐，將歸見夫婿。

There are a small group of poems in the Hanshan corpus that deal with beautiful women and their appeal to men. Here the expression *pini* 睥睨 in line seven may mean "to look with askance at" someone, here it seems to mean "to look at out of the corner of one's eyes." The role of beautiful women to distract men from the proper path is a well-known trope in Buddhism, but here the poem, thought charming, seems out of sync with the rest of the Hanshan poems.

> My mind resembles the full autumn moon,
> Or a jade-green lake, clear, bright and pure.
> There is nothing that bears comparison—
> Tell me, how can I explain it?

吾心似秋月，碧潭清皎潔。
無物堪比倫，教我如何說。

The poem may be comparing the poet's to both the moon and the lake. However, the second line may also be understood as "in" or "on the jade-green lake" suggesting that the image of the moon here is that which appears reflected on the water. If this reading is correct, and the moon is only a reflection, then the it suggests that the nature of the mind, too, is illusory and empty, thus inexplicable.

BIBLIOGRAPHY

Editions:
Chen Yaodong 陳耀東. *Hanshan shi ji banben yanjiu* 寒山詩集版本研究. Beijing: Shijie Zhishi, 2007.
Hanshan shi ji 寒山詩集. Beijing: Xianzhuang, 2001.
Hanshanzi shiji 寒山子詩集. *SBCK*.
Hanshanzi zhuanji ziliao 寒山子傳記資料. Taibei: Tianyi, 1982.
Quan Tang shi, 12: 9160–87, 14: 11105.
Ye Zhuhong 葉珠紅. *Hanshan shi ji jiao kao* 寒山詩集校考. Taibei: Wenshizhe, 2005.

Annotations:
Guo Peng 郭鵬. *Hanshan shi zhushi* 寒山詩註釋. Changchun: Changchun, 1995.
Hanshan shi pinggu 寒山詩評估. Taibei: Tianyi, 1982.
Hanshan shi zhu 寒山詩注. Beijing: Zhonghua, 2000.
Hanshanzi shi: fu Shide shi 寒山子詩: 附拾得詩. Taibei: Taiwan Shangwu, 1967.
Li Yi 李誼. *Chanjia Hanshan shi zhu* 禪家寒山詩注. Taibei: Zhengzhong, 1992.
Qian Xuelie 錢學烈. *Hanshan shide shi jiaoping* 寒山拾得詩校評. Tianjin: Tianjin Guji, 1998.
___. *Hanshan shi jiaozhu* 寒山詩校注. Guangdong: Guangdong Gaodeng Jiaoyu, 1991.
Shi Yuanpeng 史原朋. *Hanshan shide shi shangxi* 寒山拾得詩賞析. Beijing: Zhongguo Shehui Kexue, 2004.
Xiang Chu 項楚. *Hanshan shi zhu, fu Shide shi zhu* 寒山詩注, 附拾得詩注. Beijing: Zhonghua, 2000.
Xu Guangda 徐光大. *Hanshanzi shi jiaozhu: fu shide shi* 寒山子詩校注: 附拾得詩. Xi'an: Shanxi Renmin, 1991.

Biographical Sources:
Zan Ning, 19.484–85.

Translations:
Birch, *Anthology*, pp. 194–202.
Carré, Patrick. *Le mangeur de brumes, l'oeuvre de Han-shan, poète et vagabond*. Paris: Phébus, 1985.
Collet, Hervé and Cheng Wing-fan. *Han Shan: 108 poèmes*. Millemont: Moundarren, 1985.
Egan, *Clouds*, pp. 3, 39–40, 45–47, 61–64.
Henricks, Robert G. *The Poetry of Hanshan: A Complete, Annotated Translation of Cold Mountain*. Albany: State University of New York, 1990. See also Stephen R. Bokenkamp's review in *CLEAR* 3 (1991): 619–24 and the review by Victor H. Mair (below under Studies).
Kahn, Paul. *Han Shan in English*. Buffalo, New York: White Pine, 1989.
Kusumoto Bunyū 久須本文雄. *Zayūban, Kanzan, Jittoku* 座右版, 寒山, 拾得. Tokyo: Kabushiki Kaisha, 1995.
Mair, "Tang Poems," p. 340.
Minford and Lau, pp. 975 and 979–83.
New Directions, pp. 53–57.
Owen, Anthology, pp. 404–06, 620.
Pimpaneau, Jacques. *Li Clodo du Dharma, 25 poems de Han Shan, calligraphies de Li Kwokwing*. Paris: Centre de publication Asie orientale, 1975.
Red Pine. *The Collected Songs of Cold Mountain*. Post Townsend, Washington: Copper Canyon, 1983.
Rouzer, Paul. *On Cold Mountain: A Buddhist Reading of the Hanshan Poems*. Seattle: University of Washington, 2015.
___. *The Poetry of Hanshan (Cold Mountain), Shide, and Fenggan*. Boston/Berlin: Walter de Gruyter, 2017.
Schumacher, Stephan. *Hanshan. 150 Gedichtevom Kalten Berg*. Düsseldorf and Köln: Diedrichs, 1974.

Snyder, Gary. "Cold Mountain Poems," *Evergreen Review*, 2.6 (Autumn 1958), 69–80; reprinted in *Riprap & Cold Mountain Poems*, San Francisco, 1965.

Tobias, Arthur. "Han Shan," in Seaton, Jerome P. and Denni Maloney, eds. *A Drifting Boat: An Anthology of Chinese Zen Poetry*. Fredonia, NY: White Pine Press, 1994, pp. 29–35.

Waley, Arthur. "Twenty-seven Poems by Hanshan," *Encounter*, 3.3 (1954): 3–8.

Watson, Burton. *Cold Mountain. 100 Poems by the Tang Poet Han Shan*. New York: Grove, 1962. See also David Hawkes' review, *JAOS* 82.4 (Dec. 1962): 596–99.

Studies:

Chen Huijian 陳慧劍. *Hanshanzi yanjiu* 寒山子研究. Taibei: Xingwen, 1974.

Cheng Zhaoxiong 程兆熊. *Hanshanzi yu hanshanshi* 寒山子與寒山詩. Taibei: Dalin, 1974.

Chung Ling. "The Reception of Cold Mountain's Poetry in the Far East and the United States," in *China and the West: Comparative Literature Studies*. William Tay, Ying-hsiung Chou and He-hsiang Yuan, eds. Hong Kong: The Chinese University, 1980, pp. 85–96.

Cui Xiaojing 崔小敬. *Hanshan: yizhong wenhua xianxiang de tanxun* 寒山：一種文化現象的探尋. Beijing: Zhongguo Shehui Kexue, 2010.

Halperin, Mark Robert. "Pieties and Responsibilities: Buddhism and the Chinese Literati, 780–1280." Ph. D. dissertation, University of California, Berkeley, 1997.

Hanshanzi ji hehe wenhua guoji yantaohui lunwen ji 寒山子暨和合文化國際研討會論文集. Hangzhou: Zhejiangdaxue, 2009.

He Shanmeng 何善蒙. *Yinyin shiren: Hanshan zhuan* 隱逸詩人：寒山傳. Hangzhou: Zhejiang Renmin, 2006.

Hobson, Peter. *Poems of Hanshan*. New York and Oxford: Rowman & Littlefield, 2003.

___. "The Far Journey': An Archaic Chinese Poem," *Studies in Comparative Religion* 15.1/2 (Spring 1983): 42–53.

___. "Introduction" in Ben Penny. *Writing Sacred Lives*. Richmond, Surrey: Curzon, forthcoming.

Hu Anjiang 胡安江. *Hanshan shi: wenben lüxing yu jingdian jiangou* 寒山詩：文本旅行與經典建構. Beijing: Qinghua Daxue, 2011.

Huang Boren 黃博仁. *Hanshan ji qi shi* 寒山及其詩. Taibei: Xinwenfeng, 1980.

___. *Hanshanzi yu Hanshan shi zhi yanjiu* 寒山子與寒山詩之研究. Xinzhu: Shanyan Wenzhai She, 1985.

Iriya Yoshitaka 入矢義高 (1910–1998). *Kanzan* 寒山. Tokyo: Iwanami, 1958. *Chūgoku shijin senki* 中国詩人選集 5.

Iritani Sensuke 入谷仙介 and Matusmara Takashi 松村昂. *Kanzan shi* 寒山詩. *Zen no goroku* 禅の語錄, 13. Tokyo: Chikuma, 1970.

Johnston, Reginal. "Han-shan (Kanzan) and Shih-te (Jittoku) in Chinese and Japanese Literature and Art," *Transactions and Proceedings of the Japan Society*, 34 (1936–37): 133–37.

Li Yi 李誼. *Chanjia Hanshan shi zhu: fu Shide shi* 禅家寒山詩注：附拾得詩. Taibei: Zhengzhong, 1992.

Li Zhongmei 李鐘美. *Hanshan shi banben xitong yuanliu kao* 寒山詩版本系統源流考. Ph. D. Dissertation, Zhejiang Daxue, 2004.

Lu Yongfeng 陸永峰. "Wang Fanzhi shi, Hanshan shi bijiao yanjiu" 王梵志詩, 寒山詩比較研究, *Sichuan Daxu xuebao (Zhexue shehui kexue)*, 1999.1: 110–13.

Mair, Victor H.. "Script and Word in Medieval Vernacular Sinitic," *JAOS* 112.2 (1992): 269–72.

Nishitani Keiji 西谷啓治 (1900–1990). "Kanzan shi" in *Zenke goroku*. Nishitani Keiji and Yanagida Seizan 柳田聖山 (1922–2006). Tokyo: Chikuma, 1974, pp. 5–112.

Pulleyblank, E. G. "Linguistic Evidence for the Date of Han-shan," in *Studies in Chinese Poetry and Poetics*, Ronald Miao, ed., San Francisco: Chinese Materials Center, 1978, pp. 763–95.

Shen Meiyu 沈美玉. "Hanshan shi yanjiu 寒山詩研究." M.A. Thesis, Zhongguo Wenhua Xueyuan, 1977.

Stalberg, Roberta. "The Poems of the Han-shan Collection." Unpublished Ph.D. dissertation, Ohio State University, 1977.
Wan Quan 萬泉. *Shishifenyun du Hanshan* 世事紛紜讀寒山. Guangzhou: Jinan Daxue, 2012.
Watson, Burton. "Buddhist Poet-Priests of the T'ang," *The Eastern Buddhist* (New Series) 25-2 (1992): 30–58.
Wu Chi-yu 吳其昱. "A Study of Han Shan," *TP*, 45 (1957), 392–450.
Xue Jiazhu 薛家柱. *Hanshan dashi* 寒山大師. Nanjing: Fenghuang, 2011.
Yamaguchi Harumichi 山口晴海地. "*Kanzanshi kō*" 寒山詩考, *Indogaku Bukkyō kenkyū* 18.2 (1970): 784–86.
Ye Zhuhong 葉珠紅. *Hanshan ziliao kao bian* 寒山資料考辯. Taibei: Xiuwei Zixun Keji, 2005.
___. *Hanshan shi ji luncong* 寒山詩集論叢. Taibei: Xiuwei Zixun Keji, 2006.
Youguan Hanshan yanjiu lunzhu ji guancang 有關寒山研究論著及館藏. Taibei: Tianyi, 1982.
Yoshida Toyoko. "Chinese Aloneness and Japanese Loneliness: The Poetry of Han Shan and Saigyō," *Transactions of the Asiatic Society of Japan*. 1981: 57–75.
Zhang Shi 張石. *Hanshan yu Riben wenhua* 寒山與日本文化. Shanghai: Shanghai Jiaotong Daxue, 2011.
Zhao Zifan 趙滋蕃. *Hanshan de shidai jingshen* 寒山的時代精神. Taibei: Zheyidai, 1970.
Zheng Wenquan 鄭文全. "Hanshan shi zai guowai de chuanbo yu jieshou" 寒山詩在國外的傳播與接收. Ph.D. Dissertation, Beijing Shifan Daxue, 2012.
Zhou Qi 周琦. *Hanshan shi yu shi* 寒山詩與史. Hefei: Huangshan, 1994.
Zhuo Anqi 卓安琪. *Hanshanzi qi ren ji qi shi zhi jianzhu yu jiaoding* 寒山子其人及其詩之箋註與校訂. Taibei: Tianyi, 1971.

Wolfgang Kubin and William H. Nienhauser, Jr.

He Zhizhang 賀知章 (*zi*, Jizhen 季真, *hao*, Shichuang 石窗, 659–744), will always be remembered as the first of the notorious "Eight Immortals of the Wine Cup" (Yinzhong Baxian 飲中八仙) eulogized by Du Fu 杜甫 (712–770)* in a poem of the same name. As Du Fu's now famous appellation suggests, He Zhizhang is primarily remembered as an eccentric figure. While such caricatures have only served to heighten his status as renowned poet and celebrated calligrapher, they have to an extent suppressed attention to his lengthy career as an influential statesman and dedicated academic.

Born in Yongxing 永興 county, in Yuezhou 越州 (modern Xiaoshan 蕭山 district in Hangzhou), charitable, intelligent, fond of conversation and laughter, the young He Zhizhang is said to have won a reputation for his literary talents from the very beginning. He spent his boyhood in the shadows of Mount Kuaiji 會稽, and it is easy to imagine that as a young scholar-in-training, he harbored dreams of equaling the great poets and calligraphers who tread the same paths centuries before him. His family appears to have been reasonably well-off but not particularly well-connected, and history remembers only a distant cousin of three generations prior who served the then heir apparent. Even so, He passed the prestigious *jinshi* examination with distinction in 694 and embarked on a career in the civil service. He would never wield any significant political influence, but his presence in the capital was felt, and he would eventually come to be associated with three other literati from the lower reaches of the Yangzi, Zhang Xu 張旭 (ca. 675–ca. 750), Zhang Ruoxu 張若虛 (ca. 660–ca. 720),* and Bao Rong 包融 (695–764), who were collectively known as the "Wuzhong sishi" 吳中四士 (The Four Scholars from Wu). His first appointment was to the position of Academician in the School of Four Gates of the Directorate of Education, and soon after he was promoted to Erudite in the Court of Imperial Sacrifice, a role which saw him consulted by Emperor Xuanzong (685–762, r. 712–756) on the solemn *feng* 封 and *shan* 禪 sacrifices in honor of Mount Tai 泰山, the empire's Eastern Marchmount. When the emperor finally undertook the journey to perform these rarely witnessed rites, He Zhizhang was in tow, providing lyrics for the musical accompaniments to the Shan sacrifices at Mount Dushou 杜首. During his time in the imperial capital Chang'an, He would also compose a number of panegyrics at imperial command, matching the sovereign's verse with lines of his own. Three such poems have been preserved. Despite the weight of such occasions, He's poetic replies to Xuanzong manage to conform to the technical precision expected of court poets while revealing a singular flair.

As He approached old age, he was ordered in 723 by the Grand Councilor Zhang Yue 張說 (667–731)* to take part in a number of editorial projects at the Imperial Archives, including the assembly of a conspectus of administrative law which would come to be known as the *Tang liudian* 唐六典 (Compendium of the Six Tang Government Branches). However, he would not remain at this post long enough to see the project through to its completion. Three years later, then in his mid-sixties, He Zhizhang received the title of Academician in the Academy of Scholarly Worthies, was made Advisor to the Heir Apparent, and appointed Vice-minister of the Ministry of Rites. It was in this, his penultimate official position, that his career and his life were momentarily jeopardized when He apparently botched the funeral services of the posthumously titled Heir Apparent Huiwen 惠文 (Li Fan 李範, d. 726), whose untimely death had grieved the emperor deeply. Nevertheless, He managed to escape official reprimand, and was instead transferred to the position of Director of the Palace Library and appointed Advisor to the new Heir Apparent, Li Heng 李亨 (711–762), the future emperor Suzong (r. 756–762).

Despite the many civic and scholarly achievements of a career that spanned some five decades, He Zhizhang the man is instead remembered for a series of anecdotes and appellations which fit the all too familiar archetype of the "bizarre genius." Held in awe by their contemporaries for supramundane peculiarities of character and "unlearnable" abilities, such men are often presented to posterity as the untamed artist or mad poet, and in this respect He's legacy is reminiscent of that other figure whose "bizarreness" he himself influenced. Tradition has that upon meeting the poet Li Bo 李白 (701–762)* in the capital, He Zhizhang read Li's famous "Shudao nan" 蜀道難 (The Road to Shu is Hard) and immediately christened his junior the "Zhexian" 謫仙 (Banished Transcendent), setting in motion a powerful leitmotif that would come to dominate Li's considerable legacy. Ironically, the same fate awaited He himself, as official history portrays him as a man partial to acting upon strange dreams and visions, fond of issuing abnormal commands, and according to the *Jiu Tangshu*, suffering from mental illness. This was no doubt helped along by He's own self-styled pseudonym "Siming Kuangke" 四明狂客 (The Mad Sojourner from Siming), and his later appearance as a stock character in a number of Daoist texts and anecdotes, some of which assert that he achieved immortal transcendence through the practice of Daoist alchemy.

One of He Zhizhang's enduring contributions to *belles lettres* was his skill for putting pen to paper, and his name still finds a place in the pantheon of China's most celebrated calligraphers. Among the surviving examples of his penmanship, his steady and yet ethereal *caoshu* 草書 (grass script) rendering of the *Xiaojing* 孝經 (Classic of Filial Piety) is most admired. Tragically only nineteen of He Zhizhang's poems, a pithy few of what must have been a corpus numbering in the hundreds, have come down to us today. Standing in opposition to the persona crafted by official history, what remains of He's literary corpus presents readers with a starkly different figure given to pensive contemplation, and prone to severe melancholy as expressed in "Yong liu" 詠柳 (Of the Willow I Sing):

> A beauty dressed in jasper jade, one tree tall:
> myriad tendrils weeping down in green, silken cords.
>
> Not known, of these thin leaves, who has cut them out–
> the second month's spring winds like scissors.
>
> 碧玉妝成一樹高，萬條垂下綠絲條。
> 不知細葉誰裁出，二月春風似剪刀。

The poem opens with a comparison of the willow to a graceful girl (*biyu* 碧玉), then transitions to describe the tender leaves of the willow seemingly formed by the warm spring winds. Commentators have suggested that He was metaphorically lamenting his own fate having been slandered by unknown parties. This reading gains support from a line in the second of He's poems titled "Hui xiang ou shu" 回鄉偶書 (Lines on Returning Home): "Recently in affairs of men I've been half worn down" 近來人事半消磨.

By the 740's He Zhizhang's many years began to weigh heavily upon him, and it has been suggested that illness had compromised his ability to carry out his official duties. He petitioned the throne to be ordained as a *Daoshi* 道士 (Daoist Priest) and begged leave to retire from public life. How familiar He was with Daoist liturgy, and how seriously he practiced it, remain a mystery forever shrouded by the eclectic legacy crafted around him. His request was nonetheless granted. The old scholar was bestowed with a poem from the emperor's own hand as a parting gift, and a farewell banquet was held in his honor with the heir apparent presiding. Not long thereafter, he set out on the long journey back to the Yangzi River Delta. The year was 744, and He Zhizhang would not live to see the next. However, the aged poet still had one final masterpiece left in him. In China's long history of homecomings, He Zhizhang's bittersweet return to the land of his youth has become one of the most famous thanks to a pair of quatrains titled "Huixiang oushu" 回鄉偶書 (Lines on Returning Home). Here the first of the pair which reads:

> When young I left home, having grown old I've returned;
> My village dialect unchanged, yet the hair on my temples has thinned,
> The children I come upon, they know naught of me,
> laughing they ask, "Stranger, where are you from?"
>
> 少小離家老大回，鄉音無改鬢毛衰，
> 兒童相見不相識，笑問客從何處來。

BIBLIOGRAPHY

Editions:
Feng Zhenqun 馮貞群, Zhang Shouyong 張壽鏞, eds. *He Mijian ji* 賀祕監集. Shanghai: Shanghai Shudian, 1994. Most useful modern edition.
___. *He Mijian yishu* 賀祕監遺書. Taibei: Xinwenfeng, 1985.
Quan Tang shi, 2: 1145–49, 13: 9919, 14: 11069.
Quan Tang wen, 300.3393–99.

Annotations:
Wang Ruoxing 王興, Zhang Hong 張虹, eds. *He Zhizhang, Bao Rong, Zhang Xu, Zhang Ruoxu shizhu* 賀知章, 包融, 張旭, 張若虛詩注. Shanghai: Shanghai Guji, 1986. An annotated collection of the poetry written by the "Four Scholars from Central Wu," it is appended by a useful assemblage of materials concerning each figure ranging from poems and essays to scholarly biographies and popular anecdotes.

Biographical Sources:
Fu, *Tang caizi*, 1:451–60, 5:85–87.
Jiu Tang shu, 190B.5033–35.
Xin Tang shu, 196.5606–07.

Translations:
Barnstone, *Chinese Poetry*, p. 94.
Bynner, *Jade Mountain*, p. 26.
Demiéville, *Anthologie*, p. 230.
Mair, *Anthology*, p. 191.
Margoulies, *Anthologie*, pp. 230, 372.
Miao, "T'ang Quatrains," pp. 70–74.
Minford and Lau, p. 823.
New Directions, p. 60.
Owen, *Early T'ang*, p. 368.

Studies:
Cao Xu 曹旭. *Li Bo yu He Zhizhang* 李白與賀知章. *Shanghai Shifan Xueyuan xuebao* 1 (1981): 152–53.
Chen Shangjun 陳尚君. "He Zhizhang de wenxue shijie" 賀知章的文學世界. *Hangzhou Shifan Daxue xuebao* 3 (2012): 23–29.
Feng Menglong 馮夢龍 (1574–1645), ed and comp. "Lai Bai the Banished Immortal Writes of Drunkenness to Impress the Barbarians," in *Stories to Caution the World, Volume 2*. Yang Shuhui, Yang Yunqin, trans. Seattle: University of Washington, 2005. pp. 124–41. A translation of one of the more famous accounts of He's relationship with Li Bo from Feng's famous 1620 collection, *Yushi mingyan* 喻世明言.
He Shengdai 賀聖逮. "Yuhan yunhai, ciyin *jinshi*: He Zhizhang de daojiao shengya yu wenyi chuangzuo" 興涵雲海, 詞韻金石: 賀知章的道教生涯與文藝創作. *Shanghai Daojiao* 1 (1993): 17–19.
Kirkland, Russell. "From Imperial Tutor to Taoist Priest: Ho Chih-chang at the T'ang Court." *Journal of Asian History* 23.2 (1989): 101–33.
___. "The Making of an Immortal: The Exaltation of Ho Chih-chang." *Numen* 38.2 (1992): 214–30.
___. "Three Entries for a T'ang Biographical Dictionary: Wang Hsi-i, Huang Lingwei, Ho Chih-chang." *T'ang Studies* 10–11 (1993): 160–65.

He Zhizhang

Lin Maoyi 林懋義. "Cong Tang shi kan He Zhizhang de shufa" 從唐詩看賀知章的書法. *Shufa* 3 (1986): 18.

Ma Junqing 馬俊青. "He Zhizhang ji qi Caoshu xiaojing" 賀知章及其草書孝經 *Zhongguo shufa* 4 (2012): 45–51.

Wen Xingshan 聞性善 et al. *Tang He Jian jilüe* 唐賀監紀畧. Tainan: Zhuangyan Wenhua Shiye Youxian Gongsi, 1996.

Thomas Donnelly Noel

Huangfu Ran 皇甫冉 (*zi*, Maozheng 茂政, ca. 714–ca. 767), immortalized as one of the *Dali shi caizi* 大歷十才子 or "Ten Talents of the Dali Reign," occupies a curious place in the history of Tang literature. A talented lyricist and aspiring civil servant, his poetry and its reception remain largely obscure to modern audiences. For much of his life he was witness to the halcyon reign of Xuanzong, a compeer to dynasty's greatest poets, and a confidant to prominent members of the body politic. Yet Huangfu Ran remains an outsider, a latecomer, and a man largely out of time and place both then and now.

A scion of an influential house that had served on China's northwestern periphery for centuries as generals, physicians, and scholars, his family hailed from the region Anding 安定, a county straddling the northern Silk Road near the eastern terminus of the famed Hexi Corridor. While they remained proud of their frontier origins, the Huangfu Clan eventually scattered during the fifth and sixth centuries as they sought positions throughout the reunified empire's growing bureaucracy. Huangfu Ran was raised in Danyang 丹陽 on the southern banks of the Yangtze, in the former homeland to emperors when China was ruled from Jiankang 建康 (modern Nanjing). The official histories suggest that Huangfu Ran enjoyed the benefits of a classical education, as both he and his younger brother Huangfu Zeng 皇甫曾 (d. ca. 785) were recognized for their skill in poetic composition from an early age. Huangfu Ran soon gained attention from those in power, and no less than the then Grand Councilor Zhang Jiuling (678–740)* himself marveled at the young Huangfu Ran's literary talents. His youthful promise was however slow to bear fruit and little more is remembered of Huangfu Ran's childhood, much less the first two decades of his majority. Huangfu Ran would not enjoy any success in public life during his early years. After many failures he was ultimately successful in the prestigious *jinshi* examination, ranking highly among his peers, though the honor had not come until 756 when he already passed his fortieth year. His career, moreover, began in disappointment with punitive demotion in the southeast. His frustration continued in appointments to minor positions in the clerical retinues of the more powerful men of his generation, often as an aide to military governors. Near the end of his life Huangfu Ran rose as high as the imperial palace, first in the position of Reminder of the Left and later in a similar role as Right Rectifier of Omissions.

What survives in present from the hand of Huangfu Ran the poet are some two hundred thirty poems, a comparably small corpus that has largely thwarted attempts at thematic or historiographic classification. Though his life is roughly contemporary with those of Du Fu 杜甫 (712–770)* or Cen Shen 岑參 (715–770),* Huangfu Ran has occasionally been described as a Mid-Tang poet, a possible consequence of his highly eclectic corpus and equally abundant intellectual interests. There little agreement in appraisals of his poetry beyond widespread recognition of his mastery of regulated pentasyllabic verse, a form which accounts for more than a third of his surviving works. When his works are anthologized in the premodern and contemporary collections, critics have tended to reinforce his status as an outcast in favoring verse devoted to description of natural scenery and the ephemeral wanderings of literati moving between official appointments. One of his more frequently celebrated heptasyllabic octaves, "Chun si" 春思 (Longings in Springtime), was chosen for inclusion in the *Three Hundred Tang Poems* anthology.

> Orioles twitter and swallows chatter, announcing a New Year;
> To Mayi and Longdui the road is thousands of leagues.
> My home is below the capital's walls, by the Han Gardens,
> my heart follows bright moon, reaching the Tartary Skies.
> On a loom brocaded words discourse on everlasting regret,
> by my chamber, flowering sprigs laugh at my sleeping alone.
> I ask after Marshal Dou, General of Chariot and Horse,
> when will those banners return for the carving at Yanran?

> 鶯啼燕語報新年, 馬邑龍堆路幾千.
> 家住層城臨漢苑, 心隨明月到胡天.
> 機中錦字論長恨, 樓上花枝笑獨眠.
> 為問元戎竇車騎, 何時返旆勒燕然.

The persona here, as in many "Longings in Springtime" poems is a wife whose husband is serving at the frontier in the Northwest. The poem opens with sounds that suggest the pairing of bird at the New Year when families usually gathered together. Line 2 depicts Mayi (Horsetown) and Longdui (Dragon Hill) located in the western part of modern Shaanxi and Xinjiang respectively, where the husband may be serving. The second couplet reveals the wife to be living near the palace (Han Gardens) in the capital, Chang'an. The moon that can be viewed by both husband and wife serves to send along her love. The loom in line 5 alludes to the story of Su Hui 蘇蕙 (late fourth century) whose husband was banished to Longsha 龍沙 in the Northwest. Pining for him she wove a palindrome into a piece of silk and sent it to him. *Xiao* 笑, "to laugh at," in line 6 has a double meaning since it was also a metaphoric expression for "bloom" in Tang verse. Marshal Dou Xian 竇憲 (d. 92) defeated the Xiongnu in 89 and then returned to Mount Yanran where he had an inscription carved in rock to commemorate the event. Despite Huangfu Ran's erudite allusions, the poem still allows the emotion of his persona to come through.

By the late 760s, a more prestigious promotion in the capital seemed likely for Huangfu Ran. The emperor had however assented to first send him back to the Yangtze River Delta on official business, and he found occasion to return home on a brief leave of absence to visit relatives. Perhaps Huangfu Ran already knew that his days had grown few. Not long after he arrived back in Danyang, he died at home at the age of fifty-four.

Huangfu Ran

BIBLIOGRAPHY

Editions:
Er Huangfu ji 二皇甫集. Liu Runzhi 劉潤之, editor and compiler. Beijing: Beijing Airusheng Shuzihua Jishu Yanjiu Zhongxin, 2009. A collection including the poetry of Huangfu Ran's younger brother, Huangfu Zeng.
Fu, *Tang caizi zhuan*, 3.45–46.
Huangfu Ran shiji 皇甫冉詩集. Beijing: Beijing Tushuguan, 2003.
Quan Tang shi, 4: 2786–827.
Quan Tang wen, 451.4615.

Biographical Sources:
Xin Tang shu, 202.5771.

Translations:
Bynner, *Jade Mountain*, p. 41–42. Offers a fairly loose, though not wholly inaccurate, translation of the same piece rendered above.
Kroll, "Recalling Xuanzong," p. 6. Includes a translation and brief discussion of "Huaqing gong" 華清宮 (the Huaqing Palace).

Studies:
Chen, Jinhua. "One Name, Three Monks: Two Northern Chan Masters Emerge from the Shadow of Their Contemporary, the Tiantai Master Zhanran 湛然 (711–782)" *The Journal of the International Association of Buddhist Studies*, 22 (1999): 1–92. Discussion of Huangfu Ran's later life and poetry, especially his association with prominent Buddhist monks.
Chu Zhongjun. "Huangfu Ran kaolun" 皇甫冉考論. Unpublished PhD Dissertation, Pudong Nanshi Normal College, 1991.
Huang Qiaoxi. ""Huangfu Ran liju shengping kaobian" 皇甫冉里居生平考辯. *Wenxue yi chan*, 1 (1990): 120-121.
Owen, *High T'ang*, pp. 267-8. Provided a translation and brief reading of "Wushan gao" 巫山高 (Wu Mountain High) in the context of a larger survey of later eighth century court poets.
Yu, Pauline. "Poems for the Emperor: Imperial Tastes in the Early Ninth Century." *Rhetoric and the Discourses of Power in Court Culture: China, Europe, and Japan*. David R Knechtges and Eugene Vance, editors. Seattle: University of Washington, 2005, pp. 73–93. Includes a discussion (pp. 9–12) the influence of Huangfu Ran's "Wu Shan Gao" on later poets.
Zhang Ruijun. "Li Jiayou Huangfu Ran shenping shiyi buzheng" 李嘉祐皇甫冉生平事蹟補証." *Shanxi Shida xuebao*, 4 (1992): 54–55.

Thomas Donnelly Noel

Huangfu Shi 皇甫湜 (*zi*, Chizheng 持正, ca. 777–ca. 835) was one of the more notable Chinese prose stylists of the late eighth and early ninth centuries, and a disciple of one of the Tang Dynasty's greatest literary figures, Han Yu 韓愈 (768–824).*

The exact dates of his birth and death remain unclear, and little is known of his childhood and adolescence. Hailing from Muzhou 睦州 (modern Zhejiang) He spent his youth in the bustling port region of Yangzhou hoping to gain entrance in the imperial civil service. It appears that he sat for the *jinshi* examinations at least three times, and after initial disappointment spent time wandering the regions east and south of the capital in search of patronage. We are certain that Huangfu Shi was among the first cohort of *jinshi* graduates under the reign of the Emperor Xianzong (778–820, r. 805–820) in 806, and that he then struggled to join an imperial bureaucracy during the cataclysmic upheaval that defined Tang polity at the beginning of the ninth century. Despite his youth and relative obscurity, Huangfu Shi would to soon find himself in a minor scandal when he sat for the Worthy and Excellent, Straightforward and Upright examination in 808 that invited frank criticism of the new regime. Huangfu's performance was among those singled out for praise by the examiners but condemned by the then Grand Councilor Li Jifu 李吉甫 (758–814) for its biting criticism of his policies. As a result, he was assigned to the minor post of Commandant, then banished to Luling 廬陵 County (south of modern Jian 吉安 County in Jiangxi). His political career was hampered for years, though he would eventually manage to attain the rank of Director of Ministry of Works; the accomplishments of Huangfu Shi the civil servant are considerably less illustrious than the man of letters. Part of his public failures are also seen as the due consequence of a host of character flaws. Both the dynastic histories and popular accounts present him as a masterful literary talent harboring grand and unrealized political aspirations; he also was known for a fondness of drinking and sudden outbursts of haughty rage.

The defining aspect of his literary career came with increasingly close association with Han Yu, who had welcomed him into an inner circle of literary talents that would include many of the preeminent prose essayists of the era. Huangfu's talents as a *guwen* 古文 (ancient-style prose) writer would thrive under the guidance of Han. Although there were occasional claims that his writing was often too cryptic and difficult, his steady and balanced prose won him many admirers, in spite of his apparent penchant for self-aggrandizement. Huangfu Shi became in his own time a much sought after literary panegyrist, acclaim due in large part to the skill in *guwen* he acquired under the tutelage of the form's most celebrated master, Han Yu. The most widely read of Huangfu's tomb inscriptions which have survived are two poignant elegies written in memory of his departed teacher entitled: "Han Wengong shendao bei" 韓文公神道碑 (An Epitaph for the Spirit Road of Han Yu) and "Changli Han Xiansheng mu zhiming" 昌黎韩先生墓誌铭 (An Epitaph for Master Han of Changli). The much-revered conclusion of his preface to the later inscription reads:

> The Master was with people both candid and magnanimous and did not make use of personal attendants. If there were any among his relatives, his affinities, friends, or old acquaintances who could not support themselves, he was sure to take it upon himself to then clothe them, feed them, make arrangements for their marriages, and provide for their funerary rites. Whenever he slept or ate, he would not set aside his books; when tired they served as his pillows, and when eating supper made his food tastier. He was diligent in offering lectures to hone his many students, fearing that they would not find perfection. When the students were relaxing he bantered and chanted songs with them, causing all to become enthralled with his ideas and to forget to return home. Alas! It may be said that he was a joyous and amiable gentleman, a great man and a figure of veneration. His wife is of the prominent Lu Clan of Fanyang (near modern Beijing), he orphans the *jinshi* Chang (799–855), his sons-in-law, Li Han (ca. 790–ca. 860), Reminder on the Left, and [subsequently] Fan Zongyi, Subeditor for the Academy of Collected Worthies [his eldest

daughter was divorced from Li Han and remarried to Fan Zongyi], a second daughter betrothed to the Chen Clan, and three daughters not yet full-grown.

先生與人洞朗軒辟，不施戟級。族姻友舊不自立者，必待我然後衣食嫁娶喪葬。平居雖寢食，未嘗去書，怠以為枕，飡以飴口。講評孜孜，以磨諸生，恐不完美。遊以詼笑嘯歌，使皆醉義忘歸。嗚呼！可謂樂易君子，鉅人長者矣。夫人高平郡君範陽盧氏，孤前進士昶，婿左拾遺李漢、集賢校理樊宗懿，次女許嫁陳氏，三女未笄。

The relative fame he won in his own time has partially faded in later eras as Huangfu Shi's work has often been described as derivative of his teacher, a fate that would somewhat understandably befall many of Han Yu's most gifted pupils and associates. For students of literature, this is particularly unfortunate because while there are a great many stylistic and thematic resonances between the two, Huangfu wrote with very much his own voice and rhythms and these can provide even the most knowledgeable readers of Tang *guwen* with a unique, fulfilling experience. In addition to prose, he is said to have authored a large amount of poetry and though only three pieces have managed to survive, they offer glimpses of a gifted and remarkably original lyricism. One such piece, an appraisal of a stele inscription entitled "Ti Wuxi shi" 題浯溪石 (Written on the Stone at Wu Creek) is extolled as an intriguing meditation on the correlations running between a number of major Tang literary figures including Chen Zi'ang 陳子昂 (659–ca. 699),* Li Bo 李白 (701–762),* Du Fu 杜甫 (712–770),* and Han Yu. It begins with the couplet: "Cishan [i.e. Yuan Jie 元結 (719–772)*] has a strength in composing prose, / What a pity he only indulged in trifling subjects" 次山有文章，可惋只在碎. Indeed, more balanced traditional appraisals Huangfu's own place in this greater tradition have in turn remarked that two aspects of Han Yu's genius was imparted to two of his most gifted devotees: Li Ao 李翱 (774–836)* retained Han's *zheng* 正 (rectitude), Huangfu Shi inherited his *qi* 奇 (sense of the marvelous). This notion of the strange or the marvelous as a quality not only of literary content but also of style was a matter of great importance to Huangfu, and the chief concern of some his most celebrated prose works. Among these, a series of three letters written to Li Ao titled "Da Lisheng shu" 答李生書 (Letters in Response to Master Li) serve not only as splendid examples of mid-Tang epistolary *guwen*, but also represent important pieces of literary criticism that offer fascinating hints at what might have been a vast, philosophically driven correspondence between two luminaries of the genre. The first of the three letters, and still the most widely read, is a telling commentary on the literary trends of Huangfu's time. In their struggle to equal the already growing legacy of the High Tang, Huangfu cautions Li Ao that many of their contemporaries had misguided notions of what the "marvelous," the "novel" (*xin* 新), and "the uncanny" (*guai* 怪) meant to prose composition, stressing that they were not the only means to recognition in their own times. More important for Huangfu however was a sentiment echoed by the generations that would follow in calling for a return to the classics, and for bold declarations of genuine intentions.

What ultimately became of Huangfu Shi remains unknown, as any mention of him in the historical record ceases after the midpoint of his life. While many have speculated that he met his end sometime after reappointment as the Administrative Assistant to Pei Du 裴度 (765–839) who was at the time serving as Metropolitan Governor of Luoyang, in truth it is as if Huangfu Shi simply vanished from memory. Indeed, despite the penchant of traditional Chinese critics to view literature through the prism of biography, his own story has become ancillary to the challenging, crisp, and cadenced style for which Huangfu Shi was admired, and the intellectual concerns that informed his life and the lives of those with whom he most closely identified.

BIBLIOGRAPHY

Editions:
Huangfu Chizheng ji 皇甫持正集. Shanghai: Shanghai Guji, 1987.
Huangfu Chizheng wen ji 皇甫持正文集. Shanghai: Shanghai Guji, 1994.
Huangfu Chizheng wen ji 皇甫持正文集. Taibei: Taiwan Zhonghua, 1968.
Quan Tang shi, 6: 4164.
Quan Tang wen, 685–87.7755–82.

Biographical Sources:
Xin Tang shu, 176.5267–68.

Studies:
Guozhen Jiang 江國貞. *Huangfu Chizheng xueshu yanjiu* 皇甫持正學術研究. Taibei: Youshi Wenhua Shiye Gongsi, 1975.
Huang Guoan 黃國安. "Li Ao, Huangfu Shi liangjia sanwen bijiao yanjiu" 李翱, 皇甫湜兩家散文比較研究, Unpublished M.A. Thesis, Furen Daxue, 1968.
Liu Xinzheng 劉新征. "Huangfu Shi yanjiu" 皇甫湜研究, Unpublished Ph. D. dissertation, Huazhong Keji Daxue, 2012.
___. "Huangfu Shi yanjiu zongshu" 皇甫湜研究綜述, *Hunan Daxue xuebao* 3 (2012): 44–47
___. "Lun Huangfu Shi sanwen de yishu tese" 論皇甫湜散文的藝術特色, *Zhongguo wenxue yanjiu* 3 (2011): 9–11.
Qian Jibo 錢基博 (1887–1957), *Han Yu wen du* 韓愈文讀. Shanghai: Shangwu, 1934. A famous study of prose selections written by Han Yu and his disciples, it appends most selections with light annotation and useful introductions.
Yao Jishun 姚繼舜. "Huangfu Shi shengcui nian zhushuo banzheng" 皇甫湜生卒年諸說辨正, *Wenxue yichan* 2 (1992): 51–54. Suggests the earlier, though still somewhat suspect, date of 830 for Huangfu's death.
Zhao Shaohong 趙曉紅 and Liu Zhenfeng 劉振峰. "Huangfu Shi qinshu guanxi" 皇甫湜的親屬關係, *Shehui zhanxian* 2 (2010): 278–80.

Thomas Donnelly Noel

Jia Dao 賈島 (*zi*, Langxian 浪仙, *dharma* name Wuben 無本, 779–843) was among a group of poets that gathered around Han Yu 韓愈 (768–824)* in the early ninth century, attracted by Han's advocacy of a literary "return to antiquity" (*fugu* 復古). Members of this circle, which included Meng Jiao 孟郊 (751–814),* Zhang Ji 張籍 (ca. 776–829),* and Zhu Qingyu 朱慶餘 (b. 791), encouraged each other to experiment in a wide variety of poetic styles, all of which exhibited a self-conscious belief in the moral efficacy of literature and an affirmation of the poet's own role

Jia Dao

as a protector of traditional values. They sought to achieve poetic "sincerity" by broadening the range of diction, vocabulary, and themes allowable in a poem.

We have no detailed knowledge about Jia Dao's early life. He was born in Fanyang 範陽 (between modern Baoding City 保定市 and Beijing in Hebei). Early in life, he entered a Buddhist order, presumably a Chan sect. He left his monastic order around 810 when he met Han Yu in Luoyang and accompanied him to Chang'an; he remained in Chang'an for most of the rest of his life. In the capital Jia Dao successfully established a reputation as a poet but did not meet similar success in his attempt to embark on an official career. He repeatedly failed the *jinshi* examinations and remained on the fringes of political life. To pass the *jinshi* examination in the early ninth century one needed both literary talent and political connections. Jia seems to have prepared his appearance on the examination grounds in 821 with two poems he addressed to Yuan Zhen 元稹 (779–831),* then a Hanlin Academician and a favorite of Emperor Muzong (r. 821–824). Jia Dao's attempts to win favor through Yuan Zhen may have led to his embarrassing failures in the examinations of 822. Yuan Zhen's rapid rise had won the enmity of other high officials. Even former friends like the powerful minister Pei Du 裴度 (765–835) were alienated. Their squabbling enabled a common enemy, Li Fengji 李逢吉 (758–835) to bring about their downfall. Thus Jia attempted to take the examinations at a markedly inopportune time. Although we know little of Jia's activities after 822, his problems with Yuan Zhen in the early 820s may have eventually caused Jia to attempt late in life to gain affiliation with a rival faction by sending the following poem to Linghu Chu 令狐楚 (766–837),* an enemy of Yuan Zhen:

> Supported by a walking stick, hurrying from post to mountain post,
> He asks everyone he meets about Zizhou.
> But Changjiang, how could he ever reach it?
> Fellow travelers all feel his sorrow.

策杖馳山驛，逢人問梓州。
長江那可到，行客替生愁。

The poem, perhaps written in 837, starts with the trope of "supported by a walking stick," which recalls Cao Zhi's 曹植 (192–232) "Gusi xing" 苦思行 (Bitter Thoughts; also titled "Fu Changjiang daozhong" 赴長江道中 [Written on the Road to Changjiang]); that poem concludes "Supported by his walking stick an old hermit wanders with me, / teaching me to seek to forget the words" 策杖從我游，教我要忘言. It was used by many poems between Cao and Jia to suggest a poet's withdrawal from the mundane world. Here, however, Jia is on his way to take up an official position in Changjiang (a county in Suizhou 遂州, modern Suining 遂寧 County in Sichuan). He hurries in part because the roads between Chang'an and Zizhou are dangerous. To understand lines 2-3 something of the geography of the region is needed: Zizhou was a small, out of the way prefecture and even it was difficult to find. But Changjiang, beyond Zizhou, was so small and remote that Jia didn't even dare to ask the way to it. This technique is sometimes referred to as "shadow-sketching" (*ying lüe* 影略) a line. The fact that he was heading into such a backwater is what evoked sorrow in those he met. Jia was possibly in a hurry to reach Changjiang where Yang Rushi 楊汝士 (778–ca. 839) was serving as Prefect and Military Commissioner, since Yang seems to have been become a patron of sorts for Jia. Jia's poem was intended to let Linghu Chu know of

Jia's difficulties and his location and perhaps to appeal to both Linghu and Yang for help. These lines are dominated by verbs—hurry, ask, reach, feel sorrow—which suggest both the motions and emotions of a traveler. The poem emphasizes Jia's own unworldly stance through the topos of the recluse leaning on a walking stick as well as his desire to reach the protection he hopes Yang Rushi will provide.

Whatever patronage Yang may have provided, Jia was transferred three years later to Puzhou 普州, north of Suining, and in 843 was appointed Revenue Administrator for the same district. He died before he could assume the post. Throughout his life, he maintained close relationships with "poet-priests" (*shiseng* 詩僧) and other Buddhist adepts and monks.

Jia Dao's poetry shows little stylistic development and is written in one of two markedly different modes–the discursive or the lyric. His discursive poetry, mostly in old-style forms, praises Confucian virtues and complains about society's rejection of the honest man. Jia's lyric poetry, at which he particularly excelled, is mostly in the five-syllable regulated-verse form. These poems evoke a muted, though powerful, mood through skillfully balanced couplets and judicious use of the colloquial constructions that also dominate his discursive poems. Although they may seem to lack overt intellectual content, diffuse Buddhist resonances may often be ascertained as in the following "Chun xing" 春行 (Setting out in Spring):

Moving on and on, a traveling man gains distance,
Dust follows his horse, with no end in sight.
A traveler's feelings, once the sun's rays have slanted;
Spring colors, in the morning mist.
The sound of flowing waters thread through the empty inn,
Languring flowers open in the old palace.
I think of home a thousand *li* away,
Where a green-willow wind stirs on the pond.

去去行人遠，塵隨馬不窮。
旅情斜日後，春色早煙中。
流水穿空館，閑花發故宮。
舊鄉千里思，池上綠楊風。

This poem can be read simply as a depiction of Jia Dao's emotions as he sets out on a spring day. But *chen* 塵 (dust) in the second line suggests the mundane world from which Jia hoped to escape. As with other Tang poets (most notably Du Fu) Jia identifies with the horse who is unable to emerge from this dusty world. Yet the persona here realizes that worldly matters are no more than momentary feelings that fade with the night, spring colors that last only as long as the morning mist. The next couplet emphasizes the ephemeral and impermanent nature of the dusty world, the emptiness of the inn revealed by the sound of the water, the flowers replacing the beauties who once dwelt in the palace. Even the thoughts of home seem as transient as the light wind on the pond Jia left there.

A clearer sense of Jia's attachment to Buddhism can be seen in his "Sung Wuke Shangren" 送無可上人 (Seeing off Monk Wuke):

Jia Dao

The sky freshened blue at Jade-point Peak,
As I see off this man of Grass-hut Temple.
A fly-whisk in your hand as we leave the grounds,
Amid the cries of crickets, we hesitate to part.
Your special shadow walks the bottom of the pond alone,
I rest now and again beside the tree.
In the end we'll meet in the colored clouds and haze,
I'll be your closest neighbor on Mount Tiantai.

圭峰霽色新，送此草堂人。
麈尾同離寺，蛩鳴暫別親。
獨行潭底影，數息樹邊身。
終有煙霞約，天臺作近鄰。

Wuke 無可 (fl. 825–827)* was Jia's younger cousin, a man with his own considerable reputation as a poet-monk. One might expect that a poem between these two men would reflect both their close feelings for each other and their religious backgrounds. The poem opens by setting the scene in a mountain temple. Meeting in the grounds before departing, Jia Dao identifies Wuke as a monk, noting the fly-whisk in his hands—a common Buddhist motif. The third couplet is famous in part because Jia Dao claimed he worked on the lines for three years. *Du xing* 獨行 in the context of eremitic life suggests the "independent" or "unique" behavior of men of high moral standards who removed themselves from the mundane world. Wuke becomes in line five a "shadow" moving across the bottom of the pond as seen through the clear waters, suggesting the unreality of the perceivable world and Wuke's purity as in the first line of another of Jia's poems, "Chou Cien Si Wenyu Shangren" 酬慈恩寺文郁上人 (A Reply to Monk Wenyu of Cien Temple): "The shadow of priestly robes enters the mirror-pond's purity." In line six of the poem for Wuke, *shu xi* 數息 can also mean "to count breaths," a form of meditation. *Shu bian* 樹邊 (beside the tree) is possibly related to *shu xia* 樹下, the ninth of the twelve Dhūta (Toutuo 頭陀) methods to get rid of the trials of life. Thus this line could also mean "In a few breaths of meditation, I transport my body to the states of being beneath the tree." The "tree" here may also recall the Bodhi Tree, under which Sakyamuni Buddha realized nirvana, now serving as an occasional respite for Jia Dao as he sojourns with his cousin through the world of dust. The final couplet points to a meeting Jia predicts beyond their current worldly life when both men can retire to the mountains and enjoy the colors of the clouds and haze.

Besides his poetic corpus, Jia Dao has also been credited with the authorship of a text entitled the *Ernan mizhi* 二南密指, a primer of metaphor for apprentice poets. The body of this work defines certain common poetic images as metaphors for phases in the relationship between ruler and subject. However, the attribution to Jia Dao is uncertain.

Though Jia Dao professed the ideal of writing poems whose plainness reflected universal truths, traditionally his poetry has been seen as limited in intellectual and emotional range and too dependent on literary artifice. Su Shi 蘇軾 (1037–1101) criticized both Jia Dao and Meng Jiao in his "Ji Liu Ziyu wen" 祭柳子玉文, terming Jia "lean" (*shou* 瘦) and Meng "cold." (*han* 寒). These epithets have persisted. Jia Dao's attention to detail has been seen as evidence of a petty talent. However, others have praised Jia's technical artistry.

BIBLIOGRAPHY

Editions:
Changjiang ji 長江集. *Sibu beiyao* 四部備要. Shanghai: Zhonghua, 1936.
Li Jiayan 李嘉言. *Changjiang Ji xinjiao*長江集新校. Shanghai: Shanghai Guji, 1983. Appends chronological biographies and a study of Jia's friends.
Mao Jin 毛晉, comp. *Tangren bajia shi* 唐人八家詩. Shanghai: Hanfen Lou, 1926.
Quan Tang shi, 9: 6674–747, 11: 9006, 14: 10657, 15: 11295.

Annotations:
Chen Yanjie 陳延傑, annotator. *Jia Dao shizhu* 賈島詩注. Shanghai: Shangwu, 1937.
Huang Peng 黄鹏. *Jia Dao shiji jianzhu* 贾岛诗集笺注. Chengdu: Ba Shu, 2002.
Li Jiankun 李建崑. *Jia Dao shiji jiaozhu* 賈島詩集校注. Taibei: Liren, 2002.
Qi Wenbang 齊文榜. *Jia Dao jijiaozhu* 贾岛集校注. Beijing: Renmin Wenxue, 2001.

Biographical Sources:
Fu, *Tang caizi*, 1:544, 2:314–36, 5:220–22.
Xin Tang shu, 176.5268.

Translations:
Articulated Ladies, pp. 299.
Demiéville, pp. 332–33.
Egan, *Clouds*, pp. 80–82.
Fuller, Michael A. *An Introduction to Chinese Poetry: From the* Canon of Poetry *to the Lyrics of the Song Dynasty*. Cambridge: Harvard University Press, 2018, pp. 307–11.
Kroll, "Recalling Xuanzong," pp. 9–10.
Mair, *Anthology*, p. 233.
Minford and Lau, pp. 867–69.
New Directions, p. 140.
O'Connor, Mike and Red Pine, eds. *The Clouds Should Know Me by Now: Buddhsit Poet Monks of China*. Boston: Wisdom Publications, 1998. pp. 16–40.
O'Connor, Mike. *When I Find You Again, It Will Be in Mountains: Selected Poems of Chia Tao*. Boston: Wisdom Publications, 2000.
Owen, *Anthology*, p. 373.
Pimpaneau, p. 457.
Seaton, Jerome P., "Wu Pen (Chia Tao)," in Seaton, Jerome P. and Denni Maloney, eds. *A Drifting Boat: An Anthology of Chinese Zen Poetry*. Fredonia, NY: White Pine Press, 1994, pp. 60–63.
Sunflower, pp. 226–27. Five poems.
Watson, *Lyricism*, pp. 117–18.
Yu, *Imagery*, p. 200.
See also Witzling below.

Studies:
Arai, Ken 荒木健康. "Ka Tō" 賈島, *Chūgoku bungaku hō* 10 (1959): 52–95.
Ashidate Ichirō 芦立一郎. "Ka Tō shi shitan" 賈島詩誠探, *Yamagata Daigaku kuyō-Jinbun kagaku* XIII.1 (1996): 147–62.
Dong Beiji 董培基. "Jia Dao shi chongchu chenbian" 賈島詩重出甄辨, *Henan Daoxue Xuebao* 60 (1985): 44–49.

Fang Rixi 房日晰. "Jia Dao kaocheng er ze" 賈島考證二則, *Wenxue yichan* 6 (1992): 106–08.

Jia Dao Juan 賈島卷. In *Quan Tang shi suoyin* 全唐書索引. Beijing: Xiandai, 1994.

Jing Kaixuan 景凱旋. "Jia Dao shiji kaobian" 賈島事跡考辨, *Wenshi* 37 (1993): 213–28.

Li Jiayan 李嘉言. *Jia Dao nianpu* 賈島年譜. Rpt. Taibei: Da Xiyang Tushu Gongsi, 1974.

Liu Zhuqing 劉竹青. *Meng Jiao, Jia Dao yanjiu* 孟郊, 賈島研究. Taibei: Wenshizhe, 1986.

Mazanec, Thomas J. "Jia Dao's Rhythm, Or, How to Translate the Tones of Medieval China," *Journal of Oriental Studies*, 49 (2016): 27–48.

Nienhauser, William H., Jr. "The Other Side of the Mountain: A New Translation of Chia Tao," (Review Article on *Selected Poems of Chia Tao*, by Mike O'Connor), *CLEAR* 24 (2002): 161–73.

O'Connor, Mike and Red Pine, see above, pp. 12–15.

Owen, *Meng Chiao*, pp. 212–13, 225–27, 240–44.

Qi Wenbang 齊文榜. *Jia Dao yanjiu* 賈島研究. Taibei: Renmin Wenxue, 2007.

Watson, Burton. "Buddhist Poet-Priests of the T'ang," *The Eastern Buddhist* (New Series) 25-2 (1992): 30–58.

Wen Yiduo 聞一多. "Jia Dao," in his *Tangshi zalun*, included in *Wen Yiduo quan ji* 聞一多全集. Shanghai: Kaiming, 1948. v. 3, *neiji* 丙集, pp. 37–43.

Witzling, Catherine. "The Poetry of Chia Tao: A Re-Examination of Critical Stereotypes," Unpublished Ph.D. dissertation, Stanford University, 1980. Contains numerous translations.

Wu Ruyu 吳汝煜 and Xie Rongfu 謝榮富. "Li Jiayan, Jia Dao nianpu dingbu" 李嘉言賈島年譜訂補, *Liaoning Guangbo Dianshi Daxue xuebao* 3 (1987): 1–6.

Yixilamu 益西拉姆. "Jia Dao zhi shiren xingxiang: zai yu shi zhijian" 賈島之詩人形象:在虛與實之間, *Zhonghua wenshi luncong* 1 (2013): 351–73, 399.

Yu, *Imagery*, pp. 183–85.

Zhou Yukai 周玉凱. "Jia Dao shige yu Chanzong guanxi zhi yanjiu" 賈島詩格與禪宗關係之研究. *Shibian yu chuanghua: Han-Tang, Tang-Song zhuanhuanqi zhi wenyi xianxiang* 世變與創化: 漢唐, 唐宋轉換期之文藝現象. Lo-fen I 衣若芬 and Liu Yuanru 劉苑如, eds. Taibei: Zhongyuan Yanjiuyuan, Zhongguo Wenzhe Yanjiusuo, 2000, pp. 425–58.

Catherine Witzling and William H. Nienhauser, Jr.

Jia Zhi 賈至 (*zi*, Youji 幼幾 or Youlin 幼鄰, 718–772) has a place in literary history of the basis of his reputation as an author of rescripts, his reformist views on literary practice, and his verse. Hailing from Luoyang, Jia Zhi was the son of a prominent literary official. He passed the *mingjing* examination (ca. 740) and served as Editor in the Palace Library and Commandant of Shanfu 單父 (modern Shan County 單縣, Shandong). By the mid-750s he was a Secretariat Drafter and he held this post again, following a period of political reverses and provincial service, after the accession of Emperor Daizong (r. 762–779) in 763. His later posts included those of Vice-minister of the Ministry of Rites controlling *jinshi* examinations in the eastern capital, Vice Director of the Ministry of War, and, from 770 until his death, Metropolitan Governor.

The office of Secretariat Drafter, which Jia's father, Jia Zeng 賈曾 (d. 727), had also held, carried the duty of drafting rescripts in the name of the emperor, to provide, in the oft-cited phrase from the *Lunyu*, "proper elegance and finish" (*runse* 潤色) to the emperor's words. Rescript-writing had enormous prestige in the Tang literary world, for it involved both recognition by the emperor himself of literary skill and a high level of political responsibility. Collections of rescripts by secretariat drafters and rescript-writers circulated widely in literary society and biographies of successful rescript-writers, like Jia and his father, were often represented in the literary sub-section of the dynastic history. Jia Zhi's documentary style was highly praised; moreover, of a group of scholars later recognized as forerunners of the *Guwen yundong* 古文運動 (Ancient-style Prose Movement), Jia Zhi was the only one who composed rescripts. He was also the only one to have received the coveted canonization of Wen 文.

Jia had strong views on the literary climate of his day. After the An Lushan Rebellion (756–763) he especially criticized the prestige that literary skill commanded in the *jinshi* examination. When in 763 there were discussions of the content of the *jinshi* examination, he condemned obsession with tonal patterning and euphuistic diction. Elsewhere he emphasized the preeminence of the Confucian canons as models for literary practice and the progressive decline in standards that he and other reformist critics believed had taken place since the time of Confucius. Jia and his friend of Dugu Ji 獨孤及 (725–777),* one of the most influential of these critics, were cited as forerunners of the much better known, more innovative, and more productive *guwen* writers of the next generation, Han Yu 韓愈 (768–824)* and Liu Zongyuan 柳宗元 (773–819).*

Jia Zhi also wrote well-turned regular verse, such as his "Bai ma" 白馬 (The White Horse):

> White horse, figured with purple patterns,
> Neighing before the crimson palace towers.
> Listen to the bridle ornaments sound as it prances,
> There's no need to apply the golden whip.

> 白馬紫連錢，嘶鳴丹闕前。
> 聞珂自踥蹀，不要下金鞭。

The white horse—with spots that resemble copper coins—is an imperial steed shown here performing before the emperor himself. The horse proudly displays its talents all without the need of the rider's whip. As in many Tang poems, the horse here could be identified with the poet. Jia Zhi's family had for generations served at court and he himself was a long-serving high official who was noted for his loyalty and literary merits. Like the white horse, Jia was both proud and eager to serve the emperor.

A three-year period of exile at Yuezhou 岳州 on Lake Dongting was the indirect result of his membership with Du Fu 杜甫 (712–770)* and others in a losing faction at court. There he compiled a small anthology, the *Baling shiji* 巴陵詩集 (Baling Anthology of Poetry), containing extant poems which express nostalgia for the life of the capital and interest in the company of fellow exiles, as well as impressions of the landscape and river journeys on the Yangzi. Li Bo 李白 (701–762),* Du Fu and Dugu Ji all knew Jia during this period and praised his poetry. "Dongting song Li Shier fu Lingling" 洞庭送李十二赴零陵 (At Dongting Lake Seeing Off Li the Twelfth [i.e. Li Bo] who Was Heading to Lingling) was written as Li Bo was heading south to Yongzhou 永州 in 759:

> Today we meet before the falling leaves,
> The waters of Dongting stretching so far they touch the skies.

Jia Zhi

> We each spoke of those places we wandered through the Golden Splendor Hall,
> Turning to look at the Big Dipper in the north, both about to break into tears.

今日相逢落葉前，洞庭秋水遠連天。
共說金華舊游處，回看北斗欲潸然。

The poem is no tour de force, but a personal reminder to Li Bo of their time together in Xuanzong's court in the early 740s. The Golden Splendor Hall was actually part of the Han-dynasty palace, but the use of Han people and places to refer indirectly to their Tang counterparts was a commonplace, as was a reference to constellations in the northern part of the sky.

Earlier, Jia had composed verse with two other celebrated writers of the period, Wang Wei 王維 (692–761 or 699–759)* and Cen Shen 岑參 (715–770).* Of his original collection of thirty-five *juan* only three *juan* of prose, mainly rescripts, and one *juan* of poetry are now extant. These owe their survival in almost all cases to their inclusion in the main Song literary and documentary anthologies. Jia was also a scholar of genealogy, but his work in this field has not survived.

BIBLIOGRAPHY

Editions:
Quan Tang shi, 4: 2587–95.
Quan Tang wen 366–68.4237–60.
Tangwen shiyi, juan 22, fol. 12.

Biographical Sources:
Fu, *Tang caizi*, 1:480–92.
Jiu Tang shu, 190B.5027–29.
Xin Tang shu, 119.4297–99.

Studies:
Bol, pp. 114–22.
Fu, *Shiren*, pp. 171–91.
Ju Yan 鞠岩. "Jia Zhi zhongshu zhigao yu Tangdai guwen yundong" 賈至中書制誥與唐代古文運動, *Beijing Daxue xuebao (Zhexue shehui kexue)* 4 (2010): 74–80.

David L. McMullen and William H. Nienhauser, Jr.

Jiao Ran 皎然 (secular name, Xie Zhou 謝晝, *zi*, Qingzhou 清晝, 720–799) dominated the literary scene on the lower Yangzi in the late eighth century with his versatility as a poet and his adeptness as a conversationalist, equally well-read in Buddhist, Confucian, and Daoist thought. But he is best known for provocative literary criticism that reflects the High Tang Style. A tenth-generation descendant of Xie Lingyun 謝靈運 (385–433), Jiao Ran resolved the traditional conflict between literature and Buddhist quietism by making poetry an intellectual instrument. Born and raised in Changcheng 長城 (modern Zhejiang 浙江) he took ordination at Lingyin Temple 靈隱寺 before the An Lushan Rebellion, was indoctrinated in *vinaya* teachings, traveled widely to study at monasteries throughout the country, and remained a Buddhist all his life.

His reputation as a poet probably first spread through poems for social entertainment that were composed by several hands and a considered the true beginnings of "linked verse." These were written between 773 and 776 in company with several prominent figures in Huzhou 湖州, including Yan Zhenqing 顏真卿 (709–785), the noted calligrapher who was then Military Commissioner 節度使 of the area. It was also in this period that Jiao Ran, Yan Zhenqing, Lu Yu 陸羽 (733–804), author of the *Chajing* 茶經 (Classic of Tea, 760), and other associates made a compilation of poetry extracts arranged by rhyme known as the *Yunhai jingyuan* 韻海鏡原 (360 *juan*). In the 770s and early 780s he also exchanged verse with leading contemporary poets and served as a mentor for younger Buddhist poets such as Yuanhao 元浩 and Lingche 靈澈 (746–816).* Unfortunately, neither the *Yunhai jingyuan* nor any of Jiao Ran's apparently quite voluminous philosophical and anecdotal writing dating from this period survives.

In 785 Jiao Ran went into semi-retirement near the city of Wuxing 吳興 (modern Huzhou 湖州 City in Zhejiang). Immediately thereafter, he was engaged in the writing of his two major critical works, the *Shishi* 詩式 and *Shiping* 詩評, and literary figures continued to find their way to him. Wei Yingwu 韋應物 (737–ca. 791)* wrote: "Vainly his literary fame spreads across the land, / While his dharma mind remains at peace." It is likely that contact with the poet Meng Jiao 孟郊 (751–814)* at this time resulted in the influence of Jiao Ran's theory of active reaction to the literary past upon the poetry and prose of the Ancient-style Prose Movement (*Guwen yundong* 古文運動) at the turn of the ninth century. In 793 Yu Di 于頔 (d. 818) oversaw the compilation of Jiao Ran's complete works (in 10 *juan*) at the behest of Tang Emperor Dezong (r. 779–805) and submitted them for imperial preservation.

Although his reputation as a poet was founded largely upon work in regulated verse that grew out of the tradition of Wang Wei 王維 (692–761 or 699–759)* and *Dali shi caizi* 大曆十才子 (Ten Talents of the Dali Era), Jiao Ran was also respected for his old-style verse and literary ballads. His poems often develop the melancholic, *vanitas vanitatum* themes of a Chan Buddhist's perspective on life, unfolding images of tranquil beauty which are then rejected as earthly illusions. Esteem for Jiao Ran's poetry in his own time was considerable. His work was included in a contemporary anthology, the *Nan xun ji* 南熏集, a collection of thirty poets of the Dali 大曆 period (766–780) edited by Dou Chang 竇常 (746–825) in the 780s, and in several later Tang anthologies. In 833 Liu Yuxi 劉禹錫 (772–842)* praised Jiao Ran as the only poet of the lower Yangzi in the late eighth century who truly had depth and range in all styles.

Although later critics, most notably Yan Yu 嚴羽 (Southern Song dynasty) in his *Canglang shihua* 滄浪詩話, continued to rank him high among Buddhist poets of the Tang, few of his poems are common anthology pieces. His poetry often ties the aesthetic to the philosophical as in "Xi yun" 溪雲 (Clouds above the Creek), one of five "Nanchi zayong" 南池雜詠五首 (Miscellaneous Songs from Southern Creek):

> Stretching and coiling, what do you end up with?
> Twining above the stream or surrounding the skies.
> You have form but are not a thing of substance.

Leaving no trace you go off following the wind.
Don't blame me for always chasing after you,
Floating about, you're no different than I.

舒卷意何窮，縈流複帶空。
有形不累物，無跡去隨風。
莫怪長相逐，飄然與我同。

Clouds are an oft-used metaphor for the spontaneous wandering lifestyle of a Chan monk who were sometimes called "cloud and water monks" 雲水僧. "Stretching and coiling" implies beginning or leaving affairs of the secular world. The style and structure of the poem are, however, more reminiscent of the philosophical poems of Tao Qian 陶潛 (365–429).

Of more interest today than any of his other work, however, is the literary criticism of Jiao Ran's *Shishi* 詩式 (5 *juan*), *Shiping* 詩評 (3 *juan*), and *Shiyi* 詩議 (1 *juan*). The former two works were probably substantially completed in 785. The *Shiyi* may be a simplification of the *Shiping* or, what seems more likely, is the series of critical essays Jiao Ran wrote in conjunction with the *Yunhai jingyuan* 韻海鏡原 in the mid-770s. All three were well known by the early ninth century. Extracts from the *Shiyi* appear in the *Bunkyō hifuron* 文鏡秘府論, an anthology of criticism collected by the Japanese monk Kūkai (774–835). The five-*juan* text of the *Shishi* in the *Shiwan juan lou congshu* 十萬卷樓叢書 (1879) must be close to the original, but the numerous passages scattered there that begin with the words "*Ping yue*" 評曰 (the [Shi]ping says) probably only partially represent the full original text of the *Shiping*.

The *Shishi* ranks verse selected from Han to Tang dynasty poets in five levels of accomplishment. Jiao Ran follows the earlier critics Zhong Rong 鐘嶸 (468–518), Shen Yue 沈約 (441–513), Liu Xie 劉勰 (fl. 5th c.), and Wang Changling 王昌齡 (ca. 690–ca. 756)* in the quest for poetry that "fully expresses the poet's emotions through his description of scene" (*qiongqing xiewu* 窮情寫物) without the adulteration of allusions, archaisms, or any other literary or historical accoutrements. The progression from *juan* one to *juan* five is from immediacy and effectiveness to some rather dramatic examples of writing that are marred by literary fatuousness and lack of genuine feeling. The "Nineteen Words Discerning Style" 十九字辨體, introduced in *juan* 1 and drawn upon for comments on selections in the first three *juan*, influenced the terminology of later critics such as Sikong Tu 司空圖 (837–908)* and Yan Yu, but also occasionally led to castigation of Jiao Ran as a technical reductivist.

The *Shiping* consists of interpretive and theoretical expositions on style, literary history, and the nature of poetic creation. Not only in poetic images, but also in writing in general, and in the material world we are always dealing, says Jiao Ran, merely with *traces*. What is beyond them or what they effect is more important. Great poetry therefore transcends the traces to lead to enlightenment, and when Jiao Ran talks of "the dharma of poetry" (*shidao* 詩道), he really means something that supersedes Buddhist, Daoist, and Confucian teachings. The poetry of the Jian'an poets, Tao Qian 陶潛 (365–427), Shen Quanqi 沈佺期 (656–716),* Song Zhiwen 宋之問 (656–ca. 712),* Meng Haoran 孟浩然 (689–740),* Wang Wei, and above all Xie Lingyun is immediate and reflects personal experience at a specific place and time. Contrary to contemporary opinion, Jiao Ran argues that a good poem does not reject embellishment, parallelism, or intellectual struggle (*kusi* 苦思), although the end-product must *appear* effortless (*ziran* 自然). It is typified by "lines in which the appearance of scenery conveys emotion" (*wuse daiqing ju* 物色帶情句). Close to Wang Changling's arguments in his *Shige* 詩歌 (Poems and Songs) composed a decade or two earlier, Jiao Ran's literary theory remains the best abstract exposition of the High Tang Style and was the first extensive statement of the juxtaposition of Chan Buddhism and the arts that became so important in later criticism.

The freshness of both the *Shiping* and the *Shiyi* arises from Jiao Ran's zest for radical inversions of commonly held opinions. Usually denigrated in the eighth century (and later), the poetry of the Qi 齊 and Liang 梁 dynasties should be recognized, he argues, as the source of much that comprises the High Tang Style. Furthermore, radical "transformation that sustains continuity" (*tongbian* 通變) with earlier literature is superior to imitatively "returning to the past" (*fugu* 復古) precisely because it along can breed freshness and immediacy. When Jiao Ran criticizes the use of colloquialisms and literary clichés, he is also attacking the Fugu School's infatuation with adaptations from the countryside vernacular in the literary ballad and with archaisms. Yet he simultaneously recognizes the potential for weakness in the new regulated verse, if overpowered by technical and rhetorical considerations. For Jiao Ran, great poets are "geniuses of change" (*bianzhicai* 變之才).

BIBLIOGRAPHY

Editions:

Gan Shengtong 甘生統, ed. *Jiao Ran shixue yuanyuan kaolun* 皎然詩學淵源考論. Beijing: Renmin, 2012.

Guo Shaoyu 郭紹虞, ed. Qian Zhonglian 錢仲聯, comp. and annot., in *Zhongguo lidai wenlun xuan* 中國曆代文論選. Beijing: Zhonghua, 1962. Selections from the first half of *juan* one and the "Fugu tongpian" section of *juan* five. Other unannotated selections, including material from the *Shixue zhinan* are appended.

He Wenhuan 何文煥, comp. *Lidai shihua* 歷代詩話, 1770; rpt. Taibei: Muduo, 1974. One *juan*; the material only reflects the first half of *juan* one of the *Shiwan juan lou* text.

Konishi Jinichi 小西甚一, "*Shiyi* 詩議," in, *Bunkyō hifuron kō* 文鏡秘府論考. V. 3. Tokyo: Kodansha Ltd., 1953. *Shiyi* selections in sections 121–24.

Lu Xinyuan 陸心源 comp. *Shiwan juan lou congshu* 十萬卷樓叢書 1979; rpt., in *Baibu congshu jicheng*. Taibei: Yiwen, 1968. The only full, five-*juan* text of *Shishi* 詩式.

Quan Tang shi, 12: 9252–352, 14: 11161, 15: 11655.

Quan Tang wen, 917–18.12533–49.

Wuxing Zhou shangren ji 吳興晝上人集. Yü Di 于頔, comp., 793. SBCK. 10 *juan*. Photo-reprint of a handwritten Song dynasty text; complete poetry and prose, exclusive of critical writings.

Zhou Weide 周維德, ed. "*Shiyi* 詩議," in Kūkai 空海, comp. *Bunkyō hifuron kō* 文鏡秘府論考. Beijing: Renmin Wenxue, 1975. *Shiyi* material runs from p. 141 ("Huo yue...") to p. 149; the most readily available text.

Biographical Sources:

Fu, *Tang caizi*, 1:183–206, 5:199–201.

Zan Ning, 29.728–30.

Jiao Ran

Translations:

Bodman, Richard. "Poetics and Prosody in Early Medieval China: A Study and Translation of Kūkai's *Bunkyō hifuron*." Unpublished Ph.D. dissertation, Cornell University, 1978. Pp. 404–24 provide translation and notes for *Shiyi* material in section 121–24 of Kūkai's collection.

Egen, *Clouds*, pp. 72–77.

Nielson, Thomas P. "The Tang Poet-Monk Jiao Ran," *Occasional Paper No. 3*. Tempe, Arizona, 1972. Includes translation of over thirty poems.

Owen, Stephen. "How Did Buddhism Matter in Tang Poetry?" *TP* 103 (2017): 393–94.

Seaton, Jerome P. "Chiao Jan," Seaton, Jerome P. and Denni Maloney, eds. *A Drifting Boat: An Anthology of Chinese Zen Poetry*. Fredonia, NY: White Pine Press, 1994, pp. 52–56.

Watson, *Lyricism*, pp. 117–18.

Studies:

Chen Xiaoqiang 陳曉薔. "Jiao Ran yu *Shishi*" 皎然與詩式, *Tonghai xuebao* 8 (1967): 113–25.

Ichihara Kōkichi 市原享吉. "Chū Tō shoki ni okeru Kōsa no shisō ni tsuite" 中唐初期におけける江左の詩僧について, *Tōhō gakuhō* 28 (1958): 219–48.

Inui Mototoshi 乾源俊. *Shisō Kyōnen shūchū* 詩僧皎然集注. Tokyo: Kyūko, 2014.

Iriya Yoshitaka 入矢義高, annot. "Tang Huzhou Zhushan Jiao Ran zhuan" 唐湖州杼山皎然傳, in Ogawa Tamaki 小川環樹, ed. *Tōdai no shijin: Sono denki* 唐代の詩人: その傳記, Tokyo: Taishūkan, Shōwa 50, 1975, pp. 625–35. Text, translation, and notes for the Jiao Ran biography by Zan Ning 贊寧 in the *Song gaoseng zhuan* 宋高僧傳 (988), which is also available in the *Taishō shinshū daizōkyō* 大正新修大藏經 (Tokyo, 1924–1932), 50, entry 2061, and is probably based on an epitaph written in 809 by Lingche and/or Fan Chuanzheng 范傳正.

Jia Jinhua 贾晋华. *Jiao Ran nianpu* 皎然年谱. Xiamen: Xiamen Daxue, 1992.

Konishi Jinishi 小西甚一. *Bunkyō hifuron kō* 文鏡秘府論考. I (Kyoto, 1948), pp. 52–55 and II (Tokyo: Kodansha Ltd., 1951), pp. 130–32. Good, though polemical, summary of Jiao Ran's critical position.

Williams, Nicolas Morrow. "The Taste of the Ocean: Jiao Ran's Theory of Poetry." *TS* 31 (2013): 1–27.

Xu Lianjun 许连军. *Jiao Ran "Shishi" yanjiu* 皎然《诗式》研究. Beijing: Zhonghua, 2007.

Xu Qingyun 許清雲, ed. *Jiao Ran shishi yanjiu* 皎然詩式研究. Taibei: Wenshizhe, 1988.

___. *Jiao Ran shishi jijiao xinbian* 皎然詩式輯校新編. Taibei: Wenshizhe, 1984.

Yu, *Imagery*, pp. 182–83.

Craig Fisk

Judun 居遁 (*xing*, Guo 郭, *hao*, Zhenkong Dashi 證空大師 also known as the Longya Heshang 龍牙和尚 [Monk of Mount Longya], 835–923) was a poet-monk active in the late Tang and early Five Dynasties. He was from Nancheng 南城 County in Fuzhou 撫州 (in modern Jiangxi). At the age of fourteen, he entered the Putian Monastery 蒲田寺 in Jizhou 吉州 (modern Ji'an city in Jiangxi) and later was ordained in Mount Song 嵩山. He learned from the Chan masters Cuiwei Wuxue 翠微無學 (739–824) and Deshan Xuanjian 德山宣鑒 (780–865) and was eventually was recognized as enlightened by Dongshan Liangjia 洞山良價 (807–869). At the start of the Later Liang dynasty (907) he was invited by Ma Yin 馬殷 (r. 907–930), King of Chu, to stay at the Miaoji Cloister 妙濟院 in Mount Longya 龍牙山 of Tanzhou 潭州 (modern Changsha city in Hunan). In 915 he was bestowed the title of Zhengkong Dashi (Master of Realizing Emptiness). He passed away in the ninth month of 923 at the age of eighty-nine. The *Zutang ji* 祖堂集 (Collection from the Patriarchs'

Hall), *Song Gaoseng zhuan* 宋高僧傳 (Biographies of Eminent Monks of the Song), and *Jingde chuandeng lu* 景德傳燈錄 (*Jingde* Era Record of the Transmission of the Lamp) include accounts of his life. Judun composed many *gāthās* (*jisong* 偈頌, Buddhist poetic verses), which were broadly circulated. His disciples compiled his verses into a collection, and the fellow poet-monk Qiji 齊己 (fl. 881)* wrote a preface for it. This collection was lost, but the *Quan Tang shi bubian* 全唐詩補編 (Supplementary Compilation to the *Complete Poetry of the Tang Dynasty*) includes ninety-six of Judun's *gāthās*. Most of the verses illustrate Buddhist teachings and Chan thought and practice, while some pieces also describe daily monastic life and feelings.

The relationship between *gāthā* and poetry is complicated, and there have been arguments about whether *gāthā* can be viewed as poetry. This may be the reason why Judun was not seen as a poet-monk in the past and his verses were not collected into the *Quan Tang shi*. Judun's *gāthās*, however, do present a certain degree of literary achievement. He was adept in applying vernacular language, accounts of daily life, and fresh metaphors to elaborate on Chan ideas; Qiji argued that "he relies on images to express marvelous ideas which always imply greater meanings" 托像寄妙, 必含大意, as in the following example:

Studying the Dao is like striking a flint for fire,
Don't stop just when smoke arises.
Wait for the golden sparks to appear,
Only then do you come to the end and hit home.

學道如鑽火, 逢煙且莫休.
直待金星現, 歸家始到頭.

In this *gāthā* attaining Dao/enlightenment is compared to striking a flint. When one strikes a flint, smoke first appears. However, this is not yet true fire, and therefore one should not stop striking the flint until sparks emerge and one then truly attains fire/enlightenment and returns to his original home—the Buddha nature inherently in his mind.

BIBLIOGRAPHY

Editions:
Chen Shangjun 陳尚君, ed. *Quan Tangshi bubian* 全唐詩補編. Beijing: Zhonghua, 1992.
Daoyuan 道原 (fl. 1004), eds. *Jingde chuandeng lu* 景德傳燈錄. *Sibu congkan* 四部叢刊 ed.
Jing 靜 (fl. 952) and Yun 筠 (fl. 952), comp., Sun Changwu 孫昌武, Kinugawa Kenji 衣川賢次, and Nishiguchi Yoshio 西口芳男, collators. *Zutang ji* 祖堂集. Beijing: Zhonghua, 2007.
Quan Tang shi, 15: 11668–75.
Zisheng 子昇 and Ruyou 如祐, comps. *Chamen zhuzu shijie song* 禪門諸祖師偈頌. Rpt. Taibei: Wenshu, 1990.

Biographical Sources:
Zan Ning, 13.305.

Studies:

Chen Shangjun 陳尚君. "Judun," in Zhou Zuzhuan 周祖譔 ed., *Zhongguo wenxuejia dacidian: Tang Wudai juan* 中國文學家大辭典: 唐五代卷. Beijing: Zhonghua, 1992, p. 541.
Chen Zuolong 陳祚龍. *Jianjie Litang Judun chanshi de xingyi yu jisong* 簡介李唐居遁禪師的行誼與偈頌, in *Zhonghua Fojiao wenhuashi sance chuji* 中華佛教文化史散策初集. Taibei: Xinwenfeng, 1978, pp. 248–57.
Gao Huaping 高華平. "Tangdai de shiseng yu sengshi" 唐代的詩僧與僧詩, *Minnan foxue* 3 (2004): 468–504.
Jia Jinhua 賈晉華 and Fu Xuancong 傅璇琮. *Tang Wudai wenxue biannianshi: Wudai juan* 唐五代文學編年史: 五代卷. Shenyang: Liaohai, 1998.
Wang Fanzhou 汪泛舟. "Dunhuang shici buzheng yu kaoyuan" 敦煌詩詞補正與考源, *Dunhuang yanjiu* 3 (1997): 105–13.
Xiang Chu 項楚. *Tangdai baihua shipai yanjiu* 唐代白話詩派研究. Chengdu: Ba Shu, 2005.
Zha Minghao 查明昊. *Zhuanxing zhong de Tang Wudai shiseng qunti* 轉型中的唐五代詩僧群體. Shanghai: Huadong Shifan Daxue, 2008.

Jinhua Jia and Chunli Yu

Li Ao 李翱 (*zi*, Xizhi 習之, 774–836) was an official and literatus of the mid-Tang period whose contribution toward an intellectual and practical synthesis of Buddhism and Confucianism laid a solid foundation for the Neo-Confucianism of the eleventh century. He associated for many years with Han Yu 韓愈 (768–824),* and his philosophical speculations had important implications for the theory of literary style.

Li Ao was born in Bianzhou 汴州 (modern Kaifeng) to a family of literati who traced its origins to Six Dynasties aristocracy. But Li Ao's immediate forebears held only minor posts. He was an only son. He arrived in the capital in 793 to sit for the *jinshi* examination, for which he secured the support of Liang Su 梁肅 (753–793).* The latter died several months later, however, and Li Ao did not obtain the degree until 798. He met Han Yu in 796 in Bianzhou where Han was serving on the staff of the Military Commissioner. The pair associated there with Meng Jiao 孟郊 (751–814),* and Zhang Ji 張籍 (ca. 776–829),* this quartet forming the initial nucleus of the "Han Yu circle." In 800, Li Ao married the daughter of Han Yu's cousin.

Li Ao served in over twenty different positions during the course of a long and stormy official career: his major positions were in 817–818 in the Directorate of Education, 823–825 in the Ministry of Rites, 827–831 in the Censorate, and 834 a brief tour as Vice Director of the Ministry of Justice. His straightforward personality and outspoken directness made it impossible for him to remain long in the capital and he spent most of his life in the central and southern provinces. He died in 836 as Military Commissioner of Shannan East at Xiangzhou 襄州 (modern Hubei).

Li Ao's three "Fu xing shu" 復性書 (Letters to Bring Back Nature) are the most important of his extant work; they articulate his thoughts on the problem of "human nature" (*xing* 性). The first letter defines the perfection of "human nature" as the attainment of "sagehood" (*sheng* 聖) through the stilling of the seven passions (*qing* 情). The second outlines the proper methods used to cultivate and attain this goal. In the third letter Li stresses its importance and affirms it as his own goal. The letters quote heavily from the *Zhongyong* and from *Meng Zi* and did much to focus attention on these works as basic texts of Neo-Confucianism. Yet the main tenor of the letters, although expressed in Confucian terms, is Buddhist, specifically Tiantai and Chan, and there are textual affinities to the writings of Liang Su. Although his best-known Chan teacher was Yaoshan

Weiyan 藥山惟儼 (751–834), whom he met in Langzhou 郎州 in 820, Li Ao had maintained extensive relations with other followers of the Chan patriarch Mazu 馬祖 at least since 790.

It is more difficult to assess Li Ao's role as a man of letters. Although eighteen *juan* of his writings survive, most of his poetry is lost. One of the poems that has been passed down, perhaps his best known, is titled: "Zeng Yaoshan Gaoseng Weiyan" 贈藥山高僧惟儼 (Presented to Weiyan, the Eminent Monk of Mount Yao):

> The shape of your body resembles the shape of a crane,
> Under thousands of pines: two cases of scriptures;
> I came and asked about the Way, you said nothing but:
> "The clouds in the blue sky and the water in the bottle."

> 練得身形似鶴形，千株松下兩函經
> 我來問道無餘說，雲在青天水在瓶.

According to the backstory in the *Song Gaoseng zhuan* 宋高僧傳 (Song-dynasty Biographies of Eminent Monks) Li Ao had tried to visit Weiyan several times. When he finally saw him he asked about the Dao 道. Wei Yan simply pointed upwards and then downwards with his finger. Li Ao didn't understand and then Wei Yan uttered the words in the final line. In response Li Ao wrote this poem.

Many of Li Ao's prose pieces are official and formal compositions included as models in the ninth-century anthologies. Li Ao postulated a reciprocal connection with personal moral cultivation (*yi* 義) and literary expression (*wen* 文), whereby stylistic effectiveness was a result and a reflection of the author's moral cultivation. Such a theory has obvious Chan affinities: the closer the adept comes to attaining this spiritual goal of enlightenment, the more natural become his behavior and expression. This critical stance was related to Liang Su's emphasis on vitality (*qi* 氣) in literature and to Han Yu's dictum to "expunge clichés" 陳言務去 as artificial and unnatural.

It is difficult to judge the degree of agreement between Li Ao and Han Yu. A joint commentary by the two authors, the *Lunyu bijie* 論語筆解 (Penned Explanations of the *Analects*), in which the infusion of Chan concepts into the old Confucian text is readily apparent, suggests the agreement was considerable. It is probably the case that the dissimilar personalities of the two men caused them to emphasize different facets of their common goal to create a vibrant, contemporary Confucianism. Towards this goal, Li Ao's contributions were more philosophical, Han Yu's more literary, as can be seen in the following "Guoma shuo" 國馬說 (Parable on the Horse from the Imperial Stables), which, although it adopts a genre Han Yu favored, lacks the humor and bite of Han Yu's *shuo* 說:

> There was a man riding a horse from the state stables who was traveling on the same road as a man riding a noble steed. The noble steed nipped the mane of the horse from the state stables and blood flowed onto the ground. The horse from the state stables kept his pace as before, his vigor also as before. He did not look back because of it as if he were unaware of it. After the noble steed had returned home he would not eat hay and would not drink water, but for two days stood there trembling with fear. The rider of the noble steed told the rider of the horse from the state stables and the later replied, "He [the noble steed] must feel ashamed. I shall have my horse go to encourage him and then things will be good."

Only then did he take his horse there. Thereupon the horse from state stables saw the noble steed and nuzzled with him. In the end he shared the stable and hay with him. In no time the noble horse's problems resolved themselves. Those who have four legs and eat hay are classified as horses; those with two legs who are able to speak are classified as human beings. Thus the horse from the state stables, with four legs and eating hay, is a horse. His ears, eyes, nose and mouth are also those of a horse. His four limbs and hundred bones are also those of a horse. In not being able to speak when he makes a sound it is also that of a horse. If you observe how his heart acts, then he is a human being. Therefore offended against but not retaliating [*Analects* 8.5], this was the horse from the state stables. Making a mistake and being able to correct it [variation of *Analects* 7.3], this was the noble steed. Among the people, there are many who indulge their anger by riding others, unaware that these others must bear this. If you observe that they have two legs and speak, they are human beings. Their ears, eyes, noses, and mouths are also those of human beings. Their four limbs and hundred bones are also those of human beings. [But] if one seeks that by which they act as human beings he will not find it. These human beings are human beings by means of their bodies and bones. The horse from the state stables is a horse by means of its body and bones. When those people ride a horse from the state stables, everyone thinks it is a human being riding a horse, but I'm not sure you can't claim it is a horse who is riding a human being. Is this not lamentable!

有乘國馬者，與乘駿馬者並道而行。駿馬齧國馬之鬃，血流於地，國馬行步自若也，精神自若也，不為之顧，如不知也。既駿馬歸，芻不食，水不飲，立而栗者二日。駿馬之人以告，國馬之人曰：「彼蓋其所羞也，吾以馬往而喻之，斯可矣。」乃如之。於是國馬見駿馬而鼻之，遂與之同櫪而芻，不終時而駿馬之病自已。夫四足而芻者，馬之類也；二足而言者，人之類也。如國馬者，四足而芻，則馬也；耳目鼻口，亦馬也；四支百骸，亦馬也；不能言而聲，亦馬也；觀其所以為心者，則人也。故犯而不校，國馬也；過而能改，駿馬也。有人焉，恣其氣以乘人，人容之而不知者，多矣。觀其二足而言，則人也；耳目鼻口，亦人也；四支百骸，亦人也；求其所以為人者，而弗得也。彼人者，以形骸為人；國馬者，以形骸為馬。以彼人乘國馬，人皆以為人乘馬，吾未始不謂之馬乘人。悲夫！

BIBLIOGRAPHY

Editions:
Hao Runhua 郝潤華. "*Li Ao ji* banben yuanliu kaobian" 李翱集版本源流考辨, *Tushu yu qingbao* 圖書與情報, 1992.4.
Li Ao 李翱. *Li Ao ji* 李翱集. Hao Runhua 郝潤華 et al., eds. Lanzhou: Gansu Renmin, 1992.
___. *Li Wengong ji* 李文公集. 18 *juan*. *SBCK* reprints Ming edition of 1475.
___. *Li Wengong ji*. Shanghai: Shanghai Guji, 1993.
___. *Li Xizhi Xiansheng wenji* 李習之先生文集. Shanghai: Huiwentang, 1911.
___ and Han Yu 韓愈 (768–824). *Lunyu bijie* 論語筆解. Taibei: Zhongguo Zixue Mingzhu Jicheng Bianyin Jijihui 中國子學名著集成編印基金會, 1977.
___. *Zhuo yi ji* 卓異記. Taibei: Yiwen, 1966.
Quan Tang shi, 6: 4162–63, 15: 11279.
Quan Tang wen, 634–640.7161–225.

Biographical Sources:
Jiu Tang shu, 160.4205–09; *Xin Tang shu*, 177.5280–82.

Translations:

Kunugi Tadashi 功刀正. *Ri Kō no Kenkyū, shiyōhen* 李翱の研究, 資料編. Tokyo: Hakuteisha 白帝社, 1987. Japanese translation (unannotated) of the eighteen *juan* of *Li Wengong ji*.

Strassberg, *Inscribed Landscapes*, 127–32.

See also Timothy Barrett, Reinhard Emmerich and Madeline Spring in Studies below.

Studies:

Barrett, Timothy Hugh. "Buddhism, Taoism and Confucianism in the Thought of Li Ao." Unpublished Ph.D dissertation, Yale, 1978. Contains a complete, annotated translation of the "Fu xing shu" and an appendix on the bibliography of Li's *Collected Works*.

___. *Li Ao: Buddhist, Taoist, or Neo-Confucian?* Oxford: Oxford University Press, 1992.

Bian Xiaoxuan 卞孝萱 et al. *Han Yu pingzhuan, fu Li Ao pingzhuan* 韓愈評傳, 附李翱評傳. Nanjing: Nanjing Daxue, 1998.

Bol, pp. 136–40.

Emmerich, Reinhard. *Li Ao (ca. 772–ca. 841): Ein Chinesisches Gelehrtenleben*. Wiesbaden: Harrassowitz, 1987.

Fukushima Shunnō 福島後翁. "Li Kō no gakuzen to 'Fukusei-sho'" 李翱の學禪と復性書, *Zengaku kenkyū* 禪學研究, 51 (February 1961): 32–44.

Hao Runhua 郝潤華. "Li Ao yu *Li Wengong ji*" 李翱與李文公集, *Xibei Shifan Daxue bao (Shehui Kexue ban)*, 1992.2.

He Zhihui 何智慧. *Li Ao nianpu gao* 李翱年譜稿. Chengdu: Sichuan Shifan Daxue, 2002.

Huang Aiping 黃愛平. *Li Ao yanjiu* 李翱研究. Shanghai: Fudan Daxue, 2007; Rpt. Taibei: Huamulan Wenhua, 2013.

Li Guangfu 李光福. "Li Ao nianpu dingbu" 李翱年譜訂補, *Sichuan Daxue xuebao* 1985.4.

Li En-p'u 李恩溥. "Li Ao nien-p'u" 李翱年譜, *Chung-yang jih-pao*, 15 May 1948.

Lo Lien-t'ien 羅聯添. Li Ao nianpu" 李翱年譜, in *Tangdai shiwen liujia nianpu* 唐代詩文六家年譜. Taibei: Xuehai, 1986.

___. "Li Ao yanjiu" 李翱研究. *Guoli bianyi guan guankan* 國立編譯館館刊, 2.3 (December 1973): 55–89. Contains information for family background, biography, and a chronological list of debatable Li Ao writings.

Spring, Madeline. "Roosters, Horses, and Phoenixes: A Look at Three Fables by Li Ao." *Monumenta Serica* 39 (1900–91): 199–208.

Tan Shaohong 潭紹紅. *Li Ao* 李翱. Kunming: Yunnan Jiaoyu, 2012.

Yang Lihua 楊立華. "Lun Songxue jinyu quxiang de genyuan jiqi zai sixiang shi shang de jieguo: song Han, Li yitong shuoqi" 論宋學禁欲取向的根源及其思想史上的結果：從韓，李異同說起. *Zhongguo zhexue shi* 中國哲學史, 2000.

Charles Hartman and William H. Nienhauser, Jr.

Li Bo 李白 (*zi*, Taibo 太白, 701–762; also known as Li Bai, Li Taibai) generally shares or competes with Du Fu 杜甫 (712–770)* for the honor of being the greatest of the Tang poets. Li's birthplace is uncertain, perhaps in Central Asia, and a minor branch of Li Bo studies centers on the irresolvable question of whether Li was of Turkic origin. Whatever his background, Li grew up in west China (modern Sichuan), and the conventions of the Sichuanese "type" exerted a strong influence on his self-image. The bravura of his poetic voice belonged to a long tradition of poets from the Sichuan region, from Sima Xiangru 司馬相如 (179–117 BC) in the Western Han to Chen

Zi'ang 陳子昂 (659–ca. 699)* in the Early Tang, and, after Li, to Su Shi 蘇軾 (1037–1101) in the Northern Song. He studied ca. 720 with the Daoist Zhao Rui 趙蕤 (ca. 660–ca. 742), an eclectic scholar who emphasized political topics in his *Fan jing* 反經 (Against the Classics), under whom he also practiced swordsmanship.

In the mid-720s Li Bo traveled down through the Yangzi Valley, seeking the social connections necessary to gain public recognition. His "Du Jingmen songbie" 渡荊門送別 (A Farewell While Travelling Past the Gateway to Jing) is dated by scholars to 724 and marks his emergence from the mountain-ringed stronghold of traditional Shu 蜀 into the plains of what was once the ancient state of Chu 楚 (also referred to as Jing):

> Having travelled far, I'm beyond the Gateway to Jing,
> Come to wander through Old Chu;
> The mountains follow the flat plains, and vanish,
> The River enters into this vast wasteland, and flows.
> The moon descends, a mirror flying from the sky,
> Clouds rise, forming images of city walls.
> I still cherish these waters from my hometown,
> That for ten-thousand miles see off my little boat.

> 渡遠荊門外，來從楚國游。山隨平野盡，江入大荒流。
> 月下飛天鏡，雲生結海樓。仍憐故鄉水，萬里送行舟。

Jingmen 荊門 (The Gateway to Jing) was one of the two mountains (Jingmen on the south bank of the Yangzi and Huya 虎牙 [Tiger's Fang] on the north shore) which framed the final narrow valley leading downstream from the precipitous terrain of Sichuan into the region traditionally known as Jing 荊 or Chu 楚 (centered on modern Hubei). The poem is written from the perspective of a native of Sichuan (and echoes an earlier poem by his fellow Sichuanese, Chen Zi'ang, titled "Du Jingmen wang Chu" 度荊門望楚 [Passing the Gateway to Jing and Gazing out on Chu]). Li Bo's poem reveals his youthful perception of the unfamiliar landscape of Chu that he is seeing for the first time. His depiction of Chu as a "vast wasteland" (line 4), turns the table on the normal view of Shu as the border region with little culture. The verbs *jin* 盡 (stop) and *liu* 流 (flow) suggest the lines may be parsed 2-2-1, the unusual line-break mirroring the disruption of the landscape (mountains to plains) and the river (torrent to flow). The third couplet portrays the night scene metaphorically: the moon descends slowly, but appears in the mirror-like Yangzi from the perspective of the moving boat to be flying; the clouds seem to weave a mirage-city such as those often seen near the sea (the *locus classicus* is the "Tianguan shu" 天官書 in the *Shiji*), perhaps suggesting the cityscapes the young poet expects to see as he continues his descent down the river. Yet the final couplet reveals the complex feelings of the poet. He sees the river's waters as both connecting him to his homeland upstream (some editions read *reng lian* 仍連, "still connect me," in line 7), while also rapidly seeing off his boat further and further from that homeland. This reading of the poem suggests it is the waters of the Yangzi which usher Li Bo into this new environment. But some critics believe that Li Bo is seeing off a friend in the final couplet ("I still cherish these waters from my hometown, as I see *your* little boat off on its ten-thousand-mile journey"). Yet other readings interpret the last four lines as dominated by the setting moon, which creates the cloud-illusion and, having also accompanied Li Bo downriver, both cherishes his hometown and takes leave of him as it sets.

After lingering for some time at Jingmen (where he wrote several poems) and sojourning a bit longer in Chu, Li Bo moved further downriver where he gradually made contacts which would lead him to Chang'an and the court. But during the late 720s after moving to Anzhou 安州 (near modern Anlu 安陸 fifty miles northwest of Wuhan in Hubei), he lived in reclusion, staying for some time at Taohua Yan 桃花巖 (Peach-flower Cliff) on Mount Baizhao 白兆山. "Shanzhong wenda" 山中問答 (Question and Response in the Mountains) is dated to 727 and describes Bi shan 碧山 (Azure Mountain), another name for Mount Baizhao, where the poem is thought to be written:

> Asking me why I dwell on the Azure Mountain?
> I smile, yet do not reply, my heart content and at ease.
> Peach blossoms are carried far into seclusion by flowing waters:
> to another world, beyond the human domain.

> 問余何意棲碧山？笑而不答心自閑。
> 桃花流水窅然去，別有天地非人間。

This short poem is framed as a dialogue between Li Bo and a local man, since an alternate version of the poem's title is "Shanzhong da suren" 山中答俗人 (Replying to a Commoner in the Mountains). Whoever the questioner is, he asks for the poet's motivation in choosing a life in the secluded mountains. Even though the poet is evasive and does not respond, the last two lines depict a scene which provides clues to the poet's state of mind. The landscape imagery is reminiscent of Tao Qian's 陶潛 (365–427) utopian "Peach Blossom Spring" 桃花源. It seems that the poet finds himself to be part of a similarly beautiful otherworldly realm. He smiles at the question because his surroundings speak for themselves. Expressing something without saying as well as the images of the Azure Mountain and its arcadian setting reflect the poet's interest in Daoist rhetoric. Li Bo here may be echoing the famous Daoist Tao Hongjing's 陶弘景 (456–536) response to an imperial summons while he was living on Mao Shan titled "Zhao wen shanzhong hesuo you fushi yida" 詔問山中何所有賦詩以答 (Responding to a Summons 'Asking What Do the Mountains Possess' by Writing a Poem):

> "What do the Mountains Possess?"
> Atop ridges midst so many white clouds.
> One can only naturally rejoice,
> It won't bear carrying along to give to you.
> 山中何所有，嶺上多白雲。
> 只可自怡悅，不堪持寄君.

It was probably also at this time that Li wrote "Chang xiang si" 長相思 (Endless Longing), a poem which has been read either as a love song sung by a female persona or as an allegory of Li Bo's desire to win favor with Emperor Xuanzong (the latter interpretation supports a later date for the poem):

Li Bo

Endless longing for you, in Chang'an.
Crickets autumnal chirp by the golden well-railing,
Light frost chills sadly, the bamboo mat's color is cold,
The lonely lamp's dim threads of longing almost cut.
Rolling up the curtain to gaze at the moon, I sigh for you in vain.
The lovely one, like a flower, distanced at clouds' edge.
Above an endless sky, azure and abyssal,
Below rippling waves of clear, green waters;
Heaven is distant, the way is far–my soul struggles to fly to you,
Even in dreams my soul cannot cross the mountain passes;
Endless longing shatters my heart!

長相思，在長安。絡緯秋啼金井欄，
微霜淒淒簟色寒。孤燈不明思欲絕，
卷帷望月空長歎，美人如花隔雲端。
上有青冥之長天，下有綠水之波瀾。
天長路遠魂飛苦，夢魂不到關山難。
長相思，摧心肝。

The poem implies a distant lover or friend, long parted. But it is one of three Li Bo wrote to this traditional *yuefu* tune pattern. Although the diction borrows clouds, flowers and the moon from earlier *yuefu*, Li Bo's imagistic use of them is fresh. The synesthesia of the "cold color" in line 3 and the trope of the "lamp's dim threads of longing" in line 4 have been widely praised.

Li Bo's sights, however, were set on the court in Chang'an. Through one of his acquaintances of this period, Wu Yun 吳筠 (d. 778),* a failed examination candidate turned wizard, Li was summoned to the court of Xuanzong (r. 713–756) in 742 and given a post in the new Hanlin 翰林 Academy (an appointment that lay outside the channels of usual bureaucratic advancement). One of his most famous poems, "Yujie yuan" 玉階怨 (Lament on the Jade Staircase), depicts a lonely palace lady and was probably written in 743:

On jade stairs dew arises,
as night lengthens soaks her gauze stockings.
Still she drops the crystalline blinds
gazing at the diaphanous autumn moon.

玉階生白露, 夜久侵羅襪。
卻下水晶簾, 玲瓏望秋月。

Although Li Bo uses some of the imagery of an early poem on this *yuefu* title by Xie Tiao 謝朓 (464–499), this quatrain turns on the second line with the dew-soaked stockings marking the length and intensity of the female persona's loneliness,

While serving in court, Li Bo traded on his reputation for drunken insouciance and became the subject of numerous anecdotes. However, the favor that he enjoyed rested on unstable ground, and in 744 he was expelled from court. Thereafter, Li first went to Luoyang, where he met Du Fu and then Gao Shi 高適 (700–765),* then wandered in the east and southeast, proclaiming himself an unappreciated man of genius who had been driven from court by powerful enemies. Arriving in Xuanzhou 宣州 (modern Xuancheng 宣城 in extreme southeastern Anhui just west of Lake Tai 太湖), Li Bo wrote some of his most famous poems including "Xuanzhou Xie Tiao Lou jianbie Jiaoshu Shu Yun" 宣州謝朓樓餞別校書叔雲 (At the Xie Tiao Pavilion in Xuanzhou, a Farewell Dinner for the Editor, Uncle Yun [Xie Tiao, mentioned just above, was a favorite poet of Li Bo and other High Tang poets]):

> What are abandoned and distanced now are
> Those bygone days that could not be retained;
> What unsettles my mind are
> These present days, full of troubles and worries.
> The long wind stretches thousands of miles, escorts the autumn wild geese—
> Faced such a scene, we can drink deep on this lofty pavilion.
> Your writings at Penglai have the bones of Jian'an poetry,
> My poems, like those of Xie Tiao, are fresh and elegant.
> We both have unrestrained enthusiasm, our sturdy thoughts are flying,
> Wishing to rise up to the blue sky to gaze at the bright moon.
> As I draw my dagger to cut the waters—the waters flow faster,
> When I lift my goblet to melt away sorrows—sorrows grow deeper.
> Life in this world does not satisfy our desires,
> Tomorrow dawn let's let down our hair and sail off in a small boat.

> 棄我去者，昨日之日不可留；
> 亂我心者，今日之日多煩憂。
> 長風萬里送秋雁，對此可以酣高樓。
> 蓬萊文章建安骨，中間小謝又清發。
> 俱懷逸興壯思飛，欲上青天覽明月。
> 抽刀斷水水更流，舉杯銷愁愁更愁。
> 人生在世不稱意，明朝散髮弄扁舟。

This poem was written when Li Bo had been cast out of the palace by the emperor and came to Xuanzhou. There he met Li Yun 李雲 and saw him off at the Xie Tiao Pavilion (Li Yun was returning to the capital). Although the title reveals it was written at "a farewell dinner," the poem is solely about Li Bo, his desires and worries. Letting down one's hair (removing an official cap and hairpin) and sailing a small boat are tropes of the hermetic life.

After the outbreak of the An Lushan Rebellion (756), he became implicated in a secondary revolt led by Prince Yung 永王 (Li Lin 李璘, ca. 720–757). Whether Li's complicity was voluntary remains uncertain, but when the revolt was crushed, Li was arrested for treason. After a year moving slowly to exile in Yelang 夜郎 (in modern Guizhou), he was released in 758 and spent his last years wandering in the Yangzi Valley, vainly seeking patrons to restore him to favor with the central government. The most outstanding of these appeals is his "Wei Song Zhongcheng zijian biao" 為宋中丞自薦表 (A Memorial Written for Vice-censor Song Recommending Myself), essentially a clever ruse intended to spur Song Ruosi 宋若思, the official who had been instrumental in having Li Bo released from prison in 757), to further assist him:

> Your servant has heard that when the feudal lords of ancient times recommended a worthy man, they received superior rewards, when they hid a worthy man, they received public

execution. If they three times suitably praise admirable qualities of someone, they will certainly be granted the nine marks of imperial favor, to be handed down a norm as a model for perpetuity. This Li Bo, in your servant's charge, has according to the facts been verified as free of guilt, is possessed of administrative talents, a match for the moral standards of Chaofu and Xuyou, his literary talents capable of transforming habits and customs, his learning can exhaust the boundaries of man and heaven. If he does not receive preferment, all within the four seas will proclaim it an injustice.

臣聞古之諸侯，進賢受上賞，蔽賢受顯戮。若三適稱美，必九錫光榮，垂之典謨，永以為訓。臣所管李白，實審無辜，懷經濟之才，抗巢、由之節。文可以變風俗，學可以究天人，一命不霑，四海稱屈。

Here Li Bo displays both his classical knowledge and his ever-present creativity. He essentially recommends himself, suggesting that he is writing this on behalf of Song Ruosi (for whom he has written other memorials) to be submitted to the Emperor. This is the height of hubris and perhaps desperation. The first line is a variation of a line in the "Wudi ji" 武帝紀 (Annals of Emperor Wu) in the *History of the Han*. The nine marks of imperial favor include a chariot and horses, state robs, musical instruments, the right to have a vermillion gate, the right to have one hundred armed attendants, bows and arrows, battle-axes, an sacrificial wines. Chaofu 巢父 and Xuyou 許由 are famous recluses who refused to take the throne offered them by the sage Emperor Yao. The implication here is that Li Bo has also refused high position out of moral rectitude, though now it seems he is ready to serve the court.

Of the 1004 poems ascribed to Li in the *Quan Tang shi* (additional attributions in other sources bring the number to around 1100), many are probably spurious. Some scholars argue less than 900 poems are definitely from his hand. Li Bo was an easy poet to imitate, and since most of his *yuefu* 樂府 and songs circulated orally, his name became a convenient one on which to hang poems of unknown authorship.

Although Li Bo's corpus contains about sixty pieces of prose and eight *fu* 賦, it is as a poet that Li is known. The first part of his poetic collection contains fifty-nine pentasyllabic "old-style" poems collectively entitled *Gufeng* 古風 (In the Old Manner). They are written in the thematic and stylistic tradition of the poetry of the Jian'an 建安 and Wei 魏 eras, as it was understood in the Tang. These works date from various periods of Li's life and include a number of concealed references to topical events. In the *Gufeng*, Li Bo often adopts the voice of a Confucian moralist, a voice entirely proper for the style in which he was writing, but one contrasting his usual pose as inebriate eccentric.

After the *Gufeng* in Li's collected works, there is a body of *yuefu* and songs (*gexing* 歌行). These two categories are only loosely differentiated, the former tending to adopt the personae of various *yuefu* "types," the latter tending to be the poet speaking in his own voice. Li was best known to his contemporaries for these *yuefu* and songs, and on them his later reputation was founded. "Shudao nan" 蜀道難 (Hard Road to Shu), anthologized in Yin Fan's 殷璠 *Heyue yingling ji* 河嶽英靈集 (753), is an excellent example of Li Bo's *yuefu* in the most extravagant manner. Using wildly irregular line lengths, Sichuanese exclamations, and long subordinate clauses normally excluded from both poetry and literary prose, Li hyperbolically describes the difficulties of the mountain journey from Chang'an to Chengdu 成都 (here the opening lines):

Oho! Behold! How steep and high!
How the roads to Shu are hard, harder than climbing up to the sky!
...
To the west stands Mount Taibo and its bird-track paths,
cutting across the top of Mount E'mei.
Earth collapsed, a mountain crumbled, five strongmen died,
but thereafter for the first time, through the heavenly ladders and plank roadways,
    Shu was joined with us.
The peak so high the Six-dragon chariot carrying the sun has to turn back;
Below one meets tortuous rivers, roaring torrents, rushing and swirling.

Even yellow cranes awing cannot cross;
Apes and gibbons helpless to clamber and climb.

噫吁戲！危乎高哉！
蜀道之難難於上青天！
...
西當太白有鳥道，可以橫絕峨眉巔。
地崩山摧壯士死，然後天梯石棧方鉤連。
上有六龍回日之高標，下有衝波逆折之迴川。
黃鶴之飛尚不得過，猿猱欲度愁攀援。

In reference to poems such as this, Li's contemporary Yin Fan described the poet's work as "strangeness on top of strangeness" 奇之又奇. Li Bo's *yuefu* and songs used folk motifs, fantastic journeys, mythic beings, and evocations of moments in history and legend to create a poetry of extreme and intense situations. The reference to strongmen comes from a story that tells when King Hui of Qin sent five beautiful girls to the King of Shu the five men sent to meet them were killed when their attempts to pull a snake from a hole caused a landslide which killed them all (the girls climbed the mountain and turned into stone). Yet even in such wild flights of fancy there is a strong undercurrent of irony, and his conscious excesses are such that the poet's stance is revealed as merely playful.

Occasional poems occupy the largest part of Li's collected works. A few of the more famous are merely intentional applications of the style of Li's *yuefu* and songs, but most are formally more conventional. Li wrote such poems with great facility, and even though he frequently achieved a simple felicity beyond the reach of his more cautious contemporaries, his occasional works are often marred by carelessness. In general, Li Bo lacked the carefully controlled craft that came so readily to his contemporaries, who were raised in the upper-class circles of the capital.

Following Li's occasional poems in the collected works, there is a small group of private poems containing many of Li's most famous pieces composed in even line-lengths. Poems such as "Yuexia duzhuo" 月下獨酌 (Drinking Alone by Moonlight [the first, and most famous, of four under this title], dated to 744) celebrate the self-image of drunken insouciance in which Li took pride:

Among the blossoms with a pot of wine,
I pour for myself, no friends at hand.
Raising my cup, I invite the bright moon,

Li Bo

    Facing my shadow, we become a threesome.
    Now the moon has never understood my drinking,
    And my shadow has only followed my outward self.
    Momentary companions, the moon and my shadow,
    We find pleasure that must keep pace with spring.
    I sing and the moon sways to the beat,
    I dance and my shadow follows helter-skelter.
    Getting high we share our enjoyment,
    Once drunk we scatter each on his own.
    Joined forever to revels beyond human feelings,
    We've arranged to meet in the far Milky Way.

花間一壺酒，獨酌無相親。
舉杯邀明月，對影成三人。
月既不解飲，影徒隨我身。
暫伴月將影，行樂須及春。
我歌月徘徊，我舞影凌亂。
醒時同交歡，醉後各分散。
永結無情游，相期邈雲漢.

Readers of classical poetry have always valued a poem's ability to embody a strong and identifiable personality; in the case of Li Bo, personality becomes the subject rather than the involuntary mode of the poem. Even Li's most speculative fantasy points more strongly to the poet's imaginative capacity than to the otherworldly objects of his vision.

Li Bo's poetry caused something of a literary sensation in the 740s and early 750s, but his stature as a contemporary poet was probably lower than that of Wang Wei 王維 (692–761 or 699–759)* or Wang Changling 王昌齡 (ca. 690–ca. 756).* As is the case with Du Fu, little attention was given to Li's work in the conservative atmosphere of the later part of the eighth century. The honor accorded Li by mid-Tang poets such as Han Yu 韓愈 (768–824)* and Bo Juyi 白居易 (772–846)* first raised Li, along with Du Fu, to preeminence among all the poets of the dynasty. Evaluation of the relative merits of Li Bo and Du Fu later became a minor critical genre, and while Du Fu had perhaps the larger following, Li Bo has had his partisans, from Ouyang Xiu 歐陽修 (1007–1072) to the modern scholar Guo Moruo 郭沫若 (1892–1978).

Li Bo was one of the first major figures in what was to become a cult of spontaneity in Chinese poetry. Li proclaimed, and others admired, his capacity to dash off poems in the heat of wine or inspiration. In the case of Li Bo, the interest in rapid and spontaneous composition was linked to a belief in innate genius that found its purest expression when untainted by the reflective considerations of craft. Such a concept of individual and innate genius, inimical to plodding poetic craft, is a historical growth within civilization; and the development of such a concept of artistic genius in China owes much to Li Bo, who so often made his own genius the true topic of his poetry.

Stylistic simplicity was a natural consequence of spontaneous composition (or of the desire to give the appearance of spontaneity). Not only is the diction and syntax of Li's poetry generally less bookish, but his poetry is noticeably more straightforward than that of his contemporaries.

Li Bo often referred to persons and events of legend and history, but he did not use textual allusions with the same frequency or precision as his younger contemporary, Du Fu.

Li Bo pays Daoist esoterica considerable attention, but this was perhaps less a satisfaction of genuine spiritual interests than appreciation of a source of delightful material for poetic fantasy. It is Li Bo's capacity for fantasy which, more than any other quality, sets him apart from his contemporaries and won him the admiration of later generations. Most Tang poets (with exceptions such as Li Bo's spiritual descendent Li He 李賀 [791–817]*) were most comfortable treating the world before their eyes; Li Bo greets the immortals and watches their flights with greater ease and familiarity than when he bids farewell to a friend.

BIBLIOGRAPHY

Editions:

Guo Yunpeng 郭雲鵬, ed. *Fenlei buzhu Li Taibo shi* 分類補註李太白詩. *SBCK*. Guo's Commentary includes earliest efforts by the Yuan scholars Yang Qixian 楊齊賢, and Xiao Shiyun 蕭士贇. This edition also includes Li Bo's prose. The most extensive commentary is that of Wang Qi 王琦 (1696–1774); it is the most frequently reprinted, under a number of titles. Wang draws from the commentaries of Yang and Xiao as well as from notes by other scholars, but he also corrects them and adds his own commentary on Li Bo's prose.

Hanabusa Hideki 花房英樹 *A Concordance to the Poems of Li Po*, Kyoto: Kyoto Daigaku Jinbun Kagaku Kenkyujo, 1957. Pages 6–30 contain an introduction to early editions.

Hiraoka Takeo 平岡武夫. *Ri Haku no sakuhin* 李白の作品. Tokyo: Tokyo Daigaku Jinbun Kagaku Kenkyujo, 1958. Contains the Song-dynasty edition of Li Bai's works held in the Seikadō Bunko 靜嘉堂文庫.

Li Bo 李白. *Li Bo shiji* 李白詩集. Changchun: Jilin Daxue, 2011.

___. *Li Hanlin ji: dangtu ben* 李翰林集: 當塗本. Hefei: Huangshan Shushe, 2004.

___. *Li Taibo ji* 李太白集. Beijing: Shangwu, 1930.

___. *Li Taibo jizhu* 李太白集註. Shanghai: Shanghai Guji, 1992.

___. *Li Taibo quanji* 李太白全集. Shanghai: Shanghai Shudian, 1988.

___. *Li Taibo quanji* 李太白全集. Beijing: Beijing Tushuguan, 1998.

___. *Li Taibo quanji* 李太白全集. Beijing: Zhonghua, 1977, 2003.

___. *Li Taibo wenji* 李太白文集. Lanzhou: Lanzhou Daxue, 2003.

___. *Li Taibo wenji: [30 juan]* 李太白文集: [30卷]. Beijing: Beijing Tushuguan, 2003.

___. *Li Taibo wenji* 李太白文集. Shanghai: Shanghai Guji, 1994.

Liu Kaiyang 劉開揚, ed. *Li Bo shi xuanzhu* 李白詩選注. Shanghai: Shanghai Guji, 1989.

Quan Tang shi, 3: 1673–1899, 11: 8970, 13: 10045, 14: 10624.

Quan Tang wen, 347–50.3970–4001.

Song Minqiu 宋敏求. *Li Taibei wenji: [sanshi juan]* 李太白文集: [三十卷]. Chongqing: Xinan Shifan Daxue; Beijing: Renmin, 2008.

Wang Qi 王琦. *Li Taibo quanji* 李太白全集. Beijing: Zhonghua, 2011.

Wang Xinlong 王新龍. *Li Bo wenji* 李白文集. Beijing: Zhongguo Xiju, 2009.

Xiong Lihui 熊禮匯. *Li Bo shi* 李白詩. Beijing: Renmin Wenxue, 2005.

Yang Qixian 楊齊賢. *Fenlei buzhu Li Taibo shi: [25 juan]* 分類補註李太白詩: [25卷]. Beijing: Beijing Tushuguan, 2003.

Ying Song kan ben Li hanlin ji 景宋刊本李翰林集. Beijing: Xianzhuang, 2001.

Yu Xianhao 郁賢皓. *Xin yi Li Bo shi quanji* 新譯李白詩全集. Taibei: Sanmin Shuju Faxing, 2011.

___. *Li Bo ji* 李白集. Nanjing: Fenghuang, 2006.
Zhan Ying 詹鍈. *Li Bo quanji jiaozhu huishi jiping* 李白全集校注匯釋集評. 8v. Tianjin: Bohua Wenyi, 1996.
Zhang Ruijun 張瑞君. *Li Bo ji* 李白集. Taiyuan: Sanjin, 2008.

Annotations:
An Qi 安旗. *Xinban Li Bo quanji biannian zhushi* 新版李白全集編年註釋. Chengdu: Ba Shu Shushe, 2000.
Ge Jingchun 葛景春. *Li Bo shi xuan* 李白詩選. Beijing: Zhonghua, 2005.
Lin Donghai 林東海. *Li Bo shi xuanzhu* 李白詩選注. Shanghai: Shanghai Yuandong, 2011.
Luan Rui 欒睿. *Li Bi shi ci xiang zhu* 李白詩詞詳注. Wulumuqi: Xinjiang Renmin, 2000.
Min Jing 閔靜. *Li Bo yu ju Anlu si shiwen xuanzhu* 李白寓居安陸司詩文選注. Wuhan: Huazhong Shifan Daxue, 2008.
Qu Tuiyuan 瞿蛻園 and Zhu Jincheng 朱金城. *Li Bo ji jiaozhu* 李白集校注. Shanghai: Guji, 1980.
Song Xulian 宋緒連 and Chu Xu 初旭, eds. *San Li shi jianshang cidian* 三李詩鑑賞辭典. Changchun: Jilin Wenshi, 1992. Contains numerous close readings of poems by Li He, Li Bo and Li Shangyin as well as short biographies and useful bibliographies for these three important poets.
Yu Xianhao 郁賢皓, ed. *Li, Du shi xuan* 李, 杜詩選. Taibei: Sanmin, 2001.
___. *Li Bo xuan ji* 李白選集. Shanghai: Shanghai Guji, 1990.
Zhou Qinying 周沁影 and Chi Naipeng 遲乃鵬. *Li Bo shi xuan* 李白詩選. Chengdu: Ba Shu Shushe, 2008.
Zhu Jian 朱諫. *Li shi bian yi* 李詩辨疑. Jinan: Qi Lu Shushe, 2005.

Biographical Sources:
Fu, *Tang caizi*, 1:380–95.
Jiu Tang shu, 190A.5053
Xin Tang shu, 202.5762–64.

Translations:
Alley, Rewi and Pan Jiezi. *Li Pai: 200 Selected Poems*. Hong Kong: Joint Publishing Co., 1980.
Articulated Ladies, pp. 293.
Birch, *Anthology*, pp. 225–34 and 335.
Cooper, Arthur. *Li Bo and Tu Fu*. Baltimore: Penguin, 1973.
Demiéville, *Anthologie*, pp. 220–46.
Eide, Elling O. *Poems by Li Bo,* with a separate volume, *Translator's Note and Finding Lists*. Lexington, Kentucky: The Anvil Press, 1984. Elegant translations of fifty poems. A phonograph record of reconstructed Tang music enclosed in the back cover.
Fuller, Michael A. *An Introduction to Chinese Poetry: From the* Canon of Poetry *to the Lyrics of the Song Dynasty*. Cambridge: Harvard University Press, 2018, pp. 204–19.
Hamill, Sam. "Li Po," in Seaton, Jerome P. and Dennis Maloney, eds. *A Drifting Boat: An Anthology of Chinese Zen Poetry*. Fredonia, NY: White Pine Press, 1994, pp. 47–48.
Hinton, David. *The Selected Poems of Li Po*. New York: New Directions, 1996.
Hu-Sterk, Florence. *L'Apogeé de la poésie chinoise—Li Bai et Du Fu*. Paris: Éditions You-feng, 2000.
Jakob, Paul. *Li Bai—Florilège*. Connnaissance de l'Orient 58. Paris: Gallimard, 1985.
Kubo Tensui 久保天隨. *Ri Taihaku*. Tokyo, Kokumin Bunko Kankōkai, 1928. Complete Japanese translation.
Mair, "Tang Poems," pp. 345–47.
Margoulies, *Anthologie*, pp. 231, 279, 316, 349, 361, 375, 392–93, 414, 425, 436.
Matsuura Tomohisa 松浦友久. *Ri haku shisen* 李白詩選. Tokyo: Iwanami, 1997.
Miao, "T'ang Quatrains," pp. 75–86.
New Directions, pp. 73–93.

Obata Shigenyoshi. *The Works of Li Po, the Chinese Poet*. London: Dent, 1923. Rpt. New York: Paragon, 1965.

Owen, *Anthology*, pp. 122–3, 213–14, 244, 247, 284–5, 376–8, 381–2, 397–404, 411–2, 463–5, 487–8.

___, *High T'ang*, pp. 109–43.

___, *Late Tang*, pp. 195–96, 313–14.

___, *Omen*, pp. 98–100, 138–41, 196–99, 201–02, 212–18.

___, *Remembrances*, pp. 77–79.

Pimpaneau, pp. 419–26.

Stoces, Ferdinand. *Le ciel pour couverture, la terre pour oreiller—la vie et l'œuvre de Li Po (701–762)*. Paris: Philippe Picquier, 2003.

Sunflower, pp. 101–14.

Von Zach, Erwin. *Li T'ai-po: gesammelte Gedichte*. Hartmut Walravens and Lutz Bieg, eds. 3v. Wiesbaden: Harrassowitz, 2000, 2005, and 2007.

Xiong Zhirui 熊智銳. *Li Bo youxianshi yanjiu* 李白遊仙詩研究. Taibei: Huamulan, 2020.

Xu Yuanchong 許淵沖. *Li Bo shi xuan* 李白詩選. Changsha: Hunan Renmin, 2007.

Yang Xianyi, *Poetry and Prose*, pp. 17–36.

Yu, *Imagery*, pp. 190–94.

Studies:

These are more numerous than Li Bo's poems: for bibliographies of articles see *Li Bo yanjiu lunwen ji* 李白研究論文集. Beijing, 1964, pp. 417–25; *Chūgoku koten kenkyū*, 16 (1968): 78–84; as well as Kroll and Nienhauser (below).

An Qi 安旗. *Li Taibo bie zhuan* 李太白別傳. Xi'an: Xibei Daxue, 2005.

___. ed. *Li Bo quanji biannian zhushi* 李白全集編年注釋. Chengdu: Ba Shu Shushe, 2000.

___ and Xue Tianwei 薛天緯. *Li Bo nianpu* 李白年譜. Jinan: Qi Lu, 1982.

Aoki Masaru 青木正児. *Ri haku* 李白. Tokyo: Shūeisha, 1996.

Benary-Isbert, Margot. *Das Ewige Siegel, eine Legende um den Dichter Li Tai Pe*. Frankfurt: Josef Knecht, 1974.

Cao Fanglin 曹方林. "Lun Li Bo de xiandao sixiang" 論李白的仙道思想, *Zhongguo wenxue yanjiu*, 1989. 4.

Chan, Timothy Wai Keung. "Engulfing and Embracing the Vast Earth: Li Bai's Cosmology in His 'Ballad on the Sun Rising and Setting,'" *Tang Studies* 37 (2019): 30–58.

Chen Dakang 陳大康. *Shuo Li Bo* 說李白. Shanghai: Cishu, 2007.

Chen Jingjie 陳敬介. *Li Bo shi yanjiu* 李白詩研究. Taibei: Hua Mulan Wenhua, 2009.

Chen Minxiang 陳敏祥. *Li Bo shan shui shi yanjiu* 李白山水詩研究. Gaoxiong: Chunhui, 2004.

Chen Wenhua 陳文華. *Shi jiu Li Taibo* 詩酒李太白. Beijing: Zhonghua, 2004.

Chen Xiang 陳香. *Kuangshi shixian Li Bo ping zhuan* 曠世詩仙李白評傳. Taibei: Guojia, 2010.

Chen Xuanxu 陳宣諭. *Li Bo shige hai yixiang* 李白詩歌海意象. Taibei: Wanjuanlou Tushu Gufen Youxian Gongsi, 2011.

Debon, Günther. *Li Tai-bo, Rausch und Unsterblichkeit*. Munich, Vienna and Basel: Kurt Desch, 1958.

Ding Zhihong 丁稚鴻. *Li Bo yu Ba Shu ziliao huibian* 李白與巴蜀資料彙編. Ba Shu Shushe, 2011. *20 shiji Li Bo yanjiu lunwen jingxuan ji: Ji nian Li Bo danchen 1300 zhou nian* 20世紀李白研究論文精選集: 紀念李白誕辰1330周年. Taibei Wenyi, 2000.

Eide, Elling O. "On Li Bo," in *Perspectives on the T'ang*, Arthur Wright and Denis Twitchett, eds., New Haven, 1973, pp. 367–403.

Fang Rixi 房日晰. "Li Bo shi yu sheng Tang qixiang" 李白詩與盛唐氣象, *Xibei Daxue Xuebao*, 1987. 2.

Fukuchi Jun'ichi 福地順一. *To ho ri haku haku rakuten: chūgoku no sandai shijin sono shi to shōgai* 杜甫, 李白・白楽天: 中国の三大詩人その詩と生涯. Tokyo: Chōeisha, 2007.

Fu Shaoliang 傅紹良. "Li Bo de gexing yishi yu beiju xintai" 李白的個性意識與悲劇心態, *Shanxi Shida Xuebao*, 1992. 1.

Ge Jingchun 葛景春. *Wenhua sheng Tang de shixian Li Bo* 文化盛唐的詩仙李白. Hefei: Anhui Daxue, 2013.

Guan Shiguang 管士光. "Lun Li Bo zhengzhi sixiang de zhudao yinsu ji qi fazhan licheng" 論李白政治思想的主導因素及其發展歷程, *Zhongguo Renmin Daxue Xuebao*, 1987.6.

Guo Moruo 郭沫若. *Li Bo yu Du Fu* 李白與杜甫. Beijing: Renmin Wenxue, 1971. Many reprints.

Ha Jin 哈金. *The Banished Immortal: A Life of Li Bai (Li Po)*. New York: Pantheon, 2019.

Hargett, James. M. "Li Bo (701–762) and Mount Emei," *Cahiers d'Extrême-Asie* 8 (1995): 67–85.

He Nianlong 何念龍. *Li Bo wenhua xianxiang lun* 李白文化現象論. Wuhan: Hebei Renmin, 2009.

He Qizhu 何騏竹. *Li Bo yuefu shi zhong de "wenxuexing"* 李白樂府詩中的"文學性". Taibei: Huamulan Wenhua, 2011.

Hou Yanshuang 侯延爽. *Li Bo shi yu yue* 李白詩與樂. Chengdu: Sichuan Renmin, 2009.

Hu Guorui 胡國瑞. *Li Bo zai Anlu xu* 李白在安陸序. Wuhan: Huazhong Shida, 1986.

Hu Sui 胡遂. "Daojiao yu Li Bo shige de xiangxiang yishu" 道教與李白詩歌的想象藝術, *Zhongguo wenxue yanjiu*, 1990.2.

Hu Zhenlong 胡振龍. *Li Bo shi guzhuben yanjiu* 李白詩古注本研究. Xi'an: Shaanxi Renmin, 2006.

Huang Xigui 黃錫珪. *Li Taibo nianpu: fu Li Taibo biannian shi mulu* 李太白年譜：附李太白編年詩目錄. Beijing: Zuojia, 1906 (rpt. 1958).

Ichikawa Momoko 市川桃子. *Ri haku: sono hito to bungaku* 李白：その人と文学. Tokyo: Nitchū, 1992.

Ichikawa Momoko 市川桃子 and Iku Kenkō 郁賢皓. *Shinpen ri haku no bun: sho shō no yakuchū kōshō* 新編李白の文: 書・頌の譯注考證. Tokyo: Kyūko, 2003.

Ichikawa Momoko 市川桃子 and Katsu Gyōon 葛曉音. *Ri haku no bun : jo hyō no yakuchū kōshō* 李白の文: 序, 表の譯注考證. Tokyo: Kyūko, 1999.

Inui Mototoshi 乾源俊. *Seisei suru ri haku zō* 生成する李白像. Tokyo: Kenbun, 2020.

Ji Wenbin 吉文斌. *Li Bo yue ci shu lun* 李白樂辭述論. Nanjing: Fenghuang, 2011.

Ji Zhun 紀準. *Li Bo shi shang du* 李白詩賞讀. Beijing: Xianzhuang, 2007.

Jia Jinhua 賈晉華. "Li Bo Gufeng xinlun" 李白古風新論, in *Zhongguo Li Bo yanjiu* 中國李白研究. Nanjing: Jiangsu Guji, 1990, pp. 142–48.

___. "Shu wenhua yu Chen Zi'ang, Li Bo" 蜀文化與陳子昂、李白, in *Tangdai Wenxue yanjiu* 唐代文學研究, 1992.

Jiang Zhi 蔣志. *Li Bo yu diyu wenhua* 李白與地域文化. Chengdu: Ba Shu, 2011.

Jin Taosheng 金濤聲 and Zhu Wencai 朱文采. *Li Bo ziliao huibian (Tang, Song zhibu)* 李白資料彙編（唐宋之部. Zhonghua, 2007

Kang Huaiyuan 康懷遠. *Li Bo shi shi xinian kaobian* 李白事詩系年考辨. Chengdu: Xinan Jiaotong Daxue, 2006.

___. *Li Bo piping lun* 李白批評論. Chengdu: Ba Shu Shushe, 2004.

___. "Li Bo Donghai zhi xing he ta dui daojiao taidu de bianhua" 李白東海之行和他對道教態度的變化, *Zhongguo wenxue yanjiu*, 1989.4.

Kong Fan 孔繁. "Li Bo he Daojiao" 李白和道教, *Shijie Zongjiao yanjiu*, 1991.4.

Kroll, Paul W. "Bibliography of Li Po Studies." Manuscript, Department of Oriental Languages, University of California, Berkeley, 1981.

___. "Lexical Landscapes and Textual Mountains in the High T'ang," *TP*, 84 (1998): 62–101. Contains readings of both poems and a prose text.

Li Bo yanjiu luncong 李白研究論叢. Chengdu: Ba Shu Shushe, 1991.

Li Changzhi 李長之 (1910–1978). *Li Bo zhuan* 李白傳. Tianjin: Bohua Wenyi, 2010.

___. *Dao jiaotu de shiren Li Bo ji qi tongku* 道教徒的詩人李白及其痛苦. Tianjin: Renmin, 2008.

Li Limin 李利民. *An Shi zhi luan yu san da shiren yanjiu* 安史之亂與三大詩人研究. Beijing: Zhongguo Shehui Kexue, 2010.

Li Xiemin 李協民. *Li Bo xin tan* 李白新探. Beijing: Zhongguo Wenlian, 2000.

Li Yongxiang 李永祥. *Li Bo shi ci* 李白詩詞. Jinan: Jinan, 2007.

Li Congjun 李從軍. *Li Bo kaoyi lu* 李白考異錄. Jinan: Qi Lu Shushe, 1986.

Lin Bangjun 林邦鈞, "Li Bo de zonghengjia sixiang yu fengge" 李白的縱橫家思想與風格. *Beijing Shifan Daxue Xuebao*, 1986.1.

Lin Geng 林庚. *Shiren Li Bo* 詩人李白. Shanghai: Shanghai Guji, 2000; rpt. Beijing: Qinghua Daxue, 2011.

Liscomb, Kathlyn. "Iconic Events Illuminating the Immortality of Li Bai," *MS* 54 (2006): 75–118.

Luo Zongqiang 羅宗強. "Li Bo yu Daojiao" 李白與道教, *Wenshi zhishi*, 1987.5.

Ma'anshan Li Bo yanjiusuo 馬鞍山李白研究所. *Taibo xian zong* 太白仙蹤. Hefei: Huangshan, 2010.

Ma Zhao 馬昭. *Li Bo zhuan* 李白傳. Taiyuan: Beiyue Wenyi, 1996.

Ma Zili 馬自立. "Li Bo shi yu furen ji jiu-jian tan Wang Anshi ping Li Bo shi" 李白詩與婦人及酒—兼談王安石評李白詩, *Nanjing Shehui Kexue*, 1990.3.

Maeno Naoaki 前野直彬. "Anriku no Ri Haku" 安陸の李白, *Chūgoku koten kenkyū*, 16 (1969): 9–22,

Margini, Maria Attards. *I Grandi poeti cinesi, Li Po*. Milan: Italian-Chinese Cultural Institute, 1956.

Matsuda Satomi 松田聡美. "Ri Haku–To Ho no shifu no tokucho: Dobutsu byosha o toshite" 李白-杜甫の詩風の特徴：動物描写を通して. *Chikushi gobun* 筑紫語文 22 (2013.10): 1–16.

Matsuura Tomohisa 松浦友久. *Ri Haku denkiron: kakugū no shisō* 李白伝記論: 客寓の詩想. Tokyo: Kenbun, 1994.

___. *Ri Haku shisen* 李白詩選. Tokyo: Iwanami, 1997.

___. *Ri Haku kenkyū* 李白研究. Tokyo: Sanseito, 1976.

___. "*Ri Haku—shi to shinshō* 李白—詩と心象. Tokyo: Shakai Shishōsha, 1984.

Minami Shinbō 南伸坊. *Ri Haku no tsuki* 李白の月. Tokyo: Chikuma, 2006.

Moore, Paul Douglas. "Stories and Poems About the T'ang Poet Li Bo." Ph.D. dissertation, Georgetown University, 1982.

Nienhauser, William H., Jr. 倪豪士. "Li Bo yanjiu Xiwen lunzhu mulu" 李白研究西文論著目錄, in You Xianhao 郁賢皓, ed., *Li Bo da cidian* 李白大辭典. Nanning: Guangxi Jiaoyu, 1995, pp. 378–86.

Ōno Jitsunosuke 大野實之助. *Ri Taihaku kenkyū* 李太白研究. Tokyo, 1959.

Pei Fei 裴斐. and Liu Shanliang 劉善良. *Li Bo ziliao huibian (Jin, Yuan, Ming, Qing zhibu)* 李白資料彙編 (金元明清之部). Beijing: Zhonghua, 2004.

Qi Weihan 戚維翰. *Li Bo yanjiu* 李白研究. Taibei: Huashi, 1975.

Ruan Tingyu 阮廷瑜. *Li Bo shi lun* 李白詩論. Taibei: Guoli Bianyiguan, 1986.

Shanghai cishu chubanshe wenxue jianshang cidian bianzuan zhongxin 上海辭書出版社鑑賞辭典編纂中心. *Li Bo shige jianshang cidian* 李白詩歌鑑賞辭典. Shanghai: Shanghai Cishu, 2012.

Shi Fengyu 施逢雨. *Li Bo shengping xintan* 李白生平新探. Taibei: Xuesheng, 1999.

___. "Li Bo: A Biographical Study." Unpublished Ph.D. dissertation, University of British Columbia, 1983.

___. *Li Bo shi de yishu chengjiu* 李白詩的藝術成就. Taibei: Daan, 1992.

Sō Rojin 莊魯迅. *Ri haku to to ho hyōhaku no shōgai* 李白と杜甫漂泊の生涯. Tokyo: Taishūkan, 2007.

Sun Gongfa 孫功發. "Shi lun Li Bo de youhuan yishi" 試論李白的憂患意識, *Zhongguo wenxue yanjiu*, 1989.4.

Takashima Toshio 高島俊男. *Ri Haku to To Ho: sonokodo to bungaku* 李白と杜甫：その行動と文學. Tokyo: Hyoronsha, 1972.

___. *Ri Haku to to ho* 李白と杜甫. Tokyo: Kōdansha, 1997.

Tong Yiqiu 童一秋. *Zhongguo shi da wenhao. [Li Bo]* 中國十大文豪. [李白]. Changchun: Jilin Wenshi, 2004.

Toroptsev, Sergey A. *Kniga o velikoi belizne. Li Bo: poeziya i jizn'*. Moscow: Natalis, 2002. The author has published numerous works on Li Bo, including translations and a biography of the poet.

Uno Naoto 宇野直人. *Ri Haku* 李白. Tokyo: Nihon Hōsō, 2007.

Uno Naoto 宇野直人 and Ebara Masashi 江原正士. *Ri Haku: kyodainaru nohōzu* 李白: 巨大なる野放図. Tokyo: Heibonsha, 2009.

Varsano, Paula M. "Drinking Alone beneath the Moon: Li Bai and the Poetics of Wine," in *Stories of Chinese Poetic Culture*. Zong-qi Cai, ed. New York: Columbia University, 2017.

___. "Immediacy and Allusion in the Poetry of Li Bo," *HJAS* 52.2 (June 1992): 225–61.

___. "Transformation and Imitation: The Poetry of Li Bo." Ph.D. diss. Princeton University, 1988.
___. *Tracking the Banished Immortal, The Poetry of Li Bo and Its Critical Reception*. Honolulu: University of Hawai'i Press, 2003.
Wada Hidenobu 和田英信. *Ri Haku* 李白. V. 1. Tokyo: Meiji, 2019.
Waley, Arthur. *The Poetry and Career of Li Bo*. London, 1950.
Wang Boxiang 王伯祥. *Zengding Li Taibo nianpu* 增訂李太白年譜. Chengdu: Sichuan Renmin, 1981.
Wang Dingchao 王定超. "Li Bo sixiang lun lue" 李白思想論略, *Zhongguo wenxue yanjiu*, 1989. 4.
Wang Guowei 王國巍. *Dunhuang ji haiwai wenxian zhong de Li Bo yanjiu* 敦煌及海外文獻中的李白研究. Chengdu: Ba Shu Shushe, 2010.
Wang Hongxia 王紅霞. *Songdai Li Bo jieshou shi* 宋代李白接受史. Shanghai: Guji, 2010.
Wang Jingzhi 汪靜之. *Li Du yanjiu* 李杜研究. Taizhong: Wentingge, 2011.
Wang Yunxi 王運熙. *Li BoYanjiu* 李白研究. Beijing: Zuojia, 1962.
___. *Li Bo jingjiang* 李白精講. Shanghai: Fudan Daxue, 2008.
Wang Yunzhao 王運照. "Lun Li Bo de pingjiao wanghou sixiang" 論李白的平交王侯思想, in *Zhongguo Li Bo yanjiu 1990 nian ji·shang* 中國李白研究 1990 年集·上. Nanjing: Jiangsu Guji, 1990.
Weng Wenxian 翁文嫻. *Li Bo shiwen timao zhi toushi* 李白詩文體貌之透視. Taibei: Hua Mulan Wenhua, 2010.
Williams, Nicholas Morrow. "The Pity of Spring: A Southern Topos Reimagined by Wang Bo and Li Bai," in Williams and Wang Ping, eds. *Southern Identity and Southern Estrangement in Medieval Chinese Poetry*. Hong Kong: Hong Kong University, 2915, pp. 137–63.
___. "Li Bai's 'Rhapsody on the Hall of Light': A Singular Vision of Cosmic Order," *TP* 101 (2015): 35–97.
Wong Siu-kit. *The Genius of Li Bo*. Hong Kong: Centre of Asian Studies, University of Hong Kong, 1974.
Wu Mingxian 吳明賢. *Li Bo yu Sichuan* 李白與四川. Chengdu: Sichuan Daxue, 2010.
Xie Chufa 謝楚發. *Shi jiu rensheng Li Bo* 詩酒人生李白. Shijiazhuang: Hebei Renmin, 2003.
Xie Yuzheng 謝育爭. *Li Bo gufu yanjiu* 李白古賦研究. Taibei: Wenjin Chubanshe Youxian Gongsi, 2010.
Xu Donghai 許東海. *Shiqing fubi hua zhexian: Li Bai shi fu jiaorong de duo miangxiang kaocha* 詩情賦筆話謫仙—李白詩賦交融的多面向考察、. Taibei: Wenjin, 2000.
Xu Yongzhang 許永璋. "Li Bo shige de shidai jiazhi" 李白詩歌的時代價值, in *Li Bo yanjiu luncong* 李白研究論叢. Chengdu: Ba Shu Shushe, 1987.
Xue Tianwei 薛天緯. *Li Bo, Tangshi, Xiyu* 李白, 唐詩, 西域. Shanghai: Guji, 2011.
Yamaguchi Naoki 山口直樹. *Ri Haku: honpō no shijin shisen ten'i muhō o utau* 李白: 奔放の詩人詩仙、天衣無縫を詠う. Tokyo: Gakushū Kenkyūsha, 1995.
Yan Qi 閻琦. *Li Bo shi xuan ping* 李白詩選評. Xi'an: Sanqin, 2010.
Yang Xusheng 楊栩生. *Li Bo shengping yanjiu kuangbu* 李白生平研究匡補. Chengdu: Ba Shu Shushe, 2000.
Yang Yi 楊義. *Li, Du shixue* 李杜詩學. Beijing: Beijing, 2002.
Yin Guohong 尹國宏. *Li Bo* 李白. Beijing: Kunlun, 2008.
Yu Xianhao 郁賢皓, ed., *Li Bo da cidian* 李白大辭典. Nanning: Guangxi Jiaoyu, 1995.
___. *Li Bo yu Tang dai wenshi kao lun* 李白與唐代文史考論. Nanjing: Nanjing Shifan Daxue, 2008.
___. *Li, Du shi xuan* 李, 杜詩選. Taibei: Sanmin, 2001.
___. "Lun Li Bo zuopin de shidai tezheng ji yishu tedian" 論李白作品的時代特徵及藝術特點, *Tianfu xinlun*, 1990. 5.
Yu Yuan 于元. *Li Bo* 李白. Changchun: Jilin Wenshi, 2011.
Yuan Xingpei 袁行霈. "Li Bo shige yu sheng Tang wenhua" 李白詩歌與盛唐文化, in *Zhongri Li Bo yanjiu lunwen ji* 中日李白研究論文集. Bejing: Zhanwang, 1986.10.
Zhan, *Daojiao*, pp. 261–86.
Zhan Furui 詹福瑞. "Tang Song shiqi Li Bo shige de jingdianhua" 唐宋時期李白詩歌的經典化, *Wenxue yichan* 2017.4: 51–64.
Zhan Ying 詹鍈. *Li Bo shiwen xinian* 李白詩文繫年. Beijing: Zuojia, 1958.
Zhang Houyu 張厚余. *Taibo shi zhuan* 太白詩傳. Changchun: Jilin Renmin, 2000.

Zhang Renqing 張仁青. *Li Bo shi chun* 李白詩醇. Taibei: Tiangong, 2003.

Zhao Changping 趙昌平. *Li Bo shi xuan ping* 李白詩選評. Shanghai: Shanghai Guji, 2003.

Zhongguo Li Bo yanjiu (2010–2011 nian ji) 中國李白研究 (2010–2011 年集). Hefei: Huang Shan Shushe, 2011.

Zhong Ri Li Bo yanjiu lunwen ji 中日李白研究論文集. Zhongguo Zhanwang, 1989.

Zhou Xiaoyou 周曉佑. "Qian lun Li Bo dui Jian'an fenggu de jicheng yu fazhan" 淺論李白對建安風骨的繼承與發展, *Xuexi yu Tansuo*, 1991.1.

Zhou Xunchu 周勛初. *Li Bo pingzhuan* 李白評傳. Nanjing: Nanjing Daxue, 2011.

___. *Li Bo* 李白. Nanjing: Nanjing Daxue, 2010.

___. *Li Bo yanjiu* 李白研究. Wuhan: Hubei Jiaoyu, 2003.

___. *Shixian Li Bo zhi mi* 詩仙李白之謎. Taibei: Shangwu, 1996.

Zhu Fengjuan 祝鳳娟. *Shixian Li Bo yu langman zhuyi shige* 詩仙李白與浪漫主義詩歌. Changchun: Jilin Wenshi, 2010.

Stephen Owen and William H. Nienhauser, Jr.

Li Deyu 李德裕 (*zi*, Wenrao 文饒, 787–850) was an important statesman poet of the mid-late Tang. Li served as a Grand Councilor under two emperors and was involved in the "Niu-Li factional rift" as the leading figure of the Li faction. Li Deyu was born into the Zhaojun Li 趙郡李 clan (modern Zhaoxian 趙縣 of Hebei province), one of the five great "Noble Shandong Houses" 山東士族. His father, Li Jifu 李吉甫 (758–814) served as Grand Councilor during the Yuanhe reign period (806–820), thus Li Deyu entered officialdom as Editor in the Palace Library, a fast-track entry post, through the protection privilege instead of the *jinshi* examination in 813. Yet, he soon resigned from that position and took appointments on the staffs of provincial governors. In 817, he was employed as a Recorder by Zhang Hongjing 張弘靖 (760-824), Military Commissioner in Hedong 河東). With the succession of Emperor Muzong (r. 820–824), Li Deyu's political career took off at the capital. In 820, Li Deyu was summoned to the court and appointed as an Academician of the Hanlin Academy. Along with Yuan Zhen 元稹 (779–831)* and Li Shen 李紳 (772–846),* Li Deyu was included as one of the *Sanjun* 三俊 (The Three Perfections)." Li was known for the sublimity of his writing and drafted many major proclamations from the Forbidden Palace during his two years at the Hanlin Academy.

Li Deyu was forced out of the capital in 822 by the then Grand Councilor Li Fengji 李逢吉 (758–835). Li Fengji later empowered Niu Sengru 牛僧孺 (ca. 779–ca. 848) and Li Zongmin 李宗閔 (d. 846), who were to become Li Deyu's life-long political rivals and the leading figures of the Niu faction. For the next decade, Li Deyu was in and out of the capital several times—his major positions during this time include Surveillance Commissioner at Zhexi 浙西 (commandery seat at Runzhou 潤州, modern Zhenjiang 鎮江, Jiangsu province), and then Military Commissioner of Xichuan 西川 (commandery seat at modern Chengdu 成都, Sichuan province). In 833, Li Deyu made a comeback as Grand Councilor under Emperor Wenzong 文宗 (r. 827–840). However, Li Deyu had to step down from the position after a year and a half under pressure from both the Niu faction and a new faction headed by Zheng Zhu 鄭注 (d. 835) and Li Xun 李訓 (d. 835), which had gained imperial favor through eunuch connections. After six years in the provinces, Li Deyu was reinstated as Grand Councilor when Emperor Wuzong (r. 840–846) succeeded the throne in 840. With the support of the emperor, Li Deyu pacified rebellious military

Li Deyu

commissioners, suppressed the expanding power of the eunuchs, and resisted the invasions of the Uighurs and other peoples. The Huichang reign period (841–846), which was regarded in retrospect as a brief revival of the great Tang prosperity, saw Li's rise to the summit of his professional life as he became Duke of Wei 衛 and Defender-in-Chief. But this glorious time quickly faded when Emperor Xuanzong (r. 846–859) took the throne. Under the new emperor, the Niu faction, now headed by Bo Minzhong 白敏中 (792-861), regained power. As a consequence, Li Deyu was exiled to far-off lands, serving first in Chaozhou 潮州 (modern Chaoan 潮安, Guangdong province) as Vice Prefect and then as Revenue Manager in Yazhou 崖州 (modern Qiongshan 瓊山, Hainan province), where he eventually died in 850.

Li Deyu's thoughts on writing and its role influenced later authors. He advocated writings that are "precise and logical" 簡而當理. As for the originality, he did not strive for unprecedented invention, but valued innovation based on traditional words and ideas. As he put it in a metaphor, the originality of writing is just like the "newness" of the sun and moon, in the sense that the sun and moon are "commonly seen throughout history, but their illuminations are constantly new" 雖終古常見，而光景常新. That is to say, Li believed that writings can "illuminate" the world afresh with old materials. In seeking originality in writing, one does not need to be cut off from traditional roots.

Modern scholars generally divide the entire corpus of Li Deyu's writings into three groups, which correspond to the rises and falls of his career. The first category is generally referred to as the "Huichang Writings," which consists of memorials to the throne, orders or instructions for officials, and state letters to rulers of border states. These writings, now preserved in his twenty-*juan Huichang yipin ji* 會昌一品集, have long been considered exemplars for documentary writing, along with those by Lu Zhi 陸贄 (754–805).* The second group includes poems and rhapsodies that Li Deyu composed during his exiles and retreats. During his stay in Yuanzhou 袁州 (modern Yichun 宜春, Jiangxi province), Li Deyu wrote more than ten rhapsodies that are fused with homesickness and political aspirations. Among these poems of retreat and exile, there is an entire *juan* of eighty-eight poems written in nostalgia for the Pingquan Mountain Estate 平泉山莊, Li Deyu's magnificent mansion in Luoyang. Li Deyu's occasional poems, those that he composed during idle moments as military commissioner in various regions, form the third group of his writings. During his last years in exile, Li Deyu composed a series of essays, titled *Record of Utmost Sorrow* (Qiongchouzhi, 窮愁志). According to his official biography in the *Jiu Tang shu*, he also compiled records and accounts of the past events, including *Ci liushijiu wen* 次柳氏舊聞 (Sequenced Old Stories from the Lius), a collection of stories concerning Emperor Xuanzong's reign. The loss of official accounts during the An Lushan Rebellion (755–763) afforded the post-rebellion generation an opportunity to fix and reshape the collective memory of the recent past. Li Deyu was one of those who had direct access to rare materials through family ties and broader social connections and was, therefore, able to ride an early tide in his generation's re-writing of the Kaiyuan-Tianbao era. These accounts were first presented to the throne in 834 and later incorporated into official histories after the fall of the Tang dynasty, thus further becoming fertile soil for the growth of even more anecdotes. The anecdote translated below is very typical of the stories collected in *Ci Liushi jiuwen*:

Yuan Qianyao's 源乾曜 (?–731) memorials always pleased the emperor, and, consequently, His Highness became very fond of Yuan and promoted him all at once from the position of Vice Director of Ministry of Revenue, Metropolitan Governor, all the way to Grand Councilor. One day, His Highness confided to his close attendant Gao Lishi, "Do you know why I promoted Qianyao so fast?" Lishi replied, "I am afraid that I really don't know." His Highness then explained, "I advanced him because he so closely resembles Xiao Zhizhong 蕭至忠 (?–713) in appearance and speech." Lishi asked, "But didn't Zhizhong betray Your Majesty? Why does Your Majesty still remember him so favorably?" His Highness said, "It was only in Zhizhong's later years that he blundered [by attaching himself to Princess Taiping]. When he first served at the court, can you say that he was not a worthy Grand Councilor?" His Highness always cherished the talents of his ministers and was tolerant of their mistakes. All those who heard this story about Yuan Qianyao were deeply touched and filled with joy.

源乾曜因奏事稱旨，上悅之，於是驟拔用，歷戶部侍郎、京兆尹，以至宰相。異日，上獨與力士語曰：「爾知吾拔用乾曜之速乎？」曰：「不知也。」上曰：「吾以其容貌、言語類蕭至忠，故用之。」力士曰：「至忠不嘗負陛下乎，陛下何念之深也？」上曰：「至忠晚乃謬計耳。其初立朝，得不謂賢相乎？」上之愛才宥過，聞者無不感悅。

This anecdote addresses the "puzzle" as to why and how Yuan achieved a high status in view of his mediocrity. Through a purported "private conversation" with his close attendant, this anecdote claims to reveal the emperor's reflections on this revolt and its participants. It downplays the cruelty of this political struggle and highlights the emperor's tolerance and forgiveness of disloyal ministers.

Li Deyu has also been credited with "Wang Jiangnan" 望江南 (Gazing at the Southland), a *ci* lyric tune which he was said to have composed in memory of a courtesan or concubine he met when he was stationed in Zhexi. The following poem, "Deng Yazhoucheng zuo" 登崖州城作 (Written on Climbing the Yazhou City Wall), was composed in exile during his late years:

I climb the tall tower alone, gaze towards the imperial capital;
Even for a bird in flight, the journey is still half a year.
Green mountains seem to invite one to stay and settle down,
Their hundreds of turns and myriad curves encircle the city walls.

獨上高樓望帝京，鳥飛猶是半年程。
青山似欲留人住，百匝千遭繞郡城。

This poem is simple and devoid of literary allusions or strong emotion. The poem is in traditional poetic mode of "climbing high and looking afar." The old imperial capital the poet was so eager to see again is now out of sight, but not for a moment out of his mind. The poet also places "the bird in flight," a symbol of freedom, in sharp contrast to the poet marooned in this far-off land. Yet, as if to comfort himself, the poet does not conclude his verse in low spirits, for, in the second couplet, the mountains separating the poet from the imperial capital are now personified as a host warmly inviting the poet to "stay and settle down."

In the end, Li Deyu did not make it back to the imperial capital in his remaining years. In 850, he passed away in Yazhou, thousands of miles away from the imperial capital. Two years later, his son, Li Ye 李燁 (826-860), escorted his coffin back to Luoyang where he reinterred him in the family plot. In time, the Tang court reversed the unjust verdict on Li Deyu and in 860 reinstated him posthumously.

BIBLIOGRAPHY

Editions:

Fu Xuancong 傅璇琮 and Zhou Jianguo 周建國, eds. *Li Deyu wenji jiaojian* 李德裕文集校箋. Shijiazhuang: Hebei Jiaoyu, 2000.

Li Deyu 李德裕. *Li Weigong Huichang yipin ji* 李衛公會昌一品集. Beijing: Zhonghua, 1985. *Congshu jicheng chubian* 叢書集成初編 edition.

___. *Huichang yipin ji* 會昌一品集. Shanghai: Shanghai Guji, 1994. *Siku tangren wenji congkan* 四庫唐人文集叢刊.

___. *Huichang yipin zhi ji* 會昌一品制集. Beijing: Beijing Tushuguan, 2004. Photocopied from on a Song edition.

Quan Tang shi, 7: 5423–49, 14: 10663, 15: 11313–14.

Quan Tang wen, 696–711.7923–8075.

Wang Shizhen 王世貞 (1526–1590). "Du *Huichang yipin ji*" 讀會昌一品集 [On Reading the *Huichang yipin ji*], in *Yanzhou shanren sibugao* 弇州山人四部稿 1577 edn., rpt. Taibei: Weiwen, 1976, 112.19b.

Biographical Sources:

Jiu Tang shu, 174.4509–31.

Xin Tang shu, 180.5327–44.

Translations:

See Zhou Jianguo (Jonathan Pease, translator) and Zou Xin below in Studies.

Studies:

Dong Naibin 董乃斌. "Li Deyu de shi he shizhong de Li Deyu" 李德裕的詩和詩中的李德裕. *Tangdai wenxue luncong* 唐代文學論叢 6. Xi'an: Shanxi Renmin, 1985, pp. 70–83.

___. "*Huichang yiping ji* ji Li Deyu de sixiang he chuangzuo" 會昌一品集及李德裕的思想和創作. *Wenxue pinglun congkan* 文學評論叢刊 18. Beijing: Zhongguo Shehui kexue, 1983: 310–35.

Drompp, Michael Robert. *Tang China and the Collapse of the Uighur Empire: a Documentary History*. Leiden: Brill, 2005.

Fu Xiren 傅錫壬. *Niu Li dangzheng yu Tangdai wenxue* 牛李黨爭與唐代文學. Taibei: Dongda Tushu Gongsi, 1984.

Fu Xuancong 傅璇琮 (1933-2016). *Li Deyu nianpu* 李德裕年譜. Beijing: Zhonghua, 2013.

Knight, David A. "Plain Becomes Patterned: Li Deyu and the White Lotus." *CLEAR* 39 (2017): 55–78.

Liu Peng 刘鹏, "Li Deyu yu 'Zhao Ming wenxuan'" 李德裕与"昭明文选," *Zhongguo wenxue yanjiu* 3 (2012): 70–73.

Luo Manling. "Remembering Kaiyuan and Tianbao: The Construction of Mosaic Memory in Medieval Historical Miscellanies." *T'oung Pao*, 97 (2011): 263-300.

Ouyang Xiu 歐陽修 (1007–1072). "Tang Li Deyu 'Dagushan fu'" 唐李德裕大孤山賦 [Li Deyu's Rhapsody on the Dagushan from the Tang Dynasty]. *Jigu lu bawei* 集古錄跋尾, ch. 9, *Ouyang Xiu quanji* 歐陽修全集. Taibei: Shijie, 1971, p. 1198.

Qu Jingyi 曲景毅. "Li Deyu yi wenzhang zhi tianxia" 李德裕以文章治天下, in Qu Jingyi, *Tangdai 'Dashou bi' zuojia yanjiu* 唐代大手筆作家研究. Beijing: Zhongguo Shehui Kexue, 2015, pp. 167–222.

Schafer, Edward H. "Li Te-yü and the Azalea," *Études Asiatiques, Asiatische Studien*, 18–19 (1965): 105–14.

Sun Min 孫敏. *Li Deyu yu Niu Li dangzheng: Qiongchou zhi yanjiu* 李德裕與牛李黨爭: 窮愁志研究. Chengdu: Sichuan Daxue, 2004.

___. "Li Deyu *Wenzhang lun* kaozhen jiqi wenxue guan" 李德裕《文章论》考证及其文学观, *Sichuan Shifan Xueyuan Xuebao (Zhexue Shehui Kexue Ban)* 2 (2003).

Tang Chengye 湯承業. *Li Deyu yanjiu* 李德裕研究. Taibei: Xuesheng, 1973.

Zhou Jianguo 周建國. "Consider the Sun and Moon: Li Te-yü and the Written Word," Jonathan Pease, trans. *TS* 10–11 (1992–1993): 81–110.

___. "Lun zhongwan Tang wenxue yu Niu Li dangzheng, jianping *Li Deyu nianpu*" 論中晚唐文學與牛李黨爭—兼評李德裕年譜. *Wenxue yichan* 文學遺產 3 (1987): 130–37.

___. "Considering the Sun and Moon: Li Te-yu and the Written Word." Jonathan Pease trans. *T'ang Studies* 10–11 (1992–1993): 81–109.

Zou Xin. "Collecting Memories of a Fading Glory: A Translation of Li Deyu's (787-850) *Ci Liushi jiuwen*." *T'ang Studies* 36 (2018): 121–49.

Xin Zou

Li Duan 李端 (*zi*, Zhengji 正己, d. ca. 785) is reputed to have studied poetry with the poet-monk Jiao Ran 皎然 (720–799).* He was a nephew of Li Jiayou 李嘉祐 (*jinshi* 784, d. ca. 779), a celebrated poet of the same period who is sometimes counted as one of the "Ten Talents of the Dali Era" (see also the entry on Lu Lun [748–ca. 798]).* Li Duan was a native of Zhaozhou 趙州 (modern Zhaoxian 趙縣 in Hebei); he studied as a youth at Lushan 廬山 and passed the *jinshi* examination in 770, becoming an Editor in the Palace Library. He resigned this position due to illness and went to live and study in the Caotang Si 草堂寺 (Grass-hut Monastery) on Zhongnan Shan 終南山 south of the capital. Sometime later he became Vice Prefect of Hangzhou. There he bought some land south of the Huqiu 虎丘; later he moved to Hengshan 衡山 (modern Hunan) where he went into reclusion. At some time in his career he also visited Shu 蜀 (modern Sichuan).

His poetry (over 250 poems are extant) has been compared to, but ranked below, that of Sikong Shu 司空曙 (ca. 720–790),* because of his less skillful use of prosody. He also used the heptasyllabic meter with some success, both in occasional verses and in songs and ballads. His friends included a number of literati including many of the "Ten Talents," as well as Liu Zhongyong 柳中庸 (fl. 770) and Zhang Fen (fl. 767). His son, Li Yuzhong 李虞仲 (772–836), was also skilled in poetry.

"Ting Zheng" 聽箏 (Listening to the Zither) is one of his most widely read poems:

> Strumming a zither with the cassia-wood pegs,
> Her hands so white in her jade-like chamber.
> Wanting to attract the attention of Zhou Yu,
> She plays a wrong note from time to time.

> 鳴箏金粟柱，素手玉房前。
> 欲得周郎顧，時時誤拂絃。

Li Duan

The poem revolves on the clever allusion to Zhou Yu 周瑜 (175–210), a handsome general and statesman during the Three Kingdoms era. He was so sensitive to classical music that if a musician played a wrong note, he would remind the player of his error with a glance. The persona who is playing the zither in the first two lines is obviously hoping to flatter a man in her company by comparing him to Zhou Yu, while also attracting his glance.

Li Duan, besides the associations noted above, was often together with other important literati in the capital from about 768 until he passed the *jinshi* in 770 including Dugu Ji 獨孤及 (725–777),* Gu Kuang 顧況 (727–ca. 814),* and Huangfu Ran 皇甫冉 (ca. 717–ca. 771).*

BIBLIOGRAPHY

Editions:
Quan Tang shi, 5: 3229–77, 14: 11144.

Annotations:
Zhang Dengdi 張登第, Jiao Wenbin 焦文彬 and Lu Anshu 魯安澍. *Dali shi caizi shixuan* 大曆十才子詩選. Xi'an: Shaanxi Renmin, 1988.

Biographical Sources:
Fu, *Tang caizi*, 1:71–82; 5:177–81.

Translations:
Margoulies, *Anthologie*, pp. 350, 415, 437.
Owen, *High Tang*, pp. 274–80.

Studies:
Guo Dianchen 郭殿忱, "Lulun 'Song Li Duan' shi kaoyi" 盧綸《送李端》詩考異, *Yuncheng Xueyuan xuebao* 1 (2014): 29–30.
Jiang Yin 蔣寅. "Caizi zhongde caizi—Li Duan"才子中的才子—李端, *Hebei Daxue xuebao (Zhexue Shehui Kexueban)* 3 (1993): 59–66.
___. *Dali shiren yanjiu* 大曆詩人研究. Beijing: Zhonghua, 1995.
Li Na 李娜, "Li Duan yu Fojiao zhi guanxi lüeshu" 李端與佛教之關係略述, *Anhui wenxue* 5 (2008).
Ogawa Shoichi 小川昭一. "Taireki no shijin" 大曆の詩人, *Shibun*, 24 (1959): 22–33.
Owen, *High Tang*, pp. 274–80.
Peng Jieying 彭洁莹, "Lun Tang Dali Caizi Li Duan de shige tishi jiqi meixue fengge"論唐大歷才子李端的詩歌體式及其美學風格, *Guandong Haiyang Daxue xuebao* 33.5 (Oct. 2013): 44–49.
Zhang Guohao 张国浩, "Lüelun Li Duan de shengping ji shige chuangzuo" 略論李端的生平及詩歌創作, *Zhongwen zixue zhidao* 4 (2007): 43–45.

William H. Nienhauser, Jr.

Li Gongzuo 李公佐 (*zi*, Chuanmeng 顓蒙, ca. 770–ca. 848), was one of the principal writers of literary-language tales during the Tang dynasty. His ancestral home was Longxi 隴西 (modern Gansu), but he seems to have spent most of his long life in central and south China. There is also evidence that he was distant kin to the Tang imperial family. He was a successful *jinshi* examination candidate, probably in the mid-790s, and he subsequently held several rather low-ranking positions in various administrative offices in what are now the provinces of Guangdong, Jiangxi, and Jiangsu. Many of his positions were under officials associated with the court faction of Li Deyu 李德裕 (787–850),* and in the early 840s he was clerk to Li Shen 李紳 (772–846),* then Military Commissioner of Huainan 淮南 (seat at modern Yangzhou), who was one of Li Deyu's principal supporters. When Emperor Xuanzong assumed the throne in mid-846, Li Deyu's faction fell from favor (a posthumous investigation of corruption involving Li Shen provided the final excuse for their dismissal), and in the sweep Li Gongzuo was also stripped of his official status. Wording in the memorial denouncing Li Shen and the others involved in the case is understood by some to indicate that Li Gongzuo was already dead when it was presented in 848.

Only four of Li Gongzuo's short stories survive, but they show his work to be remarkable for its variety. The longest, entitled "Nanke Taishou zhuan" 南柯太守傳 (The Governor of Southern Bough), is an expanded treatment of a theme seen in Shen Jiji's 沈既濟 (ca. 740–ca. 800)* earlier "Zhenzhong ji" 枕中記 (The World Inside a Pillow); as in "The World inside a Pillow," the protagonist here, Chunyu Fen 淳于棼, dreams a whole lifetime, complete with fame, fortune, and highly-placed marriage, in a brief, drunken nap. Like Shen's earlier work, Li's story carries a message concerning the ultimate vanity of striving for worldly fame and fortune; but unlike Shen, Li tied his story more closely to the real world, his dream world being identified with an ant colony located beneath the "southern bough" of a nearby locust tree.

> When Chunyu awakens, he remembered the events of Sandalwood Creepers' campaign against him and again asked his two friends to look for traces of the campaign outside. Not a mile to the east of his home was an old dried-up brook. On its bank was a huge sandalwood tree heavily entwined with vines and creepers, so that looking up one couldn't see the sun. There was a small hole to the side of the trunk in which indeed a colony of ants was hiding together. The state of Sandalwood Creepers must have been here! At that time when Fen's drinking companions Zhou Bian and Tian Zihua, who both lived in Liuhe County, had not come by to visit for ten days, Feng quickly sent his servant-boy to ask after them. Mr. Zhou had suddenly taken ill and passed away and Mr. Tian was also bedridden with a disease. Feeling even more the transience of the Southern Bough and understanding that man's life was only a sudden moment, Chunyu Fen then settled his mind in the school of the Dao, giving up wine and women. Three years later in the *dingchou* year [797] Chunyu indeed died in his home at the age of forty-seven....

> 復念檀蘿征伐之事，又請二客訪跡於外。宅東一里，有古涸澗，側有大檀樹一株，藤蘿擁織，上不見日，旁有小穴，亦有群蟻隱聚其間，檀蘿之國，豈非此耶！時生酒徒周弁、田子華，並居六合縣，不與生過從旬日矣，生邊遣家僮疾往候之。周生暴疾已逝，田子華亦寢疾於床。生感南柯之浮虛，悟人世之倏忽，遂棲心道門，絕棄酒色。後三年，歲在丁丑，亦終於家，時年四十七....

Li Gongzuo

The second of Li's stories, "Xie Xiao'e" 謝小娥 (the heroine's name), is one of the first treatments in Chinese literature of a crime and its solution. In the story a murderer is identified when riddles involving the characters of his name are solved. Although plays on the component parts of characters appear in works as early as the *Zuozhuan*, this seems to be the first appearance of the device in a fictional setting. It is seen frequently in more modern fictional works.

Li's other two surviving stories are of lesser interest. "Lujiang Feng'ao" 廬江馮媼 (Old Mrs. Feng from the Lu River), which tells of an encounter with a woman who turns out to have died the previous year, is quite similar in content and style to the strange tales (*zhiguai* 志怪) collected and recorded earlier during the Six Dynasties period. "Gu Yuedu jing" 古岳瀆經 (The Ancient Classic of Peaks and Rivers) is a tale concerning a huge monkey-like river creature and tells of Li Gongzuo later finding confirmation of the creature's existence in an ancient scripture which he discovered in a remote mountain grotto. The scripture appears to be completely fictional, most likely intended to bring to mind the *Shanhai jing* 山海經, an actual early book of fantastic geographical lore.

Li Gongzuo is known to have associated with other contemporary writers of tales, and his stories circulated widely already during the Tang dynasty. "The Governor of Southern Bough" and "Xie Xiao'e" especially have become standard anthology selections.

BIBLIOGRAPHY

Editions:

Li Fang 李昉 (925–996) *et al*. *Taiping guangji* 太平廣記. Beijing: Zhonghua, 1961, 343.2718–19 [Feng'ao], 467.38453846 [Yuedu jing], 475.3910–15 [Nanke], 491.4030–32 [Xie Xiao'e].
Lu Xun 魯迅. *Tang Song chuanqi ji* 唐宋傳奇集. Rpt. Hong Kong: Xinyi, 1967, pp. 75–90 [all four tales].
Quan Tang Wen, 725.8380–86.
Wang Pijiang 汪辟疆. *Tangren xiaoshuo* 唐人小說. Rpt. Shanghai: Shanghai Gudian Wenxue, 1955.

Annotations:

Pindu cidian, pp. 265–79.
Wang Meng'ou 王夢鷗. *Tangren xiaoshuo yanjiu erji* 唐人小說研究二集. Taibei: Yiwen, 1973, pp. 153–54 [Feng'ao], 193–95 [Yuedu jing], 201–08 [Nanke], 226–29 [Xie Xiao'e].

Translations:

Edwards, *Prose Literature*, v. 2, pp. 150–54 [Xie Xiao'e], 206–12 [Nanke].
Lévy, André. "La vieille Feng de Lujiang" [Lujiang Feng Ao zhuan], in Lévy, *Histoires*, v. 1, pp. 93–100; "Rêve de fourmis. Biographie du préfet de Rameau-Sud" [Nanke], v. 2, pp. 77–100.
Maeno Naoaki 前野直彬. *Tōdai denkishu* 唐代傳奇集. Tokyo: Heibonsha, 1964, v. 1, pp. 120–49 [all four].
Nienhauser, William H., Jr. "The Governor of the Southern Bough," in Nienhauser, *Tang Tales*, pp. 130–83.
Uchida Sennosuke 內田泉之助 and Inui Kazuo 乾一夫. *Tōdai denki* 唐代傳奇. Tokyo: Meiji, 1971, pp. 211–51 [Nanke and Xie Xiao'e, in modern Japanese with Chinese text; extensive, useful annotation].
Wang, Elizabeth T. C. *Ladies of the Tang*. Taibei: Heritage, 1961, pp. 239–61 [Nanke], 323–30 [Feng'ao].
Wang, C. C. *Traditional Chinese Tales*. New York: Columbia University, 1946, pp. 87–92 [Xie Xiao'e].
Yang, *Dragon King's Daughter*, pp. 44–56 [Nanke].

Studies:

Knechtges, David R. "Dream Adventure Stories in Europe and Tang China," *TkR*, 4.2 (October 1973): 101–19.

Kondo Haruo 近藤春雄 (1914–2014). "Tōdai shōsetsu ni tsuite, Chinchuki, Nanka taishu den, Sha Shoga den" 唐人小說について–枕中記・南柯太守傳・謝小娥傳, *Aichi Kenritsu Joshi Daigaku kiyō*, 15 (1964): 40–58.

Liu Kairong 劉開榮. *Tangdai xiaoshuo yanjiu* 唐代小說研究. Rev. Hong Kong: Shangwu, 1964, pp. 163–75.

Uchiyama Chinari 內山知也. *Zui Tō shōsetsu kenkyū* 隋唐小說研究. Tokyo: Mokujisha, 1977, pp. 377–411.

Wang Meng'ou 王夢鷗. *Tangren xiaoshuo yanjiu erji* 唐人小說研究二集. Taibei: Yiwen, 1973, pp. 46–56.

Douglas Gjertson and William H. Nienhauser, Jr.

Li Guan 李觀 (*zi*, Yuanbin 元賓, 766–794) is best known as a friend of Han Yu 韓愈 (768–824)* and a prose writer whose life and ideals paralleled those of Li He 李賀 (790–816).* Li was born in Suzhou 蘇州 to a family originally from Longxi 隴西 (modern Gansu 甘肅). It has been argued that he was a nephew of the essayist Li Hua 李華 (715–774),* but this seems to have been an incorrect attribution. In 782 at 18 he was recommended as a provincial candidate for the national examinations, but stayed in Suzhou, presumably for further study. Several of his works mention his devotion to books and wide reading. It was perhaps for this reason that he claimed not to have made any close friends until he went to the capital.

Arriving in Chang'an in 790–seven years after he had first been made a provincial candidate–he described his wonderment with the city: "In the days of the first month, I set myself up with the landlord of an inn, saw the imperial palace with its twin gate towers stretching to the sky, craning my neck as I went back and forth, as if I had trod through the dust to stop at the heights of the Five Sacred Mountains" 一之日舍逆旅主人，仰見帝居，雙闕入天，顧身仿佯，若游塵止於五岳之高. Shortly thereafter he began to prepare for the examinations by attempting to find a patron: "In the days of the second month, I took my incomparable writings to several well-known gentlemen, hoping they would carefully read them and perceive their truth But when I went to see them, their gates were shut" 二之日持無似之文，干有名者數公，望其刮目以鑒真，作致身之椎輪，客去門掩. Although he was unsuccessful in the examinations of 790, he continued to seek influential friends (about a fourth of his prose pieces are letters appealing to potential sponsors).

Perhaps through these appeals Li Guan was able to enter the Directorate of Education and study there. The *Tang zhi yan* 唐摭言 claims he was at the Guangwen Dian 廣文殿 (Hall for Extending Literary Arts). After his failure in 790, Li was encouraged by the selection of Du Huangshang 杜黃裳 (738–808) as examiner the following year. Du had a reputation for honesty and Li Guan was brimming with confidence, as can be seen in his "Ye Fuzi Miao wen" 謁夫子廟文 (On Visiting the Confucian Temple), probably written about this time. The "purified object" referred was of course Li Guan's essay:

> Among those who have carried down the Confucian teachings through the ages, I, this descendant of the Longxi Li's, have rectified my writings as a means of purification and, holding up this purified object in offering, reverently present it to you.

世載儒訓者，隴西李氏子觀，正詞為潔，執潔為奠，恪以上薦。

Li Guan

After failing the examination in 790, as did fellow students Liu Zongyuan 柳宗元 (773–819),* and Liu Yuxi 劉禹錫 (772–842),* he seems to have lived on in what he described as impoverished circumstances, failing again in 791, but continuing to study, write, and seek a patron. Li shows in numerous letters that he was clearly under the influence of the *Fugu* 復古 "Returning to Antiquity" school of writers, the most famous of whom was Han Yu. In 792, therefore, those talented young writers in this group must have been buoyed by the news that Lu Zhi 陸贄 (754–805)* would examine them, assisted by Liang Su 梁肅 (753–793)* and Cui Yuanhan 崔元翰 (725–795), both *Fugu* advocates. In the spring of that year, Li Guan attained the fifth rank on the list of successful *jinshi* graduates, above Han Yu and several other notable Tang figures who passed that year. Because of the subsequent fame of the 792 graduates in literature and politics (five became grand councilors), and in part because of the reputations of the examiners themselves, this group soon became collectively known as the Longhu Bang 龍虎榜 (Dragons and Tigers List).

Shortly after passing the examinations, Han Yu and Li Guan exchanged poems. In Han's verse he compares himself to the gigantic mythical fish *kun* 鯤 and Li Guan to the *peng* 鵬 (roc) bird which measures over a thousand miles across its back. Li Guan was also close to another fellow-graduate, Feng Su 馮宿 (767–837).* Li and Feng shared geographical backgrounds, too– Feng was also a Southerner (from Wuzhou 婺州, modern Zhejiang). In a poem Li wrote for Feng titled "Zeng Feng Su" 贈馮宿 (Presented to Feng Su), probably in the winter before their success, he reveals his state of mind:

> From the cold city-wall I ascend to the plains of Qin,
> A wanderer with thoughts flying in the wind.
> Black clouds block the view of a myriad miles,
> Hunting fires burn from their midst.
> A long trail of smoke steams into the dark void,
> The aura of death alone will not disperse.
> Pieces of ice interlock—stones about to split;
> The winds crazed—mountains seem to sway.
> These days no hearts steadfast as the green pines,
> How can I alone not wither and fade?

> 寒城上秦原，遊子意飄飄。
> 黑雲截萬里，獵火從中燒。
> 陰空蒸長煙，殺氣獨不銷。
> 冰交石可裂，風疾山如搖。
> 時無青松心，顧我獨不凋。

Aside from avowing his loyalty to Feng Su, this poem discloses Li Guan's pessimism about contemporary politics and society. The language shares much with frontier poems, but it also exhibits the "harsh diction" (*se* 澀) reminiscent of the poetic style usually associated with Han Yu and Meng Jiao 孟郊 (751–814),* especially in the second, third and fourth couplets. The final two lines allude to *Analects* 9.28 where Confucius says: "When the year becomes cold, then we know how the pine and the cypress are the last to lose their leaves" 歲寒，然後知松柏之後彫也.

Li Guan's prose prior to 792 embodies the contradiction of employing a haughty, intransigent style to express his requests for assistance in his career–this interspersed with references to his own moral superiority. Despite passing the more advanced examination of Erudite Literatus ranked second of four candidates later that spring, Li Guan seems to have won few friends in the government. Meng Jiao's "Zeng Li Guan" 贈李觀 (Presented to Li Guan) suggests that his success in the examinations aroused jealousy. Nevertheless, he was offered the post of Gentleman in Charge of Collating Books for the Heir Apparent, a sinecure often given to recent graduates who displayed literary talent. Li Guan seems to have been disappointed with this position and went home to Suzhou during the summer of 792. On his return to Chang'an later that year he suggests that he was still not employed (in works such as "Shang Jia Puye shu 上賈僕射書 (Letter to Vice Director [of the Department of State] Jia). Often ill during his years in the capital, his health deteriorated in 793 and he died the following year. Han Yu wrote an epitaph which praised Li Guan's literary talents and his moral behavior.

Li's literary reputation today is based on four poems (of an original thirty) and about fifty works of prose. This may seem an insignificant corpus, but it is a larger number of works than either Han Yu or Liu Zongyuan had written by their late twenties and presents a broad spectrum of genres and subjects. Moreover, although clearly infused with the Confucian spirit of "return to antiquity" (*fugu*), works like Li Guan's "Tong Ru Dao shuo" 通儒道說 (Discourse on the Compatibility of Confucianism and Daoism) reveal an eclectic mind which might have added another dimension to mid-Tang thought, had Li lived longer.

Despite admiration from peers and success in the examinations, Li Guan seems never to have found contentment. His "Jiao nan shuo" 交難說 (Discourse on the Difficulty of Making Friends) reveals the paradoxical approach he took to life, and the mood in which he undoubtedly faced his too-early death. The spider in the last line cited below was often seen in Tang literature as a creature frustrated by nature, as its intricate webs were broken so easily; perhaps not unlike Li Guan's attempts at friendship:

> In ancient times men regarded it unsound not to have friends [but] friends are something you must have . . . . Making friends is difficult. A casual union based on profit leads to indignation and loud cursing. I often admonish myself not to recklessly speak of making friends. How much more does this apply to the men of today, who truly suffer from the poison of snakes and lizards. For this reason, I keep to myself, and grieve for the lonely spider [in his web].

> 昔人病於無友，嗟友不可以已矣 . . . 交之難兮。以利苟合，忿深咆哮。余常誡之，不妄語交。矧今之人兮實蒙虺蜥，是故獨處兮而悲蕭蛸。

BIBLIOGRAPHY

Editions:
Li Yuanbin wenji wenbian 李元賓文集文編. 3 *juan*. *Waibian* 外編. 2 *juan*. *Xubian* 續編. 1 *juan*. In *Tangren sanjia ji* 唐人三家集. Qin Yinfu 秦因復 (1760–1843), ed. 1818
Li Yuanbin wenbian 李元賓文編. 3 *juan*. *Waibian* 外編.2 *juan*. SKQS.
Quan Tang shi, 5: 3599–600.
Quan Tang wen, 532–35.6845–93.

Li Guan

Translations:

Nienhauser, William H., Jr. "Among Dragons and Tigers: Li Guan (766–794) and His Role in the Late 8th Century Literary Scene," *Proceedings of the 2nd International Sinological Conference, Sect. on Lit.* Taibei: Academia Sinica, 1988, 1: 243–87.

Studies:

Guo Yuheng 郭預衡. "Li Guan" 李觀, in *Zhongguo sanwen shi* 中國散文史. Shanghai: Shanghai Guji, 2000, pp. 195–98.
Kawachi Shōen 河內昭圓. "Futari no Ri Kan" 二人の李観, *Bungei ronsō* 文藝論叢 2000, (55): 1–14.
Luo Liantian 羅聯添. *Han Yu yanjiu* 韓愈研究. Taibei: Xuesheng, 1977: 138–40.
Nienhauser. "Among Dragons and Tigers" (see "Translations" above).
Saitō Shigeru 齋藤茂. "Ri Kan ronmou hitori no yōsetsu no saishi" 李觀論—もう一人の夭折の才子, *Bungei ronsō* 文藝論叢, 2007 (68): 352–36.
Sun Lina 孫麗娜. *Li He pingzhuan* 李賀評傳. Shenyan: Liaohai, 2019.
Wang Nanbing 王南冰. "Li Guan nianpu ji zuopin xi'nian" 李觀年譜及作品繫年, *Guji zhengli yanjiu xuekan* 古籍整理研究學刊, 2008 (3): 86–90.
Zhan, *Daojiao*, pp. 350–58.

William H. Nienhauser, Jr.

Li He 李賀 (*zi*, Changji 長吉, 791–817) was a tragic-romantic poet of the late Tang. Born to a distant branch of the imperial clan, talented and with every prospect and desire for a prominent career, he achieved no material success in his short life. It is a truism that the poets of the Tang did not measure their life's worth by their poetry, this was a matter for posterity. Rather it was high office in the government which counted as the essential measure of one's impact on the world. Li He's poetry reflects frustration and bitterness, offering sharp sarcasm, irony, and satire about political matters, and giving uncompromisingly precise details in erotic contexts. For the unusual richness of his diction, his simultaneous bluntness and allusiveness, and his courting of the macabre–the unlikely, unlucky image–he earned a reputation as a difficult poet to read and perhaps a dangerous one to befriend.

This characterization is drawn from the events of Li He's life and from the prefaces to his collected poems written by his near-contemporaries Du Mu 杜牧 (803–ca. 852)* and Li Shangyin 李商隱 (ca. 813–858).* In his influential "Preface," Du Mu argues, ostensibly, that Li He goes to excess in his diction and loses the sense of proportion between medium and message, and that he is in fact an eccentric poet whom the reader can choose not to understand. Li Shangyin wrote a "short biography" in which he makes legend of the life, rendering both poet and poetry as fictional. The intent of both prefaces is to defuse the poetry, to present it as safe to enjoy and preserve. It is telling that some twenty years after Li He's death his life and work were still dealt with circumspectly.

In 809 Li He took the provincial examination in Luoyang. His father had died some years before, thus he was the hope of a family consisting of his mother, sister, and younger brother; it is not supposed that he ever married. Two prominent albeit controversial figures, Han Yu 韓愈 (768–824)* and Huangfu Shi 皇甫湜 (776–ca. 835),* were his sponsors. He easily passed and went on to Chang'an to prepare for the *jinshi* examination, but he was not allowed to take it. The complaint was that he would violate the taboo against using his father's name should he participate, since the *jin* was pronounced similarly to the first character in his father's given name, [Li] Jinsu 晉肅. The practice of the time was also to avoid homophones, and on this basis the charge stuck. It is not known who made the case against Li He or why.

In poems on his return to Changgu 昌谷, the family home located in modern Henan, Li He contrasted the richness and fertility of place with the desolation of self. He had no choice but to go back to Chang'an in 811 to take the placement examination: his father had reached the fifth rank, first class, and by heredity he was entitled to any position up to the eighth rank, third class. His "Renhe li za xu Huangfu Shi" 仁和里雜序皇甫湜 (Assorted Comments for Huangfu Shi from the Renhe Quarter) expresses on various levels his feelings during this period. Between 811 and 814 he had the title Court Gentleman for Ceremonials; in effect, he was an usher.

The years in Chang'an are undoubtedly the period of Li He's many portraits of the materially rich, emotionally difficult lives of courtesans. With extraordinary diction he captures the opulence of the high-class houses and the fragile, fugitive beauty of the women, often in ironic contrast to their commercial functions, as in his "Yelai le" 夜來樂 (Joys of the Night) and "Meiren shutou ge" 美人梳頭歌 (Song of a Beauty Combing Her Hair):

> Xi Shi is dreaming at dawn, her gauze curtains are cold;
> Fragrant locks of a fallen chignon, wafting aloes and rose wood.
> As a well windlass turns, creaking like twinkling jade;
> The roused lotus-like beauty awakens, having slept just enough.
> A pair of phoenixes opens a mirror clear like autumn waters;
> She loosens her tresses before the mirror stand by an ivory bed.
> Fragrant plaits spread cloud-like on the ground;
> A jade brush glides silently through lustrous hair.
> Delicate hands bind coils black as an old rook;
> So sleek and glossy a jeweled hairpin cannot hold.
> Spring breezes unconfined, vex its languished beauty;
> At eighteen, hair so full it now collapses.
> Her toilet complete, the chignon slanted just right.
> Done up, she takes several steps—a goose treading the sand.
> Turning away in silence, where is she heading?
> Down the steps to pick herself a spring of cherry blossoms.

> 西施曉夢綃帳寒，香鬟墮髻半沈檀。
> 轆轤咿啞轉鳴玉，驚起芙蓉睡新足。
> 雙鸞開鏡秋水光，解鬟臨鏡立象床。
> 一編香絲雲撒地，玉釵落處無聲膩。
> 纖手卻盤老鴉色，翠滑寶釵簪不得。
> 春風爛漫惱嬌慵，十八鬟多無氣力。
> 妝成欹鬌欹不斜，雲裾數步踏雁沙。
> 背人不語向何處？下階自折櫻桃花。

Li He thus continues the tradition of boudoir poetry, his work reminiscent of Li Bo's 李白 (701–762)* poems on women, here. A persona overlooks a young beauty, compared to the most famous beauty in Chinese history, Xi Shi, as she awakes to the sound of a maid drawing water for the well—probably for her morning toilet—then combing and arranging her hair. The pair of phoenixes in line 5 (on the cover of the mirror) suggest liaisons of the human kind. The description of her hair in its various states of readiness in the lines that follow brings out its luster and the aromas that could only be sensed close up. *Nao* 惱 "vex" in line 11 may refer to the girl who is troubled by spring breezes which suggest an absent or longed-for lover; the subject might also be her hair which is difficult to manage in these light winds. In line 12 the expression *wu qi li* 無其力 (literally: "having no strength") might refer either to the delicate young eighteen-year old woman who is exhausted from the mere effort of fixing her hair or to her chignon which has been plaited eighteen times (the line would then read "bound eighteen times or more, her strength has gone"). Either way this kind of fragile exhaustion was seen as appealing to male suitors. In the final couplet the reader almost senses that rather than a voyeur, the persona has actually entered her bedchamber as the girl wanders outside into the garden, thus enhancing the erotic sense that pervades the entire poem.

His career stillborn, Li He grew increasingly conscious of his chronic illness and of the immediacy of death. This fueled his interest in the question of immortality, in images of death and the afterworld, and in the deceit of mythology: Li is known as the *Shigui* 詩鬼 or "Ghost of Poetry." With a skeptical eye he measured immortality and found it an endless series of deaths, as seen in the third of his "Ganfeng, wushou" 感諷五首 (Moved to Satirize, Five Poems):

> South Mountain, so full of sorrow!
> Its ghostly rain spattering the lonely grass.
> In Chang'an this autumn midnight,
> How many men have grown old in your winds?
> Dim and uncertain are these footpaths in the yellow dusk,
> Writhing upward the dark oaks along the way.
> When the moon is high the trees have no shadows—
> Over the entire mountain a white dawn.
> Dulled torches welcome the newly arrived
> As fireflies swirl over these lonely tombs.

> 南山何其悲，鬼雨灑空草。
> 長安夜半秋，風前幾人老。
> 低迷黃昏徑，裊裊青櫟道。
> 月午樹無影，一山唯白曉。
> 漆炬迎新人，幽壙螢擾擾。

South Mountain was the site of many graveyards during the Tang. Here the poet imagines winding up the ghost-filled paths—or is this an actual trip there? The sorrow of the first line causes him to view even the autumn grass as lonely, bereft not only of the foliage of spring and summer, but without the visitors who must come more often in the spring (at Qingming) and summer. Perhaps he turns back to look at Chang'an in the second couplet and imagines that even the winds from South Mountain bring people closer to death. In the third couplet nature closes in as the poet picks his way through the dim light of dusk darkened by the oak trees lining the path. The most striking couplet is the fourth. *Wu* 午, literally "midday" or "noon," is always associated with the sun, but Li He depicts a "moon noon" in which the trees lose their shadows as the moon is directly overhead, resulting in a mountainscape so white it seems to be the broad daylight, this reverse chiaroscuro effect enhancing the ghostly effect of the scene. The final couplet, however, darkens again. The "dulled torches" are actually red-and-black lacquered torch-holders that because of their colors absorb light. The newly arrived refers to those recently buried on South Mountain as well as perhaps the poet himself. In the again diminished light of the final couplet fireflies provide the only company for the inhabitants of the tombs.

In his "Shen xian" 神絃 (Spirit Strings) poems he witnesses shamanistic performances but places more magic in metaphor than in medium. Like many of his contemporaries he read the *Diamond Sutra*, yet the extent of Buddhist influence in his poetry remains uncertain. One instance might be found in his "Yaohua yue" 瑤華樂 (Jasper Flower Music), a narrative poem on the legendary visit of King Mu to the Queen Mother of the West (Xi Wang Mu 西王母), which is also a retelling of the tragic romance of Xuanzong (r. 712–756) and Yang Guifei 楊貴妃. The last couplet bears a striking resemblance to descriptions of the annual ritual of bathing the Buddha. Evidently, religion offered him little solace, and, mythology was itself a medium for allegory.

For all that distinguishes Li He from more conventional poets, he is a product of the innovators he follows. Unusual syntax, a penchant for dissimilar, discordant parallels, the delight in ambiguity, the freedom to fill his poems with intensity, all reflect the achievements of Du Fu 杜甫 (712–770)*, the forbidding-imagery of Meng Jiao 孟郊 (751–814),* and the influence of Han Yu. But the romanticism, irony, bitter wit, delight in countering traditional expectations, all belong to the poet. He saw the world in colors, fragrances, sounds, textures, and he made no pretense of doing other than interpreting his experiences. His landscapes often project a state of mind, where flowers weep, the mist has laughing eyes, and nature is measured in human terms. Repetition, onomatopoeia, alliteration, allusion–the most extensive borrowing from the *Chuci* 楚辭 since Xie Lingyun 謝靈運 (385–443)–and multiple levels of meaning in individual poems characterize Li He's poetry. And given his fondness for narratives, his best efforts tend to be old-style verse. It is said that he when riding about he would stop and dash off some lines which were then collected in tapestry bag by a servant boy.

Li He spent his last years seeking a position outside the court, on the staff of a general. Unsuccessful, he returned home in 817 quite ill and died. His collected surviving poems total about 240; legend has it that a spiteful cousin got hold of the collection and threw a large part of it into a privy–such was Li He's luck in life and legend.

BIBLIOGRAPHY

Editions:
Huang Shizhong 黃世中. *Li He shi* 李賀詩. Beijing: Renmin Wenxue, 2005.
Li He geshi bian 李賀歌詩編. *Sibu congkan* ed.
Li He shige bian 李賀歌詩編. Shanghai: Shanghai Guji, 2005.
Luan Guiming 欒貴明 et al., eds. *Quan Tang shi suoyin: Li He juan* 全唐詩索引:李賀卷. Beijing: Zhonghua, 1992.
Quan Tang shi, 6: 4405–455, 14: 10656.

Sanjia pingzhu Li Changji geshi 三家評注李長吉歌詩. Shanghai: Shanghai Guji, 1998; Yangzhou: Guangling, 2013. Includes the standard commentary by Wang Qi 王琦 (preface dated 1760) along with those by Fang Shiju 方世舉 (1675–1759) and Yao Wenxie 姚文燮 (1628–1692, preface 1657).

Tang Wen 唐文 *et al.*, eds. *Li He shi suoyin* 李賀詩索引. Jinan: Qi Lu Shushe, 1984.

Ye Congqi 葉蔥奇, ed. *Li He shiji* 李賀詩集. Beijing: Renmin Wenxue, 1984.

Annotations:

Feng Haofei 馮浩菲 and Xu Chuanwu 徐傳武, eds. *Li He shi xuanyi* 李賀詩選譯. Chengdu: Ba Shu, 1991.

Li He shixuan 李賀詩選. Beijing: Renmin, 1978.

Liu Sihan 劉斯翰. *Li He shi xuan* 李賀詩選. Taibei: Yuanliu, 2000.

Liu Yan 劉衍. *Li He shi jiao jian zhengyi* 李賀詩校箋証異. Changsha: Hunan, 1990

Song Xulian 宋緒連 and Chu Xu 初旭, eds. *San Li shi jianshang cidian* 三李詩鑑賞辭典. Changchun: Jilin Wenshi, 1992. Contains numerous close readings of poems by Li He, Li Bo and Li Shangyin as well as short biographies and useful bibliographies for these three important poets.

Suzuki Torao 鈴木虎雄. *Ri Chōkichi kashishū* 李長吉歌詩集. Tokyo, 1961.

Wu Qiming 吳企明, ed. *Li Changji geshi biannian jianzhu* 李長吉歌詩編年箋注. Beijing: Zhonghua, 2012.

Biographical Sources:

Fu, *Tang caizi*, 2:282–95.

Jiu Tang shu, 137.3772

Xin Tang shu, 203.5787–88

Translations:

Birch, *Anthology*, pp. 281–84.

Frodsham, J. D. *Goddess, Ghost and Demons: The Collected Poems of Li He (790–816)*. London: Anvil, 1983.

___. *The Poems of Li Ho (790–816)*. Oxford: Oxford University, 1970.

Fuller, Michael A. *An Introduction to Chinese Poetry: From the* Canon of Poetry *to the Lyrics of the Song Dynasty*. Cambridge: Harvard University Press, 2018, pp. 312–22.

Graham, Angus Charles. *Poems of Late Tang*. Baltimore: Penguin, 1965, pp. 89–119.

Harada Kenyū 原田憲雄. *Ri Ga kashi hen* 李賀歌詩編. Tokyo: Heibonsha, 1998–99.

Hinton, *Anthology*, pp. 286–95.

Kurokawa Yōichi 黑川洋一, ed. *Riga shisen* 李賀詩選. Tokyo: Iwanami, 1993.

Lambert, Marie-Thérèse and Guy Degen. *Li He, Les visions et les jours*. Paris: La Différence, 1994

Liu Wu-chi (1907–2002) and Irving Yucheng Lo. *Sunflower Splendor: Three Thousand Years of Chinese Poetry*. Bloomington: Indiana University, 1990, pp. 228–36.

Minford and Lau, pp. 904–15.

Owen, *Anthology*, pp. 199–200, 289, 471, 489–96.

___, *Late Tang*, pp. 156–82.

___, *Middle Ages*, pp. 22–23, 40–47, 110–14.

___, *Remembrances*, pp. 70–73.

Saitō Shō 齋藤晌. *Li Ga* 李賀. Tokyo: Shūeisha, 1967.

Suzuki Torao 鈴木虎雄. *Ri Chokichi kashishu* 李長吉歌詩集. 2v. Tokyo: Iwanami, 1962.

Wu Qiming 吳企明 ed. *Li He ziliao huibian* 李賀資料匯編. Beijing: Zhonghua, 1994.

Varon, Jodi. *The Rock's Cold Breath: The Selected New Poems*. La Grande, Oregon: Ice River, 2004.

Yang Xianyi, *Poetry and Prose*, pp. 179–90.

Yu, *Imagery*, pp. 199–200.

Studies:

Chen Yunji 陳允吉. "Li He: Shige tiancai yu bingtai jiling'er de jiehe 李賀:詩歌天才與病態畸零兒的結合" *Fudan xuebao* 6 (1988): 1–9.

___. and Wu Haiyong 吳海勇. *Li He shi xuanping* 李賀詩選評. Shanghai: Shanghai Guji, 2004

Chen Zhiguo 陳治國. *Li He yanjiu ziliao* 李賀研究資料. Beijing: Beijing Shifan Daxue, 1983.

Debon, Günther. "Das Gedicht von Ch'ang-kuh des Li Ho." Herbert Franke, ed. *Studia Sino-Altaica: Festschrift für Erich Haenisch zum 80. Geburtstag*. Wiesbaden: Franz Steiner, pp. 39–46.

Fish, Michael B. "Mythological Themes in the Poetry of Li He 791–817." Unpublished Ph.D. dissertation, Indiana University, 1973

___. "The Tu Mu and Li Shang-yin Prefaces to the Collected Poems of Li He" in *Chinese Poetry and Poetics*, v. 1, R. C. Miao, ed. San Francisco: Chinese Materials Center, 1978, pp. 231–86

___. "Yang Kuei-fei as the Hsi Wang Mu: Secondary Narrative in Two T'ang Poems," *MS* 32 (1976): 337–54.

Fu Jingxun 傅經順. *Li He shige shangxi ji* 李賀詩歌賞析集. Chengdu: Ba Shu, 1988.

Harada Kenyū 原田憲雄. *Ri Ga ronkō* 李賀研究. Kyoto, 1981.

___. *Ri Ga kashihen* 李賀歌詩編. Tokyo: Heibonsha, 1998.

Hsu, C.Y. "The Queen Mother of the West: Historical or Legendary? (Part I)" *Asian Culture Quarterly* XVI.2 (Summer 1988): 29–42. Includes a translation and discussion of a poem by Li.

LaFleur, Frances Ann. "The Evolution of a Symbolist Aesthetic in Classical Chinese Verse: The Role of Li Ho Compared with That of Charles Baudelaire in Nineteenth-century French Poetry." Unpublished Ph.D. dissertation, Princeton University, 1993.

Lang-tan, Goat Koei. "Traditionelles und Individuelles in der Bild und Versgestaltung des T'ang-Dichters Li Ho (790–816)." In *Ganz Allmaehlich, Festschrift fur Gunther Debon*. Heidelberg: Heidelberger Verlagsanstalt und Druckerei, 1986, pp. 132–45.

Li Dehui 李德輝. *Li He shige yuanyuan ji yingxiang yanjiu* 李賀詩歌淵源及影響研究. Nanjing: Fenghuang, 2010.

Li Wenbin 李文彬. "Li Ho's Poetry through Transformational-Generative Grammar." *Zhengda xuebao* 56 (1987): 1–19.

___. "The Imagery in Li Ho's Poetry." *Zhengda xuebao* 60 (1989): 1–18.

Li Zhoufan 李卓藩. *Li He shi xintan* 李賀詩新探. Taibei: Wenshizhe, 1997.

Liu Ruilian 劉瑞蓮. *Li He* 李賀. Beijing: Zhonghua, 1981.

Liu Yan 劉衍. *Li He shi zhuan* 李賀詩傳. Taiyuan: Shanxi Renmin, 1984.

Lu Mingyu 盧明瑜. *San Li shenhua shige zhi yanjiu* 三李神話詩歌之研究. Taibei: Guoli Taibei Daxue Chuban Weiyuanhui, 2000.

McCraw, David. "Hanging by a Thread: Li He's Deviant Closures," *CLEAR* 18 (1996): 23–44.

Nakata Shōei 中田昭榮. *Kisai Ri Ga: yōsetsu hakkō no Tōdai shijin* 鬼才李賀：夭折薄幸の唐代詩人. Tokyo: Shinpūsha, 1998.

Owen, Stephen. *The Late Tang: Chinese Poetry of the Mid-Ninth Century (827–860)*. Cambridge, MA: Harvard University Press, 2006, pp. 156–83.

Peng Guozheng 彭國忠. *Xinyi Li He shiji* 新譯李賀詩集. Taibei: Sanmin Shuju Gufen Youxian Gongsi, 2008.

Ri Ga kenkyū 李賀研究, 1–13 (1971–1975), Kyoto: Hokōsha Mimeographed journal (sold by Hōyū 朋友).

Robertson, Maureen. "Poetic Diction in the Works of Li He (891–917 [sic])." Unpublished Ph.D. dissertation, University of Washington; 1970.

Tao Erfu 陶爾夫. "Li He shige de tonghua shijie" 李賀詩歌的童話世界. *Wenxue pinglun* 3 (1991): 36–47.

Teng Xueqin 騰學欽. *Li He shige quanji jianshu jinyi* 李賀詩歌全集簡疏今譯. Beijing: Zhongguo, 2010.

Tu Kuo-ch'ing. *Li Ho*. Boston: Twayne, 1979.

Wu Qiming 吳企明. *Li Changji geshi biannian jianzhu* 李長吉歌詩編年箋注. Beijing: Zhonghua, 2012.

Li He

___. *Li He* 李賀. Shanghai: Shanghai Guji, 1986.
Yang Qiqun 楊其群. *Li He yanjiu lunji* 李賀研究論集. Taiyuan: Beiyue Wenyi, 1989.
Yang Wenxiong 楊文雄. *Li He yanjiu* 李賀研究. Taibei: Wenshizhe, 1983.
Yin Zhanhua 尹占華. "Li He shige chuangzuo zhong de xintai" 李賀詩歌創作中的心態 *Tangdai wenxue yanjiu* 4 (1993).
Zhang Zongfu 張宗福. *Li He yanjiu* 李賀研究. Chengdu: Ba Shu, 2009.

Michael B. Fishlen and William H. Nienhauser, Jr.

Li Hua 李華 (*zi*, Xiashu 遐叔, 715–774) was one of the most influential prose writers, critics, and literary patrons of the middle decades of the eighth century. His official career was crucially affected by the An Lushan (703–757) Rebellion of 755. He had passed the *jinshi* examination in 735, succeeded in a palace examination, and held high office. He was also connected with some of the leaders of intellectual opinion in Chang'an in the 740s and early 750s and was by then considered an established literary figure. During the rebellion, however, he was captured and forced to collaborate. He presumably wrote edicts. After the recovery of the capital he retired to the southeast, declining imperial summons and living in self-imposed exile until his death.

Like most mid-eighth century men of letters, Li composed in the euphuistic, ornamental, antithetical style (*pianwen* 駢文 or parallel prose), as well as in the free, ancient-style prose (*guwen* 古文) that he is traditionally held to have advocated. Two of his early and best-known works demonstrate this. His "Hanyuan Dian fu" 含元殿賦 (Prose-poem on the Han-yuan Palace) was compared by his friend Xiao Yingshi 蕭穎士 (717–760)* to two *fu* 賦 on palaces contained in the prestigious *Wenxuan* 文選. It was, Xiao said, not as good as one by He Yan 何晏 (d. 249), but better than that of Wang Yanshou 王延壽 (ca. 118–ca. 138). Another of Li's well-known works "Diao Gu zhanchang wen" 弔古戰場文 (Dirge on an Ancient Battlefield) is also a highly rhetorical composition, using imagery from the period of Han frontier expansion and evoking the combination of romantic fascination and pity that literary men felt for those who died in battle on the northern and western border:

> How vast! In this endless wilderness of sand,
> no one to be seen.
> The Yellow River crawls like a belt,
> the hills interlace, somber and cheerless,
> the wind moans sadly and the sun dims.
> Tumbleweed snap their roots and grasses wither.
> The chill is like the frost of early morning.
> Birds soar past, never landing;
> stray beasts run through quickly.

The head of the local outpost told me: "This is an ancient battlefield, where great armies of old were overwhelmed. Ghosts often cry out which you'll hear as the skies darken." Heartbreaking! Was it in Qin, in Han, or in more recent dynasties? I have heard that

> Qi and Wei sent forth garrisons,
> Chu and Han levied troops,
> racing across then thousand miles,

year after year exposed to the dew.
Midst sand-filled grasses they pastured their horse in the morning,
at night they forded the frozen rivers.
The land is endless,
the skies go on and on,
and they did not know the way home.
They trusted their lives to sharp blades,
with no one to tell of their pent-up sorrow.

Since the Qin and the Han, we've had many troubles with the northern tribes. The central prefectures are worn and ruined, not a single generation free of this. . . .

There had to be years of famine,
the people put to flight.
Alas and woe!
Is this brought on by the times?
Or is it fate?
Since antiquity it has been like this.
What can be done!
Guard well against the northern tribes.

浩浩乎!
平沙無垠, 敻不見人.
河水縈帶, 群山糾紛.
黯兮慘悴, 風悲日曛.
蓬斷草枯, 凜若霜晨.
鳥飛不下, 獸鋌亡群.
亭長告余曰: "此古戰場也. 嘗覆三軍; 往往鬼哭, 天陰則聞." 傷心哉! 秦歟? 漢歟? 將近代歟? 吾聞夫齊魏徭戍, 荊韓召募.
萬里奔走, 連年暴露.
沙草晨牧, 河冰夜渡.
地闊天長, 不知歸路.
寄身鋒刃, 腷臆誰訴?
秦漢而還, 多事四夷.
中州耗斁, 無世無之 . . .
必有凶年, 人其流離.
嗚呼噫嘻! 時耶?
命耶? 從古如斯.
為之奈何? 守在四夷.

This piece is famous in part because it has been collected in anthologies much read in later eras. It was composed in parallel prose and rhymed couplets but borrows the technique of using a local person to comment on some social or political problem from the ancient-style prose writers.

Li's views on literary practice and theory were given mainly in prefaces to the collected works of friends. He held that literature was both the expression of an individual's ethical life and a reflection of the moral and social climate of the age. He also emphasized that the Confucian canon embodied the highest standards of literary excellence, which contemporary literature failed to approach.

Despite his disgrace and departure from Chang'an after the An Lushan Rebellion, Li maintained wide contacts with important figures of his day. He continued to write commemorative texts for Buddhist clergy, records for local institutions, epitaphs, sacrificial prayers, and occasional verse. He also composed essays, one of his most substantial being an analysis of history in terms of the traditional polarity of *wen* 文 (refinement) and *zhi* 質 (austerity) that indicted his own time for its excess of *wen*. Another essay argued against the practice of divination using tortoise shells. A third commemorated three of his deceased friends, Xiao Yingshi, Liu Xun 劉迅 (a son of the historian and critic Liu Zhiji 劉知幾 [661–721]),* and Yuan Dexiu 元德秀 (696–754), a cousin and teacher of the prose writer Yuan Jie 元結 (719–772).*

Most of Li Hua's early works were lost in the An Lushan Rebellion. A second collection was given a preface by Dugu Ji 獨孤及 (725–777),* one of his most important followers, in about 769, shortly before Li's death. Nearly all that is extant from this collection has been preserved by virtue of its inclusion in the general anthologies compiled in the early Song. Li's other followers include: Han Yunqing 韓雲卿, an uncle of the great prose writer Han Yu 韓愈 (768–824),* and Han Hui 韓會 (738–780), Han Yu's elder brother; Cui Yufu 崔裕福 (721–780), a Grand Councilor and director of the dynastic history in the 770s; and Liang Su 梁肅 (753–793),* another literary figure, historian and scholar who also influenced Han Yu. The interest of these men, prepared as they were to overlook his crime of collaboration, helped ensure that his post-rebellion works were preserved and that his reputation for learning and literature remained high.

BIBLIOGRAPHY

Editions:
Li Xiashu wenji 李遐叔文集. Taibei: Taiwan Shangwu, 1972.
Quan Tang shi, 3: 1588–94, 14: 1116.
Quan Tang wen, 314–21.4027–122.

Biographical Sources:
Jiu Tang shu, 190 C.5047–48; *Xin Tang shu*, 203.5775–79.

Translations:
Giles, Herbert, in Minford and Lau, pp. 99–193.
Kroll, Paul W., "Lexical Landscapes and Textual Mountains in the High T'ang." *TP* 84.1–3 (1998): 87–88.
Owen, *Anthology*, pp. 475–77.

Studies:
Bol, pp. 110–25.
Jiang Guangdou 薑光鬥. "Li Hua, Xiao Yingshi shengzunian xinkao" 李華蕭穎士生卒年新考. *Wenxue yichan*, 1990.3: 65–67.
___. "Li Hua zunian buzheng" 李華卒年補證. *Wenxue yichan*, 1991.1: 18–19.
Ji Yougong 計有功. *Tangshi jishi* 唐詩紀事, *juan*. 21. Shanghai: Shanghai Guji, 2008, pp. 309–10.
Li Dan 李丹. *Tangdai qianguwen yundong yanjiu* 唐代前古文運動研究. Beijing: Zhongggguo Shehui Kexue, 2012, pp. 123–243.
Liu, Sanfu 劉三富. "Ri Ka no shiso to bungaku 李華の思想と文學" *Chūgoku bungaku ronshu*, 4 (1974): 62–71.

McMullen, David L. "Historical and Literary Theory in the Mid-Eighth Century," in *Perspectives on the T'ang*, Arthur F. Wright and Denis Twitchett, ed. New Haven: Yale University, 1973, pp. 307–44.

Owen, Stephen. "*Fugu* Revival," in *High Tang*, pp. 243–46.

Vita, Silvio. "Li Hua and Buddhism," in *Tang China and Beyond, Studies on East Asian from the Seventh to the Tenth Century.* Antonino Forte, ed. Kyoto: Italian School of East Asian Studies, 1988, pp. 97–124.

Zhang Shimin 張世敏. "Lun Li Hua de wenxue guannian ji qi Guwen yundong de yingxiang" 論李華文學觀念及其古文運動的影響, *Gansu Lianhe Daxue xuebao*, 28 (July 2012): 52–56.

David L. McMullen and William H. Nienhauser, Jr.

Li Jiao 李嶠 (*zi*, Jushan 巨山, ca. 644–ca. 714) was an influential officer and a renowned man of letters during the reigns of Empress Wu (690–705) and Emperor Zhongzong (705–710). He was a native of Zanhuang 贊皇, Zhaozhou 趙州 (modern Hebei). Li's family, the Zhaojun Li 趙郡李, had been prominent in public life for generations, although his father, Li Zhen'e 李鎮惡, only served as a Magistrate of Xiangcheng 襄城 (southwest of modern Xuchang in Henan). His father died when he was just a boy. Li Jiao gained a reputation for filially serving his mother and for his mastery of the classic, winning praise from Xue Yuanqi 薛元起 (623–684). Li was successful in the *jinshi* examinations at nineteen and rose through the ranks to become an Investigating Censor. His work in helping to quell rebellion in two southern prefectures won the notice of Emperor Gaozong (r. 649–684). Li was promoted to become Supervising Secretary, but in defending Di Renjie 狄仁傑 (630–700) and others against false charges ran afoul of Lai Junchen 來俊臣 (651–697), who enjoyed Empress Wu's 武后 (r. 690–705) favor. Li Jiao was thus sent out as Vice Prefect of Runzhou 潤州. He soon returned to court where the Empress entrusted him with composing many important documents. In 698 he and Yao Chong 姚崇 (650–721) were made Grand Councilors and assigned to work on the dynastic history (*guoshi* 國史). Because he had been attached to the Empress's favorite, Zhang Yizhi 張易之 (655–705), he was sent out from court briefly in 705 when Emperor Zhongzong (r. 684 and 705–710) was re-enthroned, but later returned to enjoy a succession of high positions. In all he held the rank (or title) of Grand Councilor several times during the latter part of his life and in 707 was given the title of Duke of Zhaoguo 趙國公. When Ruizhong (r. 684–690 and 710–712) took the throne in 710 he was exiled, then with the accession of Emperor Xuanzong (r. 712–756) in 713 he was further demoted to Administrative Aide of Lüzhou 廬州 (modern Hefei in Anhui) where he died.

Li Jiao's poetry is characterized by the "Court Style" which had flourished in the Six Dynasties–many of his verses were also written at court. He is also well-known for his *yongwu shi* 詠物詩, poems on objects, which deal with an encyclopedic spectrum of subjects, from the sun, various musical instruments, and household items, to flora and fauna. The following poem, "Feng" 風 (Wind), is typical of his style:

> It knows how to cause leaves to fall in late autumn,
> Is able to bring buds to bloom in early spring.
> Crossing the river, it raises waves of a thousand feet;
> In the bamboo, it makes ten thousand stalks slant.

> 解落三秋葉，能開二月花。
> 過江千尺浪，入竹萬竿斜。

Here the wind is personified as knowing how to effect nature's changes of season (*jie* 解, "to know how," parallel to *neng* 能, "be able"). The strength of the poem lies in this clever use of language and in its hyperbolic imagery.

Of the 209 poems attributed to Li Jiao in the *Quan Tang shi*, 120 are *yongwu shi*. These 120 poems were collected independently and entitled *Li Jiao baiyong* 李嶠百詠 or *Li Jiao zayong* 李嶠雜詠. This collection was brought to Japan during the Heian Period. There manuscript copies of the collection were made and preserved. Lost in China, they were reintroduced during the Qing in a collection found in the *Itsuzon sōsho* 佚存叢書 edited by Hayashi Kō 林衡 (1768–1841). Recently two short fragmental copies of this volume were found among the Dunhuang Manuscripts (Pelliot 3738 and Stein 555).

Li was also a well-known prose writer. His extant corpus of over 150 pieces suggest his connection with the court—most are *pan* 判 (judgments), a popular court genre of the era.

BIBLIOGRAPHY

Editions:

Ishitobi Hakkō 石飛博光. *Rikyō zatsuei, Ito naishinnō gammon, Rirakujō* 李嶠雜詠, 伊都内親王願文, 離洛帖. Tokyo: Geijutsu Shinbunsha, 2010.

Li Jiao ji 李嶠集. *Tang Wushi jia shiji* 唐十五家詩集. Shanghai: Shanghai Guji, 1981. A reprint of the Ming typeset edition.

Li Jiao zayong 李嶠雜詠. 2v. Shanghai: Shanghai Guji, 2002.

Li Jiao zayong 李嶠雜詠. *Itsuzon sōsho* 佚存叢書 edition (see above). Also found in the *Zhengjuelou congkan* 正覺樓叢刊 and the *Yihai zhuchen* 藝海珠塵.

Li Jushan yongwushi (*Ri Kyozan eibutsu shi*) 李巨山詠物詩. Japanese edition, 1761. This edition revised by Ishikawa Tei 石川貞 with his *kunten* readings is reprinted in *Wakokubon kanshi shūsei* 和刻本漢詩集成, v. 1, Tokyo, 1975.

Quan Tang shi, 2: 687–728, 14: 11077.

Quan Tang wen, 242–49.3093–192.

Ricang guchao Li Jiao yongwu shi zhu 日藏古抄李嶠詠物詩注. Zhang Tingfang 張庭芳 and Hu Zhiang 胡志昂, ed. Shanghai: Shanghai Guji, 1998.

Annotations:

Li Jiao shi zhu, Su Weidao shi zhu 李嶠詩注，蘇味道詩注. Xu Dingxiang 徐定祥, comm. Shanghai: Shanghai Guji, 1995.

Zhang Tingfang 張庭芳 and Hu Zhi'ang 胡志昂, eds. *Ricang guchao Li Jiao yongwushi zhu* 日藏古抄李嶠詠物詩注. Shanghai: Shanghai Guji, 1998.

Biographical Sources:

Fu, *Tang caizi*, 1:119–30, 5:17–19.

Jiu Tang shu, 94.2992–95.

Xin Tang shu, 123.4367–71

Translations:

Owen, *Early T'ang*, pp. 119–21, 258–59, 266, 296, 298, 314–15.

Schafer, *Vermilion Bird*, p. 249.

Studies:

Chen Guanming 陳冠明. *Su Weidao, Li Jiao nian pu* 蘇味道, 李嶠年譜. Beijing: Zhongyang Wenxian, 2000.

Duan Liping 段莉萍. "Cong Dunhuang canben kao Li Jiao *Zayong shi* de banben yuanliu" 從敦煌殘本考李嶠《雜詠詩》的版本源流, *Dunhuang yanjiu* 敦煌研究 2004.5: 74–78.

Fukuda Toshiaki 福田俊昭. *Ri Kyō to zatsueishi no kenkyū* 李嶠と雜詠詩の研究. Tokyo: Kyūko, 2012.

Hu Zhi'ang 胡志昂. "*Ri Kyō hyakuei* josetsu—sono seikaku, hyōka to juyō o megutte" 『李嶠百詠』序説—その性格・評価と受容をめぐって, *Wakan hikaku bungaku*, 32 (2004): 1–13.

Ikeda Toshio 池田利夫. "*Hyakuei waka*" to *Ri Kyō hyakuei* 百詠和歌と李嶠百詠, in his *Nitchū hikaku bungaku no kiso kenkyū: hon'yaku setsuwa to sono tenkyo* 日中比較文学の基礎研究：翻訳説話とその典拠. Tokyo: Kasama, 1974.

Jiang Yiqiao 蔣義喬. "Cong jutishi kan *Li Jiao Baiyong* zai riben de jieshou qingkuang" 從句題詩看《李嶠百詠》在日本的接受情況, *Riyu xuexi yu yanjiu* 2005.2: 59–63.

Kanda Kiichirō 神田喜一郎. "*Ri Kyō hyakuei* zakkō" 李嶠百詠雜考, *Biburia* 1 (1949): 42–53.

___. "Tonkōbon *Ri Kyō hyakuei* ni tsuite" 敦煌本『李嶠百詠』について, *Tōhōgakkai sōritsu jūshūnen kinen Tōhōgaku ronshū* 東方学会創立10周年記念東方学論集, Tokyo, 1962, pp. 63–70.

Liu Yi 劉藝. "Li Jiao *Zayong shi*: puji wulü de qimeng jiaocai" 李嶠《雜詠詩》：普及五律的啓蒙教材, *Sichuan Daxue xuebao* 四川大學學報 2002.1: 135–44.

Takashima Kaname 高島要. "Nihon koten ni okeru *Ri Kyō hyakuei* o megutte" 日本古典における『李嶠百詠』をめぐって, in Kawaguchi Hisao 川口久雄, ed. *Koten no hen'yō to shinsei* 古典の変容と新生. Tokyo: Meiji, 1984.

Xu Dingxiang 徐定祥. *Li Jiao shi zhu, Su Weidao shi zhu* 李嶠詩注, 蘇味道詩注. Shanghai: Shanghai Guji, 1995.

Yanase Kiyoshi 柳瀬喜代志, ed. *Ri Kyō hyakunijūei sakuin* 李嶠百二十詠索引. Tokyo: Tōhō, 1991.

___. "*Hyakuei waka, Mōgyū waka* o botai to suru no gunki shosai no kankoji—jumei no kun to chūshinzō no hen'yōtan nisandai o megutte." 『百詠和歌』『蒙求和歌』を媒体とするの軍記所載の漢故事—受命の君と忠臣像の変容譚二、三題をめぐって, *Waseda Daigaku kyōiku gakubu gakujutsu kenkyū Kokugo Kokubungaku hen* 45 (1996): 55–65.

Zhang Jiazhuang 張家壯. "Wu Zetian shidai de xuanju yu jintishi de tuiguang—cong Li Jiao de gelüshi tanqi" 武則天時代的舉選與近體詩的推廣—從李嶠的格律詩談起, *Wenshi zhishi*, 2001.3: 19–24.

Tamotsu Satō and William H. Nienhauser, Jr.

Li Jilan 李季蘭 (*zi*, Jilan, *ming*, Ye 冶, after 731–784) was a Daoist poet-priestess active in Huzhou 湖州 (modern Zhejiang) and the surrounding lower Yangzi region during the reigns of Emperor Suzong (756–762) and Daizong (762–779). Early in the reign of Emperor Dezong (r. 779–805), possibly in 783, she was summoned to the capital to stay in the palace convent Yuchen 玉晨. In the tenth lunar month of 783, the general Zhu Ci 朱泚 (742–784) rebelled and occupied the capital, forcing Emperor Dezong to flee. Li Jilan was caught by the rebels and forced to compose a congratulatory poem. In the seventh lunar month of 784, after the rebellion was crushed and the emperor returned to the capital, he condemned Li for the congratulatory poem and had her beaten to death.

Song-dynasty catalogues record Li Jilan's poetic collection as one *juan*, and there are sixteen poems transmitted to the present day. Meanwhile the rediscovery of fragments of the *Yaochi xinyong ji* 瑤池新詠集 (Collection of New Songs from the Turquoise Pond), an anthology of Tang

Li Jilan

female poets' works compiled by Cai Xingfeng 蔡省風 (fl. 9th century), along with other Dunhuang manuscripts provide three more of her poems.

Most of the nineteen extant poems express Li Jilan's feelings of love and friendship. In several poems addressed to southern literati such as Li Shu 李紓 (731–792) and Lu Yu 陸羽 (b. 733), Li skillfully conveys her loneliness and longing for company, and her deep concern for her friends. For example, Li Jilan's "Ji shiqixiong jiaoshu" 寄十七兄校書 (Sent to the Editor, My Seventeenth Elder Brother), is a poem sent to Li Shu, who was a friend rather than a relative.

> In Wucheng district, with nothing to do,
> more than a year wasted.
> I wonder what you, the Palace Library official
> feel about loneliness.
> Distant rivers float your immortal boat,
> cold stars accompany the envoy's carriage.
> When you pass the Great Thunder Bank,
> don't forget to send just a few lines.

> 無事烏程縣, 蹉跎歲月餘.
> 不知芸閣吏, 寂寞意何如.
> 遠水浮仙棹, 寒星伴使車.
> 因過大雷岸, 莫忘幾行書.

This five-syllabic regulated verse opens with the poet's situation since parting from Li Shu: she has been in Wucheng idle for more than a year. She then expresses her loneliness and longing for company and, although it is not properly parallel according to regulated-verse rules, the direct appeal to Li Shu perhaps emphasizes her feelings for him. Allusions dominate the third couplet. The immortal boat in line 5 refers to a legend in which people who lived by the sea saw a floating raft traveling between the sea and the Heavenly River (Milky Way) each August. Line 6 alludes to the Han-dynasty account of Li He 李郃 (fl. 79–106) in the Later Han observing two stars in the heavens moving into a section of the sky that suggested his own location, adumbrating the arrival of two imperial envoys who were on their way to investigate his governance. Li Jilan must hope that she too will see some sign of Li Shu's travels. Even without recognizing the allusions, however, the well-matched antithetical images of the two lines—seas and stars, human and heavenly dimensions, boat and carriage—construct a visible, three-dimensional scene describing Li Shu's voyage in grandiose terms. They also reveal Li Jilan's concern for him—she imagines that the stars he watches will be cold, suggesting his loneliness. The closing couplet again employs an allusion fitting their 'brother-sister' relationship: like the famous Southern-dynasty poet Bao Zhao 鮑照 (414–466) who wrote a letter to his sister when he passed by the seaside on a trip, her friend and 'elder brother' Li Shu should not forget to send her a letter as well. These references have been especially praised by later critics.

Li's many poems written for her lover Yan Shihe 閻士和 (zi, Bojun 伯均, fl. 756–779), another southern literatus, are full of passion and represent her best work, here exemplified in "Dengshan wang Yan zi bu zhi" 登山望閻子不至 (Climbing a Mountain to Gaze Far after Master Yan, Who Never Arrives):

I climb the mountain and try to gaze afar,
mountains high, lakes also wide.
I long for you day and night,
I wait for you year after year.
Densely the mountain trees flourish;
Thickly the wildflowers bloom.
Of my boundless affection since parting
I will tell when we meet again.
望遠試登山, 山高湖又闊.
相思無曉夕, 相望經年月.
鬱鬱山木榮, 綿綿野花發.
別後無限情, 相逢一時說.

This five-syllabic old-style verse passionately expresses the poet's feelings during a long separation. In male-authored love poems beginning in the Six Dynasties, the female image is often eroticized and objectified as the object of desire—glamorously helpless and emotionally dependent. Li Jilan's love poems transform the desired object into a desiring subject. Although she too mixes sorrow, anxiety, and solitude in these poems, these feelings are no longer helpless and dependent cries, but active, independent, and self-empowered pursuits of her own true love and desire. Because such experience, some critics of Song dynasty onward have labeled Li Jilan as a "courtesan." However, Emperor Dezong's summons of Li Jilan as a palace Daoist priestess clearly define her identity. Of the nineteen poems extant, many have been included in traditional and modern anthologies and translated into English. Li Jilan was most skillful in writing five-syllabic verse, both regulated and old style, though she also composed some excellent seven-syllabic quatrains and songs. She expressed erudite allusions in plain language and fresh imagery, and her style was graceful without any trace of artifice. Traditional critics also evaluated her highly. Her works were placed at the beginning of the *Yaochi xinyong ji* 瑤池新詠集. The compilers of the *Siku quanshu* claimed her five-syllabic regulated poems to be as outstanding as that of the contemporary "Dali shicaizi" 大曆十才子 (Ten talents of the Dali reign-period) and asserted that her style far surpassed that of Xue Tao 薛濤 (768–831).*

BIBLIOGRAPHY

Editions:

Chen Wenhua 陳文華. *Tang nüshiren ji sanzhong* 唐女詩人集三種. Shanghai: Shanghai Guji, 1984.
Chen Yingxing 陳應行 (fl. 1194), ed. *Yinchuang zalu* 吟窗雜錄. Beijing: Zhonghua, 1997.
Gao Zhongwu 高仲武, ed. *Zhongxing jian qiji* 中興間氣集. In Fu, *Tangren*.
Hu Zhenheng 胡震亨 (1569–1645), ed. *Tangyin tongqian* 唐音統簽. *Xuxiu Siku quanshu* 續修四庫全書 ed.
Rong Xinjiang 荣新江 and Xu Jun 徐俊. "Xinjian E cang Dunhuang Tangshi xieben sanzhong kaozheng ji jiaolu" 新見俄藏敦煌唐詩寫本三種考證及校錄, *Tang yanjiu* 唐研究 5 (1999): 59–80.
___. "Tang Cai Xingfeng bian *Yaochi xinyong* chongyan" 唐蔡省風編瑤池新詠重研, *Tang yanjiu* 7 (2001): 125–44.
Wei Hu 韋縠 (fl. 947), ed. *Caidiao ji* 才調集. In Fu, *Tangren*.
Wei Zhuang 韋莊 (ca. 836–910), ed. *Youxuan ji* 又玄集. In Fu, *Tangren*.

Li Jilan

Xu Jun. *Dunhuang shiji canjuan jikao* 敦煌詩集殘卷輯考. Beijing: Zhonghua, 2001.
Xue Tao, Li Ye shiji 薛濤, 李冶詩集. *SKQS*.
Zhong Xing 鍾惺 (1574–1625), *Mingyuan shigui* 名媛詩歸. *Xuxiu Siku quanshu* ed.

Biographical Sources:
Fu, *Tang caizi*, 1:326–33.

Translations:
Jia, Jinhua. "The Life and Poetry of Li Jilan." In Jinhua Jia, *Gender, Power, and Talent, the Journey of Daoist Priestesses in Tang China*. New York: Columbia University, 2018, pp. 140–54.
___. "New Poetry from the Turquose Pond: Women Poets in Eight and Ninth-century China," *Tang Studies*, 37 (2019): 59–80.
___. "The *Yaochi ji* and Three Daoist Priestess-Poets in Tang China." *Nan Nü: Men, Women and Gender in China* 13 (2011): 205–43.
Kelen, Christopher et al., trans. *Fragrance of Damask: Women Poets of the Tang Dynasty*. Macau: Association of Stories in Macau, 2009.

Studies:
Cahill, Suzanne. "Resenting the Silk Robes that Hide Their Poems: Female Voices in the Poetry of Tang Dynasty Taoist Nuns." In Deng Xiaonan 鄧小南, Gao Shiyu 高世瑜, and Rong Xinjiang, eds., *Tang-Song nüxing yu shehui* 唐宋女性與社會. Shanghai: Shanghai Cishu, 2001, pp. 519–66.
Chen Wenhua, "Tangdai nüguan shiren Li Ye shenshi ji zuopin kaolun" 唐代女冠詩人李冶身世及作品考論. *Nanjing Daxue xuebao* 39.5 (2002): 119–25.
Idema, Wilt and Beata Grant. *The Red Brush: Writing Women in Imperial China*. Cambridge: Harvard University Asia Center, 2004, pp. 180–81
Jia, Jinhua 賈晉華. *Jiao Ran nianpu* 皎然年譜. Xiamen: Xiamen Daxue, 1992.
___. "The *Yaochi ji* and Three Daoist Priestess-Poets in Tang China." *Nan Nü: Men, Women and Gender in China* 13 (2011): 205–43.
Sun Changwu 孫昌武. *Daojiao yu Tangdai wenxue* 道教與唐代文學. Beijing: Renmin Wenxue, 2001.
Zhou Lei 周蕾, "Zhongxing jian qiji Li Jilan pingyu shuzheng" 中興間氣集李季蘭評語疏證, *Zhongguo shige yanjiu* 2008: 220–32.

Jinhua Jia

Li Pin 李頻 (*zi*, Dexin 德新, (814–ca. 876) a native of Shouchang 壽昌 in Muzhou 睦州 (modern Zhejiang), was a poet and politician who lived during the late Tang dynasty. The earliest account of his life comes from a short biography included in the "Wenyi" 文藝 (Literature and Arts) chapter of the *Xin Tang shu* (New History of the Tang). Derivatives of his biography can also be found in many later collective works, including the *Tang caizi zhuan* 唐才子傳, the *Tang shi jishi* 唐詩紀事, and the *Xu tongzhi* 續通志, to name a few.

The compilers of the *Xin Tang shu* tell us only little about Li Pin's life as a poet. Apart from providing details on his literary education and style, they mention only two artistic influences that shaped the poet in his early life: he was on good terms with Fang Gan 方干 (809–899) who hailed from the same village, and also studied with Yao He 姚合 (ca. 779–ca. 849),* to whom he had to walk "a thousand *li*." Yao He is said to have been so impressed by his student's efforts that he gave Li Pin his daughter's hand in marriage; a number of poems Yao He and Li Pin exchanged testify to their close relationship. Apart from this, the short account in the *Xin Tang shu* does not include any further information on Li Pin's life as a poet or his connections to other writers. However, recent work by Yang Qiujin 楊秋瑾 suggests Li also would have been in close contact with Zheng Gu 鄭谷 (ca. 849–ca. 911), Xue Neng 薛能 (d. ca. 880) and other poets of his time.

After passing the *jinshi* in 855, Li Pin enjoyed a successful political career starting with his first post as Editor in the Palace Library. He was later promoted to various posts in and out of the capital, including Recorder of Nanling 南陵 (modern Anhui), Magistrate of Wugong 武功 (modern Shaanxi), Attendant Censor, and Vice Director of Criminal Administration. His last official appointment was as Regional Inspector of Jianzhou 建州 (modern day Jian'ou 建甌 in northwestern Fujian), where he is said to have died serving his post. His remains were brought home and he was buried in Yongluo Prefecture 永洛州 (modern Jiangle 將樂, Fujian) where an ancestral temple was built for him at Lishan 梨山. Noted along with the official details concerning Li Pin's career, the biographers of the *Xin Tang shu* also included several anecdotes illustrating his exemplary behavior and merit while serving various offices. Li Pin's achievements were worthy enough to garner the admiration of Emperor Yizong (r. 859–873).

Li Pin's biography found in the *Xin Tang shu* does not give any explicit dates except for when he passed the *jinshi* examination, and thus it remains difficult to date events in Li Pin's life with any certainty. The *Jiu Tang shu* (Old History of the Tang), which itself does not contain a biography of Li Pin, does however supply an exact date for Li's final promotion from Vice Director of Criminal Administration to Regional Inspector of Jianzhou as the second year of the Qianfu reign (875). As the modern scholar Wu Zaiqing 吳在慶 has argued, that same office is taken over by someone else in 876. Therefore we have to assume that this was the year of Li Pin's death.

Li Pin's poems seem to have mostly survived the long transmission process into current times. The literary catalogues allow us to reconstruct their fate to some extent. In its treatise on literature the *Xin Tang shu* lists the collected works of Li Pin as "one bundle of Li Pin's poems" 李頻詩一卷. From there on, the length of the collection always stays the same. The literary catalog of the *Song shi*, Chen Zhensun's 陳振孫 *Zhihzhai shulu jieti* 直齋書錄解題 and the authors of the *Tang caizi zhuan*, for example, also speak of one *juan*. It is therefore unlikely that significant number of pieces were lost. The poems were then included in the *Siku quanshu* 四庫全書 under the title *Liyue ji* 黎嶽集 (The Mount Li Collection). The editors of the *Zongmu tiyao* explain that this name is based on the fact that Liyue is an alternative name for the Lishan, the site where an ancestral temple was erected for Li Pin. In all, the collection contains 195 poems and it is extant today. A handful of additional poems is contained in other sources.

Assessing Li Pin's reception and importance is possible through the comments made by other authors. Many of them found his pentasyllabic poems worthy of great praise. His style reminded Yan Yu 嚴羽 and other later critics of the mid-Tang poet Liu Zhangqing 劉長卿 (726–ca. 787).* He was a technician whose ability to portray sadness weighed upon readers, many admiring this ability while others have found it unconvincing (as the modern scholar **Wei Yuxia** 魏玉俠 recently pointed out).

Li Pin

Li Pin's most widely known poem, due to its inclusion among the collection *Tangshi sanbaishou* 唐詩三百首 (Three Hundred Poems of the Tang), is "Du Hanjiang" 渡漢江 (Crossing the Han River). The piece deals with the emotional turmoil that is brought forth by being cut off from one's home and then returning in an era of turmoil that may have touched on family and friends. It reads:

> South of the ranges, cut off from news and letters,
> winters pass, the onset of spring has come again.
> Approaching my home village, more and more anxious,
> I don't dare ask the people coming towards me.

> 嶺外音書絕，經冬復立春。
> 近鄉情更怯，不敢問來人。

The poem's authorship is problematic, however, as it has also been attributed to Song Zhiwen 宋之問 (656–ca. 712)*, who had actually been exiled to Lingnan. The attribution to Li Pin seems to have originated in the early Qing when the *Tangshi sanbaishou* was published.

Li Pin's relationship with Yao He can be seen in his "Xiari Zhouzhi jiao juji Yao shaofu" 夏日盩厔郊居寄姚少府 (Having Spent the Summer Days in the Suburbs of Zhouzhi as a Guest of Chamberlain of the Palace Revenues Yao [He]). In it, the poet thinks with longing and melancholy of the days he spent in Zhouzhi 盩厔 (modern day Zhouzhi 周至 in Shanxi) with his friend and father-in-law. The poem contrasts the memory of warm summer days spent in joyful discussions with friends to various images of the encroaching autumn and winter cold:

> The ancient trees cast cool shadows,
> the cold springs have deep currents.
> The cicadas have been chirping since the first hot period,
> now towards nightfall their songs [already] cool down.
>
> But the bright sun still deceives my black temple hair,
> and the cold-blue Jiang river carries away my plain heart.
> I think with longing of our conversations that went into the middle of the night,
> what road allows us to seek each other out again?

> 古木有清陰，寒泉有下深。
> 蟬從初伏噪，客向晚涼吟。
> 白日欺玄鬢，滄江負素心。
> 甚思中夜話，何路許相尋.

BIBLIOGRAPHY

Editions:
Liyue ji 黎嶽集, Li Pin 李頻. Taibei: Taiwan Shangwu Yinshuguan, 1979 (*SKQS*).
Liyue ji 黎嶽集, Li Pin 李頻. Shanghai: Shanghai Guji Chubanshe, 1987.
Quan Tang shi, 9: 6864–901, 14: 10683, 15: 11361–62.

Biographical Sources:
Fu, *Tang* caizi, 3:380–88, 5:393–97.
Xin Tang shu, 203.5794–95.

Translations:
Bynner, *Jade Mountain*, p. 39.
Harris, Peter. *Three Hundred Tang Poems*. New York: Alfred A. Knopf, 2009, p. 138. *Everyman's Library Pocket Poets*.

Studies:
Liu Yunfeng 劉雲峰, "Riben huiliu zhi Qing dai Chen Yuanlong shu Li Pin shi zhou" 日本回流之清代《陳元龍書李頻詩軸》, *Shouzang* 11 (2015).
Wei Yuxia 魏玉俠. "Li Pin shi jianyi" 李頻詩簡議, *Wen shi zhe*, 1990.6.
___. "Wan Tang shiren Li Pin shengping bukao" 晚唐詩人李頻生平補考, *Huazhong Shifan Daxue xuebao (Zhexue Shehui Kexue ban)*, 1991.4.
Wu Zaiqing 吳在慶. "Wan Tang Wudai Shi guo shiren shengzunian congkao" 晚唐五代十國詩人生卒年叢考, *Ningbo Daxue xuebao (Renwen Kexue ban)*, 1989 (2.2).
Yang Qiujin 楊秋瑾. "Li Pin jiaoyou xiaokao" 李頻交游小考, *Sichuan Shifan Daxue xuebao (Shehui Kexue ban)*, 1996.1.
Zhou Rong 周蓉. "Tangmo Jiangnan shiren qun de shicheng jiaoyou yu chuangzuo de qutonghua" 唐末江南詩人群的師承交游與創作的趨同化, *Xibei Shida xuebao (Shehui Kexue ban)*, 2013.5.

Sebastian Eicher

Li Qi 李頎 (690–751) was a descendant of the Zhaojun 趙郡 (modern Zhao County in Hebei) Li Clan, one of the prominent noble families of the early Tang. Li was known for his good looks and led a profligate youth. He then turned to books and retired to Yingyang 潁陽 (about twenty-five miles south of Luoyang) where he spent over a decade in study. In 735 he passed the *jinshi* examination. His first and seemingly only position was that of Commandant of Xinxiang 新鄉 County (modern Xinxiang City in Henan), for in 751 went into retirement again. He was for a time a member of the social network which included High Tang capital poets such as Wang Wei 王維 (692–761 or 699–759),* Cui Hao 崔顥 (d. 754),* Gao Shi 高適 (700–765),* and Wang Changling 王昌齡 (ca. 690–ca. 756).* However, he rarely wrote regulated verse in the conventional style of this group. Instead, Li Qi is noted for his poems in song style and heptasyllabic old-style, and his work is dominated by the eremitic, the supernatural, and the hyperbolic. His eccentric approach suggests the influence of Li Bo 李白 (701–762).*

When obliged to use verse to commemorate an occasion, Li Qi would characteristically loosen the form—as in the banquet poem entitled "Qin ge" 琴歌 (Zither Song), which extends to ten lines its celebration of the musical performance at an evening banquet:

> Our host with wine to mellow this evening,
> Asks his guest from Guangling to play the zither.
> As the moon shines on the city wall, crows take flight;
> Frost freezes a myriad trees, the wind blows through our coats.

Li Qi

> In the copper stove's smoke, flowery candles all the brighter.
> First he plays Green Waters, then the Lady of Chu;
> With the first note played, everything is silent.
> The whole company speechless, as the stars grow dim.
> It's hundreds of miles to my post on the clear Huai
> But I daresay this evening I would depart for the cloudy mountains.

> 主人有酒歡今夕，請奏鳴琴廣陵客。
> 月照城頭烏半飛，霜淒萬樹風入衣。
> 銅爐華燭燭增輝，初彈淥水後楚妃。
> 一聲已動物皆靜，四座無言星欲稀。
> 清淮奉使千餘裡，敢告雲山從此始。

This poem, perhaps written in 751, is read as though Li Qi wrote it en route to his position as Commandant of Xinxiang. If that is the case, then he claims he was inspired to leave the position and return to the eremitic left because of this performance. Regardless of the context for the poem, the images of the second couplet and the poet's insistence that the world silenced to hear this performer are typical of his extreme imagery. The performance he witnessed lasted until the stars grew dim in the light of dawn, the listeners all clearly captivated by the music. The "guest from Guangling" alludes to Xi Kang 嵇康 (ca. 223–ca. 263) and the identification here both flatters him and perhaps suggests the mode or style which he should play.

In "Song Chen Zhangfu" 送陳章甫 (Farewell to Chen Zhangfu), written for a friend who had just been dismissed from office, Li praises him for his erudition, disdain of the political world, loyalty to friends, and love of wine:

> In the fourth month the southern winds turn the barley yellow,
> The date flowers have yet to fall and the paulownia leaves lengthen.
> The green hills you left this morning you can still see this evening.
> Your horses neighed as they left the gate, intent on heading home.
> Lord Chen you've established yourself, a self-contained man—
> With your curly beard, tiger brows and broad forehead.
> In your heart you've stored away ten thousand volumes,
> Not willing to bow your head in the wild fields of politics.
> At the east gate you bought wine and gave all of us to drink;
> Lighthearted you take mundane affairs like lifting a feather.
> Lying back tipsy you're unaware that the bright sun has set,
> Now and then you gaze at solitary clouds on high.
> As the waves of the Long River meet the black of the sky,
> Even the ferryman cannot get across.
> So the wanderer from the state of Zheng has not yet reached home,
> And this traveler from Luoyang sighs in vain.
> I have heard about the many friends you have made at your woodland home,
> Having just been dismissed from your position, how will things with them be now?

> 四月南風大麥黃，棗花未落桐葉長。
> 青山朝別暮還見，嘶馬出門思舊鄉。
> 陳侯立身何坦蕩，虯須虎眉仍大顙。

188

腹中貯書一萬卷，不肯低頭在草莽。
東門酤酒飲我曹，心輕萬事如鴻毛。
醉臥不知白日暮，有時空望孤雲高。
長河浪頭連天黑，津吏停舟渡不得。
鄭國遊人未及家，洛陽行子空歎息。
聞道故林相識多，罷官昨日今如何。

Chen Zhangfu was a native of Jiangling 江陵 (near modern Jingzhou City 荊州市 in Hubei) who had studied in retirement for over twenty years at Mount Song 嵩山, one of the five great marchmounts of China, located about forty miles east-southeast of Luoyang. When Li Qi retired to Yingyang they must have become friends. This poem seems to have been written after Chen lost his position and was returning to his home in the south. "Self-contained man" (*tandang* 坦蕩) in line five alludes to the *Confucian Analects* (7.37) where it depicts the ideal gentleman as someone who exhibits such qualities. The east gate in line 7 is that of Luoyang. In the following couplet the wanderer from Zheng refers to Chen, while the traveler is Li Pin himself. Line 18 may be read together with the preceding line as referring to the difficulty facing Li Pin in his attempt to go home, but the two lines can also be read allegorically as a warning to Chen Zhangfu of the obstacles that will face him should he desire to return to official life. The final line could be understood as Li Qi expressing concern over the villages near Chen's hometown or as his unease wondering whether the people in his hometown will continue to respect Chen now that he has be dismissed.

Aside from other occasional poems, Li Qi's wrote often on music, the border, and his eccentric friends; 124 poems are extant, 7 in the *Tangshi sanbaishou*.

BIBLIOGRAPHY

Editions:
Li Qi ji 李頎集 in *Tang Wushijia shiji* 唐五十家詩集. Shanghai: Shanghai Guji, 1980. Reproduction of a moveable type Ming edition.
Quan Tang shi, 2: 1338–67, 14: 11077.

Annotations:
Li Qi 李頎. *Li Qi ji jiaozhu* 李頎集校注. Zhengzhou: Henan Renmin, 2007.
Liu Baohe 劉寶和, ed. *Li Qi shi pingzhu* 李頎詩評注. Taiyuan: Shanxi Jiaoyuan, 1990.

Biographical Sources:
Fu, *Tang caizi*, 1:351–58, 5:69–70.

Translations:
Bynner, *Jade Mountain*, pp. 33–38. Includes seven of Li Qi's poems.
Demiéville, pp. 241–42.
Gundert, *Lyrik*, p. 71.
Minford and Lau, pp. 828–29.
Owen, *High T'ang*, pp. 103–18.

Studies:

Fu Xuancong 傅璇琮. "Li Qi kao" 李頎考, in his *Tang dai shiren congkao* 唐代詩人叢考. Beijing: Zhonghua, 1980, pp. 88–102.

Li Wei 李維. "Li Qi biansaishi de huyue yixiang yu renxia qingjie" 李頎邊塞詩的胡樂意象與任俠情結. *Haerbin Gongye Daxue xuebao (Shehui Kexueban)* 哈爾濱工業大學學報 (社會科學版), 2006.5: 140–44.

Liu Baohe 劉寶和. "Jianlun Li qiji qi shi" 簡論李頎及其詩, *Zhengzhou Daxue xuebao* 鄭州大學學報 1989.2: 7–12.

Luo Qin 羅琴 and Hu Sikun 胡嗣坤. *Li Qi ji qi shige yanjiu* 李頎及其詩歌研究. Chengdu: Ba Shu, 2009.

Sui Xiuling 隋秀玲. "Li Qi jiguan kaobian" 李頎籍貫考辨, *Zhengzhou Hangkong Gongye Guanli Xueyuan (Shehui Kexueban)* 鄭州航空工業管理學院 (社會科學版), 2007.2: 45–47.

Wang Yousheng 王友勝. "Li Qi shi zhong renwu xingxiang jianlun" 李頎詩中人物形象簡論, *Zhongguo wenxue yanjiu* 中國文學研究 64 (2002.1): 35–38.

Yao Dianzhong 姚奠中. "Li Qi liju shengping kaobian he shige chengjiu" 李頎里居生平考辯和詩歌成就, *Shanxi Daxue xuebao* 山西大學學報 1983.1: 12–18.

Marsha Wagner and William H. Nienhauser, Jr.

Li Rong 李榮 (*hao*, Renzhenzi 任真子, fl. 660–669) was a Daoist poet-priest and a theorist active in the early Tang. He was a native of Baxi 巴西 (modern Mianyang City 綿陽市 in Sichuan) and received his Daoist training on Mount Fule 富樂山 (Sichuan). During Emperor Gaozong's (r. 649–683) reign, he was summoned to the capital city Chang'an where he engaged actively in court debates between Buddhists and Daoists. He was very eloquent in these debates and was praised as "Number One in Daoism" (Laozong kuishou 老宗魁首). In 660, however, Li Rong lost to the monk Jingtai 靜泰 in a debate and was ordered to return to Sichuan. In 663, he was summoned to Chang'an again and debated the monk Lingbian 靈辨 and others. These debates are collected in the *Fayuan zhulin* 法苑珠林 (The Pearl Forest of the Dharma Garden) and the *Fozu lidai tongzai* 佛祖歷代通載 (Comprehensive Records of Buddhist Patriarchs over Generations). As a poet, Li Rong exchanged poems with well-known poets such as Lu Zhaolin 盧照鄰 (ca. 634–ca. 689)* and Luo Binwang 駱賓王 (640–684).* He had a love affair with the priestess Wang Lingfei 王靈妃, whose story was written into a long poem by Luo Binwang. In 669, Li Rong composed a poem on a fire at Xingshan Monastery 興善寺.

According to Song-dynasty catalogues, Li Rong 李榮 authored the *Zhuangzi zhu* 莊子注 (Commentary on *Zhuangzi*), the *Daode jing zhu* 道德經注 (Commentary on *Daode jing*), and the *Xisheng jing zhu* 西昇經注 (Commentary on the Scripture of the Ascent to the West) among other works. All three texts were lost. Fragments of *Daode jing zhu* are seen in several Dunhuang manuscripts, in Qiang Siqi's 強思齊 (fl. 920) *Daode zhenjing xuande zuanshu* 道德真經玄德纂疏 (Compendium of Commentaries on the Mysterious Virtue of the *Daode jing*), and in the *Daozang*. Meng Wentong 蒙文通 (1894–1968) collated these fragments and published them as "Jijiao Li Rong *Daodejing zhu*" 輯校李榮道德經注 (Collection and Collation of Li Rong's Commentary on *Daode jing*). Yan Lingfeng 嚴靈峰 (1903–1999) also compiled a version of the *Daode zhenjing zhu* 道德真經注 (Commentary on *Daode zhenjing*). Chen Jingyuan's 陳景元 (d. 1094) *Xisheng jing jizhu* 西昇經集注 (Collected Commentaries on the Scripture of the Ascent to the West) includes some fragments from Li Rong's *Xisheng jing zhu*. The *Quan Tang shi* preserves two of Li Rong's poems, one linked with Fagui 法軌.

Li Rong was one of the most important representatives of the philosophical tendency in the early Tang called Twofold Mystery School of Thought (Chongxuanxue 重玄學). The theory of "twofold mystery" (*chongxuan*), based on Wang Bi's 王弼 (226–249) concept of *xuan* ("mysterious"), developed from commentaries on the *Daode jing* and *Zhuangzi* that discuss the Dao in terms of being and emptiness through the application of the four propositions of the Buddhist Mādhyamika philosophy. First attested to by the Cheng Xuanying 成玄英 (fl. 631–650), the Two-fold Mystery School of Thought is more of a shared philosophical concern than any specific lineage, and its questions informed many thinkers of the Tang. Li Rong illumined his theory of *chongxuan* through his commentary to the *Daode jing*. He interpreted the phrase *xuan zhi you xuan* 玄之又玄 ("mystery of the further mysterious") in chapter one as follows:

> The virtue of Dao is ineffable and ultimate nonbeing, and its principle is impossible to grasp in image or designate with language. Its true doctrine is void and limpid, and its matter transcends both being and nonbeing. To entrust it beyond language and image, and to place it beyond being and nonbeing, is to go through the deep path. Therefore, [Laozi] speaks of the "mysterious." Still, he is afraid that those who lose their directions and principles may act with a one-track mind and be hindered by this mysteriousness, taking it as the true Dao. Therefore, he speaks of it trickily as neither being nor nonbeing and defines its name as the "mysterious." Using the mysterious to eliminate both being and nonbeing, and after eliminating both being and nonbeing, the mysterious itself is eliminated too. Therefore, [Laozi] speaks of the "further mysterious."

> 道德杳冥, 理超於言象; 真宗虛湛, 事絕於有無. 寄言象之外, 託有無之表,以通幽路, 故曰玄之. 猶恐迷方者膠柱, 失理者守株, 即滯此玄, 以為真道,故機言之, 非有無之表, 定名曰玄. 借玄以遣有無, 有無既遣, 玄亦自喪, 故曰又玄 ("Jijiao Li Rong *Daodejing zhu*").

In keeping with questions of being and nonbeing that pervade the literature associated with "Two-fold Mystery" thought, Li Rong argues here that in order to understand the Dao, one needs to use the concept of the "mysterious" to get beyond the duality of being that had been the focus of other *chongxuan* thinkers. However, that would not be enough. One must also be aware of the danger of using concepts to describe the ineffable. Thus, he cautions that one should be careful not to hold fast to the concept of the "mysterious" as a way to understand the Dao, lest one fall into the same trap of thinking in terms of being and nonbeing (i.e. the Dao *is* mysterious). His commentary on the *Laozi* shows that only by eventually leaving the idea of the "mysterious" behind, can one truly reach the "gate of all subtleties" (i.e. the Dao), where the true mystery behind even the "mysterious"—that which is "further mysterious"—may be revealed.

BIBLIOGRAPHY

Editions:
Qiang Siqi 強思齊 (late 9th–early 10th century), ed. *Daode zhenjing xuande zuanshu* 道德真經玄德纂疏. *DZ* 711.
Quan Tang shi, 13: 9909, 14: 10926.

Annotations:
Chen Jingyuan 陳景元 (d. 1094), ed. *Xishengjing jizhu* 西昇經集注. *DZ* 726.
Fan Jingyuan 范應元 (fl. 1265–1275), ed. *Laozi Daodejing guben jizhu* 老子道德經古本集注. *Xuxiu Siku quanshu* ed., 954.
Li Rong 李榮. *Daode zhenjing zhu* 道德真經注. *DZ* 722
Meng Wentong 蒙文通 (1894–1968). "Jijiao Li Rong *Daodejing zhu*" 輯校李榮道德經注, in *Mengwentong quanji* 蒙文通文集, vol.6, *Daoshu jijiao shizhong* 道書輯校十種. Chengdu: Ba Shu, 1987.
Yan Lingfeng 嚴靈峰 (1903–1999), ed. *Daode zhenjing zhu* 道德眞經注. *Wuqiubeizhai Laozi jicheng chubian* 無求備齋老子集成初編 ed. Taibei: Yiwen, 1965.

Translations:
Assandri, Friederike. *Beyond the Daode jing: Twofold Mystery in Tang Daoism*. Magdalena: Three Pines, 2009.

Studies:
Assandri, Friederike. *Beyond the Daode jing: Twofold Mystery in Tang Daoism*. Magdalena: Three Pines Press, 2009.
Dong Enlin 董恩林. *Tangdai Laozi quanshi wenxian yanjiu* 唐代老子詮釋文獻研究. Jinan: Qi Lu Shushe, 2003.
Fujiwara Takao 藤原高男. "Dōshi Ri Ei no *Dōtokukyō* chu ni tsuite" 道士李榮の道德経注について, *Kagawa daigaku kyōiku gakubu kenkyū hōkō* 香川大学教育学部研究報告 47 (1979): 1–30.
____. "Saishōkyō Ri Ei chu" 西昇経李榮注, *Kagawa daigaku ippan kyōiku kenkyū* 香川大學一般教育研究 23 (1983): 117–50.
Kohn, Livia. *Taoist Mystical Philosophy: The Scripture of Western Ascension*. Albany: State University of New York, 1991.
____. "Li Rong." In *Encyclopedia of Taoism,* ed. Fabrizion Pregadio. London: Curzon Press, 2000, 641–43.
Kohn, Livia and Russell Kirkland. "Daoism in the Tang." In Livia Kohn, ed., *Daoism Handbook*. Boston and Leiden: Brill, 2004, pp. 339–83.
Li Dahua 李大華, Li Gang 李剛, and He Jianming 何建明. *Suitang daojia yu daojiao* 隋唐道家與道教. Guangzhou: Guangdong Renmin, 2003.
Lin Junhong 林俊宏. "Li Rong de chongxuan sixiang yu zhengzhi lunshu: yi *Laozizhu* wei hexin" 李榮的重玄思想與政治論述: 以老子注為核心, *Zhengzhi kexue luncong* 政治科學論叢 6 (2009): 1–42.
Lu Guolong 盧國龍. *Zhongguo chongxuanxue* 中國重玄學. Beijing: Renmin Zhongguo, 1993.
Robinet, Isabelle. *Les commentaries du Tao to king jusqu'au VIIe siècle*. Paris: Collège de France, Institut des Hautes Études Chinoises, 1977.
Sharf, Robert H. *Coming to Terms with Chinese Buddhism: A Reading of the Treasure Store Treatise*. Honolulu: University of Hawaii, 2002.
Sunayama, Minoru 砂山稔. *Zui Tō Dōkyō shisōshi kenkyū* 隋唐道教思想史研究. Tokyo: Hirakawa, 1990.

Wang Zhongmin 王重民. "Laozi Daodejing shu" 老子道德經義疏, in *Dunhuang guji xulu* 敦煌古籍敘錄,. Beijing: Shangwu, 1958, pp. 236–42.

Yan Lingfeng 嚴靈峰. *Jingzi congzhu* 經子叢著. Taibei: Guoli Bianyiguan, 1983.

Jinhua Jia and Zhaojie Bai

Li Shangyin 李商隱 (*zi*, Yishan 義山, *hao*, Yuxisheng 玉谿生, also Fannansheng 樊南生, ca. 813–858) was born in Huojia 獲嘉 (modern Henan), where his father was then the magistrate. He grew up in Zhengzhou 鄭州 and Luoyang after his father's death in 821. In 829, Linghu Chu 令狐楚 (766–837),* the Military Commissioner of Tianping 天平, admired Li's literary skills and appointed him an Inspector on his staff and taught him *pianwen* 駢文 (parallel prose) together with his son, Linghua Tao 令狐綯 (ca. 795–ca. 872). With the support of Linghu Tao, Li Shangyin passed the *jinshi* examination in 837, and served in the retinue of Wang Maoyuan 王茂元 (d. 843), Military Commissioner of Jingyuan 涇源. Wang also recognized Li's literary talent and married his daughter to him. Li subsequently served as Editor in the Palace Library and held a number of junior posts both in the capital and in various prefectures, but never attained high rank and died without office in Zhengzhou.

Li Shangyin's 598 extant poems can be divided into four groups. The first consists of ambiguous poems, either labeled "Wuti" 無題 (Without Title) or bearing titles that are simply the first words of the opening line. Apparently concerned with clandestine love, these poems are subjects of controversy. Some scholars interpret them as autobiographical poems about secret love affairs with court ladies and Daoist priestesses. It seems fruitless to read them as *poèmes à clef* and try to identify the supposed prototypes of the *dramatis personae*; instead, it is more rewarding to reconstruct, from the text of each poem, a dramatic context which allows a consistent reading, without necessarily identifying the speaker with the author. Seen in this light, these poems are effective explorations of various facets of love: including desire, hope, joy, frustration, jealousy, tenderness, and despair. They are unusual among Chinese poems for their intensity and complexity of emotion and as well as for their density and richness of language. Replete with sensuous imagery and recondite allusions, they are structurally tight and syntactically compact. Some of them, such as "Jin se" 錦瑟 (The Ornamented Zither), his most famous poem, actually deal with more than love, using several levels of reality and fusing the past with the present, the real with the imaginary, and the historical with the mythical:

The ornamented zither unreasonably has fifty strings;
each string and each peg recall a blossoming year.
Master Zhuang's daybreak dream: bewildered about being a butterfly;
Emperor Wang's passionate heart: entrusted to the cuckoo.
In the bright moonlight on the vast sea pearls have tears
on Lantian warmed under the sun jade emits a mist.
These feelings could have waited to become a memories—
it's just that at the time I already felt so disoriented.

錦瑟無端五十弦，一弦一柱思華年。
莊生曉夢迷蝴蝶，望帝春心托杜鵑。

Li Shangyin

滄海月明珠有淚，藍田日暖玉生煙。
此情可待成追憶，只是當時已惘然。

The poem like the zither is ornamented—by allusions. In the first couplet the poet is berating the zither for reminding him of the days of his youth. In line 3 Li Shangyin shifts the mood by speculating on the reality of his memories by referring to the famous story in *Zhuang Zi* in which Master Zhuang relates his dream of being a butterfly and then ponders whether he was dreaming of being a butterfly or is actually a butterfly dreaming he is Master Zhuang. But line 4 reconfirms the poet's recollections by evoking the legendary ruler of Shu. He had a love affair with the wife of his minister, died of regret, and had his soul transformed into a cuckoo—the cuckoo's cry sounds like his own name, Du Yu 杜宇. The point is Emperor Wang never wavered from his love. What commitment Li Shangyin is suggesting here remains vague but could refer to either a love entanglement or his political career. Lines 5 and 6 depict an illusionary world, invoking (in line 5) the belief that when the moon is full pearls would appear as well as the story of a mermaid whose tears turned to pearls as well as (in line 6) the figure of Jade, the daughter of the King of Wu in the fifth century BC, who died when her father would not let her marry the man she loved. Her spirit subsequently visited the king and then turned to smoke. The final lines show the poet reflecting on his reactions which the zither put into motion, unable to accept his fate and left to puzzle his future.

To the second group belong personal and social poems of a more conventional kind, including fond recollections of the poet's deceased wife, affectionate descriptions of his children, sad valedictions as well as playful jibes addressed to friends, and polite eulogies presented to patrons. They tend to be more straightforward in manner and simple in diction than the ambiguous poems, but they are by no means merely perfunctory. On the contrary, they are often fresh and limpid, treating conventional themes with new insight. One of his most famous poems is "Ye yu, ji bei" 夜雨寄北 (Night Rain, to be Sent North) which many commentators feel was written while Li Shangyin was in Sichuan and intended for his wife in the capital:

> You ask what date I'll return—no date is yet set;
> In the mountains of Ba the night rain causes autumn pools to rise.
> When will we together trim the candles by the western window,
> And still speak of this time of the night rain on the mountains of Ba.

君問歸期未有期，巴山夜雨漲秋池。
何當共剪西窗燭，卻話巴山夜雨時。

This little poem is amazing what it compacts into twenty-eight Chinese characters. Lines one and two offer both the scene and the setting. The first line also suggests that Li Shangyin is hopeful to return. Line two, besides placing the poet in far-off Sichuan, only suggests the sadness the poet feels through the image of the autumnal rain. The time here is the present. But in the third line the reader and the recipient of the poem are invited to flash forward and imagine a time in the future when together with the poet they can reflect on this very moment which will then be part of the past. The circular logic of the poem is supported by the chiasmic repetition of "the night rain in the mountains of Ba."

The third group comprises poems on historical or contemporary events. Sometimes he comments on history to draw a lesson for the present; at other times he openly voices his indignation against the abuses of power by court officials, eunuchs, and provincial warlords. Although his analysis of political and social conditions may not be original or even accurate, these are successful poems of protest. His sarcasm concerning high officials and even the emperor is biting and witty, and his use of historical analogies both ingenious and innovative. "Mawei" 馬嵬 (Mawei) is a good example:

> Horses of Ji, armor of Yan came quaking the earth;
> Alone they buried the pink rouge, alone it turned to ash.
> If the lord king had understood she could topple kingdoms,
> How would the Jade Palanquin have needed to pass by Mawei?

> 冀馬燕犀動地來，自埋紅粉自成灰。
> 君王若道能傾國，玉輦何由過馬嵬。

This poem refers to the beloved consort Yang Guifei 楊貴妃 whom Emperor Xuanzong (r. 713–756) doted on, allowing her relatives to gain power and influence, resulting in the rebellion led by An Lushan in 755 which drove the imperial party into exile in Sichuan. On their way, at the Mawei Slope just outside of Chang'an, the imperial troops demanded that Yang Guifei be executed. The key term in the poem is the repeated *zi* 自 in line 2. It can mean "naturally" or "of itself," but here seems to emphasize the sudden isolation Yang Guifei felt as she was removed from the imperial entourage and forced to commit suicide. It emphasizes the fear she must have felt after years of being pampered in the palace to falling into the hands of the imperial troops as they fled. The juxtaposition from pink-rouged beauty to mere ashes in an unmarked grave is striking. Li Shangyin suggests that had the emperor realized the danger that Yang Guifei presented to his rule, the rebellion and his flight would never have taken place.

To the last group maybe assigned poems on objects (*yongwu shi* 詠物詩), which also have been interpreted allegorically. In fact, the poems are heterogeneous in nature: some may contain specific references, others may be symbolic in a general way, still others may be *jeux d'esprit* or poetic conundrums. For instance, the willow (*liu* 柳) may refer to a girl named Willow Branch (Liuzhi 柳枝)–Li wrote a number of poems about her, with a preface explaining the circumstances in which he met her but failed to have a love affair with her. Yet in other poems the willow may symbolize any beautiful woman, and in still others it may be a pun on the surname of one of Li's patrons, Liu Zhongying 柳仲郢 (d. 864). Each poem in this category has to be treated on its own terms as the following "Liu" 柳 (Willows) illustrates:

> Stirring spring, what end to its leaves;
> Approaching dawn, so many branches.
> Does it understand that I have such a longing?
> It must be that its dancing never stops.
> Floss flies hiding the white butterflies,
> Fronds droop revealing yellow orioles.
> A kingdom-toppling beauty should encompass the whole body,
> Who comes to admire only her brows?

Li Shangyin

動春何限葉，撼曉幾多枝。
解有相思否，應無不舞時。
絮飛藏皓蝶，帶弱露黃鸝。
傾國宜通體，誰來獨賞眉。

The poem has been interpreted as written for Liuzhi 柳枝, "Willow Branch," a girl with whom Li Shangyin had an affair. But it does not need this context. The willow itself was associated with singers and courtesans and here could be depicting the poet's longing for any young woman. The poem is linked nicely by the willow leaves in the first line which are a common metaphor for the eyebrows of an attractive girl as shown in the final line. It is one of dozens of poems Li Shangyin wrote on this favorite subject of his.

Li Shang-yin's poetry embodies passion, commitment, and conflict. It contains elements of Confucianism, Buddhism, and Daoism without reaching a complete synthesis of the three. There are signs of a conflict between Confucian puritanism and Buddhist asceticism, on the one hand, and sybaritic hedonism associated with the popular Daoist quest for the elixir of life, on the other. There is also a conflict between the Confucian ideal of public service and the wish to withdraw from society, prompted by both Buddhism and Daoism. These conflicts remain unresolved in Li's poetry, although towards the end of his life he embraced Buddhism and wrote a *gāthā* on his deathbed.

In general, Li Shangyin extended the scope of Chinese poetry by exploring spheres of experience previously untouched by poets, or by exploring familiar worlds with a new intensity and a self-awareness that often led to irony. It is perhaps this last quality, together with his striking use of language, that makes him particularly appealing to sophisticated modern readers. At the same time, his exploitation of the potentials of the Chinese language has exerted a profound influence on later poetry.

Apart from being a major poet, Li Shangyin was also a master of *pianwen* 駢文 (parallel prose). He made two collections of his works in this genre, although he apparently never compiled a collection of his poetry. His *pianwen* pieces show some of the characteristics of his poetry: skillful use of allusions, exact parallelism, and elaborate phraseology. Less read than his poetry, they nonetheless remain superb specimens of this style.

BIBLIOGRAPHY

Editions:

Qian Zhenlun 錢振倫, et al., eds. *Fannan wenji bubian* 樊南文集補編. Taibei: Taiwan Zhonghua, 1965.
Quan Tang shi, 8: 6194–310, 14: 10674, 15: 11325.
Quan Tang wen, 771–82.9187–327.
Zhu Heling 朱鶴齡, ed. *Li Yishan shiji* 李義山詩集. 1659. Rpt., 1870. Commentaries by Zhu Yicun 朱彝尊 (1629–1709), He Zhuo 何焯 (1661–1722), and Ji Yun 紀昀 (1724–1805), with the words *ji ping* 輯評 added to the title. Valuable as a collection of traditional criticism of Li's poetry.

References:
Luan Guiming 欒貴明 et al., eds. *Quan Tang shi suoyin: Li Shangyin juan* 全唐詩索引:李商隱卷. Beijing: Zhonghua, 1991.

Annotations:
Chen Bohai 陳伯海. *Li Shangyin shi xianzhu* 李商隱詩先注. Shanghai: Shanghai Guji, 1982.
Chen Yongzheng 陳永正, annot. *Li Shangyin shi xuanyi* 李商隱詩選譯. Chengdu: Ba Shu, 1991.
Deng Zhonglong 鄧中龍, ed. *Li Shangyin shi yizhu* 李商隱詩譯註. Changsha: Yuelu, 2000.
Fannan wenji 樊南文集. 2v. Including *Fannan wenji xiangzhu* 樊南文集詳注, Feng Hao 馮浩 (1719–1801), annot., and *Fannan wenji bubian* 樊南文集補編, Qian Zhenlun 錢振倫 (1816–1879) and Qian Zhenchang 錢振常 (1825–1898), annot. Shanghai: Shanghai Guji. 1988.
Feng Hao 馮浩 (1719–1801), ed. *Yuxisheng shiji jianzhu* 玉谿生詩集箋注. 1780. Rpt. Shanghai: Shanghai Guji, 1979.
Liu Xuekai 劉學鍇 and Yu Shucheng 餘恕誠, eds. *Li Shangyin shige jijie* 李商隱詩歌集解. 5v. Beijing: Zhonghua, 2004.
Nie Shiqiao 聶石樵 and Wang Rubi 王汝弼. *Yuxisheng shi chun* 玉谿生詩醇. Beijing: Zhonghua, 2008.
Song Xulian 宋緒連 and Chu Xu 初旭, eds. *San Li shi jianshang cidian* 三李詩鑑賞辭典. Changchun: Jilin Wenshi, 1992. Contains numerous close readings of poems by Li He, Li Bo and Li Shangyin as well as short biographies and useful bibliographies for these three important poets.
Xu Shugu 徐樹穀, et al., eds. *Li Yishan wenji jianzhu: [10 juan]* 李義山文集箋注: [10 卷]. Taibei: Taiwan Shangwu, 1973.
Ye Congqi 葉蔥奇, annot. *Li Shangyin shiji shuzhu* 李商隱詩集疏注. Beijing: Renmin Wenxue, 1985.
Zhou Zhenfu 周振甫. *Li Shangyin xuanji* 李商隱選集. Shanghai: Shanghai Guji, 2012.
Zheng Zaiying 鄭在瀛. *Li Shangyin shiji jinzhu* 李商隱詩集今注. Wuhan: Wuhan Daxue, 2001.

Biographical Sources:
Fu, *Tang caizi*, 3:264–81, 347–49.
Jiu Tang shu, 190C.5077–78.
Xin Tang shu, 203.5792–93.

Translations:
Articulated Ladies, pp. 294–98, 301–04.
Birch, *Anthology*, pp. 324–29.
Bonmarchand, Georges. *Li Yi-chan*. Notes and preface by Pascal Quignard. Paris: Gallimard, 1992 (rpt. of Tokyo: Maison Franco-Japonaise, 1955).
Chan Kwan-Hung 陳鈞洪. *The Purple Phoenix: Poems of Li Shangyin*. West Conshohocken, PA: Infinity, 2012.
Fuller, Michael A. *An Introduction to Chinese Poetry: From the* Canon of Poetry *to the Lyrics of the Song Dynasty*. Cambridge: Harvard University Press, 2018, pp. 323–33.
Hervouet, Yves. *Amour et politique dans la Chine ancienne, Cent poems de Li Shangyin (812–858)*. Paris: De Bocard, 1995.
Liu, James J. Y. *The Poetry of Li Shang-yin*. Chicago: University of Chicago, 1969.
Minford, John and Joseph S.M. Lau. *Classical Chinese Literature*. New York: Columbia University, 2000, pp. 920–29.
Owen, *Anthology*, pp. 454, 510–7.
___, *Mi-Lou*, pp. 166–7.
___, *Omen*, pp. 47–50.
___, *Late Tang*, pp. 335–526.

___, *Remembrances*, pp. 77–79;
Takahashi, Kazumi 高橋和巳. *Ri Shoin* 李商隱. Tokyo: Iwanami, 1958.
von Zach, Erwin, *Han Yu poetische Werke*, Cambridge, Mass.: Harvard University, 1952, pp. 353–73.
Yeh Chia-ying. "Li Shang-yin's 'Four Yen-t'ai Poems'" in *Studies in Chinese Poetry* Cambridge, Mass.: Harvard University, 1998, pp. 56–115. Translated into English by James R. Hightower.

Studies:
Anhui Shifan Daxue Zhongwenxi Gudai Wenxue Jiaoyanzu 安徽師範大學中文系古代文學教研組, ed. *Li Shangyin shixuan* 李商隱詩選. Beijing: Renmin Wenxue, 1978.
Bai Guanyun 白冠雲. *Li Shangyin yanqing shi zhi mi* 李商隱艷情詩之謎. Taibei: Mingwen, 1991.
Chang, Shuxiang 張淑香. *Li Shangyin shi xilun* 李商隱詩析論. Taibei: Yiwen, 1985.
Dong Naibin 董乃斌. *Li Shangyin de xinling shijie* 李商隱的心靈世界. Shanghai: Shanghai Guji, 1992.
___. *Li Shangyin zhuan* 李商隱傳. Xian: Shanxi Renmin, 1981.
Ge Zhaoguang 葛兆光 and Dai Yan 戴燕. *Wan Tang fengyun–Du Mu yu Li Shangyin* 晚唐風韻－杜牧與李商隱. Nanjing: Jiangsu Guji, 1991.
Geng Zhonglin 耿仲琳. *Li He, Li Shangyin nanshi pojie* 李賀李商隱難詩破解. Shanghai: Shanghai Sanlian, 2010.
Gu Yiqun 顧翊羣. *Li Shangyin pinglun* 李商隱評論. Taibei: Zhonghua, 1958.
Hervouet, Yves. "Short Titles in the Poetry of Li Shangyin." In *Zhongyang yanjiu yuan guoji hanxue huiyi lunwen ji* 中央研究院國際漢學會義論文集. Taibei: Academia Sinica, 1981, pp. 289–317.
___. Hervouet, Yves. Review of *The Poetry of Li Shang-yin, Ninth-Century Baroque Chinese Poet* by James J. Y. Liu, TP 57 (1971): 220–28.
Huang Shengxiong 黃盛雄. *Li Yishan shi yanjiu* 李義山詩研究. Taibei: Wenshizhe, 1987.
Huang Shizhong 黃世中. *Li Shangyin shixuan: cha tu ban* 李商隱詩選:插圖版. Beijing: Zhonghua, 2009.
___. *Li Shangyin wutishi jiaozhu jianping* 李商隱無題詩校注箋評. Nanchang: Jiangxi Renmin, 1987.
Kako Riichirō 加固理一郎, ed. *Ri Shōin shibunron* 李商隱詩文論. Tokyo: Kenbun, 2011.
Kawai, Kōzō 川合康三. *Chūgoku no koi no uta: shikyō kara ri shōin made* 中国の恋のうた：「詩経」から李商隱まで. Tokyo: Iwanami, 2011.
___. *Ri shōin shisen* 李商隱詩選. Tokyo: Iwanami, 2008.
Kirishima Kaoruko 桐島薰子, ed. *Ban Tō shijinkō: Ri Shōin, On Teiin, To Boku no hikaku to kōsatsu* 晚唐詩人考：李商隱・温庭筠・杜牧の比較と考察. Fukuoka: Chūgoku, 1998.
Klein, Lucas. "Pseudo-pseudo Translation: On the Potential for Annotation in Translating Li Shangyin," *JOS*, 49 (2016): 49–72.
Li Changqing 李長慶, Zhang Fulin 張輔麟 and Mi Zhiguo 米治國. *Li Shangyin ji qi zuopin* 李商隱及其作品. Changchun: Shitai Wenyi, 1989.
Li Miao 李淼. *Li Shangyin shi sanbaishou yishang* 李商隱詩三百首譯賞. Taibei: Liwen Wenhua, 1988.
Liu Wan. "Poetics of Allusion: Tu Fu, Li Shang-yin, Ezra Pound, and T.S. Eliot." Unpublished Ph.D. dissertation, Princeton University, 1992.
Liu Xuekai 劉學鍇 and Yu Shucheng 餘恕誠, et al., eds. *Li Shangyin shige jijie* 李商隱詩歌集解. Beijing: Zhonghua, 1988.
___. "Yishan qijue santi." 義山七絕三題 *Tangdai wenxue yanjiu* 2000.8: 608–19.
___. *Li Shangyin wen biannian jiaozhu* 李商隱文編年校注. Beijing: Zhonghua, 2002.
Liu Xuekai 劉學鍇, Yu Shucheng 餘恕誠, and Huang Shizhong 黃世中, eds. *Li Shangyin ziliao huibian* 李商隱資料彙編. Beijing: Zhonghua, 2001.
Lu Kunceng 陸昆曾, ed. *Li Yishan shijie* 李義山詩解. Shanghai: Shanghai Shudian, 1985.
Lü Mingtao 呂明涛. *Li Shangyin* 李商隱. Beijing: Zhonghua, 2011.

Mi Yanqing 米彥青. *Qing dai Li Shangyin shige jieshou shigao* 清代李商隱詩歌接受史稿. Beijing: Zhonghua, 2007.

Owen, Stephen. *The Late Tang: Chinese Poetry of the Mid-Ninth Century (827–860)*. Cambridge, MA: Harvard University, 2006, pp. 335–527.

___. "What Did Liuzhi Hear? The 'Yan Terrace Poems' and the Culture of Romance." *TS* 13 (1995): 81–118.

Rigisan, Shichiritsu Chushakuhan 李義山七律注釋班. "Rigisan shichiritsu shuko." 李義山七律集釋稿. *Tōhō gakuhō* 66 (1994): 381–424.

Sen, Mitsue 詹滿江. *Ri Shōin kenkyū* 李商隱研究. Tokyo: Kyūko, 2005.

Su Xuelin 蘇雪林. *Yuxi shimi zhengxu hebian* 玉溪詩迷正續合編. Taibei: Taiwan Shangwu, 1988.

Takahashi Kazumi 高橋和巳. *Ri Shōin* 李商隱. Tokyo: Kawade Shobō Shinsha, 1996.

Wang Meng 王蒙, "Li Shangyin de tiaozhan" 李商隱的挑戰, *Wenxue Yichan* 2 (1997).

___,"Hundun de xinlingchang—tan Li Shangyin wutishi de jiegou" 混沌的心靈場—談李商隱無題詩的結構, *Wenxue Yichan* 3 (1995).

Wang Pijiang 汪辟疆. "'Yuxi shijian juli' bulu." 《玉谿詩箋舉例》補錄. *Zhonghua wenshi luncong*, 2007.3: 121–55.

Wang Yiyun 王怡雲. "Li Shangyin shi zhong de niaolei yinyu tanxi." 李商隱詩中的鳥類隱喻探析. *You feng chu ming* 2009.4: 1–16.

Wu Tiaogong 吳調公. *Li Shangyin yanjiu* 李商隱研究. Beijing: Zhonghua, 2010.

Yan Kunyang 顏崑陽. *Li Shangyin shi jianshi fangfa lun* 李商隱詩箋釋方法論. Taibei: Xuesheng, 1991.

Yang Liu 楊柳. *Li Shangyin pingzhuan* 李商隱評傳. Beijing: Dangdai Zhongguo, 1997.

Yu, Teresa Yee-Wah. "Li Shangyin: The Poetry of Allusion." Unpublished Ph.D. dissertation, University of British Columbia, 1990.

Yu Xianhao 鬱賢皓 and Zhu Yian 朱易安. *Li Shangyin* 李商隱. Shanghai: Shanghai Guji, 1985.

Zhan, *Daojiao*, pp. 358–71.

Zhang Ertian 張爾田 (1874–1945). *Yuxisheng nianpu huijian* 玉溪生年譜會箋. Taibei: Taiwan Zhonghua, 1979. Together with *Li Yishan shi bianzheng* 李義山詩辯正.

Zhang Renqing 張仁青. *Li Shangyin shi yanjiu lunwen ji* 李商隱詩研究論文集. Taibei: Tiangong, 1995.

Zheng Zaiying 鄭在瀛. *Li Shangyin shi quanji: huibian jinzhu jianshi* 李商隱詩全集: 彙編今注簡釋. Wuhan: Chongwen, 2011.

James J.Y. Liu and William H. Nienhauser, Jr.

Li Shen 李紳 (*zi*, Gongchui 公垂, 772–846), known as "Duan Li" 短李 (Little Li) by his contemporary Bo Juyi 白居易 (772–846)* due to his slight stature, led a tumultuous life of officialdom that saw him reach the heights of Grand Councilor during the reign of Emperor Wuzong (r. 840–846). Coming from an old, aristocratic clan, Li's family had fallen on hard times by the time he was born in Bozhou 亳州 (modern Anhui). His father, Li Wu 李晤, served as a county official and eventually settled his family in Wuxi 無錫 (modern Jiangsu), where Li Shen would grow up. Shen's father died when he was only five or six years old, leaving his mother to oversee his education. In 802, at the age of twenty, Shen sat the *jinshi* examination in Chang'an. Though he did not pass, Li Shen did make the acquaintance of Han Yu 韓愈 (768–824),* who, in turn, recommended him to the powerful official Lu Chen 陸修 (fl. ca. 802). However, Shen did not receive any official appointment, and thus traveled on to Suzhou. In the first year of Emperor Xianzong's reign (806), Shen would return to Chang'an and succeed in his second attempt sitting the *jinshi* examination.

Li Shen

After passing the *jinshi*, Li Shen was appointed as an Instructor in the National University but found it not to his liking and journeyed south to Jinling 金陵 (modern Nanjing) in search of a patron and official position. Eventually, Li Qi 李錡 (741–807), Military Commissioner of Zhenhai 鎮海 (modern Yangzhou, Jiangsu), took on Shen as his secretary. When Li Qi rebelled against the court, Li Shen proved his loyalty to the Tang court by admonishing his patron's aggressions, and thereby endangering his own life in the process. Nonetheless, Li Shen was captured and imprisoned when Li Qi's rebellion was quelled, and only after the subsequent execution of Li Qi in 807, was Li Shen released from prison and allowed to return to Wuxi. Two years later (809) at age thirty-eight, Li Shen was recalled to the capital and appointed to the position of Editor of the Palace Library, marking the start of a long series of appointments that witnessed his ascent within palace political circles. In 820, Li Shen was made a scholar of the Hanlin academy, where he and his two colleagues, Li Deyu 李德裕 (787–850)* and Yuan Zhen 元稹 (779–831),* would become known as the "Sanjun" 三俊 (Three Gentleman). His association with the political faction led by Niu Sengru 牛僧孺 (ca. 779–ca. 848) caught the attention of the adversarial Grand Councilor Li Fengji 李逢吉 (758–835), who oversaw Li Shen's demotion in 823 to the position of Vice Censor-in-Chief in the capital, and eventually in 824 the further demotion to Marshal of Duanzhou 端州 (modern Zhaoqing City 肇慶市, in Guangdong).

In 833, Li Shen's old colleague, Li Deyu, became Grand Councilor and promoted Li Shen to a number of higher positions throughout the provinces. In 841, Li Shen was recalled to the capital and made Grand Councilor himself, where he was enfeoffed with the honorary title, "Duke of Zhao" 趙國公. Shen served as Grand Councilor for Emperor Wuzong for four more years, resigning due to illness. After his subsequent recovery, Li Shen once again took up an official position in the provinces, this time serving as both the Administrator of Henan 河南 and the Military Commissioner of Huainan 淮南 (in modern Anhui). It would be the last position in the long and illustrious career of the man affectionately known as "Little Li." Two years later (846), he would succumb to illness while in Yangzhou 揚州 (modern Jiangsu).

Throughout his tumultuous political career, Li Shen would leave behind a literary legacy that blends social commentary with subtle artistry in both poems and prose, many of which empathized with the lowly and the downtrodden. Among his most famous poems are two pieces entitled "Gufeng" 古風 (Ancient Airs), each regarded today as examplars in the newly emerging movement of poetry known as *Xin yuefu* 新樂府 (New Music Bureau Poems) that sought to provide social and political insight through lyrical engagement with the plight of the common people. Li Shen may have submitted the two "Ancient Airs" to Lü Wen 呂溫 (772–811)* early in his career in order to gain patronage. Lü praised both Shen the poet and Shen the man, prophesizing that Li Shen would doubtless become the Grand Councilor in the future. These two poems still enjoy a wide readership today thanks to their simple elegance and moving depictions of everyday life of the Chinese farmer during the Tang.

    "Ancient Airs" No. 1
One grain of millet sown in spring,
Will in autumn a myriad kernels bring.
Within the four seas not a field unfarmed,
Yet peasants still starve to death.

春種一粒粟，秋成萬顆子。
四海無閒田，農夫猶餓死。

"Ancient Airs" No. 2
Hoeing millet in midday heat,
Sweat dripping to the earth beneath.
Who recognizes that the food on their plate,
Was grain by grain produced by such hard work?

鋤禾日當午，汗滴禾下土。
誰知盤中餐，粒粒皆辛苦。

Li Shen also holds a place in the development of literary innovation and critique during the Tang for his instrumental part in establishing the poetic genre of New *Yuefu* as well as redefining the poet's role in collecting and commentating on their own literary corpus. After returning to the capital in 809, Li Shen wrote twenty New *Yuefu* poems. That same year, his colleague at the Hanlin academy, Yuan Zhen, followed with twelve New Yuefu poems of his own. Bo Juyi, who would craft fifty New *Yuefu* poems himself that year, considered Li Shen's first twenty poems to be responsible for establishing the form. The New *Yuefu* style would soon develop into its own literary movement and leave an indelible mark on Tang literary culture. Unfortunately, the majority of Li Shen's earlier poems, including the twenty New *Yuefu* from 809, were lost, with only "Gufeng, ershou" and "Yingying ge" 鶯鶯歌 (Song of Yingying) surviving.

Li Shen's endeavor to collect and comment on his own works distinguished him from many of his contemporaries. The *Xin Tang shu* notes that at the age of sixty-seven (838), Li Shen compiled his own works into three *juan* entitled *Zhuixi youji* 追昔游集 (Roaming in Search of the Past). However, the collection only remains as fragments scattered across other compilations: the *Quan Tang shi* organizes Li Shen's poetry in four *juan*; the *Quan Tang wen* contains only twelve pieces.

Most poems that remain appear to have been written around the year 838, offering a retrospective in verse that covered the events of his life between 820 and 836. The poems, arranged chronologically, are supplied with internal notes explaining the circumstances of their composition—thus clarifying what would have otherwise remained obscure for later readers. Li Shen's own commentary belies a degree of self-awareness and consideration of the poet's own place in posterity not often found among earlier poets. His efforts to collect, preserve, and document his own literary legacy would influence literary practice of later generations. His "Zhenniang mu" 真娘墓 (Tomb of the True Lady), written in reference to the burial site of the famous Tang imperial courtesan, along with his own commentary, offers an excellent example of how Li Shen's notes elucidate his deft poetic style:

Branches of voluptuous color cover the whole city wall;
A Compassion Gate of paired trees suffers the plants to grow.
Her bright charm extinguished like a candle in the wind,
Her passionate heart never as light as the flowers in rain.
The moon-shaped painted brows gone, leaving just the shadow moon in the sky;
Her songs won't stir the dust on the beams, there are only the Sanskrit chants.

She is also like Su Xiaoxiao of Qiantang:
We can only look back on her, that sweet little thing.

一株繁艷春城盡，雙樹慈門忍草生。
慧態自隨風燭滅，愛心難逐雨花輕。
黛消波月空蟾影，歌息梁塵有梵音。
還似錢塘蘇小小，祇應回首是卿卿。

[Commentary]: The True Lady was a courtesan from Wu famous for her singing and dancing. When she died, she was buried in front of the Wuqiu Temple in Wu. The young men of Wu in accordance with her wish [buried her there]. Many flowers grow on her tomb, covering the whole top. In Jiangxing County there is also the tomb of the Wu singing girl Su Xiaoxiao. On rainy, windy nights, some hear songs and pipes above them.

吳之妓人歌舞有名者，死葬於吳武丘寺前，吳中少年從其志也。墓多花草，以滿其上。嘉興縣前亦有吳妓人蘇小小墓，風雨之夕，或聞其上有歌吹之音。

The poem plays on the contrast between the True Lady's life as a courtesan and her continued hold on the memories of her admirers who visit the temple where she is buried. The image of the two trees that constitute the temple's Gate of Compassion yields to the fleeting beauty of flowers, that, as we learn from Li Shen's commentary, were known to cover the whole of her shrine. The wind and rain that are said by some to still carry her songs at night here evoke classic Buddhist imagery—the wind that extinguishes the candle of her charms resonates with the image of extinguishing the flame of one's rebirth (i.e. *nirvana*); while the weight of her passionate heart contrasts with the ephemerality of life. Her enticing glances once compared to the beauty of the moon are here juxtaposed to the illusion of the moon's shadow that serves to remind us of the illusory nature of what we take at first glance to be real. Indeed, her alluring songs that once enticed many young men can no longer even stir the dust, they are now replaced by the chants of mantras in Sanskrit. In the end, she is like other famous courtesans from Wu, but the allure that continues to bring the young men to her shrine, now articulated in the trope of Buddhist holiness, makes her memory uniquely worthy of celebrating.

BIBLIOGRAPHY

Editions:
Mao Jin 毛晉 (1599–1659), *Wu Tangren shiji* 無唐人詩集. Shanghai: Hanfenlou, 1926.
Quan Tang shi, 8: 5495–533, 15: 11308.
Quan Tang wen, 694.7873–79.

Annotations:
Lu Yanping 盧燕平 ed. *Li Shen ji jiaozhu* 李紳集校注. Beijing: Zhonghua, 2009.
Wang Boxuan 王伯旋, ed. *Li Shen shizhu* 李紳詩註. Shanghai: Guji, 1985.
Zhu Jian 朱諫, ed. *Li Shen shi xuanzhu, Gufeng xiaoxu* 李紳詩選注, 古風小序. Shanghai: Guji, 2002.

Biographical Sources:
Fu, *Tang caizi*, 3:40–52, 5:272–73
Jiu Tang shu, 173.4497–500.
Xin Tang shu, 181.5347–50.

Translations:
Field, "Taking Up the Plow," pp. 134–35.
Owen, *Late Tang*, pp. 76–88.
Schafer, *Vermilion Bird*, p. 188.

Studies:
Akai Masuhisa 赤井益久. "Ri Shin shi gi" 李紳詩臆説, *Kanbun gakkai kaihō* 11 (1979): 23–32.
Bian Xiaoxuan 卞孝萱. "Li Shen nianpu" 李紳年譜, *Anhui shixue* 3 (1960): 40–60.
___. *Liu Yuxi congkao* 劉禹錫從考. Chengdu: Ba Shu, 1988, pp. 285–87.
Feng Tao 馮濤. "Lun Li Shen qianhou shiqi shige fengmaode butong ji chengyin" 論李紳前後時期詩歌風貌的不同及成因, *Liaoning Jiaoyu Xingzheng Xueyuan xuebao* 5.22 (2005).
Hang Jianwei 杭建偉. "Li Shen yanjiu zongshu" 李紳研究綜述. *Hubei Zhiye Jishu Xueyuan xuebao* 14.1 (2011): 57–59.
Lu Yanping 盧燕平. *Li Shen jijiao zhu* 李紳集校注. Beijing: Zhonghua, 2009.
___. "Li Shen xinbian" 李紳新論, *Wenxue yichan* 2004.4: 44–50.
Tou Takagi 高木達 and Ueki Hisayuki 植木久行, "Benkoken *Ri Shin nenpu* hotei chu" 卞孝萱「李紳年譜」補訂-上, *Chūgoku koten kenkyū* 12 (1993): 70–83.
Wang Xuanbo 王旋伯. *Li Shen shizhu* 李紳詩注. Shanghai: Shanghai Guji, 1985.
Wen Ge 文閣. "Li Shen shi meixue sixiang tanwei" 李紳詩美學思想探微, *Xinyang Shifan Xueyuan xuebao*, 1987.3: 65–71.
Yan Zhengdao 严正道. "Zhong Tang shiren Li Shen xianshi shenfen kao" 中唐詩人李紳先世身份考, *Neijiang Shifan Xueyuan xuebao* 28.11 (2013): 48–51.
Zhao Zhiqiang 趙志強. "Li Shen yu xinyunfu yundong guanxi de kaocha" 李紳與新樂府運動關係的考察, *Hubei Dianli Daxue xuebao* 1 (2005): 109–13.
___. "Li Shen shi zaoqide tongsuhua qingxiang yu houqi shifeng de yahua" 李紳詩早期的通俗化傾向與後期詩風的雅化, *Jiangxi Shifan Daxue xuebao* 38.5 (2005): 66–70.
___. "Li Shen shige yanjiu" 李紳詩歌研究, Unpublished M.A. Thesis, Peking University, 1994.
Zhu Zixiao 祝子笑. "Li Shen jiaoyou jiqi chouzengshi yanjiu" 李紳交友及其酬贈詩研究, *Anhui wenxue* 1 (2005): 149–53.

Li Kun and Michael E. Naparstek

Li Yi 李益 *(zi,* Junyu 君虞, 748–ca. 827), one of the leading poets of his day, belonged to the clan of Li Kui 李揆 (711–784), who attained the office of Grand Councilor during the reign of Emperor Suzong (r. 756–763). Li Yi was born in Zhengzhou 鄭州 (modern Henan) province, although the family home appears to have been in Longxi 隴西 (modern Lintao County 臨洮縣 or Wuwei County in Gansu). After passing the *jinshi* examination at twenty-one and the Remonstrance and Mastery of Literary Skills Exam two years later, Li was first posted to a Guard 衛 in Zheng 鄭 County, then promoted to be Recorder in the same county. Frustrated in these menial positions, he resigned in 780 to accept service on the secretarial staff of a military unit on the frontier. In 783

Li Yi

after passing the Preeminent Talent Examination he became Attendant Censor at court. In 788 he began a decade of service for military commissioners in the northern marches. By 797 he was back at court as Assistant Agriculture Commissioner. Nine years later he served as Military Director of the Criminal Administrator Bureau. With the exception of two years (810–812) when he was Vice Governor of Henan during the Emperor Xianzong's reign (r. 806–820), he served in the capital as Vice Director and then Director of the Palace Library and in several positions attending on the Heir. Liu was also one of the examiners (along with Wei Guanzhi 韋貫之 [760–821] and Yang Yuling 楊於陵 [753–830]) of the imperial examinations in 808 in which three of the examinees, Niu Sengru 牛僧孺 (ca. 780–ca. 848), Li Zongmin 李宗閔 (ca. 787–843), and Huangfu Shi 皇甫湜 (776–ca. 835),* criticized the central administration. As a result, and at the urging of the Grand Councilor Li Jifu 李吉甫 (758–814), the examiners were all demoted. But the emperor quickly reversed his demotion and Li Yi became a Scholar in the Academy of Scholarly Worthies beginning in 812. He attained his highest-ranking position as Director of the Ministry of Rites in 827 and died a year or two thereafter.

According to the official histories, Li Yi was known for his meanness of spirit and cruel treatment of the women in his life. These rather unattractive personality traits, whether real or not, gained even wider currency because of the well-known classical tale "Huo Xiaoyu zhuan" 霍小玉傳 (The Story of Huo Xiaoyu) by Jiang Fang 蔣防 (fl. early ninth century), in which Li Yi is portrayed as a self-indulgent, unfeeling man who tyrannized his wives and concubines. Like many Tang classical tales this story is an amalgam of fact and fiction. Li's suspicious and jealous tendencies were evidently so pronounced that unreasonable jealousy came to be called "Li Yi's disease." By the end of the tale, the protagonist Li Yi is suffering from this disease—suggesting that the story may have been partly the result of speculation into the causes of the poet's affliction or that the tale influenced the historical accounts of Li Yi.

The narrative begins with Li Yi's search for a suitable match. A go-between introduces him to a prince's daughter, Huo Xiaoyu, now living in Chang'an in reduced circumstances—she has become a courtesan. Li Yi is charmed by her and pledges his eternal love. He is then appointed to an official post and leaves the capital, promising to send for her later. But before he can do so, his mother forces him to marry another woman. Meanwhile Xiaoyu languishes, seeking in vain information about Li Yi. When Li returns to Chang'an for his wedding, he attempts to avoid his former lover. But the author reunites the pair through a *deus ex machina*—a knight-errant appears to Xiaoyu in a dream and then brings Li Yi to her. The knight-errant later appears before Li Yi and compels Li to follow him to Xiaoyu's residence. There she reproaches Li Yi, swears to haunt him and his wives after her death, and dies. She apparently fulfills her oath: each of Li Yi's three marriages fail.

Jiang Fang may have been influenced by a similar story, Yuan Zhen's 元稹 (779–831)* "Yingying zhuan" 鶯鶯傳, composed in 804—about four years before "Huo Xiaoyu zhuan." The two stories not only have similar plots, but even make use of similar poems. Like its predecessor, "Huo Xiaoyu zhuan" is a source of later drama: Tang Xianzu's (1550–1617) 湯顯祖 *Zichai ji* 紫釵記 (The Purple Hairpin). The two stories, however, do have one major difference. Li Yi's counterpart in Yuan Zhen's story, Scholar Zhang, feels morally justified in deserting the courtesan who loves him and the narrator seems to agree with him. The narrator's praise of Zhang seems inconsistent with the sympathetic portrayal of the courtesan, Yingying. This discrepancy has stimulated some debate over whether Zhang's justification is intended seriously or ironically. If "Huo Xiaoyu zhuan" was written as a commentary on "Yingying zhuan," it would seem that some Tang readers took Zhang's moralizing seriously. The end of Jiang Fang's tale can be interpreted as giving Zhang, in the guise of Li Yi, his due.

Unlikable though he may have been, the *Jiu Tangshu* (Old Tang History) states that he was skilled in song and poetry and that his poems were popular, some being set to music by members of the *Jiaofang* 教坊 (Music Office) for performance at court. It was even claimed that he sold poems to the Music Office. Members of the upper class also had his poems inscribed on decorative panels for display in their homes. While still a relatively young man Li Yi was associated in the public mind with the "Dali shi caizi" 大歷十才子 (Ten Talents of the Dali Era). Still later, he was sometimes mentioned together with Li He 李賀 (790–816),* although there is little resemblance between their poetic styles. That he was highly esteemed as a poet in his own day is revealed by the prominence accorded him in the *Yulan shi* 御覽詩, an anthology compiled under imperial auspices in the later eighth century by Linghu Chu 令狐楚 (766–837),* in which his poems outnumber those of any other poet.

Li Yi is much admired for his mastery of the quatrain, which in diction and tone recalls the occasional social verse of the pre-Tang era. He also excelled in *biansai shi* 邊塞詩 (frontier verse). Approximately one-third of his extant corpus of over 160 poems belongs to that category. After years of frontier duty, when he was about forty, he compiled a small collection of his poems under the title *Congjun shi* 從軍詩 (Poems on Following the Army) and presented them to a certain Lu Jingliang 盧景亮 (d. 806). The title of the collection is a variation on the well-known *yuefu* song pattern, one that had previously been employed by such famous poets as Wang Can 王粲 (177–217) and Wang Changling 王昌齡 (ca. 690–ca. 756)* for their frontier poems. Steeped in that tradition, it is not surprising that Li Yi's frontier pieces follow well-established conventions in depicting the world of the northern border. That world is described as a cold and barren one, forbidding in its desolation, both physically and culturally repellant to the civilized people who live within the Great Wall. His poem "Ye shang Shoujiang Cheng wen di" 夜上受降城聞笛 (Ascending at Night the Triumphal Tower and Hearing a Flute) represents his typical style:

Below the Huile Watchtower lies sand like snow white;
Beyond the Triumphal Fortress, moonbeams like frost.
Nobody knows from where comes the wafting flute,
Making those on campaign homesick all night long.

回樂峰前沙似雪，受降城外月如霜。
不知何處吹蘆管，一夜征人盡望鄉。

In poems of this type, Li typically evokes a brooding sense of death, desolation, and despair. Along the border life is difficult and death is common among those men who have been sent to defend China against invasion. The world of the northern frontier could however evoke other visions, and in some cases it is portrayed as serene. Bathed in moonlight, it possesses an ethereal beauty, with only the plaintive sounds of tribal pipes to remind the border guard of home and hearth. In still other poems in this mode, Li Yi occasionally sounds a heroic note. Examples of this type describe battles or narrate the story of a young warrior of martial prowess, and in the process celebrate the ideals of personal honor and duty to country. Taken all together, Li Yi's *biansai* verse is richly diverse and representative of the best of that tradition. His "Congjun beizheng" 從軍北征 (Following the Army on a Northern March):

> Beyond the snows of the Tian Range the winds off the lake are cold;
> The tartar flute can be heard everywhere playing "The Hardships of Travel."
> Midst the desert all our three hundred thousand men
> Turn their heads as one to gaze up at the bright moon.

天山雪後海風寒, 橫笛偏吹行路難。
磧裡征人三十萬, 一時回首月中看。

The Tian Range stretches north and west of the Taklamahan Desert in modern Qinghai hundreds of miles west from a Chinese settlement. Its highest peak reaches nearly 7500 meters and there are snows on the major peaks year round. "The Hardships of Travel" was a *yuefu* tune which focused on the difficulties faced by travelers and the suffering of separation caused by long journeys—in this case by men on a military campaign. With their homes so distant even gazing towards them seemed futile, in Li Yi's vision the soldiers all suddenly seem gaze towards the moon, a substitute for their homes and loved ones since they realize that the moon shines simultaneously there. The physical detail and the exact figure of the number of soldiers lends verisimilitude to this powerful scene—it may indeed have been written on one of Li Yi's northern marches in the early years of the ninth century.

BIBLIOGRAPHY

Editions:
Fan Zhilin 范之麟, ed. *Li Yi shi zhu* 李益詩注. Shanghai: Shanghai Guji, 1984.
"Huo Xiaoyu zhuan," in *Tangren xiaoshuo*, pp. 77–84. A reliable, punctuated text with useful background material.
Li Junyu shiji 李君虞詩集. SBCK.
Luan Guiming 欒貴明, ed. *Quan Tang shi suoyin: Li Yi, Lu Lun juan* 全唐詩索引：李益盧倫卷. Tianjin: Tianjin Guji, 1997.
Quan Tang shi, 5: 3197–3228, 11: 8980–82..
Quan Tang wen, 481.5688.
Zhang Shu 張樹, ed. *Li Shangshu shiji* 李尚書詩集. Lanzhou: Lanzhou Guji Shudian, 1990.

Annotations:
Wang Yijun 王亦君 and Pei Yumin 裴豫敏, eds. *Li Yi ji zhu* 李益集註. Lanzhou: Gansu Renmin, 1989.

Biographical Sources:
Fu, *Tang caizi*, 2:91–106, 5:185–88.
Jiu Tang shu, 137.3771–72.
Xin Tang shu, 203.5785–86.

Translations:

Bynner, *Jade Mountain*, pp. 87–88.
Kroll, "Recalling Xuanzong," pp. 7–8.
Sunflower, p. 157.
Wang Jizhen. "Huo Xiaoyu," in *Traditional Chinese Tales*. New York: Columbia University Press, 1944, pp. 48–59.
Zhang Zhenjun. "The Tale of Huo Xiaoyu," in Nienhauser, *Tang Dynasty Tales*, pp. 233–76.

Studies:

Bian Xiaoxuan 卞孝萱. "Li Yi nianpu gao" 李益年譜稿, *Zhonghua wenshi luncong* 中华文史论丛, 1979.2.
Chan, Marie. "The Life of Li Yi (748?–827)," *MS* 38 (1988–89): 173–89.
Hao Runhua 郝潤華 and Hu Dajun 胡大浚, eds. *Li Yi shige jiping* 李益詩歌集評. Lanzhou: Gansu Renmin, 1997.
Ichikawa Kiyoshi 市川清史. "Chūtō no hanchin seisaku to Ri Eki" 中唐の藩鎮政策と李益. *Gakuen*, 785 (2006): 100–7.
___. "Ri Eki to chūtō shidan" 李益と中唐詩壇. *Gakuen*, 771 (2005): 113–22.
Kroll, Paul W. "Recalling Xuanzong and Lady Yang: A Selection of Mid- and Late Tang Poems," *Tang Studies*, 35 (2017): 1–19.
Ohashi Kenichi 大橋賢一. "Ri Eki hensai shiron" 李益邊塞詩論. *Tsukuba Sinological Studies* 20 (2000): 1–28.
Tan Youxue 谭优学. "Li Yi xingnian kao" 李益行年考, in Tan's *Tang shiren xingnian kao* 唐诗人兴年考. Chengdu: Sichuan Renmin, 1981.
Wang Meng'ou 王夢鷗. "Huo Xiaoyu zhuan zhi zuozhe ji gushi beijing" 霍小玉傳之作者及故事背景, *Shumu jikan* 書目集刊, 7.1 (1972): 3–10.
___. *Tang shiren Li Yi shengping ji qi zuopin* 唐詩人李益生平及其作品. Taibei: Yiwen, 1973.
Wang Shengming 王勝明. *Li Yi yanjiu* 李益研究. Chengdu: Ba Shu, 2004.
Yu Zhengsong 余正松 and Wang Shengming 王勝明. "Li Yi shengping ji shige yanjiu bianzheng" 李益生平及詩歌研究辨證, *Wenxue yichan*, 2004.3: 43–53.

Wilfried Spaar, Cordell Yee, and William H. Nienhauser, Jr.

Liang Su 梁肅 (*zi*, Jingzhi 敬之 and Kuanzhong 寬中, 753–793) was an important figure in intellectual and literary circles during the last quarter of the eighth century. He was a key transitional figure linking the pre-An Lushan generation of scholars such as Xiao Yingshi 蕭穎士 (717–760)* and Li Hua 李華 (715–774* with Han Yu 韓愈 (768–824)* and Liu Zongyuan 柳宗元 (773–819)* in the Yuanhe period (806–820). Liang is representative of that generation of thinkers who first began to contemplate the possibility of the Buddhist-Confucian synthesis that later developed into Neo-Confucianism.

Liang was descended from an aristocratic family of the Six Dynasties period originally based in Anding 安定 (modern Pingliang 平涼 in Gansu). Early in the Tang, the family still produced officials for the central government, but several generations before Liang Su his immediate ancestors had moved to Henan where they occupied only local posts. Liang was born in Hanguan 函關 (modern Xin'an 新安 in Henan). In 761, the family fled to the Changzhou 常州 area in the Southeast to avoid the military aftermath of the An Lushan Rebellion in Henan. In 770, at age seventeen, Liang became acquainted with Li Hua and Dugu Ji 獨孤及 (725–777),* both established literary leaders of the time, who praised his early writings. He departed the next year for the Tiantai 天台 Mountains where he probably began his lifelong study of the Tiantai School of Buddhism with the master Zhanran 湛然 (711–782). In 774, Dugu Ji was appointed Prefect of Changzhou, and Liang returned there to study formally with him. When Dugu died in 777, Liang edited his works in twenty *juan* and added a postface.

In 780, by virtue of his outstanding literary ability, Liang was summoned to Chang'an and passed the beauty-in-literary-style examination to serve as Editor for the Heir Apparent. During the early 780s he received several appointments, but left them twice to return to the Southeast, the second time to attend his aging mother. In 784 he became Chief Secretary to Du You 杜佑 (735–812) who was then serving as Military Commissioner of Huainan. In 791 he was recalled to the capital to become Reader-in-waiting to the Heir Apparent and concurrently a Hanlin Scholar. His literary prestige and influence were now at their peak, as an unusually high percentage of the candidates he supported for the *jinshi* examinations was successful. He supervised the 792 *jinshi* examinations which graduated Han Yu and a slate of other literary and political leaders of the early ninth century. Liang Su died in Chang'an in 793.

In his Confucian studies, Liang Su was an adherent of the "new school" of textual commentary associated with Dan Zhu 啖助 (725–770), which advocated increased attention to the "general meaning" (*dayi* 大義) of the Confucian classics rather than to textual detail. This "general meaning," of course, was found to be relevant to contemporary social and political issues. Thus these scholars advocated "reverence for the classics" not as objects of adoration but as texts profound with meaning for their own age.

Liang Su's *Shanding zhiguan* 刪定止觀 (The Abridged Great Concentration), a condensation of *Mohe zhiguan* 摩訶止觀 (The Great Concentration and Insight), written by Zhiyi 智顗 (539–597), the founder of the Tiantai School, reaffirmed the school's basic eclectic and syncretistic tendencies. This made it possible for thinkers to interpret certain passages in Confucian texts as rudimentary expositions of Buddhist metaphysical principles, thus laying the ground for Neo-Confucian philosophy.

In the literary domain, Liang Su inherited from Xiao Yingshi and Li Hua an impatience with *pianwen* 駢文 (parallel prose) as a vehicle for the kind of literary discourse they envisioned as necessary for their time: a literature that recaptured the fundamental Confucian link between literary and moral-political activity. Liang Su wrote, for instance, that he believed the *dao* of literature was closely connected with the *dao* of good government. The final paragraph of his essay, "Zhou Gongjin muxia shixu" 周公瑾墓下詩序 (A Preface for a "Poem Written beside Zhou Gongjin's Tomb"; the poem is no longer extant) is a typical expression of this thought:

> Poets write poems, as their minds are influenced by things, and their hearts are moved by affections. They not only express [their aspirations] in their poems, but also manifest them in their careers. Those who succeed in their careers have flowery writings, those who have great ambitions have deep feelings. Therefore Zhongshan [Wang Qiu 王丘 (d. 743)] has this passing-the-tomb [poem]. How grand are the thoughts; how brilliant is the passage! It can function as an outlook on the *dao* when one cannot advance and of the will when one's ambition cannot be realized. All those who want to respond should attach [their poems] to this piece!

詩人之作，感於物，動於中，發於詠歌，形於事業。事之博者其辭盛，志之大者其感深，故仲山有過墓之什。廓然其慮，粲乎其文！可以窺盤桓居貞之道，梁父閑吟之意。凡有和者，當系於斯乎！

Liang Su carried the realization of a *guwen* 古文 style forward by postulating the concept of *qi* 氣 (spirit or vitality) as an intermediate stage between a piece of writing's *dao* 道 (moral power) and its *ci* 辭 (diction). *Qi* had been used earlier in Six Dynasties' criticism to designate an author's inherent mode or style of writing. Liang Su's use of the term, however, seems to derive from *Mencius*, where *qi* means something like "moral character." Thus, for Liang Su, the moral power of a piece of writing is tied to the moral character of its author, and this quality in turn affects the diction and style of a piece 道能兼氣，氣能兼辭. In modern terms, this means that a text's power to influence its readership is a function of the author's rhetorical skills, which themselves are a product of his own self-cultivation, both as a writer and as a member of society.

Although Liang Su was active as a teacher in Chang'an during the last several years of his life, it is unlikely that he had any meaningful, direct contact with either Han Yu or Liu Zongyuan. Rather his ideas on scholarship and literature were probably already part of the general anti-establishment literary world in which these famous *guwen* authors matured.

BIBLIOGRAPHY

Editions:
Liang Su 梁肅, ed. *Shanding zhiguan* 刪定止觀. Tainan: Zhanransi, 1998.
Liang Su Wen ji 梁肅文集. Hu Dajun 胡大浚, Zhang Chunwen, ed., 張春雯. Lanzhou: Gansu Renmin, 2000.
Nakano Gorōzaemon 中野五郎左衛門, ed. *Santeishikan* 刪定止觀, 1661.
Pi Ling ji: 20 juan, houxu. 毘陵集: 20 卷, 后序. Dugu Ji 獨孤及, Liang Su 梁肅. Changchun: Jilin Chuban Jituan Yousian Gongsi, 2005.
Quan Tang wen, 517–22.6655–730.

Biographical Sources:
Xin Tang shu, 202.5774.

Studies:
Bol, pp. 118–22.
Kanda Kiichirō 神田喜一郎. "Ryō Shuku nempu" 梁肅年譜, in *Tōhō gakkai sōritsu 25 shūnen kinen Tōhōgaku ronshū* 東方学会創立二十五周年記念東方学論集, Tokyo, 1972, pp. 259–74.
Ono Shihei 小野四平. "Ryō Shoku kara Ryū Sōgen e—'Tōdai kobun no genryū' hosetsu" 梁肅から柳宗元へ—「唐代古文の源流」補説, *Shūkan Tōyōgaku* 集刊東洋學 66 (1992): 83–101.
Sudo Kentaro 須藤健太郎. "Ryō Shuku no bundoron to butsugaku" 梁肅の文道論と佛學. *Zhongguo wenxue yanjiu* 中國文學研究, 26 (2000): 46–61.

Charles Hartman and William H. Nienhauser, Jr.

Lingche

Lingche 靈澈 (also written as Lingche 靈徹, surname Tang 湯, *zi*, Yuancheng 源澄, also *zi*, Mingyong 明泳, 746–816) was a poet-monk active in the mid-Tang period. He was a native of Guiji 會稽 (or Kuaiji, modern Shaoxing City in Zhejiang) and entered the Yunmen Monastery 雲門寺 in Guiji at a young age. He learned from the Buddhist master Shenyong 神邕 (710–788), who was famous in Vinaya, Tiantai theory, and poetry. Lingche also studied poetry with the famous poet Yan Wei 嚴維 (fl. 757). His poetry became well known during the Dali reign (766–779). By the end of the reign, he left his hometown and traveled extensively, exchanging poems with literati and other poet-monks, and was praised by famous poets such as Liu Zhangqing 劉長卿 (726–ca. 787)* and Huangfu Zeng 皇甫曾 (d. 785). In 780, he visited Huzhou 湖州 (modern Zhejiang) and discussed and composed poetry with the poet-monk Jiao Ran 皎然 (720–799).* There the nine-year old Liu Yuxi 劉禹錫 (772–842)* would come to study poetry with the two monks. In 781, on the recommendation of Jiao Ran, Lingche went to Jiangzhou 江州 to visit Bao Ji 包佶 (ca. 727–792), and then possibly traveled to Hongzhou 洪州 to visit Quan Deyu 權德輿 (761–818)* and Mazu Daoyi 馬祖道一 (709–788). In about 785, Lingche returned to Guiji, and Quan Deyu wrote an essay seeing him off. During the Zhenyuan reign-period (785–805), Lingche went to Chang'an and exchanged poems with Liu Yuxi, Liu Zongyuan 柳宗元 (773–819),* Lü Wen 呂溫 (772–811),* and others. In 801, Mazu Daoyi's disciples compiled the *Baolin zhuan* 寶林傳 (Biographies of the Baolin Monastery), and Lingche wrote a preface for it. In about 805, he was banished to Tingzhou 汀州 (modern Changting 長汀 County in Fujian) because of rumors made by other monks. He was pardoned in 809 and went to reside on Mount Lu 廬山 for a while. Then, he visited Jiao Ran's portrait-hall in Huzhou to mourn for him. From 810 to 814, he stayed in his hometown and associated with Li Ao 李翱 (774–836),* who was then serving in the office of Surveillance Commissioner of Zhedong. He died in 816 at the Kaiyuan Monastery of Xuanzhou 宣州 at the age of 71. Liu Zongyuan wrote a poem to mourn him. The *Song Gaoseng zhuan* 宋高僧傳 includes his biography.

Lingche composed about two thousand poems during his lifetime. His disciple Xiufeng 秀峰 (ca. 9th century) selected three hundred pieces to be compiled into an anthology titled *Che Shangren wenji* 澈上人文集 (Literary Anthology of Venerable [Ling]che) in ten *juan*, and Liu Yuxi wrote a preface for it. Xiufeng also selected the poems Lingche exchanged with others to compile another anthology titled *Chouchang ji* 酬唱集 (Anthology of Exchanged Poems) in ten *juan*. Both anthologies were lost. The *Quan Tang shi* preserves seventeen of his poems, and the *Quan Tangshi bubian* adds one poem and two couplets. Lingche also composed a Buddhist text titled *Lüzong yinyuan* 律宗引源 (A Guide to the Origin of Vinaya) in twenty-one *juan*, which was lost as well.

Lingche's extant poems are mainly occasional and travel pieces. He is adept at heptasyllabic quatrains and can be seen in his most famous poem "Donglinsi chou Wei Dan cishi" 東林寺酬韋丹刺史 (In Response to Prefect Wei Dan at the Donglin Monastery):

> An old man his mind at ease with no external concerns,
> A hempen garment and grass hassock good enough to accommodate my body.
> Everyone I meet says better to resign from office,
> But here 'beneath the trees' I never see anyone.

年老心閒無外事, 麻衣草座亦容身.
相逢盡道休官好, 林下何曾見一人.

The first half of the quatrain describes the poet's state of mind after returning from banishment. His detachment to worldly matters is contrasted with the second half of the poem which mocks the insincerity of many literati-official who posture about giving up their positions and retiring. *Linxia* 林下 'under the trees' is a trope suggesting retirement. This kind of direct satirical poem is seldom seen in Tang poetry.

BIBLIOGRAPHY

Editions:
Chen Shangjun 陳尚君, ed. *Quan Tangshi bubian* 全唐詩補編. Beijing: Zhonghua, 1992.
Hu Zhenheng 胡震亨 (1569–1645), ed. *Tangyin tongqian* 唐音統簽. *Xuxiu Siku quanshu* 續修四庫全書 ed.
Li Gong 李龏 (b. 1194), ed. *Tangseng hongxiu ji* 唐僧弘秀集. *SKQS* ed.
Quan Tang shi, 14: 10631.

Biographical Sources:
Fu, *Tang caizi*, 1:612–21.
Song Gaoseng zhuan, 15:369–70.

Translations:
Minford and Lau, pp. 984–85.

Studies:
Chen Shangjun 陳尚君. "Lingche" 靈澈, in Zhou Zuzhuan 周祖譔 ed., *Zhongguo wenxuejia dacidian: Tang, Wudai juan* 中國文學家大辭典: 唐五代卷. Beijing: Zhonghua, 1992, pp. 403–404.
Chu Zhongjun 儲仲君. "Lingche" 靈澈, in Fu Xuancong 傅璇琮 ed., *Tang caizi zhuan jiaojian* 唐才子傳校箋. Beijing: Zhonghua, 1987, 1: 612–21.
Ichihara Kōkichi 市原亨吉. "Chū Tō shoki ni okeru kōhidari no shisō ni tsuite" 中唐初期における江左の詩僧について. *Tōhō gakuhō*, 28 (1958): 219–48.
Jia Jinhua 賈晉華. *Jiao Ran nianpu* 皎然年譜. Xiamen: Xiamen Daxue, 1992.
___. "The Hongzhou School of Chan Buddhism and the Tang Literati." Ph.D. diss., University of Colorado, 1999.
Jiang Yin 蔣寅. *Dali Shiren Yanjiu* 大曆詩人研究. Beijing: Beijing Daxue, 2007.
Kawachi Shoen 河内昭円. "Tetsu shōnin bunshō jo kanken: shisō Reitetsu no shōgai" 徹上人文集序管見: 詩僧霊徹の生涯, *Ōtani daigaku kenkyū nenhō* 大谷大学研究年報 26 (1974): 79–134.
Liu Weilin 劉衛林. "Xinming kongwu, jiji wenzi: Zhongtang shiseng Lingche shengping ji shige kaolun" 心冥空無 跡寄文字: 中唐詩僧靈澈生平及詩歌考論. *Pumen xuebao* 普門學報 25 (2005): 115–43.
Peng Yaling 彭雅玲. *Tangdai shiseng de chuangzuolun yanjiu: shige yu Fojiao de zonghe fenxi* 唐代詩僧的創作論研究: 詩歌與佛教的綜合分析. Taibei: Huamulan Wenhua, 2009.
Tao Min 陶敏, Li Yifei 李一飛, and Fu Xuancong 傅璇琮. *Tang Wudai wenxue biannianshi: Zhongtang juan* 唐五代文學編年史: 中唐卷. Shenyang: Liaohai, 2012.
Tozaki Tetsuhiko 戶崎哲彦. "*Hōrinden* no josha Reitetsu to shisō Reitetsu" 宝林伝の序者霊徹と詩僧霊徹. *Bukkyō shigaku kenkyū*, 30.2 (1987): 28–55.
Watson, Burton. "Buddhist Poet-Priests of the T'ang," *Eastern Buddhist* 25.2 (1992): 1–22.

Zha Minghao 查明昊. *Zhuanxing zhong de Tang Wudai shiseng qunti* 轉型中的唐五代詩僧群體. Shanghai: Huadong Shifan Daxue, 2008.

Jinhua Jia and Chenxi Huang

Linghu Chu 令狐楚 (*zi*, Keshi 殼士, 766–837) is better known as a patron of Li Shangyin 李商隱 (ca. 813–858)* and an admirer of the poets of the Dali era (766-779), many of whom appeared in the anthology *Yulan shi* 御覽詩 (Poems for the Emperor's Perusal) which Linghu compiled for the Emperor Xianzong in 817, and a nexus figure in the literary world from about 815–830. He was also noted for his skill in composing official documents in the elaborate *pianti* style, a factor contributing to his rise in politics.

Linghu was a native of Huayuan 華源 (modern Yaoxian 耀縣 in Shaanxi) and the descendant of an illustrious line of scholar-officials stretching back to Linghu Zheng 令狐整 (513–578), but his father was only a minor provincial official. According to a preface Liu Yuxi 劉禹錫 (772–842)* wrote to a collection of Linghu's works, he was a child prodigy, compiling verse at the age of five. He passed the *jinshi* examination in 791 and during his time in the capital got to know a number of poets including Lu Lun 盧綸 (739–799),* Liu Yuxi, Bo Juyi 白居易 (772–846),* and Yang Juyuan 楊巨源 (755–after 833) as well as important officials such as Li Fengji 李逢吉 (757–835; Linghu was through his relationship with Li associated with the Niu Faction in the Niu-Li controversies). For the next dozen years he was a secretary to the successive Military Commissioners of Taiyuan 太原, Li Shuo 李說 (740–800), Zheng Dan 鄭儋 (741–801), and Yan Yuan 嚴綬 (746–822). The drafts he wrote for their correspondence with the court including memorials, works he compiled into a collection of ten *juan* himself, won him the notice of Emperor Dezong who was said to be able to recognize Linghu's excellent *pianwen* 駢文 (parallel-prose) style. In 810, in his late thirties, Linghu first took a position in the capital either as Erudite of Imperial Sacrifices or as Vice Director of the Ministry of Rites. By 814, he was a Hanlin Academician and in the next several years rotated through a series of court posts. In 816, he presented his *Yulan shi* to the emperor, but was sent out to be Prefect of Huazhou 華州 (modern Hua County 華縣 about thirty miles east of Xi'an) the following year. In 819 he was recalled and made 中書侍郎, and concurrently 忠恕門脇平章事, de facto one of the grand councilors. After Emperor Xianzong was killed by eunuchs in 820, Linghu was sent out from court to become Prefect of Xuanzhou 宣州 (modern Xuancheng County 宣城縣 in Anhui). For the next two years he would spend some time in the provinces but by 822 was Adviser to the Heir Apparent. With Emperor Muzong's death in 824, Li Fengji 李逢吉 (758–835) came to power and raised Linghu to be Censor in Chief. In 825 he became Military Commissioner of the Xuanwu in Bianzhou 汴州 (modern Kaifeng) where he remained until 828 when he was made Minister of the Ministry of Revenue. The following year he was sent out to be Prefect of Yunzhou 鄆州 (northeast of modern Dongping 東平 in Shandong) and Military Commissioner of the Tianping Army 天平軍. At this time, he had first noticed Li Shangyin who was then only in his teens. In 832 he became the Administrator of Taiyuan and Military Commissioner of Hedong 河東 and was joined by Li Shangyin who had just failed the *jinshi* examination. Linghu became Minister of the Ministry of Rites. In 833 he became Left Vice Director of the Department of State Affairs. After the failed attempts to assassinate the eunuchs in 835 (Sweet-dew Incident), Linghu was sent to Hanzhong 漢中 and appointed Military Commissioner of Shannan Xidao 山南西道. In 837 he died while serving at this post and was granted the posthumous title "Wen" 文.

Linghu Chu was particularly appreciated for his great achievements in composing quatrains and traditional *yuefu*, often choosing to write about women in the palace or soldiers on the northern frontier. He composed a number of such poems with Wang Yai 王涯 (ca. 764–835) and Zhang Zhongsu 張仲素 (ca. 769–819) during the Yuanhe era, poems that are still preserved in *Yuanhe san sheren ji* 元和三舍人集 (Collection of the Three Grand Councilors of the Yuanhe Era). Three of his "Shaonian xing" 少年行 (The Rowdy Youth) poems stand out:

> My bow shining morning-bright, my sword sparkling like frost.
> Into the autumn wind I drive my horse, heading out from Xianyang.
> Until we recover the Emperor's lands between the Yellow and the Huang,
> I don't plan to look back towards my hometown.

> 弓背霞明劍照霜，秋風走馬出咸陽。
> 未收天子河湟地，不擬回頭望故鄉。

"The Rowdy Youth" is a traditional *yuefu* title. Although the poem is placed in the Han period by referring to the Han capital Xianyang, it clearly depicts one of the Tang capital gallants, as a *shaonian* at home in the lanes of the Chang'an brothels as on the battlefields. Here he leaves the capital bedecked with his brand-new weapons intent on recovering the lands to the northwest near Koko Nor between the Yellow and Huang rivers, at that time held by the Tibetans. Other than the metaphors of the first line, which may also suggest his youth, the poem is rather conventional. But in combination with the other poems of this series, it takes on added meaning. Another poem in the series reads:

> My home's in Qinghe, but I live in the Five Cities,
> Depending on bow and arrows to seek a merit and fame.
> Effortlessly I let the reins fly on autumn plains,
> Heading alone under cold clouds, trying to shoot at sounds.

> 家本清河住五城，須憑弓箭得功名。
> 等閒飛鞚秋原上，獨向寒雲試射聲。

This poem further characterizes the young man who rode out with his shining sword. Qinghe (in Hebei, sixty miles northwest of modern Jinan) was the home of noble families like the Boling Cui 博陵崔, suggesting the persona may come from an aristocratic line. At present, however, he is living on the border among the "Five Cities," three of which were retaken from the Tibetans. Despite his origins, he has only gained merit through his skill with the bow. The final two lines attribute his horsemanship and his skill with the bow. The final image shows him attempting to master the skill of shooting at what he could only hear rather than at what he could see—the highest skill a bowman can achieve. The language here, as in many of Linghu's *yuefu* is bordering on the colloquial. The cold clouds are seen often in frontier poetry, and with the autumn plain, although the season for military maneuvers, suggest desolation of the region.

> When I was young in the border regions I was used running wild,
> Riding tartar horses bareback and shooting antelope;
> Now that I've grown old and no longer strong,
> I still lean on the gate to camp, counting the geese fly by.

少小邊州慣放狂, 騧騎蕃馬射黃羊。
如今年老無筋力, 猶倚營門數雁行。

The third poem in this series finds the trooper grown old, reflecting on his youthful feats. The imagery of the first two lines is original. *Fang kuang* 放狂, "running wild" or "going crazy," is a favorite expression of Bo Juyi 白居易 (772-846),* but used exclusively when Bo has been drinking. Here the persona is drunk on daring, stealing enemy horses and riding them saddleless. The "antelope" (*huang yang* 黃楊) here is also nearly unique in Tang verse, referring to the "Mongolian antelope" (*Procapra gutturosa*), now an endangered animal. After depicting youthful revelry on the frontier, the poem switches to a meditate tone. The wild campaigning past, the soldier can only watch the geese who can fly south to the Han Chinese homeland and muse about returning home.

The "Yiwen zhi" 藝文志 (Bibliographic Treatise) of the *Xin Tang shu* records Linghu's collection titled *Qilian ji* 漆奩集 (Collection in a Lacquered Vanity Case) in one hundred and thirty *juan*, his *Liangyuan wenlei* 梁苑文類 in three *juan*, his *Biaozou ji* 表奏集 in ten *juan*, and his *Yuanhe bianbang lüe* 元和辨謗略 in ten chapters that he compiled together with Shen Chuanshi 沈傳師 (769–827). These works suggest a broad spectrum of private and official writings to rival the most prolific Tang writers of that era, but all are unfortunately lost. The *Quan Tang wen* does contain 140 of his prose works and the *Quan Tang shi* preserves sixty of his poems.

BIBLIOGRAPHY

Editions:
Linghu Chu 令狐楚. *Linghu Chu ji* 令狐楚集. Yin Zhanhua 尹占華 and Yang Xiaoai 楊曉靄, eds. Lanzhou: Gansu Renmin, 1998.
___. *Yulan shi* 御覽詩. Shanghai: Shanghai Guji, 1987.
___. *Yulan shi*. Zhao Shixiu 趙師秀, ed. Taibei: Shangwu, 1979. *SKQS zhenben* edition.
___. *Yulan shi*. *Tangren xuan Tang shi* 唐人選唐詩. Beijing: Kunlun, 2005, pp. 173–229.
Quan Tang shi, 5: 3748–57, 15: 11282–84; *Quan Tang wen*, 539–43.6251–93.

Biographical Sources:
Fu, *Tang caizi*, 2:379–99, 5:233–34.
Jiu Tang shu, 172.4459–69; *Xin Tang shu*, 166.5098–104.

Studies:
Bian Xiaoxuan 卞孝萱. *Liu Yuxi congkao* 劉禹錫從考. Chengdu: Ba Shu, 1988, pp. 166–74.
Jiang Jianyun 姜劍雲. "Linghu Chu nianpu jianbian" 令狐楚年譜簡編, *Shanxi Daxue xuebao* 3 (1999): 35–42.
___. "Linghu Chu shengzu yu liji kao" 令狐楚生卒與里籍考, *Wenxue yichan* 1996.4: 112–14.

___. "Youguan Linghu Chu de jidian kaobian" 有關令狐楚的幾點考辨, *Shanxi Daxue Shifan Xueyuan Xuebao (Zonghe Ban)* 4 (1992): 28–32.

Jiang Weiyin 蔣瑋茵. "A Study of Linghu Chu (776–837)," M.A. Thesis, University of Hong Kong, 2011.

Li Qingshi 李青石, "Linghu Chu zhenshou Hanzhong qijian de shige chuangzuo" 令狐楚鎮守漢中期間的詩歌創作, *Shaanxi Ligong Xueyuan Xuebao* 30 (Feb. 2012): 12–14.

Tao Min 陶海, "'Quan Tangshi' Linghu Chu *juan*ji Li Fengji shi zhengli chuyi" '全唐詩' 令狐楚卷及李逢吉詩整理芻議, *Hunan Keji Daxue Xuebao (Shehui Kexue ban)* 2 (1987): 22–30.

Wu Jinhui 武錦輝, "Qianlun Linghu Chu de wenxue chuangzuo" 淺論令狐楚的文學創作, *Beifang Wenxue* 11 (Nov. 2012): 14–15.

Yang Jie 楊洁, "Xin chutu Tang Linghu Chu jiazu liangfang muzhi tanze" 新出土唐令狐楚家族兩方墓誌探賾, *Wenbo* (2011.05): 30–33.

Yang Xiao'ai 楊曉靄. "Linghu Chu jianlun" 令狐楚簡論, *Lanzhou Daxue xuebao* 6 (2002): 45–54.

Yin Chubing 尹楚兵. *Linghu Chu nianpu; Linghu Tao nianpu* 令狐楚年譜·令狐綯年譜. Shanghai: Shanghai Guji, 2008.

William H. Nienhauser, Jr. and Chen Wu

Lingyou 靈祐 (*hao*, Guishan 溈山, *hao*, Gui Yang Zongzu 溈仰宗祖, *hao*, Guishan Dayuan 溈山大圓, *shi*, Chan-master Dayuan 大圓禪師, secular surname, Zhao 趙, 771–853), whose name literally means "Aide of the Divine," was a famous monk from Changxi 長溪 (modern Xiapu 霞浦, Fujian) who became the founding patriarch of the Gui-Yang School 溈仰宗, one of the so-called Five Houses 五家 of Chan Buddhism in the late Tang Dynasty.

Lingyou's early years are remembered for having been marked by several predictions of his future achievements. He entered the local Jianshan Monastery 建善寺 at around age fifteen to study Vinaya scriptures with the Vinaya-master Faheng 法恆 (or Fachang 法常). Later on, he took the precepts, likely at the Longxing Monastery 龍興寺 in Hangzhou 杭州. Doing so partially fulfilled the prophecy his family was given when he was a young child: one day, when he was playing in outside his home, auspicious clouds gathered above him; heavenly music was heard, and an old man suddenly appeared foretelling that this child was destined to make the teachings of the Buddha shine anew.

When he was twenty-three years old, Lingyou journeyed to the famous Tiantai Mountain 天台山 after having decided that the answers he sought were not to be found just by reading the Buddhist scriptures. On his way, he encountered a hermit who greeted him with a smile and told him enigmatically:

> In your later life, fate has something in store for you,
> with age you will shine ever more.
> When you meet Tan, stop.
> When you encounter Gui, dwell there.

> 余生有緣，老而益光；逢潭則止，遇溈則住.

Lingyou

According to a later source, the stranger told him rather:

> Among the thousand mountains and ten thousand rivers,
> if you encounter Tan, then stop.
> You will obtain a priceless treasure,
> and help to relieve all the various Masters.

千山萬水，遇潭即止；獲無價寶，賑贍諸子.

In both cases, as the story goes, Lingyou had no idea what these verses meant—nor that he had just met Hanshan 寒山,* the legendary poet recluse. Upon arriving at the Guoqing Monastery 國清寺 on Tiantai Mountain, Lingyou also met Shide 拾得, the equally famous companion of Hanshan, who told him to leave and seek the guidance of Baizhang Huaihai 百丈懷海 (720–814) in Jiangxi 江西. When Huaihai first saw Lingyou, he immediately accepted him and made him the head of his students. One day, when Lingyou was waiting in attendance, Huaihai asked him: "Who are you?" He said: "Lingyou." Huaihai then asked him: "Poke in the oven, is there fire or not?" Lingyou replied: "There is no fire." Huaihai got up and poked deep to find a little fire, he held it up to show him, and said: "Is this not fire!" At that moment, Lingyou awakened to enlightenment.

In the last year of the Yuanhe era (820), Lingyou was given the opportunity to move to the Da Gui Mountain 大潙山 in Tanzhou 潭州 (near modern Ningxiang 寧鄉, Hunan). There he lived as a recluse until the local people built a temple for him, later granting it the name Tongqing Monastery 同慶寺 upon the request of Li Jingrang 李景讓 (fl. 840–846). On this mountain, Lingyou spread his teaching, taught many famous students, and received esteemed guests such as the high official Pei Xiu 裴休 (791–846). His relationships with ranking officials proved beneficial. Mainly through the support of the prominent official Cui Shenyou 崔慎由 (fl. 856–858) he was allowed return to his former monastery after the official abolishment of Buddhism during the Huichang era (841–846). Lingyou passed away in the seventh year of the Dazhong 大中 era (853). His stupa was named Qingjing 清淨 (Pure and Quiet), where a stele was erected and the poet Li Shangyin 李商隱 (ca. 813–858)* dedicated a plaque honoring him.

Before he passed away, Lingyou presented his followers with the following question, now preserved in *juan* 16 of the large Chan compendium, *Zutang ji* 祖堂記 [Anthology from the Patriarchs' Hall]:

> When this old monk has died, he will go down the mountain and become a water buffalo, on its flanks will be written two rows of characters reading: "Monk Guishan, His Insignificance." At that time, would you call it "water buffalo," or would you call it "Monk Guishan, His Insignificance"? If you called it "Monk Guishan," it would still be a water buffalo. If you called it "water buffalo," it would still be "Monk Guishan, His Insignificance." All of you, what would you do?

老僧死后，去山下作一頭水牯牛，脅上書兩行字云：潙山僧某專甲。與摩時，喚作水牯牛，喚作潙山僧某專甲？若喚作潙山僧，又是一頭水牯牛。若喚作水牯牛，又是潙山僧某專甲。汝諸人作摩生？

The memory of Lingyou's teachings is mainly preserved in his recorded sayings, a corpus that shifted over time until it was edited during the Ming by Yuanxin 圓信 (1571–1647) and Guo Ningzhi 郭凝之 and given the title *Tanzhou Guishan Lingyou chanshi yulu* 潭州溈山靈祐禪師語錄 (Recorded Sayings of Chan Master Lingyou from Guishan, Tanzhou). Many of the incidents recorded therein tell of celebrated encounters between him and his successor Huiji 慧寂 (807–883), who would later move to Yang Mountain 仰山 at Yuanzhou 袁州 (near modern Yichun 宜春, Jiangxi) to continue his teachings—what would eventually come to be called the Gui-Yang School. According to a commentary in the *Song shi* 宋史 (History of the Song Dynasty), the now lost *De Shan ji* 德山集 in one *juan* was believed to contain the sayings of both Lingyou from Guishan and Huiji from Yangshan.

Lingyou's only surviving work, the *Guishan Dayuan chanshi jingce* 溈山大圓禪師警策 (Admonitions of Chan-master Dayuan from Guishan) has survived as a Dunhuang fragment (P.4638) as well as preserved in part in several other collections. It is also was transmitted separately with a Song-dynasty commentary by Shousui 守遂 (1072–1147) and in two commentated Ming editions.

BIBLIOGRAPHY

Editions:

Harada Tokinosuke 原田時之助, ed. *Isan daien zenji kyōsaku* 溈山大円禅師警策. Kyoto: Bukkyō Gokoku Enjōkai, 1908. Hongzan 弘贊 (1611–1685), comm. *Guishan jingce jushi ji* 溈山警策句釋記. Guangzhou: Haichuangsi Jing Fang, 1660.

___, comm., Kaixiong 開詗 (1634–1676), ed. *Guishan jingce jushi ji* 溈山警策句釋記. *Shinsan Dainihon Zokuzōkyō*, No. 1240, vol. 63.

Quan Tang wen, 919.12550–53.

Yuanxin 圓信 (1571–1647) and Guo Ningzhi 郭凝之 (Ming), ed. *Tanzhou Guishan Lingyou chanshi yulu* 潭州溈山靈祐禪師語錄. *Taishō shinshū Daizōkyō*, No. 1989, vol. 47.

Annotations:

Daxiang 大香 (fl. 1634), comm. *Guishan jingce zhu* 溈山警策註. *Shinsan Dainihon zokuzōkyō*, No. 1294, vol. 65.

Shousui 守遂 (1072–1147). *Guishan jingce zhu* 溈山警策註. *Shinsan Dainihon zokuzōkyō*, No. 1239, vol. 63.

Biographical Sources:

Zanning, 11.264.

Translations:

Kirchner, Thomas. "The Admonitions of Zen Master Guishan Dayuan." *Hanazono Daigaku Kokusai Zengaku Kenkyūjo ronshū* 1 (2006): 1–18.

Studies:

Abe Chōichi 阿部肇一. "Tōdai no igyōshū ni tsuite" 唐代の溈仰宗について. *Komazawa shigaku* 16 (1969): 1–13.

Cai Rixin 蔡日新. "Daochang longsheng de Guiyang shan chan shu ping" 道场隆盛的沩山禅述评. *Chuanshan xuekan* 1996.2: 226–41.

Huijing 會靜. *Guishan jingce wen shi* 溈山警策文釋. Jilong: Fayan, 2000.
Ishii Shūdō 石井修道. "Igyōshū no jōsui" 溈仰宗の盛衰. *Komazawa daigaku bukkyō gakubu ronshū* 18 (1988): 111–62; 19 (1988): 96–138; 20 (1989): 28–76; 21(1990): 85–110; 22 (1991): 87–123; 24 (1993): 83–122.
___. "Isan kyōdan no dōkō ni tsuite" 溈山教団の動向について, *Indogaku bukkyōgaku kenkyū* 79 (1991): 90–96.
___. "Hyakujō kyōdan to Isan kyōdan" 百丈教団と溈山教団, *Indogaku bukkyōgaku kenkyū* 81 (1992): 106–12; 83 (1993): 289–95.
Ozaki Shōzen 尾崎正善. *Isan: Igyō no oshie to wa nani ka* 溈山: 溈仰の教えとは何か. Kyoto: Rinsen, 2007.
Suyama Chōji 須山長治. "Isan Reiyū no jishū" 溈山靈祐の示衆. *Philosophia* 74 (1986): 159–76.
Suzuki Tetsuo 鈴木哲雄. "Isan goroku seiritsu no haikei toso no seikaku" 溈山語錄成立の背景とその性格. *Indogaku bukkyōgaku kenkyū* 40 (1972): 230–36.
Wang Jianxing 王建星. "Lingyou chanshi foxue sixiang chutan" 靈祐禪師佛學思想初探. *Fujian sheng shehui zhuyi xueyuan xuebao* 4 (2008): 89–91.
Wu Yansheng 吳言生. "Gui Yang zong chan shi yanjiu" 溈仰宗禪詩研究. *Huaiyang Shifan Xueyuan xuebao* 2 (2000): 69–74.
Xuliang Kann 闞緒良. *Weiyang zong kaizong zushi. Weishan Lingyou Dashi zhuan* 溈仰宗開宗祖師. 溈山靈祐大師傳. Taibei Xian: Foguang, 2000.
Yamada Kōdō 山田孝道 (1863–1928). *Isan kyōsaku kōgi* 溈山警策講義. Tokyo: Kōyūkan, 1909.
Yanagida Seizan 柳田聖山 (1922–2006). "Isanshū no tekisuto" 溈仰宗のテキスト. *Yanagida Seizan shū* 柳田聖山集. Kyoto: Hōzōkan, 2001. Vol. 2: 627–793.

Marc Nürnberger

Liu Cha 劉叉 (fl. 806–820) is one of the most influential poets of the Yuanhe style (*Yuanhe ti* 元和體). Known for his fondness for 'chivalry' (*renxia* 任俠) and his brash disposition, Liu Cha's poetry affects a sense of unrestrained freedom that earned him renown among his contemporaries for his personality as much as for his literary achievement. His given name is unknown and details of his upbringing are unclear. He would at times refer to himself as Pengcheng zi 彭城子 (The Master of Pengcheng), perhaps an indication that he was from Pengcheng (modern Xuzhou 徐州 in Jiangsu Province). However, the *Tang caizi zhuan* 唐才子傳 claims that he was from Heshuo 河朔 (generally referring to territories north of the Yellow River in modern Hebei Province). The confusion surrounding Liu Cha's origins is further obfuscated by the fact that his name is sometimes confused with "Liu Yi" 劉乂/劉义.

During his early years, Liu Cha lived in Wei 魏 (northeast of Daming 大名 County of modern Handan 邯鄲 in Hebei Province) and associated with other like-minded men. Liu Cha was said to be tall and strong and would show up in the marketplace to take part in various martial encounters and "carry out acts of chivalrous justice" 任氣行俠. He is thought to have once killed a person while drunk, and thus had to change his name and flee. Following a general amnesty, he went to live in the Qi-Lu 齊魯 area (modern Shandong Province), determined to forsake his old habits and dedicate himself to studying. It was then that he first began composing poetry.

Later Liu Cha traveled the Ba Shu 巴蜀 region (modern Sichuan Province) and then north to Sanggan 桑乾 (northern modern Hebei and Shanxi Province). During the Yuanhe reign period of Emperor Xianzong (806–820), having heard that Han Yu 韓愈 (768–824)* was accepting literati as retainers, Liu went to join them. Two of Liu Cha's poems, "Bingzhu" 冰柱 (Icicle) and "Xueche"

雪車 (Snow Carriage), earned him a reputation among the coterie of Lu Tong 盧仝 (ca. 775–ca. 815)* and Meng Jiao 孟郊 (751–814),* and won him the admiration of Fan Zongshi 樊宗師 (fl. 806–820). During his time with Han Yu's coterie, Liu Cha also studied the *Chunqiu* 春秋 with Lu Tong. The following lines taken from his famous "Bingzhu" shows the typical flights of imagination found throughout his verse; here they depict ordinary objects in grandiose terms of historical significance. As he looks at the hanging icicles sparkling in the sun, the poet sees dragons with their teeth and claws descending to the earth; then he envisions the founding emperor of the Han, Liu Bang, on his way to establish and pacify his land:

> Slight snowflakes dance chaotically in vain—
> they drop, then exposed to the sun melt.
> among the eaves the icicles drop to crossing each other;
> Some drooping, some soaring, small and large glittering clear,
> they follow no discernable trend;
> At first I thought jade dragons had descended from their realm to come to the world of humans,
> all pointing to the thatch eaves spreading their teeth and claws.
> Then I thought it was Emperor Gao of the Han coming West to behead the serpent.
> If people did not recognize him,
> They would ask who braves the wind brandishing the Moye sword?

纖片亂舞空紛拏。
旋落旋逐朝暾化，檐間冰柱若削出交加。
或低或昂，小大瑩潔，隨勢無等差。
始疑玉龍下界來人世，齊向茅檐布爪牙。
又疑漢高帝，西方來斬蛇。
人不識，誰爲當風杖莫邪。

The "Moye" sword mentioned in the last line recalls the story of the two famous swordsmiths, the couple Gan Jiang 干將 and Mo Ye 莫邪, who each forged a sword to make a pair for the King of Wu, Helü 吳闔閭 (r. 514–496 BC). Gan Jiang was put to death by the covetous king over his famous sword, spurring their son, Chi 赤, to seek vengeance. The story concludes when an unknown traveler presents the king with the sword and Chi's head. The traveler then slices off the king's head which falls into a boiling cauldron before cutting off his own head. The three severed heads were boiled beyond recognition and had to be entombed together in the "Tomb of the Three Kings." Liu Cha's allusion to the tale in the final lines of the poem presented here recalls the noble mission of the wandering stranger, whose identity remains unknown but who was able to find justice for Gan Jiang.

Later, due to quarrels within the group, possibly over Han Yu's insistence on employing the ancient-writing style (*guwen* 古文), Liu Cha left and absconded with money Han Yu had earned by writing epitaphs, claiming that since this was earned by flattering the dead. Liu Cha then returned to wandering through Qi and Lu. In 819, when Han Yu was exiled to Chaozhou 潮州 (modern Guangdong) due to his critique of the courts' willingness to receive a Buddhist relic, Liu Cha sent him a poem as a gift to show his support.

Liu Cha remained proud of his talent to the point of audacious hyperbole, claiming his poetic skills were greater than Heaven. His poetry is elusive, arrogant, and exotic, often cynical and highly critical of society and the court. His seemingly unrefined style belies a sense of freedom and lack of restraint colored with a sense of desolation that many of his contemporaries came to admire. Meng Jiao, for example, praised Liu Cha's poetry as though it were filled with "qiongyao ci" 瓊瑤辭 (words as precious as jade). "Duyin" 獨飲 (Drinking Alone) is exemplary of his playful, humorous style tinged with a sense of loneliness:

> Exhausting my desire to blend the five-flavored broth,
> Since ancient times no one has been skilled at this.
> And so, I became a man in the mountains,
> just giddily drinking my wine.

> 盡欲調太羹。自古無好手。
> 所以山中人。兀兀但飲酒。

Here, Liu Cha alludes to the resonance between culinary skill and political prowess—exhausting his talents to "blend the five-flavored broth" in an attempt perhaps to emulate the famous minister of the Shang dynasty, Yi Yin 伊尹 (fl. ca. 1600 BC). Early historical texts record accounts that the first ruler of the Xia, Tang 湯, was so impressed by Yi Yin's ability to bring together culinary harmony in his cooking that he judged him worthy of governing the land. Liu Cha's first two lines not only evoke the correlation between politics and cooking, but also reveal his own recognition that a political career is unattainable and thus he will seek solace in the life of a mountain recluse, finding joy in his own brew.

Liu Cha's literary bravado and poetic style was part of what came to be known as the Yuanhe Style. He would leave behind his own reflections on the process of poetry in verse in "Zuo shi" 作詩 (Writing a Poem):

> I'm composing a poem without knowing the tune,
> Not composing is better than composing.
> I've yet to come upon someone to answer my poems;
> this road is long and lonely.
> Youyu is now done and gone,
> upon those who come, whom can I depend?
> By loudly chanting I clear my mind
> brush strokes and tears fall together.

> 作詩無知音, 作不如不作.
> 未逢廣載人, 此道長寂寞.
> 有虞今已矣, 來者誰為託.
> 朗詠豁心胸, 筆與淚俱落.

While the poem is structured around the familiar trope of not having a bosom friend "to know the tune," it smacks of the self-aggrandizing that made Liu Cha stand out amongst his peers. Wandering the roads alone, no one can answer his poems. One is left to ponder whether this is due to missing a compatriot, or whether Liu Cha doubts there is anyone his equal. The fifth line recalls the legendary emperors of China, Shun whose clan name was Youyu. According to legend,

Shun was exemplary in his righteousness and valued the same in others. When choosing his successor, Shun found his own son to be lacking and instead selected the virtuous Yu 禹 to be his heir. Here in the poem, Liu Cha laments that the days of rulers who could recognize and thus reward the righteous and valiant have long passed. Now, with no one upon whom he can rely, Liu Cha is left to weep for his art.

Liu Cha gained renown during his own time for his unrestrained verse, a quality that seemed to reflect the story of his own life. Just as with his birth, the details surrounding his death remain obscure, with some accounts speculating that he died under mysterious circumstances due to a strange illness. Liu Cha's work has been collected in traditional anthologies, with the majority of his extant poems being preserved in one *juan* of the *Quan Tang shi*. A late nineteenth century compilation organizes his work in two *juan* under the title *Liu Cha shiji* 劉叉詩集 (Collected Poems of Liu Cha).

BIBLIOGRAPHY

Editions:
Li Shangyin 李商隱, "Qi Lu er sheng" 齊魯二生 [Two People of Qi Lu Region]. *Li Yishan wenji* 李義山文集 [The Collective Works of Li Yishan], *juan* 4, in *Sibu congkan chubian* 四部叢刊初編. Shanghai: Shangwu, 1919.
Liu Cha shiji 劉叉詩集. 2 *juan*. Suzhou: Lingjiange Guangxu, 1895.
Quan Tang shi, 6: 4456–61.

Biographical Sources:
Fu, *Tang caizi*, 2:278–82, 5:214.
Xin Tang shu, 176.5268–69.

Studies:
Matsumoto Hajime 松本肇 and Kawai Kōzō 川合康三. *Chū Tō bungaku no shikaku* 唐文学の視角. Tokyo: Sōbunsha, 1998.
Wang Lizeng 王立增. "Lun Han-Meng shipai de xingcheng" 論韓孟詩派的行程, *Zhengzhou Daxue xuebao (Zhexue Shehui Kexueban)* 3 (May, 2003): 104–07.
Wang Xiang 王香. "Liu Cha" 劉叉, *Wenshi yuekan* 2013.8: 37.
Zhang Tianjian 張天健. "Gangchang xiashi hua Liu Cha" 剛腸俠詩話劉叉, *Shehui Kexue yanjiu* 1989.3: 122–27.

Wenting Ji and Michael E. Naparstek

Liu Fangping 劉方平 (726–ca. 758) was a native of Henan and was known for his abilities as a painter of landscapes as well as for his skill as a poet. Liu Fangping's family traced their origins to the Xiongnu, but by the Tang, the family had settled in Luoyang enjoying high social status and having gained a noble repute. Liu Fangping's great-great-grandfather was the famous statesman Liu Zhenghui 劉政會 (d. 635), who helped found the Tang dynasty, and Fangping's grandfather, Liu Qi 劉奇, served as the Vice Director of the Ministry of Personnel during the reign

Liu Fangping

of Wu Zetian 武則天 (r. 690–705). Liu Qi would be killed in 697 as a result of his involvement in a failed coup, but Liu Wei 劉微, Fangping's father, was able to continue the family tradition of officialdom, serving as the Investigation Commissioner of Jiangnan Province 江南. Liu Fangping himself sat the *jinshi* examination in 750 but did not pass. Soon thereafter, he joined the army to pursue a career in the military but would find little success. Liu Fangping left the army to retire to live the rest of his days as a hermit on the banks of the Ru River 汝水 in the Yingyang 潁陽 valley (modern Henan and Anhui) among the landscape of his father's old official circuit.

Liu Fangping had already gained a reputation as a poet in his twenties and was friends with literati such as Yuan Dexiu 元德秀 (696–754), Huangfu Ran 皇甫冉 (ca. 717–ca. 771), Yan Wu 嚴武 (726–765), and Li Qi 李頎 (690–751).* Li Qi praised Liu Fangping's skill, claiming that at twenty, he was an expert in *ci* 詞 (lyrics) and *fu* 賦 and was the only one who deserved his sterling reputation. Xiao Yingshi 蕭穎士 (717–760)* also thought highly of Fangping and would praise him for his talent and uniqueness. Based on his reputation, the Grand Councilor Li Mian 李勉 (717–788) wanted to recommend Liu Fangping to the imperial court, but Fangping would refuse, choosing instead to continue his life in relative seclusion.

Liu Fangping was known for his broad-ranging artistic abilities. In addition to his landscape paintings (*shanshui* 山水), Liu Fangping was celebrated for his literary skill in presenting objects as still life in verse. His *yongwu* 詠物 (describing objects) poems, for example, are noted for their portrayal of homesickness or women's passion through the description of everyday things. The trope of taking on a female voice of lament is often employed by male poets to express their frustration over the failure of their own career. The following take on the theme of "Chunyuan" 春怨 (Spring Lament) exemplifies how Liu Fangping focuses on the elements of a scene to express emotional bitterness through the guise of an imperial concubine having fallen out of favor.

> By her silken window the sun sets, gradually turning to dusk,
> In her Golden Chamber with no one to see her tears pour out.
> From the deserted courtyard spring about to end,
> With pear blossoms littering the ground, she won't open her door.

> 紗窗日落漸黃昏，金屋無人見淚痕。
> 寂寞空庭春欲晚，梨花滿地不開門。

This seven-syllable poem utilizes imagery of light and nature to paint a scene of loneliness and despair among the trappings of decadence. It opens by focusing on an object, a silken window, from which the palace lady can only see the fading light of dusk pass by from her place inside. The departing glow illuminates her room where she weeps alone, emphasizing her isolation amidst golden luxury. The "Golden Chamber" alludes to the famous narrative describing the betrothal of Princess Guantao's 館陶 teenage daughter, A'Jiao 阿嬌, to the five year-old prince, Liu Che 劉徹 (156–87 BC), who would eventually grow to ascend the throne as Emperor Wu of the Han 漢武帝 (r. 141–87 BC). While his father, Emperor Jing 景 (r. 157–141 BC), first disapproved of their union based on their young age, the precocious Liu Che boasted that he would build for A'Jiao a golden room (*jinwu* 金屋) were they to marry. The "Golden Chamber" would also later come to refer to keeping a mistress in luxury. The imagery of the "Golden Chamber" here in the poem takes on a more somber tone, as it is linked to the deserted courtyard of the next line.

Shifting her gaze from within her gilded prison to the world outside, the lady notices the Spring soon to depart, much like as the favor of her lord who has left her alone. Her view is then cut off by the door, shut and never to open again.

The short poem "A Moonlit Night" ("Yue Ye" 月夜) stands among Liu Fangping's most recognized examples of 'painting' a landscape in verse:

> In the deepest of night, the moon colors in half the homes,
> The Northern Dipper slanting, the Southern Dipper tilting.
> On this night though I know of the warm air of spring,
> The sound of insects penetrates my green-muslin window.

> 更深月色半人家, 北斗闌干南斗斜.
> 今夜偏知春氣暖, 蟲聲新透錄窗紗.

The poem paints a scene of stillness in the deepest and darkest time of night. Its first two lines identify the time by position of nocturnal astral bodies: the two dippers already slanting and the moon angled such that its light illuminates only half the houses of the village leaving the rest in darkness. Here in the coldest depths of the night, the perspective shifts from the sky to the immediate environs around the poet's home. As the only soul awake, he can hear the stirring of insects—the tiniest of creatures whose muffled sounds reach him through the muslin window—emphasizing the otherwise complete and utter stillness that surround him. "A Moonlit Night" thus not only paints "night" through its adept visual imagery, but like the best landscape paintings, also brings the reader into the visceral world of the poet where one can almost hear the faint sounds of insects and shudder at the sense of cold, dark solitude.

While equally well-known in the biographies of painters, Liu Fangping's extant literary works were first collected by his contemporaries and a number of poems still remain as part of larger compilations such as the *Quan Tang shi* and the *Tangshi sanbaishou*.

BIBLIOGRAPHY

Editions:
Quan Tang shi, 4: 2828–32.

Biographical Sources:
Fu, *Tang caizi*, 1:587–92.

Translations:
Bynner, *Jade Mountain*, p. 75.
Giles, Herbert A. *Chinese Poetry in English Verse*. London: B. Quaritch, 1898, p. 154.
Margoulies, *Anthologie*, p. 375.

Studies:
Chen Qiaosheng 陈桥生, "'Bu guanmen' yu 'Bu kaimen'—du Liu Fangping 'Chunyuan'" '不關門' 與 '不開門'—讀劉方平 "春怨," *Lanzhou Jiaoyu Xueyuan xuebao* (1994.1): 10–12.

Li Yuanlin 李源林, "Xini de bichu youshen de jingjie—Li Fangping 'Yueye' yishu meitan" 細膩的筆觸幽深的境界—劉方平《月夜》藝術美談, *Nei Menggu Diandaxue kan* (1993.3): 44–45.

Shao Bowen 邵伯溫. *Henan Shaoshi wenjian qianlu* 河南邵氏聞見前錄. Taibei: Guangwen, 1970.

Wen Zhonglan 溫中兰 and Ma Dasen 马大森, "Tangdai shiren Liu Fangping 'Yue Ye'—shide Yingyi pinping" 唐代詩人劉方平《月夜》一詩的英譯品評 [critique of Bynner' translation], *Ningbo Gongcheng Xueyuan xuebao* (2009.3).

Xin Wenfang 辛文房. *Tang caizi zhuan* 唐才子傳. Shanghai: Gudian Wenxue, 1957.

You Xingbo 由兴波. "Ruowen xianqing duji xu—cong Lu Fangping 'Yue Ye' he Zhao Shixiu 'Yue Ke' guankui Tang Song shi" 若問閒情都幾許—從劉方平《月夜》和趙師秀《約客》管窺唐宋詩, *Ha'erbin Xueyuan xuebao* (2005.8).

Zhang Yanyuan 張彥遠 (fl. 9th c.). *Lidai minghua ji* 歷代名畫記, *j.* 10. Beijing: Renmin Meishu, 1963, p. 192.

Han Yan and Michael E. Naparstek

Liu Mian 柳冕 (*zi*, Jingshu 敬叔, d. 804) was a scholar-official with a strong interest in ritual who enjoyed close relations with many of the most important literary figures at the end of the eighth century. He used these ties to advocate the *Fugu* 復古 (Return to Antiquity) and *Guwen* 古文 (Ancient-Prose) movements.

The Lius were a family of scholar-officials from Puzhou 蒲州 (modern Yongji 永濟 County in Shanxi). Liu's father, Liu Fang 柳芳 (ca. 710–ca. 785), was a noted genealogist and historian who had worked with Wei Shu 韋述 (d. 757). He was involved in a number of important projects in the 750s and 760s including work on the *Guo shi* 國史 (History of the [Tang] State). Liu Mian's predilection for ancient-style prose can probably be traced to Liu Fang, who passed the *jinshi* in 735 together with Li Hua 李華 (715–774)* and Xiao Yingshi 蕭穎士 (717–760)* under the examiner Sun Ti 孫逖 (fl. 735), a scholar who rejected the rote memorization of passages and commentary from the Chinese Classics in favor of the careful study and discussion of the canon.

There is no record of Liu Mian taking the *jinshi* or any other examination. He began his career as a Right Rectifier of Omissions of in the College of Assembled Worthies and worked as a Senior Compiler in the Historiography Institute. In 780, Liu Mian was sent to the provinces to take up a minor post in remote Bazhou 巴州 (modern Bazhong City 巴中市 in Sichuan), because of his friendship with the financial doyen Liu Yan 劉晏 (d. 780) who had just fallen from power. In 785 he was recalled to the capital as Erudite in the Court of Imperial Sacrifices. It was in this position that he became embroiled in the controversy over royal burial and the appropriate type of mourning (this controversy was part of a larger discussion of ritual which often occupied the court in the late eighth century). After having been transferred to Director of the Board of Civil Office and spending some time at court, he was again appointed to provincial posts, rising to Surveillance Commissioner of Fujian in 797. Recalled in 805, he died en route to the capital.

Liu Mian is best known to modern readers through the lengthy discussion of his prose and prose theories in Liu Dajie's 劉大杰 (1904–1977) standard *Zhongguo wenxue fazhan shi* 文學發展史 (A History of the Development of Chinese Literature). Liu Dajie devotes almost as much space to Liu Mian as he does to Liu Zongyuan 柳宗元 (773–819),* and emphasizes the importance Liu Mian gave to expressing the Dao in literature. Indeed, the fourteen prose writings remaining from what was once certainly a larger collection, reveal two important literary contributions: (1) Liu

Mian stresses the importance of the Dao in literature and outlines a history of literature which closely follows the Confucian tradition, thereby preparing the way for the theories of Han Yu 韓愈 (768–824)* and other return-to-antiquity advocates of the ninth century; (2) Liu Mian seems to have spread the ancient-style-prose gospel more than most writers through an active correspondence with some of the most influential literary figures of the 780s and 790s, men who were patrons or advisors to Han Yu and his associates, including Pei Du 裴度 (765–839), Quan Deyu 權德輿 (761–818),* Du You 杜佑 (735–812), and Zhang Jianfeng 張建封 (735–800).

Liu wrote in none of the genres that typify the writings of the later ancient-style-prose masters (such as *zhuan* 傳 "accounts", *shuo* or *shui* 說 "persuasions," *lun* 論 "essays on"), but his five extant letters which discuss various aspects of literature and its history are important pieces of literary criticism. Although he disparaged his own prose, these letters present strong arguments in a cogent style. An excerpt from his letter to Zhang Jianfeng reveals many of the problems that continued to trouble ancient-style-prose writers through the end of the Tang:

> Literary writings are rooted in moral teachings and civilizing transformations expressed according to one's emotions and nature. The Dao of [the sage rulers] Yao and Shun was rooted in moral teachings and civilizing transformations; the words of the sages were expressed according to their emotions and nature. Since the deaths of kings Cheng 成 and Kang 康 [at the start of the Zhou dynasty], the music of the laudes has ceased, the *sao* 騷 poets began to compose, licentious beauty arose, and literary writings and moral teachings separated into two. Those who were not adequate produced literary writings by force, thus they did not understand the Dao of the superior man; those who understood the Dao of the superior man were ashamed by their literary writings. To write and to understand the Dao–these two things are difficult to unite. To unite them is the task of the grandly superior man.

> 夫文章者，本於教化，發於情性。本於教化，堯舜之道也；發於情性，圣人之言也。自成康歿，頌聲寢，騷人作，淫麗興，文与教分為二：不足者強而為文，則不知君子之道；知君子之道者，則恥為文。文而知道，二者兼難，兼之者大君子之事．

Liu Mian here presents the contradiction he and many subsequent *guwen* writers faced: literature was a personal thing, "expressed according to one's emotions and nature," but it was also meant to be combined with politics, to serve society. The difficulty of combining literary skills and Confucian didacticism eluded all but a few (such as Han Yu), leading to the bifurcation of these writers into two schools of ancient-style-prose writers in the late ninth century, one stressing Dao, the other *wen* 文 (literary skills).

Liu's letter to Lu Qun 盧群 (742–800) reiterates the role of the superior man (*junzi* 君子) in literature, touched on the passage cited above, and also explains the relationship between literature and government:

> Literature arises from emotions, emotions arise from sorrow and joy, sorrow and joy arise from order and chaos. Therefore, when the superior man is moved by sorrow and joy to compose literary writings, he thereby comes to understand the root of order and chaos.

> 夫文生於情，情生於哀樂，哀樂生於治亂。
> 故君子感哀樂而為文章，以知治亂之本。

Finally, in his letter to Du You, Liu Mian applies some of his ideas to the development of early Chinese literature:

> The writings of today and the writings of antiquity differ in how they establish their meaning. Why is this? The writers of antiquity, according to whether the government was ordered or chaotic, were moved to sorrow or joy; according to whether they felt sorrow or joy, they came to chant or sing; according to whether they chanted or sang, they engendered comparisons and stimuli. For this reason when the Greater Elegentiae [of the *Classic of Poetry*] were composed, the Royal Way flourished, when the Lesser Elegentiae were composed, the Royal Way was damaged, when the Elegentiae became the [*Classic of*] *Poetry*, the Royal Way was in decline, and when poems like those in the [*Classic of*] *Poetry* were no longer composed, the Royal Grace was exhausted. As for the sorrowful laments of Chu Yuan and Song Yu [whose works are included in the *Songs of the South*], who because of their thoughts were exiled and yet did not rebel, they are all the sounds of a kingdom about to perish.
>
> 且今之文章，與古之文章，立意異矣。何則？古之作者，因治亂而感哀樂，因哀樂而為詠歌，因詠歌而成比興。故《大雅》作，則王道盛矣；《小雅》作，則王道缺矣；《雅》變《風》，則王道衰矣；詩不作，則王澤竭矣。至於屈宋，哀而以思，流而不反，皆亡國之音也。

Although there is some repetition in the themes and language of these letters, the multifarious subjects and daring arguments expressed in them suggest that Liu Dajie's assessment of Liu Mian as the most important precursor to Han Yu and Liu Zongyuan is to be taken seriously.

BIBLIOGRAPHY

Editions:
Quan Tang wen, 527.6783–94.

Biographical Sources:
Jiu Tang shu, 149.4030–33.
Xin Tang shu, 132.4536–38.

Studies:
Bol, pp. 144–45.
Guo Shaoyu 郭紹虞. *Zhongguo wenxue piping shi* 中國文學批評史. Shanghai: Shanghai Guji, 1979, pp. 148–152.
Liu Dajie 劉大杰 (1904–1977). *Zhongguo wenxue fazhan shi* 中國文學發展史 (A History of the Development of Chinese Literature). Shanghai: Shanghai Shudian, 1990, pp. 10–11.
Luo Genze 羅根澤. *Zhongguo wenxue piping shi* 中國文學批評史. Shanghai: Shanghai Gudian Wenxue, 1994, pp. 130–33.
Luo Zongqiang 羅宗強. *Sui Tang Wudai wenxue sixiang shi* 隨唐五代文學思想史. Beijing: Zhonghua, 2003.
McMullen, David L. *State and Scholars in Tang China*. Cambridge: Cambridge University Press, 1988, pp. 246–47.

Ming Yuezhao 明月熙. "Lun Liu Mian yu Han Yu wenlun sixiang de yitong" 論柳冕與韓愈文論思想的異同. *Qiusuo* 10 (2011): 193–94.

Obi Koichi 小尾郊一. "Ryū Ben no bunron" 柳冕の文論, *Shinagaku kenkyū*, 1962.3: 27–37.

William H. Nienhauser, Jr.

Liu Yuxi 劉禹錫 (*zi*, Mengde 夢得, 772–842) came from a clan that originated in Pengcheng 彭城 (modern Xuzhou 徐州, Jiangsu), but Liu himself was born in Luoyang. As a youth he lived with his father in Jiaxing 嘉興 and then Wuxing 吳興, studying poetry with the poet-monks Jiao Ran 皎然 (720–799)* and Lingche 靈澈 (746–816).* After passing the *jinshi* in 793, Liu became a Editor for the Heir Apparent in 795. In 801, he followed Du Yu 杜預 (735–812), serving as his Chief Secretary, at first to put down rebellious troops in Xuzhou, and then to serve under Du in Huainan 淮南. In 803 he became the Recorder of Weinan County 渭南縣 near the capital. On account of his participation in the reform faction led by Wang Shuwen 王叔文 (735–806) which sought to restrain the power of the eunuchs, local army commanders, and aristocratic families, he was sent into the provinces as Vice Prefect of Langzhou 朗州 (modern Changde 常德, Hunan) in 805 and spent the next decade there among minorities. Liu was called back to court in 815, but supposedly because of his satirical poem "Xizeng kanhua zhu junzi" 戲贈看花諸君子 (Presented to and Mocking Those Flower-Viewing Noblemen) he was banished for another ten years to Lianzhou 連州 (modern Lianxian 連縣, Guangdong; see text below).

By 821 he had become Prefect of Kuizhou 夔州 (modern Sichuan) and three years later Liu was transferred to the same post in Hezhou 和州 (modern He County in Ma'anshanshi 馬鞍山市, Anhui). In 826 he left official life to return to Luoyang. The following year he was made Director of the Bureau of Receptions in Luoyang and then an Academician in the Academy of Scholarly Worthies. In 831 because of his close ties to Pei Du 裴度 (765–839) he was sent out of the capital and began serving successively as Prefect of Suzhou 蘇州 (modern Jiangsu) and Ruzhou 汝州 (modern Henan) where his efforts to relieve famine were noted. By 836, because of a problems with his feet, he returned to the capital and was made Advisor to the Heir Apparent. Despite his advanced age he continued to serve in several other court positions until in 842 he passed away of illness in Luoyang. His collected works bear the name *Liu Binke wenji* 劉賓客文集 (Collected Writings of Advisor to the Heir Apparent Liu).

Liu Yuxi, who was a close friend of Liu Zongyuan 柳宗元 (773–819)* and Bo Juyi 白居易 (772–846),* is important both as a poet and as an essayist. His most famous essay is his philosophical dissertation, "Tianlun" 天論 (On Heaven), which discusses the relationship between Heaven and man. This text, which belongs to the tradition of Xunzi 荀子, develops a materialistic and dialectical conception of nature and was written in opposition to the idealistic theory of Han Yu 韓愈 (768–824).*

Though as a poet Liu Yuxi is generally regarded as an equal to Liu Zongyuan and Han Yu, neither his poetry nor his essays have received equal attention. Only four of his poems are included in the *Tangshi sanbaishou*. But Liu's most essential contributions to Chinese poetry are his political poems and his poems that reflect the influence of non-Chinese folk literature. In his poetry, most of which was written after 805, new topics and stylistic innovations are noteworthy.

Liu Yuxi

Liu shares with his contemporaries reflections on history's steady decline in "Yangliuzhi ci" 楊柳枝詞 (Willow Branch Songs), on loneliness in "Guiyuan ci" 閨怨詞 (A Boudoir Plaint), and on the transitory nature of man in "Shitou cheng" 石頭城 (Stone City) one of a five-poem series called "Jinling" 金陵 which depicts the old capital (modern Nanjing) in its various guises through the Six Dynasties:

> Surroundings of the mountain-ringed former capital remain;
> Tides strike the empty city-wall, then solitarily recede.
> East of the Qinhuai River hangs the moon of old,
> Still crossing the parapets deep in the night, as it always has.

> 山圍故國周遭在，潮打空城寂寞回。
> 淮水東邊舊時月，夜深還過女牆來。

"Stone City" was the name given the city by Sun Quan 孫權 (182–252), the ruler of the Wu 吳 Kingdom, which had by Liu Yuxi's time become an abandoned ruin. The loneliness of the city is enhanced by the image of the tide receding by itself from its cold walls. Only the moon and the Qinhuai river have endured the ravages of time. They are also the links in the poet's imagination to the flourishing city that once was: the banks of the Qinhuai River were formerly the center of the pleasure quarters. The message here is that all things mortal must pass.

In his nature and love poetry, besides traditional tropes, there are also fresh ideas. For example, in the poem "Shi daohuan ge" 視刀環歌 (Song of Looking at a Sword Handle), Liu considers the limitations of language and its inability to express the depth of the inner heart.

> I have always regretted the shallowness of words,
> They don't measure up to the depth of human hearts.
> Today the we two look at one another,
> Silently, but with feelings a hundredfold.

> 常恨言語淺，不如人意深.
> 今朝兩相視，脈脈萬重心.

This poem is considered to be a "new *yuefu*," that is a poem with a political message. Liu Yuxi wrote this poem during his years in exile when he longed to return to the capital, Chang'an. The message the poem aims to express is embedded in an allusion to the Han-dynasty general, Li Ling 李陵 (d. 74 BC). Li Ling had led an army against the Xiongnu and was captured alive in 99 BC, making Emperor Wu 武帝 (r. 141–86 BC) furious that he had allowed himself to be taken captive. But when Emperor Zhao 昭帝 (r. 94–74 BC) took the throne, two of his generals, Huo Guang 霍光 (d. 68 BC) and Shangguan Jie 上官桀 (ca. 140–80 BC), had been on good terms to Li Ling and wanted to bring him home. They send Ren Lizheng 任立政 to the Xiongnu to see if this would be possible. The Chanyu feasted Ren Lizheng and two other envoys who came with him but gave him no opportunity to speak with Li Ling in private. Ren touched the ring (*huan* 環) that topped his sword handle and rubbed his foot. *Huan* suggests *huan* 還, "to return," and rubbing the foot meant Li Ling could go back to the Han with no fear of punishment. In the end, Li Ling would not return. Here Liu Yuxi—perhaps addressing his poem to an envoy from the capital—

turns the story on its head and makes his intent clear by touching his own sword handle that he hopes to be able to return to Chang'an.

Many other political poems directed against autonomous tendencies among the local military commanders, the growing influence of the eunuchs at court, and the old aristocracy, set forth a view of history as a process leading to something new. This view finds its expression in the poem "Juwen yao" 聚蚊謠 (Song of the Gathering Mosquitoes), which attacks those greedy for power who, like mosquitoes, do mischief in the darkness and leave with the dawn. In his poem "Xisaishan huaigu" 西塞山懷古 (Longing for the Past at Western Pass Mountain), Liu writes against the movement for autonomy by certain military commanders. Giving the example of the Kingdom of Wu and its capital, Jinling 金陵, which was conquered by Wang Jun 王濬 (206–286) in 230, he relates that after the unification of China nothing was left of the autonomous kingdoms but ruins blown by the autumn wind. Here history is not transfigured as often happens in *huaigu* (longing for antiquity) poetry but understood in the sense of *Historical docet*.

Fine examples of Liu's political poems are two pieces he wrote on visits to the Xuandu Temple 玄都觀 in Chang'an, written in 816 and 828. Each poem supposedly led to the banishment of the poet. The first poem, "Yuanhe shiyinian zi Langzhou zhaozhi jing xizeng kanhua zhu junzi" 元和十一年自朗州召至京戲贈看花 (Presented to and Mocking Those Flower-Viewing Noblemen in the Eleventh Year of the Yuanhe Reign after Being Summoned Back from Langzhou) describes the peach trees, which were planted by a Daoist priest in the Xuandu Temple after Liu's first banishment (805), and are now being enjoyed by those in power. That poem reads:

> On purpled roads a red dust in their faces;
> Everyone sure to mention they were returning from flower-viewing.
> Inside the Xuandu Temple, one thousand peach trees,
> All of which were planted after Gentleman Liu had left.

紫陌紅塵拂面來，無人不道看花回。
玄都觀裡桃千樹，盡是劉郎去後栽。

The first four words have become a fixed expression that, in the spirit of this poem, decries the hustle and bustle of early-ninth-century urban society. In the poem, however, these words refer to the purple flowers along the road and the dust thrown up by the throngs of people, noveau riche all, who have come to view them. This practice seems to have begun with this class of people in the early ninth century—Bo Juyi also wrote criticizing such flower viewing (see his entry above). For the viewers, however, the trip marks their status: "everyone was sure to mention it." The entire poem invites a reading beyond mere flower viewing. The flowers at the Xuandu Daoist Temple south of the city wall represent the excesses of the wealthy confronted with the "red dust" the everyday life of the common people. Moreover, these noblemen are newly promoted since Liu Yuxi left the capital ten years earlier—like the peach trees, none of them were in place when Liu Yuxi was exiled in 805. By suggesting that imperial favor had led to the rise of a group of powerful officials, who often had nothing better to do than view flowers, the poet offended the entire power structure of Emperor Xianzong's reign (805–820) and found himself, after only a short time in Chang'an, exiled once again.

The second poem, "Zai you Xuandu Guan" 再遊玄都觀 (Visiting Xuandu Temple Again), written twelve years later when Liu was again back in the capital, reports the decay of the temple and its garden: moss and weeds have replaced the peach trees. The peach trees as in the first poem symbolize the courtiers who in 816 had dominated the capital, but now, with the chance of emperors and political fortunes, were themselves gone. The pair of poems combine to satirize the factional politics of the era. The final line may self-confidently suggest that the author himself may now come to exert more influence on the political scene:

> Acres of courtyard, half of it moss;
> Not a peach blossom left--the wild weeds bloom.
> Where has that Daoist who planted the peach trees gone?
> Young Master Liu who passed by before has come once again.

> 百畝庭中半是苔，桃花淨盡菜花開。
> 種桃道士歸何處？前度劉郎今又來。

The banishments into aboriginal regions allowed Liu contact with non-Chinese folk literature. Like Qu Yuan 屈原, Liu felt himself bound to write new words to the shamanistic, ritual texts to make them more suitable for Confucian sacrificial ceremonies. Still extant are the "Zhuzhi ci" 竹枝詞 (Bamboo Branch Songs), and the eight "Yang liu zhi ci" 楊柳枝詞 (Willow Branch Songs). Breaking off a willow (*zhe liu* 折柳) was a tradition at the parting of friends or lovers, *liu* "willow" was a homophone of *liu* 留, "to detain," and breaking a branch from the tree was thought to delay the traveler. Based on this convention a *yuefu* tradition arose. Liu plays on this tradition in the first of the "Willow Branch Songs," written in 834 while in Suzhou, reads:

> At the palace dike by the Blue Gate, you hang sweeping the ground—
> One thousand strands of golden thread, ten thousand fronds of silk.
> I'll tie you up to make a love knot,
> Later to send to a traveler—will he know or not?

> 禦陌青門拂地垂，千條金縷萬條絲。
> 如今綰作同心結，將贈行人知不知。

The Blue Gate was the popular name for the three gates in the eastern city wall during the Han dynasty. Outside the gate was the Ba Bridge 灞橋 where willows grew in profusion and travelers were traditionally sent off. During the Tang it was a bustling area with wine shops, temples, and entertainments of many kinds. The female persona may have gone there to part with her lover or husband. The poem is addressed to one of the willows there. In her eyes its yellow branches and fronds resemble the thread she uses for weaving. Extending this image she imagines tying them into a love-knot to send to her departed beau, wondering whether he will share her feelings. It is also possible to read the poem as intended for a close friend whom Liu was seeing off (in which case line three could be read: "I'll tie you up to knot our kindred feelings"). In yet another of these willow poems Liu Yuxi promotes the appeal of this new style of poem in his final lines: "Play no more tunes, sir, of bygone dynasties, But hear the new Willow Ballads" 請君莫奏前朝曲，聽唱新翻楊柳枝. The poems were indeed imitated by late Tang poets such as Niu Jiao 牛嶠 (fl. 890).

BIBLIOGRAPHY

Editions:
Gao Er'shi 高二適. *Gao Er'shi pijiao Liu Yuxi ji* 高二適批校《劉禹錫集》. Nanjing: Fenghuang, 2011.
Liu Yuxi. *Liu Yuxi ji* 劉禹錫集. Bian Xiaoxuan 卞孝萱, ed. 2 vols. Beijing: Zhonghua, 1990.
___. *Liu Mengde wenji* 劉夢得文集. *SBCK*.
___. *Liu Binke wenji* 劉賓客文集. *SBBY*.
——. *Liu Binke jiahua lu* 劉賓客嘉話錄. *TDCS*.
___. *Liu Yuxi ji* 劉禹錫集. Zhu Zheng 朱澂, ed. Shanghai: Shanghai Guji, 1975. A modern typeset edition based on the *Liu Binke wenji* in the *Jieyilu shengyu congshu* 結一盧賸餘叢書.
Quan Tang shi, 6: 3973–4142, 11: 8988, 13: 9894, 14: 10654, 15: 11290–91.
Quan Tang wen, 599–610.6802–909.

Annotations:
Jiang Weisong 蔣維崧, ed. *Liu Yuxi ji biannian jianzhu* 劉禹錫集編年箋注. Jinan: Shandong Daxue, 1997.
Liang Shouzhong 梁守中, ed. *Liu Yuxi shixuan* 劉禹錫詩選. Hong Kong: Sanlian Shudian, 1986.
Qu Tuiyuan 瞿蛻園, ed. *Liu Yuxi ji jianzheng* 劉禹錫集箋證. Shanghai: Shanghai Guji, 1989.

Biographical Sources:
Fu, *Tang caizi*, 2:481–501.
Jiu Tang shu, 160.4210–13.
Xin Tang shu, 168.5128–32.

Translations:
Bynner, *Jade Mountain,* pp. 100–1.
Chinese Literature, 1975.6: 87–93.
Gundert, *Lyrik,* pp. 118–19.
Demiéville, *Anthologie,* p. 311.
Frankel, *Palace Lady,* pp. 97–98.
Kroll, "Recalling Xuanzong," pp. 10–11.
Margoulies, *Anthologie,* 247–48, 343.
Owen, *Anthology,* p. 505.
Owen, *Late Tang,* pp. 67–76, 187–90.
Sunflower, pp. 196–201.
Waley, *Po Chü-i,* p.168.
Yang Xianyi, *Poetry and Prose,* pp. 99–106.

Studies:
Bian Xiaoxuan 卞孝萱 and Wu Juyu 吳汝煜. *Liu Yuxi* 劉禹錫. Shanghai: Shanghai Renmin, 1980.
___. *Liu Yuxi congkao* 劉禹錫從考. Chengdu: Ba Shu, 1988, pp. 166–74.
___. *Liu Yuxi shiwen xuan zhu* 劉禹錫詩文選注. Nanjing: Jiangsu Renmin, 1980.
___. *Liu Yuxi nianpu* 劉禹錫年譜. Beijing: Zhonghua, 1963.

___ and Bian Min 卞敏. *Liu Yuxi pingzhuan* 劉禹錫評傳. Nanjing: Nanjing Daxue, 1996.
Gao Zhizhong 高志忠. *Liu Yuxi shiwen xinian* 劉禹錫詩文繫年. Nanjing: Guangxi Renmin, 1988.
Hong Yinghua 洪迎華 and Shang Yongliang 尚永亮. "Ershi shiji yilai Liu Yuxi yanjiu zongshu—yi shengping, zuopin ji wenji de wenxian xue kaosuo wei zhongxin" 二十世紀以來劉禹錫研究綜述—以生平、作品及文集的文獻學考索為中心, *Wenxian* 2 (2009).
Kemura Sanshigo, 木村三四吾. "Sōhan Ryū Mutoku bunshu kaidai" 宋版劉夢得文集解題, *Tenri biburia*, 4 (1955): 36–37.
Kroll, Paul W. "Recalling Xuanzong and Lady Yang: A Selection of Mid- and Late Tang Poems," *Tang Studies*, 35 (2017): 1–19.
Liu Weilin 劉衛林. *Song kan Liu Yuxi wenji banben yanjiu* 宋刊劉禹錫文集版本研究. Taibei: Hua Mulan Wenhua, 2008.
Luo Liantian 羅聯添, "Liu Binke jiahua lu jiaobu ji kaozheng" 劉賓客嘉話錄校補及考證 (1 & 2), *Youshi xueji*, 2.1 (January 1963): 1–39, 2.2 (April 1963): 1–50.
___. "Liu Mengde nianpu" 劉夢得年譜, *Wenshizhe xuepao*, 8 (1958): 181–295.
Luo Xiaoyu 羅筱玉. "Shilun zhong Tang shifeng tuishan zhi ji de Liu Yuxi" 試論中唐詩風蛻嬗之際的劉禹錫, *Qi Lu xuekan*, 3 (2011).
Ogawa Shōichi 小川昭一. "Ryū Ushaku ni tsuite" 劉禹錫について, *Tōyō bunka fukukan*, 10 (April 1965): 34–45.
Qu Shouyuan 屈守元 and Bian Xiaoxuan 卞孝萱. *Liu Yuxi yanjiu* 劉禹錫研究. Guiyang: Guizhou Renmin, 1989.
Richardson, Tori. "*Liu Pin-ko chia-hua lu* [A Record of an Adviser to the Heir Apparent Liu (Yü-hsi's) Fine Discourses: A Study and Translation." Unpublished Ph. D. dissertation, University of Wisconsin-Madison, 1994.
Spaar, Wilfried. "Liu Yuxi (772–842), An Annotated Bibliography of Editions, Translations, and Studies," *Bochumer Jahrbuch zur Ostasiaenforschung, Sonderdruck, 1986*, pp. 1-81.
Sun Siwang 孫思旺. "Liu Yuxi, Yuan Zhen zhenbian change shi xinian jishi bianzheng" 劉禹錫元稹枕鞭唱和詩繫年紀事辨正, *Wenxue yichan*, 2012.5.
Tang Lan 唐蘭. "*Liu Binke jialu* de jiaoji yu bianwei" 劉賓客嘉話錄的校輯與辨偽, *Wenshi* 4 (1965): 75–106.
Tao Min 陶敏 and Tao Hongyu 陶紅雨, eds. *Liu Yuxi quanji biannian jiaozhu* 劉禹錫全集編年校注. 2 vols. Changsha: Yuelu, 2003.
Wu Ruyu 吳汝煜. *Liu Yuxi zhuanlun* 劉禹錫傳論. Xi'an: Shanxi Renmin, 1988.
Xiao Ruifeng 肖瑞峰. *Liu Yuxi shi lun* 劉禹錫詩論. Hangzhou: Zhejiang Daxue, 2013.

Wolfgang Kubin and William H. Nienhauser, Jr.

Liu Zhangqing 劉長卿 (*zi*, Wenfang 文房, *hao*, Suizhou 隨州, 726–ca. 787) was one of the most important poets of his day and is the most representative poet of the period immediately following that of the major High Tang figures Wang Wei 王維 (692–761 or 699–759),* Li Bo 李白 (701–762),* and Du Fu 杜甫 (712–770).* Liu was also acquainted with a great number of other fellow writers.

He was born in Xuanzhou 宣州 (modern Xuancheng 宣城 in Anhui), but the exact year of his birth is unknown. In his youth he studied at Songshan 嵩山 (in the central part of modern Henan), but several times failed to pass the *jinshi* examination. He then became a student in the Directorate of Education. Sometime in the early 750s he passed the examination, but when the An Lushan Rebellion broke out in 756 he fled to the Southeast. In 757 he was made Commandant of

Changzhou 長州 (located in what is today the northern part of Vietnam) and the following year joined the newly organized Salt Administration. His checkered career—he was imprisoned or banished and subsequently restored to office several times—during this latter period seems to reflect the changing fortunes of his sponsors in the central government, rather than any particular merit or demerit of his own. He was generally in comfortable economic circumstances, for he owned a number of rural estates in various parts of the empire. By 780 he had been appointed to his most important official post, Prefect of Suizhou 隨州 (modern northern Hubei). He had evidently retired from this post by the last datable occurrence in his life, but it is not known where or when he died.

Over five hundred of Liu's poems are extant. Many of them are occasional pieces of no great literary interest, but they also include a number of fine landscape poems in a style that owes much to both Tao Qian 陶潛 (365–427) and Wang Wei. Although he is not included among the "Dali shi caizi" 大曆十才子 (Ten Talents of the Dali Reign), a grouping of typical—and generally mediocre—younger contemporaries, his style has much in common with theirs in its concentration on bucolic subjects and a cultivated casualness of manner. One of his poems representing this style is "Tan qin" 彈琴 (A Zither Song):

> Clear and melodious sound the seven-strings,
> To listen attentively to "Wind in the Pines" is chilling.
> Such an old tune yet I love it,
> These days people seldom play it anymore.

> 泠泠七弦上，靜聽松風寒。
> 古調雖自愛，今人多不彈。

"Wind in the pines" in line 2 could also be read as a description of the scene. As a tune title it is obviously moving for Liu Zhangqing. Tang music was in the process of a sea-change during the late eighth century as music from Central Asia gained favor and the pipa became the main instrument. So this apparently naive quatrain suggests that the poet has not followed popular taste but prefers the traditional in music and perhaps also in life.

Only a decade younger than Wang Wei and Li Bo, he clearly belongs to a very different generation. That difference was compounded by his long life and his obscurity as a younger man. Indeed, he scarcely emerged as a poet at all until after the An Lushan Rebellion, and most of his extant poems were probably written after the deaths of all the major High Tang poets except Du Fu. The persistence of the High Tang landscape manner in his work is perhaps due to his prolonged absence from the capital and his lack of involvement with advanced literary circles in the provinces. He is often grouped with Wei Yingwu 韋應物 (737–ca. 791),* but it is not certain that the two men were acquainted.

BIBLIOGRAPHY

Editions:
Chu Zhongjun 儲仲君. *Liu Zhangqing shi biannian jianzhu* 劉長卿詩編年箋註. Beijing: Zhonghua, 1996.

Liu Zhangqing

Liu Suizhou ji 劉隨州集. 10+1 *juan*. SBCK. The former is the best edition, the latter the most readily accessible.
Luan Guiming 欒貴明. *Quan Tang shi suoyin: Liu Zhangqing juan* 全唐詩索引：劉長卿卷. Beijing: Xiandai, 1995.
Quan Tang shi, 3: 1481–583.
Ruan Tingyu 阮廷瑜. *Liu Suizhou shiji jiaozhu* 劉隨州詩集校注. Taibei: Wunan Tushu, 2012.
Yang Shiming 楊世明. *Liu Zhangqing ji biannian jiaozhu* 劉長卿集編年校注. Beijing: Renmin Wenxue, 1999.

Biographical Sources:
Fu, *Tang caizi*, 1:311–26, 5:57–60.

Translations:
Bynner, *Jade Mountain*, pp. 70–74.
Gundert, *Lyrik*, p. 98.
Minford and Lau, pp. 831–34.
Owen, *High Tang*, pp. 258–61, 265–66, and 281–82.
Sunflower, pp. 116–17.
Watson, *Columbia*, p. 276.

Studies:
Akai Masuhisa 赤井益久. "Ryū Chōkei shiron—Chōshū ken I toki no sataku o chūshin ni" 劉長卿詩論—長洲縣尉時の左謫を中心に, in his *Chūtō shidan no kenkyūu* 中唐詩壇の研究. Tokyo: Sōbunsha, 2004.
Chen Shunzhi 陳順智. "*Liu Zhangqing ji* banben kaoshu" 劉長卿集版本考述, *Tangdai wenxue yanjiu* (2002): 396–406.
___. "Lun Liu Zhangqing shige de fengge" 論劉長卿詩歌的風格, *Shehui kexue yanjiu* 3 (2000): 134–39.
Chen Xiaoqiang 陳曉薔. "Liu Zhangqing shengping shiji chukao" 劉長卿生平事跡初考, *Dalu zazhi*, 29.3–5 (1964): 81–84, 129–34, 170–75. Thorough study of Liu's biography with a collection of comments by traditional critics appended.
Du Shuifeng 杜水封. "Suizhou qilü shangxi" 隨州七律賞析, *Xueshu lunwen jikan*, 3 (1976): 97–134. Discussion of thirty of Liu's heptasyllabic regulated verse poems, preceded by a detailed gathering of biographical and critical materials.
Fang Rixi 房日晰. "Liu Zhangqing jiguan wei Luoyang buzheng" 劉長卿籍貫為洛陽補證, *Zhongzhou xuekan* 5 (1982): 95.
Fu Xuancong 傅璇琮. "Liu Zhangqing shiji kaobian" 劉長卿事跡考辯, in his *Tang dai shiren congkao* 唐代詩人叢考. Beijing: Zhonghua, 1980, pp. 238–68.
Gao Lintao 郜林濤. "Liu Zhangqin beibian Nan Ba shiji" 劉長卿被貶南巴事跡, *Zhongguo dianji yu wenhua* 1 (2002): 16–19.
He Jianping 何劍平. "Liu Zhangqing yu Fojiao xiangguan shiji kao" 劉長卿與佛教相關事跡考, *Wuhan Daxue xuebao (Renwenke Xueban)*, 62.4 (Sept. 2009): 528–33.
Jiang Yin 蔣寅. "Liu Zhangqing yu Tangshi fanshi de yanbian" 劉長卿與唐詩範式的演變, *Wenxue pinglun* 1 (1994): 41–52.
Kominami Ichirō 小南一郎. "Ryū Chōkei" 劉長卿, in Ogawa, *Tōdai*, pp. 266–70. A heavily annotated translation of the biography of Liu in the *Tang caizi zhuan*.
Lee, Oscar. "The Critical Perception of the Poetry of Wei Yingwu (737–792): The Cretation of a Poetic Reputation." Unpublished Ph.D dissertation. Columbia University, 1986, pp. 108–18.
Liu Qian 劉乾. "Liu Zhangqing shi zakao" 劉長卿詩雜考, *Wenxian* 1 (1989): 3–15.

Takahashi Yoshiyuki 高橋良行. "Ryū Chōkei shū tembon kō" 劉長卿集伝本考, *Chūgoku bungaku kenkyū (Waseda Daigaku)*, 3 (1978): 52–71. A thorough study of the textual history of Liu's works.

Daniel Bryant, Yiwen Shen, and William H. Nienhauser, Jr.

Liu Zhiji 劉知幾 *(zi,* Zixuan 子玄, 661–721), *jinshi,* ca. 680, primarily known as a critic of historical writing, was a scholar-official whose service in the metropolitan academic institutions of the Tang spanned the period from 699 until he was banished from the capital in the year of his death. He compiled or took part in the compilation of at least twelve works, was briefly a rescript writer, and participated in scholarly debates on Confucian canonical texts, on their commentaries, and on state ritual prescriptions. He also wrote verse. One of his highest posts was that of Commandant of the Heir Apparent's Guard Command after which he was transferred to become Vice Director of the Palace Library. He was posthumously canonized "Wen" 文.

Liu Zhiji's *Shitong* 史通 (Generalities on Historiography), the work that has given him his reputation, was completed in 710. Attempting to do for the discipline of history what Liu Xie's *Wenxin diaolong* 文心雕龍 did for that of belles lettres, it critically surveyed all aspects of historical scholarship from its origins in Confucian canonical texts to the compilations by the early Tang official historians who were Liu's immediate predecessors in the history office. Comprising thirty-six "inner sections" and thirteen "outer sections," it opens with a description of six schools of history writing in antiquity, and then focuses on two of them, *biannian* 編年 (chronicle) and *jizhuan* 紀傳 (composite), as the models followed in later times. Then it reviews in detail the constituent parts of the composite model, principally the *benji* 本紀 (basic annals), *liezhuan* 列傳 (biographies), and *shuzhi* 書志 (treatises). After this come a number of sections on technical matters, such as the appropriate span of a history, terms by which figures in it should be referred to, titles, and commentaries. A group of sections is concerned with style, narrative imitation, the technique, the problems of imitation, the desirability of concise diction, and the need for moral objectivity. The "outer" portion of the work opens with an account of the history office, first founded as a separate institution by the Tang itself in 629. It follows with an description of its precursors, reviews the sequence of "orthodox" (*zheng* 正) histories produced for successive dynasties, and goes on to collect Liu's criticisms of Confucian canonical historical texts, the *Shujing* 書經 and the *Chunqiu* 春秋 and to plead the special value as history of the *Zuozhuan* 左傳. Further sections gather Liu's miscellaneous judgments and his criticisms of the "Wuxingzhi" 五行志 (Monograph on the Five Phases) in the *Han shu,* a piece that he considered undisciplined and unreliable. Liu's letter of 708 to Xiao Zhizhong 蕭至忠 (d. 713), director of the dynastic history, attempting to resign from the history office, is appended as a final section.

The *Shitong* is a work of wide erudition and brave critical insight, for Liu draws from, or refers to, nearly three hundred works and cites an even larger number of authors. Despite a highly moralistic perspective, it conveys a sense of romantic enthusiasm for history writing and for the role of the individual historian. Liu's independent imagination also led him to believe that classical antiquity, despite differences in dress, speech, and mores, was not radically different from his own time and was by no means as utopian as convention accepted it to be. His belief in the function of history as a register of change led him to suggest, from within the discipline of

Liu Zhiji

history as Tang scholars understood it in its broadest sense, new topics for treatises in composite-form histories.

Yet for all his strikingly organic understanding of the past, he believed that the compilation of histories was a discipline governed by strict formal rules and capable of great precision and consistency, and he never broke free of the classificatory, schematic approach to learning that characterized official scholarship in Tang times.

Liu's sense of compartmentalization led him to demarcate history from literary composition or belles lettres, and the importance of the *Shitong* to the literary historian, an incidental result of Liu's main purpose, derives from the concern he expressed in it for the concise narrative style and diction. Probably no other writer of the medieval period stated so clearly what he considered desirable in narrative prose.

Running through Liu's critique of style is a demand that only the essential be included. He seems to have been exhilarated by brevity and condemned any hint of wordiness. Conjunctions, interjections, and other particles were to be considered carefully. Parenthetical or editorial remarks were to be included only if they contributed substantially to the sense. Liu was known to consider the laconic writer to be already comprehensive within a single expression. Liu identified four basic narrative techniques: describing a man's qualities directly; letting his actions speak for themselves; letting the facts be known through direct speech; and expounding them in supplementary essays or assessments.

If his comments were restricted to narrative in official histories, it was precisely this category of writing, commanding great prestige in the medieval scholarly world, that set the tone for other narrative genres—the countless biographies, epitaphs, and reports of conduct, and beyond them the less formal sources, collections of vignettes and anecdotes, and even *chuanqi* 傳奇 (tales).

Some of his ideas on historiography can be found in his letter written to resign his post as a historiographer towards the end of his life. This passage is the first of his obstacles to continuing to serve in the position:

> The histories of states in ancient times all were produced by one scholar, like [Zuo] Qiuming of Lu and Zichang[Sima Qian (145–ca. 86 BC], Dong Hu of Jin and the anonymous Qi author of the *History of the Southern Dynasties*, they were all able to expound their ideas in an immortal work of history, and deposit leave it for transmission to posterity. No one has heard of a text that was the effort of a number of men, that was a superb work. Only with the East Belvedere of the Later Han (i.e., the *Notes on the Han from the East Belvedere*), was there a gathering of a group of scholars who wrote without one master, and there were no rules of composition established. Because of this Li Fa (fl. 100) criticized its lack of truth and Zhongchang Tong thought that it might well be burned, Zhang Heng and Cai Yong denounced it in (180–220) its own age and Fu Xuan (217–278) and Fan Ye (398–445) jeered it in later ages. Now our Bureau of Historiography has chosen as many **sc**holars as in the Eastern Capital [who compiled the *Notes on the Han from the East Belvedere*] and each of use regards himself as having the talent of a Xun Yue (148–209) or a Yuan Hong (328–376), the learning of Liu Xiang (77–6 BC) or Liu Xin (25–1 BC) Whenever we want to write down an event, or record a statement, we all stop writing and look around at each other, moistening our brushes without stop. Thus we may expect our hair to turn white and the green strips (early histories were written on bamboo strips) of our histories will never be finished.

古之國史,皆出自一家,如魯、漢之丘明、子長,晉、齊之董狐、南史,鹹能立言不朽,藏諸名山。未聞藉以眾功,方雲絕筆。唯後漢東觀,大集群儒,著述無主,條章靡立。由是伯度譏其不實,公理以為可焚,張、衡。蔡邕。二子糾之於當代,傅、玄。 范曄。兩家嗤之於後葉。今者史司取士,有倍東京。人自以為荀、袁,家自稱為政、駿。謂劉向、歆。每欲記一事,載一言,皆擱筆相視,含毫不斷。故頭白可期,而汗青無日。

The Tang began with the goal of compiling official histories for the many dynasties after the Three Kingdoms, each an imperial ordered work (see Xu Jingzong*). Liu Zhiji here rehearses the great historians of antiquity (Zuo Qiuming, Sima Qian, etc.), then points to the critics of the first compilation by a group of scholars before arguing that the Tang has codified this faulty method of writing history.

Although the following poem, "Du *Han shu* zuo" 讀漢書作 (Written on Reading the *History of the Han*), is undated, it was possibly written sometime after Emperor Xuanzong took the throne in 712, and Liu Zhiji may have intended for his own relationship to Xuanzong to be seen as comparable to that of Zhang Liang 張良 under Emperor Gaozu:

> The King of Han possessed all under heaven,
> Rising suddenly from among commoners.
> Spreading his wings to fly from a grass-filled pond,
> Roaring loudly he drove a band of heroes.
> Han Xin having attached himself to the phoenix,
> Qing Bu and Peng Yue also held to his dragon scales.
> In a single morning they encountered their fortune—
> When he faced South they all became kings and marquises.
> Once the fish was caught, he naturally forgot about the traps,
> When the birds were gone, he was sure to put away the bow.
> Those who reprimand met with boiling pot and chopping block.
> Clans wiped out clans without a trace.
> How wise was Zhang Zifang!
> Who alone was skilled at adjusting to circumstances.
> For his merit achieved merit he received little love,
> He raised himself high to follow Red Pine.
> He understood when to stop, his trustworthiness unstained.
> His body at ease, his Way became popular.
> Now after a thousand long years
> I beat out this song and look up to his legacy.

漢王有天下, 欻起布衣中。
奮飛出草潭, 嘯咤馭群雄。
淮陰既附鳳, 黥彭亦攀龍。
一朝逢運會, 南面皆王侯。
魚得自忘筌, 鳥盡必藏弓。
咄嗟罹鼎俎, 赤族無遺蹤。
智哉張子房, 處世獨為工。
功成薄愛賞, 高舉追赤松。
知正信無辱, 身安道亦隆。
悠悠千載後, 擊抃仰遺風。

Liu Zhiji

The poem is based on the basic annals of Han Gaozu and the biographies of Han Xin 韓信, Qing Bu 黥布, Peng Yue 彭越, and Zhang Liang 張良 (i.e. Zhang Zifang) as they appear in the *History of the Han*; it contains a number of shared passages with these biographies or allusions to them. Liu Zhiji distinguishes the former three generals who were all made kings by Gaozu and who subsequently revolted against the emperor, to Zhang Liang who chose to follow the famous recluse Red Pine (Chisong 赤松) who withdrew from the affairs of the world and eventually achieved immortality.

BIBLIOGRAPHY

Editions:
Gagnon, G. and E. Gagnon. *Concordance combinée du Shitong et du Shitong Xiaofan*. 2v. Paris: A. Maisonneuve, 1977.
Liu Zhiji. *Shitong* 史通. Li Yongqi 李永圻 and Zhang Genghua 張耕華, eds. Shanghai: Shanghai Shiji, 2008. Incorporates the commentaries of Pu Qilong 浦起龍 (1679–1762).
___. Shitong 史通 and *Shitong zhaji* 史通札記. Sun Yuxiu 孫毓修 (1871–1922), ed. Rpt. of 1602 edition. *SBCK*.

___. *Shitong tongshi* 史通通釋. Edited with commentary by Pu Qilong 浦起龍 (1679–1762), ed. Revised by Pu Xiling 浦錫齡, 1893, *SBBY*.
Quan Tang wen, 274.3105–17.

Annotations:
Cheng Qianfan 程千帆 (1913–2000), comm. *Shitong jianji* 史通箋記. Beijing: Zhonghua, 1980.
Liu Zhanshao 劉占召. *Shitong pingzhu* 史通評注. Beijing: Zhuangyang Bianyi, 2010.
Zhang Sanxi 張三夕 and Li Cheng 李程, annot. *Shitong* 史通. Nanjing: Fenghuang, 2013.
Zhang Zhenpei 張振珮. *Shitong jianzhu* 史通箋注. Guiyang: Guizhou Renmin, 1985.

Biographical Sources:
Jiu Tang shu, 102.3168–76.
Xin Tang shu, 132.4519–25.

Translations:
Chaussende, Damien. *Liu Zhiji, Traité de l'historien parfait, Chapitres intérieurs*. Paris: Les Belles Lettres, 2014.
Masui Tsuneo 増井經夫. *Shitsū: Tōdai no rekishikan* 史通，唐代の歷史觀. Tokyo: Heibonsha, 1966. With introduction and index.
Nishiwaki Tsuneki 西脇常記. *Shitō naihen* 史通內篇. Tokyo: Tokyo Daigaku, 1989.
___. *Shitō gaihen* 史通外篇. Tokyo: Tokyo Daigaku, 2002.
Sargent, Stuart H. "'Understanding History: The Narration of Events,' by Liu Chih-chi (661–721)," in *The Translation of Things Past: Chinese History and Historiography*, George Kao, ed., Hong Kong: Renditions, 1982.
Xiong, Victor Cunrui, *A Thorough Exploration in Historiography* (Shitong 史通) by Liu Zhiji 劉知幾 (661-721): Annotated translation with an introduction. Seattle: University of Washington, forthcoming.
Yao Song 姚松 and Zhu Hengfu 朱恒夫. *Shitong quanyi* 史通全譯. Guiyang: Guizhou Renmin, 1990.
Yi Yun-hwa 이윤화. *Sat'ong t'ongsŏk* 史通通釋, 4 vols. Seoul: Somyŏng Ch'ulp'an, 2012.

Studies:

Chaussende, Damien. "Un historien sur le banc des accusés: Liu Zhiji sur Weishou," *Études chinoises*, 29 (2010): 141–80.

Fu Zhenlun 傅振倫. *Liu Zhiji nianpu* 劉知幾年譜. 3rd ed. Rpt. Beijing: Zhonghua, 1963 (1934).

___. *Shitong zuozhe Liu Zhiji yanjiu* 史通作者劉知幾研究. Taibei: Wenxing Shudian, 1963.

___. *Tang Liu Zixuan Xianshen Zhiji nianpu* 唐劉子宣先生知幾年譜. Taibei: Shangwu, 1982.

Gagnon, Guy. "La Notion d'histoire chez Liu Zhiji (661–721), fonctionnaire-historien à l'époque des Tang." Unpublished Ph.D. dissertation, University of Paris-VII, 1988.

___. "La postface personnelle de Liu Zhiji au *Shitong*: un easai d'ego-histoire," in Jean-Pierre Drège, ed. *De Dunhuang au Japon, Études chinoises et bouddhiques offertes à Michel Soymié*. Paris: Droz, 1996, pp. 337–69.

Hung, William. "A Bibliographical Controversy at the T'ang Court A.D. 719," *HJAS*, 20 (1957), 74–134.

___. "*Shitong* 'Dianfan pian' yibu" 史通點煩篇臆補, *Shixue nianbao* 史學年報, 2.2 (1935): 149–60.

___. "A Tang Historiographer's Letter of Resignation," *HJAS*, 29 (1969), 5–52.

Koh, Byongik. "Zur Werttheorie in der chinesische Historiographie auf Grund des *Shih t'ung* des Liu Chih-chi (661–721)," *OE*, 4 (1957): 5–51, 125–81.

Liu Weisheng 劉衛生. "Liu Zhiji cifu de shijia lichang ji qi yiyi" 劉知幾辭賦的史家立場及其意義, *Zhongguo yunxue xuekan* 中國韻學學刊, 2015.3: 78–83.

Ma Tiehao 馬鐵浩. *Shitong yu xian Tang dianji* 史通與先唐典籍. Beijing: Xueyuan, 2010.

___. *Shitong yinshu kao* 史通引書考. Beijing: Xueyuan, 2011.

Masui Tsuneo 增井經夫. "Liu Chih-chi and the *Shih t'ung*," *Memoirs of the Research Department of the Toyo Bunko*, 34 (1978): 113–62.

Peng Yaling 彭雅玲. *Shitong de lishi xushu lilun* 史通的歷史敘述理論. Taibei: Wenshizhe Chuabanshe, 1993.

Pulleyblank, E. G. Chinese Historical Criticism: Liu Chih-chi and Ssu-ma Kuang," in W. G. Beasley and E. G. Pulleyblank, eds., *Historians of China and Japan*. London: Oxford University, 1961, pp. 135–66.

Quirin, Michael. "Beitrage zur Erforschung von Liu Zhiji's *Shi Tong*." Unpublished M.A. thesis, Rheinischen Friedrich-Wilhelms-University, Bonn, 1980.

___. *Liu Zhiji und das Chun Qiu*. Frankfurt: Peter Lang, 1987.

Schinköthe, Ailika. "Liu Zhiji's *Shitong* and its Revival in Ming Dynasty—Pacing Historiography Anew." Ph. D. dissertation, University of Tübingen, 2018.

Wang Jiachuan 王嘉川 (2013), *Qingqian Shitong xue yanjiu* 清前《史通》学研研究. Beijing: Shehui Kexue Wenxian, 2013.

Xu Guansan 許冠三. *Liu Zhiji de shilu shixue* 劉知幾的實錄史學. Hong Kong: Zhongwen Daxue, 1983.

Xu Lingyun 許凌雲. *Liu Zhiji pingzhuan* 劉知幾評傳. Nanjing: Nanjing Daxue, 1994.

Yeung Man Shun 楊文信. "*Shitong* shanben zongshu: yi Ming Qing liangdai kanben, chaoben wei zhongxin" 史通善本綜述：以明清兩代刊本，鈔本為中心, in *Ming Qing shi jikan* 明清史季刊, 5(2001): 269–321.

___. "Shixue pinglun yu zhengzhi—cong Qingchao de *Shitong* xue tanqi" 嗜血評論與政治—從清朝的史通學談起, in Shan Zhouyao 單周堯, ed., *Ming Qing xueshu yanjiu* 明清學術研究. Beijing: Zhongguo Shehui Kexue, pp. 297–320.

Zhang Sanxi 張三夕. *Pipan shixue de pipan: Liu Zhiji ji qi Shitong yanjiu* 批判史學的批判：劉知幾及其史通研究. Taibei: Wenjin, 1992.

Zhuang Wanshou 莊萬壽. *Shitong tonglun* 史通通論. Taibei: Wanjuanlou Tushu Gongsi, 2009.

David L. McMullen and William H. Nienhauser, Jr.

Liu Zongyuan

Liu Zongyuan 柳宗元 (*zi*, Zihou 子厚, also known as Liu Liuzhou 柳柳州 and Liu Hedong 柳河東, 773–819) is traditionally recognized as a master essayist of the *Guwen yundong* 古文運動 (Ancient-style Prose Movement) and one of the most eclectic minds of his era. His ancestry as a member of the Hedong Liu Clan (based near modern Yuncheng 運城 in Shanxi) goes back to officials of the Jin dynasty (317–421). His great-great uncle, Liu Shi 柳奭 (d. 659) served as Grand Councilor under Tang Gaozong until he was executed in 659 after opposing Wu Zetian's elevation to empress.

Liu was born and spent his first ten years in the Tang capital, Chang'an. Thereafter he went with his father, Liu Zhen 柳鎮 (d. 793), a graduate of the *mingjing* (clarifying the classics) examination (756), to several provincial locations before he was recommended at age nineteen as a prefectural nominee for the *jinshi* examination. He passed that examination in 793 at age twenty to much acclaim. Later that year Liu Zhen died and Liu went into mourning. Returning to official life in 796, he passed the special Literatus Examination under Lü Wei 呂渭 (735–800, Lü Wen's 呂溫 [772–811]* father), married a daughter of Yang Ping 楊憑, and was appointed Editor in the Palace Library to work on the imperial diary, a choice position for new graduates. Later that same year he was made Commandant of Lantian 藍田 (about 20 miles southeast of the capital). Under the aegis of Wang Shuwen 王叔文 (753–806) and his faction who were strongly supporting reducing the power of the eunuchs with the support of Li Song 李誦 (761–806), the imperial Heir, Liu was promoted rapidly to be Investigating Censor in 803 and later that year Vice Director of the Ministry of Rites, in charge of court rituals and the *jinshi* examination. After Emperor Dezong died in 805, Liu's career reached its height under the new Emperor Shunzong (r. 805). Shunzong, however, was forced to abdicate because of a severe illness after ruling only a few months (he died early in 806) and the new Emperor, Xianzong (r. 805–820), banished all members of Wang's clique. Assigned to be Vice Prefect (a sinecure at the time) in Yongzhou 永州 (modern Lingling 零陵 county in Hunan) in 805, he was recalled to the capital a decade later, only to be reassigned immediately as Prefect in the aboriginal region of Liuzhou 柳州 (modern Guangxi) where he died in 819.

His earliest writings (before his exile to Yongzhou) are primarily bureaucratic, but they served to mark him as a stylist of documentary prose and to win him a reputation among his colleagues in the capital. This group may also have provided Liu's first contacts with members of the Ancient-style Prose Movement. Many of these colleagues joined him in promoting the studies of what has been called "Neo-Legalism" based on the iconoclastic *Chunqiu* 春秋 scholarship of Lu Chun 陸淳 (d. 806). Their influence can be seen in Liu's numerous textual studies such as his critiques of the authenticity of *Kangcang Zi* 亢倉子 or *Heguang Zi* 鶡冠子, and his determination that the *Lunyu* 論語 was compiled by disciples of Zeng Zi 曾子. A similar approach can be seen in the "Fei *Kuoyu*" 非國語 (Contra *Conversations of the States*), an attack on the superstitions and unfounded traditions of this early "history." Indeed, Liu himself claims that during this period he considered literature only a means to forward his career.

It was not until he was exiled that literature began to dominate his life. About 400 of his over 500 prose pieces were written in Yongzhou. Before he arrived in Yongzhou, however, Liu began to adopt the literary garb of a neglected or banished official in works like "Diao Qu Yuan wen" 弔屈原文 (A Lament for Qu Yuan), written when he arrived in Tanzhou 潭州 (near modern Changsha City 長沙市 about 120 miles north of Yongzhou in Hunan). While in Yongzhou he perfected the euphuistic style of prose in numerous *fu* 賦, *sao* 騷, and landscape essays. The later corpus, most notably the "Yongzhou baji" 永州八記 (Eight Records [of Excursions] in Yongzhou) established the *youji* 遊記 (records of excursions) as a subgenre and gained Liu a position as a major stylist in Chinese literary history. The fourth of these essays, "Zhi Xiaochiu xi Xiaoshi Tan ji" 至小丘西小石潭記 (A Record of Reaching the Little Rock Pond West of the Little Hillock), dating probably to 810, is typical:

> If you walk one hundred twenty paces west of the Little Hillock, separated by a copse of bamboo, you will hear the sound of water, like the sound of jade pendants tinkling, and I took pleasure in it. I had the bamboo cut down to open a path and below saw a small pond. The water was clear and pure. One entire rock made up the bottom; as it approached the bank the rock emerged [from the surface], curling up to form bars, islets, peaks and pinnacles. Verdant creepers wrap the green trees, entwining branches shade and sway together as they bob in the breeze.
>
> There are more than one hundred fish in the pond, all seeming to swim along in empty space with nothing to support them. The rays of the sun penetrate deep into the water, spreading their shadows on the rocky [bottom], contentedly suspended in motion–all of a sudden distancing themselves, rapidly coming and going, as if sharing their pleasure with we wanderers.
>
> Looking off southwest of the pond, its waters bend like the Big Dipper or a snake moving– where they shine or disappear quite clear. Its banks shaped like the teeth of a dog, so [jagged and winding] that I could not realize its source. Sitting down above the pond, I was completely surrounded on four sides by bamboo and trees. It was lonely with no one there, my spirit turned cold and my bones were chilled, saddening me deeply. I considered this scene too pure and could not stay there long, so I recorded this and left.
>
> Those who went wandering with me were [the literatus] Wu Wuling, Gong Gu, and my younger brother Zongxuan. Those who came along and served us were the two young men of the Cui household, called Shuji and Fengyi.

> 從小丘西行百二十步，隔篁竹聞水聲，如鳴佩環，心樂之。伐竹取道，下見小潭，水尤清冽。全石以為底，近岸卷石底以出，為坻為嶼，為嵁為巖。青樹翠蔓，蒙絡搖綴，參差披拂。潭中魚可百許頭，皆若空遊無所依。日光下澈，影布石上，怡然不動；俶爾遠逝，往來翕忽，似與遊者相樂。
> 潭西南而望，斗折蛇行，明滅可見。其岸勢犬牙差互，不可知其源。坐潭上，四面竹樹環合，寂寥無人，淒神寒骨，悄愴幽邃。以其境過清，不可久居，乃記之而去。
> 同遊者吳武陵龔古，予弟宗玄。隸而從者崔氏二小生，曰恕己，曰奉壹。

Here is the standard style Liu uses for these records: first he situates the location precisely in terms of his previous records, then in a splendid style reminiscent of parallel prose and replete with metaphors he describes the location; then comes Liu's emotional reaction to the scene; finally, in a coda he notes his fellow travelers. This combination served to mentally transport countless readers in both the Tang and thereafter to these eight scenic spots.

In addition to his musings on the local landscape, Liu's interest in the didactic functions of literature grew during this exile, as can be seen in various letters on the subject. Many of his epistles are, however, tied to his personal political misfortunes, such as his letter to his cousin Xiao Mian 蕭俛 (d. 842), "Yu Xiao Mian shu" 與蕭翰林俛書 (A Letter to Hanlin Academician Xiao

Liu Zongyuan

Miao) in which he first congratulates Xiao on being selected to serve in the Hanlin Academy and then relates his own dismal situation in exile. Those who "sought to advance but withdrew" are probably members of the Wang Shuwen clique who were able to deny their relationship to Wang and to Liu. This may explain why during Liu's ten years of exile in Yongzhou he was never recalled:

> Your humble servant has been unfortunate and in the past in an unstable and unsafe situation I have dwelt at peace behind a closed gate, speaking little, and even less have I been able to enjoy the company of old friends, let alone risk going to their gates. As for those who sought to advance but withdrew [from court], they have all joined together in hatred, creatively hiding the truth, increasingly unrestrained.

> 僕不幸,向者進當脆瓠不安之勢,平居閉門,口舌無數,況又有久與遊者,乃岌岌而造其門哉。 其求進而退者,皆聚為仇怨,造作粉飾,蔓延益肆。

In more public writings Liu was more cautious, showing himself to be a master of general allegories. The "Bushezhe shuo" 捕蛇者說 (Discourse of a Snake-catcher) tells of a man who prefers snaring poisonous snakes and presenting their venom to court to paying taxes (so onerous were the taxes!); "Zhongshu Guo Tuotuo zhuan" 種樹郭橐駝傳 (Hunchback Guo the Gardener) suggests that the effective, albeit passive, techniques of this old gardener might serve as a model for high-ranking politicians in their treatment of the common people. Both are masterpieces of this form. In other allegorical works such as "Niu Fu" 牛賦 (Prose-poem on the Ox), "Linjiang zhi mi" 臨江之麋 (Deer of Linjiang), or "Fuban zhuan" 蝜蝂傳 (Account of the Dung Beetles), a strong Daoist influence, especially from *Zhuang Zi*, can be seen. Primarily on the basis of this exile corpus Liu Zongyuan was later included, along with Han Yu 韓愈 (768–824), as one of two Tang dynasty members of the Eight Great Prose Masters of the Tang and Song (Tang Song bada sanwenjia 唐宋八大散文家).

His poetry (only 180-some pieces) is considered to have been influenced by earlier "nature poets": Xie Lingyun 謝靈運 (385–433), Wang Wei 王維 (692–761 or 699–759) * Meng Haoran 孟浩然 (689–740),* and Wei Yingwu 韋應物 (737–ca. 791).* Although clearly a Mid-Tang poet, Liu's verse is atavistic, resembling that of the High Tang–little influence of early ninth century poetic movements such as Han Yu's "prosification" of poetry, the *Xin Yuefu* 新樂府 (New Music-Bureau Verse), or the proto-*ci* 詞 (lyric), can be seen in his verse. *Yuefu* titles such as "Gu Dongmen xing" 古東門行 or "Xinglu nan" 行路難 become allusive and allegorical in Liu's hands. Nature and historical themes were his primary concerns. Though he is accorded the status of a minor poet, his "Jiangxue" 江雪 (River Snow), which depicts a solitary fisherman clad in wet-weather gear, is a poem known to every literate Chinese:

> Over a thousand peaks, flight of birds is stopped,
> On ten thousand paths, tracks of men wiped out.
> In a single boat an old man in a straw hat and coat
> Fishes alone in the cold river snow.

千山鳥飛絕，萬徑人踪滅，
孤舟蓑笠翁，獨釣寒江雪.

This simple poem has a complex structure. The first two lines set the scene: a limitless snow scape in which neither the foreground nor the horizon can be clearly seen. The birds and men that occupy day to day life are suddenly obliterated. This is no diurnal landscape, but a word painting of purity. The verbs of the first two lines, *jue* 絕 "stop" or "cut off" and *mie* 滅 "wipe out," cleanse both the natural and secular. The third line contains no verbs which allows the reader to focus on what can be seen: the old fisherman in his straw raincoat who appears backgrounded by the river where the snow is of course melting as it touches the surface of the water. In juxtaposition to the thousand peaks and ten thousand paths of the first two lines, here there is only a single boat and a fisherman alone. But by focusing on this solitary image, the expanse of the snow is heightened. Given the resolve of this fisherman to persevere in such surroundings, it may be that Liu Zongyuan is suggesting his own condition in distant exile in Yongzhou. The resonances with the last lines of the seventh poem of Du Fu's 杜甫 (712–770) "Qiu xing" 秋興 (Autumn Meditations) series— „"Over the pass, all the way to the sky, a road for none but the birds / On rivers and lakes to the ends of the earth, one old fisherman" 關塞極天唯鳥道, 江湖滿地一漁翁—enhances such a reading.

Another well-known piece, "Xiju" 溪居 (Dwelling Brookside), which extols the free and easy lifestyle Liu sometimes enjoyed in exile:

> Long pinned and strapped to official life,
> It was fortune that exiled me to these Southern tribes.
> Leisure has me neighbor to farms and gardens,
> Chance made me resemble a guest of the mountains and forests.
>
> In the morning my plow turns over the dewy grasses,
> In the evening my oars splash echoing off rocks in the brook.
> Coming or going I meet no one
> Belting out my song in the blue skies of Chu.

> 久為簪組束，幸此南夷謫。
> 閑依農圃鄰，偶似山林客。
> 曉耕翻露草，夜榜響溪石。
> 來往不逢人，長歌楚天碧.

This piece might be read ironically in view of the countless poems and letters surrounding it in the text, poems and letters which lament life in the provinces, which appeal to friends for assistance in having him reassigned to the capital, or which portray his longing for his home in the northwest. "Yu Haochu Shangren tong kanshan ji jinghua qingu" 與浩初上人同看山寄京華親故 (Viewing Mountains with His Reverence Haochu to Send to Old Friends and Relatives in the Capital):

> These coastal jagged mountains, like sword points,
> Since autumn's come, they always cleave my grieving heart.

> If I could transform my body into millions of selves,
> I would scatter them atop the peaks to gaze towards home.

海畔尖山似劍芒，秋來處處割愁腸。
若為化作身千億，散向峰頭望故鄉。

Some of these appeals were also allegorical, ostensibly describing a bird or an animal–"Fang zhegu ci" 放鷓鴣詞 (Releasing the Chukar) is typical. Other Buddhist-influenced poems such as "Chen ye Chao Shi yuan du Chan jing" 晨謁超師院讀禪經 (Paying an Early Morning Visit to Priest Chao's Courtyard to Study the Chan Sutras) indicate again that Liu found solace at times during his long banishment.

Although his Buddhist and even Daoist learnings are sometimes stressed, Liu Zongyuan approached both religions in the spirit of a Confucian. That is to say, he was a precursor of the Neo-Confucians of the early Song who were also not averse to Daoist or Buddhist notions. In works such as his "Tian shuo" 天說 (Discourse on Heaven), in which he argued his views of heaven with Liu Yuxi 劉禹錫 (772–842),* or the "Xiao shicheng shan ji" 小石城山記 (Record of [an Excursion to] the Mountain of Little Stone City Walls), in which he speculates on the existence of a "creator," Liu shows himself more concerned with developing a valid philosophy, than in adhering to any particular established school.

BIBLIOGRAPHY

Editions:

Guxun Liu Xiansheng wenji 詁訓柳先生文集. *Siku quanshu zhenben* ed. Descends from corpus as put together by Liu's literary executor, Liu Yuxi–most complete traditional edition.

Liu Hedong ji 柳河東集. 2v. Shanghai: Zhonghua, 1961; rev. rpt., 1974. Includes Liu's official biography; based on Song *Hedong Xiansheng ji* 河東先生集 printed by Shicai Tang 世綵堂. Punctuated in traditional fashion; reliable and easily available.

Liu Zongyuan ji 柳宗元集. Wu Wenzhi 吳文治, ed. 4v. Beijing: Zhonghua, 1979. An excellent critical edition which combines the traditional commentaries with extensive textual notes. Contains a preface and two appendixes–a list of all traditional commentaries and a colophon which discusses editions.

Liu Zongyuan jiaozhu ji 柳宗元校注集. Yin Zhanhua 尹占華 and Han Wenqi 韓文奇, eds. 10v. Beijing: Zhonghua, 2013. Includes extensive textual notes and adds twelve prose works in a *waiji bu* 外集補 section along with the text of the *Longcheng lu* 龍城錄; a *nianbiao* 年表 (chronological biography), an extensive bibliography, and an index to works cited by Liu Zongyuan are appended.

Luan Guiming 欒貴明, et al., eds. *Quan Tangshi suoyin, Liu Zongyuan juan* 全唐詩索引，柳宗元卷. Beijing: Xiandai, 1995.

Quan Tang shi, 6: 3926–72.

Quang Tang wen, 569–93.6520–754.

Wu Wenzhi 吳文治. *Liu Zongyuan shiwen shijiuzhong shanben yiwen huilu* 柳宗元詩文十九種善本異文匯錄. Hefei: Huang Shan Shushe, 2004.

___. *Liu Zongyuan ziliao huibian* 柳宗元資料彙編. Beijing: Zhonghua, 2006.

___. and Xie Hanqiang 謝漢強, ed. *Liu Zongyuan dacidian* 柳宗元大辭典. Hefei: Huang Shan Shushe, 2004.

Zengguang zhushi yinbian Tang Liu Xiansheng ji 增廣註釋音辨唐柳先生集. *SBCK*. An important early edition based upon three earlier Song commentaries; noted for its glosses of difficult words.

Annotations:

Gao Wen 高文 and Qu Guang 屈光, eds. *Liu Zongyuan xuanji* 柳宗元選集. Shanghai: Shanghai Guji, 1992.
Gu Yisheng 顧易生 and Hu Shiming 胡士明. *Liu Zongyuan jiqi zuopin xuan: Liu Zongyuan; Liu Zongyuan shiwen xuanzhu* 柳宗元及其作品選：柳宗元；柳宗元詩文選注. Shanghai: Shanghai Guji, 1998.
Meng Erdong 孟二冬. *Han Yu, Liu Zongyuan shixuan* 韓愈，柳宗元詩選. Beijing: Zhonghua, 2006.
Shang Yongliang 尚永亮. *Liu Zongyuan shiwen xuanping* 柳宗元詩文選評. Shanghai: Shanghai Guji, 2003.
Wang Guoan 王國安, ed. *Liu Zongyuan shiji jianshi* 柳宗元詩集箋釋. Shanghai: Shanghai Guji, 1993.
Wang Xiandu 汪賢度, ed. *Liu Zongyuan sanwen xuanji* 柳宗元散文選集. Shanghai: Shanghai Guji, 1997.
Wang Yunxi 王運熙. *Liu Zongyuan sanwen jingxuan* 柳宗元散文精選. Shanghai: Dongfang Chuban Zhongxin, 1998.
Wu Wenzhi 吳文治. *Liu Zongyuan xuanji* 柳宗元選集. Beijing: Renmin Wenxue, 1998.
___. *Liu Zongyuan shiwen xuanping* 柳宗元詩文選評. Xi'an: Sanqin, 2004.

Biographical Sources:

Fu, *Tang caizi*, 2:456–74.
Jiu Tang shu, 160.4213–14; *Xin Tang shu*, 168.532–42.

Translations:

Bian Xiaoxuan 卞孝萱 and Zhu Chongcai 朱崇才. *Xinyi Liu Zongyuan wenxuan* 新譯柳宗元文選. Taibei: Sanmin, 2006.
Birch, *Anthology*, pp. 258–59.
Chang, H. C. "Liu Tsung-yüan (773–819)," in *Chinese Literature 2, Nature Poetry*, New York: Columbia University, 1977, pp. 93–124. Poetry and prose. Free, uneven translation.
Kakei Fumio 筧文生. *Kan Go, Ryū Sōgen* 韓愈柳宗元. Tokyo: Chikuma, 1973.
Liu, Shih-shun. "Liu Tsung-yüan (773–819)," in *Chinese Classical Prose, The Eight Masters of the T'ang Sung Period*. Hong Kong: Chinese University, 1979, pp. 98–131. Relatively free versions of some texts otherwise not translated.
Margoulies, *Anthologie*, pp. 112–13, 120–24, 129–34, 167–71, 180–81, 241, 361–62, 401–02.
Miao, "T'ang Quatrains," pp. 58–65.
New Directions, p. 139.
Owen, *Anthology*, pp. 601–03, 611–12, 617–18.
___. *Middle Ages*, pp. 29–33, 48–54, 61–67, 127–28.
___. *Late Tang*, p. 3.
Strassberg, Richard. *Inscribed Landscapes: Travel Writing from Imperial China*. Berkeley: University of California Press, 1994, pp. 141–49.
Takeda Akira 竹田晃編. *Ryū Sōgen kobun chūshaku: Setsu den sō chō* 柳宗元古文注釈：説, 伝, 騒, 弔. Tokyo: Shinten, 2014.
Wang Songling 王松齡 and 楊立揚, eds. *Liu Zongyuan shiwen xuanyi* 柳宗元詩文選譯. Chengdu: Ba Shu Shushe, 1991.
Yang Xianyi, *Poetry and Prose*, pp. 135–78.

Studies:

Bol, pp. 140–44.
Chen Jo-shui 陳弱水. *Liu Tsung-yüan and Intellectual Change in T'ang China, 773–819*. Cambridge: Cambridge University Press, 1992. A solid study of the intellectual stage as Liu found it in the late eighth century and Liu's role as a political, philosophical, and literary player upon it.

___, Guo Yingjian 郭英劍 and Xu Chengxiang 徐承嚮. *Liu Zongyuan yu Taidai sixiang bianqian* 柳宗元與唐代思想變遷. Nanjing: Jiangsu Jiaoyu, 2010.

Chen Yu-shih. "Liu Tsung-yüan: The Individual in History," *Images and Ideas in Chinese Classical Prose: Studies of Four Masters*, Stanford: Stanford University, 1988, pp. 71–107.

Crump, James I., Jr. "Lyǒu Dzūng-ywán," *JAOS*, 67 (1947), 161–171.

Duan Xingmin 段醒民. *Liu Zihou yuyan wenxue tanwei* 柳子厚寓言文學探微. Taibei: Wenjin, 1978.

Gentzler, J. M. "A Literary Biography of Liu Tsung-yüan." Unpublished Ph.D. dissertation, Columbia University, 1966. An excellent, still relevant study containing over thirty translations (all but one of prose).

Hajime Matsumoto 松本肇. *Ryū Sōgen kenkyū* 柳宗元研究. Toyko: Sobunsha, 2002.

Hartman, Charles. "*Alieniloquium*: Liu Tsungyüan's Other Voice," *CLEAR*, 4.1 (January 1982): 23–73.

He Shuzhi 何書置. *Liu Zongyuan yanjiu* 柳宗元研究. Changsha: Yuelu, 1994.

Koike Ichirō 小池一郎. "Ryūshi chūyaku" 柳詩注訳 [六部], *Gengo bunka* 言語文化 (Doshisha Daigaku 同志社大學) (6 parts), 8.2 (2005): 409–451; 8.4 (2007): 791–817; 9.1 (2006): 117–160; 9.3 (2007): 509–563; 10.1 (2007): 141–175; 10.2 (2007): 297–332.

Kurada Mamiko 黒田真美子. "Ryū Sōgen no gijinhō" 柳宗元詩の擬人法, *Hosei Daigaku bungakubu kiyō* 法政大學文學部紀要, 2003: 67–108.

Lam Lai-kwan 林麗君. "Messianic Elements in Mid-Tang Thought: The Case of Liu Zongyuan (773–819)," 唐中葉淑世思想探討：柳宗元研究. Unpublished M.A. Thesis, University of Hong Kong, 2001.

Lamont, H. G. "An Early Ninth Century Debate on Heaven, Part I," *AM*, NS, 19 (1974): 37–85.

Liang Huiru 梁惠如. "Liu Zongyuan tingchiji yanjiu" 柳宗元 (773–819) 亭池記研究 (A Study of Liu Zongyuan's Essays on Pavilions and Ponds). Unpublished M.A. thesis, Hong Kong University, 2009.

Lien, Y. Edmund. "The Moral High Ground: Two Admonitory *Fu* by Liu Zongyuan [*Fu* on the Pitcher and *Fu* on the Water Buffalo]," *Tang Studies* 23–24 (2005–2006): 169–186.

Luo Liantian 羅聯添, ed. *Liu Zongyuan shiji xinian ji ziliao leibian* 柳宗元事跡繫年暨資料類編. Taibei: Guoli Bianyi Guan, 1981. A collection of previous comments of Liu's genealogy, life, prose writings and editions of his collected works.

Nienhauser, William H., Jr., et al. *Liu Tsung-yüan*. New York: Twayne, 1973. Also contains translations of fables (Lloyd Neighbors), poetry (Jan B. Walls), and prose (Nienhauser).

___. "Floating Clouds and Dreams in Liu Tsung-yüan's Yung-chou Exile Writings," *JAOS* 106 (1986): 169–81. Study of two dominant motifs in the Yongzhou corpus.

Nienhauser, William H., Jr. "A Selected Bibliography of Liu Tsung-yüan," *Shumu jikan* 書目季刊, 20.1 (June 1986): 204–43.

Ono Shihei 小野四平. *Kan Ko to Ryū Sōgen: Tōdai kokubun kenkyū shōsetsu Ryū Sōgen kenkyū* 韓愈と柳宗元: 唐代古文研究序說. Tokyo: Iwanami, 1995.

Shields, Anna M. *One Who Knows Me: Friendship and Literary Culture in Mid-Tang China*. Cambridge and London: Harvard University Asia Center, 2015, pp. 202–04 and passim.

Shimosada Masahiro 下定雅弘. *Ryū Sōgen: Gyakkyō o ikinuita utsukushiki tamashii* 柳宗元：逆境を生きぬいた美しき魂. Tokyo: Bensei, 2009.

___. *Haku Kyoi to Ryū Sōgen: konmei no yo ni sei no sanka o* 白居易と柳宗元：混迷の世に生の讚歌を. Tokyo: Iwanami, 2015.

Shinkai Hajime 新海一. *Ryū bun kenkyū shosetsu* 柳文研究序説. Tokyo: Iwanami, 1997.

Soejima Ichirō 副島一郎. "Sōjin no mieta Ryū Sōgen" 宋人の見えた柳宗元, *Chūgoku bungakuhō*, 47 (1993): 103–45.

Spaar. Wilfried. *Liu Zongyuan's Works in Translation: A Bibliography*. Berlin: Staatsbibliothek, 2003.

Spring, Madeline Kay. *Animal Allegories in T'ang China*. New Yale: American Oriental Society, 1993.

___. "A Stylistic Study of Tang *Guwen*: The Rhetoric of Han Yu and *Liu Zongyuan*." Unpublished Ph. D. dissertation, Seattle: University of Washington, 1983.

Shi Ziyu 施子愉. *Liu Zongyuan nianpu* 柳宗元年譜 (A Chronology of Liu Zongyuan's Life and Works). Wuhan: Hubei Renmin, 1958.

Shimizu Shigeru 清水茂. "*Ryū Sōgen no seikatsu taiken to so no sansuiki*" 柳宗元の生活体験とその山水記 (Liu Zongyuan's Life Experience and His Records of Excursions in Nature), *Chūgoku bungaku hō*. 2 (April 1955): 45–74.

Sun Changwu 孫昌武. *Liu Zongyuan zhuanlun* 柳宗元傳論. Beijing: Zhonghua, 1982. The best available biographical account.

___. *Liu Zongyuan pingzhuan* 柳宗元評傳. Rpt.; Nanjing: Nanjing Daxue, 2007 [1998].

Tosaki Tetsuhiko 戶崎哲彥. Jin Peiyi 金培懿 譯. "Liu Zongyuan de mingdao wenxue: qi yu Lu Chun *Chunqiu* xue zhi guanxi"柳宗元的明道文學:其與陸淳《春秋》學之關係. *Zhongguo wenzhe yanjiu tongxun* 中國文哲研究通訊 11:2 (2001): 1–131.

___. *Ryū Sōgen: Ajia no Rusō* 柳宗元: あしあのルソ. Tokyo: Yamakawa, 2018.

Wang Dequan 王德權. "Weishi zhidao: Liu Zongyuan shiren lun de kaocha" 為士之道:柳宗元士人論的考察, *Zhonghua wenshi luncong* 中華文史論叢 2007.3: 251–300.

___. "'Shiren rushi' de zai quanshi: Liu Zongyuan 'Fengjian lun' de yige cemian" 「士人入仕」的再詮釋:柳宗元〈封建論〉的一個側面, *Hanxue yanjiu* 漢學研究 26:2 (2008): 71–100.

Wang Jilun 王基倫. "*Yi* [*jing*] yu Liu Zongyuan guwen biaoxian fengge zhi guanxi xilun" 《易》與柳宗元古文表現風格之關係析論. *Guowen xuebao* 國文學報 2002: 155–174.

Wang, Richard G. "Liu Tsung-yüan's 'Tale of Ho-chien' and Fiction," *TS* 14 (1996): 21–48.

Wang Wanxia 王晚霞. *Liu Zongyuan yanjiu* 柳宗元研究 (2006–2014). Changsha: Hunan Renmin, 2015.

Whitfield, Susan. "Politics against the Pen: History, Politics and Liu Zongyuan's (773–819) Literary Reputation." Unpublished Ph.D. dissertation, University of London, 1995.

Wu Wenzhi 吳文治. *Liu Zongyuan juan* 柳宗元卷. 2v. Beijing: Zhonghua, 1964. Collection of traditional comments on Liu and his works.

Wu Zhenhua 吳振華. "Lun Liu Zongyuan Tangya de xianshi yiyi ji qi yishu tedian" 論柳宗元唐雅的現實及其藝術特點, *Wenxue yichan* 2014.3: 57–66.

___. *Liu Zongyuan shi wen xuanping* 柳宗元詩文選評. Xian: San Qin, 2004.

Xie Hanqiang 謝漢強, Yang Ben 楊奔 and Lu Yongliang 魯永良, eds. *Liu Houze hui: Liu Zongyuan zai Liuzhou* 柳侯澤惠：柳宗元在柳州. Beijing: Guangming Ribao, 2006.

Yang Xiaoshan. "Naming and Meaning in the Landscape Essays of Yuan Jie and Liu Zongyuan," *JAOS* 120 (2000): 82–96.

Zhang Shizhao 章士釗. *Liuwen zhiyao* 柳文指要. 3v. Beijing: Zhonghua, 1974.

Zhang Yong 張勇. *Liu Zongyuan ru-fodao sanjiaoguan yanjiu* 柳宗元儒佛道三教觀研究. Hefei: Huangshan, 2010.

___. *Liu Zongyuan ru fo dao sanjiao guanxin lun* 柳宗元儒佛道三教觀心論. Beijing: Zhonghua, 2020.

Zheng Sexing 鄭色幸. *Liu Zongyuan cifu yanjiu* 柳宗元辭賦研究. Taibei: Wenjin, 2004.

William H. Nienhauser, Jr.

Lu Guimeng 陸龜蒙 (*zi*, Luwang 魯望, 836–881), was a native of Wu County 吳縣, Suzhou. Lu's father, Lu Binyu 陸賓虞 (826 *jinshi*), had been a minor local official. Lu Guimeng was a precocious student of the classics, Yang Xiong 楊雄 (53 BC–18 CE), and *Mencius* with special insight into the *Chunqiu*, for all of which he was known throughout the region. Little is known of his early life until in 865 he paid a visit to Lu Yong 陸墉 who was serving as Prefect of Muzhou 睦州 (about fifty-five miles southeast of modern Hangzhou at the confluence of the Xinan 新安 and Lan 蘭

rivers). Lu Yong sent him to study at the nearby Laojun Yuan 老君院 (Laozi Academy) in the Longxing Guan 龍興觀, noted for the Chan master, Daoming 道明 (780–877), who lived there. A few years later he was recommended to take the *jinshi* examination but failed and retired to a village near his hometown. He was, therefore, with good reason treated by the *Xin Tang shu* as a Daoist: his biography is in the section called "Yin yi" 隱逸 (The Hidden and Uninhibited), along with those of the learned physicians Sun Simiao 孫思邈 (ca. 581–682)* and Meng Shen 孟詵 (621–713), the ecstatic poet Wu Yun 吳筠 (d. 778),* and Pan Shizheng 潘師正 (ca. 584–ca. 682) and Sima Chengzhen 司馬承禎 (647–735),* the eleventh and twelfth Maoshan Patriarchs respectively. Most of Lu's life was spent in the village of Fuli 甫里, near Songjiang 松江 in the Wu region, hence his byname Fuli Xiansheng 甫里先生 (he was also sometimes styled Tiansuizi 天隨子 and Jianghu Sanren 江湖散人). In this pleasant land adjacent to the Taihu 太湖 (Grand Lake) and Maoshan 茅山 he wrote prolifically, much of the time in the company of his poetic friend Pi Rixiu 皮日休 (ca. 834–ca. 883)* and the scholarly Daoist Zhang Ben 張賁 (fl. 850–875),* both of whom are frequently addressed in the titles of his poems.

Lu Guimeng is reported to have been a brooding, melancholy person, who suffered much from illness and poverty. But this official characterization seems inadequate: he was fond of good company and laughter, by no means a despondent hypochondriac, and it is difficult to understand how a pauper could have amassed a fine library of more than ten thousand scrolls. In fact, he led the life he chose to lead, away from the turmoil of urban and political life and the winds of fashion. His library contained many fine manuscripts, and he was himself a conscientious editor, collator, and restorer, who did not hesitate to repair the rare books he borrowed from his friends. The notion that he suffered from poverty seems to be based on the observation that he loved the land and was constantly to be seen laboring in his extensive fields–where he also owned a large house. Having abandoned winebibbing to become a tea fancier, he made tea one of his favorite crops. He did not like to travel about on horseback, preferring to go everywhere in his watery realm by boat, carrying his own bedding, desk, bundles of books, angling gear, and tea stove. In short, he played the role of a sophisticate who stripped himself of worldly pleasures and ambitions.

The subjects of his poems are often trees, flowers, birds, insects, and clouds—all manner of natural things—with which he felt an intimacy that he enjoyed with few men. His "Bailian" 白蓮 (White Lotus) is well-known:

> White blooms are often outweighed by flowers of more seductive hues,
> These flowers should be planted in a jade pool.
> Heartless they may seem, but who can know their deep grief?
> They will fall when moonlight fades and the morning wind blows.

素花多蒙別豔欺，此花端合在瑤池。
無情有恨何人覺？月曉風清欲墮時。

Although the poem can be read as a literal—and rather effective—depiction of a white lotus, it is often seen as a personal plaint, Lu Guimeng comparing himself, as pure as the white lotus, but not able to attain the recognition that the men of more seductive hues find theirs.

He frequently wrote of landscapes in the Wu area, especially temple precincts, haunted grottoes, holy mountains, and numinous springs, and also of the seasons and such daily activities as walking, sitting, sleeping, and eating. He particularly liked to write of rural technologies in which he could claim mastery: he left a sequence of twenty poems on the art of fishing, including vignettes of weirs, moles, traps, boats, reels, and the like; a set of ten on wood-cutting and wood-gathering; another set of ten on wine and winemaking; and still another ten on tea, all written in a knowledgeable, affable, good-humored tone. He also produced many verses on his experiences in the company of boon-companions and on such admirable producers as farmers and fishermen, presenting a face different from that which he showed to the rest of the world.

Many of his poems tell of the tropical south–although there is no record that he ever visited the region. A poem addressed to an acquaintance in Hainan, referring to sorcery and pearl-fishing, suggests a probable source for his exotic imagery, which includes dragon-haunted Hanoi, the non-Chinese aborigines of Guangdong, and local taxes paid in cowrie shells there.

His familiarity with nature extended to the supernal world. Such preoccupations were related to his familiarity with Daoist rites, especially those at Maoshan, and his close acquaintance with priests and adepts. He is confident of the divinity of nature and familiar with the rites due the moon and the Northern Dipper. Among the pleasures of visits to Maoshan he enumerates the opportunities to take rubbings from ancient incised texts, to find and collate old manuscripts, to participate in alchemical demonstrations, to search for invigorating herbs and sacred mushrooms, and to explore mysterious grottoes in the company of learned ecclesiastics.

Lu Guimeng has also left us many skillful and imaginative *fu* 賦, on themes such as moss, lice, and mythical animals, not to mention living in obscurity. A small number of prose writings show similar preoccupations. Two pieces have been regularly anthologized: "Xiaoming lu" 小名錄 (Register of Little Names), about the juvenile names of persons of antiquity (it survives only in part), and "Jinqun ji" 錦裙記 (Record of a Damask Apron).

There is also a short but witty autobiography, composed as if about a stranger of unknown antecedents. This alter-ego has been described as rustic and uninhibited and fond of reading the writings of the incomparable men of antiquity. So Lu Guimeng liked to represent himself–but his writings are far from being rustic and uninhibited. Their well-flavored language is as carefully contrived as was the man himself.

BIBLIOGRAPHY

Editions:
Bai Juncai 柏俊才, ed. *Lu Fuli Xiaopin* 陸甫里小品. Beijing: Wenhua Yishu, 1997.
Jinqun ji 錦裙記, in *Tangdai congshu*. 1 *juan*.
Leisi jing 耒耜經, in *CSJC*. 1 *juan*.
Lize congshu 笠澤叢書. Shanghai, 1914. 4 *juan*.
Quan Tang shi, 9: 7158–282, 14: 10695.
Quan Tang wen, v. 17, *j*. 800–801, pp. 10585–618.
Songling ji 松陵集. Reprint of a Song ed. in *Jiguge* 汲古閣. 10 *juan*.
Tang Fuli Xiansheng wenji 唐甫里先生文集. *SBCK*. 20 *juan*.

Lu Guimeng

Xiaoming lu 小名錄, in *CSJC*. 2 *juan*.
Yuju yong 漁具詠, in *Shuofu* 說郛 (Wanwei Shantang 宛委山堂 ed.).

Annotations:
Lu Guimeng quanji jiaozhu 陸龜蒙全集校注. He Xiguang 何錫光, ed. 2v. Nanjing: Fenghuang, 2015.

Biographical Sources:
Fu, *Tang caizi*, 3:508–17, 5:433–35.
Xin Tang shu, 196.5612–13.

Translations:
Davis, *Penguin*, p. 30.
Edwards, E. D. "The Embroidered Skirt," in *Chinese Prose Literature*, v. 2, pp. 311–13.
Nienhauser, William H., Jr. *P'i Jih-hsiu*. Boston: Twayne Publishers, 1979, pp. 70–71, 89–90, 106–7 and 112. Several *shi* and one *fu*.
Owen, *Late Tang*, p. 239.
Schafer, *Golden Peaches*, p. 67.
___. *Mao Shan in Tang Times* (Society for the Study of Chinese Religions, Monograph No. 1), University of Colorado, 1980, pp. 31–32, 37–38, 41.
Sunflower, pp. 255–59.

Studies:
Cao Lifang 曹麗芳. "Lu Guimeng shiwen ji banben yuanliu ji buyi kaoshu" 陸龜蒙詩文文集集版本源流補遺考述, *Guji zhengli yanjiu xuekan* 古籍整理研究學刊, 4 (2015): 43–47.
Hu Shanlin 胡山林 and Xu Hun 許揮. "Lu Guimeng yinju kao" 陸龜蒙隱居考, *Huazhong Shifan Daxue xuebao* 華中師範大學學報 (*Renwen Shehuikexue ban* 人文社會科學版) 7 (1998): 57–63.
Li Fubiao 李福標. *Pi, Lu Nianpu* 皮陸年譜. Guangzhou: Sun Yat-sen University Publishing House, 2011.
Maegawa, Yokio 前川幸雄. "*Shōryōshū* sho shū shi no kenkyū (1)" 松陵集所收詩の研究, *Fukui kōhyō kōtō semmon gakkō kenkyū kiyō (Jimbun shakai kagaku)* 11 (1978): 1–29.
Marney, John. *Chinese Anagrams and Anagram Verse*. Asian Library Series, Taibei: Chinese Materials Center, 1993. Traces the history of anagrams in literature; three chapters devoted to exchanges between Lu Guimeng and Pi Rixiu.
Miller, David Charles. "Self-presentations in the Poetry of Lu Kuei-meng (d. 881?)." Ph.D., Stanford University, 1990.
Nienhauser. *P'i Jih-hsiu*, passim.
Wang Maofu 王茂福. *Pi, Lu Shi zhuan* 皮陸詩傳. Changchun: Jilin Renmin, 2000.
Wang Xijiu 王錫九. *Pi, Lu Shige Yanjiu* 皮陸詩歌研究. Hefei: Anhui Daxue, 2004.
Xiao Difei 蕭滌非. "Qianyan" 前言, in *Pizi wensou*, Beijing: Zhonghua, 1959, pp. 1–21, pp. 407–30.
Xiong, Yan'e 熊豔娥. *Luguimeng Yanjiu* 陸龜蒙研究. Xi'an: Shaanxi Normal University Publishing House, 2012.
Yao Yao 姚垚. "Pi Rixiu, Lu Guimeng changhe shi yanjiu" 皮日休陸龜蒙唱和詩研究. Unpublished M.A. thesis, National Taiwan University, 1980.

Edward H. Schafer and William H. Nienhauser, Jr.

Lu Lun 盧綸 (*zi*, Yunyan 允言, 748–ca. 798) is known as a leading member of the group of poets known as the *Dali shi caizi* 大曆十才子 (Ten Talents of the Dali Era [766–779], a dozen or so poets at various times including Qian Qi 錢起 (720–ca. 780)* and Li Yi 李益 (748–827).* A native of Puzhou 蒲州 (modern Yongji xian 永濟縣 in Shanxi), he took the examinations in the mid-750s but failed, withdrawing to Zhongnan Shan 終南山 south of the capital to study. When the An Lushan Rebellion broke out in 755, he spent several years in Poyang County 鄱陽 with his uncle (about 25 miles southwest of modern Jingdezhen in Jiangxi). Thereafter, he sat again several times for the *jinshi* examination during the Dali era but never passed it. Consequently, he was dependent on his literary talents to obtain employment. Those talents seemed to have sufficed, however.

His first position came in 771 at the recommendation of the Grand Councilor Yuan Zai 元載 (d. 777), under whose sponsorship he was appointed Commandant of Wenxiang County 閿鄉縣 (modern Lingbao City 靈寶市 in western Henan); that same year he was made Magistrate of Mi County 密縣 (modern Xinmi City 新密市 about twenty miles southwest of Zhengzhou in Henan). Three or four years later (about 775) with Wang Jin's 王縉 (700–782) support he was called to the capital to become an Academician in the Academy of Scholarly Worthies and Editor of the Palace Library. During this time he befriended the poets Qian Qi and Li Duan 李端 (d. ca. 785)* and was for a time in the company of Guo Ai 郭曖 (752–800), husband to one of the imperial princesses. Lu also knew a number of the powerful men of the day, including Lu Zhi 陸贄 (754–805),* Jia Dan 賈耽 (730–805), and Ma Sui 馬燧 (726–795). Lu's poems seem to have even caught the attention of Emperor Dezong 德宗 (r. 779–805). In 777, following Yuan and Wang's precipitous downfall, he lost both of his posts and was imprisoned for a time. He was still in the capital during its occupation by the rebel Zhu Ci 朱泚 (742–784) in 783. Freed in 784 by Hun Jian 渾瑊 (736–799), the Military Commissioner of Hezhong 河中, Lu joined the latter's staff until he was summoned in late 797 at the emperor's request to an audience in the palace and made Director of the Ministry of Revenue. A year or two later he died.

Lu Lun's poetry (over 300 poems are extant) reveals a variety of thematic material, a reflection of his broad experiences and extensive travels. His "Wanci Ezhou" 晚次鄂州 (Mooring at Night in Ezhou) is an early example of his imagistic powers, written while in the South during the An Lushan Rebellion.

> Clouds disperse, Hanyang City appears in the distance,
> Still another day's sail away;
> Sleeping in the daytime, the merchants enjoy the calm,
> Talking at night, the boatmen feel the tide.
> My greying sideburns contrast the autumn colors of Xiang River region,
> My nostalgic heart faces the bright moonlight.
> Years of battles and upheavals ruined my old enterprises,
> Harder to bear are the sounds of war drums along the river.

> 雲開遠見漢陽城，猶是孤帆一日程。
> 估客晝眠知浪靜，舟人夜語覺潮生。
> 三湘愁鬢逢秋色，萬里歸心對月明。
> 舊業已隨征戰盡，更堪江上鼓鼙聲。

Lu Lun

The six quatrains comprising "He Zhang Pu ye saixia qu" 和張僕射塞下曲 (Frontier Songs: Matching Rhymes with Assistant Executive Secretary Zhang), a product of his years in Hun Jian's camp, are some of the best-known examples of "frontier poetry." His "Saixia qu" 塞下曲 (Song Beneath the Great Wall) is the most famous:

The woods are dark, the grass startled by the wind,
The general draws his bow at night.
At dawn he looks for his white-plumed arrow,
And finds it sunk into the face of a rock.

林暗草驚風，將軍夜引弓。
平明尋白羽，沒在石棱中。

The poem alludes to the biography of the great Han-dynasty general Li Guang 李廣 (d. 119 BC) in the *Shiji*, which tells that Li Guang went hunting and shot at a rock mistaking it for a tiger (presumably in the fading light of dusk). Unable to find the tiger the next day, he however discovered that his arrow had penetrated the rock. The poem thus recalls the many generals since the Han who have fought on the northern borders and displayed their gallantry and skills. Since Li Guang also went from being a favorite of the emperor to disgrace through no fault of his own, [the poem] it may also suggest Lu Lun's own lament for his political downfall.

However, like the work of the other "Ten Talents," his consists mainly of social and occasional poetry written in the favored pentasyllabic, regulated-verse form. Indeed, it is such verses with which the group is traditionally identified.

The name of the group itself refers to a number of poets who resided in the capital and enjoyed great popularity among the social elite at about 770, a time of stability at court brought about by the autocratic Yuan Zai, Grand Councilor from 762 to 777. The roster of the "Ten Talents," however, began changing during the Northern Song as poets whose works had been lost in transmission came to be replaced by others. The original "Ten Talents," based on near contemporary sources, were Lu Lun, Sikong Shu 司空曙 (ca. 720–790),* Li Duan, Geng Wei 耿湋 (d. ca. 785),* Han Hong 韓翃 (fl. 754),* Qian Qi, Miao Fa 苗發 (d. 786), Xiahou Shen 夏侯審 (*jinshi* 780), Ji Zhongfu 吉中孚 (*jinshi* ca. 775, d. ca. 790), Cui Tong 崔峒 (*jinshi* ca. 770, d. after 785).

While critics often mention a *Dali ti* 大曆體 (Dali style), there is no evidence to show that the "talents" ever consciously espoused any literary ideals or that they even considered themselves a literary clique. This term, however, has become a stylistic designation referring, at its best, to the polished (if undistinguished) pentasyllabic verses of the "talents" and, at its worst, to wholly derivative mediocre poetry lacking in moral and ethical concerns.

Besides revealing contemporary poetic tastes, modern literary historians tend to view the role of the "Ten Talents" as helping to set the background for the reactions that gave rise to the various styles of the Mid-Tang or as "transitional poets" between the High and Mid-Tang.

BIBLIOGRAPHY

Editions:

Han Hong shiji jiaozhu 韓翃詩集校注. Chen Wanghe 陳王和, ed. Taibei: Wenshizhe, 1973. Contains the photolithographic reprint of the text of Han Hong's poems in the *Quan Tang shi* (1707 edition), which is used as the basic text for collation; with extensive annotation.

Liu Chutang 劉初棠, ed. *Lu Lun shiji jiaozhu* 盧綸詩集校注. Shanghai: Shanghai Guji, 1989.

Luan Guiming 欒貴明, ed. *Quan Tang shi suoyin: Li Yi, Lu Lun juan*. Beijing: Zhonghua, 1997.

Quan Tang shi, 5: 3119–185.

Zhang Dengdi 張登第, Jiao Wenbin 焦文彬 and Lu Anshu 魯安澍. *Dali shi caizi shixuan* 大曆十才子詩選. Xi'an: Shaanxi Renmin, 1988.

Biographical Sources:

Fu Xuancong 傅璇琮. "Lu Lun kao" 盧綸考, *Tangdai shiren congkao* 唐代詩人叢考. Beijing: Zhonghua, 1980, pp. 469–92.

___, *Tang caizi*, 2:1–13, 5:155–61.

Jiu Tang shu, 163.4268–74.

Xin Tang shu, 203.5785.

Translations:

Kao Yu-kung and Mei Tsu-lin, "Meaning, Metaphor and Allusion," *HJAS* 38 (1978): 305.

Minford and Lau, p. 846.

Owen, *High Tang*, pp. 274–80.

Sunflower, p. 157.

Studies:

Bian Xiaoxuan 卞孝萱 and Qiao Zhangfu 喬長阜. "Lu Lun de shengping yu chuangzuo" 盧綸的生平與創作, *Sichuan Shifan Daxue xuebao*, 1988.2: 22–27.

Huang Qingfa 黃清發. "Xinchu shike yu Lu Lun yenjiu 新出石刻與盧綸," *Wenxue yichan*, 2016.1: 72–80.

Jiang Yin 蔣寅. "Dali shi caizi zhi qiaochu: Lu Lun" 大曆十才子之翹楚—盧綸. *Gudian wenxue zhishi* 古典文學知識, 2 (1994): 66–70.

___. *Dali shiren yanjiu* 大曆詩人研究. Beijing: Zhonghua, 1995.

___. "Lun Lu Lun shi ji qi dui Zhong Tang shitan de yingxiang" 論盧綸詩及其對中唐詩壇的影響, *Wenxue yichan*, 1993.6: 42–51.

Ogawa, Shoichi 小川昭一. "Taireki no shijin" 大曆の詩人, *Shibun*, 24 (1959): 22–33.

Owen, *High Tang*, pp. 253–80.

Shi Guangzhao 史廣超 and Tu Xianjing 涂顯鏡. "Lu Lun jiashi, shengping bukao" 盧綸家世, 生平補考, *Guiyang Xueyuan xuebao* 貴陽學院學報, 2008.3: 68–70.

Zhao Lintao 趙林濤. *Lu Lun yanjiu* 盧綸研究. Baoding: Hebei Daxue, 2010.

Oscar Lee and William H. Nienhauser, Jr.

Lu Tong 盧仝 (ca. 775–835) gained renown for his verse early in life, a life which has *also* been assigned various datings. Born in Jiyuan 濟源 County (modern Jiyuan City, Henan), he styled himself Yuchuan Zi 玉川子 (Master of the Jade Stream), an epithet he took from the stream near his home which supplied the water he used to make tea. Lu Tong is also famous for the many poems he wrote related to tea and tea drinking. One of the most popular was "Qi wan shi" 七碗詩 (Seven Bowls of Tea). Another well-known poem was written by Lu Tong for Grand Master of Remonstrance, Meng Jian 孟簡 (d. 824), thanking him for a large package of exceptionally rare tea.

Lu came from a poor family whose most valuable possessions were their books. He went into reclusion at Mount Shaoshi 少室山 (also known as Mount Song 嵩山, about twenty miles east-southeast of Luoyang in Henan) before he was twenty-years old. He later moved to Luoyang, where he lived in extreme poverty (with a toothless old maidservant and a unkempt male slave) and was said to have had to beg for rice from his neighbors. Fortunately, Han Yu 韓愈 (768–824),* who was Magistrate of Luoyang at that time (810), appreciated Lu Tong and his verse, often using his own salary to support him. Han was impressed with Lu's scholarship on the *Chunqiu* which seems to have been in the iconoclastic mode of eighth century scholars like Lu Chun 陸淳 (d. 806) and Dan Zhu 啖助 (724–770; see Han Yu's poem "Ji Lu Tong" 寄盧仝 [To Lu Tong]). Lu Tong's "Yue shi" 月蝕 (Lunar Eclipse), a poem which was interpreted as a topical allegory attacking the power that the eunuch Tutu Chengcui 吐突承璀 (d. 820) had gained over the court of Emperor Xianzong 獻宗 (r. 806–820), was likely written in 810 as well. Han Yu particularly admired this poem and wrote his own poem on the same subject imitating Lu Tong. Over one thousand words in all, Lu's poem opens:

> The fifth year after the new Son of Heaven took his place,
> The cyclic year *gengyin*,
> The Dipper's handle has penetrated the Zi position
> And the pitch pipe is now Yellow Bell.
> Tens of thousands of trees stood rigid in the night,
> The cold air intense but windless.
> A glittering silver plate rose from the bottom of the sea,
> And lit the east side of my thatched cottage.
> The sky turned purple as it froze motionless,
> Its icy rays flashing in the cold moonrise.
> At first, I thought the moon was a white lotus,
> Floating up from the Dragon King's Palace.
> This Mid-Autumn night
> could not be matched by other nights:
> At this time a strange thing happened,
> Something had come to devour the moon . . . .

> 新天子即位五年，歲次庚寅。
> 斗柄插子，律調黃鐘。
> 森森萬木夜殭立，寒氣鑿鑿頑無風。
> 爛銀盤從海底出，出來照我草屋東。
> 天色紺滑凝不流，冰光交貫寒朣朧。
> 初疑白蓮花，浮出龍王宮。
> 八月十五夜，比並不可雙。
> 此時怪事發，有物吞食來 . . . .

In 811 Lu went to Yangzhou to sell the old family residence in that city, then returned to Luoyang with the books that had been kept in Yangzhou and purchased a residence there. Meng Jiao 孟郊 (751–814)* eulogized this in his "Hu bu pin xi Lu Tong shu chuan gui Luo" 忽不貧喜盧仝書船歸洛 [Suddenly Feeling Better, Pleased that Lu Tong's Boat and His Books Returned to Luoyang]). He was especially close to Meng Jiao, but also on good terms with Jia Dao 賈島 (779–843)* and Ma Yi 馬異 (ca. 799–ca. 869) and he was regarded as a member of the Han Meng Shipai 韓孟詩派 (The Poetic school of Han Yu and Meng Jiao). Known for his lifelong study of the "Tea Culture," his surprising, risky, strange poems (almost one hundred are extant) gave rise to the term "Lu Tong Style."

Tradition has it that sometime after 810 Lu Tong refused an invitation from the government to be a Grand Master of Remonstrance, but modern scholars have questioned this. Another account of Lu's life, possibly based on the fact that Lu's poem had attacked the growing eunuch power, claims that in the eleventh lunar month of 835, Lu Tong was a guest in the home of Wang Yai 王涯 (764–835), a Grand Councilor at that time. Lu was thereby drawn into the Ganlu zhi Bian 甘露之變 (Ganlu Incident) in which Wang Yai and his associates attempted to enter the palace and kill a number of eunuchs. The plot failed, and as result both Lu and Wang were put to death by the eunuchs and their followers. Yet another tradition says he died in of illness in Yangzhou. Jia Dao lamented his death in his poem "Ku Lu Tong shi" 哭盧仝詩 (Crying for Lu Tong).

BIBLIOGRAPHY

Editions:
Lu Tong ji 盧仝集. Taibei: Taiwan Shangwu, 1966.
Quan Tang shi, 6: 4390–404, 15: 11266.
Quan Tang wen, 683.7709.
Yuchuanzi shiji 玉川子詩集. 5 *juan*. Taibei: Shangwu, 1965.

Biographical Sources:
Fu, *Tang caizi*, 2:267–74, 5:211–14.
Xin Tang shu, 176.5268.

Translations:
Birch, *Anthology*, pp. 285–87 (from Graham, see below).
Graham, *Late T'ang*, pp. 81–88.

Studies:
Bian Xiaoxuan 卞孝萱. *Liu Yuxi congkao* 劉禹錫從考. Chengdu: Ba Shu, 1988, pp. 53–55.
Chen Zhenpeng 陳振鵬. "Lu Tong shengnian jieyi" 盧仝生年解疑. *Cishu yanjiu*, 1981.2: 250.
Kong Qingmao 孔慶茂, Wen Xiuwen 溫秀雯. "Lu Tong xingnian kao" 盧仝行年考. *Nanjing Shida xuebao*, 1990.4: 96–101.
Wang Lizeng 王立增. "Lu Tong ji qi shige chuangzuo jianlun" 盧仝及其詩歌創作簡論, *Xuchang Xueyuan xuebao*, 2003.3: 59–62.
Wu Qiming 吳企明. "Lu Tong" 盧仝, in *Tang caizizhuan jiaojian* 唐才子傳校箋. Fu Xuancong 傅璇琮, ed. 5v. Beijing: Zhonghua, 1989, v. 2, pp. 267–74.

Xiao Bo 肖波. "Tonghua shiren de gexing xiezuo: lun 'Lu Tong ti'" 童話詩人的個性寫作–論"盧仝體, *Xiezuo*, 2010.5: 7–10.

Yan Qi 閻琦. "Lu Tong shengnian zhiyi" 盧仝生年質疑. *Cishu yanjiu*, (1981.2: 248–50.

Yu Cailin 余才林. "*Zuanyi ji* he Lu Tong siyin" 纂異記和盧仝死因. *Wenxue yichan*, 2004.1: 71–76.

Zheng Huixia 鄭慧霞. "Lu Tong shiji banben yanjiu" 盧仝詩集版本研究, *Henan Daxue xuebao (Shehui Kexueban)*, 2008.1: 144–49.

___. "Lu Tong Yanjiu" 盧仝研究. Ph. D. dissertation, East China Normal University, 2007.

___. *Lu Tong zonglun* 盧仝綜論. Beijing: Guangming Ribao, 2010.

Thomas Donnelly Noel and William H. Nienhauser, Jr.

Lu Zhaolin 盧照鄰 (*zi*, Shengzhi 昇之, ca. 634–ca. 686) is along with Luo Binwang 駱賓王 (ca. 640–684),* Wang Bo 王勃 (650–676)* and Yang Jiong 楊炯 (650–694),* traditionally regarded as one of the *Chu Tang sijie* 初唐四傑 (Four Eminences of the Early Tang). These writers, however, did not constitute a real coterie; the social contacts between the four were rare and fleeting, and indeed Lu Zhaolin and Luo Binwang were nearly a generation older than Wang Bo and Yang Jiong. It is better to examine each of these authors individually, rather than regard them as representatives of a homogeneous seventh-century "school" or "period-style."

Lu Zhaolin was a native of Fanyang 范陽 (near modern Beijing). In his youth he studied under the famous classical scholars Cao Xian 曹憲 (541–645) and Wang Yifang 王義方 (615–669) and was early given a position in the private archive of Li Yuanyu 李元裕 (d. 665), Prince of Deng 鄧, seventeenth son of the founding emperor of the Tang. A fine scholar, Lu was said to have exhausted the resources of the prince's extensive library; this erudition is evident in the many uncommon allusions employed in his poems. It is not certain how long Lu remained in the entourage of Li Yuanyu, but he appears to have been at court through at least 666, when he was a member of the party accompanying the third Tang emperor–Gaozong 高宗 (r. 649–683–on the latter's pilgrimage to Mount Tai for the sacred *fengshan* rites. Shortly thereafter Lu was posted to Xindu 新都 in the province of Shu (near modern Chengdu, Sichuan), as a district Defender.

During the last four of the five years he spent in Shu, he suffered from what seems to have been progressive rheumatoid arthritis, a debilitating disease that eventually left him lame of foot and palsied in one hand. This physical disability led to his resignation from official service. For some time around the year 673 he became an avid disciple of the great physician 'and alchemist Sun Simiao 孫思邈 (ca. 581–682),* both at the latter's retreat on Mount Taibo 太白山 and his official lodgings in Chang'an. It was at this time that Lu took for himself the sobriquet Youyou Zi 幽憂子 (Master of Shrouded Sorrow) and seems to have begun the experiments with drugs to abate his disease that were to be an important part of his remaining years. Later he shifted his residence to the Dong Longmen Shan 東龍門山 near Luoyang and then finally to Mount Quci 具茨山 (in modern Yu 禹 county, Henan). When his chronic physical agony became unbearable, he drowned himself in the river Ying 潁. While we can firmly date several of the events of Lu's life and some of his poems, the dates of his birth and death are uncertain. When internal evidence and statements in his works are correlated with known social and political incidents, a span of 634–686 seems the most reliable supposition. But, in any case, the commonly accepted dates of 641–680, based on Lu's laconic official biography in the *Jiu Tangshu*, cannot be upheld: Lu was definitely nearer to fifty years old than to forty when he died, and he probably just outlived Gaozong.

Although only about one hundred of his compositions remain, Lu's *shi* 詩 and *fu* 賦 show him to have been an exceptionally gifted writer, with a total command of the classical literary heritage and tradition. While he was a practiced hand at composing courtly poems and one of the earliest Tang authors to write "frontier" verse, his real achievements lie in other areas. His three most famous works are the philosophical "Bing lishu fu" 病梨樹賦 (Prose-poem on the Diseased Pear Tree), the vibrant, recondite *yuefu* poem "Chang'an guyi" 長安古意 (Chang'an, Thoughts on Antiquity), and the allegorical poem also set to an old *yuefu* title, "Xinglu nan" 行路難 (Hardships of the Road). The latter two works were written in the heptasyllabic meter—an old song-style form—that was beginning to find favor during the second half of the seventh century in *shi* poems of a decidedly narrative bent; Lu was one of the first writers to master the form for use in long poems. "Xinglu nan" has forty lines, "Chang'an guyi" contains sixty-eight lines. It begins:

> The great roads of Chang'an connect to alleys and lanes—
> Crowded with black oxen, white horses, and seven-fragrance carriages.
> Jade palanquins crisscross, stop at princesses' residences,
> Golden whips in an unbroken string, head to marquises' homes.
> From dragon mouths, posts propping precious baldachins, also hold the morning sun,
> Spit from phoenix beaks, tassels lit by sunset clouds.
> A thousand feet of gossamer struggle to wrap the trees,
> A single flight of graceful birds joins their songs midst the flowers.
> Songs midst the flowers, playful butterflies beside the thousand gates,
> Jade-green trees, silvery towers, ten thousand different hues . . . .

> 長安大道連狹斜，青牛白馬七香車。
> 玉輦縱橫過主第，金鞭絡繹向侯家。
> 龍銜寶蓋承朝日，鳳吐流蘇帶晚霞。
> 百丈遊絲爭繞樹，一羣嬌鳥共啼花。
> 啼花戲蝶千門側，碧樹銀臺萬種色 . . .

This opening sets the tone of the luxury and licentious behavior of the capital city elite. The narrow alleyways are part of the motif of the pleasure quarters. The second line echoes one of the four poems titled "Wu qi qu" 烏棲曲 (Crow-nesting Tunes) written by Xiao Gang 蕭綱 (503–551; i.e., Emperor Jianwen of the Liang, r. 550–551): "Black oxen, crimson wheel-hubs, a seven-fragrance carriage / How lovely, tonight I stay over in a singing-girl's house. / In the tall tree of the singing-girl's house a crow's about to nest; / The gauze curtains and azure covers I'll trouble you to lower" 青牛丹轂七香車．可憐今夜宿娼家．娼家高樹鳥欲棲．羅帷翠帳向君低. The golden whips of the fourth line were plied by the young gallants who visited the courtesan houses. But unlike Xiao Gang's poem, "Chang'an guyi" evolves through several scenes to portray the impermanence both of the Spring's flourishing and the sensual pursuits of these young men:

> Seasonal vistas and sights wait for no one;
> The mulberry groves and fields change into jade-green seas in a moment.

Lu Zhaolin

> From those golden staircases and white jade halls of old,
> We see today only the green pines remain.

> 節物風光不相待，桑田碧海須臾改。
> 昔時金階白玉堂，即今惟見青松在。

The final section, which alludes to the great literatus of the Han, Yang Xiong 揚雄 (53 BC–18 AD), reads:

> Silent and alone, Master Yang dwelt,
> Year after year after year, his whole bed filled with books.
> Only when the cassia flowers bloom on Southern Mountain
> Do they fly hither and yon, invading the lapels of one's robe?

> 寂寂寥寥揚子居，年年歲歲一床書。
> 獨有南山桂花發，飛來飛去襲人裾。

These last two couplets allude to the traditional account in which Yang Xiong dwelt in seclusion during his final years, untainted by the politics of his time, a role that Lu Zhaolin sees as his own. This closing resonates with the last lines of Luo Binwang's "Dijing pian" 帝京篇 (Composition on the Imperial Capital), another lengthy verse narrative that juxtaposes Han times with those of the late seventh century and ends with Luo invoking another famous avatar of the unappreciated courtier and literatus, Jia Yi 賈誼 (201–169 BC). Lu Zhaolin's combination of resonance, allusion and imagery produces a powerful depiction of the city, its history, and its politics.

Despite his success with these septasyllabic works, the great majority of his *shi*, however, are written in the prevalent pentasyllabic meter; his most memorable works were composed during the final fifteen years of his life, beginning from the time of his residence in Shu. Many of these poems are allegories of solitary birds or blighted trees, containing harsh and cutting images played off against a general tone of melancholy and frustration. During his last years he created two lengthy and remarkable works in the *sao* style, "Wu bei" 五悲 (Five Griefs) and "Shiji wen" 釋疾文 (Text to Dispel Illness), which are artfully contrived and often painful meditations on fate, flux, and existence, composed in varying prosodic schemes borrowed from different sections of the *Chuci* 楚辭 (particularly those of the "Li sao" 離騷 as well as the "Jiuge" 九歌, and "Jiu zhang" 九章 sections).

Among his prose writings, perhaps the most interesting are his entreating letter to several courtiers in Luoyang, requesting high-quality cinnabar granules for use in his medicinal concoctions, and his fictional "Dui Shu fulao wen" 對蜀父老文 (Response to the Question of an Elder Father of Shu) in which he seeks to explain why he is not ashamed that he holds no influential position at court.

BIBLIOGRAPHY

Editions:
Youyoutzi ji 幽憂子集. *SBCK*. A late Ming edition; typeset and punctuated, collated with the texts printed in *Quan Tang shi* and *Quan Tang wen,* and selections included in *Wenyuan yinghua* and *Yuefu shiji,* in *Lu Zhaolin ji, Yang Jiong ji* 盧照鄰集，楊炯集. Xu Mingxia 徐明霞, ed. Beijing: Xinhua Shudian, 1980.

Annotations:
Li Yunyi 李雲逸, ed. *Lu Zhaolin ji jiaozhu* 盧照鄰集校注. Beijing: Zhonghua, 1998.
Ren Guoxu 任國緒. *Lu Zhaolin ji biannian jianzhu* 盧照鄰集編年箋註. Harbin: Heilongjiang Renmin, 1989.
Zhu Shangshu 祝尚書, ed. *Lu Zhaolin ji jiaozhu* 盧照鄰集校注. Shanghai: Shanghai Guji, 1994.

Biographical Sources:
Fu, *Tang caizi*, 1:44–55, 5:6–7.
Jiu Tang shu, 90A.5000; *Xin Tang shu*, 201.5742.

Translations:
Frankel, *Palace Lady*, pp. 130–43.
Kroll (see below).
Minford and Lau, pp. 681–88.
New Directions, p. 58.
Nienhauser (see below).
Owen, *Anthology*, p. 461.
Owen, "Deadwood," 160–62 ("Bing Lishu fu" 病梨樹賦 [Rhasody on a Sick Pear Tree]).
Owen, *Early T'ang*, pp. 83–103.

Studies:
Furukawa Sueyoshi 古川末喜. "Sho-Tō shiketsu no bungaku shisō" 初唐四傑の文學思想, *Chūgoku bungaku ronshū*, 8 (1979): 1–27.
Ge Xiaoyin 葛曉音. "Guanyu Lu Zhaolin Shengping de ruogan wenti" 關於盧照鄰生平的若干問題. *Wenxue yichan* 1989.6: 68–73.
Han Chengwu 韩成武. "Lu Zhaolin yanjiu de xin chenguo—ping Wang Minghao de *Lu Zhaolin yanjiu*" 盧照鄰研究的新成果—評王明好的《盧照鄰研究》, *Hebei xuekan*, 2013.6.
Hu Kexian 胡可先. "Xin chutu 'Lu Zhaoji muzhi' ji xiangguan wenti" 新出土《盧照己墓誌》及相關問題, *Zhongguo dianji yu wenhua*, 2008.2.
Kroll, Paul W. "Aid and Comfort: Lu Zhaolin's Letters," in *The History of Letters and Epistolary Culture in China*. Antje Richter, ed. Boston and Leiden: Brill, 2015, pp. 827–52.
___. "The Memories of Lu Chao-lin," *JAOS* 109.4 (1989): 581–92.
Li Yunyi 李雲逸. "Guanyu Lu Zhaolin shengping de ruogan wenti" 關於鹿趙林生平的若干問題, *Xibei Daxue xuebao*, 1988.7: 24–31.
Liu Chengji 劉成紀. "Lu Zhaolin de bingbian yu wenbian" 盧照鄰的病變與文變. *Wenxue yichan*, 1994.5: 43–49.
Luo Xiangfa 駱祥發. *Chu Tang sijie yanjiu* 初唐四傑研究. Beijing: Dongfang, 1993.
Lü Shuangwei 呂雙衛. "Lun Lu Zhaolin shiwen chuangzuo de 'sao yuan' jingshen" 論盧照鄰詩文創作的'騷怨'精神, *Yunmeng xuekan* 2002.5: 55–58.
Ma Qingzhou 馬慶洲. *Chu Tang sijie* 初唐四傑. Beijing: Zhonghua, 2010.

Nienhauser, William H., Jr. "Chang'an on My Mind: A Reading of Lu Zhaolin's 'Chang'an, Thoughts on Antiquity'," *Sungkyun Journal of East Asian Studies*, 10.1 (April 2010): 121–52.

Ren Guoxu 任國緒. *Lu Zhaolin ji nianpu* 盧照鄰年譜. Harbin: Heilongjiang Renmin, 1991.

___. "Lu Zhaolin shengping shiji xinkao" 盧照鄰生平事跡新考. *Wenxue yichan*, 1985.2: 51–56.

___. "Luelun Lu Zhaolin Luo Binang de qiyan gexing" 略論盧照鄰駱賓王的七言歌行. *Beifang Luncong*, 1985.3: 38–43

___. "Lu Zhaolin sixiang shuping." 盧照鄰思想述評. *Beifang Luncong*, 1993.6: 66–72.

Shang Ding 尚定. "Lu Luo gexing de jiegou moshi yu yishu yuanyuan" 盧駱歌行的結構模式與藝術淵源. *Wenxue pinglun*, 1993.6: 94–104.

Takagi Masakazu 高木正一. "Ryo Shōrin no denki to bungaku" 盧照鄰の傳記と文學, *Ritsumeikan bungaku*, 196 (October 1961), 777–809.

Wang Minghao 王明好. *Lu Zhaolin yanjiu* 盧照鄰研究. Beijing: Renmin, 2013.

Wen Dongmei 文冬梅. "Lun Lu Zhaolin de jingshen kunao" 論盧照鄰的精神苦惱. Ph.D. dissertation, Haerbin Shifan Daxue, 2011.

Wen Yiduo 聞一多. "Si Jie" 四傑, in Wen, *Tangshi zalun* 唐詩雜論, in *Wen Yiduo quanji*, Rpt. Beijing: Guji, 1956, v. 1, pp. 23–29.

Xie Jiujuan 謝久娟. "Qianxi Lu Zhaolin shige de yixiang" 淺析盧照鄰詩歌的意象. *Yangzhou Chiye Daxue xuebao* 揚州職業大學學報 2010.14 : 15–18.

Xu Ping 徐平. "P'ing Lu Zhaolin ji qianzhu 評《盧照鄰集箋注》," *Zhongguo wenxue yanjiu*, 1996.3.

Zhan, *Daojiao*, pp. 228–32.

Zhang Zhilie 張志烈. *Chu Tang sijie nianpu* 初唐四傑年譜. Chengdu: Ba Shu, 1992.

Zhu Shangshu 祝尚書. "'Lu Zhaolin shengping shiji xinkao' shangdui" 《卢照邻生平事迹新考》商兑, *Sichuan Shifan Daxue xuebao (Shehui Kexueban)*, 1988.1.

___. "Ping *Lu Zhaolin ji* jiaodu zhayi" 評盧照鄰校讀扎迻, *Sichuan Daxue xuebao (Zhexue Shehui Kexueban)*, 1988.3.

Paul W. Kroll and William H. Nienhauser, Jr.

Lu Zhi 陸贄 (*zi*, Jingyu 敬輿, 754–805) was one of the most influential inner-court politicians of his time and master of a polemical *pianwen* prose-style which anticipated the *siliu* 四六 *pianwen* of the eleventh century. His extant prose works are official documents written over a fifteen-year period (779–794) during which he served as a key adviser to Emperor Dezong (r. 779–805).

Lu was born into one of the four leading southern clans. His immediate family came from Jiaxing 嘉興 (modern Zhejiang). At the age of nineteen, he placed sixth (out of thirty-four) in the *jinshi* examination and began a meteoric climb to the center of political power. Having spent the intervening six years in provincial posts, he was called to Chang'an in 779 to serve as a censor. Emperor Dezong, impressed with Lu's judgment and prose style, had Lu made a Hanlin Academician the next year. In this capacity, Lu Zhi developed an extremely close relationship with Dezong through a position that was outside the normal bureaucratic chain. Dezong had come to the throne with the intention of wresting control from rebellious northeastern military leaders who then ruled large parts of the empire with virtual independence. The emperor's actions provoked a series of rebellions in the early 780s. One rebel group forced him to flee to Fengtian 奉天, where he became most dependent on the advice and support of Lu Zhi and a few other officials who accompanied him there. Many of Lu's extant memorials date from 783 and 784 and seem to have been influential in determining the direction of imperial policy. The rest were written from 792 through 794 when he was a Grand Councilor, attempting to convince the emperor to carry out economic reforms and to restrain his own avarice.

The following memorial, written ca. 784 to advise Emperor Dezong on how to reward peasants who had presented melons to him, exhibits some of the key principles in his writing of his early career, namely righteousness (*yi* 義) and expediency (*quan* 權):

> The way to establish a state lies solely in righteousness and expediency. The method to lead people lies solely in fame and profit. Fame is close to emptiness but is important in moral teaching; profit is close to substance, but is light in virtue. All those measures used to consider and decide right and wrong and to set up legal institutions are dependent upon righteousness.
>
> As for considering when to employ fame or profit, judging the degree of their moral importance, making them coexist without harming each other, adopting them alternately without contradiction, following the multitude's desire, estimating the appropriateness of the time and hence practicing proper administration in prosperous or declining times so as not to exhaust the people—all of these things depend upon expediency.
>
> If the ruler relies exclusively on substantial profits without the aid of emptiness [i.e., fame], these profits will then be wasted and deficient, and the resources [of the state] will be insufficient. If the ruler relies exclusively on empty fame without supplementing it with substance [profit], this fame will then be deemed absurd and deceptive and people will not be motivated to pursue it. The reason the state formulates a code of awards, grants money, and goods, and bestows grain emoluments is to make manifest the substance [profit]; the reason it differentiates between official ranks and makes distinctions in the adornment of their clothes is to beautify the emptiness [fame].

> 夫立國之道，惟義與權，誘人之方，惟名與利。 名近虛而於教為重，利近實而於德為輕，凡所以裁是非立法制者，則存乎其義。
>
> 至於參虛實，揣輕重，並行而不傷，迭用而不悖，因眾之欲，度時之宜，消息盈虛，使人不倦者，則存乎其權。
>
> 專實利而不濟之以虛名，則耗匱而物力不給；專虛名而不副之以實利，則誕謾而人情不趨。故國家之制賞典，錫貨財，賦秩廩，所以彰實也；差品列，異服章，所以飾虛也

Lu upheld righteousness as the moral basis of a state. Without it there would be no standard upon which moral judgments could be made. Expediency was a complementary principle which allowed the state institutions to operate within the moral framework.

During most of his fifteen years of service, Lu Zhi enjoyed the emperor's companionship and protection. However, after the recovery of the capital in 784, and especially after Lu Zhi became Grand Councilor in 792 (and was no longer an imperial adviser), his remonstrations of imperial actions led to strained relations with Dezong. In 792 he was the examiner for the famous Dragon-Tiger Slate 龍虎榜 of *jinshi* that included Han Yu 韓愈 (768–824),* Li Guan 李觀 (766–794),* and Ouyang Zhan 歐陽詹 (ca. 755–ca. 801).*

Lu's vitriolic attack on another adviser, Pei Yanling 裴延齡 (738–796), finally provoked the emperor to demote Lu. But for the intervention of Lu Zhi's influential friends, including the heir apparent, he would have been executed. In 795 he was exiled to a post at Zhongzhou 忠州 (modern Zhongxian 忠縣, Sichuan). Ten years later, in 805, both the emperor and Lu Zhi died. By the end of the year, Lu Zhi was granted the posthumous title Xuan 宣.

Lu's writings have been traditionally cited as examples of straightforward, loyal remonstrations of a monarch. Indeed, his memorials, especially those of 783 and 784, are unusually frank. At least three times during the bureaucrat-dominated eleventh and twelfth centuries, copies of Lu Zhi's memorials were presented to Song emperors as polite reminders that officials be allowed to speak their minds on public issues.

Lu Zhi's *pianwen* style was different from the style of the Six Dynasties which had continued to influence prose through the early eighth century. To a certain extent Lu's style was an outgrowth of the changes brought about by Zhang Yue 張說 (667–731)* and Su Ting 蘇頲 (670–727)* during the early eighth century. It was used to compose official rather than personal prose pieces and contained fewer historical allusions than the older style, but it adhered more strictly to the *pianwen* format of parallel four- and six-syllable lines. Lu Zhi's prose diction is unique. The polemical qualities of his writing, using a relatively uncomplicated vocabulary to appeal directly to the emperor's reasoning powers and emotions, like a modern political speech, are also noteworthy.

Lu Zhi's prose seems to have survived nearly intact since first published, but little of his poetry is extant. Modern editions of his prose writings can be traced to at least three different Song textual traditions, all including the same writings. According to the *Xin Tang shu*, his prose was originally published in two works, a twelve-*juan* collection of memorials, both official (*zhongshu zouyi* 中書奏議) and private (*zoucao* 奏草), and a ten-*juan* anthology of edicts (*zhigao* 制告) he wrote on the emperor's behalf. An extant preface to the latter collection by his follower Quan Deyu 權德輿 (761–818)* says that the memorials were published in fourteen *juan*. However, all extant editions of his prose include the same eighty-three edicts and fifty-six memorials.

BIBLIOGRAPHY

Editions:
Lang Ye 郎曄 (fl. 1132–1187). *Pingzhu Lu Xuangong ji* 評註陸宣公集. Taibei: Taiwan Zhonghua, 1970. Original title: *Zhu Lu Xuangong zouyi* 註陸宣公奏議. Chronologically the second of three textual traditions; includes Lang Ye's 1191 memorial and annotations. A photocopy of Liu Tieleng 劉鐵冷 1925 collation of a 1354 edition with other versions, including one with punctuation.

___. *Tang Lu Xuanggong ji* 唐陸宣公集. 22 *juan*. SBCK. The oldest text tradition; includes Su Shi's 蘇軾 memorial of 1193. No annotations. Reprint of Song edition.

___. *Tang Lu Xuangong hanyuan ji zhu* 唐陸宣公翰苑集注. 24 *juan*. Taibei: Shijie, 1964. Based on a sixteenth-century edition, includes Xiao Sui's 蕭燧 memorial (1186) and annotations by Zhang Peifang 張佩芳 (1732–1793). This is the only modern annotated edition with both the edicts and the memorials.

Quan Tang shi, 5: 3282–83, 14: 10639.
Quan Tang wen, 460–75.5414–556.
Wang Su 王素, ed. *Lu Zhi ji* 陸贄集. 2v. Beijing: Zhonghua, 2006. Modern critical edition.

Biographical Sources:
Jiu Tang shu, 139.3791–819.
Xin Tang shu, 157.4911–36.

Studies:

Ding Yan 丁晏 (1794–1875). *Tang Lu Xuangong nianbu* 唐陸宣公年譜. Beijing: Beijing Tushuguan, 1999.

Jiang Yin 蔣寅. "Lu Zhi he ta de zhengzhi wen" 陸贄和他的政治文. *Gudian wenxue zhishi*, 1990.2: 71–75.

Liu Xuepei 劉學沛. "Lu Zhi lun zhiguo zhi dao" 陸贄論治國之道. *Fujian luntan* 24 (1985): 56–60.

Lu Shen 陸申. *Lu Xuangong nianpu* 陸宣公年譜. Beijing: Beijing Tushuguan, 1999.

Shen Shirong 沈時蓉. "Shi lun Lu Zhi dui Han Yu ji Tang guwen yundong de yingxiang" 試論陸贄對韓愈及唐古文運動的影響. *Sichuan Shifan Daxue xuebao* 1991.1 (1991): 22–27.

Twitchett, Denis. "Lu Chih (754–805): Imperial Adviser and Court Official," in Arthur F. Wright, ed. *Confucian Personalities*. Stanford: Stanford University, 1962. pp. 84–122.

Ueki Hisayuki 植木久行. "Tōdai kakka shin ginen roku (5)–Gi Chō, Gu Seinan, Jōkan Shōyō, Tei Ryōshi, Haku Kyoi, Haku Gyōkan Gō Hō, Ra In, Ri Riran, Raku Shi, Ryū Ushaku" 唐代作家新疑年錄 (5)– 魏徵, 虞世南, 上官昭容, 鄭良士, 白居易, 白行簡, 鮑防, 李李蘭, 陸贄, and 劉禹錫, *Bunkei ronsō* XXXVII, 3, 1992.

Yan Yiping 嚴一萍. *Lu Xuangong nianpu* 陸宣公年譜. Taibei: Yiwen, 1975.

Yang Ximen 楊希閔. *Tang Lu Xuangong nianbu* 唐陸宣公年譜. Beijing: Beijing Tushuguan, 1999.

Yu Jingxian 于景祥. *Lu Zhi yanjiu* 陸贄 研究. Shenyang: Liaoning Renmin, 1998.

C. Bradford Langley and William H. Nienhauser, Jr.

Lü Wen 呂溫 (*zi*, Heshu 和叔 and Huaguang 化光, 772–811) was a gifted author whose literary achievements are often outshone by those of his more illustrious contemporaries, and forever overshadowed by the political intrigue that haunts his intellectual legacy. Born in Hedong 河東 County (modern Yongji 永濟 Municipality in Shanxi), Lü's youth and adolescence were spent in a world struggling to make sense of the cataclysm that recently had befallen it. Like so many others born into privileged families of Tang society, Lü's boyhood was spent in study. His father, Lü Wei 呂渭 (735–800) trained him to read classical texts like the *Shijing* and the *Liji*. He learned to interpret the *Chunqiu* with the distinguished academic Lu Zhi 陸質 (754–805),* and he later honed his skill in creative composition under the watchful eye of Liang Su 梁肅 (753–793),* a celebrated man of letters and exemplar for the then emerging *Guwen yundong* 古文運動 (Ancient-style Prose Movement). Lü most likely sat for the *jinshi* examinations in 798, passing with distinction, and following in the footsteps of a number of renowned literati earlier in the decade that included Han Yu 韓愈 (768–824)* and Liu Zongyuan 柳宗元 (773–819).* At the same time he also successfully sat for the Erudite Literatus examination. Soon after he began to serve in an imperial bureaucracy that had been revitalized by an efflorescence of artistic genius not seen since the reign of Xuanzong (r. 712–756).

Lü Wen's rise to political prominence was meteoric. First appointed Editor in the Academy of Scholarly Worthies, within five years was promoted to the position of Reminder of the Left. During this period he befriended other prominent scholars like Liu Zongyuan and Liu Yuxi 劉禹錫 (772–842).* Lü had quickly become the favorite of Wang Shuwen 王叔文 (ca. 735–806), an ambitious politician who had been slowly grooming a stable of young talents to take over the reins of the Tang imperium after his patron, the Heir Apparent Li Song 李誦 (761–806, later Emperor Shunzong, r. 805), ascended the throne.

Lü Wen

In 804, Lü and Zhang Jian 張薦 (744–804) were sent as emissaries to Tibet. When the aging Zhang died before reaching their destination, Lü pressed onward, spending more than a year away from the capital he had worked so hard to reach. The poetry which remains from this period offers one of the few glimpses of ninth century Tibet through the eyes of a Tang literatus. Though one might expect that the brooding majesty of the Himalaya would have spurred a talent like Lü Wen to pen contributions to the growing corpora of *shanshui* 山水 (mountains and waters) and *biansai* 邊塞 (frontiers and fortresses) poetry, Lü found little solace in such conventions; his spirits perhaps faltered in the thin, frigid airs of the world's highest plateau. In one surviving quatrain from this period, he writes with resentment for even the moonlight in his bedchamber, as if the natural world itself had become too much for him to bear. At the same time, the harshness of his experience left a lasting impression on Lü, instilling him with a sense of spiritual reaffirmation and renewal as seen in his "Tufan bieguan song Yang Qi lushi xiangui" 吐蕃別館送楊七錄事先歸 (At a Tibetan Inn, Seeing off the Recorder, Yang the Seventh, Who Is Returning Before Me):

Sorrowful clouds once more brush the ground,
whirling snows blur the distant road.
Don't be distressed by the gloom in mountains ahead,
as you return you'll see your way clear.

愁雲重拂地，飛雪亂遙程。
莫慮前山暗，歸人正眼明。

His surviving literary corpus of one hundred or so poems and a number of prose essays, is dominated by resolute, vigorous works in this vein. He wrote poetry almost exclusively in the prosodically intricate regulated verse forms typical of his day, and of these Lü favored pentasyllabic octaves and especially the septasyllabic quatrain. It is primarily for the latter that he is most remembered as a poet, and his preference for these dense, terse poetics gave rise to a lyrical style that is unusually bold and at times almost wild. He was particularly fond of meditating on the past in his writings, as if looking for portents of the future through the echoes of deep antiquity. However, his work is often underlain by epidictic commentary on the political tides of his life and times, though his appetite for rebuking his faction's rivals and his personal enemies would eventually lead to political hardship. Moreover, as a political theorist he was ruthless and authoritarian, frequently drew upon Legalist thought for inspiration. He wrote a number of influential treatises on governance including "Ren wenhua cheng lun" 人文化成論 (A Treatise on the Civilizing of Men) and "Zhuge Wuhou miao ji" 諸葛武侯廟記 (A Record of the Temple of Zhuge [Liang], the Martial Marquis) which are celebrated for their literary artistry as much as for the ideas they espouse. The literary legacy of Lü Wen is in many ways emblematic of his era as it bears all the marks of a man determined to avoid the disasters of previous generations. "Zhenyuan shisinian hanshen jian quanmen yi shaoyao hua" 貞元十四年旱甚見權門移芍藥花 (On Seeing an Aristocrat's Transplanted Peonies as the Drought of the Fourteenth Year of the Zhuanyuan Era [798] Worsens), which attacks the lack of concern for the common good in many officials of the time, is one of his better known works:

Green plateaus and verdant barrows slowly become dust,
Drawing water from wells to revive his garden day after day.
The fourth month brings flowers and transplanted peonies,
I don't know anyone who might still be concerned for the state.

綠原青壠漸成塵，汲井開園日日新。
四月帶花移芍藥，不知憂國是何人。

Though Lü Wen might have initially rued his transfer to Tibet that made the capital seem so remote, it was this distance which shielded him from the conspiracy that would soon engulf court politics. Emperor Shunzong, his faction's patron, who had only just ascended the throne, was stricken by a sudden and mysterious illness and was forced to abdicate. His staunchest supporters were scattered to the four winds. By the time the smoke had cleared in 806, Emperor Shunzong and Wang Shuwen were dead and allies like Liu Zongyuan and Liu Yuxi were banished to the far reaches of the empire. While the surviving members of his faction languished in exile, Lü, by virtue of his distance, emerged unscathed and upon his return to the capital he was promoted to Vice Director of the Ministry of Revenue, Vice Director of the Bureau of Honors, and later Director of the Ministry of Justice. However, in 808 his unyielding nature and a bizarre political struggle at court earned him the ire of the then grand councilor Li Jifu 李吉甫 (758–814), and he was demoted and sent to modern-day Hunan Province to serve as the new Prefect of Daozhou 道州, a position he would take up in Hunan again at Hengzhou 衡州 two years later. The news of his demotion had been painful for his allies and friends, as he had become their man in the capital, a surrogate for their collective political will and their greatest hope for redemption. But such dreams would soon wither for, within a year of arriving at Weizhou in the fall of 811, Lü Wen was dead. The news of his death was particularly devastating for Liu Zongyuan who grieved him in a piece entitled "Hengzhou Cishi Lü Jun lei" 衡州刺史呂君誄 (An Eulogy for Mr. Lü, Prefect of Hengzhou).

BIBLIOGRAPHY

Editions:
Lü Hengzhou ji 呂衡州集, 10 *juan*. SKQS.
Lü Heshu wen ji 呂和叔文集. 10 *juan*. SBCK..
Quan Tang shi, 6: 4170–90, 13: 9922.
Quan Tang wen, 625–31.7067–131.
Tan Ying 譚瑩, ed. *Lü Hengzhou ji: fu kaozheng* 呂衡州集：附考證. Taibei: Yiwen, 1965. Annotated reprint based on the *Siku quanshu* edition
Wu Chongyao 伍崇曜, ed. *Lü Hengzhou ji kaozheng* 呂衡州集考證. Taibei: Hualian, 1965. Heavily annotated reprint of the *Siku quanshu* edition.

Biographical Sources:
Fu, *Tang caizi*, 2:537–52, 5:256–58.
Jiu Tang shu, 137.3768–70.
Xin Tang shu, 160.4967.

Studies:
Bol, pp. 145–46.
DeBlasi, Anthony. *Reform in the Balance: The Defense of Literary Culture in Mid-Tang China*. New York: SUNY Press, 2012. Contains discussions of Lü's thoughts on education and literary culture throughout.
Deng Chuanrui 鄧傳銳 and Yu Shucheng 余恕誠. "Tangren chu Tufan de shishi: Lun Lü Wen shi Fan shi 唐人出使吐蕃的詩史: 論呂溫使蕃詩. *Minzu wenxue yanjiu*, 2012.4
Ip Po-chung, Danny 葉寶忠. *Lü Wen shengping yu sixiang yanjiu* 呂溫的生平與思想研究. Unpublished Ph. D. Thesis, University of Hong Kong, 1995.
Liu Chengqun 劉成群. *Lü Hengzhou kaolun* 呂衡州考論. Unpublished Ph.D. Thesis, Fudan University, 1995.
Ma Chengsu 馬承驌. *Lü Heshu xuepu* 呂和叔學譜. Taibei: Hongshi, 1977.
Zhang Shizhao 章士釗. "Lü Wen," in Zhang, *Liuwen zhiyao* 柳文指要. Rpt. Shanghai: Wenhui, 2000, pp. 1283–96.
Zhao Rongwei 赵荣蔚. *Lü Wen nian pu* 呂溫年譜. Xi'an: Sanqin, 2003.
___. *Lü Wen yanjiu* 呂溫研究. Xi'an: Sanqin, 2003.

Thomas Donnelly Noel

Luo Binwang 駱賓王 (ca. 640–684) was a master of Six-Dynasties-style *pianwen* 駢文 prose and an important early reformer of Qi-Liang-style 齊梁體 court poetry. He, Lu Zhaolin 盧照鄰 (ca. 634–ca. 689),* Wang Bo 王勃 (650–676),* and Yang Jiong 楊炯 (650–694)* were called the *Chu Tang sijie* 初唐四傑 (The Four Eminences of the Early Tang).

Luo Binwang, unlike the other three "Eminences," did not attempt to seek a simplicity in his poetic diction, but rather carried over to his poetry all the complex prosodic rules and allusive language of his *pianwen*. He attempted to divorce himself from the superficial sentiments found in Qi-Liang-style poetry and to enter the world of deep emotional expression without forgoing his desire to display his erudition.

Luo Binwang's family was from Yiwu 義烏 (modern Zhejiang), but he was raised mostly in North China (modern Shandong), where his father was an official. Sometime during the 650s he was recommended to the court as a companion for Prince Dao 道王, Li Yuanqing 李元慶 (636–664), and probably served the prince until the latter's death in 664.

Between 665 and 670, Luo drafted documents in Chang'an. However, in 670 he was banished to the remote post of Anxi Xizhen 安西西鎮 (modern Turfan in Xinjiang), and later traveled with the imperial army to Yaozhou 姚州 (modern Yao'an 姚安) in another remote district (modern Yunnan). During these years Luo wrote many detailed and emotional descriptions of these desolate regions and of his exile.

By 674 Luo's political fortunes had improved and he was made a Recorder at Wugong 武功, not far from Chang'an; in 677 or 678 he was made a recorder in Chang'an itself. Concurrently he was appointed to the Censorate, but he was soon thrown in jail for criticizing the growing power of Empress Wu (r. 690–705). In 679 he was released during an amnesty and appointed a magistrate at Linhai 臨海 (modern Zhejiang). Finding himself at odds with Empress Wu (she had deposed the new emperor), he resigned and joined the rebellion of Xu Jingye 徐敬業 (d. 684; also known as Li Jingye 李敬業) at Yangzhou. Luo Binwang contributed to the rebels' cause by submitting a dispatch addressed to Empress Wu explaining their motives (see below). In 684 the rebellion was crushed and Luo is presumed to have been one of thousands who perished. In the sixteenth century Luo's grave was rediscovered and he became the object of veneration by late Ming scholars. One of these men successfully petitioned the emperor to grant Luo the posthumous title Wenzhong 文忠.

Luo is best known for his old-style poetry–it makes up the bulk of his extant verse corpus. During his lifetime his "Di jing pian" 帝京篇 (Poem on the Imperial Capital), written in five-syllable lines, was well known. However, later critics tend to agree that his "Chou xi pian" 疇昔篇 (Poem on Former Times), a very long autobiographical poem (over 1300 characters) written in both five- and seven-syllable lines, far surpasses it. In fact this poem is an example of early narrative poetry and as such occupies an important place in Chinese literary history. Another of Luo's well-known poems is "Zai yu yong chan" 在獄詠蟬 (In Prison Chanting about Cicadas), a five-syllable poem in regulated verse written in 678. This piece was anthologized by many popular collections of Tang poetry, such as the *Tangshi sanbaishou* and has also been frequently translated into English (see bibliography below):

> The sun tracks west: autumn and the cicada sings,
> As prisoner, my longing for home deepens.
> How can I endure the image of my black wings
> That cause me to face my own 'Song of White Hair'?
> Under heavy dew it's difficult to fly here.
> In the strong wind voices are easily suppressed.
>
> If no one believes in my lofty purity,
> Who will express for me what is in my heart?

> 西陸蟬聲唱，南冠客思深。
> 那堪玄鬢影，來對白頭吟。
> 露重飛難進，風多響易沉。
> 無人信高潔，誰為表予心。

Luo compares himself throughout the poem to the cicada, associating both with autumn, old age, and purity of song and purpose. "The Song of White Hair" (*Baitou yin* 白頭吟) was the plaint that Zhuo Wenjun 卓文君 sang when she was abandoned by her husband, Sima Xiangru 司馬相如 (179–117 BCE). Luo's song is addressed to the Gaozong (r. 649–683) who has similarly renounced him. But by alluding to white hair, Luo is also certainly referring to his own advancing age. The heavy dew and strong western winds of autumn retard the cicadas' ability to escape as they also depict Luo's plight in prison. In the final couplet Luo sees his own poetic appeal as similar to the cicada's cries to which no one pays close attention. The subject might also be understood as Luo himself: "If no one believes in my lofty purity, / Who will express what is in my heart?").

In the realm of prose, his essay "Wei Xu Jingye tao Wu Zhao xi" 為徐敬業討武曌檄 (A Dispatch on Behalf of Xu Jingye Condemning [Empress] Wu Zhao) is an excellent example of parallel prose and one of the representative pieces of this genre from the early Tang period. It is likely that Luo's training and expertise in writing parallel prose influenced his later poetry, often resulting in a highly ornamental and somewhat artificial effect. Whereas his adept skill at couching literary allusions in elaborate language is quite appropriate in his prose, the same is not always applicable to his verse. Nonetheless it is significant that he attempted to expand the acceptable limits of poetry by using this format to express his personal experiences and sentiments. In this way Luo provided a precedent for later Tang poets who further developed the use of poetry for self-expression.

Luo's writings were probably proscribed during Empress Wu's reign. Subsequently Emperor Zhongzong (r. 705–710) issued an appeal to collect whatever survived. The task fell to Xi Yunqing 郗雲卿 whose preface still appears in some editions. Xi's collection of Luo's works eventually consisted of ten *juan* and may be substantially the same collection we have today. During the Ming, several fairly complete annotated editions of Luo's works were published in four *juan*, including that of Yan Wen 顏文 in 1615; they were based largely on writings copied from general anthologies of Tang writers.

BIBLIOGRAPHY

Editions:
Luo Binwang. *Luo Binwang wenji* 駱賓王文集. 10 *juan*. SBCK. Photocopy of a Ming reprint of a Yuan edition.
Luo Binwang. *Luo Binwang wenji* 駱賓王文集. Beijing: Zhonghua, 1986.
Luo Binwang. *Luo Binwang wenji* 駱賓王文集. Beijing: Zhongguo Shudian, 1988.
Luo Binwang. *Luo Cheng ji* 駱丞集. 1615, 4 *juan*. In *Sikuquanshu zhenben*, Series 4. Taibei: Taiwan Shangwu, 1974. Annotated by Yan Wen 顏文.
Quan Tang shi, 2: 7588–683.

Annotations:
Luo Binwang. *Luo Linhai ji jianzhu* 駱臨海集箋注. 10 *juan*. 1953; rpt. Beijing: Zhonghua, 1961. Modern, punctuated edition with text annotated by Chen Xijin 陳熙晉 (1791–1851); includes extensive biographical materials.
Luo Xingfa 駱祥發. *Luo Binwang shi pingzhu* 駱賓王詩評注. Beijing: Beijing Chubanshe, 1989.
Wang Guoan 王國安 and Wang, Youmin 王幼敏, eds. *Chu Tang Sijie yu Chen Zi'ang shiwen xuanzhu* 初唐四傑與陳子昂詩文選注. *Zhongguo gudian wenxue zuopin xuandu congshu*. Shanghai: Shanghai Guji, 1995.

Biographical Sources:
Fu, *Tang caizi*, 1:55–66, 5:7–8.
Jiu Tang shu, 190C.5006–07.
Xin Tang shu, 201.5742–43.

Translations:
Bynner, *Jade Mountain*, p. 80.
Frankel, *Flowering Plum*, p. 91.
Margoulies, *Anthologie*, pp. 218–20.
Minford and Lau, pp. 688–90.
Owen, "Deadwood," pp. 163–65.
Owen, *Early T'ang*, pp. 111–15, 138–50.
von Zach, *Han Yü*, p. 312.

Studies:

Chen Xijin 陳熙晉. "Xubu Tangshu Luo Binwang shiyu zhuan" 續補唐書駱賓王侍御傳. In *Luo Linhai ji jian zhu*, pp. 387–94.

Chen Yu 陳瑜 and Du Xiaoqin 杜曉勤. "Cong Eshino zhong muzhi kao Luo Binwan congjun xiyu shishi" 從阿史那忠墓誌考駱賓王從軍西域事實. *Wenxian* (2008.3): 29–37.

Furukawa, Sueyoshi 古川末喜. "Sho-Tō shiketsu no bungaku shisō" 初唐四傑の文學思想, *Chūgoku bungaku ronshū*, 8 (1979), 1–27.

Klöpsch, Volker. "Luo Binwang's Survival: Traces of A Legend." *TS* 6 (1988): 77–97.

Liu Kaiyang 劉開揚. "Lun Tang sijie ji qi shi" 論初唐四傑及其詩, in *Tang shi lunwen ji* 唐詩論文集, Shanghai: Zhonghua Shuju Shanghai Bianjisuo, 1961, pp. 1–28.

Liu Weichong 劉維崇. *Luo Binwang pingzhuan* 駱賓王評傳. Taibei: Liming Wenhua Shiye Gongsi, 1978.

Luo Xiangfa 駱祥發. *Luo Binwang quanzhuan* 駱賓王全傳. Shanghai: Shanghai Renmin, 2011.

___. *Chu Tang sijie yanjiu* 初唐四傑研究. Beijing: Dongfang, 1993.

___. "Luo Binwang jianpu" 駱賓王簡譜, *Zhejiang Shifan Xueyuan xuebao (Shehui Kexue ban)*, 1984.2: 81–90.

Owen, *Early T'ang*, pp. 1–14.

Takagi, Masakuzu 高木正一. "Raku Hinnō no denki to bungaku" 駱賓王の傳記と文學, *Ritsumeikan bungaku* 245 (1965): 95–117.

Tanemura Yukiko 種村由季子. "Raku Hinō 'Teikyo hen' to sokuten buko no rakuyochuren" 駱賓王「帝京篇」と則天武后の洛陽駐輦. *Nihon Chūgoku-gaku kaihō* 64 (2012): 67–81.

Wang Zengbin 王增斌. "Lun Luo Binwang shi" 論駱賓王詩, *Jinyang xuekan* 晉陽學刊 1994.5: 91–95.

Yang Encheng 楊恩成. "Luo Binwang shengzu niankao bian" 駱賓王生卒年考辨, *Renwen zazhi*, 1981.2: 108–11.

Yang Liu 楊柳, Luo Xiangfa 駱祥發. *Luo Binwang pingzhuan* 駱賓王評傳. Beijing: Beijing Chubanshe, 1987.

Zhan, *Daojiao*, pp. 232–35.

Zhang Zhilie 張志烈. *Chu Tang sijie nianpu* 初唐四傑年譜. Chengdu: Ba Shu Shushe, 1992.

Zhejiangsheng Gudai Wenxue Xuehui 浙江省古代文學學會, ed. *Luo Binwang yanjiu lunwenji* 駱賓王研究論文集. Hangzhou: Hangzhou Daxue, 1993.

C. Bradford Langley, Madeline Spring and William H. Nienhauser, Jr.

Luo Yin 羅隱 (original name Heng 橫, *zi*, Zhaojian 昭諫, 833–909) was a native of Yuhang 餘杭 (some say of Xincheng 新城) in Hangzhou. He and his kinsmen Luo Qiu 羅虬 and Luo Ye 羅鄴, also talented writers, were collectively styled "The Three Luos" 三羅. Luo Yin aspired to a career in government but failed the metropolitan examinations six times, despite the support of important persons, notably the minister Zheng Tian 鄭畋 (825–883). Unfortunately his censorious character, which often showed itself in a mocking and sarcastic manner, alienated other highly placed men whose favor was necessary for preferment. Despite his ugly visage, which is said to have spoiled a promising alliance with Zheng Tian's daughter, a physiognomist prophesied that he would ultimately find success in the Wu 吳 area (near modern Suzhou). Bitter because of his failure at court, he left Chang'an in 880. It appears that another factor in this decision was the chaos attendant upon the military successes of the revolutionist Huang Chao 黃巢 (d. 883), who occupied the capital and, on January 6, 881, inaugurated the reign "Binding [Authority] of Metal" (Jintong 金統) over the new state of Qi 齊. Luo Yin appears to have found peace and profit in his pleasant old homeland, fortunate in its wealth of such resources as cinnabar, ginger, clams, and silk. He spent the rest of his life as the loyal servant of Qian Liu 錢鏐 (852–932), who eventually became prince of the semi-independent state of Wu Yue 吳越 during the waning years of the Tang.

Luo Yin was a prolific writer, but the greater part of his production is now lost. What survives of his prose is scattered through a number of short texts, some of them, for example the *Chan shu* 讒書 (Defamatory Writings), mixed with pieces of poetry. In that collection the author offers revisions of Confucian notions about antiquity and novel opinions about society and history. Elsewhere are his reflections on kingship, duty, and public morality (in the *Liang tong shu* 兩同書). He also wrote wonder tales and stories of adventure. Examples are preserved in *Guangling yaoluan zhi* 廣陵妖亂志. Some official correspondence, prefaces to literary works, descriptions of town and country, and a fair number of reflective essays on many subjects–matters of belief and tradition preponderate–usually infused with a moral tone, also survive.

The themes of Luo Yin's poems fall into readily definable groups. One is made up of verses about the capital city, especially the Qujiang 曲江 (Serpentine River), the pleasure park of the aristocracy; others focus on Luoyang, Hunan, the Yangzi River, and, above all, the Wu area, including Hangzhou, Jiangdu 江都 (Yangzhou), and Gusu 姑蘇 (Suzhou). His poems on the former homes and the tombs of eminent men form another category. There are references to his correspondence with such distinguished contemporaries as Guanxiu 貫休 (823–912)* and Lu Guimeng 陸龜蒙 (836–881).* Many of his poems tell of religious events and festivals and visits to temples and monasteries. He sometimes displays a longing for the world above, as when he wistfully addresses a Daoist priest ("Ji Diwu Zunshi" 寄第五尊師: "I wish to visit you, Prior Born, to ask about the scriptures and the oral arcana. In *this* world it is hard to gain anything which does not spring from yourself" 欲访先生问经诀, 世间难得不由身. He also wrote of such popular celebrations as Qixi 七夕 (Seventh Evening) and Qingming 清明 (Clear and Bright) and about the goddess of the Xiang River (Xiang Fei 湘妃).

There are a great many poems about the natural world, including peonies, chrysanthemums, swallows, goshawks, snow fireflies, the moon, bees, wildflowers, and the blooms of the peach, the apricot, and the paulownia. Characteristically he showed a strong preference for wilted flowers, red leaves, and other aspects of autumn, along with ghosts, dust, and other tokens of the transience and decay that eat away at the living world. But he found many other subjects suitable to his pen, among them incense, embroidery, music, pictures, and even horoscope astrology. In all of these topics he found occasion for a cultural analogy or moral allegory–usually a pessimistic one. A caged parrot leads him to comment that plain speech tends to stand in the way of advancement in the world of men, as he knew well from his own experience. Many of his poems are undisguised attacks on public practice; one such is his treatment of "Snow," in which he finds the supposedly auspicious character of a heavy snowfall a sorry mockery, since the poor folk of Chang'an are freezing to death:

> Everyone says this snow's an auspice of a bumper harvest.
> What good will a bumper harvest do?
> Chang'an has many poor people,
> For them to be auspicious, it shouldn't snow much.

盡道豐年瑞，豐年事若何。
長安有貧者，為瑞不宜多。

Although he has a reputation as a writer on historical themes (*yongshi* 詠史), he shows his contempt for cherished views of historical process; an example is his poem about the beauty Xi Shi 西施, in which he attacks the traditional notion that a kingdom can be subverted by the gift of an enchanting woman to its ruler: "If Xi Shi knew how to subvert the Kingdom of Wu, who then was it that brought about the downfall of the Kingdom of Yue?" 西施若解傾吳國, 越國亡來又是誰. Here, in effect, he was refuting the "great man" theory of history.

In addition to these lyric effusions, Luo Yin wrote a number of *fu* 賦, of which five survive. They treat the subjects of spider webs, drifting snow, screens, markets, and the labyrinthine palace of Emperor Yang of the Sui. Like his *shi* 詩, these also contain strong allegorical elements.

Traditional accounts of Luo Yin and his writing say little more than that he was a "satirist." But he was much more than that. He was an honest man with a well-developed sense of ethics, and capable of making penetrating insights through shallow conventions. His style favored parable more than true satire.

BIBLIOGRAPHY

Editions:
Chan shu 讒書. *Shaowu Xushi congshu* 邵武徐氏叢書, 1886.
Chan shu 讒書. Collected by Wu Qian 吳騫 (1733–1813). *Congshu jicheng chubian*. Beijing: Zhonghua, 1985.
Chan shu 讒書. 5 *juan*, appendix 1 *juan*. Luo Yin 羅隱. Shanghai: Shanghai Guji, 2002.
Jiayiji 甲乙集. *SBCK*.
Jiayiji 甲乙集: 10 *juan*. Luo Yin 羅隱. Beijing: Beijing Tushuguan, 2003.
Liang tong shu 兩同書, in Yang Jialuo 楊家駱 ed., *Sui Tang zishu shizhong* 隋唐子書十種, v. 2. Taibei: Shijie, 1962; also included in *BBTSJJ*, series 18: *Baoyan tang miji* 寶顏堂秘笈, v. 146.
Lingbizi 靈璧子 in *Zhuzi huihan* 諸子彙函, from *Juying Tang cangban* 聚英堂藏板, ca. 1660.
Luo Yin ji 羅隱集. Yong Wenhua 雍文華, ed. *Zhongguo gudian wenxue jiben congshu*. Beijing: Zhonghua, 1983.
Luo Yin shifeng jiuxi 羅隱詩風究析. Huang Zhigao 黃志高. Taibei: Xuehai, 1981.
Luo Yin shiji jianzhu 羅隱詩集箋注. Luo Yin 羅隱. Li Zhiliang, comm. 李之亮. Changsha: Yuelu Shushe, 2001.
Quan Tang shi 10: 7588–683, 14: 10742.
Quan Tang wen, v. 19, ch. 894–97, pp. 11769–819.
Shi jiazinian shi 拾甲子年事 in *Jiu xiaoshuo* 舊小說, Shanghai: Shangwu, 1921, v. 2, pp. 155–56.
Shuo Shi lie shi 說石烈士 in *Jiu xiaoshuo*, pp. 156–57.
Wang Xiaoning 王小寧, ed. *Luo Zhaojian xiaopin* 羅昭諫小品. Beijing: Wenhua Yishu, 1997.
Zhao Ji 趙季 and Ye Yancai 葉言材, ed. *Luo Shaojian xiaopin* 羅邵諫小品. Beijing: Wenhua Yishu, 1997.

Annotations:
Luo Yin shiji jianzhu 羅隱詩集箋注. Luo Yin 羅隱. Li Zhiliang, comm. 李之亮. Changsha: Yuelu Shushe, 2001.

Biographical Sources:
Fu, *Tang caizi*, 4:112–31, 5:456–57.
Jiu Wudai shi, Xue Juzheng 薛居正 (921–981). Beijing: Zhonghua, 2015, 24.375–76 and textual note on p. 380.

Translations:
Kroll, Paul. "The Egret in Medieval Chinese Literature," *CLEAR*, 1.2 (July 1979): 186.

Sunflower, pp. 266–67.

Yang Xianyi, trans. "Selections from 'Slanderous Writings,'" *Chinese Literature*, (Feb. 1982): 119–22.

Studies:

De Meyer, Jan. "Confucianism and Daoism in the Political Thought of Luo Yin," *TS* 10-11 (1992–1993): 67–80.

___. "'Listing the Past to Disparage the Present: Luo Yin and his *Slanderous Writings*," *Chinese Culture* 37 (1996): 69–85.

Deng Guiying, trans. by Yang Xianyi. "The Late Tang Writer Luo Yin," *Chinese Literature* (Feb. 1982): 113–18.

Li Dahua 李大華 et al. "Luo Yin Daojiao shehui lishi guan" 羅隱的道教社會歷史觀 in *Sui Tang Daojia yu Daojiao* 隋唐道家與道教. Beijing: Renmin, 2011, pp. 581–603.

Pan Huihui 潘慧惠. "Lun Luoyin ji qi shiwen" 論羅隱及其詩文, *Wenshizhe* 226 (1995): 76–80.

Wang Dezhen 汪德振. *Luo Yin nianpu* 羅隱年譜. Shanghai: Shangwu, 1937.

Zhang Qiugui 張丘奎. *Tangmo Du Fu shige yanjiu yi Luo Yin, Wei Zhuang, Han Wo sanren wei tantao* 唐末杜甫詩歌研究以羅隱韋莊韓偓三人為探討. Taibei: Huamulan, 2020.

Edward H. Schafer

Ma Dai 馬戴 (*zi*, Yuchen 虞臣, ca. 799–ca. 869) was a poet best known for his five-syllable regulated poetry (*wulüshi* 五律詩) and his poetry about his travels to the frontier *biansaishi* 邊塞詩. He also wrote many political allegories (*ganyu shi* 感遇詩) and leisure poems (*xianyi shi* 閒逸詩). Little is known about his personal life. Even the date of his birth is contested. He was born in Quyang 曲陽 (in modern Jiangsu). However, as he frequently visited Huazhou 華州, scholars sometimes refer to him as a Huazhou native. He tried the *jinshi* examination several times before he passed it in 844, the same year as Zhao Gu 趙嘏 (ca. 806–ca. 850).* In the beginning of the Dazhong reign (847–859) he became the Chief Secretary of the Office of the Army Commander in Taiyuan 太原. He was later demoted to the position of Commandant in Longyang County 龍陽縣 in Langzhou 朗州 (modern Changde City 常德市 northwest of Changsha). His final post was as an Erudite of the National University. He was acquainted with and exchanged poetry with many of the more known poets of his day such as Yao He 姚合 (ca. 779–ca. 849),* Jia Dao 賈島 (779–843),* Yin Yaofan 殷堯藩 (780–855), and Gu Feixiong 顧非熊.

Although little known today, Ma Dai was well received in his lifetime. Yan Yu 嚴羽 (ca. 1195–after 1245), claimed that Ma Dai is a better poet than all others from the Late Tang. His reputation lasted throughout the Ming and Qing, but thereafter lost popularity. Modern scholars focus on his frontier poetry, which captures various images of life in China's frontier regions, quite different from more familiar scenes of Chang'an or other centers of Chinese culture. Take "She diaoqi" 射鵰騎 (A Rider Shooting an Eagle) as an example.

> The foreign-visaged general wears a marten-fur coat,
> Singing merrily he dashes through the snow in this border region.
> Still hunting through Mount Black, still riding his horse:
> A cold vulture shot down without turning his head.

蕃面將軍著鼠裘，酣歌衝雪在邊州.
獵過黑山猶走馬，寒鵰射落不回頭.

This poem ostensibly depicts a Tujue (Turkic) general such as those who commanded Tang troops. Whether he is fighting for the Tang or for the Turks is unclear, but Mount Black (Hei shan 黑山) is the site of an important Tang victory of the Turks in a prolonged campaign from 679–680 and from the overall context of the poem it seems he is a Tang commander. Marten fur (*shu qiu* 鼠裘 is an abbreviation for *diaoshu qiu* 貂鼠裘) is expensive and precious and wearing it shows the status and extravagance of this general. Ma Dai's sketch on the surface praises his striking apparel, unconstrained moves, and superior marksmanship of this border-defender, but he imbues every line with a certain irony, suggesting the problems of the Tang depending on such men. Cen Shen 岑參 (ca. 715–770)* has a similar poem: "Hu ge" 胡歌 (Song of a Tartar), which depicts one of the leaders of the Western Turk Hei (Kara Turgesh or Black Bone) Clan 黑姓, may support the idea that Ma Dai too was implying a less favorable extended meaning:

> A Black Clan Tartar-king in marten-fur coat—
> Drunk, he offers a palace-style grape-embroidered headband [to a dancer].
> While west of the pass the old generals able to fight bitter battles,
> At seventy still sending forth troops, they are yet to rest.

黑姓蕃王貂鼠裘，葡萄宮錦醉纏頭.
關西老將能苦戰，七十行兵仍未休.

The *chantou* 纏頭 was a headband or a turban often awarded to excellent dancers at parties attended by female entertainers. The grape was a motif favored by Turkic military leaders. Cen Shen depicts the elegant dress and misbehavior of a Turk commander who had won favor with the Tang to the life of the "old generals," Chinese generals who are enduring a difficult life on the northwestern frontier (the pass here is probably Yang Pass 陽關, forty miles southwest of modern Dunhuang).

BIBLIOGRAPHY

Editions:
Quan Tang shi, 14: 10677.

Annotations:
Yang Jun 楊軍 and Ge Chunyuan 戈春源, eds. *Ma Dai shizhu* 馬戴試注. Shanghai: Shanghai Guji, 1987. A collection of all of Ma Dai's poetry with annotations. The appendices also provide helpful biographical data.

Translations:
Owen, *Late Tang*, pp. 137–39.

Studies:

Fang Qi 方奇. "Ma Dai kaolun" 馬戴考論. Unpublished M.A. Thesis. Huazhong Shifan Daxue, 2012.

Han Jinfeng 韓金風. "Ma Dai ji qi shige yanjiu" 馬戴及其詩歌研究. Unpublished M.A. Thesis. Xiamen University, 2006.

Hua Yan 華岩. "Guanyu Ma Dai ji qi shige chuangzuo" 關於馬戴及其詩歌創作, in *Tangdai wenxue luncong* 唐代文學論叢. Xi'an: Shaanxi Renmin, 1986, pp. 39–54.

Shi Haijun 師海軍. "Ma Dai biansai manyou kaolue" 馬戴邊塞漫遊考略. *Xibei Daxue Xuebao*, 38.5 (Sept. 2008): 110–12.

Josiah Stork

Meng Haoran 孟浩然 (689–740) ranks among the most renowned poets who lived during the reign of Emperor Xuanzong (r. 712–756), an age blessed with a host of gifted writers whose works constitute one of the chief treasures of Chinese literature. Meng was a decade or more older than most of the other famous poets–Li Bo 李白 (701–762),* Wang Wei 王維 (692–761 or 699–759),* Du Fu 杜甫 (712–770)*–who were active during this period. He may thus be regarded, along with Zhang Jiuling 張九齡 (678–740),* as a senior representative of the so-called High Tang poets.

Meng's tie to his natal place, Xiangyang 襄陽 (in modern north-central Hubei) was exceptionally strong, and he seems to have spent all but a decade of his life there. Xiangyang's historical heritage–especially as the home of many of the most famous recluses of the late Han and early Three Kingdoms (such as Zhuge Liang 諸葛亮 [181–234], Pang Tong 龐統 [179–214], Xu Shu 徐庶 [fl. 220], Sima Hui 司馬徽 [fl. 200], and Pang Degong 龐德公 [fl. 200])–was both rich and illustrious. Abundant references to the local lore, legends, and history of the area are found in Meng's numerous poems on the lovely hills and streams of Xiangyang. Two sites may be noted as being of especial importance to him. The first is his family seat, a place called "Nan yuan" 南園 (South Garden), located near Fenghuang shan 鳳凰山 (Phoenix Mountain), about three miles south of the city. This site is also often referred to in Meng's poems as "Nan shan" 南山 (South Mountain). It is this spot–not the Zhongnan Mountains south of Chang'an, as commonly asserted—that is the locus of his well-known poem "Suimu gui Nanshan" 歲暮歸南山 (Returning to South Mountain on the Eve of the Year). The other place with which Meng was most closely associated is Lumen Shan 鹿門山 (Deer Gate Mountain), ten miles southeast of Xiangyang. Although the evidence is scant, it appears that at some time Meng briefly established a hermitage for himself on the slopes of this mountain, in conscious imitation of Pang Degong who secluded himself there five centuries earlier. Meng celebrated his habitation on Deer Gate Mountain and his self-identification with Pang Degong in the famous poem "Ye gui Lumen ge" 夜歸鹿門歌 (A Song on Returning at Night to Deer Gate). Later writers invariably link Meng's name with this mountain, although his period of residence there was short.

In contrast to most writers of his day, Meng Haoran did not enjoy a career in government service. In 728, at the relatively advanced age of thirty-nine, he sat for—and failed—the *jinshi* examination. However, a year-long stay in Chang'an at this time, as well as earlier and later visits to Luoyang, put him on familiar terms with several of his more successful contemporaries. In the autumn of 737 the influential statesman and writer Zhang Jiuling, who had recently been ousted from his high position at court and rusticated to central China, appointed Meng as his assistant, thus allowing Meng for the first and only time in his life to don the garb of a Tang official (his rank was but one step from the bottom of the thirty-rung bureaucratic ladder). But any exhilaration Meng may have felt over this was fleeting, for he resigned this post less than a year later. Two years afterward he died at home in Xiangyang.

It has long been a cliché of traditional criticism to pair Meng Haoran and Wang Wei as the two exemplars of a "school" of Tang "nature poetry." But this facile and somewhat reductive characterization, based primarily on a dozen or so "anthology pieces," does justice to neither poet. In Meng's case, an examination of his entire *oeuvre* reveals him to be a poet of more parts than is customarily acknowledged. Many of his verses, for example, display elegantly allusive turns of phrase that remind one strongly of the work of Six Dynasties poets or exhibit his scholarly command of pre-Tang literature and history.

Comparing his so-called "nature poems" with those of Wang Wei, reveals striking differences in the diction, tone, and viewpoint of the two writers. Meng's depictions of natural scenes are usually precise and individualized, with most attention given to foreground objects – in contrast to Wang Wei, whose landscapes are more generalized and non-specific, focusing often on large, background images. This difference is reflected in the range of vocabulary employed in each poet's work: the various kinds of flora, fauna, and topographic features presented by Meng–and the detail with which he describes them–far exceed what one finds in Wang Wei's verses. A notable human presence, or at least the unmistakable persona of the poet, is another feature common to Meng Haoran's landscapes. He is a warm poet, who does not often lose himself totally in his scenes. Meng is, however, an extremely moody and erratic poet, whose peaks of verbal excellence are sometimes commeasured by vales of unremarkable platitudes. In this regard, he is perhaps the least consistent of the major poets of the period.

His quatrain "Chun xiao" 春曉 (Daybreak in Spring) is one of the best-known poems, perhaps because it was included as the first poem in *Qianjia shi* 千家詩 (Poems of a Thousand Authors), a primer for aspiring poets used from late Song times on:

> Dozing in spring and unaware of daybreak—
> 'Til all around one hears the chittering of birds!
> During the night, the sound of wind and rain—
> But of the blossom's falling, how much do we know?

春眠不覺曉，處處聞啼鳥。
夜來風雨聲，花落知多少。

It bears mention that this poem is not just a lyrical vignette of waking up late to the raucous cries of birds and dimly recalling the storm of the preceding night (although it *is* primarily this); it is also a miniature portrait of our human, superficial, and uncertain perception of the ways of life in this world. We know as much, and as little, about our own existence and passing away as about the falling of nature's blossoms.

BIBLIOGRAPHY

Editions:
Ke Baocheng 柯寶成, ed. *Meng Haoran quanji* 孟浩然全集. Wuhan: Chongwen, 2013.
Kroll, Paul W. and Joyce Wong Kroll. *A Concordance to the Poems of Meng Hao-jan*. San Francisco: Chinese Materials Center, 1982. Keyed to the *SBCK* text.
Meng Haoran ji 孟浩然集. Changsha: Yuelu Shushe, 1990.
Meng Haoran ji 孟浩然集. *SBCK*. The standard text of the poems; copy of a Ming woodblock edition.
Meng Haoran shiji 孟浩然詩集. Beijing: Beijing Tushuguan, 2003.
Meng Haoran shiji 孟浩然詩集. Shanghai: Shanghai Guji, 1982.
Quan Tang shi, 3: 1622–72, 14: 11055.

Annotations:
Cao Yongdong 曹永東, ed. *Meng Haoran shiji jianzhu* 孟浩然詩集箋註. Tianjin: Tianjin Guji, 1989.
Chen Yixin 陳貽焮, ed. and comm. *Meng Haoran shixuan* 孟浩然詩選. Beijing: Renmin Wenxue, 1983.
Li Hua 李華, ed. and comm. *Meng Haoran shi baishou* 孟浩然詩百首. Zhengzhou: Zhongzhou Guji, 1990.
Li Jingbai 李景白, ed. and comm. *Meng Haoran shiji jianzhu* 孟浩然詩集箋注. Chengdu: Ba Shu Shushe, 1988. Contains biographical and critical materials, and Meng's preface.
Tong Peiji 佟培基, ed. *Meng Haoran shiji jianzhu* 孟浩然詩集箋註. Shanghai: Shanghai Guji, 2000.
Wang Dajin 王達津, ed. and comm. *Wang Wei, Meng Haoran xuanji* 王維, 孟浩然選集. Shanghai: Shanghai Guji, 1990. Includes biographical material.
Wang Peilin 王沛霖, ed. and Cao Yongdong 曹永東, comm. *Meng Haoran shiji jiaozhu* 孟浩然詩集校注. Tianjin: Tianjin Guji, 1989. Appends Meng's preface, critical materials, and a *nianpu*.
Xiao Jizong 蕭繼宗. *Meng Haoran shishuo* 孟浩然詩說. Taibei: Taiwan Shangwu, 1985.
Xu Peng 徐鵬, comm. *Meng Haoran ji jiaozhu* 孟浩然集校注. Beijing: Renmin Wenxue, 1989.
You Xinli 游信利, annot. *Meng Haoran ji jianzhu* 孟浩然集箋注. Taibei: Jiaxin Wenhua Jijinhui 嘉新文化基金會, 1968. The most thorough and best annotated edition, based on the *SBBY*. However, frequent typographical errors require one always to check these versions against the *SBCK* text.
Zhao Guifan 趙桂藩, comm. *Meng Haoran jizhu* 孟浩然集注. Beijing: Lüyu Jiaoyu, 1991.

Biographical Sources:
Fu, *Tang caizi*, 1:362–75, 5:70–72.
Jiu Tang shu, 190C.5050.
Xin Tang shu, 203.5779–80.

Translations:
Chang Hsin-chang. "Meng Hao-jan," in his *Chinese Literature, Volume 2: Nature Poetry*. New York: Columbia University Press, 1977, pp. 81–96.
Demiéville, *Anthologie*, pp. 213–15.
Hinton, David. *The Mountain Poems of Meng Hao-jan*. New York: Archipelago Books, 2004.
___, *Anthology*, pp. 147–56.
Fuller, Michael A. *An Introduction to Chinese Poetry: From the* Canon of Poetry *to the Lyrics of the Song Dynasty*. Cambridge: Harvard University Press, 2018, pp. 190–92.
Kosho Hiroshi 公庄博. *Mo konen zen'yaku shishu: haru no nemuri no kokochiyosa* 孟浩然全訳詩集:春の眠りの心地よさ. Kyoto: Sobunsha, 2008.
Kroll, Paul W. *Meng Hao-jan*. Boston: Twayne, 1981.
___, "The Quatrains of Meng Hao-jan." *MS* 31 (1974–75): 344–74.

Margoulies, *Anthologie*, pp. 188, 373–74, 392.
Miao, "T'ang Quatrains," pp. 65–70.
Minford and Lau, pp. 825–27.
New Directions, pp. 61–64.
Owen, *Anthology*, pp. 33, 373, 375, 395–97.
___, *High Tang*, pp. 71–88. Translation with short readings of the poems.
___, *Remembrances*, pp. 24–25.
Pimpaneau, pp. 416–18.
Sunflower Splendor, pp. 92–96.

Studies:

Aoyama Hiroshi 青山宏校閲. *Mo Konen shi sakuin* 孟浩然詩索引. Tokyo: Kyūko, 1981.
Bryant, Daniel. "The High T'ang Poet Meng Hao-jan: Studies in Biography and Textual History." Unpublished Ph.D. dissertation, University of British Columbia, 1978.
Chen Xinzhang 陳新璋. *Meng Haoran Lunxi* 孟浩然論析. Guangzhou: Guangdong Renmin, 2004.
Chen Yixin 陳貽焮 (1924–2000). "Meng Haoran shiji kaobian" 孟浩然事跡考辨. *Wenshi* 4 (1965): 41–74.
___, "Tan Meng Haoran de yinyi" 談孟浩然的陰逸. *Tangshi yanjiu*: 46–52.
Ding Xixian 丁錫賢, "Meng Haoran 'You Tiantaishan' kao" 孟浩然游天台山考. *Dongnan wenhua* 6 (1990): 302–4.
Field, "Taking Up the Plow," pp. 124–25.
Frankel, Hans H. *Biographies of Meng Hao-jan*. Berkeley: University of California Press, 1952.
Fu Xuancong 傅璇琮. "Tangdai shiren kaolue Meng Haoran" 唐代詩人考略孟浩然, *Wenshi* (1980.3).
Kroll, Paul W. *Meng Hao-jan*. Boston: Twayne, 1981.
___. "The Quatrains of Meng Hao-jan." *MS* 31 (1974–75): 344–74. Contains translations.
___. "Wang Shih-yüan's Preface to the Poems of Meng Hao-jan" *MS* 34 (1979–80): 349–69.
Liu Ning 劉寧. *Wang Wei, Meng Haoran shi xuanping* 王維孟浩然詩選評. Shanghai: Shanghai Guji, 2011.
Liu Wengang 劉文剛. *Meng Haoran nianpu* 孟浩然年譜. Beijing: Renmin Wenxue, 1995. Contains the official biographies of Meng Haoran as well as Tang dynasty prose pieces and poems concerning Meng.
Liu Yang 瀏陽. *Meng Haoran yanjiu wenji* 孟浩然研究文集. Beijing: Renming Ribao, 2001.
Miller, James Whipple. "The Poetry of Meng Hao-jan: Translations and Critical Introduction for the Western Reader." Unpublished Ph.D. dissertation, Princeton University, 1972.
Qu Delai 曲德来. *Meng Haoran and Wang Wei* 孟浩然王維. Shenyang: Chunfeng Wenyi, 1999.
Rust, Ambros. *Meng Hao-jan, 691–740: sein Leben und religiöses Denken nach seinen Gedichten*. Ingenbohl: Theodosius Buchdruckerei, 1960.
Suzuki Shuji 鈴木修次. *Tōdai shijin ron* 唐代詩人論. Tokyo: Otori, 1973, v. 1, pp. 75–137.
Taniguchi Akio 谷口明夫. "Mo Konen jiseki kō: jokyo oshi o megutte" 孟浩然事跡考: 上京應試をあぐって. *Chūgoku chusei bungaku kenkyū* 11 (1976): 48–65.
Wang Congren 王從仁. *Wang Wei he Meng Haoran* 王維和孟浩然. Shanghai: Shanghai Guji, 1984.
Wang Huibin 王輝斌. *Meng Haoran da cidian* 孟浩然大辭典. Hefei: Huang Shan Shushe, 2008.
___. *Meng Haoran yanjiu* 孟浩然研究. Lanzhou: Gansu Renmin, 2002.
Yang Yinshen 楊陰深. *Wang Wei yu Meng Haoran* 王維與孟浩然. Shanghai: Shangwu, 1936.
Zha Zhengxian 查正賢, "Mugui de shixue: Meng Haoran de shiyi xide yu chaoyue" 暮歸的詩學：孟浩然的詩藝習得與超越. *Wenxue yichan* (2006.4): 65–73.
Zhongguo Meng Haoran Yanjiuhui 中國孟浩然研究會. *Meng Haoran yanjiu luncong* 孟浩然研究論叢. Hefei: Huangshan, 2015.

Paul W. Kroll and William H. Nienhauser, Jr.

Meng Jiao

Meng Jiao 孟郊 (*zi,* Dongye 東野, 751–814) was the eldest and most difficult of the *fugu* 复古 writers who gathered around Han Yu 韓愈 (768–824)* at the turn of the ninth century. Meng was from Huzhou 湖州 (modern Wuxing in Zhejiang), and during his younger years he seems to have had contact with the Jiao Ran 皎然 (720–799)* Circle, then active in the region. However, it was not until 791, when Meng went to the capital to take the examination and met the young Han Yu, that he began to write poetry in the harsh, idiosyncratic style for which he was later famous.

Meng Jiao twice failed the examination for the *jinshi*, in 792 and 793, and those failures occasioned angry, disillusioned lyrics that were to win Meng the shocked contempt of many later readers. His "Lao hen" 老恨 (Frustrations of Old Age), although written later in life is typical:

> I have no child to take down my writings—
> what an old man chants mostly falls away lost.
> Sometimes I blurt them into my bed,
> but my pillow and mat don't understand.
> Battles of ants on the tiniest scale,
> yet in sickness I hear them so clearly.
> To tell no difference between large and small
> is the true nature of things, Heaven's gift.

> 無子抄文字，老吟多飄零。
> 有時吐向床，枕席不解聽。
> 鬥蟻甚微細，病聞亦清泠。
> 小大不自識，自然天性靈。

Here, Meng Jiao's frustration over his own failing is expressed in the melancholy of others' disregard. The poem's first several lines direct his lament outward at the lack of those who could appreciate his work—the absence of children to heed his words, the inanimate objects of his bed that offer no comfort in the middle of the night. The poem pivots with the realization that in the miniscule world of ants, conflicts of life and death go equally unrecognized. Realizing the profundity of being disregarded, the final lines turn inward to revisit his own concern for achieving recognition.

In 796 Meng took the examination for the third time and passed. At least for a time he was gleeful, expressing his joy as he celebrated in a short poem titled "Dengke hou" 登科後 (After Passing the Examination):

> Of the wretchedness of my former years I have no need to brag:
> Today's gaiety has freed my mind to wander without bounds.
> Lighthearted in the spring breeze, my horse's hooves run fast;
> In a single day I've seen all the "flowers" of Chang'an.

> 昔日齷齪不足誇，今朝放蕩思無涯。
> 春風得意馬蹄疾，一日看盡長安花。

Line three could also be read as Meng attaining his goal (*deyi* 得意) by passing the examination after several unsuccessful attempts and receiving the imperial favor (*chunfeng* 春風) that goes along with it. The "flowers" of the final line may also refer to the beautiful young entertainers who often accompanied the parties thrown by successful candidates.

Despite this success, Meng Jiao lacked necessary support from powerful patrons in the government; he did not receive a position until 800, and then it was the lowest provincial post in the official hierarchy. By 806 Meng had given up official life and settled in Luoyang, where he spent the rest of his life.

With the exception of two letters and one brief encomium, Meng Jiao's extant work consists of just over five hundred poems, almost all pentasyllabic old-style verse. As Meng himself so proudly claimed, his style was out of harmony with the gracious occasional poetry of his contemporaries. In Meng's own occasional poetry, even when he aspired to simple graciousness, there is almost always some jarring note: whether he erred in excessive directness or in excessive obliquity, he always erred. His *yuefu* 樂府 and non-occasional poems are often straightforward and consciously rough, sometimes developing complex conceits, but usually avoiding the polish and ornament of contemporary poetics. Meng Jiao conceived of his work as being in the "ancient style," and ethical messages, associated with the mid-Tang revival of Confucian values, occur throughout his poetry. Yet even in his ethics there is discord, and such poems often possess a shrill stridency that undermines and complicates the magisterial calm of the would-be didactic poet.

Meng Jiao's most interesting and difficult works are his remarkable poem-sequences: among these are the fifteen "Qiuhuai" 秋懷 (Autumn Meditations), the ten poems of "Shicong" 石淙 (Stone Run), the nine poems of "Hanxi" 寒溪 (Cold Creek), the twelve "Diao Yuan Lu shan" 弔元魯山 (Elegies for Mount Yuanlu), ten "Xia'ai" 峽哀 (Laments of the Gorges), nine poems on "Xingshang" 杏殤 (The Death of Apricots), and ten "Diao Lu Yin" 弔盧殷 (Elegies for Lu Yin). These sequences contain some of the most difficult and disturbing poetry of the Tang, at times verging on madness. "The Death of Apricots," for example, explores the correspondences and reciprocal relations between the early death of Meng's infant sons and the destruction of blossoms in a late-spring frost. The theme might have been a merely convenient analogy for another poet; in Meng Jiao the correspondences provoke the suspicion of an invisible and malicious order governing the world's operations. "Cold Creek" and "Laments of the Gorges" likewise concern encounters with cosmic malice embodied in landscapes. Through such poems many later readers came to hate the poetry of Meng Jiao, but the explications of his verse preserved in *shihua* 詩話 often attest to the disturbing power of Meng Jiao's best work. The first of the "Cold Creek" poems, which depicts the little stream than runs before Meng's home village, exemplifies that praise and that malice:

> Frost washes the water's color out,
> In Cold Creek tiny fish can be seen.
> As I regally inspect this empty mirror,
> It shines back a ruined, haggard body.
> What would sink away cunningly can't hide itself,
> Its bottom revealed, the luster fresher and fresher.
> Clarity seeming to be a good man's heart,

Meng Jiao

> Was in truth a treacherous trap for men.
> For now I see clearly the shallow common soul,
> At night it froze, by dawn already fordable.
> Rinsed pure by two hands of emerald green,
> Melting far from me the foulness of a thousand cares.
> Now I know that a stream that muddies feet,
> Will never be a neighbor to the mountain spring.

霜洗水色盡，寒溪見纖鱗。
幸臨虛空鏡，照此殘悴身。
潛滑不自隱，露底瑩更新。
豁如君子懷，曾是危陷人。
始明淺俗心，夜結朝已津。
淨漱一掬碧，遠消千慮塵。
始知泥步泉，莫與山源鄰。

The poem, an introduction to the sequence of nine poems, is about revelation of the creek's treacherous winter nature and the moral ambivalence of nature itself, which Meng Jiao proceeds to lay out in the following eight poems of the series. The entire poem can be read as a comment on the purity of reclusion versus the turbid world and false pretense of Tang political life. Lines seven and eight warn of the true nature of the current which, perhaps like those embroiled in court politics, appears to act as a gentlemen only to reveal an unfeeling disregard toward others. The final four lines seem to suggest a ritual of ablution as Meng washes away the dusty world and dedicates himself to life by Cold Creek—at least for the time being.

Meng Jiao's linked verses, written always with Han Yu and sometimes including several other participants, show Meng in a different light. Speculative buffoonery, erudite word games, and stylistic *tours de force* make such poems a delight to read. "Chengnan lianju" 城南聯句 (Linked Verse, South of the City), written on an excursion south of Chang'an, remains the greatest linked-verse in the language.

Yet one of his most famous poems is a touching rendering of a son's maternal love titled "Youzi yin" 游子吟 (Song of a Traveling Son), which concludes in a couplet that compares this love to that of many years of the warm spring sun:

> From the threads in a mother's hands,
> A coat for the traveling son's back.
> Sewn stitch by stitch as he's about to leave,
> Her only concern that his return might be delayed.
> Who would claim that the heart of a tiny sprout of grass
> Would be able to repay the warmth of many spring's sun?
> Who could say that the heart of such a tiny sprout
> Could repay what it received from the warmth of an entire spring?

慈母手中線，遊子身上衣。
臨行密密縫，意恐遲遲歸。
誰言寸草心，報得三春暉。

For two centuries after his death, Meng Jiao's reputation remained very high. However, a pair of famous poems by Su Shi 蘇軾 (1037–1101), "Du Meng Jiao shi" 讀孟郊詩 (On Reading Meng Jiao's Poetry), attacked Meng with a directness that only the brash Su Shi would dare. The second of these poems begins baldly: "I detest the poems of Meng Jiao" 我憎孟郊詩 (an outrageous inversion of a conventional opening of panegyric, "I love . . .") and continues with a memorable parody of Meng's easily parodied style. The careful reader of Su Shi will note, however, that Su borrowed extensively from the poet whose work he so abhorred. Between this attack and the growing literary-historical orthodoxy that freely damned the whole mid-Tang style, Meng was placed back among the second rank of Tang poets, and his work continues to be generally unpopular.

BIBLIOGRAPHY

Editions:
Hua Chenzhi 華忱之, ed. *Meng Dongye shiji* 孟東野詩集. Beijing: Renmin Wenxue, 1959.
___ and Yu Xuecai 喻學才, eds. *Meng Jiao shiji* 孟郊詩集. Beijing: Renmin Wenxue, 1995.
Kazuo Noguchi 野口一雄. *Mō Kō shi sakuin* 孟郊詩索引. Tokyo: Tokyo Daigaku, 1984.
Luan Guiming 欒貴明 et al., eds. *Quan Tangshi suoyin, Meng Jiao juan* 全唐詩索引: 孟郊卷. Beijing: Xiandai, 1995.
Meng Dongye wenji 孟東野文集. Shanghai: Shanghai Guji, 1994.
Meng Dongye wenji: wujuan 孟東野文集: 五卷. Beijing: Beijing Tushuguan, 2006.
Quan Tang shi, 6: 4191–289; *Quan Tang wen*, 684.7726–27.

Annotations:
Chen Yanjie 陳延傑, ed. and comm. *Meng Dongye shizhu* 孟東野詩注. Shanghai: Shangwu, 1939.
Han Quanxin 韩泉欣. *Meng Jiao jijiao zhu* 孟郊集校注. Hangzhou: Zhejiang Guji, 1995.
Hao Shifeng 郝世峰. *Meng Jiao shi ji jianzhu* 孟郊詩集箋注. Shijiazhuang: Hebei Jiaoyu, 2002.
Liu Sihan 劉斯翰. *Meng Jiao, Jia Dao shixuan* 孟郊, 賈島詩選. Hong Kong: Sanlian, 1986.
Xia Jingguan 夏敬觀 (1875–1953). *Meng Jiao shi xuanzhu* 孟郊詩選注. Taibei: Taiwan Shangwu, 1965.

Biographical Sources:
Fu, *Tang caizi*, 2:502–18, 5:245
Jiu Tang shu, 160.4204–05; *Xin Tang shu*, 176.5265.

Translations:
Demiéville, *Anthologie*, p. 304.
Graham, *Late Tang*, pp. 57–69.
Hinton, David. *The Late Poems of Meng Jiao*. Princeton: Princeton University, 1997.
___, *Anthology*, pp. 237–49.
Mair, "Tang Poems," pp. 347–48.

Margoulies, *Anthologie*, pp. 233, 301, 317–18, 416–17.
McCraw, David. "Yuanhe Poetry Sequences: A New Look." *JAOS* 136 (2016): 69–97.
New Directions, pp. 120–22.
Owen, *Anthology*, pp. 288, 478–84.
___, *Middle Ages*, pp. 13–15, 70–75.
___, *Omen*, pp. 270–72, 277–78, 284–85.
___, *Remembrances*, pp. 18–19.
Sunflower, pp. 157–64.

Studies:

Dai Jianye 戴建業. *Meng Jiao lun gao* 孟郊論稿. Shanghai: Shanghai Guji, 2006.
Fan Xinyang 范新阳, "Meng Dongye zaonian shenghua kaolüe" 孟東野早年生化考略, *Jiangxi Shifan Daxue Xuebao (Zhexue Shehui kexue ban)* (2007.06).
___, "'Meng Dongye shiji' yishi kaobian" '孟東野詩集' 疑詩考辨, *Huaiyin Shifan Xueyuan Xuebao (Zhexue Shehui Kexue Ban)* (2013.06).
Hu Yu 胡蔚, "'Meng Dongye shiji' deng Tang ji de ji shouwu shoushi kao" '孟東野詩集' 等唐集的几首誤收詩考 *Wenxian* (July 2007.03): 25–31.
Hua Chenzi 華忱之. *Tang Meng Jiao nianpu* 唐孟郊年譜. Beijing: Guolu Beijing Daxue Tushuguan, 1940.
Li Deshan 李德山, "Ming keben 'Meng Dongye shiji' kaoshu" 明刻本'孟東野詩集'考述, *Guji Zhengli Yanjiu Xuekan* (1998.04): 42–46.
Liu Zhuqing 劉竹青. *Meng Jiao, Jia Dao yanjiu* 孟郊, 賈島研究. Taibei: Wenshizhe, 2003.
Owen, *Meng Chiao*. Contains numerous translations.
Shang, Wei. "Prisoner and Creator: The Self-Image of the Poet in Han Yu and Meng Jiao." *CLEAR* 16 (1994): 19–40.
Shields, Anna M. *One Who Knows Me: Friendship and Literary Culture in Mid-Tang China*. Cambridge and London: Harvard University Asia Center, 2015, pp. 101–15, 159–72 and passim.
Xie Jianzhong 謝建忠. "Daojiao yu Meng Jiao shige" 道教與孟郊詩歌. *Wenxue yichan* 1992.2 (1992): 42–50.
You Xinxiong 尤信雄. *Meng Jiao yanjiu* 孟郊研究. Taibei: Wenjin, 1984.

Stephen Owen and William H. Nienhauser, Jr.

Ouyang Zhan 歐陽詹 (*zi*, Xingzhou 行周, ca. 755–ca. 800) was one of the first natives of Min (modern Fujian) to pass the *jinshi* examination. He was born into a family of minor local officials in Panhu 潘湖 Village (in modern Jinjiang 晉江 County about ten miles west-southwest of Quanzhou 泉州 in Fujian) who claimed descent from the early Tang academician, Ouyang Xun 歐陽詢 (557–641). Zhan was said to have been a studious, contemplative youth who gained a reputation for his writing. He studied with several friends including Lin Zao 林藻 (*jinshi* 791) whose younger sister he married in 780. When Chang Gun 常袞 (729–783)* was made Surveillance Commissioner of Fuzhou in 780, he and his colleague Xue Bo 薛播 (d. 787), then Prefect of Quanzhou, were impressed with Ouyang and recommended him for the *jinshi*. Ouyang remained at home, however, debating whether he should go north for the examinations. Three sons were born between 781 and 785, the year he finally decided to go to the capital. He sat for the *jinshi* six times before passing in 792 under the chief examiner Lu Zhi 陸贄 (754–805).* Zhan ranked second ahead of Han Yu 韓愈 (768–824),* who was third, Li Guan 李觀 (766–794),* Cui Qun 崔群 (772–832), Li Jiang 李絳 (764–830; both Cui and Li became Grand Councilors) and other future notable officials (they were collectively known as the Longhu Bang 龍虎榜 or Dragon and Tiger List). About a year after passing the examination, Ouyang returned to Jinjiang in part to care for his aging parents, but also to enjoy his accomplishment among his family members. As a man with few connections in the capital, he may also have gone home to plan his next career move. By the end of 793 he was back in the capital bringing eight provincial candidates for the examination with him. The following year he went to what is now modern Gansu for unknown reasons. In 795 he took the Erudite Literatus Examination but failed. Later that year he headed north to Taiyuan, where the Military Commissioner of Hedong 河東, Li Yue 李說 (740–800), was based. During his stay with Li Yue, he is said to have met a singing girl and have fallen in love with her.

Nevertheless, in 796 he returned to his home in Panhu where he built a new residence for his family. Returning yet again to Chang'an, he remained in the capital but lived in relative poverty until he passed the placement examination in 798 and was appointed Instructor in the School of the Four Gates in the Directorate of Education. That same year he wrote to Zheng Yuqing 鄭餘慶 (748–820), then a Grand Councilor, seeking a higher position, but nothing came of this. While serving in the Directorate of Education he recommended Han Yu for the position of Erudite (i.e. Professor) there. He died most likely in 800 from unknown causes, although rumors circulated attributing his death to remorse over his ill-fated love affair with the singing girl from Taiyuan.

Han Yu praised Ouyang Zhan for his *guwen* 古文 (ancient-style prose) and wrote a eulogy upon Zhan's death. Ouyang's "Ergong ting ji" 二公亭記 (A Record of the Pavilion of Two Gentlemen) written for the Prefect of Quanzhou, Xi Xiang 席相 (fl. 790), and the former Grand Councilor, Jiang Gongfu 姜公輔 (730 or 731–805), during Zhan's return home in 793, is one of his better known pieces in this style.

While his poetry included a number of pieces written in response to other poets, his verse is also noteworthy for its deftness in portraying his sadness. The following "Yuxing" 寓興 (An Allegory) is typical:

> Peach and plum have wonderful wood,
> Ailanthus and chestnut–oak with no marvelous form.
> All owe fertility to the felicitous clouds,
> With the same spring wind to blow on them.
> The beautiful and the ugly, if they are really no different
> All our bustling about in vain.
> To become a grand councilor or a general depends on the creator,
> For now, goblet in hand, I might as well get drunk.

> 桃李有奇質，樗櫟無妙姿。
> 皆承慶雲沃，一種春風吹。
> 美惡苟同歸，喧嚚徒爾為。
> 相將任玄造，聊醉手中巵。

The poem seems to criticize the arbitrary appointments of high officials and generals, perhaps even appointments of those with whom Ouyang took the *jinshi* examination who found more success in their official careers. Zhan evokes the common trope of peach and plum with their connotation of excellent qualities to contrast the utter lack thereof found in ailanthus and chestnut–oak as a way to distinguish worthiness. Attributing each of their successes to the whim of outside forces, there becomes little point in struggling to prove oneself worthy, especially while the rationale becomes lost in the mystery of the creator. One can feel Ouyang Zhan's sense of frustration as it ultimately turns to resignation in the last line, when all he can do for the time being is drink his sorrows away.

The prose and verse Ouyang Zhan left were first collected under the title *Ouyang Zhan ji* 歐陽詹集 by Li Yisun 李貽孫 (fl. 850), a relative of Zhan's, as well as calligrapher in his own right who served as Prefect of Fuzhou.

BIBLIOGRAPHY

Editions:
Tangshi jishi 唐詩紀事, *juan* 203.
Ouyang Xingzhou ji 歐陽行周集. 10 *juan*. SBCK.
Ouyang Xingzhou ji 歐陽行周集. 10 *juan*. SKQS.
Quan Tang shi, 6: 3909–25; *Quan Tang wen*, 595–98.6766–801.

Annotations:
Liao Yuanquan 廖淵泉, ed. *Ouyang Simen ji* 歐陽四門集. Shanghai: Shanghai Cishu, 2011.
Yang Yiqi 楊遺旗, ed. *Ouyang Zhan wenji jiaozhu* 歐陽詹文集校注. Wuhan: Huazhong Keji Daxue, 2012.

Biographical Sources:
Xin Tang shu, 203.5786–87.

Translations:
Nienhauser (see Studies below)

Studies:
Dai Xianqun 戴顯群. "Ouyang Zhan yu guwen yundong" 歐陽詹與古文運動, *Fujian xuekan*, 1989.4" 45–62, 65.
___. "*Ouyang Xingzhou wenji* banben kaoshu" 歐陽行周文集版本考述, *Guli zhengli yanjiu xuekan*, 1989.6: 29–33.
Huang Jiliang 黃潔琼. "Lun Ouyang Zhan yu Tangdai Fujian wenhua de fazhan" 論歐陽詹與唐代福建文化的發展, *Haerhbin Xueyuan xuebao*, 2004.2: 1–6.
Huang Xinxian 黃新憲. "Ouyang Zhan yu keju" 歐陽詹與科舉, *Xuzhou Shifan Daxue xuebao*, 2005.6: 60–63.
Luo Liantian 羅聯添. "Ouyang Zhan" 歐陽詹, in *Han Yu yanjiu* 漢語研究. Taibei: Student Book Company, 1977, pp. 140–45.
Nienhauser, William H., Jr. "Literature as a Source for Traditional History: The Case of Ou-yang Chan," *CLEAR* 12 (1990): 1–14.
Song Qi 宋祁 (998–1061). "Ouyang Zhan zhuan" 歐陽詹傳, *Xin Tang shu* 新唐書. Beijing: Zhonghua, 1975, *juan* 201, p. 5726.
Wang Chunting 王春庭. "Du *Ouyang Zhan ji* zhaji 讀歐陽詹集札記, *Quanzhou Shifan Xueyuan xuebao*, 2006.3: 67–70.
___. "Manhu zhi ying, wen wei qingjin—Ouyang Zhan yu Zhongyuan wenhua 縵胡之纓, *Zhangzhou Shiyuan xueyuan xuebao*, 2006.3: 60–64.

Yang Qiqun 楊其群. "Shilun Han Yu 'Huibian' sheji de si wenti" 試論韓愈諱辯涉及的四問題, *Shanxi Daxue xuebao*, 1983.3: 41–50.

Yang Weigang 楊偉民. *Ouyang Zhan yanjiu* 歐陽詹研究. Xi'an: Shanxi Shifan Daxue Tushuguan, 2004.

Yang Yiqi 楊遺旗. "'Hanmen dizi' Ouyang Zhan yanjiu zongshu" 韓門弟子歐陽詹研究綜述, *Zhoukou Shifan Xueyuan xuebao*, 2011.4: 27–31.

___. "*Ouyang Xingzhou wenji* shi*juan*ben banben yuanliu kaoshu" 歐陽行周文集十卷本版源流考述, *Guji zhengli yanjiu xuekan*, 2010.1: 25–31.

___. "Ouyang Zhan shengping kaobian sanze" 歐陽詹生平考辨三則, *Hunan Keji Xueyuan xuebao*, 2011.6: 41–43.

___. "*Ouyang Xingzhou wenji* ba*juan*ben banben yuanliu kaoshu" 歐陽行周文集八卷本版源流考述, *Hunan Keji Xueyuan xuebao*, 2010.1: 25–31.

___. "Ouyang Zhan wenyou 'Li Ping shi' kao" 歐陽詹文友李評事考, *Hunan Keji Xueyuan xuebao*, 2009.6: 27–28.

Zhang Changping 張晶平. "Lun Zhong Tang Zhenyuan shifeng" 論中唐貞元詩風. Shanghai: Fudan Daxue Tushuguan, 2005.

Zhang Weimin 張偉民. *Ouyang Zhan nianpu ji zuopin xinian* 歐陽詹年譜及作品繫年. Wuhan: Huazhong Keji Daxue Tushuguan, 2006.

William H. Nienhauser, Jr.

Pei Xing 裴鉶 (ca. 825–ca. 880), whose *zi*, native place, and dates all remain uncertain, was known for composing Tang *chuanqi* 傳奇 (Tang Tales) during the Xiantong era 咸通 (860–874) of Emperor Yizong's 懿宗 reign (r. 859–874). What little is known of his public life places him under the patronage of Gao Pian 高駢 (d. 887), Military Commissioner of the Jinghai Army 靜海軍. As an official, Pei Xing served as the Prefectural Secretary for Gao Pian, who would later make him an Attendant Censor Auxiliary. In the fifth year of the Qianfu 乾符 era (878), he was appointed as the Vice Military Commissioner of Chengdu.

The scant details of his official career stand in contrast to Pei Xing's renown for his literary skill in producing Tang tales, especially those involving the world of divinities, immortals and the anomalous. Early commentaries on Pei Xing's tales like those found in Chao Gongwu's 晁公武 (1105–1180) *Junzhai dushu zhi* 郡齋讀書志 find a political agenda that appealed to his benefactor's predilections toward the marvelous. Later studies such as Wang Pijiang's 汪辟疆 (1887–1966) *Tangren xiaoshuo xulu* 唐人小說敘錄 would hold Pei Xing up as an exemplar of the knight-errant genre (*wuxia xiaoshuo* 武俠小說), focusing on the ornate and evocative aspects of Xing's narratives that would influence later generations.

Among his collections, three tales stand out in part for their influence on later iterations of the knight-errant genre. "Kunlun nu" 昆侖奴 (Slave from Kunlun), "Nie Yinniang" 聶隱娘 (Lady of Whisper and Secret), and "Pei Hang" 裴航 have each found their way into works of later writers of traditional *zaju* 雜劇 (poetic drama). "Kunlun nu" itself serves as the basis for famous adaptations such as *Hongxiao ji* 紅綃記 (The Story of Hongxiao) by Liang Chenyu 梁辰魚 (ca. 1519–ca. 1593) and *Kunlun nu jianxia chengxian* 昆侖奴劍俠成仙 (The Knight-errant Kunlun Slave Becomes an Immortal) by Mei Dingzuo 梅鼎祚 (1549–1615). It continues to inform numerous modern renditions as well, including *Yedao Hongxiao ji* 夜盜紅綃記 (The Story of the Night Theft of Hongxiao) by Nan Shanyan 南山燕 (1919–1982) and adaptions for feature-length films.

Pei Xing

Pei Xing's skill at describing martial-arts action combined with his talent for seductive foreshadowing lends an air of suspense and excitement to his tales that still appeal to a modern audience. In "Kunlun nu," the first meeting between the protagonist Scholar Cui and object of his obsession Hongxiao at the residence of the ranking official Guo Ziyi ends with a mysterious sign from the silent singing girl:

> The ranking official [Guo Ziyi] ordered the singing girl Hongxiao to feed [Cui] with a spoon, so that he had no choice but to eat. The singing girl smiled about it and thereupon bid him farewell and took her leave... [Guo Ziyu] ordered Hongxiao to see him [Cui] off in the courtyard. At that time, the young scholar turned his head to see that the singing girl had raised three fingers. She then turned her palm three times and afterward pointed at the little mirror worn on her chest, saying: "Bear this in mind." There were no further words.

> 一品命紅綃妓以匙而進之，生不得已而食。妓哂之，遂告辭而去...命紅綃送出院，時生回顧，妓立三指，又反三掌者，然後指胸前小鏡子，云："記取。"餘更無言。

Appearing at the very start of the story, this short scene sets the stage for the developing obsession Cui has over this mysterious beauty compelling the audience to wonder along with the protagonist about this provocative girl and the implications of her mysterious message. When the titular Slave from Kunlun named Mole 磨勒 offers to interpret the sign for his master, the Scholar Cui, the details for a daring abduction emerge:

> Raising three fingers means that in the residence of the first-rank official (i.e. Guo Ziyi), there are ten courtyards of singing girls, and this is just the third courtyard. Turning the palm three times amounts to fifteen fingers, also indicating the number of fifteen days. The little mirror on her chest implies that on the night of the fifteenth day, the moon will be as round as the mirror. Isn't this asking you to come?

> 立三指者，一品宅中有十院歌姬，此乃第三院耳。返掌三者，數十五指，亦應十五日之數。胸前小鏡子，十五夜月圓如鏡，令郎來也？

With the solution of the mysterious riddle the singing girl's favor toward Scholar Cui as well as the final and daring theft of Hongxiao from the residence of Guo Ziyi are prepared. Mole first offers that he alone should sneak in and kill the ferocious dog guarding the residence. After succeeding in vanquishing the beast, he takes both Scholar Cui and Hongxiao on his back to escape from the compound:

> Mole said, "I fear it is slowly getting light." Thereupon, he put the scholar and the Singing Girl on his back and flew over and out of more than ten high walls. None of the Ranking Officials' guards were alerted. Thereupon they returned to the scholar's study and hid her... [Guo Ziyi] ordered fifty armored warriors gripping weapons tightly to encircle Cui's study in order to capture Mole. Mole thereupon grabbed his dagger and flew out over the high wall, darting as though he had wings, with a sickening speed like a falcon. Arrows came down like rain, but none could hit him. In the space of no time at all, they did not know which direction he went.

然後曰：恐遲明，遂負生與姬。而飛出峻垣十餘重。一品家之守禦。無有警者。遂歸學院而匿之... 命甲士五十人，嚴持兵仗圍崔生院，使擒磨勒。磨勒遂持匕首，飛出高垣。瞥若翅翎，疾同鷹隼。攢矢如雨，莫能中之。頃刻之間，不知所向。

The seemingly supernatural ability of Mole to evade physical harm by leaping tall buildings resonates with narrative traditions about Daoist immortals and their suprahuman talent for ascending, inspiring later iterations of the story like Mei Dingzuo's account of Mole becoming an immortal. This combination of action and suspense found in Pei Xing's narratives such as "Kunlun nu" and his other tales would accord him reverence as a master of the knight-errant genre. Thus Pei Xing's corpus of *chuanqi* would come to be recorded in multiple sources. The *Yiwen zhi* 藝文志, *Xin Tang shu* 新唐書, and the *Junzhai dushu zhi* record his tales arranged in three-chapters, while the *Zhizhai shulu jieti* 直齋書錄解題 records them in six-chapter editions with the comment that "people in later generations found its chapters too long, and so divided them" 後人以其卷帙多而分之也. Neither the three-chapter version nor the six-chapter version is extant; however, several tales are preserved individually in the *Taiping guangji*. Zhou Lengqie's 周楞伽 (1911–1992) modern annotated edition of Pei Xing's collected *chuanqi* derives from a wide variety of sources.

In addition to his *chuanqi* corpus, Pei Xing also has one extant piece of prose preserved in the *Quan Tang wen* and a single poem in the *Quan Tang shi*. Events and matters from his life are recorded in chapter three of the "Yiwen zhi" of the *Xin Tang shu* as well as in chapter sixty-seven of the *Tangshi jishi* 唐詩紀事.

BIBLIOGRAPHY

Editions:
Pei Xing 裴鉶 (ca. 825–ca. 880). *Zheng Delin zhuan* 鄭德璘傳. Taibei: Yiwen, 1966.
Quan Tang shi, 9: 6964.
Quan Tang wen, 805.9826–28.
Taiping guangji 太平廣集, *juan*: 34, 152, 194, 356, 445. *SKQS*.
Wang Gongwei 王公伟, comp. Pei Xing 裴鉶. *Chuanqi* 傳奇. Beijing: Beijing Chubanshe, 2000.
Wang Meng'ou 王夢鷗. *Tangren xiaoshuo yanjiu* 唐人小說研究. Taibei: Yiwen, 1971.
Zhou Lengqie 周楞伽, comp. *Pei Xing Chuanqi* 裴鉶傳奇. Shanghai: Shanghai Guji, 1980.

Translations:
Edwards, E. D. *Chinese Prose Literature of the T'ang Period, vol. II*. London: Probsthain, 1938, pp. 101–106.
Kao Karl S. Y. *Classical Chinese Tales of the Supernatural and the Fantastic Selections from the Third to the Tenth Century*. Bloomington: Indiana University Press, 1985, pp. 321–362.
Liu, James J. Y. *The Knight-Errant*. London: Routledge, 1967, pp. 88–90. Synopsis of "Kunlun Nu" and "Nie Yinniang" with brief introduction.
Owen, *Anthology*, pp. 198–199. Translation of opening section of "Xiao Kuang."
Wang, C. C. *Traditional Chinese Tales*. New York: Columbia University Press, 1944, pp. 93–103.
Yang Xianyi 楊憲益 (1915–2009) and Gladys Yang (1919–1999), trans. *Chuanqi xuan* 傳奇選. Beijing: Xinshijie, 2002.

Studies:

Altenburger, Roland. *The Sword or the Needle: The Female Knight-Errant (xia) in Traditional Chinese Narrative.* Bern: Peter Lang, 2009, pp. 57–81.

Bian Xiaoxuan 卞孝萱, "Lun 'Qiuranke zhuan' de zuozhe zuonian ji zhengzhi beijing" 論虬髯客傳的作者作年及政治背景, *Dongnan Daxue xuebao* 3 (2005): 93–8.

Chen Junmou 陳君謀, "Pei Xing jiqi Chuanqi" 裴鉶及其傳奇, *Suzhou Daxue xuebao* 1 (1982): 17–25.

Wang Meng'ou 王夢鷗. *Tangren xiaoshuo yanjiu: Zuanyi ji yu Chuan qi jiaoshi* 唐人小說研究: 纂異記與傳奇校釋. Taibei: Yiwen, 1971.

Wang Yiwen 王怡文. *Pei Xing Chuanqi zhong shi de yanjiu* 裴鉶傳奇中詩的研究. Taibei: Hua Mulan Wenhua Gongzuofang, 2008.

Zhu Chuanyu 朱傳譽. *Pei Xing yu Chuanqi* 裴鉶與傳奇. Taibei: Tianyi, 1982.

Chen Wu and Michael E. Naparstek

Pi Rixiu 皮日休 (*zi*, Ximei 襲美, ca. 834–ca. 883) is known for his poetry which depicted the social injustices of his era, for his advocacy of *Mencius* and Han Yu 韓愈 (768–824),* and for his association with a literary Suzhou coterie centered around Lu Guimeng 陸龜蒙 (836–881).* By virtue of the breadth of his literary interests and the variety of his work, Pi Rixiu's reputation since his death has been mercurial, closely tied to the transmission of the several distinctive collections of his works that suggest different images of the poet. Pi's *Wensou* 文藪 (Literary Marsh, 866), which contains primarily prose (the influence of *guwen* 古文 [ancient-style prose] is prevalent) along with a few "socially conscious" poems, seems to have been much more widely circulated than the three hundred euphuistic poems (collected in the *Songlingji* 松陵集, *ca.* 870) which he wrote with Lu Guimeng in a single year. Although his work is well represented in several Song-dynasty anthologies, including the *Tang wen cui* 唐文萃, the better-known poems (all didactic) were not in concert with the tastes of the compiler of the *Tangshi sanbaishou*. Thus, Pi is known to the modern reader primarily through his series of ten poems titled "Zheng yuefu" 正樂府 (Orthodox Music-bureau Poems) and from the praise Lu Xun gave his essays which led to a subsequent reassessment in China.

One of the major preoccupations of early PRC critics has been to claim that he was of peasant stock, a claim which seems specious, since records tell us he was born into a local gentry family based in Xiangzhou 襄州 (Xiangyang, Hubei). At an early age he withdrew to the hermitage on Lumen shan 鹿門山 (Deer-gate Mountain) nearby to prepare for the literary examinations. Although he certainly studied the classics, he seems to have had a special predilection for the *Chuci* 楚辭, for the poetry of Bo Juyi 白居易 (772–846),* and for the prose of Han Yu. He traveled widely in his late teens, perhaps seeking a patron. Provincial life kept him in close touch with the people and much of his early verse reflects their concerns and hardships. "Xiang'ao tan" 橡媼嘆 (Lament of an Old Acorn-gatherer) may represent this corpus:

> Deep into autumn the acorns ripen,
> Scattering as they fall into the hillside scrub.
> Hunched over, a hoary-haired crone
> Gathers them, treading the morning frost.
> After a long time she's got only a handful,

An entire day just fills her basket.
First she suns them, then steams them,
To use in making late-winter provisions.
At the foot of the mountain she has ripening rice,
From its purple spikes a fragrance pervades.
Carefully she reaps, then hulls the grain.
Kernel after kernel like jade earrings.
She takes the grain to offer as government taxes,
In her own home are no granary bins.
How could she know that well over a picul of rice
Becomes only five pecks in the officials' measure?
Those crafty clerks don't fear the law,
Their greedy masters won't shun a bribe.
In the growing season she goes into debt,
In the off-season sends grain to government vaults.
From winter even into spring,
With acorns she tricks her hungry innards.
I've heard that Tian Chengzi
By feigning goodness made himself a king.
Ah, in meeting this old woman acorn-gatherer
Tears come uncalled to moisten my robe.

秋深橡子熟，散落榛蕪崗。
傴僂黃髮媼，拾之踐晨霜。
移時始盈掬，盡日方滿筐。
幾曝復幾蒸，用作三冬糧。
山前有熟稻，紫穗襲人香。
細穫又精舂，粒粒如玉璫。
持之納於官，私室無倉箱。
如何一石余，只作五斗量！
狡吏不畏刑，貪官不避贓。
農時作私債，農畢歸官倉。
自冬及于春，橡實誑飢腸。
吾聞田成子，詐仁猶自王。
吁嗟逢橡媼，不覺淚沾裳。

Although many of these ballads were based in hyperbole, the Japanese monk Ennin (793–864) reports that in the early 840s he encountered famine conditions in what is now Shandong province such that acorns were a staple. The "fragrance" and "earrings" in lines 10 and 12 may be intended to contrast the physical rigors of this woman's life with the norms of the female presence in palace-poems. The allusion to Tian Chengzi in the penultimate couplet refers to Tian's winning the hearts of the people of the state of Qi by distributing rice in large ladles and collecting rice required in taxes in smaller ladles; shortly thereafter, however, he assassinated his lord and usurped power. Here the unstated implication is that the Tang government's practices were worse than those of Tian's—"well over a picul of rice, becomes only five pecks in the officials' measure"—and was therefore even more corrupt than the Qi government under Tian.

During this period he also composed the *Lumen yinshu* 鹿門隱書 (Writings of a Recluse at Deer-gate), a collection of sixty pasquinades in which the government and society of the times comes under sharp attack, often in comparison to some model from antiquity:

> Those who withdrew from society in ancient times did so of their own free will; those who withdraw from society today do so in order to gain advancement in rank through it (number 26).
> Those who killed men in ancient times did so in a rage; those who kill men today do so with a smile (number 55).
> In ancient times a worthy man was employed for the benefit of the state; today he is employed for the benefit of a single family (number 56).
> In ancient times drunken rages were caused by wine; today they are caused by the state of mankind (number 57).
> In ancient times officials were appointed to drive off bandits; today they are appointed to become bandits (number 58).

> 古之隱也，志在其中。今之隱也，爵在其中。
> 古之殺人也怒，今之殺人也笑。
> 古之用賢也為國，今之用賢也為家。
> 古之酗酱也為酒，今之酗酱也為人。
> 古之置吏也，將以逐盜。今之置吏也，將以為盜。

Although the style and ideas of these pieces were not destined to mark Pi as a major writer or thinker, his commitment to improving the lot of his fellow man is impressive for someone barely twenty. He wrote numerous other prose works including ten imitations of Han Yu's *yuan* 原 ("On the Origin of...") and four *fu* 賦. Although his work was obviously influenced by Mencius and Han Yu, his style never attains their clarity.

Yet another side of Pi's personality can be seen in his early writings. They reveal a haughty, often self-indulgent man. Apparently conscious of this, Pi once compared himself to the notoriously impudent Mi Heng 禰衡 (173–198), who ran afoul of Cao Cao 曹操 (155–220) and was summarily executed.

Having been in the capital off and on since 864, Pi passed the *jinshi* examination in 867. He seems to have never been comfortable in the capital city, which was indeed not the mecca for young graduates it had been several generations earlier. Unable to find either patron or position–the two went hand in hand in the late Tang–he went to Suzhou and attached himself to the coterie of the Prefect, Cui Pu 崔璞 (fl. 870). In a matter of months he and Lu Guimeng, a scion of a prominent local clan, had become fast friends. In the next year Pi was to write over three hundred poems, many in concert with Lu. Taking advantage of a virtual sinecure, he frequented the homes of several literati with large personal libraries, reading widely in many fields including local Suzhou history. In the security of his new home and the lushness of the environs of the Taihu 太湖 (The Great Lake) his literary and personal styles quickly changed. From man's sufferings which had been so evident in his travels, his eye had turned to the natural beauty and past greatness of Suzhou. He had withdrawn from the everyday world. The didacticism and prose of the once pragmatic young graduate gave way to the ornamental, occasional poem of the aesthete as can be seen in his "Chongti qiangwei" 重題薔薇 (Again on the Rose):

Thick like an orangutan's blood just smeared on a white cloth,
Light as the swallows intending to fly to the empyrean—
What a pity this delicate beauty can scarcely stand the sun;
It throws its rays upon the deep reds, fading their hues.

濃似猩猩初染素，輕如燕燕欲淩空。
可憐細麗難勝日，照得深紅作淺紅。

The Daoist Zhang Ben 張賁 (fl. 850–875)* also exchanged poems with Pi during this period. "Ji Runqing Boshi" 寄潤卿博士 (Send to the Erudite [Zhang] Runqing [Ben]) reflects Pi's interest in the Daoist tradition:

Living in leisure one can want for black and crimson silks,
A magpie-tail bronze censer will burn for a generation.
A villager beyond this dusty world, you've become Officer Xu,
The landlord of the mountains, you're a Lord Mao.
To gather numinous mushrooms, in case of snow,
Wanting to sun your charts and books, no way to handle the clouds.
If you allow yourself to recline in Huayang Grotto,
Whose texts will the Han family use for the *feng* and *shan* rites?

高眠可為要玄纁，鵲尾金爐一世焚。
塵外鄉人為許掾，山中地主是茅君。
將收芝菌唯防雪，欲曬圖書不奈雲.
若使華陽終臥去，漢家封禪用誰文。

This seven-word regulated poem balances between praising Zhang Ben for his attainments in seeking the Dao while also suggesting Zhang might still serve at court. The silks of the first line are those which were in ancient times offered as tribute to Yu 禹 (as noted in the *Shang shu* 尚書), and which later rulers would give to invite worthy men in retirement to take office. Line 2 refers to a magpie-tail censer owned by the famous Daoist Tao Hongjing 陶弘景 (456–536) and suggests a lifetime in Daoist pursuits. The third couplet first alludes to Xu Xun 許詢 (fl. 358), a recluse poet (and disciple of the famous Buddhist scholar Zhi Dun 支盾 [314–366]) who lived in the Zhejiang hills and steadfastly refused public office. The second reference to Lord Mao, the early Shangqing Daoist adept Mao Ying 毛盈, suggests Zhang Ben's already considerable progress in Daoism. Lines six and seven turn to portray the tribulations of a recluse's life, searching high on the mountains for the divine mushrooms and battling the weather even to just air out one's personal collection of books. The last two lines urge Zhang Ben to reconsider leaving the official life for good (Huayang is located at Mount Mao and is one the grotto caves that subterraneously link the Daoist sacred mountains) and rather to make himself available to the Tang court (for Zhang Ben's response to this poem, see his entry below). The implications are that the Tang government with Zhang Ben in office would improve to the point that they could offer the *feng* 封 and *shan* 禪 sacrifices, rituals reserved only for virtuous regimes. This poem is also an example of Pi's theoretical transformation which paralleled the changes in his personal life. Living in reclusion he abandoned didacticism for a kind of formalism, advancing the theory that poetry had evolved from the prosodically simple old-style to the complex regulated verse. The next form to dominate, he maintained, would be the *zati shi* 雜體詩 (verse of miscellaneous forms). By this he meant the literary exercises including *huiwen* 迴文 (palindromes) or *zasheng yun* 雜聲韻 (alliterative verse).

Leaving Suzhou after a sojourn of just over a year, Pi traveled back to the capital and served in the government there, attaining the rank of Erudite of the National University. His family may have stayed in the South. When he returned there in 880 with an appointment to a post in Changzhou 長洲 he encountered Huang Chao 黃巢 (d. 883) and his rebel horde. Apparently swept up by the possibility of replacing the corrupt Tang regime, Pi joined the rebels and upon their arrival in Chang'an was made a Hanlin Academician in the short-lived Da Qi 大齊 dynasty. It soon became apparent that Huang Chao was not receptive to advice from his courtiers; many of them were persecuted for admonishing him. Although there are several accounts of Pi's death (this is the other major concern of modern critics), it seems most likely that Pi offended Huang Chao and was put death by the rebel leader.

Pi Rixiu's poetic legacy represents the two major tendencies of the late Tang (didactic and baroque) and perhaps illustrates by its inadequacies some of the reasons for the prominent place of the new lyrics (*ci* 詞) on the literary stage of the Five Dynasties and early Song. The inner drive which seems to have steered Pi through his capricious career–from avid reformer, to recluse-poet, to rebel—in addition to the large and varied corpus he has left, make him one of the most fascinating minor literary figures of the late Tang. But his adherence to ancient-style prose, his advocacy of Mencius, his interest in philosophy, and his lowly social origins tie him more closely to the intellectual milieu of the early Song.

BIBLIOGRAPHY

Editions:

Pi Lumen Xiaopin 皮鹿門小品. Mo Daocai 莫道才 and Shen Weidong, 沈偉東, eds. Beijing: Wenhua Yishu, 1997.

Pi Zi wensou 皮子文藪 (Literary Marsh of Master Pi). Edited by Xiao Difei 蕭滌非 and Zheng Qingdu 鄭慶篤. Beijing: Zhonghua, 1959; rpt. Shanghai: Guji, 1982.

___. SBCK. Photolithic reprint of a Ming edition then in the possession of Mr. Yuan 袁 of Xiangtan 湘潭, probably first printed during the Hongzhi era (1488–1506).

Quan Tang shi, 9: 7068–152, 11: 9011–19, 13: 9930, 14: 10694.

Quan Tang wen, 796–799.10523–584.

Songling ji 松陵集 (Pine Knoll Anthology). *Hubei Xianzheng yishu* 湖北先正遺書 ed.

Xiang Zhenxiang 項貞詳, ed. (Ming dynasty). *Xiangshi Pingshengxie xinke Pi Ximei shi* 橡氏瓶笙榭新刻皮襲美詩, in the Rare Book Collection of the Beijing Library.

Annotations:

Shen Baokun 申寶昆, ed. *Pi Rixiu shiwen xuanzhu* 皮日休詩文選注. Shanghai: Shanghai Guji, 1991.

Biographical Sources:

Fu, *Tang caizi*, 3:497–508, 5:430–33.

Translations:

Nienhauser, William H., Jr. *P'i Jih-hsiu*. Boston: Twayne Publishers, 1979. Nearly 40 poems and 13 prose pieces are rendered–see pp. 151–52 ("Finding List of Translations").

Schafer, *Golden Peaches*, pp. 99, 123 and 129.

Sunflower, pp. 259–66.

Studies:

Li Fubiao 李福標. *Pi, Lu Yanjiu* 皮陸研究. Changsha: Yuelu Shushe, 2007.

Li Shude 李叔德. *Jingshi haisu Pi Rixiu* 驚世駭俗皮日休. Hubei: Hubei Renmin, 2011.

Masuda Kiyohide 增田清秀. "Hi Jitsukyu no 'Seigakufu' to jiji hihan" 皮日休の正樂府と批判, in *Gakufu no rekishiteki kenkyū* 樂府の歷史的研究, Tokyo: Sōbunsha, Shōwa, 1975.

Miao Yue 繆鉞. "Pi Rixiu te shiji sixiang ji qi zuopin" 皮日休的事蹟思想及其作品, in *Tangshi yanjiu lunwen ji* 唐詩研究論文集. Beijing: Renmin Wenxue, 1959, pp. 371–89.

Nakajima Chōbun 中島長文. "Hi Jitsukyū" 皮日休, in *Tōdai no shijin: sono denki* 唐代の詩人：その傳記, Ōgawa Tamaki 小川環樹, ed., Tokyo: Taishūkan, Shōwa, 1975, pp. 581–89.

Nienhauser. *P'i Jih-hsiu*.

Wang Maofu 王茂福. *Pi, Lu Shi zhuan* 皮陸詩傳. Changchun: Jilin Renmin, 2000.

Wang Xijiu 王錫九. *Pi, Lu Shige Yanjiu* 皮陸詩歌研究. Hefei: Anhui Daxue, 2004.

Xiao Difei 蕭滌非. "Qianyan" 前言, in *Pizi Wensou*, Beijing: Zhonghua, 1959, pp. 1–21. pp. 407–30.

Yao Yao 姚垚. "Pi Rixiu, Lu Guimeng changhe shi yanjiu" 皮日休陸龜蒙唱和詩研究. Unpublished M.A. thesis, National Taiwan University, 1980.

Zhou Liankuan 周連寬. "Pi Rixiu de shengping ji qi zuopin" 皮日休的生平及其作品, *Lingnanxuebao*, 12.1 (June 1952), pp. 113–44.

William H. Nienhauser, Jr.

Qiji 齊己 (secular name Hu Desheng 胡得生, fl. 881), was a native of Changsha 長沙. Orphaned at the age of seven, he found refuge in a Buddhist monastery at Mount Dagui 大溈 in Hunan, where he was first employed as a cowherd. He was precocious, and it is said that he scratched verses on the backs of his cows with a bamboo stick. Eventually he was ordained as a monk and wandered far and wide, traveling on lakes and rivers and visiting sacred mountains and other holy places. His name is particularly associated with Heng Shan 衡山 in the south, and he styled himself "Sramana of Mount Heng."

The scenery around Lake Dongting 洞庭湖, especially views of its magic island, Jun Shan 君山, and that along the numinous reaches of the Xiang River, exalted and inspired him. He also spent several years in the vicinity of Chang'an. But his career was centered in and around Jiangling 江陵 (modern Jiangling County about 15 miles south-southeast of Jingzhou City 荊州市 in Hubei) which early in the tenth century was the capital of a small kingdom called Nanping 南平 (sometimes known as Jingnan 荊南) in a prosperous region commanding the river route where the Yangzi flows out of its gorges. Nanping was noted for its fine damasks, citrus fruits, medicinal herbs, and fish. It was fortunate enough to escape incorporation into the northern domains ruled by the ephemeral Five Dynasties. Its king, Gao Zonghui 高從誨 (r. 927–934), welcomed the poetic priest and gave him a position of authority in a monastery, the Longxing si 龍興寺. He became the friend of some of the most eminent poets of the age, among them Cao Song 曹松 (828–903),

Qiji

Fang Gan 方干 (809–888), and Zheng Gu 鄭谷 (ca. 849–ca. 911). Sun Guangxian 孫光憲 (d. 901 or 901–968), an important official of Nanping, a notable poet, and author of *Beimeng suoyan* 北夢瑣言, wrote a preface to Qiji's collected poems, which he titled *Bailian ji* 白蓮集 (The White Lotus Collection). The preface is dated April 3, 938, and in it Sun reports that the talented monk was regarded by his contemporaries as one of the great Buddhist poets, comparable to Guanxiu 貫休 (832–912)* and Jiao Ran 皎然 (720–799).* Qiji's contemporary and fellow-believer Xichan 棲蟾 (fl. 896) described him in a poem as "The Literary Star That Lights Up the Sky of Chu" 文星照楚天. Besides his verses, Qiji wrote two critical typologies of early poetry, the *Xuanji fenbie yaolan* 玄機分別要覽 and the *Shi ge* 詩格 (one *juan* each), neither of which appears to be extant.

The poems themselves are readily classified according to theme. Qiji wrote frequently about his own experience. He wrote about his close friends, most often Zheng Gu, to whom he addressed many verses in his lifetime and whose death he lamented. He wrote more than once about the great prelate Guanxiu, who was in Nanping for a period before the height of his career in the court of the King of Shu. The poetry refers repeatedly to Buddhist monks, Daoist recluses, and ghosts and tells of visits to monasteries, highland retreats, sacred mountains, and the homes of deceased worthies. Qiji was haunted by Lake Dongting and the watershed of the Xiang River to the point of obsession.

He even took sympathetic note of the ancient deities who presided over these divine waterways. He wrote several poems on the dilapidated site of Zhu Gong 渚宮 (The Strand Palace), the old Chu palace overlooking the Yangzi. He was fond of drinking tea and often wrote about the pleasure it gave him. Nature was dear to him–but he had his preferences. Above all he loved old pines: the image of their gnarled and gnomish forms is constantly present in his verses. "Xiao song" 小松 (Little Pines) can represent these poems:

> Sprouting from the ground barely above my knees—
> Already a spirituality in their coiled roots.
> Though harsh frost has turned all the grasses white,
> deep in the courtyard, one grove of green!
> Late at night spiders rustle about;
> crickets call from the empty staircase.
> A thousand years and more from now
> Poems will be intoned on these entwined 'ancient dragons.'

> 發地才過膝，蟠根已有靈。
> 嚴霜百草白，深院一林青。
> 後夜蕭騷動，空階蟋蟀聽。
> 誰于千歲外，吟繞老龍形。

Besides the pines, wilting and fallen flowers were ever on his mind. His favorite flowers were the red rose and the white lotus. For him, the roses were not just symbols of transient earthly beauty, but also of blood (as he plainly says in one poem) and so of both life and death. The lotus, on the other hand, represented perfection and purity unknown to this world. Among animals, he gave special attention to flying creatures: butterflies, fireflies, crickets, and birds. Water birds in particular fascinated him: cranes, herons, wild geese, kingfishers, and gulls populate the poems. He shows his Buddhist concern for living things in a set of verses telling how he released a captive monkey and a number of caged birds, including a sacred crane. He was entranced by the evanescent forms of water and snow and the phantoms visible in reflections and shadows. He gives due attention to indications of holy power and sacred scenes, objects, and odors—as of sandalwood and incenses. Permeating everything is an atmosphere of transience and fragility, subtly conveyed: the setting sun, the tokens of autumn, the brevity of life. A characteristic poem, "Riri qu" 日日曲 (Song of Sun on Sun), distinguished by strange internal sonorities, an untypical meter, and the sextuple presence of the graph for "sun/day" in the first two verses, may serve to illustrate his writing:

> Sun on sun—the sun goes up in the east:
> Sun on sun—the sun sinks into the west.
> Even though he may have the appearance of a Divine Transcendent,
> Still, he will turn to rotten bones.
> Drifting clouds are snuffed out—but born again;
> Fragrant plants will die—then emerge again.
> This I do not know: the men of a thousand ages, a myriad ages past,
> Buried over there in the blue-green hills—what things are they now?

> 日日日東上，日日日西沒。
> 任是神仙容，也須成朽骨。
> 浮雲滅復生，芳草死還出。
> 不知千古萬古人，葬向青山為底物。

The first two lines could be read "day by day—the sun goes up in the east; day by day the sun sinks into the west." Whatever the sense of these lines, the repetition of the same character three times in succession must have shocked the Tang reader. Beyond the aural effects, however, the poem contains the themes of all conquering time, the vain hopes of the Daoists (to become a Divine Transcendent), the resurrection or revitalization of some parts of nature, the unavoidable doom of men—and the question, "are the unnumbered dead alive in other forms, or escaped into nirvana?"

For all of his preoccupation with uncanny atmospheres and spectral apparitions, Qiji's writing has a quality of equanimity and resignation—of fortitude in tranquility. The stream of time flows by him, and he is fully conscious of mortality—indeed he sees fit to admonish his readers of the implications of this: the motif of *memento mori* is recurrent. But he retains his composure. Inevitably he is skeptical about the possibility of eternal life and the efficacy of theriacs and elixirs. He scorns the seemingly invincible optimism of the Daoists. At the same time, he regards them less as doctrinal enemies than as deluded friends. But once he went so far as to compose a poem, "Hua dao" 話道 (Speaking of the Dao), which begins: "The Great Dao is a great laugh!" 大道多大笑.

BIBLIOGRAPHY

Editions:
Bailian ji 白蓮集. SBCK.

Quan Tang shi, 12: 9517–663.
Quan Tang wen, 921.12629–30.
Qiji 齊己. *Fengsao zhi ge yi juan* 風騷旨格一卷. Taibei: Yiwen, 1965.

Annotations:
Wang Xiulin 王秀林, ed. *Qiji shi ji jiao zhu* 齊己詩集校注. Beijing: Zhongguo Shehui Kexue, 2011.

Biographical Sources:
Fu, *Tang caizi*, 4:173–87, 5:460–61.
Song gaoseng zhuan, 30.751–52.

Translations:
Egan, *Clouds*, pp. 94–98.
Owen, Stephen. "How Did Buddhism Matter in Tang Poetry?" *TP* 103 (2017): 388–406.
Schafer, E. H. *The Divine Woman, Dragon Ladies and Rain Maidens in Tang Literature*. Berkeley: University of California Press, 1973, pp. 84–85.
___. *Pacing the Void: Tang Approaches to the Stars*. Berkeley: University of California Press, 1977, pp. 155–56.
Watson, Burton. "Ch'i-chi," in O'Connor and Red Pine, eds. *The Clouds Should Know Me by Now: Buddhist Poet Monks of China*. Boston: Wisdom Publications, 1997. pp. 46–74.

Studies:
Cao Xun 曹汛. "Qiji shengzu nian kaozheng" 齊己生卒年考證, *Zhonghua wenshi luncong* 1983.3.
Cheng Yalin 程亞林. "Shi Chan guanxi renshi shi shang de zhongyao huanjie–du Jiao Ran Qiji shi" 詩禪關係認識史上的重要環節—讀皎然、齊己詩. *Wenxue yican* 1989.5.
Cui Liannong 崔煉農. "Qiji *Bailian ji* de shi chan guan" 齊己《白蓮集》的詩禪觀. *Zhongguo yunwen xuekan* 2002.2.
He Lintian 何林天. "Qiji chutan" 齊己初探. *Shanxi Shida xuebao* 1992.2.
Li Jiangfeng 李江峰. "*Fengsao zhi ge* yu Qiji de shige chuangzuo–shige yu shige chuangzuo de ge'an kaocha zhiyi" 《風騷旨格》與齊己的詩歌創作–詩格與詩歌創作的個案考察之一. *Qianyan* 2009.2.
Pan Dingwu 潘定武 et al. *Qiji shizhu* 齊己詩注. Heifei: Huangshan, 2014.
Tian Daoying 田道英. "Qiji jiaoyou kao" 齊己交遊考. *Sichuan Shifan Xueyuan xuebao (Zhexue shehui kexue ban)* 2003.2.
___. "Qiji xingnian kaoshu" 齊己行年考述. *Tianjin Daxue xuebao (Shehui kexue ban)* 2001.3.
Watson, Burton, see above, pp. 44–45.
Xia Lian 夏蓮. "Shiseng Qiji" 詩僧齊己. *Wenshi zhishi* 1992.2.
Yin Chubin 尹楚彬. "Hu Xiang shi seng Qiji yu Guiyang zong" 湖湘詩僧齊己與溈仰宗. *Hunan Daxue xuebao (Shehui kexue ban)* 2001.4.

Edward H. Schafer

Qian Qi 錢起 (*zi*, Zhongwen 仲文, 720–780) was the most celebrated figure in the group of poets known as the "Dali shi caizi" 大曆十才子 (Ten Talents of the Dali Era). He was a native of Wuxing 吳興 (modern Zhejiang). Little is known of his early years, since his fame and the vast majority of his works postdate the outbreak of the An Lushan Rebellion in 755. He passed the *jinshi* examination in 750 or 751 and lived most of his adult life near Chang'an, first as a minor official in Lantian 藍田 (about 10 miles southeast of Chang'an), rising within the central bureaucracy to the post of Director of the Bureau of Evaluations. More than four hundred of his poems are extant.

Qian was generally considered the poetic successor to Wang Wei 王維 (692–761 or 699–759).* His relationship with the older writer probably began during his tenure in Lantian, where Wang Wei's famous Wang River estate was situated. Qian Qi's "Lantian Xi zayong, ershier shou" 藍田溪雜詠, 二十二首 (Twenty-two Poems on Lantian Creek), which explicitly imitate Wang Wei's "Wangchuan ji" 輞川集 (Wang River Collection), are especially well-known. "Yuanshan zhong" 遠山鐘 (Bell at a Faraway Mountain) in that series reads:

> The wind brings the sound from the mountain bell,
> The rosy clouds ford the water's shallows.
> If you want to know where the sound will disappear:
> It's far beyond the sky where no bird exists.

> 風送出山鐘, 雲霞度水淺.
> 欲知聲盡處, 鳥滅寥天遠.

Although Qian Qi was the most popular poet in capital society after Wang Wei's death, his reputation has not fared well. Indeed, his connection with Wang Wei may actually have worked against him in the eyes of later critics: many of Qian's works invite comparison with Wang's, and as regards Buddhist themes, for instance, Qian's works lack the profundity and intellect which animates Wang's poems.

Qian was a poetic craftsman who continued to write in a style harkening back to the court and nature poetry of the High Tang; the lack of distinguishing individual characteristics is probably what led to his lowered reputation. Thus, later critics often singled out couplets for admiration, but he was never regarded as a major poet. Nonetheless, his mastery at imagistic evocation of a scene, as in "Sheng shi: Xiangling guse" 省詩: 湘靈鼓瑟 (Examination Poem: On the Xiang River Spirits Strum Their Zithers) shows Qian Qi's creativity in this famous example of a poem written for the *jinshi* examinations in 751 when Qian passed as the second name on a list of successful candidates that included Jia Zhi 賈至 (718–772)* and Jia Dan 賈耽 (730–805). The piece is centered on the story of the legendary emperor Shun who died during his visit to Cangwu Mountain. His two wives, Ehuang 娥皇 and Nüying 女英, on hearing of his death played dirges on their zithers and then drowned themselves in the Xiang River. The spirits became goddesses of the Xiang. The zither played here seems to have been made on Cloud-harmony Mountain:

> In the skilled strumming on a Cloud-harmony zither,
> Are often heard the spirits of the imperial daughters—
> Feng Yi [the River God] begins to blindly dance on his own,
> The sojourner in Chu cannot bear to listen.
> The sad melody grieves the bells and stone chimes,
> Crystal tones rise up to the sky and spread it further.
> The sound reaches Cangwu Mountain, Emperor Shun's spirit is touched,
> White angelicas set the aromatic fragrance in motion.
> The rushing waters send the music past the shores of the Xiang,
> Melancholy winds blow it over Lake Dongting.

Qian Qi

> The song ends, no one's to be seen—
> On the river, a few mountain peaks of green.

善鼓雲和瑟，常聞帝子靈。
馮夷空自舞，楚客不堪聽。
苦調淒金石，清音入杳冥。
蒼梧來怨慕，白芷動芳馨。
流水傳瀟浦，悲風過洞庭。
曲終人不見，江上數峰青。

The language here is reminiscent of another great tradition of the Chu region, that of the ancient poet Qu Yuan 屈原 (traditionally dated ca. 340–278 BC; here he is the "sojourner in Chu") who also mused: "I made the Xiang goddesses play on their zithers, / and I bade the Hairuo [The Sea God] dance with Feng Yi [The River God]" 使湘靈鼓瑟兮，令海若舞馮夷 (in his "Yuan you" 遠遊 from the *Chuci* 楚辭). The River God doesn't understand the magical music of this zither from Cloud-harmony Mountain so he must dance "emptily" (*kong* 空) or blindly. This music conjures up for Qian Qi a landscape peopled with mythical figures out of the Chu tradition, a landscape which returns to reality when the music ends and the poet can see just "a few peaks of green."

Qian's name was often linked with that of Lang Shiyuan 郎士元 (fl. 766), especially as writers of occasional social poetry. In reading these works, one must remember that they were written for an audience that, despite greatly altered political conditions, retained tastes cultivated during the preceding reign of Emperor Xuanzong. Qian was above all fully conscious of his role as a master of the style of the occasional social poetry necessary for the preservation and continuation of the social and cultural life of his times. However, the pessimism and anxiety of the times is evident in some of his works, for instance, "Dongcheng chuxian yu Xue Yuanwai, Wang Buque mingtou Nan shan Fo si" 東城初陷與薛員外王補闕暝投南山佛寺 (Fleeing in the Night to a Buddhist Temple in the Southern Mountains with Auxiliary Secretary Xue and Rectifier of Omissions Wang, when the Eastern City Walls [of Chang'an Began to Fall to the Tibetans]), written in 763 when Tibetan forces overran and sacked the capital:

> The sun sinks into the gap between the two halves of the stone door,
> A wind blows among the pine forest and a chill rises up.
> The fragrant clouds lie silent on the ground,
> A becalmed stream has no torrents.
> Washing my feet to shed the dust of the secular world,
> I suddenly feel the sky becomes wider.
> The sound of the bell resounds in the empty valley,
> The waning moon deepens the outlines of mountain peaks.
> I sigh that my generation is like the morning dew,
> We bob and sink on the great waves of change.
> My destiny having now encountered this anxious situation:
> Why should I linger in the secular world?
> All these things are but images seen in a mirror,
> Because after all there is no birth or death.

日昃石門裡，松聲山寺寒。
香雲空靜影，定水無驚湍。
洗足解塵纓，忽覺天形寬。
清鐘揚虛谷，微月深重巒。
噫我朝露世，翻浮與波瀾。
行運邁憂患，何緣親盤桓。
庶將鏡中象，盡作無生觀。

This poem was written when Qian Qi had taken refuge along with Wang Wei in a temple high in the Zhongnan Mountains south of the capital; it resonates with Buddhist imagery as befits the surroundings. Fragrant clouds often surround temples in part from the incense burned in them. The stream also absorbs the quietude of the place and is becalmed. The purity of the temple life imbues all the surroundings and leads Qian in the final lines to consider the alternative of a life of contemplation.

Part of one of Qian Qi's poems, "Xiao Guqiu ye chang" 效古秋夜長 (In Imitation of the Ancient Poem 'Autumn Nights Are Long'), was used by Gustav Mahler for the second movement of his *Das Lied von der Erde*. The lyric laments the dying of flowers and the passing of beauty. The inclusion of Qian Qi's poetry in Mahler's work joins him into the company of the other Tang poets whose works Mahler drew upon: Li Bo 李白 (701–762),* Wang Wei, and Meng Haoran 孟浩然 (689–740).*

BIBLIOGRAPHY

Editions and References:
Luan Guiming 欒貴明 et al., eds. *Quan Tang shi suoyin: Qian Qi juan* 全唐詩索引: 钱起卷. Tianjin: Tianjin Guji, 1997.
Qian Qi 錢起. *Qian Kaogong ji: 10 juan* 錢考功集10卷. Beijing: Beijing Airusheng Shuzi Hua Jishu Yanjiu Zhongxin, 2009.
___. *Qian Zhongwen ji* 錢仲文集. Shanghai: Shanghai Guji, 1993.
Quan Tang shi, 4: 2596–682, 14: 10636, 11129.
Tabei Fumio 田部井文雄, ed. *Sen Ki shi sakuin* 錢起詩索引. Tokyo: Kyūko, 1986.
Zhang Yuanji 張元濟 et al., comp. *Qian Kaogong ji* 錢考功集. In *Sibu congkan* 四部叢刊 (Shanghai: Hanfen Lou, 1919–1936). Contains misattributions, however, such as the series of quatrains "Jiangxing wuti yibai shou" 江行無題一百首 (Traveling on the Yangzi: One Hundred Untitled Poems), which were actually written by his great-grandson Qian Xu 錢珝 (fl. 900).

Annotations:
Ruan Tingyu 阮廷瑜, ed. *Qian Qi shiji xiaozhu* 錢起詩集校注. Taibei: Xinwenfeng, 1996.
Wang Dingzhang 王定璋, ed. *Qian Qi shiji jiaozhu* 錢起詩集校注. Hangzhou: Zhejiang Guji, 1992.

Biographical Sources:
Fu, *Tang caizi*, 2:35–46, 5:167–70.
Jiu Tang shu, 168.4382–86.
Xin Tang shu, 203.5786.

Qian Qi

Translations:

Bynner, *Jade Mountain*, pp. 12–13.
Demiéville, *Anthologie*, p. 295.
Gundert, *Lyrik*, pp. 98–99.
Minford and Lau, pp. 839–41.
New Directions, p. 117.
Owen, *Omen*, pp. 92–93.
___, *High T'ang*, pp. 254–65, 261–66, and 273–76.

Studies:

Ashidate Ichirō 芦立一郎. "Sen Ki no shisaku–taireki shi e no apurōchi" 錢起の詩作–大歷へのアプローチ. *Yamagata Daigaku kiyō* 山形大学紀要, 13.3 (1994): 404–18.
Chen Qinghui 陳慶惠. "Qian Qi he ta de shi" 錢起和他的詩. *Zhejiang Shifan Xueyuan xuebao*, 1983.3.
Duan Ying 段瑩. "Qian Qi de xue Dao jingli yu dui Dao jiao fei shengming wuzhi shige meixue de kaituo" 錢起的學道經歷與對道教非生命物質詩歌美學的開拓. *Hebei Shifan Daxue xuebao (Zhexue shehui kexue ban)*, 2013.5.
Fu Xuancong 傅璇琮. "Qian Qi kao" 錢起考, *Tangdai shiren congkao* 唐代詩人叢考. Beijing: Zhonghua, 1980, pp. 427–48.
Jiang Yin 蔣寅. "Qian Qi shengping xi shi buzheng" 錢起生平繫詩補正. *Hebei daxue xuebao (Zhexue shehui kexue ban)*, 1995.1.
Kubo Takuya 久保卓哉. "Hayashi Fumiko kura Ro Jin shinpitsu Sen Ki 'kigan' uta ni tsuite—kore made no teisetsu to shin kenkai" 林芙美子蔵 魯迅親筆 錢起「帰雁」詩について—これまでの定説と新見解. *Fukuyama Daigaku, Jimbunken Bungakubu kiyō* 福山大学人間文化学部紀要. 10 (2010.3): 1–16.
Lee, Oscar. "The Critical Perception of the Poetry of Wei Yingwu (737–792): The Creation of a Poetic Reputation." Unpublished Ph.D dissertation. Columbia University, 1986, pp. 81–91.
Lei Sha 雷莎. "Lun Qian Qi de shanshui shi: Jian lun Tangdai shanshui shi de shengzhong dai bian" 論錢起的山水詩–兼論唐代山水詩的盛中代變. *Shehui kexue luntan*, 2010. 04.
Ma Zhijin 馬汁金. "Guanyu Qian Qi de dengdi shijian yu zuozhu" 關於錢起登第時間與主. *Jianghai xuekan*, 1991.5.
Tabei Fumio 田部井文雄, ed. *Sen Ki shi sakuin* 錢起詩索引. Tokyo: Kyūin, 1986.
___. "Sen Ki shōron—Aida Kei zatsuei o chūshin to shite" 錢起小論--藍田溪雜詠を中心として. *Kanbun gakai kaihō* 漢文学会会報. (1976.7): pp. 25–37.
Wang Dingzhang 王定璋. "Ping Qian Qi shige" 評錢起詩歌. *Yancheng Shizhuan xuebao (Shehui kexue ban)*, 1987.3.
___. "Qian Qi bufen shige xinian" 錢起部份詩歌繫年. *Wenxian* 文獻, 1984.4.
___. "Qian Qi jianpu" 錢起簡譜. *Zhongguo wenxue yanjiu (ji kan)*, 2002.2.
___. "Qian Qi jiaoyou kao" 錢起交遊考. *Chengdu Daxue Kexue xuebao (Shehui kexue ban)*, 1987.4.
___. "Qian Qi jiaoyou xu kao" 錢起交遊續考. *Hunan Shifan Daxue shehui kexue xuebao*, 1989.3.
___. "Qian Qi shige xinian buyi" 錢起詩歌繫年補遺. *Wenxian* 文獻, 1988.1.
___. "Qian Qi shige xinian xukao" 錢起詩歌繫年續考. *Wenxian* 文獻, 1986.4.
___. "Qian Qi shige yishu fengge chutan" 錢起詩歌藝術風格初探. *Nanchong Shiyuan xuebao (Zhexue shehui kexue ban)*, 1985.3.
Wu Qiming 吳企明. "Qian Qi, Qian Xu shi kaopian" 錢起錢珝詩考辯. *Wenxue pinglun congkan*, 13 (May 1982): 169–87.
Xie Taofang 謝桃坊. "Dali caizi Qian Qi zhi shi de yanjiu yu zhengli: ping *Qian Qi shiji jiaozhu*" 大曆才子錢起之詩的研究與整理—評《錢起詩集校注》. *Sichuan she ke jie*. 1993.2.

Yamada Teppi 山田哲平. "Gokan no higan jōken—sen ki shiron" 五感の彼岸常建-錢起試論. *Meiji Daigaku kyōyō ronshū* 明治大学教養論集 (1997.1): 95–144.

Yi 毅. "Wang Wei yu Qian Qi shifeng de tongyi" 王維與錢起詩風的同意, *Wenxue yichan*, 1989.5: 113.

Zhou Zhou 周舟. "Jian ping Wang Dingzhang *Qian Qi shiji jiaozhu*" 簡評王定璋《錢起詩集校注》. *Wenshi zazhi*, 1993.1.

___. "Yi xiang tianbu kongbai zhi ju: ping *Qian Qi shiji jiaozhu*" 一項填補空白之舉—評《錢起詩集校注》. *Qinghai Minzu Xueyuan xuebao*, 1994.2.

William H. Nienhauser, Jr.

Qingjiang 清江 (d. ca. 806) was a poet-monk active in the mid-Tang period. He was a native of Guiji 會稽 (or Kuaiji, modern Shaoxing city in Zhejiang), and entered the Kaiyuan monastery 開元寺 in Guiji at a young age to follow the Vinaya master Tanyi 曇一 (692–771). He was such a good student of Buddhist teachings that he was praised as "a Buddhist thousand-mile colt" 釋門千里駒.

In the early Dali reign period (766), he went to Tianzhu Monastery 天竺寺 in Hangzhou 杭州 (modern Zhejiang) and studied with Shouzhen 守真 (700–770), who was excellent in Vinaya, Tiantai, Huanyan, Chan, and Tantric doctrines. Then, he returned to Guiji to study Vinaya with Tanyi again. During the Dali and Zhenyuan reign periods (766–805), Qingjiang wandered to many places, and exchanged poems with Lu Lun 盧綸 (739–799),* Jiao Ran 皎然 (720–799),* Yan Wei 嚴維 (ca. 8th century), Fazhao 法照 (fl. 766), and others. In 773 he met the Chan master Nanyang Huizhong 南陽慧忠 (d. 775) in Ruzhou 汝州, who transmitted Chan mind-essence to him. By 776 Qingjiang was in Luoyang where he composed an epitaph for the Vinaya master Qingyuan 清源 (fl. 821–824). From 779 to 780, he was in the capital city Chang'an and exchanged poems with Yan Wei and Zhang Bayuan 章八元. In his old age, Qingjiang moved to the Bianjue Monastery 辨覺寺 in Xiangzhou 襄州 (modern Xiangyang city in Hubei), and died there about 806. His biography appears in the *Song Gaoseng zhuan* 宋高僧傳 and the *Quan Tangshi* preserves twenty-one of his poems, though some of the attributions to him are questionable.

Qingjiang and Jiao Ran were equally famous and together called "The Two Pure Ones in Guiji" (Guiji erqing 會稽二清). His extant works are mostly occasional poems, in which he often expresses melancholic feelings about social chaos or some personal experience. Perhaps referring to this kind of work, the *Song gaoseng zhuan* praises his writings as "a record of the discourse of a Confucius in an elegant style and diction" 儒家筆語, 體高辭典. He was good at pentasyllabic regulated verse and his style was considered close to that of the famous "Dali shicaizi" 大曆十才子 (Ten Talents of the Dali Era).

Interestingly, Qingjiang's best known work is a love poem titled "Qixi" 七夕 (Night of the Seventh Day in the Seventh Month) which treats the spirits of the two stars Cowherd and Weaving Maid who were legendary lovers separated by the Milky Way, allowed to meet only one night in a year on the seventh day of the seventh month:

> Far, far away, the night scene of the seventh day—
> They meet there, but only for one night.
> The moonlight serves as a candle in the open bedcurtains;

Clouds form a bridge over the Milky Way stream.
Reflected in the waters, her golden cap trembles;
Facing the wind, his jade pendant swings.
Their only worry the night watch and the water clock:
Urging them to part with the next morn.

七夕景迢迢, 相逢只一宵.
月為開帳燭, 雲作渡河橋.
映水金冠動, 當風玉珮搖.
惟愁更漏促, 離別在明朝.

This pentasyllabic, regulated verse describes the lovers' reunion. The first couplet sets the scene and the second depicts how nature itself assists in their rendezvous. Lines 5 and 6 depict the couple reunited, the sexual tension expressed through the trembling of her cap and the swinging of his girdle pendant. The final couplet brings home the carpe diem theme underlining the sadness of the lovers' imminent parting. The Tang-dynasty *Yunxi youyi* 雲溪友議 points to this poem as one of four by different authors who went against common sense, since Qingjiang, though a monk, composed a love poem. However, Zanning 贊寧 (919–1001), the author of the *Song gaoseng zhuan,* defended Qingjiang, noting that poet-monks had been writing love poems since the Southern Dynasties and that this poem could be read as a metaphor for the transciency of human life.

BIBLIOGRAPHY

Editions:
Hu Zhenheng 胡震亨 (1569–1645), ed. *Tangyin tongqian* 唐音統籤. *Xuxiu Siku quanshu* 續修四庫全書.
Li Gong 李龏 (b. 1194), ed. *Tangseng hongxiu ji* 唐僧弘秀集. *Siku quanshu* ed.
Quan Tang shi, 12: 9228–32.
Wei Hu 韋縠 (fl. 947), ed. *Caidiao ji* 才調集. In Fu Xuancong 傅璇琮, ed., *Tangren xuan Tangshi xinbian* 唐人選唐詩新編. Xi'an: Shaanxi Renmin Jiaoyu, 1996.

Biographical Sources:
Fu, *Tang caizi*, 1:537–540.
Zan Ning, 15.368–69.

Studies:
Ichihara Kōkichi 市原亨吉. "Chūtō shoki ni okeru kōhidari no shisō ni tsuite" 中唐初期における江左の詩僧について. *Tōhō gakuhō* 東方学報 28 (1958): 219–248.
Jiang Yin 蔣寅. *Dali Shiren Yanjiu* 大曆詩人研究. Beijing: Beijing Daxue, 2007.
Kawachi Shōen 河內昭円. "Shisō Seikō ni tsuite" 詩僧清江について, *Bungei ronsō* 文芸論叢 12 (1979): 43–56.
Peng Yaling 彭雅玲. *Tangdai shiseng de chuangzuolun yanjiu: shige yu Fojiao de zonghe fenxi* 唐代詩僧的創作論研究: 詩歌與佛教的綜合分析. Taibei: Huamulan Wenhua, 2009.
Watson, Burton. "Buddhist Poet-Priests of the T'ang," *Eastern Buddhist* 25.2 (1992): 1–22.

Zha Minghao 查明昊. *Zhuanxing zhong de Tang Wudai shiseng qunti* 轉型中的唐五代詩僧群體. Shanghai: Huadong Shifan Daxue, 2008.

Jinhua Jia and Chenxi Huang

Qiwu Qian 綦毋潛 (*zi*, Xiaotong 孝通 or Jitong 季通, ca. 692–ca. 756), was born into an undistinguished family in Qianzhou 虔州 (modern Nankang 南康 in Hubei), and was one of the group of minor court poets during the Tianbao era (742–755) of Emperor Xuanzong. When he was fourteen years old Qiwu came to Chang'an to study and gained a reputation for his poetic skills. Around 720 he took the *jinshi* examination and failed, then returned to his home in the south. Six years later in 726 he passed the *jinshi* examination and was appointed Editor in the Palace Library but seems to have returned to the south thereafter. In 729 he composed the poetic inscription for a stele at the Longxing Temple 龍興寺 in Suzhou. When Chu Guangxi 儲光羲 (ca. 706–ca. 762)* left office in 733 and went into retirement, Qiwu Qian followed. In the early 740s he returned to the capital seeking a position and by 748 he was made Commandant of Yishou 宜壽 County (modern Zhouzhi 周至 in Shaanxi) about thirty miles west of the capital. In 752 he became Reminder on the Right and then in 754 was concurrently first appointed Academician in the Academy of Scholarly Worthies and subsequently Erudite in the Institute for the Extension of Literary Arts. His final position was Editorial Director in the Palace Library, fifth level. In 755 or 756 following the start of the An Lushan Rebellion he fled south from the capital into the Huai River Valley; the rest of his life is not known.

During his years in the capital he became part of the social network of capital poets which clustered around Wang Wei 王維 (692–761 or 699–759).* He exchanged poems with Zhang Jiuling 張九齡 (678–740),* Li Qi 李頎 (*jinshi* 725),* Chu Guangxi, Wei Yingwu 韋應物 (737–ca. 791),* Wang Wei, Meng Haoran 孟浩然 (689–740),* Gao Shi 高適 (700–765),* and others.

Qiwu Qian is noted for his sophisticated, graceful style. His poetry is also noted for its finely crafted structure. His old-style poem entitled "Chun fan Ruoye Xi" 春泛若耶溪 (Drifting on Ruoye Creek in Spring), written while boating beneath Mount Ruoye (southeast of modern Shaoxing 紹興 in Zhejiang), illustrates this talent:

> My elation at finding seclusion is unbounded,
> From here I'm ready to meet whatever comes along.
> The evening wind pushes my boat forward,
> Through a path of flowers into the mouth of the stream.
> As night falls I turn into the Western Valley,
> And gaze across the mountains at the Southern Dipper.
> A mist over the pool hovers and spreads
> As the moon backs lower and lower into the trees.
> Now in daily tasks so immersed,
> I wish to become an old man still holding a fishing-pole.

幽意無斷絕，此去隨所偶。
晚風吹行舟，花路入溪口。
際夜轉西壑，隔山望南斗。

Qiwu Qian

潭煙飛溶溶，林月低向後。
生事且瀰漫，願為持竿叟。

Other than the allusion to the Southern Dipper, which marks the celestial boundary of the ancient state of Yue (the Ruoye Creek lies within that boundary on earth), the poem evolves through natural images, the persona taking on the motif of the reclusive fisherman in the final couplet. The metaphoric use of *miman* 瀰漫 (to inundate) to depict the effect of *shengshi* 生事 (daily affairs) ties together this traditional theme to the watery setting and was perhaps the reason the poem was selected as one of the *Tangshi sanbaishou*.

Besides this famous poem, only twenty-five of Qiwu Qian's compositions are still extant, and four are of dubious attribution. Six verses were included in the *Heyue yingling ji* 河嶽英靈集 (753). Most of his works are pentasyllabic, regulated poems seeing off colleagues such as the following "Song Zhang Yi xiadi" 送章彝下第 (Seeing Off Zhang Yi Who Has Failed the Examinations):

On the road from Chang'an to the Wei River Bridge,
Feeling deeply our separation before you set out.
You have presented poems but the Warm Springs are finished,
But with no intermediary the palace gates seem deeper.
As the dawn oriole sings you take to your horse,
In bright sunshine you darkly return to groves of home.
At thirty your name still not established
You should all the more cherish every moment.

長安渭橋路，行客別時心。
獻賦溫泉畢，無媒魏闕深。
黃鶯啼就馬，白日暗歸林。
三十名未立，君還惜寸陰。

Qiwu Qian here laments the examination woes of one of his fellow students as he sees the Zhang Yi off, apparently heading to his home somewhere north of the Wei River. The Warm Springs refers to the Lishan 驪山 Palace a few miles northeast of the capital that Emperor Xuanzong loved to visit and the poems (literally *fu* 賦 or prose-poems) may indicate those in Zhang Yi's examination papers. Here the emperor has apparently finished his visit and is back in the capital. But without someone to introduce his poems to the emperor, the palace gates seem all the more distant. Line 6 reveals the darkness of Qiwu Qian's mood (and possibly that of the groves at his home). The reference to thirty recalls Confucius saying, "at thirty I was established" (*Analects*, 2.4).

Another frequent theme was Daoist or Buddhist temples such as the following "Ti Linyin Si shanding chanyuan" 題靈隱寺山頂禪院 (Written on the Wall of the Mountain Top Zen Hall in the Lingyin Temple):

The monastery atop this mountain,
Has no contact with the vulgar world below.
The Milky Way seems to hang from the pagoda;
The sound of bells mixes with the white clouds.

Beholding emptiness, the meditation chamber is shut,
Following the way, surrounded by burning incense.
I halt my carriage come from the west
Sensing the ties between heaven and man before the sun sets.

招提此山頂，下界不相聞。
塔影掛清漢，鐘聲和白雲。
觀空靜室掩，行道眾香焚。
且駐西來駕，人天日未曛。

The images of the second couplet are what distinguishes this poem as one of Qiwu's best. As the persona looks skyward, the tall pagoda seems to reach to the Milky Way which then appears to hang from it. The temples' bells raise their sound skyward to blend with the clouds. The fifth and sixth lines are ambiguous: *guankong* 觀空 can mean "looking up to the sky" but also is a Buddhist concept of regarding all things as illusory; *xingdao* 行道 can literally mean "to walk a path" but also to follow the Buddha-truth. These lines cause the reader to pause and contemplate, much as the persona himself does, thus preparing the reader for the final couplet in which the Qiwu Qian looks out towards the west, takes in the sunset view that the temple is so known for, and contemplates the symbiosis between the Chan world of the temple and the mortal realm below. The connection between man and heaven refers to the two highest *gati* or states of sentient beings: man and heaven.

But Qiwu Qian is perhaps better known for poems written to him. Wang Wei's "Song Qiwu Qian luodi huanxiang" 送綦毋潛落第還鄉 (Seeing off Qiwu Qian Returning Home Having Failed in the Examinations), Li Qi's "Ji Qiwu San" 寄綦毋三 (Sent to Qiwu Qian), and Wang Wan's 王灣 (fl. 722) "Ku Qiwu buque shi" 哭綦毋補闕時 (A Lament for Rectifier of Omissions Qiwu), trace Qiwu's career through its several successes and failures.

BIBLIOGRAPHY

Editions:
Quan Tang shi, 2: 1368–72.
Quan Tang wen, 333.3813.

Biographical Sources:
Fu, *Tang caizi*, 1:244–50, 5:47–50.

Translations:
Bynner, *Jade Mountain*, p. 62.
Owen, *High Tang*, pp. 58–59.

Studies:
Fu Ruyi 傅如一. "Qiwu Qian shengping shiji kaobian" 綦毋潛生平事跡考辨, *Zhongguo shehui kexue*, 1984.4: 217–23.

Jiang Fang 蔣方. "Tang ren Qiwu Qian shengping zhong jige wenti de kaobian" 唐人綦毋潛生平中幾個問題的考辨, *Hubei Daxue xuebao*, 1990.4.

Jiang Lingling 蔣玲玲. "Qiwu Qian jiqi shige chuangzuo yanjiu" 綦毋潛及其詩歌創作研究. M.A. Thesis, Shanghai Normal University, 2013.

Liu Jiajia 劉珈珈. "Qiwu Qian shengping kaobian" 綦毋潛生平考辨, *Jiangxi Jiaoyu Xueyuan xuebao*, 1989.3: 15–19.

Liu Kongfu 劉孔伏. "Qiwu Qian liguan Ganzhou bian" 綦毋潛里貫贛州辨, *Wenxue yichan*, 1992.6.

Wei Jingbo 魏景波 and Wei Gengyuan 魏耕原. "Sheng Tang qianqi Wang Wan, Zu Yong, Cui Shu yu Qiwu Qian ji Liu Shenxu helun" 盛唐前期王灣、祖詠、崔曙與綦毋潛及劉眘虛合論, *Fuzhou Daxue xuebao (Zhexue shehui kexue ban)*, 2011.2.

William H. Nienhauser, Jr.

Quan Deyu 權德輿 (*zi*, Zaizhi 載之, 761–818) was born in Lüeyang 略陽 in Tianshui 天水 (modern Qin'an 秦安 in Gansu Province) and lived in Danyang 丹陽 in Ruizhou 潤州 (modern Jiangsu Province). The son of Quan Gao 權皋 (724–766), a famous minister in the Tang court during the An Lushan Rebellion, Quan Deyu was said to possess a preternatural ability for poetry, already composing poems at four years of age. By the time he reached fifteen, he was reputed to have already written hundreds of poems and prose pieces, thus earning him renown among literary circles at an early age.

Quan Deyu served various posts as a minor local official under Han Hui 韓洄 (732–794), Du You 杜佑 (735–812) and Bao Ji 包佶 (ca. 727–792) throughout the Jianzhong reign (780–784). In the eighth year of the Zhenyuan reign (792), Quan Deyu entered the court with the position of Erudite in the Court of Imperial Sacrifice. Over the course of the next decade, he would attain the position of Left Rectifier of Omissions and would eventually rise to the post of Secretariat Drafter within the office of the Grand Secretary. In 802, Quan Deyu was appointed as Director of the Ministry of Personnel and held the position of Chief Examiner of the *jinshi* examination on three separate occasions. Over the next several years, Quan was appointed as Vice Director of the Ministry of Revenue, Vice Director of Ministry of the War and Vice Director of Ministry of Personnel. By the fifth year of the Yuanhe reign (811), he rose to the position of Jointly Manager of Affairs with the Secretariat-Chancellery (i.e. Grand Councilor), a position he held for three years.

It was during his time at court that Quan gained influence within literati circles. Over the course of his career, he developed a reputation for being forthright in his assessment of other's works—a trait that led many of his contemporaries to admire his honesty and seek out his critique of their own work. Renowned contemporaries such as Liu Yuxi 劉禹錫 (772–842)* and Liu Zongyuan 柳宗元 (773–819)* submitted their work for his appraisal and would credit his influence on their own writing. Quan would come to be regarded as a master in his own right, and many high officials and celebrated scholars would request his hand in writing prefaces for their memorials and other literary works.

Quan himself would write extensively, commenting on works ranging in topic from noble houses and stele inscriptions to literary collections of fellow authors. Even his own work would come under his exacting scrutiny, as Quan left behind critical reflections of his own pieces. Quan would promote the stance that prose should benefit society, and as such, tended to disregard what he saw as the more extravagant styles of writing. The following essay, "Liang Han bianwang lun" 兩漢辨亡論 (A Discussion of the Fall of the Western and Eastern Han Dynasties), serves to highlight his straightforward style and his unique insights:

> It is said that those who caused the fall of the Western and Eastern Han were called [Wang] Mang and [Dong] Zhuo. I consider Mang and Zhuo to be rebels. That they defiled the throne and caused chaos among the people, courting their own ruin is clearly understood by everyone with ears and eyes. [Yet] if one calmly seeks out evidence, then the one who caused the fall of the Western Capital was Zhang Yu and the one who caused the fall of the Eastern Capital was Hu Guang. By means of their Confucian learning they both achieved their vile goals, seeking to establish their fame in their own time and to reach the highest ministerial posts. The words that they spoke destroyed or enhanced careers, while in many ways pleasing and flattering [the emperor] to maintain their own positions and salaries. They either encouraged the path of their lord toward disaster making the sovereign fall into misfortune or depended on foul disharmony to lead him to future trouble. Therefore a motivation to subvert [their rulers], and their use of portents to allow usurpation, guided them both. Although the years they lived were far apart from the great disorders that happened many years after them, it seems that the disasters were handed down via their own hands and guided via their own jaws. How could the devastation caused by Mang and Zhuo compare to this?

> 言兩漢所以亡者，皆曰莽、卓。予以為莽、卓篡逆．污神器以亂齊民，自賈夷滅，天下耳目，顯然聞知。靜征厥初，則亡西京者張禹，亡東京者胡廣，皆以假道儒術，得申其邪心，徼一時大名，致位公輔。詞氣所發，損益系之。而多方善柔，保位持祿。或陷時君以滋厲階，或附凶邪以結禍胎。故其盪覆之機，篡奪之兆，皆指導之、馴致之。雖年祀相遠，猶手授頤指之然也。其為賊害，豈直莽、卓之比乎？

Quan's argues here that the two famous rebels, Wang Mang 王莽 (46 BC–AD 23) and Dong Zhuo 董卓 (d. 192), were less to blame for the fall of the Han dynasties than the Confucian ministers Zhang Yu 張禹 (ca. 85–5 BC) and Hu Guang 胡廣 (91–172). Zhang Yu was a noted classical scholar who wrote one of the earliest commentaries on the *Lunyu* 論語 (*Analects*). He became Chancellor in 25 BC under Emperor Cheng (r. 33–7 BC) and through imperial favor was able to live an extravagant lifestyle. He advised Emperor Cheng to disregard warnings about the Wang family's increasing power thereby allowing Wang Mang to overthrow the Former Han shortly after the Emperor's death. Hu Guang shared control of the court with Chen Fan 陳蕃 (d. 168) in the transitional years between Emperor Huan (132–167, r. 146–167) and Emperor Ling (156–189, r. 168–189). The reference here may be to the abortive attempt by Hu and Chen to eliminate the power of the palace eunuchs in 149. The plan ultimately backfired after defeat in a palace battle allowed the eunuchs a victory and even more power. As a result the eunuchs were able to direct the youthful Emperor Ling into a decadence that led indirectly to the rebellion of the Yellow Turbans in 184 and the fall of the dynasty. Or it may go back to Hu's recommendation in 131 that Emperor Shun (r. 126–144) should select Liang Na 梁妠 (116–150) as empress, setting in motion the dominance that the Liang family held over the throne for the next three decades, a dominance which led to internecine court battles that also provided motives and opportunities for the Yellow Turbans. In any case Hu Guang has been generally faulted for the ease with which he switched loyalties throughout his career. As in so many Tang works, however, reference to Han dynasty events could always be read as referring to the contemporary Tang situation. Since Quan was an acknowledged opponent of Pei Yanling 裴延齡 (728–796) the piece may have been intended as criticism of Pei's actions.

Quan would also gain renown for his poetry, most notably for his five-syllable verse. Yan Yu 嚴羽 (fl. 1200) in his *Canglang shihua* 滄浪詩話 compares Quan's style to the bucolic poetry of Wei Yingwu 韋應物 (737–ca. 791)* and Liu Zhangqing 劉長卿 (726–ca. 787).* In the following example entitled "Lingshang feng jiubeizhe youbie" 嶺上逢久別者又別, Quan expresses a profound melancholy in very simple words:

> Ten years ago we parted,
> on this campaign road we chance to meet.
> Where shall my horse's head turn?
> In the setting sun are countless peaks.

> 十年曾一別，征路此相逢。
> 馬首向何處？夕陽千萬峰。

Further details of Quan's life can be found in Han Yu's 韓愈 (768–824)* "Tang guxiang Quan Gong mubei" 唐故相權公墓碑 (Funerary Stele of the Tang Former Grand Councilor Master Quan), his biographies are in chapter 148 of the *Jiu Tang shu* and Chapter 165 of the *Xin Tang shu*.

BIBLIOGRAPHY

Editions:
Guo Guangwei 郭廣偉. *Quan Deyu shiwen ji* 權德輿詩文集. 2v. Shanghai: Shanghai Guji, 2008.
Jiang Yin 蔣寅 et al., eds. *Quan Deyu shi wen ji biannian jiaozhu* 權德輿詩文集編年校注. Shenyang: Liaohai, 2013.
Quan Deyu (761–818) 權德輿. *Lu Xuan'gong wenji* 陸宣公文集. Taibei: Xinan, 1973.
___. *Quan Zaizhi wenji* 權載之文集. 50 juan. Taibei: Taiwan Shangwu, 1965.
Quan Tang shi, 5: 3606–87, 14: 10645.
Quan Tang wen, 483–509.4933–5181.
Quan Zaizhi wenji 權載之文集. SKQS.

Biographical Sources:
Fu, *Tang caizi*, 2:575–605, 5:261–63.
Jiu Tang shu, 148.4001–06.
Xin Tang shu, 165.5076–80.

Translations:
Shields, Anna M. "Entombed Funerary Inscription for My Daughter, the Late Madame Dugu (785–815) and Entombed Record for My Grandson Who Died Young (Quan Shunsun, 803–815)," in *The Lives of Men and Women over Two Millennia, Recorded in Stone: Chinese Funerary Biographies*. Patricia Buckley Ebrey, Ping Yao and Cong Ellen Zhang. Seattle: University of Washington, 2019, pp. 66–74.

Studies:

Bol, pp. 110–11, 122f.

Chen Yiqiu 陳彝秋. "Quan Deyu dui Chu Sao de jieshou yu ZhongTang wenxue sixiang de bianqian 權德輿對楚騷的接受與中唐文學思想的變遷, *Huanan Shifan Daxue xuebao*, (2006.2).

DeBlasi, Anthony. "Quan Deyu (759–818) and the Spread of Elite Culture in Tang China," in Kenneth J. Hammond, ed. *The Human Tradition in Premodern China*. Wilmington, Delaware: Scholarly Resources, Inc., 2002.

___. *Reform in the Balance: The Defense of Literary Culture in Mid-Tang China*. Albany: State University of New York Press, 2002.

___. "Striving for Completeness: Quan Deyu and the Evolution of the Tang Intellectual Mainstream," *HJAS* 61 (2001): 5–36.

Ditter, Alexei Kamran. "Genre and the Construction of Memory: A Case Study of Quan Deyu's 權德輿 (759–818) Funerary Writings for Zhang Jian 張薦 (744–804)." In *Memory in Medieval China: Text, Ritual, and Community*. Wendy Swartz and Robert Ford Campany, eds. Leiden: Brill, 2018, pp. 193212.

Duan Chengxiao 段承校. "Shilun Jiao Ran shixue dui Quan Deyu shilun ji shizuo de yinxiang" 試論皎然詩學對權德輿詩論及詩作的影響, *Nanjing Shifan Daxue xuebao* 5 (2000).

___, "Quan Deyu yu Han Yu guanxi tanwei" 權德輿與韓愈關係探微, *Xi'an Lianhe Daxue xuebao* (2002.2).

Guo Guangwei 郭廣偉. "Quan Deyu nianpu jianben" 權德輿年譜簡編, *Xuzhou Shifan Daxue xuebao*, 3 (1994).

___. "Quan Deyu nianpu jianben xu" 權德輿年譜簡編續, *Xuzhou Shifan Daxue xuebao* 4 (1994).

___. "Quan Deyu yu Zhenyuan houqi shifeng" 權德輿與貞元後期詩風, *Tangdai wenxue yanjiu* (1994).

Hu Sui 胡遂 and Xiong Ying 熊. "Quan Deyu shige chuangzuo yu Mazu Hongzhou Chan" 權德輿詩歌創作與馬祖洪州禪, *Hunan Daxue xuebao* 4 (2006).

Huo Xudong 霍旭東. "Quan Deyu he shige chuangzuo" *Shehui zongheng* 社會縱橫 2 (1994).

Jiang Yin 蔣寅. "Quan Deyu yu Tangdai zengxu wenti zhi queli" 權德輿與唐代贈序文體之確立, *Beijing Daxue xuebao* (2010.2).

___. "Quan Deyu yu cengneishi" 權德輿與贈內詩, *Shanxi Shifan Daxue xuebao* 山西師範大學學報, (1999.1).

Mao Guohua 茅國華. "Lun Quan Deyu de renge fengbao yu shige fengge" 論權德輿的人格風范與詩歌風格, *Hebei Daxue xuebao* (2007.3).

Wang Chaoyuan 王朝源. "Lun Quan Deyu de beizhi sanwen" 論權德輿的碑志散文, *Sichuan Shifan Daxue xuebao*, 2006.5.

Wang Hongxia 王紅霞. *Quan Deyu yanjiu* 權德輿研究. Chengdu: Ba Shu Shushe, 2009.

___. "Shilun Quan Deyu de guwen chuangzuo" 試論權德輿的古文創作, *Xinan Minzu Daxue xuebao*, 11 (2003).

___. "Lun Quan Deyu de Ru, Shi, Dao guan" 論權德輿的儒、釋、道觀, *Sichuan Shifan Daxue xuebao* (2002.2).

Wu Ruyu 吳汝煜. "Quan Deyu shiren mingkao zheng" 權德輿詩人名考證, *Xibei Shifan Daxue xuebao* 5 (1989).

Yan Guorong 嚴國榮. *Quan Deyu yanjiu* 權德輿研究. Beijing: Zhongguo Shehui, 2006.

___. "Quan Deyu shengping yu jiaoyou kaolüe" 權德輿生平與交游考略, *Tangdu xuekan*, 4 (1997).

___. "Quan Deyu yu guwen yundong–Jianlun Quan Deyu de wenlun zhuzhang" 權德輿與古文運動—兼論權德輿的文論主張, *Tangdu xuekan* 4 (1998).

___. "Quan Deyu shige 'Chengzhong youbian' de lishi gongji" 權德輿詩歌"承中有變"的歷史功績, *Journal of Peking University* (2003.3).

Jingyi Qu and Michael E. Naparstek

Rong Yu 戎昱 (744–800) was a poet active in the Dali period (766–779). Growing up in the tumultuous time surrounding the An Lushan rebellion, scholars debate whether he hailed from Jingnan 荊南 (Jiangling 江陵 in modern Hubei) or Fufeng 扶風 (in modern Shanxi). The famous calligrapher and statesmen, Yan Zhenqing 顏真卿 (709–785), was the first to appreciate Rong Yu's talent and from 759 to 760 had him assigned as a Retainer in his bureau in Zhexi 浙西 (modern southern Jiangsu and northern Zhejiang Provinces). Impressed by his capability, Yan would go on to recommended him multiple times.

Rong Yu left his position in 760 and travelled to Chang'an to take the examinations. It took six years and several attempts to eventually pass the *jinshi*, during which time Rong Yu would travel between Luoyang, Qi, Zhao, Jingzhou, and Longxi (modern Gansu). During this period, Rong Yu would exchange poems with Wang Jiyou 王季友 (714–794) and wrote a series of five poems named "Ku zai xing" 苦哉行 (What Bitterness), depicting the social conflicts and hardships of the common people due to the court's policy to use troops to put down domestic turmoil (see below). After Rong Yu passed the *jinshi* in 766, he left Chang'an and traveled to Shu 蜀 (modern Sichuan) where he met Cen Shen 岑參 (715–770)* in Chengdu. For the next fifteen years, Rong Yu would travel between positions in one provincial administration to another, gaining a sense of the way of life throughout southern China.

In 767, Rong Yu became a Retainer to the Military Commissioner, Wei Boyu 衛伯玉 (d. 776) appointed him Retainer to the Military Commission of Jinnan 荊南 (based in Jiangling in modern central Hubei). The following year proved momentous for his literary development as he met Du Fu 杜甫 (712–770)* in Jiangling. In 769, he went to Hunan and joined the staff of Surveillance Commissioner Cui Guan 崔瓘 (fl. 770). The local military upheaval continued for a year until it abated in 772, when Rong Yu sojourned down to the Xiangzhong 湘中 region of Hunan. In 773 he went to Guizhou 桂州 (modern Guilin in Guangxi), where he found a position with Surveillance Commissioner, Li Changkui 李昌夔. There, he was forced to temporarily leave his position due to slander in 775 but returned to it shortly after.

Rong Yu's fifteen-year journey in the four provincial governments finally led him to a position in court in 782, where he served in the Censorate. The following year, when Emperor Dezong (r. 779–805) was forced to leave the capital during the Jingyuan Mutiny 涇原兵變, Rong Yu fled the court and was appointed Prefect of Chenzhou 辰州 (modern Huaihua 懷化 County in Hunan). When Emperor Dezong regained the throne, Rong Yu returned to court in 787 until where he remained until 791, when he was made Prefect of Qianzhou 虔州 (modern Ganzhou 贛州 in Jiangxi), and would then serve in the same capacity seven years later in Yongzhou 永州 (modern Hunan). The circumstances surrounding his death are unknown.

The fluctuations of Rong Yu's political career lent a melancholy and desolate tone to his poems, in which he described historical events and major social conflicts of the time. As a great admirer of Du Fu, many of his poems also depict the suffering of the vulnerable, common people and criticize the ruling class which brought on such calamities. Like Du Fu, Rong Yu's poetry often frames his critique in an expression of his deepest concerns for the fate of his county. However, his poems never reached the artistic depths of Du Fu's. Nevertheless, during his own lifetime, Rong Yu's poems impressed his supervisors and served him well in facilitating his career. At the same time, Rong Yu's verse also served as a means for expressing criticism through personal passion. When an entertainer he favored was summoned to court, Rong Yu found an opportunity to reflect on the hardships of those dispossessed and left wandering by war. The following poem is the second of his "Ku zai xing" 苦哉行:

When the government troops took back Luoyang,
my family dwelt in Luoyang.
My husband and my brothers,
before my eyes I watched them wounded and dying.
I swallowed my sobs not permitted to weep,
and still dressed in embroidered silk.
Mounting a horse I followed the Xiongnu,
countless autumns in the yellow dust.
Born as a girl from an honored family,
I will die as a ghost on the border wall.
Without hope of returning to my homeland,
at Heaven's End Bridge they must weep into a flowing river.

官軍收洛陽，家住洛陽裏。
夫婿與兄弟，目前見傷死。
吞聲不許哭，還遣衣羅綺。
上馬隨匈奴，數秋黃塵裏。
生為名家女，死作塞垣鬼。
鄉國無還期，天津哭流水。

In this, the second of a series of poems in which Rong Yu takes up a female persona to depict the bitter reality of those caught between political conflicts, he voices the internal lament of woman from a well-to-do family who now suffers in silence having watched the Tang army destroy her home and family. Set in the context of the An Lushan Rebellion, when the army she longs for takes back Luoyang, her family nevertheless is shattered by the pillaging troops. Forced to live an iterant life following the Xiongnu, the finery of her outward appearance stands in poignant contrast to the harsh reality she now endures. Now dead inside, she has become a ghost of her former self. The final line has the poet imagining her relatives weeping for her at the Tianjin 天津 or Heaven's End Bridge, overlooking a main thoroughfare back in Luoyang. By voicing her internal lament, Rong Yu exposes the unseen costs of war, and can be read as a reproach of the ruling class who carelessly brings suffering and agony to the common people as a result of their political ambition.

BIBLIOGRAPHY

Editions:
Fu *Shiren*, pp. 336–57
Fu, *Caizi zhuan*, p. 664.
Quan Tang shi, 4: 2998–3019.
Rong Yu shiji 戎昱詩集, Puban Collection. Shanghai: Lingjian ge, 1895.
Shi Qiyu 席啓寓, ed. *Rong Yu shi ji : 1 juan, bu yi 1 juan* 戎昱詩集 一卷, 補遺一卷. Dongshan Xishi Qinchuan shuwu, 1708 reprint. Shanghai: Saoye Shanfang, 1920; Electronic reproduction. Cambridge, Mass. Harvard Library Preservation, 2015. (Harvard-Yenching Library Chinese Rare Books Digitization Project-Collected Works). Copy digitized: Harvard-Yenching Library: T 5237.48 0233 (14). M-1
___. *Tang shi baimingjia quanji* 唐詩百名家全集 (Qing).

Tang shiji shi 唐詩紀事, *juan* 28.

Tang caizi zhuan jiaojian 唐才子傳校箋, *juan* 3.

Xi Qiyu 席啓寓 (d. 1703). *Rong Yu shiji: yijuan, buyi yijuan* 戎昱詩集一卷, 補遺一卷. Dongshan Xishi Qinchuan Shuwu, 1708.

Annotations:

Zang Weixi 藏維熙. *Rong Yu shizhu* 戎昱詩注. Shanghai: Shanghai Guji, 1982.

Biographical Sources:

Fu, *Tang caizi*, 1:660–72.

Studies:

Chen Wenli 陳文麗. "Rong Yu rumi kao jiqi rumi xintai fenxi" 戎昱入幕考及其入幕心態分析, *Wenxie jie (Lilun ban)* 2002.1: 113–17.

Guo Rui 郭睿. "Rong Yu shige yongyun kao" 戎昱詩歌用韻考, *Suihua Xueyuan xuebao* 33.2 (Feb., 2013): 42–45, 147.

He Xu 何旭. "Zhong Tang shiren Rong Yu jiguan kao" 中唐詩人戎昱籍貫考, *Yanchen Shifan Xueyuan xuebao (Renwen Shehui Kexueban)* 2013.4: 62–65.

Huang Gui 黃圭. "Lüelun Rong Yu de shige" 略論戎昱的詩歌, *Shehui Kexue xuebao* 1987.2: 89–94.

Jiang Yin 蔣寅. "Rong Yu de shipin yu renpin" 戎昱的詩品與人品, *Zhongguo Yunwen xuekan* 1993.7: 22–28.

Ziyun Liu and Michael E. Naparstek

Shangguan Wan'er 上官婉兒, also known as Shangguan Zhaorong 上官昭容 (664–710), was born in Shan County 陝縣, Shanzhou 陝州 (modern Shan County in Henan). She was the granddaughter of the courtier and poet Shangguan Yi 上官儀 (ca. 607–ca. 665).* After her father, Shangguan Tingzhi 上官庭芝 (d. 665), and grandfather were executed for plotting against Empress Wu (Wu Zetian, 624–705, r. 690–705), Shangguan and her mother, Lady Zheng 鄭, became slaves in the Palace Discipline Service. In her childhood, Shangguan studied with her mother and demonstrated talents in writing poetry and prose as well as a sensitivity to political matters. In 678, barely into her teens, the Empress recognized her exceptional literary talents and released Shangguan from her bondage. Little is known of the next two decades of her life, but by the time she reached her early thirties, Shangguan was in charge of drafting imperial edicts and participated in the discussions of official memorials. On one occasion she faced the death penalty for disobeying Empress Wu, but once again, in recognition of her talents, the Empress reduced Shangguan's sentence to tattooing of her face. Thereafter, Shangguan's political influence rapidly increased and she became the Empress's personal secretary.

In 705, Emperor Zhongzong (656–710, r. 684 and 705–710) was restored to the throne after the death of Empress Wu, and he promoted Shangguan Wan'er to the rank of Consort of Shining Countenance, the sixth rank among imperial consorts. Due to her political prominence, her mother was given the title of the Lady of the State of Pei (Peiguo Furen 沛國夫人) and her grandfather, Shangguan Yi, was posthumously conferred the title of Duke of Chu (Chuguo Gong 楚國公). In 707, Prince Li Chongjun 李重俊 (d. 707) initiated a coup, accusing Shangguan of having an affair with Emperor Zhongzong's cousin, Wu Sansi 武三思 (649–707). After this coup attempt, Shangguan concentrated more on the affairs of the state, forcefully advocating the expansion of Literary Institute. Every year, she brought numerous poets to the palace, including noted bards like Li Jiao 李嶠 (ca. 644–ca. 714),* Shen Quanqi 沈佺期 (656–716),* Song Zhiwen 宋之問 (656–ca. 712)* and Du Shenyan 杜審言 (ca. 645–708).* Her influential position in both politics and public literary life enabled her to exert great power under both Empress Wu and Emperor Zhongzong.

Zhongzong's sudden death in 710 caused a political upheaval. Empress Wei 韋皇后 (d. 710) attempted to seize power, but Zhongzong's nephew, Li Longji 李隆基 (685–762), the future Emperor Xuanzong 玄宗 (r. 712–756), was able to have Empress Wei and her clan members killed and eventually took the throne. During the coup Shangguan came out from her residence holding the original will of Emperor Zhongzong to show her readiness to serve the new powers. But since she was considered to be part of the Empress Wei clique, she was executed. Her title of the Consort of Shining Countenance was resumed posthumously.

After Shangguan Wan'er's death, her poetry and prose were collected in twenty *juan*. Zhang Yue 張說 (667–731)* wrote a preface to the collection. Traditionally, the compilation order is ascribed to Emperor Xuanzong, but some recent studies conclude that it may have happened earlier after Shangguan's death in 710 when Princess Taiping 太平 (ca. 665–713) obtained permission from Emperor Ruizong (662–717, r. 684–690 and 710–712), the father of Xuanzong. The original collection was lost and only thirty-two of her poems are collected in *Quan Tang shi*. These poems can be roughly classified into three categories: lyric poems, court poems, and landscape poems. The majority of the topics in the extant corpus are on court activities, a highly conventional genre at the time featuring rigid structure and stock phrases. Despite her predilection for court poetry, her style is dynamic and straightforward; she presented new ways of expression foreshadowing trends of High Tang poetry to come. Moreover, her experience in political and literary activities of the Early Tang are comparable to even the most successful male poets of the era.

Her best-known lyric poem "Cai shu yuan" 彩書怨 (A Lament Written on Colored Paper) stands out from the poet's extant corpus by having a distinctive female voice and diction strongly reminiscent of boudoir poetry. The poem expresses a wife's grief of parting in what seems to be an unsophisticated style:

> Leaves start to fall on Lake Dongting,
> I long for you, a thousand miles away.
> The dew becomes heavy, the scented quilt feels cold,
> As the moon sets, the embroidered screen empties.
> I want to play a "melody from down South,"
> And strive to seal a letter for you at the northern border.
> The letter has no other intent but
> To express the disappointment at living long apart.

> 葉下洞庭初，思君萬里餘。
> 露濃香被冷，月落錦屏虛。
> 欲奏江南曲，貪封薊北書。
> 書中無別意，惟悵久離居。

Shangguan Wan'er

Some critics read the poem biographically and think it was written when Shangguan was a teenager; moreover, they believe that it was addressed to Prince Li Xian 李賢 (655–684), for whom Wan'er had a secret love. Others read it as simply expressing Shangguan's loneliness in the palace. However, the poem describes a wife in South China missing her husband who is guarding the frontier in the north, which does not correspond to the lives of Li Xian and Shangguan Wan'er.

The first couplet is reminiscent of Qu Yuan's 屈原 (ca. 340–ca. 278) lyric poem "Xiang Furen" 湘夫人 (Lady of the Xiang River) and uses similar imagery to describe the season and location. "Gently the wind of autumn whispers; / On the waves of the Dongting lake the leaves are falling" 嫋嫋兮秋風，洞庭波兮木葉下. Both poems set a tone of sadness caused by an absent lover. The character *si* 思 (long for) in the second line reveals the theme of the whole poem. The second couplet is most vivid, depicting her bedroom as cold and suggesting that she remains awake late into the night watching the details on the brightly embroidered screen disappear from sight as the light from the setting moon dims. The author sets a contrast between symbols of the opulent life and feelings of emptiness and coldness. Lines five to six describe two daily details: playing a Jiangnan melody and writing letters to her absent husband. The *Jiangnan qu* 江南曲 (Melody from Down South) refers to the Southern style of *yuefu* poems, dominated by expressions of love between separated lovers. The particular melody contrasts the woman's situation as it describes the admiration of beautiful scenery and seeking pleasure. The woman in her loneliness thinks of the melody and strives to write a letter to her loved one. The last couplet in simple and direct language exposes both the depth of her longing and the frustrations she must feel: she has nothing to say other than to share her sadness. It echoes two lines from Xiao Gang's 蕭綱 (503–551) "Zhe yangliu" 折楊柳 (Breaking off Poplar and Willow Branches): "The melody has no other intent, other than it being mutual longing" 曲中無別意，並是為相思.

The second group of Shangguan's poems are poems on topics designated by the emperor. They often describe extravagant palace activities or glorify the emperor's accomplishments. Generally speaking, such poems are monotonous in pattern and light in content; Shangguan's poems, however, represented her best work, containing original observations of natural beauty and cultural activities, and the harmony between them. The poem "Fenghe shengzhi lichunri shiyan neidian chu jiancaihua yingzhi" 奉和聖制立春日侍宴內殿出剪彩花應制 (Written upon Imperial Command to Match a Poem by the Emperor: Presenting Colored Paper-Cut Flowers at a Royal Banquet in the Inner Palace on the 'Establishing Spring' Day) is an example:

> Dense leaves come into bloom from trimming;
> New flowers unroll from cutting.
> Even though you are not mistaken by pulling on a branch,
> You unexpectedly discover the flaw when plucking a bud.
> From the time when spring comes, flowers start to bloom;
> In autumn they are still unwilling to wither.
> May I ask the blossoms of peaches or plums,
> What would happen if I mix paper and real flowers together?

密葉因裁吐，新花逐剪舒。
攀條雖不謬，摘蕊詎知虛。

春至由來發，秋還未肯疏。
借問桃將李，相亂欲何如。

The poem was probably written in early spring of 709 during the gathering in which palace ladies presented paper-cut blossoms to Emperor Zhongzong. The Emperor ordered Shangguan Wan'er and six other Academicians to write poems on the occasion. Although this poem ostensibly describes the routine palace activity of "paper flower-cutting," Shangguan's agile language adds an erotic dimension by enlivening paper flowers and personifying plants.

The third group comprises poems on natural scenes and famous sights. Twenty-five extant poems of this group are titled "You Changning Gongzhu Liubeichi" 遊長寧公主流杯池 (Visiting Princess Changning's Pond of Floating Cups). The estate poem genre became particularly popular during Zhongzong's second reign. Shangguan wrote this collection under the Emperor's orders to extol the beauty of looking out over the pond; these poems are written from various perspectives and together constitute a gorgeous image of a Chinese garden. They include natural scenes that typically appear in *shanshui* poems: the moon, the wind, mountains, forests, springs, and frosts. However, unlike Wang Wei 王維 (692–761 or 699–759),* who is famous for his *shanshui* quatrains with little human presence, Shangguan prefers to describe the harmonious relationship between humans and nature. The twenty-first poem of this collection is a good example:

> Sitting at the pond, I slightly test the brush,
> Leaning on the rock, I quickly compose a poem.
> Planning to play "High-mountain" or "Flowing-river" melodies,
> To the end I intend to follow Zhong Qi.

傍池聊試筆，倚石旋題詩。
豫彈山水調，終擬從鐘期。

This short poem describes three outside literary activities: preparing the writing brush by the pond, inscribing poems on the rock, and playing the zither in nature. The literary persona finds inspiration in interacting with the surroundings, eventually finding peace with them. The last two lines of the quatrain become clear only through the story of Yu Boya 俞伯牙 and Zhong Zi Qi 鐘子期. Boya was a master of the zither and when he played on Mount Huang 黃山 the woodcutter Zi Qi could recognize what Boya was thinking through his musical presentation of the "High mountain" and "Flowing river" melodies. But Shangguan Wan'er could not find someone like Zi Qi who could understand her feelings. This allusion may express Shangguan's desire to find a soulmate who could assist her in the palace. Overall, in this group of poems she paralleled palace activities with natural scenes finding a retreat in opulent palace gardens as if she were a hermit while still at court. Due to a variation of similar vocabulary and themes throughout the series, the modern scholar Wu Jie argues that the poems as a whole might have been composed by a group of poets rather than by Shangguan Wan'er hand alone.

Shangguan greatly influenced palace literary initiatives and promoted early Tang poetry development. She oversaw most of the singing and writing activities attended by the Emperor and his officials. She is said to have ghostwritten poems for the Emperor, collected responding poems from palace officials, and judged poetry competitions. Such efforts promoted the development of Tang poetry away from the conventionality of the Early Tang.

BIBLIOGRAPHY

Editions:
Chen Bohai 陳伯海. *Tangshi huiping* 唐詩匯評. Hangzhou: Zhejiang Jiaoyu, 1995.
Ji Yougong 計有功. *Tangshi jishi* 唐詩紀事. Shanghai: Shanghai Guji, 2008, pp. 3.25–28.
"Shangguan zhaorong ji xu" 上官昭容集序 in *Wenyuan yinghua* 文苑英華. Beijing: Zhonghua, 1986, 700.4b–6a.
Quan Tang shi, 5: 60–64.
Quan Tang wen, 225.2274–75.
Wang Lusheng 王盧生, ed. *Datang cainu Shangguan Wan'er shiji* 大唐才女上官婉兒詩集. Shanghai: Shanghai Guji, 2011.

Translations:
Chang, *Women Writers,* pp. 50–51, 722–25.
Fuller, Michael A. *An Introduction to Chinese Poetry: From the* Canon of Poetry *to the Lyrics of the Song Dynasty.* Cambridge: Harvard University Press, 2018, pp. 184–85.
Idema, Wilt and Beata Grant. *The Red Brush. Writing Women of Imperial China.* Cambridge, Mass.: Harvard University Asia Center, 2004, 68–70, 71–72.
Larsen, Jeanne. *Willow, Wine, Mirror, Moon: Women's Poems from Tang China.* Rochester, New York: BOA Editions, 2005, 26–31.

Studies:
Chen Bohai 陳伯海 and Zhu Yi'an 朱易安. *Tangshi shulu* 唐詩書錄. Jinan: Qi Lu Shushe, 1988.
Cheng Ya-ju 鄭雅如. "Chongtan Shangguan Wan'er de siwang, pingfan yu dangdai pingjia" 重探上官婉兒的死亡、平反與當代評價 in You Jianming 游鑑明, ed., *Zhongguo funü shi lunji* 中國婦女史論集. Xinbei: Daoxiang, 2014, pp. 7–40.
Doran, Rebecca. *Transgressive Typologies: Constructions of Gender and Power in Early Tang China.* Cambridge, Mass: Harvard University Asia Center, 2016.
Du Wenyu 杜文玉. "Bei wudu de Shangguan Wan'er" 被誤讀的上官婉兒. *Wenshi zhishi* 1 (2014): 69–74.
Hu Kexian 胡可先, "Shangguan shi jiazu yu chu Tang wenxue—jianlun xin chutu 'Shangguan Wan'er muzhi' de wenxue jiazhi" 上官氏家族與初唐文學—兼論新出土《上官婉兒墓誌》的文學價值. *Qiushi xuekan* 41.5 (2014): 163–72.
Idema, Wilt and Beata Grant. *The Red Brush. Writing Women of Imperial China.* Cambridge, Mass.: Harvard University Asia Center, 2004, pp. 61–67, 71–72.
Li Haiyan 李海燕. "Shangguan Wan'er yu chu Tang gongtingshi de zhongjie" 上官婉兒與初唐宮廷詩的終結. *Qiusuo* 求索 2 (2010): 165–66.
Li Ming 李明 and Geng Qinggang 耿慶剛. "'Tang zhaorong Shangguan shi muzhi' jianshi—jiantan Tang zhaorong Shangguanshi mu xiangguan wenti"《唐昭容上官氏墓誌》箋釋—兼談唐昭容上官氏墓相關問題. *Kaogu yu wenwu* 6 (2013): 86–91.
Lee, Lily Xiao Hong and Sue Wiles, eds. *Biographical Dictionary of Chinese Women, Tang through Ming 618–1644.* Armonk, NY: M.E. Sharpe, 2014, pp. 336–40.
Lu Yang 陸揚. "Shangguan Wan'er he ta de zhizuozhe" 上官婉兒和他的製作者. In *Qingliu wenhua yu Tang diguo* 清流文化與唐帝國. Beijing: Beijing Daxue, 2015.

Luo Shijin 羅時進 and Li Ling 李淩. "Tangdai nüquan wenxue de shenhua: Shangguan Wan'er de gongting shige chuangzuo jiqi wenxueshi diwei" 唐代女權文學的神話：上官婉兒的宮廷詩歌創作及其文學史地位. *Jiangsu Daxue xuebao* 7.6 (2005): 63–65.

Owen, Stephen. "The Formation of the Tang Estate Poem." *HJAS* 55.1 (1995): 39–59.

Qiu Luming 仇鹿鳴, "Beizhuan yu shizhuan: Shangguan Wan'er de shengping yu xingxiang" 碑傳與史傳：上官婉兒的生平與形象. *Xueshu yuekan* 46.5 (2014): 157–68.

Rothschild, Norman Harry. "'Her Influence Great, Her Merit beyond Measure': A Translation and Initial Investigation of the Epitaph of Shangguan Wan'er." *Studies in Chinese Religions* 1.2 (2015): 131–48.

Shen Wenfan 沈文凡 and Zuo Hongjie 左紅傑. "Jin bainian Wu Zetian yu Shangguan Wan'er shige yanjiu zongshu" 近百年武則天與上官婉兒詩歌研究綜述. *Xihua Daxue xuebao (Zhexue shehuikexue ban)* 31.2 (2012): 1–11, 17.

Tang Tuanjie 唐團結 "Shangguan Wan'er shengping kaoshu" 上官婉兒生平考述. *Henan Jiaoyu Xueyuan xuebao* 5 (2004): 34–38.

Wu, Jie. "A Study of Group Compositions in Early Tang China (618–713)." Ph.D. Dissertation. University of Washington, 2008.

___. "Vitality and Cohesiveness in the Poetry of Shangguan Wan'er (664–710)." *Tang Studies* 34 (2016): 40–72.

Xie Zhen 謝榛(明). *Siming shihua* 四溟詩話, Beijing: Zhonghua, 1985.

Yuan Fengqin 袁风琴. "Fengya zhi sheng liu yu laiye—Tangdai gongting nüshiren 風雅之聲流于來葉—唐代宮廷女詩人, *Wuhu Zhiye Jishu Xueyuan xuebao* 9 (2003): 54–57.

Zhen Zhouya 甄周亚. "Zhongri gongting nüshiren Shangguan Wan'er yu Etian wang shige chuangzuo bijiao yanjiu" 中日宮廷女世人上官婉儿與额田王詩歌創作比較研究. *Xiandai yuwen* 7 (2013): 69–73.

Zheng Yaru 鄭雅如. "Chongtan Shangguan Wan'er de siwang, pingfan yu dangdai pingjia" 重探上官婉兒的死亡、平反與當代評價. *Zaoqi Zhongguo shi yanjiu* 早期中國史研究, 4.1 (2012): 111–45.

Zhou Shufang 周淑舫. *Zhongguo nüxing wenxue fazhan lanlun* 中國女性文學發展覽論. Jilin: Jilin Daxue, 2012.

Masha Kobzeva and Xue Bai

Shangguan Yi 上官儀 (*zi*, Youshao 游韶, ca. 607–ca. 665) is regarded as the most representative court-style poet of the time. He was born in Shan County 陝縣, Shanzhou 陝州 (modern Henan). His father, Shangguan Hong 上官弘 (573–618), was a Deputy Director of the Palace in Jiangdu during the Sui dynasty. At the end of Daye era (605–618), he was killed by general Chen Leng 陳稜 (d. 619). At that time Shangguan Yi was still young, and he managed to escape by secretly obtaining ordination as a Buddhist monk.

Since he immersed himself in reading Buddhist sutras, focusing on the scriptures of the School of Three Treatises (Sanlunzong 三論宗), it is likely his motives were genuine. He was also studying Confucian classics as well as working on literary composition. At the beginning of the Zhenguan era (627–650), recommended by the influential Yang Gongren 楊恭仁 (d. 639), Shangguan Yi passed the *jinshi* examination and was summoned as an Auxiliary Academician in the Institute for the Advancement of Literature. Later he was promoted to Assistant in the Palace Library. It is said that Emperor Taizong (598–649, r. 626–649) sent draft versions of poetic compositions for Shangguan to review. Shangguan was frequently invited to banquets and court gatherings where he was skilled at matching poems and extemporaneous composition. He was later transferred to the position of Imperial Diarist and was part of the editorial group revising the *Jin shu* 晉書 (History of Jin). After Emperor Gaozong (628–683, r. 650–683) ascended the throne,

Shangguan Yi

Shangguan became Vice Director of the Palace Library. In 662 he was promoted to Vice Director of the Secretariat (i.e. one of the Grand Councilors).

At the time, due to court intrigues, Empress Wang 王皇后 was demoted, replaced by the Primary Consort Wu Zetian 武則天 (624–705, r. 690–705). The court split into two factions, one represented by Li Yifu 李義府 (614–666) and Xu Jingzong 許敬宗 (592–672),* wanted the Empress removed. The other, including Zhangsun Wuji 長孫無忌 (d. 659), Chu Suiliang 褚遂良 (596–658) and the demoted former heir-apparent, Li Zhong 李忠 (643–664), supported her continuing as Empress. When the eunuch Wang Fusheng 王伏勝 learned that Wu Zetian had secretly brought a Daoist sorcerer into the palace, he reported it to the Emperor, who in turn asked Shangguan Yi's advice. In a decisive moment, Shangguan Yi recommended that Gaozong demote Wu Zetian. The ailing Emperor, however, was already under Wu Zetian's influence, and when confronted by Wu Zetian, revealed Shangguan Yi's recommendation to her. In response Wu Zetian made Xu Jingzong falsely accuse Shangguan Yi, Li Zhong, and Wang Fusheng of plotting against the Emperor.

In the first year of the Linde era (664), Shangguan Yi's property was seized, and he was imprisoned where he soon died. Historical sources are not clear whether Shangguan Yi was arrested and sentenced to death on the same day, or whether he first spent some time in prison, thus it is difficult to determine the exact date of his death. In addition to Shangguan Yi, others thought to be involved were also purged one after another, including Shangguan Yi's son, Shangguan Tingzhi 上官庭芝 (d. 665), who was murdered. However Tingzhi's wife, Lady Zheng 鄭, and his daughter, Shangguan Wan'er 上官婉兒 (664–710),* were taken as palace servants and survived. Shangguan Wan'er was favored by Empress Wu and later became a consort of Emperor Zhongzong (656–710, r. 684, 705–710). Emperor Zhongzong posthumously conferred Shangguan Yi with the title of Duke of the Chu 楚國公 and reburied him with honors.

It was said that Shangguan Yi's successful political career was not due to his family background, but to his great literary talent. He excelled at writing pentasyllabic verse, and his poetic diction adhered to the Qi-Liang style. Others would come to imitate his poetry after he became eminent at court, giving rise to a style known as the Shangguan Ti 上官體 (Shangguan Style). He described principles of poetic composition, most famously rules of parallelism: *liu dui* 六對 and *ba dui* 八對, in his treatise *Bizha hualiang* 筆札華梁 (The Ornamented Ridgepole of Written Tablets). The work, which today only exists in fragments, also expounded on versification rules, such as *ba jie* 八階 (eight steps) and *ba bing* 八病 (eight maladies). His works and theories influenced the development of regulated verse, *lüshi* 律詩. The poet himself often followed these guidelines of poetic composition in writing his own verses and is thought to have provided the examples in the treatise. Only twenty of his poems out of the original thirty *juan*, as recorded in the "Yiwen zhi" 藝文志 of the *Xin Tang shu* 舊唐書, remain today, most written upon imperial command. The courtly banquet poem "Zaochun Guilin Dian yingzhao" 早春桂林殿應詔 (Written upon Imperial Command on Early Spring in Guilin Hall) is representative of his style:

> A sedan chair emerges from the Pixiang Palace,
> a clear song draws near to the Taiye pond.
> Morning trees are filled with warbling orioles,
> Spring banks are strewn with fragrant grasses.
> The scenery reflected in the luster of the dewdrops,

petals of snow rise up to the azure void.
Colorful butterflies appear without end,
the mountain's glow dims with the approaching sunset.

步輦出披香，清歌臨太液。
曉樹流鶯滿，春堤芳草積。
風光翻露文，雪華上空碧。
花蝶來未已，山光曖將夕。

The poem was written some time before 635. The first lines, reflecting the conventions of court poetry, use Han place names to set the occasion; thus the Pixiang Palace of the Han dynasty metaphorically refers to the Guilin Hall of the Tang imperial palace. Following these conventions, the poem despite the lack of personal emotions works because of its imagery. The imperial palanquin is a metonym for the emperor as the clear song represents the accompanying female musicians. In the following couplets the poet uses scenes from nature to describe the magnificence and splendor of the courtly gathering, drawing the refreshing and ambient atmosphere of the beginning of spring to reflect the joyful and lavish nature of the imperial outing. The description of the beginning of spring is a typical trope for court poetry. Shangguan's attentiveness to detail fills the stillness with various sounds and movements, bursts of light and color. In addition to the exploration of space, the last three couplets become framed by the time of the occasion. The third line commences with the character *xiao* 曉 (morning), and the last line of the poem ends with *xi* 夕 (evening). The gathering starts at dawn and the setting sun signifies that the occasion is over, as is the poem. The last couplet draws a stark contrast between its first and second halves. While the first line features fluttering of the multitude of colorful butterflies, the final line abruptly turns to a still and dark panoramic view of the mountains. The day inadvertently draws to an end following the natural flow of events. Nature's celebration, just like the imperial festive occasion, must come to an end sooner or later.

Some of his verses, however, neither followed the rules and ornamental rhetoric of court style, nor strictly followed the rhyme-pattern regulations. For example, "Ruchao Luo ti bu yue" 入朝洛堤步月 (Strolling Beneath the Moon along Luo Riverbanks before Entering Court:

Tacit and steady the vast stream flows,
I spur my horse to cross the long embankment.
Magpies fly from the mountain moon and dawn breaks,
cicadas chirp in the wild wind bringing the autumn.

脈脈廣川流，驅馬歷長洲。
鵲飛山月曙，蟬噪野風秋。

The poem was written in 660s at the apogee of the poet's career and describes a moment when he was waiting with other officials outside to enter the imperial palace of Luoyang. The audience was granted early in the morning and the officials had to arrive before dawn when the Tianjin Bridge 天津橋 (i.e. the long embankment) lowered and let them in. In the first couplet the poet describes his immediate physical surroundings; in the second, the time of the day, the season and the natural scene, actual or imagined. The presence of different perspectives enlarges the spatial realm and provides a more panoramic view, rather than focusing on one spot in space. The steady flow of the Luo River reflects the stability and peace of the state and of the poet's mind; the poet feels at ease and urges his horse on. Unlike the "Written upon Imperial Command on Early Spring in Guilin Hall," this description of the natural scenes allow the reader to probe the poet's feelings: the tacit flow of the stream, the unhurried pace of the horse lets the poet pause and enjoy the view in a pensive state. The magpies, harbingers of good news, fly from the mountains to bring the light of the new day. The sounds of birds and cicadas break the silence and stillness of the landscape. The poet depicts the transition from dark and quiet to light and vivacity reflecting the awakening of nature. On the other hand, cicadas signify the advent of autumn and, consequently, winter, the season of loneliness, worry, and inertia.

Shangguan Yi and Xu Jingzong were literary representatives of the two threads of the Longshuo 龍朔 style, as well as members of opposite political cliques. Shangguan Yi lost his life for adhering to his political principles. After his death his poetry and ornate style were ridiculed and criticized by Wang Bo 王勃 (650–676),* Chen Zi'ang 陳子昂 (659–ca. 699)* and many more who were against flowery diction as a remnant of the Qi-Liang style. But despite all that, his works, especially his guidelines on parallelism, had a significant influence on the subsequent period and left clear traces in the literary history of the Early Tang.

BIBLIOGRAPHY

Editions:
Fu Xuancong 傅璇琮, ed. *Tangren xuan Tang shi xinbian* 唐人選唐詩新編. Xi'an: Shaanxi Renmin Jiaoyu, 1996. In *Hanlin xueshi ji* 翰林學士集 are six matching poems written by Shangguan Yi.
Masahiro Murata 村田正博. *Kanrin gakushi shū. Shinsen ruirin shō: honbon to sakuin* 翰林學士集. 新撰類林抄: 本文と索引. Tokyo: Izumi, 1992.
Quan Tang shi, 1: 509–13, 13: 10242, 14: 10928.
Quan Tang wen, 154–55.1780–92.
Zhou Weide 周維德, ed. *Bunkyō hifuron* 文鏡秘府論. Beijing: Renmin, 1975, pp. 58–63, 123–27.
Wei Qingzhi 魏慶之, ed. *Shiren yuxie* 詩人玉屑. Shanghai: Shanghai Guji, 1978, v.1, j. 7, pp. 165–66.

Biographical Sources:
Jiu Tang shu, 80.2743–45.
Xin Tang shu, 105.4035–36.

Translations:
Owen, *Early T'ang,* pp. 74–76, 240–45.

Studies:
Chan, Tim Wai-keung. "In Search of Jade: Studies of Early Tang Poetry." Unpublished Ph. D. Dissertation. University of Colorado, 1999.
Chen Bohai 陳伯海. "Tang *juanzi* ben *Hanlin xueshi ji* kaosuo" 唐卷子本翰林學士集考索. *Zhonghua wenshi luncong* 29 (1984): 67–77.

Chen, Jack Wei. *The Poetics of Sovereignty: on Emperor Taizong of the Tang Dynasty*. Cambridge: Harvard University Asia Center, 2010. Includes translation and discussion of one of the matching poem in a court poem collection.

Deng Ping 鄧屏. "Luelun 'Shangguan Ti' xingcheng de yuanyin" 略論上官體行程的原因. *Gannan Shifan Xueyuan xuebao* 5 (1999): 24–28.

Du Xiaoqin. *Qi Liang shige xiang sheng Tang shige de shanbian* 齊梁詩歌向盛唐詩歌的嬗變. Beijing: Beijing Daxue, 2009.

___. "Lun Longshuo chuzai de shifeng xinbian" 論龍朔初載的詩風新變. *Wenxue yichan* 5 (1999): 34–42.

Ge Xiaoyin 葛曉音. "Lun gongting wenren zai chu Tang shige yishu fazhan zhong de zuoyong" 論宮廷文人在初唐詩歌藝術發展中的作用, in *Shiguo gaochao yu sheng Tang wenhua* 詩國高潮與盛唐文化. Beijing: Beijing Daxue, 1998, pp. 29–32.

Gong Zupei 龔祖培. "Shangguan Yi: Tongji shuju yu shenglü lilun de beilun - yu Du Xiaoqin shangque" 上官儀：統計數據與聲律理論的悖論 - 與杜曉勤商榷. *Sichuan Daxue xuebao* 5 (2009): 113–20.

Gu Yu 穀雨 and Zhou Jingting 周婧婷. "Chong ping Shangguan Yi shige chuangzuo ji qi yingxiang" 重評上官儀詩歌創作及其影響. *Chang cheng* 5 (2010): 45–46.

Hong Jin 洪進. "'Shangguan Ti' shengcheng lun" 上官體生成論. *Anhui Guangbo Dianshi Daxue xuebao* 4 (2004): 113–16.

Hu Yulan 胡玉蘭. "Fojiao yu Shangguan Yi ji qi shiwen quangzuo zhi guanxi" 佛教與上官儀及其詩文創作之關係. *Qiusuo* 10 (2012): 145–46, 159.

Jia Jinhua 賈晉華. *Tangdai jihui zongji yu shirenqun yanjiu* 唐代集會總集與詩人群研究. Beijing Daxue, 2001.

Kato Satoshi 加藤敏. "Jōkan Gi no shi ni tsuite" 上官儀の詩について. *Chiba Daigaku Kyōiku Gakubu kenkyū kiyō* 49 (2001): 165–74.

Li Jun 李軍. "Lun 'Shangguan Ti' de yishu tezheng" 論上官體的藝術特徵. *Huaihua Xueyuan xuebao* 25 (2006): 74–77.

Li Xiaoqing 李曉青. "Yujie liang shibi, jinma shan tiancai - lun Shangguan Yi de shige lilun yu jiqi gongxian" 玉階良史筆，金馬掞天才—論上官儀的詩歌理論及其貢獻. *Beijing Ligong Daxue xuebao* 10 (2008): 70–73.

Meng Xianshi 孟憲實. "Shangguan Yi yanjiu santi" 上官儀研究三題. *Tang yanjiu* 20 (2014): 209–28.

Nie Yonghua 聶永華. *Chu Tang gongting shi fengliu bian kaolun* 初唐宮廷詩風流變考論. Beijing: Zhongguo Shehui Kexue, 2002.

___. "'Shangguan Ti' kaobian er ti" 上官體考辨二體. *Zhengzhou Daxue xuebao* 34.3 (2001): 94–99.

___. "'Shangguan Ti' shixue lilun jiyi" 上官體詩學理論輯議. *Zhengzhou Daxue xuebao* 36.6 (2003): 11–15.

___. "Shangguan Yi shige chuangzuo chulun" 上官儀詩歌創作芻論. *Luoyang Daxue xuebao* 18 (2003): 36–39.

Nishi Yoshikazu 西義一. "Jōkan Gi to Jōkan Shoyo" 上官儀と上官昭容. *Shibun* 斯文 10 (1971): 8–12.

Owen, *Early T'ang*, pp. 72–77.

Shang Yongliang 尚永亮. "Chu Tang shenglülun de shenhua jiqi tedian—yi Shangguan Yi, Yuan Jing de shixue lilun wei zhongxin" 初唐聲律論的深化及其特點—以上官儀，元競的詩學理論為中心. *Hunan Minzu Zhiye Xueyuan xuebao* 6 (2006): 28–32.

Wang Meng'ou 王夢鷗. *Chu Tang shixue zhushu kao* 初唐詩學著述考. Taibei: Taiwan Shangwu, 1977, p. 19–61. Provides information on the poet and his poetry as well as traces textual history and reconstructs the *Bizha hualiang* based on the *Bunkyō hifuron* edition.

Wen Yiduo 聞一多 (1899–1946) and Ziqing Zhu 朱自清. *Wen Yiduo quan ji*. Beijing: Xinhua, 1982, p. 164.

Wu, Jie. "A Study of Group Compositions in Early Tang China (618–713)." Unpublished Ph. D. Dissertation. University of Washington, 2008.

Yu Shucheng 余恕誠. "Chu Tang shige de jianshe yu qidai" 初唐詩歌的建設與期待. *Wenxue yichan* 5 (1996): 42–51.

Zhao Changping 趙昌平. "Shangguan Ti jiqi lishi chengdan" 上官體及其歷史承擔. *Wenxue shi* 1 (1993): 117–37.

Masha Kobzeva

Shen Jiji 沈既濟 (ca. 740–ca. 800) is known principally for his authorship of two perennially popular literary-language short stories, "Renshi zhuan" 任氏傳 (Miss Ren) and "Zhenzhong ji" 枕中記 (The World Inside a Pillow). He was a member of the Shen family of Wuxing 吳興 (modern Zhejiang), which also produced the famous Six Dynasties historian, poet, and literary theorist, Shen Yue 沈約 (441–513), and another writer of literary-language short stories, Shen Yazhi 沈亞之 (781–832).* Shen Jiji's grandfather had been an official at court and later served as a provincial official in what is now Fujian. His father had held a comparatively low official position in what is now Zhejiang. All that is known of Shen Jiji's early years is that his son, Shen Chuanshi 沈傳師, was born in 769 (d. 827), and that he resided in Zhongling 鐘陵 (modern Nanchang 南昌 in Jiangxi) during the mid-770s, before traveling to Chang'an in 778 to take a position in the Court of Imperial Sacrifices.

A new emperor, Dezong (r. 779–805), ascended the throne in the summer of 779 and, in an attempt at political and fiscal reform, made Yang Yan 楊炎 (727–781), a financial expert, his chief minister. Yang Yan had heard of Shen Jiji's skill at historical writing and had him appointed to a position in the Chancellery and concurrently made an Senior Compiler in the Historiography Institute, where he was in charge of the compilation of the records concerning the emperor's daily actions. Although Yang Yan and his party introduced a number of important reforms, they also rapidly made enemies and soon fell from power. Yang Yan was demoted, exiled, and sentenced to death in mid-781, and Shen Jiji was transferred to a minor position at Chuzhou 處州 (modern Zhejiang). He seems to have been pardoned as part of the general amnesty of 785, for he returned to the capital to serve as a Vice-director in the Ministry of Personnel before his death. The two short stories and seven brief pieces of official prose are all that have survived of Shen's writing.

Shen was one of the first writers of literary-language tales to combine an interest in supernatural events that pervaded accounts of the Six Dynasties period with a more elaborate plotting, characterization, and incidental detail that helped to raise the Tang tales to new levels of literary art. The plots of both of Shen's surviving tales were drawn from Six Dynasties sources. "Miss Ren" is based on an earlier tale which tells of a beautiful young woman who, after having lived with a young man for some time, was killed by hunting dogs and shown to have been a fox spirit in human form. Shen elaborated this simple plot into a story of considerable length, providing his characters with well-rounded personalities and motivation for their acts and enlivening his narration with scenes of vigorous action and suspense. That he endowed his fox spirit, Miss Ren, with qualities more admirable than those seen in her human acquaintances is thought to be an ironic commentary on contemporary society.

In a sense, Shen's second tale, "The World Inside a Pillow," also deals with the irony implicit in the human condition. Again taking its basic plot from an earlier work, it tells of a man who dreams an entire lifetime while napping with his head on a porcelain pillow. The man gains a highly-placed marriage, imperial favor, and powerful position—marked realistically with occasional setbacks. His sons go on to successful careers and provide him with numerous grandchildren. The man awakens, however, to find that this entire lifetime had taken place in the time needed to cook a bowl of gruel. Below is an excerpt from the end of the story:

> "Scholar Lu yawned, stretched, and awakened to see that he was just then lying down in the rest-lodge. Old Man Lü was sitting by his side and the host of the lodge was steaming millet which was not yet cooked. [Everything] that he sensed was as before. The Scholar was startled, but got up, saying, "Could it all have been a dream in my sleep?" The old man said to the Scholar, "The contentments of human life are surely like that." The Scholar was lost in thought for a great while. Then he thanked the old man and said, "Now, the ways of favor and disgrace, the fatefulness of failure and success, the principles of gain and loss, and the emotions of death and life—I have thoroughly known them. This is how you, Venerable sir, have checked my desire. Dare I not accept this lesson?" He touched his forehead to the ground, bowed twice, and left."

> 盧生欠伸而悟，見其身方偃於邸舍，呂翁坐其傍，主人蒸黍未熟，觸類如故。生蹶然而興，曰：「豈其夢寐也？」翁謂生曰：「人生之適，亦如是矣。」生憮然良久，謝曰：「夫寵辱之道，窮達之運，得喪之理，死生之情，盡知之矣。此先生所以窒吾欲也。敢不受教！」稽首再拜而去。

The story is usually interpreted in light of contemporary Buddhist and Daoist ideas concerning the illusory nature of life and the vanity of striving after worldly gain. Some also see connections between the tales's message and the major setback experienced by the author in his own career. Other tales expanding the same theme appeared not long after Shen's death (see Li Gongzuo 李公佐 [ca. 770–ca. 848]*), and his own tale has been used as the basis for dramatic works in both China and Japan.

BIBLIOGRAPHY

Editions:
Quan Tang wen, 476.5563–71.
"Zhenzhong ji" in Li Fang 李昉, et al. *Taiping guangji* 太平廣記. Beijing: Zhonghua, 1986, ch. 82 (526–28).
___. in Wang Bijiang 汪辟疆. *Tangren xiaoshuo* 唐人小說. Hong Kong: Zhonghua, 1958, pp. 37–42.
___. *Tangren xiaoshuo yanjiu erji*. 唐人小說研究二集. Wang Mengou 王夢鷗, comp. Taibei: Yiwen, 1973, pp. 196–200.
___. *Wenyuan yinghua*. Rpt.; Taibei: Huawen, 1965, 883.7b–10a (4395–97).
"Renshi zhuan." *Taiping guangji*, ch. 452 (3692–97).
___. *Tangren xiaoshuo*, pp. 43–48.
___. *Tangren xiaoshuo yanjiu erji*, pp. 186–92.

Biographical Sources:
Xin Tang shu, 132.4538–40.

Translations:

Contes choisis de la dynastie des Tang. Beijing: Waiwen, 2003.

Fishman, Olga and A. Tishkova. *Tanskie novelli*. Moscow: Goslitizdat, 1960. (both tales)

Knickerbocker, Bruce J. "Record within a Pillow" in William H. Nienhauser, *Tang Dynasty Tales: A Guided Reader*. Singapore: World Scientific Publishing Company, 2010, pp. 73–131.

Lange, Clemens-Tobias, trans. *Die Geschichte des Fräulein Ren: eine chinesische Fuchsgeistergeschichte aus der Tang-Zeit*. Hamburg: CTL, 1992.

Lévy, André. *Histoires extraordinaires et récits fantastiques de la Chine ancienne*. Paris: Aubier, 1993, pp. 57–68.

Nienhauser, William H., Jr. "Miss Jen," in Y. W. Ma and Joseph S. M. Lau, eds. *Traditional Chinese Stories: Themes and Variations*. New York: Columbia University Press, 1978, pp. 339–45.

___. "The World Inside a Pillow." *Traditional Chinese Stories*, pp. 435–38.

___. Tsai, Frederick C. "Miss Jen." *Renditions* 8 (Autumn 1977), 52–58.

Wang, C.C. *Traditional Chinese Tales*. New York: Columbia University Press, 1944, pp. 20–34 (both).

Wang, Elizabeth T.C. *Ladies of the T'ang*. Taibei: Heritage Press, 1961, pp. 203–23 (both).

Studies:

Bian Xiaoxuan 卞孝萱. "'Zhenzhong ji' zhujiao yuanxing sanshuo zhiyi" 枕中記主角原型三說質疑. *Xibei Shida xuebao* 6 (1993): 49–55.

He Manzi 何滿子. "Shen Jiji 'Renshi zhuan' dude" 沈既濟任氏傳讀得. *Mingzuo xinshang* 2 (1987): 36–37.

Hsieh, Daniel. "Induced Dreams, Reading, and the Rhetoric of 'Chen-chung chi.'" *TkR* 27.1 (Autumn 1996).

Knechtges, David R. "Dream Adventure Stories in Europe and T'ang China." *TkR* 4.2 (October 1973): 101–19.

Kondō Haruo 近藤春雄 (1914–2014). "Tōdai shōsetsu ni tsuite, Tōjō rōfu den, Jitsu den, Ri Shōbu den" 唐代小說について東城老父傳任氏傳李章武傳. *Aichi Kenritsu Daigaku bungakubu ronshū (Gogaku, bungaku)* 18 (1967): 63–81.

___. "Tōdai shōsetsu ni tsuite, Chinchūki, Nanka taishu den, Sha Shōga den" 唐代小說について，枕中記，南柯太守傳，謝小娥傳. *Aichi Kenritsu Joshi Daigaku kiyō* 15 (1964): 40–58.

Li Jianguo 李劍國, ed. *Tang Wudai zhiguai chuanqi xulu*. 唐五代志怪傳奇敘錄. Tianjin: Nankai Daxue, 1993, 269–73.

Lin Boqian 林伯謙. "Tangren xiaoshuo 'Renshi zhuan' xintan" 唐人小說任氏傳新探. *Zhonghua wenhua fuxing yuekan* 20.4 (1987): 65–72.

Liu Kairong 劉開榮. *Tangdai xiaoshuo yanjiu* 唐代小說研究. Hong Kong: Shangwu, 1964, revision of 1947 edition, pp. 163–75.

Liu Ying 劉瑛. *Tangdai chuanqi yanjiu* 唐代傳奇研究. Taibei: Lianjing, 1994. Studies of "Renshi zhuan" and "Zhenzhong ji" are found on pp. 299–313 and pp. 350–56.

Mei Jialing 梅家玲. "Lun 'Du Zichun' yu 'Zhenzhong ji' de rensheng taidu" 論杜子春與枕中記的人生態度. *Zhongwai wen xue* 15.12 (1987): 122–33.

Uchiyama, Chinari 內山知也. *Zui Tō shōsetsu kenkyū* 隋唐小說研究. Tokyo: Mokujisha, 1977, pp. 326–49. Also translated in Chinese and published by Shanghai: Fudan Daxue, 2010.

Wang Mengou, ed. and annot. *Tangren xiaoshuo jiaoshi* 唐人小說校釋. Taibei: Zhengzhong, 1983. A study of "Zhenzhong ji" is found on pp. 23–57.

___. *Tangren xiaoshuo yanjiu erji*, pp. 37–46.

___. "Du Shen Jiji 'Zhenzhong ji' bukao" 讀沈既濟枕中記補考. *Zhongguo wenzhe yanjiu jikan* 1 (1991): 1–10.

___. "'Zhenzhong ji' ji qi zuozhe" 枕中記及其作者. *Youshi xuezhi* 5.2 (1966): 1–28.

Zhu Chuanyu 朱傳譽. *Shen Jiji yanjiu ziliao* 沈既濟研究資料. Taibei: Tianyi, 1981.
___. *Shen Jiji yu Zhenzhong ji* 沈既濟與枕中記. Taibei: Tianyi, 1982.

Donald Gjertson and Masha Kobzeva

Shen Quanqi 沈佺期 (*zi*, Yunqing 雲卿, 656–716) is usually paired with Song Zhiwen 宋之問 (*zi*, Yanqing 延清, (656–ca. 712).* Their works are traditionally taken as the epitome of the poetry that marked the transition from the Early to the High Tang.

Both men passed the *jinshi* examinations in 675 and were associated with the government of Empress Wu, specifically with the literary salon of her favorite Zhang Yizhi 張易之 (d. 705). They were both exiled to the provinces when this government fell in 705. A general amnesty returned them to the capital soon afterwards.

Both men were schooled in the late seventh-century traditions of court poetry, a tradition where wit and decorum were paramount. Many of their poems were *yingzhi shi* 應制詩 (poems composed according to imperial command) for formal state occasions. It was in this atmosphere that the tonal requirements *lüshi* 律詩 (regulated verse) assumed their final shape, and the works of Shen and Song represent the earliest major body of Chinese verse to contain sizable amounts of standard *lüshi* forms.

At the same time as they were perfecting the formal aspects of *lüshi,* Shen and Song both expanded the parameters of it subject matter by personalizing the stereotyped guises of seventh-century court verse. Shen Quanqi, for example, wrote fine poetry in the *yuefu* 樂府 style. "Du bujian" 獨不見 (Alone and Not Seeing Him), one of his two poems included in the *Tangshi sanbaishou*, employs the *yuefu* motif of the solitary wife's lament for her husband away on the king's business, yet the form is close to a standard seven-character *lüshi*, complete with parallelism and tonal euphony:

> The young wife of Lu family in a turmeric-infused hall,
> Where swallows nest in pairs on tortoise-shell beams.
> In the ninth month the sound of pounding clothes on cold stones urges the leaves to fall,
> For ten years arousing thoughts of her husband, guarding the Liaoyang frontier.
> News or letters from north of White Wolf River have been cut off;
> In the south within vermillion palace walls the autumn nights extend.
> Who causes her to harbor sorrow for the one unseen—
> And all the more has the bright moon shine on the yellow silks of her loom?

> 盧家少婦鬱金堂，海燕雙棲玳瑁梁。
> 九月寒砧催木葉，十年徵戍憶遼陽。
> 白狼河北音書斷，丹鳳城南秋夜長。
> 誰為含愁獨不見，更教明月照流黃。

Like many *yuefu* some knowledge of earlier poems on the same theme helps to understand the poem. A boudoir lament, Shen's poem resonates with Xiao Yan's 蕭衍 (464–549; i.e., Emperor Wu of the Liang 梁武帝, r. 502–549) "Hezhong zhi shui" 河中之水 (Song of the Waters in the Midst of the River), which also limns the longing of a wealthy wife of the Lu family for her absent husband.

The first couplet of Shen's poem draws on the setting for the Lu wife that Xiao's poem establishes, the walls infused with a clay-turmeric mixture, the tortoise shells on the beams overhead in gleaming yellow set off by their black patterns. The sound of washing clothes by pounding them on stones is conventionally associated with a wife waiting for her husband. The moon, which can be seen by both this young woman and her husband, delivers the final reminder of the one "she cannot see." An ironic twist, that same moonlight shines upon the silken threads she is futilely weaving either for her husband (who cannot receive them) or herself (who has no one to appreciate them). Shen Quanqi was able to modify the rhetorical excesses of the court style and thereby provide a working prototype of the development *lüshi* in later generations.

BIBLIOGRAPHY

Editions:
Quan Tang shi, 2: 1016–50, 14: 11023.
Shen Zhanshi ji chi 沈詹事集. 7 vols., preface by Wang Tingxiang 王廷相 dated 1518.
Tao Min 陶敏 and Yi Shuqiong 易淑瓊, eds. *Shen Quanqi, Song Zhiwen ji jiaozhu* 沈佺期宋之問集校注. Beijing: Zhonghua, 2001.

Annotations:
Lian Bo 連波 and Cha Hongde 查洪德, ed. *Shen Quanqi shi ji jiaozhu* 沈佺期詩集校注. Zhengzhou: Zhongzhou Guji, 1991.

Biographical Sources:
Fu, *Tang caizi*, 1:75–85, 5:8–10.
Jiu Tang shu, 190B.5017.
Xin Tang shu, 202.5749–50.

Translations:
Minford and Lau, p. 696.
Owen, *Early T'ang*, pp. 339–64.

Studies:
Cha Hongde 查洪德. "Chu Tang shitan de yida zongshi—Shen Quanqi xinlun" 初唐試探的一代宗師—沈佺期新論, *Tangdu xuekan*, 1991.3: 26–32.
Cheng Youqing 程有慶. "Shen Quanqi de yiwen de faxian" 沈佺期的佚文的發現, *Wenxian*, 1995.2.
Chu Yaowen 儲姚文. "Lun Du Shenyan, Shen Quanqi, Song Zhiwen de shanshui shi" 論杜審言、沈佺期、宋之問的山水詩. *Tangdu xuekan*, 1999.1.
Hu Wei 胡偉. "Shen Quanqi jinti shiyun yanjiu" 沈佺期近體詩韻研究. *Yuwen xuekan* 21 (2006): 57–59.
Liu Kaiyang 劉開揚. "Guanyu Shen Quanqi, Song Zhiwen de pingshu" 關於沈佺期宋之問的評述, *Shenhui Kexue yanjiu*, 1981.4.
Liu Minghua 劉明華. "Shen Quanqi yanjiu de xin shouhuo: du Shen Quanqi shiji jiaozhu" 沈佺期研究的新收獲—讀沈佺期詩集校注. *Zhongguo dianji yu wenhua* 2 (1993): 54–55.
Li Yunyi 李雲逸. "Shen Quanqi 'kaogong shouqiu' kao" 沈佺期"考功受賕"考. *Xueshu luntan*, 1983.3.
___. "Shen Quanqi 'peiliu Lingbiao' kao" 沈佺期配流領表考. *Xueshu luntan*, 1981.4.

Matsuoka Eiji 松岡榮志. *Chin Senki shi sakuin* 沈佺期詩索引. Tokyo: Tokyo Daigaku Tōyō Bunka Kenkyūjo Fuzoku Tōyōgaku Bunken Senta, 1987.

Tao Min 陶敏 and Yi Shuqiong 易淑瓊. "Shen Song lunlue" 沈宋論略. *Xiangtan Shifan Xueyuan xuebao* 2 (1996): 6–10.

Xu Zhiyin 許智銀. "Shen Quanqi, Song Zhiwen songbie shi yanjiu" 沈佺期,宋之問送別詩研究, *Pingdingshan Xueyuan xuebao*, 2006, 21.4: 23–26.

Zha Hongde 查洪德. "Chu Tang shitan de yidai zongshi—Shen Quanqi xinlun" 初唐詩壇的一代宗師—沈佺期新論. *Tangdu xuekan*, 1991.3: 26–32.

___. "Shen Quanqi nianpu" 沈佺期年譜. *Tangdu xuekan* 3 1989.3: 34–39.

Zhan, *Daojiao*, pp. 241–48.

Charles Hartman and William H. Nienhauser, Jr.

Shen Yazhi 沈亞之 (*zi*, Xiaxian 下賢, 781–832) was descended from the well-known Shen family of Wukang 武康 in Wuxing 吳興 (modern Huzhou 湖州) which also produced the poet Shen Yue 沈約 (441–513) and Yazhi's cousin, Shen Jiji 沈既濟 (ca. 740–ca. 800),* a historian and writer of tales. Shen Yazhi was distantly related to Daizong's (r. 762–779) Empress Shen, the mother of Dezong (r. 779–805).

Shen was born, however, in Longzhou 隴州 (modern Long County in western Shensi) where his father was stationed. Shortly after his birth his father died and the family returned to the southeast; Shen probably remained in the capital with his uncle, Shen Chuanshi 沈傳師 (769–827). Shen married a woman named Yao 姚 and in 803, while still in his early twenties, he arranged to take a concubine from a good family in Chang'an, Lu Jinlan 盧金蘭 (789–814) who bore him a son and a daughter. In 805 Shen returned to the southeast, taking wife and concubine with him.

For the next few years Shen presumably studied. Then in 809, he did two things that he would continue in later years. First, he stopped at a monastery in Hangzhou and inquired about the history of a statue of the Buddha that was being moved; then he recorded the tale that the monks told him ("Yi Fo Ji" 移佛記 [Record of Moving the Buddha]). Throughout the rest of his life Shen would remain interested in listening to and recording stories. Second, he (with his wife and concubine) retraced the long route to Chang'an where he was to take the *jinshi* examination the following spring. His subsequent years were also beset by arduous travel, as he searched for a position early in his career and later was called upon to move from one post to another.

In the spring of 810, and again in 811, Shen failed the *jinshi* examination. During this period he met Li He 李賀 (790–816)* and Nan Zhuo 南卓 (ca. 791–854), also examination candidates. Frustrated with his lack of success, Shen left Chang'an in the summer of 811 in search of a sponsor. He went from Fuzhou 鄜州 (modern Fu 富 County in Shensi, north of the capital) to Luoyang and finally to Pengcheng 彭成 (modern Xuzhou 徐州 City in Jiangsu). On this trip, possibly at Li He's suggestion, he met Han Yu 韓愈 (768–824),* who was in Luoyang.

After failing the *jinshi* in 812, Shen Yazhi went home; both Li He and Jia Dao 賈島 (779–843)* wrote poems seeing him off. The following spring Shen went to Jingzhou 涇州 (modern Jingzhou County in west-central Shanxi); that summer he was in Luzhou 潞州 (modern Changzhi Shi 長治市 in Shanxi). In 814 he again eschewed the examinations, travelling first to Handan 邯鄲 and then to his home. On his return later that year he passed through Huazhou 滑州 (modern Hua

County in Henan) and visited the Military Commissioner, Xue Ping 薛平 (d. 830), a well-connected scion of an old military family. Shen's concubine and then his wife died during this same year.

In 815, Shen Yazhi passed finally the *jinshi* with Cui Qun 崔群 (772–832), Han Yu's fellow-graduate, as examiner. He then joined the staff of Li Hui 李彙, the son of the Prince of Linhuai 臨淮王, Li Guangbi 李光弼 (708–764), as a Record Keeper. Li Hui was married to one of Shen's cousins and had just been made Military Commissioner of Jingyuan 涇原. That summer Li Hui entertained his officials and guests with a story about a dream his mentor, Xing Feng 邢鳳, had enjoyed. In the dream Xing met a beautiful woman who exchanged poems with him. When he awoke and changed his clothes, he found the poems in one of his sleeves. Another guest told a similar story. The party agreed that these tales should be preserved, so Shen fashioned them into an account titled "Yimeng lu" 異夢錄 (Account of Dreams of the Extraordinary). The fact that he among the various literati present was asked to record this shows that he already had a reputation as a skilled storyteller. Li passed away later that summer, leaving Shen unemployed.

From 815 to 818 Shen traveled through the East and the South. Back in Chang'an, he visited nearby prefectures to expand his network of possible patrons. His poem "Bianzhou chuanxing fu anbang suojian" 汴州船行賦岸傍所見 (Depicting What I see Along the Shore from a Moving Boat at Bianzhou) was probably written on a trip to Sishang:

> Ancient trees in the early light have gone grey—
> The autumn forest brushes the bank with fragrance.
> Pearls of dew, a "spider's web" so fine,
> Threads of gold, a "rabbit's hair" so long.
> Autumn waves from time to time return frothed,
> Startled fish suddenly bump against the boat.
> The milkweed's mist catches hold of green willow threads,
> The sour jujube's fruit is stitched into red sacks.
> Riotous ears of grain wave like flying-squirrels' tails,
> Drooping roots hang down like phoenix entrails.
> I'm merely holding one washed foot—
> Who says I could be compared to the Canglang poet?

> 古木曉蒼蒼，秋林拂岸香。
> 露珠蟲網細，金縷兔絲長。
> 秋浪時迴沫，驚鱗乍躅航。
> 蓬煙拈綠線，棘實綴紅囊。
> 亂穗搖鼯尾，垂根挂鳳腸。
> 聊持一濯足，誰道比滄浪。

"Rabbit's hair" is a euphemistic name for a plant which grows by winding up a tree; "spider's web" may have a similar reference. This type of imagery, along with verses like "Riotous ears of grain wave like flying-squirrels' tails, / Protruding roots hang down like phoenix entrails" reflect the difficult diction and figurative language of Han Yu. The final couplet alludes to Qu Yuan 屈原 (ca. 340–278 BC), and is Shen's attempt to excuse his failure to find a position by suggesting that he would not want to serve a government as unenlightened as that then in Chang'an.

In 819 Shen revisited Huazhou and recorded an account he heard from Liu Yuanding 劉元鼎 (*jinshi* 789) about a knight-errant named Feng Yan 馮燕 ("Feng Yan zhuan" 馮燕傳). Feng had served the Grand Councilor, Jia Dan 賈耽 (730–805) when the latter was military commissioner of the area from 786–793. The story tells how Feng killed his lover when she suggested he stab her husband. When the husband was accused of the murder, Feng turned himself in. Jia Dan oversaw the case and successfully petitioned the emperor to pardon Feng. At the end of the story Shen added a "historian's comment" imitating Sima Qian 司馬遷 (145–ca. 86 BC) in which he praised Feng for his righteousness. These events may well have actually happened (Lu Xun 魯迅, 1881–1936, does not include the story in his *Tang Song chuanqi ji* 唐宋傳奇集 suggesting he believed it related to a historical incident). In his adaptation, Shen created a moral tale, which may also have been intended to flatter a relative or an associate of Jia Dan and thereby establish another possible connection for Shen in his search for a position.

For most of 820 Shen seems to have remained in Chang'an. In the spring of 821 he passed an advanced placement examination and was appointed Proofreader in the Palace Library. In late summer of 822 he was made Commandant of Liyang 櫟楊 (25 miles northeast of modern Xi'an), a position he held for almost two years. Although this was a minor position, it kept him close to the capital and to the contacts he had established.

In 824 he received a promotion to Assistant Military Training Commissioner of Fujian 福建 and neighboring prefectures and was sent to serve under the Surveillance Commissioner of Fujian, Xu Hui 徐晦 (d. 838), headquartered in Fuzhou 福州 (modern Fuzhou). Xu Hui was recalled to court in the early autumn of 826 and Shen Yazhi presumably returned to Chang'an with him. Shortly after returning to the capital, probably with Xu Hui's assistance, Shen was appointed Aide to the Royal Scribe in the Palace and subsequently Palace Attendant. In 827 while traveling west of the capital, Shen wrote "Qin meng ji" 秦夢記 (Record of a Dream of Qin), which tells how Shen dreamt that he married a daughter of Duke Mu 穆 (r. 659–621 BC), who would shower him with favor. After a year, however, his wife dies and he decides to return home. Shen is accompanied to the Hangu 函谷 Pass where he wakes up. There he realizes that the inn where he stayed was near the place where Duke Mu was buried. This plot bears a strong resemblance to another well-known Tang tale, Li Gongzuo's 李公佐 (ca. 770–ca. 848)* "Nanke Taishou zhuan" 南柯太守傳 (Account of the Governor of Southern Branch) and Shen Jiji's 沈既濟 "Zhenzhong ji" 枕中記 (A Record of [Events] within a Pillow).

The year 828 was a watershed for Shen. After finally securing a position at court, events beyond his control adumbrated the end of his career and his life. In the early fall the Military Commissioner of Hebei, Yanhai 兗海, Li Tongjie 李同捷 (d. 829), rebelled. Shen was assigned to the staff of Bai Qi 柏耆 who had been sent to put down the rebellion. In early 829 while a compromise plan calling for Li Tongjie to surrender was being negotiated, Bai rushed into Li's camp, arrested the rebel leader, and set out for the capital with him. Upon learning of a plot to free Li en route to Chang'an, Bai Qi on his own authority executed Li Tongjie. As a result Emperor Wenzong came under pressure from Bai Qi's jealous colleagues and a group of eunuchs allied with provincial forces to punish Bai Qi. In late spring Shen was therefore exiled to become Commandant of Nankang 南康 (modern Nankang in Jiangxi). Zhang Hu 張祜 (792–ca. 853)* and Yin Yaofan 殷堯藩 (780–855) wrote poems to see him off. He spent three years in Nankang and then was transferred to Yingzhou 郢州 (modern Zhongxiang 鍾祥 in Hubei) in 831 as Revenue Administrator. Not long after arriving in Yingzhou, Shen became ill and died.

Although he had a reputation as a poet in his own day cited along with Wei Yingwu 韋應物 (737–ca. 791)* and others in the preface to the literati chapter in the *Xin Tang shu*, only two dozen of his poems remain today. What should interest the modern reader more are the variety of narratives in Shen's corpus and the development of his narrative art that can be seen in his prose (eighty such pieces are extant).

BIBLIOGRAPHY

Editions:
Quan Tang shi, 8: 5620–26, 13: 9895, 14: 10662.
Quan Tang wen, 734–38.9585–654.
Shen Xiaxian wen ji 沈下賢文集, 9 *juan*. SBCK.
Tangren xiaoshuo, pp. 157–68 (standard edition of "Xiangzhong yuanjie," "Yimeng lu," "Qingmeng ji," and "Feng Yan zhuan").
Yu Jiaxi 余嘉錫. "*Shen Xiaxian ji* shi'er *juan*" 沈下賢集十二卷. In Yu's *Siku tiyao bianzheng* 四庫提要辨證. Beijing: Zhonghua, 1974, *juan* 20, pp. 1294–96.

Annotations:
Tang Song sanwen xuanzhu 唐宋散文選注. Shen Ping, comm. Taibei: Zhengzhong, 1968, p. 117. Lightly annotated version of "Bieqian Qishan Ling Zou Jun xu" 別前岐山令鄒君序.
Xiao Zhanpeng 肖占鵬 and Li, Boyang 李勃洋. *Shen Xiaxian ji jiaozhu* 沈下賢集校注. Tianjin: Nankai Daxue, 2003.

Biographical Sources:
Fu, *Tang caizi*, 3:86–93.

Translations:
Hartman, Charles. *Han Yu and the T'ang Search for Unity*. Princeton: Princeton University Press, 1986, p. 165.
Kao, *Chinese Classical Tales*, pp. 205–8 ("Xiangzhong Yuanjie").
Ma and Lau, *Traditional Chinese Stories*, pp. 50–51 ("Feng Yan zhuan").
Nienhauser, William H., Jr. "Creativity and Storytelling in the *Ch'uan-ch'i*: Shen Ya-chih's T'ang Tales," *CLEAR* 20 (1998): 31–70.
___. "Shen Yazhi 沈亞之, 'An Account of Feng Yan' 馮燕傳," in Nienhauser, ed. *Tang Tales: A Guided Reader, Volume 2*. Singapore: World Scientific, 2016, pp. 163–80.
___. "Shen Yazhi 沈亞之, 'A Record of the Dream of Qin' 秦夢記," *Tang Tales: A Guided Reader, Volume 2*. Singapore: World Scientific, 2016, pp. 181–206.

Studies:
Allen, Sarah M.,"Tales Retold: Narrative Variation in a Tang Story" *HJAS*, 66 (2006): 105–43.
Cheng Yizhong 程毅中. "Shen Yazhi ji qi 'Qinmeng ji'–Tangdai xiaoshuo suoji" 沈亞之及其秦夢記－唐代小說瑣記, *Tangdai wenxue luncong*, 5 (1984).
Fukunaga Ichitaka 富永一登. "Chin Ashi no shidenteki sakuhin" 沈亞之の史伝的作品. In *Obi Hakushi taikuyū kinen Chūgoku bungaku ronshū* 小尾博士退休記念中國文學論集. Tokyo, 1976.

Hu Wanchuan 胡萬川. "'Feng Yan zhuan' ji qi xiangguan xilie gushi de lijie" 馮燕傳及其相關系列故事的理解. In *Xiaoshuo xiqu yanjiu* 小說戲曲研究. Taibei: Lianjing, 1995.

Li Jianguo 李劍國. *Tang, Wudai zhiguai chuanqi xulu* 唐五代志怪傳奇敍錄. Tianjin: Nankai Daxue, 1993, v. 2, pp. 380–95 and 404–10. See especially the fine discussion of Shen's life, pp. 380–95.

Lin Chen 林辰. "Lu Xun yu Tangdai chuanqi zuojia Shen Yazhi" 魯迅與唐代傳奇作家沈亞之, *Lu Xun yanjiu*, 2 (1984).

Liu Yan 劉衍. "Shen Yazhi yu Shen zi mingbian" 沈亞之與沈子明辨, *Hunan Shiyuan xuebao*, 1983.2.

Lu Xun 魯迅. *Zhongguo xiaoshuo shilue* 中國小說史略. Beijing: Renmin Wenxue, 1973 (rpt. of 1925), ch. 8, pp. 59–60.

Uchiyama Chinari 內山知也. "Chin Ashi to 'Shinmuki' sono hoka ni tsuite" 沈亞之と秦夢記その他について. In Uchiyama, *Zui Tō shōsetsu kenkyū* 隋唐小說研究. Tokyo: Mokujisha, 1978, pp. 489–546.

___. "Chin Ashi to shōsetsu" 沈亞之と小說, *Chūgoku bungaku hō* 12 (1960): 85–134.

Wang Meng'ou 王夢鷗. "Shen Yazhi zhi shengping ji qi xiaoshuo" 沈亞之之生平及其小說. In Wang's *Tangren xiaoshuo yanjiu* 唐人小說研究. Taibei: Yiwen, 1973, v. 2, pp. 97–106.

Wu Qiming 吳企明, annot. "Shen Yazhi." In *Tang caizi zhuan jiaojian* 唐才子傳校箋. Fu Xuancong 傅璇琮, ed. Beijing: Zhonghua, 1990, v. 3, pp. 86–93.

Yang Shengkuan 楊勝寬. "Quan Tangshi waibian suo shou Shen Yazhi yiju de zhenwei wenti" 全唐詩外編所收沈亞之逸句的真偽問題, *Shehui kexue* (Lanzhou), 1986.3: 82–84.

William H. Nienhauser, Jr.

Shi Jianwu 施肩吾 (*zi*, Xisheng 希聖, *hao*, Qizhenzi 棲真子, Qingxu Dongtian Huayang Zhenren 清虛洞天華陽真人, fl. 820) was a poet and a Daoist active in the mid-Tang period. He was a native of Fenshui 分水 County in Muzhou 睦州 (modern Tonglu 桐廬 County in Zhejiang). In his early years, he secluded himself on Mount Siming 四明山 to practice Daoist techniques of longevity. In 816 he went to the capital as an examination candidate and presented a poem to the influential official Li Cheng 李程 (ca. 761–ca. 837) but did not pass the *jinshi* examination until 820. However, he was not interested in seeking office, and Zhang Ji 張籍 (ca. 776–829)* wrote a poem to see him off as he returned to the Southeast. He then lived in seclusion on Mount Xi 西山 in Hongzhou 洪州 (modern Nanchang City in Jiangxi), practicing alchemy and cultivating the Dao.

Song-dynasty catalogues record Shi Jianwu's works as *Shi Jianwu shiji* 施肩吾詩集 (Collected Poetry of Shi Jianwu) in 10 *juan* (also as *Xishan ji* 西山集 [Collection from Mount Xi] in 5 *juan*), and *Bianyi lun* 辨疑論 (Treatise on Discerning Doubts) in 1 *juan*. Both texts were lost. Song-Yuan catalogues also attribute several Daoist texts on inner alchemy (*neidan* 內丹) to Shi, such as the *Zhong Lü chuandao ji* 鐘呂傳道集 (Collection of Zhong [Li Quan] Transmission of the Dao to Lü [Yan]), the *Huayang zhenren bijue* 華陽真人秘訣 (Secret Formulas of the True Man of Huayang), and the *Xishan qunxian huizhen ji* 西山群仙會真記 (Record of the Immortals of the Huizhen [Hall on Xishan), which appears in the Daoist Canon. All these works were probably written by Daoists of the Song dynasty or later, and many of the attributions were already being questioned during the Song. Some scholars assume there were two Shi Jianwu during the Tang-Song period, but they have not presented convincing evidence. Nonetheless, over two-hundred extant poems along with nine essays are attributed to Shi.

Shi Jianwu's verse presents a wide range of topics, including occasional poems, poems on hermitages, Daoist practice, on depicting the landscape, and on describing objects; also including

Shi Jianwu

on records of travel, new *yuefu*, and boudoir laments. He was noted for his work in heptasyllabic style, especially heptasyllabic quatrains. In his *Shiren zhuke tu* 詩人主客圖, Zhang Wei 張為 (late Tang) listed Shi Jianwu as a capable "disciple" of Bo Juyi 白居易 (772–846).* Originally Shi had a two-hundred line, heptasyllabic, extended regulated poem titled "Baiyun shanju" 百韻山居 (Mountain Dwelling, in One Hundred Rhymes), which described his life in seclusion and was widely circulated. However, only two couplets of this long poem remain.

Shi Jianwu was at his best when adopting a female persona, sophisticatedly describing a woman's longing for her absent husband. Some of his poems, such as the following "Qingye yi Xiangong zi" 清夜憶仙宮子 (On a Clear Night I Recall the Immortal's Palace), may be based on relationships he had with Daoist priestesses:

> Quiet night, deep inside the gate, among the mists of the purple grotto,
> I walk alone, sit alone, thinking of an immortal.
> Inside the Palace of Three Clarities, moon as bright as daylight;
> Among the Twelve Palace Towers, in which do you sleep?
> 夜靜門深紫洞煙, 孤行獨坐憶神仙.
> 三清宮裏月如晝, 十二宮樓何處眠.

Daoist priestesses were often referred to as *xianzi* 仙子 (immortals) or *xiannü* 仙女 (female immortals). The "purple cave" refers to Shi's own secluded residence and the "Palace of Three Clarities" to a Daoist abbey. The poet wanders anxiously at night, missing his priestess-lover, hoping for a reunion. Although there is no clear allusion to an earlier text, Sanqing originally referred to the three realms of the Daoist immortals, Yuqing 玉清, Taiqing 太清 and Shangqing 上清, but came to be used generally to refer to Daoist temples or monasteries; moreover, the deity Xiwang mu 西王母 was said to have had twelve jade towers in her palace. The imagery of the Palace of the Three Clarities (also the three highest gods of the Daoist pantheon) and the Twelve Palace Towers also conjures visions associated with the meditative journeys detailed in the practice of inner alchemy.

BIBLIOGRAPHY

Editions:
Dong Fen 董棻. *Yanling ji* 嚴陵集. Changsha: Shangwu, 1937.
Hong Mai 洪邁 (1123–1202), ed. *Wanshou Tangren jueju* 萬首唐人絕句. Beijing: Shumu Wenxian, 1983.
Quan Tang shi, 8: 5627–57, 13: 9945, 14: 10667, 15: 11292.
Quan Tang wen, 739.8576–80
Wei Hu 韋縠 (fl. 947), ed. *Caidiao ji* 才調集. In Fu Xuancong 傅璇琮, ed., *Tangren xuan Tangshi xinbian* 唐人選唐詩新編. Xi'an: Shaanxi Renmin Jiaoyu, 1996.
Wei Zhuang 韋莊 (ca. 836–910), ed. *Youxuan ji* 又玄集. In *Tangren xuan Tangshi xinbian*.
Xishan qunxian huizhen ji 西山群仙會真記 (Record of the Immortals of the Huizhen [Hall] on Xishan). DZ 246.

Biographical Sources:
Fu, *Tang caizi*, 3:139–44.

Studies:

Baldrian-Hussein, Farzeen, "*Xishan qunxian huizhen ji* 西山群仙會真記" in Kristofer Schipper and Franscisus Verellen, eds. *The Taoist Canon: A Historical Companion to the Daozang* (Chicago: University of Chicago Press, 2005), pp. 804–05.

Chen Caizhi 陳才智. *Baipai jimen dizi Shi Jianwu* 白派及門弟子施肩吾, in *Yuanbai shipai yanjiu* 元白詩派研究. Beijing: Shehui Kexue Wenxian, 2007, pp. 325–33.

Seiichi Watanabe 渡辺精一. "Chū Tō no shijin Shi Kengo to sono shi" 中唐の詩人施肩吾とその詩. *Kanbun gakkai kaihō* 漢文學會會報 25 (1966) : 33–41.

Tao Min 陶敏, Li Yifei 李一飛, and Fu Xuancong 傅璇琮. *Tang Wudai wenxue biannianshi: Zhongtang juan* 唐五代文學編年史: 中唐卷. Shenyang: Liaohai, 2012.

Wu Qiming 吳企明. "Shi Jianwu" 施肩吾, in Fu Xuancong ed., *Tang caizi zhuan jiaojian* 唐才子傳校箋, Beijing: Zhonghua, 1987, 3: 6.139–46.

Wu Ruyu 吳汝煜. "Shi Jianwu" 施肩吾, in Zhou Zuzhuan 周祖譔 ed., *Zhongguo wenxuejia dacidian: Tang Wudai juan* 中國文學家大辭典: 唐五代卷. Beijing: Zhonghua, 1992, p. 594.

Jinhua Jia and Chunli Yu

Sikong Shu 司空曙 (*zi*, Wenming 文明, also Wenchu 文初, ca. 720–790) was a native of Guangping 廣平 County (about 20 miles southeast of modern Handan in Hebei) and one of the better poets of the *Dali shi caizi* 大曆十才子 (Ten Talents of the Dali Era [766–779]); see also the entry for Sikong's cousin, Lu Lun 盧綸 [748–ca. 798]*). Coming from a relatively poor family, he passed the *jinshi* examination in the early 750s, then spent the years of the An Lushan Rebellion in the South, returning to Chang'an around 767. During these years he was ill and his family often went hungry. He lived for a time in Changsha then moved into what is now modern Jiangxi.

He knew many of the other Ten Talents and was also acquainted with Chang Kun 常袞 (729–783),* Wei Yingwu 韋應物 (737–ca. 791),* Miao Fa 苗發 (fl. 756) and Dugu Ji 獨孤及 (725–777).* After his return to Chang'an he was soon called to court and appointed Reminder on the Left. Although the dating of his appointment remains undetermined, he also served as Recorder of Luoyang and Director of the Bureau of Waterways and Irrigation. He was well acquainted with the Imperial Son-in-Law Guo Ai 郭曖 (752–800), a son of Guo Ziyi 郭子儀 (697–781), but apparently did not use this connection to foster his career.

In 782 he was banished to Changlin 長林 (near modern Jingmen County 荊門縣 in Hubei) as an Assistant Magistrate. Late in life (but before 788) Sikong Shu served under Wei Gao 韋皋 (745–805), Military Commissioner of Jiannan 劍南 (central and western Sichuan). Thereafter he was Director of the Bureau of Forestry and Crafts. Presumably he died in the latter position.

His regulated verses, mostly pentasyllabic, are especially noted for the precise yet natural use of antithesis, as in the well-known "Zei ping hou song ren beigui" 賊平後送人北歸 (Sending off Someone Returning North after the Rebels Were Subdued):

> When the chaos came we fled south together,
> Now that it's peaceful you return north alone.
> Our hair turned white here in another land,
> The green mountains still to be seen in our old hometown.
> Under the morning moon you will pass the ruined ramparts,

> Beneath the stars you will sleep at the former frontier passes.
> Chill birds and withered grass
> Will everywhere accompany your saddened face.

> 世亂同南去，時清獨北還。
> 他鄉生白髮，舊國見青山。
> 曉月過殘壘，繁星宿故關。
> 寒禽與衰草，處處伴愁顏。

This poem was likely written in 763 after the An Lushan Rebellion finally collapsed. Although it ostensibly addresses a friend from Sikong Shu's hometown, the poem may simply be a lament on what Sikong imagines was left of his hometown in modern Hebei, an area that had been deep inside rebel territory.

Despite his many travels, it seems that most of Sikong Shu's poetic output—over 170 poems—remains. Reflecting his peripatetic life, many of them are intended to see off friends or express his nostalgia for his hometown.

BIBLIOGRAPHY

Editions:
Quan Tang shi, 5: 3304–334.

Annotations:
Zhang Dengdi 張登第, Jiao Wenbin 焦文彬 and Lu Anshu 魯安澍. *Dali shi caizi shixuan* 大曆十才子詩選. Xi'an: Shaanxi Renmin, 1988.

Biographical Sources:
Fu, *Tang caizi*, 2:146–57, 5:36–37.
Xin Tang shu, 203.5786.

Translations:
Demiéville, *Anthologie*, p. 296.
Mair, *Anthology*, p. 221.
Owen, *High Tang*, p. 274.
Watson, *Chinese Lyricism*, p. 119.
___. *Columbia*, pp. 278–79.

Studies:
Chen Qinghui 陈庆惠, "Dali Shiren Sikong Shu de shengping jiqi chuangzuo" 大曆詩人司空曙的生平及其創作, *Zhejiang Shifan Xueyuan xuebao* 4 (1984): 67–73.
Fu Xuancong 傅璇琮. "Sikong Shu kao" 司空曙考, *Tangdai shiren congkao* 唐代詩人叢考. Beijing: Zhonghua, 1980, pp. 502–14.
Hu Rong 胡蓉 and Jia Yanguo 贾彦国, "Lun Tangdai shiren Sikong Shu de shige" 論唐代詩人司空曙的詩歌, *Wenxue Jiaoyu* 10 (2010): 11–12.

Ji Ping 季平, "Sikong Shu shengping yu chuangzuo kaolun" 司空曙生平與創作考論, *Xinxiang Shifan Gaodeng Zhuanke Xuexiao xuebao* 14.3 (Aug. 2000): 21–27.

Jiang Yin 蔣寅. *Dali shiren yanjiu* 大曆詩人研究. Beijing: Zhonghua, 1995.

Lee, Oscar. "Lu Lun," in *Indiana Companion*, p. 607.

Liu Yanyan 刘燕燕, "Dali Shicaizi de shige chuangzuo" 大曆十才子的詩歌創作, *Qianyan* 7 (2008): 182–184.

Ogawa, Shoichi 小川昭一. "Taireki no shijin" 大曆の詩人, *Shibun*, 24 (1959): 22–33.

Owen, *High Tang*, pp. 274–80.

Wen Hangshen 文航生, "Sikong Shu shige de yishu yinwei yu biaoda" 司空曙詩歌的藝術意味與表達, *Changchun Ligong Daxue xuebao* 6.3 (Mar. 2011): 60–68.

Zhang Shengyi 張聲怡, "Lun Sikong Shu de shige chuangzuo ji yingxiang" 論司空曙的詩歌創作及影響, *Zhongguo yunwen xuekan* 23.1 (Mar. 2009): 14–21.

Zhang Youliang 张幼良 and Cheng Pei 程佩, "Lun Sikong Shu jilüshi de qingan zhixiang yishu biaoxian" 論司空曙羇旅詩的情感指向及藝術表現, *Changshu Ligong Xueyuan xuebao* 5 (Sept. 2013): 76–81.

Zhou Shaoliang 周紹良, ed. "Sikong Shu" 司空曙, *Tang caizi zhuan jianzheng* 唐才子傳箋證. Beijing: Zhonghua, 2010, v. 2, pp. 683–93.

William H. Nienhauser, Jr.

Sikong Tu 司空圖 (*zi*, Biaosheng 表聖, *hao*, Zhifeizi 知非子 and Nairu Jushi 耐辱居士, 837–908), one of the major poets of the late Tang period, owes his place in literary history to the "Ershisi shipin" 二十四詩品 (The Twenty-four Moods of Poetry), commonly considered to be one of the most important works of Tang literary criticism.

Reliable biographical data on Sikong Tu is sparse. He was probably born in Sishui 泗水 (modern Anhui), although some sources give Yuxiang 虞鄉 (modern Yongji 永濟 in Shanxi where his father had been assigned) as his birthplace. His family had a long tradition of government service. His father, Sikong Yu 司空輿, held important posts as Salt Monopoly Commissioner and as Director of the Ministry of Revenue. After years of study, perhaps in one of the Buddhist temples located in the Zhongtiao 中條 Mountains (south and east of Yuxiang), Sikong Tu passed the *jinshi* examination in 869. When the Chief Examiner Wang Ning 王凝 (821–878) was accused of favoritism and banished, Sikong Tu followed him. For the next decade there is no record of what Sikong was doing. Perhaps he had returned to his estate in Wangguan Gu 王官谷 (Royal Official's Valley) in the Zhongtiao Mountains. Nevertheless, in 878 he was made Recorder in the Court of Imperial Entertainments in Luoyang. There he was noticed by the Grand Councilor Lu Xie 盧攜 (d. 880) and made Vice Director of the Ministry of Rites, then Director. Sikong's career was interrupted by the siege and capture of Chang'an by Huang Chao's 黃巢 (d. 883) rebels in 880 and although Huang summoned him, Sikong fled to join Emperor Xizong (r. 873–888) in Fengxiang 鳳翔 (near modern Baoji 寶雞 in Shaanxi). There he was made Participant in the Drafting of Proclamations and Secretariat Drafter. The following year when Xizong fled further to Baoji 寶雞, Sikong Tu returned to his estate in Wangguan Gu 王官谷. He then retired to the Huanyin 華陰 district, south of Mount Hua 華山 (in modern Shaanxi about sixty miles southwest of Yuxiang). In the preface to his collected works he justifies his retirement by emphasizing the impossibility of realizing his social and political ambitions. When summoned to court a few years later was reluctant to resume office, turning to Buddhist and Daoist pursuits instead. The monk Xuzhong 虛中 (fl. 897–942)* would describe Sikong Tu's life in in retreat in two poems entitled

Sikong Tu

"Ji Huashan Sikong Tu" 寄華山司空圖 (Sent to Sikong Tu of Mount Hua). The opening lines of the second poem depict Sikong Tu in terms of a Daoist practitioner:

> You wander about in a coarse cloth jacket,
> With a wave of your sword stirring up the spirits.
> Midday dream of the immortal isles,
> Early morn ritually read the Daoist classics.

> 逍遙短褐成，一劍動精靈。
> 白晝夢仙島，清晨禮道經。

The image of Sikong Tu as a religious practitioner may have well influenced the many anecdotes that would come to grow around his persona. It is said that when he heard that the last Tang emperor had been murdered and the throne usurped, he stopped eating and died.

Although Sikong Tu would gather to him a varied group of intellectuals (scholar-officials, Daoists, and Buddhist monks), he did not belong to any of the poetic groups of the time and had no connections with other contemporaries such as Pi Rixiu 皮日休 (ca. 834–ca. 883)* or Lu Guimeng 陸龜蒙 (836–881).* Likewise, Sikong Tu's own poetry does not appear in the contemporary Tang anthologies.

"Ershisi shipin," a series of twenty-four poems, is in the tradition of "poems about poetry." This form of critical engagement—unlike Zhong Rong's 鐘嶸 (ca. 465–518) earlier prose work also called *Shipin*—tries to embody the principles of its critique within the composition of a poem itself. Sikong Tu's "Ershisi shipin" does not classify or evaluate specific poets, nor does it construct any artistic kinship between them. Rather than take the poet as the point of comparison, the "Ershisi shipin" focuses on formal relationships between the poems themselves. More than any other work of Chinese literary criticism of its time, the "Ershisi shipin" attempts to penetrate into the realm of poetry itself. However, given its lack of concrete examples and explicit critique, a certain vagueness often results from such an intuitive method that makes up the work.

The structure and the form of the collection's twenty-four poems is remarkably simple: twelve ancient-style four-syllable verses make up one poem; each poem has one rhyme occurring at the end of the even-numbered lines. The twenty-four pieces describe literary "qualities," "modes," and "moods" (*pin*) in a highly artistic language. The sixth poem "Dianya" 典雅 (Classic Refinement) is an example of this formula:

> Purchasing spring in a jade bottle;
> Appreciating rain on a thatched hut.
> Sitting inside, a fine scholar,
> All about, the tall bamboo.
> White clouds in newly sunny skies;
> Dark birds come chasing each other.
> A resting zither in the green shade;
> Above there is a flying waterfall.
> Falling flowers do not speak;
> This man as limpid as the chrysanthemums.

He writes of the seasons' splendors,
What he says worthy to be read.

玉壺買春，賞雨茅屋。
坐中佳士，左右修竹。
白雲初晴，幽鳥相逐。
眠琴綠陰，上有飛瀑。
落花無言，人淡如菊。
書之歲華，其曰可讀。

The poem suggests a category of verse and a kind of poet rather than depict a real scene (the green shade of summer and the chrysanthemums of fall share only their refinement). The mode is of passive quietude. The line "falling flowers does not speak" evokes such fixed expressions as "though the peach and plum do not speak, paths naturally form beneath them," often a metaphor bespeaking the quite communion with nature of this "fine gentleman."

Among his extant poems outside "Ershisi shipin," and more typical of Sikong Tu's own expressive verse, however, are the following poems written while in reclusion:

Oxhead Temple 牛頭寺
From my favorite spot in the Zhongnan Mountains,
The chanting of sutras emerges into the dark heavens.
A clump of trees stands out secluded and lonely,
Wisps of mist float in the vast void.

終南最佳處，禪誦出青霄。
群木澄幽寂，疏煙泛沉寥。

In the Mountains 山中
All birds love to chatter in a place one wants quiet;
Idle clouds seem jealous when the moon shines forth.
The myriad problems of the world of men are not my affair!
I'm only shamed that autumn has come and I have made no poems.

凡鳥愛喧人靜處，閑雲似妒月明時。
世間萬事非吾事，只愧秋來未有詩。

Here, trees that stand out "secluded and lonely" and the serenity of the mountains disturbed by chattering birds reflect themes of reclusion, loneliness, and isolation that recur throughout Sikong Tu's work. Most of the nearly four hundred extant poems found in later collections are in the *jueju* 絕句 form and express a life and an attitude that place Sikong Tu in the tradition of Tao Qian 陶潛 (365–427), Wang Wei 王維 (692–761 or 699–759),* and Wei Yingwu 韋應物 (737–ca. 791).*

Beyond his published works, Sikong Tu's ideas on poetry can also be found in letters like "Yu Jipu shu" 與極浦書 (Letter to Jipu [i.e. Wang Ji 王極], *jinshi* 891), in which he describes his concept of "an image beyond the image" (*xiangwai zhi xiang* 象外之象), or "Yu Li Sheng lunshi shu" 與李生論詩書 (Letter to Master Li on Poetry) in which he extorts this certain Master Li to aim for "a meaning beyond flavor" (*weiwai zhi zhi* 味外之旨):

> Prose is difficult and poetry more difficult—from ancient to modern times there have been many explanations of this... satire, instruction, meter, rhythms, the straightforward, the subtle, the profound and the elegant are all within it [poetry]. Yet for it to directly achieve success, it must be in a mode that naturally becomes wondrous. Those poetry collections of former ages were not all skilled in this, how much more must it be so for their followers. Wang Wei and Wei Yingwu are tranquil and exquisite, this mode is a part of them. How could they avoid being acclaimed? Jia Dao truly has startling lines, but when you look at a whole piece, its meaning is rather empty.... Your poetry shares the unattractive qualities of that time. If you could return to making overall beauty your goal, then you would come to understand the significance that lies beyond flavor.

> 文之難而詩尤難，古今之喻多矣... 諷諭抑揚，渟蓄淵雅，皆在其中矣。 然直致所得，以格自奇。前輩諸集，亦不專工於此，矧其下者耶？ 王右丞、韋蘇州，澄澹精緻，格在其中，豈妨於道學哉？ 賈閬仙誠有警句，然視其全篇，意思殊餒。... 足下之詩，時輩固有難色。 儻復以全美為上，即知味外之旨矣。

More than his own poetic style, it would be Sikong Tu's literary criticism that would impact later generations. His "Ershisi shipin" and his letters on the craft of poetry would influence critics such as Mei Yaochen 梅堯臣 (1002–1060), Yan Yu 嚴羽 (fl. 1200), and Wang Shizhen 王士禛 (1634–1711), and as result, Sikong Tu holds a prominent place in the tradition of literary criticism.

BIBLIOGRAPHY

Editions:
Lau, D.C. 劉殿爵, Chen Fangzheng 陳方正 and He Zhihua 何志華, eds. *Shipin zhuzi suoyin* 詩品逐字索引. Hong Kong: Zhongwen Daxue, 2007.
Quan Tang shi, 10: 7292–340, 14: 10695.
Quan Tang wen, 807–810.9927–68.
Sikong Biaosheng shi ji 司空表聖詩集. 5 *juan*. SBCK.
Sikong Biaosheng shi wen ji 司空表聖詩文集. Beijing: Wenwu, 1982. *Jiayetang Congshu* 嘉業堂叢書 ed.
Sikong Biaosheng wenji 司空表聖文集. 10 *juan*. SKQS.
Sikong Biaosheng wenji 司空表聖文集. *Song Shu keben Tangren ji* 宋蜀刻本唐人集. V. 24. Shanghai: Shanghai Guji, 2012.
Sikong Shipin 司空詩品. 1 *juan*. BBCS.

Annotations:
Cai Naizhong 蔡乃中, Wu Zonghai 吳宗海, and Luo Zhongding 羅仲鼎, eds. *Shipin jinxi* 詩品今析. Nanjing: Jiangsu Renmin, 1983.
Du Lijun 杜黎均. *Ershisi Shipin yizhu pingxi* 二十四詩品譯注評析. Beijing: Xinhua Shudian, 1988.
Gao Zhongzhang 高仲章, et al., eds. *Sikong Tu xuanji zhu* 司空圖選集注. Taiyuan: Shanxi Renmin 1989.
Guo Shaoyu 郭紹虞, ed. *Shipin jijie* 詩品集解. Hong Kong: Shangwu, 1965.
Wang Jiheng 王济亨. *Sikong Tu xuanji zhu* 司空圖選集注. Taiyuan: Shanxi Renmin, 1989.
Yang Tingzhi 楊廷芝 et al. *Sikong Tu Shipin jieshuo erzhong* 司空圖詩品解說二種. Jinan: Qi Lu Shushe, 1980.

Biographical Sources:
Fu, *Tang caizi*, 3:517–29 5:436–37.
Jiu Tang shu, 190C.5082.
Xin Tang shu, 194.5573–75.

Translations:
Giles, Herbert, trans. "The Twenty-Four Modes of Poetry." *A History of Chinese Literature*. London: Heinemann, 1901.
Guo Lingyuan 郭令原. *Baihua Shipin* 白話詩品. Changsha: Yuelu Shushe, 1997.
Kadowaki Hirofumi 門脇博文. *Nijūshi Shihin* 二十四詩品. Tokyo: Meitoku, 2000.
Owen, *Anthology*, p. 508.
___, *Remembrances*, p. 125.
Sunflower, pp. 285–86.
Woon, Yoon Wah. *Sikong Tu's Shih-p'in*. Singapore: Department of Chinese Studies, 1994. Includes an introduction.
Yang Xianyi, *Poetry and Prose*, pp. 191–206.
___. "The Twenty-four Modes of Poetry," *Chinese Literature*, 1963.7: 65–77.
Yu, *Imagery*, p. 208.

Studies:
Alekseev V.M. *Kitajskaja poema o poete. Stansy Sykun Tu (837–908)* [Chinese Poem about a Poet. Stanzas of Sikong Tu]. Moscow: Vostochnaya literatura, 2008. Translation and analysis.
Cao Lengquan 曹冷泉, comm. *Shipin tongshi* 詩品通釋. Xian: Shanxi Shifan Daxue, 1989.
Chen Guoqiu 陳國球. "Sikong Tu yanjiu lunzhu mulu" 司空圖研究論著目錄. *Shumu jikan* 21.3 (1987): 93–100.
Chen Shangjun 陳尚君 and Wang Yonghao 汪涌豪. "Sikong Tu *Ershisi shipin* bianwei" 司空圖二十四詩品辨偽. *Zhongguo guji yanjiu* 中國古籍研究. V. 1. Shanghai: Shanghai Guji, 1996, pp. 39–73.
Du Lijun 杜黎均. *Ershisi shipin yizhu pingxi* 二十四詩品譯注評析. Beijing: Beijing, 1988.
Fang Zhitong 方志彤. "*Shiping* zuozhe kao" 詩品作者考, *Wenxue yichan*, 2001.5.
Fei Yunhua 非雲華. "Lun Sikong Tu 'Weiwai zhi Zhi' dui Shiwei Lun de Fazhan 論司空圖 "味外之旨" 對詩味論的發展, *Kunming xueyuan xuebao* 4 (2009).
Hong Zheng 弘征. *Sikong Tu Shipin jinyi jianxi fuli* 司空圖詩品今譯簡析附例. Yinzhuan: Ningxia Renmin, 1984. Rpt. Nanchang: Jiangxi Renmin, 1993.
Jiang Guozhen 江國貞. *Sikong biaosheng yanjiu* 司空表聖研究. Taibei: Wenjin, 1985.
Journeau, Véronique A. *L'art poétique de Sikong Tu: Ershisi Shipin: 24 poèmes*. Paris: You-Feng, 2006.
Kadowaki, Hirofumi 門脇博文. *Nijushin shihin* 二十四詩品. Tokyo: Meitoku, 2000.
Lin Hua 林華. *Sikong Tu 'Ershisi Shipin' qujie jizhu* 司空圖二十四詩品曲解集注. Shanghai: Shangha Yinyue XueYuan, 2019.
Liu Ning 刘宁. "Wan Tang Shixue Shiye zhongde You Cheng Si—Sikong Tu dui Wang Wei de Jiedu 晚唐詩學視野 中的右丞詩—司空圖對王維的解讀, *Beijing Daxue xuebao (Zhexue Shehui Kexue ban)* 51.6 (Nov. 2014): 69–78.
Liu Yuchang 劉禹昌. *Sikong Tu Shipin yizheng ji qita* 司空圖詩品義證及其它. Wuhan: Wuhan Daxue, 1993.
Lu Yuanchi 陸元熾. *Shi de zhexue, zhexue de shi* 詩的哲學哲學的詩. Beijing: Beijing, 1984.
Ma Xiancheng 馬現誠. "Sikong Tu shi lunji shige de Fo Chan neiyun" 司空圖詩論及詩歌的佛禪內蘊, *Guangxi Minzu xueyuan xuebao (Zhexue Shehui Kexue Ban)* 24.1 (Jan. 2002): 118–123.
Owen, Stephen. "The Twenty-four Categories of Poetry." In *Readings in Chinese Literary Thought*. Cambridge: Harvard University Press, 1992, pp. 299–357.
Qiao Li 喬力. *Ershisi shipin tanwei* 二十四詩品探微. Jinan: Qi Lu Shushe, 1984.

Robertson, Maureen A. "To Convey What is Precious: Ssu-k'ung T'u's Poetics and the *Erh-shih-ssu Shih P'in*," in *Transition and Permanence: Chinese History and Culture*. David C. Buxbaum and Frederick W. Mote, eds. Hong Kong: Cathay Press, 1972, pp. 323–57.

Shi Zhenping 石振平. "Sikong Tu 'Ershisi shibin' meixue qianxi 司空圖《二十四詩品》美學思想淺析, *Puyang Zhiye Jishu Xueyuan xuebao* 20.1 (Feb. 2007): 67–68.

Tao Litian 陶禮天. *Sikong Tu nianpu huikao* 司空圖年譜匯考. Beijing: Huanwen, 2002.

Wang Bugao 王步高. *Sikong Tu pingzhuan* 司空圖評傳. Nanjing: Nanjing Daxue, 2006.

Wang Hong 汪泓. "Sikong Tu *Ershisi Shipin* zhenwei bian zongshu" 司空圖二十四詩品真偽辨綜述. *Fudan xuebao* 2 (1996): 32–37.

Wang Hongyin 王宏印. *Shipin zhuyi yu Sikong Tu shixue yanjiu* 詩品注譯與司空圖詩學研究. Beijing: Beijing Tushuguan, 2002.

Wang Runhua 王潤華. *Sikong Tu xinlun* 司空圖新論. Taibei: Dongda Tushu Gongsi, 1989.

Wei Junling 魏俊玲, "Sikong Tu 'Ershisi shipin' de jiben meixue sixiang" 司空圖《二十四詩品》的基本美学思想, *Xinxiang Jiaoyu Xueyuan* 2009.4:

Wong Yoon Wah 王潤華. *Sikong Tu xinlun* 司空圖新論. Taibei: Dongda Tushu Gongsi, 1989.

___. *Ssu-K'ung T'u: Poet-Critic of the T'ang*. Hong Kong: The Chinese University of Hong Kong, 1976.

Yu, Pauline. "Ssu-k'ung T'u's 'Shih-p'in': Poetic Theory in Poetic Form" in Ronald C. Miao, ed., *Studies in Chinese Poetry and Poetics*. San Francisco: Chinese Materials Center, 1978, v. 1, pp. 81–103.

Zhan Youxing 詹幼馨. *Sikong Tu Shipin yanyi* 司空圖詩品衍繹. Hong Kong: Hua Feng, 1983.

Zhang Guoqing 張國慶. *Ershisi shipin shige meixue* 二十四詩品詩歌美學. Beijing: Zhongyang Bianyi, 2008.

Zhang Shaokang 張少康. *Sikong Tu ji qi shilun yanjiu* 司空圖及其詩論研究. Beijing: Xueyuan, 2005.

___. "Qingren lun Sikong Tu 'Ershisi shipin'" 情人論司空圖《二十四詩品》, *Nanyang Shifan Xueyan Xuebao (Shehui Kexue ban)* 1.5 (2002 Oct.): 32–37.

Zhao Futan 趙福壇. "Sikong Tu 'Ershisi shipin' yanjiu jiqi zuozhe bianwei zongxi 司空圖《二十四詩品》研究及其作者辨偽綜析, *Guangzhou Shiyuan Xuebao (Shehui Kexue Ban)* 1.5 (Oct. 2002).

___. *Shipin xinshi* 詩品新釋. Canton: Huacheng, 1986.

Zu Baoquan 祖保泉. *Sikong Tu de shige lilun* 司空圖的詩歌理論. Shanghai: Shanghai Guji, 1984. Rpt. Taibei: Guowen Tiandi Zazhi, 1992.

___. *Sikong Tu shiwen yanjiu* 司空圖詩文研究. Hefei: Anhui Jiaoyu, 1999.

___ and Tao Litian 陶禮天. *Sikong Biaosheng shi wen ji jian jiao* 司空表聖詩文集箋校. Hefei: Anhui Daxue, 2002.

___. *'Ershisi Shipin' jiaozhu yiping* 二十四詩品校注譯評. Wuhu: Anhui Shifan Daxue, 2018.

Volker Klöpsch, Masha Kobzeva, and William H. Nienhauser, Jr.

Sima Chengzhen 司馬承禎 (*zi*, Ziwei 子微, 647–735), the twelfth patriarch of the Shangqing 上清 (Highest Clarity) school of Daoism, was one of the most eminent religious figures of the Tang dynasty and an important member of the literary world during Emperor Xuanzong's reign (r. 712–756). A grandson of Sima Yixuan 司馬裔玄, a former local official in Jinzhou 晉州 (modern Shanxi), Chengzhen was said to be from Wenxian 溫縣 (modern Henan). As a young man he served as a functionary for a time, then began religious studies with Pan Shizheng 潘師正 (587–684) at the sacred mountain Songshan 嵩山. He was so proficient a student that he was eventually chosen as Pan's successor. Later (precisely when is not known), he left Songshan, traveled to many sacred sites, and finally settled at Tiantaishan 天台山 (in modern Zhejiang).

Sima Chengzhen

Sima Chengzhen was summoned to court from Tiantai by Wu Zetian 武則天 (r. 690–705), Ruizong (r. 684–690, 710–712), and Xuanzong. His relationship with the latter was especially close. In 721 he ordained Xuanzong as an official Daoist. The two worthies collaborated on an edition of *Laozi* with a fixed length of 5380 graphs, penned in three different styles by Sima. A few years later, when Sima's new abode at Wangwushan 王屋山 was completed, Xuanzong presented him with a horizontal plaque on which he had personally written Yangtai Fuan 陽臺觀 (Belvedere of the Solar Terrace) along with three hundred bolts of silk. Sima spent the remainder of his days at Wangwushan. His biographies state that he died in 727 at the age of 89. Other, earlier sources claim he died in 735.

Sima's many extant works show him to have been a man of great versatility. They include poetry and meditation manuals. One of the more interesting texts is the "Shangqing hanxiang jianjian tu" 上清含象劍鑑圖, an illustrated description of swords and mirrors—important liturgical implements—attributed to Sima Chengzhen and found in the Daoist canon. Sima was said to have presented the work to Emperor Xuanzong, who responded with a poem that is now included in the text itself. Likewise, the canonical "Zuowang lun" 坐忘論 (Treatise on Sitting and Forgetting) and the "Tianyin zi" 天隱子 (Master Hidden in the Heaven) are also attributed to Sima Chengzhen, each of which outline meditative techniques and practices based on the famous passage of "sitting and forgetting" from the *Zhuang Zi*. In addition to being known for his works on Daoist practice, Sima was also known to be a skilled painter and calligrapher.

The importance of the texts he wrote are matched by the lives he touched and impressed with his piety. Some evidence of this may be found in Tang literature. The *Quan Tang shi* preserves two poems written to him by the Emperor Xuanzong, as well as a number of verses in his honor by noted Tang poets–Song Zhiwen 宋之問 (656–ca. 712),* Li Jiao 李嶠 (ca. 644–ca. 714),* and Zhang Jiuling 張九齡 (678–740).* To one such poem Sima Chengzhen wrote a reply, "Da Song Zhiwen" 答宋之問 (Replying to Song Zhiwen):

> Time is about up—the season just about spring;
> The mountain forest is quiet, embracing the recluse.
> Ascending marvelous peaks, gazing at the white clouds;
> Saddened by their remoteness, images are about to scatter.
> The white clouds leisurely drift and do not come back;
> A cold wind blows rustling till day is done.
> Not seeing you, with whom can I talk?
> I return to sit and play my zither, my thoughts far away.

> 時既暮兮節欲春，山林寂兮懷幽人。
> 登奇峰兮望白雲，悵緬邈兮象欲紛。
> 白雲悠悠去不返，寒風颼颼吹日晚。
> 不見其人誰與言，歸坐彈琴思逾遠。

The time in the first line of this poem can refer simply to the end of the year but may simultaneously also refer to the end of a person's life. The white clouds in lines three and four evoke the distance between the poet and Song Zhiwen—while the clouds can easily cover this distance, the two men cannot. Sima Chengzhen can only reach his friend in his thoughts and eventually through this poem. Some critics have sensed that meditation may figure in the final line, but it seems likely that it may suggest the classic story of friendship between the woodcutter Zhong Ziqi 鐘子期 who was the only person who could understand Boya's 伯牙 meaning when he played the zither. After Zhong died, Boya gave up the zither knowing that there will never be another to truly understand his tune. In his final line to Song Zhiwen, Sima Chengzhen may be suggesting that he too was missing his friend, a soulmate who could understand his innermost feelings.

Sima also met Li Bo 李白 (701–762),* who recorded their meeting in the allegorical and rather satirical "Da peng fu" 大鵬賦 (Prose-poem of the Great Roc). The poet-official Chen Ziang 陳子昂 (661–702)* also wrote of an encounter with him.

The life of Sima Chengzhen is one of contradictions. A Shangqing Patriarch who rarely spent time at the center of Shangqing activity on Maoshan 茅山 (Jiangsu Province), he was a hermit who hobnobbed with poets and princes. Yet he always retained an aura of holiness that commanded respect leading to a description of him as having a body like a cold pine and a heart like a bright mirror.

BIBLIOGRAPHY

Editions:
DZ 277 *Xiuzhen jingyi zalun* 修真精義雜論.
DZ 1026 *Tianyin zi* 天隱子.
DZ 1036 *Zuowang lun* 坐忘論.
Quan Tang shi, 12: 9699, 14: 11042.
Quan Tang wen, 924.12696–708.
Wang Shouju 吳受琚, ed. *Sima Chengzhen ji* 司馬承禎集. Beijing: Shehui Kexue Wenxian, 2013.
Zhong Zhaopeng 鐘肇鵬, ed. *Zuo wang lun* 坐忘論. Beijing: Beijing Tushuguan, 1998.

Biographical Sources:
Jiu Tang shu, 192.5127–29.
Xin Tang shu, 196.5606–06.

Translations:
Demiéville, *Anthologie*, pp. 257–58.
Minford and Lau, pp. 835–37.
Zhang Songhui 張松輝. *Xinyi Zuo wang lun* 新譯坐忘論. Taibei: Sanmin, 2005.

Studies:
Engelhardt, Ute. *Die klassisches Tradition der Qi-Übungen (Qigong), eine Darstellung anhangend des Tangzeitlichen Textes 'Fu Qijingyi lun' von Sima Chengzhen*. Stuttgart: Franz Steiner, 1987. *Münchener Ostasiatische Studien*, v. 44. Translation and study of the *Fu Qijingyi lun* 服氣精義論, prefaced by a study of Sima Chengzhen's life and related sources.
Jülch, Thomas. *Der Orden des Sima Chengzhen und des Wang Ziqiao: Untersuchungen zur Geschichte des Shangqing-Daoismus in den Tiantai-Bergen*. Munich: Utz, 2011.
Kirkland, Russell. "Ssu-ma Ch'eng-chen and the Rule of Taoism in the Medieval Chinese Polity." *Journal of Asian History* 31 (1997): 105–38.

___. "Taoists of the High T'ang: An Inquiry into the Perceived Significance of Eminent Taoists in Medieval Chinese Society." Ph. D. dissertation, Indiana University, 1986, pp. 43–71.

Koffler, Pauline Bentley, "Shangqing hanxiang jianjian tu," in in Kristofer Schipper and Fransiscus Verellen, eds. *The Taoist Canon*. Chicago: University of Chicago Press, 2005, pp. 617–18.

Kohn, Livia. *Seven Steps to the Tao: Sima Chengzhen's Zuowanglun*. Nettetal: Steyler Verla-Wort und Werk Monumenta Serica Monograph 20, 1987.

Kroll, Paul W. "Notes on Three Taoist Figures of the T'ang Dynasty." *Bulletin of the Society for the Study of Chinese Religions*, 9 (1981): 19–41.

___. "Ssu-ma Ch'eng-chen in T'ang Verse." *Bulletin of the Society for the Study of Chinese Religions*, 6 (1978): 16–30.

___. *Sitting in Oblivion: The Heart of Daoist Meditation*. Dunedin, Florida: Three Pines, 2010.

Li Dahua 李大華 et al. "Sima Chengzhen de Daojiao zhexue sixiang" 司馬承禎哲學思想 in *Sui Tang Daojia yu Daojiao* 隋唐道家與道教. Beijing: Renmin, 2011, pp. 252–316.

Pregadio, Fabrizio, ed. *Encyclopedia of Taoism*. London; New York: Routledge, 2008, v. 2, pp. 911–14.

Qing Xitai. "The Place of Daoist Culture Within Traditional Chinese Culture: A Reappraisal." *Contemporary Chinese Thought* 29 (Spring, 1998): 72–80.

Robinet, Isabelle "Zuowang lun," in Kristofer Schipper and Fransiscus Verellen, eds. *The Taoist Canon*. Chicago: University of Chicago Press, 2005, pp. 306–07

Douglas Nielson, Masha Kobzeva, and Michael E. Naparstek

Song Zhiwen 宋之問 (*zi*, Yanqing 延清, also named Shaolian 少連; 656–ca. 712) is usually paired with Shen Quanqi 沈佺期 (656–716).* Their works are traditionally taken as the epitome of the poetry that marked the transition from the Early to the High Tang.

Song's hometown is disputed: he was either from Fengzhou 汾州 (modern Fenyang 汾陽 in Shanxi) or from near modern Lingbao 靈寶 in Henan). Song passed the *jinshi* examinations with Shen Quanqi in 675 and both men were associated with the government of Empress Wu, specifically with the literary salon of her favorite Zhang Yizhi 張易之 (d. 705). They were both exiled to the provinces when this government fell in 705. A general amnesty returned them to the capital the following year, but Song Zhiwen apparently could not refrain from involvement in the politics of imperial succession. In 710 he was banished further to the south. When Xuanzong (r. 712–755) ascended the throne, returning firm control of the state once again into the hands of the Li family, the new emperor ordered Song Zhiwen to commit suicide.

Many of Song's poems were *yingzhi shi* 應制詩 (poems composed to imperial command) for formal state occasions. It was in this atmosphere that the tonal requirements of *lüshi* 律詩 (regulated verse) assumed their final shape, and the poetry of Song—together with that of Shen Quanqi—represent the earliest major body of Chinese verse to contain sizable amounts of standard regulated poetry.

Song was also instrumental in introducing new, more personal matters into early Tang verse. He was also noted for his revival of the old "Chu Songs" 楚歌, a precursor of the *yuefu* that had been popular in the Han dynasty. One of his best-known poems in this mode was "Du Hanjiang" 渡漢江 (Crossing the Han River), which shares language and sentiment with some of Shen Quanqi's *yuefu*, although the theme is more personal:

>Beyond the Southern Range letters stopped;
>I pass through winter and again undergo spring.
>As I near home my heart the more anxious—
>Not venturing to ask news of those coming from there.

>嶺外音書斷，經冬復歷春。
>近鄉情更怯，不敢問來人。

This poem was written when Song was recalled to Luoyang from Longzhou 瀧州 (modern Guangdong) in 706. It is a forerunner of the complex psychological poems of the High Tang, here revealing the nervousness Song felt on approaching his home and family from the distant south, realizing that they, like him, may have suffered under the changing scene at court. Line two is an interesting depiction of the distance he traveled portrayed in seasonal change: he moved from spring in Longzhou, through the wintry mountains, and then back into spring again. Despite the optimism spring and homecoming would normally bring, this poem reveals the many tensions of those literati whose lives changed greatly with the restoration of the Li family on the throne in 712.

BIBLIOGRAPHY

Editions:
Quan Tang shi, 1: 621–60, 13: 10040, 14: 10598–11003.
Quan Tang wen, 240–41.2713–27.
Song Zhiwen ji 宋之問集. 2 *juan*. SBCK. Rpt. of a Ming edition, probably of the Jiajing 嘉靖 (1522–1566) period.
Zhang Shunye 張遜業, ed. *Song Zhiwen ji* 宋之問集. 2 *juan*. Hongchun Dongbi Tushufu 黃埻東壁圖書府, 1552.

Annotations:
Yi Shuqiong 易淑瓊, et al., eds. *Shen Quanqi, Song Zhiwen ji jiaozhu* 沈佺期,clev集校注. Beijing: Zhonghua, 2001.

Biographical Sources:
Fu, *Tang caizi*, 1:85–96, 5:10–14.
Jiu Tang shu, 190B.5025–26.
Xin Tang shu, 202.5750–51.

Translations:
Bynner, *Jade Mountain*, p. 107.
Fuller, Michael A. *An Introduction to Chinese Poetry: From the* Canon of Poetry *to the Lyrics of the Song Dynasty*. Cambridge: Harvard University Press, 2018, pp. 182–83.
Margoulies, *Anthologie*, pp. 230, 435.
Minford and Lau, p. 695.
Owen, *Early T'ang*, pp. 364–80.

Studies:

Chu Yaowen 儲姚文. "Lun Du Shenyan, Shen Quanqi, Song Zhiwen de shanshui shi" 論杜審言、沈佺期、宋之問的山水詩. *Tangdu xuekan* 唐都學刊, 1999.1.

Hu Zhenlong 胡振龍. "Song Zhiwen Songgongzhai song Ning jianyi shi de zuodi" 宋之問《宋公宅送寧諫議詩》的作地. *Wenxue yichan* 1990.2: 26.

Liu Kaiyang 劉開揚. "Guanyu Shen Quanqi, Song Zhiwen de pingshu" 關於沈佺期宋之問的評述, *Shehui kexue yanjiu* 社會科學研究, 1981.4.

Liu Zhenya 劉振婭. "Song Zhiwen liang zhe Lingnan xinkao" 宋之問兩謫嶺南新考. *Wenxue yichan* 1988.6: 75–84.

Ma Menquan 馬鬥全. "Song Zhiwen de jiguan ji 'Du Hanjiang' shi" 宋之問的籍貫及《渡漢江》詩, *Zhongzhou xuekan* 中州學刊 1982.6: 91–97.

Tao Min 陶敏 and Yi Shuqiong 易淑瓊. "Shen, Song lunlue" 沈宋論略. *Xiangtan Shifan Xueyuan xuebao* 1996.2: 6–10.

Tao Min 陶敏. *Song Zhiwen ji* kaobian 宋之問集考辨, *Tangdai wenxue yanjiu* 6 (1996): 631–40.

Wang Qixing 王啟興. "Song Zhiwen shengping shiji kaobian" 宋之問生平事蹟考辨, *Guizhou Daxue xuebao (Shehuikexueban)* 貴州大學學報（社會科學版）1987.4: 41–47.

Xu Zhiyin 許智銀. "Shen Quanqi, Song Zhiwen songbie shi yanjiu" 沈佺期,宋之問送別詩研究, *Pingdingshan Xueyuan xuebao* 平頂山學院學報, 21.4 (2006): 23–26.

Yu Xianhao 郁賢皓. "Song Zhiwen shiji he jiaoyou wuti kaobian" 宋之問事蹟和交遊五題考辨. *Wenxue yichan* 1993.1: 26–31.

Zhou Bin 周斌 and Shang Yongliang 尚永亮. "Song Zhiwen shige yishu jieshou shulun" 宋之問詩歌藝術接受述論. *Tangdu xuekan* 2005.3: 5–8.

Charles Hartman and William H. Nienhauser, Jr.

Su Ting 蘇頲 (*zi*, Tingshuo 廷碩, ennobled as Xuguo Gong 許國公, 670–727) was a high official and literary arbiter at the courts of emperors Zhongzong (r. 684 and 705–710) and Xuanzong (r. 713–756). Together with Zhang Yue 張說 (667–731)* he was among the earliest of *pianwen* 駢文 (parallel-prose) writers to devote his energies to writing official, imperial documents. The writings of both men are said to have begun the trend towards the limitation of *pianwen* style to bureaucratic writings, and they set the standard of prose writing in their time: their names, since at least the eleventh century, have been linked together in the accolade, *Yan Xu Dashoubi* 燕許大手筆 (The Great Penmen, Dukes of Yan and Xu).

Su Ting was from Wugong 武功, just west of the capital. His father, Su Gui 蘇瓌 (639–710), was a noted scholar-official who had passed the special-degree examination *Yousu ke* 幽素科 in 666 along with Wang Bo 王勃 (650–676).* The elder Su held high offices under Empress Wu (r. 684–705) and served as a Grand Councilor under Xuanzong. Su Ting passed the *jinshi* examination in 690 and served as an Vice Prefect in Wucheng 烏程 (modern Wuxing 吳興, Zhejiang). In 696 he passed the Worthy and Excellent, Straightforward and Upright special-degree examination and was eventually promoted to the post of Investigating Censor.

With the accession of Zhongzong (705), and with Su Gui's appointment as Grand Councilor, Su Ting was promoted to Reviewing Policy Advisor and Academician in the Institute for the Veneration of Literature, the institute which served as a reservoir of literary talent for Zhongzong's entourage. Su participated, with other leading poets of the day, in the excursions organized by Zhongzong, on which he would elicit cycles of poems from his courtiers. Many of the poems from these occasions are still extant. Su also became an important drafter of imperial edicts at this time.

When his father died in 710, Su Ting was offered higher posts but declined to serve, probably to mourn his father's death. Su Ting was back at the court following Xuanzong's accession and in 713 was given the high post of Vice Minister of Works. In early 714, he was further promoted to the office of Secretariat Drafter and also made Participant in the Drafting of Proclamations. Together with Li Yi 李乂 (649–716), Su was in charge of drafting all official edicts from 713 through 716. In the latter year, he was named Grand Councilor, and worked closely with Song Jing 宋璟 (663–737) until both were demoted in 720. Su Ting's demotion was to the office of Minister of the Ministry of Rites, a position he held until his death in 727. In 720 he was also sent to Sichuan as an Chief Scribe at Yizhou 益州 (modern Chengdu 成都) and is credited with preventing an alliance of the Man people with the Tibetans. According to one account, he also interviewed the young Li Bo 李白 (701–762)* at this time and likened his poetry to that of Sima Xiangru 司馬相如 (179–117 BCE).

By 724, Su Ting was back at the court where he, Zhang Yue and Zhang Jiuling 張九齡 (678–740)* were leading court poets and edict writers for Xuanzong. After his death, Su Ting was granted the posthumous name Wenzhen 文貞.

Although prominent in his own day, very little was said about Su Ting's writings subsequently. However, much of his work was, and is, extant. In the literary history of the years 705 to 730, he is overshadowed by many political peers, Song Zhiwen 宋之問 (656–ca. 712),* Li Jiao 李嶠 (ca. 644–ca. 714),* Zhang Yue, and Zhang Jiuling, among others. Most of his extant 102 poems date from Zhongzong's reign. They were set to rhymes determined by the emperor and, generally speaking, were *yingzhi shi* 應制詩 (poems composed at imperial command), among which is the widely known "Fenghe chunri xing Wangchun Gong yingzhi" 奉和春日幸望春宮應制 (Written at Imperial Command on the Royal Visit to the Gazing at Spring Palace on a Spring Day):

> Eastward gazing at Gazing at Spring [Palace], the spring so lovely;
> All the more on a sunny day, willows shrouded in mist.
> Looking down from the palace the Southern Mountains all in view,
> At eye level the Big Dipper hangs over the palace walls.
> Slender grasses all bear traces of the royal cart,
> Light flowers float down before toasting wine cups;
> The imperial progress through this setting offers limitless views,
> Every sound the birds sing resonating with the wind and string instruments.

> 東望望春春可憐，更逢晴日柳含煙。
> 宮中下見南山盡，城上平臨北斗懸。
> 細草徧承回輦處，輕花微落奉觴前。
> 宸遊對此歡無極，鳥哢聲聲入管絃。

The repetition of *wang* 望 (gazing) and *chun* 春 (spring) in the first line, although it goes against poetic convention, results in a clever trope: although it is clearly speaking of the palace the emperor was visiting, the line could also be read as referring to spring in general: "Eastward gazing, gazing at spring, spring so lovely." The majesty of the palace itself can be seen in lines three and four in which the distant Zhongnan Mountains 終南山 are all visible from the heights of its towers, its walls so high they intersect with the stars of the Northern Dipper, itself an oft used metaphor from the imperial palace (both are at the center of their worlds). But the poetic vision is contrived, mixing daylight and nighttime scenes. Still the overall effect is that of a collage of powerful images of that make spring almost tangible.

Almost all of Su Ting's 290 extant prose pieces are edicts he wrote on the emperor's behalf. This figure alone assures Su Ting's place in the history of Chinese prose. During the early eighth century there was an enhanced imperial interest in acquiring skilled prose writers for civil servants, and in promoting these men to top offices. Whereas prior to this time *pianwen* 駢文 prose writers (from Wang Bo 王勃 [650–676]* back to Xu Ling 徐陵 [507–583]) used the style primarily personal writings, subsequently writers applied the style to official documents. For a time, this had the effect of broadening the applications of *pianwen* from purely literary to utilitarian purposes. Imperial interest in prose led to new norms and standardizations (promoted in some examinations), and eventually divorced the *pianwen* style from belles lettres altogether, since it was seen as an "official" style.

Thus, Su Ting is one of the earliest *pianwen* writers after the Six Dynasties to have made a reputation solely for his official edicts, anticipating later masters such as Lu Zhi 陸贄 (754–805),* Quan Deyu 權德輿 (761–818),* and Li Deyu 李德裕 (787–850).* In terms of style, Su Ting's *pianwen* followed most of the prosodic features of earlier, belletristic *pianwen*. Because of its official applications, however, there was a tendency to limit the breadth of vocabulary, and allusive passages were held within the bounds of history and politics.

BIBLIOGRAPHY

Editions:
Chu Tang Su Ting shiji 初唐蘇頲詩集. 1608. *Shijia Tangshi* 十家唐詩 ed.
Quan Tang shi, 2: 794–815, 14: 11029.
Quan Tang wen, 250–58.2803–97.
Su Ting shuo wen ji 蘇頲碩文集. 20 *juan.* An early manuscript copy. In the Rare Book Collection of Peking University.
Su Xugong wenji 蘇許公文集. 11 *juan. Su Ting yu keben* 蘇頲玉刻本 (1842), now held in Beijing Shifan Daxue library.

Biographical Sources:
Jiu Tang shu, 88.2880–84.
Xin Tang shu, 125.4399–04.

Translations:
Owen, *Early T'ang,* pp. 259, 282.

Studies:
Chen Jun 陳鈞. *Li Bo yu Su Ting lunkao* 李白與蘇頲論考. Taiyuan: Shanxi Guji, 2001.
___. *Su Ting shi wen ji biannian kaojiao* 蘇頲詩文集編年考校. Taiyuan: Shanxi Guji, 2001.

Chen Yaodong 陳耀東, "Tang *Su Ting ji* zhijian lu" 唐蘇頲集知見錄, *Wenxian* 文獻, 1994.1: 37–44.
Lin Dazhi 林大志. *Su Ting, Zhang Yue yanjiu* 蘇頲張說研究. Jinan: Qi Lu Shushe, 2007.
Qu Jingyi 曲景毅. "Shengshi qixiang: Zhang Yue yu Su Ting" 省市氣象: 張悅與蘇頲, in Qu Jingyi, *Tangdai 'Dashou bi' zuojia yanjiu* 唐代大手筆作家研究. Beijing: Zhongguo Shehui Kexue, 2015, pp. 70–116.
Yu Xianhao 郁賢皓. *Su Ting shiji kao* 蘇頲事跡考. Guilin: Guangxi Shifan Daxue, 1992.

C. Bradford Langley and William H. Nienhauser, Jr.

Sun Qiao 孫樵 (*zi*, Kezhi 可之, Yinzhi 隱之, *jinshi* 855) hailed from Guandong 關東 or "East of the [Hangu 函穀] Pass," a region of vital strategic importance, located to the south of Lingbao 靈寶 Municipality in modern Henan Province. However all other details of his youth, including the name of his father, where he spent his childhood, and even the year and place of his birth, have been lost in the passage time. In the semi-autobiographical preface to his collected works, he tells us that the Sun clan originated in Guandong and had for generations maintained a tradition of public service where the achievements and positions of the young were inherited from their fathers. Sun Qiao appears to have quickly proven a worthy heir to this legacy. The first reliable date concerning his life is 855, when Sun passed the *jinshi* examination. Sometime thereafter he was appointed Secretariat Drafter and eventually attained the position of Director of the Bureau of Operations. His influence as a civil servant was largely insignificant, though it is said that his highest position was won during the ten-year rebellion of Huang Chao 黃巢 (d. 884) in part for having accompanied Emperor Xizong (r. 873–888) in flight from Chang'an during the winter of 880.

His surviving works give ample evidence to a life devoted to the art of letters, deep contemplation, and active engagement in the body politic. Thus, while Sun deserves recognition as a prose stylist and rhetorician of distinction, many of the issues he concerned himself with were representative of literati as a whole during the Late Tang. Moreover, due to the influence of Han Yu 韓愈 (768–824)* and his disciple Huangfu Shi 皇甫湜 (776–ca. 835),* Sun was also deeply invested in the *Guwen yundong* 古文運動 (Ancient-style Prose Movement). He referred to himself with pride as one of Han's disciples, though his work has often been described as largely imitative of the more prominent figures in the movement. Of his surviving prose works, two have played the largest role in shaping Sun's legacy. One is titled "Shu He Yiyu" 書何易於 (On He Yiyu), a touching account of a devoted literatus which would find its way into a larger series of similar biographies in the *Xin Tang shu*. The other is the "Shu Baocheng Yi bi" 書褒城驛壁 (Written on the Walls on the Way Station at Bao), a biting critique of governmental negligence and corruption which, while it may be a product of its time, nonetheless resonates with our own:

> The Bao City Way Station has been dubbed "First Under Heaven." [Yet] when seen with one's own eyes, looking at its pools, they are found shallow, tangled, and mired; when looking at its boats, they are found stranded, foundered, and run aground. Its courtyards heavily overgrown, its halls and terraces in great ruin; what can be seen of its so called "surpassing beauty?"

I asked a functionary at the way station, and he said: "The Steadfast Duke Mu [Li Zhong 李忠 (643–665), Gaozong's 高宗 eldest son] in the past had been Prefect of Liangzhou, and because Baocheng was placed under the control of two Military Commissioners there were dragon tallies and tiger standards, hard-ridden post-horses and rushing carriages were coming and going, wheels turned and hooves pounded, and because of this they expanded their way station to give witness to their greatness. All at that time, when viewing against other way stations, called it 'majestic.' And so for a year those who came as guests were no less than several hundred in number, and they carelessly shared in its shelter for the night and took their fill of its table, and all would at dawn's arrival depart; had they any sense of appreciation? When it came to the rowboats, only when it was certain that the oars were snapped, the bulwarks broken, and the bows wrecked would they then stop; and as for fishing, only when it was certain that the springs were dry, the mud churned up, and the fish exhausted would they then stop. Even more so was the feeding of horses on the veranda and the lodging of flacons in the halls, and all of the rooms and chambers were thus sullied and broken by varying tools and means of destruction. Of those officials who were lowly, though their underlings were fierce, they could be thwarted. Of those officials who were exalted, their underlings were mindlessly violent and wayward, and they themselves were difficult to impede. Because of this there was wanton damage and destruction, and it is not as it was once was. The eight or nine of us here, though we serve food during our leisure time, and one or two strive to solve these issues, could it possibly make up for the violence of several hundred people?"

His words were yet unfinished when there was an old farmer who laughed at our side, and then said: "All counties and townships are now way stations. I have heard that in the Kaiyuan Era (713–742), the World was then flourishing, and it was called 'The Ordered and Pacified,' and those traveling on foot for a thousand miles needn't carry grains, and those raising sons and grandsons knew not of soldering. At present, the World is without the sounds of metal strings, and families grow fewer by the day, the border regions that haven't been taken suffer catastrophe, and plowed fields grow more abandoned each day, the living are in greater hardship each day, and our wealth grows more depleted each day. What is the reason for all this? Now officials under command of the Imperial Court, they already take lightly the responsibilities of an official posting in the provinces, and moreover they are constantly transferring and replacing one another. As for these officials with postings in the provinces, those with a longer period will be transferred once in three years, those with a shorter period will be transferred every one or two years. For this reason the governance of the counties and townships, if it should not benefit the people, they can thereby give suggestions to reform or abolish such major issues, but at that the officials will say, 'Tomorrow I will have already left, what use is there in this?' and the county magistrate will also say, 'Tomorrow I will have already left, what use is there in this?' When they are anxious they get drunk on brew, and when hungry full on fresh meats." After having bowed and taken leave of the old farmer, I revised his words, and wrote them on the chambers and walls of the Bao City Way Station.

襃城驛號天下第一。及得寓目，視其沼，則淺混而汙；視其舟，則離敗而膠；庭除甚蕪，堂廡甚殘，烏睹其所謂宏麗者？

訊於驛吏，則曰：忠穆公曾牧梁州，以襃城控二節度治所，龍節虎旗，馳驛奔軺，以去以來，轂交蹄劇，由是崇侈其驛，以示雄大。蓋當時視他驛為壯。且一歲賓至者不下數百輩，苟夕得其庇，饑得其飽，皆暮至朝去，寧有顧惜心耶？至如棹舟，則必折篙破舷碎鷁而後止；漁釣，則必枯泉汨泥盡魚而後止。至有飼馬於軒，宿隼於堂，凡所以汙敗室廬，糜毀器用，官小者，其下雖氣猛，可制；官大者，其下益暴橫，難禁。由是日益破碎，不與曩類。某曹八九輩，雖以供饋之隙，一二力治之，其能補數十百人殘暴乎？

> 語未既，有老甿笑於旁，且曰：舉今州縣皆驛也。吾聞開元中，天下富蕃，號為理平，踵千里者不裹糧，長子孫者不知兵。今者天下無金革之聲，而戶口日益破，疆場無侵削之虞，而墾田日益寡，生民日益困，財力日益竭，其故何哉？凡與天子共治天下者，刺史縣令而已，以其耳目接於民，而政令速於行也。今朝廷命官，既已輕任刺史縣令，而又促數于更易。且刺史縣令，遠者三歲一更，近者一二歲再更，故州縣之政，苟有不利於民，可以出意革去其甚者，在刺史則曰：'明日我即去，何用如此。在縣令亦曰：明日我即去，何用如此。當愁醉醲，當饑飽鮮，囊帛檀金，笑與秩終。嗚呼！州縣真驛耶？矧吏代之隙，黠吏因緣恣為奸欺，以賣州縣者乎。如此而欲望生民不困，財力不竭，戶口不破，墾田不寡，難哉。予既揮退老甿，條其言，書於襃城驛屋壁。

Whether Sun Qiao actually met this insightful, gregarious farmer is debatable but placing extraordinary political criticism in the mouths of the ordinary people was a literary motif common to essays of the *Guwen yundong* (Ancient Prose Movement). Sun's musings on a government waystation, which apart from temples or the homes of friends were the only available housing to traveling officials, is exemplary of the terse, melodious prose he crafted over a lifetime. This, perhaps Sun Qiao's finest prose work, provides ample evidence to the decadence, ineptitude, and moral decay he believed had infested the elite classes of the empire. Many of his works deal with moral and intellectual decline. Apart from the essays, letters, prefaces, and inscriptions written in this archaized prose style, Sun has also left a number of poems, though they lack the power and sophistication of his prose. Sun will no doubt remain a somewhat neglected figure having followed in the footsteps of men more deserving of recognition in the same disciplines to which he chose to devote himself. However Sun's corpus offers us not only a selection of exceptional Late Tang prose written in the "ancient style," but also insight into the development of socio-political and philosophical ideals which would eventually reemerge to be counted among the chief concerns of Chinese political and intellectual life during the Song.

BIBLIOGRAPHY

Editions:

Quan Tang wen, 794–95: 9638–58.
Sun Kezhi Xiansheng wenji 孫可之先生文集. Shanghai: Huiwen Tangcui ji, 1910.
Sun Kezhi wenji 孫可之文集. Shanghai: Shanghai Guji, 1979.
Sun Qiao ji 孫樵集. Shanghai: Shangwu, 1929.
Tang Sun Qiao ji 唐孫樵集. Taibei: Taiwan Shangwu, 1967.

Studies:

Ding Enquan 丁恩全. "Sun Qiao de shixue sixiang ji qi sanwen de jingshen shizhi" 孫樵的史學思想及其散文的精神實質. *Henan Daxue xuebao* 2009.2: 84–88.
___. "Sun Qiao yanjiu" 孙樵研究. Unpublished Ph.D. dissertation, Huanzhong Kezhi Daxue, 2009.
___. "Sun Qiao 'Yubian guancha panguan shu' de xiezuo niankao." *Wenxue yichan* 2009.1: 50.
Li Guangfu 李光富. "Sun Qiao shenping ji Sunwen xinian" 孫樵生平及孫文系年. *Sichuan Daxue xuebao* 1987.1: 64–67.
Qian Jibo 錢基博 (1887–1957), *Han Yu wen du* 韓愈文讀. Shanghai: Shangwu yinshu guan, 1934. A famous study of prose selections written by Han Yu and his most prominent followers, it includes light annotation and useful introductions to authors and notable works.

Wang Zhikun 王志昆. "Sun Qiao ji banben yuanliu kao" 孫樵集版本源流考. *Chongqing Shifan Daxue xuebao* 1988.1: 66–68.

Thomas Donnelly Noel

Sun Simiao 孫思邈 (ca. 581–682) was a Daoist-physician in the Sui and early Tang. He was a native of Huayuan 華原 (modern Yao 耀 county in Shaanxi). There is no record of his ordination, but Livia Kohn and others have surmised that Sun might have received the Zhengyi 正一 (Orthodox Unity) ordination according to his works on Daoist alchemy. He lived in seclusion in Mount Taibo 太白山 (on the border between modern Taibo and Mei 眉 counties in southwestern Shaanxi). His biographies in the *Jiu Tangshu* and *Xin Tangshu* (New Tang History) say that he was summoned during the Northern Zhou dynasty (561–581), but this seems unlikely as he died in 682. Emperor Taizong (r. 627–649) summoned him to the capital city Chang'an and bestowed on him an official position, but he declined. In 659, Emperor Gaozong (r. 649–683) again summoned and offered him a high official position, but he declined once more. In 674, he pleaded illness and asked to return to the mountains. The emperor allowed him to live in Princess Poyang's 鄱陽公主 residence. Sun associated with many literati including Song Lingwen 宋令文 (fl. 650–683), Meng Shen 孟詵 (621–713), and Lu Zhaolin 盧照鄰 (ca. 634–ca. 689).* Emperor Huizong of the Song (r. 1100–1126) granted him the posthumous title Miaoying Zhenren 妙應真人 (Realized Man of Marvelous Response). Later generations have worshipped him as Yaowang 藥王 (King of Medicine).

Sun Simiao had an excellent command of the *Laozi*, *Zhuangzi*, and Daoist alchemy, was versed in Buddhist scriptures, pre-Qin philosophers, and techniques of *yin-yang* magical calculation of numbers and divination and was especially expert in medical theory. He authored many works, with the *Beiji qianjin yaofang* 備急千金要方 (Essential Priceless Prescriptions for All Urgent Ills) in 30 *juan* (652) and *Qianjin yifang* 千金翼方 (Priceless Supplementary Prescriptions) in 30 *juan* (682) as the most influential. Song-dynasty catalogs record other works attributed to him, such as *Laozi zhu* 老子注 (Commentary on *Laozi*) and *Zhuangzi zhu* 莊子注 (Commentary on *Zhuangzi*), but most were lost. The *Yunji qiqian* 雲笈七籤 (Cloudy Bookcase with Seven Labels) includes under his name the *Taiqing Danjing yaojue* 太清丹經要訣 (Essential Formulas of the Elixir Scripture of Great Clarity), and the *Daozang* also lists the *Cunshen lianqi ming* 存神煉氣銘 (Inscription on Concentrating the Spirit and Refining Breath) as his compositions. Other works which are attributed to him, such as *Yinhai jingwei* 銀海精微 (Essential Subtleties on the Silver Sea) and *Sun zhenren haishang fang* 孫真人海上方 (Prescriptions of the Sea by Realized Man Sun), were later creations. The *Quan Tangshi* collections preserve six of his poems and the *Quan Tang wen* eight essays. The poems are in part simple exhortations to good health like the following:

> Every day I eat three dates,
> I don't chew but let them dissolve.
> My five organs are of a fine brocade,
> Though what I wear is a filthy dirty robe.

日食三個棗，不嚼而自消。
錦繡為五臟，身著糞掃袍。

The poem stresses the importance of maintaining inner health in contrast material wealth in order to maintain a healthy, long life.

Sun Simiao's *Qianjin yaofang* and *Qianjin yifang* are broad and profound, epitomizing all medical works before the Tang dynasty. He combined traditional medical theory with Daoist thought and longevity techniques, and illumined and developed many significant ideas and formulas, which have greatly influenced the Chinese medical tradition. At the same time, he helped to shape Chinese practical prose, borrowing many allusions from early works such as the *Shijing* (Book of Poetry) and *Chuci* (Songs of the South).

Sun Simiao was the first to discuss Chinese medical ethics. He defined a great physician as follows (in the best four-six euphuistic style):

> Whenever a great physician treats diseases, he has to be mentally calm and his disposition firm. He should not give way to wishes and desires but has to develop first a marked attitude of compassion. He should commit himself firmly to the willingness to take the effort to save every living creature.
>
> If someone seeks help because of illness, or on the grounds of another difficulty, a great physician should not pay attention to status, wealth, or age; neither should he question whether the particular person is attractive or unattractive, whether he is an enemy or a friend, whether he is Chinese or a foreigner, or finally, whether he is uneducated or educated. He should meet everyone on equal ground; he should always act as if they were his closest family. He should not desire anything and should ignore all consequences; he is not to ponder over his own fortune or misfortune or cherish his own life. He should look upon those who have come to grief as if he himself had been struck, and he should sympathize with them deep in his heart. Neither dangerous mountain passes nor the time of day, and neither weather conditions nor hunger, thirst, nor fatigue, should keep him from attempting to save people with his whole heart, without the intention of chasing fame. Whoever acts in this manner is a great physician for the living. Whoever acts in this way can be a great physician of all humanity, while whoever acts contrary to this will be a great traitor with a bitter taste in his mouth.

> 凡大醫治病, 必當安神定志, 無欲無求, 先發大慈惻隱之心, 誓願普救含靈之苦. 有疾厄來求救者, 不得問其貴賤貧富, 長幼妍媸, 怨親善友, 華夷愚智,普同一等, 皆如至親之想. 亦不得瞻前顧後, 自慮吉凶, 護惜身命. 見彼苦惱, 若己有之, 深心淒愴. 勿避嶮巇, 晝夜, 寒暑, 飢渴, 疲勞, 一心赴救, 無作功夫形跡之心. 如此可為蒼生大醫. 反此則是含靈巨賊 (*Qianjin yaofang*; translation adapted from Paul U. Unschuld, *Medical Ethics in Imperial China*).

In addition, Sun Simiao promoted the Daoist concept of cherishing life, indicating that "human life is the most valued and *priceless*; to help a man with a prescription, there is no virtue surpassing this, so I titled my work with it" 人命至重, 有貴千金, 一方濟之, 德逾於此, 故以為名也. It is the concept of cherishing life that encouraged him to practice the duties of a physician, to research medical theory and prescriptions, and to include the word "priceless" in his two books.

Sun Simiao's contribution to Chinese pharmacology is outstanding. He emphasized the importance of gathering herbs at the right time and from a genuine source and of preparation by the physician himself. He examined traditional pharmaceutical works and described more than one thousand medicinal materials, including some chemical materials from Daoist alchemy. He collected from past and contemporary physicians numerous formulas, including those of minority groups and foreigners. In terms of medical treatment, he paid special attention to women and children.

Based on traditional medicine and Daoist theories and techniques, Sun Simiao discussed the importance and methods of nourishing life. He believed that the most important thing was the cultivation of moral sentiments, as a kindhearted person is peaceful in both mind and body. Next, he emphasized the significance of prevention and health care, "to cure the disease before it emerges" 治未病之病. Third, he indicated that besides longevity techniques of taking elixirs and drugs there were many other ways methods discussed in his *Qianjin yaofang,* including physical exercise, massage therapy, breathing exercises, a medicated diet, and sexual practices.

BIBLIOGRAPHY

Editions:
Li Jingrong 李景榮 et al., eds. *Beiji Qianjinyaofang jiaoshi* 備急千金要方校釋. Beijing: Renmin Weisheng, 1997.
Quan Tang shi, 12: 9779, 14: 10939.
Quan Tang wen, 158.1822–26.
Sun Simiao 孫思邈. *Beiji Qianjin yaofang* 備急千金要方. (1) 1065 ed., preserved in Uesugi Bunko 上杉文庫 in Yonezawa 米澤, Japan; **(2)** *Daozang* ed., No.1162; (3) Xiaoqiushan 小丘山房 (1543) ed; (4) Edo igaku 江戶醫學 (1848 reprint of North Song edition) ed.; (5) Beijing: Renmin Weisheng, 1955 (reprint of Edo Igaku ed.).
____. *Beiji qianjin yifang* 備急千金翼方. Beijing: Renmin Weisheng, 1955 (reprint of a Yuan ed).
____. *Taiqing danjing yaojue* 太清丹經要訣, in Zhang Junfang 張君房 (fl. 1001), ed., *Yunji qiqian* 雲笈七籤. Beijing: Zhonghua, 2003, pp. 1568–97.
____. *Cunshen lianqi ming* 存神煉氣銘, *Daozang* ed., No. 833.
Zhu Bangxian 朱邦賢 et al., eds. *Qianjin yifang jiaozhu* 千金翼方校注. Shanghai: Shanghai Guji, 1999.

Biographical Sources:
Jiu Tang shu, 191.5094–97.
Xin Tang shu, 196.5596–98.

Translations:
Kohn, Livia. *Sitting in Oblivion* (translation of *Cunshen lianqi ming*). Dunedin, Florida: Three Pines, 2010.
____. *Chinese Hearing Exercises* (translation of parts of *Qianjin yaofang*). Honolulu: University of Hawai'i Press, 2008.
Kovacs, Jürgen and Paul U. Unschuld. *Essential Subtleties on the Silver Sea: the Yin-hai jing-wei: A Chinese Classic on Ophthalmology*. Berkeley: University of California Press, 1998.
Sivin, Nathan. *Chinese Alchemy: Preliminary Studies* (translation of *Taiqing danjing yaojue*). Cambridge, Mass.: Harvard University Press, 1968.
Unschuld, Paul Ulrich. *Medical Ethics in Imperial China: A Study in Historical Anthropology*. Berkeley: University of California Press, 1979.
____. *Medicine in China: A History of Pharmaceutics*. Berkeley: University of California Press, 1986.

Wile, Douglas. *Art of the Bedchamber: Chinese Sexual Yoga Classics Including Women's Solo Meditation Texts* (translation of parts of *Qianjin yaofang*). Albany: State University of New York Press, 1992.

Studies:
Cao Jianbo 曹劍波. *Zuohu zhenlong: jishi jiuren de yaowang Sun Simiao* 坐虎針龍:濟世救人的藥王孫思邈. Beijing: Zongjiao Wenhua, 2009.
Cleary, Thomas F. *Taoist Meditation: Methods for Cultivating a Healthy Mind and Body*. Boston: Shambhala, 2000.
Engelhardt, Ute. "Qi for Life: Longevity in the Tang," in Livia Kohn, ed., *Taoist Meditation and Longevity Techniques*. Ann Arbor: Center for Chinese Studies, The University of Michigan, 1989, pp. 263–296.
Furth, Charlotte. *A Flourishing Yin: Gender in China's Medical History, 960–1665*. Berkeley: University of California Press, 1999.
Gan Zuwang 幹祖望. *Sun Simiao pingzhuan* 孫思邈評傳. Nanjing: Nanjing Daxue, 2011.
Hsu, H. Y. and C. S. Hsu. *Commonly Used Chinese Herbal Formulas Companion Handbook*. 2nd ed. Long Beach: Oriental Healing Arts Institute, 1997.
Kohn, Livia. *The Taoist Experience*. New York: State University of New York Press, 1993.
____. *Chinese Healing Exercises: the Tradition of Daoyin* (see above).
____. *Sitting in Oblivion: the Heart of Daoist Meditation* (see above).
Lei Zishen 雷自申, Zhao Shilin 趙石麟, Zhang Wen 張文 et al. *Sun Simiao Qianjinfang yanjiu* 孫思邈千金方研究. Xian: Shanxi Kexue Jishu, 1995.
Miyashita Saburō 篠原孝市, ed. *Senkinhō kenkyū shiryōshu* 千金方研究資料集. Osaka: Oriento, 1989.
Qian Chaochen 錢超塵 and Wen Changlu 溫長路, eds. *Sun Simiao yanjiu jicheng* 孫思邈研究集成. Beijing: Zhongguo Guji, 2006.
Sass, Hans-Martin. "Emergency Management in Public Health Ethics: Triage, Epidemics, Biomedical Terror and Warfare," *Eubios Journal of Asian and International Bioethics* 15 (September 2005), 161–67.
Sivin, Nathan. *Chinese Alchemy: Preliminary Studies*. Cambridge, Mass.: Harvard University Press, 1968.
Unschuld, Paul Ulrich. *Medical Ethics in Imperial China: A Study in Historical Anthropology* (see above).
____. *Medicine in China: A History of Pharmaceutics* (see above).
____. *Medicine in China: A History of Ideas*. Berkeley: University of California Press, 1985.
____. *Medicine in China: Historical Artifacts and Images*. Munich: Prestel, 2000.
Watanabe Kozo 渡邊幸三. "Son Shibaku Senkin yōhō shokuchihen no bunkengaku no kenkyū" 孫思邈千金要方食治篇の文獻學的研究, *Nihon Tōyō igaku kaishi* 日本東洋醫學會誌 5-3 (1955): 21–34.
Yang Zhongwu 楊忠武, ed. *Zhongguo Sun Simiao zhongyiyao wenhua tansuo yu shijian* 中國孫思邈中醫藥文化探索與實踐. Xi'an: Sanqin, 2012.
Zhang Jingwei 張經緯. *Zhongyixue sixiangshi* 中醫學思想史. Changsha: Hunan Jiaoyu, 2006.

Jinhua Jia and Zhaojie Bai

Wang Bo 王勃 (*zi*, Zi'an 子安, 650–676) was a master of Six-Dynasty-style *pianwen* 駢文 prose and an important early reformer of Qi-Liang-style 齊梁體 court poetry. Though there is little evidence of close association between him, Luo Binwang 駱賓王 (ca. 640–684),* Lu Zhaolin 盧照鄰 (ca. 634–ca. 689),* and Yang Jiong 楊炯 (650–694),* they were all included in the literary grouping *Chu Tang sijie* 初唐四傑 (Four Eminences of the Early Tang), because they (especially Wang and Luo) have been traditionally considered among the best *pianwen* prose writers of the 660s through 680s.

The Six-Dynasties-style *pianwen* written by the Four Eminences used parallelism between lines and couplets, end rhyme, and numerous historical allusions; the style was applied to all forms of prose. In the late seventh century, *pianwen* prose had not yet been limited to the writing of government documents and civil-service examination essays. The Four Eminences were perhaps the last generation of scholars to successfully use the style in purely literary endeavors. Wang Bo's best-known prose pieces, for example, are prefaces to poems. Though their prose styles were similar, each of these four men had a different approach to the reform of court poetry, that style best exemplified in the works of their predecessor, Shangguan Yi 上官儀 (ca. 607–ca. 665).* They brought personal feelings into the court-style verse, experimented with stylistic changes, and used new (or revived old) themes such as description of frontier garrisons and poems of farewell. Nonetheless, their writings were still within the accepted context of court poetry and contrast sharply with those of the late seventh-century poet Chen Zi'ang 陳子昂 (659–ca. 699),* who broadened the scope of poetry by dropping the court style altogether. The Four Eminences anticipated the gradual change in themes and style made by the late seventh-century court poets Song Zhiwen 宋之問 (656–ca. 712),* Shen Quanqi 沈佺期 (656–716)* and Du Shenyan 杜審言 (ca. 645–708).* The formalization of these changes became the style since known as "regulated verse" (*lüshi* 律詩), a style most closely associated with the great eighth-century poets.

Wang Bo was probably born in Longmen 龍門 (modern Hejin 河津, Shanxi) into a family originally from Qi 祁 County near Taiyuan. His grandfather was the noted Confucian scholar Wang Tong 王通 (584–617) and his granduncle the poet Wang Ji 王績 (584–644).* His biographers describe him as a child prodigy who, at the age of ten or eleven, wrote a critique of a *Han shu* commentary and was presented to the emperor along with Yang Jiong and several other talented sons of officials. Shortly afterwards, Wang was attached to the household of the even younger Tang prince, Li Xian 李賢 (655–686) as a Reader-in-waiting.

While with the boy prince, Wang also studied medicine with Cao Yuan 曹元 and began to write prose pieces that would attract the attention of elder literati such as the Grand Councilor, Liu Xiangdao 劉祥道 (596–666), to whom he wrote a letter. Some biographers claim that he wrote his best-known piece, "Tengwang Ge xu" 滕王閣序 (A Preface to the Poem "Pavilion of Prince Teng"), at this time, though others say it was written a decade later. The poem itself reads:

The Prince of Teng's high pavilion overlooks the river isles;
Tinkling jade-pendants, jingling harness bells have ceased, dancing and singing stopped.
Dawn clouds from the southern banks fly across painted roofbeams,
Evening rains from the western hills roll up the beaded curtains.
Idle clouds, reflected in deep pools, stretch far day after day.
But things change, the stars move–how many autumns have passed?
Where is that Prince of the pavilion now?
Beyond its railings, the Long River alone flows on and on.

滕王高閣臨江渚，珮玉鳴鸞罷歌舞。
畫棟朝飛南浦雲，珠簾暮捲西山雨。
閒雲潭影日悠悠，物換星移幾度秋。
閣中帝子今何在，檻外長江空自流。

Wang Bo

Wang addresses here the passage of time and its ravages on human ventures. The poet depicts the majesty of the pavilion in lines 1, 3, and 4 (the evening rains, though far off, can be seen from the pavilion). In the second line the verb *ba* 罷 (to cease, stop) refers to both the bells on the carriage horses that would bring guests and the girls with their tinkling pendants who would dance and sing for the Prince. In line 3 the verbs *fei* 飛 and *juan* 捲 reanimate the poem: the ceiling of the pavilion is so high it seems the clouds race across the roofbeams; the power of the evening rains seems to roll up the curtains. In the second half of the poem the emphasis is on time. While the clouds and the river remain, the Prince and his retinue are gone.

In 666, Emperor Gaozong announced a special examination, the *Yousu ke* 幽素科 (Examination for the Deep Feeling and Pure-minded). Wang was invited to take part and by passing it officially entered the civil service. In 667 or 668, Wang's appointment in the prince's household was terminated because he had written a composition lampooning cockfighting, a sport enjoyed by the prince and his brothers.

Unable to obtain another post, Wang Bo took himself to Sichuan in 669. During the next three years he traveled widely in that region, writing prose and poetic descriptions of his experiences and observations. He also visited Lu Zhaolin and the two "Eminences" exchanged poems. By 672, Wang Bo had returned to Chang'an and sought a post in an area known for its medicinal herbs, Guozhou 虢州 (near modern Lingbao County 靈寶縣, Henan). In 674, he murdered a slave whom he had first attempted to harbor. Wang was sentenced to death, then released following a general amnesty in late 674. The next year he set out to join his father in Jiaozhi 交阯 (modern Vietnam near Hanoi). The elder Wang had been exiled there as a magistrate following his son's arrest. Wang wrote many descriptions of his travels to Vietnam, including one in which he mentions leaving Canton in December 675, presumably to go by boat to Jiaozhi. Wang's biographers say he drowned during his passage to Vietnam. However, Yang Jiong, in a preface to Wang's works, says that Wang died about eight months later in 675 at the age of twenty-seven and makes no mention of drowning.

Although his *pianwen* prose is nearly like that of the other three "Eminences," Wang Bo attempted to avoid using an overabundance of allusive expressions in developing a lively, extemporaneous style. In his poetry, he was famous as a master of the parallel couplet, which critics say seemed less contrived than those written by his contemporaries. It was then usual in court-style poetry to express a moral or a summary in the last line, but Wang eschewed the practice, leaving the last line open-ended and demanding that the reader find their own conclusion, as in the following poem "Jiangting yeyue songbie, Ershou dier" 江亭夜月送別二首第二 (Parting by Moonlight at a River Pavilion, The Second of Two Poems):

> A swirling mist shrouds the emerald stairs,
> A flying moon heads toward the southern horizon.
> In silence the door of the pavilion where we parted closes—
> Mountains and rivers, this night, turn cold.

亂煙籠碧砌，飛月向南端。
寂寂離亭掩，江山此夜寒。

Once again the poet is at a pavilion. In the aftermath of parting from a friend the night turns dark and cold. Although the poet is inside the pavilion (lines 1 and 3), he looks out to see the last light in the sky—the moon—racing towards setting. The final line ties the poet to his departed friend: while Wang Bo's loneliness causes him to perceive a special ("*this* night") coldness in the mountains and rivers his departed friend is actually experiencing the cold night landscape.

As in the poems seem above, most of Wang Bo's thematic innovations were made while away from court and the influence of court-style poetry. The poems he wrote in Sichuan or during travels to other parts of the country deal with thoughts of exile and include descriptions of a less-than-benign natural world, subjects foreign to the "court" tradition. At court, however, Wang Bo and the other three Eminences wrote the sort of court poetry considered most characteristic of the seventh century. Wang's tentative steps toward another kind of verse were little appreciated by later generations who had access to works of the great eighth-century poets. Only Du Fu 杜甫 (712–770)* admired Wang Bo, but he, ironically, appreciated Wang for his genius as a court poet.

The original edition of Wang Bo's anthology is lost, though most of what it contained appears to be extant today; it appeared shortly after his death and included Yang Jiong's preface. Several complete texts were reported to have existed between the eighth and thirteenth centuries, but none of these is extant. An edition of his poetry and *fu*, published in 1007, seems to have survived until the sixteenth century and served as the basis of a reprinted edition in 1552 (original copies still extant). Zhang Xie 張燮 (1574–1640) gathered many pieces of Wang's prose writing from the *Wenyuan yinghua* 文苑英華 and, using the 1552 edition of poetry and *fu*, edited a relatively complete collection of Wang's writings in 1640.

In 1781, Xiang Jiada 項家達 (*jinshi* 1771) filled in some lacunae in the prose sections of Zhang's edition and published a more complete anthology of Wang's prose together with prose writings of the other Eminences in a work entitled *Chu Tang sijie ji* 初唐四傑集.

BIBLIOGRAPHY

Editions:

Chen Dongbiao 湛東飈, ed. Wang Bo ji 王勃集. Changsha: Yuelu Shushe, 2001.

He Lintian 何林天, ed. and comm. *Chongding xinjiao Wang Zi'an ji* 重訂新校王子安集. Taiyuan: Shanxi Renmin, 1990.

Luan Guiming 欒貴明 et al., eds. *Quan Tang shi suoyin: Wang Bo juan* 全唐詩索引: 王勃卷. Beijing: Zhonghua, 1992.

Quan Tang shi, 2: 671–86, 13: 10299, 14: 10599–601, 10938.

Shiomi Kunihiko 塩見邦彦. *Ō Botsu shi ichiji sakuin* 王勃詩一字索引. Nagoya: Konron, 1986.

Wang Bo. *Shōsōinbon Ō Botsu shi jo yakuchū* 正倉本王勃詩序訳注.Tokyo: Kanrin, 2014.

___. *Tang Wang Zi'an ji zhu* 唐王子安集注 (title also listed as *Wang Bo quanji jianzhu* 王勃全集箋注). Wu xian, 1883. Text annotated by Jiang Qingyi 蔣清翊 (late 19th c.); most complete, and annotated, edition.

___. *Tō shohon Ō Botsu shu* 唐抄本王勃集. Tokyo: Nigensha 二玄社, 1970.

___. *Wang Zi'an ji* 王子安集 (1640). *SBCK*. Edition compiled by Zhang Xie 張燮; no annotations, more readily available than Jiang Qingyi's edition.

___. *Wang Zi'an yiwen* 王子安佚文, in *Yongfeng xiangren zazhu xubian* 永豐鄉人雜著續編, n.p., 1918. Reprinted in *Luo Xuetang xiansheng quanji chubian* 羅雪堂先生全集初編, Taibei: Wenhua, 1968. Largest collection of writings not found in other editions; compiled by Luo Zhenyu 羅振玉.

Wang Guoan 王國安 and Wang Youmin 王幼敏, eds. *Chu Tang Sijie yu Chen Zi'ang shiwen xuanzhu* 初唐四傑與陳子昂詩文選註. Shanghai: Shanghai Guji, 1995.

Annotations:
Wang Bo. *Tang Wang Zi'an ji zhu* 唐王子安集注 (title also listed as *Wang Bo quanji jianzhu* 王勃全集箋注). Shanghai: Guji, 2002. Text annotated by Jiang Qingyi 蔣清翊 (late 19th c.).

Biographical Sources:
Fu, *Tang caizi*, 1:23–34, 5:2–5.
Jiu Tang shu, 190C.5004–06.
Xin Tang shu, 201.5739–41.

Translations:
Jade Mountain, p. 152.
Chan, Tim Wa Keung. "Dedication and Identification in Wang Bo's Compositions on the Gallery of Prince Teng," *MS* 50 (2002): 215–55.
Fuller, Michael A. *An Introduction to Chinese Poetry: From the* Canon of Poetry *to the Lyrics of the Song Dynasty*. Cambridge: Harvard University Press, 2018, pp. 180–81.
Mair, Victor H. *Mei Cherng's "Seven Stimuli" and Wang Bor's "Pavilion of King Terng:" Chinese Poems for Princes*. Lewiston: Edwin Mellen, 1988. *Studies in Asian Thought and Religion*, 11.
Margoulies, *Anthologie*, pp. 372.
Minford and Lau, p. 690.
Owen, *Early T'ang*, pp. 123–37.
Owen, *Late Tang,* pp. 192–93.
Strassberg, Richard E. *Inscribed Landscapes: Travel Writing from Imperial China*. Berkeley: University of California Press, 1994, pp. 105–10.

Studies:
Chan, Tim Wa Keung. "Beyond Border and Boudoir: The Frontier in the Poetry of the Four Elites of Early Tang." *Reading Medieval Chinese Poetry: Text, Context and Culture*. Paul W. Kroll, ed. Leiden: Brill, 2015, pp. 130–68.
___. "Dedication and Identification in Wang Bo's Compositions on the Gallery of Prince Teng," *MS* 50 (2002): 215–55.
___. "In Search of Jade: Studies of Early Tang Poetry." Unpublished Ph.D. dissertation, University of Colorado at Boulder, 1999.
___. "Restoration of a Poetry Anthology by Wang Bo," *JAOS* 124 (2004): 493–515.
Furukawa, Sueyoshi 古川末喜. "Sho-Tō yonketsu no bungaku shisō" 初唐四傑の文學思想. *Chūgoku bungaku ronshū*, 8 (1979): 1–27.
Liu Kaiyang 劉開揚. "Lun Chutang sijie jiqi shi" 論初唐四傑及其詩, in *Tangshi lunwen ji* 唐詩論文集. Beijing: Zhonghua, 1961, pp. 1–28.
Liu Ruiqing 李瑞卿. "Wang Bo Yixue ji qi shixue sixiang" 王勃易學及其詩學思想 *Wenxue yichan* 2010.6: 65–74.
Lo Xiangfa 駱祥發. *Chu T'ang sijie yanjiu* 初唐四傑研究. Beijing: Dongfang, 1993.
Nien Wenyu 聶文郁. *Wang Bo shijie* 王勃詩解. Xining: Qinghai Renmin, 1980.
Owen, "Wang Po: A New Decorum," in *Early T'ang*, pp. 123–37.
Shen Huiyue 沈惠樂 and Qian Huikang 錢惠康 ed. *Chu Tang sijie he Chen Zi'ang* 初唐四傑和陳子昂. Shanghai: Shanghai Guji, 1987.

Suzuki Torao 鈴木虎雄. "Ō Botsu nempu" 王勃年譜, *Tōhō gakuhō*, 14.3 (1944): 1–14.
Tian Zongyao 田宗堯. "Wang Po nien-p'u" 王勃年譜, in *Ta-lu tsa chih*, 30.12 (June 1965): 379–389.
Warner, Ding Xiang. "'A Splendid Patrimony': Wang Bo and the Development of a New Poetic Decorum in Early Tang China," *TP* 98 (2012): 113–44.
___. "An Offering to the Prince: Wang Bo's Apology for Poetry," in Paul W. Kroll, ed. *Reading Medieval Chinese Poetry: Text, Context, Culture*. Leiden: Brill, 2015, pp. 90–129.
Williams, Nicholas Morrow. "The Pity of Spring: A Southern Topos Reimagined by Wang Bo and Li Bai," in Williams and Wang Ping, eds. *Southern Identity and Southern Estrangement in Medieval Chinese Poetry*. Hong Kong: Hong Kong University, 2915, pp. 137–63.
Wu Ke 吳可. "Cong qihe dao xingqi: shilun Wang Bo wuyan jueju zhi xinbian" 從綺合到興寄：試論王勃五言絕句之新變. *Mingzuo xinchang* 35 (2012): 4–6.
Wu Zhenhua 吳振華. "Lun Wang Bo de shixu" 論王勃的詩序, *Zhongguo wenxue yanjiu*, 2010:2: 48–53.
Zhan, *Daojiao*, pp. 222–25.
Zhang Zhilie 張志烈. *Chu Tang sijie nianpu* 初唐四傑年譜. Chengdu: Ba Shu Shushe, 1992.
___. "Wang Bo za kao" 王勃雜考. *Sichuan Daxue xuebao* 2 (1983): 70–78.

C. Bradford Langley and William H. Nienhauser, Jr.

Wang Changling 王昌齡 (*zi*, Shaobo 少伯, ca. 690–ca. 756), one of the pre-eminent literary figures of the first half of the eighth century, is best known today for his mastery of seven-syllable *jueju* 絕句 (quatrains). His themes varied from parting to recounting the hardships of the soldier on the frontier to laments of the lonely soldier's wife or neglected palace lady. His newly rediscovered critical works, moreover, reveal him to be unique in Chinese literary history as a poet able to explain both the aesthetics and the techniques of poetry in relatively simple language and with an abundance of useful examples.

Born in Chang'an around 690, Wang passed the *jinshi* (727) and Erudite Literatus (ca. 734) examinations late in life but never held an important post. He served in the Secretariat under Zhang Jiuling 張九齡 (678–740)* and as a county official in Sishui 汜水 (near modern Xingyang 滎陽 in Henan). He seems to have traveled extensively on the northern and western frontiers of the Tang from 723 to 725. After a brief banishment to Guangdong in 738 following the fall of Zhang Jiuling, Wang returned to serve in the administration of Jiangning 江寧 County (modern Nanjing). He thus acquired his subsequent sobriquet of "Wang Jiangning." He was killed early on during the An Lushan Rebellion. His friends include the best-known poets of the day as well as many Buddhist and Daoist priests. He is credited with an anthology in five *juan* (lost), with a work on *yuefu* 樂府 poetry entitled the *Yuefu gujin tijie* 樂府古今題解 in three *juan* (also lost), and with a work of criticism in one *juan* entitled the *Shige* 詩格 (Poetic Form).

The peak of Wang's fame as a poet came in the last two decades of his life and is marked by his inclusion in two anthologies: the mid-eighth century *Guoxiu ji* 國秀集 and *Heyue yingling ji* 河嶽英靈集. In the latter, the editor Yin Fan 殷璠 cites more of his poems than even Wang Wei 王維 (692–761),* Li Bo 李白 (701–762),* or Meng Haoran 孟浩然 (689–740).* He praises him for continuing the "forceful style" (*fenggu* 風骨) of Cao Zhi 曹植 (192–232), Liu Zhen 劉楨 (d. 217), Lu Ji 陸機 (261–303), and Xie Lingyun 謝靈運 (385–433), and selects for praise examples of lines that startle the ear and surprise the eye. Among his best-known poems are "Furong Lou song Xinqian" 芙蓉樓送辛漸 (Farewell to Xinqian at Hibiscus Tower) and "Changxin qiu ci" 長信秋詞 (Autumn in the Palace of Eternal Faith [five poems]). Both are seven-syllable *jueju*. The first of "Autumn in the Palace of Eternal Faith," written on the theme of Lady Ban Jieyu 班婕妤, the forsaken Consort of the Emperor Cheng of Han (r. 33–7 BC), reads:

> Autumn leaves of the paulownia turn yellow by the golden well;
> beaded curtains are not rolled up, with night comes the frost.
> Her censer and jade pillow have lost their color—
> as she lies listening to water drip in the Southern Palace.

> 金井梧桐秋葉黃，珠簾不卷夜來霜。
> 熏籠玉枕無顏色，臥聽南宮清漏長。

The lines contrast the mood of Lady Ban between when she was the emperor's favorite and after she lost favor. In the former, all was yellow and gold. But now she lies in a darkened chamber where even the colors of her censer and pillow cannot be seen in the dim light (or perhaps are not perceived in her dark mood). The ennui of her new life is paralleled by the steady dripping of the clepsydra.

Wang is also known for two ancient-style poems in five-syllable meter entitled "Saishang qu" 塞上曲 (Above the Pass) and "Saixia qu" 塞下曲 (Below the Pass), probably written in 724 when Wang was traveling westward in what is now modern Gansu (between Tang and Tibetan territory). Here is "Above the Pass":

> Cicadas hum in deserted mulberry groves,
> in the eighth month, on the road through the Xiao Pass.
> Out of the pass we go, in we come again;
> everywhere just the reedy yellow grasses.
> Since long ago those bravos from You and Bing
> have all grown old together with the sand and dust.
> Don't imitate those young wandering knights
> or boast that your mighty steed is best.

> 蟬鳴空桑林，八月蕭關道。
> 出塞入塞寒，處處黃蘆草。
> 從來幽並客，皆共沙塵老。
> 不學遊俠兒，矜誇紫騮好。

Although Wang may have been traveling near the border, this poem is not merely a poetic description of his trip. While the Xiao Pass seems to be where Wang was—about 150 miles northwest of Chang'an near modern Guyuan 固原 in Ningxia—the fifth line literally reads "since long ago those bravos in Youzhou and Bingzhou," both prefectures on the northeastern frontier of the Tang that were noted for producing courageous knight-errants. The mulberry groves, where the women worked and thus a symbol of social normality, are empty, suggesting the local populace has fled before the threat of foreign incursions. The only company the soldiers have are the yellow grasses and the sand and dust. In the final couplet the poem warns young men not to romanticize military life (the "mighty steed" here was actually the stallion Ziliu 紫騮 who was praised in Han *yuefu*).

"Below the Pass," written later that year, reads:

> I water my horse and cross the autumn river;
> The water's cold, wind cuts like a knife.
> Across the level sands, the sun has not yet sunk;
> Dimly in the distance I make out Lin-tao.
> Of all who fought along the Great Wall in other days,
> Everyone says their spirits were high.
> There's yellow dust enough for both past and present,
> And white bones lying scattered in the grass.

飲馬渡秋水，水寒風似刀。
平沙日未沒，黯黯見臨洮。
昔日長城戰，咸言意氣高。
黃塵足今古，白骨亂蓬蒿。

Here Wang Changling—or his imagination—has reached Lintao (now a county, then a fortification in Gansu on what was then the Tibetan border). Once again grass and dust dominate the landscape: line 7 reads literally "the yellow dust has filled both past and present." This poem contains a warning not unlike that of the previous one, ending with a vision of the bones of those filled with high spirits who kept the vigil, but also a lament for the all the soldiers who have lost their lives on the frontier.

Wang's major critical work, the *Shige*, is innovative in its style, philosophy, and attention to technique. Its informal organization, semi-vernacular language, and abundance of examples set it apart from the highly abstruse literary criticism of the preceding Six Dynasties, setting the stage for Song *shihua* 詩話. His work is more concerned with the psychology of composition and with the poem as a fusion of the author's mind with the world than it is with questions of defining genres or ranking poets. Wang prefers the short poem which crystallizes a mood through the poet's observation of nature and which acts as a catalyst for the reader's continuing pleasure. Wang is innovative in adopting a critical vocabulary with borrowings from Buddhism. He uses the metaphor of the mind as a mirror, traces the history of "northern" and "southern" schools of poetry, and defines poetic worlds (*jing* 景). For Wang, a poem is a living creature, with a "head," "belly," and "tail," each part of which requires a certain kind of couplet and use of language so that the whole will work together. In reviewing examples of fine couplets and fine lines he seems to be aware of the central importance of verbs in creating the "world" of a poem. The *Shige*, long-lost in China, has fortunately been preserved by quotation in the *Bunkyō hifuron* 文鏡秘府論 of the Japanese monk Kūkai.

After having been lost in the late T'ang, Wang's complete works have never been collected in full. However, a relatively complete edition of 190 poems has been collated and annotated by Li Guosheng. His prose works and criticism must be sought elsewhere. The *Quan Tang wen* preserves six prose pieces, while the *Wenyuan yinghua* 文苑英華 contains an examination *fu* 賦.

BIBLIOGRAPHY

Editions:

Luan Guiming 欒貴明, ed. *Quan Tangshi suoyin: Wang Changling juan* 全唐詩索引：王昌齡卷. Beijing: Zhonghua, 1997.

Quan Tang shi, 2: 1420–54, 13: 9918–19, 10244–45, 10316, 11084–85, 14: 10619.

Quan Tang wen, 331.3778–81.

Yoshimura, Hiromichi 芳村弘道, ed. *Ō Shorei shi sakuin* 王昌齡詩索引. Kyoto: Hoyu, 1983.

Annotations:

Huang Ming 黃明, ed. and comm. *Wang Changling shi ji* 王昌齡詩集. Nanchang: Jiangxi Renmin, 1981. Rpt. Beijing: Bohuazhou Wenyi, 1993.

Li Guosheng 李國勝, ed. *Wang Changling shi jiaozhu* 王昌齡詩校注. Taibei: Wenshizhe, 1973.

Li Yunyi 李雲逸, ed. and comm. *Wang Changling shizhu* 王昌齡詩注. Shanghai: Shanghai Guji, 1984.

Biographical Sources:

Fu, *Tang caizi*, 1:250–58, 5:50–51.

Jiu Tang shu, 190C.5050.

Xin Tang shu, 203.5789.

Translations:

Articulated Ladies, pp. 290–91.

Bodman, "Poetics and Prosody" (see below), *passim*.

Bynner, *Jade Mountain*, pp. 147–49.

Demiéville, *Anthologie*, pp. 218–19.

Gundert, *Lyrik*, p. 85.

Margoulies, *Anthologie*, pp. 230, 343, 349, 373.

Minford and Lau, pp. 829–30.

New Directions, p. 95.

Owen, *Middle Ages*, pp. 111–15, 123–25.

Owen, *Late Tang*, pp. 197–98,

Shields, Anna. *Crafting a Collection, The Cultural Contexts and Poetic Practice of the Huajian ji* 花間集 *(Collection from Among the Flowers)*. Cambridge: Harvard University Asia Center, 2006, pp. 49–40.

Sunflower, p. 10.

Watson, *Lyricism*, p. 116.

White Pony, p. 224.

Studies:

Bi Shikui 畢士奎. *Wang Changling shige yu shixue yanjiu* 王昌齡詩格與詩學研究. Nanchang: Jiangxi Renmin, 2008.

Bodman, Richard W. "Poetics and Prosody in Early Mediaeval China." Unpublished Ph.D. dissertation, Cornell University, 1978. See especially Chapter I, "The Poetics of Wang Ch'ang-ling" pp. 22–98 and translations from his criticism, pp. 363–403.

Chen Bizheng 陳必正. *Wang Changling shilun yanjiu* 王昌齡詩論研究. Taibei: Huamulan Wenhua, 2009.

Fu Xuancong 傅璇琮. "Wang Changling shiji kao lue" 王昌齡事跡考略, in *Tangdai shiren congkao* 唐代詩人叢考. Beijing: Zhonghua, 1980, pp. 103–141. A critical attempt to reconstruct Wang's biography.

Hu Wentao 胡問濤. "Lun Wang Changling de biansaishi" 論王昌齡的邊塞詩. *Sichuan Shiyuan xuebao* 1 (1991): 75–81.

___. *Wang Changling ji biannian jiaozhu* 王昌齡集編年校注. Chengdu: Ba Shu Shushe, 2000.

Huang Yiyuan 黃益元. "Wang Changling shengping shiji bianzheng" 王昌齡生平事跡辯證. *Wenxue yichan* 2 (1992): 31–34.

Lee, Joseph J. *Wang Ch'ang-ling*. Boston: Twayne, 1982.

Li Houpei 李厚培. "Wang Changling liangci chusai luxian kao" 王昌齡兩次出塞路線考. *Qinghai shehui kexue* 5 (1992): 75–80.

Li Zhenhua 李珍華. *Wang Changling yanjiu* 王昌齡研究. Nanchang: Taibo Wenyi, 1994.

___ and Fu Xuancong 傅璇琮. "Tan Wang Changling de 'shige'" 談王昌齡的詩格. *Wenxue yichan* 6 (1988): 85–97.

Liu Kaiyang 劉開揚. "Lun Wang Changling de shige chuangzuo" 論王昌齡的詩格創作, in his *Tang shi lunwenji* 唐詩論文集, Hong Kong: Zhongguo Yuwenxueshe, 1963, pp. 38–51. Uses Wang's own critical terms to discuss his poetic achievements.

Okada Mitsuhiro 岡田充博. "Ō Shorei kenkyū bunken mokuroku ko" 王昌齡研究文獻目錄稿. *Nagoya Daigaku Chūgoku gogaku bungaku ronshū* 6 (1993): 39–53.

Owen, Stephen. *The Great Age of Chinese Poetry: The High Tang*. New Haven: Yale University Press, 1981, pp. 91–108.

Suzuki Shuji 鈴木修次. *Tōdai shijin ron* 唐代詩人論. 2v. Tokyo: Otori, 1973, pp. 139–82.

Tan Youxue 譚優學. *Wang Changling xingnian kao* 王昌齡行年考. Beijing: Zhonghua, 1963.

Varsano, Paula. "Whose Voice Is it Anyway? A Rereading of Wang Changling's 'Autumn in the Palace of Everlasting Faith: Five Poems," *Journal of Chinese Literature and Culture*, 3.1 (April 2016): 1–25.

Wang Jingfen 王競芬. "Wang Changling shengping xingyi ji yishi xinian kao" 王昌齡生平行誼及遺詩繫年考. *Si yu yan* 25.1 (1987): 63–84.

Wang Yunxi 王運熙. " Wang Changling de shige lilun" 王昌齡的詩格理論. *Fudan xuebao* 5 (1989): 22–29.

Xie Chufa 謝楚發. "Wang Changling qijue meili chutan" 王昌齡七絕魅力初探. *Jianghan luntan* 56 (1985): 50–55.

Xu Fangming 许方铭. *Wang Changling* 王昌齡. Beijing: Wuzhou Chuanbo 五洲传播, 2008.

Yoshikawa, Kojiro 吉川幸次郎. "Ō Shorei shi" 王昌齡詩, in *Yoshikawa Kojiro zenshū*, v. 11, Tokyo: Chikuma, 1968–1970, pp. 189–221. Written in 1948, it discusses several of Wang's most famous seven-syllable *jueju*.

Zeng Yalan 曾亞蘭, ed. *Wang Changling ji, Gao Shi ji, Cen Shen ji* 王昌齡集, 高市集, 岑參集. Changsha: Yuelu, 2000.

Richard Bodman and Masha Kobzeva

Wang *Fanzhi* 王梵志 (Wang the Zealot) is the name associated with a sizable corpus of Tang vernacular poetry, the vast majority of which exists only in manuscript copies found at Dunhuang in the early part of this century. *Fanzhi* is not a given name, but a title, a Chinese equivalent of Sanskrit *brahmacarin,* which designates a lay Buddhist zealot (thus Paul Demiéville's translation "Wang le Zélateur)."

A paragraph in the *Taiping guangji* 太平廣記 records that Wang *Fanzhi* was born from a tumescence on a crabapple tree in the garden of one Wang Dezu 王德祖, a Sui dynasty resident of Henan. The myth of magical birth is probably a folk etymology to explain *Fanzhi* and testifies to the popularity of the poems in the latter half of the Tang. The language of the poems is the

Wang *Fanzhi*

vernacular of the eighth century. The earnest references to Wang *Fanzhi* also suggest that the poems began to be popular in Buddhist educational circles in this period. The *Lidai fabao ji* 歷代法寶記, a history of the Chan sect completed about 780, quotes a poem by Wang *Fanzhi* and explains that such verses were often used for instructional purposes in Buddhist institutions. The late ninth-century *Yunxi youyi* 雲谿友議 has a similar remark and quotes nineteen poems. This practice is perhaps confirmed by the fact that several Dunhuang manuscripts containing "Wang *Fanzhi* poems" are obviously schoolboy calligraphy exercises (notably P2842). Finally, the *Shishi* 詩式 manuscripts divide into two distinct collections of verse, each attributed to Wang *Fanzhi*, yet different in form, content, and tone. A single *juan* collection of ninety-two pentasyllabic *jueju* was obviously the most common of the two, being represented by five complete manuscripts (P2718, P3558, P3656, P3716, and S3393) and six fragments. The quatrains in this "Ninety-two Poem Collection" are all didactic and gnomic, emphasizing such basic moral virtues as filial piety, social manners, fiscal responsibility, and abstinence from alcohol. A few of the later poems stress Buddhist piety. The first quatrain in this collection reads:

> Brothers should live in harmony,
> Cousins shouldn't mistreat each other.
> Put all valuables in a common chest,
> Don't hoard up possessions in your own room.

> 兄弟須和順，叔侄莫輕欺。
> 財物同箱櫃，房中莫蓄私。

And the last reads:

> Renounce evil deeds,
> Don't resist good ones.
> The wise who seek the Good Law
> will surely behold the *Tathagata*.

> 惡事總須棄，善事莫相違。
> 知意求妙法，必得見如來。

Such verses were probably composed by Buddhist monks to instruct the lay children in their schools and are of little intrinsic literary interest.

Quite otherwise is the much longer and varied collection in three *juan*. Although no single copy of the entire "Three *Juan* Collection" survives, most of its contents can be reconstructed from seven manuscripts (S778 and S5796—*juan* 1; P3211, S5441, and S5641—*juan* 2, and P2914 and P3833—*juan* 3). The poems are preceded by a preface, unfortunately undated and anonymous, which states that the collection contains "over three hundred poems." Together with the ninety-two quatrains in the single *juan* collection, this figure brings the total number of poems attributed to Wang *Fanzhi* to about four hundred. The poems in the "Three *Juan* Collection" are marked by melancholy meditations on the vanity of human life and on the impermanence and nonreality of worldly existence. There is an almost macabre fascination with death, evident from the first poem in the collection:

I watch from afar the people of the world
in villages and peaceful towns.
When a family has a death in the house,
the whole town comes to weep.
With open mouths they bewail the corpse,
not understanding that bodies go fast.
Actually we're ghosts of the long sleep,
come for a time to stand on the earth.
It's almost like babies' diapers
at once dry then wet in turn.
The first to die is buried deep,
the later ones are thrown in on top.

遙看世間人，村坊安社邑。
一家有死生，合村相就泣。
張口哭他屍，不知身去急。
本是長眠鬼，暫來地上立。

欲似養兒氈，廻乾且就濕。
前死深埋卻，後死續即入。

The poems in both collections are written without allusions in a vigorous, colloquial language that intensifies the immediacy and simplicity of the content.

Both Demiéville and Iriya Yoshitaka have suggested that Wang *Fanzhi*—"Wang the Zealot"—may never have existed as a historical person and that the poems now attributed to him were collected together by virtue of their common didactic origin and colloquial language. Both scholars see in this process a parallel to that which shaped the present Hanshan 寒山 collection (see Hanshan 寒山), which linguistic evidence has demonstrated comprises poems whose dates of composition span at least a century. In the case of Wang *Fanzhi* it seems probable that the "Ninety-two Poem Collection" arose in this way. The texts in the "Three *Juan* Collection," on the other hand, reveal a dynamic yet basically cohesive personality which suggests they are more likely to be the work of a single hand. The value of both collections for the history of Chinese poetry is considerable: they provide as close a glimpse as is likely to be obtained of Tang dynasty popular poetry, and thus constitute an important measure against which to judge the "orality" of traditionally transmitted Tang poetry. In the same vein, a detailed study of the colloquialisms in the Wang *Fanzhi* corpus will probably suggest that the normative language of Tang poetry contains more colloquial elements than has hitherto been suspected. Finally, these fragmentary Wang *Fanzhi* texts provide a vivid picture of the didactic use of poetry at lower, nonliterate and semiliterate levels of Tang society. This picture suggests that this ubiquity of poetry provided an important background for the creation of the enduring poetic masterpieces of the period.

BIBLIOGRAPHY

Editions:

Demiéville, Paul. *L'oeuvre de Wang le Zélateur (Wang Fan-tche). Poèmes populaires des T'ang, VIII–IX siècle.* Paris, 1982. The definitive work on Wang Fanzhi.

Quan Tang shi, 13: 10383–93, 14: 10605–07, 10953–79.

Wang Fanzhi shi jiaoji 王梵志詩校輯. Zhang Xihou 張錫厚, ed. Beijing: Zhonghua, 1983.

Annotations:

Wang Fanzhi shi jiaozhu 王梵志詩校注. Xiang Chu 項楚, ed. Shanghai: Shanghai Guji, 1991.

Zhao Heping 趙和平 and Deng Wenkuan 鄧文寬. "Dunhuang xieben Wang Fanzhi shi jiaozhu" 敦煌寫本王梵志詩校注, *Beijing Daxue xuebao (Zhexue Shehui kexue ban)* 1980.5: 64–81.

___. "Dunhuang xieben Wang Fanzhi shi jiaozhu (xu)" 敦煌寫本王梵志詩校注(續), *Beijing Daxue xuebao (Zhexue shehui kexue ban)* 1980.6: 32–37.

Translations:

Minford and Lau, pp. 977–78 (translated by C. H. Kwock and Vincent McHugh).

Tatsumi Masaaki 辰巳正明. *Ō Bonshi shishū chūshaku: tonkō shutsudo no bukkyōshi o yomu* 王梵志詩集注釈 : 敦煌出土の仏教詩を読む. Tokyo: Kasama, 2015.

Studies:

Demiéville, Paul. *Annuaire du Collége de France*, 1957, pp. 253–357; 1958, pp. 386–391; 1959, pp. 436–39. Short, work-in-progress notes on Demiéville's reading of the Wang Fanzhi corpus. Superseded by his 1982 book (see above, Translations), but still useful.

___. "Le Tch'an et la poésie chinoise," *Hermès* 7 (1970): 123–36.

Iriya Yoshitaka 入矢義高. "Ō Bonshi ni tsuite" 王梵志について, *Chūgoku bungakuhō* 3 (1955): 50–60; 4 (1956): 19–56.

Lu Yongfeng 陸永峰. "Wang Fanzhi shi, Hanshan shi bijiao yanjiu" 王梵志詩，寒山詩比較研究, *Sichuan Daxu xuebao (Zhexue Shehui Kexueban)*, 1999.1: 110–3.

Ma Jiandong 馬建東. "Wang Fanzhi de diceng shenghuo jingyan" 王梵志的底層生活經驗, *Dunhuang yanjiu* 敦煌研究, 2008.2: 97–101.

Miao Yu 苗昱. "Wang Fanzhi shi, Han Shan shi (fu Shide shi) yongyun bijiao yanjiu" 王梵志詩, 寒山詩(附拾得詩)用韻比較研究, *Yuyan yanjiu* 2004.4: 42–46

Wang Zhipeng 王志鵬. "Wang Fanzhi jiqi shige de xingzhi xianyi" 王梵志及其詩歌的性質獻疑, *Dunhuang yanjiu* 2011.5: 61–66.

Zhang Xihou 張錫厚. "Guanyu Donghuan xieben Wang Fanzhi shi zhengli de ruogan wenti" 關於敦煌寫本王梵志詩整理的若干問題, *Wenshi* 15 (September 1982), 185–202.

Zhu Fengyu 朱鳳玉. *Wang Fanzhi shi yanjiu* 王梵志詩研究. Taibei: Xuesheng, 1987.

Charles Hartman and Masha Kobzeva

Wang Ji 王績 (*zi*, Wugong 無功, *hao*, Donggaozi 東皋子, 585–644) was a native of Longmen 龍門 in Jiangzhou 絳州 (Shanxi). His brother Wang Tong 王通 (584–617) was a famous and well-respected scholar in the Sui dynasty. Another brother, Wang Ning 王凝, was appointed to work on the compilation of the Sui dynastic history but died before the work was completed.

Unlike his brothers, Wang Ji did not attain contemporary success. His life closely paralleled that of Tao Qian. He was well known for his eccentricity and his capacity for wine. He held several insignificant posts under the Sui before retiring to his farm during the chaos at the end of the dynasty. There he heard of a recluse named Zhongchang Ziguang 仲長子光 who lived alone and had supported himself by his own labor for thirty years. Wang Ji was greatly impressed by Zhongchang's way of life and moved his entire family closer to the hermit. However, Wang became an official again when he took a minor post in the early Tang period. Later he asked to be transferred to the Imperial Music Office because he discovered that the director there brewed a good wine. After the death of the director, Wang resigned from the post. There is no record that he ever took a government position again. This episode is similar to the story that Ruan Ji requested a military appointment because three hundred jugs of good wine were stored in the cellar of the headquarters. Likewise it recalls the story in which Tao Qian applied for a position because the government land there would provide crops for him to make wine. These resemblances suggest that historical motifs may have shaped the extant account of Wang's life.

Wang also composed several prose works, including "Wudou Xiansheng zhuan" 五斗先生傳 (The Biography of Mr. Five Dippers), an autobiographical sketch, modeled on Tao Qian's "Wuliu Xiansheng zhuan" 五柳先生傳 (The Biography of Mr. Five Willows). The title alludes to the fact that Wang could remain sober even after drinking five large dippers of wine. He also wrote his own obituary, as Tao Qian did. There, however, he revealed a bitterness and arrogance not found in the writings of the other Six Dynasty tippler-hermits:

> This man Wang Ji had father and mother but no friends. He called himself "Wugung" [No Merit]. People asked him the meaning [of this appellation], but he simply sat there with outstretched legs not caring to answer. [Because he believed] he had the Way, even though he had no achievements in his time.... He had great talents but occupied low positions. [What he pursued was] only to avoid denunciation. The Son of Heaven did not know him. The senior officials and ministers could not recognize him. In his forties and fifties, he was still insignificant. Thereupon, he resigned himself and returned, roaming about in his village with his "wine virtue."
>
> 王績者，有父母，無朋友，自為之字曰無功焉。人或問之，箕踞不對。蓋以有道於己，無功於時也。...才高位下，免責而已。天子不知，公卿不識。四十五十，而無聞焉。於是退歸，以酒德游於鄉里。

This attitude was perhaps one of the reasons why Wang did not enjoy as great a reputation as, for example, Tao Qian 陶潛 (365–427). Nevertheless, the naturalness and simplicity of his work, at a time when an over-decorative style was in vogue, lends it a historical importance. Opting for simplicity and directness in the fashion of Tao Qian whom, together with Ruan Ji 阮籍 (210–263), he admired greatly. The following four-line poem, "Ti jiudian bi" 題酒店壁 (Written on the Wall of a Wineshop), is typical of his style:

> Only last night the bottle was emptied,
> Immediately this morning a new jug was opened.
> After finishing dreaming in another dream,
> I, again, return to the wine shop.

> 昨夜瓶始盡，今朝甕即開。
> 夢中占夢罷，還向酒家來。

Although his eight-line poems do not always conform to the regulated-verse style, they anticipate this later poetic form.

BIBLIOGRAPHY

Editions:
Donggao xiasheng ji 東皋先生集. SBBY.
Donggaozi ji 東皋子集. SBCK.
Quan Tang shi, 1: 480–89, 13: 10038–39, 10379, 14: 10897–904, 10905–10.
Quan Tang wen, 131–32.1466–80.
Wang Wugong wenji 王無功文集. Han Lizhou 韓理洲, ed. 5 *juan*. Shanghai: Shanghai Guji, 1987.
Wang Wugong wenji, fu buyi 王無功文集, 附補遺. CSJC ed.

Annotations:
Wang Ji shiwen ji jiaozhu 王績詩文集校注. Jin Ronghua 金榮華, ed. Taibei: Xinwenfeng, 1998.
Wang Ji shi zhu 王績詩註. Wang Guoan 王國安, ed. Shanghai: Shanghai Guji, 1981.

Biographical Sources:
Fu, *Tang caizi*, 1:4–9, 5:1–2.
Jiu Tang shu, 192.5116–17.
Xin Tang shu, 196.5594–96.

Translations:
Ditter, Alexei Kamran, "Self-offered Epitaph, by Wang Ji (590? –644)," in *The Lives of Men and Women over Two Millennia, Recorded in Stone: Chinese Funerary Biographies*. Patricia Buckley Ebrey, Ping Yao and Cong Ellen Zhang. Seattle: University of Washington, 2019, pp. 47–52.
Margoulies, *Anthologie*, pp. 229, 391–92.
Owen (see Studies below).

Studies:
Jia Jinhua 賈晉華. "Wang Ji yu Wei Jin fengdu" 王績與魏晉風度, *Tang dai wenxue yanjiu* 唐代文學研究, 1990.
Kang Jinsheng 康金聲 and Xia Lianbao 夏連保 eds. *Wang Ji ji biannian jiaozhu* 王績集編年校注. Taiyuan: Shanxi Renmin, 1992.
Lang Ruiping 郎瑞萍. *Wang Ji kaolun* 王績考論. Beijing: Zhongguo Jingji, 2015.
Lin Xuejiao 林雪嬌. "Luelun Wang Ji shi zhong diangu" 略論王績詩中典故, *Qinzhou Xueyuan xuebao* 2015.12: 11–15.
Ono Jitsunosuke 大野實之助. "Ō Seki to sono shifū" 王績とその詩風, *Chūgoku koten kenkyū* 18 (1971): 64–92.
Owen, *Early T'ang*, pp. 60–71.
Takagi Masakazu 高木正一. "Ō Seki no denki to bungaku" 王績の伝記と文学, *Ritsumeikan bungaku* 124 (1955): 40–70.

Warner, Ding Xiang. "Mr. Five Dippers of Drunkenville: The Representation of Enlightenment in Wang Ji's Drinking Poems," *JAOS* 118 (1998): 347–55.

___. *A Wild Deer amid Soaring Phoenixes: The Opposition Poetics of Wang Ji*. Honolulu: University of Hawai'i Press, 2003.

Ye Qingbing 葉慶炳. "Wang Ji yanjiu" 王績研究, *Fujian Daxue renwen xuebao* (1970): 167–89.

You Xinli 游信利. "Wang Ji yinian lu" 王績疑年錄, *Zhonghua xueyuan* 8 (1971): 149–85.

Zhan, *Daojiao*, pp. 218–22.

Zhang Xihou 張錫厚. "Wang Ji de shiwen ji qi wenxue chengjiu" 王績的詩文及其文學成就. *Wenxue yichan* 1984.6: 116–26.

___. *Wang Ji yanjiu* 王績研究. Taibei: Xin Wenfeng Chuban Gongsi, 1995.

Zheng Chaolin 鄭朝琳. "Tao Yuanming he Wang Ji de yinyi zhi bie" 陶淵明和王績的隱逸之別, *Gudian wenxue zhishi* 2005.1.

Marie Chan and William H. Nienhauser, Jr.

Wang Jian 王建 (*zi*, Zhonghe 中和; also probably in error known as Zhongchu 仲初, ca. 766–ca. 830) gained some renown as a poet in the first three decades of the ninth century, primarily because of his composition of new *yuefu* verse and his close relationship with Zhang Ji 張籍 (ca. 766–829).* Although the Tang official histories did not afford him a biography, his more than five hundred extant poems, many addressed to prominent politicians, writers, and generals, allow the modern reader to gain an accurate picture of his life.

The *Tang caizi zhuan* 唐才子傳 entry on Wang is the earliest independent biographical source and the origin of a number of errors in depicting his life. That entry claims Wang Jian was a native of Yingchuan 潁川 (modern Xuchang 許昌 in Henan), but Yingchuan was most likely his ancestral home and Wang was probably born in Chang'an. That same source records Wang's success in the *jinshi* examinations in 775, but modern scholarship has shown that the Wang Jian involved was a namesake who later became Prefect of Guangzhou 廣州 (modern Guangzhou in Guangdong). Wang himself left Chang'an for Shandong 山東 in 783; he spent a number of years learning the Daoist arts, part of the time in the company of Zhang Ji. About 797 he joined the staff of Li Ji 李濟 (757–810), the Military Commissioner of Youzhou 幽州 (modern Beijing). Three years later he traveled south and found an assignment under the Military Commissioner of Lingnan 嶺南 (based in modern Guangzhou). The following poem, "Jiangnan za ti" 江南雜體 (其一) (Occasional Poem Written South of the Yangzi, Number 1), was probably written on his way south:

> The river wind rustles the trees,
> Through the bamboo the Xiang River flows.
> Day and night the cassia flowers fall,
> The traveler has left and gone afar.
> When I look back at the place we parted:
> Only the sounds of insects, rain on a gloomy autumn.

Wang Jian

江上風翛翛，竹間湘水流。
日夜桂花落，行人去悠悠。
復見離別處，蟲聲陰雨秋。

The poem depicts the reactions of the persona on a sleepless night. Troubled by the departure of a friend, he stirs to the sound of the wind and the water flowing, perhaps even sensing the fall of the cassia flowers. The piling up of images of insects chirping, dark rain, and autumn in the final line add to his gloom.

By 803 Wang had made his way back north to Jingzhou 荊州 (northeast of modern Changde City 常德市 in Hunan) where he remained for three years. While there he met the former Grand Councilor Du Yuanying 杜元穎 (775–838) who held a position in Jingzhou. The next reliable information places Wang in Weibo 魏博 (northeast of modern Handan City 邯鄲市 in Henan) where he was on the staff of yet another general, Tian Hongzheng 田弘正 (764–821), for part of that year, before being appointed Assistant Magistrate of Zhaoying 昭應 County (modern Lintong 臨潼, a few miles east of Xi'an), possibly at the recommendation of Pei Du 裴度 (765–839). It was probably at this time that he met Han Yu 韓愈 (768–824).* From poems he addressed to other literati it is clear that he knew Jia Dao 賈島 (779–843),* Linghu Chu 令狐楚 (766–837),* and Yang Juyuan 楊巨源 (ca. 755–after 833)* among others. But it was perhaps his relationships with politicians such as the Grand Councilors Li Jifu 李吉甫 (758–814), Pei Du, and Cui Qun 崔群 (772–832) that enabled him to find positions such as Aide to the Court of the Imperial Treasury and Aide to the Chamberlain for Ceremonials in the early 820s. After nearly a decade at court, Wang was sent out to become Vice Prefect of Shanzhou 陝州 (near modern Sanmengxia 三門峽 in Henan), but retired soon after to live at Xianyang 咸陽 northwest of the Tang capital.

He is also known for his new *yuefu* poetry that gained popularity during the early ninth century. These works are characterized by the belief that poetry should serve as a vehicle for the expression of moral values. Although major literary figures such as Bo Juyi 白居易 (772–846)* and Yuan Zhen 元稹 (779–831)* were more instrumental in applying these principles to this subgenre, Wang Jian, Zhang Ji, and other less known figures also played significant roles in the movement. Wang's "Dang chuang zhi" 當窗織 (Weaving at the Window) is typical:

> Heaving a sigh and again a sigh—
> In the garden are dates craved by passers-by.
> A girl of a poor family for a rich one must weave,
> Her mother-in-law beyond the wall can give her no help.
> Cold water, clumsy hands—the fine thread breaks so easily;
> Stitch in, stitch out, it wears at her heart.
> Crickets in the grasses cry beneath her loom;
> In two days they urge her to do a bolt and a half.
> When each tax is paid, only odd pieces are left.
> Her mother-in-law has no new dress—how could she wear one?
> From her window she even envies those green-bower girls,
> Their ten fingers idle, while clothes fill their hamper.

歎息復歎息，園中有棗行人食。
貧家女為富家織，翁母隔牆不得力。

水寒手澀絲脆斷，續來續去心腸爛。
草蟲促促機下啼，兩日催成一匹半。
輸官上頂有零落，姑未得衣身不著。
當窗卻羨青樓倡，十指不動衣盈箱

The poem opens with resonances to traditional *yuefu* poems. The first line is a formulaic depiction of a weaving girl as found in earlier poems. The dates in the second line allude to the traditional *yuefu* poem "Zhe yangliu zhi" 折楊柳枝 (Breaking the Willow Branch) which begins "in front of the gates there stands a date tree / that never grows old though it lives on year after year" 門前一株棗，歲歲不知老. The unspoken comparison is to the girl who is growing older and, unlike the date tree, has no visitors. The cries of the crickets of line 7 are supposed to resemble the sounds of the loom, thus here they seem to chirp out a rhythm that spurs on the young girl efforts. Silk was collected as part of the Tang tax burden. The green-bower girls are the courtesans.

Wang is, however, perhaps better known for his more than one hundred palace-style poems ("Gong ci" 宮詞), which were quite popular among his contemporaries and have been frequently included in collections of Tang poetry. It is said that he learned much about the palace from the powerful eunuch Wang Shoucheng 王守澄 (d. 835), who served in the court of Emperor Xianzong (r. 806–820). Yet many of the poems have no specific historical context, rather taking typical palace courtiers or palace women as personae as the following two:

> Hoping to accompany the emperor to go flower viewing
> I come down the golden stairs, but regret setting out;
> Afraid we'll see that old courtyard of those who have lost his favor
> When I return to reflect up to the sounds of a zither.

> 欲迎天子看花去，下得金階卻悔行。
> 恐見失恩人舊院，回來憶著五弦聲。

This poem depicts a palace girl who hopes to attract the emperor's attention by accompanying him to view flowers but then realizes (in the second line) that they will pass the old courtyard where he has relegated former favorites. Upon her return she in fact is able to hear the sad melodies of those women, causing her to reflect upon imperial vagaries and her own future. Another reading of the poem claims the persona is worried that the emperor may also hear the zither music and rekindle a former love.

> A spring breeze blows the rain, sprinkles the flagstaff;
> Out from the depths of the palace, I'm not afraid of the cold.
> Boasting that I can run a horse,
> I barge through the garden to catch his eye.

> 春風吹雨灑旗竿, 得出深宮不怕寒。
> 誇道自家能走馬, 園中橫過覓人看。

Wang Jian

Once again this poem depicts the desperation of a palace woman. Despite the rain, she braves the cool weather for the chance to attract imperial attention by bursting into the garden where the emperor is astride his horse.

BIBLIOGRAPHY

Editions:
Mao Jin 毛晉 (1599–1659). *Sanjia gongci* 三家宮詞. Rpt. Shanghai: Shangwu, 1936. Includes the palace poems by Wang Jian, Huarui Furen 花蕊夫人 (935–965) and Wang Gui 王桂 (1019–1085).
Quan Tang shi, 5: 3355–444, 13: 10126–27, 14: 11251.
Quan Tang wen, 129.1441–45.
Wang Jian shiji 王建詩集. Beijing: Zhonghua, 1959.
Zhang, Wang yuefu 張王樂府. Xu Chengshou 徐澄守, ed. Shanghai: Shanghai Guji, 1957.

Annotations:
Wang Zongtang 王宗堂, ed. *Wang Jian shiji jiaozhu* 王建詩集校注. Zhengzhou: Zhongzhou Guji, 2007.
Yi Zhanhua 尹占華. *Wang Jian shiji jiaozhu* 王建詩集校注. Chengdu: Ba Shu Shushe, 2006.

Biographical Sources:
Fu, *Tang caizi*, 2:150–62, 5:196.

Translations:
Bynner, *Jade Mountain*, p. 184.
Frankel, *Palace Lady*, p. 153.
Kroll, "Recalling Xuanzong," pp. 8–11.
Margoulies, *Anthologie*, pp. 349–50.
Sunflower, pp. 191–95.
Schafer, *Golden Peaches*, pp. 160, 162, 205–06.
Waley, Arthur. *Chinese Poems*, p. 119.
___. *Translations*, pp. 314–15.
Watson, *Lyricism*, pp. 119–20.
Yang, Hsien-yi and Gladys Yang. "Tang Dynasty 'Yüeh-fu' Songs—Chang Chieh [sic] and Wang Chien," *Chinese Literature* 1 (1965): 77–84.
___, "Wang Chien: Songs," *Chinese Literature*, 1965.1: 80–84.

Studies:
Bian Xiaoxuan 卞孝萱, "Guanyu Wang Jian de jige wenti" 關於王建的幾個問題, in *Tang shi yanjiu lunwen ji* 唐詩研究論文集. Chen Yixin 陳貽焮, ed. Hong Kong: Zhongguo Yuwen Xueshe, 1969, v. 2, pp. 193–205.
Chi Naipeng 遲乃鵬. *Wang Jian yanjiu conggao* 王建研究叢稿. Chengdu: Ba Shu Shushe, 1997.
Higashi Kei 東褧 (Aoyama Hakki 青山伯頎). *Tang Wang Jian gongci yibai shou* 唐王建宮詞一百首. Kyoto: Kyoto University Department of Literature, 1953 [reviewed in *HJAS*, 16 (1953), 491].
Miyazaki Ichisada 宮崎市定. "Ō Ken no shi sairon" 王建の詩再論, *Tōyshi kenkyū* 18.3 (December 1959): 26.
Nagata, Natsuki 長田夏樹. "Hakuwa shijin Ō Ken to sono jidai: Tō, Godai kōshō bungaku hattatsushi no ichisokumen toshite" 白話詩人王建とその時代—唐五代講唱文學發達史の一側面として, *Kōbe gaidai ronsō*, 7.1–3 (June 1956): 141–65.

___. "Ō Ken shiden keinen hikki" 王建詩傳繫年筆記, *Kōbe gaidai ronsō* 12.3 (August 1961): 35–52.

Nienhauser, William H., Jr. "The Imperial Presence in the Palace Poems of Wang Chien (ca. A.D. 768–833)," *Tamkang Review* 8.1 (1977): 111–22.

Sun Hong 孫紅. "Wang Changling 'Gongyuanshi' he Wang Jian 'Gongci' bijiao" 王昌齡宮怨詩和王建宮詞比較. *Mingzuo xinshang* 名作欣賞, 2015.2.

Wang Junze 王君澤. "Wang Jian yuefushi de yishu yinzi jianxi" 王建樂府詩的藝術因子簡析. *Taiyuan Daxue xuebao* 太原大學學報, 2007.6.

Wang Yuhong 王育紅. "Wang Jian 'Gongci' baishou shici yu zaru pianzhang kao" 王建宮詞詩次與雜入篇章考, *Nantong Daxue xuebao (Shehui kexueban)*, 2006.1.

___. "Wang Jian 'Gongci' baishou zuoshi kao" 王建宮詞作時考, *Zhongguo yunwen xuekan*, 2007.3.

Xie Minghui 謝明輝. *Wang Jian shige yanjiu* 王建詩歌研究. Taibei: Hua Mulan Wenhua, 2008.

Xu Lijie 徐禮節. *Zhang Ji, Wang Jian shige yanjiu* 張籍王建詩歌研究. Hefei: Huang Shan Shushe, 2015.

Madeline Spring and William H. Nienhauser, Jr.

Wang Wei 王維 (*zi*, Mojie 摩詰, 692–761 or 699–759) is one of the major poets of the Tang dynasty, acclaimed in particular for his limpid depictions of nature. Born into an influential family in Qi County 祁縣 (thirty miles south of modern Taiyuan in Shanxi), though he was the eldest child and eventually the most remembered by later generations, it was in fact his younger brother Wang Jin 王縉 (700–872) who would go on to represent their family at the highest levels of Tang government, serving as Grand Councilor during the reign of Emperor Daizong (r. 762–779). Nevertheless, Wang Wei distinguished himself as poet, painter, and musician at an early age and passed the *jinshi* examinations in 721. From his subsequent appointment as Vice Director of the Imperial Music Office, he enjoyed a slow but steady rise through government ranks which took him through various offices in the court at Chang'an and several provinces to his highest position, Right Assistant Director of the Department of Affairs, attained in 759. His career was interrupted only three times: by an unknown infraction committed at his first post, which led to a brief but virtual exile as an official in modern Shandong, by the death of his mother around 750, and by the An Lushan Rebellion of 755–757, during which he was captured and forced to serve under the puppet government. Only the intercession of his powerful younger brother, Wang Jin, who offered to have himself demoted as ransom for his elder brother's freedom, led to Wang Wei's pardon after the return of the imperial family to the capital.

Of his relatively small poetic corpus—about four hundred poems in all—those for which Wang Wei is best known present scenes from various retreats enjoyed at different periods throughout his life. Perhaps the most famous of these were written at his country home on the Wang River in Lantian 藍田, southeast of Chang'an, especially the quatrains of his *Wang Chuan ji* 輞川集 (Wang River Collection), which describe twenty different spots on his estate. (He is also said to have painted a long handscroll of the same scenes, but this work is no longer extant, although there are numerous imitations by later artists.) The quatrain entitled "Lu zhai" 鹿柴 (The Deer Paling) is one of the most widely read and admired pieces from this collection:

Wang Wei

> In empty mountains seeing not a man,
> only heard are the sounds of a man's voice.
> Returning sunbeams enter deep forests,
> again to shine atop the green moss.

> 空山不見人，但聞人語響。
> 返景入深林，復照青苔上。

"Lu zhai" is an epitome of the metaphysic and aesthetic problems Wang Wei often struggled with, but never seemed willing to resolve. A moment of concentration is broken briefly, but not wholly unpleasantly, providing occasion for reflection on the ambiguities of the senses. An emptiness of vision is deepened by fleeting sound, only for sight's return to then obscure the passage of time and the boundaries between civilization and the wilds.

Equally well known are the quatrains written in response to each of Wang Wei's by his friend Pei Di 裴迪, a minor poet who eventually attained the post of Prefect of Shuzhou 蜀州 (modern Chongzhou City 崇州市 in Sichuan) after the An Lushan Rebellion. Their friendship as revealed through their collaboration and correspondence was clearly regarded by both as one of equals, but Pei Di often played the role of interlocutor for his more talented companion. He responded to "The Deer Paling" with the following, more grounded reading of an enclosed meadow favored by deer.

> Day and night seeing cold mountains
> I've become a lonely sojourner.
> I don't understand the affairs of deep forests,
> only that there are tracks of stags.

> 日夕見寒山, 便為獨住客。
> 不知深林事, 但有麀麚跡。

Wang Wei spent much of his leisure time with Pei Di, and his corpus contains several other poems written to or about his friend; his "Shanzhong yu Pei Xiucai Di shu" 山中與裴秀才迪書 (Letter from the Mountains to Candidate Pei Di) is his most famous prose evocation of the pleasures of life in retreat:

> Of late at the twelfth month's end, the country and its airs are peaceful and pleasant, and so the mountains could be crossed. You were in the midst of reviewing the classics, and I did not dare to trouble you. So I went into the mountains, resting at the Ganpei Temple, supping with the mountain monks, and then departing.
>
> Wading northward over the darkened River Ba, a clear moon was reflected on the city walls. By night I had ascended Huazi Hill, and the Wheel's waters rolled and churned, rising and falling with the moon. On the cold mountains were distant fires, brightening and fading beyond the forests. In deep lanes cold dogs barked with a sound like leopards. The villagers pounded grain in the night, time and again, alternating with the dim ringing of bells. At this time I sit alone, my servants are silent and still, and I often think of how before, hand in hand and composing poems, we walked out of the way paths and overlooked clear streams.

We should wait for spring, for grasses and trees growing and blooming, when spring mountains can be gazed upon and when brook minnows leap from the waters, when white gulls straighten their wings, dews dampen green shores, and roosters crow from wheat fields in the mornings. This time is not far off; will you be able to wander with me then? If you were not one of the Great Mystery's pristine marvels, how could I, with such trivial matters, dare summon you? Rather, it is that, in such things, there is deep appeal; do not overlook this. I rely on a man who carries cork bark to send this, and I shall say no more.

Respectfully yours, Wang Wei, a dweller in the mountains.

近臘月下，景氣和暢，故山殊可過。足下方溫經，猥不敢相煩。輒便往山中，憩感配寺，與山僧飯訖而去。

北涉玄灞，清月映郭。夜登華子岡，輞水淪漣，與月上下。寒山遠火，明滅林外。深巷寒犬，吠聲如豹。村墟夜舂，復與疏鍾相間。此時獨坐，僮僕靜默，多思曩昔攜手賦詩，步仄徑，臨清流也。

當待春中，草木蔓發，春山可望，輕鰷出水，白鷗矯翼，露濕青皋，麥隴朝雊。斯之不遠，倘能從我游乎？非子天機清妙者，豈能以此不急之務相邀？然是中有深趣矣，無忽。因馱黃檗人往，不一。

山中人王維白。

Wang Wei's appreciation of nature was no doubt fostered by his involvement with Buddhism. He studied for ten years with the Chan master Daoguang 道光 (d. 739). After his wife's death around 730 he remained celibate and later converted part of his Lantian estate into a monastery. He wrote stele-inscriptions honoring both Daoguang and the Chan patriarch Huineng 惠能 (638–713), as well as more general essays in praise of Buddhism and Amida, the Buddha of the Western Paradise. Particularly illuminating is his choice of style name (zi), for, together with his given name, it forms the Chinese transliteration of the name of Vimalakīrti (Weimojie 維摩詰), the contemporary of Sakyamuni Buddha who was said to have spoken a sutra affirming the layman's practice of the religion. Indeed, Wang Wei's commitment to Buddhism is evident not so much in explicit doctrinal argument or vocabulary, of which there is little, as in the attitudes implicit in his poetry. For example, his contemplative, dispassionate observations of the sensory world affirm its beauty at the same time that they put its ultimate reality into question, by emphasizing its vagueness, relativity, and "emptiness," as well as problems of perception in general. The quatrain "Xinyi wu" 辛夷塢 (Magnolia Glen), remembered for its haunting and yet cunningly ironic imagery, is emblematic of Wang's distrust of mundane perception:

On the treetops are hibiscus flowers,
in the mountains red blossoms bloom.
The brookside gate is quiet, no one there,
they open pell-mell set to fall.

木末芙蓉花，山中發紅萼。
澗戶寂無人，紛紛開且落。

The poem is held together by the image of the hibiscus flowers which traces the short lives of the hibiscus from lines 1 through 4. In contrast to the lack of a human presence (except for the poet), the flowers bloom in profusion. Here we have the moment of silence before they fall. The simple, natural diction and syntax here and in much of his poetry suggests the illusion of effortlessness that is analogous to that moment of enlightenment masking the care taken to achieve it. This subtle or "bland" aspect of his style led to his later elevation as the "father" of the Southern School of literati (as opposed to professional) painters. For all Wang Wei's religious devotion, he never abandoned the engagement with the bureaucratic world expected of any good Confucian. Several of his works are court compositions, and, indeed, his very style is heavily indebted to the conventions of court-poetry established during the seventh century.

Some modern biographers have seen nothing but contradiction in his ties to both court and country, secular activity and religious retreat. In fact, such dual allegiances were not so much the exception as the rule at the time. The primary thrust of Wang Wei's poetry—on this question as elsewhere—is one of compromise and balance between potentially opposing forces or issues. Just as his landscape scenes evince a harmony of self and world or even the submergence of man in nature, so his work and life as a whole display a tendency toward integration rather than conflict, a disposition readily apparent in what remains one of most his most popular octaves, "Shan ju qiu ming" 山居秋暝 (Staying in the Mountains on an Autumn Eve):

Empty mountains after fresh rains,
Heaven's airs are by evening autumnal.
A bright moon shines amongst pines,
a clear spring flows upon rocks.
Bamboo hums with washer girls' return,
lotuses move as fishing boats pass.

Of their own accord spring's fragrances ease,
and princelings might allow themselves to linger.

空山新雨後，天氣晚來秋。
明月松間照，清泉石上流。
竹喧歸浣女，蓮動下漁舟。
隨意春芳歇，王孫自可留。

This well-known poem depicts the quiet scene of an empty mountain on a moonlight night when the first sense of autumn can be felt. The last four lines remind the reader of the opening lines of Wang Wei's "Lu zhai" 鹿寨: "On the empty mountain there is no one, but human voices can be heard echoing" 空山不見人, 但聞人語響. Here the quiet is broken by the women who emerge from within the bamboo grove and the boats which come forth out of the lotus—both unexpected. Whether the poem was written in the spring (line 7) with the feeling of autumn (line 2), or in the autumn depicting fragrances so vivid they suggest the spring, is impossible to tell. The final line alludes to the "Zhaoyin shi" 招隱士 in the *Chuci* which ends "Oh Prince return, in the mountains you cannot remain long" 王孫兮歸來, 山中兮不可久留. Wang Wei turns the reference on its head by expressing hopes that he would be able to remain away from court life.

BIBLIOGRAPHY

Editions:
Chen Kang 陳抗, et al., eds. *Quan Tang shi suoyin: Wang Wei juan* 全唐詩索引: 王維卷. Beijing: Zhonghua, 1992.
Gu Qijing 鼓起經, ed. *Leijian Wang Youcheng quanji* 類箋王右丞全集. 2v. 1557; rpt. Beijing, 1957, Taibei, 1970.
___ed. *Wang Wei shiji* 王維詩集. Photo-reproduction of 1590 ed. Kyoto, 1975.
Harada Ken'yū 原田憲雄. *Ō I shishū* 王維詩集. Tokyo: Kadokawa, 1972.
Ō I shi sakuin 王維詩所引. Kyoto: Kyoto Daigaku Chūgoku Gogaku Chūgoku Bungaku Kenkyūshitsu, 1952.
Quan Tang shi, 2: 1235–1309, 13: 10243, 14: 11094.
Quan Tang wen, 324–27.3667–703.
Tsukuru Haruo 都留春雄 et al. *Ō I shi sakuin* 王維詩所引. 1952; rpt. Nagoya, 1971.

Annotations:
Chen Tiemin 陳鐵民 ed. *Wang Wei ji jiaozhu* 王維集校注. Rpt. Beijing: Zhonghua, [1997] 2005. Appends selected biographical materials and traditional criticism of Wang's verse.
Chen Wenpeng 陳文鵬. *Wang Wei shige shangxi* 王維詩歌賞析. Nanning: Guangxi Jiaoyu, 1991.
Chen Yixin 陳貽焮. *Wang Wei shi xuan* 王維詩選. Shijiazhuang: Hebei Jiaoyu, 1999.
Deng Ansheng 鄧安生, et al., eds. and comms. *Wang Wei shi xuanyi* 王維詩選譯. Chengdu: Ba Shu Shushe, 1990. *Gudai wenshi mingzhu xuanyi zongshu*. Reprinted in Taibei as *Wang Wei shi* 王維詩 by Jinxiu in 1993.
Fu Donghua 傅東華, ed. *Wang Wei shixuan* 王維詩選. 1933; rpt. Hong Kong: Daguang, 1973.
Liu Ning 劉寧. *Wang Wei, Meng Haoran shi xuan ping* 王維, 孟浩然詩選評. Shanghai: Shanghai Guji, 2002.
Tao Wenpeng 陶文鵬. *Wang Wei shige shangxi* 王維詩歌賞析. Nanning: Guangxi Jiaoyu, 1991.
Wang Dajin 王達津, ed. and comm. *Wang Wei, Meng Haoran xuanji* 王維, 孟浩然選集. Shanghai: Shanghai Guji, 1990.
Yang Wensheng 楊文生. *Wang Wei shiji jianzhu* 王維詩集箋注. Chengdu: Sichuan Renmin, 2003.
Zhao Diancheng 趙殿成 (1683–1756), ed. *Wang Youcheng ji jianzhu* 王右丞集箋注. Introduction by Wang Yunxi 王運熙. 2v. Shanghai: Shanghai Guji, 1984 (1961).

Biographical Sources:
Fu, *Tang caizi*, 2:285–304, 5:56–57.
Jiu Tang shu, 109C.5051–53.
Xin Tang shu, 202.5764–66.

Translations:
Articulated Ladies, pp. 293.
Barnstone, Tony, et al. *Laughing Lost in the Mountains: Poems of Wang Wei*. Hanover: University Press of New England, 1991.
Birch, *Anthology*, pp. 219–24.
Bynner, *Jade Mountain*, pp. 153–67.
Carré, Patrick. *Les Saisons bleues: L'oeuvre de Wang Wei, poète et peintre*. Paris: Editions Phebus, 1989.
Chang Hsin-chang. "Wang Wei." *Chinese Literature, Volume 2: Nature Poetry*. New York: Columbia University Press, 1977, pp. 58–79.
Chang Wei-penn and Lucien Drivod. *Paysages: Miroirs du Cœur*. Connaissance de l'Orient, 71. Paris: Gallimard, 1990.
Chang Yin-nan and Lewis C. Walmsley. *Poems by Wang Wei*. Rutland, Vermont: Charles E. Tuttle Co., 1958.

Ch'en, Jerome and Michael Bullock. *Poems of Solitude*, London: Abelard-Schuman, 1960, pp. 47–79.

Cheng Wing-fun and Herve Collet. *Wang Wei, le plein du vide*. 2nd revised ed. Millemont, France: Moundarren, 1986.

Diény, J.-P. Review of the *Poetry of Wang Wei* by Pauline Yu, *TP* 68 (1982): 359–66.

Demiéville, *Anthologie*, pp. 247–54.

Fuller, Michael A. *An Introduction to Chinese Poetry: From the* Canon of Poetry *to the Lyrics of the Song Dynasty*. Cambridge: Harvard University Press, 2018, pp. 193–201.

Harada Ken'yu. *Ō I* 王維 Tokyo: Shūeisha, 1967.

Hinton, David. *The Selected Poems of Wang Wei*. New York : New Directions Books, 2006.

Hsieh, Daniel. "The Nine Songs and the Structure of the 'Wang River Collection,'" *CLEAR* 35 (2013): 1–30.

Kobayashi Taiichirō 小林太市郎 (1901–1963) and Harada Ken'yū. *Ō I* 王維. Tokyo: Shūeisha, 1964.

Lisowski, Joseph. "Wang Wei and P'ei Ti," in Seaton, Jerome P. and Denni Maloney, eds. *A Drifting Boat: An Anthology of Chinese Zen Poetry*. Fredonia, NY: White Pine Press, 1994, pp. 40–46.

Mair, "Tang Poems," pp. 341–42 , 347.

Margoulies, *Anthologie*, pp. 230, 251–52, 315–16, 373, 413, 436.

Minford and Lau, pp. 699–720.

New Directions, pp. 65–72.

Owen, *Anthology*, pp. 371–74, 385–95, 462–64.

___. *High T'ang*, pp. 27–51.

___. *Late Tang*, pp. 103, 306–09.

___. *Omen*, pp. 63–65, 134–37, 153–54, 219–20.

Robinson, G. W. *Poems of Wang Wei*. Baltimore: Penguin, 1973.

Rouzer, Paul. *The Poetry and Prose of Wang Wei*. Boston and Berlin: Walter de Gruyter, 2020.

Strassberg, Richard E. *Inscribed Landscapes: Travel Writing from Imperial China*. Berkeley: University of California Press, 1994. pp. 111–14.

Tsuge, Keiichirō 柘植敬一郎. *Ō I no fūi Shiga bunshu* 王維の風姿 詩画文集. Tokyo: Shoshi Yamada, 1993.

Tsukuru Haruo et al. *Ō I* 王維. Tokyo: Iwanami, 1958.

Waley, *Translations*, pp. 116–17.

Yang Xianyi, *Poetry and Prose*, pp. 7–16.

Yang Xianyi 楊憲益 and Li Shiji 李士俶. *Han Ying duizhao huitu ben Wang Wei shi xuan* 漢英對照繪圖本王維詩選. Beijing: Zhongguo Wenxue, 1999.

Yip Wai-lim. *Hiding the Universe*: Poems by Wang Wei. New York, 1972.

Yu, Pauline. *The Poetry of Wang Wei: New Translations and Commentary*. Bloomington: Indiana University Press, 1980.

___. *The Reading of Imagery in the Chinese Poetic Tradition*. Princeton: Princeton University Press, 1987, pp. 187–90.

___. "Wang Wei: Seven Poems," *The Denver Quarterly*, 12.2 (Summer 1977): 353–55.

Studies:

Ang, A.C 洪惜珠. "Taoist-Buddhist Elements in Wang Wei's Poetry." *Chinese Culture* 30.1 (1989): 79–89.

Cao Zuoya. "Poetry and Zen: A Comparison of Wang Wei and Basho." *TkR*, 24.2 (Autumn 1993): 23–41.

Chen Tiemin. "Wang Wei nianpu" 王維年譜. *Wenshi*, 16 (November 1982): 203–27.

___. *Wang Wei lun gao* 王維論稿. Beijing Shi: Renmin Wenxue, 2006.

___. *Xinyi Wang Wei shi wenji* 新譯王維詩文集. Taibei: Sanmin, 2009.

___. "Wang Wei shengnian xintan" 王維生年新探. *Wenshi* 28 (1988): 185–94.

___. "Wang Wei xinlun" 王維新論. Beijing: Beijing Shifan Xueyuan, 1990.

___. "Wang Wei yu Daojiao." 王維與道教. *Wenxue yichan*. 1989.5: 56–63

Chen Yunji 陳允吉. "Wang Wei 'Zhongnan bieshu' ji 'Wang chuan bieshu kao'" 王維終南別墅即輞川別墅考. *Wenxue yichan* 1985.1: 45–54.

___. "Wang Wei Wangchuan 'Huazi Gang' shi yu Fojia 'fei niao yu'" 王維輞川華子岡詩與佛家飛鳥喻. *Wenxue yichan*, 1988.2: 63–70.

Chou Shan. "Beginning with Images in the Nature Poetry of Wang Wei." *HJAS*, 42.1 (June 1982), 117–37.

Cleaves, Francis Woodman. "Additional Data on Sung Lien, Wang Wei, and Chao Hsi.in." Appended to "The 'Postscript to the Table of Contents of the *Yuan shih*.'" *JSYS* 23 (1993): 13–18 (1–18).

Dagdanov, G. B., "Vliianie chan'buddizma na tvorchestvo tanskikh poetov. Na primere Van Veia (701–61) i Bo Tsziu-ii (772–846) [The Influence of Ch'an Buddhism on the Writings of the T'ang Poets: The Cases of Wang Wei (701–761) and Po Chu-I (772–846)]." Unpublished Ph. D. dissertation, Institut vostokovedeniia Akademii nauk SSSR, 1980.

Feinerman, James Vincent, "The Poetry of Wang Wei." Unpublished Ph.D. dissertation, Yale University, 1979.

Field, "Taking Up the Plow," pp. 117–24.

Gao Ming 高明, et al., eds. *Wang Wei* 王維. Taibei: Jinxiu, 1992.

Gong Shu. "The Function of Space and Time as Compositional Elements in Wang Wei's Poetry: A Study of Five Poems." *LEW*, 15.4 (April 1975): 1168–93.

Hsieh, Daniel. "Wang Wei, 'The Nine Songs,' and the Structure of the 'Wang River Collection.'" *CLEAR*, 35 (2013): 7–35.

Iritani Sensuke 入谷仙介. *Ō I kenyu* 王維研究. Tokyo: Sōbunsha 1976 (Chinese translation: *Wang Wei yanjiu jieyi ben* 王維研究節譯本. Lu Yanping 盧燕平, trans. Beijing: Zhonghua, 2005).

Jin Xuezhi 金學智, "Wang Wei shizhong de huihuamei" 王維詩中的繪畫美. *Wenxue yichan* 1984.4: 55–66.

Juhl, R. A., "Patterns of Assonance and Vowel Melody in Wang Wei's Yüeh-fu Poems." *JCLTA*, 12.2 (May 1977): 95–110.

Kong Haili, "The Point of View—The Narrative Quality in Wang Wei's Poems," in *TkR*, 24.2 (Winter 1993): 2–18.

Liao Chiahui. "A Critical Study of the Reception and Translation of the Poetry of Wang Wei in English." Ph. D. Dissertation, University of Warwick, 2011.

Liou Kin-ling. *Wang Wei le poéte*. Paris: Jouve, 1941.

Liu Chengjun 柳晟俊. *Wang Wei shi bijiao yanjiu* 王維詩比較研究. Guilin: Guangxi Shifan Daxue, 1997.

____. *Wang Wei* 王維詩研究. Taibei: Liming Wenhua Gongsi, 1987.

Liu Weichong 劉維崇. *Wang Wei pingzhuan* 王維評傳. Taibei: Zhengzhong, 1972.

Lu Yu. *Wang Wei zhuan* 王維傳. Taiyuan: Shanxi Renmin, 1989.

Luk, Thomas Yuntong, "A Cinematic Interpretation of Wang Wei's Nature Poetry." *New Asia Academic Bulletin*, 1 (1978): 151–61.

___, "A Study of the Nature Poetry of Wang Wei in the Perspective of Comparative Literature." Unpublished Ph.D. dissertation, University of Michigan, 1976.

___, "Wang Wei's Perception of Space and His Attitude Towards Mountains." *TkR*, 8.1 (April 1977), 89–110.

Owen, Stephen, "Wang Wei: The Artifice of Simplicity," in *The Great Age of Chinese Poetry: The High T'ang*. New Haven: Yale University Press, 1981, pp. 27–51.

Pollack, David, "Wang Wei in Kamakura: A Consideration of the Structural Poetics of Mishima's *Spring Snow*."*HJAS*, 48. 2 (December 1988): 383–402. Traces the role of Wang Wei's verse in the on Mishima Yukio's novel *Spring Snow*.

Stepien, Rafal, "The Imagery of Emptiness in the Poetry of Wang Wei (699–761)," *Interdisciplnary Literary Studies* 16.2 (2014): 207–38.

Wagner, Marsha L., "The Art of Wang Wei's Poetry." Unpublished Ph.D. dissertation, University of California at Berkeley, 1975.

___, "From Image to Metaphor: Wang Wei's Use of Light and Color." *JCLTA*, 2 (May 1977): 111–17.

___. *Wang Wei*. Boston: Twayne Publishers, 1982.

Walmsley, Lewis C. and Dorothy B. *Wang Wei the Painter-Poet*. Rutland, Vermont: Charles E. Tuttle Co., 1968.

Watanabe Hideki 渡部英喜. *Shizen shijin Ō I no sekai* 自然詩人王維の世界. Tokyo : Meiji, 2010.

Wang Congren 王從仁. *Wang Wei he Meng Haoran* 王維和孟浩然. Shanghai: Shanghai Guji, 1984. *Zhonguo gudian wenxue jiben zhishi congshu*, 34. Reprinted in Taiwan in 1992.

Wang Wei yanjiu 王維研究. Xian: Sanqin, 1996– . Journal appearing annually.

Wang Wei Yanjiu Hui 王維研究會, ed. *Wang Wei yanjiu* 王維研究. Beijing: Zhongguo Gongren, 1992– . Various articles on the life, thought and writings of Wang Wei. Subsequent volumes have appeared irregularly through v. 6 in 2013.

Warner, Ding Xiang, "The Two Voices of the *Wangchuanji*: Poetic Exchange between Wang Wei and Pei Di." *Early Medieval China*, 10–11.2 (2005): 57–72.

Wei Zuqin 魏祖欽, "Lun Wang Wei qiyan gushi de yishu tese" 論王維七言古詩的藝術特色. *Wenxue yichan*, 2007.1: 130–32.

Weinberger, Eliot and Octavio Plaz. *Nineteen Ways of Looking at Wang Wei: How a Chinese Poem is Translated*. Mount Kisco: Moyer Bell, 1987.

Williams, Nicolas Morrow. "Quasi-Phantasmal Flowers: An Aspect of Wang Wei's Mahāyāna Poetics." *CLEAR*, 39 (2017): 27-54.

Wong Yoon-wah 王潤華. *Wang Wei shi xue* 王維詩學. Hong Kong: Xianggang Daxue, 2009.

Yang Jingqing. *The Chan Interpretations of Wang Wei's Poetry: A Critical Review*. Hong Kong: Chinese University Press, 2007.

Yang Wenxiong 楊文雄. *Shifo Wang Wei yanjiu* 詩佛王維研究. Taibei: Wenshizhe, 1988.

Yang Yinshen 楊蔭深. *Wang Wei yu Meng Haoran* 王維與孟浩然. Shanghai: Shangwu, 1936.

Yip Wai-lim, "Wang Wei and the Aesthetic of Pure Experience," *TkR*, 2.2 (April 1972): 199–208.

Yu, Pauline, "Hidden in Plain Sight? The Art of Hiding in Chinese Poetry." *CLEAR* 30 (Dec., 2008): 179–86. Much of the discussion deals with Wang's eremitic verse.

___,"Wang Wei: Recent Studies and Translations." *CLEAR*, 1.2 (July 1979): 219–40. Review article.

___, "Wang Wei's Journeys in Ignorance," *TkR*, 8.1 (April 1977): 73–87.

Zhan, *Daojiao*, pp. 254–58.

Zhang Qinghua 張清華. *Shifo Wang Mojie zhuan* 詩佛王摩詰傳. Zhengzhou: Henan Renmin, 1991.

___. *Wang Wei nianpu* 王維年譜. Shanghai: Xuelin, 1988.

Zhang Yi 張毅, "Wang Wei yu sheng Tang shanshui shi de ming xiu kong jing zhi mei" 王維與盛唐山水詩的明秀空靜之美. *Nankai xuebao*, 1997.5: 31–36.

Zhang Yong 張勇, ed. *Wang Wei shi quanji: huijiao, huizhu, huiping* 王維詩全集: 匯校, 匯注, 匯評. Wuhan: Chongwen, 2017.

Zhu Lixia 朱麗霞, "Wang Wei shanshui shi de chanjing yu kongjing" 王維山水詩的禪境與空境. *Song Liao xuekan*, n.74 (1996): 37–41.

Zhuang Shen 莊申. *Wang Wei yanjiu* 王維研究. V. 1. Hong Kong: Wanyou Tushu Gongsi, 1971.

Pauline Yu and Thomas Donnelly Noel

Wang Zhihuan 王之渙 (*zi*, Jiling 季陵, 679–742), who is known today primarily as an accomplished writer of *juezhu* 絕句 (quatrains), was a native of Bingzhou 幷州 (modern Taiyuan in Shanxi). Wang's family were all officials at least from his ancestor Wang Longzhi 王隆之 who is said to have been Prefect of Jiangzhou 絳州 (modern Xinjiang County 新絳縣 in Yuncheng City 運城市 in southwestern Shanxi) under the Later Wei dynasty (386–534). Wang Zhihuan's father,

Wang Yu 王昱, was a minor official who last served as Magistrate of Zhunyi County 浚儀縣 in Bianzhou 汴州 (modern Kaifeng in Henan). Wang Zhihuan himself first served as Assistant Magistrate of Hengshui County 衡水縣 in Jizhou 冀州 (modern Heshui City in Hebei, about sixty-five miles east-southeast of Shijiazhuang), obtaining the position through *yin* privilege. Because of a lawsuit that supposedly originated from a certain Li Di 李滌 giving his three daughters in marriage to Wang Zhihuan, Wang left his position and spent the next fifteen years out of office. He traveled to Luoyang, Yunmen Guan 雲門關 (Jade Gate Pass), and around 722 to the capital, Chang'an. There he met Gao Shi 高適 (700–765)* and Wang Changling 王昌齡 (ca. 690–ca. 756).*

A well-known anecdote involving the three poets suggests Wang's contemporary reputation. While they were drinking in a wine shop, singing girls sang verses by Gao Shi and then Wang Changling, who then jocularly boasted to Wang Zhihuan of their prominence. Wang entreated them to wait to see what the most beautiful of the girls sang, and, of course, it turned out to be one of his songs, "Liangzhou ci" 涼州詞 (Song of Liangzhou). Liangzhou occupied the narrow strip of land controlled by the Tang running from south of modern Lanzhou in Gansu to west of Dunhuang—thus the northern frontier of the Tang. This poem was set to a tune brought to court by Guo Zhiyun 郭知運 (667–721) during the early years of the Kaiyuan era (713–742). Zhang Ji 張籍 (ca. 776–829)* and Xue Feng 薛逢 (fl. 841–866) both wrote lyrics to the song, but Wang Zhihuan's is the most famous, praised by later critics as the ultimate in the quatrain form:

> Yellow sands rise up among distant white clouds,
> A strip of lonely wall along a thousand-foot hill.
> Must the Tartar flutes cause me to resent "Breaking the Willow"?
> The spring winds will never cross Jade Gate Pass.

> 黃沙直上白雲間，一片孤城萬仞山。
> 羌笛何須怨楊柳，春風不度玉門關。

The poem depicts the barren landscape of Liangzhou from the perspective of a solider stationed there. Breaking willow branches was part of the Tang custom of seeing off someone who was traveling away from home. But it was also a *yuefu* of the northern regions in pre-Tang times which went:

> He mounted his horse but didn't hold the whip,
> Instead broke a branch from the willow tree.
> Stamping his foot he played the long flute,
> The sorrow tearing apart the traveler's heart.

> 上馬不捉鞭，反折楊柳枝。
> 蹀座吹長笛，愁殺行客兒。

Wang Zhihuan may have been playing upon this song which again depicts someone parting from loved ones. In Wang's version the song is played by foreigners on the frontier making it doubly poignant: the spring winds suggesting the wife that the soldier had left behind were insurmountably distant. According to Yang Shen 楊慎 (1488–1559) the poem is an allegory which suggests that imperial favor and concern stopped, like the spring winds, somewhat short of the area.

Wang Zhihuan's other well-known quatrain is "Deng Guanque Lou" 登鸛雀樓 (Ascending the Tower of the Red Crowned Crane) which, like "Liangzhou ci," has been included in numerous anthologies. The form is strictly regular (a five-syllable *juezhu* with no violations in pattern), the poem is of interest because of its philosophic tone:

> The bright sun leans on the mountains, then is gone;
> The Yellow River flows into the sea.
> If you want to see out to a thousand miles,
> Climb one more story of this tower.

> 白日依山盡，黃河入海流。
> 欲窮千里目，更上一層樓

The Tower of the Red Crowned Crane was located in what is now modern Puzhou Zhen 蒲州鎮 west of Yuncheng City 運城市 in Shanxi—thus not far from where Wang held office at the start of his career. It overlooks the Yellow River and was built as a lookout tower by the Northern Zhou general Yuwen Hu 宇文護 (513–572) when he was stationed there. Here the setting sun and the flowing of the Yellow River both suggest the passing of time. The ascent of the tower in the last two lines builds on the Tang topos that allowed the poet to rise above the limitations of his present situation. By viewing temporal as well as spatial distance, poet and reader are invited to ponder the future.

In 742 Wang Zhihuan was appointed Commandant of Wen'an County 文安縣 (modern Langfang City 廊坊市 thirty miles southeast of Beijing in Hebei) where he died of illness.

BIBLIOGRAPHY

Editions:
Quan Tang shi, 4: 2841–42.

Biographical Sources:
Fu, *Tang caizi*, 1:446–51, 5:82–85.

Translations:
Debon, *Mein Haus*, pp. 157–58.
Fuller, Michael A. *An Introduction to Chinese Poetry: From the* Canon of Poetry *to the Lyrics of the Song Dynasty*. Cambridge: Harvard University, 2018, pp. 188–89.
Lin and Owen, *Vitality*, pp. 325–6.
Mair, *Anthology*, p. 193.
Owen, *High Tang*, pp. 247–8.
Pimpaneau, pp. 456.

Studies:

Bian Xiaoxuan 卞孝萱. "Wang Zhihuan pingzhuan" 王之渙評傳. *Huaiyang Shizhuan xuebao (Shehui Kexue ban)*, 1983.10.

Chen Shangjun 陳尚君. "Ba Wang Zhihuan zufu Wang Debiao, Qi Lishi muzhi" 跋王之渙祖父王德表，妻李氏墓誌, *Wenxue yichan*, 1987.5.

Fu, *Shiren*, pp. 56–65.

Li Ximi 李希泌, "Sheng Tang shiren Wang Zhihuan jiashi yu shiji kao" 盛唐詩人王之渙家世與事跡考. *Jinyang xuekan* 晉陽學刊, 1988.6.

Ma Maoyuan 馬茂元, "Wang Zhihuan shengping kaolue" 王之渙生平考略. *Zhonghua wenshi luncong* 中華溫室論叢, 4 (1979).

Shi Tieliang 史鐵良, "Ye tan Wang Zhihuan de 'Liangzhou ci'" 也談王之渙的'涼州詞.' *Wenxue pinglun*, 1980.12.

Wang Yuanming 王元明. *Wang Zhihuan 'Liangzhou' ci xintan* 王之渙《涼州詞》新探. Nanjing: Jiangsu Jiaoyu, 1994.

Yishan 宜珊, "Wang, Cen, Gao de biansai shi" 王岑高的邊塞詩. *Jinji Zhongguo*, 57 (January 1976).

Tamotsu Satō, Po-hui Chuang, and William H. Nienhauser, Jr.

Wei Yingwu 韋應物 (735–ca. 792) was a Tang poet whose verses are best known for their tranquil settings and clear diction. A native of Duling 杜陵 near Chang'an, he was born into an illustrious clan (his great-grandfather Wei Daijie 韋待階 [d. 689] was Grand Councilor under Empress Wu) and served in his youth as an imperial guard in the retinue of Emperor Xuanzong. He never obtained or even sat for any degree, but he did hold through *yin* privilege a number of posts in the capital and in Luoyang including that of Personnel Evaluator (774) and Vice Director of the Bureau of Review (782) before being appointed in 783 to the first of the three Prefectships in the south: Chuzhou 滁州 (783; modern Chuzhou City in Anhui), Jiangzhou 江州 (785; modern Jiujiang City 九江市 in Jiangxi), and Suzhou 蘇州 (798; modern Jiangsu). In 787 he was made Director of the Left Office of the Department of State Affairs, and then District Baron of Fufeng County 扶風縣 (modern Fufeng County about 65 miles west of Xian) with a fief of three hundred households. He probably died shortly after resigning the third Prefectship, that of Suzhou, in 791.

His poetry (the only other extant works being a single *fu* and two funerary inscriptions) is often associated with that of the earlier "nature poets," due to the great number of pieces that treat nature and personal themes, often in the High Tang style of Wang Wei 王維 (692–761 or 699–759)* and Meng Haoran 孟浩然 (689–740).* Examples are "Chuzhou xijian" 滁州西澗 (West Torrent at Chuzhou), his most famous poem, written in 781:

I alone love the secluded grasses growing along the mountain stream.
Above the torrent orioles warble deep in boughs.
The spring swell bearing rain turns rapid as it grows late.
No one at the rural ferry, but the boat by itself shifts askew.

獨憐幽草澗邊生, 上有黃鸝深樹鳴.
春潮帶雨晚來急, 野渡無人舟自橫.

Following the tendency of traditional critics, these first four lines have been read in the context of the poet's biography. The first two lines, focusing on *du* 獨, "I alone," suggest that the poet identifies with the grasses and the orioles, both far from the mundane world and a life of politics. The boat which finds itself "askew" (*heng* 橫) resonates with the world in which petty men are in positions of power while gentlemen slave away in lowly posts. Regardless of the potential for social commentary this poem offers, critics agree that it presents a splendid depiction of a rural scene and is exemplary for its use of imagery to paint a picture in these four lines. It comes as no surprise then, that Wei Yingwu was also known to be an admirer of Xie Lingyun 謝靈運 (385–433): such pieces as "Ting ying qu" 聽鶯曲 (Song: Listening to the Orioles) contain descriptive passages in the "mountains and waters" tradition of landscape poetry.

But the poet most commonly linked with him is the putative originator of "fields and gardens" poetry, Tao Qian 陶潛 (365–427), not only because of shared Daoist leanings, but also from the meditative tone and relaxed diction that Wei adopted from him, especially in his pentasyllabic verses. Wei was also adept at writing old-style verse and composed many pieces in imitation of earlier poetry, such as "Ni gu" 擬古 (Imitations of Old [Poetry]), inspired mainly by the "Gushi shijiu shou" 古詩十九首 (Nineteen Ancient Poems). As such, he became a recognized master of pentasyllabic ancient-style verse, with the direct, unmannered, and yet dignified style especially apparent in pieces treating complex personal themes, such as "Song Yangshi nü" 送楊氏女 (Seeing My Daughter off [upon Her Marriage] to the Yang Family) or the set of poems mourning the death of his wife. The discursive tone and the clarity of diction no doubt account for his popularity with Bo Juyi 白居易 (772–846)* and many Song-dynasty poets, including Mei Yaochen 梅堯臣 (1002–1060) and Su Shi 蘇軾 (1037–1101). In his own lifetime, however, he was not especially renowned, perhaps precisely because of the qualities which set him apart from contemporary tastes as exemplified by the clever, if unexceptional, verses of the Dali Shi Caizi 大曆十才子 (Ten Talents of the Dali Era).

While he derived much of his personal style from earlier poetry, Wei was not blind to contemporary events and developments. Many pieces, including *gexing* 歌行 (songs and ballads), realistically depict the economic and social disorder following the An Lushan Rebellion; they also reveal his own complex responses: outrage at military abuses, sympathy for the victims, and nostalgia for the cultural and material wealth of his courtier days. Of interest are his "Tiaoxiao ling" 調笑令 (Song of Flirtatious Laughter), several lyrics set to contemporary music which are regarded both as *yuefu* poems and as early examples of the *ci* lyric. Twelve of his poems were included in the *Tang shi sanbaishou* 唐詩三百首 (Three Hundred Poems of the Tang).

BIBLIOGRAPHY

Editions:

Liu Chenwen 劉辰翁 (1232–1297), collator and commentator. *Yuan kan Wei Suzhou ji* 元刊韋蘇州集. Fuzhou: Fujian Renmin, 2008.

Luan Guimin 欒貴明. *Quan Tangshi suoyin: Wei Yingwu juan* 全唐詩索引: 韋應物卷. Tianjin: Tianjin Guji, 1997.

Nielson, Thomas Peter. *A Concordance to the Poems of Wei Yingwu*. San Francisco: CMC, 1975. Keyed to *SBBY* edition of *Wei Suzhou ji*. Includes a biographical study.

Quan Tang shi, 3: 1900–2015, 13: 10126, 10421, 14: 11151–52.
Quan Tang wen, 375.4329–31.
Sun Wang 孫望. *Wei Yingwu shiji xinian* 韋應物詩集繫年. Beijing: Zhonghua, 2002.
Wei Jiangzhou ji 韋江州集. SBCK. Not as carefully edited as *Wei Suzhou ji*, but has appendix with all prefaces, colophons, and biographies from previous editions.
Wei Suzhou ji 韋蘇州集. SBBY is the most reliable edition, but lacks the eight poems in the *shiyi* 拾遺 (omissions) section of other editions.

Annotations:

Liu Yisheng 劉逸生 and Li Xiaosong 李小松, ed. *Meng Haoran, Wei Yingwu shixuan* 孟浩然, 韋應物詩選. Hong Kong: Sanlian, 1983.
Ruan Tingyu 阮廷瑜. *Wei Suzhou shi jiaozhu* 韋蘇州詩校註. Taibei: Huatai, 2000.
Tao Min 陶敏 and Wang Yousheng 王友勝, eds. *Wei Yingwu shixuan* 韋應物詩選. Beijing: Zhonghua, 2005.
___. *Wei Yingwu ji jiaozhu* 韋應物集校註. Shanghai: Shanghai Guji, 1998.

Biographical Sources:

Fu, *Tang caizi*, 2:163–82, 5:196–97.

Translations:

Bynner, *Jade Mountain*, pp. 169–74.
Debon, *Mein Haus*, p. 111.
Demiéville, *Anthologie*, pp. 278–84.
Field, "Taking Up the Plow," pp. 125–27.
Red Pine. *In Such Hard Times: the Poetry of Wei Yingwu*. Port Townsend, Washington: Copper Canyon Press, 2009.
Sunflower Splendor, pp. 153–54.

Studies:

Ceng Zhaomin 曾昭岷, ed. *Wen, Wei, Feng ci xin jiao* 溫韋馮詞新校. Shanghai: Shanghai Guji, 1988.
Chu Zhongjun 儲仲君. "Wei Yingwu shi feiqi de tantao" 韋應物詩分期的探討. *Wenxue yichan* 1984.4: 67–75.
Fang Rixi 房日晰. "Wei Yingwu yuefu gexing lun lue" 韋應物樂府歌行論略. *Xibei Daxue xuebao* 1996.3: 49–51.
Fukazawa Kazuyuki 深澤一幸. "I Ōbutsu no kakō" 韋應物の歌行. *Chūkgoku bungakuhō*, 1974. 24: 48–74.
Jiang Guangdou 姜光斗 and Gu Qi 顧啓. "Wei Yingwu ren Suzhou cishi shi de jianshu he wannian gaikuang" 韋應物任蘇州刺史時的建樹和晚年概況. *Suzhou Daxue xuebao* 1986.4: 122–26.
Kuroda Mamiko 黑田真美. *I Ōbutsu shiron: Tōbōshi o chūshin to shite* 韋應物詩論: 悼亡詩を中心として. Tokyo: Iwanami, 2017.
Lee, Oscar. "The Critical Perception of the Poetry of Wei Yingwu (737–792): The Creation of a Poetic Reputation." Unpublished Ph.D dissertation. Columbia University, 1986.
Li Shiying 李世英 and Hou Runzhang 侯潤章. "Jinnian lai Wei Yingwu yanjiu zhi jianlun" 近年來韋應物研究之檢論. *Lanzhou Daxue xuebao*, 1988.2: 100–05.
Lim Chooi Kua 林水檺. "The Artistic Achievement and Style of Wei Yingwu's Poetry." *Chinese Culture: A Quarterly Review*, 1994.3: 25–44.
Luo Liantian 羅聯添. "Wei Yingwu shiji xinian" 韋應物事蹟繫年. *Youshi xuezhi* 幼獅學志, 1969.8. 1: 72.
Nielson, Thomas Peter. "The Tang Poet Wei Yingwu and his Poetry." Unpublished Ph.D. dissertation. University of Washington, 1969.

Ren Lili 任莉莉. "Wei Suzhou ji xulu" 韋蘇州集敍錄. *Gugong wenwu xuekan* 故宮文物學刊, 1989. 70: 128–33; 71: 130–37.

Suzuki Toshio 鈴木敏雄. "I Ōbotsu no zatsugishi ni tsuite" 韋應物の雜擬詩について: 模倣の樣式とその意味. *Nihon Chūgoku Gakkaihō*, 1990. 42: 125–40.

____. "I Ōbotsu gikoshi nijusshu kō" 韋應物「擬古詩十二首」考. *Chūgoku chūsei bungaku kenkyū*, 1991.20: 159–78.

Tao Min 陶敏. "Wei Yingwu shengping zai kao" 韋應物生平再考. *Wenxue yichan*, 2010.1, pp. 136–38.

Varsano, Paula M. "The Invisible Landscape of Wei Yingwu (737–792)." *HJAS* 54.2 (1994): 407–35.

Wan Man 萬曼. "Wei Yingwu zhuan" 韋應物傳. *Guowen xuekan* 國學學刊, 1958.60: 23–32; 1958. 61: 23–28.

Wang Xiyuan 王熙元, *et al.* eds. *Wei Yingwu* 韋應物. Taibei: Jinxiu, 1992.

Xia Ji'an 夏濟安 (1916–1965). "Wei Ying-wu," in *Zhongguo wenxue shi lunji* 中國文學史論集, v. 1, Taibei: Zhonghu Wenhua Chuban Shiye Weiyuanhui, 1958, pp. 331–37.

Xie Yongfang 謝永芳. *Wei Yingwu quanji: huijiao, huizhu, huiping* 韋應物全集: 匯校, 匯注, 匯評. Wuhan: Chongwen, 2019.

Xu, C. Y. "The Stone Drums." *Asian Culture Quarterly* 13.1 (1985): 87–109. A study of poems inscribed on ancient drum-shaped stelae and of Wei Yingwu, Han Yu and other later poets' verses on them.

Yoshikawa Kojiro 吉川幸次郎. "I Ōbutsu no shi" 韋應物的詩. *Chūgoku shishi* 中國詩史, Tokyo: Chikuma, 1967, pp. 80–84.

Yoshimura Hiromichi 芳村弘道. "I Ōbutsu no shōgai" 韋應物の生涯. *Gakurin* 7–8 (1986) 7: 53–69; 8: 66–84.

Oscar Lee, Ma Nan, and William H. Nienhauser, Jr.

Wei Zhuang 韋莊 (*zi*, Duanji 端己, ca. 836–910), a high government official, poet, and anthologist, was a native of Duling 杜陵, a district in the Chang'an metropolitan area, and a member of a once powerful and prominent clan which counted the Grand Councilor Wei Jiansu 韋見素 (687–762) among its members. By Wei Zhuang's time his immediate family had apparently fallen on hard times. Although he was orphaned when quite young, he managed to obtain an education and prepare himself for the civil-service examinations. Little is known about his activities until he went to Chang'an in 881 to take the *jinshi* examination shortly before the city was captured and plundered by the rebel armies of Huang Chao 黃巢 (d. 884). His moving depiction of those momentous events in the famous narrative poem "Qinfu yin" 秦婦吟 (The Lament of the Lady of Qin) brought him fame and attention. But the chaotic events of the time forced him into a long period of wandering in the south and in the east, and it was more than a decade later (894) before he was able to compete successfully for the highest examination degree. Although nearly sixty years of age, he was given an appointment as a minor official in the capital and three years later posted to what is now Sichuan on the staff of a senior official. There he met and became an adviser to Wang Jian 王建 (847–918). When the Tang collapsed in 907, Wang Jian proclaimed the founding of the Qian Shu 前蜀 (Former Shu) dynasty in his own name and called upon Wei Zhuang to join the new regime. As a result, Wei Zhuang played a key role in the formation of the government and followed the Tang model in defining the institutions for the Former Shu. Until his death three years later, he held a succession of high offices, culminating in that of Grand Councilor. He is said to have been responsible for drafting many of the official documents of state. Because of the Former Shu's relative stability in politically troubled times, Wang Jian was successful in attracting to his regime many of the leading literary figures of the day.

After taking up permanent residence in the city of Chengdu, Wei Zhuang purchased and restored the Huanhua Xi Caotang 浣花溪草堂 (The Thatched Hut of Flower-washing Brook), the former home of Du Fu 杜甫 (712–770).* Thus, when his younger brother Wei Ai 韋藹 compiled and edited his poems for publication in 903, the collection was given the title *Huanhuaji* 浣花集 (The Collection of Flower-washing). In a poem probably written rather late in life, Wei Zhuang stated, perhaps somewhat hyperbolically, that he had written a thousand songs and poems. The modern edition of his collected works is much smaller. It contains about three hundred *shi* poems and includes neither the "Qinfu yin" poem, which was apparently deleted from the collection at his express wish, nor his *ci* poems. Fortunately, several manuscript versions of the former poems were recovered early in the twentieth century from the cave-temples of Dunhuang. Most of his extant *ci* have been preserved in the *Huajianji* 花間集.

"The Lament of the Lady of Qin," one of Wei Zhuang's best loved works then and now, is a unique example of a genre only occasionally practiced in pre-modern times—namely, the long narrative poem. It is remarkable for its sheer length (238 lines in the heptasyllabic mode), its rather realistic depiction of the capture and brutal sack of Chang'an by the rebel armies of Huang Chao, and its dramatic power and intensity. Few writers of the past cared, or perhaps dared, to express their feelings about contemporary political events so openly. But in this instance Wei Zhuang chose to do so with clarity and detail, perhaps best exemplified by the famous couplet "The Inner Treasury consumed in ashes of embroidery and brocade, / Along imperial avenues nowhere to walk but on the bones of high officials" 內庫燒為錦繡灰，天街踏盡公卿骨.

Compared with the "Qinfu yin" poem and his *ci* verse, Wei Zhuang's *shi* poems have been little studied except for several well-known anthology pieces (two poems appear in the *Tangshi sanbaishou*. When his *shi* poems are discussed, they are usually cited as evidence of his travels and personal experiences or his attitude toward social classes. It can be said, however, that Wei had a strong preference for the longer line-length (approximately three-fourths of the collection is in the heptasyllabic form) and regulated-verse patterns in the pentasyllabic and heptasyllabic line lengths predominate. His concerns as a *shi* poet are more often personal than public, although echoes of the turbulent times so dramatically described in the "Lament" poem are occasionally heard. A muted pathos informs his verse on such time-tested themes as separation and parting or contemplations of the past, and these are expressed in a diction less given to artifice than was characteristic of the times.

As a contributor to the then emerging literati *ci* 詞-lyric tradition, Wei Zhuang stood between the generation of Wen Tingyun 溫庭筠 (ca. 812–870)* and that of Feng Yansi 馮延巳 (ca. 903–960) and Li Yu 李煜 (937–978). These four men are often considered as the four early masters of the form, and comparisons of their respective styles have proven to be particularly illuminating. Generally speaking, traditional criticism usually regarded Wen Tingyun and Wei Zhuang as differing little in matters of style, but modern analytical methods have enabled scholars to uncover important distinctions between these two men. Both poets share a similar thematic range—namely, the so-called "bedroom topos" and the personal plaint. And both poets also wrote exclusively in the *xiaoling* 小令, or short-lyric patterns. But in other respects, as Kang-i Sun Chang in particular has demonstrated, their styles are fundamentally different. Wei Zhuang characteristically employs a rhetoric of explicit meaning, by which means he speaks directly to the listener/reader, carefully maintaining a sequential narrative progression, both within and between the stanzas. He adopts a language logically consistent with his chosen stance as the explicit narrator, one which retains elements of colloquialism and is hypotactically expressive. Thus, Wei Zhuang is closer stylistically to the popular Dunhuang *ci* than is Wen Tingyun or his imitators among the *Huajian* Poets. It is also similar to the work of the post-*Huajian* poets of the mid-tenth century who were to carry the form to new heights, as Wei's poem "Pusa man" 菩薩蠻 (Bodhisattva Barbarian) illustrates:

> Everyone says the South is good.
> A sojourner should just grow old in the South.
> Springtime waters bluer than the sky,
> In painted boats you listen to the rain and doze.
> Beside the wine shop, a girl like the moon—
> On her pale wrists frost and snow congeal.
> Until you grow old, don't go home.
> Go home and your heart is bound to break.

> 人人盡說江南好，遊人只合江南老。
> 春水碧於天，畫船聽雨眠。
> 墟邊人似月，皓腕凝霜雪。
> 未老莫還鄉，還鄉須斷腸。

This poem is thought to have been written after Wei Zhuang had fled to the South during the Huang Chao Rebellion. The beauty depicted in lines 5–6 may be intended to invoke the image of Zhuo Wenjun 卓文君 who eloped with Sima Xiangru 司馬相如 (179–117 BC) and then ran a wine shop with him. The heartbreak of the final lines would be that experienced on leaving the idyllic South to go back north to homes that had been destroyed by the rebellion.

During his later years Wei Zhuang compiled a large anthology of Tang-dynasty verse, the *Youxuanji* 又玄集 (Collection of Restoring the Mystery), which contains selections from 150 poets of the era. The title chosen for this work suggests that Wei Zhuang regarded it as a kind of continuation to the *Jixuanji* 極玄集 (The Supreme Mystery Collection), a much smaller compilation by Yao He 姚合 (ca. 779–ca. 849).*

BIBLIOGRAPHY

Editions:

Huanhuaji 浣花集. *SBCK*.

Fu, *Tangren*, pp. 571–684.

Luan Guiming 欒貴明, comp. *Quan Tangshi suoyin: Wei Zhuang juan* 全唐詩索引·韋莊卷. Tianjin: Tianjin Guji, 1997.

Nagasawa Kikuya 長沢規矩也 (1902–1980), ed. *Wakokubon Kanshi shūsei, sōshiken* (1) 和刻本漢詩集成. 総集篇 1 輯. Tokyo: Kyūko, 1978. Three *juan* of Wei Zhuang's *Youxuanji* originally published in the third year of the Xianghe 享和 Era (1803).

Quan Tang shi, 10: 8066–132, 13: 10143–49, 10322–26, 15: 11725.

Quan Tang Wudai ci huibian 全唐五代詞彙編. 2v. Taibei, Shijie, 1967. Rpt. Of the Lin Dazhuang 林大椿 compilation *Tang Wudai ci*. Contains 54 *ci* attributed to Wei Zhuang.

Zeng Zhaomin 曾昭岷, ed. *Wen, Wei, Feng ci xinjiao* 溫韋馮詞新校. Shanghai: Shanghai Guji, 1988.
Zhao Chongzuo 趙崇祚, ed. *Huajianji* 花間集. *SBBY*.

Annotations:
Jiang Congping 江聰平. *Wei Duanji shijiao zhu* 韋端己詩校注. Taibei: Zhonghua, 1969.
Li Yi 李誼, ed. *Wei Zhuang ji jiaozhu* 韋莊集校注. Chengdu: Sichuansheng Shehui Kexueyuan, 1986.
Nie Anfu 聶安福, annot. *Wei Zhuang ji jianzhu* 韋莊集箋注. Shanghai: Shanghai Guji, 2002.
Xia Chengtao 夏承燾, ed. and Liu Jincheng 劉金城, comm. *Wei Zhuang ci jiaozhu* 韋莊詞校注. Beijing: Zhongguo Shehui Kexue, 1981.

Biographical Sources:
Fu, *Tang caizi*, 4:322–33, 5:473–74.

Translations:
Birch, *Anthology*, pp. 339–41.
Demiéville, *Anthologie*, pp. 324, 331–32.
Fusek, Lois. *Among the Flowers: The Hua-chien chi*. New York: Columbia University Press, 1982.
Levy, *Narrative Poetry*, pp. 138–49.
Nakata Yūjirō 中田勇次郎. *Rekidai meishi sen* 歷代名詞選. Tokyo: Shūeisha, 1997. Selected some of Wei Zhuang's *ci* poems.
Owen. *Late Tang*, pp. 204–05.
Soong, Stephen C. *Song Without Music: Chinese Tz'u Poetry*. Hong Kong: The Chinese University Press, 1980, pp. 45–56.
Shields, Anna. *Crafting a Collection, The Cultural Contexts and Poetic Practice of the Huajian ji* 花間集 *(Collection from Among the Flowers)*. Cambridge: Harvard University Asia Center, 2006, pp. 179, 196, 214–15, 246–48, 250.
Sunflower, pp. 267–84.
Wixted, John Timothy. *The Song-Poetry of Wei Chuang (836–910)*. Temple, Arizona: Center of Asian Studies, Arizona State University, 1979. Translation of 48 *ci* with an introduction.
See also Chang Kang-I Sun below.

Studies:
Ashidate Ichirou 芦立一郎. "Isoushi no goinitsuite" 韋莊詞の語彙について. *Yamagata Daigaku Jinbun Gakubu Kenkyū nenpō* 山形大学人文学部研究年報, 5(2008): 101–15.
Cao Lifang 曹麗芳. "Wei Zhuang *Huanhuaji* banben yuanliu ji buyi kaoshu" 韋莊浣花集版本源流及補遺考述. *Wenxian* 文獻, 2003.2: 135–49.
___. "Bainianlai Wei Zhuang yanjiu shuping" 百年來韋莊研究述評. *Tangdu xuekan* 唐都學刊 no. 3 (2002): 29–31.
Chang Kang-I Sun. "Wen T'ing-yün and Wei Chuang: Towards a Formation of Conventions." In *The Evolution of Chinese Tz'u Poetry: From Late T'ang to Northern Sung*. Princeton: Princeton University Press, 1980, pp. 33–62.
Diény, J. P. "Review of J. T. Wixted's The Song Poetry of Wei Chuang," *T'oung Pao*, 67 (1981), 111–16.
Giles, Lionel. "The Lament of the Lady of Ch'in." *T'oung Pao* 24.4/5 (1925–1926): 305–80.
Levy, Dore J. *Chinese Narrative Poetry: The Late Han Through T'ang Dynasties*. Durham: Duke University Press, 1988. Study of Wei Zhuang's "Qinfu yin."
Li Yi 李誼, ed. *Wei Zhuang ji zhu* 韋莊集注. Chengdu: Sichuan Daxue, 2017.

Wei Zhuang

Matsuura Tomohisa 松浦友久 (1935–2002). *Kōchū Tōshi kaishaku jiten (Zoku)* 校注唐詩解釈辞典（続）. Tokyo: Taishūkan, 2001. Selected some of Wei Zhuang's poems.

Mo Lifeng 莫礪鋒. "Lun Wan Tang Wudai cifeng de zhuanbian—jianlun Wei Zhuang zai cishishang de diwei" 論晚唐五代詞風的轉變—兼論韋莊在詞史上的地位. *Wenxue yichan* 文學遺產, 1980.5.

Mori Hiroyuki 森博行. *Shijin to namida: Tō Sō shishiron* 詩人と涙：唐宋詩詞論. Tokyo: Hatsubo Seiunsha, 2002.

Nakata Yoshikatsa 中田喜勝. "Kakansyuu to Isou" 花間集と韋莊. *Nagasaki Daigaku Kyōyōbu kiyō* 長崎大學教養部紀要. 1980, 20.2: 17–40.

Nugent, Christopher M. B. "The Lady and Her Scribes: Dealing with the Multiple Dunhuang Copies of Wei Zhuang's 'Lament of the Lady of Qin,'" *AM* 20 (2007): 25–73.

Qi Tao 齊濤. "Wei Zhuang shengping xinkao" 韋莊生平新考. *Wenxue yichan* 文學遺產, 1996.3: 39–44.

Ren Haitian 任海天. *Wei Zhuang yanjiu* 韋莊研究. Beijing: Renmin Wenxue, 2005.

Tang, Raymond Nai-wen. "The Poetry of Wei Zhuang (836–910)." Unpublished Ph.D. dissertation, Stanford University, 1982.

Wagner, Marsha. *The Lotus Boat: The Origins of Chinese Tz'u Poetry in Tang Popular Culture*. New York: Columbia University Press, 1984.

Xia Chengtao 夏承燾. *Tang Song ciren nianpu* 唐宋詞人年譜, Shanghai: Gudian Wenxue, 1955, pp. 1–33. A chronological account of Wei Zhuang's life.

Yan Tingliang 顏廷亮 and Zhao Yiwu 趙以武. *Qinfu yin yanjiu huilu* 秦婦吟研究彙錄. Shanghai: Shanghai Guji, 1990.

Yates, Robin D.S. *Washing Silk: The Life and Selected Poetry of Wei Chuang (ca. 834–910)*. Cambridge, Massachusetts: Harvard University Press, 1988. *Harvard-Yenching Monograph Series*, 26. Detailed scholarly study of Wei's biography, background and poetry followed by annotated translations of *shi* (110 poems) and *ci* (55).

Ye Jiaying 葉嘉瑩. *Wen Tingyun, Wei Zhuang, Feng Yansi, Li Yu* 溫庭筠韋莊馮延巳李煜. Taibei: Da'an, 1992. *Tang Song mingjia ci shangxi* 唐宋名家詞賞析, 1.

Zhang Qiugui 張丘奎. *Tangmo Du Fu shige yanjiu yi Luo Yin, Wei Zhuang, Han Wo sanren wei tantao* 唐末杜甫詩歌研究以羅隱韋莊韓偓三人為探討. Taibei: Huamulan, 2020.

Zhao Huaide 趙懷德. *Wei Zhuang pingzhuan* 韋莊評傳. Xi'an: Shaanxi Renmin Jiaoyu, 2001.

Wilfried Spaar and Wu Chen

Wen Tingyun 溫庭筠, sometimes Tingyun 廷筠 or Tingyun 庭雲, original *ming*, Qi 歧 (*zi*, Feiqing 飛卿; ca. 812–870), a versatile and innovative poet and writer, was a native of Taiyuan 太原 (Shanxi), and a lineal descendant of Wen Yanbo 溫彥博 (575–637), a Grand Councilor during the reign of Emperor Taizong (r. 627–650). His was an illustrious family, as the older brother of Wen Yanbo, Wen Daya 溫大雅 (574–629), was the author of the well-known *Da Tang Chuangye Qiju Zhu* 大唐創業起居注 (Record of Activity and Repose of the Founding of the Great Tang) and also influential at the Tang court. Wen Tingyun's grandfather and father both had modestly successful official careers. Because of numerous references in his poetry to the lower Yangzi Valley region, it is thought that Wen Tingyun may have spent his youth there. He traveled widely in the area in his later years.

When Wen Tingyun arrived in Chang'an in his early twenties to participate in the *jinshi* examination, he was already regarded as a promising literary talent and a skilled performer on the flute and various stringed instruments. Frequent mention is also made in the historical sources of his practiced skill in the examination-style *fu* 賦. Two of his compositions in that genre are contained in the *Quan Tang wen*, both elegant displays of word magic. Nonetheless, he failed to pass the examinations, apparently disqualified on one occasion for assisting eight fellow candidates with their papers. Although it seems that he never received the coveted *jinshi* degree, he was appointed to a minor provincial post on the basis of personal connections. Some sources also indicate that he was ultimately made a tutor in the Imperial Academy because of his friendship with the powerful official Linghu Tao 令狐綯 (ca. 795–ca. 872). His failure to distinguish himself in the examinations or later in public service may have resulted from his personal habits and mannerisms, for the historical sources describe him as an arrogant non-conformist, a decadent ne'er-do-well, and an habitué of the gay quarters. He apparently formed a temporary liaison with the famous female poet Yu Xuanji 魚玄機 (ca. 844–868)*—their relationship was later fictionalized by the Japanese novelist Mori Ogai 森鷗外 (1862–1922). Wen Tingyun's familiarity with the world of popular entertainment had other important consequences, for it was in that environment that the new musical and *ci* (lyric) patterns were then much in vogue. Inspiration gained in that milieu, along with his own talents as a musician, explain why he was the first literati poet to seriously explore the potentials of the *ci* form as a medium of polite verse.

Although other writers before him, such as Li Bo 李白 (701–762),* Liu Yuxi 劉禹錫 (772–842),* and Bo Juyi 白居易 (772–846),* had rather infrequently experimented with *ci* verse-patterns, their efforts actually differed little in either form or content from the traditional *shi* modes. Wen Tingyun, however, elected to follow a bolder course in distinguishing between *shi* and *ci* and in making extensive use of the latter. As a result, two collections of his *ci* poems were in circulation during his lifetime: the *Wolan ji* 握蘭集 (Plucking the Orchid Collection) in three *juan*, and the *Jinquan ji* 金荃集 (The Golden Fish-trap Collection) in ten *juan*. Both of these works were subsequently lost, but seventy of his *ci* survive, most of which have been preserved in the famous ninth-century anthology *Huajian ji* 花間集. Because of Wen Tingyun's vital contribution to the development of the *ci* as a new literati verse-form and his pervasive influence on many of the other authors represented in his anthology, he was accorded more space than any other figure.

Critical reaction to Wen Tingyun's *ci* has varied enormously over the centuries. Some critics have found them morally objectionable because of their exotic and sensuous imagery and their bedchamber topoi. On the other hand, there are those who admired their obvious aesthetic qualities. The influential critic Zhang Huiyan 張惠言 (1761–1802), for instance, praised Wen's *ci* style for its profundity and beauty. More recently, specialists writing on the early history of the form and its major practitioners have sought to go beyond the traditional impressionistic generalities to discover the underlying elements of form and style. Zheng Qian 鄭騫, for instance, has stressed the objective point-of-view in Wen's poems, and Chia-ying Yeh Chao 葉嘉瑩 has called attention to the pictorial quality of his *ci*. Kang-i Sun Chang has carried the analysis forward by focusing on what she calls his "rhetoric of implicit meaning," while drawing attention to the important differences between the single- and two-stanza *xiaoling* (short lyric) poems. The former tend to be explicit in manner, linguistically hypotactic, and normally concerned with the depiction of a young woman and her lover. The latter, on the other hand, are more complex, where meaning is usually implied. The persona in these poems is typically the neglected woman, who seems to be immobilized by her loneliness. She is seen to be languishing in bed, sitting before her mirror, or leaning disconsolately against a balustrade. Her inner feelings are suggested metaphorically by the physical environment which she inhabits, an opulent world of crystal curtains, incense burners, figured embroideries, and the like. Visual, aural, and olfactory images invest the scene with color and movement and meaning. Thus Wen Tingyun's song-lyrics represent a sharp break with earlier examples of the form, whether popular *ci* from Dunhuang with their vernacular language, their open and direct manner, and their greater variety of subject matter, or the relatively unimaginative *ci* of his literati predecessors. Thus, it is to Wen Tingyun's credit that the *ci* form achieved a new stature and began to move in new directions. The following "Pusa man" 菩薩蠻 (Bodhisattva Barbarian) is typical of his *ci* style:

> Blue-feathered headdress stitched with gold—a pair of mandarin ducks;
> Ripples on the greenish-blue waters of the spring pond.
> By the pond a crabapple tree—
> Rain-washed, red fills the branches.
>
> A brocade collar hides a dimpled cheek;
> Misted grasses cling to flying butterflies.
>
> Blue-patterned doors open on the fragrant scene,
> But not a word is heard from the Jade Pass.
>
> 翠翹金縷雙鸂鶒，水紋細起春池碧。
> 池上海棠梨，雨晴紅滿枝。
> 繡衫遮笑靨，煙草粘飛蝶。
> 青瑣對芳菲，玉關音信稀。

The female persona is placed in a familiar setting here—that of a garden whose bright colors reflect her headdress of kingfisher feathers (line 1). The penultimate line depicts a noble house and a garden fit for a tryst, but the poems closes by revealing that the persona's husband (or lover) is campaigning on the frontier.

As a poet of ancient and modern style *shi* verse forms, Wen Tingyun was linked in his own day with his contemporaries Li Shangyin 李商隱 (ca. 813–858)* and Duan Chengshi 段成式 (d. 863), although the only real connection between these men seems to have been the marriage of Wen's daughter to Duan's son. Their differences as individuals and men of letters are greater than their similarities. It is more useful to compare Wen's *ci* with his poems written to the traditional forms. The following poem, "Shangshan zaoxing" 商山早行 (Setting Out Early from Mount Shang), is typical of his style:

> Up at break of day, I start to the jingle of bells on the reins—
> A traveler setting out, missing his hometown.
> A cock's crow, the moon over the thatched inn;
> Footprints of others on the frosted plank bridge.
> Oak leaves fall on the mountain road,
> Hedge thorn blossoms brighten the wall of the inn—

Out of my thoughts comes a dream of Duling,
Ducks and geese filling the winding ponds.

晨起動征鐸，客行悲故鄉
雞聲茅店月，人跡板橋霜 。
槲葉落山路，枳花明驛牆 。
因思杜陵夢，鳧雁滿回塘 。

This poem was written in 856 when Wen was on his way to exile in Sui 隋 County (in modern Shaanxi) following an examination scandal the previous year. What is striking in the poem is not the diction or sound patterns, but the syntax. The poem is distinguished by noun images such as in lines 3 and 4 (literally): "cock sound thatched-room inn moon / others' footprints plank bridge frost." Despite the lack of active verbs, the lines nevertheless create a vibrant scene with all of the typical elements of an early morning departure present: the sounds of the bells on the horse, the cock's crow, the setting new moon, and the frosted planks on the bridge leading to the open road. In contrast, the first lines use sound to rouse poet and reader, while the third couplet brings in the fledgling morning light revealing green leaves falling and the white hedge thorn blossoms reflecting onto the walls of the inn where the poet has spent the night before. In the final couplet, the poet, now fully awake, realizes that the peaceful ponds of his hometown in Du Ling he saw in his dream now reflect his current concerns as he heads further south. Unlike the ducks and geese of the dream, however, Wen cannot migrate back home.

Generally speaking, his *shi* poems reveal a greater range of diction, mood, and theme than is the case with his *ci*. Among his three hundred-odd extant *shi*, there is a slight preference for the longer heptasyllabic line; nonetheless, at one time or another he adopted all of the major forms. Variety of form is matched by diversity of language and style. For instance, "Su Wu miao" 蘇武廟 (The Temple of Su Wu), is classical in its restraint and concision. Similarly, many of his regulated-verse poems depict in approving terms the simple, bucolic existence of the rustic farmer or fisherman, and the untrammeled happiness of reclusion in nature. Still other poems belong to the *yongshi* 詠史 (on history) subgenre; among these are celebrations of the grandeur and affluence of former political leaders which are notable for their absence of critical comment. These and other themes lend his *shi* a degree of richness and diversity generally lacking in his *ci*.

In addition to the *fu, ci,* and *shi* already mentioned, a number of letters from his hand are to be found in the *Quan Tang wen*. Other prose writings on a variety of subjects are also preserved in various collectanea.

BIBLIOGRAPHY

Editions:
Iwama Keiji 岩間啓二. *On Teiin kashi sakuin* 溫庭筠歌詩索引. Kyoto: Hōyu, 1977.
Luan Guiming 欒貴明 et al., eds. *Quan Tang shi suoyin: Wen Tingyun juan* 全唐詩索引：溫庭筠卷. Qinhuangdao: Xiandai, 1994.
Quan Tang shi, 9: 6748–820, 13: 10133–39, 10255, 14: 10680, 15: 11343.
Quan Tang wen, 786.9362–71.

Wen Tingyun

Wen Feiqing shi ji 溫飛卿詩集. Taibei, 1967. A photolithographic reprint of the edition with Zeng Yi's annotation and Gu Yuxian's supplementary notes, with a post-face by Gu Sili dated 1696.

Zhao Chongzuo 趙崇祚, ed. *Huajian ji*. SBBY.

Annotations:

Liu Xuekai 劉學鍇. *Wen Tingyun quanji jiaozhu* 溫庭筠全集校注. Beijing: Zhonghua, 2007.

___. *Wen Tingyun shici xuan* 溫庭筠詩詞選. Zhengzhou: Zhongzhou Guji, 2011.

Liu Yisheng 劉逸生 and Liu Sihan 劉斯翰, eds. and comms. *Wen Tingyun shici xuan* 溫庭筠詩詞選. Hong Kong: Sanlian, 1986.

Wen Feiqing ji jianzhu 溫飛卿集箋注. Annotated by Zeng Yi 曾益 with supplementary notes by Gu Yuxian 顧予咸 and Gu Sili 顧嗣立. Rpt. Shanghai: Shanghai Guji, 1980.

Zeng Zhaomin 曾昭岷, ed. *Wen, Wei, Feng ci xin jiao* 溫、韋、馮詞新校. Shanghai: Guji, 1988.

Biographical Sources:

Fu, *Tang caizi*, 3:433–48, 5:415–16.

Jiu Tang shu, 190C.5078–79.

Xin Tang shu, 91.3787–88.

Translations:

Birch, *Anthology*, pp. 336–39.

Chaves, Jonathan, "The *Tz'u* Poetry of Wen T'ing-yün." Unpublished M.A. thesis, Columbia University, 1966. Includes translations of all 70 extant *ci*.

Demiéville, *Anthologie*, pp. 321–22, 330.

Fuller, Michael A. *An Introduction to Chinese Poetry: From the* Canon of Poetry *to the Lyrics of the Song Dynasty*. Cambridge: Harvard University Press, 2018, pp. 341–46.

Fusek, *Among the Flowers*, pp. 37–54.

Margoulies, *Anthologie*, p. 376.

Owen, *Late Tang*, pp. 465–66, 527–65.

Shields, Anna. *Crafting a Collection, The Cultural Contexts and Poetic Practice of the Huajian ji* 花間集 *(Collection from Among the Flowers)*. Cambridge: Harvard University Asia Center, 2006, pp. 178, 191–92, 203–04, 233–34, 325–26.

Sunflower, pp. 244–54.

Studies:

Chang Kang-I Sun. "Wen T'ing-yün and Wei Chuang: Towards a Formation of Conventions." In *The Evolution of Chinese Tz'u Poetry: From Late T'ang to Northern Sung*. Princeton: Princeton University Press, 1980, pp. 33–62.

Fang Yu 方瑜. *Zhongwan Tang Sanjia shixi lun* 中晚唐三家詩析論. Taibei, 1975.

Gao Ming 高明, et al., eds. *Wen Tingyun* 溫庭筠. Taibei: Jinxiu, 1992. *Tang shi xinshang*, 13.

Gu Xuexie 顧學頡, "Xinjiu *Tang shu* Wen Tingyun zhuan dingbu" 新舊唐書溫庭筠傳訂補, *Guowen yuekan* (December 1947): 19–26.

Guo Juanyu 郭娟玉. *Wen Tingyun bianyi* 溫庭筠辨疑. Taibei: Guojia, 2012.

___. *Wen Tingyun jieshou yanjiu* 溫庭筠接受研究. Taibei: Wanjuanlou, 2013

Huang Kunyao 黃坤堯. *Wen Tingyun* 溫庭筠. Taibei: Guojia, 1984.

Liu Xuekai 劉學鍇. *Wen Tingyun zhuan lun* 溫庭筠傳論. Hefei: Anhui Daxue, 1994.

Lu Yi. *Wen Fei-ch'ing und seine literarische Umwelt*. Würzburg: Aumühle, 1939.

Mou Huaichuan 牟懷川, "Wen Tingyun shengnian xinzheng" 溫庭筠生年新證, *Shanghai Shifan Xueyuan xuebao* 1984.1.

Murakami Tetsukmi 村上哲見. "On Hikyō no bungaku" 溫飛卿の文学, *Chūgoku bungakuhō*, 5 (1956): 19–40.

Rouzer, Paul E., "Wen Tingyun." Unpublished Ph. D. dissertation, Harvard University, 1989.

___. "Watching the Voyeurs: Palace Poetry and the *Yuefu* of Wen Tingyun," *CLEAR* 11 (1989): 13–34.

___. *Writing Another's Dream: The Poetry of Wen Tingyun*. Stanford: Stanford University Press, 1993.

Wan Wenwu 萬文武. *Wen Tingyun bianxi* 溫庭筠辨析. Xi'an: Shanxi Renmin, 1992. *Zhongguo gudai zuojia yanjiu congshu*.

Wu Hongyi 吳宏一. *Wen Tingyun 'Pusa man' ci yanjiu* 溫庭筠菩薩蠻詞研究. Xinzhu: Guoli Qinghua Daxue, 2009.

Xia Chengtao 夏承燾. *Wen Feiqing xinian; Wei Duanji nianpu* 溫飛卿繫年; 韋端己年譜. Taibei: Shijie, 2012.

___. *Tang Song ciren nianpu* 唐宋詞人年譜. Shanghai, 1955, pp. 383–434.

Ye Jiaying 葉嘉瑩. "Wen Tingyun ci gaishuo" 溫庭筠詞概說, in *Jialing tanci* 迦陵談詞, Taibei, 1970, pp. 13–54.

___. *Wen Tingyun, Wei Zhuang, Feng Yansi, Li Yu* 溫庭筠韋莊馮延巳李煜. Taibei: Daan, 1992.

Zheng Qian 鄭騫. *Cong shi dao qu* 從詩到曲. Taibei, 1961.

___. "Wen Tingyun, Wei Zhuang yu ci de chuang shi" 溫庭筠, 韋莊與詞的創始, in *Jingwu congbian* 景午叢編, v. 1, Taibei: Zhonghua, 1972, pp. 103–09.

Wilfried Spaar, Shen Yiwen and William H. Nienhauser, Jr.

Wuke 無可 (secular surname Jia 賈, fl. 825–827) was Jia Dao's 賈島 (779–843)* paternal cousin and wrote Buddhist-inspired poetry in a similarly limpid style. Yuan-period scholar Xin Wenfang 辛文房, compiler of *Tang caizi zhuan* 唐才子傳 (Biographies of Talented Men of the Tang [published 1304]) counted him among the eight most important *shiseng* 詩僧 (poet-monks) of the Tang, along with Lingyi 靈一 (727–762), Lingche 靈澈 (746–816),* Jiao Ran 皎然 (720–799),* Qingsai 清塞 (a.k.a. Zhou He 周賀, fl. mid-9th ca.), Xuzhong 虛中 (fl. 897–942),* Qiji 齊己 (fl. 881),* and Guanxiu 貫休 (832–912).* He Yisun 賀貽孫 (1605–ca. 1688) in *Shifa* 詩筏 (Raft of Poetry) ranks him among the top five (with Jiao Ran, Qingsai, Qiji, and Guanxiu), but does so with something of a backhanded compliment: "… because these men's poems lack the odor of the begging bowl" 缽盂氣, by which he meant their poems avoided Buddhist and Chan terminology and proselytizing.

Wuke was a native of Fanyang 范陽 (the region around modern Zhuozhou City 涿州市 in Hebei, southeast of Beijing). Though his birth and death dates are not recorded, he was younger than Jia Dao, and outlived his elder cousin. Brief biographical sketches in various sources are not entirely in accord, but the general arc of his life and career is clear. He left home to become a monk when very young, as did Jia Dao (Buddhist name Wuben 無本). For a time both lived at the Qinglong Si 青龍寺 just southeast of the capital Chang'an, until Jia Dao returned to secular life. Wuke's works include poems dedicated to several monks there.

Wuke moved frequently and traveled widely—he was a typical itinerant "clouds and waters monk" 雲水僧, but the majority of his activities were in the capital region. During the Yuanhe period (806–820) he resided for a time at the Xiantian Si 先天寺 (an alternate name for the Baochang Si 寶昌寺) in the southeastern part of the capital, and then moved to the Zhongnan Mountains 終南山 (approximately 30 miles southeast of the city), where he joined the Caotang Si

Wuke

草堂寺 community on Guifeng Peak 圭峰. While his biographies do not mention Wuke's Buddhist training, his association with the Caotang Si is telling. His residence there coincided with that of the major Buddhist scholar-monk Guifeng Zongmi 圭峰宗密 (780–841), who became simultaneously the fifth patriarch of Huayan 華嚴 Buddhism and a patriarch of the Heze 菏泽 lineage of Southern Chan. A poem among Wuke's works, "Zeng Guifeng Chanshi" 贈圭峰禪師 (Presented to Chan Master Guifeng), describes Zongmi's fame: "All morning, visitors arrive with admiring hearts; / Like a stream, monks come to study the Way" 朝滿傾心客，溪連學道僧.

During the Dahe period (827–835), Wuke moved to the "Baige si" 白閣寺 – probably a reference to the Xicao Tang 西草堂 on nearby Boge Peak, also in the Zhongnan Mountains. He also traveled far, to Yuezhou 越州 (modern Shaoxing, Zhejiang), Mount Tiantai 天台山 (in Zhejiang), Hu Xiang 湖湘 (in Hunan), Mount Lu 廬山 (in Jiangxi), and perhaps Mount Song 嵩山 (in Henan). In his final years, he lived on Mount Hua 華山 (approximately 70 miles east of Xi'an, Shaanxi), where he called himself the "Shugu Seng" 樹谷僧 (Monk of Tree Valley). He died sometime in late Huichang (841–846) or early Dazhong (847–859) period.

Wuke's poetry collection is noted in multiple records of private libraries from the Southern Song to the Ming, which reflects its broad dissemination. The great majority of the poems are occasional: Wuke carried on poetic exchanges with many of the eminent poets of the age, including Yao He 姚合 (ca. 779–ca. 849),* Xue Neng 薛能 (*jinshi* 846), Fang Gan 方干 (809–888), Zhu Qingyu 朱慶餘 (*jinshi* 826), Yu Fu 喻鳧 (*jinshi* 840), Ma Dai 馬戴 (ca. 799–ca. 869),* Zhang Ji 張籍 (ca. 776–829),* and Li He 李賀 (790–816).* He primarily utilized the *wulü* form, and created harmonious and delicate descriptions of the natural world to encourage Buddhist reflection. "Ji Qinglong Si Yuan Shangren" 寄青龍寺原上人 (Sent to Monk Yuan at Qinglong Temple) is a good example:

> I slow my steps, and enter cold bamboo;
> Quiet meditation: clepsydra sounds pass by.
> From a tall pine, the last cone falls;
> In the deep well, ice traces grow.
> Chimes come to an end; branches move in the wind;
> Lamps are hung; the room is bright in snow.
> When will you summon me for a visit?
> By moonlight I'll climb to your mountain temple.

> 斂屨入寒竹。安禪過漏聲。
> 高杉殘子落。深井凍痕生。
> 罷磬風枝動。懸燈雪屋明。
> 何當招我宿。乘月上方行。

While such poems suggest placidity, this should not be taken as weakness or lack of poetic technique. In the context of a quiet scene, the introduction of a subtle shift in tone or action can be startling. Thus Hu Zhenheng 胡震亨 (1569–1645) in *Tangyin guiqian* 唐音癸簽 wrote that like Jia Dao, Wuke at times times "produces powerful lines" 雄句, like "a sudden fiery attack" 咄咄火攻. He has also been praised for his gift of indirect expression, for "lines that project beyond the images" 象外句 (the term is based on lines in Sikong Tu's 司空圖 [837–908]* *Ershisi Shipin* 二十四詩品: "Project beyond images to gain the center" 超以象外，得其環中). Huihong 惠洪 (1071–1128)

explains in *Lengzhai yehua* 冷齋夜話 (Night Talks from the Cold Study) that "to compare objects to express meaning, but not directly name the objects" 比物以意，而不指言某物 can be exemplified Wuke's lines, "Listening to the rain, the cold watch comes to an end; / Opening the door, fallen leaves are deep" 聽雨寒更盡，開門落葉深.

The multiple poems Wuke and Jia Dao exchanged over the years reflect their very close relationship. When the latter died in Shu (modern Sichuan), Wuke was grief-stricken, and movingly wrote ("Diao Congshu Dao" 弔從兄島 [Lament for Elder Cousin Dao]):

> All day I've drowned in sadness for you—
> Jieshi, you were so lofty and alone.
> Your poetic name will linger through the ages,
> Yet as exile you passed through this life.
> Did you revise the poems you wrote in Shu?
> And now, only the slapdash funeral rites of Ba.
> By the dark gate I read your old scrolls—
> I wish to see you, but never will again.

> 盡日歎沉淪，孤高碣石人。
> 詩名從蓋代，謫宦竟終身。
> 蜀集重編否，巴儀薄葬新。
> 青門臨舊卷，欲見永無因。

Sorrow over the death of his cousin echoes throughout the poem, where multiple references to Jia Dao's poetic legacy indicate that Wuke laments losing a literary confidant as much as the passing of a close family member. The setting for the poem is revealed in the last line, where the "dark gates" (*qingmen* 青門) indicate the entrance to the burial grounds where Jia Dao now lies. In the preceding line, Wuke complains of this undeserved end, where provincial funerary rites performed far from home underscore the contrast with Jia Dao's refined verse. In this moment of great personal grief, impermanence is forgotten and Wuke is left only to mourn the loss of his close friend as darkness descends on the scene.

Wuke's calligraphy in the standard (*kaishu*) form compares well with that of his younger contemporaries Liu Gongquan 柳公權 (778–865) and Pei Xiu 裴休 (791–864). The stele of Duan Chengshi's 段成式 (803–863) "Jizhao Heshang bei" 寂照和上碑 (Stele Inscription for Monk Jizhao, now in the Xianyang Museum) is done in his hand.

BIBLIOGRAPHY

Editions:

Jiang Biao 江標, ed. *Seng Wuke shiji erjuan* 僧無可詩集二卷, *Tangren wushijia xiaoji* 唐人五十家小集 13. Suzhou: Jiangshi Lingjiange, Guangxu 21 [1895].

Quan Tang shi, 12: 9233–51, 15: 11310.

Shen Yucheng 沈玉成 and Yin Jiliang 印繼梁, eds. *Zhongguo lidai shiseng quanji: Jin, Tang, Wudai juan* 中國歷代詩僧全集: 晉、唐、五代卷, 3 vols. Beijing: Dangdai Zhongguo, 1997.

Wuke 無可. *Seng Wuke shiji erjuan* 僧無可詩集, 二卷. Taibei: Guoli Gugong Bowuyuan, 1997.

Biographical Sources:
Fu, *Tang caizi,* 3:74–77, 5:285–87.

Translations:
Barnstone, Tony and Chou Ping. *The Anchor Book of Chinese Poetry: From Ancient to Contemporary, The Full 3000-Year Tradition.* New York: Random House, 2005.
Egan, *Clouds,* pp. 82–85.
Owen, *Late Tang,* p. 137.

Studies:
Gao Huaping 高華平. "Tangdai shiseng yu sengshi" 唐代詩僧與僧詩, *Minnan Foxue* 1 (2004).
Li Junbiao 李俊標. "'Shiseng Wuke de shige chuangzuo" "詩僧"無可的詩歌創作," *Zhongguo yunwen xuekan,* 2 (2004).
Zhong Mingshan 鍾明善. "Seng Wuke shu 'Jizhao heshang bei' de shufa yishu" 僧無可書《寂照和上碑》的書法藝術, *Wenbo,* 1 (2001).

Charles H. Egan

Wu Yuanheng 武元衡 (*zi,* Bocang 伯蒼, 758–815), was born into a noble family in Goushi 緱氏 (modern Yanshi 偃師 in Henan) and became one of the few poets to serve as Grand Councilor during the Tang. He was born into a lineage of famous officials. His great grandfather, Wu Zaide 武載德, was a younger cousin of the Empress Wu (r. 690–705). Yuanheng's grandfather, Wu Zuyi 武祖一 served as Vice Director of Bureau of Evaluation, and as an Academician of Institute for the Cultivation of Literature. Yuanheng's father, Wu Jiu 武就 (713–790), served as a Palace Censor.

Wu began his official career after passing the *jinshi* examination 783, serving in the frontier provinces, and then taking the post of Investigating Censor. Later, Wu became the District Magistrate of Huayuan County 華原 near the capital (southeast of modern Yao County 耀縣 in Shaanxi). He came to resent the meddling of the local Military Commissioner and resigned his position on the excuse of illness. However, Wu's talent for poetry and political skills would garner the attention of Emperor Dezong (r. 780–805), who recruited Wu to serve as Vice Director of Bureau of Review. In 804, Wu was promoted to Vice Censor-in-Chief, but his rise was halted with the death of the emperor a year later.

When the sickly Emperor Shunzong (r. 805) ascended the throne in 805, his courtier, Wang Shuwen 王叔文 (735–806) played a central role in state affairs and soon launched a political reformation at court. When Wu Yuanheng refused to join Wang's faction, he was demoted, only to be later reinstated as Vice Censor-in-Chief when Emperor Xianzong (r. 806–820) ascended the throne the following year. In the first month of 807, Wu received a series of promotions, eventually becoming a Grand Councilor. Wu was then later appointed Military Commissioner of Jiannan Xichuan 劍南西川 (modern Sichuan) and sent back to the provinces. In 813 he was recalled to court, where he was restored to the position of Grand Councilor. Resituated at court, he sought revenge on former political enemies, starting with the demotion and exile of those from Wang Shuwen's faction, including the poets Liu Yuxi 劉禹錫 (772–842)* and Liu Zongyuan 柳宗元 (773–819).*

During Wu Yuanheng's time as Grand Councilor, Military Commissioners held great political power, and often directly interfered with imperial government on matters of state. Perhaps an result of the conflicts during his early days as a District Magistrate, Wu had been a lifelong advocate for restraining the power of the Military Commissioners, and promoted a plan to use the army to pacify powerful figures like Wu Yuanji 吳元濟 (783–817) of Huaixi 淮西 (in modern Henan). This proactive stance against local power, along with his actions taken against the former clique of Wang Shuwen, would lead to many more enemies and increased resentment. The danger mounting against Wu Yuanheng reached its breaking point in 815, when an assassin hired by the Military Commissioner Wang Chengzong 王承宗 (d. 820) assassinated Wu on the street. Following his death, the court granted Wu with the title of Situ 司徒 (Head of the Ministry of Education) and honored him with the posthumous name "Zhong Min" 忠愍.

Wu's lifelong engagement in politics and administration lends his poetry an embellished and florid style. When composing poems, Wu maintains a special affection for certain images like valuable jewelry and bright colors, which matches his notable status as a high official. Wu is also known for his ingenious use of color, as in the following couplet, "White dew hurts red leaves, cool breeze cuts green aureum vines" 白露傷紅葉, 清風斷綠蘿. Wu's meticulous word choice is also well-known as in "The wind flips over the cold leaves into disorder" 風翻涼葉亂 where the wind is personified as turning over (*fan* 翻) the leaves as one would turn pages in a book.

Wu's military service and experience on the frontier are also reflected in his poetry. A portion of his works were designated by later critics as frontier style (*biansai ti* 邊塞體). Inheriting this theme from the High Tang poets, Wu's works depict the bleak vistas of battlefields and the homesickness of the soldiers there. For example, "The gloaming horn sounds in the fortress among the clouds, the setting sun casts light on flags at the ends of the earth" 暮角雲中戍，殘陽天際旗. In Wu's vision the garrison sits on a height "among the clouds," and their flags seem to be at "the ends of the earth," hyperbola that emphasizes the isolation of the troops there. Both soldiers and readers turn nostalgic when they hear some mournful tune played by the horn.

Wu wrote a number of quatrains and the following "Ti Jialing yi" 題嘉陵驛 (Written on the Wall of the Jialing Post Station) is typical:

Long flowing banners wind their way through mountains and rivers,
A mountain post station blurred by a misty rain.
In Jialing, halfway to Chengdu, my hair is already turning white;
The way west to the Shu Pass is much closer to the blue sky.

悠悠風旆繞山川, 山驛空濛雨似煙.
路半嘉陵頭已白, 蜀門西上更青天.

Jialing (modern Nanchong 南充 in Sichuan) is about 120 miles east of Chengdu. Wu wrote the poem on his way to take up his position as Military Commissioner in Chengdu. He has been demoted from the position of Grand Councilor and must have been wondering what the future held for him. The opening word, *youyou* 悠悠 "far reaching" or "drawn out" may refer to the banners or to the lengthy road he traveled. *Rao* 繞 (to wind) here suggests the arduous journey through roads that led up and down canyons. The misty rain in line two reminds him of his unclear future sent to a region that was far from the capital and rife with unrest among the various peoples who lived there. The last line plays on the famous couplet written by Li Bo 李伯 (701–762),* "The road to Shu is hard, harder than climbing up to the sky!" 蜀道之難, 難於上青天. Wu is perhaps suggesting it is even harder (*geng* 更) than Li Bo claimed, suggesting as well how he viewed the problems of his new position.

Later, Xue Tao 薛濤 (ca. 768–ca. 813)* was touched by this poem and wrote a responding one in which she took Wu's last line as her line. Xue was only one of many local literati and exiled officials in Shu who were drawn to Wu. His sojourn in Chengdu contributed greatly to the development of literati culture in Sichuan in the early ninth century.

BIBLIOGRAPHY

Editions:
Hu Zhenheng 胡震亨 et al., eds. *Tangyin tongjian* 唐音統籤, Section 4, *juan* 312–15, xerographically printed by Hainan chubanshe, 2000. Volume 5, 56–78.
Tang wushi jia shiji 唐五十家詩集, Shanghai: Shanghai guji chubanshe, 1981. volume 8: 4375–468.
Quan Tang shi, 5: 3544–82, 11: 8983, 13: 10436.
Quan Tang wen, 531.6167-6171.
Wu Yuanheng. *Linhuai shi ji* 臨淮詩集. 1 *juan*. In *Tangshi baimingjia quanji* 唐詩百名家全集. Shanghai: Saoye Shanfang 掃葉山房, 1920.
___. *Wu Yuanheng ji* 武元衡集. 3 *juan*. Huang Guanzeng 黃貫曾 (Ming dynasty), ed. Fuyu Shanfang 浮玉山房, 1554, 1708.

Biographical Sources:
Fu, *Tang caizi*, 2:206–10, 5:201–03.
Jiu Tang shu, 158.4159–62.
Xin Tang shu, 152.4833–35.

Studies:
Fu Xuancong 傅璇琮. *Tang caizi zhuan jiaojian* 唐才子傳校箋, *juan* 4. Beijing: Zhonghua, 1987, pp. 207–10.
Li Ningjuan 李寧娟, "Shiren zhuke tu zhi guiqi meili pai yanjiu" 詩人主客圖之瑰奇美麗派研究, M.A. Thesis, Shanxi Shifan Daxue, 2014.
Ruan Yi 阮怡, and Wu Xianming 吳明賢. "Wu Yuanheng ru Shu jiqi dui Shuzhong chuangzuo de yingxiang" 武元衡入蜀及其對蜀中創作的影響, *Chengdu Daxue Xuebao* (2nd ser., 2013).
Ruan Yi 阮怡 and Wu Mingxian 吳明賢, "Wu Yuanheng rushu jiqi dui shuzhong chuangzuo de yingxiang" 武元衡入蜀及其對蜀中創作的影響, *Chengdu Daxue Xuebao*, (February 2013): 14–18.
Smilack, Jascha Isaac. "'Peach Blossom Spring' and allusion in Chinese poetry," Ph.D. Dissertation, Harvard University, 2010.
Wang Qin 王秦. "*Jiu Tang shu* Wu Yuanheng yuci shijian zhi kanpo" 舊唐書武元衡遇刺時間之勘破, *Chengde Minzu Shizhuan Xeubao* (vol. 30. 2, 2010).
Xin Wenfang 辛文房. *Tang caizi zhuan* 唐才子傳, *juan* 4. Shanghai: Gudian Wenxue, 1957, pp. 69–70.
Xu Feng 徐峰, "Jianlun Wu Yuanheng shige yixiang de dijin jiegou" 簡論武元衡詩歌意象的遞進結構, *Jiannan Wenyuan* (August 2011): 42.
Yu Cailin 余才林, "Liu Yuxi, Liu Zongyuan, yu Wu Yuanheng guanxi lunlüe" 劉禹錫劉禹錫與武元衡關係論略, Tangdu Xuebao, 15.2 (April 1999): 15-19.
Zhao Junbo 趙俊波, "Wu Yuanheng shi chutan" 武元衡詩初探, *Leshan shifan xueyuan* (no.3, 2002).

Zhao Muzhen 趙目珍, "Shiren zhuke tu guiqi meili zhu Wu Yuanheng kaolue" 詩人主客圖'瑰奇美丽主'武元衡考略, *Zhongguo Yunwen Xuekan* (no. 10, 2011).

___, "Shiren zhuke tu guiqi meili zhu Wu Yuanheng nianpu" 詩人主客圖'瑰奇美丽主'武元衡年譜, *Zhejiang Shehui kexue* (vol. 27 no. 2, 2013).

Ji Wang, Michael E. Naparstek, and William H. Nienhauser, Jr.

Wu Yun 吳筠 (*zi*, Zhenjie 貞節; posthumous title Zongxuan Xiansheng 宗玄先生, d. 778) played two important roles in Chinese intellectual history: as a Daoist master and as a poet. The biographical details for Wu Yun are clouded by discrepancies of various sources. The preface to Wu's collected works penned by Quan Deyu 權德輿 (761–818),* a contemporary who knew Wu, has been considered more credible than Wu's biographies in the two dynastic histories. The *Jiu Tangshu* claims Wu was from the Lu 魯 area (modern Shandong province), while in Quan's preface Wu he is said to be a native of Huayin 華陰 district, Huazhou 華州 (in modern Shaanxi province). Quan's preface also relates that Wu set his mind to the study of Daoism at the age of fifteen, living in reclusion on Mount Yidi 倚帝山 near Nanyang 南陽 (in modern Henan) before he was summoned by an imperial order to the capital in the early Tianbao reign-period, around 745. This biographical sketch is supported by Wu's three extant poems on the mountain. Below is a rendition based on Jan De Meyer's translation of the second of his "You Yidishan" 遊倚帝山 (Roaming on Mount Yidi), in which Wu expresses his enjoyment of the natural scene and his reclusive life:

> How uniquely graceful is this mountain!
> Eighty thousand feet high it leans against the vast azure sky.
> At daybreak I clamber up to the foot of mist and clouds,
> At dusk I rest in the field of the numinous immortals.
> Bowing down I behold the moon above the sea,
> Sitting down I toy with the drifting clouds that roam about.
> The wind shakes a refined melody from the pine trees,
> The dew upon the cassia contains the glow of the clear sky.
> Without having to pass beyond the six realms,
> I reach transcendence and the myriad ties are forgotten.
> I put my faith in those gentlemen of days long gone,
> Roosting among cliffs, the Way entirely manifests itself.

> 茲山何獨秀，萬仞倚昊蒼。
> 晨躋煙霞趾，夕憩靈仙場。
> 俯觀海上月，坐弄浮雲翔。
> 松風振雅音，桂露含晴光。
> 不出六合外，超然萬累忘。
> 信彼古來士，巖棲道彌彰。

The poem depicts Mount Yidi with imagery found among the kind of *shanshui* 山水 ("landscape") paintings often associated with expressing the search for the Way (Dao 道). Here, the sheer grandeur of the peak set against the symbolically rich azure sky (azure being the color associated with divine attendants as well as with elixirs of immortality) alludes to the mountain abodes of Daoist immortals. Rising above the sea like the immortal realm of Penglai 蓬萊, Wu Yun describes his ascent to Mt. Yidi's peak in terms of convening among powerful transcendents (*lingxian* 靈仙), as he himself seeks to go beyond the six-directions that map the mundane world. In the end, the dusty world below is forgotten as the poet follows the path of past immortals whose spirits now roost among the lofty cliffs where he finds the Dao.

Outside of his sojourn on Mount Yidi, two other episodes in Wu's life remain uncertain. The first is the *Jiu Tangshu* account that Wu once recommended Li Bo 李白 (701–762)* to the imperial court. Although this oft retold legend was argued to be a fabrication by Yu Xianhao in the early 1980s, some scholars present strong evidence in support of the legend's veracity. The second unsettled issue concerns whether Wu took and failed the imperial *jinshi* examination before heading into seclusion in Nanyang. This episode, recorded also in *Jiu Tangshu*, might have been intentionally omitted in Quan's preface. Most hagiographies of Wu also do not mention the incident. Leading some scholars to the supposition that this kind of craving for honor and power would have tarnished Wu's image as a Daoist prelate. That it was Wu's disciple, Shao Jixuan 邵冀玄, who invited Quan to pen the preface, supports the idea that Wu would not have been tempted by renown or profit.

Wu Yun was summoned to the imperial court on two occasions as a result of Emperor Xuanzong's (r. 712–56) zeal for Daoism. In the first summons in 745, Wu made a request to Xuanzong for a Daoist ordination, thereby becoming a Daoist adept. Wu studied the Zhengyi 正一 (Orthodox Unity) Daoist tradition with Feng Zhengqi 馮整齊, a disciple of Pan Shizheng 潘師正 (586–684), at Songyang Abbey in Song Mountains 嵩山嵩陽觀 (in modern Henan province). The second summons took place in 754, when Wu was appointed Hanlin Scholar. The presentation of his *Xuangang lun* 玄綱論 (On the Essentials of the Arcana) in three chapters, a treatise on Daoist philosophy written in Song Mountains, won him the praise of the emperor. However, these good days did not last. He requested to return to his mountain hermitage shortly before the An Lushan Rebellion broke out in the autumn of 755. In his two poems "Hanlinyuan wang Zhongnanshan" 翰林院望終南山 (Gazing at Mount Zhongnan from the Hanlin Academy), written during his Hanlin tenure, he expresses his eager wish for a carefree life that would be possible in one of the retreats on the mountain. Here is the first:

> Intimately I yearn for the Dao of hiding and immersing.
> That in which I take pleasure is living amidst cliffs and caves.
> Who would expect that I ashamedly took the fine appointment,
> And in the end entered the Hut of Received Brilliance?
> Yet my disposition may not be changed;
> Nor may it be set free in this confinement.
> Fortunately I can see Mount Zhongnan—
> Towering and soaring, it pierces the Great Void.

竊慕隱淪道，所歡巖穴居。
誰言忝休命，遂入承明廬。
物情不可易，幽中未嘗攄。
幸見終南山，岩嶤凌太虛。

The Hut of Received Brilliance was attached to the Han-dynasty Chengmingdian 承明殿 (Hall of Received Brilliance), where officials who could were to be summoned by the emperor were supposed to wait. Lines 3-4 suggest that although Wu took an imperial appointment, he found himself neglected. His wish for leaving the palace post is more patently expressed final couplet of the second poem: "How may I untie the trammels, / Forever entrusting myself to the realm of the carefree?" 何當解維縶，永託逍遙墟。

There have been speculations about Wu's motives and his eventual decision to leave the capital. Wu may have been reacting to the antagonism incurred by envy the emperor's attention to Wu leading to his vehement opposition to Buddhism and his renouncement of court life. When Xuanzong's asked Wu about how to achieve immortality, as he discouraged the emperor from believing in Buddhist doctrine. As a result, Buddhist monks allied with Gao Lishi 高力士 (684–762), a powerful official and pious believer of Buddhism, and slandered Wu. This in turn ignited Wu's anti-Buddhist sentiments, which became a prominent theme in his "Si huanchun fu" 思還淳賦 (Rhapsody on My Longings to Recover Purity). In addition to this background, dynastic histories ascribe his departure from the capital to his foresight of the devastation of the An Lushan Rebellion. The emperor reluctantly let Wu return to the Song Mountains, where he had commissioned the construction of a Daoist abbey for Wu.

During the Rebellion, Wu sojourned in eastern and southern China. He visited Mount Mao 茅山 (in modern Jiangsu province), the sacred place for Shangqing 上清 (Highest Clarity) Daoism, and later around 761 reached Mount Lu 廬山 (in modern Jiangxi province). His large number of writings on this famous mountain reveals his fondness for the locale. His "Yanqi fu" 巖棲賦 (Rhapsody on Roosting on Cliffs) most typically outlines the enjoyment of his contented reclusive life in the mountains. Here is a stanza of this poem, as translated by Paul W. Kroll:

> Observe here
> The winding and lofty tors, cross-angled and lifted valleys;
> The welling and gushing springs, thick-set and enveloping trees.
> Behind, erratically arrayed, thrusting up and huddled low.
> I pursue the summer coolness of shaded straths,
> Rest in the winter warmth of sun-lit scarps.
> I admire sturdy composure in pine-tree and bamboo-culm,
> Enjoy the especial fragrances of mum and thoroughwort.
> Attenuated pipings purify the ear,
> And languid clouds bedazzle the eye.
> I depend on the seagoing crane to advise me of nightfall,
> Trust in the painted stork to let me know of sunup.
> Apprehensions are subdued in a want of excitement,
> And spirit is calmed in a lessening of desires.

> 觀其
> 繚崇巒，橫峻谷，
> 激泌泉，羅森木，
> 後巍峨以縈紆，前參差而筲伏。
> 追陰壑之夏涼，偃陽崖之冬燠，
> 美勁節於松筠，翫幽芳於蘭菊。

虛籟清耳，閑雲瑩目，
因海鶴以警夜，任鷗雞以知旭，
慮靜於無擾，神恬於寡慾。

After his stay on Mount Lu, Wu Yun arrived in eastern China no later than 770. He took part in gatherings for poetic composition and was associated with literati such as Yan Zhenqing 顏真卿 (709–85), Jiao Ran 皎然 (720–799),* and Yan Wei 嚴維 (d. 780). In 778, Wu passed away in a Daoist Abbey in Xuancheng 宣城 (in modern Anhui province).

Wu Yun's religious belief and passion distinguishes his writing in content and style from the works on similar themes by others. His religio-philosophical views are mainly expressed in his treatises such as the *Xuangang lun* and *Shenxian kexue lun* 神仙可學論 (That Transcendence May Be Achieved through Learning). In Wu's theory, one principal method of meditation is the cultivation of mental quietue and the abandonment of personal interests and desires. This philosophy gave direct rise to the representation of his serious attitude toward transcendence in his poetic works, the most representative of which are his "Youxian shi" 遊仙詩 (Poems on Roaming to the Transcendent Realm). Unlike most traditional "Youxian" poems, Wu's works do not focus on political allegory, but are devoted to the vivid depiction of the magnificent scenes of his meditative roaming based on a clear "roadmap" of his celestial journeys. These striking descriptions of the fantastic realm are abundant in Daoist scriptures, especially those in the Shangqing tradition. This kind of representation of wondrous scenes is common in Wu's poems "Buxu ci" 步虛詞 (Pacing the Void) written for Daoist rituals.

Wu's religious beliefs do not overshadow his lyrical voice in his poetic works. He continued the legacy of "meditation on the ancients" (*huaigu* 懷古) and "expression of inner feelings" (*yonghuai* 詠懷). His representative works of the former tradition are his fourteen-poem suite entitled "Langu shi" 覽古詩 (Viewing the Past). The deep-rooted poetic tradition of *yonghuai* has infiltrated most of his "Langu shi," poems on journeying, and dedicatory poems. His poetry contains a synthesis of Daoist and Confucian thought as even his reclusive sentiments are colored with social criticism. However, the trope of Daoist carefree roaming remains prominent. In his fifteen poems collectively entitled "Gaoshi yong" 高士詠 (In Praise of High-minded Scholars), Wu expresses his admiration for the conduct of these figures. His lyrical voice was heard through beautiful scenic descriptions as well as fantastic Daoist lore. For example, in the poem on ascending the Beigu 北固 Mountains (in modern Zhenjiang, Jiangsu province) gazing at the sea ("Deng Beigu shan wang hai" 登北固山望海), Wu alludes to the legend of Anqi 安旗 and that of Wangzi Qiao 王子喬, two iconic figures who left the human world and transcended.

BIBLIOGRAPHY

Editions:

Chen Shangjun 陳尚君, ed. *Quan Tangwen bubian* 補編. Beijing: Zhonghua, 2005, 48.574–75. Contains the preface to the *Nantong dajun neidan jiuzhang jing*, which has been identified by Chen as a forgery.
___. *Quan Tangshi bubian* 補編. Beijing: Zhonghua, 1992, pp. 296–97, 355, 891.
Li Fang 李昉 (925–96) et al., comps. *Wenyuan yinghua* 文苑英華. Beijing: Zhonghua, 1982, 36.4a–5a, 98.2a–3a, 134.8a–9a, 146.1b–3a, 739.9a–14a, 822.2b–3b.

Quan Tang shi, 12 : 9704–13, 13: 10110–11, 10567, 14: 10622, 11125.
Quan Tang wen, 925–26.12709–27.
Wu Yun. DZ 1051, *Zongxuan Xiansheng wenji* 宗玄先生文集.
___. DZ 1052, *Zongyuan Xiansheng Xuangang lun* 玄綱論.
___. DZ 1054, *Nantong dajun neidan jiuzhang jing* 南統大君內丹九章經.
___. *Neidan jiuzhang jing* 內丹九章經 in 1 *juan*, SKQS.
___. *Zongxuan ji* 宗玄集, in 3 *juan*, SKQS.
Zhou Shaoliang 周紹良, ed. *Quan Tangwen xinbian* 全唐文新編. Changchun: Jilin Wenshi, 2000, vol. 18, pp. 12709–27 (*juan* 925–26).

Biographical Sources:
Fu, *Tang caizi*, 2:148–56, 5:24–26.
Jiu Tang shu, 192.5129–30.
Xin Tang shu, 196.5604–05.

Translations:
Kroll, Paul W., "Lexical Landscapes and Textual Mountains in the High T'ang." *TP* 84.1–3 (1998): 96–100. Annotated translation of the first few stanzas of Wu Yun's "Yanqi fu."
See also De Meyer, Kohn, and Schafer below.

Studies:
Barrett, Timothy Hugh. *Taoism under the T'ang: Religion & Empire during the Golden Age of Chinese History*. London: Wellsweep Press, 1996, pp. 70–71.
___, "Wu Yun." In Pregadio, Fabrizio, ed. *Encyclopedia of Taoism*. London; New York: Routledge, 2008, pp. 1048–49.
De Meyer, Jan. "A Daoist Master's Justification of Reclusion: Wu Yun's Poems on 'Investigating the Past'." *Sanjiao wenxian: Matériaux pour l'étude de la religion chinoise* 2 (1998): 9–40.
___. "Linked Verse and Linked Faiths: An Inquiry into the Social Circle of an Eminent Tang Dynasty Taoist Master." In De Meyer and Peter M. Engelfriet, eds. *Linked Faiths: Essays on Chinese Religions and Traditional Culture in Honour of Kristofer Schipper*. Leiden: Brill, 2000, pp. 148–83.
___. "Mountainhopping: The Life of Wu Yun." *T'ang Studies* 17 (1999): 171–211.
___. *Wu Yun's Way: Life and Works of an Eighth-century Daoist Master*. Leiden and Boston: Brill, 2006.
Huang Junming 黃君名. "Wu Yun shiji chutan" 吳筠事跡初探, *Daojiaoxue tansuo* 道教學探索 5 (December 1991): 194–205.
Jiang Yin 蔣寅, "Wu Yun: Daoshi shiren yu daojiao shi" 吳筠：道士詩人與道教詩, *Ningbo Daxue xuebao (renwen kexue ban)*, 7.2 (1994): 29–35.
___. *Dali shiren yanjiu* 大曆詩人研究. Beijing: Zhonghua, 1995, pp. 312–22.
Jiang Zhenhua 蔣振華. *Tang Song daojiao wenxue sixiang shi* 唐宋道教文學思想史. Changha: Yuelu Shushe, 2009, pp. 163–87.
Kamitsuka Yoshiko 神塚淑子. "Go Un no shōgai to shiso" 吳筠の生涯と思想, *Tōhō shukyō* 54 (November 1979): 33–51.
Kirkland, J. Russell. "Taoists of the High T'ang: An Inquiry into the Perceived Significance of Eminent Taoists in Medieval Chinese Society." Ph.D. dissertation, Indiana University, 1986, pp. 96–111.
Kohn, Livia. "Mind and Eyes: Sensory and Spiritual Experience in Daoist Mysticism." *Monumenta Serica* 46 (1998): 129–56. Includes English translation of Wu's "Xinmu lun" 心目論, *Xinmu lun: On Mind and Eyes* (pp. 146–51).

Li Baojun 李寶鈞, "Wu Yun jianju Li Bo ru Chang'an xinbian" 吳筠薦舉李白入長安新辨, *Wenshizhe* 1981.1: 71–74.

Li Dahua 李大華 et al. "Wu Yun de Daojiao zhexue sixiang" 吳筠哲學思想 in *Sui Tang Daojia yu Daojiao* 隋唐道家與道教. Beijing: Renmin, 2011, pp. 376–414.

Li Gang 李剛, "Lun Wu Yun de daojiao zhexue sixiang" 論吳筠的道教哲學思想, *Zhongguo zhexue shi* 2000.1: 94–100.

Li Shenglong 李生龍, "Li Bo yu Wu Yun jiujing youwu jiaowang" 李白與吳筠究竟有無交往, *Li Bo yanjiu luncong*, vol. 2. Chengdu: Ba Shu Shushe, 1990, pp. 251–59.

Liu Huanling 劉煥玲, "Wu Yun de 'Buxu ci'" 吳筠的步虛詞, *Daojiaoxue tansuo* 5 (December 1991): 174–93.

Lu Guolong 盧國龍. *Zhongguo chongxuan xue: lixiang yu xianshi de shutu yu tonggui* 中國重玄學——理想與現實的殊途與同歸. Beijing: Renmin Zhongguo, 1998, pp. 380–408.

Luo Mingyue 羅明月, "Wu Yun daojiao shige tanxi" 吳筠道教詩歌探析, *Mingzuo xinshang*, 2011.22: 119–22.

Owen, *High T'ang*, pp. 143–46.

Qing Xitai 卿希泰, ed. *Zhongguo daojiao shi* 中國道教史, revised edition, vol. 2. Chengdu: Sichuan Renmin, 1996, pp. 234–50.

Schafer, Edward H. "Empyreal Powers and Chthonian Edens: Two Notes on T'ang Taoist Literature," *JAOS* 106.4 (October–December 1986): 667–78.

___. "Wu Yün's 'Cantos on Pacing the Void,'" *HJAS* 41 (1981): 377–415.

___. "Wu Yün's Stanzas on 'Saunters in Sylphdom,'" *Monumenta Serica* 34 (1981–83): 1–37.

___. *Pacing the Void: T'ang Approaches to the Stars*. Berkeley: University of California Press, 1977, pp. 244–46.

Wang Xue 王雪, "Lun Wu Yun de daoxue sixiang tese" 論吳筠的道學思想特色, *Xibei daxue xuebao (zhexue shehui kexue ban)*, 34.5 (2004): 133–36.

Wei Chunxi 韋春喜 and Zhang Ying 張影, "Shilun Tangdai daojiao shiren Wu Yun de yongshi zushi" 試論唐代道教詩人吳筠的詠史組詩, *Nanchang daxue xuebao (Renwen shehui kexue ban)* 37.6 (2006): 154–59, 164. This article is also published under the title of "Lun Tangdai daoshi Wu Yun de yongshi zushi" 論唐代道士吳筠的詠史組詩, in *Zongjiao xue yanjiu* 宗教學研究 2006.4: 41–46.

___, "Tangdai daojiao shiren Wu Yun shengping kao shu" 唐代道教詩人吳筠生平考述. *Guizhou daxue xuebao (shehui kexue ban)*, 24.3 (2006): 112–14.

Xu Jiafu 許嘉甫. "Wu Yun jian Li Bo shuo zhengbu" 吳筠薦李白說徵補, *Linyi shizhuan*, 17.4 (August 1995): 68–72.

Yan Jinxiong 顏進雄. *Tangdai youxianshi yanjiu* 唐代遊仙詩研究. Taibei: Wenjin, 1996, pp. 225–47.

Yu Xianhao 郁賢皓. "Wu Yun jian Li Bo shuo bianyi" 吳筠薦李白說辨疑. *Nanjing Shida xuebao (Shehui kexue ban)*,1981.1: 40–46.

Zhan Shichuang 詹石窗. "Wu Yun shicheng kao" 吳筠師承考, *Zhongguo daojiao*, 1994.1: 26–28.

___. *Daojiao wenxueshi* 道教文學史. Shanghai: Shanghai Wenyi, 1992, pp. 206–17.

Zhou Shaoliang 周紹良, comm. *Tang caizi zhuan jianzheng* 唐才子傳箋證. Beijing: Zhonghua, 2010, 1.146–55.

Zhuang Hongyi 莊宏誼. "Tangdai daoshi Wu Yun de xiandao sixiang" 唐代道士吳筠的仙道思想, *Furen zongjiao yanjiu*, 19 (Sept. 2009): 107–26.

Timothy Wai Keung Chan

Xiao Yingshi 蕭穎士 (*zi*, Maoting 茂挺, 717–760) enjoyed a considerable reputation in Tang times for his prose. He also gained renown as a teacher of literature and for his strict Confucian views: he was, for example, critical of Sima Qian's 司馬遷 *Shiji* 史記. In this mode, he refused to bend to his enemies in power, often at the expense of furthering his own official career. He was a lifelong friend of Li Hua 李華 (715–774),* and the two are often considered the forerunners of the *Guwen yundong* 古文運動 (Ancient-Style Prose Movement).

Xiao was the seventh-generation descendant of Xiao Hui 蕭恢 (476–526), a prince during the Liang dynasty. Little is known about Xiao's early life in Ruyin 汝隱 in Yingzhou 穎州 (modern Fuyang 阜陽 County, Anhui). He grew up, according to his own words, in relative poverty. Yet his literary prowess was evident from an early age. Xiao sat the *jinshi* in 735 and placed first overall. His official career within the capital, however, would not live up to the promise of his achievements in the examination.

Xiao Yingshi served first in the provinces. During the Tianbao reign of Emperor Xuanzong (742–756), Xiao was made a Subeditor in the Academy of Scholarly Worthies. Running afoul of Chancellor Li Linfu 李林甫 (683–752) in 749, Xiao went to serve as an secretary to the Military Commissioner of Guangling 廣陵 (Yangzhou 揚州, Jiangsu) before being recalled the following year to the capital as an Edict Attendant in the Historiography Institute. In 751 he became adjutant to the Military Commissioner in Henan. In the first year of Suzong's reign (756), Xiao became Chief Secretary on the staff of the Military Commissioner in Shannan 山南 (modern Tibet). Later, the Military Commissioner of Huainan 淮南 appointed Xiao Personnel Evaluator of his army. In 760, Xiao Yingshi set off to return to his ancestral home at Nan Lanling 南蘭陵 (modern Changzhou in Jiangsu) in order to bury his parents but died in Runan 汝南 (Henan Province) before completing the journey. His followers honored him with the posthumous title "Wenyuan Xiansheng" 文元先生 (Master First among Letters), and he was often referred to as "Xiao Gongcao" 蕭功曹 (Personnel Evaluator Xiao) in the writing of friends and admirers, including Li Hua.

In his early years Xiao's search for a patron led him to write to Wei Shu 韋述 (d. 757), the prominent official historian and compiler of over one hundred chapters of the 'National History' (*Guoshi*) 國史). In what would stand as one of the most extensive self-apologies from the mid-eighth century, Xiao's "Zeng Wei Siye shu" 贈韋司業書 (Letter to Director of Studies Wei), Xiao describes himself as a single-minded, isolated, and austere scholar, in contrast to the ambitious, opportunistic, and morally lax horde against whom he was forced to compete. He also questions the very validity of the examinations, in which he himself had been highly successful, as a valid test of a scholar's true abilities. Both of these attitudes were to become established themes in later reformist writing. The letter reads in part:

> I was born in Ruying. In my youth I suffered from poverty. But I was industrious and diligently studied and achieved my goal when I was twenty. I took the examinations and passed the presented-scholar examination and was praised by officials at court. At present, I wield my brush like a flying phoenix, writing my mind and airing my own views. . . . Not to mention that day after day, year by year, I have wasted almost half of my life as a low-ranking officer in distant regions. If I ponder what I feel in my heart, unconsciously anger arises in my chest. My great accomplishments of back then—of what use are they now? This is something I cannot discuss with those who do not understand me.
>
> All my life I have composed pieces in my own style, not the popular fashion, but in each looking up to the ancients [of the Pre-Qin and Han eras]. I did not pay attention to what came after the Wei and Jin periods . . . . I was also obsessed with writing and indulged myself in history.

Xiao Yingshi

> Since I can recall there have been few things that attracted me. Besides the Confucian Classics nothing can stir my mind. When in my youth I first studied texts, I was taught the *Analects* and the *Exalted Documents*. Although I could understand their subtleties, yet I saw the explanations they relied on are not different from those of today. Because of this my mind was opened and I felt at ease, in one day reciting and memorizing more than one thousand words. The threat of the teacher's rod never touched my body. . . .

> 僕生于汝穎，幼而苦貧，孜孜強學，業成冠歲。射策甲科，見稱朝右。當此之時，為奮筆飛鸞鳳，摛論吐雲煙 … 何言日損一日，年貶一年，蹉跎半紀，乃殊方一下吏耳。興言念此，不覺氣之交胸。從來事業，復何所用；未可為不知己者論也。
> 僕平生屬文，格不近俗，凡所擬議，必希古人。魏晉以來 . . . . 又溺志著書，放心前史，. . . . 僕有識以來，寡于嗜好，經術之外，略不嬰心。幼年方小學時，受《論語》、《尚書》，雖未能究解精微，而依說與今不異。由是心開意適，日誦千月余言。榎楚之威，不曾及體……

This essay in five thousand words is the longest in Xiao Yingshi's extant corpus and best expresses his feelings of indignation. Here, Xiao Yingshi treats Wei Shu as a confidante, pouring out his thoughts, feelings, and ambitions in this personalized essay.

Other major events in Xiao's life, however, would be described in *fu* 賦. His choice of this genre, for both narrative and analytical accounts of his own experience, belies the conventionally accepted view that by mid-Tang times the *fu* was moribund as a creative literary form. Xiao's *You Liang xinji* 遊梁新集 (New Collection of Work about Travels in Liang [modern Henan]), now lost, likely contained several verses of this kind.

Xiao's main scholarly focus was history and genealogy. He was particularly interested in problems of dynastic legitimacy as they affected the orthodox line of succession (*zhengtong* 正統) from the Liang dynasty, from whose imperial house he was descended, to the Tang. His highly moralistic attitude toward historical compilation was justified by appeal to the *Chunqiu* 春秋 (Spring and Autumn Annals); but he probably never completed the chronicle-style general history he planned. After the An Lushan Rebellion, his knowledge of history served him in the strategic advice he gave to officials as retainer and adjutant in the modern Henan and Jiangsu areas.

Xiao was particularly influential as a teacher and during the Tianbao period helped a number of students who had left the metropolitan schools to prepare under him for the examinations, gaining the sobriquet of Master Xiao 蕭夫子. Like other reformist critics of his period, he emphasized the moral function of literature and condemned writing that showed mere technical virtuosity or powers of description. He also stressed, both explicitly and implicitly in his own sometimes densely allusive prose style, the primacy of Confucian canonical texts as models. Besides Li Hua, he was often in the company of Jia Zhi 賈至 (713–772), Gao Shi 高適 (700–765), and Yen Zhenqing 顏真卿 (709–785).

Xiao Yingshi's arrogance towards the dictatorial Grand Councilor of the Tianbao period, Li Linfu, inspired one of his best known compositions, the "Fa Yingtao shu fu" 伐櫻桃樹賦 (Prose-poem on Falling a Cherry Tree), an allegorical attack on Li written in 749 after Li removed him from the Academy of Assembled Worthies.

Most of Xiao's writing had already been lost by the end of the An Lushan Rebellion. That his friend Li Hua and some of his own former pupils promoted his reputation after his death, and that the great ancient-style prose writer Han Yu 韓愈 (768–824)* knew his son, helped maintain his reputation in mid-late Tang times. What now survives of Xiao's writing is preserved by virtue of its inclusion in early Song anthologies.

BIBLIOGRAPHY

Editions:
Quan Tang shi, 3:1595–1601, 13: 10043–44.
Quan Tang wen, 322–23.4123–50.
Sheng Xuanhuai 盛宣懷 (1844–1916) comp. *Xiao maoting ji*. Taibei: Yiwen, 1971.
Song Liu Fangping Shen Zhongchang xiucai tong guan suo shi zawen 送劉方平沈仲昌秀才同觀所試雜文, In Chen Shangjun 陳尚君 eds., *Quan Tang wen bubian* 全唐文補編, Beijing: Zhonghua, 2005, p. 472.
Tang gu yizhou cheng xianling Jia jun(Qinhui) muzhiming bingxu 唐故沂州丞縣令賈君（欽惠）墓誌銘, in *Zhou Shaoliang* 周紹良 (1917–2005), ed. *Tangdai muzhi huibian* 唐代墓誌匯編. Shanghai: Shanghai guji, 1992, p. 1689.
Tangshi jishi 唐詩紀事, ch. 21: includes Li Hua's "Yangzhou Gongcao Xiao Yingshi wenjixu" 揚州功曹蕭穎士文集序.
Xiao Maoting ji 蕭茂挺集, in Sheng Xuanhuai 盛宣懷 (1844–1916), compliler. *Changzhou xianzhe yishu* 常州先哲遺書, Section 1. Rpt. Taibei: Yiwen, 1971. Drawn from the *Wenyuan yinghua* 文苑英華 and *Tang wen cui* 唐文粹.
Xiao Yingshi 蕭穎士 *Xiao Maoting wenji* 蕭茂挺文集. Taibei: Taiwan Shangwu, 1983.

Biographical Sources:
Jiu Tang shu, 190C.5048–49.
Xin Tang shu, 202.5767–69.

Studies:
Bol, pp. 111–22.
Chen Tiemin 陳鐵民. "Xiao Yingshi xinian kaozheng" 蕭穎士系年考證, *Wenshi*, 37 (1993).
Fang Qingxu 房慶旭. "Xiao Yingshi wen jiaozhu" 蕭穎士文校注. Ph.D. dissertation, Liaoning Shifan Daxue, 2015.
Hiraoka Takeo 平岡武夫. "Shikan no ishiki to kotenshūgi no bungaku" 史官意識と古典主義の文學, in *Keisho no dentō* 經書の傳統. Tokyo: *Iwanami* 岩波書店, 1951, ch. 2, pp. 92–139.
Jiang Guangdou 薑光鬥. "Li Hua Xiao Yingshi shengzunian xinkao" 李華蕭穎士生卒年新考, *Wenxue yichan*, 1990.3: 65–67.
Li Dan 李丹. *Tangdai qianguwen yundong yanjiu* 唐代前古文運動研究. Beijing: Zhongguo Shehui Kexue, 2012, pp. 123–243.
McMullen, David L. "Historical and Literary Theory in the Mid-Eighth Century," in Arthur F. Wright and Denis Twitchett, eds. *Perspectives on the T'ang*. New Haven and London: Yale University, 1973, pp. 307–42.
Owen, *High T'ang*, pp. 225–46.
Pan [Lü] Qichang 潘[呂]棋昌. *Xiao Yingshi yanjiu* 蕭穎士研究. Taibei: *Wenshizhe*, 1983.
Qiao Changfu 喬長阜, "Xiao Yingshi shiji xinian kaobian" 蕭穎士事跡系年考辨, *Jiangnan Xueyuan Xuebao*, 2000 (03).
Sima Zhou 司馬周, "Xiao Yingshi yu Zhong Tang wenfeng" 蕭穎士與中唐文風, *Chuanshan Journal*, 2010 (02).

Tōno Haruuki 東野治之. "Tō no bunjin Shō Eishi no shōsei to Tenpyō shōho no I Tō shi" 唐の文人蕭穎士の招請と天平勝宝の遣唐使, in Hiroshi Ito 伊藤博 and Idea Itahen 井手至, eds. *Kotengaku sō: Kojima Noriyuki Hakushi koki kinen ronbunshū* 古典学藻：小島憲之博士古稀記念論文集. Tokyo: Hanaba, 1982.

Yu Jidong 俞紀東, "Xiao Yingshi shiji kao 蕭穎士事跡考," *Zhonghua wenshi luncong* 中華文史論叢, 1983.2.

Zhang Siqi 張思齊, "Lun Xiao Yingshi de Sixiang he Shige Chuangzuo" 論蕭穎士的思想和詩歌創作, in Feng Tianyu 馮天瑜 ed., *Renwen Luncong* 人文論叢. Wuhan: Wuhan University, 1999.

Zhang Weihong 張衛宏, "Xiao Yingshi Yanjiu" 蕭穎士研究, Ph.D. diss., Xibei University, 2007.

Zhao Yinshang 趙殷尚, "Lun Xiao Yingshi Li Hua de wenxue sixiang" 論蕭穎士, 李華的文學思想, *Tangdu xuekan*, 2008.6.

David L. McMullen and Jingyi Qu

Xu Hun 許渾 (*zi*, Yonghui 用晦, Zhonghui 仲晦, ca. 788–ca. 858) was a native of Anlu 安陸 in An Prefecture 安州 (modern Hubei), though some sources place his origins in Luoyang. Later, he would sojourn to Danyang 丹陽 in Run Prefecture 潤州 (modern Jiangsu), and subsequently was regarded as a native of Danyang. His residence was close to the Dingmao Bridge 丁卯橋, and he would eventually title the anthology of his work *Dingmao ji* 丁卯集 (Collection by the Dingmao [Bridge]). Thus, Xu Hun also came to be known as Xu Dingmao 許丁卯.

Although a descendant of Xu Yushi 許圉師 (d. 679), a Grand Councilor under Emperor Gaozong (r. 649–683), Xu Hun grew up in relative poverty. It is said that his assiduous study left him frail and sickly. In his youth, he traveled around Dongting Lake 洞庭湖 and the Xiang River 湘江 for nearly a decade, continuing to live in poverty and poor health. However, in 832, Xu passed the *jinshi* examination, but it was only in 838 that he was appointed to his first post as Magistrate of Dangtu 當涂 County (modern Anhui), and then as Magistrate of Taiping 太平 County (modern Jingxian 涇縣, Anhui) in 841. In the winter of 841, Xu was promoted to Investigating Censor, but he resigned his post in 843 pleading illness. At the beginning of the Dazhong reign (847), Xu Hun was once again promoted to Investigating Censor, but claimed to be too ill to go to court and resigned, returning to his home place. The following year he was employed again, serving as Vice Prefect of Runzhou 潤州 (modern Wuxi 無錫, Jiangsu). In 850, while still was living in Danyang, he compiled his own collected works. He later served as the Vice Director of the Bureau of Forestry and Crafts 虞部員外郎. In 854, he was appointed Prefect of Yingzhou 郢州 (modern Wuchang 武昌, Hubei). Four years later, he was appointed as Prefect of Muzhou 睦州 (modern Changyang 長陽, Hubei), where he would die at his post.

Throughout his official career, Xu Hun befriended and exchanged poetry with several significant poets including Du Mu 杜牧 (803–ca. 852),* Li Pin 李頻 (814–ca. 876),* and Li Yuan 李遠 (d. ca. 860). While some critics such as Sun Guangxian 孫光憲 (900–968) would claim that the general opinion of Xu Hun's contemporaries was that Xu's poetry was unimpressive, Xu Hun's work increasingly won admirers such as Wei Zhuang 韋莊 (ca. 836–910)* and Lu You 陸遊 (1125–1210), and his reputation grew steadily from the end of the ninth century into the Song dynasty.

Xu is the best known for his *lüshi* 律詩 (regulated verse), especially his heptasyllabic verses, and is also celebrated for his poems meditating on the past (*huaigu* 懷古), as well as those on traveling and sojourning (*jilü* 羈旅). His use of tonal patterns was considered well balanced, and his elegant style and dexterous poetic syntax also won praise. Xu enjoyed natural beauty, and thus many of his most renowned poems are about visiting famous mountains or places and reflecting on an ancient event. His most quoted lines can be found in his "Xianyang cheng Donglou" 咸陽城東樓 (The East Turret on the City Wall of Xianyang) and the following "Xianyang Cheng Xilou wantiao" 咸陽城西樓晚眺 (Gazing Afar at Dusk at the West Turret on the City Wall of Xianyang):

Once atop the high city wall, I am faced with melancholy spreading thousands of miles,
Reeds and rushes, poplars and willows, look like beaches and isles;
Clouds above the creek just rising, as the sun sets into the pavilion;
The mountain rain about to arrive, winds overflow the turret.
Birds alight on green thicket grass in the Qin garden evening;
Cicadas sing among yellow leaves in the autumn of the Han Palace.

Travelers, do not ask about the affairs of those days—
Heading eastward from the old capital the Wei River flows on.

一上高城萬里愁, 蒹葭楊柳似汀州.
溪雲初起日沉閣, 山雨欲來風滿樓.
鳥下綠蕪秦苑夕, 蟬鳴黃葉漢宮秋.
行人莫問當年事, 故國東來渭水流.

Written around 849 when the Tang empire was shaken by political and military turmoil, the poem opens with a sense of impending crisis and far-reaching melancholy. The fourth line, depicting such tension and anxiety through the image of looming rain and a rising wind, has since become the most quoted line of Xu Hun. The poet's anxiety over loss and ruin in the present is echoed, and intensified, by his concern over the loss of the great dynasties of the past. Birds and cicadas enjoy the wilderness where Qin gardens and Han palaces used to be, and nothing more is left than the Wei River flowing eastward from the old capital city of Xianyang. The past has thus faded beyond the reach of inquiries.

Other famous poems by Xu Hun are "Qiuri fu que ti Tongguan Yilou" 秋日赴闕題潼關驛樓 (Setting out for the Capital on An Autumn Day and Inscribing A Poem on the Post Station Tower at the Tong Pass), "Jinling huaigu" 金陵懷古 (Meditating on the Past in Jinling), and "Gu Luo cheng" 故洛城 (The Old City Wall of Luo). Wei Zhuang, in his "Ti Xu Hun shi*juan*" 題許渾詩卷 (Inscription on Xu Hun's Poetry Scrolls), commented "In the poetry of Xu Hun, the talent from the south of the Yangzi River, each word is fresh and new, every line is marvelous. Ten *hu* of radiant pearls are not enough to measure [the value of his poetry], Huixiu, [on the other hand,] had composed his Emerald Clouds song in vain" 江南才子許渾詩，字字清新句句奇。十斛明珠量不盡，惠休空作碧雲詞. Ranking Xu Hun's poetic talent above Huixiu, a rather influential poet during the Liu Song (420–479) of the Southern Dynasties, is indeed a high evaluation.

The Song dynasty *Xuanhe shupu* 宣和書譜 (Catalogue of Calligraphic Styles during the Xuanhe Reign, 1119–1125) notes that Xu Hun was also good at calligraphy. The *Xuanhe shupu* also notes that his poetic style was similar to that of Du Mu. The Qing-dynasty poet Tian Wen 田雯 (1635–1704) also commented that "[when it comes to] the skillfulness in the regulated schemes of poetry, there is no one who can be compared to [Xu] Hun" 詩律之熟，無如渾者.

Critics have noticed that Xu's poems have many references to water. The *Tongjiang shihua* 桐江詩話 (The Tong River Poetry Remarks), acknowledging this interesting feature with a pun on *shi*, both "wet" 濕 and "poems" 詩, playfully switches the two words in noting "Xu Hun's one thousand pieces of wetness" 許渾千首濕 (i.e., Xu Hun's one thousand poems are all wet).

Xu Hun included five hundred poems in his three-*juan* anthology, the *Collection by the Dingmao [Bridge]*, in 850. Different editions of his anthology are listed in the "Yiwen zhi" of the *Xin Tang shu*, the *Junzhai dushu zhi*, and the *Zhizhai shulu jieti* 直齋書錄解題 (Annotated Bibliography of the Book Catalog at the Zhi Study). Most of his poetry is collected in eleven chapters in the *Quan Tang shi*.

BIBLIOGRAPHY

Editions:

Dingmao ji 丁卯集, 2 vols.; *Dingmao ji xu gao* 丁卯集續藁, 2 vols.; *Dingmao ji xu buji* 丁卯集續補集; *Dingmao ji wai yishi gao* 丁卯集外遺詩藁. Zhu Defu 祝得甫 ed. Qing dynasty edition published sometime between 1644 and 1795.

Dingmao ji 丁卯集, 2 vols. Xi Qiyu 席啓寓 (d. 1703), ed. Shanghai: Saoye Shanfang 掃葉山房, 1920.

Dingmao ji 丁卯集, in *Changshu Weng shi shicang guji shanben congshu* 常熟翁氏世藏古籍善本叢書. Beijing: Wenwu, 1996.

Dingmao ji 丁卯集, 3 vols. Mianyang Lushi Shenshiji Zhai 沔陽盧氏慎始基齋, 1923.

Dingmao shiji 丁卯詩集., in Liu Tui 劉蛻 (*jinshi* 850), ed. *Wenquan zi ji* 文泉子集. Shanghai: Shanghai Guji, 1994.

Dingmao shiji 丁卯詩集, 2 vols., and *Xu ji* 續集, *Xu bu* 續補, *Ji wai yi shi* 集外遺詩. Xi Qiyu 席啓寓 (d. 1703), ed. Dongting, China: Dongshan Xishi Qinchuan Shuwu, 1708.

Junzhai dushu zhi 郡齋讀書志, *j.* 18.

Luo Shijin 羅時進, ed. *Dingmao ji jianzheng* 丁卯集箋證. Nanchang: Jiangxi Renmin, 1998.

____, ed. *Dingmao ji jianzheng* 丁卯集箋證. Beijing: Zhonghua, 2012.

Quan Tang shi, 8: 6086–193, 13: 10064, 10253, 10498, 14: 10674.

Quan Tang wen, 760.8993.

Song kan Xu Yonghui wenji 宋刊許用晦文集. Shanghai: Hanfenlou 涵芬樓, 1922.

Xu Cishi shiji 許刺史詩集, 7 vols. Li Zhizhen 李之楨, ed. Ming dynasty edition, published between 1522 and 1620.

Xu Yonghui wenji 許用晦文集. Shanghai: Shanghai Guji, 1994, 2013.

Xu Yonghui wenji 許用晦文集, 2 vols.; *Shiyi* 拾遺, 2 vols. Shanghai: Shangwu Yinshuguan Hanfenlou, 1923.

Yuankan Dingmao shiji 元刊丁卯詩集. Zhu Dezi 祝德子, ed. Fuzhou: Fujian Renmin, 2008.

Ying Song ben Dingmao ji 景宋本丁卯集, 2 vols. Zhenjiang: Hanpaoyi 寒匏簃, 1936.

Zengguang yinzhu Tang Yingzhou Cishi Dingmao ji 增廣音註唐郢州刺史丁卯集, 2 vols., and *Xu ji* 續集. Beijing: Beijing Tushuguan, 2005.

Annotations:

Dingmao ji jianzheng 丁卯集箋證. Luo Shijin 羅時進, ed. Nanchang: Jiangxi Renmin, 1998.

Dingmao ji jianzhu 丁卯集箋注. Xu Peirong 許培榮 et al. In *Xu xiu Siku quanshu* 續修四庫全書, vol. 1311.1756.

Dingmao ji jianzhu 丁卯集箋注. Annotated by Xu Peirong 許培榮, commented by Lei Qijian 雷起劍, collated and carved by Xu Zhongde 許鍾德 and Xu Zhonglin 許鍾霖, 1756. Shanghai: Shanghai Guji, 1995, 1999.

Xu Hun shi jiaozhu 許渾詩校注. Jiang Congping 江聰平, ed. Taibei: Taiwan, Zhonghua, 1973.

Biographical Sources:

Fu, *Tang caizi*, 3:231–43, 5:330–45.

Translations:

Bynner, *Jade Mountain*, pp. 37–38.
Owen, *Late Tang*, pp. 202, 226–36, 280, 334.
___, *Omen*, pp. 70–75.

Studies:

Ayscough, Florence. *Mi Yüan-Chang Writes Poems by Hsü Hun: A Hand-Scroll. Mi Yüan-Chang Hsü Hun Shih Chüan*. Extr. de : M.S. IV. 1940: 627–37.

Dong Naibin 董乃斌. "Tang shiren Xu Hun shengping kaosuo" 唐詩人許渾生平考索, *Wenshi* 26 (1986): 265–79.

He Xiuming 賀秀明. "Lun Xu Hun shi zhong de shui" 論許渾詩中的水, *Huazhong Shifan Daxue xuebao: Renwen Shehui Kexue Ban* 39.6 (Nov. 2000): 88–92.

Li Lipu 李立樸. *Xu Hun yanjiu* 許渾研究. Guiyang: Guizhou Renmin, 1994.

Luo Shijin 羅時進. *Tangshi yanjin lun* 唐詩演進論. Nanjing: Jiangsu Guji, 2002, pp. 138–72.

___. *Wan Tang shige geju zhong de Xu Hun chuangzuo lun* 晚唐詩歌格局中的許渾創作論. Xi'an: Taibo Wenyi, 1998.

___, "Lun Xu Hun shi zai wan Tang de dianxing yiyi" 論許渾詩在晚唐的典型意義, *Wenxue yichan*, 1997.5: 62–71.

___, "Xu Hun zunian zai kaobian" 許渾卒年再考辨, *Xueshu yuekan* 1996.8: 47.

___, "Xu Hun shengnian kao" 許渾生年考, *Shanxi Shida xuebao* 4 (1988): 56–57.

Tan Youxue 譚優學. *Tang shiren xingnian kao* 唐詩人行年考. Chengdu: Ba Shu Shushe, 1987, pp. 132–67.

Tetsuhiko Tosaki 戶崎哲彥, "Xu Hun yu Li Jue: Dui Guilin Huajing dong shike Xu Hun 'Ji Li xianggong' liang shou shi ji Niu Li dangzheng yanjiu de qishi" 许浑与李珏: 对桂林华景洞石刻许浑《寄李相公》两首诗及"牛李党争"研究的启示, *Shehui kexue jia* 17.1 (Jan 2002): 93–97.

Wang Jiannan 王見楠, "Xu Hun yanjiu shuping (1980–2007)" 許渾研究述評, *Huaiyin Shifan Xueyuan xuebao: Zhexue Shehui Kexueban* 31.4 (2009): 531–37.

Wang Yan 王艷, "Xu Hun shige jufa moshihua de tanxi" 許渾詩歌句法模式化的探析, *Jiujiang Xueyuan Xuebao: Shehui Kexueban* 134.1 (2006): 74–77.

Xu Jun 徐俊, "Shilun 'Xu Hun qian shou shi'" 試論"許渾千首湿." *Wenxue yichan* 1 (1989): 52–58.

Xu Yongli 徐永麗, "Shilun Wei Zhuang dui Xu Hun shige de jieshou" 試論韋莊對許渾詩歌的接受, *Hefei Xueyuan xuebao: Shehui Kexueban* 25.6 (Nov. 2008): 63–65.

Yang Weigang 楊為剛 and Wu Chen 吳晨, "Xu Hun zaonian xingji zai kao" 許渾早年行跡再考, *Xuchang Xueyuan xuebao* 27 (2008.3): 66–67.

Ying Qin and Shuxiang You

Xu Jingzong 許敬宗 (*zi*, Yanzu 延族, 592–672), along with Shangguan Yi 上官儀 (ca. 607–ca. 665),* was one of the two most important court poets of the 630s and 640s. Born in Xincheng 新城 (modern Fuyang 富陽 in Zhejiang near Hangzhou 杭州), Xu came from an elite family with ancestors from Gaoyang 高陽 (modern Xushui 徐水 County in Hebei). His father, Xu Shanxin 許善心 (558–618), and great-grandfather, Xu Mao 許懋 (446–532), had served the Liang and Sui dynasties.

Xu Jingzong

Xu passed the *xiucai* 秀才 examination under the Sui and gained a reputation as a writer while young. After his father had been killed by the rebel general Yuwen Huaji 宇文化及 (d. 619), Xu became a secretary to the general Li Mi 李密 (582–619). When Li Mi surrendered to the Tang, Xu became a scholar in the camp of the heir and Prince of Qin 秦王, Li Shimin 李世民 (598–649). After Li Shimin ascended the throne, posthumously titled Taizong (r. 626–649), Xu worked on compiling a national history and was one of the eighteen academicians at court who made up the Institute of Literary Attendants along with other scholars of note such as Kong Yingda 孔穎達 (547–648) and Yao Silian 姚思廉 (d. 637). Xu was exiled, supposedly for laughing on the day Empress Zhangsun's funeral, to be the Vice Prefect of Hongzhou 洪州. Soon after returning to the capital, he began serving the heir, Li Zhi 李治 (628–683). He compiled two important accounts of Taizong's reign, *Wude shilu* 武德實錄 (The Veritable Records of the Wude Era) and *Taizong shilu* 太宗實錄 (Veritable Records of Emperor Taizong). When Li Zhi became emperor, posthumously titled Gaozong (r. 650–683), Xu was made Director of the Ministry of Rites and became a strong supporter of Empress Wu (r. 690–705), helping the Empress to rid the court of Zhangsun Wuji 長孫無忌 (594–659) and Shangguan Yi, both of whom were eventually killed. In 657 he was made Grand Councilor and supplanted Zhangsun Wuji in the Empress's favor. In 658 he was ennobled as Duke of Jun 郡 and replaced Li Yifu 李義府 (614–666) as Director of the Secretariat. In 662 Xu again became a Grand Councilor, holding other honorary titles until his retirement in 670. At his death two years later at age 81 the Emperor honored him in various ways including suspending court for three days.

Many of the nearly thirty poems he left were written on imperial command (*yingzhi shi* 應制詩) or at court on a specific theme, such as the following piece, "Qixi fuyong chengpian" 七夕賦詠成篇 (A Piece Completed on the Seventh Night [of the Seventh Month] to Express My Feelings). Composed in response to the legends surrounding the seventh day of the seventh month when the separated lovers, the Herder Boy and Weaving Girl, are allowed to meet for a single night, the poem reads:

> After one year of disappointment, I sigh over the long separation,
> On this seventh night restrained we speak of reunion.
> So lightly in silk stockings you step through heaven's gleam,
> So brightly newly made up you mirror the moon's splendor.
> Love pained, as you coyly smile, dimples appear,
> Not hesitating to reveal, as you undo your cloud gown.
> We sigh that we must follow the clepsydra's deadline,
> Covering our tears as you return to work your loom of past nights.

> 一年抱怨嗟長別，七夕含態始言歸。
> 飄飄羅襪光天步，灼灼新妝鑒月輝。
> 情催巧笑開星靨，不惜呈露解雲衣。
> 所歎卻隨更漏盡，掩泣還弄昨宵機。

Although the poem expresses sincere feelings, it is but an exercise that matched a number of other poets who must have written on the same theme on the same occasion. This lack of concern for appeal to reality or moral comment in Xu's verse hindered both the appreciation of his works in later ages and the study of his poetry in English, but it was his skill in matching verse that enhanced the esteem he won from his royal patrons.

Under Xu's influence, following the completion of a number of dynastic histories from the Northern and Southern Dynasties in the 640s and 650s, the Emperor sponsored a number of new works, including Li Shan's 李善 (630–689) commentary to the *Wenxuan* 文選 (Selections of Refined Literature) and the literary collection (now lost) *Leibi* 累璧 (An Accumulation of Precious Jade Discs). Perhaps Xu's most important work, however, was the editing of the *Wenguan cilin* 文館詞林 (Forest of Writings from the Hall of Literature) in one thousand *juan* compiled under imperial auspices in 658. It seems to have been lost as early as the Southern Song period. During the next few centuries, this work was virtually forgotten. However, in the late eighteenth century, surviving manuscripts were discovered in Japan. So far about twenty-seven *juan* (some fragmentary) are known and have been published in various editions. Judging from the surviving portions, this work seems to have included both private writings and official documents, such as imperial edicts, from the early Han through the early Tang. Even though less than one-tenth of it has survived, the importance of the extant portion need hardly be stressed. Many poems and documents, long presumed to be lost, now appear here for the first time. Many are not found in the two earlier "complete" collections: the *Han Wei Liuchao baisan mingjia ji* 漢魏六朝百三名家集 compiled by Chang Pu 張溥 (1602–1641) and the *Quan Shanggu Sandai Qin Han Sanguo Liuchao wen* 全上古三代秦漢三國六朝文 by Yan Kejun 嚴可均 (1762–1843). The work is one of a series of similar anthologies going back to the Northern Qi era. Its purpose, similar to these precursors, was to define a corpus of traditional genres and works—the selection of genres herein seems to fall between that of the earlier *Wenxuan* 文選 and its Song-dynasty sequel, the *Wenyuan yinghua* 文苑英華 (Blossoms and Flowers from the Literary Garden).

BIBLIOGRAPHY

Editions:
Bunkan shirin 文館詞林. Abe Ryūichi 阿部隆一, ed. Tokyo: Koten Kenkyūkai, 1969. Facsimile reprint of an MSS. copy dated 823. Includes a lengthy study by Abe.
Luo Guowei 羅國威, ed. *Ercang Hongren ben Wenguang cilin jiaozheng* 日藏弘仁本文館詞林校證. Beijing: Zhonghua, 2001.
Quan Tang shi, 1: 464–70, 13: 10039, 14: 10595–96, 10933–36.
Quan Tang wen, 151–52.1734–55.
Wenguan cilin 文館詞林. Yang Baochu 楊葆初 (fl. 1890–1920), ed., 1893. Includes 6 *juan*.
___, in *Yicun congshu* 佚存叢書 (1800), contains 4 *juan*; in *Guyi congshu* 古佚叢書 (1884), contains 14 *juan*. These two (in all, 18 *juan*) are incorporated into *BBCSJC*, series 75, v. 50–57.
___, in *Shiyuan congshu* 適園叢書. 1914. Contains 23 *juan* including several earlier published versions.

Biographical Sources:
Jiu Tang shu, 82.2761–65.
Xin Tang shu, 223A.6335–39.

Xu Jingzong

Translations:
Owen, *Early T'ang*, pp. 35, 42, 52, and 73.

Studies:
Li Xiaoqing 李曉青. "Lun Xu Jingzong ji qi shige chuangzuo" 論許敬宗及其詩歌創作. *Anhui Ligong Daxue xuebao (Shehui Kexueban)*. 2007.4: 31–33.

Meng Sen 孟森. "*Wenguan* cilin jiaoji" 文館詞林校記, *Beiping Tushuguan guankan*, 7.1 (February 1933): 81–102.

Niu Zhigong 牛致功. "Xu Jingzong dui Tangdai shixue de gongguo" 許敬宗對唐代史學的功過, *Shixue yuekan*, 1987.3: 12–16.

Shi Shufang 石樹芳. "*Hanlin xueshi ji* timing zhiguan yu shege biannian xinkao" 《翰林學士集》題名職官與詩歌編年新考, *Xinan Jiaotong Daxue xuebao (Shehui Kexueban)*, 2013.2: 19–24.

Yang Chunqiao 楊春俏 and Que Jianhua 闕建華. "Xu Jingzong zouqing Qiyun zhayun 'he er yongzhi' kaobian" 許敬宗奏請《切韻》窄韻「合而用之」考辨, *Shandong Shifan Daxue xuebao (Renwen Shehui Kexue ban)*, 2011.1: 21–26.

Yue Cunzhi 岳純之. "Ye tan Xu Jingzong cuangai Tangdai shilu, guoshi wenti" 也談許敬宗篡改唐代實錄, 國史問題, *Yantai Daxue xuebao (Zhexue Shehui Kexue ban)*, 2001.1: 89–94.

S. F. Lai and William H. Nienhauser, Jr.

Xuanjue 玄覺 (*zi*, Mingdao 明道, *hao*, Shendao 神道, *hao*, Great Teacher Zhenjue 真覺大師, *hao*, Great Teacher from Yongjia 永嘉大師, *hao*, Yisu Jue 一宿覺, posthumous name Wuxiang 無相, secular surname Dai 戴, 665 or 675–713) was a monk from Yongjia 永嘉 (modern Wenzhou 溫州) famous for his broad learning. As a small child, he was given to a monastery—some say Kaiyuan Monastery 開元寺, some say Longxing Monastery 龍興寺.

There are several accounts of his family background and his quest for enlightenment. One day he and his sister offered a passing elder monk called Shence 神策 (a possible reference to Huineng's 慧能 [638–713] disciple Xuance 玄策) some tea. The guest soon realized Xuanjue's excellence and suggested that he should visit the Chan master Huineng in the South, pay him homage as his teacher, and receive his seal of approval. With the blessing of his elder sister and his abbot, he set off to Mount Caoxi 曹溪山. At the age of 31, he met the famous patriarch and earned—in an extraordinary dialogue—Huineng's praise for his unshakeable insight into the matters of life and death. Afterwards, he was invited to stay for the night, a fact well memorialized by his name Yisu Jue 一宿覺, i.e. "Awakened in One Night's Stay," and the incorporation of this anecdote into the Song edition of the *Platform Sutra*. Famous over night, he spread his teaching upon his return far beyond the local community. His sister then started to collect his literary works which she continued to do until his death in 713. The record of a *younger* sister, a nun known by the name Xuanji 玄機 (*hao*, Jingju 淨居 [Pure Abode], d. 713?), who authored a commentary to one of Xuanjue's works, evinces the possibility that Xuanjue had more than one sister.

A slightly later account, possibly accessing a now lost stele inscription by Li Yong 李邕 (678–747), offers a more detailed account of his family background, while omitting the references to sisters. Apparently, his ancestor, a certain Dai Lie 戴烈, who was a descendant in the fifth generation of Dai Kan 戴侃 and in the ninth generation of Dai Yan 戴燕, had come to Yongjia after crossing the Yangzi river at the end of the Later Han dynasty (25–200). Xuanjue's elder brother, Dharma-master Xuan 宣, was a famous monk, too, and his two nephews also donned the cloth. When the young Xuanjue discovered a beautiful spot outside the monastery, he built himself a hermitage beyond a cliff. Yet having no teacher, he decided to join the company of Chan-master Ce 策 from Dongyang 東陽 (a possible reference to the above-mentioned Xuance). His wanderings would culminate once more in his intense encounter with Huineng, but not without relating that Shenxiu 神秀 (ca. 605–706), the prominent rival of Huineng (as later history would have it), had not been able to adequately quench his thirst for enlightenment. Huicao 惠操, Huite 惠特, Cideng 等慈, and Xuanji 玄寂 are presented as Xuanjue's students, who handed down his teachings, while finally Zuoxi Xuanlang 左溪玄朗 (673–754), known as the eighth Patriarch of the Tiantai School, has a short appearance as a close friend with whom Xuanjue exchanged letters that are still preserved in his works.

In the Yuanhe era (806–820), Du Ben 杜賁 (fl. 813), the Grand Protector of Yongjia, discovered during the renovation of Xuanjue's grave that his corpse had not withered. Upon his report to the court, Emperor Xianzong (r. 805–820) ordered the erection of a stupa, that was bestowed the name "Jingguang" 淨光 (Pure Splendor) by Emperor Xizong (r. 873–888), and later on expanded by an additional stupa garden with a plaque by Emperor Zhaozong (r. 888–904) reading "Jingguan chanyuan" 淨光禪院 (Chan Courtyard of Pure Splendor). After several reconstructions, Xuanjue's stupa was destroyed in the year 1499, only to be re-erected in the year 2001—which ultimately led to the re-discovery of Xuanjue's śarīra (shelizi 舍利子) in an earthen pot beneath the foundations of the stupa. His relics have since then been kept at Wenzhou's Miaoguo Monastery 妙果寺.

Due to his fame, various Buddhist denominations laid claims on Xuanjue as a historical figure, especially during the Song dynasty, when he was eventually not only counted as a disciple of Huineng, the sixth Chan Patriarch, but also of Huiwei 慧威 (634–713 or 714), the seventh Patriarch of the Tiantai school. Thus, some of his later biographies asserted that he not only mastered the *Tripiṭaka* but was especially versed in the Tiantai doctrine of Buddhist meditation, i.e., "cessation" and "observation" (*zhi guan* 止觀). However, a different source specifically attributed his enlightenment to his reading of the *Vimalakīrti Sūtra*, a *Mahāyāna* scripture that enjoyed prominence among the emerging Chan schools. These interdenominational struggles and constructions of an authoritative lineage of transmission that are part of the development of Buddhism in China are important, not only in regard to the biographical sources, but also for an adequate appraisal of Xuanjue's oeuvre itself.

According to the *Xin Tang shu*, there was a *Xuanjue Yongjia ji* 玄覺永嘉集 (The Yongjia Collection of Xuanjue) in ten *juan*, compiled by a certain Wei Jing 魏靖/静, Prefect of Qingzhou 慶州. The transmitted version of his works, known as the *Chanzong Yongjia ji* 禪宗永嘉集 (The Chan School's Yongjia Collection) in one *juan* included a preface by the aforementioned Wei Jing, and was first canonized into the *Hongwu nan zang* 洪武南藏 (1372–1398). It is still preserved in Korean separate editions, featuring Yongsheng's 永盛 (1275–1347) commentary, dating from the late 14th and 15th century. The *Yongjia ji* is presented as a gradual approach to the attainment of Buddhahood, exemplified by the ten pieces of the collection. The resonance of Tiantai teachings in this work justified, at least in the eyes of the Ming Dynasty monk Chuandeng 傳燈 (1554–1628),

a reorganization of the whole collection to bring it in proper accordance with the structure of the *Mohe zhiguan* 摩訶止觀 (The Great Cessation and Observation), a core text of the Tiantai School.

The *Yongjia ji* made its entrance into the Buddhist canon with Xuanjue's second independently transmitted work, the "Yongjia zhengdao ge" 永嘉證道歌 (Yongjia's Song of Realization of the Way)—a vigorous, long poem about Xuanjue's insight into the Chan way that pays a flaming tribute to Huineng and the Southern school of sudden enlightenment, as its opening lines already reveal:

> *Kun* (Milord), have you not seen,
> Beyond learning and without any makings, the man of the Way at ease,
> Who neither discards erring thoughts, nor seeks the truth?
> The real nature of ignorance is the Buddha-nature;
> The illusory void body is the Dharma-body.
> In the final awakening of the Dharma-body there is not a thing;
> Turning to the origin of the self-nature is the heavenly true Buddhahood.
> The Five Darkeners are floating clouds, void in their coming and goings;
> The Three Poisons are water bubbles, empty in their appearing and vanishing.
> Realizing the aspects of reality, there is no person or dharma,
> And in an instant even karma leading to the *Avici* Hell is destroyed.
> If I makeup lies to deceive sentient beings,
> I shall bring upon myself the Hell, where tongues are pulled out for *kalpas* as uncountable as dust and sand.

> 君不見，
> 絕學無爲閒道人，不除妄想不求眞。
> 無明實性即佛性，幻化空身即法身。
> 法身覺了無一物，本源自性天眞佛。
> 五陰浮雲空去來，三毒水泡虛出沒。
> 證實相，無人法，刹那滅却阿鼻業。
> 若將妄語誑衆生，自招拔舌塵沙劫。

Several likely anachronisms have prompted a long line of critics to doubt Xuanjue's authorship beginning as early as the Song dynasty. Yet what to some presents irreconcilable differences in content and style has not prevented others from attempting a (mostly diachronic) synthesis of Xuanjue's thought. Regardless of its disputable provenance, the "Zhengdao ge" received an overwhelming reception from the late Tang dynasty on, as several travelogues of Japanese monks, Dunhuang manuscripts (S.2165, S.4037, S.6000, P.2104, P.2105, and P.3360), and the legendary anecdote of its translation by an Indian monk into Sanskrit (under the title "Dongtu Dasheng jing" 東土大乘經 [*Mahāyāna Sutra of the Eastern Soil*]) attest.

BIBLIOGRAPHY

Editions:

Faquan 法泉 (Song), comm. *Zhengdao ge song* 證道歌頌. *Taishō Shinshū Daizōkyō*, no. 1291, vol. 65.

Hamhŏ Tŭkt'ong 涵虛得通 (1376–1433), comm., and Jingyuan 淨源 (1011–1088), ed. *Sŏnjŏng yŏnggajip kwajŭ sŏrui* 禪宗永嘉集科註説誼. *Han'guk pulgyo chŏnsŏ* 韓國佛教全書, 7: 170–216. Print from 1464, reprint: *Sŏnjong yŏnggajip ŏnhae* 禪宗永嘉集諺解. Seoul: Hongmungak, 1983.

Jingju 淨居 (d. 710–712), comm. *Yongjia Zhenjue dashi zhengdao ge* 永嘉眞覺大師證道歌. *Hyosŏng Sŏnsaeng p'alsip songsu Koryŏ Pulchŏk chibil* 曉城先生八十頌壽高麗佛籍集佚. Ed. Cho Myŏng-gi 趙明基 (1905–1988). Seoul: Tongguk Taehakkyo Ch'ulp'anbu, 1985.

Quan Tang shi, 14: 11014–17.

Quan Tang wen, 913.12402–05.

Wei Jing 魏静, ed. *Chanzong Yongjia ji* 禪宗永嘉集. *Taishō Shinshū Daizōkyō*, no. 2013, vol. 48.

Xuanjue. *Yongjia zhengdao ge* 永嘉證道歌. *Taishō Shinshū Daizōkyō*, no. 2014, vol. 48.

Annotations:

Chuandeng 傳燈 (1554–1628), ed. and comm. *Yongjia chanzong ji zhu* 永嘉禪宗集註, *Shinsan Dainihon Zokuzōkyō*, no. 1242, vol. 63.

Xingjing 行靖 (Song), comm. *Chanzong Yongjia ji zhu* 禪宗永嘉集註. *Wan zheng zang jing*, no. 1592, vol. 64.

Yanqi 彥琪 (Song), comm. *Zhengdao ge zhu* 證道歌註. *Shinsan Dainihon Zokuzōkyō*, no. 1241, vol. 63.

Yongsheng 永盛 (1275–1347), comm., and Dehong 德弘, ed. *Zhengdao ge zhu* 證道歌註. *Shinsan Dainihon Zokuzōkyō*, no. 1293, vol. 65.

Zhine 知訥 (1079–1158), comm. *Zhengdao ge zhu* 證道歌註. *Shinsan Dainihon Zokuzōkyō*, no. 1292, vol. 65.

Biographical Sources:

Zan Ning, 8.184–85.

Translations:

Liebenthal, Walter (1886–1982). "Yung-chia's Song of Experiencing the Tao." *MS* 6.1/2 (1941): 1–39.

Luk, Charles [Lu Kuanyu 陸寬昱] (1898–1978). "Yong-chia's Song of Enlightenment." *Ch'an and Zen Teaching*. London: Rider, 1969, vol. III, pp. 103–145.

Shengyan 聖嚴 (1931–2009). *The Sword of Wisdom: Lectures on 'The Song of Enlightenment.'* Elmhurst, NY: Dharma Drum Publications, 1990.

Studies:

Bai Chin-Hsien 白金銑. "Yongjia Xuanjue chanfa zhong de chanhui sixiang" 永嘉玄覺禪法中的懺悔思想. *Xin shiji zongjiao yanjiu* 7.2 (2008): 103–144.

Chang Yŏng-gil 장영길, comm. *Yŏkchu Sŏnjong yŏnggajip ŏnhae* 역주선종영가집언해. Seoul: Hanul, 2007.

Cheng Shenggang 陳盛港. "'Yongjia zhengdao ge' yuan zuozhe suyuan bing gewen bijiao" 永嘉證道歌'原作者溯源併歌文比較. *Zhonghua Fojiao yanjiu* 5 (2001): 163–204.

Furota Bonsen 古田梵仙 (fl. 19. cent.), and Issen 一線 (fl. 1736); comms. *Zōchū Shōdokā jikisai* 增註證道歌直截. Kajita Kansuke: Urisabakinin Miura Kensuke, 1881.

Hong Qisong 洪啟嵩. *Yongjia de dunwu: Chanzong de qianqu juechang* 永嘉的頓悟：禪宗的千古絕唱. Beijing: Zhongguo Shehui, 2004.

Hongxue 弘學. *Yongjia Xuanjue dashi "Zhengdao ge" jiangxi* 永嘉玄覺大師《証道歌》講析. Chengdu: Ba Shu Shushe, 2006.

Hu Shi 胡適 (1891–1962). "Suowei 'Yongjia zhengdao ge'" 所謂『永嘉證道歌』. *Hu Shi wen cun* 胡適文存. Taibei: Yuandong Tushu Gongsi, 1961. Vol. 3, 4.356–358.

Huang Yi-hsun 黃繹勳. "A Critical Study of Yongjia Xuanjue's Biographies." *Ryūkoku Daigaku bukkyō bunka kenkyūjo shohō* 33 (2009): 26–23[!].

Jia Jinhua 賈晉華. *The Hongzhou School of Chan Buddhism in Eighth- through Tenth-century China*. Albany, NY: State University of New York, 2006, pp. 89–95.

Jiang Jiusi 蔣九愚, comm. *Xinyi Yongjia Dashi zhengdaoge* 新譯永嘉大師證道歌. Taibei: Sanmin, 2005.

Kazama Toshio 風間敏夫. "Yōka shū no shisō ni tsuite"永嘉集の思想について. *Indogaku bukkyōgaku kenkyū* 71 (1987): 101–10.

Kazama Toshio 風間敏夫. "'Zenshū Yōka shū' no kōzō shisō" 『禅宗永嘉集』の構造と思想. *Shūkyō kenkyū* 282 (1989): 1–29.

Katō Totsudō 加藤咄堂 (1870–1949). "Shōdōka kōgi" 證道歌講義. *Hekiganroku daikōza* 碧巖錄大講座. Tokyo: Heibonsha, 1939–40. Vol. 9–11.

Li Bichun 李碧純, "Yongjia xuanjue chanfa yanjiu" 永嘉玄覺禪法研究. Master thesis. Xuanzhuang Renwen Shehui Xueyuan 玄奘人文社會學院, 2004.

Nie Qing 聶清. "'Zhengdao ge' zuozhe kao" 《証道歌》作者考. *Zongjiaoxue yanjiu* 1 (2000): 131–37.

Sawaki Kōdō 澤木興道 (1880–1965). *Zen no satori: Shōdōka o kataru* 禅のさとり—証道歌を語る. Tokyo: Daihōrinkaku, 1999.

Sengoku Keisho 仙石景章. "Chitotsu no 'Shōdōka chū' ni tsuite" 知訥の『証道歌註』について. *Indo tetsugaku bukkyōgaku* 16 (2001): 125–36.

___. "'Zenshū Yōka shū' saikō" 『禅宗永嘉集』再考. *Indo tetsugaku bukkyōgaku* 6 (1991): 273–87.

Shōdō 摂道. *Yōka daishi shōdōka: Gōtō* 永嘉大師証道歌: 鼇頭. Mitsubuchimura (Aichi): Ōnami Chōsui, 1878.

Tanxu 倓虛 (1875–1963), comm. *Yongjia Dashi zhengdao ge lüe jie* 永嘉大師證道歌略解. Jiulong: Zhonghua Fojiao Tushuguan, 1959.

Ui Hakuju 宇井伯寿. *Zenshūshi kenkyū* 禪宗史研究. Tokyo: Iwanami, 1966. Vol. 2: 269–81.

Washisaka Sōen 鷲阪宗演. "Yōka Genkaku no zenkan" 永嘉玄覚の禅観. *Zen bunka kenkyūjo kiyō* 7 (1975): 53–68.

Xu Wenming 徐文明. "'Yongjia zhengdao ge' yu ershiba zu shuo de yuanqi" 《永嘉証道歌》與二十八祖說的緣起. *Zhongguo chanxue* 1 (2006): 127–38.

You Liru 游麗茹. "Yongjia Xuanjue de chanxue sixiang" 永嘉玄覺的禪學思想. Diss. Donghai Daxue 東海大學, 2011.

Zhang Liaokai 張子開. "Yongjia Xuanjue ji qi 'Zhengdao ge' kaobian'" 永嘉玄覺及其《証道歌》考辨. *Zongjiaoxue yanjiu* 1 (1994): 53–57.

Marc Nürnberger

Xuantai 玄泰 (*hao*, Taibuna 泰布納, *hao*, Nanyue Xuantai 南嶽玄泰, ca. 850–ca. 912) was a monk of unknown origin at the end of the Tang Dynasty who was famous for his austere life and literary talents. Xuantai is counted as a Dharma heir of the Chan-master Shishuang Qingzhu 石霜慶諸 (807–888), who also fostered two other famous poet monks, Qiji 齊己 (fl. 881)* and Guanxiu 貫休 (832–912).* Before meeting his final master, he may have also visited the Chan-master Deshan Xuanjian 德山宣鑑 (782–865).

In the end, however, Xuantai decided to have no students of his own. Whoever came to him, he treated as a friend. Some stayed, some left again. Taciturn, he never donned fine clothes, and hence was also called Taibuna 泰布納 (Tai, Who Wears Rags). Xuantai dwelled in an abode called Qibaotai 七寶臺 (Seven Treasures Terrace; also known as: Qibao Monastery 七寶寺) in the seclusion of Mount Heng 衡山 (north of modern Hengyang 衡陽, Hunan), one of the five holy mountains, also known as Nanyue 南嶽 (Southern Peak), to which Xuantai owed his later name. Yet, as poems dedicated to him attest, he must have been in contact with other poet monks like the aforementioned Qiji, as well as Xiumu 修睦 (fl. 898–928), Qichan 栖蟾 (fl. 900), and the unsuccessful examinee Li Xianyong 李咸用 (fl. 859–872).

With death approaching and no monk around him, he had to leave his abode to summon someone to prepare a pile of firewood to burn his body. He then wrote down two *gāthās* (*ji* 偈):

> This year, at sixty-five,
> The Four Great Elements are about to leave their master.
> His way is by itself subtler than subtleties,
> Yet therein are neither Buddhas nor Patriarchs.

> 今年六十五，四大將離主.
> 其道自玄玄，箇中無佛祖.

The Four Great Elements are earth, water, fire and wind.

> No need to shave my head,
> Not necessary to wash me.
> A pile of fierce fire,
> Will thousand fold suffice, ten thousand fold suffice?

> 不用剃頭，不須澡浴.
> 一堆猛火，千足萬足.

After the immolation, his remains were collected and buried in a small stupa on the left side of Chan-master Jiangu's 堅固 stupa.

During his lifetime he not only exchanged verses with other poet monks, but was also asked to prepare the now lost stele inscriptions for his Dharma uncle, Daowu Yuanzhi 道吾圓智 (769–835), the famous Caoshan Benji 曹山本寂 (840–901), and Yantou Quanhuo 巖頭全豁 (828–887), a disciple of Deshan Xuanjian. He was even asked to collect the sayings and deeds of his master, Shishuang Qingzhu. After his death, his literary oeuvre was edited into a popular collection, but it has likewise not survived. Probably Xuantai's most influential (and the only other surviving) piece is the "She shan yam" 畬山謠 (Ditty about the Slash-and-Burn Farming on the Mountain). When the local farmers were about to irrevocably destroy the whole ecosystem of Mount Heng (and probably thereby endanger the abodes of the monks), Xuantai composed a highly critical song that, once heard at court, prompted the prohibition of this invasive farming method. This outcome earned Xuantai even further fame and has made him a welcome reference point for early ecological awareness within the Buddhist clergy:

> Mountain slash-and-burners, mountain slash-and-burners, they know not a thing,
> Year after year, chopping down the eyebrows of the green mountain.
> Right at the most beautiful spots of Heng's peaks,
> Sharp axes destroy upright branches of firs and pines.
> Divine birds and wild cranes have no place to rest;
> The white clouds withdraw, as blue smoke flies.
> The ways of the apes and macaques are cut off, leaving the cliffs in open sight,
> Lingzhi mushrooms and boshu have lost their roots, while the grass grows fat.

Year after year, when the chopping is done, there is still the planting and weeding,
After a thousand autumns, the mountain will hardly recover.
And they even say that this year's sowing was not much,
Next year they will chop down yet more on the south-facing slopes.
If even the Mountain of Longevity (i.e., Mount Heng) of the State is like this,
How could one not see where this rationale will lead?!

畲山兒，畲山兒，無所知。年年斫斷青山嵋。
就是最好衡岳色，杉松利斧摧貞枝。
靈禽野鶴無因依，白雲回避青煙飛。
猿猱路絕岩崖出，芝朮失根茆草肥。
年年斫罷仍栽鋤，千秋終是難復初。

又道今年種不多，來年更斫當陽坡。
國家壽岳尚如此，不知此理如之何。

Boshu thistles are a medicinal ingredient that in combination with the Lingzhi mushrooms provide longer life. However, in his flaming critique of those "mountain slash-and-burners" Xuantai unfolds a gruesome picture to persuade readers of the unlawfulness of this practice: not only will the most beautiful scenic spots eventually all be ruined, but also the auspicious inhabitants of the mountains and even the rain-bearing clouds, signs of virtue and grace, will be robbed of their home. The imminent damage reaches symbolically far beyond the loss of the natural habitat of these rare plants. If the original nature of Heng Mountain, or, as the last line has it, the "Mountain of Longevity," is hurt too deeply, it will be beyond recovery—and, by extension, the health of the whole Empire (which is, of course, linked to the life of the Ruler), too.

BIBLIOGRAPHY

Editions:
Chen Tianfu 陳田夫 (12th cent.). *Nanyue zong sheng ji* 南岳總勝集. *SKQS. juan* zhong, 497a.
Gu Hongyi 顧宏義, comm., *Jingde chuandeng lu yi zhu* 景德傳燈錄譯注. Shanghai: Shanghai Shudian, 2009. Vol. 3:16.1180–1184.
Quan Tang shi, 15: 11437–38.

Biographical Sources:
Jing, Yun Er Chanshi 靜, 筠二禪師, eds. *Zutang ji* 祖堂集. Beijing: Zhonghua, 2007. Vol. 1: 9.444–445.
Zan Ning, 17.429–430.

Studies:
Benn, James A. *Burning for the Buddha: Self-immolation in Chinse Buddhism.* Honolulu: University of Hawai'i Press, 2007, pp. 139–40, 143.
San Baojing 桑宝靖, "Niannian zaoduan qingshan mei—du Nanyue Xuantai 'She shan yao'" 年年鑿斷青山嵋—讀南岳玄泰《畲山謠》, *Shijie zongjiao wenhua* 2001.3: 34–35.

Marc Nürnberger

Xue Tao 薛濤 (*zi*, Hongdu 洪度, ca. 768–ca. 831) was one of the two most distinguished women poets of the Tang dynasty, the other being Yu Xuanji 魚玄機 (ca. 844–868).* She was born to an ordinary family in Chang'an. Her father, Xue Yun 薛鄖, was a minor government official who died in Sichuan, leaving his family stranded there with no means of support. Xue Tao, fourteen or fifteen at the time, was known for her talent in versification. To support herself and her widowed mother, she became a sing-song girl.

It is said that when Xue Tao was barely seven or eight, her father, to test her talent, asked her to finish a quatrain which he began with these lines: "In the garden an ancient *tong*-tree, / Towering, its trunk thrusting into the clouds" 庭除一古桐，聳干入雲中. Without hesitation the child responded, "Its branches welcome birds from north or south; / Its leaves bid adieu to winds that come and go" 枝迎南北鳥，葉送往風來. Although impressed with his daughter's precociousness, Xue Yun was chagrined at the symbolic meaning of her imagery, which seemed to prognosticate her future as a courtesan welcoming men who would come and go.

In 785, when Xue Tao's literary fame had spread throughout Chengdu, the capital of Sichuan, Wei Gao 韋皋 (745–805), the Military Commissioner at the time, had her registered as an official courtesan to entertain honored guests at public functions. She served a series of new Military Commissioners who came to Chengdu after Wei's death in 805 in this capacity. Wu Yuanheng 武元衡 (758–815)* proposed recommending her to the throne to become an Editor, but that proved impossible, so she came to be called Nü shulang 女書郎 (The Female Editor).

During these years, Xue Tao had occasion to meet many celebrities from Chang'an. She was on intimate terms and exchanged poetry with no fewer than twenty eminent Tang poets, among them, Pei Du 裴度 (765–839), Linghu Chu 令狐楚 (766–837),* Liu Yuxi 劉禹錫 (772–842),* Bo Juyi 白居易 (772–846),* and in particular Yuan Zhen 元稹 (779–831).* When Yuan Zhen went to eastern Sichuan in 809 on an inspection tour as Investigating Censor, he expressed his desire to meet this renowned poetess. His host complied by sending Xue Tao to him, and a lasting, close relationship developed between them. After Yuan Zhen returned to the capital, Xue Tao continued to send him poems written on colorful tablets with fir and flower patterns which she designed and manufactured herself. The poem "Ji jiushi yu Yuan Weizhi" 寄舊詩與元微之 (Sending an Old Poem to Yuan Weizhi) is one of them:

> The style and mood of poems, everyone has his own—
> But the delicacy and subtlety of a scene, only I understand.
> To extol flowers in the moonlight, I show my love of the pale;
> To write of willows in the rain, I make branches droop.
> For long I've been told to hide away these pieces of green jasper,
> But after all I carry them along on red paper that I made.
> Old age makes it impossible to collect all my verses,
> I send some to you as if teaching a young boy.

詩篇調態人皆有，細膩風光我獨知。
月下詠花憐暗澹，雨朝題柳為欹垂。
長教碧玉藏深處，總向紅箋寫自隨。
老大不能收拾得，與君開似教男兒。

The poem explains Xue's ideas about the sources of poetry: human emotions and the physical environment. Green jasper may refer to a young girl who was the concubine of the King of Runan 汝南王 during the Liu Song dynasty known for her unassuming ways. But it could just as easily be a metaphor stressing the purity of Xue's verse, or even a reference to the paper on which the poem was written. The final line seems to show Xue's pride, but some critics have argued it may refer to a son she bore to Yuan Zhen.

In her lifetime, Xue Tao had a collection of over five hundred poems in circulation; only about ninety of them have survived. Most are love poems addressed to her male patrons in their absence, or occasional poems celebrating their brief unions. Her poems are noted for the rich, sensuous imagery and melodious rhythm, suitable for singing. Critics tend to dismiss Xue Tao's poetry as mere erotic, occasional verse of no significance. They overlook the subtle satire and hidden metaphors. Sadness pervades many of her poems. Regardless of subject matter, her poetry often reflects her own life and her melancholy.

After retirement, Xue Tao moved to the outskirts of Chengdu. There she spent her remaining years composing poetry and practicing calligraphy. Aside from the information in her poems, little else is known about her life.

BIBLIOGRAPHY

Editions:
Chen Wenhua 陳文化. *Tang nüshiren ji sanzhong* 唐女詩人集三種. Shanghai: Shanghai Guji, 1984. Contains works of Xue Tao, Yu Xuanji 魚玄機 and Li Ye 李冶.
Kuang Yanzi 鄺龑子. *Wu Zetian, Li Ye, Xue Tao, Yu Xuanji shi zhuzi suoyin* 武則天、李冶、薛濤、魚玄機詩逐字索引. Nanjing: Fenghuang, 2011.
Quan Tang shi, 12: 9131–43, 13: 10452, 14: 11249.
Xue Tao, Li Ye shi 薛濤李冶詩. Taibei: Taiwan Shangwu, 1983.
Xue Tao 薛濤. *Xue Tao shi* 薛濤詩. Beijing: Beijing Tushuguan, 2002.
___. *Hongdu ji* 洪度集. Lanzhou: Lanzhou Daxue, 2003.
___ et al. *Jiezhongji, Xue Tao, Li Ye shiji jie zhong ji* 篋中集, 薛濤, 李冶詩集. *SKQS*.

Annotations:
Zhang Pengzhou 張篷舟. *Xue Tao shi jian* 薛濤詩箋. Rpt. Beijing: Renmin Wenxue, 1983.

Biographical Sources:
Fu, *Tang caizi*, 3:102–13.

Translations:
Chang, *Women Writers*, pp. 59–66.
Larsen, Jeanne. *Brocade River Poems, Selected Works of the Tang Dynasty Courtesan Xue Tao*. Princeton: Princeton University Press, 1987.
Mair, *Anthology*, pp. 224–25.
Orchid Boat, pp. 21–23.
Sunflower, pp. 190–91.

Studies:

Feng Guanghong 馮廣宏. "Tangdai Xi Shu nüshiren Xue Tao shiji jichen" 唐代西蜀女詩人薛濤事跡稽沈. *Wenshi zazhi*, 2015.3: 74–77.

Huang Yan 黃豔. "Xue Tao, Yu Xuanji zengshi zhi bijiao yanjiu" 薛濤、魚玄機贈詩之比較研究, *Mingzuo xinshang* 名作欣賞, 2011 (2): 153–55.

Karashima, Takeshi 辛島驍. *Gyo Genki, Setsu Tō* 魚玄機, 薛濤. Tokyo: Shueisha 集英社, 1964.

Liu Tianwen 劉天文. "Xue Tao shiliao kaobian" 薛濤史料考辨. *Chengdu Daxue xuebao (Shehui Kexueban)*. 2004.3: 47–57.

Su Shanyu 蘇珊玉. *Xue Tao ji qi shi yanjiu* 薛濤及其詩研究. Taibei: Hua Mulan Wenhua, 2008.

Wang Huixiu 汪輝秀. "Cong Xue Tao shizuo kan qi chushi taidu de zhuangbian" 從薛濤詩作看其處世態度的轉變. *Chengdu Daxue xuebao (Shehui Kexueban)*. 2011.4: 42–45.

___. "Lun Xue Tao shi zhong de yongdian tedian" 論薛濤詩中的用電特點. *Zhonghua wenhua luntan*, 2014.4: 40–43.

Wang Yangling 王揚靈. *Da Tang nüshi Xue Tao zhuan* 大唐女史薛濤傳. Beijing: Zhongguo Minzhu Fazhi, 2019.

Wimsatt, Genevieve B. *A Well of Fragrant Waters: A Sketch of the Life and Writings of Hung Tu*. Boston: John W. Luce Co, 1945.

Wu Ke 吳柯 and Wu Weijie 吳維杰. *Xue Tao zhi mi* 薛濤之謎. Beijing: Zuojia, 2010.

Xie Wuliang 謝無量. *Zhongguo funü wenxue shi* 中國婦女文學史. Rpt. Zhengzhou: Zhongzhou Guji, 1992, pp. 205–14.

Xiong Faxue 熊發學. "Shilun Xue Tao shi de fenqi huadai" 試論薛濤詩的分期劃代. *Chengdu Daxue xuebao (Shehui Kexueban)*. 2013.2: 47–49.

Zhang Shaocheng 張紹誠. *Xue Tao 'Choubian Lou' shi yu Li Deyu jian Choubian Lou* 薛濤籌邊樓與李德裕建籌邊樓. English and Chinese text. Chengdu: Sichuan Renmin, 1995.

Zhang Yunjing 張雲錦 and Duan Jiquan 段吉泉. *Yidai nü shiren—Xue Tao* 一代女詩人—薛濤. Chengdu: Chengdu Daxue, 2006.

Zhou Zhengju 周正舉, ed. *Xue Tao yanjiu lunwen ji* 薛濤研究論文集. Chengdu: Sichuan Renmin, 1999.

Angela Jung Palandri and William H. Nienhauser, Jr.

Xuzhong 虛中 (fl. 897–942) was a poet-monk active in the late Tang and early Five Dynasties. He was a native of Yichun 宜春 district in Yuanzhou 袁州 (modern Yichun city in Jiangxi). He entered a monastery at a young age and seems to have started writing poetry at that time. For many years he lived on Mount Yusi 玉笥山 in Jizhou 吉州 (modern Ji'an city in Jiangxi). By the end of the Tang, he was wandering in what is modern Hunan.

Around 897 he sent a poem to Sikong Tu 司空圖 (837–908)* which Sikong later praised. The following year he went to Mount Lu 廬山 to study poetry with Chen Hang 陳沆 (*jinshi* 908). In 921 he was living in the Zongcheng Temple 宗成寺 in Changsha 長沙 (modern Hunan). From 935 to 942, he exchanged poems with Ma Xizhen 馬希振 (d. 942), the son of Ma Yin 馬殷 (852–930), King of Chu 楚. Xuzhong also exchanged poems with Zheng Gu 鄭谷 (ca. 849–ca. 911), Guanxiu 貫休 (823–912),* Qiji 齊己 (fl. 881),* Shang Yan 尚顏 (fl. 881), Qichan 棲蟾 (fl. 900), Shen Bin 沈彬 (853–957), Liao Kuangtu 廖匡圖 (fl. 932–947), Liu Zhaoyu 劉昭禹 (fl. 909), Li Honggao 李宏皋 (d. 951), and Xu Zhongya 徐仲雅 (b. 893). The *Shiguo chunqiu* 十國春秋 includes his biography.

Song-dynasty catalogues record his poetic collection in one *juan*, titled *Biyun shi* 碧雲詩 (Poetry of Cyan Clouds) or *Xuzhong shi* 虛中詩 (Poetry of Xuzhong); the *Tang caizi zhuan* 唐才子

傅 gives the titles as *Biyun ji* 碧雲集 (Collection of Cyan Clouds). The separate collection(s) are lost, but the *Quan Tang shi* preserves fourteen of his poems and six couplets, and the *Quan Tangshi bubian* adds one poem and three couplets. Song catalogues also mention his work of poetics titled *Liulei shoujian* 流類手鑒 (Handbook of Similes and Metaphors; also titled *Shi wuxiang liulei shoujian* 詩物象流類手鑒, Handbook of Similes and Metaphors of Poetic Objects and Images) in 1 *juan*, which was also lost, although a few entries are preserved in the *Yinchuang zalu* 吟窗雜錄 and the *Shixue zhinan* 詩學指南. These extant entries reveal that Xuzhong highly appreciated the poetry of Jia Dao 賈島 (779–843)* and Qiji, and he emphasized basing similes and metaphors on natural objects, as he said, "those who are good in composing poems have the creator of nature in their minds and a myriad images in their words" 善詩之人, 心含造化, 言令萬象.

Xuzhong's extant poems are all regulated verses, including works on travel, on landscapes, and for various occasions. His "Bo Dongting" 泊洞庭 (Mooring in the Dongting Lake) is an example of a poem using the natural scene to reflect the poet's emotions:

> Pagoda trees and willows unaware of autumn's coming,
> Still supple and tender above the inn.
> Travelers' hearts all long to be far away,
> But the seasonal rains hold them back.
> Waves flood fish markets,
> Sails are taller than wine shops.
> I toss and turn through the night:
> My homeland is in the southern lands.
>
> 槐柳未知秋, 依依館驛頭.
> 客心俱念遠, 時雨自相留.
> 浪沒貨魚市, 帆高賣酒樓.
> 夜來思輾轉, 故里在南州.

This pentasyllabic, regulated poem depicts a night Xuzhong spent at an inn by Lake Dongting. The first couplet describes the scene surrounding the inn as autumn is imminent. Unlike the pagoda and willow, *yiyi* 依依 "supple and tender," the poet plays on the other meaning of *yiyi* as "the feeling of regret at parting." The far-away goals of the travelers in line three may vary, but they must all be connected with return to some family members or loved ones. Like the trees of the first line, the rains here are personified. It is they who detain the poet. The clever images of the third couplet emphasize how cut off the poet is. The fish markets, near the lake, are flooded, and the boats on the lake now have risen on the surging waters to that they top even the two-story wine shops. The final lines not only reflect the poet's concern to move on towards home, but also his fears that perhaps even his hometown is flooded.

BIBLIOGRAPHY

Editions:
Hu Zhenheng 胡震亨 (1569–1645), ed. *Tangyin tongqian* 唐音統簽. *SKQS* ed.
Li Gong 李龏, ed. *Tangseng hongxiu ji* 唐僧弘秀集. *SKQS*.

Quan Tang shi, 12: 9670–72, 15: 11676.

Wang Zhongyong 王仲鏞, ed. *Tangshi jishi jiaojian* 唐詩紀事校箋. Chengdu: Ba Shu Shushe, 1989, 2:1952–54.

Biographical Sources:

Fu, *Tang caizi*, 3:530–34.

Studies:

Duan Shuangxi 段雙喜. *Tangmo Wudai jiangnan xi dao shige yanjiu* 唐末五代江南西道詩歌研究. Shanghai: Shanghai Guji, 2010.

Jia Jinhua 賈晉華. *Tang Wudai jihui zongji yu shirenqun yanjiu* 唐代集會總集與詩人群研究. Beijing: Beijing Daxue, 2001.

___ and Fu Xuancong 傅璇宗. *Tang Wudai wenxue biannianshi: Wudai juan* 唐五代文學編年史: 五代卷. Shenyang: Liaohai, 1998.

Luo Genze 羅根澤. *Zhongguo wenxue pipingshi* 中國文學批評史. Shanghai: Shanghai Shudian, 2003.

Peng Yaling 彭雅玲. *Tangdai shiseng de chuangzuolun yanjiu: shige yu fojiao d zonghe fenxi* 唐代詩僧的創作論研究：詩歌與佛教的綜合分析. Taibei: Huamulan Wenhua, 2009.

Sun Changwu 孫昌武. *Tangdai wenxue yu Fojiao* 唐代文學與佛教. Xi'an: Shaanxi Renmin, 1985.

Watson, Burton. "Buddhist Poet-Priests of the T'ang," *Eastern Buddhist* 25.2 (1992): 1–22.

Wang Xiulin 王秀林. *Wantang Wudai shiseng qunti yanjiu* 晚唐五代詩僧群體研究. Beijing: Zhonghua, 2008.

Zha Minghao 查明昊. *Zhuanxing zhong de Tang Wudai shiseng qunti* 轉型中的唐五代詩僧群體. Shanghai: Huadong Shifan Daxue, 2008.

Zhang Bowei 張伯偉. *Quan Tang Wudai shige jiaokao* 全唐五代詩格校考. Xi'an: Shaanxi Renmin Jiaoyu, 1996.

Jinhua Jia and Gonghuang Liu

Yan Shigu 顏師古 (*ming*, Zhou 籀, 581–645) was born in Wannian (萬年, modern Xi'an), although his family patria was Langye (琅邪, near modern Linyi 臨沂 in Shandong). Yan's grandfather, Yan Zhitui 顏之推 (531–597), was the author of the well-known *Yanshi jiaxun* 顏氏家訓 (Family Instructions of Mr. Yan) and an official under the Northern Qi (550–577). After the fall of Northern Qi, Zhitui became an official of the Northern Zhou, and moved his family to Guanzhong (the capital area). His son Yan Silu 顏思魯, Yan's father, was also an official, and served in the residence of Li Shimin 李世民 the future emperor Taizong. Yan's brother, Yan Qinli 顏勤禮, was a noted calligrapher.

Yan was well-read during his youth and studied philology (many modern Chinese studies refer to him as a "linguist"). Recommended by Li Gang 李綱 (547–631), he was given a post at Anyang County 安陽 (modern Xiangyang 襄陽, Hubei) during the reign of Emperor Wen of the Sui (r. 581–604). One of his father's friends, Xue Daoheng 薛道衡 (540–609), was impressed by Yan's talent and served as an early patron. In 617, Yan Shigu accompanied his father to pay a visit to Li Yuan 李淵 (566–635) who had just joined the rebellion against the Sui. After this meeting, Li appointed Yan as Grand Master for Closing Court. About a year late Yan was made Instructor of Household Li Shimin (then Heir). Later, he was promoted become Drafter in the Secretariat in charge of imperial edicts. When Li Shimin took the throne Yan was named Vice Director of the Secretariat and granted a fief in Langye 瑯琊. Between 622 and 633, he was demoted twice for

Yan Shigu

unknown reasons but exempted from severe punishment because of his literary talent and scholarship. Yan became Vice Director of the Palace Library in 633, ordered to revise the *Five Classics*. He also wrote commentaries on several histories including the *Shiji* 史記 and the *Han shu* 漢書 and compiled the annals and memoirs for the *Sui shu* 隋書.

When Emperor Taizong's composed the following poem, "Zhengri linchao" 正日臨朝 (On the First Day of the Year Overlooking the Court), Yan was commanded to respond:

>The east wind opens the offerings to the ancestors' festival;
>The ash-filled pipes stir in the first month.
>The hundred tribes present tribute from afar,
>The myriad states attend court in the Weiyang Palace.
>Although I have no deeds to match Shun and Yu,
>I have the fortune to enjoy peace on heaven and earth.
>The chariot roads unite to the eight extremities,
>So texts and scripts flow to the four corners.
>Awe-inspiring the majestic caps and baldachins,
>Robes and patterns lend a sumptuousness.
>Feathers and banners fly down the imperial highway,
>Bells and drums shake the palace corridors.
>Cavalry and foot soldiers gleam in bright clouds of dawn,
>Frosted halberds shine in the morning light.
>Morning to night I think of how best to govern,
>Finally shamed that I have yet to foster the far-away borderlands.

>條風開獻節，灰律動初陽。
>百蠻奉遐贐，萬國朝未央。
>雖無舜禹跡，幸欣天地康。
>車軌同八表，書文混四方。
>赫奕儼冠蓋，紛綸盛服章。
>羽旄飛馳道，鐘鼓震巖廊。
>組練輝霞色，霜戟耀朝光。
>晨宵懷至理，終愧撫遐荒。

The title actually refers to holding court audience, but the literal rendition seems apt since it was written by the emperor who was actually "overlooking the court," but given the text of the poem the title might have another meaning of "overlooking the dawn" on the first day of the year. Taizong here congratulates himself on uniting the empire and overwhelming neighboring peoples (the "myriad states" in line 4) allowing the written culture of the Tang to extend to the ends of the earth (echoing the "Basic Annals of the First Emperor of Qin" in the *Shiji* 史記 [Grand Scribe's Records]). Lines 10–14 depict the scene of the officials, civil and military, who gather for the ceremony.

Yan Shigu's response is his only extant poem:

>Presented to Match "On the First Day of the Year Overlooking the Court"
>The Dipper's handle begins to point horizontal,
>The Three Beginnings of the year renew the imperial throne.

Before the royal screen the invited hundred officials,
The hanging tassels of the imperial nine ranks.
In fine order like pheasants or herons,
In great crowds of hairpins and belts,
From the ends of the earth your words are translated over and over,
As regions where the sun rises offer rare treasures.

奉和正日臨朝
七府璿衡始，三元寶曆新。
負扆延百辟，垂旒禦九賓。

肅肅皆鵷鷺，濟濟盛簪紳。
天涯致重譯，日域獻奇珍。

After pointing to the astronomical signs of the New Year in the first couplet (the Three Beginnings are year, month and day), Yan also pictures the vast assembly of officials, perhaps best in the third couplet. In the final lines he echoes Taizong's claim to control all under Heaven by emphasizing the reach of the imperial word and the wealth of foreign tribute that was collected. However, Wei Zheng 魏徵 (580–643) and Li Baiyao 李百藥 (564–648) were also in attendance and their poems both contain sixteen lines, suggesting that what we have in twelve lines is only a fragment of Yan's reply.

According to his biography in the *Xin Tang shu* he died on the road during an expedition to Goguryeo in 645. Yan Yuansun 顏元孫 and the calligrapher-scholar Yan Zhenqing 顏真卿 (709–785; Yuansun's nephew), were among Yan Shigu's descendants.

BIBLIOGRAPHY

Biographical Sources:
Jiu Tang shu, 73.2594–96; *Xin Tang shu*, 198.5641–43.

Editions:
Quan Tang shi, 30.434; *Quan Tang wen*, 347–50.3970–4001.
Yan Shigu 顏師古. *Dengcisi bei* 等慈寺碑. Changsha: Hunan Meishu, 1991
___. *Sui yilu* 隋遺錄. Beijing: Zhonghua, 1991.
___. *Kuang miu zhengsu* 匡謬正俗: Beijing: Zhonghua, 1985.

Annotations:
Luo Xianglin 羅香林. *Tang Yan Shigu Xiansheng zhou nianpu* 唐顏師古先生籀年普. Taibei: Shangwu Yinshuguan, 1982.
Shentu Luming 申屠爐明. *Kong Yingda, Yan Shigu pingzhuan* 孔穎達 顏師古評傳. Nanjing: Nanjing Daxue, 2011.
Yan Shigu 顏師古. *Kuangmiu zhengsu pingyi* 匡謬正俗平議. Liu Xiaodong 劉曉東, ann. Jinan: Qilu, 2016.

Studies:

Poon Ming Kai [Pan Mingji] 潘銘基. *Yan Shigu jingshi zhushi luncong* 顏師古經史注釋論叢. Hong Kong: D. C. Lau Research Centre for Chinese Ancient Texts, 2016.

Sun Xianbin 孫顯斌. *Hanshu Yan Shigu zhu yanjiu* 漢書顏師古注研究. Nanjing: Jiangsu Fenghuang, 2018.

Wang Guang 王廣. *Yan Shigu xueshu sixiang yanjiu* 顏師古學術思想研究. Jinan: Shandong Renmin, 2013.

Wang Zhiqun 王智群. "Ershinian lai Yan Shigu *Han shu zhu* yanjiu shulue" 二十年來顏師古漢書註研究述略. *Guji zhengli yanjiu xuekan* 古籍整理研究學刊, 2003.7: 58–61.

Zhang Jinxia 張金霞. *Yan Shigu yuyanxue yanjiu* 顏師古語言學研究. Jinan: Qilu Shushe, 2006.

William H. Nienhauser, Jr.

Yang Jiong 楊炯 (650–694) was a poet, scholar, and sometime official of the late seventh century. He came to court a prodigy, passing in 659 the *Shentong* 神童 (Examination for Divine Lads) in which youthful candidates of nine years or under were tested in their knowledge of the *Lunyu* 論語, the *Xiaojing* 孝經, and one other classic text of their own choosing. Following his success in this examination, Yang was given a place in the Institute for the Advancement of Literature at the capital. In 676 following his success in a special recruitment examination, he was made Editor in the Palace Library. In 682 at the recommendation of Xue Yuanchao 薛元超 (622–683), he became Rectifier in the Household Administration of the Heir Apparent, Li Xian 李憲 (679–742), and a Scholar in the Institute for the Veneration of Literature. His life seems to have been a privileged and pleasant one until the year 685, when he was rusticated to Zizhou 梓州 (near modern Santai 三台 District in Sichuan) as a Judicial Administrator in punishment for his relationship to a paternal uncle who had been involved in an abortive rebellion the year before. By 690 he had been recalled to the capital and given a teaching post in the Palace School. But late in 693 he was again sent to the provinces, this time to Yingchuan 盈川 (near modern Qu 衢 District in western Zhejiang) as Magistrate. He died there, sometime during the next year or two; the precise date of his death is uncertain.

Yang Jiong is today the least widely read of the quartet of writers known collectively as the *Chu Tang sijie* 初唐四傑 (Four Distinguished Ones of the Early Tang), the other three being Wang Bo 王勃 (650–676),* Lu Zhaolin 盧照鄰 (ca. 634–ca. 689),* and Luo Binwang 駱賓王 (ca. 640–684).* He is best remembered for his preface to the works of Wang Bo. This relative disregard is due in part to the fact that only thirty-four of Yang's *shi* 詩 poems have been preserved. All but four of these are pentametric *lüshi* 律詩 or *pailü* 排律, and most are exercises on standard themes, occasionally with striking effects. Yang is noted for his frontier-style poems, such as "Congju xing" 從車行 (A Song of a Convoy Chariots):

> Beacon-fires illuminate the Western Capital;
> my mind naturally becomes restless.
> An ivory tally is dispatched from the imperial palace;
> crack cavalry surround the enemy stronghold.
> Snow's heavy haze withers banners' hues;
> wind's heavy clamor mixes with sounds of drums.
> I would rather become a head of hundred soldiers;
> better than serving as a single pedant.

烽火照西京，心中自不平。牙璋辭鳳闕，鐵騎繞龍城。
雪暗凋旗畫，風多雜鼓聲。寧為百夫長，勝作一書生。

However, Yang's true skill as a writer is best exhibited in his eight remaining *fu* 賦. These compositions—undeservedly neglected today—are rich confections of scholarly lore and effusive wordplay; here one sees the lavish talent that won Yang the respect of his contemporaries and prompted Zhang Yue 張說 (667–731),* the literary arbiter of the succeeding generation, to compare his works to "the gushing waters of a precipitate stream—pouring down, never drying up" 楊盈川文思如懸河注水，酌之不竭. Among Yang's *fu*, especially notable are the "Huntian fu" 渾天賦 (The Enveloping Sky) and the "Laoren xing fu" 老人星賦 (The Old Man Star; i.e., the exceptionally bright and auspicious star known to us as Canopus), both of which contain much fascinating information about Tang astral beliefs. Equally interesting is the *fu* on the grand Buddhist Ulambana festival ("Yulanpen fu" 盂蘭盆賦) held under Empress Wu's (r. 690–705) direction in Luoyang in 692. A large quantity of Yang's prose writings, mostly memorial inscriptions, has also been preserved.

BIBLIOGRAPHY

Editions:

Chen Dongbiao 諶東飈. *Chu Tang sijie ji* 初唐四傑集. Changsha: Yuelu, 2001.
Luan Guiming 欒貴明 et al., eds. *Quan Tang shi suoyin: Yang Jiong juan* 全唐詩索引:楊炯卷. Beijing: Zhonghua, 1992.
Quan Tang shi, 14: 10985.
Xu Mingxia 徐明霞, ed. *Yang Jiong ji* 楊炯集. Beijing: Zhonghua, 1980. Appends materials pertinent to the study of Yang's life.
Yang Yingchuan ji 楊盈川集. 10 *juan*. *SBCK*. This is a Ming edition, from the Wanli period (1573–1620), compiled by Tong Pei 童珮. A typeset and punctuated revision of this text, collated with the versions appearing in *Quan Tang shi* 全唐詩 and *Quan Tang wen* 全唐文, and early anthologies such as *Tangwen cui* 唐文粹 and *Wenyuan yinghua* 文苑英華, is included in *Lu Zhaolin ji* 盧照鄰集, *Yang Jiong ji* 楊炯集.
Yingchuan ji 盈川集. Taibei: Shangwu, 1983. *SKQS* ed.

Annotations:

Zhu Shangshu 祝尚書. *Yang Jiong ji jianzhu* 楊炯集箋注. Beijing: Zhonghua, 2016.

Biographical Sources:

Fu, *Tang caizi*, 1:34–4, 5:5–6.
Jiu Tang shu, 190A.5000–04.
Xin Tang shu, 201.5741.

Translations:

Hart, Henry H. *A Garden of Peonies*. Stanford: Stanford University, 1947, p. 73
Owen, *Early T'ang*, pp. 80, 295, 298–99.
Schafer, Edward H. *Pacing the Void, T'ang Approaches to the Stars*. Berkely: University of California, 1977, pp. 38, 86–87, and 163.

Studies:

Chen Yuquan chen 陳于全. *Yang Jiong yanjiu* 楊炅研究. Wuhan: Huazhong Keji Daxue, 2011.

Deng Wenkuan 鄧文寬. "Xin faxian de Dunhuang xieben Yang Jiong 'Huntian fu' can*juan*" 新發現的敦煌寫本楊炯渾天賦殘卷, *Wenwu* 5 (1993): 61–65.

Fu, *Shiren*, pp. 1–20.

Furukawa, Sueyoshi 吉川末喜. "Shō Tō shiketsu no bungaku shisō" 初唐四傑の文學思想 *Chūgoku bungaku ronshū* 8 (1979): 1–27.

Jiang Jinshen 蔣金珅. "Yang Jiong zaonian renguan kaozheng" 楊炯早年任官二則, *Wenxue yichan* 2019.3: 182–84.

Luo Xiangfa 駱祥發. *Chu Tang sijie yanjiu* 初唐四傑研究. Beijing: Dongfang, 1993.

Ma Qingzhou 馬慶洲, Li Feiyue 李飛躍 and Guo Jinxue 郭金雪. *Chu Tang sijie* 初唐四傑. Beijing: Zhonghua, 2010.

Nie Wenyu 聶文郁. *Yang Jiong shijie* 楊炯詩解. Xining: Qinghai Renmin, 2000.

Ren Guoxu 任國緒. *Chu Tang sijie shixuan* 初唐四傑詩選. Xian: Shaanxi Renmin, 1992.

Shen Huiyue 沈惠樂 and Qian Huikang 錢惠康. *Chu Tang sijie he Chen Ziang* 初唐四傑賀陳子昂. Shanghai: Shanghai Guji, 1987.

Takagi Shigetoshi 高木重俊. *Shotō bungaku ron* 初唐文學論. Tokyo: Kenbun, 2005.

Tao Min 陶敏. "Yang Jiong zunian qiushi" 楊炯卒年求是, *Wenxue yichan* 1995.6: 114–15.

Wu Jie. "A Political Eulogy that Dazzles: Yang Jiong's (650–ca. 694) '*Fu* on the Old Man Star,'" *AM* 31 (2018): 47–89.

Yang Chengzu 楊承祖. "Yang Jiong nianpu" 楊炯年譜, *JOS* 13 (1975): 57–72.

Zhan, *Daojiao*, pp. 225–28.

Zhang Zhilie 張志烈. *Chu Tang sijie nianpu* 初唐四傑年譜. Chengdu: Ba Shu Shushe, 1993.

Paul W. Kroll and Masha Kobzeva

Yang Juyuan 楊巨源 (*zi*, Jingshan 景山, 755–after 833) was a native of Hezhong 河中 (just west of modern Yongji 永濟 in Shanxi). Not much is known about his life. He placed second in the *jinshi* examination of 789 under chief examiner Liu Taizhen 劉太真 (d. 725–789), the same year as his lifelong correspondent Pei Du 裴度 (765–839). He likely served several Military Commissioners starting in the early 800s, until in 814 he became Investigating Censor under Zhang Hongjing 張弘靖 (760–824), the Military Commissioner of Yang's native Hezhong. Probably because of his experiences during those times, Yang's poems often incorporate themes of life in military encampments and at the borders. When Zhang was recalled to court in 814, Yang followed him and was made Assistant in the Palace Library. Around 816 he was transferred to the post of Erudite of the Court of Imperial Sacrifices and in 818 to that of Vice Director of the Bureau of Forestry and Crafts. Shortly afterwards he left the capital and became Vice Governor of Fengxiang 鳳翔 prefecture (modern Fengxiang County in Shaanxi). Sometime before 823, possibly in 821, he was once again recalled to court to become Director of Studies at the Directorate of Education. After having reached the age of 70 in 824 he asked to be dismissed to return to his hometown. Because the acting Grand Councilor was fond of him, he was made Vice Governor of his native Hezhong and was allowed to keep his official salary. He died sometime after 830.

Throughout his life he maintained a wide and active circle of friends and correspondents, including Han Yu 韓愈 (768–824),* Bo Juyi 白居易 (772–846),* Liu Yuxi 劉禹錫 (772–842),* Yuan

Zhen 元稹 (779–831),* Zhang Ji 張籍 (776–829),* Wang Jian 王建 (ca. 766–ca. 830),* Jia Dao 賈島 (779–843),* and Linghu Chu 令狐楚 (766–837).* Many of his extant poems consequently are pieces written in response to other poets or on the occasion of parting with friends. A good example can be seen in his "Che yangliu" 折楊柳 (Breaking the Willow):

On the water's edge the willows like threads of pale-yellow wine;
I stop my horse and trouble you, Sir, to break off a twig.
The spring breeze alone shows the strongest affection.
Ardently it blows ever harder into my hands.

水邊楊柳麴塵絲。立馬煩君折一枝。
惟有春風最相惜。殷勤更向手中吹。

The willow is a symbol both of spring and of separation. It is an old custom to break of a small branch of a willow to give to a parting traveler. The setting in early spring is emphasized by the leaves of the willow being still of a fresh, pale yellow color. The Chinese words used here literally describe the color of yeast in the process of fermenting wine. Wine of course is also associated with parting. After setting up this farewell scene, the third and fourth lines suddenly relate the traveler to the twig that he now is holding in his hands. Like the twig which is now dead but is still moved, and thus revived, by the loving spring wind, so, too, the parting person in his sorrow relies solely on the affections of his friend.

Yang Juyuan's extant works belong principally to the genre of modern-style poetry of five- or seven-characters per line. He was held in high regard by his contemporaries. Zhang Ji and Liu Yuxi spoke highly of his art, and later Wang Fuzhi 王夫之 (1619–1692) praised his seven-character poems as being the most superbly crafted of the middle Tang period. Besides his poetry there is a Tang tale attributed to him by one tradition, although his authorship is doubtful (compare Nienhauser under translations, below).

BIBLIOGRAPHY

Editions:
Han Yu 韓愈. "Song Yan shaoyin xu" 送楊少尹序, in: *Quan Tang wen*, juan 556, v. 12, p. 7139.
Quan Tang shi, 5: 3717–47.
Tangshi jishi 唐詩紀事, juan 35.

Biographical Sources:
Fu, *Caizi zhuan*, 2:400–12, 5:234–39.

Translations:
"Hongxian" 紅線, Cao Weiguo, tr. In: Nienhauser, *Tang Dynasty Tales*, 1–47. [Attribution unclear, see appended "Translator's Note."]
Payne, *White Pony*, p. 239.

Pine, Red. *Poems of the Masters: China's Classic Anthology of T'ang and Sung Dynasty Verse*, Red Pine, tr. Port Townsend, Wash.: Copper Canyon Press, 2003, 186–7.

Schafer, Edward H. "Notes on T'ang Geisha," *Schafer's Sinological Papers*, 4 (3 March 1984), p. 12.

Studies:

Hu Kexian 胡可先 and Wei Na 魏娜. "Tangdai shiren shiji xin zheng" 唐代詩人事蹟新證. *Zhejiang Daxue xue bao (Renwen Shehui Kexueban)*, 2010.5: 27–35.

Li Jun 李俊. "Yang Juyuan shiji xiao kao" 楊巨源詩集小考. *Wenxue yichan*, 2006.3: 143–46.

Li Lili 李麗黎. "Lun Yang Juyuan de biansai shi" 論楊巨源的邊塞詩. *Xinan Nongye Daxue xuebao (Shehui Kexueban)*, 2013.1: 136–37.

___. "Yang Juyuan shige de yishu tese" 楊巨源詩歌的藝術特色. *Yunnan Shehui Zhuyi Xueyuan xuebao*, 2012.4: 295–96.

Liu Lihua 劉麗華. "Lun Yang Juyuan de chouzeng songbie shi" 論楊巨源的酬贈送別詩. *Shanxi dang'an*, 2014.5: 30–34.

Meng Zixun 孟子勛. "Yang Juyuan shige yanjiu" 楊巨源詩歌研究. *Ezhou Daxue xuebao*, 2014.5: 35–37.

Sun Qian 孫茜. "Lüelun Yang Juyuan shi zhong de chanxing" 略論楊巨源詩中的禪性. *Huabei Dianli Daxue xuebao (Shehui Kexueban)*, 2004.3: 70–72.

Sun Qin'an 孫琴安. "Tangdai qilüshi de jige zhuyao paibie" 唐代七律詩的幾個主要派別. *Xueshu jikan*, 1988.2: 185–92.

Ueki Hisayuki 植木久行. "Tōdai sakka shin ginen roku (6)" 唐代作家新疑年録(6). *Bunkei ronsō*, 28.3 (1993): 95–140.

___. "Tōdai sakka shin ginen roku (10)" 唐代作家新疑年録(10). *Bunkei ronsō*, 32.3 (1997): 127–74.

Xie Weiping 謝衛平. "Lun Yang Juyuan de shige" 論楊巨源的詩歌. *Wenxue yichan*, 2005.4: 137–40.

___. "Lun Yang Juyuan shige shenmei tezheng" 論楊巨源詩歌審美特徵. *Qiye daobao*, 2014.14: 184, 186.

___. "Yang Juyuan shige secai yu yijing de jiaorong" 楊巨源詩歌色彩與意境的交融. *Nantong Daxue xuebao (Shehui Kexueban)*, 2014.9: 61–65.

Yan Wenjing 閆文靜. "Tangdai shiren Yang Juyuan shige yong yun yanjiu" 唐代詩人楊巨源詩歌用韻研究. *Yuwen xuekan*, 2014.2: 26–27, 69.

Yang Sheng 楊勝. "Lun Yang Juyuan shige zhong de rujia sixiang" 論楊巨源詩歌中的儒家思想. *Liuzhou Shizhuan xuebao*, 2010.1: 50–51, 108.

Zhao Qian 趙謙. "Zhong Tang houqi qilü lun" 中唐後期七律論. *Huazhong Shifan Daxue xuebao*: 1990.2, 85–91.

Zuo Hong 佐宏. "Lun Yang Juyuan shige de sixiang neirong" 論楊巨源詩歌的思想內容. *Xiandai yuwen (Wenxue Yanjiuban)*, 2007.6: 23–24.

___. "Yang Juyuan shengping zhushi kao" 楊巨源生平諸事考. *Xihua Shifan Daxue xuebao (Zhexue Shehui Kexue ban)*, 2008.1: 35–39.

___. "Yang Juyuan shige xuanben kao" 楊巨源詩歌選本考. *Wenjiao ziliao*, 2007.18: 66–67.

___. "Yang Juyuan wu chong shi kaobian" 楊巨源誤重詩考辨. *Qiusuo*, 2005.8: 138–39, 146.

___. "'Zhe yangliu' zuozhe kao" 《折楊柳》作者考. *Yibin Xueyuan xuebao*, 2005.4: 53–54.

Jakob Pöllath

Yang Ning 楊凝 (*zi*, Maogon 懋功, fl. 780–802) was a noted statesman-poet active through the Dali (766–779) and Zhenyuan (785–805) periods. Losing his father at an early age, Yang lived with his mother and brothers in Hongnong 弘農 county in Guozhou 虢州 (between modern Lingbao

靈寶 county and Sanmenxia 三門峽 in Henan). Later, they fled to Suzhou, seeking refuge from An Lushan Rebellion (755–763). Yang Ning was a scion of the Yang family of Yongning 永寧, a brunch of the Yang clan that rose in Hongnong during the Han dynasty. From the mid-Tang onward, this clan produced more than fifty *jinshi* graduates, some of whom were important members of Niu Sengru 牛僧孺 (779–848) faction.

Yang Ning and his two brothers each started their political career through these imperial examinations. His elder brother, Yang Ping 楊憑 (fl. 774), achieved the highest rank on the list of *jinshi* graduates in 774 and Yang Ning matched this accomplishment in 777. Their younger brother, Yang Ling 楊凌 (fl. 790), also entered officialdom through the examinations in 778. Their success in the examinations combined with their literary talents won them great acclaim and the label "The Three Yang" 三楊.

Yang Ning served first as an Editor in the Place Library, and in 784 was appointed as Prefectural Secretary for the Military Commissioner of Eastern Shannan Circuit 山南東道. Some years later, Dong Jin 董晉 (723–799), the Military Commissioner of Xuanwu 宣武 (commandery seat at modern Kaifeng 開封, Henan), appointed Yang Ning as his Administrative Assistant; then, when a vacancy for Regional Chief in Bozhou 亳州 (modern Anhui) occurred, Dong moved Yang there. While in Bozhou, Yang reclaimed wasteland, dredged riverbeds, and built dams to tame a persistent problem with floodwaters. But when Meng Shudu 孟叔度 (d. 799), then Administrative Assistant in Bozhou, challenged Dong's authority, Yang reputedly withdrew and turned to drink. After Dong Jin's death, his troops killed Meng Shudu. Yang Ning returned to the capital city and lived in seclusion for three years. He was appointed as the Director of Bureau of Military Appointments in 802 and the following year died from a disease.

Yang Ning had a close relationship with Liu Zhen 柳鎮 (fl. 769–793), and married his daughter to Liu Zhen's son, Liu Zongyuan 柳宗元 (773–819).* In the epitaph written for Yang Ning, Liu Zongyuan praised Yang for both his moral virtue and literary merit. After his death from a chronic disease, Yang Ning's works were compiled by Yang Ping and with a preface by Quan Deyu 權德輿 (759–818).* Yet this twenty-volume anthology was lost. The twenty-nine poems that survived in the *Yulan shi* 御覽詩 (Poems for the Emperor's Perusal) compiled by Linghu Chu 令狐楚 (ca. 766–837) are all we have of Yang Ning's writings today.

This farewell song dedicated to a friend, "Song ke ru Shu" 送客入蜀 (Sending off a Traveler to Sichuan), is perhaps his best-known poem:

> Jiange Pass is far away, haunting dreams and mind,
> The traveler's road home winds through Mount Liang.
> Tomorrow morning on horse, whip in hand, you will go,
> In autumn rain, sophora flowers fill Ziwu pass.

劍閣迢迢夢想間, 行人歸路繞梁山.
明朝騎馬搖鞭去, 秋雨槐花子午關.

In many farewell verses, the persona stands grieving until the traveler vanishes from his sight. Depiction of this scene, usually follows the persona's gaze, beginning at the place of parting and then moving with the traveler into distant hills or wide waterways. Yang's poem, however, depicts an imagined journey in a reverse order. The starting point is the most remote place, Jiange, a military pass and stronghold in Shu (as depicted in Li Bai's "Shudao nan" 蜀道難 [The Way to Shu is Arduous]). Then, Yang leads readers to withdraw through the winding roads in Mount Liang which lies midway on the journey, to finally stop at Ziwu Pass, gateway to the south of Chang'an. The traveler, in the third line, is silhouetted against the vast landscape between the destination and his first stop. The poet imagines how his friend will ride into the rainy mountains alone. The sophora (*huai* 槐) in the last line may imply that the traveler has failed in imperial examination. In the Tang dynasty, the name list of *jinshi* graduates was published in early summer, but scholars who failed still had chance to study all summer and enter officialdom through the supplementary examination in early autumn, the time when the sophora flowers bloom, as in the old saying popular in the Tang times: "As sophora flowers turn yellow the examination candidates are busy" 槐花黃舉子忙." The sophora also symbolizes high social rank as in the expression "Three Scholar Trees" (*Sanhuai* 三槐) which referred to the "Three Eminent Officials" (Sangong 三公) in early Chinese texts. Seen in this light, the last line of this poem not only expresses Yang's sympathy for the traveler's failure, but also conveys a fervent hope that he may succeed in near future.

Yang Ping 楊憑 (*zi*, Xushou 虛受 or Siren 嗣仁, fl. 774-819) had a more successful official career than his brothers. He was appointed Surveillance Commissioner of Hunan in 802 and transferred to the same position in Jiangxi in 805. Two years later, he was recalled back to the court. Holding the title Cavalier Attendant-in-ordinary, he was in charge of Bureau of Punishments.

In 809, Yang Ping assumed the office of Governor of the Capital. However, he was soon impeached by Li Yijian 李夷簡 (757-823) for taking bribes and constructing a villa on a scale incompatible with his social rank. Judicial investigation attested to his crime, but he was exempted from confiscation and death due to the intersession of his friends. Considering Yang's political achievements when he was in charge of the capital area, Emperor Xianzong (r. 806–820) mitigated his punishment and demoted him to District Defender of Lihe 臨賀 (modern He 賀 County in Guangxi). Later, he was promoted to the Senior Scribe of Hangzhou and finally died at the post of Supervisor of the Heir Apparent. Nineteen of his poems remain.

Yang Ling 楊凌 (*zi*, Gonglü 恭履, fl.778-790), the youngest of the three Yang siblings, lived a much shorter life than his brothers. He died no later than the sixth year of the reign of Yuanhe, 790. His early death circumscribed his political achievement but did not affect his literary fame at the time. Yang Ling was considered a prodigy who showed skill in writing at very young age. Like his elder brother nineteen of his poems are extant.

BIBLIOGRAPHY

Editions:
Quan Tang shi, Yang Ping 5:3289–3292; Yang Ning, 5:3293–3299; Yang Ling, 5:3300–3303.
Quan Tang wen 478.4884–86.

Biographical Sources:
Fu, *Tang caizi*, 2:91–106, 5:185–88.
Jiu Tang shu, 146.3967–3968 (Yang Ping).

Xin Tang shu, 160.4970–72 (Yang Ping, Yang Ning; Yang Ling's son, Yang Jingzhi).
Tangshi jishi, juan 28, 436 (Yang Ling).

Studies:
Hu Kexian 胡可先. "Yangshi jiazu yu Zhong-wan Tang wenxue shengtai" 楊氏家族與中晚唐文學生態, *Beijing Daxue xuebao zhexue shehuikexue ban* no.5, vol.47, 9(2010): 41-49.
Xu Yougen 許友根. "Tangdai Yangshi keju jiazu de chubukaocha" 唐代楊氏科舉家族的初步考察, *Shangqiu Shifan Xueyuan xuebao* 7(2017): 69–73.
Yan Yinchun 嚴寅春. "Yang Ning chaozheng kao" 楊凝朝正考, *Shanxi Shida xuebao* 1(2005): 79–80.

Ji Wang and William H. Nienhauser, Jr.

Yao He 姚合 (ca. 779–ca. 849) was a native of the Shan Prefecture 陝州 (in modern Henan); his lineage can be traced to Wuxing 吳興 (in modern Zhejiang). He was a great-grandnephew of Yao Chong 姚崇 (650–721), a Grand Councilor during the Kaiyuan (713–741) reign. Yao He passed the *jinshi* examination in 816 and successively served as Retainer in Weibo 魏博, Assistant Magistrate in Wugong 武功, and District Defender in Fuping 富平. Therefore, he was also known as Yao Wugong 姚武功 (Yao of Wugong), and his poetic style was known as the "Wugong Style" (*Wugong ti* 武功體). In 826, he was appointed Investigating Censor and put in charge of the Eastern Capital, Luoyang. During this period he also served as Prefect of Jin Prefecture 金州 (modern Ankang 安康 in Shaanxi). In 828 he was called back to the court and made Palace Censor, later he received a series of promotions to Attendant Censor, Vice Director of the Bureau of Punishments, and then Vice Director and then Director of the Census Bureau. In 834, he again was dispatched from court to be the Prefect of Hangzhou 杭州. In the spring of 836, he returned to court to serve as Grand Master of Remonstrance, and in 839 he was dispatched from the post of Supervising Secretary to be the Surveillance Commissioner of Shanguo 陝虢 (in modern Henan). During the years of the Huichang reign (841–846), he came back to court to serve as Vice Director of the Palace Library. Toward the end of the Huichang reign, he died while serving as Director of the Palace Library and was awarded the posthumous title Yi 懿. Thus he was also known as Yao Bijian 姚秘監 (Yao the Director of the Palace Library) or Yao Shaojian 姚少監 (Yao the Vice Director). He has biographies in both the *Jiu Tang shu* and the *Xin Tang shu*.

Yao He was famous for his regulated verse in the five-syllable line. His "Wugong xian zhong zuo, sanshi shou" 武功縣中作三十首 (Composed in Wugong County, Thirty Poems) are representative of his poetic style; the third poem of the series reads:

> Insignificant officials are like the hooves of horses,
> They merely exist amidst dust and dirt.
> Wherever I go, poverty follows me,
> Throughout the year, old age pursues a man.
> Accounting books deplete the strength of my eyes,
> Wine in cups consumes the spirit of my heart.
> Early will I plan on retiring and resting,
> In deep seclusion shall I dwell and nourish this life.

Yao He

微官如馬足，只是在泥塵。
到處貧隨我，終年老趁人。
簿書銷眼力，杯酒耗心神。
早作歸休計，深居養此身.

As can be seen from the biographical sketch above, this poem was written just as Yao began what was a long official career. The discussion of old age and retirement are more formulaic than reflective of Yao's actual circumstances—it is the person Yao imagines he will be decades later. The metaphor the first two lines is typical of the striking comparisons of mid-Tang poets like Han Yu 韓愈 (768–824). The personification of "poverty" (*pin* 貧) and "old age" (*lao* 老) and the active verbs in the second couplet—*sui* 隨 "to follow" and *chen* 趁 "to pursue"—are also conceits typical of the poets who advocated "painstaking chanting" (*kuyin* 苦吟). The third couplet also turns the previously positive image of wine and books into things which assail the poet in the dull routine of his everyday life—account books and wine as something which affects his health. This careful selection of words is also typical of the *kuyin* style, concluding with the image of "nourishing" (*yang* 養) himself. This attention to small details is also typical of mid-Tang poetics.

Jia Dao 賈島 (779–843),* another poet who took the *kuyin* approach to poetic composition, is often matched with Yao both in poetic style and fame; they were known together as "Yao and Jia" 姚賈 during their time. Compared to Jia Dao, Yao He's poetry is simpler and easier to access. The late Tang and Five Dynasties monk and poet Qiji 齊己 (fl. 881)* comments that "the cold, subdued [verses] are heard from Yao the Director; the refined and unusual [verses] are seen in Langxian's [Jia Dao's poetry]" 冷淡聞姚監，精奇見浪仙.

Yao He exchanged poetry with famous poets of his time, such as Bo Juyi 白居易 (772–846),* Liu Yuxi 劉禹錫 (772–842),* Li Shen 李紳 (772–846),* Linghu Chu 令狐楚 (766–837),* and Zhang Ji 張籍 (ca. 776–829).* His poetry influenced many late Tang poets such as Li Pin 李頻 (814–ca. 876),* Zheng Chao 鄭巢 (fl. 867), as well as the "Yongjia siling" 永嘉四靈 (Four Lings of the Yongjia Reign) poets of the Song dynasty, and the "Jingling" 竟陵 style poets of the Ming dynasty. Zhao Shixiu 趙師秀 (1170–1220), one of the "Four Lings" of Song, published a combined collection of Yao He's and Jia Dao's poetry entitled *Er miao ji* 二妙集 (Anthology of Two Exquisite Ones).

Yao He admired Wang Wei's 王維 (692–761 or 699–759)* poetry. He selected one hundred poems from twenty-one Tang dynasty poets, from Wang Wei to Dai Shulun 戴叔倫 (732–789) and compiled the *Ji xuan ji* 極玄集 (Anthology of Extreme Subtlety). Yao He's own poetry fills seven chapters in the *Quan Tang shi* 全唐詩 (Complete Poetry of the Tang). The "Yiwen zhi" 藝文志 (Treatise on Literature) of the *Xin Tang shu* records Yao He's works as the *Yao He shiji* 姚合詩集 (Poetry Collection of Yao He) in ten chapters, the *Ji xuan ji* in one chapter, the *Shi li* 詩例 (Poetry Examples) in one chapter, and the *Yao Shaojian shiji* 姚少監詩集 (Poetry Collection of Yao the Vice Director) in ten chapters.

BIBLIOGRAPHY

Editions:

Er miao ji 二妙集. Zhao Shixiu 趙師秀 (1170–1220) ed. Manuscript edition by Xiushitang 繡石堂, 1536. Rpt. Kyoto: Kyoto Hoyu, 1970. Combined anthology of poetry by Jia Dao and Yao He.

Ji xuan ji 極玄集, 2 vols. Taibei: Shangwu, 1980. Rpt. 1983, 1986.

Ji xuan ji xuan 極玄集選, 1 vol. Wang Shizhen 王士禎 (1634–1711), ed. Published by Nanzhitang 南芝堂, 1692.

Quan Tang shi: 8: 5664–757.

Shizhong Tang shi xuan 十種唐詩選. Wang Shizhen 王士禎 (1634–1711), ed. Published by Puban Shulou 蒲坂書樓, 1687.

Tang liu mingjia ji 唐六名家集. Chang Jian 常建 ed. Shanghai: Hanfenlou 涵芬樓, 1866. Rpt. 1926.

Yao He shiji jiaokao 姚合詩集校考. Liu Yan 刘衍, ed. Changsha: Yuelu Shushe, 1997.

Yao He shiji jiaozhu 姚合詩集校注. Wu Heqing 吳河清, ed. 2v. Shanghai: Shanghai Guji, 2012.

Biographical Sources:

Fu, *Tang caizi*, 3:114–28, 5:297–301.

Xin Tang shu, 124.4388.

Translations:

Owen, *Middle Ages*, pp. 119–21.

Studies:

Cao Fanglin 曹方林. *Yao He kaolun* 姚合考論. Chengdu: Ba Shu Shushe, 2001.

Matsubara Akira 松原郎. *Bantōshi no yōran: Chō Seki, Yō Hō, Ka Tō ron* 晚唐詩の搖籃: 張籍, 姚合, 賈島論. Tokyo: Senshū Daigaku, 2012.

Shen Wenfan 沈文凡 and Zhou Feifei 周非非. "Tang dai shiren Yao He yanjiu zongshu" 唐代詩人姚合研究綜述. *Dongbei shida xuebao: Zhexue shehui kexue ban*, 2007.3: 124–32.

Xu Yumei 徐玉美. *Yao He ji qi shi yanjiu* 姚合及其詩研究. Taibei: Huamulan Wenhua Gongzuofang, 2009.

Zhang Zhenying 張震英. "Lun Wugong ti" 論武功體. *Lanzhou Daxue xuebao: Shehui kexue ban*. 31.3 (May 2003): 31–37.

Ying Qin

Yu Shinan 虞世南 (*zi*, Boshi 伯施, also known as Yu Qi 虞七, Yu Jian 虞監, Yu Mijian 虞祕監, Yongxing Gong 永興公, Yu Yongxing 虞永興, and Yu Gong 虞公 558–638) was an influential statesman, calligrapher, and poet of the early Tang. Yu's nascent career was shaped by the vagaries of the Southern Chen (557–589) and Sui (581–619) dynasties. After serving as a princely administrator under Emperor Xuan of the Chen (陳宣帝, 530–582), Yu was appointed Assistant in the Palace Library by Emperor Yang of the Sui (隋煬帝, 541–604), and with full access to the imperial collections, compiled the first *leishu*, the *Beitang shuchao* 北堂書鈔, a groundbreaking compilation of quotations from pre-Tang texts on a number of topics, many of which were political in nature. By the time Yu was brought into Li Shimin's 李世民 (posthumously known as Taizong 太宗 598–649, second emperor of the Tang) retinue during the Sui-Tang transition, he was already a scholar of some renown, and was promoted swiftly from Administrator of the Princely Establishment of Qin to Scholar of the Institute for the Advancement of Literature and eventually to Director of the Palace Library. Yu was a close personal advisor to the Emperor Taizong during the first decade of his reign. In addition to submitting a number of memorials making recommendations about the emperor's moral conduct during that time, he also wrote a short treatise, *Diwang luelun* 帝王略論 (Discourse on Ruling), which explicated various proscriptive and prescriptive examples of imperial behavior throughout Chinese history.

Yu Shinan was especially well known for his masterful calligraphy. He has been called one of the foremost calligraphers of the early Tang, and is often paired with his contemporary, fellow scholar of the Institute, Ouyang Xun 歐陽詢 (557–645). Having studied under the Buddhist monk Zhiyong 智永 (fl. ca. 557–617, seventh generation descendent of the famous calligrapher Wang Xizhi 王羲之 (303–361), Yu was a crucial link in the transmission of Wang's lineage of calligraphic style into the Tang dynasty.

Yu Shinan was also a skilled poet and a key transmitter of Southern Dynasties court poetry to the Tang as the leading southern poet in Taizong's literary clique. Yet he occupied an uneasy position as a Confucian moralist diametrically opposed to the "decadent" qualities with which the Southern Dynasties courtly style had come to be associated. An oft–quoted anecdote from the *Tang shi jishi* 唐詩紀事 records how Yu, when asked to compose a matching poem to the Emperor's in the palace style, refused. Yu linked the overindulgence of palace-style poetry with the moral failings of the Southern Dynasties, failings which had led to a loss of mandate and regime change.

Yu Shinan's evocative "Poems on Things" (*Yong wu shi* 詠物詩), especially "Chan" 蟬 (Cicada) and "Yong ying" 詠螢 (Firefly Ode), frontier *yuefu* poems, and matching poems have been the subject of critical discussion. In contrast, Yu Shinan's landscape poetry is often overlooked. For example, in Yu's "Ling chen zao chao" 凌晨早朝 (Early Court in the Predawn) offers a dynamic poetic description of the Tang capital cityscape:

> Night's light breaks to dawn on a myriad households,
> Evening mists collect around hanging eves"
> Jade flowers cease their nightly flickering,
> Golden vases send off the dawn tallies.
> Sunlight glows on azure-latticed halls,
> Rosy mist rises to weave patterned towers.
> Layered gates open to corresponding roads,
> Official placards beckon to lords and princes.

> 萬戶宵光曙, 重簷夕霧收.
> 玉花停夜燭, 金壺送曉籌.
> 日輝青瑣殿, 霞生結綺樓.
> 重門啓應路, 通籍引王侯.

This piece begins with a wide perspective, envisioning the dwellings which house the innumerable imperial subjects of the capital and perhaps even the entire realm, all illuminated by the same glow of dawn. The perspective draws in closer, to household timepieces (candles [jade flowers] and water clocks [golden vases]), then moves toward the center, to the azure latticed administrative buildings within the palace complex, and finally to the roads which lead even farther inward, toward the imperial court. This dynamic description of the political landscape has resounding echoes in later Tang poems, especially those of Du Fu 杜甫 (712–770).*

Yu Shinan's literary production was certainly influential during the Tang, but he was seldom remembered as a poet in later dynasties. Instead, it was his influence as an exemplar of an accomplished calligrapher and loyal official that remained far–reaching, especially in Japan. He is even mentioned in the famed medieval Japanese *Tale of Heike* 平家物語 as an upright minister. In addition, his calligraphic style in the lineage of Wang Xizhi, remains well studied and emulated today, especially in Mainland China.

BIBLIOGRAPHY

Editions:
Chen Hu 陳虎 ed. *Diwang luelun* 帝王略論. Beijing: Zhonghua, 2008. A new critically annotated edition of the text, which was partially pieced together from fragments found at Dunhuang and quotations found in other sources.
Chen Yumo 陳禹謨 ann. *Beitang shuchao* 北堂書鈔, *SKCS*. rpt. Taibei: Taiwan Shangwu, 1983–86.
Huang Yongwu 黃永武 ed. "Diwang luelun" 帝王略論. *Dunhuang baozang* 敦煌寶藏 伯 2736. Taibei: Xin Wenfeng, 1986. A reprint of the Dunhuang version of the text, which is fragmentary.
Hu Hongjun 胡洪軍 and Hu Xiaji 胡遐 eds. *Yu Shinan shiwen ji* 虞世南詩文集. Hangzhou: Zhejiang, 2012. The most readily available and complete version of Yu Shinan's collected works.
Ke Xiaogang 柯小剛 ed. *Yu Shinan bi sui lun zhu* 虞世南筆髓論注. Shanghai: Huadong Shifan Daxue, 2015.
Kong Guangtao 孔廣陶 ann. *Beitang shuchao* 北堂書鈔. 1888. 2v. rpt. Shanghai: Shanghai Guji, 2002.
___. ann. *Beitang shuchao* 北堂書鈔. 1888. 2v. rpt. Taibei: Wenhai, 1972.
Kongzi miaotang bei, you ming, Fuzi miaotang bei 孔子廟堂碑, 又名, 夫子廟堂碑. Changchun: Jilin Wenshi, 1999. A reproduction of this influential inscription by Yu Shinan in *kaishu* script.
Quan Tang shi, 1: 473–79.
Quan Tang wen, 138.1558–78.
Yamada Hideo 山田英雄 ed. *Hokudō shoshō insho sakuin* 北堂書鈔引書索引. Nagoya: Saika shorin, 1973.
Zhang Shouyong 張壽鏞 ed. *Yu mijian ji* 虞秘監集. rpt. Taibei: Xin Wenfeng, 1989. A reprint of a woodblock edition included in the *Siming congshu* 四明叢書, printed between 1932 and 1948.

Biographical Sources:
Jiu Tang shu, 72.2565–71.
Xin Tang shu, 102.3969–73.

Translations:
Allen, Joseph. *In the Voice of Others: Chinese Music Bureau Poetry*. Ann Arbor: Center of Chinese Studies Publications, 1992. Translates a series of "Yin ma" 飲馬 *yuefu*, including a rendition composed by Yu Shinan.
Owen, *Early T'ang*, p. . A translation of "Chan" 蟬 (Cicada).
Wu Fusheng. *Written at Imperial Command: Panegyric Poetry in Early Medieval China*. Albany: State University of New York Press, 2008. This critical text includes several translations of Yu Shinan's matching poems to those of Emperor Yang of the Sui.
Wu Fusheng. *The Poetics of Decadence: Chinese Poetry of the Southern Dynasties and Late Tang Periods*. Albany: State University of New York Press, 1998.

Studies:

Ge Zhaosheng 葛兆生. "Yu Shinan shufa de yuanyuan yu yingxiang" 虞世南書法的淵源與影響摭談, *Zhongguo shufa* 中國書法 17 (2016): 131–33.

Ruan Aidong 阮愛東. "Tang yin zhi shi: Yu Shinan shige xinlun" 唐音之始：虞世南詩歌新論, *Xinjiang daxue xuebao* 39.2 (2011.3): 114–18.

Wechsler, Howard. "The Confucian Impact on Early T'ang Decision–Making," *T'oung Pao, Second Series*, 66 1/3 (1980): 1–40.

Yu Xin 俞欣. "Fumi shi feng de chedi qingsao—lun Yu Shinan shige de kaichuangxing" 浮靡詩風的徹底清掃—論虞世南詩歌的開創性. *World Literature Studies* 世界文學研究 1 (2013): 35–42.

Wu Fusheng. *Written at Imperial Command: Panegyric Poetry in Early Medieval China.* Albany: State University of New York Press, 2008.

——. *The Poetics of Decadence: Chinese Poetry of the Southern Dynasties and Late Tang Periods.* Albany: State University of New York Press, 1998.

___, "The Concept of Decadence in the Chinese Poetic Tradition." *Monumenta Serica* 45 (1997): 39–62.

Christine Welch

Yu Xuanji 魚玄機 (*zi*, Youwei 幼微 and Huilan 蕙蘭, ca. 844–868), born in Chang'an, is one of the best-known women poets of the Tang period (see also Xue Tao 薛濤 [768–832]*). Chinese women have written good poetry during every period of literary history from the *Shijing* 詩經 down to modern times. Anthologies of poems from any given period usually contain, at the back of the collection, a small number of works by women, ghosts, clergymen, and others whose efforts might provide amusement, if not enlightenment, following the more serious writings that form the bulk of the collection proper.

Most women poets are remembered primarily as someone's wife or concubine, or as a courtesan or a nun, although there are notable exceptions such as Li Qingzhao 李清照 (1084–1155). Yu Xuanji is known to have been a talented courtesan, the concubine of a government official, and a Daoist nun who entertained gentlemen in her quarters at the Convent of Gathered Blessings in Chang'an, the Tang capital. As a courtesan, she has no official biography and anecdotal sources are all that are available.

According to these sources, early in life Yu became a public courtesan (the lowest rank) and entertained Wen Tingyun 溫庭筠 (ca. 812–870)* with whom she had a relationship for a time (two of her poems are addressed to Wen). It was he who supposedly introduced her to Li Yi 李億, about whom little is known; Li who took Yu as his concubine back to his home in what is now Shansi in 858, the same year that he was the top graduate in the *jinshi* examination. Li's wife is said to have become jealous, Li's ardor lessened, and Yu was left with little opportunity other than to return to Chang'an and enter a convent as a Daoist novice. She is said to have gone to the Xianyi Guan 咸宜觀 (Convent of Gathered Blessings), a noted nunnery that was known for its murals by many of the famous artists of the day. The remainder of her life is open to speculation, but, according to the account in the *Beimeng suoyin* 北夢瑣言, she was sentenced to death by Wen Zhang 溫璋 (d. 870), the Governor of the Capital, for having killed a serving maid.

Her fifty extant poems give ample evidence of her activities in each of the three roles and ways of life. The earliest biographical account states that she was executed in the year 868 (at the age of twenty-four) for the murder of her maid, whom she suspected of carrying on with one of her gentleman callers. The account of this murder, which appears in the *Sanshui xiaodu* 三水小牘 (A Little Tablet from Three Rivers) of Huangfu Mei 皇甫枚 (fl. 880), is told in such dramatic detail that its historical accuracy becomes suspect. The many activities of her short life are richly reflected in her extant poems. The topics touched upon include the joys of banqueting, love poems to her absent husband, poem-letters to friends, elegies, travel poems, poems on historical sites, introspective poems, poems to fellow Daoists and fellow courtesans, allegorical poems reflecting the courtesan's trade, and several boudoir laments.

Since many of Yu's allegorical poems have erotic overtones, it is perhaps best to first read her rather explicit account of a polo match, "Da qiu zuo" 打球作 (A Polo Match Composition):

> Firm, round, clean, slick,
>   a single shooting star,
> A crescent club struggling
>   to strike without pause.
> When there is no opponent
>   to move to and fro,
> Where there is a barrier,
>   keep it as a lure.
> Do not shy from rolling around,
>   always keeping it handy.
> But fear that you are not on the point of
>   reaching the end of the game.
> Only when finally entering the gate
>   should then be finished,
> Hoping that your efforts will take
>   the very best score.

堅圓淨滑一星流，月杖爭敲未擬休。
無滯礙時從撥弄，有遮欄處任鉤留。
不辭宛轉長隨手，卻恐相將不到頭。
畢竟入門應始了，願君爭取最前籌。

If this poem does not make clear to the reader Yu's skills at suggesting a metatext, this same reader will struggle to fully understand her other poems. One such is her "Fu de 'Jiangbian liu'" 賦得江邊柳 (Composed on the Theme 'Riverside Willow') which according to was commissioned by Wen Tingyu:

> An azure hue all along the desolate riverbank,
>   their misty shapes stretching to a distant tower.
> Their shadows overspread the autumn-clear water,
>   their catkins fall on the angler's head.
> Old roots form hollows for hiding fish,
>   limbs reach down to tie up the traveler's boat.
> Soughing, sighing in a night of wind and rain,
>   startled from my dreams my gloom compounded.

Yu Xuanji

翠色連荒岸，煙姿入遠樓。
影鋪秋水面，花落釣人頭。
根老藏魚窟，枝低系客舟。
蕭蕭風雨夜，驚夢復添愁。

A misty, barren landscape is a trope seen in other Tang poems, such as Chen Ziang's "Wan ci Leixiang Xian" 晚次樂鄉縣 (Stopping in the Evening at Lexiang County) which reads "At the garrison post in the wilderness a desolate mist breaks off, / Deep in the mountains the ancient trees all the same height" 野戍荒煙斷, 深山古木平. Chen's poem, written at Lexiang (in the southern suburbs of modern Baoding in Hebei), stresses the poet's isolation. Yu's emphasis is similar, but she has constructed a poem that at first reading seems to be about a lonely fisherman plying an autumn stream. However, the title tells us the poem is rather about willows, *liu* 柳, an image closely associated with courtesans like Yu herself in phrases such a "flowery willow" (*hualiu* 花柳). The first four lines set up a possible secondary reading. The autumn willow still green may suggest Yu herself, now older but still vital. Although she is her looks remain verdant, she is clearly alone. *Mian* 面 in line three is translated as "surface," but it could also suggest Yu's clear visage. As the studies of the modern scholar Wen Yiduo 聞一多 (1899–1946) have pointed out, the angler (*diaoren* 釣人) in line four could be a patron (perhaps Wen Tingyun himself is meant) searching for the courtesan—here the "fish" (*yu* 魚) or Yu herself (*yu* occurs six times in Yu's extant works; *diao* four times). In line five Yu like the fish has hidden herself away in the convent, yet she, as willow, still reaches out (with this poem) her branches to tie up the traveler's boat, this figure again standing for the courtesan-visitor relationship. Line seven may depict the persona's dream of a meeting in which fish and angler make love as *fengyu ye* 風雨夜 might suggest, only to be startled awake by the literal "wind and rain" to the realization that this has all been a dream.

Another poem that plays on the word "fish" is "Ji Liu Shangshu" 寄劉尚書 (To Minister Liu):

The Eight Offices have sent fierce troops to garrison,
songs of the people fill the road anew;
Rains of the third month on the River Fen,
the hundred flowers made spring on the River Jin.
Jails are forever locked up and empty,
shield and sword have long been covered with dust.
Scholar and bonze watch Midnight perform,
travelers drunk on the scarlet mats.
Brush and ink close at hand as you travel,
poems and histories surround you in your seat.
Even lesser talents are well cared for
and able to be men who dine on fish.

八座鎮雄軍，歌謠滿路新。
汾川三月雨，晉水百花春。
囹圄長空鎖，干戈久覆塵。
儒僧觀子夜，羈客醉紅茵。
筆硯行隨手，詩書坐繞身。
小材多顧盼，得作食魚人。

This poem is a *pailü* 排律 or extended regulated verse. As Jan Walls has shown, Minister Liu was probably Liu Zhuan 劉瑑 (796–858) who was acting head (Shangshu 尚書) of the Ministry of Rites and Military Commissioner of Taiyuan 太原 (modern Shani) in 857. The Eight Offices, literally "Eight Seats" (*Bazuo* 八座), refers to the heads of the six ministries and the director and vice director of the Department of State Affairs. Thus Yu suggested the armies which had been often under the control of provincial leaders were now controlled by the proper civilian authorities including Liu himself. The people's songs would have been ditties (*minge* 民歌) praising this situation. Both the Fen and the Jin in the second couplet are rivers in what is now modern Shansi, suggesting that this poem may have been written in 858 when Li Yi took Yu Xuanji to his home in that province. The third couplet concludes the setting and again emphasize the then current good government of which Liu was a part. In the second half of the poem Yu alludes to Ziye or Midnight, the famous fourth-century courtesan about whom nothing is known except that she wrote subtly suggestive poems. Here Ziye stands for Yu Xuanji, the fourth couplet speaking directly to Yu's popularity. In line nine the focus shifts to Minister Liu, depicting his life as a sojourner, possibly in Taiyuan. "Eating fish" is an allusion to the story of Feng Xuan 馮諼 who served the Lord of Mengchang 孟嘗 and brazenly demanded fish for his meal before eventually proving that he was the most talented retainer. So these last two lines may refer to Yu's hope that she could become a "retainer" of Minister Liu. Or they may suggest the flattering idea that Liu was not valued highly enough by the emperor. Or it may even suggest that Yu sees herself as the "minor talent" who could serve as a dish of fish for Liu—once again a possible play on her surname and the trope in which eating fish is a euphemism for sexual relations.

The following poem titled "Ch'ou si, di yi" 愁思 (Anxious Thoughts) also features an evening rain in autumn, but finds Yu in a much less sanguine mood:

> Leaves flutter confusedly down
>   mingling with the evening rain;
> Strumming over scarlet strings alone
>   I sing myself a pure song.
> Setting free my feelings,
>   I cease to resent my heartless mate.
> I nourish true nature,
>   toss off the waves of the bitter sea.
> Carriages of the well-to-do
>   can be heard outside my gate;
> Volumes of Daoist scrolls
>   lie by my pillow;
> Once a cotton-clad layperson,
>   now a traveler of the highest clouds,
> Those times of green waters and verdant hills
>   have passed by in a flash.

落葉紛紛暮雨和，朱絲獨撫自清歌。
放情休恨無心友，養性空拋苦海波。
長者車音門外有，道家書卷枕前多。
布衣終作雲霄客，綠水青山時一過。

Yu Xuanji

Here the first line provides both setting and tone—autumnal. Whereas nature is in harmony, with the leaves and evening rain mingling, the poet can only sing her song to herself. The red strings are those she has played for male companions many times before. The "bitter sea" (*ku hai* 苦海) is a Buddhist term for this life of suffering which is as boundless as the sea. Here it perhaps refers to Yu's entering the convent. The heartless mate may be Li Yi, but it could just as well be another of her lovers. Line five alludes to the Han-dynasty minister and general Chen Ping 陳平, who began living in poverty but was known for his good looks—both like Yu. Chen was only able to marry the girl he chose after his future mother-in-law noticed the tracks of carriages of people of position and means outside his hut. Yu must have attracted a similar clientele. These last four lines, which on the surface describe Chen Ping, must therefore also refer to Yu's background and her current hopes that on entering the convent her status would be elevated like the clouds in the sky, while perhaps lamenting that the freedom to roam she previously enjoyed was now gone.

Another feature of Yu Xuanji's collected poems which distinguishes her from other Chinese women poets is the relative variety of verse types and line lengths employed. Her collection includes verses of four, eight, twelve and twenty-four lines, written not only in the standard five- and seven-character lines, but in the rare six-character line as well. This is noteworthy, since most female poets excelled in a single verse form and only on certain themes. Here one of her six-word poems entitled "Yu yan" 寓言 (An Allegory):

> Red peaches, everywhere the scene is spring,
> green willows, every house in moonlight.
> Upstairs, freshly made-up, waiting for night,
> seated alone in the boudoir, brimming with passion.
> Fish sport beneath moonlit lotus leaves,
> sparrows twit under a distant rainbow.
> This world is a dream of grief and joy:
> how can one be able to achieve a Perfect Pairing?

> 紅桃處處春色，碧柳家家月明。
> 樓上新妝待夜，閨中獨坐含情。
> 芙蓉月下魚戲，蟠蜘天邊雀聲。
> 人世悲歡一夢，如何得作雙成。

The poem moves in the first two couplets from a description of spring and its associations with romance to a woman in her chamber filled with love for someone. The third couplet depicts the lovemaking among nature—fish (again Yu!) and sparrows before concluding with the persona's Realization that finding the ideal mate is the most difficult task. The title asks the reader to look beyond the surface meaning. Accordingly the peach and willow in the first couplet must refer to a beautiful woman and the world of the courtesan as can be seen in the opening couplet of another of Yu's poems, "Dai ren dao wang" 代人悼亡 (An Elegy for Someone's Wife): "The sight of a tender peach recalls her lovely face, / Willow leaves in the breeze retrace her moth-brows" 曾睹夭桃想玉姿，帶風楊柳認蛾眉. The first four lines then tell us of a lovely courtesan seductive as spring who is awaiting in her upstairs chamber filled with desire. Line five resonates with a *yuefu* poem and suggests a couple dallying in amorous play, here made even clearer when we recall Yu's surname. Similarly the rainbow has been associated since the *Shijing* 詩經 (Classic of Poetry) with improper pairings and extra-marital relationships. The extended meaning of this third couplet is that the courtesan persona seeks the kind of amorous dalliance she sees around her. A variant reading of line six suggested by several modern scholars—*he sheng* 鶴聲 "cranes cry" instead of *que sheng* "sparrows twit"—would tie the line to the following couplet and suggest that Yu was wavering between her life as a Daoist priestess and that of her former status. But this seems to go against the sentiments of the majority of her poems. Whichever reading is correct, the last line contains a play on words: Shuang Cheng 雙成 is both the name of a handmaid to the mythical goddess Hsi-wang-mu 西王母 who refines a pill of immortality and ascends to heaven on the back of a crane as well as (literally) "a perfect" or "complete pair." Thus our courtesan longs for that perfect mate with whom she can have a more permanent liaison. In both this poem, that addressed to Minister Li, and "Anxious Thoughts," however, we can sense the feeling that Yu may have regretted that she was not born a male.

BIBLIOGRAPHY

Editions:

Chen Wenhua 陳文華, comm. and ed. *Tang nü shiren ji sanzhong* 唐女詩人集三種. Shanghai: Shanghai Guji, 1984. Collects poems by Yu Xuanji, Xue Tao 薛濤 and Li Ye 李冶.

Kuang Yanzi 鄺龑子 (Charles Yim-tze Kwong). *Wu Zetian, Li Ye, Xue Tao, Yu Xuanji shi zhuzi suoyin* 武則天、李冶、薛濤、魚玄機詩逐字索引. Nanjing: Fenghuang, 2011.

Quan Tang shi, 12: 9145–54.

Tang nülang Yu Xuanjii shi 唐女郎魚玄機詩. Nanjing: Fenghuan, 2011.

Annotation:

Peng Zhixian 彭志憲 and Zhang Yi 張毅, eds. *Yu Xuanji shi bian nian yizhu* 魚玄機詩編年譯注. Urumqi: Xinjiang University, 1994.

Biographical Sources:

Fu, *Tang caizi*, 3:448–53.

Huangfu, Mei 皇甫枚. "Yu Xuanji chibi lüqiao zhilu" 魚玄機笞斃綠翹致戮, in *Sanshui xiaodu* 三水小牘, see *Datang xinyu waiwuzhong* 大唐新语外五种. Beijing: Zhonghua, 2012, pp. 213–14.

Sun Guangxian 孫光憲, "Yu Xuanji" 魚玄機, in *Beimeng suoyan* 北夢瑣言, with annotations by Jia Erqiang 賈二強. Beijing: Zhonghua, 2002, pp. 194–95.

Translations:

Chang, *Women Writers*, pp. 66–75.

Hinton, pp. 321–30.

Sunflower, pp. 286–88.

Takeshi Karashima 辛島驍. *Gyo Genki, Setsu Tō* 魚玄機, 薛濤. Tokyo: Shūeisha, 1979.

Young, David, and Jiann I. Lin *The Clouds Float North: The Complete Poems of Yu Xuanji*. Hanover: Wesleyan University Press: Published by University Press of New England, 1998.

Yu Xuanji

Studies:

Cahill, Suzanne. "Material Culture and the Dao: Textiles, Boats, and Zithers in the Poetry of Yu Xuanji (844–868)," in *Daoist Identity: History, Lineage, and Ritual*. Honolulu: University of Hawaii, 2002, pp. 102–26.

___, "Smell Good and Get a Job," in Sheryl J. Mou, ed. *Presence and Presentation: Women in the Chinese Literary Tradition*. New York: St. Martin's, 1999, pp. 174–76; 180–81.

Huang Yan 黃豔. "Xue Tao, Yu Xuanji zengshi zhi bijiao yanjiu" 薛濤、魚玄機贈詩之比較研究, *Mingzuo xinshang* 名作欣賞, 2011 (2): 153–55.

Jia, Jinhua. "Unsold Peony, The Life and Poetry of the Priestess-Poet Yu Xuanji," in Jinhua Jia. *Gender, Power, and Talent, The Journey of Daoist Priestesses in Tang China*. New York: Columbia University, 2018, pp. 164–87.

Karashima, Takeshi 辛島驍 *Gyo Genki-Setsu Tō* 魚玄機 薛濤. Tokyo: Shueisha, 1964.

Kuhn, Dieter. *Yu Xuanji. Die Biographie der T'ang-Dichterin, Kurtisane und taoistischen Nonne*. Privately printed by Habilitationsvortrag, Heidelberg, 1985.

Li Zhizhong 李致忠. "Yu Xuanji ji qi shiji" 魚玄機及其詩集. *Beijing Tushuguan guankan* 北京圖書館館刊, 1992.2: 68–70.

Liang Chaoran 梁超然. "Yu Xuanji kaolue" 魚玄機考略. *Xibei Daxue xuebao (Zhexue Shehui Kexueban)*, 1997.3: 18–25.

Peng Zhixian 彭志憲. *Yu Xuanji shi biannian yizhu* 魚玄機詩編年譯注. Wulumuqi: Xinjiang Daxue, 2006.

Qu Wenjun 曲文軍. "Yu Xuanji kaozheng santi" 魚玄機考證三題. *Tangdu xuekan* 唐都學刊, 8 (1992.2): 49–51.

Ren Qiang 任強. "Yu Xuanji yanjiu wenxian kaosuo" 魚玄機研究文獻考索. *Chuxiong Shifan Xueyuan xuebao* 楚雄師範學院學報, 2 (March 2017): 99–106.

Sang Baojing 桑寶靖. "Nüguan caiyuan Yu Xuanji: Zhongguo Daojiao wenhua shi de guangcai yiye" 女冠才媛魚玄機: 中國道教文化史的光彩一頁. *Shijie zongjiao yanjiu* 世界宗教研究, 2002.1: 48–57.

Tan Zhengbi 譚正璧. "Yu Xuanji he nü daoshi" 魚玄機和女道士. *Zhongguo nüxing wenxueshi* 中國女性文學史. Tianjin: Baihua Wenyi, 2001, pp. 138–47.

Walls, Jan W. "The Poetry of Yu Xuanji: A Translation, Annotation, Commentary and Critique." Unpublished Ph.D. dissertation, Indiana University, 1972. Contains translations and comments on all her poems.

Wang Xueji 王雪枝 and Liu Dongling 劉冬玲. *Youlan yi lu hong: Yu Xuanji zhuan* 幽蘭泡露紅: 魚玄機傳. Shijiazhuang: Huashan Wenyi, 2001.

Wimsatt, Genevieve B. *Selling Wilted Peonies*. New York: Columbia University Press, 1936.

Yokoyama, Eisan 橫山勇三. "Gyo Genki ni tsuite" 魚玄機 について. *Chūgokukei ronsetsu shiryō*, 10 (July-December 1968), 218–25.

Jan W. Walls, Ji Wang, and William H. Nienhauser, Jr.

Yuan'an 元安 (*hao*, Luopu Yuan'an 洛浦元安, *hao*, Luopu Heshang 樂普和尚, secular surname Dan 淡, 835–899) was a Chan monk from Linyou 麟游 in Fengxiang 鳳翔 County (modern Shaanxi) who was famous for his poetic replies. As a young child, Yuan'an would follow his brother, the Vinaya-master You 祐, into the local Huai'en Monastery 懷恩寺 at Qiyang 岐陽 (near modern Baoji 寶雞, Shaanxi) to be ordained as a monk and study the scriptures. Later, he would study with Cuiwei Wuxue 翠微無學, a Dharma heir of Xiashan Tianran 霞山天然 (739–824), and the famous Linji Yixuan 臨濟義玄 (767–866). He stayed with his final teacher, Jiashan Shanhui 夾山善會 (805–881), until the master's demise, after which Yuan'an would leave to dwell on Luopu

Mountain 樂普山 (also 洛浦山, near modern Li 澧 County, Hunan), and then eventually would move on to Suxi 蘇溪 (near modern Changde 常德, Hunan).

Yuan'an was well known for his single verses that he often used as obfuscating answers to the questions posed to him, in the Chan tradition of employing non-logical responses to provoke deeper understanding (*gong'an* 公案). On one occasion, a monk approached Yuan'an with the following question (*Zutang ji* 祖堂集, *juan* 9):

> "What is the meaning of Bodhidharma coming to the West?"
> The Master said: "Shhh shhh—the tall bamboo braves the wind, enduring frost without feeling cold." When it seemed that the monk would ask again, the Master said: "He only hears the sound of the wind hitting; he does not know how many thousand stalks."

> 如何是西來意。師曰：「颯颯當軒竹，經霜不自寒。」僧擬再問，師曰：「只聞風擊響，不知幾千竿。」

Apart from the short verses found among Yuan'an's biographical records, only two longer songs have survived: The "Fu'ou ge" 浮漚歌 (Song of the Floating Bubbles), elaborating on the illusory nature of the everyday world, and the "Shenjian ge" 神劍歌 (Song of the Sword of the Spirit). Each reveals Yuan'an's use of vivid imagery to reflect his Buddhist ideals. His "Shenjian ge" presents Buddhist allusions in an idiom of martial and often wildly violent combat:

> How odd, the sword of the spirit indeed bears strange marks,
> Since ancient times, those seekers who found it are few.
> In a box, it is called lusterless,
> Only in use, one realizes the radiance it conveys.
> Shattering hesitation, eliminating doubt,
> It strengthens the heart and the liver and calms the spirit.
> Once the Six Thieves are removed through it,
> All the eighty thousand defilements are thus wiped away.
> Beheading the heterodox believers, eliminating the evil bastards,
> It determines all life and death, blossoming and withering once and for all.
> A three-foot divine snake upsets the green pool,
> Where, a fleck of bright glare, the cold moon shines.
> Forgetting the sword, a fool notched the boat for the quest,
> To dash through the turbid waves, flying with a longing heart.
> Renouncing the clear well, he chased the murky stream,
> How could he know that the sword of the spirit does not follow the flow?
> The swords of others bear the stink of blood,
> My sword harbors a divine ring.
> Others have their swords to wound the life of sentient beings,
> I have my sword to save their living souls.
> Once attained, a nobleman leaves all sophistry behind,
> On the spot, a petty man will himself despise his life.
> Other houses do not use the sword of my house,
> Elseways the highs and lows of this world would sooner or later be leveled out.
> One must know, the merits of the sword of the spirit are hard to put to record,

Intimidating the demonic powers, settling life and death.
For those who have not attained it, the simple becomes difficult.
For those who have attained the sword, the difficult is just simple.
Draw it, and all around is contained in the Dharma-world,
Sheath it, then all turns into a single grain of dust.
If you would use this sword to secure the Heaven above and the Earth below,
There would never rise another front of clouds within the four passes of this world.

異哉神劍實標奇，自古求人得者稀。在匣謂言無照耀，用來方覺轉光輝。
破猶豫，除狐疑，壯心膽兮定神姿。六賊既因斯剪拂，八萬塵勞盡乃揮。
斬邪徒，盪妖孽，生死榮枯齊了決。三尺靈蛇覆碧潭，一片晴光瑩寒月。
愚人忘劍剋舟求，奔馳濁浪徒悠悠。拋棄澄源逐渾派，豈知神劍不隨流。
他人劍兮帶血腥。我之劍兮含靈鳴。他人有劍傷物命，我之有劍救生靈。
君子得時離彼此，小人得處自輕生。他家不用我家劍，世上高低早晚平。
須知神劍功難紀，懾魔威兮定生死。未得之者易成難，得劍之人難卻易。
展則周遍法界中，收乃還歸一塵裏。若將此劍鎮乾坤，四塞終無陣雲起。

The imagery of a sword to cut through the illusory nature of the mundane world appears throughout Buddhist literature and is often related in esoteric practice to the *vajra* (*jingang* 金剛). Here, the song starts in a pseudo-narrative form resonant with anomaly tales (*zhiguai* 志怪) that employs a combination of Buddhist motifs of enlightenment and allusions to exorcistic practice. The tone of the song shifts when it describes the sword as 'mine,' where the Chan-trained Yuan'an deploys sword-imagery to reflect his own particular insight into enlightenment and the ways in which it may benefit the world. He uses the familiar trope of juxtaposing the mundane and the ultimately true as found throughout Chinese religious contexts: the common sword 'stinks of blood,' while Yuan'an's resounds with a 'divine ring'; others kill, while Yuan'an saves all living beings. The imagery of the sword also bears the marks of the practical functions of Chinese ritual: purifying the land by chasing demons and setting right the wrongs of the world. In the end the sword is revealed to be an instrument for enlightenment, that once attained transforms the difficult to simple. The song concludes with the serene cessation of clouds arising within the four passes of the world, perhaps alluding to the end of codependent arising as used in Mahayana traditions to explain existence and the suffering that comes with it. Even as only one of two extant songs, "Shenjian ge" stands as a clear example of Yuan'an's skill in blending popular narrative tropes with Buddhist themes to reveal his own particular perspective on enlightenment.

BIBLIOGRAPHY

Editions:
Gu Hongyi 顧宏義, comm. *Jingde chuandeng lu yi zhu* 景德傳燈錄譯注. Shanghai: Shanghai Shudian, 2009. Vol. 3: 16.1184–97.
Jing, Yun er chanshi 靜, 筠二禪師, eds. *Zutang ji* 祖堂集. Beijing: Zhonghua, 2007. Vol. 1: 9.410–21.

Biographical Sources:
Zan Ning, 12.289.

Studies:

Gong Jigang 龔積剛. "Changde Tang Song shiqi chanzong zhi lüe" 常德唐宋時期禪宗志略. *Hunan Wenli Xueyuan xuebao* 34.2 (2009): 75–79, 122.

Zhang Zikai 張子開. "'Fu'ou ge kao'" 浮漚歌考. *Zongjiaoxue yanjiu* 3 (1996): 47–49.

Marc Nürnberger and Michael E. Naparstek

Yuan Chun 元淳 (*zi*, Chunyi 淳一, ca. 720–ca. 779) was a Daoist poet-priestess. She was from a gentry family in Luoyang (modern Henan) and was well-educated from a young age. She entered the Daoist order because of a strong desire to pursue immortality. She was ordained around 742 and soon became the abbess of the Zhide 至德 Convent in the capital city Chang'an. She stayed in this position for thirty-six years, often practicing alchemy. She died around 779 about the age of sixty.

Only six poems are extant, three as a result of the rediscovery of sections of the *Yaochi xinyong ji* 瑤池新詠集 (Collection of New Songs from the Turquoise Pond), an anthology of Tang female poets' works compiled by Cai Xingfeng 蔡省風 (fl. 9th century) along with other Dunhuang manuscripts. Yuan Chun's extant poems present various styles and themes including three written for her sisters and fellow priestesses. These are among the earliest examples of poems exchanged between female writers or at least between female writers and female readers. In a seven-syllabic old-style poem titled "Xianju ji Yang nüguan" 閑居寄楊女冠 (Leisurely Dwelling: Sent to Priestess Yang), Yuan describes her monastic life and feelings: she enjoys practicing meditation and being away from the noisy secular life, but she also feels lonely and longs for friendship. In a five-syllabic regulated verse titled "Ji Luoyang zimei" 寄洛陽姊妹 (Sent to My Sisters in Luoyang), she expresses her strong feelings toward her sisters back in their hometown during the chaos of the An Lushan Rebellion:

> Leaving our old estate for so long,
> I yearn for the city and the river far off.
> Writing letters, I rely on the feet of wild geese;
> gazing at the moon, I think of your beautiful brows.
> My hair seems whiter when I grieve,
> only dreams know the heart tends home.
> Who can endure such disorder?
> I cover my face and sob towards the southern branches.

> 舊業經年別, 關河萬里思.
> 題書憑雁足, 望月想蛾眉.
> 白髮愁偏覺, 鄉心夢獨知.
> 誰堪離亂處, 掩淚向南枝.

"Southern branches" is a traditional image for one's hometown, as in the "Gushi shijiu shou" 古詩十九首 (Nineteen Ancient Poems). The poet's homesick feelings are intensified by the temporal and physical space that separated her from her family and the great chaos caused by the wars. The sad tone and use of exquisite antitheses represent the typical style of the rebellion period.

BIBLIOGRAPHY

Editions:

Chen Yingxing 陳應行 (fl. 1194), ed. *Yinchuang zalu* 吟窗雜錄. Beijing: Zhonghua, 1997.

Peng Dingqiu 彭定求 (1645–1719) et al., eds. *Quan Tangshi* 全唐詩. Beijing: Zhonghua, 1960; 805.9060–61.

Rong Xinjiang 荣新江 and Xu Jun 徐俊. "Xinjian E cang Dunhuang Tangshi xieben sanzhong kaozheng ji jiaolu" 新見俄藏敦煌唐詩寫本三種考證及校錄. *Tang yanjiu* 唐研究 5 (1999): 59–80.

___. "Tang Cai Xingfeng bian *Yaochi xinyong* chongyan" 唐蔡省風編瑤池新詠重研. *Tang yanjiu* 7 (2001): 125–44.

Quan Tang shi, 12: 9158.

Wei Hu 韋縠 (fl. 947), ed. *Caidiao ji* 才調集. In *Tangren xuan Tangshi xinbian*.

Wei Zhuang 韋莊 (ca. 836–910), ed. *Youxuan ji* 又玄集. In *Tangren xuan Tangshi xinbian*.

Xu Jun. *Dunhuang shiji canjuan jikao* 敦煌詩集殘卷輯考. Beijing: Zhonghua, 2001.

Biographical Sources:

Fu, *Tang caizi*, 1:335.

Translations:

Cahill, Suzanne. "Resenting the Silk Robes that Hide Their Poems: Female Voices in the Poetry of Tang Dynasty Taoist Nuns." In Deng Xiaonan 鄧小南, Gao Shiyu 高世瑜, and Rong Xinjiang, eds. *Tang-Song nüxing yu shehui* 唐宋女性與社會. Shanghai: Shanghai Cishu, 2001, 519–66.

Jia, Jinhua 賈晉華. "The Life and Poetry of Yuan Chun." In Jinhua Jia, *Gender, Power, and Talent, the Journey of Daoist Priestesses in Tang China*. New York: Columbia University, 2018, pp. 154–58.

Studies:

Cahill, Suzanne (see Translations above).

Jia Jinhua. "New Poetry from the Turquose Pond: Women Poets in Eight and Ninth-century China," *Tang Studies*, 37 (2019): 59–80.

___. "The *Yaochi ji* and Three Daoist Priestess-Poets in Tang China." *Nan Nü: Men, Women and Gender in China* 13 (2011): 205–43.

Sun Changwu 孫昌武. *Daojiao yu Tangdai wenxue* 道教與唐代文學. Beijing: Renmin Wenxue, 2001.

Jinhua Jia

Yuan Jie 元結 (*zi*, Cishan 次山, 719–772) was among the most innovative writers of the mid-eighth century. His family was from Henan and claimed descent from the Xianpi rulers of the Later Wei 後魏 dynasty (386–534), but they had lived for generations in Taiyuan. He spent his early years on Mount Shangyu 商餘山 in Lu County 魯縣 (modern Lushan 魯山 County in Henan). As a youth he was outspoken and unrestrained, but at seventeen devoted himself to study under his cousin, Yuan Dexiu 元德秀 (696–754). Like others of his generation, he also had emphatic views on the literary practice of his day. His literary career divides into three main stages. Common to all three was a sense of indignation, a directness of style, and an occasional eccentricity. The first period extended from his youth in Henan to the outbreak of the An Lushan Rebellion in 755.

Over this first period his writing was colored by his failure to obtain official status and by his reaction to the corrupt political world in Chang'an, dominated by the autocratic Li Linfu 李林甫 (683–753). He wrote brief autobiographical vignettes, satirical anecdotes, Daoist inspired condemnations of decadent metropolitan life, and a few *yuefu* style verses describing the sufferings of the general populace. In his essay "Gai lun" 丐論 (On Begging), he told how friendship with a beggar in Chang'an led him to conclude that mendicancy was preferable to the corruption of official life; it is one of his best prose sketches.

The second period spans the rebellion itself and his early official career, which was late in starting. After withdrawing with his family to Yiyu Dong 猗玗洞 (on Mount Donghui 東回山 in modern Daye 大冶 in Hubei) during the early years of the rebellion, Su Yuanming 蘇源明 (d. 764) recommended Yuan to Emperor Suzong (r. 756–762) in 759 and he was appointed Adjutant in the Military Service Section of the Imperial Insignia Guard. Because of merit in suppressing Shi Siming 史思明 (703–761), he became Vice Director of the Bureau of Waterways and Irrigation, and in 760 Administrative Assistant to Lü Yin 呂諲 (712–762), Military Commissioner of Jingnan 荊南. In 762 after Lü's death, he was summoned back to the capital to become an Editorial Director in the palace library but resigned this position and retired for a time. During this period, old-style verse, sometimes eremitic in its setting, alternates with official writing. The following cycle of four poems titled "Shi gong, si yong" 石宮四詠 (A Palace of Rocks, Four Songs) is typical:

> At the palace of rocks, spring clouds white—
> white clouds suit green moss best.
> Brush apart the clouds, tread the rocky path:
> what ordinary man could come along?
>
> 石宮春雲白，白雲宜蒼苔。
> 拂雲踐石徑，俗士誰能來。
>
> At the palace of rocks, summer waters cold—
> cold waters suit the tall grove best.
> A distant wind rustles ivy and vine:
> the rustic delights in the cool shade.
>
> 石宮夏水寒，寒水宜高林。
> 遠風吹蘿蔓，野客熙清陰。
>
> At the palace of rocks, autumn air clear—
> clear air suits the mountain vale best;
> Falling leaves chase the frosty wind:
> the hermit loves bamboo and pine.
>
> 石宮秋氣清，清氣宜山谷。
> 落葉逐霜風，幽人愛松竹。

Yuan Jie

> At the palace of rocks, winter sun warm—
> warm sun suits the hot springs best;
> Morning rays silence a watery fog:
> the recluse still sleeps soundly.

> 石宮冬日暖，暖日宜溫泉。
> 晨光靜水霧，逸者猶安眠。

The language here is simple and the repetition typical of folksongs. The poems all turn on a type of anastrophe where the nouns-adjectives that end the first line, become adjectives-nouns in the second.

The third period covers the last years of his official career. He was twice appointed (first in 763 and then in 766) Prefect of Daozhou 道州 (modern Dao County 道縣 in Hunan) and finally in 768 Prefect of Rongzhou 容州 (modern Beiliu City 北流市 in Guangxi). At Daozhou the local Chinese population had suffered badly from incursions by the non-Chinese tribes to the south and were further oppressed by rapacious tax collectors sent by the central government. Two old-style poems of this period describe how he mediated this situation: "Chongling xing" 舂陵行 (Ballad of Chongling) and "Zei tui shi guanli" 賊退示官吏 (Shown to My Staff on the Withdrawal of the Insurgents) have traditionally been considered among his best verse. The latter piece, presumably written in 764 when he first arrived in Daozhou indicates in its preface that it was intended to be shown to the tax collectors. The poem reads:

> In former years I encountered the Great Peace—
> In mountains and forests for twenty years.
> A wellspring at the courtyard gate,
> Deep valleys right before my door.
> Field taxes were due at regular times,
> When the sun set one could still get to sleep.
> Suddenly we're met with changing times
> And I've served several years under battle flags.
> Now as I come to take charge of this commandery,
> The mountain barbarians are again rising up.
> Our city is small, so the raiders did not sack it,
> But its people are poor, their losses to be pitied.
> For this reason when the neighboring districts fell,
> This prefecture along remained whole.
> Commissioners come bearing royal commands,
> Could they be less burdensome than the raiders?
> Now those who exact and collect taxes
> Pressure them as if they are frying them in a fire.
> Who could be able to put an end to men's lives
> Just to be known as a worthy of the age?
> I long to cast aside my symbols of office,
> Pull on pole and punt my boat away.
> Take my family to where there are fish and grain,
> To live till I'm old midst the Rivers and Lakes.

昔歲逢太平，山林二十年。
泉源在庭戶，洞壑當門前。
井稅有常期，日晏猶得眠。
忽然遭世變，數歲親戎旃。
今來典斯郡，山夷又紛然。
城小賊不屠，人貧傷可憐。
是以陷鄰境，此州獨見全。
使臣將王命，豈不如賊焉。
今彼征斂者，迫之如火煎。
誰能絕人命，以作時世賢。
思欲委符節，引竿自刺船。
將家就魚麥，歸老江湖邊。

The poem could be read as a synopsis of Yuan's life prior to this time, alternating from a period of peace and contentment before the great rebellion, the peaceful period under Emperor Xuanzong's reign, followed by turmoil and strife, leading to the poet's renewed hope to withdraw from the political world. Over the same period he depicted the landscape in and around Daozhou in both prose and verse; these works evinced a much more tranquil mood, lauding the pleasures of drinking and making excursions.

Like Xiao Yingshi 蕭穎士 (717–760)* and Li Hua 李華 (715–774),* with whom he was connected through their admiration for his cousin and teacher Yuan Dexiu, Yuan Jie condemned literary practice for failing to fulfill its responsibility to promote moral standards. In a preface to the *Qiezhong ji* 篋中集 (Anthology from a Literary Box), a collection of verse by friends on the periphery of official life, and in an introduction to his own collection, Yuan emphasized that literature must not be merely euphuistic or descriptive, nor should it be obsessed by technical rules of tonality or antithesis and should return to the standard exemplified by the Confucian Canon. If Yuan overemphasized this message, his directness, his occasional humor, and his ability to innovate, rescue his writing from unrelieved moralizing. Well-known contemporaries lauded his work. Yuan Jie was connected throughout his life with the famous calligrapher, lexicographer, and loyalist, Yan Zhenqing 顏貞卿 (709–784). After Yuan's death, Yan himself composed and wrote out the text for a commemorative stele which still exists today. Du Fu 杜甫 (712–770)* knew Yuan and enthusiastically commended his Daozhou verses. Han Yu 韓愈 (768–824)* and other literary figures of the early ninth century also praised him. His links with these men, combined with his record for courage as Prefect of Daozhou, kept his standing high in Tang times.

Some of the works in the three collections Yuan compiled in his own lifetime did not survive the disapproval of Song scholars. But in the Ming his writings were collected and republished. In recent years, his humanitarian attitudes have again found favor, and his collected works have been collated and republished.

BIBLIOGRAPHY

Editions:
Quan Tang shi, 4: 2683–707, 14: 11114.
Quan Tang wen, 380–83.4877–930.

Yuan Jie

Yang Jialuo 楊家駱, ed. *Xinjiao Yuan Cishan ji* 新校元次山集. Taibei: Shijie, 1964.
Yuan Cishan ji 元次山集. Sun Wang 孫望, ed. Beijing: Zhonghua, 1960.
Yuan Jie 元結. *Qiezhong ji* 篋中集. *SKQS* ed.

Biographical Sources:
Fu, *Tang caizi*, 1:513–22, 5:103.
Xin Tang shu, 143.4681–86.

Translations:
Minford and Lau, p. 838.
Nienhauser, "'Twelve Poems Propagating the Music Bureau Ballad': A Series of *Yüeh-fu*, by Yüan Chieh," in *Critical Essays*, pp. 135–46.
Owen, *High Tang*, pp. 228–37.
Sunflower, pp. 149–50.
Waley, *Translations*, p. 115.

Studies:
Di Mangui 翟滿桂. "Yuan Jie Xiangnan shiwen lunlue" 元結湘南詩文論略, *Hunan Shehui Kexue*, 2010.2: 137–41.
Ichikawa Momoko 市川桃子. "Gen Ketsu shakai shi kō" 元結社會詩考, *Chūtetsubun Gakkai hō*, 2 (1976), 88–108.
___. "Gen Ketsu 'Shunryo kō' kō" 元結'舂陵行'考, *Tōhōgaku*, 60 (July 1980): 45–61.
Itō Masafumi 伊藤正文. "To Ho to Gen Ketsu: *Kūchū shū* no shijintachi" 杜甫と元結: 篋中集の詩人たち, *Chūgoku bungakuhō*, 17 (1962): 123–47.
Kawakita Yasuhiko 川北泰彥. "Gen Ketsu ni okeru bungakuteki kiseki" 元結における文學的軌跡, in *Mekada Makoto Hakushi koki kinen Chūgoku bungaku ronshū* 目加田誠博士古稀記念中國文學論集. Tokyo: Ryūkei Shosha 龍溪書舍, 1974, pp. 255–75.
Liu Fasui 劉法綏. "Du Yuan Jie zuopin xiaoshi" 讀元結作品小識. *Wenxue yichan*, 1981.1: 143.
Long Gong 龍龔. "Shiren Yuan Jie" 詩人元結, in *Wenxue yichan zengkan*, 2 (1956): 128–40.
McMullen, David. "Literary Theory," pp. 307–30.
___, "Yüan Chieh and the Early *Ku-wen* Movement." Unpublished Ph.D. dissertation, Cambridge University, 1968.
Nie Wenyu 聶文郁. *Yuan Jie shi jie* 元結詩解. Xian: Shaanxi Renmin, 1984.
Owen, *High Tang*, pp. 225–38.
Peng Xiaodong 彭小東. "Yuan Jie de guwen gexin yu Tangdai Guwen yundong" 元結的革新於唐代古文運動, *Wenhua luntan* (2015.9): 168–73.
___. "Yuan Jie 'yi wen wei shi' lun" 元結以文為詩論, *Shangqiu Shifan Xueyuan xuebao*, (2015.10).
Sun Wang 孫望, *Yuan Cishan nianpu* 元次山年譜. Shanghai: Zhonghua 1957.
___. "*Qiezhong ji* de zuozhe shiji" 篋中集的作者事跡, *Jinling xuebao*, 8.1–2 (1930): 37–66.
Wei Lai 魏來. "Yijiujiusi nian yilai Dalu Yuan Jie yanjiu shuping" 一九九四年以來大陸元結研究述評. *Kaoshi zhoukan*, (2010.11): 27–29.
Yang Chengzu 楊承祖. "Yuan Jie nianpu" 元結年譜, *Danjiang xuebao*, 5 (1963): 25–69.
___. "Yuan Jie nianpu bianzheng" 元結年譜辨正, *Danjiang xuebao*, 7 (1966): 277–92.
___. *Yuan Jie yanjiu* 元結研究. Taibei: Guoli Bianyiguan, 2002.

David L. McMullen and William H. Nienhauser, Jr.

Yuan Zhen 元稹 (*zi,* Weizhi 微之, 779–831) was one of the most celebrated poets and statesmen of the mid-Tang period. He was a complex person with a complicated family background. According to the Tang dynastic histories, Yuan Zhen was a native of Luoyang and a tenth-generation descendant of the royal house of Tuoba Wei 拓跋魏, which ruled northern China during the fifth and sixth centuries. One of its rulers, Emperor Xiaowen 孝文帝 (r. 471–495), adopted the Chinese surname Yuan after he moved the capital from Pingcheng 平城 (modern Datong 大同, in Shanxi) to Luoyang. After the unification of China, the offspring of the Tuoba house chose to remain in Luoyang; they were generally referred to as "Luoyang ren" 洛陽人 (natives of Luoyang). Yuan Zhen, however, was born in Chang'an, where his father held a minor post on the Ministry of Justice. When Yuan Zhen was seven years old his father died and the family was left destitute. He passed the examinations under the *Mingjing* 明經 (Clarification of the Classics) category in 793, but it was not until after he passed the *Bacui* 拔萃 (Preeminent Talent) examination in 803 that he received an appointment, along with Bo Juyi 白居易 (772–846),* his lifelong friend, as Editor in the Palace Library.

Between 803 and 806 Yuan Zhen and Bo Juyi prepared themselves for a special examination to be monitored by the emperor. They anticipated all possible questions concerning current national affairs and attempted their solutions. Having personally experienced poverty in their youth and witnessed the sufferings of common people caused by official corruption and wars, Yuan Zhen and his friend were intent on changing the status quo. Upon passing the examination with the highest score, Yuan Zhen was the first to be appointed, as Reminder of the Left. Taking advantage of the proximity to the emperor, Yuan Zhen offered a ten-point proposal, suggesting political reform, beginning with the court. For this presumption he was banished from the capital. By coincidence, his mother died at about this time, and Yuan Zhen retired to observe the period of mourning. In 809 he was appointed a censor to inspect eastern Sichuan. There he exposed local government corruption, making enemies in high places. Once more he was banished, this time for ten years. His talent was finally recognized and he was made a Secretariat Director in 822, only to be removed from office in less than four months, because of factional struggles. Although he held several high offices in the provinces, he was unable to carve out the political reforms he had envisioned before he died.

Yuan Zhen was more successful in bringing about literary reform. When he was a member of the Hanlin Academy in charge of drafting imperial rescripts, he was responsible for changes in the documentary language, stressing a classical simplicity. Although generally attributed to Bo Juyi, it was in reality Yuan Zhen and Li Shen 李紳 (772–846)* who initiated the New *Yuefu* Movement. As early as 809, Yuan Zhen wrote twelve *yuefu* with new titles to harmonize the twenty by his friend, Li Shen, and sent them to Bo Juyi, who then composed fifty of his own. It was their conscious effort to liberate poetry from the rigid rules of prosody practiced by most Tang poets at the time. It is true that the *yuefu* form had been revived by earlier poets, such as Li Bo 李白 (701–762)* and Du Fu 杜甫 (712–770),* but Yuan Zhen and his friends went beyond the structural freedom of meter and rhyme advocated by others and stressed simplicity of language and seriousness of purpose. They firmly believed that poetry could affect social and political changes.

One of the most exemplary of Yuan Zhen's political poems is "Lianchang gong ci" 連昌宮詞 (The Lianchang Palace), a new *yuefu* in ninety seven-character lines. It voices an anti-military

Yuan Zhen

attitude and questions the government's responsibility for causing war. The criticism is typically veiled in the recent past, the time of the An Lushan Rebellion (755–763). It was said that Yuan Zhen's poems were the steppingstones for him to climb to the lofty height of Secretariat Director, for the new emperor, Muzong (r. 821–825), sought him out from relative obscurity after reading this poem. Here are the first few verses of "The Lianchang Palace" in which Yuan Zhen's persona encounters an old man who wistfully recalls the glories of the palace before the An Lushan Rebellion:

> Lianchang Palace was overgrown with bamboo,
> Long years untended, it turned into a thicket.
> The double-flowering peach trees, towering above the walls,
> Shed red showers when the wind stirred.
> By the palace gate an old man with tears told me:
> "Once in my youth I was there to bring food to the palace.
> The Grand Emperor was in the Fairy-viewing Hall,
> Taizhen leaned against the railing by his side.
> Above the hall and in front, whirled jade and pearls;
> Sparkling, they reflected heaven and earth.
> I returned as in a dream, and with my senses gone.
> How could I relate in full these palace affairs?"

> 連昌宮中滿宮竹，歲久無人森似束。
> 又有牆頭千葉桃，風動落花紅蔌蔌。
> 宮邊老翁為余泣，小年進食曾因入。
> 上皇正在望仙樓，太真同憑闌干立。
> 樓上樓前盡珠翠，炫轉熒煌照天地。
> 歸來如夢復如癡，何暇備言宮裡事。

The poem then describes the remnants of the deserted imperial palace after the Rebellion from the perspective of the old peasant. He like many people had fled the capital when the rebels ruled it, but his narration goes on to depict how the palace looked when he revisited it circa 816–817 when the poem was probably written:

> "Last year an order came to cut down the palace bamboo,
> By chance I found the gate open and stepped in:
> Thorns and brambles thickly closed the imperial pond,
> Proud foxes and doltish hares capered around trees;
> The dance pavilion had collapsed, its foundation still there;
> The ornamented windows were dim, but the screens still green;
> Dust covered the old filigrees on painted walls;
> Crows had pecked the wind chimes, scattering pearls and jade."

> 去年敕使因斫竹，偶值門開暫相逐。
> 荊榛櫛比塞池塘，狐兔嬌癡緣樹木。
> 舞榭欹傾基尚在，文窗窈窕紗猶綠。
> 塵埋粉壁舊花鈿，烏啄風箏碎珠玉。

When the old man has told his tale, Yuan Zhen's persona breaks into the narration in the final two lines in an appeal to end all wars:

I am deeply moved by the old man's thoughts;
Let's spare no effort to put an end to all wars.

老翁此意深望幸，努力廟謀休用兵。

Aside from the vivid imagery which brings the court life alive, the poem is notable for its indirect characterization of the old man, and for the manipulation of the point-of-view from the persona to the peasant and back again. Such creative encounters the peasants—it is unlikely a such a man could speak so fulsomely about the palace—played a role in both new *yuefu* and the fictional biographies penned by ancient-style prose authors such as Han Yu 韓愈 (768–824) and Liu Zongyuan 柳宗元 (773–819).

During his long exiles and less strenuous appointments at outlying districts, Yuan Zhen had ample time for literary pursuits. He exchanged poems constantly with his friends; special messengers were assigned to deliver the poems Yuan and Bo wrote to each other when they were governors of neighboring provinces. In 823, Yuan Zhen completed his own collected works in one hundred *juan* and titled it *Yuanshi Changqing ji* 元氏長慶集 (Mr. Yuan's Collection from the Changqing Reign). Then he edited Bo Juyi's collected works in fifty *juan* and gave it a similar title: *Boshi Changqing ji* 白氏長慶集 (Mr. Bo's Collection from Changqing Reign).

There is also a *chuanqi* tale known as "Huizhen ji" 會真記 (A Tale of an Encounter with an Immortal) or more famously as "Yingying zhuan" 鶯鶯傳 (The Story of Yingying) written by Yuan Zhen, which had a great influence on subsequent literature. It concerns the love affair between the young scholar Zhang 張 and an enigmatic maiden, Cui Yingying 崔鶯鶯, while both were staying temporarily in a monastery. As perhaps the finest example of *chuanqi* fiction, this story was later modified and expanded into a *zhugongdiao* 諸宮調 (all keys and modes) by Dong Jieyuan 董解元 in the thirteenth century. Eventually, this latter version evolved into the famous Yuan-dynasty drama *Xixiang ji* 西廂記 (The West Chamber). Because of the sustained popularity of the original story and of the two subsequent versions, it is probable that "Yingying" was the single best-known love story in traditional China.

Scholars who have studied this story, however, have tended to take the historical/biographical approach rather than to assess the reasons for its undeniable appeal. In the usual case, they either assume (as does the modern scholar Chen Yinke 陳寅恪 [1890–1969]) or attempt to show (as does James R. Hightower) that the hero Zhang and the putative author Yuan Zhen are essentially one and the same. For this reason, the fictiveness of the tale is played down in favor of Yuan's biography as a necessary guide to its understanding. Discussion tends to dwell on why Chang does not simply arrange to marry Yingying, or why he so casually leaves her. In either reading, the rationale provided in the tale itself is less than convincing.

Such an apparent shortcoming, however, has clearly not detracted from the story's manifest ability to capture and sustain a reader's interest, and the reasons for this are more crucial than historical or biographical circumstance. The story does not really concern itself with the rounded portrayal of Zhang; nor is it actually a self-confession on the part of the author. Rather, as either of its titles suggests, it is essentially a portrait of its fascinating heroine Yingying. How this portrait is presented constitutes the basis of its meaning and artistic merit.

The reader first meets Yingying through Zhang's startled eyes, as she comes out with great reluctance to greet him. The narrator notes her everyday dress, her lack of makeup, her look of resentment, and her utter refusal to be drawn into conversation. It is this very negative manner that marks her as uncommon and brings about an overwhelmingly positive response in Zhang (and, through him, in the reader). He finds her to be uniquely captivating and radiantly beautiful, and he falls madly in love.

This kind of ironic reversal characterizes the entire portrayal of the heroine and, in large measure, accounts for the enduring hold the story has over the imagination. She sends Zhang a verse which appears to be a coy invitation, but she rebuffs him with cold formality when he arrives. Then, without explanation, she goes to him herself, blushing and leaning weakly on her maid's arm. Even as Zhang rejoices in the initial fulfillment of their love, she says nothing. When Zhang first leaves her, she makes no open objection, though the narrator is careful to note that her usually impassive face shows traces of pain. There is also mention of her literary and musical skills, along with her stubborn refusal to display them to others. When she realizes that Zhang is overhearing her as she plays the zither alone at night, she abruptly stops.

Internal irony is therefore the most prominent feature of Yingying's character. Moreover, because irony permeates the way the character is described, the reader becomes thoroughly stimulated and is drawn into active participation. When the narrator says that Yingying is silent during stressful situations, the reader is conditioned to formulate on his own a greater depth of feeling than direct telling could possibly convey.

Because of this, the tale is charged with emotional tension in spite of its terse and understated classical prose. Toward the end of the story, Yingying attempts to express her grief directly by agreeing to play her zither as a parting gift for her lover. As she proceeds, however, she finds her feelings too intense for her music to express and so she stops and runs to her mother's quarters in tears. The incident itself is related in a line and a half of text; like her music, it breaks off because what is left unsaid is, in context, more profound and meaningful.

Like other fine works of literature in the classical mode, "The Story of Yingying" challenges the critic to take the reader into careful consideration, for it is the reader who must fill in with his imagination the empty spaces that are an integral part of the total text. Much as Yuan Zhen would have liked to be remembered for his poems of social protest, it is this story along with his romantic poems–especially his elegies–which ensure his reputation.

BIBLIOGRAPHY

Editions:

Luan Guiming 欒貴明, ed. *Quan Tangshi suoyin: Yuan Zhen juan* 全唐詩索引：元稹卷. Beijing: Zhonghua. 1997.

Quan Tang shi, 6: 4462–64.

Quan Tang wen, 647–55.7295–418.

Wu Zaiqing 吳在慶. "Shinian Yuan Zhen yanjiu shuping" 十年元稹研究述評. In *Tangdai wenxue yanjiu nianjian, 1992* 唐代文學研究年鑑, 1992. Guilin: Guangxi Shifan Daxue, 1993, pp. 219–32.

"Yingying zhuan," in *Taiping guangji, juan* 488.

___. in *Tangren xiaoshuo yanjiu er ji* 唐人小說研究二集. Wang Mengou 王夢鷗, ed. Taibei: Yiwen, 1973, pp. 255–62.

Yuan Zhen ji 元稹集. Ji Qin 冀勤, ed. V. 1 of 2. Beijing: Zhonghua, 1982.

Yuan Zhen shixuan 元稹詩選. Shanghai: Gudian Wenxue, 1957.

Yuanshi Changqing ji. SBBY.

Annotations:

Yang Jun 楊軍. *Yuan Zhen ji biannian jianzhu* 元稹集編年箋注. Xi'an: Sanqin, 2002.

Biographical Sources:

Fu, *Tang caizi*, 3:22–40, 5:271.

Jiu Tang shu, 166.4327–38.

Xin Tang shu, 174.5223–29.

Translations:

Birch, *Anthology*, pp. 279–80, 290–99.

Field, "Taking Up the Plow," pp. 143.

Hightower, James Robert. "The Story of Yingying," in *Traditional Chinese Stories*, pp. 139–45.

Owen, *Mi-Lou*, pp. 52–55.

___, *Middle Ages*, pp. 149–73, 192–204.

___, *Omen*, pp. 65–68, 199–203.

___, *Remembrances*, pp. 75–76.

Sunflower, pp. 216–26.

Waley, *Translations*, pp. 297–313 ("Yingying zhuan" and a poem).

Wu Dakui 吳大奎 and Ma Xiujuan 馬秀娟, comms. *Yuan Zhen Bo Juyi shi xuanyi* 元稹白居易詩選譯. Chengdu: Ba Shu Shushe, 1991.

Studies:

Bian Xiaoxuan 卞孝宣. *Yuan Zhen nianpu* 元稹年譜. Shandong: Qi Lu Shushe, 1980.

Ch'en, Yin-k'o 陳寅恪. "Du Yingying zhuan" 讀鶯鶯傳, *BIHP*, 10.2 (1942): 189–95.

___. *Yuan Bo shi jian zheng gao* 元白詩箋證稿. Shanghai: Shanghai Guji, 1978.

Fan Shufen 范淑芬. *Yuan Zhen ji qi yuefushi yanjiu* 元稹及其樂府詩研究. Taibei: Wenjin, 1984.

Fu Dixiu 伏滌修. *Xixiangji ziliao huibian* 西廂記資料彙編. Hefei: Huangshan, 2012.

Hanabusa, Hideki 花房英樹. *Gen Shin sakuhin shiryō* 元稹作品資料. Kyoto, 1958.

___. *Gen Shin nenpu kō* 元稹年譜考. Kyoto: Furitsu Daigaku Chūgoku Bungaku Kenkyūshitsu, 1962.

___ and Maegawa Yukio 前川幸雄. *Gen Shin kenkyū* 元稹研究. Tokyo: Ibundo shokan, 1977. Includes a genealogy, a chronological biography, textual criticisms and works, a linguistic analysis of Yuan's poetry, and a concordance.

Hightower, James Robert. "Yuan Zhen and 'The Story of Yingying,'" *HJAS*, 33 (1973): 93–103.

Hsia, C. T. "A Critical introduction" to *The Romance of the Western Chamber*, S. I. Hsiung, trans., rpt. New York: Columbia University Press, 1968, pp. xi–xxxii. Discussion of differences between the story, the *zhugong diao*, and the Yuan play.

Ikas, Ludger. *Der klassische Chinesische Vierzeiler: Das Beispiel Yuan Zhen (779–831)*. Frankfurt am Main: P. Lang, 1995.

Jian Changchun 蹇長春. *Bo Juyi ping zhuan: fu Yuan Zhen ping zhuan* 白居易評傳：附元稹評傳. Nanjing: Nanjing Daxue, 2002.

Lee, Yu-hwa. *Fantasy and Realism in Chinese Fiction: Tang Love Themes in Contrast*. San Francisco: Chinese Materials Center, 1984.

Liu Weichong 劉維崇. *Yuan Zhen pingzhuan* 元稹評傳. Taibei: Liming Wenhua, 1977.

Palandri, AngelaJung. *Yiian Chen*. Boston: Twayne, 1977.

Shields, Anna. "Defining Experience: The 'Poems of Seductive Allure' (*Yanshi*) of the Mid-Tang Poet Yuan Zhen (779–831)," *JAOS* 122 (2002): 61–78.

___. "Remembering When: The Uses of Nostalgia in the Poetry of Bo Juyi and Yuan Zhen," *HJAS* 66 (2006): 321–61.

___. *One Who Knows Me: Friendship and Literary Culture in Mid-Tang China*. Cambridge and London: Havard University Asia Canter, 2015, pp. 173–99 and passim.

Tan Mei-ah. "A Study of Yuan Zhen's Life and Verse 809–810: Two Years That Shaped His Politics and Prosody." Unpublished Ph.D. Dissertation, University of Wisconsin–Madison, 2008.

___. "Allegory as a Means to Present Political Advice: Yuan Zhen's 'Sacrificing to Spirits.'" *Journal of Chinese Studies* 54 (January 2012): 161–98.

___. "Exonerating the Horse Trade for the Shortage of Silk: Yuan Zhen's 'Yin Mountain Route.'" *Journal of Chinese Studies* 57 (July 2013): 49–96.

___. "Beyond the Horizon of an Avian Fable: 'Large-Beaked Crows' as an Allegory of Wang Shuwen's Political Reforms." *Journal of Chinese Studies* 51 (July 2010): 217–53.

___. "Monetary Policy as Key to State Authority and Income in Tang China." *Journal of Chinese Studies* 64 (January 2017): 35–109.

___. "New Music Bureau Poetry as Memorial: The True Significance of Yuan Zhen's 'Shangyang Baifa Ren,'" *TS* 35 (2017): 87–108.

___. "Decoding the Ambiguous Narrative Voice in 'Tale of Yingying': Ritual Propriety as Key," *Nan nü: Men, Women, and Gender in China* 21 (June 2019): 38–75.

Tian Enming 田恩銘. *Yuan Zhen he Zhong Tang shiren xintai* 元稹和中唐士人心態. Beijing: Zhongguo Shehui Kexue, 2020.

Wang Jisi 王季思. *Cong "Yingying zhuan" dao "Xixiang ji"* 從鶯鶯傳到西廂記. Shanghai: Gudian Wenxue, 1955.

Wang Shiyi 王拾遺. *Yuan Zhen zhuan* 元稹傳. Yinchuan: Ningxia Renmin, 1985.

Wong, Timothy C. "Self and Society in Tang Dynasty Love Tales," *JAOS*, 99 (1979): 95–100.

Wu Weibin 吳偉斌. *Yuan Zhen kaolun* 元稹考論. Zhengzhou: Henan Renmin, 2008.

Xie Yongfang 謝永芳. *Yuan Zhen shi quanji: huijiao, huizhu, huiping* 元稹詩全集: 匯校, 匯注, 匯評. Wuhan: Chongwen, 2016.

Zhang Daren 張達人. *Tang Yuan Weizhi Xiansheng Zhen nianpu* 唐元微之先生稹年譜. Taibei: Taiwan Shangwu, 1980.

Angela Jung Palandri, Timothy Wong, and William H. Nienhauser, Jr.

Zhang Ben 張賁 (*zi*, Runqing 潤卿, fl. 850–875) hailed from Nanyang 南陽 (modern Henan county 河南) and was known as the "Erudite of Nanyang" (*Nanyang boshi* 南陽博士) among the late Tang coterie of Zhang, Pi Rixiu 皮日休 (ca. 834–ca. 883)* and Lu Guimeng 陸龜蒙 (836–881).* Zhang has no biography in the dynastic histories; what little is known of Zhang's life can be gleaned from the brief sketches provided in literary compilations read in concert with the verse he and his companions composed for one another. Zhang passed the *jinshi* towards the beginning of the Dazhong 大中 era (847–860) and was made an Erudite in the Institute for the Extension of Literary

Arts at the capital. Soon thereafter, he forsook a career at court for the life of a recluse on Maoshan 茅山, the center of Shangqing 上清 (Highest Clarity) Daoism during the period. Maoshan was famous for the myriad pharmacopeia found amongst its peaks, and according to Shangqing cosmology, is considered to be the site of the eighth grotto-heaven (*dongtian* 洞天) known as Huayang 華陽 (Flourishing Yang). During his time in the mountain complex, Zhang earned the appellation "Erudite of Huayang," in reference to both his dedication to cultivation as well as his literary talent. Poems honoring Zhang by Pi Rixiu and Lu Guimeng depict an accomplished practitioner earnestly committed to pursuits beyond the mundane, such as refining his own alchemical ingredients and devoting himself to Daoist deities. Indeed, allusions found within Zhang's poetry resonate with aspects of Shangqing cosmology, as in his poem dedicated to Pi Rixiu referencing the Realized Man of Purple Yang (*Ziyang zhenren* 紫陽真人), who first bestowed Shangqing revelation to Yang Xi 楊羲 (330–386), "Chou Ximei xianjian ji daolai yun" 酬襲美先見寄倒来韻 (A Poem Responding to Rhymes of the One Ximei [i.e. Pi Rixiu] First Sent Me):

> I suspect Heaven intends to destroy this culture of ours,
> Thus I choose Mao's' Peak to entrust myself to the white clouds.
> After drink I merely await a guest of the azure seas,
> Before incense I see only the Lord of Purple Yang.
> The recent years have cut my habit of poetry and writing,
> Today both my brush and ink-stone will burn.
> For having this body I still bitterly suffer,
> Not understanding what to make of this black and crimson silk.

> 尋疑天意喪斯文, 故選茅峰寄白雲.
> 酒後只留滄海客, 香前唯見紫陽君.
> 近年已絕詩書癖, 今日兼將筆硯焚.
> 為有此身猶苦患, 不知何者是玄纁.

The poem opens by setting the scene by way of Zhang's rationale for eschewing the life of officialdom to seek quietude in the mountain temples of Maoshan 茅山. Lamenting the degradation of "this culture of ours" (*siwen* 斯文) alludes to the Confucius's defiant stance in the face of personal danger while travelling in the state of Kuang 匡. There, the master identifies with the "culture" that Heaven shall not let perish, thus proving he has nothing to fear from others. Invoking the resolve of Confucius here in the first line, Zhang may well be expressing his own personal frustration at being passed over for official service, albeit with a defiant tone. Instead, he retreats to the Daoist sanctuaries on Maoshan, the seat of Shangqing 上清 (Highest Purity) Daoism. There, he takes up the motif of drinking to toast guests from across the azure seas, describing experienced literati in language that resonates with Shangqing deities. Turning away from drink and toward the altar, Zhang finally comes to see the source of revelation itself, the Lord of Purple Yang, thus placing himself within a lineage of divine transmissions. The poem shifts in the third line to the recent past, where Zhang has demonstrably given up his "habit" of reading the classics, a move punctuated by the present promise of burning the physical accoutrements of officials (and perhaps ironically, that of poets). The lengths he goes to leave the past, even destroying the ink and brush are not enough. He is left to contemplate the crimson and black robes, symbols of office given to officials by the emperor seeking their service, unsure how they fit with his reclusive lifestyle.

Also known as the "Daoist of Huayang," Zhang would eventually leave the mountain to settle in the nearby region of Wu 吳 (home of Lu Guimeng), where he would spend the years between 869 and 871 travelling throughout Suzhou with his literary friends Pi Rixiu and Lu Guimeng. Together, they composed response poems, crafting lines in concert using "linked-verse"(*lianju* 聯句) style (see Nienhauser reference below). Each of Zhang's sixteen poems preserved in the *Quan Tang shi* were composed as a response to those of either Pi Rixiu or Lu Guimeng, or both. Though sometimes irreverent, it is clear from their poetic exchanges that Zhang was held in the highest esteem by his two fellow sojourners. The *Tangshi jishi* 唐詩紀事 contains four of Zhang's own poems, describing his work as born from inspiration that comes with traveling as a stranger, and thus, affecting a sense of wistful freedom. Zhang's "Lübo Wumen" 旅泊吳門 (Moored while Traveling at the Gate to Suzhou) reflects themes of natural imagery mixed with a sense of intoxication to express freedom from social constraint that resonate with the works of other poets often associated with Daoist influence. Here, the high-spirited combination also reveals a sense of anxiety and want for companionship that accompanies the freedom to wander:

> A single barge in the Wu River evening,
> the ills of this Erudite worthy of worry;
> With whom does the perch companion,
> while the gulls gather amongst themselves?
> The setting sun reflected on the crisscrossed waterways;
> Tilting in the sky breaks and rejoins clouds.
> Far from home with boundless wonder,
> spent I hand over the wine in helpless intoxication.

> 一舸吳江晚，堪憂病廣文。
> 鱸魚誰與伴，鷗鳥自成群。
> 反照縱橫水，斜空斷續雲。
> 異鄉無限思，盡付酒醺醺。

Zhang sets the scene of anxious desolation, as he places himself, the Erudite) floating in anxious solitude along the river in quiet evening. Likening himself to the lonely perch, he contrasts his current sense of isolation with the gathering gulls. The mention of gulls here alludes to an anecdote from "Huangdi" 黃帝 chapter of the *Liezi* 列子, where one enjoyed playing freely with the seagulls, only to have them stop coming to him once his intention was to take them home. Floating along the Wu River places the persona in Suzhou, where the sun glints off the many canals and waterways that crisscross the region, the poem then draws forth an image of the fading sunlight dancing in and out along the waves, as the distinction between the water and sky dissipates in the poet's eye. In a gesture reminiscent of Zhuang Zi, the poem shifts tenor from anxiety to ease, as the poet gives in to the undulating expanse across which he travels, and floats happily and effortlessly drunk down the river.

Though now remembered mostly through his literary engagement with his two more well-known companions, Zhang's erudition, along with his earnest attempt at a life of reclusion, inspired great admiration among his peers. Compelled to respond in verse, the work of Pi Rixiu and Lu Guimeng depict a unique talent capable of expressing the profundity of his practice with literary grace. Those examples of Zhang's own lines preserved in later collections evince a poet worthy of such praise.

BIBLIOGRAPHY

Editions:
Quan Tang shi, 10: 7283–86, 11: 8928–29.

Biographical Sources:
Ji Yougong 計有功 (fl. 1121–1161). *Tangshi jishi* 唐詩紀事 [Records of Tang Poetry] (81 *juan*) 2 vols. Beijing: Zhonghua, 1965. Vol 2, *juan* 64, p. 961.

Translations:
Nienhauser, William H. Jr. *P'i Jih-hsiu*. Boston: Twayne Publishers, 1979. pp. 106–07. "Hanye wenyan lianju" 寒夜文宴聯句 (Linked-line Verse Written at a Literary Party on the Night Before the Cold Food Festival) Zhang Ben along with Pi Rixiu 皮日休 and Lu Guimeng 陸龜蒙.

Studies:
Nienhauser, William H. Jr. *P'i Jih-hsiu*.
Schafer, Edward H. *Mao Shan in T'ang Times*. Boulder, Colorado: Society for the Study of Chinese Religions, Monograph No. 1, pp. 51–52.

Michael E. Naparstek

Zhang Hu 張祜 (*zi*, Chengji 承吉, ca. 782–ca. 853, also mistakenly known in some records as Zhang You 張祐), was a noted poet of the first half of the ninth century. He was born in Nanyang 南陽 (modern Deng 鄧 County in Henan). In his early years he wandered about and gained a reputation as a chivalrous and uninhibited young man. In 820, he traveled around Huainan 淮南 (stretching from what is now middle Jiangsu 江蘇 to southeastern Henan 河南) and fell in love with a singing girl. Later he took her as a concubine and begot a son named Qier 杞兒. That same year, at Linghu Chu's 令狐楚 (ca. 766–837)* recommendation, he went to Chang'an and presented his poems at court. However, Yuan Zhen 元稹 (779–831),* who was then in favor with the emperor, felt he was too insolent. As a result, Zhang was unable to stay at court but remained in Chang'an for three years without a position before despondently returning eastwards. In 824, he went to Hangzhou 杭州 to call on the Prefect, Bo Juyi 白居易 (772–846),* hoping that Bo would recommend him as the *jieyuan* 解元 (the scholar who ranked first in provincial imperial examinations). However, when Bo Juyi selected Xu Ning 徐凝 (fl. 806–820) as the *jieyuan*, Zhang Hu was angered and abandoned his pursuit for an official position. In his sixties, Zhang Hu moved to Jiaxing 嘉興 (modern Jiaxing in Zhejiang 浙江) and became a minor officer at Dongguayan 冬瓜堰, an appointment he soon gave up, claiming the position would corrupt him. Du Mu 杜牧 (803–ca. 852)* described him in a poem as "what man could be able to be like Master Zhang, with his thousands of poems making light of the marquises in charge of ten thousand households" 誰人得似張公子，千首詩輕萬戶侯. In his last years, he lived in seclusion in Danyang 丹陽 (modern Danyang in Jiangsu) and died in poverty. Yan Xuan 顏萱, Lu Guimeng 陸龜蒙 (ca. 836–881),* and Pi Rixiu 皮日休 (ca. 834–ca. 883)* all wrote poems grieving over his death.

Zhang Hu's *gongci* 宮詞 (palace poems) and *wulü* 五律 (pentasyllabic regulated poems) were especially admired. His *gongci* reputedly spread to the imperial palace and many palace women reputedly could sing them. Among his most famous pieces are "Gongci ershou" 宮詞二首 (Two Palace Poems):

> Three thousand miles from her old country,
> Deep in the palace these twenty years,
> At the first sound of "He Manzi"
> Pairs of tears fall in front of her lord.

> 故國三千里，深宮二十年。
> 一聲何滿子，雙淚落君前。

He Manzi was the name of a man in Cangzhou 滄州 during the Kaiyuan reign (713–742) who had been facing death for a crime he committed; he submitted a song to ransom his life. The song then became representative for music that was desolate and heartbreaking. The singer here is sad both because of the mournful tune and its associated story, but also because she has been unnoticed in the palace for so long.

Zhang Hu also wrote poems typical of a traveler heading to the South, such as his "Ti Jinling du" 題金陵渡 (Written upon Crossing the Yangzi at Jinling):

> At a hilltop tower having just crossed at the Jinling Ford,
> After just one night a traveler naturally finds sorrow.
> The slanting moon sinks on the river's tide,
> Two or three flickering lights—that's Guazhou.

> 金陵津渡小山樓，一宿行人自可愁。
> 潮落夜江斜月裡，兩三星火是瓜洲。

The Jinling Ford is near modern Zhenjiang City 鎮江市 in Jiangsu. The traveler in line two is of course the poet himself. South of the Yangzi, he looks back to the north and senses all the more the distance from his home beyond the broad expanse of the river. As the moon seems to set into the tide waters, straining his eyes he sees in the final line what appear to be two or three faint stars, then realized they are lights in Guazhou on the northern shore. The poem has been described by later critics as a landscape painting down in light ink, but there is more to it. Although the poet's feelings are never mentioned, the length of time he stares back to the north suggests his homesickness.

BIBLIOGRAPHY

Editions:
Quan Tang shi, 8: 5835–93, 11: 9007, 13: 9923, 10057, 14: 10669, 15: 11319.
Zhang Chushi shi ji 張處士詩集. Taibei: Yiwen, 1970.

Biographical Sources:
Fu, *Tang caizi*, 3:161–84.
Tang zhi yan, 2.17, 7.80, 11.221, 13.146–48.

Translations:
Kroll, "Recalling Xuanzong," pp. 12–14.
Owen, *Late Tang*, pp. 165–66, 170.
Yang Xiaoshan. "Tradition and Individuality in Wang Anshui's *Tang bai jia shixuan*," *HJAS* 70 (2002): 117–18.

Studies:
Tan Xueyou 譚學優. *Tangshiren xingnian kao* 唐詩人行年考. Sichuan: Sichuan Renmin, 1981, pp. 240–42.

Yanwen Wu and William H. Nienhauser, Jr.

Zhang Ji 張繼 (*zi*, Yisun 懿孫, fl. 753–779) was a native of Xiangzhou 襄州 (modern Xiangyang 襄陽, Hebei). He gained a reputation through his verse early in life and passed the *jinshi* in 753 under the examiner Yang Jun 楊浚 (d. ca. 760), who supervised four *jinshi* examinations in succession, but never seems to have gained access to elite Chang'an society. Perhaps as a result, Zhang spent most of his career in the provinces, serving in Suzhou 蘇州 and Hongzhou 洪州 (modern Nanchang 南昌). While in the southeast he met up with Huangfu Ran 皇甫冉 (ca. 717–ca. 771), whom he had first met probably in the early 750s in Chang'an (Huangfu's uncle, Huangfu Zeng 皇甫曾, also passed the *jinshi* in 753). During the 770s Zhang served in the capital as Acting Director of the Bureau of Sacrifices. Little is known of his final years–he died, according to one account, in Hongzhou.

Zhang Ji's extant corpus includes around forty poems, with another ten possibly from his pen. Over half are accounts of feelings and thoughts inspired by places the poet visited, from a famous historic site or well-known scenic spot to a certain outpost or an unidentified path on an autumn day. Some reflect personal concerns: homesickness, nostalgia for younger days, or grief over old age. Others express his consideration for social issues such as the destructiveness of war, the irretrievable passage of time, and the preservation of moral integrity in the face of temptation. Still others, apparently not inspired by visiting places, treat quite conventional subjects, such as friendship, separation, lovesickness, and reclusion.

Neither traditional criticism nor modern scholarship has deemed Zhang Ji a leading poet. He was not, for instance, included as one of the *Dali shi caizi* 大歷十才子 (Ten Talents of the Dali [Reign Period, 766–779]). Yet for all his apparent mediocrity, a single short poem earned him a prominence far greater than that of any of the "Ten Talents"–"Fengqiao ye bo" 楓橋夜泊 (A Night

Zhang Ji

Mooring at Maple Bridge), a seven-character *jueju*:

> The moon descends, crows cry, frost fills the sky,
> Through river maples fishermen face my sorrow in sleep.
> Outside the city walls of Suzhou is Cold-Mountain temple–
> At midnight the sound of its bell reaches a traveler's boat.

> 月落烏啼霜滿天，江楓漁火對愁眠。
> 姑蘇城外寒山寺，夜半鐘聲到客船。

For centuries this has been among the most widely known Tang poems, and its popularity has lasted to this day. It has also received much critical attention. Traditional discussions have centered on two areas: identification of the place-names in the poem (Cold-mountain Temple was one-third of a mile west of the bridge near the city walls of what is now Suzhou) and verification of the statement in the poem that bells were rung at midnight in Tang temples. Modern study of the poem, on the other hand, is prompted by interest in the interaction of the real and imagined worlds and is based on a view of the poem as an artistic organism, incorporating both the night scene (*jing* 景) and the poet's emotions (*qing* 情) as a traveler far from home. The image of the crows' caw evokes the traditional *yuefu* tune-title "Wu ye ti" 烏夜啼 [Crows Cry at Night]) which often (as in the following anonymous fifth-century poem) metaphorically expressed the sorrow of parted lovers:

> Ravens once born seem to want to fly,
> Flying, two go their own way.
> Separated in life, their hearts not at ease
> They cry through the night until day breaks.

> 烏生如欲飛，飛飛各自去。
> 生離無安心，夜啼至天曙。

BIBLIOGRAPHY

Editions:
Quan Tang shi, 4: 2709–17, 14: 11125–26.

Biographical Sources:
Fu, *Tang caizi*, 1:505–13, 5:102.

Translations:
Bynner, *Jade Mountain*, p. 3.
Margoulies, *Anthologie*, pp. 191–92, 254, 350, 375–76, 438.
Minford and Lau, p. 852.
New Directions, p. 117.
Pimpaneau, p. 456.
Watson, *Columbia*, p. 280.

Studies:

Chu Zhongjun 儲仲君. "Zhang Ji de xingji ji qita" 張繼的行跡及其他. *Wenxue yichan*, 1991.3.
Fu Shuxian 傅述先. "Du 'Fengqiao ye bo'" 讀楓橋夜泊. *Zhongwai wenxue*, 9.2 (July 1980): 110–15.
Fu Xuancong 傅璇琮. "Zhang Ji kao" 張繼考. *Tangdai shiren congkao* 唐代詩人叢考. Beijing: Zhonghua, 1980. pp. 209–19.
Gan Zhengqi 甘正氣. "Zhang Ji shi luodi xiucai ma?" 張繼是落第秀才嗎? *Yuwen yuekan*, 2016.5.
Kunst, Arthur E. "A Critical Analysis of Witter Bynner's 'A Night Mooring near Maple Bridge.'" *Tsing Hua Journal of Chinese Studies*, 7.1 (August 1968): 114–42.
Liu Yisheng 劉逸生. "Zhang Ji: 'Fengqiao ye bo'" 張繼: 楓橋夜泊, in his *Tangshi Xiaozha* 唐詩小札. Rev. ed. Canton, 1978, pp. 181–83.
Matusbara Akira 松原郎. *Ban Tōshi no yōran: Chō Seki, Yō Gō, Ka Tō ron* 晚唐詩の揺籃: 張籍・姚合・賈島論. Tokyo: Senshū Daigaku, 2012.
Nienhauser, William H., Jr. "Tied Up at Maple Bridge Once Again." *Tamkang Review*, 11.4 (Summer 1981): 421–29.
Yang Ming 楊明. "Zhang Ji shizhong Hanshan si bian" 張繼詩中寒山寺辨. *Zhonghua wenshi luncong*, 1987. 2/3: 297–304.
Zhou Ming 周銘. "Jianlun 'Fengqiao ye bo'" 簡論楓橋夜泊. *Jiangsu Jiaoyu Xueyuan Xuebao*, 1991.4.
Zhu Yinyu 朱正玉. "Zhang Ji yanjiu erti" 張繼研究二題. *Chaohu Xueyuan xuebao*, 2007.7: 46–48.

Sharon S. J. Hou and William H. Nienhauser, Jr.

Zhang Ji 張籍 (*zi*, Wenchang 文昌, ca. 776–829) authored a corpus of *yuefu* poetry whose realistic descriptions of economic ravages of warfare and administrative corruption on the populace underscored the political and social ills of his time. Both contemporary and later readers of Zhang Ji praised his *yuefu* poetry as an affirmation of the Confucian tradition of expressing social comment in verse.

Zhang was a native of Wujiang 烏江 in Hezhou 和州 (modern Anhui). The lack of any information about his immediate family, except that a younger brother passed the *jinshi* in 813, would suggest for him a humbler origin than was usual for most Tang poets and may explain his sympathy for the sufferings of the Tang lower classes. He seems to have spent the first thirty years of life at home in Hezhou. In 796, Meng Jiao 孟郊 (751–814),* while on a journey to the Southeast, met him in Hezhou, and the following year secured for him an appointment on the staff of Dong Jin 董晉 (724–799), Military Commissioner of the Xuanwu 宣吳 region, whose headquarters were at Bianzhou 汴州 (modern Kaifeng). Zhang's colleagues there were Meng Jiao, Li Ao 李翱 (774–836),* and Han Yu 韓愈 (768–824),* under whose sponsorship he passed the provincial examinations in 798 and obtained the *jinshi* the following year. After several years in mourning at Hezhou and further service attached to southern military commissioners, he returned to Chang'an in 806 as Great Supplicator in the Bureau of Imperial Sacrifices, a low-ranking ceremonial post in which he remained for ten years. Frequent references to his failing eyesight and requests to friends to write letters for him suggest that during this period Zhang's poor eyesight may have hampered his official career. He was obviously never totally blind, for in 816 Han Yu secured for him a teaching position in the Directorate of Education where he remained until 822 when he was made Vice Director of the Bureau of Waterways and Irrigation.

Zhang Ji

He left this post in the summer of 824 to stay with Han Yu, who was then mortally ill, at the latter's villa south of Chang'an.

Zhang Ji returned to service in the autumn as Director of the Bureau of Receptions and was present at Han Yu's death in 824. Zhang Ji's verse eulogy for Han Yu ("Ji Tuizhi" 祭退之 [An Offering to Han Yu]), his longest poem, is a moving tribute to their long friendship and an important source of information about Han Yu's last days. Zhang came back to the Directorate of Education to serve as Director of Studies in 827. He associated and exchanged poems with other elder literati including Bo Juyi 白居易 (772–846),* Liu Yuxi 劉禹錫 (772–842),* and Pei Du 裴度 (765–839). After a short trip home to Hezhou in 828, he died in Chang'an, probably in 829.

Zhang Ji was among the first poets to recognize the merits of Du Fu 杜甫 (712–770).* He is even reputed to have burned a copy of a Du Fu poem, mixed its ashes with oil, and ingested the mixture in order to absorb the spirit of Du Fu's poetry. Zhang Ji's own *yuefu* poetry was a conscious continuation of the tradition of verse narratives, such as Du Fu's "Shihao li" 石壕吏 (The Officer at Shihao), that depicted the sufferings of the populace during the An Lushan Rebellion. Bo Juyi acknowledged that Zhang's poems in this tradition were the immediate inspiration for his own "New *Yuefu*" poetry. In his poem "Du Zhang Ji guyuefu" 讀張籍古樂府 (On Reading the Old-style *Yuefu* of Zhang Ji), Bo Juyi wrote that Zhang "was especially skilled at *yuefu* poetry, in all the ages few were his equal" 尤工樂府詩，舉代少其倫. He attributed this excellence to Zhang's conscious emulation of the Confucian principles of verse criticism as articulated in the traditional explication of the *Shijing* (Classic of Poetry). Although his government career was unsuccessful, Zhang played an important role in the literary contacts with Han Yu's circle and with the group centering around Bo Juyi and Yuan Zhen 元稹 (779–831).* He was thus an important conduit for ideas between the two coteries, whose relations seem to have been strained by differing political viewpoints.

Zhang's surviving corpus contains over four hundred poems, only seventy of which are in the *yuefu* mode. Over twenty of these describe the hardship of incessant warfare on the peasantry. For example, the "Saishang qu" 塞上曲 (Song from the Frontier) concludes, "year after year, no rest from the wars; the border people are all dead, only empty mountains remain" 年年征戰不得閒，邊人殺盡唯空山. Zhang also portrays the effect on the poor of the taxes levied to support such wars. In the "Yelao Ge" 野老歌 (Song of the Older Farmer), an old man's harvest is taken for taxes and then rots in the government granary. The old man and his son are forced to gather acorns to survive, "while a West River merchant, with a hundred chests of pearls, feeds meat to the dogs on his boat" 西江賈客珠百斛，船中養犬長食肉. This Confucian disgust with trade, further developed in Zhang's satire "Jiake le" 賈客樂 (The Merchant's Pleasures), and indignation over the economic exploitation of the peasantry is related to the conviction that such satires can serve as moral example to persuade the evil to mend their ways. Bo Juyi, in the same poem mentioned above, wrote that Zhang's "Dong Gong shi" 董公詩 (Poem for Master Dong), a long encomium to the civil virtue of Military Commissioner Dong Jin, "would admonish greedy and cruel officials" 讀君董公詩，可誨貪暴臣, presumably by acting as a positive example. On the other hand, "Shang Gexing" 傷歌行 (A Song of Sorrow) describes in vivid detail the disgraced departure from Chang'an in 809 of the Governor of the Capital Yang Ping 楊憑 (fl. 775–815) who had been convicted of corruption and exiled to the far South: "dressed in green robes, he rides an old horse; beyond the eastern gate there is no one to see him off" 身着青衫騎惡馬，東門之外無送

者. Officials of the lowest rank wore green robes. The poem provides a negative example to potential wrongdoers. Zhang's satires in this mode are written in a simple and direct language that underlines the popular origins of the questions they discuss and that served as a base for the "New *Yuefu*" poetry of Bo Juyi and Yuan Chen. Zhang's *yuefu* were also linked with those of Wang Jian 王建 (ca. 766–ca. 830)* under the epithet "Zhang Wang *yuefu*" 張王樂府.

Zhang Ji's reputation as a *yuefu* poet, established by the praise of his contemporaries Han Yu and Bo Juyi, continued in later periods. Typical and most appropriate is the remark of the Song critic Zhang Jie 張戒 (fl. 1135): "Zhang's poetry is on par with that of Bo Juyi and Yuan Chen. He was particularly good at expressing those concerns the people had in their hearts" 張司業詩與元白一律，專以道得人心專為工.

One of his best known *yuefu* is "Xiang Jiang qu" 湘江曲 (Song on the Xiang River) in which he expresses his own feelings:

> The Xiang River wave less, autumn waters vast;
> The Xiang Moon descends as the traveler sets out.
> I see men come, I see men go—
> Over a surface of white duckweed partridges fly to and fro.
>
> 湘水無潮秋水闊，湘中月落行人發。
> 送人發，送人歸，白蘋茫茫鷓鴣飛。

The most striking feature of the poem is auditory since six words are repeated lending an almost conversational tone to the piece. The first line depicts the scene of the Xiang River, probably as it empties into Lake Dongting 洞庭湖. Line two finds the persona seeing off someone just before dawn. The third line is a conventional depiction put in unconventional language—as men pass through, Zhang Ji must remain behind. What is left for him is another lake scene in which the cry of the partridges, traditionally heard as "don't set out, dear" (*xingbude, gege* 行不得，哥哥) as if it were a wife beseeching her husband to say at home, further reminds the poet of his plight far from home.

Much of Zhang Ji's writing has been lost. Although his works were first collected in the Southern Tang and again in the Song, neither edition survives. The modern corpus derives from an early sixteenth-century Ming edition that is textually unsatisfactory. Only two prose pieces remain, extant by virtue of their inclusion in the *Wenyuan yinghua* 文苑英華. These are the famous letters criticizing Han Yu written at Bianzhou in 798. Zhang also wrote a commentary to the *Analects*, the *Lunyu zhubian* 論語注辨, which has not survived.

BIBLIOGRAPHY

Editions:
Hiraoka Takeo 平岡武夫 and Maruyama, Shigeru 丸山茂. *Chō Seki kahi sakuin* 張籍歌詩索引. Kyoto: Hōyū, 1976. A complete concordance keyed to the 1959 Beijing edition, a reprint of which is included.
Luan Guiming 欒貴明, ed. *Quan Tang Shi suoyin: Zhang Ji juan* 全唐詩索引：張籍卷. Qinhuangdao: Xiantai, 1994.

Quan Tang shi, 6: 4291–377, 14: 10656.
Quan Tang wen, 684.7738–39.
Xu Chengyu 徐澄宇 (1902–1980), ed. *Zhang Wang yuefu* 張王樂府. Shanghai, Gudian Wenxue, 1957.
Zhang Ji juan 張籍卷. in *Quan Tang shi suoyin* 全唐詩索引. Beijing: Xiandai, 1994.
Zhang Ji shi ji 張籍詩集. Beijing: Zhonghua, 1959. A modern reset edition that mainly follows the *SBCK* text.
Zhang Siye shi ji 張司業詩集. 8 *juan*. Beijing: Zhonghua, 1958. A modern critical edition based on the Ming Wanli edition.
Zhang Wenchang wenji 張文昌文集. Shanghai: Shanghai Guji, 1994.

Annotations:
Chaves, Jonathan, trans. *Cloud Gate Song: The Verse of Tang Poet Zhang Ji*. Warren, CT: Floating World Editions, 2006.
Chen Yanjie 陳延傑, ed. *Zhang Ji shi zhu* 張籍詩注. Shanghai, Shangwu, 1938: rpt, Taibei: Taiwan Shangwu, 1967.
Li Dongsheng 李冬生, comm. *Zhang Ji jizhu* 張籍集注. Hefei: Huangshan, 1988.
Li Jiankun 李建崑. *Zhang Ji shi ji jiao zhu* 張籍詩及校注. Taibei: Huatai Wenhua Shiye, 2001.
Li Shuzheng 李樹政, ed. *Zhang Ji, Wang Jian shixuan* 張籍，王建詩選. Canton: Guangdong Renmin, 1984. Rpt. Taibei: Yuan Liu, 1988.
Xu Lijie 徐禮節. *Zhang Ji ji xinian jiaozhu* 張籍集繫年校注. Beijing: Zhonghua, 2011. Rpt. Hefei: Huangshan, 2015. Includes a twenty-page bibliography.

Biographical Sources:
Fu, *Tang caizi*, 2:552–75, 5:258–59.
Xin Tang shu, 176.5266–67.

Translations:
Davis, Timothy M. "Lechery, Substance Abuse, and . . . Han Yu?" *JAOS*, 135 (2015): 71–92.
Field, "Taking Up the Plow," pp. 134–35.
Owen, *Anthology*, pp. 470–1.
Owen, *Late Tang*, pp. 99–100, 115, 119.
Pimpaneau, p. 456.

Studies:
Akai Masuhisa 赤井益久. "Chō Seki no kofū nijūnanashu" 張籍の古風而是七首. *Chūgoku kankei ronetsu shiryō*, 21.2b (1979): 151–57.
Bian Xiaoxuan 卞孝萱. "Zhang Ji jianpu" 張籍年譜. *Anhui shixue tongxun* 安徽史學通訊, 1959.4/5.
Bol, pp. 123–27.
Chow Chuen-tang. "Chang Chi the Poet." Unpublished Ph.D. dissertation, University of Washington, 1968.
Hua Chenzhi 華忱之. "Lüetan Zhang Ji ji qi yuefu shi" 略談張籍及其樂府詩, in *Yuefu shi yanjiu lunwen ji* 樂府詩研究論文集. Beijing: Zuojia, 1959, 2, pp. 157–69.
Jiao Tijian 焦體檢. *Zhang Ji yanjiu* 張籍研究. Kaifeng: Henan Daxue, 2010.
___. "Zhang Ji jiaowang sengren, daoshi kao" 張籍交往僧人道士考, *Han yuyan wenxue yanjiu*, 2010.3: 48–50.
Ji Zhenhuai 季鎮淮. "Zhang Ji er ti" 張籍二題. *Wenxue yichan*, 1996.1: 49–51.
Ji Zuoliang 紀作亮. *Zhang Ji yanjiu* 張籍研究. Hefei: Huangshan, 1986.
Li Yifei 李一飛. "Zhang Ji, Wang Jian jiaoyu kaoshu" 張籍，王建交游考述. *Wenxue yichan*, 1993.2: 54–63.
Liu Guoying 劉國盈. "Han Yu yu Zhang Ji" 韓愈與張籍, *Shoudu Shifan Daxue xuebao (Shehui Kexue ban)*, 1997.2: 57–60.

Lo Lien-t'ien 羅聯添. "Zhang Ji nianpu" 張籍年譜. *Dalu zazhi*, 25.4 (Aug. 31, 1962), 14–19; 25.5 (Sept. 15, 1962), 15–22; 25.6 (Sept. 30, 1962), 20–29.

___. "Zhang Ji zhi jiaoyu ji qi zuopin xinian" 張籍之交遊及其作品繫年. *Dalu zazhi*, 26.12 (June 30, 1963), 14–18.

___. "Zhang Ji yishi ji shihua" 張籍軼事及詩話. *Dalu Zazhi* 27.10 (Nov. 30, 1963), 13–16. Lo's articles organize most of the traditional source material on Zhang Ji.

Matsubara Akira 松原朗. *Bantōshi no yōran: chō seki yō gō ka tō ron* 晚唐詩搖籃:張籍, 姚合, 賈島. Tokyo: Senshu Daigaku, 2012.

Pan Jinghan 潘竟翰. "Zhang Ji xinian kaozheng" 張籍繫年考證. *Anhui Shida xuebao*, 1981.2.

Tong Peiji 佟培基. "Zhang Ji Shi Zhongchu Zhenbian" 張籍詩重出甄辨. *Henan Daxue xuebao* 98 (1987): 80–84.

Waley, Arthur. *The Life and Times of Po Chü-i, 772–847 A.D.* London: G. Allen & Unwin, 1949, pp. 143–46.

Wu Shuning 巫淑寧. *Zhang Ji ji qi yuefu shi yanjiu* 張籍及其樂府詩研究. Taibei: Hua Mulan Wenhua, 2009.

Zhang Guoguang 張國光. "Tang Yuefu shiren Zhang Ji shengping kaozheng: Jianlun Zhang Ji shi de fenqi" 唐樂府詩人張籍生平考證：簡論張籍詩的分期. In *Quanguo Tangshi taolunhui lunwen xuan* 全國唐詩討論會論文選. Huo Sung-lin 霍松林, ed. Xian: Shanxi Renmin, 1984. pp. 230–80.

Zhang Guowei 張國偉. "Shilun Zhang Ji shi de xianshi yiyi" 試論張籍詩的現實意義, in Hu Yunyi 胡雲翼, ed. *Tangshi yanjiu* 唐詩研究. Hong Kong: Shangwu, 1959. pp. 237–46.

Charles Hartman and William H. Nienhauser, Jr.

Zhang Jiuling 張九齡 (*zi*, Zishou 子壽, 678–740) was the most important writer and statesman of the 730s, a decade in the prosperous and serene heyday of the great Emperor Xuanzong (r. 712–756) that in many ways marked the apogee of Tang culture. Born in Qujiang 曲江 township of Shaozhou 韶州 (modern northern Guangdong), Zhang Jiuling was a native of the tropical south. The most conspicuous example of a southerner rising to fame and high influence in Tang times, he was also partly responsible through his writings for the increasing acceptance and appreciation of the southern landscape in medieval Chinese literature.

It was through the examination system that Zhang, an outsider of comparatively modest origins, made his entry into the privileged circles of Tang officialdom and elite society, placing second in the *jinshi* examination of 702 (the poet Shen Quanqi 沈佺期 [656–716]* was one of the examiners that year). Shortly thereafter, he made the acquaintance of Zhang Yue 張說 (667–731),* who agreed to regard Zhang Jiuling as a distant relative and in later years advanced the younger man's career when it was in his power to do so. In both 707 and 712 Zhang sat for and passed special-decree examinations (the disquisitions he wrote for the latter test are still extant). His success in the 712 exam, of which he is recorded to have been the only successful candidate, led to a position as Reminder of the Left on the staff of the then Heir Apparent Li Longji 李隆基 (later Xuanzong). In 716, as a result of disagreements with higher officials, Zhang resigned his position and returned to Shaozhou, where he remained for the next two years. During this time, he oversaw the construction of a new road through the daunting Dayu Pass 大庾嶺, just north of Shaozhou, which greatly facilitated trade and transportation between the North and Guangzhou 廣州 (modern Canton) and points southwest. Zhang was recalled to court in 718. He received several promotions in the following years and in 723 was made Zhang Yue's immediate subordinate in the Secretariat. In this year he was also granted ennoblement, as the Baron of

Zhang Jiuling

Qujiang 曲江男. When Zhang Yue suffered a temporary political setback in 727, Zhang Jiuling was sent out to the provinces, holding office during the next years in Hongzhou 洪州 (modern Jiangxi) and then Guizhou 桂州 (modern Guangdong). One of his most famous poems, "Wang yue huai yuan" 望月懷遠 (Looking at the Moon and Thinking of a Distant One), is considered to have been written during his banishment to Hongzhou:

A bright moon rises above the sea;
at every corner of the world this moment is shared.
Lovers bemoan the endless night;
till dawn they are up longing for one another.
Extinguishing the candle and cherishing the moonlight all around,
I slip on a jacket, feel it moisten with dew.
As I cannot give a handful of moonlight to you,
I return to bed to dream of our meeting.

海上生明月，天涯共此時。
情人怨遙夜，竟夕起相思。
滅燭憐光滿，披衣覺露滋。
不堪盈手贈，還寢夢佳期。

This poem takes on the traditional motif of a woman in her boudoir thinking about her husband far from home. In the first four lines the persona dispassionately portrays the situation that has been presented in so many previous, similar poems. But in the third couplet the woman by extinguishing the candle and slipping on a jacket, shows her intent to extend her vigil throughout the entire night. Yet in the final couplet she realizes that the only way she can come closer to her love is through dreams and thus returns to bed.

In Hongzhou Zhang was certainly also thinking of returning to court and by 731 following Zhang Yue's death that year he was back in the capital and beginning to come to power in his own right. As the emperor reposed more and more confidence in him, Zhang was rapidly promoted through a succession of important posts, attaining ministerial status and the control of the Secretariat in 734. Further ennoblement (as Patrician of Shixing District [near Qujiang]) and honors (e.g., receipt of the exalted title Auriporphyrian Great Official of Glorious Favor 金紫光祿大夫) were forthcoming. His regime became, in the eyes of later historians, the model of a "Confucian" ministership. But by the end of 736, Zhang's administration was being challenged strongly by the aristocratic faction of Li Linfu 李林甫 (683–752), and in May of 737 Zhang was demoted to office in Jingzhou 荊州 (southern Hubei), the government falling into Li Linfu's dictatorial hands for fifteen years. Zhang died on June 5, 740 in his native Qujiang, where he had recently returned on leave from his post in Jingzhou.

More than 250 of Zhang Jiuling's poems–all but a handful of which are in pentasyllabic meter–have been preserved. His style is fluid and, in general, descriptive. The greater part of Zhang's verse is devoted to depictions of natural scenes, often in the south, and the traditional responses to the exotic landscape are sometimes, quite surprisingly, reversed. In several poems, for instance, the usually mournful cries of the gibbon in fact drive away the morose thoughts of the southern poet: for him they are welcome sounds of familiar companions. An especially large number of Zhang's poems are "ascent" verses, depicting views from atop hills, storied buildings, city walls, and towers.

At his best, Zhang has a flair for capturing precise visualizations–and vitalizations–of natural objects, particularly in parallel couplets with unexpected juxtapositions of elements in the landscape. He is often vivid and exciting (as, for example, in his several poems on the famous waterfall at Mount Lu), but he does at times lapse into a rather pallid manner–the other side of inspiration. A curious feature of Zhang's diction is his common, though not invariable, substitution of either the colloquial *na* 那 or the archaic *hu* 胡 for the word *he* 何 (how?). But Zhang's poetic lexicon, while extensive, is not especially abstruse or allusive. Above all, he excels in compositions, such as his marvelous "Lizhi fu" 荔枝賦 (Prose-poem on the Lychee), in which he celebrates the unappreciated (by northerners) glories of his native region and attempts to affect a reorientation of traditional geographic prejudice.

Over two hundred of Zhang's prose pieces are also extant. Many of these are official documents drafted for Xuanzong–policy statements, letters to rulers of foreign nations, and the like. Zhang's style in these works–a number of which furnish very important material for the study of political history of the time–is, of course, much denser and more academic than in his poetic works.

Just as Zhang Yue had aided Zhang Jiuling, so Jiuling was himself a notable patron of several younger poet-bureaucrats, such as Wang Wei 王維 (692–761 or 699–759)* and Bao Rong 包融, and it was he who appointed Meng Haoran 孟浩然 (689–740)* in 737 to the only official post that poet ever held. His imposing influence on many of his contemporaries is nicely summed up in a military metaphor used by Xuanzong, who on one occasion pronounced Zhang "the commander-in-chief of the literary fields."

Zhang's tomb, situated at the foot of Mount Luoyuan 羅源山, in the northwestern suburbs of the present-day city of Shaoguan 韶關市, was excavated in 1960. The memorial inscription discovered there, along with the additional testimony of a eulogistic text preserved in the *Quan Tang wen*, has enabled us to revise the date of birth of this great writer from the previously accepted year 673 to 678.

BIBLIOGRAPHY

Editions:

Quan Tang shi, 1: 567–612, 14: 10598, 11056.

Qujiang ji 曲江集. 12 *juan*. SBBY. Taibei: Taiwan Zhonghua, 1965. Substantially the same as *Zhang Qujiang ji* below, but lacking annotation.

Qujiang Zhang xiansheng wenji 曲江張先生文集. 20 *juan*. SBCK. Shanghai: Shangwu, 1922. (Also *Guoxue jiben congshu* edition, punctuated, under the title *Qujiang ji* 曲江集). Based on a Ming edition, edited by Qiu Jun 丘濬 (1421–1495) in 1473. The most reliable text.

Zhang Jiuling. *Zhang Jiuling ji* 張九齡集. Shanghai: Shanghai Guji, 1981. Photolithic reprint of Ming-dynasty edition of the *Tang wushi jia shiji* 唐五十家詩集.

Zhang Qujiang ji 張曲江集. 12 *juan*. *Guangdong congshu* 廣東叢書. Shanghai: Shangwu, 1946. With annotations by Wen Rushi 溫汝適 (1757–1808). Based on a lost Qing (1743) edition.

Zhang Jiuling

Annotations:
Xiong Fei 熊飛. *Zhang Jiuling ji jiaozhu* 張九齡集校注. Beijing: Zhonghua, 2008.

Biographical Sources:
Jiu Tang shu, 99.3097–100.
Xin Tang shu, 126.4424–30.

Translations:
Demiéville, *Anthologie*, pp. 208–09.
Mair, *Anthology*, p. 193.
Minford and Lau, p. 824.
Owen, *Early T'ang*, pp. 414–15.

Studies:
Altiere, Daniel P. "*The Kan-yü* of Chang Chiu-ling: Poems of Political Tragedy," *TkR* 4.1 (April 1973): 63–73.
Chen Jiansen 陳建森. "Zhang Jiuling de wenhua jiazhi quxiang yu shige de meixue zhuiqiu" 張九齡的文化價值取向與詩歌的美學追求. *Wenxue yichan* 4 (2001): 41–50.
Chen Xinzhang 陳新璋. "Ji Zhang Jiuling shige de zhuti xingxiang yu yishu fengge" 記張九齡詩歌的主體形象與藝術風格, *Xueshu yanjiu* 4 (1989).
Gu Jianguo 顧建國. *Zhang Jiuling nianpu* 張九齡研究. Beijing: Zhongguo Shehui Kexue, 2005.
___. *Zhang Jiuling yanjiu* 張九齡研究. Beijing: Zhonghua, 2007.
Herbert, P. A. "The Life and Works of Chang Chiu-ling." Unpublished Ph.D dissertation, University of Cambridge, 1973.
___. *Under the Brilliant Emperor: Imperial Authority in T'ang China as Seen in the Writings of Chang Chiu-ling.* Canberra: Australian National University Press, 1978.
He Ge'en 何格恩. "Zhang Jiuling nianpu" 張九齡年譜, *Lingnan xuebao* 4 (1935): 1–21.
___. "Zhang Jiuling zhi zhengzhi shenghuo" 張九齡之政治生活, *Lingnan xuebao* 4 (1935): 22–46.
___. "Qujiang nianpu shiyi" 曲江年譜拾遺, *Lingnan xuebao* 6 (1937): 133–34.
Honey, David B. "Zhang Jiuling," in Honey, ed., *The Southern Garden Poetry Society, Literary Culture and Social Memory in Guangdong.* Hong Kong: Chinese University of Hong Kong, 2013, pp. 11–22.
Kroll, Paul W. "Zhang Jiuling and the Lychee," *TS* 30 (2012): 9–22.
Mair, Victor H. *Four Introspective Poets: A Concordance to Selected Poems by Roan Jyi, Chern Tzyy-arng, Jang Jeouling, and Lii Bor.* Tempe: Center for Asian Studies, Arizona State University, 1987.
Okazaki, Takashi 岡崎敬. "To Cho Kyurei no funbo to sono boshimei" 唐張九齡の墳墓とその墓誌銘, *Shien* 89 (1962): 45–83.
Owen, *High Tang*, pp. 22–26.
Schafer, Edward H. *The Vermilion Bird. T'ang Images of the South.* Berkeley: University of California, 1967, *passim*.
Toscano, Dominic J. "Naively Perfect: A Note on the Image of the Boat in Zhang Jiuling's Poems." *Tang Studies*, 34 (2016): 1–11.
Wang Difei 王鏑非. *Zhang Jiuling* 張九齡. Guangzhou: Guangdong Renmin, 2008.
Wen Rushi 溫汝適. "Qujiang ji kaozheng; Qujiang nianpu" 曲江集考證; 曲江年譜, appended to *Zhang Qujiang ji*.
Xiong Fei 熊飛. *Zhang Jiuling yu Jiuling wenhua* 張九齡與九齡文化. Guangzhou: Jinan Daxue, 2020.

Yang Chengzu 楊承祖. *Tang Zhang Zishou xiansheng Jiuling nianpu* 唐張子壽先生九齡年譜. Taibei: Taiwan Shangwu, 1980.

Yang Hao 楊豪. "Tangdai Zhang Jiuling mu fajue jianbao" 唐代張九齡墓發掘簡報, *Wenwu* 6 (1961): 45–52.

Paul W. Kroll and William H. Nienhauser, Jr.

Zhang Ruoxu 張若虛 (ca. 660–ca. 720) was a poet and official about whom little is known today. He was a native of Yangzhou 揚州 (modern Jiangsu) and once occupied a minor military post in Yanzhou 兖州 (modern Shandong). His literary reputation was established in the capital during the first years of the eighth century in conjunction with a group of poets, all from the Lower Yangzi Basin, which included He Zhizhang 賀知章 (659–744),* Bao Rong 包融 (695–764) and Wan Qirong 萬齊融 (fl. 711). They were known as the "Wuzhong sizi" 吳中四子 (Four Masters from Wu). His poems were first collected in the Song-dynasty compilation, *Yuefu shiji* 樂府詩集.

It is no exaggeration to say that his "Chunjiang huayue ye" 春江花月夜 (The River by Night in Spring), one of only two extant poems, made Zhang's reputation. It is a tour de force which depicts the moon in various images in almost every line:

> The tides of the spring river high as the sea's horizon,
> by the sea the bright moon rises together with the tide.
> Shimmering along the waves for a million miles—
> everywhere the spring river covered in moonlight!
>
> The river waters wind through an aromatic grassy plain,
> while the moonshine over the flowery groves like sleet.
> Frost hangs in the air imperceptively fluttering.
> above the islet's white sand, unable to be seen.
>
> River and sky blend into a whiteness unsoiled;
> a wheel-like disc hangs in the brilliant sky.
> Who first observed the moon by the riverbank?
> When did the moon over the river begin to shine upon man?
>
> Generation after generation, human life without end;
> year by year, the moon over the river just looks the same.
> For whom is the river moon awaiting?
> The Long River only sees it off in the flowing water.
>
> A swath of white cloud drifts by languidly,
> Unbearable the sorrow at the riverside islet full of green maples.
> From what family is the traveler's in that skiff tonight?
> Where is the moonlit balcony on which his wife pines for him?
>
> So miserable the moon above the balcony meanders slowly,
> it must be casting light upon her dressing table.

Zhang Ruoxu

The moonlight never leaves the curtain of her jade door,
Wiped it away with the clothes-pounding pestle, it comes right back.

We may be watching the same moon at this moment, but we cannot speak to each other.
I wish I could follow the moon corona to shed beams upon you, my beloved.
Swan geese can fly afar, but they're unable to move beyond the moonlight.
Fish and dragons spring from the deep, but they stir ripples at most.

Last night I dreamt of petals falling in our tranquil pond,
A shame that midway through spring I have not returned home.
The river waters have almost washed spring away,
The sinking moon slants once again to the west.
The slanting moon heavily hidden beneath the sea's mist;
The road between Mount Jieshi and the Xiao-Xiang rivers is too long.
Who knows how many people, traveling on this moonlight can make it home—
Trees surround the river, the descending moon stirs my heart.

春江潮水連海平，海上明月共潮生。
灩灩隨波千萬里，何處春江無月明！

江流宛轉繞芳甸，月照花林皆似霰；
空里流霜不覺飛，汀上白沙看不見。

江天一色無纖塵，皎皎空中孤月輪。
江畔何人初見月？江月何年初照人？

人生代代無窮已，江月年年望相似。
不知江月待何人，但見長江送流水。

白雲一片去悠悠，青楓浦上不勝愁。
誰家今夜扁舟子？何處相思明月樓？

可憐樓上月徘徊，應照離人妝鏡台。
玉戶簾中卷不去，搗衣砧上拂還來。

此時相望不相聞，願逐月華流照君。
鴻雁長飛光不度，魚龍潛躍水成文。

昨夜閑潭夢落花，可憐春半不還家。
江水流春去欲盡，江潭落月復西斜。

斜月沉沉藏海霧，碣石瀟湘無限路。
不知乘月幾人歸，落月搖情滿江樹。

It is one of the first successful poems of its type in the Tang (old style, seven syllables per line), one which initiated a stylistic break from Six Dynasties' verse. The poem can be divided into quatrains—nine in all. Three lines of each quatrain use the same rhyme (aaxa, bbxb, etc.). There are three major sections. The first depicts the setting: the river scene and the neighboring forests under a bright moon. The second is a lament on the ephemeral nature of life with both the river waters and the moonlight representing the transitory nature of time and thus human life. The third and final section describes the sorrow of a traveler and the loved one he has left at home—seemingly referring to the poet's own situation.

The poem has appealed to modern readers because of its universal scope. In depicting wives longing for a husband away from home, Zhang presents both a glimpse of a wealthy woman gazing at the moon through her jade door and a commoner who attempts to wash away the moonlight as she pounds clothes clean. The images of the blinds and the stone are often associated with poems on this theme. In both style and content the poem anticipates aspects of High Tang poetry such as the seven-word line and the use of an extended image.

BIBLIOGRAPHY

Editions:
Quan Tang shi, 2: 1184–85.
Wang Qixing 王啟興 and Zhang Hong 張虹, eds. *He Zhizhang, Bao Rong, Zhang Xu, Zhang Ruoxu shizhu* 賀知章，包融，張旭，張若虛詩註. Shanghai: Shanghai Guji, 1986.

Translations:
Demiéville, *Anthologie*, pp. 210–11.
Margoulies, *Anthologie*, pp. 412–13.
Minford and Lau, pp. 820–23.
Wu, John. "The River by Night in Spring," *THM*, 6.4 (1938), 358.

Studies:
Chai Feifan 柴非凡. "Lun Zhang Ruoxu 'Chunjiang huayue ye'" 論張若虛春江花月夜, *Wenxue pinglun* 文學評論, November, 1975.2: 23–80.
Cheng, Francois [Chi-hsien]. *Analyse formelle de l'oeuvre poétique d'un auteur des Tang, Zhang Ruo-xu*. Paris: Mouton, 1970. An extensive linguistic-literary analysis (and translation) of both of Zhang's extant poems.
Cheng Qianfan 程千帆. "Zhang Ruoxu 'Chunjiang huayue ye' de bei lijie he bei wujie" 張若虛春江花月夜的被理解和被誤解. *Wexue pinglun* 文學評論 1982.4.
Hu Guangwei 胡光煒. "Zhang Ruoxu shiji kaolue" 張若虛事蹟考略, *Wenxue lunji* 文學論集, Shanghai, 1929.
Nakamori Kenji 中森健二. "Chō Jakuki 'Shunkō kagetsuya" 張若虛'春江花月夜'について, *Gakurin* 22 (1995): 31–55.
Wen Yiduo 聞一多. "Gongti shi de zishu" 宮體詩的自贖, *Wen Yiduo quanji* 聞一多全集, v. 3, Shanghai: Kaiming, 1948, pp. 11–22.
Wu Xiaoru 吳小如. "Shuo Zhang Ruoxu 'Chunjiang huayue ye'" 说張若虛《春江花月夜》, *Beijing Daxue xuebao (Zhexue shehui kexue ban)*, 1985:6.
Zeng Zhi'an 曾智安. "Xiqu wuqu yu Zhang Ruoxu 'Chunjiang huayue ye' de quci jiegou" 西曲舞曲與張若虛《春江花月夜》的曲辭結構. *Wenxue pinglun* 文學評論, 2008.5.

Tamotsu Satō, Po-hui Chang, and Ji Wang

Zhang Wei

Zhang Wei 張謂 (*zi*, Zhengyan 正言, ca. 711–ca. 775), was a native of Henei 河內 (modern Qinyang 沁陽 County in Henan). In his early years, he studied on Mount Song 嵩山. In the second year of the Tianbao reign (743), he passed the *jinshi* examination and joined the army, serving on the northeast border for ten years. After his commander was sacked, in 754 or 755, Zhang joined the staff of the general Feng Changqing 封常清 (d. 756) in the Protectorate Keeping Peace in the West 安西都護府.

In the autumn of 758 he was sent out as Secretarial Court Gentlemen to Xiakou 夏口 (modern Hankou 漢口 in Hubei) as Prefect. At that time, Li Bo 李白 (701–762)* stopped by Xiaokou on his way to exile in Yelang 夜郎 (in modern Guizhou). They were old friends and drank together near the south lake at Jiangcheng 江城 (modern Wuhan) which Li Bo then named "Langguan hu" 郎官湖 (The Lake of Secretarial Official). Li also wrote a poem to commemorate their meeting. Early in 765 Zhang joined the staff of Tian Shengong 田神功 (d. 774), the Military Commissioner of Huainan (based at modern Yangzhou) where became acquainted with Yuan Jie 元結 (719–772).* Yuan's "Bie Cui Man xu" 別崔曼序 (Preface on Parting with Cui Man) touches on aspects of Zhang Wei's life. In 767 or 768 Zhang was appointed Prefect of Tanzhou 譚州 (modern Shandong). A year or two later, Zhang entered the royal court as the Mentor to the Heir Apparent on the Left where he met Chang Gun 常袞 (729–783)* who was then a Scholar in the Academy of Scholarly Worthies. He was soon promoted to be the Vice Director of the Ministry of Rites and in that position supervised the *jinshi* examinations for three years beginning in 774. The last known reference to him is in a document dated 777.

Zhang gained a reputation for his verse from an early age. Six of his poems were included in the *Heyue yinglingji* 河岳英靈集 by Yin Fan 殷璠. Xin Wenfang 辛文房, the author of the *Tang caizi zhuan* 唐才子傳 (Biography of Talented Men in the Tang), praised him as follows: "Zhang's poems have precise and rigorous metrical patterns, employ concise but profound wording, and give the reader the sense of a rhythm" 格度嚴密，語致精深，多擊節之音. Zhang was often critical of official policies. "Dai Beizhou Laoweng da" 代北州老翁答 (Reply on Behalf of an Old Man in Beizhou), for example, is set in the later years of Emperor Xuanzong (r. 713–756) and exposes the harmful effect of the then warlike policies; "Du Shiyu song gongwu xizeng" 杜侍禦送貢物戲贈 (The Playful Presenting of the Tribute by the Attendant Censor Du) satirizes the corruption among officials. These poems demonstrate that he was an avatar of the *Xin Yuefu* 新樂府 (New Music Bureau) poets who flourished in the early ninth century. Zhang also wrote about his refined tastes, his sorrow while living far from his home, pleasant banquets with family and friends, and various Buddhist themes. "Tong Wang Zheng jun Xiangzhong you huai" 同王征君湘中有懷 (Sighing with Lord Wang Zheng Midst the Xiang River) is one of his representative works.

> The eighth month is Lake Dongting's autumn—
> the Xiao and Xiang rivers flow northward.
> A dream of a thousand-mile return to home,
> brings the traveler pre-dawn sorrow.
> No need to open my book box,
> best to climb up into the tavern.
> My friends fill the two capitals,
> when will I be able to join them again?

八月洞庭秋，瀟湘水北流。
還家萬里夢，為客五更愁。
不用開書帙，偏宜上酒樓。
故人京洛滿，何日復同游？

The poem begins with the persona turned to follow the rivers flowing north, gazing in the direction of the capital. In the second couplet even his dream of a return is ruptured by sorrow awakening him. With no career or friends in sight, he abandons his resolve to study and climbs to the upper floor of the wine shop where he would normally go with friends. Although this is an oft-used set of images, the simple, nearly colloquial language of the poem (especially the third couplet) distinguish it from similar verses.

The *Quan Tang shi* includes forty of his poems. *Quan Tang wen* also include eight prose works. Information about his life can also be found in Li Bo's "Fan Mianzhoucheng nan Langguan hu xu" 泛沔州城南郎官湖序 (A Preface about Roaming on the Langguan Lake South of the City Wall of Mian Prefecture) as well as Chang Gun's 常袞 (729–783)* "Shou Zhang Wei Taizi Zuoshuzi zhi" 授張謂太子左庶子制 (An Imperial Order Granting Zhang Wei the Position of Mentor to the Heir Apparent on the Left).

BIBLIOGRAPHY

Editions:
Quan Tang shi, 14: 11124.
Quan Tang wen, 375.3806–09.

Annotations:
Chen Wenhua 陳文華. *Zhang Wei shi zhu* 張謂詩注. Shanghai: Shanghai Guji, 1997.

Biographical Sources:
Fu, *Tang caizi*, 2:137–46.

Studies:
Dou Sichao 竇思超. "Tang dai shiren Zhang Wei qi ren qi shi" 唐代詩人張謂其人其詩. In *Yanjiusheng luntan 2006*. Anhui Daxue xuebao bianjibu, 2006: 31–34.
Xiong Fei 熊飛. "Tang dai shiren Zhang Wei shengping shiji kaolue" 唐代詩人張謂生平考略. *Wenxian.* 1999.3: 54–72; 1993.4: 58–68.
___. "Li Bo, Zhang Wei jiaoyou kao" 李白，張謂交遊考. In Fu Xuancong 傅璇琮. *Tangdai wenxue yanjiu* 唐代文學研究, vol. 9, pp. 279–84.

Ma Nan and William H. Nienhauser, Jr.

Zhang Yue

Zhang Yue 張說 (*zi*, Daoji 道濟 or Yuezhi 說之, posthumously Wenzhen 文貞, 667–731) was one of the most influential writers and statesmen of the first decades of the eighth century. Although his works are now somewhat eclipsed by those of the more famous poets of the succeeding generation, such as Wang Wei 王維 (692–761 or 699–759),* Li Bo 李白 (701–762),* and Du Fu 杜甫 (712–770),* he was in his day a greatly esteemed literary figure.

Zhang came from a relatively undistinguished Luoyang family (the family seat can be traced to Fanyang 范陽, near modern Beijing). He entered court circles in 689, after placing second–out of a field of more than a thousand hopefuls–in a special examination decreed by Empress Wu (r. 690–705). He was an active figure at court during most of the years of that formidable lady's reign (enduring exile in Guangdong for the final years of her sovereignty, 703–705, owing to his opposition of her persecution of the minister Wei Yuanzhong 魏元忠 [d. 707]), as well as during the reign of Zhongzong (705–710). But it was not until the accession of Ruizong (r. 684–690, restored 710–712) in 710 that he began to come to real prominence. During the first two years of this monarch's rule, Zhang held several important positions and also was put in charge of compiling the "state history" (*guoshi* 國史), this latter being a charge that he was to maintain–even through periods of subsequent rustication, military service, and official demotion–until the end of his life. It was at this time also that Zhang became a close friend and confidante of the Heir Apparent, Li Longji 李隆基 (685–762, as Xuanzong [r. 712–756]). In 712 Zhang was instrumental in convincing Ruizong of the wisdom of formally abdicating the throne in favor of his son (with whom he in fact shared authority till his own death a year later), and in 713 was perhaps the most trusted adviser of Li Longji during that monarch's successful consolidation of his sole rule: late in that year of his first as emperor, Xuanzong enfeoffed Zhang in appreciation of his meritorious services. Zhang also enjoyed a bureaucratic promotion to the prestigious post of Secretariat Director. However, Zhang was soon demoted to a series of provincial posts which took him successively to Xiangzhou 相州 (Henan), Yuezhou 岳州 (modern Yueyang in Hunan), and Jingzhou 荊州 (Hubei), and then spent several years overseeing military operations on the northeast frontier. By 723 he was restored to his former position in the Secretariat and despite a two-year forced resignation lasting from 727 to 729, was thereafter continually in Xuanzong's good graces, eventually rising to occupy the exalted office of Left Assistant Director of the Department of State Affairs (in functional terms, Secretary of State). During the last years of his life, no official was more highly honored than he. Upon his death–on February 9, 731, two days before the New Year–the sovereign declared three days of state mourning, and cancellation of the grand New Year's court levée, out of respect for the passing of his long-time minister.

As one might expect, in light of the career sketched above, many of Zhang Yue's literary works were composed on "official" occasions–royal excursions, state banquets, and the like. Besides the obligatory pendant poems written "to accord with" (*he* 和) those of a member of the imperial family or the monarch himself, Zhang was often made responsible for turning out verses to be used at solemn ceremonies of state. In 725, for instance, he was commissioned to write new lyrics for the dignified *yayue* 雅樂 (classical music) performed at court and later that year, while supervising all aspects of the imperial progress to and encampment at Mount Tai for the awesome *feng* 封 sacrifice, composed the works for the fourteen songs designed to bring down, welcome, entertain, and finally send off the divinity of Taishan during the sacred rites on the holy peak.

But works such as these constitute only a part of the 350 poems by Zhang that remain to us. Many of his best verses are found among the scores of poems written during his various assignments to the provinces. In most of these poems the literary refinement of the courtier is blended, with surprising suppleness, with the sounds and sights confronting the poet in these less aristocratic environments. While Zhang's style is even here always controlled and elegant, it often admits an attractive emotional coloring absent in the courtly verses. This is especially so in the numerous verses written in Yuezhou. Although Zhang's poems in general rarely sparkle with the unexpected, they warm one with the persistent pleasure of carefully considered diction and their mature, steady word craft. Zhang's favored form was the pentasyllabic *lüshi* 律詩, with more than a third (122) of his extant poems being in this form. Next on the scale of formal frequency are 103 ten-line poems in pentasyllabic meter, the majority of these being *pailü* 排律. But Zhang also wrote excellent jueju such as the following quatrain "Song Liang Liu zi Dongting shan" 送梁六自洞庭山 (Seeing off Liang Liu from Mount Dongting) written in Yuezhou (i.e. Baling 巴陵):

In Baling I gaze afar on Dongting's autumn scene,
each day see its lonely peak floating its waters.
I've heard about its divine immortals, but they cannot be met,
so my heart will just follow the lake waters, stretching far into the distance.

巴陵一望洞庭秋，日見孤峰水上浮。
聞道神仙不可接，心隨湖水共悠悠。

The poem was written to see off Liang Zhiwei 梁知微, the prefect of nearby Tanzhou 潭州 (modern Changsha in Hunan), who was returning to the capital. The description of the scene as one of "autumn" and the peak of the island as "lonely" reflect the poet's own emotions as he sees off a friend. The "peak" Jun Shan 君山 (Mountain of Gentlemen), in the center of Lake Dongting, had a reputation of being the seat of unearthly beings who were difficult to encounter. The intended reference is to Emperor Xuanzong whom Zhang Yue far from the capital will not be able to meet. The compound *you you* 悠悠 in the final line is ambiguous, suggesting the vast expanse of the lake's waters, its remoteness, and the drawn-out sorrow that Zhang feels at this parting. His sorrow is because he is unable to return with Prefect Liang to the capital and continue his career there. According to a story tied to this poem, Prefect Liang took the poem to show to Zhang's friends and one of them—the famous poet Su Ting 蘇頲 (670–727)*—showed it to the emperor who then recalled Zhang.

In addition to his poems, over two hundred of Zhang Yue's prose writings have been preserved. Most of these are official documents having little more than historical interest, but some–such as his preface to Shangguan Wan'er's 上官婉兒 (664–710)* collected poems, his memorial inscription for that same lady, and his account (with rhymed lauds) of nineteen auspicious phenomena encountered by Zhongzong during various outings to Luzhou 潞州 (near modern Xiangyuan County 襄垣 in Shanxi) in the years 707–709 – have great intrinsic interest.

Such was Zhang's exceptional fame and standing during his lifetime that his conception was rumored to have been attended by uncanny circumstances: one Tang source reports that he was conceived when his mother dreamed she saw a jade swallow cast itself into her bosom (the word for "swallow" is *yan* 燕, the name of the principality with which Zhang was later to be enfeoffed).

Another popular anecdote told of a magic pearl owned by Zhang: it was phosphorescent, in hue a deep purplish-blue, and, when its owner held it in his mouth, had the virtue of calling up from the depths of his memory the details of any forgotten item he wished to recall. Regardless of the veracity of such tales, it is certain that a signal mark of imperial respect and honor was forthcoming from Xuanzong following Zhang's death, namely, the bestowal of a posthumous title–Wenzhen, meaning "Cultured (more narrowly, Literary) Probity."

BIBLIOGRAPHY

Editions:
Luan Guiming 欒貴明 et al., eds. *Quan Tang shi suoyin: Chen Ziang, Zhang Yue juan* 全唐詩索引: 陳子昂，張說卷. Beijing: Zhonghua, 1997.
Quan Tang shi, 2: 914–78, 14: 10602.
Quan Tang wen, 221–33.2508–632.
Zhang Yue. *Zhang Yangong ji* 張燕公集. 25 *juan*. Beijing: Zhonghua, 1985. Typeset and punctuated reprint of edition copied into the *Siku* collection, from the Congshu lou 叢書樓 library of the famous bibliophiles Ma Yueguan 馬曰琯 (1688–1755) and Ma Yuelu 馬曰璐 (1697–1766); based on a Ming (1537) edition, but includes numerous supplemental additions. The best text.
___. *Zhang Yuezhi wenji* 張說之文集. SBCK. 25 *juan*. Shanghai: Shanghai Shudian, 1989. Facsimile of Ming (1537) woodblock. The *juan* placement of individual works differs from that of the above edition.

Annotations:
Xiong Fei 熊飛. *Zhang Yue ji jiaozhu* 張說集校注. Beijing: Zhonghua, 2013.

Biographical Sources:
Fu, *Tang caizi,* 1:130–39, 5:21.
Jiu Tang shu, 97.3049–59.
Xin Tang shu, 125.4404–15.

Translations:
Margoulies, *Anthologie,* p. 413.
Minford and Lau, pp. 696–7.
Owen, *Early T'ang,* pp. 387–413.
(see also works by Chen Zuyan below)

Studies:
Chen Zuyan 陳祖言. "Chang Yüeh: First Poet of the High Tang." *TS* 12 (1994): 1–10.
___. "Impregnable Phalanx and Splendid Chamber: Chang Yüeh's Contributions to the Poetry of the High T'ang." Unpublished Ph.D. dissertation, University of Wisconsin, 1989.
___. "Impregnable Phalanx and Splendid Chamber: Chang Yüeh and the Aesthetics of High T'ang Poetry." *CLEAR* 17 (1995): 69–88.
___. *Zhang Yue nianpu* 張說年譜. Hong Kong: Zhongwen Daxue, 1984.
Kroll, Paul W. "The Dancing Horses of Tang." *TP* 67 (1981): 240–68.
___, "On the Date of Chang Yüeh's Death." *CLEAR* 2 (1980): 264–65.

Li Jianguo 李劍國. "Zhang Yue de chuanqi kaolun" 張說的傳奇考論. *Liaoning Jiaoyu Xueyuan xuebao* 遼寧教育學院學報 4 (1985): 38–44.

Li Jun 李軍. "Lun Zhang Yue shige de yishu tezheng" 論張說詩歌的藝術特徵, *Tangdu xuekan* 6 (2011): 27–32.

Li Lingling 李玲玲. "Zhang Yue yu Chuxue ji" 張說與《初學記, *Zhongguo guji yuwenhua* 4 (2009): 101–04.

Lin Dazhi 林大志. *Su Ting, Zhang Yue yanjiu* 蘇頲張說研究. Jinan: Qi Lu Shushe, 2007.

Ono Jitsunosuke 大野實之助. "Tōdai shidan ni okeru Chō Etsu" 唐代詩壇における張說, Part I. *Chūgoku koten kenkyū* 14 (1966): 109–30; Part II. *Chūgoku koten kenkyū* 15 (1967): 119–44.

Qu Jingyi 曲景毅. "Shiguo gaochao de qianzou: Jianlun Kaiyuan qianqi Zhang Yue ji qi zhouwei de shiren qunti chuangzuo" 詩國高潮的前奏—簡論開元前期 張說及其周圍的詩人群體創作. *Wenxue yichan* 4 (2008): 50–58.

———, "Shengshi qixiang: Zhang Yue yu Su Ting" 省市氣象: 張悅與蘇頲, in Qu Jingyi, *Tangdai 'Dashou bi' zuojia yanjiu* 唐代大手筆作家研究. Beijing: Zhongguo Shehui Kexue, 2015, pp. 70–116.

Takagi Shigetoshi 高木重俊. *Chō Etsu : Gensō to tomoni kaketa bunjin saishō* 張說：玄宗とともに翔た文人宰相. Tokyo: Taishuken, 2003.

Xu Jingzhuang 徐靜莊. *Zhang Yue yu Kaiyuan wentan* 張說與開元文壇. Taibei: Huamulan Wenhua, 2011.

Yoshikawa, Kojiro 吉川幸次郎. "Chō Etsu no denki to bungaku" 張說の傳記と文學. *Tōhōgaku* 1(1951): 54–75.

Yuan Xingpei 遠行霈 and Fang Ding 丁放. *Sheng Tang shitan yanjiu* 盛唐詩壇研究. Beijing: Beijing Daxue, 2012.

Zhang Buyun 張步雲. "Lun cong chu Tang dao sheng Tang de guodu shiren Zhang Yue" 論從初唐到盛唐的過度詩人張說. *Shanghai Shifan Daxue xuebao* 41 (1989): 15–19.

Zhang Haisha 張海沙. "Lun fojiao kongguan lilun dui Zhang Yue ji qi shige de yingxiang" 論佛教空觀理論對張說及其詩歌的影響, *Wenxue yichan* 3 (2011): 41–51.

Zhou Rui 周睿. *Zhang Shuo: chu Tang jian sheng wenxue zhuanxing guanjian renwu lun* 張說：初唐漸盛文學轉型關鍵人物論. Beijing: Zhonghua, 2012.

Zou Jinxian 鄒進先 and Zhang Anzu 張安祖. "Zhang Yue dui Tangshi fazhan de gongxian" 張說對唐詩發展的貢獻. *Qiu shi xuekan* 求是學刊 3 (1991): 57–61.

Paul W. Kroll, Masha Kobzeva, and William H. Nienhauser, Jr.

Zhang Zhuo 張鷟 (*zi*, Wencheng 文成, ca. 657–730) was a native of Luze 陸澤 County of Shenzhou 深州 Prefecture (Shen County in modern southern Hebei). A precocious child, he passed the *jinshi* examination in 679. Thereupon he became Adjutant to Prince Qi 岐王, Li Zhen 李珍 (d. 761), and then successively the Commandant of Xiangle 襄樂 County of Ningzhou 寧州 Prefecture (modern Gansu), of Luoyang, and then of Chang'an 長安. His writings were compared to "coins minted in bronze" 青銅前 (i.e. precious items), and he was known to his contemporaries as the "Bronze-coin Scholar" (Qingqian Xueshi 青錢學士). But he was notorious for his volatile disposition and loose conduct, which offended many people. The Grand Councilor Yao Chong 姚崇 (651–721), in particular, had a grudge against him. About 720 he was demoted to the far South because of his criticism of the government. Later he returned to the capital, serving as the Vice Director in the Ministry of Justice just before his death.

Zhang wrote swiftly, had a genuine sense of humor, and gained widespread fame. Neighboring countries like Silla and Japan especially treasured his literary works. Their envoys often brought back Zhang's writings from China, writings for which they had exchanged gold

Zhang Zhuo

His extant corpus includes *Chaoye qianzai* 朝野僉載 (Comprehensive Records of Affairs Within and Outside of the Court, completed in 720), a *biji*-story collection, and *Longjin fengsui pan* 龍筋鳳髓判 (Dragon Sinews and Phoenix Marrow Judgments), which was a collection of judgments (*pan* 判) pronounced by local magistrates in addition to allusions that could be used in writing such judgments. The text was important because judgments were part of the Tang system of civil-service examinations.

Among Zhang's extant works there is also a tale entitled "Youxianku," 遊仙窟 (A Dalliance in the Dwelling of Goddesses) composed about 677. It was transmitted to Japan during the Tang dynasty, but never recorded in Chinese sources. The edition transmitted to Japan contains an epigraph which reads says it was written by Zhang Wencheng, Commandant of Xiangle. From this it can be inferred that the work was written by Zhang Zhuo in his youth. It was not until the late Qing, when Yang Shoujing 楊守敬 (1839–1915) wrote *Riben fangshu zhi* 日本訪書志 (Records of a Search for Books in Japan) that the title "Youxianku" was first recorded in China. "Youxianku" was highly valued in Japan, where annotations were compiled for it quite early.

The story is narrated in the first person. The persona, Zhang Wencheng, en route to Heyuan 河源 (modern Guangdong) on an official mission seeks lodging one night in a large mansion. There he meets two women: Shiniang 十娘, a young widow, and her sister-in-law, Wusao 五嫂. Wencheng and the two women then entertain themselves with sumptuous banquets. They also compose poems and flirt with one another. Wencheng spends the night in Shiniang's chamber and then departs. The story line is very simple. It is written in parallel prose, interspersed with some Tang colloquialisms. The ending lines of "Youxianku" are considered a tour de force of parallel prose:

> That night [after parting] troubles won't allow me to sleep; In my heart I feel utterly alone, no one to rely on.
> Saddened by the cries of apes sadden me, All the more grief in the song of a parting swan.
> Choking down sobs and muffling my voice; the Way of Heaven, the emotions of men!
> How short the past days seem! How long the coming days will be!
> Like a flatfish separated from its mate, Or a mandarin duck that's lost its companion;
> Every day my clothes grow baggier, Every morning my belt is looser.
> My lips crack, My chest fills with anguish,
> Tears stream endlessly down my cheeks, My sorrowful heart broken in infinite pieces.
> I sit up, place my zither before me, As tears of blood flow onto my collar.
> A thousand longings one after another; A hundred worries mix within.
> My sad visage will never change, I hug my knees and heave a long sigh.
> I strain to see the goddesses but cannot, Heaven and earth must understand my heart.
> I long to reach the goddesses, but cannot, Seeking Shiniang, all word cut off.
> Hoping to hear something, my insides tremble, More see something, my mind awhirl.

夜耿耿而不寐，心煢煢而靡托。
既悵恨於啼猿，又淒傷於別鵠。
飲氣吞聲；天道人情。
有別必怨，有怨必盈。
去日一何短，來宵一何長！
比目絕對，雙鳧失伴，
日日衣寬，朝朝帶緩。

口上唇裂，胸間氣滿，
淚臉千行，愁腸寸斷。
端坐橫琴，涕血流襟，
千思競起，百慮交侵。
獨顰眉而永結，空抱膝而長吟。
望神仙兮不可見，普天地兮知余心；
思神仙兮不可得，覓十娘兮斷知聞；
欲聞此兮腸亦亂，更見此兮惱余心。

According to a legend which circulated in Japan, Zhang Zhuo was handsome and licentious. He composed the "Youxianku" to win Empress Wu Zetian's attention. But in the *Taiping guangji* (*juan* 255, "Zhang Zhuo") there is a satirical song written by Zhang which criticizes Empress Wu, undermining the Japanese legend.

BIBLIOGRAPHY

Editions:
Fang Shiming 方詩銘, ed. and comm. *Youxianku* 遊仙窟. Shanghai: Gudian Wenxue, 1955.
Hayasi Nozomu 林望, coll. *Yūsenkutsu shō* 遊仙窟鈔. 2v. Tokyo: Benseisha, 1981. A reprint of the 5v. Genroku 元禄 edition in 1690. Appends a comparison chart of the Genroku edition and the Edo Shoki Mukankibon edition.
Huang Chengxuan 黃承玄, Shen Dexian 沈德先, ed. *Chaoye qianzai* 朝野僉載. 6v. Taibei: Yiwen, 1965.
Kawashima 川島 [Zhang Tingqian 章廷謙], ed. and comm. Preface by Lu Xun 魯迅. *Youxianku* 遊仙窟. Shanghai: Beixin, 1929.
Kuranaka Susumu 蔵中進, ed. *Edo shoki mukankibon Yūsenkutsu: honbun to sakuin* 江戶初期無刊記本遊仙窟本文と索引. Osaka: Izumi, 1979.
Li Haowei 李豪偉, comm. *Yūsenkutsu genten* 遊仙窟原典. Yokohama: s.n., 1965.
Liu Yunpeng 劉允鵬, comm. *Longjin fengsui pan* 龍筋鳳髓判. Taibei: Taiwan Shangwu, 1983. *SKCS* edition
___, Chen Chun 陳春 comm. *Longjin fengsui pan* 龍筋鳳髓判. Beijing: Zhonghua, 1985.
Quan Tang shi, 1: 556.
Quan Tang wen, 172–74.1993–2029.
Wang Pijiang 汪辟疆, ed and comm. *Tangren xiaoshuo* 唐人小說, Shanghai: Shanghai Guji, 1978, pp. 19–36.
Yang Yifan 楊一凡, Xu Lizhi 徐立志, ed. "Longjin fengsui pan" 龍筋鳳髓判 in *Lidai panli pandu* 歷代判例判牘. 12v. Beijing: Zhongguo Shehui Kexue, 2005.
Yūsenkutsu 遊仙窟. Tokyo: Koten Hozonkai, 1927. A photocopy of the Daigoji 醍醐寺 manuscript in 1344.
Yūsenkutsu 遊仙窟. Tokyo: Kichō Kotenseki Kankōkai, 1954. A photocopy of the Shinpukuji 真福寺 manuscript in 1353.

Annotations:
Li Shiren 李時人, Zhan Xuzuo 詹緒左, eds. *Youxianku jiaozhu* 遊仙窟校注. Beijing: Zhonghua, 2010.

Biographical Sources:
Da Tang xinyu, 8.128.
Jiu Tang shu, 149.4023–26 ; *Xin Tang shu*, 161.4979–82.

Zhang Zhuo

Translations:

Fujiwara Hidefusa 藤原英房. *Yūsenkutsu* 遊仙窟. Published by Nakano Tarō Saemon 中野太郎左衛門, 1652.

Fukuda Minoru 福田稔. *Yūsenkutsu* 遊仙窟. Tokyo: Kyūko, 1989.

Imamura Yoshio 今村与志雄. *Yūsenkutsu* 遊仙窟. Tokyo: Iwanami, 1990.

Levy, Howard S. *The Dwelling of Playful Goddesses*. 2v. Tokyo: Dai Nippon Insatsu, 1965.

Maeno Naoaki 前野直彬. "Yūsenkutsu" 遊仙窟 in *Yūmeiroku, Yūsenkutsu hoka* 幽明錄/遊仙窟他. Tokyo: Heibon sha, 2007.

Ogaeri Yoshio 魚返善雄. *Kanyaku Yūsenkutsu* 完訳遊仙窟. Tokyo: Soku, 1948.

Rouzer, Paul. "A Dalliance in the Immortals' Den," in *Articulated Ladies*, pp. 313–354.

Urushiyama Matashirō 漆山又四郎. *Yūsenkutsu 313* 遊仙窟. Tokyo: Iwanami, 1949.

Yagisawa Hajime 八木沢元. *Yūsenkutsu zenkō* 遊仙窟全講. Tokyo: Meiji, 1967

Studies:

Egan, Ronald. "On the Origin of the *Yu hsien k'u* Commentary," *HJAS*, 36 (1976): 135–46.

Fukuda Toshiaki 福田俊昭. *Chōya sensai no honbun kenkyū: fu jimokuki kō* 朝野僉載の本文研究: 付耳目記考. Tokyo: Daito Bunka Daigaku, 2001.

Hirai Hidefumi 平井秀文. "Keichū to *Yūsenkutsu* kun" 契沖と「遊仙窟」訓, *Nihon bungaku kenkyū* 19 (1983.11): 205–13.

Huo Cunfu 霍存福. "*Longjin fengsui pan* panmu poyi" 龍筋鳳髓判判目破譯, *Jilin Daxue shehui kexue xuebao*, 1998.2: 19–27.

Kinugawa Kenji 衣川賢次. "*Yūsenkutsu* kyūchū kōdoku ki" 遊仙窟旧注校読記, *Hanazono Daigaku Bungakubu kenkyū kiyō* 27 (1995.3): 97–144, 28 (1996.3): 89–111, 29 (1997.3): 19–46.

Kondō Haruo 近藤春雄 (1914–2014). "*Yūsenkutsu* ni tsuite" 遊仙窟について, *Aichi Kenritsu Joshi Tanki Daigaku kiyō* 5 (1954): 34–54.

Li Shiren 李時人 and Zhan Xuzuo 詹绪左. "*Youxianku* de riben guchaoben he gukanben" 遊仙窟的日本古鈔本和古刊本, *Shanghai Shifan Daxue xuebao* 2006.3: 47–53.

Liu Zhenlun 劉真倫. "Zhang Zhuo shiji xinian kao" 張鷟事跡系年考, *Chongqing Shifan Daxue xuebao*, 1987.4: 83–88.

Okuno Shintarō 奧野信太郎. "Shinpukujibon *Yūsenkutsu* kokanki" 眞福寺本遊仙窟考勘記, *Shigaku* 14 (1936.3): 117–51.

Qian, Tony D. "Classical Learning and the Law: Erudition as Persuasion in the *Dragon Sinews, Phoenix Marrow Judgments* of Zhuang Zhuo," *Tang Studies*, 35 (2017): 20–50.

Shiraki Naoya 白木直也. "*Yūsenkutsu* chūinsho kō" 遊仙窟註引書考, *Hiroshima Daigaku Bungakubu kiyō* 2 (1952.3): 118–134.

___. "*Yūsenkutsu* ni tsuite" 遊仙窟について, *Shina gaku kenkyū* 6 (1950.10): 17–48.

Tan Shujuan 譚淑娟. "Guanyu Zhang Zhuo *Longjin fengsui pan* wenfeng wenti de tantao" 關於張鷟龍筋鳳髓判文風問題的探討 *Jianghai xuekan*, 2010.3: 182–87.

Utsunomiya Mutsuo 宇都宮睦男. "Seigidō bunkobon *Yūsenkutsu* no honbun to kunten" 成簣堂文庫本遊仙窟の本文と訓点, *Kuntengo to kunten shiryō* 53 (1973.8): 33–63.

Waley, Arthur. "Colloquial in the *Yu-hsien k'u*," *Bulletin of the School of Oriental and African Studies*, 29, (1966.3): 559–65.

Wang Zhonghan. "The Authorship of the *Yu-Hsien-K'u*," *HJAS*, 11(1948): 153–62.

Yu Tianchi 于天池. "Yingyin 'Youxianku chao tiji'" 影印遊仙窟鈔題記, *Beijing Shifan Daxue xuebao* 1992.6: 109–11.

Yu Weina 于偉娜. "Zhang Zhuo xiaoshuo de shenmei tezheng" 張鷟小説的審美特徵, *Shehui kexue luntan*, 2006.8: 176–79.

Zhang Zhejun 張哲俊. "*Youxianku* yu zhongri wenxue meixue tezhi" 遊仙窟與中日文學美學特質, *Guowai wenxue* 1998.3: 115–19.

Zhao Jinming 趙金銘. "*Youxianku* yu tangdai kouyu yufa" 遊仙窟與唐代口語語法, *Yuyan yanjiu* 1995.1: 89–100.

Zhan Ying and William H. Nienhauser, Jr.

Zhao Gu 趙嘏 (*zi*, Chengyou 承祐, ca. 806–ca. 850) was a poet renowned for both his seven-syllable and five-syllable poems that exemplified the style of his day. He is most remembered for the line, "one note from a long flute, someone leaning from the tower" 長笛一聲人倚樓 which evokes such a strong sense of loneliness. The line appears in his seven-syllable regulated poem, "Chang'an qiuwang" 長安秋望 (Gazing Far from Chang'an in Autumn) and the image of a solitary person "leaning from a tower" (*yilou* 倚樓), would become a literary sobriquet for Zhao Gu after Du Mu 杜牧 (803–852)* dubbed him "Zhao Yilou" 趙倚樓.

Zhao Gu was a native of Shanyang 山陽, Chuzhou 楚州 (modern Huaiyin 淮陰 City in Jiangsu), but would travel extensively throughout the realm. As a young man he went north to the Great Wall, and then traveled south to join the literary circle of Yuan Zhen 元稹 (779–831),* who was serving as Surveillance Commissioner of Zhedong 浙東 (the southern part of modern Zhejiang). There he lingered for several years mingling with literati until Yuan Zhen transferred to a post in Xuancheng 宣城 (modern Xuancheng in Anhui). Sometime around 832, Zhao Gu then joined the service of Shen Chuanshi 沈傳師 (777–835), the Surveillance Commissioner of Jiangxi 江西 (in parts of modern Anhui, modern Jiangxi and Hunan). It was during this time that Zhao Gu became acquainted with several poets in the service of Shen Chuanshi, including Du Mu. Zhao Gu would leave Shen for Chang'an to sit the *jinshi* examination for the first time but would not meet with initial success. He then stayed in Chang'an for the next several years before traveling to Xunzhou 循州 (modern Huizhou 惠州 in Guangdong). Zhao Gu returned to the capital in 844 to once again take the examinations and this time meet with success. He would then spend his time travelling between Zhexi 浙西 (modern Zhenjiang 鎮江 in Jiangsu) and the capital. Sometime around 852, Zhao Gu entered officialdom, serving as a Commandant in Weinan 渭南 County (Shaanxi), marking the apex of his official career. He died sometime soon after taking the post.

More than 260 of Zhao's poems survive, as well as several unfinished extant works, including an incomplete collection of heptasyllabic regulated verse, the *Biannian shi* 編年詩, which was found at Dunhuang. Much of the attention to Zhao's poetry has focused on his seven-syllable regulated verse, though his extant corpus includes more than fifty pentasyllabic poems.

"Chang'an wang qiu" 長安望秋 (Gazing at Autumn in Chang'an) is his most famous poem:

> Clouds and fog cool and clear, sweep the currents in the dawn,
> Palace towers of the Han touch the high autumn sky.
> The remaining stars—several dots, wild geese cross the pass,
> A long flute, a single note—someone leans from the tower.
> Purple voluptuousness of opening chrysanthemums by the hedge are stilled;
> Their red jackets fallen away, lotuses on the islets are saddened.

The perch are in their prime, but I do not go back,
Vainly, I wear a southern cap, following the example of the Chu prisoner.

雲霧淒清拂曙流，漢家宮闕動高秋。
殘星幾點雁橫塞，長笛一聲人倚樓。
紫豔半開籬菊靜，紅衣落儘渚蓮愁。
鱸魚正美不歸去，空戴南冠學楚囚。

Written sometime during 833 after his failed attempt to pass the *jinshi*, "Chang'an wang qiu" opens with a autumn dawn breaking over the capital, as the edifice of the imperial palace rises to meet the glowing sky. The quiet fading remnant of the night sky is juxtaposed to the rush of wild geese tearing through the morning light. The loneliness of the scene is punctuated by the single note from a long flute played by a solitary figure leaning from a tower. Beautiful flowers lose their petals as a matter of course, and the changing season moves on regardless. Feelings of bitterness mix with homesickness in the allusions that fill the final lines, as the taste of perch calls the poet to leave his ambitions at the capital and return home, evoking the image of Zhang Han 張翰 from the *Shishuo xinyu* 世說新語 (A New Account of Tales of the World), who would resign his post because he missed the taste of *gu* 菰 (wild-rice shoot) soup. But unlike the classic example, Zhao Gu does not go back. Likewise, the last line alludes to the example of Zhong Yi 鍾儀 in the *Zuozhuan*, who still wore the southern-style cap of his home in Chu even after he had been a prisoner in the state of Jin 晉 for two years. The final line, with its reference to Zhong Yi's imprisonment, reinforces the helplessness of the poet as he looks out onto the coming of a new day in an unforgiving city far from home.

Zhao Gu is often appraised by modern critics as a "typical" poet of the late Tang. His poetry evinces a subtle sense that allows him to connect images of the natural world to human emotions (in particular, sentimentality and nostalgia), which are conveyed in the refined antithesis between his lines, as well as in the metrical patterns of his regulated verse and quatrains. While for some modern critics, this sort of delicate style puts Zhao Gu closer to the larger group of poets who wrote during last years of the Tang dynasty. His mastery of wider subjects also pigeon-hole him as typical of this group. However, a review of his corpus reveals several scenes of the northern frontier (such as in "Xiang Lu" 降虜 [Vanquish the Catiffs] and "Ping Rong" 平戎 [Suppress the Barbarians]), that harken back to classical frontier poetry and are filled with the images of his days traveling as young man along the border. In this sense, Zhao Gu's life and work go beyond what was typical or his era.

BIBLIOGRAPHY

Editions:
Quan Tang shi, 9: 6383–438.
Xu Jun 徐俊, *Dunhuang shiji canjuan ji kao* 敦煌詩集殘卷輯考 (Compilation and Collation of Incomplete Poetry Collection in Dunhuang Manuscripts). Beijing: Zhonghua, 2000, pp. 522–34.

Annotations:

Tan Youxue 譚優學. *Zhao Gu shi zhu* 趙嘏詩注 (Annotation of Zhao Gu's Poems). Shanghai: Shanghai Guji, 1985.

Biographical Sources:

Fu, *Tang caizi*, 3: 297–308.
Tang zhi yan, 3.32, 7.80, 11.123, 15.163.

Translations:

Owen, *Late Tang*, pp. 243–47.

Studies:

Zha Pingqiu 查屏球. "'Zhao Yilou,' 'yidi feng' yu chanzong yuyan" "趙倚樓," "一笛風"與禪宗語言, *Wenxue yichan* 2007.4: 33-40.

Yixuan Cai and Michael E. Naparstek

Zhu Kejiu 朱可久 (*zi*, Qingyu 慶餘, generally known by his *zi*; fl. 826), was a native of Yuezhou 越 (in modern Shaoxing 紹興 County about thirty miles southeast of Hangzhou in Zhejiang). Zhu established his literary reputation largely through a poem in a letter recommending himself to Zhang Ji 張籍 (ca. 776–829),* an influential official in charge of the imperial examination during the reign of Emperor Mu (r. 820–824) and Emperor Jing (r. 824–826). Zhang liked his poem, partly because of their similar tastes and styles, and began to lionize him. Carrying a copy of twenty-six of Zhu's poems and showing them to others, Zhang started a fad among literati to transcribe Zhu's poems or to compose responding pieces. Owing to Zhang's reputation and praise, Zhu Qingyu passed the *jinshi* examination in 826 and returned to his hometown to wait for an official appointment. Before Zhu left, his friends like Jia Dao 賈島 (779–843),* Yao He 姚合 (ca. 779–849),* and Zhang Ji made him farewell presents of many poems. In replying to them, Zhu demonstrated his unmatchable talent in composing responding poems. Four years later, Zhu was awarded a position as an Editor in the Palace Library. Later he was Director of the Bureau of Waterways and Irrigation.

Unlike most of his peers, Zhu showed little enthusiasm in officialdom or politics. Of his more than 160 extant poems none concerned political affairs or his life as an official. The next known position Zhu occupied was as Chief Musician in the Imperial Music Office, again only a minor functionary. His pursuit of inner peace and adherence to personal values at times conflicted with his official career.

Zhu spent most of his life in different provinces and administrative exile. Local landscapes and historical sites served as subjects for many of his poems. Through them, one can map out his vast footprint in China, from the frontier fortresses and deserts in modern Gansu to the scenic southeastern provinces—a vagrant life destined to be accompanied by endless parting from close friends. Therefore many of his better works, circulated among his friends, were *chouda* 酬答 (companion pieces or answers) for friends who came to see him off.

Zhu Kejiu

Zhu was adept at composing classical poems in two verse forms, *qijue* 七絕 (regulated poems in four lines of seven syllables each) and *wulü* 五律 (regulated poems in eight lines of five syllables each). He is famous for his innovative use of metaphor and a style that has been considered austere and archaic. The following poem, "*Jinshi* shang Zhang Shuibu" 近試上張水部 (Submitted to Vice-minister Zhang of the Ministry of Water as the Imperial Examination Approaches), is Zhu's best-known work. The poem is thought to have been written before Zhu took the imperial examinations to win the attention of Chief Examiner, Zhang Ji. The persona depicted in this poem is a bride who is similarly worried about the impression she will give when she visits the bridegroom's parents. The language here is almost colloquial, which grants the whole poem a less refined style that is closer to the *guti* 古体 (ancient style) popularized during the Jin dynasty (265-420). "Whisper" (*di sheng* 低聲) in line three vividly depicts both the bride's nervousness and that of Zhu Qingyu himself. In the final line, Zhu utilized his persona to suggest his own uncertainty about whether his literary talents will impress his readers.

> Last night red candles were placed in the nuptial chamber,
> Early morning, I pay a visit to my parents-in-law before the hall.
> Touching up my face I whisper to my husband,
> "Have I painted my brows too dark to seem fashionable?"

> 洞房昨夜停紅燭，待曉堂前拜舅姑。
> 粧罷低聲問夫婿，畫眉深淺入時無。

While it is possible this poem helped Zhu find success in the *jinshi* examination, it is more likely that Zhang Ji's support, as noted above, launched his career such as it was.

BIBLIOGRAPHY

Editions:
Quan Tang shi, 8: 5906–36.

Annotations:
Chen Yixin 陳貽焮 et al., eds. *Zengding zhushi Quan Tang shi* 增訂注釋全唐詩, *juan* 507–8, vol. 3. Beijing: Wenhua Yishu, 2007, pp.1193–1211.
Ji Yougong 计有功 (fl. 1121), Wang Zhongyong 王仲镛 annotated, *Tangshi jishi jiaojian* 唐詩紀事校箋. Chengdu: Ba Shu, 1989, pp. 1256–57.

Biographical Sources:
Fu, *Tang caizi*, 3:189–91.

Translations:
Xu Yuanchong 許淵沖. *Tangshi sanbaishou xinyi* 唐詩三百首新譯. Beijing: Zhongguo Duiwai Fanyi, 1988, pp. 310–11.

Studies:

Fan Shu 范攄 (fl. 877). "Guifu ge" 閨婦歌, *Yunxi youyi* 雲溪友議, vol. 3. Huzhou: Jiayetang 嘉业堂. pp. 154–55.

Guo Yufeng 郭育峰, "Zhu Qingyu shige yanjiu" 朱慶餘詩歌研究. M.A. thesis. Xinjiang Normal University (Ürümchi), 2006.

Ren Dawei 任大偉. "Zhu Qingyu kaolun" 朱慶餘考論. M.A. thesis. Huadong Normal University (Wuhan), 2013.

Xu Song 徐松 (1781–1848). *Dengke jikao* 登科記考, *juan* 20. *Xuxiu Siku quanshu* 續修四庫全書, vol. 829. Shanghai: Shanghai Guji, 2002, p. 323.

Ji Wang

Appendix I: Official Titles and Ranks

The Tang administration would become the model upon which all succeeding dynasties would aspire to structure their governments. In so doing, as Charles Hucker notes in his introduction to the dynasty's governmental organization, the Tang "created a bewildering confusion of systems of official nomenclature." This Appendix is designed to serve as a reference for the official titles of many Tang literati who appear in this volume.

The Tang central government employed the Nine Rank (Jiupin 九品) system that had been the established administrative hierarchy for organizing officialdom since the end of the Han. Ranks were grouped into three tiers: upper (1–3), middle (4–6), and lower (7–9). Each rank was further delineated by an upper grade (a) and a lower grade (b) designation. Each rise in rank came with increased authority within the bureaucracy, as well as the material benefit of a commensurate increased salary indicated in bushels. Ranking Official Titles are denoted here in the second table using the convention of number indicating rank followed by the letter of grade. For example Director of the Palace Library 3b (Bishu Jian 秘書監 3b, i.e., Third-rank, lower grade).

For many, entrance into official posts came by way of the imperial examination system. Central and regional exams were administered throughout the empire on a regular basis and would provide those with the requisite aptitude (or family connections) the chance to prove themselves worthy of government service. The most prestigious exam was the *jinshi* (進士, which serves as the eponymous degree conferred) held at the capital, where roughly 1–2% of the entrants would pass. However, there were several other levels of examinations that would qualify literati for service in the central government or in the provinces. Likewise, the Directorate of Education oversaw different academies that were formed to prepare entrants for the various levels, each one administering to sons of different social strata and official status. The School for the Sons of State (Guozi xue 國子學) administered to sons of officials from the third rank or above. The National University (Taixue 太學) was open to sons of officials who ranked in the fifth degree or above, while the School of the Four Gates (Simen xue 四門學) admitted sons of official from the seventh rank and above, as well as commoners.

According to Hucker the main administrative branches of the central government were the "Three Departments" (Sansheng 三省): The Department of State Affairs (Shangshu Sheng 尚書省), the Chancellery (Menxia Sheng 門下省), and the Secretariat (Zhongshu Sheng 中書省). The Chancellery and the Secretariat shared the duties of facilitating and preserving records and communications within the bureaucracy. Much of the daily administrative duties fell to the Department of State Affairs, which had its own hierarchy of Directors (Ling 令) and Vice-Directors (Puye 僕射), who in turn presided over Six Ministries (Liubu 六部) that was headed by a Minister (Shangshu 尚書). The Ministries themselves were further broken into Bureaus (Si 司), each of which had their own Director (Langzhong 郎中), who oversaw a bureaucracy that would include a plethora of further divisions and titles to govern them. In addition to the "Three Departments", the Palace Censorate (Yushi Tai 御史臺), which was responsible for overseeing the conduct of court officials in the execution of their duties, became a powerful administrative force. Likewise, the Garrison Military (Fubing 府兵), with its own administrative organization, remained an ever-powerful political presence throughout the dynasty.

Appendix I: Official Titles and Ranks

Beyond the central government, the governance of the territories and provinces was likewise broken down into several administrative units, generally broken down by size: the largest unit was a Prefecture (Zhou 州) headed by a Prefect (Cishi 刺史), and the smallest unit was a District (Xian 縣) headed by a Magistrate (Ling 令). In turn, these units, along with Defense Commands (Zhen 鎮) and distinct functionary units such as the Salt Monopoly (Yantie 鹽鐵), each had Commissioners (Shi 使) to oversee operations, who were supported by an extensive localized bureaucracy of official serving distinct administrative roles.

For many of the figures in this volume, it was in these local administrative roles far away from home that they first began their official careers, while the highest political goal remained a position in the central government. Rising to such prestige often meant navigating an increasingly complex bureaucracy, moving across administrative units as one's career rises and falls with the temper of the times. The following Lists of Official Titles and Ranks are appended here with the intent of aiding the reader as a reference for the various titles and positions one finds in the biographies of literati within this volume. For readability, official titles mentioned within an entry only appear in translation. The first two tables appended here give both the English and Chinese (both in Pinyin and in Chinese characters) terms for all the official titles that appear in this volume. The first table list is organized alphabetically by English and the second table is organized alphabetically by Pinyin. In most cases, we have relied on Charles Hucker's work for the translations.

Official Titles, Alphabetized by English Translation

Academician in the Academy of Scholarly Worthies	Jixian Dian Xueshi 集賢殿學士
Academician in the Four Gates of the National University	Guozijian Simen Boshi 國子監四門博士
Academician in the Institute for the Cultivation of Literature	Xiuwenguan xueshi 修文館學士
Academician of the Institute for the Veneration of Literature	Chongwenguan xueshi 崇文館學士
Acting (temporary role in the position)	Jianjiao 檢校
Adjutant	Canjun 參軍
Adjutant in the Office of the Crown Prince's Bodyguard	Younei Shuifu Bingcao Canjun 右內率府兵曹參軍
Adjutant Left Militant Guard in the Military Service Section (of the Palace)	Zuo Wuwei Bingcao Canjun 左武衛兵曹參軍
Administrative Aide	Biejia 別駕
Administrative Assistant	Panguan 判官
Administrator (of a major prefecture), or Governor (of major metropolitan area)	Yin 尹
Administrator for Law Enforcement	Dali Sifa 大理司法
Administrator of the Princely Establishment of Qin	Qinfu canjun 秦府參軍
Advisor to the Heir Apparent	Taizi Binke 太子賓客
Aide to Chamberlain for Ceremonials	Taichang cheng 太常丞
Aide to Royal Scribe in the Palace	Dianzhong cheng yushi 殿中丞御史
Aide to the Court of the Imperial Treasury	Taifushi cheng 太府寺丞
Assistant Agriculture Commissioner	Yingtian fushi 營田副使
Assistant Editorial Director	Zhuzuo zuolang 著作佐郎
Assistant in the Palace Library	Bishu Lang 秘書郎
Assistant Magistrate	Cheng 承
Assistant Military Training Commissioner	Du Tuanlian fushi 都團練副使
Attendant Censor	Shi Yushi 侍御史
Attendant Censor Auxiliary	Shiyushi nei gongfeng 侍禦史內供奉
Attendant Gentleman of the Secretariat	Shu Shilang 書侍郎
Auxiliary Academician	Zhixue shi 直學士
Bibliographer of the Imperial Library	Tushu Shi 圖書使
Bureau of Honors	Sifeng 司封司
Bureau of Review	Bibu Si 比部司
Bureau of Sacrifices	Cibu 祠部
Bureau of Waterways and Irrigation	Shuibu 水部

Appendix I: Official Titles, English

Cavalier Attendant-in-ordinary	Sanji changshi 散騎常侍
Censor-in-chief	Yushi dafu 御史大夫
Censorate	Yushi 御史
Chancellor of the National University	Guozi Jijiu 國子祭酒
Chief Clerk	Zhangshi 長史
Chief Scribe	Chang shi 長史
Chief Secretary	Zhangshuji 掌書記
Chief Secretary of the Office of the Army Commander	Junmufu zhangshuji 軍幕府掌書記
Collator for the Heir Apparent	Taizi jiaoshu 太子校書
College of Scholarly Worthies	Jixianyuan 集賢院
Commandant	Wei 尉
Commandant of the Heir Apparent's Guard Command	Leigeng Ling 率更令
Commissioner Councilor	Shixiang 使相
Consort of Shining Countenance	Zhaorong 照容
Controller General	Tongpan 通判
Court Gentleman for Ceremonials	Fengli lang 奉禮郎
Court of Imperial Entertainments	Guanglusi 光祿寺
Defender-in-Chief	Taiwei 太尉
Department of Drafting Proclamations	Zhigao 制誥
Department of Worthy and Excellent, Straightforward and Upright	Xianliang fangzheng ke 賢良方正科
Director (of a Bureau)	Langzhong 郎中
Director of Astrologers	Taishi ling 太史令
Director of Bureau of Operations	Zhifang Langzhong 職方郎中
Director of Evaluations	Kaogong Langzhong 考功郎中
Director of Ministry of Rites	Libu Langzhong 禮部郎中
Director of Ministry of Works	Gongbu Langzhong 工部郎中
Director of Studies	Siye 司業
Director of Studies in the National University	Guozi siye 國子司業
Director of the Bureau of Receptions	Zhuke langzhong 主客郎中
Director of the Bureau of Waterways and Irrigation	Shuibu Langzhong 水部郎中
Director of the Crown Prince's Palace	Chungong langzhong 春宮郎中
Director of the Ministry of Personnel	Libu Langzhong 吏部郎中
Director of the Ministry of Revenue	Hubu Langzhong 戶部郎中
Director of the Palace Library	Bishu Jian 秘書監
Directorate of Education	Guozi jian 國子監
District Baron	Xiannan 縣男

497

Appendix I: Official Titles, English

District Defender	Xianwei 縣尉
District Viscount	Xianzi 縣子
Edict Attendant	Daizhi 待制
Editor	Jiaoshulang 校書郎
Editorial Director	Zhuzuo zuolang 著作郎
Editorial Director of Collating Books in the Palace Library	Bishusheng Zhuzuolang 秘書省著作郎
Erudite in the Institute for the Extension of Literary Arts	Guangwen Guan Boshi 廣文館博士
Erudite Literatus	Boxue Hongci 博學宏辭
Erudite Literatus Examination	Boxue Hongci ke 博學宏詞科
Erudite of Imperial Sacrifices	Taichang boshi 太常博士
Erudite of the National University	Guozi Boshi 國子博士
Examination for Divine Lads	Shentong 神童
Examiner	Zhusi 主司
Female Editor	Nüshulang 女書郎
Field Office	Mufu 幕府
Gentleman Collating Books in the Palace Library	Bishusheng Jiaoshulang 秘書省校書郎
Gentleman in Charge of Collating Books for the Heir Apparent	Taizi Jiaoshulang 太子校書郎
Grand Academician in the Academy of Scholarly Worthies	Jixian Dian daxueshi 集賢殿大學士
Grand Councilor	Zaixiang 宰相
Grand Guardian of the Heir Apparent	Taizi shaobao 太子少保
Grand Master of Remonstrance	Jianyi Dafu 諫議大夫
Grand Master of Remonstrance	Yushi Zhuojianyi dafu 御史擢諫議大夫
Grand Preceptor of the Heir Apparent	Taizi shaoshi 太子少師
Great Supplicator	Taizhu 太祝
Hall for Extending Literary Arts	Guangwen dian 廣文殿
Hanlin Scholar	Hanlin Xueshi 翰林學士
Historiography Institute	Shiguan 史館
Household Administration of the Heir Apparent	Zhanshi fu 詹事府
Imperial Diarist	Qiju Lang 起居郎
Imperial Diarist	Qiju Sheren 起居舍人
Imperial Music Office	Taiyue An 太樂案
Institute of Literary Attendants	Wenxue zhiguan 文學直館
Institute for the Advancement of Literature (formerly Institute of Education 文學館)	Hongwen guan 弘文館

Appendix I: Official Titles, English

Institute of Education	Wenxue guan 文學館
Instructor	Zhujiao 助教
Instructor in the Four Gates of the National University	Guozi Jian Simen Zhujiao 國子監四門助教
Investigating Censor	Jiancha Yushi 監察御史
Investigation Commissioner	Caifang shi 採訪使
Jointly Manager of Affairs with the Secretariat-Chancellery	Tong Pingzhang Shi 同平章事
Jointly Manager of Affairs with the Secretariat-Chancellery	Tong Zhongshu Menxia Pingzhangshi 同中書門下平章事
Judicial Administrator	Sifa canjun 司法參軍
Left Office of State Affairs	Zuosi 左司
Left Rectifier of Omissions	Zuo Buque 左補闕
Left Vice Director of the Dept. of State Affairs	Zuo Puye 左僕射
Libationer or Chancellor (in the Guozijian)	Jijiu 祭酒
Literary Institute	Wenguan 文館
Magistrate	Ling 令
Manager of Affairs	Pingzhang shi 平章事
Mentor to the Heir Apparent on the Left	Taizi Zuoshu lang 太子左庶郎
Metropolitan Governor	Jingzhao Yin 京兆尹
Military Commissioner	Jiedushi 節度使
Military Director of the Criminal Administrator Bureau	Duguan langzhong 都官郎中
Minister of Ministry of Rites	Libu Shangshu 禮部尚書
Minister of Rites	Da Sili 大司禮
Minister of the Ministry of Revenue	Hubu Shangshu 戶部尚書
Minister of Works	Sikong 司空
Ministry of Justice	Xingbu 刑部
Ministry of Revenue	Hubu 戶部
Ministry of Rites	Libu 禮部
Music Office	Jiaofang 教坊
Nine Classics Examination	Jiujing 九經
Palace Attendant	Nei shifeng 內室奉
Palace Bursary	Dafu Si 大府寺
Palace Censor	Dianzhong yushi 殿中御史
Palace Discipline Service	Yiting 掖庭
Palace School	Xiyi guan 習藝館
Participant in the Drafting of Proclamations	Zhizhigao 知制誥
Personnel Evaluator	Gongcao 公曹

499

Appendix I: Official Titles, English

Personnel Management Administrator	Sigong canjun 司功參軍
Prefect	Cishi 刺史
Prefectural Secretary	Jiedu zhangshuji 節度掌書記
Present Scholar Examination	Jin shi 進士
Proofreader	Zhengzi 正字
Proofreader in the Imperial Library	Xianshu Quexia 獻書卻下
Proofreader in the Palace Library	Lintai Zhengzi 麟台正字
Proofreader in the Secretariat of the Heir Apparent	Taizi zhengzi 太子正字
Reader-in-Waiting	Shidu 侍讀
Reader-in-Waiting of the Heir Apparent	Taizi shidu 太子侍讀
Recorder	Zhubu 主簿
Recorder Keeper	Jishi 記室
Rectifier	Zhongzheng 中正
Rectifier in the Court of Judicial Rule	Dalisi Sizhi, 大理寺司直
Regent	Liushou 留守
Reminder of the Left	Zuo Shiyi 左拾遺
Reminder of the Right	You Shiyi 右拾遺
Remonstrance and Mastering of Literary Skills Examination	Fengjian zhuwen ke 諷諫主文科
Retainer	Congshi 從事
Revenue Administrator	Sihu canjun 司戶參軍
Revenue Manager	Sihu 司戶
Right Assistant Director of the Department of Affairs	Shangshu youcheng 尚書右丞
Right Rectifier of Omissions	You Buque 右補闕
Right Scribe	Youshi 右史
Salt Monopoly	Yantie 鹽鐵
Salt Monopoly Commissioner	Yantie shi 鹽鐵使
Scholar in the Academy of Scholarly Worthies	Jixianyuan xueshi 集賢院學士
Secretarial Court Gentleman	Shangshu lang 尚書郎
Secretariat Chancellery	Zhongshu menxia 中書門下
Secretariat Director	Zhongshu ling 中書令
Secretariat Drafter	Zhongshu sheren 中書舍人
Secretary of the Phoenix Hall	Fengge sheren 鳳閣舍人
Senior Compiler	Xiuzhuan 修撰
Subeditor in the Academy of Scholarly Worthies	Jixian Jiaoli 集賢校理
Supernumerary in the Bureau of Evaluations	Kaogong Yuanwai 考功員外

Appendix I: Official Titles, English

Supervising Secretary	Jishizhong 給事中
Supervisor in the Salt Monopoly	Jian Yanguan 監鹽官
Surveillance Commissioner	Guanchashi 觀察使
Vice Censor-in-Chief	Yushi Zhongcheng 御史中丞
Vice Director [of a bureau]	Yuanwai lang 員外郎
Vice Director of Criminal Administration	Duguan yuanwai lang 都官員外郎
Vice Director of the Bureau of Evaluations	Kaogong Yuanwailang 考功員外郎
Vice Director of the Bureau of Forestry and Crafts	Yubu yuanwai liang 虞部員外郎
Vice Director of the Bureau of Receptions (Bo Xingjian	Zhuke yuanwailang 主客員外郎
Vice Director of the Bureau of Review	Shangshu bibu yuanwailang 尚書比部員外郎
Vice Director of the Chancellery	Menxia Shilang 門下侍郎
Vice Director of the Ministry of Personnel	Libu Shilang 吏部侍郎
Vice Director of the Ministry of Revenue	Hubu Shilang 戶部侍郎
Vice Director of the Ministry of Rites	Libu Shilang 禮部侍郎
Vice Director of the Ministry of Rites	Libu Yuanwailang 禮部員外郎
Vice Director of the Ministry of War	Bingbu Shilang 兵部侍郎
Vice Director of the Palace Library	Bishu Shaojian 秘書少監
Vice Director of the Secretariat	Xitai Shilang 西臺侍郎
Vice Director of the Secretariat	Zhongshu shilang 中書侍郎
Vice Governor	Shaoyin 少尹
Vice Military Commissioner	Jiedu fushi 節度副使
Vice Minister of the Ministry of Rites	Sili shaoqing 司禮少卿
Vice Minister of Works	Xiao sikong 小司空
Vice Prefect	Sima 司馬
Worthy and Excellent, Straightforward and Upright Examination	Xianliang fangzheng 賢良方正

Official Titles, Alphabetized by Pinyin Romanization

Bibu Si 比部司	Bureau of Review
Biejia 別駕 (rank 4b2)	Administrative Aide
Bingbu Shilang 兵部侍郎 (3a)	Vice Director of the Ministry of War
Bishu Jian 秘書監 (3b)	Director of the Palace Library
Bishu Lang 秘書郎 (6b1)	Assistant in the Palace Library
Bishu Shaojian 秘書少監 (4b2)	Vice Director of the Palace Library
Bishusheng Jiaoshulang 秘書省校書郎 (9a1)	Gentleman Collating Books in the Palace Library
Bishusheng Zhuzuolang 秘書省著作郎 (6b1)	Editorial Director of Collating Books in the Palace Library
Boxue Hongci ke 博學宏詞科	Erudite Literatus Examination
Boxue Hongci 博學宏辭	Erudite Literatus
Caifang shi 採訪使	Investigation Commissioner
Canjun 參軍 (7a–9a)	Adjutant
Chang shi 長史 (5a1–6a2)	Chief Scribe
Cheng 承 (7b1–9a2)	Assistant Magistrate
Chongwenguan xueshi 崇文館學士	Academician of the Institute for the Veneration of Literature
Chungong langzhong 春宮郎中 (5b1)	Director of the Crown Prince's Palace
Cibu 祠部	Bureau of Sacrifices
Cishi 刺史 (3b-4a2)	Prefect
Congshi 從事 (8b)	Retainer
Da Sili 大司禮	Minister of Rites
Dafu Si 大府寺	Palace Bursary
Daizhi 待制 (4b)	Edict Attendant
Dali Sifa 大理司法 (6b1)	Administrator for Law Enforcement
Dalisi Sizhi 大理寺司直 (7a1)	Rectifier in the Court of Judicial Rule
Dianzhong cheng yushi 殿中丞御史	Aide to Royal Scribe in the Palace
Dianzhong yushi 殿中御史 (7b1)	Palace Censor
Du Tuanlian fushi 都團練副使	Assistant Military Training Commissioner
Duguan langzhong 都官郎中 (5b1)	Military Director of the Criminal Administrator Bureau
Duguan yuanwai lang 都官員外郎 (6b1)	Vice Director of Criminal Administration
Fengge sheren 鳳閣舍人	Secretary of the Phoenix Hall
Fengjian zhuwen ke 諷諫主文科	Remonstrance and Mastering of Literary Skills Examination
Fengli lang 奉禮郎 (9b1)	Court Gentleman for Ceremonials
Gongbu Langzhong 工部郎中 (5b1)	Director of Ministry of Works
Gongcao 公曹	Personnel Evaluator

Appendix I: Official Titles, Pinyin

Gongmen cheng 宮門丞	Assistant Director of the Palace Gate
Gongmen cheng 宮門承	Aide to the Palace Gates
Guanchashi 觀察使 (3b)	Surveillance Commissioner
Guanglusi 光祿寺 (4b2)	Court of Imperial Entertainments
Guangwen dian 廣文殿	Hall for Extending Literary Arts
Guangwen Guan Boshi 廣文館博士 (5a1)	Erudite in the Institute for the Extension of Literary Arts
Guozi Boshi 國子博士 (5a1)	Erudite of the National University
Guozi Jian Simen Zhujiao 國子監四門助教 (7b1–8b1)	Instructor in the Four Gates of the National University
Guozi jian 國子監	Directorate of Education
Guozi Jijiu 國子祭酒 (3b)	Chancellor of the National University
Guozi siye 國子司業 (4b2)	Director of Studies in the National University
Guozijian Simen Boshi 國子監四門博士 (7a1)	Academician in the Four Gates of the National University
Hanlin Xueshi 翰林學士	Hanlin Scholar
Hongwen guan 弘文館	Institute for the Advancement of Literature (formerly Institute of Education 文學館)
Hubu Langzhong 戶部郎中 (5b1)	Director of the Ministry of Revenue
Hubu Shangshu 戶部尚書 (3a)	Minister of the Ministry of Revenue
Hubu Shilang 戶部侍郎 (3a)	Vice Director of the Ministry of Revenue
Hubu 戶部	Ministry of Revenue
Jian Yanguan 監鹽官	Supervisor in the Salt Monopoly
Jiancha Yushi 監察御史 (8a2)	Investigating Censor
Jianjiao 檢校	Acting (temporary role in the position)
Jianyi Dafu 諫議大夫 (5a1)	Grand Master of Remonstrance
Jiaofang 教坊	Music Office
Jiaoshulang 校書郎 (9b1)	Editor
Jiedu fushi 節度副使 (4a1)	Vice Military Commissioner
Jiedu zhangshuji 節度掌書記 (8b1)	Prefectural Secretary
Jiedushi 節度使 (3b)	Military Commissioner
Jijiu 祭酒 (3b)	Libationer or Chancellor (in the Guozijian)
Jin shi 進士	Present Scholar Examination
Jingzhao Yin 京兆尹 (2b)	Metropolitan Governor
Jishi 記室	Recorder Keeper
Jishizhong 給事中 (5a1)	Supervising Secretary
Jiujing 九經	Nine Classics Examination
Jixian Dian daxueshi 集賢殿大學士	Grand Academician in the Academy of Scholarly Worthies
Jixian Dian Xueshi 集賢殿學士	Academician in the Academy of Scholarly Worthies
Jixian Jiaoli 集賢校理	Subeditor in the Academy of Scholarly Worthies

Appendix I: Official Titles, Pinyin

Jixianyuan xueshi 集賢院學士	Scholar in the Academy of Scholarly Worthies
Jixianyuan 集賢院	College of Scholarly Worthies
Junmufu zhangshuji 軍幕府掌書記	Chief Secretary of the Office of the Army Commander
Kaogong Langzhong 考功郎中 (5b1)	Director of Evaluations
Kaogong Yuanwai 考功員外	Supernumerary in the Bureau of Evaluations
Kaogong Yuanwailang 考功員外郎 (6b1)	Vice Director of the Bureau of Evaluations
Langzhong 郎中 (5b1)	Director (of a Bureau)
Leigeng Ling 率更令	Commandant of the Heir Apparent's Guard Command
Libu Langzhong 禮部郎中 (5b1)	Director of Ministry of Rites
Libu Langzhong 吏部郎中 (5b1)	Director of the Ministry of Personnel
Libu Shangshu 禮部尚書 (3a)	Minister of Ministry of Rites
Libu Shilang 吏部侍郎 (4a1)	Vice Director of the Ministry of Personnel
Libu Shilang 禮部侍郎 (4a1)	Vice Director of the Ministry of Rites
Libu Yuanwailang 禮部員外郎 (6b1)	Vice Director of the Ministry of Rites
Libu 禮部	Ministry of Rites
Ling 令 (7a1–7b2)	Magistrate
Lintai Zhengzi 麟台正字 (9a2)	Proofreader in the Palace Library
Liushou 留守	Regent
Menxia Shilang 門下侍郎 (4a1)	Vice Director of the Chancellery
Mufu 幕府	Field Office
Nei shifeng 內室奉	Palace Attendant
Nüshulang 女書郎	Female Editor
Panguan 判官	Administrative Assistant
Pingzhang shi 平章事	Manager of Affairs
Qiju Lang 起居郎 (6b1)	Imperial Diarist
Qiju Sheren 起居舍人 (6b1)	Imperial Diarist
Qinfu canjun 秦府參軍 (7–9)	Administrator of the Princely Establishment of Qin
Sanji changshi 散騎常侍 (3b)	Cavalier Attendant-in-ordinary
Shangshu bibu Yuanwailang 尚書比部員外郎 (6b1)	Vice Director of the Bureau of Review
Shangshu lang 尚書郎	Secretarial Court Gentleman
Shangshu youcheng 尚書右丞 (4a1)	Right Assistant Director of the Dept. of Affairs
Shaoyin 少尹 (4b2)	Vice Governor
Shentong 神童	Examination for Divine Lads
Shi Yushi 侍御史	Attendant Censor
Shidu 侍讀	Reader-in-Waiting
Shiguan 史館	Historiography Institute

Shixiang 使相	Commissioner Councilor
Shiyushi nei gongfeng 侍禦史內供奉	Attendant Censor Auxiliary
Shu Shilang 書侍郎 (3a)	Attendant Gentleman of the Secretariat
Shuibu Langzhong 水部閣中 (5b1)	Director of the Bureau of Waterways and Irrigation
Shuibu 水部	Bureau of Waterways and Irrigation
Sifa canjun 司法參軍 (9a2)	Judicial Administrator
Sifeng 司封司	Bureau of Honors
Sigong canjun 司功參軍 (7–9)	Personnel Management Administrator
Sihu canjun 司戶參軍 (7–9)	Revenue Administrator
Sihu 司戶 (6)	Revenue Manager
Sikong 司空 (1a)	Minister of Works
Sili shaoqing 司禮少卿	Vice Minister of the Ministry of Rites
Simen zhujiao 四門助教 (8b1)	Instructor in the Four Gates of the National Univ.
Sima 司馬 (5a2–6a2)	Vice Prefect
Siye 司業 (4b2)	Director of Studies
Taichang boshi 太常博士 (6a1)	Erudite of Imperial Sacrifices
Taichang cheng 太常丞 (5b2)	Aide to Chamberlain for Ceremonials
Taifushi cheng 太府寺丞	Aide to the Court of the Imperial Treasury
Taishi ling 太史令 (5b2)	Director of Astrologers
Taiwei 太尉 (1a or 2a)	Defender-in-Chief
Taiyue An 太樂案	Imperial Music Office
Taizhu 太祝 (6)	Great Supplicator
Taizi Binke 太子賓客 (3a)	Advisor to the Heir Apparent
Taizi jiaoshu 太子校書	Collator for the Heir Apparent
Taizi Jiaoshulang 太子校書郎 (9a1)	Gentleman in Charge of Collating Books for the Heir Apparent
Taizi shaobao 太子少保 (2b)	Grand Guardian of the Heir Apparent
Taizi shaoshi 太子少師 (2b)	Grand Preceptor of the Heir Apparent
Taizi shidu 太子侍讀	Reader-in-Waiting of the Heir Apparent
Taizi zhengzi 太子正字 (9a2)	Proofreader in the Secretariat of the Heir Apparent
Taizi Zuoshu lang 太子左庶郎	Mentor to the Heir Apparent on the Left
Tong Pingzhang shi 同平章事 (1a)	Jointly Manager of Affairs with the Secretariat
Tong Zhongshu Menxia Pingzhangshi 同中書門下平章事 (1a)	Jointly Manager of Affairs with the Secretariat-Chancellery
Tongpan 通判	Controller General
Tushu Shi 圖書使	Bibliographer of the Imperial Library
Wei 尉 (9a2–9b1)	Commandant
Wenguan 文館	Literary Institute
Wenxue guan 文學館	Institute of Education

Appendix I: Official Titles, Pinyin

Wenxue zhiguan 文學直館	Institute of Literary Attendants
Xiannan 縣男 (5b)	District Baron
Xianliang fangzheng ke 賢良方正科	Department of Worthy and Excellent, Straightforward and Upright
Xianliang fangzheng 賢良方正	Worthy and Excellent, Straightforward and Upright Examination
Xianshu Quexia 獻書卻下	Proofreader in the Imperial Library
Xianwei 縣尉	District Defender
Xianzi 縣子	District Viscount
Xiao sikong 小司空	Vice Minister of Works
Xingbu 刑部	Ministry of Justice
Xitai Shilang 西臺侍郎	Vice Director of the Secretariat
Xiuwenguan xueshi 修文館學士	Academician in the Institute for the Cultivation of Literature
Xiuzhuan 修撰	Senior Compiler
Xiyi guan 習藝館	Palace School
Yantie shi 鹽鐵使	Salt Monopoly Commissioner
Yantie 鹽鐵	Salt Monopoly
Yin 尹 (2b)	Administrator (of a major prefecture), or Governor (of major metropolitan area)
Yingtian fushi 營田副使	Assistant Agriculture Commissioner
Yiting 掖庭	Palace Discipline Service
You Buque 右補闕	Right Rectifier of Omissions
You Shiyi 右拾遺 (8b1)	Reminder of the Right
Younei Shuifu Bingcao Canjun 右內率府兵曹參軍 (7–9)	Adjutant in the Office of the Crown Prince's Bodyguard
Youshi 右史	Right Scribe
Yuanwai lang 員外郎	Vice Director [of a bureau]
Yubu yuanwai liang 虞部員外郎 (6b1)	Vice Director of the Bureau of Forestry and Crafts
Yushi 御史	Censorate
Yushi dafu 御史大夫 (3b)	Censor-in-chief
Yushi Zhongcheng 御史中丞 (5a1)	Vice Censor-in-Chief
Yushi Zhuojianyi dafu 御史擢諫議大夫 (5a)	Grand Master of Remonstrance
Zaixiang 宰相 (1a)	Grand Councilor
Zhangshi 長史 (4b1)	Chief Clerk
Zhangshuji 掌書記 (8b)	Chief Secretary
Zhanshi fu 詹事府	Household Administration of the Heir Apparent
Zhaorong 照容	Consort of Shining Countenance
Zhengzi 正字 (9a2)	Proofreader
Zhifang Langzhong 職方郎中 (5b1)	Director of Bureau of Operations

Appendix I: Official Titles, Pinyin

Zhigao 制誥	Department of Drafting Proclamations
Zhixue shi 直學士	Auxiliary Academician
Zhizhigao 知制誥	Participant in the Drafting of Proclamations
Zhongshu ling 中書令 (3a)	Secretariat Director
Zhongshu menxia 中書門下	Secretariat Chancellery
Zhongshu sheren 中書舍人 (5a1)	Secretariat Drafter
Zhongshu shilang 中書侍郎 (4a1)	Vice Director of the Secretariat
Zhongzheng 中正	Rectifier
Zhubu 主簿 (8b1)	Recorder
Zhujiao 助教 (8b1)	Instructor
Zhuke langzhong 主客郎中 (5b1)	Director of the Bureau of Receptions
Zhuke yuanwailang 主客員外郎 (6b1)	Vice Director of the Bureau of Receptions
Zhusi 主司	Examiner
Zhuzuo lang 著作佐郎 (6b1)	Editorial Director
Zhuzuo zuolang 著作佐郎	Assistant Editorial Director
Zuo Buque 左補闕	Left Rectifier of Omissions
Zuo Puye 左僕射	Left Vice Director of the Dept. of State Affairs
Zuo Shiyi 左拾遺 (8b)	Reminder of the Left
Zuo Wuwei Bingcao Canjun 左武衛兵曹參軍 (7–9)	Adjutant Left Militant Guard in the Military Service Section (of the Palace)
Zuosi 左司	Left Office of State Affairs

Appendix II: Literary Timeline of the Tang

Much of the material in this timeline comes from Fu Cuanzong 傅璇琮 (1933–2016), Tao Min 陶敏 (1938–2013), and Li Yifei's 李一飛 *Tang, Wudai wenxue bianian shi* 唐五代文學編年史 as well as the *Cambridge History of the Tang*. The listing includes major political changes, publications of individual works and collections, and often just notes on the interactions between various literati which shed light on their lives. Those names in bold type have entries in this volume. Chinese characters and dates are given on first occurrence only.

618   In the fifth lunar month after taking the position of emperor, Li Yuan 李淵 (Emperor Gaozu 高祖, 566–635, r. 618–635) founded the Tang Dynasty; he ordered the National University 太學, the School for the Sons of State 國子, and the School of the Four Gates 四門生 to be established, staffed by 300 scholars; schools in the provinces were also established.

About this time Wang Du 王度 (fl. 620) completed his tale "Gu jing ji" 古鏡記 (Record of an Ancient Mirror).

Li Shimin 李世民 (598–649, Emperor Taizong 太宗, r. 636–649) was made Prince of Qin 秦王 age 21.

Yan Shigu 顏師古 (581–645) was made Imperial Diarist.

In these years the heir, Li Jiancheng 李建成 (589–626), Li Yuanji 李元吉 (603–626), the Prince of Qi 齊王, and Li Shimin competed to gain the support of important ministers including many literati. Scholars allied with Li Shimin included Fang.

Xuanling 房玄齡 (579–648), **Yu Shinan 虞世南 (558–638),** Yao Silian 姚思廉 (557–637), and **Yan Shigu**. The power of these three grew quickly with Li Yuanji supporting Li Jiancheng against Li Shimin, leading to the events of 626.

621   Li Shimin established his own literary institution, the Institute of Education 文學館 with eighteen scholars including **Yu Shinan**, **Xu Jingzong 許敬宗 (592–672),** and Yao Silian.

622   The first attempts to compiled official histories for several previous dynasties were initiated with **Yan Shigu**, Ouyang Xun 歐陽詢 (557–641), Linghu Defen 令狐德棻 (583–666), Wei Zheng 魏征 (5806–43) and others involved; but after some time these efforts were abandoned.

The first examinations resulting in 4 presented scholars and 143 classicists (*mingjing*) took place.

623   Gaozu visited lectures by Xu Wenyuan 許文遠 (ca. 560–ca. 623), a *Zuo zhuan* specialist, lectures on the *Spring and Autumn Annals* in the National University.

There were 4 presented scholars.

Appendix II: Literary Timeline of the Tang

624	Ouyang Xun, Linghu Defen, Yuan Lang 袁朗 and others completed work on the encyclopedic *Yiwen leiju* 藝文類聚 (Literary Works Collected in Categories) in 100 *juan*.
	There were 6 presented scholars and 2 *xiucai* cultivated talents.
625	**Wang Ji 王績 (586–644)** became ill while living in the quarters of Li Yanji, Prince of Qi.
	Five presented scholars and two cultivated talents.
626–684	Reigns of Taizong 太宗 and Gaozong 高宗, apex of Court Poetry.
626	In the sixth lunar month Li Shimin ambushed and killed his brothers, Li Jiancheng and Li Yuanji in an ambush at the Xuanwu Gate 宣武門 (called the Xuanwu Gate Incident).
	In the eighth month Li Shimin became emperor and shortly afterwards ordered more than 20,000 *juan* of texts to be collected in the Institute for the Advancement of Literature.
	Following Li Shimin's ascension he was forced to agree to buy off the Eastern Turk leader Ashina Shibobi 啊史那什缽苾 (602–631) whose troops came to the far side of the Wei River threatening Chang'an.
	Fang Xuanling, an early supporter of Li Shimin, became Secretariat Director; he remained a force in the Tang court often as Grand Councilor or the near equivalent through his death in 648.
	There were 17 presented scholars and 2 cultivated talents.
627	Buddhist monk Xuanzang 玄奘 (602–664) sets off for India to collect sutras.
	Shangguan Yi 上官儀 (ca. 607–ca. 665) and 3 others succeeded in the *jinshi*.
630	Li Jing 李靖 (571–649) defeated the Eastern Turks after which all the northwestern tribes acknowledged Taizong as Khagan of Heaven 天可汗.
631	**Yan Shigu** ordered to produce a critical edition of the *Wujing* 五經 (Five Classics)
636	Wei Zheng 魏征 (580–643) in his *Suishu* 隋書 (History of the Sui) criticized verse of preceding Southern dynasties.
637	Fang Xuanling revised the penal code and, with Wei Zheng, compiled a code of ritual.
	Taizong granted Daoist priests precedence over Buddhist monks.
638	**Yu Shinan**, poet, calligrapher, courtier, dies.
641	**Yan Shigu** submitted his *Han shu zhu* 漢書注 (Commentary on the *History of the Han*) that had been ordered by the crown prince, Li Chengqian 李承乾 (619–645).
642	Kong Yingda 孔穎達 (574–648) presents *Wujing zhengyi* 五經正義 (Corrected Meaning of the Five Classics) to the throne (these sub-commentaries were used as basis for the *mingjing* 明經 examination).
	Li Tai 李泰 (620–653), Prince of Wei 魏王, submitted *Kuo di zhi* 括地誌 (Monograph on All the World) to the throne.
643	Among the 24 portraits of those who contributed to the Tang in the Lingyange 凌煙閣 were those of Fang Xuanling, Wei Zheng, Li Jing, **Yu Shinan**, and Zhangsun Wuji 長孫無忌 (594–659).
645	**Xu Jingzong** appears among the top officials.
	Xuanzang returns and is ordered to translate the sutras he brought back; Taizong urges him to renounce his vows and take up office, before finally accepting him as his spiritual mentor.

Appendix II: Literary Timeline of the Tang

	Yan Shigu, commentator on the classics and editor of *Han shu* 漢書 (*History of the Han*), dies.
649	Li Shimin, Emperor Taizong, dies and Gaozong takes the throne.
650	**Yang Jiong 楊炯 (650–694)** and **Wang Bo 王勃** (650–676) born.
655	Wu Zetian 武則天 made empress.
656	Three successful candidates in the *jinshi* 進士 (presented scholar) examination.
	Song Zhiwen 宋之問 (656–ca. 712) and **Shen Quanqi 沈佺期** (656–716) born.
657	**Xu Jingzong 許敬宗** (592–672) presents *Wenguan cilin* 文館詞林 in 1000 *juan* (no longer extant).
	Gaozong wrote "Xue shi" 雪詩 (Poem on Snow) with poetic responses from Zhangsun Wuji, **Xu Jingzong**, and others.
658	Li Shan 李善 (630–689) presents his *Wenxuan zhu* 文選注 (Notes on Selections of Refined Literature).
	Luoyang is made the Eastern Capital.
659	**Xu Jingzong** and others compiled a *Shilu* 實錄 (Veritable Record) of Gaozong's first years on the throne.
	Twenty successful candidates in the *jinshi* examination.
660	Li Rong 李榮 (fl. 660–669) and Jingtai 靜泰 (fl. 636-670) debated before Gaozong in Luoyang.
	Gaozong's ill health (a stroke) cause him to yield decision-making power to Wu Zetian.
661	**Xu Jingzong** presents the *Lei bi* 累璧 in 630 *juan* (encyclopedia now lost).
663	Daminggong 大明宮 (Great Enlightenment Palace) is completed.
	Fanglin yaolan 芳林要覽, an anthology in 300 *juan*, completed by **Xu Jingzong, Shangguan Yi** and others.
664	Xuanzhang dies having compiled *Da Tang xiyou ji* 大唐西域記 (A Record of the Western Regions in the Great Tang) and translated 75 sutras.
665	Wu Zetian becomes de facto ruler.
668	**Daoshi 道世** (597–683) living in Ximingsi 西明寺 in the capital completed *Fayuan zhulin* 法苑珠林 (A Grove of Pearls in the Dharma Garden) in 100 *juan*.
670	Tibetans raid 18 prefectures.
	Du Shenyan 杜審言 (ca. 645–708) and 53 others passed the *jinshi* examination.
672	Gaozong returned to Chang'an from a decade living in Luoyang.
673	Guo Yuanzhen 郭元珍 (656–713) was one of 97 successful *jinshi* candidates.
675	Wu Zetian dissolves the Beimen Xueshi 北門學士 (Scholars of the Northern Gate) Gaozong had created.
677	**Zhang Zhuo 張鷟** (ca. 657–730) composed *Youxianku* 遊仙窟 (A Dalliance in the Dwelling of Goddesses).
680s-710s	Constant warfare with the Tibetan empire.
680	The Heir, Li Xian 李賢 (654–684) was demoted to be a commoner, Li Zhe 李哲 (later Zhongzong) made Heir
682	**Liu Zhiji 劉知集** (661–721) was one of 55 successful candidates in the *jinshi*.
	Droughts, floods and other catastrophes in the capital region.
683	Emperor Gaozong dies and Zhongzong succeeds.
684	Wu Zetian deposes Zhongzong and installs Ruizong.
685	Li Longji 李隆基 (Xuanzong 玄宗 685-762, r. 712–756) born (Ruizong's son).

Appendix II: Literary Timeline of the Tang

688	Wu Zetian has Tang princes and princesses killed.
690	Wu Zetian declares herself Emperor of the Zhou dynasty.
	Zhang Yue 張說 (667–731) is ranked first in the *jinshi* examination.
	At a party held in the Mingtang 明堂 (Hall of Light) hosted by Empress Wu, Li Longji and other royal children perform dances.
695	The Mingtang burned to the ground.
	He Zhizhang 賀知章 (659–744) was one of the 22 successful *jinshi* graduates.
696	The new Mingtang was completed.
697	The Zhang brothers, Zhang Yizhi 張易之 and Zhang Changzong 張昌宗 become Wu Zetian's lovers.
699	**Song Zhiwen** and **Shen Quanqi** joined the Empress in an excursion to Longmen 龍門 (one of several in the years to follow); **Li Jiao** 李嶠 (ca. 644–ca. 714), **Zhang Yue**, and **Liu Zhiji**, were also courtiers and all joined in compiling a 1300 *juan* collection of court verse, the *Sanjiao zhuying* 三教珠英 (Pearls and Petals of the Three Teachings) completed in 701.
700	**Gao Shi** 高適 (700–765) born.
701	**Li Bo** 李白 (i.e., **Li Bai**, 701–762) born.
702	**Zhang Jiuling** 張九齡 (678–740) and 20 others were successful in the *jinshi* with Song Zhiwen or Shen Quanqi as examiner.
	Li Jiao became Regent or Imperial Representative in Luoyang, after Empress Wu moved to Chang'an in 701.
703	The Empress returned to Luoyang with **Li Jiao, Du Shenyan**, and **Shen Quanqi** in her entourage.
705	Zhang Jianzhi 張柬之 (625–706) kills the Zhang brothers and restores Zhongzong.
	Li Jiao, Shen Quanqi, Du Shenyan, and **Song Zhiwen** all banished to provinces.
	Empress Wu dies of illness; **Song Zhiwen** wrote several poems lamenting her.
	With **Su Ting** 蘇頲 (670–727) as examiner 61 candidates passed the *jinshi*.
	Lotus Sutra printed.
706	**Song Zhiwen** and **Du Shenyan** both recalled to the capital; **Shen Quanqi** in 707.
707	The Institute for the Cultivation of Literature was expanded to include **Liu Zhiji, Li Jiao**, and others.
708	**Shangguan Wan'er** 上官婉兒 (664–710), **Song Zhiwen**, **Li Jiao** and others accompanied Zhongzong to visit the Sanhuisi 三會寺; many similar occasions in 709 and the early part of 710.
710	In the first and second months Zhongzong entertained Tibetan envoys and then went with the court to Mawei 馬嵬 (30 miles west of Chang'an) to see off Princess Jincheng 金城公主 who was sent to be married to the Tibetan king.
	Liu Zhiji completed his *Shitong* 史通 (Generalities on Historiography).
	In the sixth month Zhongzong is poisoned by Empress Wei 韋 and their son Emperor Shang 殤帝 succeeds.
	Then Li Longji, grandson of Gaozong, kills Empress Wei and installs Ruizong.
	Zhang Zhuo is reappointed Commandant of Chang'an.
711	Guo Yuanzhen and **Zhang Yue** made Grand Councilors.
	Zhang Yue, Shen Quanqi, and Ruizong match Li Longji's poem at Ciensi 慈恩寺.
	The position of Military Commissioner created.
712	Ruizong abdicates in favor of his son, Li Longji (Xuanzong).
	Du Fu 杜甫 (712–770) born.

Appendix II: Literary Timeline of the Tang

714	**He Zhizhang** was appointed Erudite of the Court of Imperial Sacrifices. **Su Ting** and **Zhang Jiuling** were among the courtiers.
715	Shanwuwei 善無畏 (Śubhakarasiṃha), Tantric master, arrives in Chang'an with Sanskrit texts.
716	Ruizong dies; **Su Ting** became a Grand Councilor (until early 720).
717	**Xiao Yingshi** 蕭穎士 (717–ca. 768) born.
718	**Jia Zhi** 賈至 (718–772) born.
719	**Wang Wei** 王維 (692–761) already a member of the artistic circle associated with Li Fan 李範 (717–ca. 768), the Prince of Qi 岐王 and Xuanzong's younger brother.
	Zhang Yue returns from lengthy service in the provinces to court.
	Yuan Jie 元結 (719–772) born.
720	**He Zhizhang** and **Su Ting** matched a poem by Xuanzong.
	Qian Qi 錢起 (720–ca. 783) and **Jiao Ran** 皎然 (720–799) born.
721	**Li Bo** was in Chengdu.
722	After Xuanzong sent him to gather beauties for his harem, Lü Xiang 呂向 (fl. 725), one of the five who wrote the "Wuchen zhu" 五臣注 (Five Ministers Commentary) to the *Wenxuan*, submitted the "Meiren fu" 美人賦 (Rhapsody on the Beauties) criticizing the emperor.
	Xuanzong completed his commentary on the *Xiaojing* 孝經 (Classic of Filial Piety).
723	Xuanzong toured to the north ascending the Taihang Mountains 太行山 accompanied by **Zhang Yue**, **Su Ting**, **Zhang Jiuling**, and other literati.
	Xuanzong sacrificed to the Hou tu 后土 (Queen of the Earth) at Fenyin 汾陰.
724	Xuanzong entertained the high officials in the Leyou Yuan 樂遊園 (Pleasure Jaunt Park) where the emperor as well as **Zhang Yue**, **Zhang Jiuling** and others composed poems.
	The emperor went to Luoyang.
725	Xuanzong established the Academy of Scholarly Worthies with eighteen Academicians including **Zhang Yue** (as head) and **He Zhizhang**.
	Li Bo was in the Lake Dongting area to bury his friend Wu Zhinan 吳指南.
	Xuanzong preformed the *feng* 封 sacrifice on Mount Tai 泰山;
	On the way back the emperor stopped and worshipped at Confucius' home.
	Dugu Ji 獨孤及 (725–777) was born.
726	Among the 31 successful *jinshi* candidates were **Chu Guangxi** 儲光羲 (ca. 706–ca. 762) and **Qiwu Qian** 綦毋潛 (ca. 692–ca. 756).
	The Prince of Qi died.
	Li Bo moved from Jinling (Nanjing) through Yangzhou to the Wu area.
	Liu Fangping 劉方平 (726–ca. 758) and **Liu Zhangqing** 劉長卿 (726–787) born.
727	**Wang Changling** 王昌齡 (ca. 690–ca. 756) and **Chang Jian** 常建 (fl. 727) among 19 *jinshi* successful candidates.
	Xuanzong returns to Chang'an.
	Xu Jian 徐堅 (659–729) submits the *Chuxue ji* 初學記.
	Li Bo first moves to Anlu 安陸, marries and withdraws to Mount Shou 壽山.
	Gu Kuang 顧況 (727–ca. 814) and Lingyi 靈一 (728–762) born.
728	Xuanzong composed "Xiyu fu" 喜雨賦 (Rhapsody on Timely Rains), **Zhang Yue** and other courtiers matched his piece.

Appendix II: Literary Timeline of the Tang

	Wang Wei began to study Buddhism with the Monk Dade Daoguang 大德道.
729	**Zhang Yue** made Grand Councilor again.
	Yang Chang 楊暢 (ca. 668–735) argued that standards for *mingjing* 明經 (clarifying the classics) and *jinshi* examinations be relaxed.
	Chang Gun 常袞 (729–783) born.
	Zhang Yue and others submitted a memorial to make Xuanzong's birthday (5th of the 8th month) a holiday, Qianqiu Jie 千秋節 (A Thousand Autumns Festival).
730s–760s	Constant warfare with Tibet.
730	**Li Bo** first comes to Chang'an; **He Zhizhang** praises his poems; Li lived in Princess Yuzhen's 玉真公主 country house on Zhongnanshan 终南山 (Mount Zhongnan) and sent a poem to Zhang Ji 張垍 (d. ca. 760), **Zhang Yue**'s second son, seeking a position.
	Zhang Yue died.
731	Chen Xilie 陳希烈 (d. 758) became head of the Academy of Scholarly Worthies.
733	*Laozi* added to the examination materials.
734	Because of heavy rains there was famine around Chang'an, Xuanzong went to Luoyang.
	Wang Changling passed the Erudite Literatus Examination.
735	Lin Linfu 李林甫 (683–753) begins to exert influence at court.
	Xiao Yingshi, **Li Qi** 李頎 (690–751), **Li Hua** 李華 (715–774) and 24 others successful in the *jinshi*; **Gao Shi** and **Du Fu** failed.
	Sima Chengzhen 司馬承禎 (647–735) died and Xuanzong wrote a funerary inscription.
	Xuanzong's commentary on the *Laozi* completed.
736	Li Linfu made Grand Councilor.
	Supervision of the *jinshi* transferred to the Ministry of Rites.
	Xuanzong returned to Chang'an in the tenth month.
737	Lin Linfu arranged to have **Zhang Jiuling** banished.
738	**Du Fu** around this time went to Qi and Zhao and climbed Mount Tai 泰山.
	Li Hua in these years was often in the company of **Xiao Yingshi**, **Jia Zhi**, **Gao Shi**, and Yen Zhenqing 顏真卿 (709–785).
	Hanlin Yuan 翰林院 (Courtyard of Assembled Brushes) founded.
739	*Tang liu dian* 唐六典 (Tang Institutions of Six Administrative Divisions) completed.
	Lu Lun 盧綸 (739–799) born.
741	Chongxuanxue 崇玄學 (School for Venerating the [Daoist] Mysteries) established for study of *Laozi*, *Zhuangzi*, *Wenzi*, and *Liezi* all of which were to be included in the *mingjing* examination corpus.
	Xuanzong dreamt of Laozi and had a true likeness of him distributed to all prefectures.
742	Tianbao 天寶 reign begins; period of greatest poetry.
	Li Shi 李適 (Emperor Dezong) born in the 4th month.
	Xuanzong went to the Wenquangong 溫泉宮 (Warm Springs Palace). accompanied by Li Linfu, **Wang Wei**, and **Li Bo** who had just been made a Hanlin Academician.

Wu Yun 吳筠 (d. 778) was summoned to the capital, made a Dao Priest, and went to study Dharma with Feng Qizheng 馮齊整 on Mount Song 嵩山 (30 miles southeast of Luoyang).

Bukong 不空 (i.e. Amoghavajra, 705–774) summoned to court to offer prayers for victory or an insurrection.

743 For these few years Xuanzong spent the 10th and 11th month at the warm springs at Mount Li 驪山.

About this time **Wang Wei** acquired the former country estate of **Song Zhiwen** where he and Pei Di 裴迪 wrote the poems in *Wangchuanji* 輞川集 (Wang River Collection).

744 **He Zhizhang** because of illness asked to be relieved of office and ordained a Daoist Priest; Xuanzong allowed it and arranged for a formal sendoff with many officials present.

An Lushan 安祿山 (703–757) was given a second area as Military Commissioner.

Cen Shen 岑參 (715–770) and 28 others passed the *jinshi* examination.

Li Bo asked for permission to return to "the mountains" and Xuanzong sent him off with a gift of gold.

Du Fu met **Li Bo** and **Gaoshi** in Luoyang and they traveled eastward together.

Rui Tingzhang 芮挺章 completed his collection of poetry, *Guoxiuji* 國秀集 in 3 *juan* containing 90 poets and 220 poems.

745 Shenhui 神會 (668–760) invited to settle in Luoyang and preach Huineng's 慧能 (638–713) Southern Chan doctrines.

746 Yang Guifei is now favored by Xuanzong.

Chen Xilie is made Grand Councilor and is subservient to Li Linfu.

Lingche 靈澈 (746–816) born.

747 Li Hanguang 李含光 (683–769), the 13th Patriarch of Maoshan 茅山 who had tutored Xuanzong in Daoism since 745, was allowed to return to Maoshan.

748 Yang Guifei's sisters were made ladies of Hanguo 韓國, Guoguo 虢國, and Qinguo 秦國 and given free access to the palace.

Li Hua's "Hanyuandian fu" 含元殿賦 (Rhapsody on the Hanyuan Palace) praised by **Xiao Yingshi** and **Jia Zhi**.

Jiao Ran became a Buddhist monk.

Li Yi 李益 (748–ca. 827) born.

749 **Gao Shi** after passing the Daoist examination sent poems to Li Linfu and Chen Xilie and was made Commandant of Fengqiu 封丘 County (near modern Xixiang City 新鄉市 in Henan).

Cen Shen made Administrative Assistant to Anxi 安西 under Gao Xianzhi 高仙芝 (d. 756) and with his army left for the northwestern frontier where he wrote many frontier poems.

Xiao Yingshi was removed as Subeditor in the Academy of Scholarly Worthies and wrote "Fa Yintaoshu fu" 伐櫻桃樹賦 (Cutting Down the Cherry Tree) attacking Li Linfu.

Wu Jing 吳兢 (670–749), author of *Tang chunqiu* (Annals of the Tang) in 30 *juan* and *Guyuefu* 古樂府 (Old Music-bureau Poems) in 10 *juan*, died.

750	Xuanzong founded the Guangwenguan 廣文館 (Institute for the Extension of Literary Arts) and first held court in the Huaqing Gong 華清宮 at Mount Li. **Qian Qi** and 20 other candidates passed the *jinshi*; Qian was made Editor in the Palace Library. **Du Fu** in the capital seeking a position. **Yuan Jie**, styling himself Master Yuan 元子, retired to live on Mount Shangyu 商餘山 and wrote the *Yuanzi* 元子 in 10 *juan*.
751	Xuanzong admired the "San Dali fu" 三大禮賦 (Three Rhapsodies on the Great Ritual) presented by **Du Fu**. General Gao Xianzhi, Military Commissioner of Anxi, was routed by the Arabs at the Talas River. **Cen Shen** returned to the capital from Anxi. **Yuan Jie** wrote "Xi yuefu" 系樂府 (Continuing Music-bureau Ballads), among the earliest "New Yuefu." **Meng Jiao** 孟郊 (751–814) was born;
752	Li Linfu died in the 11th month and was replaced by Yang Guozhong 楊國忠 (ca. 700–814). Around this year **Huangfu Ran** 皇甫冉 (ca. 717–ca. 771) was in Luoyang writing poetry with **Liu Fangping**, the Monk Zhanran 湛然 (711-782), and others. **Li Bo** traveling in the south.
753	**Yuan Jie** 元結 (719–772) and 55 others passed the *jinshi*. **Liang Su** 梁肅 (753–793) born. **Du Fu** wrote "Liren xing" 麗人行 (Ballad of the Beautiful) to satirize the excesses of Yang Guozhong's family members; he and **Cen Shen**, who was also in the capital, were unable to meet because of heavy rains but exchanged poems. **Li Hua** in Xuancheng 宣城 (Anhui) together with **Li Bo**. Yin Fan 殷璠 edited the collection *Heyue yingling ji* 河岳英靈集 containing 234 poems by 24 poets including **Li Bo, Wang Wei, Zhang Wei** 張謂 (ca. 711–ca. 778), **Li Qi, Gao Shi, Cen Shen, Meng Haoran** 孟浩然 (689–740), **Chu Guangxi** 儲光羲 (ca. 706–ca. 762), and **Wang Changling**. **Wei Yingwu** 韋應物 (735–ca. 792) at eighteen entered the National University.
754	**Dugu Ji** 獨孤及 (725–777) passed a Daoist examination and became Commandant of Huayin 華陰 50 miles east of Chang'an. **Wu Yun** was made a Hanlin Academician. **Li Fangping** was in Luoyang and addressed poems to Yan Wu 嚴武 (726–765), **Huangfu Ran** and others.
755	An Lushan in the 2nd month made demands to replace some of his generals; Yang Guozhong and the other Grand Councilor Wei Jiansu 韋見素 (697–762) argued against this, but Xuanzong met An's demands. General Ge Shuhan 哥舒翰 (699–757), came to court to criticize Xuanzong's decision and was put under house arrest. In the 3rd month Xuanzong entertained the court at the Qinzhenglou 勤正樓 (Tower of Diligence in State Affairs). **Chu Guangxi** as Investigating Censor in Chang'an exchanged poems with Fang Guan 房琯 (696–763). **Du Fu** was appointed Commandant of Hexi 河西 but refused the position.

Appendix II: Literary Timeline of the Tang

	In the 11th month An Lushan moved an army of more than 100,000 south from Youzhou 幽州 with the motto "Execute Yang Guozhong" beginning the rebellion that bears his name; in the 12th month he took Luoyang 33 days after he had set out.
	Gao Shi was made Investigating Censor and sent to help guard Tongguan 潼關 (Tong Pass) against the rebels.
756	On the 1st day of the year An Lushan declared himself Emperor of the Greater Yan 大燕 Dynasty.
	Huangfu Ran and 32 others passed the *jinshi* examination.
	Du Fu returned to the capital from Fengxian 奉先.
	Wang Wei (now 65 years old), Qiu Wei 丘為 (694–789), and **Huangfu Ran** all in the capital and they exchanged poems.
	Du Fu moved his family to Fuzhou 鄜州.
	Li Bo joined Prince Yong's 永王 (Li Lin 李璘, d. 757) army and after its collapse was banished to Yelang 夜郎 (modern Guizhou) in 758.
	In the 8th month the Tong Pass was taken and Xuanzong fled to Chengdu; Yang Guozhong and Yang Guifei were killed, and Chang'an fell to the rebels.
	By the 8th month **Gao Shi** and **Jia Zhi** were both with Xuanzong in Chengdu.
	Du Fu was held in Chang'an by the rebels; **Wang Wei** was also captured and confined in the Putisi 菩提寺 in Luoyang.
	Fang Guan, who had been made a Grand Councilor, led troops in the 10th month to attack the rebels but was defeated.
	Xiao Yingshi and **Liu Zhangqing** fled south and received temporary positions from local civil or military leaders.
757	In the 1st month An Lushan was murdered by his son An Qingxu 安慶緒 (723–759) in Luoyang.
	Examinations were held in the 2nd month in Fengxiang 鳳翔 (where Suzong was located), in Chengdu, and in Jiangdu 江都; **Gu Kuang** passed in Jiangdu.
	Du Fu escaped to Fengxiang and was appointed Reminder on the Left.
	Guo Ziyi 郭子儀 (697–781) recaptures Chang'an and Luoyang from the rebels.
	Cen Shen returned from the Lake Kokonor region to Suzong's court at Fengxiang.
	Qian Qi in Chang'an watches Suzong return and writes about it in a poem.
	After Luoyang was retaken in the 10th month more than 300 officials who had served An Lushan's government were taken prisoner, **Wang Wei** and others held in Yang Guozhong's former residence; **Wang Wei** demoted to be a Companion for the Heir Apparent and **Li Hua** made Personnel Manager in Hangzhou.
758	**Liu Zhangqing** visited **Gu Kuang** who was living at Hengshan 衡山; in the 6th month he was involved in an affair and wound up in prison in Suzhou 蘇州; in the 9th month he was released and became Commandant of Nanba 南巴.
	Jia Zhi was made a Secretariat Drafter wrote a poem on early morning court and **Wang Wei**, **Du Fu**, and **Cen Shen** matched it.
	Lingyi returned to the Yifengsi 宜豐寺 in Hangzhou and exchanged poems with Li Hua and **Huangfu Ran** among others.

Appendix II: Literary Timeline of the Tang

759   Shi Siming 史思明 (703–761) murders An Qingxu and retakes Luoyang.

In an examination on the *Five Classics*, the histories and the *Qieyun* 切韻, 25 candidates passed.

Du Fu traveling from Luoyang to Huazhou 華州 saw the results of fighting between Shi Siming and Guo Ziyi near Xiangzhou 相州 and wrote "Sanbie" 三別 (Three Partings) and "Sanli" 三吏 (Three Officials) poem series; later hearing of the drought and famine in the capital region he wrote "Xiari tan" 三日歎 (Lamenting Summer Days).

Rong Yu 戎昱 (744–800) joined Yen Zhenqing's 顏真卿 (709–785) staff in Zhexi 浙西.

760   **Xiao Yingshi** dies in Runan 汝南.

Jia Zhi was appointed Vice Prefect in Yuezhou 岳州 (modern Yueyang, Hunan).

Wang Wei was Assistant Director on the Right in the Department of State Affairs.

Yuan Jie was Administrative Assistant to Lü Yin 呂諲 (712–762) the Military Commissioner of Jingnan 荊南 (in Jingzhou 荊州, modern Jiangling 江陵).

Du Fu in the 9th month went to Xinjin 新津 County in Shuzhou 蜀州 and with Pei Di climbed the Xinjinsi 新津寺.

Gao Shi was moved to become Prefect of Shuzhou and **Du Fu** welcomed him with a poem.

Jiao Ran evading Liu Zhan's 劉展 rebellion in Lower Yangzi Region went to Yangzhou 揚州.

761   In the 3rd month Shi Siming killed by his son, Shi Chaoyi 史朝義 (d. 763).

Du Fu moved into his grass hut 草堂 in Chengdu then visited Pei Di in Shuzhou.

In the 7th month **Wang Wei** died.

Jia Zhi took up the position of Assistant Prefect of Yuezhou.

In the 11th month **Gao Shi** came to Chengdu and met with **Du Fu**.

762   Yan Wu is made Military Commissioner of Jiannan 劍南 based in Chengdu.

In the 4th month Xuanzong dies, aged 77; shortly thereafter Suzong dies.

Daizong takes the throne after the eunuch Li Fuguo foils a plan to have him killed.

Geng Wei 耿湋 (d. ca. 787) was in Songzhou 宋州 then besieged by Shi Chaoyi.

Yan Wu was recalled and appointed Vice Director of the Ministry of War.

In the 9th month Tang troops with Uyghur allies take Luoyang then loot the city.

Li Fuguo was killed by "robbers."

In the 10th month Lingyi died in the Longxingsi 隆興寺 in Hangzhou.

Li Bo died in the 11th month in Dangtu 當塗.

Du Fu went to Zizhou 梓州 and wrote poems for **Chen Zi'ang** and Guo Yuanzhen.

763   In the 1st month, Daizong ordered **Wang Wei**'s brother, Wang Jin 王縉 (700–781), to compiled and present **Wang Wei**'s works; Wang Jin remained an important advisor to the emperor and a promoter of Buddhism.

Du Fu moves from Zizhou 梓州 to Mianzhou 綿州 and Hanzhou 漢州 to see someone off and by the 10th month is in Langzhou 閬州.

Li Bo is summoned to serve at court but the order arrived after his death.

Gao Shi was made Military Commissioner of Jiannan 劍南 and Xichuan 西川.

Appendix II: Literary Timeline of the Tang

	In the 4th months **Qian Qi** was Commandant of Lantian 藍田; in 9th month he came to the capital and in the 10th fled to a Buddhist temple on Nanshan 南山.
	In the 10th month a Tibetan army of 100,000 took Chang'an briefly; Daizong and the court fled to Shanzhou 陝州.
	Wei Yingwu became Assistant Magistrate of Luoyang.
764	**Du Fu** hearing that Yan Wu had been made Military Commissioner in Chengdu returned to that city; he was soon in Yan Wu's employ.
	In the 3rd month **Gao Shi** was made Policy Advisor.
	Yuan Jie was Prefect of Daozhou 道州 where the members of the Xiyuanman 西原蠻 minority revolted.
765	**Gao Shi** died.
	Huangfu Ran was serving as a secretary to Wang Jin in the capital.
	Cen Shen and **Dugu Ji** were appointed to positions in the capital and were in contact with **Qian Qi, Lu Lun,** and **Rong Yu.**
	Du Fu anticipating a rebellion left Chengdu and moved down the Yangzi to Yunan.
	Jia Zhi was made Vice-minister of the Ministry of Rites and concurrently Edict Attendant in the Academy of Scholarly Worthies.
	Guo Ziyi in the 10th month persuaded Uyghur troops to join with him and defeated the Tibetans near Binzhou 邠州 (modern Bin County 彬县 in Shaanxi about 50 miles northwest of the capital).
	Chang Gun was made Secretariat Drafter.
766	**Wei Yingwu** resigned his Assistant Magistrate position to live privately in Luoyang.
	Du Fu moved to Kuizhou 夔州 and wrote "Qiuxing, ba shou" 秋興八首 (Autumn Meditations, Eight Poems).
	Li Guan 李觀 (766–794), **Zhang Ji** 張籍 (ca. 776–829), **Wang Jian** 王建 (ca. 766–ca. 830), and **Linghu Chu** 令狐楚 (766–837) born.
767	**Qian Qi, Li Duan** 李端 (d. ca. 785), **Sikong Shu** 司空曙 (ca. 720–790) all in Chang'an (known as Shicaizi 十才子, Ten Talents).
	Jiao Ran and **Lu Yu** 陸羽 (733–804) were often together in Huzhou 湖州.
768	**Du Fu** moved to Jiangling 江陵 and later that year to Gongan 公安 and Yuezhou 岳州.
	Huangfu Ran, Geng Wei, Li Duan, Qian Qi, Gu Kuang and **Dugu Ji** all often in each other's company in Chang'an.
	Han Yu 韓愈 (768–824) born.
769	**Du Fu** traveled south from Yuezhou to Tanzhou 潭州 and Hengzhou 衡州 by boat.
	Li Yi and 25 others passed the *jinshi* examination held in both Chang'an and Luoyang and was made Commandant of Zheng County 鄭縣.
770	**Li Duan** and 25 others passed the *jinshi* examination in the 2nd month.
	Du Fu moved back to Tanzhou in the 9th month and heading north in the 12th month fell ill and died in his boat age 59; his coffin was taken to Yueyang 岳陽.
	Fazhao 法照 (747–821) summoned by both Daizong and Dezong during the 770s and 780s.

Appendix II: Literary Timeline of the Tang

771	**Huangfu Ran** probably died in this year and **Dugu Ji** wrote a preface for his 350 collected poems.
	In the 4th month Daizong himself gave examinations and **Li Yi** passed the Fengjian Zhuwenke 諷諫主文科.
	Jiao Ran was with **Gu Kuang** in Huzhou.
772	In the 1st month Uyghur cavalry raided Chang'an taking captives and looting.
	Bukong presented sutras he had translated in 101 *juan*.
	Bo Juyi 白居易 (772–846), **Lü Wen** 呂溫 (772–811), **Liu Yuxi** 劉禹錫 (772–842), **Li Shen** 李紳 (772–846), and **Li Ao** 李翱 (774–836) born.
	In the 4th month **Jia Zhi** and **Yuan Jie** died.
773	Lu Zhi 陸贄 (754–805) and 33 others passed the *jinshi* in the 2nd month under examiner **Zhang Wei**.
	Yan Zhenqing, **Jiao Ran**, Lu Yu, **Wu Yun** and others wrote linked verses together in Huzhou.
	In the 10th month Guo Ziyi defeated a large Tibetan force.
	Liu Zongyuan 柳宗元 (773–819) was born.
774	In the 5th month **Li Hua** died and **Dugu Ji** wrote a preface for his collected works.
	In the 6th month **Amoghavajra** (i.e. **Bukung**) died.
775	**Zhang Wei** probably died in this year.
776	**Geng Wei**, **Sikong Shu**, and **Li Duan** all together in the capital.
	Bo Xingjian 白行簡 (776–826) and **Huangfu Shi** 皇甫湜 (776–ca. 835) born.
	Zhang Shen 張參 completed his *Wujing wenzi* 五經文字 (Model Characters of the Five Classics) which was then written on wooden panels in the Directorate of Education.
777	Twelve men passed the *jinshi* with **Chang Gun** as examiner.
	Dugu Ji died and **Liang Su** put together a collection of his works.
	Lingche traveled to Fujian and **Liu Zhangqing** wrote a poem seeing him off.
778	**Wu Yun** died in Xuancheng 宣城 and **Quan Deyu** 權德輿 (761–818) wrote a preface to his collected works.
779	In the 5th month Daizong dies of an illness and is replaced by Dezong.
	Chang Gun feuded with Cui Youfu 崔祐甫 (721–780) and as a result was demoted and sent to Chaozhou 潮州 as prefect while Cui was made a Grand Councilor.
	Shen Jiji 沈既濟 (ca. 740–ca. 800) was made Chief Musician at court.
	Yuan Zhen 元稹 (779–831) and **Jia Dao** 賈島 (779–843 both born.
780	**Chang Gun** was made Surveillance Commissioner of Fujian; he promoted literature there and discovered **Ouyang Zhan** 歐陽詹 (ca. 755–ca. 801).
	Liang Su was appointed Editing Clerk for the Heir Apparent, but declined and returned to the Wu region where his family had moved after the rebellions.
	Zhang Ji 張繼 (fl. 753–780) died in Hongzhou 洪州.
781	In the 4th month **Wei Yingwu** became Vice-director the Bureau of Review.
	Liu Zhangqing was Prefect of Suizhou 隨州.
	In the 9th month **Geng Wei** was exiled to become Administrator of Laws in Xuzhou 許州.

Appendix II: Literary Timeline of the Tang

Shen Jiji was implicated with Yang Yan 陽炎 (727–781), removed from his positions as Reminder on the Right and Senior Compiler in the Historiography Institute, and exiled to become Revenue Manager in Chuzhou 處州.

About this year **Gu Kuang** joined the office of the Military Commissioner of Zhexi Province, Han Huang 韓滉 (723–787) as an Administrative Assistant.

782
Shen Jiji visited Runzhou 潤州 and went with **Quan Deyu** to visit the Qixiasi 棲霞寺.

Zhu Tao 朱滔 (d. 785), Tian Yue 田悅 (751–784), and Wang Wujun 王武俊 (735–801) rebel against the Tang.

783
Chang Gun died in the 1st month in Fujian.

2nd month, **Wu Yuanheng** 武元衡 (758–815) is one of 27 men to pass the *jinshi*.

Rong Yu was sent out to be Prefect of Chenzhou 晨州 in the 9th month.

Major Tang-Tibetan peace treaty ending hostilities.

Zhu Ci 朱泚 (742–784) rebels and Dezong flies the capital for Fengtian 奉天.

Lingche traveled to Huzhou and wrote poems with **Jiao Ran**; together they met **Liu Yuxi** who was considered a child prodigy.

Qian Qi died in this year or slightly before.

784
Lu Lun and **Wu Yuanheng** fell into rebel hands in the 3rd month.

Many edicts written in Fengtian were from **Lu Zhi's** hand.

Zhu Ci is killed and Chang'an retaken with help of Tibetans who are promised Tang territory in return; the promise was not kept and hostilities are renewed.

Dezong returned to Chang'an in the 7th month of the year.

785
Li Duan probably died in this year.

786
Han Yu 韓愈 (768–824) and **Ouyang Zhan** were not successful in the *jinshi*; 27 men passed.

Dai Shulun 戴叔倫 (732–789) and **Quan Deyu** were together in Hongzhou 洪州 late in the year.

Liang Su completed the *Ceding Zhiguan* 測定止觀, a collection of the writings of Zhanran, the Sixth Tiantai 天台 Patriarch, and others.

787
Wei Yingwu, serving as Prefect of Jiangzhou 江州, was called in the 9th month to the capital and appointed Director of the Left Office of the Department of State Affairs.

Liu Zhangqing and **Geng Wei** both died in this year or slightly later.

788
Poets who wrote responses to Dezong's poems include (in the 3rd month) Song Ruozhao 宋若昭 (761–828), Song Ruoxian 宋若憲 (d. 830), and Bao Junwei 鮑君徽 and (in the 9th month) **Wei Yingwu**; shortly after Wei was sent to be Prefect of Suzhou 蘇州.

Indicative of a complete change in attitude, Dezong issued a number of edicts supporting the faith in the late 780s and himself wrote a preface to a new translation of the *Prajñāpāramitā* completed in 788.

Gu Kuang's home in the Xuanping Ward 宣平里 of the capital was the meeting place of various literati.

Appendix II: Literary Timeline of the Tang

Li Yi was serving in the retinue of Zhang Xianfu 張獻甫 (736–796); he compiled fifty of his poems written while in military service and presented them to Lu Jingliang 盧景亮 (d. 806).

789 **Yang Juyuan** 楊巨源 (755–after 833) and 35 other candidates were successful in the *jinshi*.

Jiao Ran completes his *Shishi* 詩式 (Poetic Forms) living at Xishan 西山 in Huzhou.

Dai Shulun dies while traveling in the South; **Quan Deyu** and **Liang Su** wrote tomb tablet inscriptions for him; his works were collected in 20 *juan*.

Bo Juyi visited **Gu Kuang** in Hangzhou 杭州; Gu praised Bo's poetry.

790 **Li Guan** and **Liu Zongyuan** did not pass the *jinshi*, 29 others did.

Wei Yingwu resigned as Prefect of Suzhou and went to live in the Yongding si 永定寺.

Han Yu traveled to Huazhou 華州 presenting his writings to Jia Dan 賈耽 (730–805).

Li He 李賀 (790–816) was born.

791 **Linghu Chu** 令狐楚 and 29 others passed the *jinshi*.

Lu Zhi because of the enmity of the Grand Councilor Dou Can 竇參 (733–792) was demoted from Hanlin Academician to Vice-director of the Bureau of Military Personnel.

Li Guan presented his writings to Lu Zhi.

Feng Yan 封演 (*jinshi* 756) completed his *Fengshi wenjian ji* 封氏聞見記 in 5 *juan*.

Lü Wen 呂溫 (772–811) studied the *Chunqiu* 春秋 with **Lu Zhi** 陸質 and literature with **Liang Su**.

Wei Yingwu died.

792 The Academy of Scholarly Worthies with the aid of the Prefect of Huzhou collected 546 of **Jiao Ran's** poems and compiled the *Zhushanji* 杼山集 in 10 *juan*.

The so-called Longhubang 龍虎榜 (Dragon and Tiger List) of candidates who passed the *jinshi* included **Li Guan**, **Han Yu**, and Feng Su 馮宿 (767–837); **Lu Zhi** was the examiner.

In the 4th month **Li Guan** passed the Erudite Literatus Examination.

Li Guan wrote a letter to **Liang Su** recommending **Meng Jiao**.

Liu Zongyuan came to the capital and in the fall presented his writings to **Quan Deyu**.

793 **Han Yu**, **Liu Zongyuan**, **Meng Jiao**, **Li Ao**, and Shi Hong 石洪 (771–812) together climbed the pagoda in the Ciensi 慈恩寺 in the 1st month.

Liu Zongyuan and **Liu Yuxi** passed the *jinshi*; **Yuan Zhen**, not yet 15-years-old, passed the *mingjing* 明經 (clarifying the classics) examination.

In the 11th month **Liang Su**, then a Hanlin Academican, died.

794 In the 1st month Tang troops allied with those of Nanzhao 南詔 (738–902) routed the Tibetans at Shenchuan 神川.

Gu Kuang returned to Maoshan 茅山.

In the 5th month **Li Guan** died in Chang'an, aged 29; **Han Yu** wrote the grave inscription.

Liu Mian 柳冕 (d. 804) was Prefect of Wuzhou 婺州 (modern Zhejiang).

Appendix II: Literary Timeline of the Tang

	Shen Jiji as Vice-director of the Ministry of Rites wrote the "Cike lun" 詞科論 (On the Literary Examinations) criticizing the ability of such examinations to produce good officials.
795	**Bo Xingjian** wrote "Li Wa zhuan" 李娃傳 (Tale of Li Wa).
	Dezong entertains his court officials increasingly often, this year on the 9th day of the 9th month at the Qujiang 曲江 (Serpentine).
	Lingche passed through the capital and met with **Liu Zongyuan**, **Lü Wen**, **Liu Yuxi**, and **Quan Deyu**.
796	In the 2nd month **Meng Jiao** and 29 others passed the *jinshi*.
	Dezong summoned Xu Dai 徐岱 (d. ca. 800) and others to discuss the Three Teachings of Confucianism, Daoism and Buddhism.
	In the 8th month **Meng Jiao** visited **Zhang Ji** 張籍 who was living in Hezhou 和州.
797	**Han Yu** was serving on the staff of Military Commissioner Dong Jin 董晉 (724–799) in Bianzhou 汴州 (modern Kaifeng); Han wrote a letter to **Feng Su** discussing literature; **Li Ao** and **Zhang Ji** were studying with Han.
	In the 7th month **Ouyang Zhan** traveled to Shu, then returned to the capital.
	On the 9th of the 9th month Dezong presented his officials with a poem; **Quan Deyu** matched it.
798	**Li Ao**, **Lü Wen**, and 18 others passed the *jinshi*.
	Liu Zongyuan became a Proofreader in the Academy of Scholarly Worthies.
799	**Zhang Ji** 張籍 and 16 others passed the *jinshi*.
	Lu Tong 盧仝 (ca. 775–ca. 835) left Yangzhou 揚州 to go to Luoyang.
	Lu Lun probably died in this year.
800	**Bo Juyi** and 16 others passed the *jinshi*.
	In the 4th month **Li Ao** married **Han Yu**'s niece.
	Rong Yu died this year while Prefect of Qianzhou 虔州.
	Huangfu Shi met **Gu Kuang** at the Xiaogansi 孝感寺 in Yangzhou.
801	**Yuan Zhen** failed the *jinshi*, then with **Yang Juyuan** and others talked about the matter of Cui Yingying 崔鶯鶯—both then wrote poems on Cui; in the 7th month Yuan first met **Bo Juyi**.
	Li Yi and **Liu Yuxi** were together in Yangzhou.
	Liu Zongyuan was transferred to be Commandant of Lantian 藍田.
	Ouyang Zhan died probably in this year.
	Liu Mian, in Fuzhou, wrote a letter on literature to Pei Zhou 裴冑 (729–803).
802	**Han Yu** became an Erudite at the School of Four Gates and assisted **Quan Deyu** in administering the examinations; 23 candidates passed.
	Jia Dan presented his *Zhenyuan shidao lu* 貞元十道錄 (Record of the Ten Provinces in the Zhenyuan Era) and **Quan Deyu** wrote a preface.
	Li Gongzuo 李公佐 (ca. 770–ca. 848) came to Luoyang from the Wu region and wrote *Nanke Taishou zhuan* 南柯太守傳 (An Account of the Governor of the Southern Branch).
	Dezong entertained the court on the 9th of the 9th month at the pavilion on the Malinchi 馬琳池 (Malin Pond) and wrote a poem; **Quan Deyu** and **Wu Yuanheng** matched it.

Appendix II: Literary Timeline of the Tang

	Liu Mian, Surveillance Commissioner of Fujian, wrote to **Quan Deyu**, who was the examiner, arguing that *shi* 詩 and *fu* 賦 should not be part of an examination that would supply officials.
803	**Bo Juyi** and **Yuan Zhen** both passed the Erudite Literatus Examination and became Editors in the Palace Library.
	Liu Zongyuan and **Liu Yuxi** were promoted to be Investigating Censors; **Han Yu** had earlier received the same position so all three served together in the Censorate.
	Lü Wen completing his mourning was mad Reminder on the Left.
	The Leshan Giant Buddha 樂山大佛 completed (Sichuan).
	Du Mu 杜牧 (803–852) was born.
804	The examinations and the feast normally held on Zhonghejie 中和節, a holiday established by Dezong to celebrate the birthday of the Daoist deity Taiyang Xingjun 太陽星君 on the 1st day of the 2nd month, were cancelled.
	The Japanese monk Kūkai 空海 (774–835) came to Chang'an and lived in the Ximingsi 西明寺.
	After conversations about Cui Yingying, **Li Shen** wrote the "Yingying ge" 鶯鶯歌 (Song of Yingying) and **Yuan Zhen** wrote *Yingyingzhuan* 鶯鶯傳 (An Account of Yingying).
	Lü Wen was sent as an envoy to the Tibetans and fell ill in Tibet in 805.
	Wu Yuanheng became Palace Aide to the Censor in Chief.
	Han Yu was at Yangshan 陽山 interacting with the monks there.
	Li He, aged 15, making a name for himself through his poetry.
	Liu Mian died in Fuzhou.
805	Dezong dies in the 1st month and is replaced by Shunzong.
	Wei Zhiyi 韋執誼 (d. ca. 807) is made Grand Councilor in the 2nd month.
	Wang Shuwen 王叔文 (793–806) was summoned to serve as a Hanlin Academician.
	Liu Zongyuan was made Vice-director of the Minister of Rites.
	Lu Zhi was summoned back to the capital but had died before the summons reached him.
	In the 5th month Wang Shuwen's mother died.
	In the 8th month Shunzong abdicated because of illness and Xianzong was enthroned; Wang Shuwen was demoted to be Revenue Manager of Yuzhou 渝州.
	Han Yu as a result of an amnesty was appointed Administrator in the Personnel Evaluation Section in Jiangling 江陵.
	Because of their ties to Wang Shuwen, **Liu Zongyuan** was sent out to be Prefect of Shaozhou 邵州 and **Liu Yuxi** to be Prefect of Lianzhou 連州; shortly after they were demoted to be Assistant Magistrates of Yongzhou 永州 and Langzhou 郎州 respectively.
	Jia Dan died in Chang'an.
	In the 11th month **Wei Zhiyi** was made Assistant Magistrate of Yazhou 崖州.
806	In the 1st month Shunzong died age 45.
	In the 2nd month **Huangfu Shi**, **Li Shen**, and 21 others passed the *jinshi*.
	Bo Juyi and **Yuan Zhen** heard the story "Yizhi hua" 一枝花 in the 3rd month.
	Kūkai returned to Japan in the 4th month.

Appendix II: Literary Timeline of the Tang

	Bo Juyi and Chen Hong 陳鴻 visited the Xianyousi 仙遊寺 in Zhouzhi County 周至縣 where the conversation turned to Xuanzong and Yang Guifei; as a result Bo wrote "Changhen ge" 長恨歌 (Song of Everlasting Sorrow) and Chen wrote *Changhen ge zhuan* 長恨歌傳 (A Prose Account of the Song of Everlasting Sorrow).
807	In the 2nd month **Bo Xingjian** and Wu Wuling 吳武陵 (d. 835) along with 26 other candidates passed the *jinshi*.
	Han Yu was made Erudite in the Directorate of Education.
	In the 11th month **Bo Juyi** was made a Hanlin Academician.
	Around this year **Li He** traveled to the Lower Yangzi Region and wrote many poems.
808	Niu Sengru 牛僧孺 (ca. 779–ca. 848), Li Zongmin 李宗閔 (d. 846), and **Huangfu Shi** initially passed the Worthy and Excellent, Straightforward and Upright Examination but because the examiners, including **Li Yi**, were found to have been too lenient in allowing criticism of the Grand Councilor Li Jifu 李吉甫 (758–814), the results were over-turned and the examiners banished.
	Pei Chun 裴均 (750–811) and Yang Ping 楊憑 (fl. 774-819) completed their collection of poems from the South titled *Jing Tan change ji* 荊潭唱和集 for which **Han Yu** wrote a preface.
	Li He went to Luoyang and presented **Han Yu** with his poems who was most impressed.
	Liu Cha 劉叉 (fl. 806–820) joined Han Yu's group of students.
809	Widespread famine in the South from the Lower Yangzi north to the Huai River.
	Bo Xingjian serving as Editor in the Palace Library wrote *Sanmengji* 三夢記 (A Record of Three Dreams).
	Liu Zongyuan in Yongzhou 永州 wrote the first four of his "Yongzhou baji" 永州八記 (Eight Records of Yongzhou's Landscape).
	Li Shen was an Editor in the Palace Library and around this time wrote a 20-poem series titled "Yuefu xinti" 樂府新題 (Ballads on New Themes); **Yuan Zhen** wrote 12 matching poems.
	Li Jifu and **Wu Yuanheng**, both serving as Military Commissioners, matched poems.
810	**Jia Dao** met with **Li Yi** in Luoyang.
	In the 6th month **Lü Wen**, then Prefect of Daozhou 道州, brought **Liu Zongyuan** a letter from Li Jifu.
	On the 15th of the 8th month **Lu Tong** wrote "Yue shi" 月蝕 (Lunar Eclipse).
	Shen Yazhi 沈亞之 (781–832) came to the capital as a tribute candidate and stayed at Bao Rong's 鮑溶 (*jinshi* 809) house.
811	**Li Gongzuo** traveling from the capital to his position in the South as a result of a story-telling session with fellow travelers wrote "Lujiang Feng'ao" 廬江馮媼 (Old Mrs. Feng from the Lu River).
	In the 8th month **Lü Wen** died in Hengzhou 衡州; **Liu Yuxi** wrote the preface to his collected works in 10 *juan*.
	Zhang Hu 張祜 (792–ca. 853) submitted his poems to **Han Yu** hoping Han would recommend him.

Appendix II: Literary Timeline of the Tang

812　　**Han Yu** returned from a provincial position became embroiled in a local conflict he encountered on the way and as a result was demoted to Erudite in the Directorate of Education.

Liu Zongyuan in Yongzhou completed the last four of his "Eight Records of Yongzhou Landscapes."

In the 11th month Du You 杜佑 (735–812) died in his Chang'an residence, leaving his massive encyclopedia, *Tongdian* 通典 in 200 *juan*.

Li He was Court Gentleman for Ceremonials.

Lu Tong died in this year or shortly afterwards.

Li Shangyin was born in this year or the next.

813　　**Han Yu** and **Bo Juyi** matched a poem **Wu Yuanheng** wrote on returning to the capital.

Li Jifu presented his *Yuanhe junxian tuzhi* 元和郡縣圖志 (Maps and Records of the Commanderies and Counties in the Yuanhe Era) in 40 *juan* along with his *Liudai lue* 六代略 (Shortcomings of Six Eras) in 30 *juan* and his *Shi daozhoujun tu* 十道州君圖 (Maps of Ten Provinces, Prefectures and Commanderies) in 54 *juan*.

Wu Yuanheng, Li Jifu, and Li Jiang 李絳 (764–830), all Grand Councilors, as well as former Grand Councilors **Quan Deyu**, and Zheng Yuqing 鄭餘慶 (745–820), all submitted poems at the emperor's request.

Meng Jiao living in Luoyang ill and impoverished wrote his series of 15 poems titled "Qiu huai" 秋懷 (Autumn Meditations).

Wang Jian as an Aide in Shaoying 昭應 sent a poem to Pei Du 裴度 (765–839).

Yuan Zhen was in Jiangling and as the request of Du Fu's grandson, Du Siye 杜嗣業 (b. 780) wrote "Du Fu muximing" 杜甫墓系銘 (Tomb Tablet Inscription for Du Fu) that also traced the history of poetry.

814　　**Yang Juyuan** was appointed Assistant in the Palace Library and **Zhang Ji** and **Jia Dao** wrote poems congratulating him on the wall of his new residence west of the city.

Liu Yuxi and the other "Ba sima" 八司馬 including **Liu Zongyuan** were recalled to the capital; during **Liu Zongyuan**'s time in Yongzhou he attracted many students.

Li Shen probably in this year was made Instructor in the National University.

815　　**Yuan Zhen** was recalled to the capital from Tangzhou 唐州; when he passed through Lantian 藍田 he left poems for **Liu Yuxi** and **Liu Zongyuan** who were also returning to the capital.

Shen Yazhi and 29 others passed the *jinshi*.

Liu Yuxi and **Liu Zongyuan** were again exiled to the distant prefectures of Lianzhou 連州 and Liuzhou 柳州 respectively; they traveled together from the capital to Hengyang 衡陽 and then went their separate ways.

Yuan Zhen was sent out to be Vice Prefect of Tongzhou 通州.

Wu Yuanheng was assassinated on the 3rd day of the 6th month by men sent by Wang Chengzong 王承宗 (d. 820) Military Commissioner of Zhenzhou 鎮州.

Han Yu presented his *Shunzong shilu* 順宗實錄 (Veritable Records of Shunzong's Reign).

Huai Hui 懷暉 (764–815) a monk at the Zhangjingsi 章敬寺 died; **Li Shen** and **Jia Dao** wrote poems lamenting his death and **Quan Deyu** composed the tomb-tablet inscription.

Bo Juyi wrote a letter to **Yuan Zhen** depicting his journey from Chang'an to Jiangxi 江西 interspersed with many poems.

816   **Yao He** 姚合 (ca. 779–ca. 849) and 32 others passed the *jinshi*.

Zhang Ji was made Instructor in the National University; **Han Yu** was Mentor to the Heir Apparent on the Right.

Li He returned to his old home at Changgu 昌谷 from Luzhou 潞州 and died, aged 26; his collected works filled 5 *juan* and **Du Mu** later wrote a preface.

Lingche died aged 70; **Liu Yuxi** wrote the preface of his works in 10 *juan*.

Gu Kuang died about this year; **Huangfu Shi** wrote the preface for his works.

817   **Li Deyu** 李德裕 (787–850) was Chief Secretary to Military Commissioner Zhang Hongjing 張弘靖 (760–824) in Taiyuan.

Linghu Chu as a Hanlin Academician compiled *Yulan shi* 御覽詩 (Poems for the Emperor to View) in 1 *juan*, collecting poems from the Dali 大曆, Zhenyuan 貞元, and Yuanhe 元和 eras.

Yao He about this time joined the staff of Tian Hongzheng 田弘正 (764–821).

818   When **Yang Juyuan** was promoted to be Vice Director of the Bureau of Forestry and Crafts, **Wang Jian** and **Bo Juyi** sent him poems congratulating him.

Quan Deyu was recalled to the capital but died on the way, age 59; **Han Yu** wrote a tomb-tablet inscription. His collected works were in 50 *juan*.

Yuan Zhen in Tongzhou probably wrote his "Liangchanggong ci" 連昌宮詞 (The Lianchang Palace) in this year

819   **Xianzong** sent men to the Famensi 法門寺 in Fengxiang 鳳翔 to receive a bone of the Buddha; **Han Yu** submitted a memorial criticizing this and was in turn banished to become Prefect of Chaozhou 潮州 in the Far South

Yuan Zhen was transferred to be Administrator in Guozhou 虢州 while Bo Juyi and his brother **Bo Xingjian** were on their way to Zhongchou 忠州 where Bo Juyi was to be prefect; the three men met at Xiazhong 峽中 and spent three days together.

Li Deyu followed Zhang Hongjing to court and was appointed Investigating Censor.

In the 10th month **Liu Zongyuan** died in Liuzhou, age 47; **Han Yu** wrote a tomb-tablet inscription; his works totaled 30 *juan* and **Liu Yuxi** wrote the preface.

820   In the 1st month Xianzong died age 42, rumored to have been poisoned by the eunuch Chen Hongzhi 陳宏志 (d. 835); his 25-year old son Muzong succeeds.

In the 2nd month **Li Shen** and **Li Deyu** were made Hanlin Academicians.

In the 5th month Xianzong was buried at Jingling 景陵; **Linghu Chu** wrote a prose elegy and **Yuan Zhen** and **Zhang Hu** wrote threnodies.

Li Yi was made Cavalier Attendant-in-Ordinary.

It was probably this year that **Zhang Ji**, at **Han Yu**'s recommendation was made Erudite in the National University.

Appendix II: Literary Timeline of the Tang

	Also about this time **Wang Jian** completed his 100 "Gongci" 宮詞 (Palace Songs) which were popular among the populace of the capital.
821	**Yuan Zhen** was made a Hanlin Academician joining **Li Shen**, and **Li Deyu**; they were popularly known as the "Sanjun" 三俊 (Three Eminences); their work in choosing successful *jinshi* candidates was judged unfair and **Bo Juyi** and Wang Qi 王起 (760–847) were ordered to reexamine the candidates; as a result several candidates, including Li Zongmin, were banished; this controversy is considered to be the start of the feud between Niu Sengru and his adherents and Li Zongmin and his party
	In the 7th month Princess Taihe 太和公主 was sent to be married to a Uyghur leader; **Zhang Ji**, **Wang Jian**, and **Yang Juyuan** sent her off with poems.
	In the 8th month **Shen Yazhi** was made Commandant of Yueyang 櫟陽 near the capital.
822	**Zhang Ji** was promoted to be Vice Director of the Bureau of Waterways and Irrigation; **Bo Juyi** wrote a poem congratulating him; later **Zhang Ji** and **Han Yu** went to the Qujiang (Serpentine) where Han wrote a poem to **Bo Juyi.**
	Yuan Zhen and Pei Du, both Grand Councilors, grew to hate one other; Pei accused Yuan of sending someone to assassinate him; as a result, both were demoted, Yuan sent out to be Prefect of Tongzhou 同州.
	Bo Juyi requested a position away from the capital and was made Prefect of Hangzhou 杭州.
	Liu Yuxi, Prefect of Kuizhou 夔州, studied local songs and wrote 9 "Zhuzhici" 竹枝詞 (Bamboo-branch Songs).
823	In the 6th month **Han Yu** was made Governor of the capital and concurrently Censor in Chief. In the 10th month Li Fengji 李逢吉 (758–835), a Grand Councilor, took advantage of an argument between Han and **Li Shen** to demote them both.
	Yuan Zhen was transferred from Tongzhou to become Prefect of Yuezhou 越州 and Military Commissioner of Zhedong 浙東.
	Yao He was made Commandant of Wannian County 萬年縣 in the capital; that fall **Jia Dao**, **Gu Feixiong**, and **Wuke** 無可 (fl. 825–827) visited his residence.
	That winter **Han Xiang** 韓湘 (794–after 823) was sent to a provincial position and **Jia Dao**, **Yao He**, Zhu Qingyu 朱慶餘 (826 *jinshi*), **Wuke** saw him off; **Shen Yazhi** wrote a *xu* 序 for him.
	Annual examinations in the *Shiji* 史記, *Han shu* 漢書 and *Hou Hanshu* 後漢書 instituted (lasting until the end of the Tang).
824	Muzong died in the 1st month and fifteen-year-old Jingzong replaced him; the new emperor indulged in various pleasures and took little interest in ruling
	Under examiner Li Zongmin 33 candidates passed the *jinshi*.
	The carving of the *Lotus Sutra* onto the walls of the Gushansi 孤山寺 in Hangzhou was completed; **Yuan Zhen** wrote a piece recording the event; possibly related was the fad for paintings of the Buddha on monastery walls in the next years.

Appendix II: Literary Timeline of the Tang

Han Yu asked for sick leave and in the 5th month moved to a villa on Nanshan; **Zhang Ji** resigned to accompany Han; **Jia Dao** also visited Han; in the 8th month he moved back to his residence in the capital; **Zhang Ji** and **Wang Jian** visited; in the 12th month he died, aged 56. **Liu Yuxi** wrote an elegy. Han's son-in-law, Li Han 李漢 (ca. 790–ca. 860), wrote a preface to Han's collected works in 40 *juan*; **Li Ao** wrote a draft biography and **Huangfu Shi** composed the tomb-tablet inscription.

Yuan Zhen compiled the 2251 poems **Bo Juyi** wrote prior to the end of the Changqing era in 50 *juan*, titled the collection *Boshi Changqing ji* 白氏長慶集, and wrote a preface for it.

825 In the first month Niu Sengru was demoted from Grand Councilor to Military Commissioner of the Wuchang 武昌 Army (in Ezhou 鄂州).

826 In the 6th month Jingzong went to the Xingfusi 興福寺 to hear the month Wenshu 文溆 expound on sutras.

Liu Yuxi and **Bo Juyi**, both returning to the capital, met in Yangzhou 揚州 and traveled together for half a month, writing and matching poems.

In the 12th month Jingzong was killed by eunuchs under orders from Liu Keming 劉克明 (d. 827), who also killed several of the royal princes, then sent for Li Han 李涵 (809–840), the Prince of Jiang 江王, who at the age of 17 succeeded as Wenzong.

In the winter **Bo Xingjian**, age 50, died in Chang'an.

827 Probably in this year **Du Mu** was traveling on the Cenyang 涔陽 Road (modern Hunan) and passed through Songzi 松滋 County where he was moved by the story of Guiniang 桂娘 and wrote *Tou Lienü zhuan* 竇列女傳 (An Account of Chaste Woman Dou).

Zhang Hu traveling through Runzhou 潤州 wrote a poem on the wall of the Beigu Xinlou 北固新樓.

Yuan Zhen and **Bo Juyi** matched 57 poems, collecting them under the title *Yinji ji* 因繼集.

Du Mu and 32 others passed the *jinshi*; subsequently Du became Editor in the Institute for the Advancement of Literature.

In the 3rd month **Bo Juyi**, **Liu Yuxi**, **Zhang Ji**, Cui Qun 崔群 (772–832) and other literati had a party in the Apricot Park at the Serpentine, drinking, boating and writing poems.

In the 9th month when **Wang Jian** was sent out to be Vice Prefect of Shanzhou 陝州, **Bo Juyi**, **Jia Dao**, **Liu Yuxi**, and **Zhang Ji** all wrote poems seeing him off.

Bo Juyi collected the poems he had written since the 3rd year of the Changqing era in a *Houji* 後集, prefaced them and sent them to **Yuan Zhen** in Yuezhou 越州; Bo regularly updated his collection in the following years.

In the 10th month **Feng Su** 馮宿 (767–837) who had been Scholar in the Academy of Scholarly Worthies was made Governor of Henan 河南 based in Luoyang; **Bo Juyi** and **Liu Yuxi** sent him off with poems.

Ma Dai 馬戴 (d. 869) and **Jia Dao** wrote poems together with **Yao He** one evening at Yao's home.

829 **Linghu Chu** in the 4th month became Regent of the Eastern Capital and he and **Bo Juyi** exchanged poems.

Appendix II: Literary Timeline of the Tang

> **Yuan Zhen**, after serving 7 years as Surveillance Commissioner of Zhedong where he entertained a number of literati, Daoists, and singers, returned to the capital as Left Assistant Director in the Department of State Affairs.
> **Cao Tang** 曹唐 (ca. 797–ca. 866) was in Chang'an; he had earlier been a Daoist priest but now was a layman again.
> **Liu Yuxi**, **Li Deyu**, and **Yuan Zhen** matched each other's poems later to be collected as *Wu Yue changhe ji* 吳越唱和集.
> Nanzhao troops take Chengdu.

830
> Niu Sengru returns to the capital as a Grand Councilor (with Li Zongmin and Pei Du).
> Linghu Tao 令狐綯 (795–879) and 24 others pass the *jinshi*; unlike in earlier times, few of those successful in the *jinshi* in the following decades made a mark on literary history; even the top graduates each year are virtually unknown today.
> **Zhang Ji**, 63 years old, was made Director of Studies in the National University.
> **Du Mu** left Shen Chuanshi's 沈傳師 (777–835) staff in Xuanzhou 宣州 to return to the capital.
> **Li Zongmin** and Niu Sengru forced **Li Deyu** out of the court; he was made Military Vice Commissioner of Jiannan and Xichuan
> It was probably this year that Niu Sengru completed his collection of tales titled *Xuanguai lu* 玄怪錄 (Records of the Mysterious and Strange).

831
> In the 2nd month Wenzong plotted with Song Shenxi 宋申錫 (d. 833), who became Grand Councilor the following month, and Wang Fan 王璠 (*jinshi* 810), Governor of the Capital, to execute some of the eunuchs, but the plan leaked out and the palace physician, Cheng Zhu 鄭注 (d. 835), along with the eunuch Wang Shoucheng 王守澄 (d. 835), foiled things, had Song arrested and charged with planning to overthrow Wenzong; Song was exiled to be Vice Prefect of Kaizhou where he died the following year.
> In the 6th month there was flooding in both the north and the south and much crop failure.
> In the 7th month **Yuan Zhen** died suddenly in his post as Military Governor of Wuchang 武昌, age 52; **Bo Juyi** wrote the tomb-tablet inscription.
> Niu Sengru who was Military Commissioner in Chengdu built the Choubianlou 籌邊樓 (Defending the Border Tower) for **Xue Tao** 薛濤 (768–832), then in her early 60s.

832
> **Xu Hun** 許渾 (ca. 788–ca. 858) and 24 other candidates passed the *jinshi*

833
> After **Li Deyu** had been made a Grand Councilor he discusses the problem of factional politics with Wenzong.
> In the 12th month Wenzong ordered that the *Nine Classics* and the *Lunyu* 論語 (*Confucian Analects*) be inscribed on a stone wall in the National University.

834
> Zheng Chuhai 鄭處海, who had earlier been a monk, passed the *jinshi* and became a layman serving as an Editor in the Palace Library; he began his *Minghuang zalu* 明皇雜錄 (Miscellaneous Records of Emperor Minghuang).

Appendix II: Literary Timeline of the Tang

        Pei Lin 裴潾 (d. 838), a scholar in the Academy of Scholarly Worthies, finished his *Taihe tongxuan* 太和通選 (A Comprehensive Selection of Literature Compiled in the Taihe Era) in 30 *juan*, intended as a sequel to the *Wenxuan* 文選 (Selections of Refined Literature).

        Yao He was made Prefect of Hangzhou; **Gu Feixiong** and **Jia Dao** wrote poems seeing him off; when he passed through Luoyang, **Bo Juyi** talked to him about his time in Hangzhou.

835   **Du Mu** returned from Yangzhou to the capital, appointed Investigating Censor; when Shen Chuanshi died later that year, Du wrote his draft biography.

        In the 11th month Li Xun 李訓 (789–835) and Zheng Zhu made plans with Wenzong to kill many of the eunuchs; at a dawn court audience it was reported that "sweet dew" had form on a pomegranate tree in the outer palace; Wenzong sent the eunuchs out to see (and into an ambush), but when the eunuchs discovered Li Xun's armed men, they fled back into the palace; then summoning the Shence Army 神策軍 that they controlled, they ordered all conspirators killed; more than 1,000 people of Chang'an were killed; this was the so-called Ganlu shibian 甘露事變 (Sweet Dew Incident).

        Huangfu Shi about this time wrote *Yuye* 諭業 (Metaphors of [Literary] Accomplishment discussing Tang literature; he died sometime after this year.

        First purge of the Buddhist church under Wenzong.

836   Wenzong discussed poetry with the new Grand Councilor, Zheng Tan 鄭覃 (d. 842); Zheng urged him to collect folksongs to gauge problems among the people, not to indulge his own feelings.

        Li Ao died in the 6th month, age 64; he was granted the posthumous title Wen 文 and left collected works in 10 *juan*.

837   **Li Shangyin** and 39 others passed the *jinshi*.

        On the 3rd day of the 3rd month the Governor of Henan, Li Jue 李珏 (785–853), hosted a day-long party on the banks of the Luo River; there were 15 guests including Pei Du, **Liu Yuxi**, and **Bo Juyi**.

        In the 11th month **Linghu Chu** died while serving as Surveillance Commissioner of Shannan Xidao 山南西道; **Li Shangyin**, on Linghu's staff at the time, **Bo Juyi** and **Liu Yuxi** all wrote elegies; Li then returned to the capital.

        An engraving of the *Nine Classics* known as the Kaicheng Era (836–840) Stone Classics 開成石經 set up in the **Directorate of Education.**

838   In the 1st month Li Shi 李石 (784–845), newly-made Grand Councilor, was attacked by bandits on his way to court but suffered only slight injury; but the capital was in a state of fear. The following day only nine officials came to court. Eventually it was determined that the assassins had been sent by the eunuch, Qiu Shiliang 仇士良 (784–845).

        In the 7th month the Japanese Monk Ennin 圓仁 (794–864) arrives in Yangzhou from Japan and meets with **Li Deyu**, Surveillance Commissioner there since 837.

        Li Jue cautions Wenzong, who is fond of poetry, that the Yuanhe Style (i.e. the poems of Yuan Zhen and Bo Juyi, including the *Yanshi* 艷詩 "**poems of seductive allure**") is despicable.

Bo Juyi wrote "Zuiyin Xiansheng zhuan" 醉吟先生傳 (An Account of the Gentleman Who Gets Drunk and Chants Verse), a playful autobiographical piece that describes the recent ten years of his life spent drinking and writing poetry.

839 Factional politics continue as Zheng Tan is replaced as Grand Councilor by Li Jue.

Guanxiu 貫休 (832–912), just 7 years old, is a novice in the Heansi 和安寺. Wuzhou 婺州 where he hears lectures on poetry from the Monk Chumo 處默 (d. after 882).

840 Wenzong died of an illness in the 1st month, age 33. The eunuchs forced Wenzong's 27-year-old younger brother, Li Yan 李炎, to replace him as emperor (Wuzong); they had the former Heir Apparent, Li Chengmei 李成美 (820–840), commit suicide. Wuzong favored Daoism and a series of edicts beginning in 842 thousands of monks and nuns in Chang'an were laicized, monasteries destroyed, and property seized.

Du Mu moved from Chang'an to Xunyang to see his younger brother who was ill.

841 In the 3rd month, the eunuch Qiu Shilang convinced Wuzong to execute two former Grand Councilors, Li Jue and Yang Sifu 楊嗣復 (783–848), but **Li Deyu** and two other current Grand Councilors protested vigorously so that Li Jue and Yang Sifu were sent out to distant places as prefects.

Wuzong favored Daoists; in 840 he had brought 81 Daoists into the palace to work on alchemical projects; this year Li Xuanjing 李玄靖 and Zhao Guizhen 趙歸真 (d. 846) were often in the palace editing Daoist texts.

Zongmi 宗密 (784–841), fifth patriarch of Huayan 華嚴 School of Buddhism, died.

842 Zheng Ying 鄭顥 (817–860), the top graduate, and 29 other candidates passed the *jinshi*.

In the 6th month many Buddhists and Daoists argued their cases before the emperor, Wuzong favoring the Daoists; Ennin was in Chang'an and recorded this situation in his diary.

In the 8th month Wuzong called on Niu Sengru and **Li Deyu** to suggest a solution to the Uyghur problem; the Kirghiz had driven the Uyghurs south into the Chinese borderlands; Niu argued for a strategy of appeasement, whereas Li urged an aggressive stance. Wuzong was convinced by **Li Deyu's** argument and put him in charge of the border.

843 In the second month 22 candidates passed the *jinshi* with Lu Zhao 盧肇 (818–882), the future author of *Tang zhi yan* 唐摭言 and *Yunxi youyi* 雲溪友議, as the top graduate.

In the 2nd month Princess Taihe, who had married the Uyghur qaghan in 821, returned to Chang'an and was admitted to the harem.

In the 7th month **Jia Dao**, age 64, died in his post at Jinzhou 晉州; **Wuke** and others wrote eulogies; Jia's works, entitled *Changjiang ji* 長江集, were in 10 *juan*.

844 In the 2nd month **Zhao Gu** 趙嘏 (ca. 806–ca. 850) and 24 others passed the *jinshi*.

In the 10th month **Du Mu** wrote a letter to **Li Deyu** with suggestions on how to handle the Uyghurs.

Appendix II: Literary Timeline of the Tang

845   In the 1st month, Wuzong, influenced by Zhao Guizhen, ordered that a Wangxiantai 望仙台 (Terrace for Watching for the Immortals) be built; **Li Deyu** remonstrated but the emperor did not listen to his criticism

           Gu Feixiong and 26 other candidates passed the *jinshi*.

           Bo Juyi collected his writings in 75 *juan* and wrote a preface depicting how he had put these writings together; at this time his poetry had already spread to Japan and other East Asian countries.

           In the 8th month Wuzong issued an edict condemning the malpractices of Buddhism and dissolving monasteries and causing monks to return to lay life; Zoroastrianism and Manichaeism were also banned.

846   Di Shensi 狄慎思 as the top graduate and 25 others passed the *jinshi*.

           In the 3rd month Wuzong died of an illness and the eunuch install the 13th son of Xianzong, Li Chen 李忱 (810–859), the future Xuanzong 宣宗.

           In the 4th month **Li Deyu** was sent out to be Military Commissioner of Jingnan, causing great concern among the populace of the capital.

           The Daoist contingent surrounding Wuzong, including Zhao Guizhen, were either executed or banished.

           Bo Juyi died in Luoyang, age 74. The emperor wrote a poem lamenting his death and he left his writings in 75 *juan*.

           Niu Sengru, Li Zongmin, Yang Sifu, and **Li Deyu** all recalled to the capital. Li Zongmin had died in Fengzhou 封州 before the recall.

847   **Wen Tingyun** 溫庭筠 (ca. 812–870), then 35-years-old, was in the capital in the company of scions of high-ranking officials; about this time he took the *jinshi* but did not pass.

           Xuanzong ordered than the bans concerning Buddhism be lifted and the monasteries restored.

848   Niu Sengru died, age 68, and was given the posthumous title Wenzhen 文貞; **Du Mu** and Li Jue wrote tomb inscriptions.

           Ban on Buddhism lifted under Xuanzhong 宣宗.

           Ennin left to return to Japan.

849   **Du Mu** was in the capital serving as Vice Director of the Bureau of Merit Titles; **Li Shangyin** sent him a poem praising Du's poetry.

           In the 2nd month, the Tibetans drove the local populace out of several border prefectures.

           Xu Hun gave up his position as Investigating Censor because of illness and was appointed Vice Prefect of Runzhou.

           Li Shangyin was appointed Administrative Assistant to Lu Hong 盧弘止 (d. 851), the Military Commissioner of Wuning 武寧.

           Li Deyu died in banishment at Yazhou 崖州, age 62; he left many varied writings including a collected works, *Huichang yipin ji* 會昌一品集 in 20 *juan* and the *Ci Liushi jiuwen* 次柳氏舊聞 (Sequenced Old Stories from the Lius), in 1 *juan*.

851   **Sun Qiao** 孫樵 (fl. 855) submitted a letter to the emperor criticizing the restoration of Buddhist monasteries.

           Li Shangyin was at court serving as Erudite in the National University; later in the year he joined the staff of the Military Commissioner of Dongchuan 東川 in Zizhou 梓州.

Appendix II: Literary Timeline of the Tang

	Luo Yin 羅隱 (833–909), then 18-years-old, presented his poetry to the Liu Jue, then the Military Commissioner of Huainan based in Yangzhou.
853	Duan Chengshi 段成式 (ca. 803–863) completed his *Youyang zazu* 酉陽雜俎 (Miscellaneous Morsels from Youyang).
854	**Xu Hun** was serving as Prefect in Yingzhou 郢州; in winter he died, age 59, leaving his *Dingying ji* 丁卯集, in 2 *juan*.
	Zhang Hu died probably in this year in Danyang 丹陽, age 62, leaving works in 10 *juan*.
855	**Sun Qiao** and 29 candidates passed the *jinshi*.
	Yao He probably died in this year leaving his *Jixuanji* 極玄集 (Collection of the Greatest Mystery) in 1 *juan*.
	Xuanzong was also fond of poetry gatherings, often summoning the Hanlin Academicians to match his poems.
856	Cui Xing 崔鉶 (826–886), the top graduate, and 29 others passed the *jinshi* (30 seems to be a quota in these years).
	Wei Xuan 韋絢 (fl. 820–860) was Vice Governor of Jiangling 江陵; about this time he completed his *Liu Gong jiahua lu* 劉公嘉話錄 (A Record of Master Liu's Excellent Talks) based on his study with **Liu Yuxi** in 821.
857	In the *jinshi* examination 30 candidates passed.
	Xuanzong's interest in spirits and the transformed increased and in the 10th month he summoned the Daoist Priest Xuanyuan Ji 軒轅集 to the palace.
	Guanxiu, who had already become a Buddhist monk at age 20, submitted his poems to the Prefect of Chuzhou 處州, Duan Chengshi.
858	Li Yi 李億, the highest-ranked candidate, and 29 others passed the *jinshi*; ca. 760 he took **Yu Xuanji** (ca. 844–868) as his concubine.
	Xuanyuan Ji returned to Luofushan 羅浮山; **Guanxiu** wrote a poem as a prayer for his safe journey and Wang Qi 王棨 (862 *jinshi*) composed a *fu* 賦 on this event.
	Li Shangyin, age 46, died of illness in the 10th month in Zhengzhou 鄭州.
859	Top-ranked Kong Wei 孔緯 (ca. 830–895), a 40th generation descendant of Confucius, and 29 others passed the *jinshi*.
	Luo Yin, age 26, failed the *jinshi* examination, then went to Tongzhou 同州 and presented his writings to Yang Hangong 楊漢公, the prefect
	Xuanzong died of illness in the 7th month; his son, Li Wen 李溫, took the throne and was posthumously titled Yizong; at the time he was 27.
	About this year **Wei Zhuang** 韋莊 (ca. 836–910) left his home in the capital to travel to the east.
860	Liu Meng 劉蒙 was the highest ranked of 30 successful candidates in the *jinshi*.
861	The top-ranked candidate in the *jinshi* was Pei Yanlu 裴延魯; two relatives of the top-ranked candidate of 859, Kong Xuan 孔絢 and Kong Lun 孔綸, also passed.
	In the 7th month Nanzhao invaded Yongzhou 邕州; several attempts to recover it were unsuccessful.
862	Xue Mai 薛邁 was the top-ranked candidate of 30 in the *jinshi*.
	Yizong revered Buddhism and neglected his court duties.
863	This year there were 35 successful candidates in the *jinshi*.
	Pi Rixiu 皮日休 (ca. 834–ca. 883), who had been living in relcusion on Lumen Shan 鹿門山 devoting himself to poetry, came to the capital for the *jinshi*;

Appendix II: Literary Timeline of the Tang

he wrote an essay urging the removal of *Zhuangzi* and *Liezi* from the examination corpus and replacing them with *Mengzi*; in the 4th month he went to Yingzhou 郢州, then in late fall to the Yuan-Xiang 沅湘 rivers region (modern Hunan); about this time he wrote a grave inscription for Liu Zaoqiang 劉棗強 in which he discussed the current fashions in poetry; his *Lumen yinshu* 鹿門隱書 (Writings of a Recluse at Lumen Mountain) in 60 sections criticized contemporary society.

Li Changfu 李昌符 (d. 884), about 40-years-old, having been unsuccessful repeatedly in the *jinshi*, circulating his fifty poems in a collection called *Pipu* 婢僕詩 (Servants), became well-known in the capital and finally passed this year.

Yu Xuanji 魚玄機 (ca. 844–868) who was in her early twenties traveled to Ezhou and sent poems to the Governor of Taiyuan 太原, Liu Tong 劉潼 and his wife, Li Yi 李億.

Guanxiu in the 8th month went to Lushan 廬山 and wrote an account of the trip in 8 poems, later he went to the Kaiyuansi 開元寺 in Hongzhou 洪州 to preach and left a poem on the wall there.

In the 12th month Nanzhao attacked Tang territories in Xichuan 西川 province.

864   Twenty-five candidates passed the *jinshi*.

Du Xunhe 杜荀鶴 (846–ca. 907), 18-years-old, came to the capital seeking a position.

865   Again there were 25 successful candidates in the *jinshi*.

866   Among the 25 successful candidates in the *jinshi*, Han Gun 韓袞 was top ranked;

Sikong Tu 司空圖 (837–908) and **Pi Rixiu** were among those who did not pass; in the summer **Pi** returned to a country residence at Feiling 肥陵.

Yu Xuanji by this time had already become a Daoist Nun in the Xianyiguan 咸宜觀 in the capital; her poetry was well known among scholar-officials and she was often in the company of Li Ying 李郢 (*jinshi* 856) and other literati.

Wen Tingyun, in his mid-60s, was serving as Instructor in the National University. In the winter **Yu Xuanji** sent him a poem and shortly thereafter he died in Chang'an; his younger brother, Wen Tinghao 溫庭皓 (d. 868), wrote a tomb-tablet inscription; Wen left various collections of his writings in various genres.

Lu Zhao was Prefect of Shezhou 歙州, but gave up his position and returned to Yichun 宜春; later he was often in the company of the Prefect of Yuanzhou 袁州, Gao Hou 高厚.

Cao Tang died suddenly around this year; he had served in minor positions on various provincial officials' staffs and wrote "Bing ma" 兵馬 (A Sick Horse) to lament his own fate; he is best known for his poems on transcendents.

Wei Xuan died probably in this year while serving as Military Commissioner of the Yiwujun 義武軍 leaving his *Rongmu xiantan* 戎幕賢談 (Opinions of A Worthy Regional Commander) and other works.

867   **Pi Rixiu** and 29 other candidates pass the *jinshi* examination; **Luo Yin** compiled his *Chan shu* 讒書 (Defamatory Writings), but again is unsuccessful in the *jinshi*; the top candidate is Zheng Hongye 鄭洪業.

	Han Wo 韓偓 (842–923), 25-years-old, left home to travel in the Jiangnan 江南 region.
868	Zhao Jun 趙峻 was the top-ranked of 30 successful candidates in the *jinshi*
	Yu Xuanji was convicted of beating a maid to death in the spring and in the autumn she was executed.
	Pi Rixiu traveled eastward out of the capital and went down the Bian Canal 汴渠 to Suzhou 蘇州.
	In the 7th month 800 of the soldiers stationed in Lingnan as part of ongoing hostilities with Annam and Nanzhao rebelled under Pang Xun 龐勛 who took Suzhou and sacked the city; in the 9th month of 869 Pang Xun was killed and the rebellion was finally suppressed.
869	**Sikong Tu** and 29 other candidates passed the *jinshi*; Gui Renshao 歸仁紹 was the top-ranked candidate; Sikong's case was advanced through Wang Ning 王凝 (821–879), the examiner, to whom he had sent his writings.
870	Because of Pang Xun's rebellion, the *jinshi* examination was cancelled.
	Pi Rixiu joined the staff of the Prefect of Suzhou, Cui Pu 崔璞, and began to write poetry together with **Lu Guimeng** 陸龜蒙 (836–881); later they were joined by **Zhang Ben** 張賁 (fl. 850–875) and other local poets; in the 11th month Honghui 弘惠, a monk from Silla, asked Pi to composed a stele-tablet inscription for the Chan master Zhou 周 of Lingjiu Shan 靈鷲山.
	Luo Yin in the fall was serving as Recorder in Hengyang 衡陽, but then resigned to return to visit his parents.
	Qiji 齊己 (fl. 881) at the age of 6 was said to have tended oxen for the monks in the Weishansi 溈山寺; while mounted on an ox he would write little poems and the monks urged him to give up the lay life and join them.
871	Forty men, headed by Li Yun 李筠, passed the *jinshi* examination.
	The poems **Lu Guimeng** composed with **Pi Rixiu** were compiled as *Songling ji* 松陵集 (A Collection from Pine Ridge) in 10 *juan*.
	Yizong, a great supporter of Buddhism, held a vegetarian feast for 10,000 monks at the palace.
872	Of the 30 successful candidates in the *jinshi*, Zheng Changtu 鄭昌圖 (d. 887) was the top ranked.
	About this time **Pi Rixiu** was appointed Editorial Director of Collating Books in the Palace Library.
	Guanxiu, age 40, was often in the company of the Prefect of Muzhou 睦州, Feng Yan 馮岩.
	In the fall **Du Xunhe** was travelling in the Hunan area.
873	Thirty men passed the *jinshi* examination
	Li Pin 李頻 (814–ca. 876), age 59, was sent to Fuzhou 鄜州 as an Attendant Censor and wrote much about this trip.
	In the 4th month Yizong, noted for his extravagant expenditures especially with regard to Buddhism, revived the ceremony of venerating the Buddha's Bone, which had not been held since 819 when **Han Yu** had denounced it; the event was conducted with the highest splendor and ceremony
	In the 7th month Yizong died, age 41, and was replaced by Li Xuan 李儇, later. Xizong, who was 11 years old, after Yizong's favorites had been banished owing to the machinations of the eunuch generals Liu Hangshen 劉行深 and Han Wenyue 韓文約.

Appendix II: Literary Timeline of the Tang

874	In the 1st month, drought and famine were reported in lower Yellow River valley.
	Of the 30 candidates successful in the *jinshi*, Gui Renyi 歸仁譯 was top ranked; one of the candidates was Choe Chiwon [Cui Zhiyuan] 崔致遠 (857–940), a 17-year-old from Silla.
	Beginning in the 12th month Wang Xianzhi 王仙芝 (d. 878) gathered several thousand men and rose in revolt at Changyuan 長垣; this uprising was joined by various bandit gangs and eventually by Huang Chao 黃巢 (835–884); by 878 they had affected large areas east of Luoyang between the Yellow and Huai rivers.
	Du Xunhe, then 28, wandered south through what is now Hunan into Guangdong, presenting the Surveillance Commissioner of Hunan, Pei Zan 裴瓚, with his writings.
875	An imperial edict ordered the feasting following the *jinshi* examination to be curtailed.
	Li Pin was moved from Vice Director of the Criminal Administration Bureau to be Prefect of Jianzhou 建州; he died in 876 and Zheng Gu 鄭谷 (849–911), **Guanxiu** and others wrote laments
876	Kong Jian 孔緘, the younger brother of Kong Wei who was the top-ranked candidate in 859, was the top ranked of 30 successful candidates in the *jinshi* this year.
	Luo Yin went to Jiangzhou 江州 and visited Lushan 廬山; he sent a poem to **Lu Guimeng.**
877	Once again there were 30 successful candidates in the *jinshi*.
	Du Xunhe, age 31, left his home in the fall to go to the capital seeking a position.
	Wei Zhuang was in Guozhou 虢州.
878	Of the 30 successful candidates in the *jinshi* Sun Wo 孫偓 (840–916) was the top ranked; **Luo Yin** again failed.
	In the 2nd month Wang Xianzhi sent two of his generals to court to negotiate, but Song Wei 宋威, the chief imperial commander, had them both killed. He then defeated Wang at Hongzhou 洪州 where Wang was killed.
	Sikong Tu was since 877 on the staff of the Surveillance Commissioner of Xuanshe 宣歙, Wang Ning (see entry in 869 above); Wang Ning died this year and Sikong wrote his draft biography.
	Pi Rixiu who was an Erudite in the Court of Imperial Sacrifices was sent out to be Vice Commissioner in Piling 毗陵 (modern Changzhou 常州 in Jiangsu just north of Lake Taihu).
	Du Xunhe was in Nanling 南陵 (in modern southeastern Anhui) and witnessed much of the fighting with the rebels; the following year he moved to the Changlin 長林 mountains to live.
879	There were 30 successful candidates in the *jinshi* examination.
	Lu Guimeng was in Suzhou on the banks of the Lize 笠澤 (i.e. Wusong River 吳淞江) where he compiled his *Lize congshu* 笠澤叢書 (Collectanea from the Li Marsh).
	In the 10th month Huang Chao took Guangzhou 廣州.
880	There were 30 successful candidates in the *jinshi* examination; Zheng Ai 鄭藹 was the top graduate.

In the 2nd month when Hou Changye 侯長業, Reminder of the Left, criticized Xizong for his fondness for horseback riding, archery, cockfighting, and polo; he was ordered to commit suicide.

When in the 7th month Huang Chao took Wuzhou 婺州 where **Guanxiu** was staying, Guan fled to Piling.

Qiji tried to join **Lu Guimeng** who was living in Fuli 甫里 (in Suzhou), but was prevented by the warfare in the area; the following year Lu fell ill and died.

In the 11th month Huang Chao captured Luoyang and attacked Tongguan 潼關 (Tong Pass) which he took the following month; in the 12th month Huang Chao took the capital founding his Great Qi dynasty, executing high officials; the emperor, the princes and the palace women fled to Fengxiang.

Sikong Tu, serving as Director of the Ministry of Personnel, and **Wei Zhuang**, awaiting the examinations early in the next year, were both in Chang'an.

Han Wo had since 860 composed almost 1000 poems, many chanted by common people or entertainers, but when he fled the capital this year the poems were all scattered and mostly lost so that later when they were edited there were only about 100 left.

Late in the year **Pi Rixiu** became a Hanlin Academician in Huang Chao's government; Huang Chao eventually killed him, probably the following year.

881   Xizong moved his court to Chengdu; **Sun Qiao** was summoned there and appointed Director of the Bureau of Operations; at the time Li Tong 李潼 and **Sikong Tu** were also with the emperor and were known as the "Xingzai Sanjun" 行在三俊 (Three Eminences of the Temporary Court).

The *jinshi* was held in Chengdu and 12 candidates passed.

Luo Yin was living in reclusion in Chizhou 池州, but in the 11th month moved to Runzhou 潤州; **Du Xunhe** was also living in Chizhou.

Xizong's court in Chengdu was dominated by eunuchs; Meng Chaotu 孟昭圖, Reminder of the Left, submitted a memorial criticizing the situation but it was blocked by the eunuchs and he was exiled to be Revenue Manager of Jiazhou 嘉州; en route to his post he drowned.

882   The *jinshi* was again held in Chengdu and 28 candidates passed; Gui Renshao, the top graduate in 869, was the examiner.

Wei Zhuang moved from Chang'an to Luoyang.

Du Xunhe traveled to Yangzhou, Xuanzhou, and the nearby region, meeting his friends Zhang Qiao 張喬 and (*jinshi* in the 860s) Gu Yun 顧雲 (d. 894), both well-known poets of the time.

Luo Yin traveled with the Monk Chumo to Beigushan 北固山 (north of modern Zhenjiang in Jiangsu) and the Qiantang 錢塘江 (Hangzhou).

883   Thirty candidates passed the *jinshi* held again in Chengdu.

The Turkish general Li Keyong 李克用 (856–908), aided by the armies of several military commissioners, initiated a series of defeats that led to Huang Chao's final defeat and death in the 6th month of 884.

884   Probably in this year the painter Chang Zhongyin 常重胤 did portraits of Xizong and his high officials for the Dasheng cisi 大聖慈寺 in Chengdu.

Appendix II: Literary Timeline of the Tang

Du Guangting 杜光庭 (850–933), age 34, serving as Music Master of the Ministry of the Pavilion of Culture and Prosperity, composed his *Lidai chong Dao ji* 歷代崇道記 (Record of Exalting the Dao throughout the Years).

885 Thirty-five candidates passed the *jinshi* held again in Chengdu.

In the 2nd month, when Xizong moved from Chengdu to Fengxiang, **Sikong Tu** was summoned to be Secretariat Drafter, but in the 9th month he resigned due to illness.

886 The *jinshi* examination was held in Xingyuan 興元 with 9 successful candidates.

887 Twenty-five candidates, including the well-known poet Zheng Gu, passed the *jinshi* held in Fengxiang 鳳翔.

Luo Yin, aged 54 was still in Hangzhou, but he had been appointed a Retainer to Qian Liu 錢鏐 (852–932), who after the end of the Tang founded the Wu-Yue Kingdom and ruled it from 908–932.

888 In the 1st month Xizong returned from Fengxiang to Chang'an; the city was devastated by Huang Chao's attack and rule as can be seen in **Wei Zhuang**'s famous poem, "Qinfu yin" 秦婦吟 (Lament of the Lady from Qin), written in 883 in Luoyang after hearing stories from those who fled the capital.

In the 2nd month 28 candidates were successful in the *jinshi* examination

In the 3rd month Xizong died, having fallen ill while in Fengxiang; his younger brother, Li Ye 李曄, then 21-years-old, was enthroned, posthumously known as Zhaozong; he respected court officials and hoped to check the power that the eunuchs had held over Xizong; he was initially successful in removing the eunuch Yang Fugong 楊復恭 (d. 894) from power.

Guanxiu was living in Dongyang 東陽 (modern Zhejiang), often in the company of **Wei Zhuang** who was living in Wuzhou about 25 miles away.

889 **Han Wo** and 24 other candidates passed the *jinshi*.

Sikong Tu declined the position of Secretariat Drafter and retired to Huayin 華陰.

890 Kong Wei, the top-graduate from 859, now one of the emperor's top advisors serving as Chancellor of the National University, proposed that officials both in the court and without should contribute funds toward rebuilding the National University and Zhaozong approved this.

Du Xunhe left Chizhou and came to the capital to take the *jinshi* examination.

Han Wo was appointed Reminder of the Right at court.

891 **Du Xunhe**, age 45, and 26 others were successful in the *jinshi*.

Du Guangting, age 41, was in Chengdu compiling records of the transmission of Daoist classics and their composition.

892 With Gui An 歸黯 as the top-ranked candidate, 30 passed the *jinshi*; Gui's uncle, Gui Renshao, had been the top candidate in 869.

893 There were 28 successful *jinshi* candidates; **Wei Zhuang**, 57 years old, did not pass.

Zhaozong, reacting to an arrogant letter from Li Maozhen 李茂貞 (856–924), the Military Commissioner of Fengxiang since 887, ordered his brother Li Zhou 李周 to lead troops to attack Li Maozhen; the government troops were defeated; Li Maozhen took advantage to seize the three bridges near the capital and threaten Chang'an; Zhaozong put the blame on the

Appendix II: Literary Timeline of the Tang

	Grand Councilor Du Rangneng 杜讓能 (841–893), whom he exiled and then ordered to commit suicide
	Luo Yin was Qian Liu's Chief Secretary, writing all the memorials for him.
894	**Wei Zhuang**, age 58, was one of 28 successful *jinshi* candidates; he returned to the Yue region for a few months, but was back in Chang'an by the 8th month.
895	The *jinshi* examination this year was held twice; the results of the first posting of 25 successful candidates were judged to be fallacious and a second examination was held which limited the success to 15 candidates; Cui Ning 崔凝, the examiner of the first round was banished to be Prefect of Hezhou 合州 (near modern Chongqing in Sichuan; like politics of these years, the literary examinations were chaotic.
	Zhaozong was rescued from an attack by three of his Military Commissioners by Li Keyong 李克用 after fleeing into the Jinling 金陵山 mountains south of the capital and then to Huazhou 華州.
896	There were 12 successful *jinshi* candidates.
	Han Wo was Vice Director of the Ministry of Justice.
897	In the 1st month, **Sikong Tu** was appointed Vice Director of the Ministry of War but declined because of problems with his feet.
	In the 2nd month 20 candidates passed the *jinshi* examination; Wang Qixia 王棲霞, a 6-year-old, passed the Examination for Divine Lads.
	Wei Zhuang was appointed Administrative Assistant to Li Xun 李洵 in Chengdu.
	Much to his dismay, **Han Wo** was appointed Chief Secretary to Li Maozhen.
898	Again 20 candidates passed the *jinshi*
	In the 8th month Zhaozong returned to Chang'an.
899	Lu Wenhuan 盧文煥 was the top graduate of 27 successful candidates in the *jinshi*.
	Sikong Shu completed his *Yi jing* 疑經 (On Doubtful Passages in the Classics).
	About this year **Qiji** came to the capital and traveled around with Zheng Gu.
900	Pei Ge 裴格 was the top candidate among 36 in this year's *jinshi*.
	Han Wo was made a Hanlin Academician and some of his poems relate stories from this experience; many poets of the time also matched his poems
	Wei Zhuang, age 64, was made Rectifier of Omissions of the Left; at this time he finished his anthology *You xuanji* 又玄集 (Another Collection of Mystery) in 3 *juan* which opens with poems by **Du Fu**, **Li Bo**, and **Wang Wei**; in the 12th month Wei submitted a memorial asking that **Li He**, **Lu Guimeng**, **Luo Yin** and other literati who did not pass the examinations be granted *jinshi* status.
	In the 11th month the eunuchs Li Jishu 李季術 and Wang Zhongxian 王仲先 removed Zhaozong, confining him in the Wen'an Gong 問安宮 in the eastern palace, and replacing him with the Heir Apparent.
901	In the 1st month, Li Jishu and Wang Zhongxian were executed and Zhaozong returned to the throne.
	Twenty-six candidates passed the *jinshi*
	In the 3rd month **Wei Zhuang** was invited to become Chief Secretary to Wang Jian 王建 (841–893) in Shu; from this time on he served Wang Jian and the state of Qian Shu 前蜀 Wang was to found in 907.

Appendix II: Literary Timeline of the Tang

	In the 11th month the eunuch Han Quanhai 韓全海 ordered Zhaozong to be moved to Fengxiang with the assistance of Li Maozhen.
	On the 3rd of the 3rd month Zhaozong feasted his Grand Councilors and high officials; **Han Wo**, as a Hanlin Academician, took part and wrote a poem depicting the event.
902	There was no *jinshi* examination this year.
	Guanxiu traveled south to Qianzhou 黔州 (modern Guizhou) and visited Yundingshan 雲頂山; then went on to Shu where he presented some of his poems to **Wang Jian**.
903	The *jinshi* examination was again suspended.
	In the 1st month Zhu Wen, now in control of most of the capital and the surrounding area, executed several hundred of the remaining eunuchs.
	Han Wo, age 61, recommended Zhao Chong 趙崇 and Wang Zan 王贊 (d. 905) as Grand Councilors; Cui Yin 崔胤 (854–904) because of this, and working with Zhu Wen 朱溫 (854–912), had Han exiled to be Vice Prefect of Puzhou 濮州 (modern Shandong).
	Guanxiu was in Western Shu and about this time wrote a poem about Wang Jian visiting the Dacisi 大慈寺 in Chengdu to listen to sutra recitation.
	Du Xunhe, age 57, had been working on the staff of Tian Jun 田頵; he was sent as an envoy to Zhu Wen and when Tian Jun was defeated, stayed with Zhu.
904	Twenty-six candidates passed the *jinshi* examination.
	In the 4th month Zhaozong was forced to move to Luoyang escorted by Zhu Wen's troops; en route over 200 of Zhaozong's attendants were killed and replaced by Zhu's men.
	In the 5th month **Han Wo** traveled to Liling 醴陵.
	In the 8th month Zhu Wen had Zhaozong killed, aged 37, and enthroned Li Zhu 李柷 (892–908), Zhaozong's 9th son, as emperor (posthumously Aidi 哀帝).
	Zhu Wen recommended **Du Xunhe** to be appointed as Vice Director of the Bureau of Receptions and a Hanlin Academician; later that year Han, then 60-year-old, took ill and suddenly died; his works were collected as *Tang feng ji* 唐風集.
905	In the 2nd month on the day of the Sacrifice to the Earth God (Sheri 社日), Zhu Wen ordered the Palace Secretary, the eunuch Jiang Xuanhui 蔣玄暉 (d. 906) to invite Zhaozong's nine sons to the Jiuquchi 九曲池 (Nine Bends Pond) for a feast; they were all strangled.
	Twenty-three candidates passed the *jinshi*.
	In the 6th month 30 palace officials who had been banished were all killed at the Baimayi 白馬驛 (White Horse Post-station) in Weizhou 渭州 and their bodies thrown in the Yellow River.
	In the 8th month **Sikong Tu**, 68-years-old, was summoned to Luoyang, but was able to extricate himself without accepting a position and returned to his mountain residence in the Zhongtiao Mountains 中條山.
906	This year 25 candidates were successful in the *jinshi*.
	Han Wo, 64-years-old, left Fuzhou 撫州 (modern Jiangxi) and traveled to Nanyue 南越 (the new, semi-independent state of Min 閩) by boat.

Appendix II: Literary Timeline of the Tang

907   Twenty candidates passed the *jinshi*.
  In the 4th Zhu Wen deposed Emperor Ai and established his own Later Liang dynasty in Bianzhou 汴州 (modern Kaifeng).
  In the 10th month **Wei Zhuang**, 71-years-old was made Assistant Pacification Commissioner in Shu.
  Qiji, 43-years-old, had moved to the Daolinsi 道林寺 in Changsha in 904 and was still living there.